Nineteenth-Century Literature Criticism

Guide to Gale Literary Criticism Series

For criticism on	Consult these Gale series
Authors now living or who died after December 31, 1999	*CONTEMPORARY LITERARY CRITICISM (CLC)*
Authors who died between 1900 and 1999	*TWENTIETH-CENTURY LITERARY CRITICISM (TCLC)*
Authors who died between 1800 and 1899	*NINETEENTH-CENTURY LITERATURE CRITICISM (NCLC)*
Authors who died between 1400 and 1799	*LITERATURE CRITICISM FROM 1400 TO 1800 (LC)* *SHAKESPEAREAN CRITICISM (SC)*
Authors who died before 1400	*CLASSICAL AND MEDIEVAL LITERATURE CRITICISM (CMLC)*
Authors of books for children and young adults	*CHILDREN'S LITERATURE REVIEW (CLR)*
Dramatists	*DRAMA CRITICISM (DC)*
Poets	*POETRY CRITICISM (PC)*
Short story writers	*SHORT STORY CRITICISM (SSC)*
Literary topics and movements	*HARLEM RENAISSANCE: A GALE CRITICAL COMPANION (HR)* *THE BEAT GENERATION: A GALE CRITICAL COMPANION (BG)* *FEMINISM IN LITERATURE: A GALE CRITICAL COMPANION (FL)* *GOTHIC LITERATURE: A GALE CRITICAL COMPANION (GL)*
Asian American writers of the last two hundred years	*ASIAN AMERICAN LITERATURE (AAL)*
Black writers of the past two hundred years	*BLACK LITERATURE CRITICISM (BLC)* *BLACK LITERATURE CRITICISM SUPPLEMENT (BLCS)* *BLACK LITERATURE CRITICISM: CLASSIC AND EMERGING AUTHORS SINCE 1950 (BLC-2)*
Hispanic writers of the late nineteenth and twentieth centuries	*HISPANIC LITERATURE CRITICISM (HLC)* *HISPANIC LITERATURE CRITICISM SUPPLEMENT (HLCS)*
Native North American writers and orators of the eighteenth, nineteenth, and twentieth centuries	*NATIVE NORTH AMERICAN LITERATURE (NNAL)*
Major authors from the Renaissance to the present	*WORLD LITERATURE CRITICISM, 1500 TO THE PRESENT (WLC)* *WORLD LITERATURE CRITICISM SUPPLEMENT (WLCS)*

ISSN 0732-1864

Volume 214

Nineteenth-Century Literature Criticism

Criticism of the
Works of Novelists, Philosophers, and Other
Creative Writers Who Died between 1800
and 1899, from the First Published Critical
Appraisals to Current Evaluations

Kathy D. Darrow
Project Editor

GALE
CENGAGE Learning

Detroit • New York • San Francisco • New Haven, Conn • Waterville, Maine • London

Nineteenth-Century Literature Criticism, Vol. 214

Project Editor: Kathy D. Darrow

Editorial: Dana Barnes, Elizabeth Cranston, Kristen Dorsch, Jeffrey W. Hunter, Jelena O. Krstović, Michelle Lee, Thomas J. Schoenberg, Lawrence J. Trudeau

Data Capture: Katrina D. Coach, Gwen Tucker

Rights and Acquisitions: Margaret Abendroth, Jacqueline Flowers, Timothy Sisler

Composition and Electronic Capture: Gary Oudersluys

Manufacturing: Cynde Bishop

Associate Product Manager: Marc Cormier

For product information and technology assistance, contact us at
Gale Customer Support, 1-800-877-4253.
For permission to use material from this text or product,
submit all requests online at **www.cengage.com/permissions.**
Further permissions questions can be emailed to
permissionrequest@cengage.com

While every effort has been made to ensure the reliability of the information presented in this publication, Gale, a part of Cengage Learning, does not guarantee the accuracy of the data contained herein. Gale accepts no payment for listing; and inclusion in the publication of any organization, agency, institution, publication, service, or individual does not imply endorsement of the editors or publisher. Errors brought to the attention of the publisher and verified to the satisfaction of the publisher will be corrected in future editions.

Gale
27500 Drake Rd.
Farmington Hills, MI, 48331-3535

LIBRARY OF CONGRESS CATALOG CARD NUMBER 84-643008

ISBN-13: 978-1-4144-3513-8
ISBN-10: 1-4144-3513-4

ISSN 0732-1864

Printed in the United States of America
1 2 3 4 5 6 7 13 12 11 10 09

Contents

Preface vii

Acknowledgments xi

Literary Criticism Series Advisory Board xiii

Preface

Since its inception in 1981, *Nineteenth-Century Literature Criticism* (*NCLC*) has been a valuable resource for students and librarians seeking critical commentary on writers of this transitional period in world history. Designated an "Outstanding Reference Source" by the American Library Association with the publication of is first volume, *NCLC* has since been purchased by over 6,000 school, public, and university libraries. The series has covered more than 500 authors representing 38 nationalities and over 28,000 titles. No other reference source has surveyed the critical reaction to nineteenth-century authors and literature as thoroughly as *NCLC*.

Scope of the Series

NCLC is designed to introduce students and advanced readers to the authors of the nineteenth century and to the most significant interpretations of these authors' works. The great poets, novelists, short story writers, playwrights, and philosophers of this period are frequently studied in high school and college literature courses. By organizing and reprinting commentary written on these authors, *NCLC* helps students develop valuable insight into literary history, promotes a better understanding of the texts, and sparks ideas for papers and assignments. Each entry in *NCLC* presents a comprehensive survey of an author's career or an individual work of literature and provides the user with a multiplicity of interpretations and assessments. Such variety allows students to pursue their own interests; furthermore, it fosters an awareness that literature is dynamic and responsive to many different opinions.

Every fourth volume of *NCLC* is devoted to literary topics that cannot be covered under the author approach used in the rest of the series. Such topics include literary movements, prominent themes in nineteenth-century literature, literary reaction to political and historical events, significant eras in literary history, prominent literary anniversaries, and the literatures of cultures that are often overlooked by English-speaking readers.

NCLC continues the survey of criticism of world literature begun by Gale's *Contemporary Literary Criticism* (*CLC*) and *Twentieth-Century Literary Criticism* (*TCLC*).

Organization of the Book

An *NCLC* entry consists of the following elements:

- The **Author Heading** cites the name under which the author most commonly wrote, followed by birth and death dates. Also located here are any name variations under which an author wrote, including transliterated forms for authors whose native languages use nonroman alphabets. If the author wrote consistently under a pseudonym, the pseudonym will be listed in the author heading and the author's actual name given in parenthesis on the first line of the biographical and critical information. Uncertain birth or death dates are indicated by question marks. Single-work entries are preceded by a heading that consists of the most common form of the title in English translation (if applicable) and the original date of composition.

- The **Introduction** contains background information that introduces the reader to the author, work, or topic that is the subject of the entry.

- The list of **Principal Works** is ordered chronologically by date of first publication and lists the most important works by the author. The genre and publication date of each work is given. In the case of foreign authors whose works have been translated into English, the list will focus primarily on twentieth-century translations, selecting those works most commonly considered the best by critics. Unless otherwise indicated, dramas are dated by first performance, not first publication. Lists of **Representative Works** by different authors appear with topic entries.

- Reprinted **Criticism** is arranged chronologically in each entry to provide a useful perspective on changes in critical evaluation over time. The critic's name and the date of composition or publication of the critical work are given at the beginning of each piece of criticism. Unsigned criticism is preceded by the title of the source in which it appeared. All titles by the author featured in the text are printed in boldface type. Footnotes are reprinted at the end of each essay or excerpt. In the case of excerpted criticism, only those footnotes that pertain to the excerpted texts are included. Criticism in topic entries is arranged chronologically under a variety of subheadings to facilitate the study of different aspects of the topic.

- A complete **Bibliographical Citation** of the original essay or book precedes each piece of criticism.

- Critical essays are prefaced by brief **Annotations** explicating each piece.

- An annotated bibliography of **Further Reading** appears at the end of each entry and suggests resources for additional study. In some cases, significant essays for which the editors could not obtain reprint rights are included here. Boxed material following the further reading list provides references to other biographical and critical sources on the author in series published by Gale.

Indexes

Each volume of *NCLC* contains a **Cumulative Author Index** listing all authors who have appeared in a wide variety of reference sources published by Gale, including *NCLC*. A complete list of these sources is found facing the first page of the Author Index. The index also includes birth and death dates and cross references between pseudonyms and actual names.

A **Cumulative Nationality Index** lists all authors featured in *NCLC* by nationality, followed by the number of the *NCLC* volume in which their entry appears.

A **Cumulative Topic Index** lists the literary themes and topics treated in the series as well as in *Classical and Medieval Literature Criticism, Literature Criticism from 1400 to 1800, Twentieth-Century Literary Criticism,* and the *Contemporary Literary Criticism* Yearbook, which was discontinued in 1998.

An alphabetical **Title Index** accompanies each volume of *NCLC*, with the exception of the Topics volumes. Listings of titles by authors covered in the given volume are followed by the author's name and the corresponding page numbers where the titles are discussed. English translations of foreign titles and variations of titles are cross-referenced to the title under which a work was originally published. Titles of novels, dramas, nonfiction books, and poetry, short story, or essay collections are printed in italics, while individual poems, short stories, and essays are printed in roman type within quotation marks.

In response to numerous suggestions from librarians, Gale also produces an annual paperbound edition of the *NCLC* cumulative title index. This annual cumulation, which alphabetically lists all titles reviewed in the series, is available to all customers. Additional copies of this index are available upon request. Librarians and patrons will welcome this separate index; it saves shelf space, is easy to use, and is recyclable upon receipt of the next edition.

Citing *Nineteenth-Century Literature Criticism*

When citing criticism reprinted in the Literary Criticism Series, students should provide complete bibliographic information so that the cited essay can be located in the original print or electronic source. Students who quote directly from reprinted criticism may use any accepted bibliographic format, such as University of Chicago Press style or Modern Language Association style.

The examples below follow recommendations for preparing a bibliography set forth in *The Chicago Manual of Style,* 14th ed. (Chicago: The University of Chicago Press, 1993); the first example pertains to material drawn from periodicals, the second to material reprinted from books:

Franklin, J. Jeffrey. "The Victorian Discourse of Gambling: Speculations on *Middlemarch* and *The Duke's Children*." *ELH* 61, no. 4 (winter 1994): 899-921. Reprinted in *Nineteenth-Century Literature Criticism*. Vol. 168, edited by Jessica Bomarito and Russel Whitaker, 39-51. Detroit: Thomson Gale, 2006.

Frank, Joseph. "*The Gambler*: A Study in Ethnopsychology." In *Freedom and Responsibility in Russian Literature: Essays in Honor of Robert Louis Jackson,* edited by Elizabeth Cheresh Allen and Gary Saul Morson, 69-85. Evanston, Ill.: Northwestern University Press, 1995. Reprinted in *Nineteenth-Century Literature Criticism*. Vol. 168, edited by Jessica Bomarito and Russel Whitaker, 75-84. Detroit: Thomson Gale, 2006.

The examples below follow recommendations for preparing a works cited list set forth in the *MLA Handbook for Writers of Research Papers,* 6th ed. (New York: The Modern Language Association of America, 2003); the first example pertains to material drawn from periodicals, the second to material reprinted from books:

Franklin, J. Jeffrey. "The Victorian Discourse of Gambling: Speculations on *Middlemarch* and *The Duke's Children*." *ELH* 61.4 (winter 1994): 899-921. Reprinted in *Nineteenth-Century Literature Criticism*. Eds. Jessica Bomarito and Russel Whitaker. Vol. 168. Detroit: Thomson Gale, 2006. 39-51.

Frank, Joseph. "*The Gambler*: A Study in Ethnopsychology." *Freedom and Responsibility in Russian Literature: Essays in Honor of Robert Louis Jackson.* Eds. Elizabeth Cheresh Allen and Gary Saul Morson. Evanston, Ill.: Northwestern University Press, 1995. 69-85. Reprinted in *Nineteenth-Century Literature Criticism*. Eds. Jessica Bomarito and Russel Whitaker. Vol. 168. Detroit: Thomson Gale, 2006. 75-84.

Suggestions are Welcome

Readers who wish to suggest new features, topics, or authors to appear in future volumes, or who have other suggestions or comments are cordially invited to call, write, or fax the Associate Product Manager:

Associate Product Manager, Literary Criticism Series
Gale
27500 Drake Road
Farmington Hills, MI 48331-3535
1-800-347-4253 (GALE)
Fax: 248-699-8054

Acknowledgments

The editors wish to thank the copyright holders of the criticism included in this volume and the permissions managers of many book and magazine publishing companies for assisting us in securing reproduction rights. Following is a list of the copyright holders who have granted us permission to reproduce material in this volume of *NCLC*. Every effort has been made to trace copyright, but if omissions have been made, please let us know.

COPYRIGHTED MATERIAL IN *NCLC*, VOLUME 214, WAS REPRODUCED FROM THE FOLLOWING PERIODICALS:

Dickens Quarterly, v. 23, December, 2006. Copyright © 2006 by the Dickens Society. Reproduced by permission.—*Eighteenth-Century Fiction,* v. 5, October, 1992; v. 15, January, 2003. Copyright © *Eighteenth-Century Fiction,* McMaster University 1992, 2003. Both reproduced by permission.—*ELH,* v. 70, spring, 2003; v. 71, winter, 2004. Copyright © 2003. 2004 by The Johns Hopkins University Press. Both reproduced by permission.—*Fabula: Zeitschrift für Erzählforschung/ Journal of Folktale Studies/Revue d'Etudes sur le Conte Populaire,* v. 46, 2005. Copyright © 2005 by Walter de Gruyter & Co., D-10785 Berlin. All rights reserved. Reproduced by permission.—*Journal of Narrative Theory,* v. 34, winter, 2004 for "'Nothing More' and 'Nothing Definite': First Wives in Elizabeth Gaskell's *Wives and Daughters* (1866)" by Joellen Masters. Copyright © 2004 by *The Journal of Narrative Technique.* Reproduced by permission of the publisher and the author.—*Marvels & Tales,* v. 20, 2006. Copyright © 2006 Wayne State University Press. Reproduced with permission of the Wayne State University Press.—*MLN,* v. 122, December, 2007. Copyright © 2007 by The Johns Hopkins University Press. Reproduced by permission.—*New Literary History,* v. 34, autumn, 2003. Copyright © 2003 by The Johns Hopkins University Press. Reproduced by permission.—*Nineteenth-Century Literature,* v. 59, March, 2005. Copyright © 2005 by The Regents of the University of California. All rights reserved. Reproduced by permission of the publisher and the author.—*Papers of the Bibliographical Society of America,* v. 98, September, 2004. Copyright © 2004 by The Bibliographical Society of America. All rights reserved. Reproduced by permission.—*Philosophy and Literature,* v. 25, October, 2001. Copyright © 2001 by The Johns Hopkins University Press. Reproduced by permission.—*Raritan,* v. 13, summer, 1993. Copyright © 1993 by *Raritan: A Quarterly Review.* Reproduced by permission.—*Scandinavian Studies,* v. 74, summer, 2002 for "Counteracting the Fall: 'Sneedronningen' and 'Iisjomfruen': The Problem of Adult Sexuality in Fairytale and Story" by Jørgen Dines Johansen. Copyright © 2002 Society for the Advancement of Scandinavian Study. All rights reserved. Reproduced by permission of the publisher and the author./ v. 78, summer, 2006 for "The Idle Spectator. Hans Christian Andersen's *Dryaden* (1868), *Illustreret Tidende,* and the Universal Exposition" by Jakob Stougaard-Nielsen. Copyright © 2006 Society for the Advancement of Scandinavian Study. All rights reserved. Reproduced by permission of the publisher and the author.—*Studies in Eighteenth-Century Culture,* v. 18, 1988. Copyright © 1988 by The Johns Hopkins University Press. Reproduced by permission.—*Studies in English Literature, 1500-1900,* v. 42, autumn, 2002; v. 47, autumn, 2007. Copyright © 2002, 2007 by The Johns Hopkins University Press. Both reproduced by permission.—*Studies in Romanticism,* v. 35, summer, 1996. Copyright 1996 by the Trustees of Boston University. Reproduced by permission.—*Studies in the Novel,* v. 32, summer, 2000; v. 34, winter, 2002; v. 38, spring, 2006; v. 39, summer, 2007. Copyright © 2000, 2002, 2006, 2007 by the University of North Texas. All reproduced by permission.—*Textual Practice,* v. 16, April, 2002 for "William Beckford's 'Sparks of Orientalism' and the Material-Discursive Orient of British Romanticism" by Diego Saglia. Copyright © 2002 Taylor & Francis Group, LLC. Reproduced by permission of Taylor & Francis, Ltd., http//:www.tandf.co.uk/journals and the author.—*Victorian Newsletter,* fall, 2004 for "Sympathy and Discipline in *Mary Barton*" by Melissa Schaub. Reproduced by permission of *The Victorian Newsletter* and the author.—*Victorian Periodicals Review,* v. 33, summer, 2000. Copyright © University of Toronto Press 2000. Reproduced by permission of University of Toronto Press Incorporated.—*Victorians Institute Journal,* v. 33, 2005. Copyright © University of Toronto Press 2005. Reproduced by permission of University of Toronto Press Incorporated.—*Women's Writing,* v. 12, 2005 for "Hysteria Repeating Itself: Elizabeth Gaskell's *Lois the Witch*" by Deborah Wynne. Copyright © 2005 Taylor & Francis Group, LLC. Reproduced by permission of Taylor & Francis, Ltd., http//:www.tandf.co.uk/journals and the author./ v. 13, October, 2006 for "Professional Frontiers in Elizabeth Gaskell's *My Lady Ludlow*" by Susan E. Colón. Copyright © 2006 Taylor & Francis Group, LLC. Reproduced by permission of Taylor & Francis, Ltd., http//:www.tandf.co.uk/journals and the author.

COPYRIGHTED MATERIAL IN *NCLC*, VOLUME 214, WAS REPRODUCED FROM THE FOLLOWING BOOKS:

Cass, Jeffrey. From "Homoerotics and Orientalism in William Beckford's *Vathek*: Liberalism and the Problem of Pederasty," in *Interrogating Orientalism: Contextual Approaches and Pedagogical Practices.* Edited by Diane Long Hoeveler

Gale Literature Product Advisory Board

The members of the Gale Literature Product Advisory Board—reference librarians from public and academic library systems—represent a cross-section of our customer base and offer a variety of informed perspectives on both the presentation and content of our literature products. Advisory board members assess and define such quality issues as the relevance, currency, and usefulness of the author coverage, critical content, and literary topics included in our series; evaluate the layout, presentation, and general quality of our printed volumes; provide feedback on the criteria used for selecting authors and topics covered in our series; provide suggestions for potential enhancements to our series; identify any gaps in our coverage of authors or literary topics, recommending authors or topics for inclusion; analyze the appropriateness of our content and presentation for various user audiences, such as high school students, undergraduates, graduate students, librarians, and educators; and offer feedback on any proposed changes/enhancements to our series. We wish to thank the following advisors for their advice throughout the year.

Hans Christian Andersen
1805-1875

(Also wrote under the pseudonym Villiam Christian Walter) Danish short story and fairy-tale writer, poet, novelist, travel essayist, autobiographer, diarist, and playwright.

The following entry presents criticism on Andersen's works from 1999 to 2007. For further information on Andersen's life and works, see *NCLC,* Volumes 7 and 79.

INTRODUCTION

Although he wrote in many genres, including novels, poems, and plays, Andersen is remembered primarily as one of the most distinguished writers of fairy tales. Many of his fairy tales—such as "Den grimme Ælling" (1843; "The Ugly Duckling"), "Keiserens nye Klæder" (1837; "The Emperor's New Clothes"), and "Den lille Havfrue" (1837; "The Little Mermaid")—are world famous. During his lifetime, Andersen wrote more than 150 tales; the majority of his tales were completely original and most were written between 1835 and 1874. Before this time, fairy tales had been part of the oral tradition of literature passed through generations and recorded in writing only for historical interest. Andersen revitalized and expanded the genre by merging the traditional folk tale with the more sophisticated literary tale. To this end he employed conversational language suitable for children, often provided sad rather than happy endings, combined an adult sensibility with a childlike simplicity, and blended into his tales aspects of his personal life.

BIOGRAPHICAL INFORMATION

Andersen was born into poverty in Odense, Denmark, to a shoemaker and his superstitious and uneducated wife. His father was an avid reader who encouraged his son's intellectual and creative aspirations by reading to him tales from Danish folklore and from such works as *The Arabian Nights* and the comedies of playwright Ludvig Holberg. The elder Andersen also built a marionette theater so that his son could write and perform plays. Just before Andersen's eleventh birthday his father died, but the elder Andersen had already instilled a love of literature and theater in his son, who particularly enjoyed the works of William Shakespeare and Sir Walter Scott. In 1819 Andersen left home, intent on joining Copenhagen's theater circle. He sought work as an actor, ballet dancer, or singer, but the only theater work he could find during the next few years was as an extra and an occasional minor character. In 1822 he wrote and submitted two plays for production: both were rejected, although one critic noted evidence of some artistry and recommended further training for the author. Eventually, Jonas Collin, a director of the Royal Theater, arranged for Andersen to obtain some basic education, which included instruction at elite private schools during the mid-1820s. By the late 1820s Andersen had passed the entrance exams for the University of Copenhagen. In the meantime, Collin had become a surrogate father to Andersen, opening his home to the young man. Andersen remained closely connected with the Collin family and never saw his own family again.

In 1829 Andersen made his dramatic debut with an original play that was performed three times at the Royal Theater: the farcical *Kjærlighed paa Nicolai Taarn, elle Hvad siger Parterret* (*Love on St. Nicholas Tower, or What Says the Pit*). Also in 1829, Andersen saw the publication of his short story, *Fodrejse fra Holmens Canal til Østpynten af Amager* (*Journey on Foot from Holmens Canal to the East Point of Amager*), a mock travel essay that describes an imaginary walk through Copenhagen. Andersen's first real success and literary breakthrough, *Improvisatoren* (1835; *The Improvisatore*), was inspired by his trip to Italy in 1833. Many scholars have contended that this trip marked a rebirth for Andersen, who turned from composing poetry to writing prose and fairy tales.

Andersen had begun his first fairy tales, published in several volumes entitled *Eventyr, Fortalte for Børn* (1835-42; *Fairy Tales Told for Children*), during his stay in Italy. Although he had originally intended the fairy tales for adults as well as children, he amended the title to "tales for children" after critics faulted the simplistic dialogue and style of the stories. After 1850, Andersen began to direct his tales more toward adults than children. Many of his early tales were adaptations of traditional folk tales, but he eventually concentrated on producing original stories; all but a dozen of his more than 150 tales are original creations. By 1837, the year his third novel, *Kun en Spillemand* (*Only a Fiddler*), was published, Andersen began to be perceived as a European celebrity and was granted an annual stipend from Denmark for the remainder of his life. Thereafter Andersen continued his travels, visiting such countries as Germany, England, Italy, Greece, and Holland. Toward the end of his life, as his health began to fail, Denmark acknowledged Andersen as its national author. He died in 1875 near Copenhagen.

MAJOR WORKS

Andersen's works that are most familiar to English-speaking readers are his early tales, written between 1835 and 1850. These include such stories as "Prindsessen paa Ærten" (1835; "The Princess and the Pea"), "Tommelise" (1835; "Thumbelina"), "Den standhaftige Tinsoldat" (1838; "The Steadfast Tin Soldier"), "Sneedronningen" (1844; "The Snow Queen"), "Stoppenaalen" (1847; "The Darning Needle"), "Den lille Pige med Svovlstikkerne" (1848; "The Little Match Girl"), and "Flipperne" (1848; "The Shirt Collar"). Although some of his tales end happily, Andersen often deviated from the "happily ever after" conclusion of the traditional fairy tale; death, for example, is the primary motif in more than three-fourths of his tales. Andersen's heroes and heroines are consumed by fire or die of cold or have to renounce their love or their ambitions. They often suffer painful ordeals in an ugly or frightening world, and even if they succeed or are transformed in a positive way, like the ugly duckling, it is often not through their own doing, as in a traditional fairy tale, but through the workings of fate or some other external agency. Among Andersen's most popular and best loved fairy tales is "The Ugly Duckling," the story of a homely cygnet who becomes the most beautiful of all swans; many biographers have commented on the autobiographical elements in the tale. In another departure from the traditional fairy tale, Andersen's stories introduce the adult theme of the role of the artist, with an emphasis on the plight of neglected artistic genius. The stories also reflect a division in Andersen between sympathy with ordinary people and distrust of authority, and a desire to be accepted by authority. In general, the stories work on several levels, combining a childlike surface and simplicity of language with serious, adult themes.

CRITICAL RECEPTION

During his lifetime, Andersen became celebrated for his tales not only in Denmark but throughout Europe and beyond. Translated into more than 150 languages, his tales have remained popular since his death, leading many critics to comment on the universality of his themes. Early scholars have pointed out the realism inherent in Andersen's tales, asserting that the tales reflect the world Andersen witnessed—which encompassed sorrow, death, evil, and man's follies. Discussing the

essential "humanness" of Andersen's tales, some commentators have found that since the tales involve everyday-life themes of love, death, nature, injustice, suffering and poverty, they appeal to all races, ideologies, classes, and genders. Other critics have noted that the appeal of Andersen's stories is based on their intrinsic optimism, which typically prevails over pessimism. In Andersen's tales, the strength of spirit of the protagonists is reaffirmed, and they prove themselves worthy of triumph.

One major trend in Andersen criticism has involved psychoanalytic studies seeking to draw connections between the suffering depicted in Andersen's stories and the troubles of Andersen's own life, including his various psychological problems and his own unrequited love affairs. Throughout his life, as biographers have recorded, Andersen was ashamed of his working-class background and as such, critics claim, was plagued by a sense of inferiority. Commentators have speculated that Andersen turned to writing fantasies as an outlet for his own frustration and embarrassment over his poverty-stricken youth and the immorality of his background. Some critics have even maintained that Andersen retold his own life story over and over again in his stories, portraying his own self as triumphing over evil, persecution, poverty, and scorn.

Critics have also examined Andersen's divided role as both an "insider" and an "outsider" in the upper reaches of society. Maintaining that Andersen's tales reveal the author's desire to be accepted by the upper classes, critic Jack Zipes has argued that the tales also depict the humiliation, pain, and suffering that "dominated" members of society must endure in order to prove their virtuosity and nobility. Such an experience, Zipes asserted, led Andersen to form an ambivalent attitude toward the aristocracy, at once aspiring to join the ranks of the higher classes while at the same time disdaining them. Other critics have commented on Andersen's feelings of being "miscast" or of not belonging. Noting that although Andersen rose from the working-class ranks to join the upper classes, critic Niels Ingwersen has pointed out that Andersen never became their equal; instead, he served those who assisted him. Andersen's tales are subversive, then, toward the audience as well as toward Andersen himself, who often despised his own efforts to gain the approval of the aristocracy.

Critical studies in recent years continue to approach Andersen's work from a variety of perspectives. As one critic observed in her analysis of one of the tales, the diverse influences on an author's final product—not only the original product but also the evolution of concepts over time—warrant more than a single approach to a work. A psychoanalytical approach continues to be popular, focusing on aspects such as Andersen's treatment of children or his relationship with his readers.

The tales have also invited recent critical attention to the complexity of the tales, Andersen's narration and narrative techniques, his influence on other writers, and the influence of contemporary culture on his work. While critics have paid some attention to Andersen's neglected plays as well as to his novels and travel writings, they, like the general public, still focus primarily on the fairy tales.

PRINCIPAL WORKS

Ungdoms-Forsøg [as Villiam Christian Walter] (novel) 1822

Fodrejse fra Holmens Canal til Østpynten af Amager [*Journey on Foot from Holmens Canal to the East Point of Amager*] (short story) 1829

Kjærlighed paa Nicolai Taarn, elle Hvad siger Parterret [*Love on St. Nicholas Tower, or What Says the Pit*] (drama) 1829

Bruden fra Lammermoor [adaptor, from the novel by Sir Walter Scott; *The Bride of Lammermoor*] (libretto) 1832

Agnete og Havmanden (verse drama) 1834

Improvisatoren [*The Improvisatore*] (novel) 1835

*Eventyr, Fortalte for Børn [*Fairy Tales Told for Children*] (fairy tales) 1835-42

O.T. (novel) 1836

Kun en Spillemand. 3 vols. [*Only a Fiddler*] (novel) 1837

De to Baronesser [*The Two Baronesses*] (novel) 1838

Den Usynlige paa Sprogø [*The Invisible Man on Sprogø*] (drama) 1839

Mulatten [*The Mulatto*] (drama) 1840

En Digters Bazar [*A Poet's Bazaar*] (poetry, short stories, and travel essays) 1842

†Nye Eventyr. 6 vols. [*New Fairy Tales*] (fairy tales) 1843-48

Den nye Barselstue [*The New Maternity Ward*] (drama) 1845

Liden Kirsten [*Little Kirsten*] (libretto) 1846

Das Märchen Meines Lebens ohne Dichtung [*The Story of My Life*] (autobiography) 1847

Eventyr [*Fairy Tales*] (fairy tales) 1850

I Sverigg [*Pictures of Sweden*] (travel essays) 1851

Historier [*Stories*] (fairy tales) 1852-55

Mit Livs Eventyr [*The Fairy Tale of My Life*] (autobiography) 1855

At være eller ikke være [*To Be, or Not To Be?*] (novel) 1857

Nye Eventyr og Historier. 10 vols. [*New Fairy Tales and Stories*] (fairy tales) 1858-66

I Spanien [*In Spain*] (travel essays) 1863

Dryaden. Et Eventyr fra Udstillingstidin i Paris 1867 [*A Tale from the Paris Exposition*] (essay) 1868

Et Besøg i Portugal [*A Visit to Portugal*] (travel essays) 1868

Lykke-Peer [*Lucky Peer*] (novel) 1870

Samlede voerker. 15 vols. (fairy tales, short stories, travel essays, novels, and poetry) 1876-80

‡Levnedsbogen [*The Book of My Life*] (autobiography) 1926

The Complete Andersen. 6 vols. (fairy tales and short stories) 1942-48

The Complete Fairy Tales and Stories (fairy tales and short stories) 1974

The Diaries of Hans Christian Andersen (diaries) 1990

*This collection includes the stories "Tommelise" (1835; "Thumbelina"), "Prindsessen paa Ærten" (1835; "The Princess and the Pea"), "Keiserens nye Klæder" (1837; "The Emperor's New Clothes"), "Den lille Havfrue" (1837; "The Little Mermaid"), and "Den standhaftige Tinsoldat" (1838; "The Steadfast Tin Soldier").

†This collection includes the stories "Den grimme Ælling" (1843; "The Ugly Duckling"), "Sneedronningen" (1844; "The Snow Queen"), "Stoppenaalen" (1847; "The Darning Needle"), "Den lille Pige med Svovlstikkerne" (1848; "The Little Match Girl"), and "Flipperne" (1848; "The Shirt Collar").

‡*Levnedsbogen* was originally written in 1832.

CRITICISM

Aage Jørgensen (essay date 1999)

SOURCE: Jørgensen, Aage. "Heroes in Hans Christian Andersen's Writings." In *Hans Christian Andersen: A Poet in Time*, edited by Johan de Mylius, Aage Jørgensen, and Viggo Hjørnager Pedersen, pp. 271-87. Odense, Denmark: Odense University Press, 1999.

[In the following essay, Jørgensen describes the various types of heroic characters that appear in Andersen's works.]

A SON OF THE PEOPLE

Let us begin in medias res: with a fabulous main character nicknamed Clod-Hans by his brothers,—which doesn't exactly suggest anything heroic. On the other hand, Clod-Hans gives his name to the text, a conventional fairy tale (from 1855) not particularly influenced by Romanticism, but clearly rooted in the art of popular storytelling.[1] As you will recall, the brothers want to ask the princess's hand in marriage. She will marry the man who has "the most to say for himself", and since the brothers are "so witty that they thought themselves too clever for words", and beyond that have impressive, supposedly useful abilities, the father willingly provides them with horses. When Clod-Hans realizes what is happening, he immediately has "a yen to get married": "If she takes me, she takes me; and if she doesn't take me, I'll take her, anyway." That's how simple Clod-Hans's life is and that's how spontaneously he tackles things. That his father refuses to lend him a horse is no problem, for Clod-Hans has his own billy-goat and is therefore mobile. So it's easy sailing for him, "halloo, here I come!" Along the way, he makes his matchless discoveries: a dead crow, an old wooden shoe with no leather top, a pocketful of the finest mud. On the back of his goat and in possession of these wonderful finds, he rides, as it is written, "right into the hall", where his brothers have just had a terrible setback, despite their abilities. They start out well enough by finding it "terribly hot" and "dreadfully warm" respectively, but when the princess explains that it is due to the fact that "my father" and "we" respectively are in the process of broiling chickens, that shuts them up. Clod-Hans also notices "a scorcher", but when she answers, "I'm roasting young chickens", he immediately scores points with clever conversation and fancy contributions to the royal cuisine. Not even the prospect of seeing the entire story verbatim in the newspaper can stop him; on the contrary, he throws what is left of his mud right in the alderman's face, to the utter delight of the princess.

In recent years, Mikhail Bakhtin's carnival concept has often proved an effective instrument in the context of literary analysis. It deals with situations in which things are stood on their heads, so to speak. Where the bottom rung of society is momentarily on the top, and where the refined and distinguished, the respectable and ideal are subjected to ridicule. Where room is given to bodily functions, to digestion and reproduction, where sexuality is for once both spoken of and allowed to speak, where bad table manners and belching undercut the show of proper etiquette, and so on. A burlesque and grotesque world of the belly unfolds itself and challenges the intellect's ability to maintain control.

Clod-Hans is in all modesty a text of that kind.[2] Its language is not exactly the most refined. It opens onto the perishable and the putrefying. The hero rides his goat right into the castle's fancy room with mirrored-ceiling (which in turning things upside down, contributes to the brothers' breakdown). And not only does he use mud in the food, but with what he has left, he also dirties the alderman's ruling-class face.

As can be seen in connection with the title, *Clod-Hans* is "an old story retold". Here, as a 50-year-old writer, Andersen returns to his popular or rather folktale point of departure. The retold folktale is found in several variants, and we do not know precisely which one Andersen knew. But in the Danish Folklore Archives, there is a transcript of a tale told by Black Grethe to her daughter, in the village Kjøng, southwest of Odense, and "given to Jens Kamp before 1904". This variant, *Klotte-Hans,* was undoubtedly in circulation in Funen in the early 19th Century.[3]

This well-turned and somewhat coarse tale, whose young lad rides a ram for the simple reason that the father only has two horses, clearly satisfies a social wish-fulfillment dream. What was not possible in the reality of the feudal social system, could be fulfilled in fiction. Not to put too fine a point on it, the hero gives the princess a turd and gets a kingdom in return.

But *Klotte-Hans* was not suitable for the fashionable urban bourgeois nursery. It differs from the literary tale in striking ways. The refined modern teller of tales—Andersen, that is—spins his story in such a way that without losing any vigour, it remains fully presentable in cultivated circles. He manages this by using several strategies. First of all, it is evident that *Clod-Hans* is invested with a powerful artistic mastery of language. The story is also expanded, refined and removed from the specifically folktale milieu and in a way transferred to "modern times". For example, in Andersen's version there aren't three brothers, but rather two and then one more, whom no one takes into account. And why not? Because the brothers have been ascribed abilities of a kind that had never been seen in a folktale, and which turn out to be utterly useless after all. To know the guild articles and the city newspaper by heart corresponds in large measure to knowing the telephone directory by heart today. The tale opposes two kinds of education: the brothers' sterile memorization which has no relation to the real world, and Clod-Hans's highly effective cunning, which brings him the fulfillment of his desires.

Clod-Hans is, in short, a popular hero. He uses his resources masterfully and achieves his goal, he is the princess's equal and indifferent to public opinion. He gets a wife, crown and throne, and the alderman gets mud in his face. The fiction rewards him and could have been rounded off in the traditional folktale manner: they lived happily ever after. However, the narrator moderates the simplicity with some ironic distance: in a story this sort of thing can happen, in the reality outside of the story is it hardly possible. So instead, Andersen sends a little greeting to the expanding bourgeois press: "we had this story straight from the alderman's newspaper—but that is one you can't always depend upon".

A MAN OF ACTION

There are few examples of this kind of folktale-retold in Hans Christian Andersen's stories, but that was what he began with,—with *The Tinder Box* at the beginning of the very first of the little booklets (1835).[4] Here, he takes up the same Oriental Aladdin story that Oehlenschläger had dramatised in the year of Andersen's birth. Oehlenschläger's Aladdin gets hold of the magic lamp because Noureddin sees at the palace square how he gets the orange in his turban by a stroke of luck, as it were. In the same manner, Andersen's Soldier gets hold of the tinder box because the old witch is in need of a helper. By means of their sources of light both get whatever their heart desires, including of course a princess. And both stand to lose her again. But Andersen turns the Soldier's story around in fairy-tale fashion, so that it ends with a wedding,—during which the dogs have a good time throwing the courtiers up in the air. Here we see a carnival element which was not present in Oehlenschläger's universal, romantic drama. On the other hand Andersen's tale omits the long hard battle through which Aladdin wins back the palace and Gulnare. The Soldier gets his tinder box back through cunning and then, with the help of the dogs, can obtain the princess and the kingdom. While Oehlenschläger tells a story of sublimation, Andersen tells one of the unfolding of drives and of self-realization. The Soldier cannot resist kissing the girl, for he is after all "a real soldier" and can apparently see that she is "a true princess". A real soldier doesn't care for nonsense, without any scruples he cuts off the witch's head,—to which his critics and the public objected, even though she obviously represents psychological states that must be overcome.

I will defy that criticism and designate the Soldier as one of Andersen's popular heroes. And not because he cuts the witch's head off, but because after he does so, which amounts to freeing himself from mother fixation, he shows that he can master his magical lamp and thereby also his drives. And note that this is mastery, not repression. Here in any event, the princess leaves the copper palace, that is liberates herself from father fixation, and becomes queen, which appeals to her. And, as written: "The wedding lasted all of a week, and the three dogs sat at the table, with their eyes opened wider than ever before."—No one need doubt that the new royal couple, acclaimed by the people, will live happily ever after.

A CHILD OF HAPPINESS

Late in his life (1870), Hans Christian Andersen wrote a little novel whose title—and the fact that the Aladdin theme is once again played out in it—makes it far more relevant than was the case with *Clod-Hans* to draw on it in an effort to clarify what might be meant by the word "hero" in the context of the author's work. *Lykke-Peer* (*Lucky Peer*) is a novel about an artist and in this respect marks a return to Andersen's first great international effort as a novelist, *Improvisatoren* (*The Improvisatore*, 1835).[5]

At precisely the same moment, two boys are born in one and the same house. The merchant's son is christened Felix, while the warehouse worker's boy is called Peer. He acquires his nickname when, while playing, he finds the merchant's wife's engagement ring in the gutter. The lucky child chooses a life in the theater, first ballet, then singing, but as an adolescent, he loses his voice. An anonymous benefactor (the theater's singing teacher, we later learn) ensures that he is sent to a provincial city and taken in as a boarder by the schoolmaster, Mr. Gabriel, whose wife—we note en passant—bids him welcome with the line: "Good heavens, how grown-up you are!" (and orders that a communicating door be nailed shut for the sake of propriety) (334).[6] She arranges for him to play Romeo in the local theater's performance of Shakespeare's tragedy, with the pharmacist's daughter as Juliet, which results in his falling in love with her. But at a ball given by the local deacon, Felix gets in the way and conquers the beauty. After two years of diligent study, Peer must return to the capital and at the final moment, during a scary dream in which the pharmacist's daughter appears as another elfmaid and tempts him to perdition, he gets his voice back. The singing teacher is still his mentor and oracle of wisdom, and Peer advances from one success to another,—while Felix enjoys life's more material pleasures and is promoted to gentleman-in-waiting. Together at a painting exhibition, they meet a young baroness, "in her sixteenth year, an innocent, beautiful child" (372), whose maternal home becomes Peer's gateway to "the great world" (373). He was "happy in his art and with the talents he possessed" (375), though with a touch of sadness at the thought of the transitory nature of all things, including the performing arts. Until the day when he marvelously improvises on the piano and brings the baroness to make a declaration, whereupon she thinks: "Aladdin!" He now writes an opera with that title, composing both lyrics and music, and rehearses it with the orchestra—and has it performed with himself in the lead role. The sounds and tones of the work "subdued all listeners and seized them with a rapture that could not rise higher when he [Aladdin] reached for the lamp of fortune that was embraced by the song of the spirits" (383). The cheering at this finale pours down upon Peer, and in this moment of triumph, he collapses, dead to the world.

We can understand that Peer is positioned between two women: the pharmacist's daughter, who plays Juliet in the provincial Shakespeare performance, and the baroness, who inspires the Aladdin opera. The pharmacist's daughter represents the petite bourgeoisie as temptation with the prospect of perdition. In Peer's feverish dream, she reveals herself to him as hollow in her back, profligate. The baroness, on the other hand, representing the aristocracy, is the one who throws him the laurel wreath, is the one who "like a spirit of beauty" leads the cheering at his triumph.

But the moment of triumph is also the moment of death. At the end Peer is called "more fortunate than millions" (384). He is spared the struggle to hold on to his luck, and possibly also for running his head into a wall in an attempt to transform the platonic relationship to a life together. Artistic fortune has its price: it doesn't simply allow itself by magic to be reconciled with a bourgeois married life. This is Andersen's version of what Georg Brandes a few decades later was to call aristocratic radicalism. The great artist is his era's seeing-eye dog.

Hans Christian Andersen's novel, as well as the main character's opera, are situated in the wake of Oehlenschläger's famous drama, in the cultural tradition established by that work. As is known, *Aladdin* appeared in the second volume of *Poetiske Skrifter* (*Poetic Writings*), as an Oriental-sanguine counterpart to the Nordic-melancholy saga pastiche, *Vaulundurs Saga.* That piece became the unavoidable lifelong assignment for the golden era's writers and artists. It taught that nature's cheerful son is as a matter of course granted happiness, but must achieve an awareness of "the ethical dimension of his task" in order to hold on to or recover it, should it be lost. "Not until after manly fight / is its full value appreciated by the owner", is it written of the lamp.[7]

Within the Aladdin figure, we can find the very core of the romantic conceptual structure, which ingeniously and organically combines philosophies of nature, personality, and aesthetics. This is brought about through the recognition that one and the same force—or spirit, as it was called at the time—flows through all of creation, though with different strengths. Schelling's well-known formulation—spirit in nature sleeps in the stone, dreams in the plant, awakens in the animal, becomes conscious in man and reaches fulfilment in the artist— beautifully illustrates this organic thinking. Its dynamic quality is also significant: everything strives for a *higher* consciousness. Man does so insofar as a seed is planted within him, which his lifelong duty is to bring to full fruition, just as an acorn is invested with the potential that can guide its growth toward becoming the most magnificent oak tree. It is called culture,—becoming cultivated and unfolding one's inherent possibilities in their pathway toward the idea. The artist, the genius, differs from ordinary people in that he consciously aims for the very source of the divine power which flows through nature and human life. When taken to its logical conclusion, Romantic philosophy is a philosophy of identity. "To embrace everything, that is love", wrote Oehlenschläger in *Sanct Hansaften-Spil* (*Midsummer Night's Play*). And in *Jesu Christi gientagne Liv i den aarlige Natur* (*The Life of Jesus Christ Symbolized in the Seasons*) Simon Peter comes to the realization that "taken in itself everything is nothing, but taken as a whole everything is everything". The mystical raises itself up to and dissolves itself into the mythic.

In the framework of a philosophy of identity, the hero can be recognized by his purposeful, exuberant growth. He is like a tree that grows up into the sky without losing connection to its roots. The ultimate hero is the great artist.

In the moment of triumph and of death, Lucky Peer undoubtedly experiences identity with the divine, with the world of the idea. But it is worth noticing that his opera does not follow Aladdin's story to the very end. It breaks off at exactly that point where he takes hold of the lamp in the underground cave. The story continues. With the lamp, Aladdin acquires the power to create a palace and win the princess, Gulnare. But it should also be noted that he becomes careless with the lamp, so that Noureddin gets hold of it,—after which he loses everything again. At one point, his spirits are so low that suicide appears to him as the only possibility. But at that very moment, there emerges within him another and higher nature, and he gets the strength to take up the battle, first with Hindbad, and later with his true counterpart, the brooding Noureddin. Out of that development, there emerges a ripened hero with his luck intact, but in a purified and ennobled form, as though spirit were added to it. Ripeness is all, as Shakespeare said.

THE CHILDLIKE HERO

Materially, **Lucky Peer** draws in several ways upon Hans Christian Andersen's so-called **Levnedsbog** (**Life Book**), his first autobiography, covering the period 1805-31, and written in 1832, that is before the great journey he undertook in 1833-34, a freer, fresher, more ingenuous and less elaborate work than the subsequent autobiographies.[8] The explicit purpose of the project is to seek clarity about himself. Although he finds his own personality or character "quite inexplicable", he nevertheless feels "that an invisible, loving hand guides all things", and "that life itself is a grand and wonderful poem" (6). Is it a hero we now see extricating himself from his infant state? And if so: a hero on the stage of life? The **Life Book** contains formulations which in fact suggest just that. As a child, he reads biographies: "[. . .] my imagination for adventure was awakened, I thought of life itself as an adventure and looked forward to appearing in it myself as a hero" (42). More and more, he relates his own life to the portrayals of heroic life in the books he reads. He decides, "just like the heroes in the many adventure stories I had read to get out—all alone—into the world" (49), that is, to the capital. Once again, however, specifically mentioning that the good Lord will see to it that things go as they should. Also when Weyse raises money and Siboni promises singing lessons, it is God who gets the credit, but Andersen is in no way surprised: "that's the way I had imagined it, and in all novels and stories the hero succeeded in the end" (62). In the end! But the year is 1819 and Andersen has just barely arrived in Copenhagen. Subsequently, and especially after his deportation to Slagelse, "heroic places" will be few and far between, while those places where he will need comforting by God and motherly ladyfriends, come one after another. He was given comfort, for example, during his visits to the Wulff family at Amalienborg. He cites from his own journal: "Oh God, this is just like Aladdin, I am also sitting in the castle and looking down. God Almighty! No, you will not abandon me" (135). The reference here is to the *final* monologue in Oehlenschläger's work; Andersen would gladly have skipped over the difficult balance sheets of existence. Later, when Meisling's lessons as well as Ludvig Müller's preparatory training for the degree examination were well behind him, he made the acquaintance of the Læssøe family.

> On many an evening, I could completely become as a child in their home. I became natural just because I did not feel shy and knew that my errors and spontaneous remarks would never be weighed without their letting the good tip the scale in my favour. While other people tried to turn me into a man of the world, they appreciated my curious, childlike character.
>
> (198f)

One can wonder why Hans Christian Andersen develops this autobiographical description at such an early point in his life. Probably above all for the purpose of legitimizing himself in relation to culture and its purveyors within the Copenhagen elite, whom he had approached, and who had in a sense invested in him,—for the purpose of giving an impression of his inner riddle, which could explain that the goal of becoming cultivated had not fully been achieved because his gift was of a most unusual nature. For that reason, the autobiography's central and most moving section becomes the one on the five accursed years—Meisling's compulsory lessons in Slagelse and finally in Helsingør.

THE LIFE'S FAIRY TALE HERO

The Fairy Tale of My Life is next on the program![9] What has been said up to this point about the artist hero and about the way the 19th Century's idea of the hero was shaped by the entire Romantic philosophy of personality and focus on culture, leads us to the question: isn't the fairy tale of life essentially Hans Christian Andersen's proposal of a contemporary hagiography? In the history of literary genres, that word refers to portrayals designed to present a person's life and deeds in so convincing a manner, that the Pope will be moved to declare the person a saint. It was not of course up to the budding saint himself—of whom it was also required that he be dead—to write the hagiography. The point is that hagiographic portrayals are written with a specific purpose in mind, and this in turn accounts for the genre's significant influence on the biographical and thereby also the autobiographical tradition in European literature. Johannes Jørgensen writes about the holy Francis of Assisi and Georg Brandes of the unholy François de Voltaire, because they want to unfold an ideal of personality,—and both are, by the way, also writers of *auto*biographies, in which they model themselves on their heroes. In the same way, Hans Christian Andersen has a task to accomplish with his autobiographical works, especially with *The Fairy Tale of My Life,* which begins with the well-known passage:

> My life is a beautiful fairy-tale, so eventful has it been and wondrous happy. Even if, when I was a boy and went forth into the world poor and friendless, a good fairy had met me and said, "Choose thy own course through life and the object for which thou wilt strive, and then, according to the development of thy mind, and as reason requires, I will guide and defend thee," my fate could not have been more wisely and happily directed. The story of my life will tell the world what it tells me:—There is a loving God who directs all things for the best.
>
> (*A,* 13)

At its conclusion, the work circles back upon itself in the following way:

> The fairy-tale of my life right up to the present hour is thus laid before me so eventful, so beautiful and so full of comfort. There came good even out of evil and joy out of pain; it is a poem more full of profound thoughts than I could possibly have written. I feel that I am a child of good fortune. So many of the noblest and best men and women of my day have dealt with me kindly and openly, and it is but seldom that my confidence in Man has been disappointed. Even the heavy days of bitterness contain the germs of blessings. All the injustice I thought I suffered and every hand which was heavy in the way in which it influenced my development brought good results after all. / As we progress towards God all pain and bitterness are dispersed, and what is beautiful is left behind. We see it like a rainbow against dark clouds. May men be mild in their judgement of me as I am in my judgement of them; and I am sure they will be. The story of a life has something of the sacredness of a confession for all noble and good men. I have told the fairy-tale of my life here openly and full of confidence as though I were sitting among cherished friends.
>
> (*A,* 346)

These concluding words are dated April 2, 1855. "Right up to the present hour" means therefore quite literally: 'in the first 50 years of my life'. Here Andersen is taking stock of his life. It is thanks to the good Lord, who guides everything for the best, together with a strongly purposeful personal commitment, that the 50th birthday does not appear to be a random pause,—for immediately before that, Andersen places a kind of acknowledgment for Grímur Thomsen's review of his collected writings. In his eyes, this discussion of his work becomes the proof that the long and arduous battle on his home grounds against every kind of small-mindedness is now finally bearing fruit. The period of rejection is over, the recognition and victories throughout Europe—which peaked in 1847—now finally makes an impact on the attitude of Danish critics. Listen carefully and notice the points that are so deftly emphasized:

Just at this present time, as I am about to complete my fiftieth year and as my **Collected Works** are being published, the *Danish Monthly Review of Literature* has published a review of it by Mr. Grímur Thomsen. [. . .] It seems almost that Heaven wished me to end this chapter of my life by seeing the fulfilment of H. C. Ørsted's words to me in those heavy days when no one appreciated me. My native land has given me the cherished bouquet of recognition and encouragement.

(*A,* 346)

It is in this way that Hans Christian Andersen organizes his life for posterity,—as a divinely guided path, along which hardships purify him in his journey toward the stars. The trials have a meaning, when viewed in retrospect from the present summit. Olympus makes a good blotting-pad, when the days of rejection are enumerated and forgiveness dispensed.

Taking stock of one's life has for all good and noble souls something of the power and sanctity of confession, as Andersen sees it; in this way he himself justifies our inscribing of this life's fairy tale in a sacred context. Glory be to God!

Andersen also makes a claim concerning cultivation. In our progress toward God beauty arises, while bitterness melts away.

It is however something of a problem that what is most decisive comes to Andersen from without. That Thomsen writes in warm and friendly tones about the fairy tales and virtually fulfills the prophecy with which H. C. Ørsted comforted the poet when he was criticized for his first fairy tales, cannot really be compared to what Aladdin experiences when a higher nature emerges from deep within him and prevents him from taking his own life in the Persian river. Aladdin is formed from within, Andersen gains recognition from without. It is the surrounding world that changes, not his own personality. It is the people who increasingly come to him in an open and loving way, not he who makes peace with existence.

He repeats this manoeuvre in 1869, when he completes the continuation of the fairy tale of his life, which he penned for the American edition of his writings. This time, the obvious culmination was the festivity at which he was proclaimed honorary citizen of Odense in December 1867. When he was approached, Andersen had proposed that they wait until September 4, 1869, the fiftieth anniversary of his departure for Copenhagen. In this case, he did not however get his way, but the proposal was presumably nothing more than an off-hand remark. After the celebration itself, but before his departure, he took part in the Lahn Foundation's annual festival. Some fuss was made over Andersen on that occasion as well. "It was as if one sunbeam after another shone into my heart, it was more than I could bear! In

such a moment one clings to God as in the bitterest hour of sorrow" (**B,** 569). And once outside of the city, Andersen finally realized what honor, joy and delight "God had endowed upon me through my native town". And further on, in conclusion:

> The greatest, the highest blessing I could attain was now mine. Now for the first time could I fully and devoutly thank my God and pray: "Leave me not when the days of trial come!"

(**B,** 569)

This final remark is essentially concerned with the future. Although allegedly his heart could not contain so much happiness, there was no occurrence of what Andersen allowed to happen to Lucky Peer a few years later:

> A fire rushed through him; his heart swelled as never before [. . .]. Dead in the moment of triumph, like Sophocles at the Olympian games, like Thorvaldsen in the theater during Beethoven's symphony. An artery in his heart had burst, and as by a flash of lightning his days here were ended, ended without pain, ended in an earthly triumph, in the fulfilment of his mission on earth. Lucky Peer! More fortunate than millions!

(383f)

Andersen spared his hero all tribulations. His own heart sighed but didn't burst when he left the scene of his triumph (which marked the fulfilment of the prophecy that Odense would some day be lit up in his honor)—on the way to awaiting trials.

If the truth be told, and it can be if the journals and letters are allowed to supplement the autobiography, then trials were an integral part of the poet's life. Some years ago, in *Flugten i sproget* (*Flight into Language*), Torben Brostrøm and Jørn Lund argued that it was precisely there, in language, that the poet occasionally overcame the experience of loneliness and coldness that came increasingly with fame. They write somewhere[10] about

> the realization that came in the final years of his life, that artistic growth was won at the expense of human development, that fame had not only cost blood, sweat and tears, but had left him with a disheartening sense of coldness, which his analytical acuity prevented him from repressing, and which he had to face head on— just before the end came.

It is Klaus P. Mortensen who sharpened the two writers'—and our—grasp of this in *Svanen og Skyggen* (*The Swan and the Shadow*), which as the title also indicates, tells "the story of young Andersen".[11] The evidence suggests that as his literary achievement was eventually honored by general European and Danish recognition, the poet understood with ever increasing clarity that success had cost a terrible price: emotional coldness.

The final chapter in Brostrøm and Lund's book is entitled "Language and poetry. The unfulfilled dream". Here, the obvious connection between *The Improvisatore* and *Lucky Peer* is drawn, in the following way:[12]

> [Andersen's] drive for poetic unfolding was also a dream of personal unfolding. He wanted both to create art and to redeem it. The improvisatore at the gateway to the literary production and Lucky Peer at the close of it, can accomplish anything, reach everyone around them, interpret shared experiences as well as individual, bound impulses and memories, see poetic possibilities and create in the here and now a kind of expression which is in harmony with eternity, with the universal poetic primitive force.

The Improvisatore was written by Hans Christian Andersen in continuation of the journey he undertook to become cultivated, during which he paradoxically and fortunately liberated himself from (or at least kept a certain distance from) the imposed and hard won cultivation. In the novel, he goes so far as to let the hero, Antonio, prevail both artistically and matrimonially. That was just before he wrote *The Tinder Box*, which he brought off with improvisational ease.

The Realization and the Price

Hans Christian Andersen produced essentially two sets of heroes: the popular (represented here by Clod-Hans and the Soldier) and the literary (represented by Lucky Peer and Hans Christian himself). His popular heroes pass their tests and win their princesses and live happily ever after. The literary heroes attune their spiritual powers to an exalted level, but have to pay dearly for that. As will be recalled, it isn't the learned man who marries the princess in the fairy tale, *The Shadow*, but precisely those shadowy properties he represses, and which ultimately kill him.

Though with social and cultural odds against him, Hans Christian Andersen achieves happiness, but specifically in the form of success: being cheered by the public, outer appearances. What he loses along the way is the popular hero's drive, and what he ultimately can only rave about is Lucky Peer's uncompromising spiritual aristocraticism. It is in the interval that, with our Lord as his guide, and thanks to an inherent stubborn tenacity, he achieves the coveted goal, *recognition*.[13]

Notes

1. "Clod-Hans", quoted from *The Complete Andersen*, translated by Jean Hersholt, illustrated by Fritz Kredel, New York 1952, Section II, pp. 175-79 [entitled "Clumsy Hans"]. (Original Danish version: "Klods-Hans", *Historier*, illustrated by Vilhelm Pedersen, 1855, pp. 114-19; cf. *H. C. Andersens Eventyr*, ed. by Erik Dal, et al., Vol. 2: *1843-55*, 1964, pp. 291-94, and Vol. 7: *Kommentar*, 1990, pp. 162-63.)

2. Cf. Jens Aage Doctor, "H. C. Andersens karneval", in *Andersen og Verden*, ed. by Johan de Mylius, et al., 1993, pp. 410-19. (The author's doctoral thesis: *Shakespeares karneval*, 1994.)

3. The version in question can be found in *Fortællerstil*, ed. by Kristian Kjær and Henrik Schovsbo, 1975, pp. 85-86. Jens Kamp was a Danish folklorist (1845-1900).

4. "The Tinder Box", quoted from *The Complete Andersen*, Section I, pp. 1-7. (Original Danish version: "Fyrtøiet", *Eventyr, fortalte for Børn*, Vol. 1:1, 1835, pp. 1-16; cf. *H. C. Andersens Eventyr*, Vol. 1: *1835-42*, 1963, pp. 23-29, and Vol. 7: *Kommentar*, 1990, pp. 19-23.)

5. *Lucky Peer* is quoted from *The Complete Andersen*, Section III, pp. 316-84. (Original Danish version: *Lykke-Peer*, 1870, 183 pp.; cf. *Romaner og Rejseskildringer*, Vol. 5, 1944, pp. 241-317.) The American edition is, despite the title, complete only as far as the fairy tales are concerned, but Hersholt may have considered Andersen's shortest novel to be rather like a fairy tale. (An English translation prior to Hersholt's appeared in *Scribner's Monthly*, Vol. 1, 1871.)—Cf. Johan de Mylius's doctoral thesis, *Myte og roman. H. C. Andersens romaner mellem romantik og realisme*, 1981, pp. 210-25 (chapter entitled "Kunst som myte").

6. The portrayal of Peer's stay with the Gabriel family can be compared with the portrayal in the so-called *Levnedsbog* (see note 8) of Hans Christian Andersen's stay with the Meisling family. Mrs. Meisling is cited in that work—as a prelude to the description of her seduction attempt—for her exclamation: "This is no real he-man" (131).

7. *Aladdin eller Den forunderlige Lampe*, ed. by Jens Kr. Andersen, 1978, p. 281 (and preface p. 7). (Cf. *Aladdin or The Wonderful Lamp*, translated by Henry Meyer, 1968, p. 222: "To grasp it dauntlessly it is your part / to fight courageously. First then you are / able to hold its value in regard".)

8. The page references in this section are to *H. C. Andersens Levnedsbog*, ed. by H. Topsøe-Jensen, 1962 (3rd impr., 1988).

9. The page references in this section are to [A] *The Fairy Tale of My Life*, translated by W. Glyn Jones, illustrated by Niels Larsen Stevns, 1954, and [B] *The Story of My Life*, translated by Horace E. Scudder, New York 1871 (= Author's Edition, Vol. 7); Scudder's translation has been slightly revised. (Cf. the Danish standard edition: *Mit Livs Eventyr*, Vols. 1-2, ed. by H. Topsøe-Jensen and H. G. Olrik, 1951 (2nd impr., 1975).)

10. Torben Brostrøm & Jørn Lund, *Flugten i sproget. H. C. Andersens udtryk,* 1991, p. 138 (in the chapter entitled "Norgesturen", by Jørn Lund).

11. Klaus P. Mortensen, *Svanen og Skyggen—historien om unge Andersen,* 1989.

12. *Flugten i sproget,* p. 155. (The chapter was written by Jørn Lund.)

13. This [essay] was presented as a paper on two occasions: first at a Hans Christian Andersen symposium held at the university in St. Petersburg on May 17, 1996, as part of the Danish-Russian festival of children's culture organized by the Danish Literature Information Center (DLIC); and subsequently at The Second International Hans Christian Andersen Conference, held at the H. C. Andersen Center, Odense University, from July 28 to August 3, 1996. The Danish version appeared in *H. C. Andersen i Rusland,* ed. by Aage Jørgensen, et al., 1997, pp. 37-48 (and in *BUM/Børne-og ungdoms-litteratur magasinet,* Vol. 14:1-2, 1996, pp. 32-38). English translation by Richard Raskin with the support of the Danish Research Council for the Humanities.

Nancy Easterlin (essay date October 2001)

SOURCE: Easterlin, Nancy. "Hans Christian Andersen's Fish out of Water." *Philosophy and Literature* 25, no. 2 (October 2001): 251-77.

[*In the following essay, Easterlin applies the theories of Darwinian criticism and evolutionary psychology to a reading of Andersen's "The Little Mermaid."*]

I

Now that Darwinian literary criticism is on the horizon, the natural human tendency to codify manifests itself in calls to summarize succinctly what such an approach entails. Though clarity is always to be praised, bioevolutionary critics need to guard against the reductiveness that has beleaguered attempts at a scientifically grounded literary criticism since the early twentieth century; most especially, we should think twice about limiting the interpretation of complex and varied works to selected sociobiological themes divorced from other biocultural considerations. David Sloan Wilson makes much the same point to students of evolution when he quotes Celia Heyes in a recent review of *Evolutionary Psychology,* David Buss's new textbook: "When I first encountered the term 'evolutionary psychology,' I thought it referred to the study of how mind and behavior evolved. But I was mistaken. In current usage, 'evolutionary psychology' refers exclusively to research on human mentality and behavior, motivated by a very specific, nativist-adaptationist interpretation of how evolution operates."[1]

If, as D. S. Wilson suggests, evolutionary psychology thus narrowly defined threatens to produce a limited understanding of human mind and behavior and, in the process, fragment the discipline of psychology further, how much less potentially productive is such an approach for those of us whose central objects of study, cultural artifacts, are as the products of behavior even further removed from the study of mind? Leda Cosmides and John Tooby are most explicit about the falsity of assuming that psychological adaptations *determine* behavior. This being so, it seems impossible that such adaptations could determine the *meaning* of artworks, which are themselves the products of complex human behaviors. As I hope this discussion of Hans Christian Andersen's **"Little Mermaid"** will demonstrate, an approach to aesthetics strictly following the lead of evolutionary psychology as currently defined, while supplying valuable general insights about the motives for artistic behaviors and the cognitive processes engaged in them, cannot by itself inform us about the *meaning* of individual artworks. This is a crucial issue, since interpretation is the fundamental pursuit of scholars in fields like mine, literary studies.

Putting the question of interpretive frutifulness aside for the moment, it can be said unequivocally that criticism that fails to be sensitive to mutation and change is not properly Darwinian. Evolutionary psychology and sociobiology themselves maintain that our psychic architecture is comprised of domain-specific competences; the result, as E. O. Wilson points out, is that the human mind is not designed to understand reality but is instead an instrument for survival and reproduction.[2] "Natural selection," says Michael Ruse, "works in a gerry-building fashion, making do with what it has at hand."[3] Though our various evolved competencies cannot be radically dissonant if the organism is to survive, neither are they logically integrated, neatly interlocking "modules." Under some environmental conditions, specific adaptations or epigenetic rules are not likely to produce a competitive advantage while other very different adaptations certainly will, and hence the flexibility of the organism ensures its survival. If, for instance, I place my coffee mug down on my desk and at that exact moment two cars collide on the street outside, familiarity with my environment militates against invocation of the causal rule, even though such a rule is incontrovertibly part of our adapted psychology.[4] Knowing, then, that we share an evolved psychic architecture whose patient excavation, so to speak, will result in a progressively better defined concept of human nature, and knowing too that the behavior of human beings as writers as well as other kinds of agents varies under divergent environmental conditions, Darwinian criticism should be sensitive to the complex relationship between individual adaptations, the total array of adaptations, subjective cognitive processes, and environmental circumstances that give literary works enduring significance. In contemplating literary meaning, as with aesthetics, we should be mindful that *epigenesis* is not simply the instantiation of *epigenetic rules*.[5] Ideally, literary interpretation should be informed by the evolution of mind, behavior, and culture, to modify Heyes's phrase, and speculation about the formal or thematic role of ancient adaptations in literature is only part of that process.

Since about 1950, attempts to explain the structure, content, and function of the arts according to biologically based psychology have yielded a variety of insights that might at first blush seem contradictory, though in the long run the seeming contradictions themselves direct us not to the invalidity of each separate insight but remind us of the piecemeal, domain-specific nature of our adapted psychology. Does art satisfy our desire for form and pattern, or does it disrupt default orientations, providing a safe arena for experimental thought and virtual action? Does it feed our need for novelty? In literature particularly, does the content derive from ancient adaptations that frame a basic structure of human motives? Do stories strengthen social groups through both the reaffirmation and opportune transgression of boundaries?[6]

So far, the broadest general thesis about the evolution of art is supplied by Ellen Dissanayake, who proposes that art attests to a general human propensity for "making special," one that manifests itself variously and develops historically in different areas of human endeavor.[7] One advantage of Dissanayake's hypothesis is that it enables us to acknowledge the validity of the foregoing insights without requiring that we choose between them. The potential disadvantage of Dissanayake's approach, that it is too broad to result in a concrete, developed definition of art, disappears if we perceive two of its important implications: (1) that art, as an evolving rather than a fixed phenomenon, is not, in fact, amenable to precise definition; and (2) that, paradoxically, exploration of separate modes of "making special" from a evolutionary perspective will in the long run contribute to our general understanding of the function of art. Some insights about the adapted mind simply have striking implications for a particular aesthetic medium but not for others. If, for instance, as part of our adapted psychology we are largely disposed to construe events causally, our attraction to novelty and our other psychic attunements at the same time enable us to recognize the unrelatedness of some consecutive events. While this understanding of our basic psychology has evident bearing on literary narrative, in which the causal rule provides the adapted foundation of plot construction but which, throughout literary history, is periodically subverted in literature, it is far less promising for the analysis of other arts, visual art being the most obvious counterexample here.

For me, Dissanayake's concept, holding as it does that art is the product of a generalized and broadly exercised impulse, suggests that we should keep in mind the complex relationship between psychology and artifact and at the same time acknowledge that there is no single approach or method that all bioevolutionary or biocultural critics should now adopt. Given the complexity of art behaviors and objects, of which literary behaviors and works form a subset, no single model or approach will do, since we may legitimately engage with the process of literary study from a variety of different vantage points. If, at one end of the spectrum, the empirical studies championed recently by Joseph Carroll and carried out by David Miall and D. S. Wilson, David C. Near, and Ralph R. Miller lead us further toward a knowledge of writer psychology and neurological processes, at the other a broad-based understanding of the conditions of human life can lead to a speculative criticism that reawakens us to the connection between words and bodily existence.[8] Given the complex array of factors that influence a final literary work, a recognition of the role of speculation seems not only advisable but essential to the practice of informed interpretation.[9]

Since fairytales are highly patterned, exhibiting a striking number of formulaic features, a literary fairytale such as **"The Little Mermaid"** stands as a useful example of what we might, in such an elementary genre, expect to be straightforward: the relationship between dominant innate propensities, environmental (e.g., cultural and historical) conditions, subjective development, and final artifact. On inspection, however, we see that even a superficially simple artwork results from enormous complexity. Major features of Andersen's story, including the mermaid herself, who descends from a rich genealogy of water deities, as well as the essential form and content of fairytale plots, are tied to central concerns in human nature. These features indeed constitute a substrate of dominant natural preoccupations and orientations which are manifested thematically and formally. The themes of childhood vulnerability, sexual maturation, pair-bonding, reproduction, and man's relation to nature, for instance, all arise from fundamental adaptive concerns, just as formal tendencies toward narrative and binary construction arise from adapted patterns of mental organization. More importantly, however, all of the main features are linked by their implications about power—its development, acquisition, abuse, or control—and by the characteristic ambivalence borne of the fundamentally conflictive nature of human existence. Nevertheless, a reading or interpretation of Andersen's tale cannot be offered on the basis of these themes alone. The literary fairytale, which probably began with the transcription of wonder tales for the middle class and aristocracy in the early Middle

Ages, developed in step with modernization and enjoyed a rich variety of influences. By the late seventeeth century, French writers beginning with Madame [Marie-Catherine] d'Aulnoy began crafting their tales to the salon culture of the times, and it was thus changes in class structure and education that made possible the institutionalization of the literary fairytale over the course of the next century and a half.[10] Written by an author who was immersed both in oral folk culture and literary romanticism and who was encouraged to take imaginative license with what was becoming a firmly established written genre, **"The Little Mermaid"** departs dramatically from some conventions and themes of oral tale traditions, and in so doing counsels against too-hasty identification of specific psychic adaptations as the determinants of *meaning* in literary works.

Careful consideration of Andersen's tale reveals, in fact, that environmental conditions—socially and economically, the development of industrialization and the ensuing movement out of rural communities; culturally, the collapse of the enlightenment and the consequent development of literary romanticism—combined with the similar trajectory of Andersen's own "fairytale" life from humble rural origins to cosmopolitan fame crucially affect the meaning of the story, bringing to the fore not sexual power or threat but our characteristic ambivalence regarding others and communal belonging. In sum, in the service of the epigenetic rule of causal organization (i.e., narrativity), the ambivalence we feel toward others and its corollary, the experience of isolation, have been selected, so to speak, from the biopsychological substrate of the story by the environment of rapidly changing nineteenth-century post-agrarian Europe, and the literary memes that concretize this ambivalence are likewise selected over those that served a simpler world and its stories of robust action and optimistically reorganized social relations.

II

Brett Cooke's recent essay on Rusalka, the mermaid figure in Hungarian opera, provides an instructive example of how environmental factors determine the significance of a specific symbol, constructing it culturally, as it were, from the ground of our adapted psychology. Identifying in Kvapil and Dvořák's mermaid operas the sexual constraint of lower-class women as a central theme borne of the evolved psychic mechanisms underlying patriarchal behavior, Cooke maintains that the half-human status of the woman is a sign of degradation, and that, finally, it is just the patriarchal bias reproduced in multiple constraints on the mermaid that so fuels the human imagination.[11]

While surely a central adaptive concern over reproductive resources and an ensuing preoccupation with female power, signified in the reproductive fertility of maiden figures, motivates our interest in the mermaid, it is one thing to conclude, as I do, that for this reason the appearance of the apparently fertile young woman in any artwork is an emotional vector and another to assume that her deployment determines *a fixed meaning or meanings* in a realized work of art. In any given case, there may be synchronicity of the mechanism of emotional arousal and semantic content, as Cooke demonstrates in these operas, or there may not. But curiously, if we assume that such unconscious mechanisms (i.e., latent contents) provide a universal key to the interpretation of specific works, evolutionary literary criticism will become nothing more than a latter-day Freudianism, performing its ritual unveilings of psychic secrets in hunter-gatherer dress.

In fact, an overview of the mermaid and like mythical creatures supports the view that the adapted mind, which has an assortment of strategies for dealing with reality, does not give birth in consciousness to emblems echoing discrete concerns. Closer inspection shows that the mermaid and her kinfolk evoke a shifting constellation of concerns, not a fixed set of meanings, a finding in keeping, I believe, with E. O. Wilson's assertion that meaning is produced by the linking of neural networks in the process of scenario building.[12] The human mind, not a machine in any sense, operates kaleidoscopically, as under certain environmental conditions various fragments are cast onto the glass of consciousness—colorful triangles, stars, and shards, torsos and fishtails and strands of hair, mingle, drift, and coalesce, and through the revolutions of culture symbolic patterns periodically emerge. Thus, if the maidenliness of the mermaid derives from our interest in her imminent fruitfulness, and if her animal qualities reveal our strong interest in animals as a salient environmental factor capable of harming or helping us, it is nevertheless the *culture,* including especially in the consideration of literature the totality of the individual work, that establishes the *meaning* of any given manifestation of the mythical creature.

The distinction between underlying adaptive mechanisms and the semantic content of cultural icons and artifacts resembles Carl Jung's definition of archetype and archetypal image in general outline—even if, in practice, Jung himself often went against his better insights and conflated the two.[13] In Jung's notion of the collective unconscious, which seems to be the intuitive precursor of evolutionary psychology, "archetypes are not determined as regards their content, but only as regards their form and then only to a very limited degree. . . . A primordial image is determined as to its content only when it has become conscious and is therefore filled out with the material of conscious experience."[14] If, as Robert Storey argues, archetypal images emerge from chief experiential nodalities and are all marked by the ambivalence of competing interests, the maiden image would be thus marked: "she is the male's companion in her benevolent aspect; when, Circe-like, she binds him to watchful domesticity, she is *la belle dame sans merci*" (p. 79). Archetypally, in other words, the maiden is at least dual, and cultural circumstances may push representation in one or another direction or toward ambiguity, or may bring other themes to the fore that overshadow or mitigate the significance of the maiden image. *Meaning,* in short, is a product of the archetypal image and its context, not of the unconscious archetypes—not, in this case, of the maiden before she is represented. While the distinction between archetype and semantically laden content warns us of the protean nature of archetypal images, it is furthermore crucial to remember that the maiden is only one portion of the mermaid, whose animal nature incorporates other archetypal concerns.

The protean nature of symbols and their meanings is reinforced by a glimpse at the mermaid and her relatives throughout cultural history. At first blush the mermaid might seem to suggest a relatively consistent and local lore, a distinct set of characteristics: she is near-mortal and lives underwater, but comes to the surface from time to time; she has a scaly tail, and often blue eyes and blond hair; she is usually seen sitting on rocks, ledges, and reefs, but sometimes swimming off-shore she holds a comb and mirror, or sometimes a magical object—usually a cap, veil, or shawl; she is frequently capable of self-transformation, and she is fond of singing and dancing (the latter, obviously, in her transformed-to-human condition).[15] Myths about her include her desire for a soul, her powers of prophecy and wish-granting, her vengeance when thwarted, and her sojourns with mortal men when her magic object is taken. These sojourns, however long, are *always* temporary, as the mermaid inevitably retrieves her magical object and returns to the sea.

Mermaid lore is additionally related to stories of seal-folk, most commonly recounted in Scandinavia and the parts of the British Isles where the Norse landed in the Early Christian Era and Middle Ages. It is not surprising that seafaring peoples would associate seals, with their sensitive, anthropoid faces, with human beings, and among Western Celts and Scandinavians a variety of beliefs make this connection. Seals figure as fallen angels condemned to live in the sea but capable of assuming human shape on land; as humans under a spell; as the souls of those who have drowned at sea; as humans that have sinned; and as the descendants of humans who have committed suicide at sea. Significantly, all of this lore, which took shape under Christianity, reflects its pronounced dualism and its attendant beliefs in sin and redemption and the immortality of the soul. This influence, apparently absent from the operas Cooke analyzes, figures centrally in Andersen's tale and in the medieval Danish ballads that he knew so well.

The mermaid's genealogy, moreover, extends well beyond this constellation of myths, for her fish tail marks her kinship with all water deities and spirits. Five thousand years ago, the Babylonians worshipped the fish-tailed god Ea/Oannes (sometimes depicted as human with a fish cloak, instead of fish-tailed), and myths of fish-tailed gods and water-dragons with prophetic and self-transformative powers are part of Indian, Chinese, and Japanese culture. In India, the lesser water nymphs and fairies loved singing and dancing and were prone to luring and seducing men, thus sharing some of the characteristics of the modern mermaid. Some other mythological sea beings and deities, such as Poseidon and the sirens, were not originally associated with water and piscine anatomy (the sirens were originally birds), indicating that divine power and womanly allure became combined with the power and promise of the sea when ancient cultures undertook maritime war and trade.

The mermaid, then, in whom many believed up through the eighteenth century, is a scaled-down descendant of these powerful water deities, a being midway between the supernatural and the human, and midway again between the human and the animal. Indeed, perhaps the emergence of the mermaid proper in European lore in tandem with the spread of Christianity attests to her essential belatedness—she is, in other words, a sign of disintegrating folk beliefs held for a number of centuries in tension with Christian mythology. If this inference is correct, then the northern European mermaid was always marked with the outsiderness that Andersen would so productively exploit. By the mid-nineteenth century, while on the one hand Matthew Arnold and perhaps Andersen himself consciously adopted merfolk as emblems of lost belief and experiential unity, on the other the mermaid had at once become literally manifest and attendantly deformed and shrunken, as fakes, often manufactured with monkey's torsos—apparently the Japanese were expert in their production—graced the circus and sideshow tents.

Both the mermaid proper and other related mythical beings have two common attributes: they are associated with water, and they are either part human or capable of temporary transformation to a human state. Studies in habitat selection indicate that water is positively correlated with emotional pleasure, its appearance in the landscape thus evoking a response that operates toward selective advantage.[16] In nearly all origin myths, creation comes from water, and many cultures have specific rituals and beliefs about its healing properties. Thus, our physiological attunement to the environment attracts us unconsciously to water, of which we are largely constituted and for which we have a great need. Bodies of water also contain and attract potential sources of nourishment, animals that live in and around them for the purposes of their own survival. While a flat plane in the environment produces emotional neutrality and even boredom, water as a sign of these potential advantages as well as an equal number of dangers provokes strong interest but, again, ambivalence. For it is also a potential place of death—a source of water-borne disease, the home of lethal and hidden creatures, the site of drowning, the origin of our identity and nonentity. Bodies of water are thus emotionally charged in the human psyche, and the mythical creatures who reside in them become variously inflected with their power, with their potent blend of threat and allure.

Jung asserts that in dreams water is the most common symbol for the unconscious and, if I understand him, his reasoning connects psychology with physiology: "water is earthy and tangible, it is also the fluid of the instinct-driven body . . . The unconscious is the psyche that reaches down from the daylight of mentally and morally lucid consciousness into the nervous system that for ages has been known as the 'sympathetic.' This does not govern perception and muscular activity like the cerebrospinal system, and thus control the environment; but, though functioning without sense organs, it maintains the balance of life and, through the mysterious paths of sympathetic excitation, not only gives us knowledge of the innermost life of other beings but also has an inner effect upon them."[17] If in dreams water is a sign of the unconscious, Jung's logic suggests that this is so only because of the isomorphism between the psyche and the body, whose fluidity connects it to the natural world. An image of resources, danger, mystery, and death, a universal and uniting element from which we are nevertheless ontologically distinct, water, like the maiden who embodies reproduction and therefore a wonderful and terrible power, is surely an omnipresent strange attractor of the human psyche.

And the sea, where the mermaids of maritime nations dwell, has special qualities: "Dwellers by the sea cannot fail to be impressed by the sight of its ceaseless ebb and flow, and are apt, on the principles of that rude philosophy of sympathy and resemblance which here engages our attention, to trace a subtle relation, a secret harmony, between its tides and the life of man, of animals, and of plants."[18] Unlike most inland waters, the sea is dynamic, apparently dictating with its ebb and flow, its own seeming life, the life of man, and so in Scandinavian mythology the waves themselves are divine. For inhabitants of seafaring cultures, the natural interest in and ambivalence toward water is exaggerated by environmental circumstance, and hence association with water carries a higher emotional charge (whether positive or negative) and melds in a psychologically coherent fashion with the maiden, who herself represents unity and life-giving reproduction or, alternatively, destruction.

If maidenliness and association with water, then, represent two glinting shards on the kaleidoscope's glass, both in themselves freighted with powerful yet shifting emotional charges, as they slide together they cohere in a being of mixed nature, half-animal and half-human, and in so doing come to embody yet another fundamental preoccupation with the relationship between the human and the natural. Like the dualistic depiction of the maiden, the human-natural dichotomy reflects the epigenetic rule of binary division or dyadic structure. Probably based in the self-other distinction and underlying much of human epistemology, cultural organization, and symbolism, binary thinking pervades human life yet functions ironically in dynamic relationship with the emotional ambivalences and cognitive ambiguities it was perhaps intended to resolve.[19] Since the origins of culture 10,000 years ago, humans have more and more "successfully" actualized the division between the human and the natural; but the awareness that this division fragments experience and, if accepted too fully, proves maladaptive because it is ultimately illusory, informs all our negotiations of this particularly problematic binary.

Myths and tales of animal transformation are one means of psychologically reconnecting what culture has worked hard to separate. In European fairytale, although the hero or heroine him/herself is human, the transformation of animals into humans and vice versa is ubiquitous, and generally represents, according to Max Luthi, the tendency of this genre to create an idealized whole by binding the human and natural worlds to one another.[20] Hedwig von Beit additionally suggests that transformation represents a mythic/holistic mode of primitive consciousness that was still to some degree prevalent during the development of the European fairytale in the Middle Ages. Even so, transformation, rather than being a pervasive feature of reality in the fairytale, is associated with curses and enchantment and therefore serves a more specialized function than in primitive culture. This specialized use of transformation signals a diminished belief in magic since primitive times and, correspondingly, a relative shift of attention to the profane world.[21]

In folklore, merfolk and seal-folk are frequently endowed with powers of transformation, and in this such stories bear witness to the psychic *recognition* that human and animal are part of a larger whole and, paradoxically but not illogically, the psychic *need* to knit the two into a more cohesive whole than the evidence of our senses indicates. Merfolk, indeed, being half-human, need not be capable of transformation to symbolize our ambivalent feelings for the natural world. Indeed, as a creature with a mixed ontology rather than metamorphic capabilities, the mermaid is an apt symbol of the individual who feels alien in either world, an obvious characteristic of Andersen's heroine in the tale to which I now turn.

III

This is how Andersen's story goes: The mermaid, the youngest of six daughters of the widower-Sea King, longs to go to the surface of the water and see the human world, a privilege allowed only at the age of fifteen. When she finally makes her first visit to the surface, she ends up saving the prince from a violent storm. Her fascination with the human world increased by this visit, she questions her grandmother and learns that humans have an immortal soul. In a deal with the sea witch, she trades her voice for legs and goes to live on land, becoming a favorite but not a lover of the prince, who does not know that she saved his life. She makes a second deal with the sea witch, requiring her to kill the prince on her wedding night; but when she can't do this she jumps into the sea and turns to sea foam, joining the little daughters of the air as they traverse the skies, performing good deeds and perhaps gaining immortal souls after several hundred years.[22]

Andersen's mermaid came to life in 1837, at a time when folk beliefs were on the wane, and it is thus not surprising that she lacks many, even most, of the characteristics of her mythological sea-sisters. She is not a siren, prophetess, or temptress; she has no special powers, including (woe betide her) powers of self-transformation. Indeed, if our attraction to the latent implications of mermaid figures is a product of our predisposition to attend to selectively advantageous but also dangerous potency, the character manifest in Andersen's tale is, by contrast, decidedly powerless and unfortunately harmless. She is depicted mostly in negative terms, for while she is not human she is defined by her desire to be so. She is consequently *other* and apart from the world to which she "naturally" belongs, the deep sea. However, the specific character of her otherness identifies her not, like the traditional mermaid, with the nonhuman mysteries of the universe, but paradoxically with human needs and desires. The story traces an important stage in her development, from child to maiden, and while she is morally good and innocent, her initiation into adulthood is marked by thoughtfulness and suffering, as she becomes progressively aware of the depths of her desires and the difficulty of fulfilling them. By contrast, the other characters in Andersen's story are one-dimensional types standard in the fairytale genre, so that, ironically, it is the mermaid's atypicality, combined with her relative complexity of character, that identifies her as the locus of humanity in the story.

Folk beliefs and traditions were all vitally alive in Odense at the turn of the nineteenth century and, although Andersen's father, a poor cobbler, was also a freethinker and man of some education, his mother was superstitious and nearly illiterate, as were her acquaintances.[23] When, at the age of fourteen, Andersen left Odense to seek his fame in the Danish Royal Theatre, a mission requiring him to take a boat between the islands of Funen and Zealand, his mother consoled herself that he would fly back to Odense as soon as he saw water. He didn't. Craigie relates tales of river men, one apparently inhabiting the waters of Odense, who take to themselves a child a year. Andersen's mother, who had tried to ward off her son's childhood illness with a mole's heart tied about his neck, could not have anticipated that the boy's desire for fame and fortune was evidently greater than his fear of the river man.

Danish ballads tells tales of merfolk of varying character, and with these Andersen was no doubt familiar. "Agnes [Agnete] and the Merman" was the basis of Andersen's verse drama *Agnete,* written in 1835, two years before **"The Little Mermaid."** This ballad tells of a human woman who willingly goes off with a merman, living with him for over eight years and bearing him seven sons. One day, she hears the church bells and asks her spouse for permission to go up to the church, which he grants. She then refuses to return; when the merman asks her to think of the children, especially the baby, she responds: "I think not of the grown ones, nor yet of the small / Of the baby in the cradle I'll think least of all."[24] So much for the mother-infant bond when the immortal soul is at stake—sociobiologically speaking, it is the presumed *unnaturalness* of her choice that constitutes the ballad's emotional power. In Matthew Arnold's version of this poem slightly more than a decade after Andersen's play, Margaret, the mother, is not without her sorrow, gazing out to the sea and searching for "the cold strange eyes of a little Mermaiden / And the gleam of her golden hair."[25] The source for "Agnes and the Merman" was a Slavic ballad that portrayed nature (personified in the merman) as a treacherous wooer, but through its adaptations to German and then to Danish it underwent a marked shift in attitude toward the merfolk, embodying in its sympathy for the merman's loss and powerlessness a nostalgia for waning folk beliefs in a culture in which Christian values had come to dominate. And Arnold's mid-century poem, adding another level of sociocultural understanding to the primal experience of loss, self-consciously reduplicates the elegiac and nostalgic mood of the original, for the grief of the "faithless" Margaret mirrors that of the abandoned sea-kings, and the medieval narrative itself, while literally depicting the loss of primitive beliefs, simultaneously symbolizes the nineteenth century's crisis of *Christian* faith.

Like "Agnes and the Merman," "The Mermaid's Spaeing [Prophesying]" Christianizes an earlier folk story, also ameliorating the transition in belief systems through a sympathetic depiction of the mermaid. Held captive by a king, the mermaid is granted her freedom by the queen after foretelling her future, which includes the prophecy that the queen will die in childbirth with her third son. But as the mermaid swims away, she tells the queen not to weep, for "The gates of Heaven stand open for thee" (*BDB,* p. 113). Here again merfolk are disempowered and spiritually inferior beings, their exclusion from Heaven foreshadowing their certain extinction. Nevertheless, they are a far cry from the type of the mermaid promoted by the Christian church and the bestiaries, which depict the mermaid as an emblem of the sins of the flesh and thus play a central historical role in shifting her toward the femme fatale image Cooke identifies with Rusalka. But though other Danish ballads show merfolk of devious and dangerous character, there are no traces of this type in Andersen's mermaid. In contrast, her temperament owes much to these characteristically nostalgic Danish ballads, which depict unfulfilled and poignantly inferior beings powerless to change their state, dwellers outside a world now more powerful than their own.

In addition to folk beliefs and traditions that, in effect, *were* Andersen's environment from an early age, he was influenced by literary romanticism, chiefly Danish and German. Bernhard Severin Ingemann, described as the Danish Sir Walter Scott, was a friend and mentor of Andersen, as well as a direct influence on his novels and poetry. Ingemann wrote a story of merfolk at one point, unfortunately not available in English translation. Additionally, Andersen scholars point to Friedrich, Baron de la Motte Fouqué's *Undine, or the Water-Spirit,* as a source.[26] Motte Fouqué's story serves as a thematic influence on Andersen, but the sensibility behind this tale about a water-spirit who desires an immortal soul is quite different from Andersen's. Undine, the changeling child of a poor fisherman and his wife, is wild and impetuous, though also delightful and innocent. She marries the knight Huldbrand who wanders into the forest, and who eventually takes her home to his castle; but gradually, Huldbrand falls out of love, replacing Undine with princess Bertalda who, it turns out, is the actual daughter of the fisherfolk. Undine returns to her watery element, but is unwittingly released above ground again when a stone is removed from a fountain, and Huldbrand ends up drowning in her embrace, although Undine does not intend to kill him. The woods are full of frightening, shape-changing and evil spirits, most particularly Undine's uncle, and thus nature, represented in the person of Undine, the other spirits, and the landscape, is presented in a starkly dichotomous fashion—at once innocent and pure (Undine and the promontory where the fisherman lives), evil, unpredictable, and antithetical to man (the woods and its spirits). Rather than choosing between the extremes suggested by maiden and natural world or resolving these extremes in images of moderation, Motte Fouqué depicts the extremes as integral qualities of Undine and her world, and the result is an unwitting *femme fatale,* dangerous to herself and others. The demonic side of nature and the prevalent elements of chivalric romance in this story are alien to Andersen's tale, from which the traces of such a distinctively German romanticism—all that *Sturm und Drang* and pageantry of the past—are absent.

That Andersen would choose to adopt the mermaid as an emblem of outsider status coheres with a biographical perspective. Indeed, as Jackie Wullschlager's important new biography makes clear, it would be difficult to imagine a set of circumstances more systematically apt to produce a constitutional outsider than those that governed Andersen's life. Denmark's first proletarian writer, Andersen received encouragement and support from a variety of sources beginning in childhood, but the difficulty of his progress was a constant reminder of the gulf between who he was and who he wanted to be. When he began serious schooling, he was almost twenty years old, and the other boys in his class were half his age. He was a gangly boy, an ugly duckling with an unusual combination of personality traits; naïve, sensitive, effeminate, and vain (from a young age, he constantly performed for people, at his own initiative), he was essentially good-natured and caring. As a child, he was doted on by his poor parents, but he had no playmates. As an adult, he was rejected repeatedly as a lover by both men and women, and never fully accepted by the middle class that had made his artistic and worldly success possible. Ironically, the massive contraction of Denmark's realm in the first sixty years of the nineteenth century resulted in a national mood of withdrawal and retreat, a mood perfectly in sympathy with the outsider theme of many of Andersen's stories.

In sum, folk tradition, literary education, and biographical circumstance together inspired Andersen to write a mermaid tale and to stamp his depiction of this figure with distinctive meanings. If through the merger of three sets of archetypal concerns, prototypically signified by maiden, animal, and water, the mermaid becomes, under modern cultural and personal circumstances in which self-other relations have become increasingly difficult, profoundly charged with our essential ambivalence, it is perhaps this ambivalence itself that Andersen most evokes as he merges it successfully with his own preoccupations. The little mermaid's psychology—her inwardness, isolation, and longing for a way of life and being other than that which is "natural" to her—is Andersen's, and the visual image of the mermaid literalizes her otherness from both the human and the natural worlds. But so too in this preoccupation with the outsider and, moreover, in the perception that a vexed relationship between individual and group is characteristically human, biography converges with the historical movement of romanticism, even while these environmental and subjective psychological factors capitalize, as it were, on an essential ambivalence embedded in our adapted psychology. We are, as Byron says, alike unfit to sink or soar—or at least as modern men and women living in too-complicated times that's what we think we are; Andersen's identification with Byron and other English, Danish, and German romantic authors and his emulation of their themes, including the romantic fascination with folk culture and the supernatural, provided additional impetus for his adoption of the mermaid as fated outsider, connected profoundly to several realms but nevertheless belonging to none.

IV

Andersen's tales were not, like those of the Brothers Grimm which revived the taste for folk stories, renditions of folk stories, but original creations derived from the folk genre. Although some of his tales, including **"The Little Mermaid,"** were not intended for children, for the most part these tales were written to be read aloud by adults to children. As such, they blend oral with writerly qualities and complicate the narratives so as to appeal to a mixed audience. Recognized as a major writer in Denmark especially for his use of a colloquial yet flexible language in stories that contain some subtlety of meaning, Andersen introduced adult themes and modern ambiguities into tales essentially childlike in their simplicity, naïveté, and humor.

In spite of this, Andersen never set out to establish himself as a writer of tales, much less a children's writer. When he began writing tales in his mid-thirties, he had already spent about ten years writing plays, poetry, and novels, and his immediate goal was probably to make a little extra money during the Christmas season—an appropriate goal, since he really did need money. In his ambitiously literary works, Andersen was drawn to the literary preoccupations of romanticism and to sophisticated literary forms. He was given to obsessive retelling of his own life, and critics claim that his novels and plays especially suffer from weaknesses in plotting. This suggests that the structural simplicity of folktales served as a felicitous constraint upon and framework for the writer's romantic themes and emotional nature. Whatever liberties Andersen took with fairytale and fable, their basic structures were rudimentary to him and, in remaining faithful to a few basic elements of structure and style, he successfully controlled his tendency toward excess.

In keeping with his romantic proclivities, Andersen's major divergence from the generic fairytale norms is a shift from external to internal action. Through the author's emphasis on the mermaid's isolation, initiation into suffering, and potential spirituality, her development becomes the main focus of **"The Little Mermaid,"** even while this inward process is often conveyed through description rather than through an abstract account of her feelings. In contrast to the standard causal operations of traditional fairytale, the actions the mermaid takes, like seeking the help of the sea witch and drinking her potion, are apparently ineffec-

tual as steps in the fulfillment of a long-term goal. However, in a further complication, this is only apparently the case, since the mermaid does not know throughout much of the story what her goal actually is. Causality, then, is complex and ambiguous in the story, consistent with the modern sensibility behind it and in contrast to the established pattern of fairytale plot.

As Luthi explains, the prototypical pattern of fairytale development has been described variously as a movement from a lack to its liquidation, from disequilibrium to equilibrium, and from need to fulfillment of need (*FAF*). The framing tensions of these stories are those of lack-to-remedy, and the conclusions of fairytales focus on rewards and elevations in rank and power. Such a definition does not distinguish fairytales appreciably from other narrative genres, though the fairytale enacts this movement with great narrative economy, usually introducing the characters and situation in a brief sentence or two. Typically, the fairytale pursues equilibrium by placing the hero on the road and requiring him to perform tasks that help him achieve his goal. He usually does not return home; however, one-dimensional character that he is, he feels no longing or loss for his home or for those associated with it.

"The Little Mermaid" does not adhere to the clear, linear causality and quick, progressive pacing typical of oral fairytale, its deviations in the pattern of action-to-achievement indicating a fundamentally different view of human agency, which is complicated not only by external constraints but by psychological conflicts of motive and desire. In marked contrast to the economy of the generic norm, which succinctly introduces the hero and the situation, Andersen's tale, beginning with two paragraphs describing the depth of the sea and the sea king's castle, works to establish mood. In this beautiful place, "the water is as blue as the petals of the loveliest cornflower and as clear as the purest glass," fish take the place of birds and the roof of the sea king's castle opens and closes to the motions of the water (*LM* ["**The Little Mermaid**"], p. 34). Far from being a lyrical exercise, the concrete realization of place in these opening paragraphs retrospectively contributes to the reader/ listener's experience of loss, for it is this home that the mermaid will leave behind. Whereas the paradigmatic fairytale focuses on the rewards attendant upon the successful completion of difficult tasks and of a corollary progress toward higher social status, Andersen's tale is preoccupied with the psychic and emotional costs of individual growth.

Andersen's leisurely method of establishing situation continues in the ensuing paragraphs. The third paragraph introduces the mermaid and her family, and identifies the little mermaid as the main character. But there is so far no drama or tension. After two further paragraphs of description, Andersen develops the little mermaid's character through a comparison of her garden with those of her sisters: "the youngest made hers perfectly round like the sun and had only flowers that shone red as the sun itself. She was a strange child, quiet and pensive, and while the other sisters decorated their gardens with all kinds of odd things they had taken from wrecked ships, the only thing she would allow in hers, besides the rosy-red flowers that looked like the sun on high, was a beautiful marble statue. It was of a handsome boy carved out of pure white stone that in a shipwreck had been sunk to the bottom of the sea" (p. 35). With this passage six paragraphs into the story, Andersen definitively identifies the mermaid as alien to the world she inhabits. Unlike her sisters—and, incidentally, the heroine of the recent Disney film—she is not interested in forks, broken crockery, and beads, the paraphernalia and trinkets of human life, but in the condition of being human itself, depicted symbolically in the statue, an idealized image of a young man. And unlike the heroes and heroines of true fairytale, she is not actually human but yearns to be so, her fascination with the sun and its light embodying her aspirations to both the physical and spiritual condition of humankind. As Bredsdorff points out, the human world matters in this story only because of its significance to the mermaid.[27] Put another way, Andersen defamiliarizes the human world by revealing it to us from the mermaid's perspective and thus asking us to think about what it means to be human; ambivalent belongers and periodic outsiders to the human project all, readers and listeners are invited to sympathize with this beautiful and charming misfit. Just as the statue is ideal to her so, in some respects, she is to us: akin to romantic conceptions of the child and the noble savage, she links the human back to the presumed purity and innocence of nature and inexperience, even as these qualities render her powerless.

Given her powerlessness, it is fitting that *waiting* constitutes a central aspect of the mermaid's development, and in the first part of the tale she waits primarily for her fifteenth birthday, the day when, like her sisters before her, she will be able to visit the ocean's surface. When she does finally visit the surface, she gains an immediate agency whose potential to realize her desires is nonetheless immediately frustrated. Saving the prince from drowning during a violent storm, she must then watch as a young girl from a nearby convent—coincidentally the princess he later marries—leans over and awakens the prince. Once again, the significant action is interior, for the mermaid returns to her home at the bottom of the sea, her sense of longing for the human world augmented and given material shape as the prince, who cannot live beneath the waves, supercedes the sunken statue. When she tells her sisters of her feelings for him, they lead her to his castle. Now watching combines with waiting as the mermaid, behind rocks

and amidst sea foam, is gradually initiated into the meaning of mature desire, the longing for an object that seems forever remote.

The statue and the young prince, while signifying heterosexual desire and possible union, furthermore symbolizes the potential for the expansion of experience and fulfillment of being, and thus Andersen's tale also resembles romantic literature in presenting sexual desire and union as a metaphor for self-completion. Though the Disney film and probably many of the early twentieth-century versions and hatchet-job "translations" of this story make the prince the final locus of the mermaid's desire, he is hardly so in Andersen's original tale. Spurred on by her growing love of humans, the mermaid asks her grandmother if they ever die. The grandmother, explaining that humans have an immortal soul, relates how "they rise up to unknown, beautiful places that we shall never see" (p. 45). Hearing this, the little mermaid no longer feels content to live her three hundred years in the sea, preoccupied as she is with the prince and the wish to "possess, like him, an immortal soul" (p. 46), and it is at this point that she seeks the help of the sea witch. In sum, whereas the traditional fairytale establishes character, conflict, and sought-after object in the first moments of the story, it is not until nearly halfway through **"The Little Mermaid"** that the central character understands the objects she desires and can therefore work actively toward her goal.

The ambiguity of her desires, the emphasis on thoughtfulness and longing—conveyed partially through direct statement, but largely through description—and the generally inward nature of the tale, all on the one hand hallmarks of romanticism, on the other stand in direct contrast to paradigmatic features of fairytale: its one-dimensional depiction of acting, not thinking, characters; its tendency to establish lack, and thus goal, immediately; and, consistent with these first two features, its logical, economical working-out of plot toward a successful attainment of the desired goal. However seemingly static in comparison to the traditional fairytale, **"The Little Mermaid"** is not without its action, constituted by the gradual realization of desires whose fulfillment is vital for self-completion, and the story's ambiguities add developmental and psychological dimension to a basically realistic depiction of the fairytale heroine/ hero (her mermaid ontology notwithstanding). The traditional fairytale isolates individuals and situations for economy and clarity, but it does not dwell on the *experience* of being alone, lonely, or other, of being an unfulfilled outsider. By contrast, in addition to **"The Little Mermaid,"** several of Andersen's best- known stories, including **"The Little Match Girl"** and **"The Ugly Duckling,"** are centrally concerned with this theme. In the shift from external to internal action and thus to the focus on isolation and loneliness, the psychological by-products of living in a democratized, developed world, Andersen demonstrates that he was not simply enamored of the trappings of romanticism but fully possessed of a romantic sensibility. Within a biocultural or Darwinian context, therefore, our innate ambivalence about belonging to social groups strongly informs literary themes and meanings when, on the one hand, as Storey points out, our relationships become depersonalized and span distances and, on the other, as culture, becoming increasingly heterogeneous and secular, no longer provides the unifying experiences and consolations it once did (*MHA*, pp. 57-62).

Just as the tale is realistic in its portrayal of the mermaid's initiation into longing and desire, it is consistent in its subtle emphasis on the inevitability of loss and suffering. When the mermaid says, "Oh, if only I were fifteen! . . . I know that I shall love the world up there and the human beings who live and dwell in it" (p. 39), the naïve words are tinged with irony, for every adult knows that where the mermaid looks for fulfillment will in fact bring an increase in desire. Like all children, she doesn't understand the nature of desire, nor does she understand that everything has costs. She must suffer the loss of her voice, traded to the sea witch for the magic potion that gives her legs; after this, she must suffer the pain of walking and dancing on legs she was never meant to have. She misses her family and the sea. When she is living in the prince's castle, she goes down in the evening and sits on the steps leading into the sea, dipping her legs in the water, assuaging both physical and mental pain—an outsider still, even if now from the other side.[28]

If the typical fairytale ends with an unequivocal increase in rank and power, **"The Little Mermaid"** tempers such optimism with ambiguity and a sense of potentiality in keeping with the tone of the story. After refusing to kill the prince on his wedding night, a method contrived by the witch at the bidding of her sisters in the hope of returning the little mermaid to the undersea world, the little mermaid plunges into the sea, turning to sea foam, but then rises up unexpectedly to meet the daughters of the air. These beings lack immortal souls but can attain them through three hundred years of good deeds. Given her basic goodness, it seems certain that the mermaid will acquire an immortal soul, but this is still different than actually having one at the end of the story (and, on one level, it can be said that her innate goodness hasn't done her much good in the story proper). Nevertheless, the magical powers of the witch are put in their place, as her instructions about how the mermaid can save herself are clearly subordinated to a greater supernatural force.

As indicated thus far, **"The Little Mermaid"** diverges significantly from many staples of the fairytale genre, but these shifts notwithstanding, many stylistic features

of fairytale are retained. For example, modified though it is, the basic pattern of lack-to-liquidation remains, just as elements of the fabulous and magical combine within a basically realistic perspective. The character constellation and patterns of repetition and variation, too, are recognizable as those of fairytale. In short, the conventions of fairytale, familiar to Andersen's contemporaneous audience because of their cultural currency but based nonetheless on innate tendencies toward linearity, binarization, and the like provide a strong formal and thematic base for Andersen's variations without determining meaning. If, for instance, the clear linear organization of traditional fairytale, in which self-contained episodes mark distinct phases in the movement toward resolution, derives from the epigenetic rule of causal organization and the attendant preference to organize narratively, their instantiation in **"The Little Mermaid"** hardly results in a story of simple and straightforward quest, unproblematic in its episodes and causes. We respond to causal organization on an emotional and unconscious level, so the semblance of it is almost always indispensable. Simply put, formal features that derive from our preference to think causality successfully attract attention, *whether or not the tale under consideration then proceeds in a clear causal fashion*. In this case, our conscious understanding of the story, of its meanings, more often than not works *against* the perception of determinate causes and logical progression.

The story is similarly exemplary in its character constellation—a father, a grandmother, six daughters, a witch, a prince, and a princess—but just as Andersen complicates the action and central themes of fairytale, so he adds complexity to the character types, usually derived from the splitting of the archetypal nodalities into binary configurations. Fairytale regularly concerns the accession of the powerless to power, since its heroes and heroines are youngest children and unwanted stepchildren, and the little mermaid, the youngest daughter, fits in this main character paradigm. That the sea king is widowed, and that the good grandmother and witch contrast with one another, are all staples of the genre. Yet the splitting of the old woman into wise woman and witch, while seeming to following the stark psychology often reproduced thematically and morally in traditional fairytale, proves to be a superficial device. In Andersen's tale, the witch fulfills her part of the bargain, even giving the mermaid a second chance when the sisters come to plead for her life. Even though the creatures surrounding her are grotesque, she is not evil; unlike Ursula, the Disney witch, she never attempts to double-cross the little mermaid. Likewise, the prince, whose delusion about who saved him from drowning is never corrected (he thinks it is the princess he marries), is a morally ambiguous character who, acknowledging the loyalty and devotion of the dumb, transformed mermaid, makes of her a kind of favorite pet while adamantly seeking the young woman he mistakenly assumes has saved his life.

Andersen's revisioning of the fairytale character constellation again constitutes a modernizing of the genre that coincides with the transition from oral to written form and with the impact of a psychologizing culture on notions of moral worth. This as well as the other traditional aspects of fairytale enables Andersen to have it both ways, for while the superficial simplicity of plot and character combined with a reality infused with magic appeal to the child's unity of experience, they also appeal to the adult who has lost that unity both developmentally and culturally.

Moreover, Andersen's use of repeated and varied actions, presented in isolation from one another, also matches paradigmatic expectations. This is most notable early in the tale, when each sister has her first opportunity to visit the surface on her fifteen birthday. Andersen presents the visits sequentially, relating the varied observations of the several sisters, and staying true to fairytale structure by isolating each episode from the others. But just as Andersen complicates the character constellation of fairytale with moral ambiguities, so he shifts the emphasis of repeated action away from its traditional function of moving the narrative toward its final goal and subsumes it under the overriding concern for the little mermaid's growing enchantment with the human world. What is important in each of these episodes is what the sister *sees,* not what she *does,* for each of the five brings back a new perspective on the world above the water, and each of these pictures feeds the little mermaid's imagination and longing. Possibly, the familiar pattern of repeated action gives the *effect* of greater forward movement in the story than is actually the case at this point, before the mermaid consciously understands her own desires. Thus the active pattern of fairytale counterbalances the potential stasis of an interior story.

In the final analysis, Andersen's **"Little Mermaid"** draws on cultural symbols and forms that derive from innate and universal preoccupations and ways of organizing, and in so doing employs elements that arouse reader/listener emotion and thus motivate interest. For the writer himself, in addition, the ascetic form of folktale placed a felicitous constraint on his emotional and highly expressive nature and enabled him as well to profit from the romantic resurgence of interest in folk culture, which had given impetus to the publication and rapid translation of the Brothers Grimm, and thus established an international audience for such tales.[29] But the *meaning* of the tale is another matter. Gazing through the lens of his romantic sensibility, his own essential loneliness and awkwardness and frustrated creativity, Andersen coaxes the colorful and glinting shards into a pattern reminiscent of the little mermaid's garden, deli-

cate and fantastic yet resonant with themes of desire, loss, loneliness, and transcendence. All of these, it seems to me, are related to the twin modern preoccupations of self-completion and communal belonging, and thus derive from our fundamental ambivalence about those others beyond the self, an ambivalence that has become more pronounced with sociocultural complexity. Even as the mermaid herself rises joyously to meet the daughters of the air in the story's conclusion, the adult listener/reader experiences a distinct poignancy, even perhaps a feeling of unfairness, on the mermaid's behalf.

Thus enchanting us while soliciting our sympathy for the outsider, **"The Little Mermaid"** is an artful reworking of an elementary folk form for the modern sensibility. As Jack Zipes puts it in his tongue-in-cheek comment, "The genuine quality of all folk and fairy tales . . . depends very much on their original contamination" (p. 869). In Andersen's tale, the spiritualization of the story, in one sense so representative of nineteenth-century culture, draws on the sense of the wonderful and marvelous that has always been central to the wonder and fairytale traditions. Though the elimination of the mermaid's desire for immortality from the recent Disney film might suggest that the original story is hopelessly dated for contemporary audiences, in the long run the human themes of the story give it a lasting significance that the fundamentally superficial film lacks. Fashioning its version to the norms of the predominant genre, Consumer Romance, Disney peels away, like a desiccated rind, unfulfilled desire, loss and suffering, loneliness and pain (Eidsvik in Haase, p. 198).[30] Although the simplifications of superficial culture, mitigated by other forms of experience and imaginative engagement, can hardly do us or our children much damage, it is the alignment of natural propensity with contemporaneous conditions, "contaminated" by original sensibility, that leaves us, in Andersen's tale, with something meaningful and lasting.

Notes

This essay is based on a paper delivered at the Twenty-First Conference on the Unity of the Sciences in Washington, D.C., November 1997. I am grateful to ICUS for its support in the research and writing of the original paper. I am also grateful to Brian Boyd, Brett Cooke, Denis Dutton, Peter McNamara, Ellen Peel, Alan Richardson, and Robert Storey for their suggestions and helpful remarks on various versions.

1. David Sloan Wilson, review of *Evolutionary Psychology: The New Science of Mind in Evolution and Human Behavior* 4 (1999): 279-87.

2. See Leda Cosmides and John Tooby, "The Psychological Foundations of Culture," in *The Adapted Mind: Evolutionary Psychology and the*

Generation of Culture, ed. Jerome H. Barkow, Leda Cosmides, and John Tooby (New York: Oxford University Press, 1992), and Edward O. Wilson, *On Human Nature* (Cambridge: Harvard University Press, 1978).

3. Michael Ruse, "The View From Somewhere: A Critical Defense of Evolutionary Epistemology," in *Issues in Evolutionary Epistemology,* ed. Kai Hahlweg and C. A. Hooker (New York: SUNY Press, 1989), p. 198.

4. Philosophy and psychology are today rife with scholars who study narrative thinking, the basis of which is the causal rule. See, for instance, Jerome Bruner, *Acts of Meaning* (Cambridge: Harvard University Press, 1990); Dan Lloyd, *Simple Minds* (Cambridge: MIT Press, 1989); Jean Matter Mandler, *Stories, Scripts, and Scenes: Aspects of Schema Theory* (Hillsdale, New Jersey: Erlbaum, 1984); and Roger C. Schank, *Tell Me a Story: A New Look at Real and Artificial Memory* (New York: Scribner's, 1990). For a discussion of how these contemporary insights contribute to a new alternative to traditional debates within epistemology, see my essay, "Making Knowledge: Bioepistemology and the Foundations of Literary Theory," *Mosaic* 32 (1999): 131-47.

5. For a discussion of how aesthetic value cannot be established on the basis of satisfying biopsychological predispositions, see my essay "Do Cognitive Predispositions Predict or Determine Literary Value Judgments? Narrativity, Plot, and Aesthetics," in *Biopoetics: Evolutionary Explorations in the Arts,* ed. Brett Cooke and Frederick Turner (Lexington: International Conference on the Unity of the Sciences, 1999), p. 242.

6. For a seminal argument that art satisfies the need for pattern, see Rudolph Arnheim, *Toward a Psychology of Art* (Berkeley: University of California Press, 1966). For an equally ground-breaking argument contemporaneous with Arnheim's that contends to the contrary, that art breaks up normative cognitive patterns, see Morse Peckham, *Man's Rage for Chaos: Biology, Behavior, and the Arts* (Philadelphia: Chilton Press, 1965). More recent discussions following Peckham include: James Ralph Papp, "Parodic Humor, Cognitive Scripts, and Neural Compromise," Literature and Human Nature, MLA Convention, Toronto, Canada, 1993; Eric Rabkin, "Imagination and Survival: The Case of Fantastic Literature," in Cooke and Turner, pp. 293-314 (n. 5); and my own "Play, Mutation, and Reality Acceptance: Toward a Theory of Literary Experience," in *After Poststructuralism: Interdisciplinarity and Literary Theory,* ed. Nancy Easterlin and Barbara Riebling (Evanston: Northwestern University Press, 1993), pp. 105-25. For discus-

sions of art and novelty, see Lee Cronk, "Gethenian Nature, Human Nature, and the Nature of Reproduction: A Fantastic Flight Through Ethnographic Hyperspace," in Cooke and Turner, pp. 205-18; and Joseph D. Miller, "The 'Novel' Novel: A Sociobiological Analysis of the Novelty Drive as Expressed Through Science Fiction," in Cooke and Turner, pp. 315-34. For a discussion of human motives and their relationship to the contents of literature, see Joseph Carroll, "The Deep Structure of Literary Representations," *Evolution and Human Behavior* 20 (1999): 159-71. For a discussion of the bonding function of stories in social groups, see Eric Rabkin, "Vegetable, Animal, Human: The Perils and Powers of Transgressing Sociobiological Boundaries in Narrative," in *Sociobiology and the Arts,* ed. Jean Baptiste Bedaux and Brett Cooke (Atlanta: Editions Rodopi-Amsterdam, 1999), pp. 83-98.

7. Dissanayake's thesis that art is a propensity for making special is developed further in each of her three books on the subject: *What Is Art For?* (Seattle: University of Washington Press, 1988); *Homo Aestheticus: Where the Arts Come From and Why* (New York: Free Press, 1992); and *Art and Intimacy: How the Arts Began* (Seattle: University of Washington Press, 2000). For an overview of the development of Dissanayake's thesis throughout the three books, see Nancy Easterlin, "Big Guys, Babies, and Beauty," Philosophy and Literature 25 (2001): 155-65.

8. For a description of the range of empirical constraint to which current literary critical activities are subject, see Joseph Carroll, "'Theory,' Anti-Theory, and Empirical Criticism," in Cooke and Turner, pp. 139-54; for a neurophysiological approach to reader response, see David S. Miall, "Anticipation and feeling in literary response: A neurophysiological perspective," *Poetics* 23 (1995): 275-98; for a study of the correlations between Machiavellian personality types and story content, see D. S. Wilson, David C. Near, and Ralph R. Miller, "Individual Differences in Machiavellianism as a Mix of Cooperative and Exploitative Strategies," *Evolution and Human Behavior* 19 (1998): 203-12.

9. For an extended discussion of the importance of speculative thinking in evolutionary literary criticism, see my essay "Voyages in the Verbal Universe: The Role of Speculation in Darwinian Literary Criticism," *Interdisciplinary Literary Studies* 2 (2001): 59-73.

10. For a discussion of the development of fairytale, see Jack Zipes, "Cross-Cultural Connections and the Contamination of the Classical Fairy Tale," in

The Great Fairy Tale Tradition, ed. Jack Zipes (New York: W. W. Norton, 2001), pp. 845-69.

11. Brett Cooke, "Constraining the Other in Kvapil and Dvořák's Rusalka," in *The Fantastic Other: Interface of Perspectives,* ed. George E. Slusser and Jaume Olivella (Amsterdam: Editions Rodopi, 1998), pp. 121-42.

12. Edward O. Wilson, *Consilience: The Unity of Knowledge* (New York: Knopf, 1998).

13. Noting the tendency in previous myth studies and linguistics to collapse meaning into structure, Claude Lévi-Strauss points to "Jung's idea that a given mythological pattern—the so-called archetype—possesses a certain meaning" as a prime example of this error. Yet at times Jung is adamant that the (unconscious) archetype alone is without content. See Claude Lévi-Strauss, "The Structural Study of Myth," in *Literary Theory: An Anthology,* ed. Julie Rivkin and Michael Ryan (Oxford: Backwell, 1998), pp. 101-15.

14. Quoted in Robert Storey, *Mimesis and the Human Animal: On the Biogenetic Foundations of Literary Representation* (Evanston: Northwestern University Press, 1996), p. 78. [hereafter referred to in text as *MHA*]

15. See Gwen Benwell and Arthur Waugh, *Sea Enchantress: The Tale of the Mermaid and Her Kin* (New York: Citadel, 1965); Horace Beck, *Folklore and the Sea* (Middletown: Wesleyan University Press, 1973); William A. Craigie, *Scandinavian Folklore: Illustrations of the Traditional Beliefs of Northern Peoples* (1896; Detroit: Singing Tree, 1970); and F. Morvan, *Legends of the Sea,* trans. David Macrae (New York: Crescent, n.d.).

16. Gordon H. Orians, "Habitat Selection: General Theory and Applications to Human Behavior," *The Evolution of Human Social Behavior,* ed. Joan S. Lockard (New York: Elsevier, 1980), pp. 49-66.

17. Carl Gustav Jung, *The Archetypes and the Collective Unconscious,* 2nd ed., trans. R. F. C. Hull (Princeton: Princeton University Press, 1971), pp. 19-21.

18. James Frazer, *The New Golden Bough,* ed. Theodor H. Gaster (New York: Mentor/New American, 1959), p. 59.

19. For discussions of the predisposition toward binary thinking, see Storey; E. O. Wilson's *Consilience,* p. 153-54; and Easterlin, *MK,* pp. 143-45.

20. Max Luthi, *The Fairytale as Art Form and Portrait of Man,* trans. John Erickson (Bloomington: Indiana University Press, 1984). [hereafter referred to in text as *FAF*]

21. For an analysis of the meaning of animal transformation, see Hedwig von Beit, "Concerning the Problem of Animal Transformation in the Fairy Tale," *Yearbook of Comparative Criticism* (1968): 48-71.

22. Hans Christian Andersen, *Tales and Stories by Hans Christian Andersen,* ed. Patricia L. Conroy and Sven Rossel (Seattle: University of Washington Press, 1990).

23. Comments on Andersen's life draw on Jackie Wullshlager's new, comprehensive biography, *Hans Christian Andersen: The Life of a Storyteller* (New York: Knopf, 2001), as well a Signe Toksvig's *The Life of Hans Christian Andersen* (New York: Harcourt Brace, 1934).

24. Axel Olrik, *A Book of Danish Ballads,* trans. E. M. Smith-Dampier (Princeton: Princeton University Press, 1939), p. 116. [hereafter referred to in text as *BDB*]

25. Matthew Arnold, "The Forsaken Merman," *The Norton Anthology of English Literature,* 6th ed., vol. 2, ed. M. H. Abrams et al. (1849; New York: W. W. Norton, 1993), pp. 1349-52, l. 105-06.

26. Baron Friedrich de la Motte Fouqué, *Undine and Other Tales* (Boston: Houghton, Mifflin, 1867).

27. Elias Bredsdorff, *Hans Christian Andersen: The Story of His Life and Work, 1805-1875* (New York: Charles Scribner's Sons, 1975), p. 314.

28. Rather than focusing on Andersen's evident identification with the mermaid and, hence, his depiction of her as a locus of sympathy, English-language interpretations of the tale emphasize, as Cooke does in his Rusalka analysis, the dangers of sexual experience and the virtue of female self-abnegation. Several find the tale misogynist in its treatment of these themes, but such readings disregard the intensity of Andersen's identification with the character as an outsider, especially evident if one takes into account biographical facts like his ambiguous sexuality, his notable sexual inhibitions, and his beautiful singing voice, which he lost at puberty. Wullschlager's assessment that Andersen is holding the mermaid up as a model of female self-denial is contradicted by her awareness that Andersen's (male) life and work are shot through with sexual revulsion and denial; see, for instance, pp. 170-76, p. 383. See also Sheldon Cashdan, *The Witch Must Die: The Hidden Meaning of Fairytales* (New York: Basic Books, 1999), pp. 163-71, and Marina Warner's discussion of this tale in the context of related lore and literature, *From the Beast to the Blonde: On Fairytales and Their Tellers* (New York: Farrar, Straus, and Giroux, 1994), pp. 387-408.

29. Cay Dollerup, "Translation as a Creative Force in Literature: The Birth of the European Bourgeois Fairy-Tale," *Modern Language Review* 90 (1995): 94-101.

30. See Donald P. Haase, "Gold into Straw: Fairy Tale Movies for Children and the Culture Industry," *The Lion and the Unicorn* 12 (1988): 193-207.

Jørgen Dines Johansen (essay date summer 2002)

SOURCE: Johansen, Jørgen Dines. "Counteracting the Fall: 'Sneedronningen' and 'Iisjomfruen': The Problem of Adult Sexuality in Fairytale and Story." *Scandinavian Studies* 74, no. 2 (summer 2002): 137-48.

[*In the following essay, Johansen examines the mechanisms by which Andersen avoids the depiction of his adult characters experiencing sexual fulfillment in his works.*]

In Andersen's works, a barrier exists that more often than not prevents the protagonists from experiencing adult sexual fulfillment. Indeed, even if this barrier is overcome by the denouement on the level of plot, somehow the reader doubts the authenticity of the putative sexual happiness because the resistance to growing up and enjoying the physical side of adult life seem to be entrenched in the texts. This is well known and serves only as my point of departure. What I want to look at here are the techniques of avoidance in two texts in which the barrier that prevents mature sexuality is openly explored: **"Sneedronningen"** [**"The Snow Queen"**] and **"Iisjomfruen"** [**"The Ice Maiden"**].

"Sneedronningen" begins with a cosmic prologue staging the opposition between God and the Devil and the latter's ability to harm the original goodness of man with the splinters of the enchanted mirror. The setting then shifts to a small idyllic ambience created by poor bourgeois parents in order to preserve benign nature within an urban milieu. Here the two children, Gerda and Kai, grow up in a humble earthly paradise. The advent of male puberty and the splinters of the mirror mean a fall/Fall and a break up of both the happy and innocent relationship between male and female children and the trust and love between the grandmother and the boy. Instead, little Kai is spellbound by the Snow Queen, a beautiful, mature woman incapable of caring and loving. Little Kai is, thus, not only kissed half to death by the Snow Queen, but her kisses also erase his memory of childhood, making it easy to hold him prisoner in the ice castle at the North Pole in Lapland. In Kai's case, the transformation is swift and irreparable as far as he is concerned since he cannot himself escape his confinement in eternal winter.

The story of Gerda's quest and rescue of Kai, on the other hand, is divided into a series of adventures. Her quest begins with the sacrifice of her red shoes, which Kai never saw, to the river, a sacrifice that in Andersen's system of images means giving up selfishness, vanity, and sexual desire. The next stop in Gerda's quest is at the old woman's house. Here the old woman tries all manner of ploys to make Gerda forget her mission, such as combing her hair with the comb of oblivion and by making the roses—the symbols of true love—disappear. She wants to hold Gerda prisoner as a child in eternal summer (all the flowers are blossoming simultaneously). However, the tears of pity that Gerda sheds make this attempt vain. Interestingly, the stories that the flowers tell her at the old woman's house are all but one—the buttercup's story about love between grandmother and grandchild—about the transitory nature of happiness, the wrong way of loving, or the damning effects of erotic desire and longing. Three of these embedded stories are, notably, blatantly erotic: the tiger lily's about a sexual desire that burns hotter than the consuming fire of a funeral pyre. But Gerda answers the lily: "Det forstaaer jeg slet ikke!" (2:58) ["I don't understand that at all" (61)]. The hyacinth's story describes the fragrance that grows even stronger; and the account of the three sisters who vanish and die in the forest is laden with erotic overtones as well. In the last story, the protagonist, the narcissus-ballerina, is described as follows: "see hvor hun kneiser paa een Stilk! jeg kan see mig selv! jeg kan see mig slev!" (2:61) ["See how she stretches out her legs, as if she were showing off on a stem. I can see myself, I can see myself" (62)]. It does not take much effort to infer what is also implied in this self-mirroring.

At this point, then, Kai is imprisoned within the eternal winter of male pride and pubescent sexuality whereas Gerda barely escapes the imprisonment in eternal female childhood, a childhood, however, beset with erotic fantasies: to wit the curious passage: "da fik hun en deilig Seng med røde Silkedyner, de vare stoppede med blaae Violer, og hun sov og drømte der saa deiligt, som nogen Dronning paa sin Bryllupsdag" (2:57) ["then she slept in an elegant bed with red silk pillows, embroidered with colored violets; and then she dreamed as pleasantly as a queen on her wedding day" (60).]

Her pure love for Kai, however, leads to escape from the entrapment of unfulfilled, pubescent longings. Her next stop at the prince and princess's castle shows two kinds of relationships that should be avoided: the stale idyll of the crows and the puerile, unconsummated relationship between prince and princess.

Her imprisonment in the robbers' castle in the woods addresses the unresolvable link between sexuality and destruction. On the one hand, there is the murder of coachman and footmen, the threat that Gerda herself is going to slaughtered and eaten, and the robber girl's sadistic treatment of animals. On the other, there is the unsavory sexuality of the robber witch and the robber girl's threats and sexual advances toward Gerda. Like the prince and princess, however, the robber girl takes pity on Gerda and facilitates her pursuit. She keeps Gerda's muff, though, as token of Gerda's continuing sacrifice.

Whereas the robber witch may be seen as a representation of the bad mother, Gerda next enters the realm of the good mothers (the Finnish woman and the Lapp woman) whose dwellings are reminiscent of wombs. By her faith, fidelity, and non-sexual love, Gerda defeats the demonic powers with the help of the angels. Gerda's tears make Kai remember, as her tears earlier made love blossom, and her love frees him of his imprisonment in intellectual pride and longing for the Snow Queen. Indeed, the pieces of ice dance and spell out the word "Eternity," which is the answer to the riddle of life.

In the present context, Gerda's and Kai's journey back to their point of departure, however is of greatest interest. First they meet or hear about some of the significant characters whom Gerda had met on her way out. Notably, both the little robber girl as well as the prince and princess have left their homes, i.e. have severed childhood ties. Second, their journey begins during the winter and continues through the spring; at the moment they enter the grandmother's drawing room though, the wholesome summer sun is shining. During the course of these events, they have matured into responsible adults but, nevertheless, sit on and fit into their little stools. They have grown up but remained children at heart.

As is well-known, an important structural homology links the fairy tale and the *Bildungsroman*: both have three sequences, often dubbed home, abroad, and at home. The name of the last phase may be a slightly misleading because the protagonists most often do not return to the home of their parents, but rather establish their own home with a spouse. **"Sneedronningen"** is a significant departure from this pattern in the literal return to the parental home. Read in conjunction with Andersen's claim that Kai and Gerda are simultaneously children and adults, it indicates that the concept of time is central to this fairy tale.

Before discussing this point, however, let us turn to **"Iisjomfruen,"** in the plot of which realism and fantasy are intertwined. A traditional realistic story, it presents a young man's maturation and efforts to qualify himself as a provider for his family, his falling in love, his overcoming of the resistance of the young woman's father, and the young couple's happiness after quarrels and misunderstandings. The end of Andersen's story is less traditional in that the protagonist drowns the day before his wedding. He, however, had become an excellent hunter and guide with the help of a talking cat that taught him to climb without becoming dizzy and afraid of heights. Hence, his upbringing had included the supernatural.

Simultaneously, the tale is about the malignant and beneficent forces of nature represented by the Ice Maiden and the daughters of the sun. The story presents a cosmic dualism juxtaposing destructive and restorative powers wherein death—in the story the Ice Maiden—takes the body but the human soul is saved by the heavenly powers. However, already as an infant Rudy had been consecrated to the Ice Maiden because she kissed him when as a mere baby he barely escaped the death on the glacier that killed his mother. Throughout the story, she longs for her son, but recovers him only when his sexuality awakens. Thus Andersen here as in **"Sneedronningen"** merges the cosmic struggle and human sexuality. Nevertheless, there are important differences between the fairy tale and the story: Kai and Rudy are different ages. Whereas Kai has just reached puberty, Rudy is an adult. Kai's imprisonment in the Snow Queen's castle occurs when he as a boy is just on the verge of becoming a young adult and adoring a highly ambiguous female whom he perceives as half mother and half beloved. Rudy, however, had already experienced sexual feelings before he met Babette, and he knows that sexuality is something that has a disturbing autonomy and that it is not inextricably bound to the beloved. Babette, moreover, is not like Gerda, she is not giving up sexuality: on the contrary, she is flirtatious, she enjoys the advances of her rich cousin, and she delights in Rudy's jealousy. Whereas Kai falls and is immediately immobilized by the destructive forces and Gerda's quest means the overcoming of various hazards by virtue of her almost angelic nature Rudy and Babette's road to union and final separation is filled with temptations that they must resist, which begin, though, before they meet. Although Rudy is in love with Babette, he kisses Annette (even the names indicate that the great leveler—lust—to a certain extent makes them interchangeable). In addition to this initial mistake, Rudy is further tempted by the Ice Maiden's maids. It is difficult not to read the second scene in which he thinks he is with the schoolmaster's Annette—whom he, by "mistake" kissed earlier—as a fall where he succumbs to the spell of the maid and to his own desire.

> *Der strømmede Livsens Glæde ind i hans Blod, den hele Verden var hans, syntes han, hvorfor plage sig! Alt er til for at nyde og lyksaliggjøre os! Livsens Strøm er Glædens Strøm, rives med af den, lade sig bære af den, det er Lyksalighed. Han saae paa den unge Pige, det var Annette og dog ikke Annette, endnu mindre Troldphantomet, som han havde kaldt hende, han mødte ved Grindelwald; Pigen her paa Bjerget var frisk som den*

nysfaldne Snee, svulmende som Alperosen og let som et Kid; dog altid skabt af Adams Ribbeen, Menneske som Rudy. Og han slyngede sine Arme om hende, saae ind i hendes forunderlige klare Øine, kun et Secund var det og i dette, ja forklar, fortæl, giv os det i Ord—var det Aandens eller Dødens Liv der fyldte ham, blev han løftet eller sank han ned i det dybe, dræbende Iissvælg, dybere, altid dybere; han saae Iisvæggene som et blaagrønt Glas; uendelige Kløfter gabede rundt om, og Vandet dryppede klingende som et Klokkespil og dertil saa perleklart, lysende i blaahvide Flammer, Iisjomfruen gav ham et Kys, der iisnede ham igjennem hans Ryghvirvler ind i hans Pande, han gav et Smertens Skrig, rev sig løs, tumlede og faldt, det blev Nat for hans Øine, men han aabnede dem igjen. Onde Magter havde øvet deres Spil.

(4:154-5)

(A living joy streamed through every vein.

"The whole world is mine, why therefore should I grieve?" thought he. "Everything is created for our enjoyment and happiness. The stream of life is a stream of happiness; let us flow on with it to joy and felicity."

Rudy gazed on the young maiden; it was Annette, and yet it was not Annette; still less did he suppose it was the spectral phantom, whom he had met near Grindelwald. The maiden up here on the mountain was fresh as the new fallen snow, blooming as an Alpine rose, and as nimble-footed as a young kid. Still, she was one of Adam's race, like Rudy. He flung his arms round the beautiful being, and gazed into her wonderfully clear eyes,—only for a moment; but in that moment words cannot express the effect of his gaze. Was it the spirit of life or of death that overpowered him? Was he rising higher, or sinking lower and lower into the deep, deadly abyss? He knew not; but the walls of ice shone like blue-green glass; innumerable clefts yawned around him, and the water-drops tinkled like the chiming of church bells, and shone clearly as pearls in the light of a pale-blue flame. The Ice Maiden, for she it was, kissed him, and her kiss sent a chill as of ice through his whole frame. A cry of agony escaped from him; he struggled to get free, and tottered from her. For a moment all was dark before his eyes, but when he opened them again it was light, and the Alpine maiden had vanished. The powers of evil had played their game.

[407-8])

This situation, so similar to and yet so different from the passage in which Kai is kissed by the Snow Queen, describes Rudy's temptation and fall. The narrator—and Andersen I presume—are giving two reasons for this fall. First, it is, according to the norms of the story, a grave sin to presume that "alt er til for at nyde og lyksaliggjøre os!" ["everything is created for our enjoyment and happiness"]. Second, the woman is first and foremost defined by her sex and her sexual nature. He is uncertain of her identity: she may be the woman he once kissed "by mistake," but she is definitely not Babette.

Likewise, her cousin's advances first tempt Babette although she resists them. Two days before her wedding, though, she has the ghastly dream of her own future

adultery and of losing Rudy. In the dream, she even prays to God that she will die on her wedding day. However, it is not she who dies, but Rudy. In the attempt to seize the boat, Rudy dives into the lake—the element of the Ice Maiden—where she finally kills him.

A twofold explanation of Rudy's death and the final separation of the young couple suggests itself. First, Rudy's death is fated because he somehow already belongs to the Ice Maiden, i.e. he is swayed by a sexuality that is linked not only to mortality, but also to active destruction. Second, however, death and the resulting sexual abstinence are explicitly conceived as a gift sent from God. There are two reasons for this interpretation: first, death is a blessing because it prevents future sins. Second, the narrator deems it a blessing to die at the verge of fulfillment, i.e. in the enjoyment of expectation in the moment when lasting happiness seems assured. Their virginal love not yet consummated is untouched by experience. Sudden death in the bloom of youth is, thus, constructed as a blessing because of its disruption of human erotic happiness: it both prevents future sinning, and the ensuing sorrow purifies Babette and leads to a quiet life in God instead of a life spent in the tribulations of desire.

In addition to ideological trends of the Danish Golden Age that might support this line of thinking, Andersen's configuration of the plot emerges from personal psychological considerations that precluded his portraying an authentic union between men and woman in erotic happiness. However, this is not the subject of this article. Here attention must remain focused on the literary reasons why Kai and Gerda both survive while Rudy and Babette are separated by his death. In order to attempt an answer, let us return to the time-space relations of the two texts and to their understanding of causality.

The question of genre—whether there is a difference between *eventyr* (fairytale) and *historie* (story)—is complicated. In one of his own observations from 1874 regarding the tales, Andersen comments on the change in their title that took place in 1852. Prior to that year, the titles of the collections of tales had been either **Eventyr fortalt for Børn** (Fairy Tales told for Children) or **Nye Eventyr** (New Fairy Tales), as in the case of the 1849 deluxe edition with 125 illustrations of his collected fairy tales published by C. A. Reitzel. Concerning this edition, Andersen goes on to say:

*Med dette Pragtbind var Eventyr-Samlingen afsluttet, men ikke min Virksomhed i denne Digtart; et nyt betegnende Navn maatte derfor tages til den nye Samling, og den kaldtes "**Historier**"—det Navn, jeg i vort Sprog anseer at være det bedst valgte for mine Eventyr i al deres Udstrækning og Natur. Folkesproget stiller den simple Fortælling og den meest dristige Phantasie-*

Skildring ind under denne Benævnelse; Ammestuehistorien, Fabelen og Fortællingen, betegnes af Barnet, Bonden og Almuen, ved det forte Navn "Historier".

(SS [*H. C. Andersens samlede Skrifter*]
1880:15:302-3)

(This edition *de luxe* concluded the collection of fairy tales, but not my work within this kind of literature. Consequently, a new name had to be given to the new collection, and it was called **Stories** [*Historier*] in our language, the name that I find most fitting for the nature and size of my tales. Vernacular language reduces the simple story and the most daring representation of fantasy to this common denominator; the child, the peasant, and common people call the cock-and-bull story the fable, and the tale "stories.")

It is difficult to see the logic of Andersen's distinction other than perhaps the wish to separate works imitating the simple folk tale from other kinds of writing. Furthermore, Andersen himself was not very consistent in applying these labels. For instance, Flemming Hovmann's commentary to the critical edition of the tales, *H. C. Andersens Eventyr I-VII 1963-1990,* shows that Andersen referred to "**Iisjomfruen**" both as a story and as a fairy tale. The reception of the collection, *Nye Eventyr og Historier* (1862) was favorable, and one of the dailies, *Fædrelandet,* calls "**Iisjomfruen**" "a kind of fantastic novelle," but, like Andersen, the critics were not consistent in their use of generic labels. Nevertheless, at that time, it seems that few critics and colleagues perceived a difference between a psychological and in some respects "realistic" work such as "**Iisjomfruen**" (which in spite of Andersen's own vacillation should be called a story) and tales modeled on the folk tale. Andersen, however, frequently altered the genre framework within which he was working. In our context, his shifting perspective is illustrated by the subtitle of "**Sneedronningen**" which is "**Et Eventyr i syv Historier**" (2:49) [**A fairy tale told in seven stories**]. And, with regard to "**Sneedronningen**," the difficulty is not only a question of the added complexity occasioned by the sequence of stories, but also involves a radical change of theme. The folk tale has little concern for the salvation of the protagonists' souls, but is preoccupied with the obstructions to achieving maturity—including sexual maturity—with making illegitimate relations between the sexes legitimate, and with social advancement. These themes are found throughout Andersen's work but always with a twist and very often turned upside down as in "**Sneedronningen**" itself. Hence, this fairy tale is very far from the folk tale. What, though, is the difference between "**Sneedronningen**" and "**Iisjomfruen**," and is the difference responsible for the very different solution to the problem of development and maturation? My answer is that the decisive difference has to do with the different handling of time and space in the two texts.

In "**Sneedronningen**" geographic references are not totally absent; there are references to Finland, Italy, and Lapland. However, this part of the world is basically treated as a mythic location of the Snow Queen's castle. As for time, it is not represented as chronology, as calendar time. It is, rather, presented cyclically, i.e. the changing and returning of the seasons and with summer and winter absolutely dominant. These two contrary seasons are strongly thematized in the fairy tale: summer is linked not only to the regenerative forces of nature, but also to innocence, faith, piety, and the love and redeeming power of Jesus and God. Winter is linked with sexuality, intellectual pride, and calculation and with destruction, the demonic powers, and damnation.

Cyclical time is, of course, a basic way of conceiving of the changes and recurrences of outward nature. Furthermore, fundamental differences between the cyclical time of outward nature and the linear time of human existence arise. Whereas nature's cyclical time is conceived as repetition, human time is seen as transitory with every moment unique and unrepeatable. The consequence of this deplorable fact is that the past cannot be changed; the most we can do is to edit its narration.

In "**Sneedronningen**," however, the time of outward nature is molded to serve the protagonists, while human time is made flexible to the extent that not only prior states of mind but even prior relationships can be restored. The basic paradox of he fairy tale is, of course, contained in the last paragraphs. As Kai and Gerda walk homewards it is spring; as they arrive in grandmother's drawing room, they realize that they have grown up. Nevertheless, they sit down hand in hand on the small chairs remaining from their childhood. In the warmth of summer, the grandmother reads the passage from Matthew 18:3, "except ye be converted, and become as little children, ye shall not enter into the kingdom of heaven." In "**Sneedronningen**" Andersen offers a literalist reading and exemplification of this passage. Hence, the formative influence of physical growth on the mind is both recognized and denied. Kai's physical and intellectual growth and the advent of puberty occasion the end of the infantile paradise. The point of Gerda's entire quest, however, has been to rescue Kai by lifting the spell of the Snow Queen and, thus, to restore him to what he was before his abduction. The flexibility of the time-space coordinates of the fairy tale universe and the necessary suspension of causal relationships render the retroaction and the consequent literalist exemplification of the sacred text, i.e. Matthew, possible.

In "**Iisjomfruen**" things are different. Despite the fourfold presence of the supernatural (as fairy tale lore, as folklore, as reminiscences of gothic tales, and as a more or less Christian allegory of opposed cosmic forces), this story has less narrative latitude to determine the level upon which the denouement will take place. The reason is its precision with regard to the space-time coordinates. It takes place in various Swiss cantons in the years before and after 1856. And according to the narrator, what is narrated ends up in the guidebooks. In fact, his reading the Baedecker for Switzerland inspired the part of the story about the drowning of the groom. He made one significant change though: in the Baedecker, the couple had just been married whereas Rudy and Babette are going to be married the next day.

Its precise setting in the immediate past of a part of a Europe known to very many people, its reference to a past event, and the realistic psychology of the protagonists make a denouement like that of **"Sneedronningen"** impossible. It would be too implausible and offend against the logic of both characters and plot. Even though there are both supernatural helpers and a powerful supernatural enemy, undoing the protagonists' realistically conceived psychosexual development would be impossible because it has been the engine of the story. In **"Sneedronningen,"** Kai suddenly falls and Gerda immediately sacrifices her own development into a maiden to save him. In **"Iisjomfruen,"** both Rudy and Babette grow, and they experience repeatedly the tribulations and temptations of desire. Furthermore, in the central passage describing Rudy's temptation and fall, he has a vision, i.e. he is endowed with an inner life, whereas this is not the case in **"Sneedronningen."** Hence, despite the fantastic elements, **"Iisjomfruen"** is a story (*historie*) not a fairy tale.

Differences of genre, then, seem to determine the different endings of the two texts. In some important respects, however, they still tell the same story: the story of the impossibility of erotic love between adults, and the story about how God's ways may be mysterious to man but nevertheless lead to salvation and true happiness. The narrator of **"Iisjomfruen"** even becomes a little insistent, quarrelsome, and didactic at the end. He first challenges the reader with the question, "Kalder Du det en sørgelig Historie?" (4:161) ["Do you think this a sad story?" (412)]. And he ends with "'Gud lader det Bedste skee for os!' men det bliver os ikke altid aabenbaret, saaledes som det blev for *Babette* i hendes Drøm" (4:162) ["'God permits nothing to happen, which is not the best for us.' But this is not often revealed to all, as it is revealed to Babette in her wonderful dream" (413)]. In **"Sneedronningen,"** we witness a miracle, the co-presence of child-like innocence and adulthood; in **"Iisjomfruen,"** it is claimed and somehow demonstrated that the wages of sin is death, but we are told that such punishment is for our own good. In **"Iisjomfruen"** too, however, time is in a sense manipulated because even if the stern necessity of linear time and individual death is not denied, it is made unimportant, almost negligible. At the moment of Rudy's death, the narrator concludes:

> *"Min er Du!" klang det i det Dybe; "min er Du!"*
> *klang det i det Høie, fra det Uendelige.*

> *Deiligt at flyve fra Kjærlighed til Kjærlighed, fra*
> *Jorden ind i Himlen.*

> *Der brast en Stræng, der klang en Sørgetone, Dødens*
> *Iiskys beseirede det Forkrænkelige; Forspillet endte for*
> *at Livs-Dramaet kunde begynde, Misklangen opløses i*
> *Harmonie.*

(4:161)

("Thou art mine," sounded from the depths below; but from the heights above, from the eternal world, also sounded the words, "Thou art mine!" Happy was he thus to pass from life to life, from earth to heaven. A chord was loosened, and tones of sorrow burst forth. The icy kiss of death had overcome the perishable body; it was but the prelude before life's real drama could begin, the discord which was quickly lost in harmony.

[412])

There, in accordance with a central tenet of Christianity, the moment of death becomes a cosmic struggle for man's soul and in Andersen, the soul's homecoming. In his review of Andersen's collection of fairy tales and stories from 1858, the Danish author Meïr Goldschmidt wrote that Andersen revealed a bent to move from a piety of nature to ecclesiastic piety, and says: "Dette Sidste kan være saare godt og gavnligt, men næppe i Længden for Eventyrpoesien. Thi det specifikt Religiøse vil være Eneherre" (*Eventyr* 6:174) [This (i.e. ecclesiastic piety)—may be very good and beneficial, but just barely in the long run for fairy tales because the specifically religious wants to be autocratic].

Even if the end of **"Sneedronningen"** is in a sense flawed as well, it abides by the logic of the tale and the unity of its universe. The universe of **"Iisjomfruen,"** however, does not possess any unity. It is fundamentally split, and its parts seem to contradict each other. Andersen, thus, does not trust the force of his own story and he directly intervenes to set things straight. Accordingly, I think Goldschmidt is right. Andersen stops narrating and starts preaching, and the sermon he gives is outrageous because one might accuse him of curing the illness by killing the patient. This response is not just the reaction of a twenty-first century reader. Even Ingemann complained that Andersen had the heart kill off Rudy to prevent their union. However, the important question is not one of sympathizing with the detractors of the story or with the young couple; it is also a question of Andersen's inability to find a narrative form congenial to his message. And I should add that I find the denouement of the latter impossible anyway.

Works Cited

Andersen, Hans Christian. *H. C. Andersens samlede skrifter*. 15 vols. Copenhagen: C. A. Reitzel, 1876-80.

———. *H. C. Andersens Eventyr*. 7 vols. Copenhagen: Reitzels Forlag, 1963-90.

————. *The Complete Hans Christian Andersen Fairy Tales.* Ed. Lily Owens. New York: Gramercy Books, 1984.

Hollis Robbins (essay date autumn 2003)

SOURCE: Robbins, Hollis. "The Emperor's New Critique." *New Literary History* 34, no. 4 (autumn 2003): 659-75.

[*In the following essay, Robbins illustrates the narrative complexity of "The Emperor's New Clothes," reading the story as a literary, social, and political commentary.*]

> "Custom," continues the Professor, "doth make dotards of us all."
>
> —Carlyle, *Sartor Resartus*

Hans Christian Andersen's **"The Emperor's New Clothes"** (1837)[1] is a tale so transparent that there has been little need for critical scrutiny. Most grownups vaguely recall that it is the story of a king who is tricked into donning imaginary clothes (encouraged by courtiers who praise his suit) and showing them off publicly until a child cries out "but he has nothing on!" Scholars well-acquainted with the tale confirm its transparency, asserting that it is a simple story of a seeing through the trappings of power to reveal "the truth" of the Emperor's vanity and the courtiers' pusillanimity. Jacques Derrida proposes that the tale's transparency is its truth; or rather that the truth of Andersen's tale is that it flagrantly stages truth as a scene of public unveiling.[2] That is, the story not only describes a scene of reading (the little boy who "reads" the absence of the Emperor's clothes) but also assigns the position of the reader in search of (and finding) truth and closes with the reader publicly pronouncing truth to general acclaim. With its notion of "truth" as a thing that can be unveiled, Andersen's tale, for Derrida, is a fantasy for analysts. With its final image of the heroic romantic child-critic, the tale seems to suggest that anyone with a little pluck and independence can see and say "the truth."

But Andersen's tale is also a critique of criticism, Derrida's criticism suggests. As tale, teller, interpreter, and critical case study all in one, it knows what it is about in offering such a transparent fantasy. Yet if it is true that the tale's very transparency is a critique of the desire to critique—or rather, the exhibitionistic desire to unveil publicly—Derrida's privileging of the themes of analysis, truth, and unveiling in his (albeit brief) reading of **"The Emperor's New Clothes"** provides evidence that the awareness of this desire does not reduce its influence. The desire to read **"The Emperor's New Clothes"** as either a fantasy of critique or a critique of the fantasy of critique is symptomatic of our assumptions about what it means to be a reader-analyst. That is, to be a reader-analyst is to occupy the position of Andersen's child and to assert that things are not as they seem—or, rather, that things are exactly as they seem, but that few can recognize this. But this critical stance requires the privileging of (and the reinvestment in) the critical stance. The critical fantasy that Andersen's tale critiques is that when there is something wrong in the world, all that is needed is a brave, insightful individual to set things right. The tale's mythic popularity suggests that something about Andersen's account of seeing and saying the truth is attractive. The tale's truth is the fantasy-desire for the kind of truth that can be revealed.

Yet to say that **"The Emperor's New Clothes"** is actually critiquing the thing that millions of readers and admirers believe the story is "about" is to risk putting myself in the position of the little boy. To critique the story at all is to step out of the mainstream; since its publication it has been read as a simple tale of aristocratic vanity that promises little beyond the obvious.[3] For Marshall McLuhan, **"The Emperor's New Clothes"** is simply a perfect illustration of how perceptive but antisocial individuals—children, poets, artists, sleuths—can see what is really going on more clearly than "well-adjusted" individuals.[4] For Sigmund Freud, who alludes to the story briefly in *The Interpretation of Dreams,* the story simply offers proof of a "typical" desire for the natural nakedness of childhood.[5] For Derrida, as noted above, the tale offers simply another example of the truth that a text is its own best critic. (For him this is true of all texts, of course; but in Andersen's tale, the ironies are richer.) **"The Emperor's New Clothes"** is a "scene of writing" that exhibits/dissimulates "the baring of the motif of nakedness" well before the analyst arrives on the scene (PT 39). (Not surprisingly, the figure of the little boy has been used in a popular critical theory textbook to describe Derrida's early acts of speaking truth to power.[6]) But none of these observations are critiques of the story *qua* story. They are accounts of the story's illustrative power.

The story would be easy enough to critique—by this I mean to read and analyze the text following one or more of the accepted critical methodologies—and I am tempted to do so. But if I take seriously Derrida's admonition that the text also already critiqued itself before I have even begun, and if I take seriously my own observation that to read the text as a plucky, independent, "unhailed" individual is to reinvest in this critical position, then my analytical project becomes complex. I do not want to play the role of the little boy and exhibitionistically unveil the tale and all those who have refused to see its truths. But what are my alternatives? Most of the traditional metaphors for reading, especially those that are medical-surgical, vegetable, or archeological, involve some sort of opening up, stripping off, peeling, probing, and focusing light on. Is there another position the critic can take in reading a text?

I suggest that we test the effect of enlisting some new verbs in analytical criticism. I propose that **"The Emperor's New Clothes"** offers several other critical positions besides that of the courageous romantic child. These positions are figured in the story by five very familiar "characters": the Emperor, the "rogue weavers," the ministers, the canopy, and the public. Each of these positions offers us critical verbs: to rule, to weave, to minister, to parade, and to applaud. In the critique that follows I will present and parade **"The Emperor's New Clothes"** by weaving the threads of the tale's often ignored characters and words, and in doing so, address and applaud its sociopolitical-literary-critical complexities.

The Emperor

> Many years ago, there was an Emperor, who was so excessively fond of new clothes, that he spent all his money in dress. He did not trouble himself in the least about his soldiers; nor did he care to go either to the theatre or the chase, except for the opportunities then afforded him for displaying his new clothes. He had a different suit for each hour of the day; and as of any other king or emperor, one is accustomed to say, "he is sitting in council," it was always said of him, "The Emperor is sitting in his wardrobe."

To review Andersen's story and its immediate historical context, recall that the central ruse of **"The Emperor's New Clothes"** is predicated on the notion of "fitness for office." The specific setting of the tale is a bustling mercantile town whose ruler cares more about clothes than the business of state. "As it was said of other kings 'he is in council,' they said 'he is in his wardrobe.'" Two rogue weavers arrive on the scene to exploit both the king's vanity and administrative insecurity. Those who are unfit for office or are "simpletons," the rogues claim, cannot see the fine cloth they will weave.[7] By wearing a suit made from this cloth, the Emperor thinks (rather uncharacteristically), "I might at once find out what men in my realms are unfit for their office, and also be able to distinguish the wise from the foolish!"

The Emperor gives the weavers gold to set up looms and begin immediately. After some time, a faithful minister is sent in to view the cloth and is shocked that he can see nothing. "What can be the meaning of this?" he asks himself. "Can it be that I am unfit for my office?" He listens carefully while the weavers describe the colors and patterns and repeats the words back to the king. Another court official is sent in, only to ask himself "am I not fit for my good, profitable office?" He too reports back that the cloth is extraordinarily magnificent. The weavers ask for more silk and gold thread, which

they put in their knapsacks.[8] Finally, the Emperor himself is shown the cloth, and he, like his ministers, is puzzled by his first deduction. "Am I unfit to be an Emperor? That would be the worst thing that could happen—Oh! The cloth is charming," he says aloud, and allows himself to be dressed in the new suit.

It is easy to make fun of this poor Emperor. Everyone does, though he is clearly the most important character, and his stature gives weight to the little boy's famous observation (*ID* 242-48).[9] Yet the Emperor seems to be practicing a kind of focused undertaking that should be just as familiar to us as the little boy's critical outburst. If one character in a story is allegorical, aren't the others equally allegorical? We often expect our leaders (and ourselves) to take risks based on instinct, desire, or philosophy and to try on for size positions that they (and we) do not, or do not yet, fully understand. If so, then we, as critics who believe all perspicacious children who publicly proclaim truths that nobody seems to see, must recognize that we are also Emperors, cloistered in our closets, often ignoring much of the world around us, sifting through and trying on new ideas—partly for display and partly for vanity, but also partly because it is what we like to do.

The Weavers

> One day, two rogues, calling themselves weavers, made their appearance. They gave out that they knew how to weave stuffs of the most beautiful colors and elaborate patterns, the clothes manufactured from which should have the wonderful property of remaining invisible to everyone who was unfit for the office he held, or who was extraordinarily simple in character.

These weavers resemble nothing so much as a new English Ph.D. on a job talk or a member of the MLA writing a proposal for a panel discussion. They are promising to create a text(ile) that will distinguish between the worthy and the unworthy; only the highly qualified will "get it." Theirs is a speculative endeavor but also a wholly critical one. Rather than pointing out truth, they are weaving a discourse that reveals truth.

The obvious (and all too familiar) critique is that these weavers are not really producing anything. They are rogues and frauds profiting from the insecurity and gullibility of others. Economic thought before Marx proposed that productive labor was only that which resulted in a material product, thus the labor of teachers and critics could not be considered productive. But for Marx all products of labor are "social things whose qualities are at the same time perceptible and imperceptible by the senses."[10] Andersen's weavers are merely insisting that the value of their labor be recognized apart from its material embodiment. Their presence in the text (and the fact that they are also coat-makers) signals an engagement with the highly charged political debate about the materiality of an artist's, craftsman's, or scholar's labor.[11] *Capital* opens with a sustained exploration of the handloom weavers' plight, investigating the social character of their labor and the mystical character of the coats they make.[12] Initially, the tale seems committed to a more optimistic future (or at least one less bleak) than Marx prophesies. In this bustling town, the handloom weavers'/tailors' work will lose neither its individual character nor its charm, artisans will be paid more than merely the objective cost of production, and they will convince the Emperor's ministers that it is in the town's best interest to appreciate the subjective value of their labor. The "truthful" child, who cannot see invisible labor, puts an end to this fantastic vision.

Moreover, the problem with the truth-telling child as a figure for the critic-analyst is that he does not labor prior to his outburst. The weavers, by contrast, succeed in selling the Emperor on their idea, and getting paid up front (like any good fellowship-recipient). They set up looms and request "the most delicate silk and the purest gold thread" (read: office and library privileges), which they promptly put in their knapsacks. Then they begin, "affecting to work very busily." The labor that the weavers/tailors will expend in turning the cloth into a coat may be invisible to some, they explain, but its beauty will appear to those who appreciate it. A "fit" minister or Emperor will fully perceive the artisans' labor in the coat. "Does not the stuff appear beautiful to you?" they ask. "Is not the work absolutely magnificent?"

The Ministers

> So the faithful old minister went into the hall, where the knaves were working with all their might, at their empty looms. "What can be the meaning of this?" thought the old man, opening his eyes very wide. "I cannot discover the least bit of thread on the looms." However, he did not express his thoughts aloud. . . .
>
> The Emperor now sent another officer of his court to see how the men were getting on, and to ascertain whether the cloth would soon be ready. It was just the same with this gentleman as with the minister; he surveyed the looms on all sides, but could see nothing at all but the empty frames.
>
> "Does not the stuff appear as beautiful to you, as it did to my lord the minister?" asked the impostors of the Emperor's second ambassador; at the same time making the same gestures as before, and talking of the design and colors that were not there.
>
> "I certainly am not stupid!" thought the messenger. "It must be, that I am not fit for my good, profitable office! That is very odd; however, no one shall know anything about it."

Any scholar-critic who does not recognize herself (from time to time) in these subalterns is as blind as . . . well, one of the Emperor's subalterns. What is the basis

for "Subaltern Studies" but the recognition that those with restricted voices speak in complicated, indirect ways? The critic or analyst who works for an institution (or within an academic field) is also a subaltern whose very dissimulation is an alternative form of critique. Literary critics are the last people who should privilege the direct speech of the little boy.

New Historicist literary critics should be especially attuned to the historical significance of the ministers' behavior. Evidently, the Emperor's court is caught up in a particularly nineteenth-century European controversy over objective qualifications for civil service. In the 1820s and '30s, the conservative Danish bureaucracy, which enjoyed power and prestige under the king's absolute rule, was under increasing pressure to respond to the needs of a growing merchant and middle class. Bourgeois liberals pressed the centralized governing structures for press freedoms, free trade, and an end to aristocratic privileges. Older bureaucrats reluctantly joined their younger, university-trained colleagues in the reform movements that would lead to a new constitutional monarchy by 1849.[13] This pattern replicated itself across Europe.[14]

Following the logic of Danish and British (as well as French and German) civil service reform, Andersen's high-level ministers and lower-level chamberlains find themselves asked to demonstrate their qualification for positions they are already holding. The old trusted minister is shocked and worried, but the reader should not be—the story suggests he and his fellow (civil) servants have proven themselves to be qualified for their jobs. The Emperor's vanity has been economically beneficial to the town: while he has been closeted with his wardrobe and ignoring his soldiers, people have prospered, and "time passed merrily in the large town which was his capital." This transparent government has been working. If the chamberlains (who are traditionally political, not sartorial) have successfully served the state by suiting the sovereign, it may be wise policy to continue.[15]

Unfortunately, however, the fashion advice that they have been used to giving has suddenly been constituted as an objective test of their fitness. They are left with a difficult choice: to acknowledge publicly that their subjective flattery has been objectively good for the capital (thus embarrassing the Emperor) or just quietly continue serving him (and keeping the peace) by admiring his clothes. All of the folk-tale precursors to **"The Emperor's New Clothes"** feature a courtier who must "see" a painting or a turban or a play or else reveal that he is illegitimate.[16] Andersen's updated version not only reflects a culture in which professional competence was quickly overtaking legitimacy and heritage as a source of aristocratic anxiety, but also weaves a new layer of complexity into the narrative. That is, while the problem of "legitimacy" follows a binary logic and is (for the most part) an objective question, professional fitness is enduringly subjective. The understandable uncertainty about the idea of "fitness" provides an incentive to admire the invisible cloth.[17] While we might indulge ourselves in picturing the Emperor's state of dishabille, the chamberlains who mime carrying the invisible train are clearly guided by their critical faculties. Their investment in the materiality of the Emperor's clothes is apparently so great that they will persist despite the public turmoil at the close of the story.

THE CANOPY

> And now the Emperor, with all the grandees of his court, came to the weavers; and the rogues raised their arms, as if in the act of holding something up, saying, "Here are your Majesty's trousers! Here is the scarf! Here is the mantle! The whole suit is as light as a cobweb; one might fancy one has nothing at all on, when dressed in it; that, however, is the great virtue of this delicate cloth. . . ."

> "How splendid his Majesty looks in his new clothes, and how well they fit!" everyone cried out. "What a design! What colors! These are indeed royal robes!"

> "The canopy which is to be borne over your Majesty, in the procession, is waiting," announced the chief master of the ceremonies. . . .

The invisible "cobweb-light" fabric shares the stage with another very material piece of cloth with objectively discernible effects: the ceremonial canopy under which the Emperor will proceed. The short narrative mentions it twice. It precedes the procession and plays a crucial role in it. Its obvious critical analogue is the diploma.

The relation of the canopy to the invisible cloth (or the diploma to the journal publication) is perhaps the same relation as the physical to the metaphysical—what Adam Smith famously called a "cobweb science."[18] But it is not a binary relation; both are fabrications whose value can only be perceived by one "in the know." Not surprisingly, nobody who reads the story "sees" the Emperor's canopy. It is part of the ceremonial text of kingship.

Oscar Wilde remarks that "the true mystery of the world is the visible, not the invisible." Likewise, the riddle of the invisible cloth's—and the story's—significance is solved by the customary visible covering of the king. Seen or unseen, it is not the cloth *qua* cloth but the position and function of the cloth within the story that determines each character and produces certain of the story's effects (to paraphrase Barbara Johnson's evaluation of a certain missing letter).[19] Until the child speaks, that is, the invisible material performs the same role as the visible. The function of the canopy is to announce that the Emperor is the emperor, whatever he happens to be wearing.[20]

In Freud's reading of **"The Emperor's New Clothes,"** the "typical" invisible cloth (*not* the canopy) is evidence of repression and thus is of interest to the analyst (as might be the modern reader's active forgetting that Marx's *Capital* begins with a discussion of coats).[21] But if the invisible textile inside the text becomes for Freud the whole text, why does it, and it alone, remain so even in Derrida's whole-cloth reconsideration of Freud's reading? Why the collective critical blindness to the visible fabric of the story—kingship and the cloth that signifies it?

THE PUBLIC

> So now the Emperor walked under his high canopy in the midst of the procession, through the streets of his capital; and all the people standing by, and those at the windows, cried out, "Oh! How beautiful are our Emperor's new clothes! What a magnificent train there is to the mantle; and how gracefully the scarf hangs!" In short, no one would allow that he could not see these much-admired clothes; because, in doing so, he would have declared himself either a simpleton or unfit for his office. Certainly, none of the Emperor's various suits, had ever made so great an impression, as these invisible ones.

In initially making manifest the social utility of the Emperor's invisible formal garments, the story exposes the invisible social conventions that bind the townspeople together and to the Emperor. The text suggests that the importance of these invisible customs is greatest in periods of social upheaval. But if the problem of invisibility engages the axes of veiled/unveiled and blindness/sight simultaneously, it is unclear whether a customary act of not seeing is an act of self-protection or self-exposure.

"The Emperor's New Clothes" dramatizes the dangers of habitual blindness in the name of social discretion. "What is perfectly correct and in order if practiced within the autonomous life of sociability," cautions Simmel, "becomes a deceptive lie when it is guided by non-sociable purposes or is designed to disguise such purposes" (*SGS* 49). The pretense of "seeing" the Emperor's invisible clothes is traditionally read as artifice at best and a lie at worst. But by foregrounding questions of sociability against a backdrop of political and economic turmoil, Andersen's tale clearly suggests that social discretion can engender democratic social solidarity. The townspeople's initial admiration for the cloth is a function of an altogether different reason. While the modern civil servant is trained to disregard (or be indifferent to) what is not in his particular purview, the townspeople remain, by contrast, fascinated with each other. "All the people throughout the city had heard of the wonderful property the cloth was to possess; and all were anxious to learn how wise, or how ignorant, their neighbors might prove to be," the narrator continues. But even while they are curious, their sense of social discretion subtly evokes bureaucratic detachment: they do not want to reveal their curiosity. Simmel observes that in all human intercourse, everyone knows more about everyone else than what is voluntarily revealed, but endeavors to be discreet about it. In general, however, "man arrogates to himself the right to know all he can find out through mere observation and reflection, without applying externally illegitimate means" (*SGS* 323). Both the townspeople and the ministers have a personal stake in admiring the invisible cloth. Their long-term economic stake, however, may be even greater.

THE LITTLE BOY

The Emperor is ecstatic, until a little boy remarks, "But the Emperor has nothing at all on!" His father exclaims, "Listen to the voice of innocence!" and the child's words are whispered from one to another. "But he has nothing at all on!" they all cry out at last. The story concludes:

> The Emperor felt most uncomfortable, for it seemed to him that the people were right. But somehow he thought to himself: "I must go through with it now, procession and all." And he drew himself up still more proudly, while the lords of the bedchamber walked after him carrying the train that wasn't there.

Ceremonies and formal performances have played a positive role in the community. The procession through the town was apparently already planned in advance of the weavers' arrival. "All [the Emperor's] retinue . . . advised his majesty to have some new clothes made from this splendid material, for the approaching procession." As Simmel notes, the sociable world—"the only world in which a democracy of the equally privileged is possible without frictions—is an *artificial* world" (*SGS* 48). These stewards of the artifice are steadfastly maintaining the "certain reserve and stylization" that Simmel suggests constitutes the social (*SGS* 48). In their steadfastness, the chamberlains are also perhaps exhibiting a rather Hegelian act of courage: "absolute obedience, renunciation of personal opinions and reasonings, in fact complete *absence* of mind, coupled with the most intense and comprehensive *presence* of mind" in order to realize and actualize a more open government.[22] They will persist in observing the proper, albeit artificial, forms despite the little boy who "sees through" it all.

Curiously, Andersen's original version had no child. The story ended this way:

> Certainly, none of the Emperor's various suits had ever made so great an impression, as these invisible ones.
>
> "I must put on the suit whenever I walk in a procession or appear before a gathering of people," said the emperor, and the whole town talked about his wonderful new clothes.
>
> (*HCA* 312)

This original version clearly registers the growing democratic political climate of the time and closes with an image of fellowship. It is a story of a successful enchantment. The townspeople simultaneously like seeing the Emperor naked (which makes them feel powerful) and like having to pretend publicly that nobody can see him naked (which keeps the crowd in check). The magical cloth enables the people's twin desires for power and security to be satisfied.

But just before publication Andersen had second thoughts about this conclusion and told the proofreader to delete the final paragraph and replace it with the final three paragraphs we are all too familiar with, hoping, he said, to give it a more satirical appearance (*HCA* 313). He succeeds. The fairy tale that we know does not end happily. The townspeople had been quite happy to ignore the Emperor's metaphoric nakedness for years, but the child's declaration abruptly ends this charade. The ceremonial fictions of sovereignty have become a problem that needs fixing. The child's words are disruptive—not for having leveled the difference between ruler and ruled, but for endangering the formal process by which it is accomplished without being openly acknowledged. While the public outside the text applauds the boy's act of disenchantment, the community inside is fractured and diminished.[23] The rogue weavers disappear from the story, the townspeople are deflated, and the chamberlains are left holding invisible robes. Read along the grain of history, the little boy whose antisocial remark is embraced as romantic insight emerges as scandalously reactionary: he calls the people fools and tells the king to get dressed. His particular version of "transparent" social interaction is intended to expose social difference rather than foster equality, and he succeeds in utterly rending the social fabric of the town by seeing through the Emperor's clothes.

That is, the Emperor is still the emperor. The townspeople's enthusiasm for his naked vanity is exposed, but (as the canopy manifests) his sovereignty is not in doubt. To paraphrase Barbara Johnson again, if the invisible cloth poses the question of its own rhetorical status, it is answered (at least initially) by a resounding "yes": "It is [visible] 'in' a *symbolic* structure, a structure which can *only* be perceived in its effects" (FR 498). The people are traumatized not by the realization that the cloth is invisible but by the public acknowledgement that they have subscribed to its visibility. They have consented to what the Emperor's accoutrements (robes, canopy), however invisible, signify. The relationship between the robes and the townspeople is only underscored by their initial blindness to their (the robes') invisibility.

The complex social desire that **"The Emperor's New Clothes"** imagines—a vision of a certain kind of economically beneficial performance that is not publicly acknowledged as simply a performance—may have been exposed, but the number of people who labored to carry it off demonstrates its materiality. I will not say that readers of **"The Emperor's New Clothes"** have been fooled when they read the text as a story of an Emperor (and a town) that has been fooled, because Andersen's text so very much wants this to be the case. The romantic idiom (a child who seems to speak the truth) is deployed precisely to create this effect. And yet this effect is wholly a function of the belief that art is objective (that there is an essential truth), that labor is invisible, and that Emperors ought to be clothed—all of which the child is somehow already socialized to believe. The pessimism of Andersen's text is located precisely in the conservatism of this child. To read him any other way is to be blind to the fact that nakedness has its "truth" in clothing—the Emperor is not naked until the child insists that he must "truly" be clothed.

THE TEXT

What is at the heart of this story's remarkable cultural/political relevance? Why is it that the allegorical "emperor's new clothes" circulates so widely even as we resist becoming on intimate terms with it? Lurking beneath our appreciation of the story's fairy-tale moral, I suggest, is an apprehension of the serious ontological and epistemological *social* problems it dramatizes. Recalling its much longer cognate text, *Sartor Resartus* (and sharing its engagement with metaphysics and fabrication), "The Emperor's" vision of invisible fabric furnishes an idiom that will to some degree underwrite the investigations of the next generation of social theorists.[24] As Ruskin will ask (putting aside "tiresome and absurd" questions of objectivity, subjectivity, and truth), what is the difference between true and false appearances when under a contemplative fancy? As Marx will ask, can something invisible have value? As Weber will ask, are individual subjectivity and bureaucratic function contradictory? As Simmel will ask, why is it that secrecy—the hiding of realities—is one of man's greatest achievements? As Wittgenstein will ask, can I ever know what someone else sees or that he sees at all, when all I have is signs of various sorts that he gives me?

The brief critical attention that Jacques Derrida pays to **"The Emperor's New Clothes"** (which is largely a critique of Freud's reading of the story) functions as a kind of dumb show for his longer and more famous critique of Jacques Lacan's reading of Edgar Allan Poe's "The Purloined Letter."[25] But although the presence of Andersen's story in a critique of critique hints that the story may have something new to say about the project of critique, Derrida never proceeds beyond descrying (or decrying) the typical project of critique and truth-telling by unveiling. In Derrida's view, both Poe's story and Andersen's feature a king whose manhood is imperiled, who is surrounded by habit-driven and blindly ineffectual civil servants, and who is saved by an individual who sees what is obvious. Both Dupin and the little boy respond to the crisis of kingly exposure with flashes of insight; both save the crown further embarrassment. Both Dupin and the boy are wholly conservative and patriotic. In their view, there is never a question that a king could or should fall from grace.

It is understandable that politics in a reading of "The Purloined Letter" should take a back burner: after all, there is a woman involved, as well as a little gold knob hanging between the cheeks of a fireplace. But **"The Emperor's New Clothes"** offers no such distractions. The tale's Zelig-like appearance at the periphery of a famous twentieth-century quarrel over the nature of truth, speech, nakedness, and disclosure is all the more remarkable for the fact that the story remains essentially unexamined. Indeed, there has been surprisingly little interest in the historical, textual, and sociopolitical agenda of Andersen's story. Unlike several of his other works (notably, **"The Shadow," "The Little Mermaid,"** and *Only a Fiddler*), **"The Emperor's New Clothes"** has provoked little academic interest.[26] Perhaps, as a noted authority of the story's many folkloric antecedents suggests, the tale resists critical scrutiny because its moral is too obvious and "too bitter a pill" (AT 17).[27]

Even this briefest of readings of **"The Emperor's New Clothes"** makes manifest that it has cultural and political relevance well beyond the popular figure of the little boy. The story quite clearly rehearses four contemporary controversies: the institution of a meritocratic civil service, the valuation of labor, the expansion of democratic power, and the appraisal of art. The story's potency, I argue, is not a function of the tale's engagement with these crises but its seductive resolution of them. We are seduced by the figure of an innocent analyst who pipes up and appears to clarify.

"Andersen's text has the text as a theme," Derrida observes (PT 37). He introduces his reading of Andersen by calling it an "apologue or parabolic pretext" for his "Purloined Letter" reading that he arrives at by opening up *The Interpretation of Dreams* "somewhere near the middle." The first two texts Derrida mentions after opening the Freud are *Oedipus Rex* and *Hamlet*. Thus we find grouped together, on one page, four stories about blindness, kingship, and threatening speech. Two of these stories, remarkably, are about Danish kings. It is a point too provocative to ignore.

The weavers' text, like the ghostly voice whispering at midnight, like the existence of a lover's letter, like the words of the prophecy, threatens to bring down a king. To their auditors, the words are "true." They sell a particular idea that the king has something to be embarrassed about, whether it is fitness for office, the right to the office, or the loyalty of his wife. The material effects of these words are the basis for these four stories, all of which are "resolved" in a manner that cleans up the office of the king.

In 1835, the Danish government, like most of its European counterparts, prohibited political meetings. But that year the Society for the Proper Employment of the Freedom of the Press was formed to resist Royal encroachment on the limited right of free speech in the country. In Germany, the Carlsbad Decrees of 1835 had killed press freedoms for the most part and sent authors such as Andersen's friend Heine into exile. Andersen, as Alison Prince suggests, could not have been unaware of the dangers of his profession.[28] In this context, Andersen's tale of an Emperor who believes in the materiality of words (who clothes himself in textual description) might also be read as an exploration of a constitutional monarchy in which the public conspires to preserve the myth of monarchial fitness. But this reform could be fraught with practical problems: the Emperor risks revealing that he has nothing on because children—the most skeptical and conservative of readers—are apt to see right through the fabrication.

Notes

I would like to thank John Fleming, Diana Fuss, Bill Gleason, and Jen Waldron for their helpful comments on an earlier version of this essay.

1. Hans Christian Andersen, "The Emperor's New Clothes," *Andersen's Fairy Tales* (E-text #1597), *Project Gutenberg,* Jan 1999, ftp://ibiblio.org/pub/docs/books/gutenberg/etext99/hcaft10.txt. All quotations of the story in this essay are from this e-text version, which is the most literal translation available.

2. Jacques Derrida, "The Purveyor of Truth," tr. Willis Domingo, James Hulbert, Moshe Ron, and M.-R.L., *Yale French Studies,* 52 (1975), 38-39; hereafter cited in text as PT.

3. First published in 1837 and translated into English in 1846, there are probably thousands of versions of "The Emperor's New Clothes" extant. It has been translated into hundreds of languages and is by now a cultural icon. See Elias Bredsdorff, *Hans Christian Andersen: The Story of His Life and Work, 1805-1875* (New York, 1975), part 2, chapter 2 for specific details of this translation history; hereafter cited in text as HCA. See also Jon Cech, "Hans Christian Andersen's Fairy Tales and Stories: Secrets, Swans and Shadows," *Touchstones: Reflections on the Best in Children's Literature,* ed. Perry Nodelman, vol. 2 (Summit, Pa., 1987), pp. 14-23. Cech quotes Andersen scholar Bo Gron-

bech: "Andersen's tales have been translated into over a hundred languages; only the Bible and Shakespeare have been translated into more" (16). The tale of the naked king and the little boy has been modernized, embellished, reimagined, and recontextualized in print, on stage, and on film. Steven Spielberg recently published a new illustrated version with himself as star. [In 2000] Disney offered a film entitled "The Emperor's New Groove." In a *New York Times Book Review* essay on the latest biography of Hans Christian Andersen, Brook Allen writes that "The Emperor's New Clothes" is "a masterpiece whose very title has become a byword for human vanity" (Brook Allen, "The Uses of Enchantment," *The New York Times,* 20 May 2001, late ed., section 7, 12). A quick database search reveals that the phrase "emperor's new clothes" is used hundreds of times every year in newspaper articles, congressional testimony, and academic journals as a tool for oppugning established policies and colleagues. Every field's iconoclasts, whistle-blowers, and revolutionaries want to see themselves as the little boy—the analyst who sees the *real* truth and proclaims it to the world.

4. Marshall McLuhan and Quentin Fiore, *The Medium is the Massage* (New York, 1967), pp. 88-89. Bredsdorff sums up: "Andersen's universally applicable tale "ridicul[es] the snobbery of people who pretend to understand or appreciate things they do not really understand or appreciate, in order not to be considered ignorant or stupid" (*Hans Christian Andersen,* p. 252).

5. Sigmund Freud, *The Interpretation of Dreams* (London, 1990), pp. 242-48; hereafter cited in text as *ID.*

6. Hazard Adams and Leroy Searle, eds., *Critical Theory Since 1965* (Tallahassee, 1986), p. 79.

7. Freud and Derrida mischaracterize the prerequisites for seeing the cloth as "virtue and loyalty."

8. In some versions, there is a suggestion that the Emperor has paid for the cloth out of his own pocket.

9. Freud recognized the Emperor's central role but stopped short of recognizing his potential as a model for the analyst. For Freud, the Emperor is a typical dreamer dreaming the typical dream of nakedness. Freud suggested that the Emperor's social predicament of being naked and yet unashamed is made sense of by the weavers' deception, which he calls "the secondary revision." That is, the dream concocts the weavers in order to "clothe" the dreamer's desire for nakedness. But although Freud acknowledges his own

dreams of nakedness, he does not perform his analysis from the position of the Emperor. Typically, he casts himself in the role of the little boy, stripping away the secondary revisions and revealing the desire for nakedness that shames the patient.

10. Karl Marx, *Capital: A Critique of Political Economy,* ed. Frederick Engels and Ernest Untermann (New York, 1906), p. 83.

11. For contemporary readers, fictional rogue weavers would resonate with their real-life counterparts who were actively petitioning their governments and demanding piecework rates, or being arrested and jailed for burning machines. In the first decades of the nineteenth century large-scale manufacture of power looms and expanding assembly-line production had devastated the rural economies of Europe and put thousands of handloom weavers and spinners out of work.

12. That is, Marx conceives of the relationship between the labor of a weaver/tailor and his final product as "imagined" but "invisible" material, beginning with the admonition that a product's utility is not a thing of air. Employing the idiom of invisible cloth, Marx "sees" the labor of these weavers and tailors. The coat produced by a weaver and tailor has value "only because human labor in the abstract has been embodied or materialized in it," and this labor is both visible and invisible (*Capital*, p. 45). The tailoring of the coat "shows" this labor, he continues, "but though worn to a thread, it does not let this fact show through" (60). The price of a commodity, he continues, is "a purely ideal or mental form," as is its value, which is made perceptible by its equality with gold, but which really exists only in one's head (107).

13. See Kenneth E. Miller, *Government and Politics in Denmark* (Boston, 1968).

14. The British transformation from aristocratic patronage to professionalism in the civil service began in earnest in 1802, when Parliament rather than the king became responsible for civil-service salaries. It continued through 1833 with the founding of Statistical Societies and with the merit-based reorganization of the India Office on John Stuart Mill's philosophy that "efficiency should be substituted for influence." It reached fruition in the famous 1854 Northcote-Trevelyan report, which recommended restructuring and centralizing the entire British civil service and instituting competitive exams for both recruitment and promotion. The discourse of fitness continued in fictional form in Charles Dickens's *Little Dorrit,* Honore de Balzac's *The Bureaucrats,* and Anthony Trollope's *The Three Clerks.*

15. A chamberlain is a king's (or queen's) private chamber attendant or administrator. The role of England's Lord Great Chamberlain is hereditary and requires attending upon and attiring the sovereign at his/her coronation, caring for various palaces and halls on formal state occasions, and attending upon peers and bishops at their creation. The Lord Chamberlain of the Household and the Mistress of the Robes share the oversight of all officers of the Royal Household. Shortly after "The Emperor's New Clothes" was published, the infamous 1839 "Bedchamber Crisis" in England provoked public debate about the political power of intimate advisors. In one of his first official acts, Tory Prime Minister Robert Peel demanded that several of Queen Victoria's Ladies of the Bedchamber and Mistress of the Robes be removed, because their husbands were Whig politicians. His fear, of course, was that each of these ladies would be looking after her own—that is, her political party's—best interest by discrediting Peel's government in the privacy of the Royal apartments. After the resignation of Melbourne's government in 1839, the new Prime Minister Robert Peel demanded this of Queen Victoria during his first meeting with her. His belief was that because their husbands were Whigs opposed to his government, these ladies-in-waiting would fill the Queen's cars with criticisms of Tory policy and compromise her confidence in Peel's government.

16. Archer Taylor, "The Emperor's New Clothes," *Modern Philology,* 25 (1927/28), 17-27; hereafter cited in text as AT. Taylor identifies a thirteenth-century, German jestbook tale about an artist whose paintings can be seen only by those who are legitimate. There is a fifteenth-century Turkish tale that turns on a silk turban. There is a seventeenth-century play by Cervantes in which not only does an individual have to be legitimate to see a theatrical spectacle, but he cannot have a single drop of Jewish blood. In the source text that Andersen acknowledged, a fourteenth-century cautionary tale by Infante don Juan Manuel, translated into German as *"So ist der Lauf der Welt,"* magic cloth woven by fraudulent weavers is similarly visible only to those who are legitimate. Taylor bases his genealogy on the shared characteristics of the "fraud," the "chain of falsehood," the disclosure of "the self-imposed deception," and the moral that "truth will out" (24). "All exemplify the idea [that] knaves will lie for their own supposed advantage, even if the act involves bold-faced deception" (17).

17. If the function of art is to make the invisible visible, both the weavers and the chamberlains prove themselves aesthetically (as well as ethically) proficient in their specific references to what the cloth

actually looks like. Their repetitive description of the cloth's immateriality paradoxically reinforces a sense of its ontological stability. "The whole suit is as light as a cobweb," the weavers say, while fitting the Emperor; "one might fancy one has nothing at all on, when dressed in it; that, however, is the great virtue of this delicate cloth." Yet despite its existence as mere fabrication, the cloth has objectively discernible effects on the individuals it touches: the two subordinate chamberlains bend down and pick up the invisible train as the Emperor prepares to parade through the town. Their dogged determination to keep holding this train even after the little boy speaks is usually considered proof positive of the ministers' lack of common sense.

18. Adam Smith, *An Inquiry into the Nature and Causes of the Wealth of Nations* (London, 1896), book 5 "Of the Revenue of the Sovereign or Commonwealth," chap. 1 "Of the Expenses of the Sovereign or Commonwealth," article 2 "Of the Expense of the Institutions for the Education of Youth," p. 292: "When metaphysics and physics are set in opposition to one another, they naturally give birth to a third, Ontology, which treats of qualities and attributes common to both." The "subtleties and sophisms" could "compose the whole of this cobweb science of Ontology." For Carlyle, metaphysical clothes are (pun intended) a physical *habit*: "Consider well, thou wilt find that Custom is the greatest of Weavers; and weaves air-raiment for all the Spirits of the Universe; whereby indeed these dwell with us visibly, as ministering servants, in our houses and workshops; but their spiritual nature becomes, to the most, forever hidden" (Thomas Carlyle, *Sartor Resartus* (London, 1896), book 3, chapter 8, p. 206). That is, we are blind to what is customary.

19. Barbara Johnson, "The Frame of Reference: Poe, Lacan, Derrida," *Yale French Studies,* 55/56 (1977), 457-505; hereafter cited in text as FR.

20. Kurt H. Wolff, ed. and tr., *The Sociology of Georg Simmel* (New York, 1964); hereafter cited in text as *SGS*. As Simmel notes, "in earlier times, functionaries of the public interests were customarily clothed with mystical authority, while, under larger and more mature conditions, they attain . . . through their distance from every individual, a certainty and dignity by means of which they can permit their activities to be public" (336). Without the "mystical authority" of visible robes, the canopy gives the Emperor, his chamberlains, and the townspeople "cover," and reminds the crowd who and what the Emperor is. As an allegory of nineteenth-century political dismantling, this preoccupation with ceremony makes sense. In the emerging democratic political movements of the 1830s, a naked king—a king divested of power—was just what people were clamoring for. (Only a decade would pass before Denmark's absolute monarchy was in fact abolished and replaced by a constitution establishing a popularly elected Parliament and guaranteeing new freedoms.)

21. Recall that for Freud, Andersen's tale enacts and *is* a disguise: the dreamer, vaguely ashamed by his public nakedness, has to clothe his dream in a secondary revision—in this case the onlookers' approbation—which the analyst/boy will pull off (*The Interpretation of Dreams,* pp. 242-48). Thus Derrida: "the baring of the motif of nakedness as secondarily revised or disguised by Andersen's fairy tale, will be exhibited/dissimulated in advance by the fairy tale in a piece of writing that therefore no longer belongs in the realm of decidable truth" ("Purveyor of Truth," p. 39).

22. *Hegel's Philosophy of Right,* tr. T. M. Knox (Oxford, 1945), part 3, chap. 2, sec. 328, pp. 211-12.

23. "In comparison with the childish stage in which every conception is expressed at once, and every undertaking is accessible to the eyes of all," Simmel argues, "the secret produces an immense enlargement of life" (*Sociology of Georg Simmel,* p. 330). The image of the naked king evokes and complicates traditionally positive metaphors of "transparent" and "open" government operating under a policy of "full disclosure." By contrast, the idea of a "cover-up" is wholly negative.

24. Carlyle's text, like Andersen's, was influenced by Goethe's writings. The similarities between the two texts are remarkable, though they are not the focus here. From *Sartor Resartus*: "Often in my atrabiliar moods, when I read of pompous ceremonials, Frankfort Coronations, Royal Drawing-rooms . . . and I strive, in my remote privacy, to form a clear picture of that solemnity, on a sudden, as by some enchanter's wand, the—shall I speak it?—the Clothes fly off the whole dramatic corps; and Dukes, Grandees, Bishops, Generals, Anointed Presence itself, every mother's son of them, stand straddling there, not a shirt on them; and I know not whether to laugh or weep. . . . What would Majesty do, could such an accident befall in reality; should the buttons all simultaneously start, and the solid wool evaporate, in very Deed, as here in Dream? *Ach Gott!* How each skulks into the nearest hiding-place; their high State Tragedy . . . becomes a Pickleherring-Farce to weep at, which is the worst kind of Farce; *the tables* (according to Horace), and with them, the whole fabric of Government, Legislation, Property, Police, and Civilized Society, *are dissolved*

in wails and howls" (*Sartor Resartus,* book 1, chap. 9, p. 48).

25. To summarize Barbara Johnson, "The Emperor's New Clothes" raises the problem of the ability of subjective "seeing" to interfere with the polarity "hidden/exposed." She alludes to Andersen's tale to critique the ways that Derrida "sees" only what is within his own sight lines—that is, in focusing on a literary text solely as a signifier of literary text, Derrida is blind to what the social circulation of text signifies ("The Frame of Reference," p. 482).

26. Otto Rank treats "The Shadow" in some depth in *The Double* [1914], tr. and ed. Harry Tucker (New York, 1979). Søren Kierkegaard's first published work is a critique of Andersen's third novel, *Only a Fiddler* (1837), written the same year as "The Emperor's New Clothes" (see Bredsdorff, *Hans Christian Andersen,* pp. 128-30, for a discussion of Kierkegaard's "From the Papers of One still Living. Published against His Will by S. Kierkegaard. About H. C. Andersen as a Novelist, with Special Reference to His Latest Work, *Only a Fiddler*").

27. See also Jack Zipes, *Fairy Tales and the Art of Subversion: the Classical Genre for Children and the Process of Civilization* (New York, 1983), pp. 71-97. Zipes claims that "the widespread, continuous reception of Andersen's fairy tales in western culture" is due to the stories' ideological embrace of "bourgeois notions of the self-made man or the Horatio Alger myth . . . [and] a belief in the existing power structure" (80-81).

28. Alison Prince, *Hans Christian Andersen: The Fan Dancer* (London, 1998).

Niels Ingwersen (essay date 2005)

SOURCE: Ingwersen, Niels. "'I Have Come to Despise You': Andersen and His Relationship to His Audience." *Fabula* 46, nos. 1-2 (2005): 17-28.

[*In the following essay, Ingwersen focuses upon Andersen's "complicated relationship" with his readers, and how the author portrayed his audience in his works.*]

The [quotation "I have come to despise you," used in the title of this essay] is from *Svinedrengen* (*The Swineherd*); it records the prince's parting words to the princess whom he initially wooed so ardently. He wanted her to be his appreciative audience, but she refused to play that role, and—like the female protagonist in the folktale *Haaken Borkenskjæg*[1]—she rejected him. That pattern was one that the young Andersen knew

well: he performed with high expectations and his audience gave him cool—if not worse—receptions. It is a pattern that haunted the successful older man, and thus he mercilessly and repeatedly replayed it in his tales. Directly or indirectly, he wrote nearly obsessively about his public. Needless to say, the relationship between Andersen and his audience was problematic. Although Andersen had become famous in his own lifetime, that relationship did not improve—on the contrary. And it was a complicated relationship, as always when love and hate mingle.

Pardon me for starting this essay with a commentary on a tale that seems to harbor little concern with the meta-matter of artist and audience. In *Svinedrengen,* Andersen uses an age-old folktale[2] but alters it drastically, for in the oral-formulaic tale, of which Andersen must have known a variant, the taming-of-the-shrew narrative ends happily, whereas Andersen concludes his text with the prince rejecting the less than perfect princess with disgust and vehemence, and consequently she is left homeless, a person rejected not only by the man who once proposed to her but also by her own father, for whom it is almost a deadly sin for a princess to kiss a filthy swineherd. In the folktale, the ending is vastly different; the prince, who truly loves the woman who cruelly rejected him, disguises himself as a pauper and educates the princess: she loses her haughtiness, becomes a genuine human being, and in the end the two of them—and their baby—can live happily forever after. That narrative, which includes the humiliation of the woman, may not strike modern readers as being a pleasant one, but the question to be posed here is why Andersen altered the plot so drastically?

My contention is that he is testing, challenging, and teasing his audience. If you agree with the priggish prince or with the utterly conventional father, then— dear member of the audience, Andersen would seem to say—you have failed to listen closely to my tale. Of course, tellers of tales could always pull that trick, but as a rule it seems that most storytellers and audiences did not find themselves in conflict with one another. I admit that we have scant information on the tellers and audiences of the nineteenth century—and that exceptions to the above claim can be found—, but it nevertheless seems rare for Nordic storytellers to challenge or insult their audiences. It appears to me that, in this case—if we can rely on Andersen's implied author— the audience would react against the macho man or men of the story and feel pity for the spoiled brat of a princess, who might well deserve a slap on the wrist but hardly exile from the two worlds ruled by men: her father's and the prince's. Andersen, through his plot changes, very likely asks his readers to get that point.

In short, Andersen uses folklore as a springboard for a sophisticated analysis—probing into the mind of his audience. He goes far beyond the 'naive' relationship between storyteller and audience in traditional folklore. Since Andersen is often considered to be a fairly traditional storyteller, at least when he seems to imitate folktales, some subtle points in his stories have been missed by his audiences—and my contention is that Andersen knew that. His intertextual play with *Svinedrengen* and *Haaken Borkenskjæg* should support this contention.

As I have argued elsewhere, in a sense this naive, selfish, but hardly callous child-woman is punished altogether too harshly by the males in her life, her father and the prince who initially wanted to marry her[3]. To abandon her alone outside the realms of both her father and the prince is a cruel punishment that is hardly commensurate with her 'crime' of kissing a swineherd to gain some fun toys. She is a child, and she is punished by narrow-minded men who fail to see that she is their victim. I know that not all readers will agree with that interpretation, but why would the non-macho Andersen cruelly abbreviate the well-known folktale with its happy ending? I prefer to interpret that as a wake-up call to his audience.

Andersen was a most sophisticated teller of tales, and, of course, he realized that he could not generalize about his readers. In fact, *Svinedrengen* suggests that he knows he is dealing with various audiences: one group will happily cheer as that awful, greedy woman is punished; one might find that the men go too far, but agree that she is a cheap woman who is willing to sell herself for insignificant toys; and yet another may feel that she is victimized by two men who are programmed to have a dim view of women; and I could go on . . . , but it is my contention that, in that masterful revision of a less-than-subtle folktale, Andersen asks his audience: where are you ideologically, dear reader; and how well do you read? It is my surmise that the perceptive reader of the story will realize that when the prince departs with a scathing pronouncement directed at the princess, "Jeg er kommet til at foragte dig, Du" (I have come to despise you)[4], he has arrived at that drastic opinion because she did not live up to his dream of how women should be. Andersen had a keen insight into the sexual politics of his day—and was aware of their unfairness.

Permit me to return to a point made earlier. I detect a pattern in Andersen's relationship to his audience. Initially, he had high hopes of approval, of being accepted, even loved, but as he gradually got to know his audience—perhaps especially the theater-goers and the critics—he felt that he was not truly understood, and with *Svinedrengen,* as well as other tales, he took revenge. I find it tempting to suggest that the prince's final statement ought to be redirected against those who fail to grasp what Andersen—the subversive social critic—really is doing with this remarkable revision of a venerable folktale. He engages himself and his audience in a sophisticated meta-game.

That Hans Christian Andersen loved and craved recognition is a well-known fact. Klaus P. Mortensen highlighted that craving in his tale of little Hans Christian singing outside a garden fence in Odense while being fully aware that the well-to-do people beyond the fence would listen to and admire his beautiful voice[5]. That scene suggests that young Andersen was fully aware of the fact that he was attracting the attention and admiration of his audience, the prosperous people sitting on the opposite side of the real and symbolic fence that separates the rich and the poor. The scene illuminates not only Andersen's ardent desire to obtain admiration, but also his employing various strategies to attract attention and applause. Andersen openly admitted that he wanted fame, and even if that fame should prove to be hollow—as he confessed later on that it was—he nevertheless could not abandon his quest for it. His striving was most certainly successful, and even if he often lamented that he was not fully appreciated—and lapsed into dour moods—he received a great many accolades that simply proved that he had achieved the fame for which he was craving in his younger years. But accolades galore do not add up to a sense of being accepted and appreciated.

If you want recognition, admiration, fame, and applause, you need the roar of an audience. Andersen loved that roar (not least from theater audiences). His early tales record the joy of receiving the approval and applause of a benign public. In *Reisekammeraten* (*The Travelling Companion*)[6] the court rejoices when virtuous Johannes answers the bewitched princess's riddles correctly and, finally, wins her hand. Audience, hero, and implied author coexist in sweet harmony. Likewise, in *Den grimme Ælling* (*The Ugly Duckling*), the protagonist, after many hardships, reaches a lovely new home in which he is appreciated by his peers, the swans, as well as by the admiring human beings who throw food to them. But already by then a perceptive audience may wonder about Andersen's view of his readers. Why? Because text and subtext seem to be at odds. The readers may seem to be reading two different tales. More to follow shortly.

Another early example deserves mention, namely, *Den lille Idas Blomster* (*Little Ida's Flowers*), for in that tale, we meet a storyteller, a humorous young student, who by creating an imaginative fiction, explains to Ida why her flowers are fading: they have been dancing all night! Ida is a wonderful audience, for she laughs and easily goes along with the student's playful narrative, which pokes fun at those who have no concept of *homo ludens*. Later, during the night, Ida has a dream, or a fantastic experience in which she witnesses her flowers joyfully dancing; they tell her that in the morning they will wither—suffer what people call death—but next year they will be reborn. In that minimalistic tale Andersen deals with the issue of children and their comprehension of mortality. But could Andersen be sure that all his readers would get that consoling message?

In both *Den grimme Ælling* and *Den lille Idas Blomster* other, less appreciative audiences make their disturbing entrances indicating that Andersen knew some members of his audience would resist the reading which his implied author strongly suggested. Before the duckling/swan reaches his idyllic, biedermeierish final home, he has encountered many crude critters who have no appreciation of him whatsoever, but tell him that he is ugly and that he ought to conform to their ways. In short, he meets others who inform him that he is a marginal individual who has no chance of succeeding, and he, the duckling—their audience—buys, at least intermittently, into their perception of him. I shall refrain from a biographical commentary; after all, there is no need to reiterate previous scholarship.

In *Den lille Idas Blomster,* an old chancellor disapproves strongly of the student's playful approach to existential issues; the act of storytelling is questioned. The chancellor, like the music master in *Nattergalen*—both caricatures of the worst aspects of the rationalist—denies imagination any authority to deal with life. In fact, they both seem jealous of those who let art guide them in their understanding of existence. The old chancellor is, of course, an esteemed member of society, whereas the young student is not. But it is early in the game, and in both tales the negative audience is clearly defeated. That was not to last. Why not?

One reason often offered for Andersen's disenchantment with his audience is his displeasure with Denmark, especially Copenhagen. That long and tortuous story readers can consult elsewhere in detail. There can be little doubt that Andersen felt that his countrymen failed to grasp his genius—whereas the English and the German-speaking people took profoundly to him. Clearly, he received more praise outside of Denmark than within, and vain Andersen needed a steady supply of appreciation, which he felt that the closed circles of Copenhagen were not always ready and willing to provide. That being said, another reason—and, as far as I am concerned, a more important reason—for Andersen's disenchantment should be suggested: he felt that his audience failed to understand him. In a plethora of stories Andersen seems to comment, covertly as well as overtly, on his audience's lack of perception. In *Den grimme Ælling,* the duckling has enticingly told about her/his joy of swimming and diving but the response is sour. Then the duckling cries, "I forstaae mig ikke!" (You don't understand me!)'. That was to foreshadow many of Andersen's feelings about the audiences who listened to/read his tales.

Let us fast forward to *Nattergalen* (*The Nightingale*). It is obvious that the song of the real nightingale is pure poetry, art with life-giving power, but how many people of the realm grasp that? (Most of them listen to the phony music-master.) And even if they name their child after the nightingale, it may well be because it is fashionable—after all the emperor seems to like the bird's singing. Only the poor and the ruler—how Romantic can you get—really fathom the beauty of the bird's song. Andersen is presenting a view that is not uncommon for Romantics, namely, that only the few will understand the exquisiteness of their poetry. Many Romanticists had a grim view of audiences as a bunch of philistines—thus, the initial address of many a book to 'the dear reader', the single individual who truly understands the author. This is a view that Søren Kierkegaard pushed to an extreme when he addressed the sole, solitary individual who was the only one to grasp what he was writing. It is with a bit of irony one recalls that Kierkegaard loved folktales, texts that presume that we all join together and enjoy the telling of stories.

Kierkegaard would be satisfied, he says, with a single, solitary, good reader, but Andersen was an author who wanted to reach the many. And he did. His novels were popular, very much so outside of Denmark; his tales won him fame, and even his plays—some of them—were quite popular in Copenhagen. He delighted in his popularity abroad and most certainly courted it. His two trips to England vouch for that. He was, and remained, an insufferable man in need of admiration. That need was nearly like a drug. Nevertheless, he became increasingly disillusioned with his audience and more and more tales dealt with his disgruntlement. That is a sad development, but not necessarily an unjustified one.

It is one that can be detected early. In his adaptation of the tale he called *Keiserens nye Klæder* (*The Emperor's New Clothes*), Andersen makes it clear that everyone, of high as well as of low standing, is corrupt, and that all are unfit for their positions. That view of audiences may, however, be caused by choice of genre, for though the jocular prose tale (or *Schwank*) tends to take a dim view of humanity, Andersen continued to imitate it freely, often using the form of trickster tales, and to reinforce that genre's less than gentle take on human activities—even if Andersen substitutes humans with animals, insects, or inanimate objects. But that misanthropic view of beings may be one that the satirist enjoys, as he depicts—and in a sense delights in—human folly. And when he uses the jocular tale, he is winking at his audience, as if saying, you and I agree, don't we, about the folly of these characters. In short, Andersen and his audience were still on the same side, enjoying a cozy relationship. In a sense, the *Schwank*-inspired tales are among Andersen's happiest, for in them the implied author assumes that author and audience are merrily and nastily giggling together. These tales convey some of the same joyful sassiness that is found in the whimsical *Fodreise fra Holmens Canal til Østpynten af Amager i Aarene 1828 og 1829* (*A Walking Tour from the*

Holmen Canal to the Eastern Point of Amager), possibly the happiest book that Andersen—the young Andersen who felt free having escaped from the straightjacket of his high-school experience, ever wrote.

But Andersen complicated the jocular tales when imitating them. Thus, the readers may not quite follow him. Even a sophisticated reader of Andersen, namely, Jens Andersen, who recently published a splendid biography of the storyteller, shows that he fails to grasp how insightful Hans Christian Andersen was of the darkness of human nature when, in hasty passing, he calls the protagonist of *Lille Claus og store Claus (Little Claus and Big Claus)*[8] "den kække, kreative lille Claus"[9], and he may be that, but he is also a coolly calculating manipulator of others and will stop at nothing to satisfy his own greed. That Andersen censored the folktale on which he based his version cannot hide the fact that the protagonist is a self-serving, gleeful crook. Late in his life, Andersen composed some jocular tales that were marvelously subversive and took a very dim view of the audience. To some of these I shall return, for they are among Andersen's best texts.

When Andersen, however, wrote stories that were close to the tale of magic—which follow a modified or obstructed Proppian pattern and tend to record the human quest for happiness—it seems that he parted ways with his audience. The audience wanted a happy ending, but Andersen often seemed to withhold it. *Svinedrengen* is just one example of a revision that Andersen undertook—one that darkened the world view of a text considerably—but it was one that he repeated several times. If, for example, one moves from *Den grimme Ælling* to *I Andegaarden (In the Duckyard)*, it seems that the outlook has become tragically grim; in the former story, the young swan escapes from a bourgeois environment that is utterly unappreciative of him and utterly conformist, but no such pleasant solution is given to the little songbird—or artist—in *I Andegaarden,* for in the end that docile creature, which is only trying to please, is pecked to death by a high-ranking member of the duckyard society. Who listens to the artist and who cares? Just as in *Gaaseurten (The Daisy)*, Andersen is venting his anger against those who do not appreciate him, and he stacks his cards well by letting the daisy and the songbird be incredibly sweet beings without a dark, unpleasant, or critical thought. In short, audiences must side with the victims. Andersen grew fond of writing tales about victims—and victimizers. The manipulative anger in *Gaaseurten,* as Klaus P. Mortensen has convincingly demonstrated, is a smart and conniving way of programming or seducing audiences[10]. Andersen asked for the compliance of his audience, but perhaps it was wise of the audience, at times, to resist Andersen's appeal to it. Andersen wrote about numerous tricksters and exposed them, but most certainly he was one himself.

In the wonderfully snide tale *Den flyvende kuffert (The Flying Trunk)*, Andersen offers an insightful study of the artist as a trickster and seducer. The protagonist is a young spend-thrift and rascal—and a person who puts his own satisfaction first and foremost. Like many protagonists of the jocular genre he is callous and manipulative. Through devious means, he gains access to the royal house of a distant kingdom and successfully woos a beautiful eligible princess; his major asset is that he can tell stories, and his main audience, the emperor and empress, want stories that are moral and entertaining. He tells his tales for the purpose of winning the hand of the princess, and he tells them well, for he is warmly accepted as a future son-in-law. That storytelling session is most revealing about Andersen's relationship to his audience: the story that the protagonist tells, one that is moralizing and entertaining—as the authoritative royal audience has requested—predicts the fall of the monarchal order and the rise of democracy; in short, the narrative ought to upset the emperor and empress profoundly, but they are clueless, an audience that completely misses the point. *Den flyvende Kuffert* gives voice to the subversive Andersen, who on the surface seems so innocent, but tends to create a subtext that undermines, and even insults, the audience who wants to believe that the story is an innocuous entertainment. Once again, when the text is close to the jocular tale, Andersen may have felt that his audience would gleefully share his insights and enjoy his sharp ridicule of the ruling class. But perhaps his readers, like the imperial couple, missed the point entirely and merely experienced the story as a nicely entertaining and moralistic tale (after all, the young man never gets to marry the princess, for chance or providence—take your pick—destroys his flying trunk and sends him packing).

Few members of any audience would, however, be able to view *Skyggen (The Shadow)* as innocent entertainment, for evil prevails and goodness is defeated. The "once upon a time" tale of magic is turned topsy-turvy, for the evil person gets the beautiful princess—who may not quite be such a wonderful person—and the good-hearted 'hero' is executed. Happy ending defunct! Once again we are close to the *Schwank* genre, but Andersen is not winking this time. In a sense, that sap, the scholar who fails to comprehend the schemes of the shadow, represents the audience of the tale, and not until the very end when it is too late, does he grasp what plot it is that has been unfolding. The shadow clearly knows that he is dealing with an audience that does not easily pick up signs of danger and that is easily fooled, deluded by ideas of what is 'true, good, and beautiful'. The audience—a learned man, to boot—is so intent on sticking to his harmonious view of the world that he ignores the shadow's ominous narratives, ideas, and behaviour. In a sense, the scholar gets what he deserves, but that outcome is most unsettling. It is as if Andersen is saying, if you do not get my points, you are a fool. Just see what happened to the scholar!

In the tales for which Andersen found inspiration in legends, his dependence on folk narratives are not easy to detect, for the fact that legend does not adhere to any given structural patterns may make the reader assume that Andersen is on his own[11]. In tales of magic and jocular tales one knows what to expect, not so in legends. To a much higher degree than the tale of magic and the jocular tale, the legend is a probing into the unknown. Perhaps that is why so many legends deal with death.

Just one example should underscore some points made in this essay. With *Historien om en Moder* (*The Story of a Mother*), Andersen most certainly created a small masterpiece that is highly original, but he relied heavily on many tales about the bereavements of mothers and on a plethora of folk beliefs. With that story, he asked his audience, once again, do you listen to me carefully enough or read me well? It is easy for readers to consider this tale as a parallel to *Barnet i Graven* (*The Child in the Grave*), for in both texts, to the consolation of the mothers, the dead child ends up with God in Paradise, or so it seems to the reader who wishes for a harmonious closure. The endings of the two tales differ drastically, however; in *Barnet i Graven,* the child happily envisions its transition to a glorious Paradise, and, thus, its mother can return to her family reconciled to the loss of her baby. In *Historien om en Moder* Death takes the child into the other world, and the mother knows that her child will now be with the Lord in Paradise. But the perceptive reader is lost in ambiguity, for the major authority on afterlife, Death himself, repeatedly calls whatever is on the other side 'the unknown land'. In fact, the last line of the tale—and that position lends authority to it—goes, "Og Døden gik med hendes Barn ind i det ubekjendte Land" (And Death went with her child to the unknown land)[12]. In short, we cannot know what awaits us as we leave this life. Perhaps it is highly understandable that, consciously or not, readers who want Andersen to be a solid Christian—as he seemed to be in the disconcerting *De røde Skoe* (*The Red Shoes*) or in the traditional *Det gamle Egetræs sidste Drøm* (*The Old Oak Tree's Last Dream*)—would overlook the ways in which Andersen undermined Christian belief in *Historien om en Moder.*

In his notes or journals Andersen did not state his misgivings—more about that peculiar omission as this essay concludes—but in some of his tales he is preoccupied with the inability of people to grasp the world around them. Andersen lamented that lack of perceptiveness in *Lygtemændene ere i Byen, sagde Mosekonen* (*The Will o' the Wisps Are in Town*) and sadly suggested that the passing of time left audiences insensitive to the spirit of the old tales; he is clearly the protagonist of the text and admits that he no longer finds any inspiration for the telling of new tales. A new muse, however, the bog witch—not a pretty creature descending from above but one who rises from the depths of the murky bog (the nasty subconscience?)—grants him new inspiration. That is, of course, a lovely development, but it is clear that the new muse will offer only dark forms of inspiration, insights that will reveal the corrupt sides of society. The protagonist can now write about what the new muse has told him, but he cannot expect anyone to listen—and one might add—to understand!

Andersen's sadness can be detected in two of his late and best tales, *Loppen og Professoren* (*The Flea and the Professor*) and *Tante Tandpine* (*Auntie Toothache*); the two are sophisticated texts, far removed from folklore, but they have touches of both the tale of magic and the jocular tale. Some form of a quest is present in each of them, however, it is undermined by a wry or glum humour. In both, however, Andersen lashes out at his audience. In *Loppen og Professoren,* the flea is representative of Andersen's art—it has a bite—but the audience nevertheless falls in love with it. That audience is embodied by the princess of the savages, and she demands total control of the flea. Andersen's view of his Copenhagen audience? In a sense, an audience that wanted Andersen to conform and relax (the artist is relegated to a pleasant hammock, is completely inactive, and is bored witless). He is rendered safe.

But artists and art cannot be domesticated. The tale is one of a rebellion against society, the status-quo society. The professor—a fake title, naturally—contrives a plan to deceive the princess and all her underlings; he pretends to work in the interest of the princess and her realm by announcing that he will create a canon—something that any aggressive country would desire. And since the majority of the people as well as their rulers, are ignorant—shades of *Keiserens nye Klæder*—the professor, a consummate trickster (i.e., a liar), manipulates the rulers of the realm to provide him with materials to make a balloon, which allows him and the flea to escape from the land of the cannibals and to live happily forever after. Art and artist are reunited, and a stupid audience is fooled and left behind. The few who understand the tale can laugh happily—or sadly, if they should deplore the fact that the cannibals were a pitiful public that could never grasp what had happened to it. The tale is a somber and whimsical take-off on the jocular tale; the public that grasps Andersen's points laughs, but perhaps cynically, for his view of the audience is totally disillusioned. *Loppen og Professoren* is a spirited, funny, and darkly weary tale. Certainly Andersen's tales invoke many different kinds of laughter from its audiences.

Even more merciless is the old Andersen's view of a sycophantic audience in *Tante Tandpine.* In that first-person narrative, Auntie is an overly sweet person who has always wanted to sugarcoat life for anyone around her. She represents *Biedermeier* at its worst: all pain of life is eliminated for the sake of harmony. She has lost all her teeth, her ability to feel the pain of toothaches, and—the tale suggests metaphorically—has lost thus her grip on reality. When her old and realistic former suitor, Brewer Rasmussen, jokingly suggests that to her, she is furious and reveals that her sunny world view is a sham. The narrator, a child then, keenly observes Auntie's psychic weaknesses but does not judge them as such. He merely renders them naively—and, of course, he likes his Auntie's inability to deny him sweets. As time moves on, Auntie becomes, it seems, more important in the narrator's life. He reads all his artistic attempts to her, and she offers her admiring, sweet reactions. The tale is a complex one that deserves thorough analysis, but it is unambiguously clear that Aunt Mille is an embodiment for Andersen of the audience—one that thoughtlessly praises the artist to the skies but fails to comprehend his deeper emotions. When the student, in his mini-tale of a leaf, records human beings' existential ignorance and anguish, Aunt Mille is exuberant over his talent. The implicit pain in that tale, she either ignores or does not grasp.

Even when Aunt Mille is somewhat critical, she misses the point. The student has written an account of a tortured, sleepless night in his rented abode—he reminds the reader of Poe's hyper-sensitive Usher—and he reads that detailed account of both physical and mental pain to her. She is exalted, praises him, compares him to Dickens, but asks him—adding insult to injury, if you know Dickens—to add unhappy people to his depiction of that sleepless night. Auntie, the utterly clueless member of the *Biedermeier* society, fails to realize that the narrator—the sufferer who is denied rest—is that tragic person. As the story concludes, after a nightmare that reveals that toothaches are metaphors for existential pain, the narrator realizes that he must keep his distance from Auntie. She wants to know whether he has made up any new stories, and that he has done through his dream, but he denies it vehemently. In short, he refuses to give in to the demands of his public.

Tante Tandpine is Andersen's farewell to his life, his career, and most certainly to his audience; and he makes it sadly obvious that he has no respect whatsoever for the last of them. If Andersen's later tales seem to strike a tragic chord, it may well be caused by his estrangement from those whose admiration he wanted so vehemently in his youth. In many ways he gained that admiration, but—at least at times—he saw it as shallow.

Various Andersen biographers have shown him to be a bundle of contradictions; the above should have supported that view. As Kierkegaard made clear, Andersen was not a man of consistency. He adored being adored, but he knew deep down that such adulation was a sham. As Klaus P. Mortensen has put it, Andersen was in a sense "a nowhere man"[13]. Andersen scholars know a good deal about him, and yet he remains illusive. Excellent—as well as poor—biographies have been written on Andersen; his journals and notebooks have found their way into print, as have numerous letters to and from Andersen. And, of course, Andersen's less than trustworthy autobiographies are available to those who want to hear from the master himself. But all this does not quite add up, and Andersen's character continues to be as slippery as one of those eels that one might try to capture in Danish streams. In spite of the fact that three new biographies have appeared fairly recently—after all Andersen turns 200 in 2005—that is still the case[14]. Why?

My tentative answer to that question is that Andersen very early established a skewed view of his audience. And quite early in the game that was his life he realized that he would be a famous man whose mere scribbles would be perused. In short, he tended to write, even when his letters and notes seemed most private, with his audience in mind. One may ask whether he was aware of it, and the answer, of course, blows in the wind. Nevertheless, a man like Andersen, who was so keenly aware of the presence of a public, could hardly express himself, whether he wanted or not, without that public in mind. In short, it is hard to find the real Andersen in his autobiographies, letters, diaries, etc. He is always hiding behind a series of masks—just like the third brother in *Noget* (*Something*), the one who protected himself by pretending that he was participating in a masquerade. That disturbing tale does not inform readers whether the strategy worked, for we do not discover whether the brother preserved his identity or lost it through his role-playing. Andersen was perfectly capable of playing some neat modernistic games with his readers. It seems to me that one only meets the real Andersen in his best tales, which is a point that even excellent biographies have failed to make. Some tales are written in sorrow, many in anger, others in pleasure, but when the tales are of quality—not all are—one detects a joy in them, a joy of creativity. And in those tales Andersen, I submit, donned his masks. In doing so, he dealt again and again with his complicated, conflicted, and eventually sad, even contemptuous, relationship with his audience. Obviously that relationship was in its nagging way an inspiration to him, yet a haunting one, for he could not leave it alone.

Notes

1. An early Norwegian variant of AaTh 900: King Thrushbird, cf. Asbjørnsen, P. Chr./Moe, Jørgen: *Norske Folke-Eventyr.* Christiania 1866, no. 45.

2. AaTh 570: The Rabbit-herd.

3. Ingwersen, Niels: Being Stuck. In: *Studies in German and Scandinavian Literature after 1500: a Festschrift to George C. Schoolfield.* Eds. James A. Parente/Richard Erich Schade. Columbia, S.C. 1991, 167-180, here 170f.

4. *Hans Christian Andersens Eventyr og Historier 1-2.* Copenhagen 1924, here vol. 2, 23.

5. Mortensen, Klaus P.: *Svanen og Skyggen-historien om den unge Andersen.* Copenhagen 1989.

6. Cf. AaTh 507 A: The Monster's Bride.

7. Cf. Andersen (above, note 4) here vol. 2, 64.

8. A version of AaTh 1535: The Rich and the Poor Peasant.

9. Andersen, Jens: *Andersen: en biografi 1-2.* Copenhagen 2003, here vol. 1, 357.

10. Interview with Klaus P. Mortensen, 1998, for the course "The Tales of Hans Christian Andersen", taught at the University of Wisconsin (Madison) through weekly television broadcasts on Wisconsin PBS.

11. Ingwersen, Niels: I Do not Understand Anything. In: *Hans Christian Andersen, a Poet in Time.* Papers from the Second International Hans Christian Andersen Conference. Eds. Johan de Mylius/Viggo Hjørnager Pedersen. Odense 1999, 451-459.

12. Cf. Andersen (above, note 4) vol. 2, 301.

13. Cf. interview (above, note 10).

14. Prince, Alison: *Hans Christian Andersen: The Fan Dancer.* London 1998; Wullschlager, Jackie: *Hans Christian Andersen: The Life of a Storyteller.* London 2000; Andersen, Jens: *Andersen: en biografi 1-2.* Copenhagen 2003.

Abbreviations

AaTh = Conventional numbering of plot types in the system for the classification of fairy tale plot types developed by Antii Amatus Aarno and Stith Thompson.

Jack Zipes (essay date 2005)

SOURCE: Zipes, Jack. "The Discourse of Rage and Revenge: Controlling Children." In *Hans Christian Andersen: The Misunderstood Storyteller,* pp. 77-101. New York: Routledge, 2005.

[*In the following essay, Zipes explores the psychological factors that shaped Andersen's depictions of children as righteous, enraged crusaders for justice in his works.*]

Children are fervent in their looking forward to things, whereas adults can lose a sense of what is there for the taking. The child, it seemed to Freud, was the virtuoso of desire, for whom the meaning of life could only be its satisfactions. And yet it was this appetite—the individual's lifeline—that seemed most under threat from within and from without: from the death instinct and from what Freud referred to rather abstractly as culture.

—Adam Phillips, *The Beast in the Nursery*

It is not generally known in North America and the United Kingdom that Andersen's fairy tales were part of a major breakthrough in Danish children's literature, part of the rise of the Danish Golden Age in the nineteenth century that produced notable writers, poets, philosophers, and artists.[1] Before Andersen created his unusual tales, important pioneer writers began introducing folk tales and fairy tales to the Danish reading public. Adam Oehlenschläger translated fairy tales by German authors in *Eventyr af forskellige digtere* (*Fairy Tales by Various Authors,* 1816). Matthias Winther published *Danske Folkeventyr* (*Danish Folk Tales,* 1823), intended more for people interested in folklore than for children. About ten years later, Christian Molbech produced *Dansk bog I Prosa, til Brug ved Sprogundervisning I Modersmålet* (*Danish Prose for Language Teaching in the Mother Tongue,* 1832), which included six of the Grimms' tales. Most important for Andersen's development were Bernhard Severin Ingemann's *De underjordiske* (*Goblins,* 1817) and *Nye Eventyr og Fortællinger* (*Fairy Tales and Stories,* 1820). There were other imaginative works for children and Danish translations of fairy tales by the Brothers Grimm and the German romantics Ludwig Tieck, Joseph von Eichendorff, Adalbert von Chamisso, Friedrich de La Motte-Fouqué, and E. T. A. Hoffmann, whose works Andersen knew. As Finn Hauberg Mortsensen makes clear:

These Golden Age efforts made children's culture visible and significant; prosperity made it possible; the new family structure made it necessary. But Andersen's discovery of childhood was more profound than that of other Danish Golden Age writers. In his fairy tales children's literature was elevated both aesthetically and psychologically to parity with literature for adults. Whereas the typical children's book throughout the rest of the century was marked by a cozy Biedermeier style, the Romanticism and the modernity in Andersen's texts brought them into dialogue with both the child and the adult, albeit on premises which were completely innocent.[2]

While it is somewhat true that Andersen "innocently" inscribed himself into children's literature, he did not realize how dangerous this inscription would be, for his "discovery" of childhood opened him up to more painful feelings of loss and rage than he realized: unfulfilled desires and needs came back to haunt him. To "save" himself he used the fairy-tale form to sublimate fomenting anxieties, disturbing desires, and furious rage: the fairy tale became his compensation for feelings of mis-recognition and lack. Andersen wrote to understand himself and to make himself understood, and he employed the figures of children and childhood as tropes to speak out against the abuse he felt—often in sympathy with children and, at the same time, to put the child in his proper "Christian" place. In the process, he voiced fervent desires and disappointments that he sought to control and regulate. [As we can see in Chapter 2 of *Hans Christian Andersen: The Misunderstood Story-teller,*] this regulation frequently led to a discourse of the dominated, especially when he sought to rationalize his outrage at the injustices he felt. Yet, there were also "rebellious" stories, sweet tales of revenge that gave him deep pleasure and set standards of moral justification that were shared by many of his readers. These were mainly stories that introduced children as the major protagonists. It is through their voice that he exposed not only social contradictions, but also his own eccentric behavior and his need to control possible outbreaks that might reveal his inner secret life. Andersen was not as innocent as he seemed when he began writing fairy tales for children. He had his own design of morality and idealism that he rationalized as the intelligent design of God, and there is something perverse in his use of children to illustrate not only how proper behavior should work, but how sexuality should be governed. Andersen cleaned up sexuality, which he regarded as messy, and his cleansing process with children as objects needs greater exploration.

Strange to say, despite all posthumous recognition of Andersen as a brilliant writer for children, few critics have taken the time to investigate what it is that made Andersen such an appealing conventional writer for children and adults. To my knowledge, few scholars have investigated Andersen's concept of childhood, how children were conceived and configured in his tales, and how they represent a tension between "civilization and its discontents," to borrow a phrase from Freud, that forms and informs the dramatic conflict of many of his best tales—and some that receive very little attention. Since it would be difficult in a short chapter to analyze all the pertinent Andersen tales that use children and childhood in significant ways, I want to focus on a select number of key texts[3] to explore how he tried to deal with his appetites to adjust to a world that denied him the fulfillment of pleasure, and I want to base my analysis in part on the work of the British child psychotherapist Adam Phillips.

Among the many books Phillips has written, *The Beast in the Nursery: On Curiosity and Other Appetites* is perhaps the most helpful for examining why Andersen's reliance on children and childhood in his fairy tales became so significant for his (mal-)adjustment to a Danish upper-class society that continually frustrated his deepest desires. Phillips argues that our appetites (understood

as interests in life) are what inspire us to enjoy life to the fullest. The difficulty for us as human beings is that we cannot always gratify our appetites the way we want, and we must learn to defer gratification—a key notion in Freud's *Civilization and Its Discontents.* As Phillips comments:

> Being realistic is a better guarantee of pleasure; it is an injunction to want sensibly. The child may expect the earth of himself and others, but if he grows up properly, he will begin to want something else. But what happens to wanting when it isn't wanting everything, and when it isn't wanting what one wants? Or, to put it another way—from an adult point of view, as it were—how do we decide what a good story about wanting is? And which stories will sustain our appetite, which is, by definition our appetite for life? Even to want death you have to be alive. Morality is the way we set limits to wanting; the way we redescribe desiring so that it seems to work for us.[4]

We tend to view childhood as a singular phase in our lives, and once we have moved through it, childhood is left behind us for good. On the contrary, Phillips argues, our very early appetites that manifest themselves in childhood, such as curiosity about sex and relish for sensual experience, remain very much essential driving forces within us. However, the civilizing process, representative of the reality principle, insists on social regulation and compliance with norms of acceptable behavior and tends to dampen the appetites—it can even kill them unless we keep the conflict between our drives for pleasure and social restraints alive. It is through creative sublimation, learning how to articulate and satisfy our drive for pleasure, Phillips suggests, that we can learn to adapt to culture's demands, to become acculturated, while fulfilling distinct desires that enable our different personalities to flourish. Phillips cogently summarizes what maturation entails:

> Growing up then becomes the necessary flight from inarticulateness, from the less affectively organized self, a self without its best behaviors to be on, a self that suffers and enjoys at a pitch that the grown-ups often find daunting. In the old, modern fable of civilization and its discontents, either the child or the culture is demonized. But if we redescribe development as not simply the progressive acquisition of linguistic, and therefore moral, competence, we may be better able to nurture in children the necessary to-and-fro between the articulate selves; a to-and-fro that might be sustainable throughout life rather than having its last gasp during adolescence, or in mystical states, which are always subject to so much fascination and suspicion by those who ironize them (so-called perversion is always a compromised mysticism).[5]

It is not easy for most human beings, however, to accept the to-and-fro of everyday life, especially when the poles that mark the boundaries of this civilizing process freeze and become rigid, making us feel trapped, disappointed, and angry. If we want more than society can afford us materially or spiritually, if we become excessive in our demands for pleasure, we can easily become psychotic in our pursuit of the impossible and may cross the moral and ethical boundaries of society. If we are severely curtailed by the social codes, laws, and customs of a restrictive society that are unjust and oppressive, we feel enraged and humiliated and will try to seek revenge by trespassing the limits. Sometimes the disparities between what we want to be and what we actually think we are become so great that we explode and vent our anger in indiscriminate ways. In each case, rage plays an important role in determining our identities, and rage can be a just expression born out of discontent. Anger and rage reveal our morality and idealism. This is indeed the case with Andersen, and there is a key passage about "just rage" in Phillips's book that reveals a great deal about the inner workings of Andersen's psyche and how his stories may have "sprouted" from this justifiably enraged psyche:

> It is as though our morality, as disclosed by our anger, is a kind of private madness, a secret personal religion of cherished values that we only discover, if at all, when they are violated. The virtues we can consciously formulate and try to abide by are, one might say, our official morality. Our unofficial, more idiosyncratic morality is only available, so to speak, through humiliation. Once you know who or what humiliates you, you know what it is about yourself that you ultimately value, that you worship. Tell me what makes you enraged—what makes you feel truly diminished—and I will tell you what you believe or what you want to believe about yourself. What, that is, you imagine you need to protect to sustain your love of life.[6]

When we explode in anger and rage, we are not really in control of ourselves. The emotions we express are inarticulate. It is through the mode or genre of revenge, Phillips maintains, that we can gain redress. "If rage renders us helpless, revenge gives us something to do. It organizes our disarray. It is one way of making the world, or one's life, make sense. Revenge turns rupture into story."[7]

Rage is important for us because it connects us to our infancy when we are confronted with primal disillusion, that is, when we are forced to realize that we are not omnipotent, that all our wishes and needs cannot be obtained through our own power, and that we are dependent on other people. The dominant tendency in the institutions of "civilized" society fosters behavior and thinking that lead toward cooperation, compliance, or amnesia. Growing up can be a numbing process. We are disposed toward minimizing pain and conflict, rationalizing humiliation, and accepting the injustices of life. It is often through humiliation and rage that we recall the sensual pleasures of our body in childhood that indicated our instinctual love of life. Returning to childhood through literate articulation, therefore, does not necessarily mean a nostalgic longing for a primal state

of innocence, but an endeavor to keep alive curiosity, imagination, interests, and a pursuit of sensual pleasure. It is an attempt to cling to lost idealism and morality. To write about and for children is not necessarily, as many critics have maintained, an act of abuse, concealment of sexuality, or manipulation of children, but it can also be an act of resistance. It is thus the figure of the outraged, enraged, and humiliated child who articulates an adult author's desire to engage society and to expose its contradictions. On the other hand, it is the punished, virtuous, and compromised child figure who articulates an adult author's desire to be accepted by society to which he delegates the right to judge and evaluate him. Either way, it is true, the author is manipulative, and the morality of the rage can easily turn to immoral acts against children and their appetites.

Andersen could go both ways as a writer and individual. He could be compliant and rebellious. He could be polite and outrageous. He was also apparently bisexual and did not know how to deal effectively with his bisexuality. Perhaps the only unifying force in his character was his discontentment and sense of just rage. It is discontentment with himself and society that drove him to become such a keen revengeful writer who set moral standards and ideal goals to which everyone should aspire. Though he often served as an apologist for the principles of domination in his narratives, he also acted out his feelings of rage that he sought to keep alive in provocative stories. At times he turned his rage against upper-class society and children, and other times he turned it against himself as though he loathed himself for not allowing his inner urges to be expressed. This tension between hatred of a superficial repressive society that constrained his urges and fear of his unfulfilled sexual desires, which he condemned as transgression, is at the basis of some of his most intriguing fairy tales in which he used children to test and play out his ideals and morals. In formulating rules of etiquette, behavior, and belief for his children figures, Andersen touched personal tensions closely wired to social tensions, and this touching may account for his wide appeal to young and adult readers, even today.

One of his earliest fairy tales, **"The Naughty Boy"** (1836), which is very rarely discussed, reads like a programmatic statement about how he would use child figures in his tales to try to tame the appetites and curiosity. At the same time, this tale reflects how Eros, the child, resists arbitrary restraints and takes revenge on the world by piercing people's hearts. This very short allegorical tale is a clear illustration about how the unsettled Andersen sought to unsettle his readership, and about the elusiveness of art and children, both of which can penetrate our hearts when we least expect to be stirred. To control the uncontrollable through art was Andersen's goal, and it is the heart of this story.

The plot is seemingly simple: An old poet sits by a cozy fire on a stormy night. All of a sudden, he hears a knocking on the door and admits a little boy, stark naked, water streaming down his golden hair. The only things he carries with him are a bow and arrows. The boy, who resembles an angel, would have certainly died if the kind poet had not let him into the house. Once the boy is resuscitated, he begins to dance about the room in joy. The old poet remarks that the boy's bow and arrows are spoiled. However, Cupid picks up the bow and arrows and proves they are fine by shooting an arrow and piercing the old poet's heart. At this point the narrator informs us:

> The old poet lay on the floor, weeping. He had really been hit right in the heart. "Oh . . . oh . . ." he moaned. "The mischievous child! I am going to tell all the other boys and girls to beware of Cupid and never to play with him, so he cannot do them any harm."

> All the boys and girls who were warned by the old poet did their best to be on the alert against Cupid; but he fooled them anyway, because he is very cunning.[8]

Nobody can stop Cupid. He shoots his arrows at young and old everywhere—in schools, parks, and churches. Finally, the narrator comments tongue in cheek:

> Cupid is a rascal! Don't ever have anything to do with him! Imagine, he once shot your poor old grandmother, right through the heart; it's so long ago that it no longer hurts, but she hasn't forgotten it. Pooh! That mischievous Cupid! Now you know what he is like and what a naughty boy he is.[9]

On one level, the story is about the toppling of "old poetry," the old order, and the rise of the young spirit, left out in the dark. The insistent Cupid, banging on the door of a poet, apparently comfortable and content with himself, takes his revenge. He wants to inspire the old poet with love. But the poet, representing the old order, resists the power of love. He is too feeble, however, to stop the force of Eros. Love and imagination triumph. But it is through the backdoor, so to speak, that love and poetry enter the hearts and souls of people who are warned to be on their guard. Cupid is supposedly dangerous and uncontrollable, and can strike at any moment.

Andersen attaches great importance to the figure of the child as Cupid, who is a menace to society and yet is so necessary for the reproduction of the species and can never be forgotten. The irony of the narrative brings out what Andersen wanted and feared most: pursuit of his powerful appetites and enjoyment of his erotic drives. Andersen associates children with these appetites and drives, and throughout all his fairy tales and stories, he places them in situations in which they must learn restraint. To act upon one's desires without the guidance of God is a sin and must be punished. Cupid is indeed naughty and should not be followed. Love should be sacred and chaste. Above all, Andersen implied in most of his fairy tales that the child should not love himself or herself, that is, should not indulge its desires, but should instead conform to Andersen's ideal of the virtuous Christian child. Andersen is surprisingly rigid in the demands he places upon his child figures. He is compassionate when the children in his tales are downtrodden and turn to God for guidance. He is severe and punitive when they pursue their dreams that involve sensual and sexual exploration. Whoever places himself or herself in God's hands and acts according to Andersen's own ideal moral principles of proper Christian behavior will be rewarded. It is through God that they will also exact revenge. Whoever seeks carnal knowledge and wants to explore his or her own sensual desires is dangerous and must be controlled or punished.

Andersen's views of children and childhood were not static. They were conflicted because he was always subconsciously drawn to the "naughty boy," and this attraction bothered him. As I have proposed above, it is exactly this unresolved conflict that forms the dramatic tension of his tales throughout his life. His constant return to this conflict indicates how vital it was for him, and in each tale he wrote, he reelaborated the problematic of fulfilling sensual desires as a moral dilemma that was and remains a moral dilemma for his readers, even today. Andersen does not become more insightful or aware of himself in the course of writing his tales: he did not come to any greater enlightenment about himself toward the end of the life. He simply became more proficient in using the genre of the fairy tale and fantastic story to express his anger against the world and take revenge through storytelling. He employed child figures to fend off erotic proclivities and create ideal possibilities that revealed both his own and society's contradictions. In the process, he left behind him tantalizing tales that need to be examined with great care for what they say about children and how they use children.

In contrast to "naughty Cupid," there are generally two models of comportment and decorum that he registers in his tales: the good girl, who is mainly self-sacrificial, and the good boy, whose zeal, innocence, and talents lead him to fame and fortune. Andersen weaves or configures these models laden with Christian symbols, if you will, throughout his tales, and they tend to be very gender specific. Given his unconscious misogynist attitudes toward women, he was bound to make distinctions between the proper roles and identities that girls and boys were to assume, as did most people in Danish society of his time—not to mention most Europeans and Americans. His girl figures are most fascinating because he clearly identified with many of them, and the punishments and tortures he created or invented for them were indications of the shame that he felt about himself, his ambivalent rage against society, and the ideal behavior that he sought to construct through the metaphorical destiny of his "heroine." Let us examine a few stories, beginning with **"The Red Shoes,"** which is among his most well-known and most egregious in its brutal treatment of children, especially girls.

To be fair to Andersen, his horrific punishments of his "naughty" child figures were not unusual for his time. Charles Dickens' works are filled with examples of how children were abused in the nineteenth century, but he generally sympathized with the children and placed the blame for their sins on adult society. On the other hand, . . . Heinrich Hoffmann in *Struwwelpeter* (1845), the most famous picture book for children in the nineteenth century, delights in the mutilation of children who are deemed sinners, and the Brothers Grimm also provided horrifying examples of children who, for example, deserved such cruel treatment as being turned into logs because of their disobedience. What makes Andersen's fairy tales slightly different are his constant sanctimonious references to Christian strictures and the ferocity of the punishments he doled out to his child figures, especially girls. There is an implosion of rage in **"The Red Shoes,"** written in 1846, that is highly disturbing.

Instead of taking revenge on society or the oppressors that restricted his movements, Andersen channels his rage in this story against his own creative spirit, against Eros, against curiosity represented by a girl, so that the explosion of his anger becomes an implosion that actually subdues a lively spirit and causes the death of instinctual curiosity. In the course of his story, he disseminates notions of childhood that call for the incarceration of the appetites and conformity to the religious penal rules of his times. Karen, his innocent victim, is selected as his exemplary figure/victim to demonstrate proper moral behavior and decorum in times of crisis. A poor village girl, she is adopted by a rich lady when her mother dies, and she is forced to abandon red shoes, which she thinks are her good luck charm that attracted the attention of the rich lady. Later, when she sees a princess dressed in a white dress and red Moroccan leather shoes, she finds them the most desirable things in the world. She deceives her foster mother and convinces her to purchase similar red shoes for her confirmation, and she even wears them to communion, despite the fact that the old lady scolds her and that they cause her to lose control of herself. She is clearly obsessed by the red shoes; they have become her fetish. When her foster mother becomes deathly ill, Karen decides to go to a ball rather than to tend the old woman. However, once she puts on the red shoes, they carry her away from the ball over fields and meadows and through the graveyard until she reaches the church door, barred by a stern angel with a shining sword (p. 292):

> "You shall dance," he said, "dance in your red shoes until you become pale and thin. Dance till the skin on your face turns yellow and clings to your bones as if you were a skeleton. Dance you shall from door to door, and when you pass a house where proud and vain children live, there you shall knock on the door so that they will see you and fear your fate. Dance, you shall dance. . . . Dance!"

And dance she does, poor Karen, for days and weeks until she comes to the executioner's cottage. She begs him to cut off her feet, which he does, and then he makes wooden feet for her. Afterward, she learns the psalm that a penitent sings and goes to live with the minister. Totally devoted to God, humble and pious, Karen joins the congregation and receives God's mercy so that "the sunshine filled Karen's heart till it so swelled with peace and happiness that it broke. Her soul flew on a sunbeam up to God; and up there no one asked her about the red shoes" (p. 294).

If total abnegation of one's self, desires, and appetites will bring about happiness, then we can imagine Karen happy in God's paradise. But what if we think children's curiosity should be encouraged and cultivated? What if we believe that we must try to keep our own childlike curiosity alive to enjoy life to its fullest? It is really not difficult to interpret the symbol of the red shoes that cause eternal movement. For Andersen, it was clearly a sign of sin, not unlike the little red riding hood or the scarlet letter, but the sign of sin is also a sign of curiosity and desire that Andersen wanted to repress and suppress. And it is from a struggle within himself that he conceives a model of the good girl: clean, often in white clothes, self-denying, obedient, respectful, shameful, industrious, devoutly religious, and God-fearing. In her upbringing, there is not one hint of pleasure. Andersen's story outlines a childhood of dread, a childhood in which the girl is to learn to dread her own desires and impulses. If naughty Cupid could not be caught in one of his first stories, Andersen made sure that the tantalizing figure of erotic desire would be caught and punished in later stories, at least, those that were apparently addressed to children and parents looking for tips on how to raise children. We can see other dreadful examples in such tales as **"The Little Mermaid,"** whose voice is taken away from her and her movement curtailed, or **"The Girl Who Stepped on Bread,"** in which a proud and arrogant girl is punished by being sent to hell for discarding some bread in order to keep her shoes clean.

There is, of course, a more positive away to analyze Andersen's tale and to view it as a critique of the socioreligious code that drives a young girl to destroy herself. In her highly insightful essay, "Red Shoes and Bloody Stumps,"[10] Erin Mackie explains how significant the red shoes can be as fetish if one acknowledges the deep powers of the fetish and gets in touch with it:

> But really getting in touch with the fetish involves not the positivist assignation of value—critical, social, and political—to concepts outside the fetish's logic, but the

recognition of the critical, even revolutionary powers of the fetish itself. Indeed, one way to talk about positivism lies in the identification of those notions it fixes against the (false) fetishized values it critiques. . . . Fetish is pitted against fetish in an interdependent logic where each is "contaminated" with the talismanic trace of the other it would displace. In Andersen's tale the red shoes become fetishes of Karen's misplaced values, the shoes operating as a counterfetish to reveal and transgress what, from the perspective of an underclass, beautiful, and ambitious young girl, is the bad juju of a socioreligious system fixed against her.[11]

The red shoes are thus similar to the figure of the recurring figure of Cupid in **"The Naughty Child"**: they are magical like our appetites, for they cannot be tamed on this earth, and Karen's obsessive appetite reveals the injustices and mortifying humiliation that any child from the lower classes must suffer for desiring to improve his or her lot. Though she is punished for her fetish, the harsh punishment does not fit the crime, and one must wonder why a girl's innocent longing for some beauty in her life is considered a sin. The ending of Andersen's tale is, as Mackie points out, clearly contrived and relies on a deus ex machina in the person of the angel. Andersen sought unsuccessfully to cap his own curiosity, attraction, and appetites aroused in his childhood by bottling them. Afraid of where they might lead him and did lead him, he enacted a kind of self-punishment on the poor girls in his tales for their transgressions and rewarded their submission to a religious code that never led to self-fulfillment.

Andersen only treated girls leniently if they were humble and devout. In **"The Little Match Girl,"** a forlorn soul is afraid to return home because she had not sold any matches and her father might beat her. As she lights the matches in an alley to keep herself warm, she has lovely visions of a pleasant home life. Though these visions do not prevent her death, they do enable the reader to see how she is rewarded for her simple piety by her grandmother, who fetches her and takes her to God. In **"What the Whole Family Said,"** little Maria celebrates her birthday by asserting how lovely it is to live, and her godfather supports this view by stating that "life was the best of all fairy tales" (p. 999). It is not clear at first what Andersen means in this little vignette, but it soon becomes evident when the godfather instructs Maria that everything that has happened or will happen was written down in the Bible. Furthermore, he adds, "the older you get the clearer you see that God is with you—both in adversity and when Fortune shines upon you—and that life is the very best fairy tale, and it is He who has given it to us for all eternity" (p. 1001).

The good girl is the pious child who will always be saved by God as long as she has faith in his omnipotence. There is hardly a girl or woman in Andersen's fairy tales who triumphs in life because she is adventurous and daring—with the possible exception of Gerda in **"The Snow Queen."** Even the shepherdess in **"The Shepherdess and the Chimney Sweep"** loses her courage in her flight from a forced marriage when she encounters the vast wide world. She returns to the parlor ready to sacrifice herself and submit to the rule of the Chinese mandarin. What is most interesting about the girl figures in Andersen's tales is that they often die and are transformed into spirits serving God. They rarely are allowed to develop, and if they do, their "realms of happiness" are associated with domesticity. A girl is to be domesticated, to become a domestic if not on earth, then in God's paradise.

It is much different with Andersen's male figures, whose tales are more often than not stories about the rise from rags to riches and fame. As is well known, Andersen was very familiar with Adam Oehlenschläger's play *Aladdin* or *The Wonderful Lamp* (1805), and one motif in his tales about boys involves the opportunism that they must embrace to survive in a class-ridden society, and the other is the decency, kindness, and trust in God that they must demonstrate to achieve what they are apparently born to achieve. In both cases, Andersen channels his rage outward in explosive ways. The fairy tale becomes his genre of just revenge.

The most obvious example of his opportunistic and somewhat violent young hero is the soldier in **"The Tinderbox."** Though he is not a boy, he is obviously very young, and as a child figure, he represents for young readers the desire for omnipotence at all costs that drives them and that they miraculously achieve. It is also clear that this young soldier has been storing a certain rage for some time. Why else does he explode and chop off the witch's head at the slightest provocation? The story is well known and quick to review. The soldier helps a witch by fetching a tinderbox from beneath the ground. He is rewarded with gold but wants to know why the tinderbox is so important. The witch refuses to tell him, and so he kills her. Then he takes the tinderbox into town and discovers its magic secret: if he strikes the tinderbox, a dog with eyes as big as teacups appears and grants him any wish he makes. So he wishes for riches and also nocturnal visits with the princess. But he is discovered by the king and queen, and they have him thrown in jail (without the tinderbox) to be hanged. Right before he is to be executed, he is granted one last wish, and he asks to smoke a pipe of tobacco. He takes out his tinderbox, which he had recovered thanks to a boy, and strikes it three times. Three dogs appear, and they attack the judge and royal council and send the king and queen flying, never to be seen again. The soldier marries the princess, and they become the new king and queen.

This is one of the few tales Andersen wrote that has no apparent moral, unless one understands that the soldier has already been mistreated in the war and has been a puppet of the king. If one assumes this mistreatment, common in related folk tales, the only morality is one based on just rage: the lower-class hero takes revenge on the upper classes. He shows no mercy because he has obviously been badly treated by his superiors, and he proves that he knows how to survive in a dog-eat-dog world. What is significant here in the portrayal of the young, Aladdin-type hero is that he is smart, ruthless, opportunistic, and decisive. The boy adventurer makes his mark in the world, and he deserves to be recognized because of his talents. Such desire for omnipotence is an infantile urge that can never be fully satisfied, and as Andersen well knew, the pursuit of omnipotence could drive a person crazy or make a man into a criminal. Therefore, he was hesitant to preach this message to young boys and often tempered his rage according to his own personal Christian code. Instead of the rebel, he often chose to portray the "good boy" in his tales.

Generally speaking, the good boy, like the good girl, must demonstrate absolute faith in God, as was demonstrated in one of Andersen's earliest fairy tales, **"The Traveling Companion."** some length. Another example, also based on the folk tradition, is **"Little Tuck,"** about a boy who is babysitting his little sister Gustava while doing his homework; he is supposed to memorize all the towns and cities of Zealand for his geography lesson. When his mother returns home, she peeks out the window and sees an old washerwoman who is laboriously carrying water from the pump in the square. She asks Tuck to help, and he graciously complies. When he returns home, it is late at night, and he goes to bed without finishing his homework assignment. As he dozes off with the geography book beneath his pillow to try to soak in the lessons through osmosis, he feels the washerwoman kissing him and saying to him, "It would be a sin and a shame . . . if you did not know your lesson tomorrow in school because you helped me. Now I shall help you and the Lord will help us both" (p. 331). Indeed, he goes on marvelous adventures in his dreams and visits the towns and cities of Zealand, learning about their history, and he also has a bright future predicted for him. The next morning he jumps out of bed, and the washerwoman comes by, thanks him for his help, and wishes that all his dreams will come true. Andersen ends with a typical wry comment: "Little Tuck didn't remember what he had dreamed; but Our Lord did" (p. 333).

Andersen based the plot of his tale on a simple folk-tale type in which a poor old woman (either a fairy or witch) appears at a well in need of water. She asks for help, generally from a good peasant maiden, and in turn for the help, the maiden returns home and pearls and diamonds come pouring from her mouth when she speaks to her stepmother, while jewels are combed from her hair. Then her stepmother sends her ugly daughter to the well to reap the same reward, except that this daughter maltreats the old woman and is punished. There are hundreds of variants of this tale, and many involve a young boy who sometimes throws a rock at an old woman carrying water or oil. Andersen's charming simple version is a didactic tale that depicts the benefits of generosity, kindness, and hard work. Throughout his tales, there are boys like little Tuck, whose determination, goodness, and innocence are recognized and blessed by God, and they are rewarded. Such tales did not emanate directly from Andersen's rage, but they did reinforce the Aladdin "revenge" motif that runs throughout many of his tales about young protagonists, who, with the help of God or magical powers, rise against all expectations to become rich and famous.

"The Bronze Pig" is another good example. It is a more complicated tale than **"Little Tuck"** and is set in Florence at the early part of the nineteenth century. A poor beggar boy, unable to earn any money, falls asleep on the back of a water fountain made in the shape of a pig. Late that night the pig becomes alive and carries the boy through the city to the gallery in the arcade of the Palazzo degli Uffizi. There he is able to see the marvelous marble statues and paintings for the first time in his life. As the boy gazes at the Medici Venus, the narrator comments, "on either side of her stood a marble statue, each proving that man's spirit and art can give life, can create it from lifeless stone. One of the figures was of a man grinding his sword; the other showed two gladiators wrestling: for beauty's sake the weapon was sharpened and the men fought" (p. 158). The boy is also struck by the painting of Agnolo Bronzino's *Jesus Descending into the Underworld* because of the innocent children waiting for Christ to lead them to paradise. After the boy and the pig view the paintings and leave the arcade, the pig says, "Thank yourself and God bless you! . . . I have helped you and you have helped me, for only when an innocent child sits on my back, do I become alive and have the strength to run as I have tonight. Yes, I even let the light from the lamp beneath the Blessed Virgin shine upon me" (p. 159).

They continue on their way to the Church of Santa Croce, where the boy is once again inspired by the art works in the church. The next morning he awakes on top of the bronze pig and realizes that he must return to his mother, who is expecting money from him. When the beggar boy shows up, his mother beats him, but he escapes and takes refuge in the Church of Santa Croce. Fortunately for him, a kind glove maker takes pity on him and brings him to his home. After speaking to the beggar boy's mother, the glove maker and his wife decide to keep the boy as an apprentice. When the boy is asked to help a painter, a neighbor, carry his paints to the Uffizi, he recognizes the paintings and marble statues and feels the urge to become a painter. Some time later the boy is blamed unfairly by the glove-maker's wife for losing her little dog, and the painter makes peace among them and gives the boy some drawings as a gift. "If you can draw," the child thinks, "then you can call the world your own" (p. 164). So he begins to teach himself how to draw. Once again he has an altercation with the glove-maker's wife because he had tied the dog to make it sit still as a model. This time he is kicked out of the house, and the famous painter takes him under his wing. We learn that, years later, the young boy became a great artist but died shortly before his work was exhibited at the Academy of Art.

There are many themes in this undeservedly neglected tale, such as the power of art and the trials and tribulations of poverty. Clearly, Andersen wants to record the salvation of an innocent child through art, especially religious art. Furthermore, he does not shy away from depicting the impoverished conditions and abuse that poor children suffered during this time. However, in contrast to the destiny that he painted for little girls, this tale shows childhood as a test that the boy can pass. As in **"Little Tuck,"** the beggar boy is saved by inspiration and determination. Nor does he have to kill anyone to gain revenge, for he instinctively becomes aware that he can make his enraged feelings beautiful, that they can serve his art, a lesson that Andersen himself had been quick to learn. The beggar boy shapes the world around him instead of allowing the world to shape him or to deform him. It is clearly this indomitable spirit in the young boys and girls that Andersen wanted to flesh out in his tales. However, it was a zest for life that had to be controlled, refined, and sanctified. If left to their own devices, children might be overcome by their feelings; they could become tarnished or be seduced by evil forces. For instance, **"The Snow Queen, a Fairy Tale Told in Seven Stories"** reveals Andersen's strong belief that children cannot survive without faith in divine powers, and in order to save themselves, they must abandon themselves to the will of God. Many of Andersen's tales have Christian imagery and references that have been eliminated in twentieth-century editions, or simply neglected. We tend to forget that many of his tales are morality plays, especially those explicitly concerned with children. This is most clear in **"Ib and Little Christina"** and **"The Snow Queen."**

To a certain extent, **"Ib and Little Christina"** is a sentimental preview of **"The Snow Queen,"** and it repeats Andersen's favorite story of chaste love, one that he never tired of telling: a boy and girl are drawn to each other in their youths, and promise each other that they will always love one another; however, they are separated. The girl appears to have more fortune than the boy, and when she is older, she marries someone else. The boy remains at home, leading a simple life and is saddened by his sweetheart's marriage. Then the tables turn: the young woman, associated with city life, falls in fortune and dies, and the young man, associated with the country, has a stroke of good luck and arrives in the city to fetch his former sweetheart only to find her dead. In **"Ib and Little Christina,"** Ib remains devoted to Christina until her death in Copenhagen. Then he takes her daughter back to the country to raise her in nature.

Andersen varied this plot in different tales, but the overall message concerns Christian charity, humility and self-sacrifice. This is apparent when Ib and Christina, lost in the woods as youngsters, meet a gypsy woman. She offers them "wishing nuts," and Christina takes two of the nuts that contain a golden carriage with golden horses and ten necklaces, dresses, stockings, and hats. But Ib is left with a little black one. From this point on, their paths will diverge because it is obvious that Christina, like the little mermaid and like Karen in **"The Red Shoes,"** values material things over the genuine country life and the deep love that Ib feels for her. She is more than happy to leave him and go to Copenhagen, where she lives in the lap of luxury. On the other hand, Ib stays in the country, and he makes his fortune because he finds a valuable relic while plowing his fields. He never overreaches. He digs into the fertile soil that provides all he needs. He even gains a measure of revenge thanks to his holding to moral principles: Christina dies impoverished, and the innocent Ib will raise her daughter named Christina. He will be in charge of her upbringing, and one can be guaranteed that he will not allow her to be attracted to luxury and the city. Andersen has a completely repressed and narrowly sentimental view of life: anyone who veers off the path of chaste love and indulges in sensuality will be punished or be hauled back on the clean right path. Boys and girls must learn to have faith, live simply, and place their destiny in the hands of the Lord.

This is the lesson to be learned in **"The Snow Queen,"** which begins with a brilliant and humorous prologue-tale that explains how evil came to the world and why little Kai is kidnapped and placed at the mercy of evil forces. The narrator tells the reader that the most evil troll in the world had once invented a huge mirror that had the power of making anything good or beautiful seem horrid in its reflection, and anything evil and worthless to appear good and worthy. The trolls decide to carry the mirror to heaven to mock God and the angels, but on the way they drop the gigantic mirror so that it shatters into millions and billions of pieces. The result is that when any one of the splinters enters a person's eyes, he would see only the flaws of the world and the faults of the people. If a splinter enters a person's heart, the heart turns to ice. All this, of course, pleases the devil.

After this prologue, the narrator introduces us to the playmates Kai and Gerda, who are about ten years old. They listen to stories by an old grandmother, who tells them about the Snow Queen, who can turn hearts to ice, and that night Kai believes that he has seen the Snow Queen outside his window. During the summer, Kai and Gerda play together in a rose garden, and they sing a song that will become a refrain throughout the tale: "In the valley where the roses be / There the child Jesus you will see" (p. 237).

Soon thereafter two splinters strike Kai in his eye and heart, and his behavior begins to change. He becomes nasty and stops playing with Gerda. That winter, he is kidnapped by the Snow Queen, who carries him off to her realm in the North. The following spring Gerda decides to go in pursuit of Kai, and her story of travails is well known. At first she is delayed by a good witch in her flower garden. Once she leaves this place, she is helped by a crow, a prince, and a princess and given a coach to travel to the Snow Queen's palace. However, the coach is attacked by ruthless robbers who kill everyone except Gerda. Fortunately, a robber girl takes a liking to her and gives Gerda a reindeer, mittens, and boots to continue on her quest to save Kai. After a Lapp woman aids her, Gerda goes to the Finnish woman near the Snow Queen's palace, and the reindeer expects her to give Gerda magic powers. But the Finnish woman explains to him (p. 257):

> I can't give her any more power than she already has! Don't you understand how great it is? Don't you see how men and animals must serve her; how else could she have come so far, walking on her bare feet? But she must never learn of her power; it is in her heart, for she is a sweet and innocent child. If she herself cannot get into the Snow Queen's palace and free Kai from the glass splinters in his heart, how can we help her?

So the reindeer carries Gerda to the Snow Queen's garden and leaves her. When Gerda says her prayers, "a whole legion of little angels stood around her. They threw their spears at the snow monsters, and they splintered into hundreds of pieces. Little Gerda walked on unafraid, and the angels caressed her little feet and hands so she did not feel the cold" (p. 258). Once she finds Kai and weeps on his breast, her tears melt the ice and glass splinters in him, and she sings their psalm:

> Our roses bloom and fade away,
> Our infant Lord abides always.
> May we be blessed his face to see
> And ever little children be.

> (p. 260)

Released from the spell of the Snow Queen, Kai rejoices, and together with Gerda they travel back to their city. As soon as they step through the doorway of the Grandmother's apartment, however, they realize that they have grown up. The Grandmother is sitting in the sunshine and reading aloud from her Bible: "Whosoever shall not receive the Kingdom of Heaven as a little child shall not enter therein" (p. 262). Gerda and Kai now understand the meaning of the psalm and sit and bask in the warmth of the summer day.

It would be interesting to compare this fairy tale to the German romantic Novalis's tale of "Roseblossom and Hyacinth," which Andersen may have known.[12] In Novalis's tale, Hyacinth is in perfect harmony with nature and Roseblossom, and when a strange man arrives and disturbs the boy's mind with a book (Reason), Hyacinth throws the book into a fire and departs on a mysterious quest. However, this quest turns out to be an existential one, and he finally arrives at the sacred dwelling of Isis. There he unveils the Egyptian goddess, only to find Roseblossom and reunite with her in eternal love. Implicit in Hyacinth's quest is that he must leave himself to find himself and the meaning of love. In the draft of another version of this tale, Hyacinth lifts the veil of Hyacinth only to find himself.

Novalis was concerned with the ontological quest of his protagonist, who is originally in touch with his feelings but suffers a breakdown when introduced to book learning. To recuperate the initial bliss he felt, he must follow his intuition and experience different environments before he is mature enough to face the truth of Isis. His growth is dependent on overcoming reason and combining his experience with a grasp of nature to uncover what he really desires in life. Novalis's tale is a recuperation of desire that forms the basis of adult action. Andersen's tale moralizes and tames desire.

"The Snow Queen" ends simply with the triumph of good over evil, and it depicts the child protagonists as adults who remain children at heart and devoted to a Christian stricture. In many ways, the tale is a baptismal ritual: Gerda and Kai must prove that they have expunged the evil in their bodies before they will be accepted in the kingdom of God. All children must prove their "innocence" if they want to be saved. Gerda is, of course, innocence incarnate, and she is one of the few female figures in Andersen's works who does not become contaminated. Moreover, she is much more active than most, perhaps because she is protected by angels. Andersen imagines that children can be infected by evil forces associated with a real devil, who holds them in his power. He also associates evil with cold reason that opposes basic good instincts. The Snow Queen's palace is on the "lake of the Mirror of Reason," and Kai is playing the "Game of Reason" when Gerda finds him. He can only learn to spell "eternity" after Gerda arrives and frees his heart. It is faith that children must learn to trust, and not reason, and it is blind trust in Christian faith that Andersen relentlessly preached in most of his fairy tales for children and adults. To be sure, his Christian faith was mystical and mixed with [Hans Christian] Ørsted's notions of divine intelligence.

As W. Glyn Jones has made clear,[13] Andersen believed in God and was a Lutheran, but he was not orthodox and never fully outlined his beliefs in his essays, diaries, or autobiographies. Nevertheless, when it came to the depiction of children and childhood in his fairy tales, it is apparent that the only good child is the Christian child, who serves God above all, and that God will punish or reward children if they keep the faith. The bond with God is somewhat mystical in the tales, although it is clear—in contrast to most folk tales and fairy tales before Andersen's time, which are secular and place fairies as the most omnipotent creatures—that the child must obey gender-specific, Christian principles of behavior to be accepted in God's paradise. What saves Andersen's tales from becoming Christian stories dripping with moral sentiments is his "innocent" depiction of the tension between the imaginative curiosity and appetites of his protagonists and the divine postulate calling upon them to submit to higher powers—and also to curb the rage that penetrates Andersen's tales.

Yet, one must also ask whether Andersen is really innocent. Was he really so guileless in how he arranged his child figures to exhibit behavior that called for reward and punishment? Do the morality and idealism of his rage excuse his manipulation of childhood and children figures? Does his innocence show his guilt? Did Andersen pander to adult conceptions of what children should be and how they should behave?

Andersen is not unlike another great writer of fantasy, namely J. M. Barrie of Peter Pan fame. Petulant, moody, disturbed, Barrie also catered to conventional notions of sexuality and childhood held by adults when he wrote about children. Moreover, there was a way in which Barrie used his fiction to conceal his desire for children and manipulate them for his own pleasure. In her controversial but convincing study *The Case of Peter Pan* or *The Impossibility of Children's Literature,* Jacqueline Rose explains how desire functions in Barrie's writings:

> Suppose, therefore, that what is at stake in Peter Pan is the adult's desire for the child. I am not using "desire" here in the sense of an act which is sought after or which must actually take place. It is not relevant, therefore, to insist that nothing ever happened, or that Barrie was innocent of any interest in sex (a point which is often made). I am using desire to refer to a form of investment by the adult in the child, and to the demand made by the adult on the child as the effect of that investment, a demand which fixes the child and then holds it in place. A turning to the child, or a circulating around the child—what is at stake here is not so much something which could be enacted as something which cannot be spoken.[14]

Though it would be unfair to both Barrie and Andersen to equate their techniques of writing and their unconscious motives behind their imaginings, there is something very similar in the fabric of their works that is disturbing. It is what Rose calls a sexual act "in which the child is used (and abused) to represent the whole problem of what sexuality is, or can be, and to hold that problem at bay."[15] In Andersen's fairy tales and stories, it is clear from the beginning in a tale like **"The Naughty Boy"** that Andersen does not know what to do with the child's appetites and his/her sexuality (polymorphous, perverse, bisexual) and thus tries to fix it and gender it in absolute terms in his writings. Andersen operated with and on all his child figures to ward off his anxieties about sex and to channel his rage. Yet by operating with principles of intelligent divine design to project how children and adults could protect their innocence (or recuperate innocence) under God's watchful eyes, Andersen sought to repress sexuality linked to the appetites, curiosity, and invention. His mode of revenge writing was chaste, and it involved not only his child figures. He also implicated all the adult figures and himself in weaving what he convinced himself was the Lord's design. Andersen was not an innocent writer. He is inculpated in his very own designs that fostered a myth of how an innocent, talented poor boy could, by God's grace, reach heavenly heights. Such a perverse myth circulates in many forms in our contemporary world and minimizes the diverse nature of human beings and the complex nature of identity formation. For Andersen, there was a formula, and if children veered from it and revealed they were not as innocent as they appeared, they would receive their just punishment and be mutilated, tortured, or put to death. Andersen, the so-called writer for children, could not tolerate the way children are in reality. What is saddest of all, however, is that he could not tolerate the child in himself.

Notes

1. See Flemming Mouritsen, "Children's Literature," in *A History of Danish Literature,* ed. Sven Rossel (Lincoln: University of Nebraska Press, 1992), 609-31. Whereas Mouritsen praises Andersen for transcending the norms of children's literature during this period, I believe that Andersen was much more conservative and conventional than most Andersen scholars admit. Certainly his writing style and themes were unusual for his time, but the ideological and didactic uses of children in his tales are very much in keeping with traditional Christian thinking of the nineteenth century.

2. Finn Hauberg Mortensen, *A Tale of Tales: Hans Christian Andersen and Danish Children's Literature,* Parts I and II (Minneapolis: Center for Nordic Studies, University of Minnesota, 1989), 44.

3. Although it is difficult to schematize which texts are "child-centered," the following tales about children reveal a great deal about Andersen's views regarding children: "The Naughty Boy," "The Storks," "The Little Mermaid," "The Ugly

Duckling," "The Bronze Pig," "The Angel," "The Red Shoes," "The Little Match Girl," "Grief," "Little Tuck," "The Snow Queen," "Five Peas from the Same Pod," "Ib and Little Christina," "The Girl Who Stepped on Bread," "Children's Prattle," "The Dead Child," "In the Children's Room," and "What the Whole Family Said."

4. Adam Phillips, *The Beast in the Nursery: On Curiosity and Other Appetites* (New York: Pantheon, 1998), xv.

5. Ibid., 56.

6. Ibid., 123.

7. Ibid., 126.

8. Hans Christian Andersen, *The Complete Fairy Tales and Stories,* trans. Erik Christian Haugaard (New York: Doubleday, 1974), 39. Note that all quotations from the fairy tales are taken from this edition, and the page references in the text refer to the Haugaard translation.

9. Ibid., 39.

10. Erin Mackie "Red Shoes and Bloody Stumps," in *Footnotes: On Shoes,* ed. Shari Benstock and Suzanne Ferriss (New Brunswick, N.J.: Rutgers University Press, 2001), 233-47.

11. Ibid., 235.

12. See "Hyacinth and Roseblossom," in *Spells of Enchantment: The Wondrous Fairy Tales of Western Culture,* ed. Jack Zipes (New York: Viking, 1991), 300-3.

13. W. Glyn Jones, "Andersen and Those of Other Faiths," in Hans Christian Andersen: *A Poet in Time,* ed. Johan de Mylius, Aage Jørgensen, and Viggo Hjørnager Pedersen (Odense: Odense University Press, 1999), 259-70.

14. Jacqueline Rose, *The Case of Peter Pan or The Impossibility of Children's Fiction,* 2nd ed. (Philadelphia: University of Pennsylvania Press, 1991), 3-4.

15. Ibid., 4.

Jørgen Holmgaard (essay date 2005)

SOURCE: Holmgaard, Jørgen. "Narration and Narrative Techniques in Andersen's Fairy Tales." In *When We Get to the End . . . : Towards a Narratology of the Fairy Tales of Hans Christian Andersen,* edited by Per Krogh Hansen and Marianne Wolff Lundholt, pp. 53-71. Odense, Denmark: University Press of Southern Denmark, 2005.

[In the following essay, Holmgaard centers on the role of the narrator in Andersen's works and the variety of narrative positions and devices employed by the author.]

Almost everywhere in Andersen's fairy tales and stories the narrator is relatively easy to locate and we can easily fix a point of view of what is narrated. So far, narration in these texts does not vary much from what we generally meet in early and mid 19th century prose fiction, i.e. before the more oblique techniques of third person narration start to flourish as they do in the later part of the century, heralded above all by the narrative techniques that [Gutave] Flaubert introduces. But as soon as we take a closer view at Andersen's tales, conventional standards of narration tend to fade away, most strikingly due to the strange but simple fact that even inside very short texts, their narrative positions and view-points defy normal kinds and levels of stability in literary prose narration.

This paper will examine the role of the narrator and the leaps between various narrative positions, devices and modes inside and in-between the entire body of his fairy tales and stories, written between 1835 and 1872.[1] Furthermore, I shall discuss whether certain patterns in his use of narrative positions and techniques can be detected. I shall not conceal from you that I am going to claim a great division located inside this body, or rather a break in the long line of fairy tales and stories. But let me start from the beginning, paraphrasing the words from **"The Snow Queen"**: "when we get to the end we shall know more than we do now".

In **"The Tinder-box"** (1835)—the first tale in the first published volume of his fairy tales—the role of the narrator is still very conventional like in a folk tale. A number of original details appear in the course of events, in the imagery of the tale and in some metaphors, but the innovations as for the role of the narrator are not so obvious. However, already in the following tale—**"Little Claus and Big Claus"** (1835)—a very personal, tongue-in-cheek sort of ironic narrator is suddenly heard. After a conventional narrative set up, in the framework of the folk tale, has been established around a hero who has transgressed social norms and has consequently been expelled from his social surroundings,[2] the narrator shall render some background information about the farmer who has been absent until then, but is now on his way to enter the scene, i.e. to take his adulterous wife and the sexton by surprise. A narrative shift of this kind is, of course, quite normal when character or other information is needed in relation to the reader's understanding of the course of events to follow. But the way this information is presented at once reveals a narrator of a more than twisted character who has not appeared in the text before: "[the farmer] was a good man," the narrator tells us, "but still he had a very strange disease [incorrectly translated "prejudice" in the English version],—he could not bear the sight of a sexton. If one appeared before him, it would put himself in a terrible rage." One might comment on this strange information about the disease of the farmer by pointing to the youngest listeners among the audience. But the very presentation of the adulterous scene tells another story, and the following explanation of the sexton's visit dismisses such a reading: "In consequence of this dislike [the farmer's disease], the sexton had gone to visit the farmer's wife during her husband's absence from home,"—a simple consideration, expression of politeness, concern for the farmer, according to this more than equivocal narrator. And in the same line, the wife treats the sexton so well simply because she is a good woman: "the good woman had placed before him the best she had in the house to eat." Still when the sexton hides, he does so—just as the wife makes all her arrangements—out of concern for the farmer: "He did so, for he knew her husband could not endure the sight of a sexton." The "disease", as is the narrator's way of explaining what happens, is maintained in a very consequent manner and with many extremely entertaining subtleties all the way through the text. For instance, when the farmer cautiously opens the lid of the chest a little, in order to peep into it and have a look at the evil one himself, he springs backwards exclaiming: "I saw him and he is exactly like our sexton".

This is not just a condescending narrator ridiculing a naive farmer who has been victimized by the shrewd hero. It is rather a more than double-bound narrative voice, subtle and ironic and far beyond any of the narrative modes we meet elsewhere in Danish literature of that period. In important parts of the fairy tale, genre and in the didactic fabliau, the narrative mode will be unambiguous, if not before, then in the conclusive moral at the end which also will anchor the position of the narrator in relation to the tale. No wonder we do not find any conclusive moral in this group of early tales.

However, an overtly moralizing narrator is heard in a series of tales following **"The Tinder-box"** and **"Little Claus and Big Claus"**. There is no overt moral in the end of these texts—**"The Princess and the Pea"** (1835), **"Little Ida's Flowers"** (1835) etc.—but intermittently the narrator steps forward addressing the audience saying, for instance, as a kind of emphatically performative utterance: "There, that is a true story", as he does in the end of **"The Princess and the Pea"**. Or he pauses in his narration and comments in a moralizing and sentimental tone how evil the villains and their deeds are, as we see in **"The Travelling Companion"** (1835). But he also picks up a special narrative device that he is going to use repeatedly later on, namely a sudden meta-fictional shift from the narrated events and fictional characters to a foregrounding of the narration itself, bridging between the two levels by way of an explanation that ironically exempts the poet from his narrative authority, like at the end of **"Little Tiny or Tumbelina"** (1835):

> "Farewell, farewell," said the swallow, with a heavy heart as he left the warm countries to fly back into

Denmark. There he had a nest over the window of a house in which dwelt the writer of fairy tales. The swallow sang, "Tweet, tweet," and from his song came the whole story.

One might label this technique "Romantic irony".

In **"The Goloshes of Fortune"** (1838), however, Andersen's use of such different narrative modes and devices inside the same text explodes into a frenzy. He sets out with a classical anecdotal narrative voice informing the reader about background and scenery: "It was in Copenhagen" etc. From the beginning a slightly ironic tone towards the actions is heard. Soon a directly satiric touch follows in the same move motivating an open leap into a "we-narrator", uniting narrator and reader in an expressive distance as objective, physical observers of the people in the scenery, who, strangely enough, at the same time are totally removed from the surrounding very realistic setting: moving from one room to another we suddenly face Fortune and Sorrow (translated Care) impersonated in two Copenhagen chamber-maidens. Thus a narrative frame around a series of new adventures is established, but not without a conclusive leap back into the sort of emphatically performative utterance we met before and which is going to be a staple in the texts: "now look, this was that conversation [not rendered very well in the English translation]", the narrator finally concludes after having referred to the exchange between Fortune and Sorrow informing us about the meta-fictitious frame of the separate stories that the Goloshes make happen.

But the framework is not going to hold at all. The clues leading from one separate story inside the framework to the next do not regularly recur in the frame, as could be expected. They may also be part of the fiction inside the fiction, i.e. when the counsellor tries to escape from the medieval depression—into which the Goloshes have brought him according to his wishes—by stooping under the table and creeping over to the door. During this effort he loses the Goloshes and is at once back in the present and so are the Goloshes. While internal—intradiegetic—devices in this way tie two of the separate parts of the narrative string together, other activities foreground the narrator. He benevolently provides an explanation to the readers from the provinces, as the narrative takes place in a specific Copenhagen setting that only some readers may be acquainted with. The story may stop for a moment while he ruminates life in general terms or assures the reader that he, by the way, has not completely forgotten a character invented some pages ago, but who has since been absent from the story because he has been transformed into an animal and the reverse metamorphosis back to human shape has not yet taken place. Add to this a series of totally anarchic leaps between narrative modes, ample satiric and humorous hints in all directions notwithstanding which level of discourse is at stake. And add eventually the fact that the conclusive stance of the overall narrative pattern in this multilayered mosaic nevertheless is extremely didactic, moralizing if not directly boring. This is a fabric woven of the most disrespectful prose experimentation in the 18th century style of [Laurence] Sterne's *Tristram Shandy,* a burlesque transgression of generic borders in the Romantic style from the early 19th century Germany and a vapid moralism on the threshold between late Biedermeier and emerging Victorianism.

"The Goloshes of Fortune" is certainly a mess, especially as it abruptly changes points of view and leaps between different narrators who are incompatible with each other. Andersen, one might guess, was aware of touching limits in his anarchic use of devices—limits that even he, all his adroitness notwithstanding, was not able to transgress without problems. Therefore, perhaps, he later made a revised version—the first one is from 1838, the latter is dated 1850. Revisions were rare exceptions in his way of working. Though never a really successful tale, it is interesting as an early text where almost all the range—and it is certainly wide—in his use of narrative techniques in the fairy tales and stories can be seen at work. Through his numerous tales written in the 1840s, 50s and 60s the bunch of devices tried out—without much control and coordination—in this early tale gradually begin to organize themselves into certain patterns. We do not see many clean types, so to say. Still, some patterns of emblematic Andersen narrative modes seem to emerge.

* * *

A stable mode is the type of narrator who explicitly addresses his reader, or preferably listener, at the very beginning of the tale, and who emphatically highlights his role and narrative set up. It is often found in fairy tales that they most obviously are meant for children, but this is no obligation. In some stories from the 1850s he occasionally seems to forget himself when he uses the same address though thematically taking up lofty questions of religion and hard-earned life experiences. This is the case in **"Paa den yderste Dag"** (1852) [not translated], **"Two Maidens"** (1855) and **"The Philosopher's Stone"** (1861). Characteristic of this narrative mode may be the introducing phrases of for instance **"The Daisy"** (**"Gaaseurten"**) (1838): "Now listen . . ." This narrator does not hesitate to foreground himself, and by his use of the inclusive first person pronoun "we" in his address to his audience, he makes no secret of how the balance of knowledge—and thus of power—between the two parts of this "we" should be counted. "Now we shall hear how Ole Lukøie . . ." it says at the end of the framing introduction to **"Ole Lukøie"** (1842). No more fooling around between incompatible modes of narration as in **"The Goloshes of Fortune"**. This narra-

tor is omniscient and very openly authoritative. In many tales the ingratiating inclusive "we"-narrator is replaced by a "you"-address which might well have a touch of being directly condescending: "In China, you know, the emperor is a Chinese, and all those about him are Chinamen also" in **"The Nightingale"** (1842), and the address is not always as amusing as here. **"The Shepherdess and the Sweep"** (1845) abruptly opens by a question to its addressee: "Have you ever seen an old wooden cupboard quite black with age, and ornamented with carved foliage and curious figures?" Not waiting for an answer he continues: "Well, just such a cupboard . . ."

The address may also and interestingly be emphatically performative, commanding the addressee to take part of the imagination that the narrator wants to produce, like in the initial frame of **"The Story of the Wind"** (1859) [elided in the English translation]: "Look how the wind up there is chasing the clouds . . . listen how the wind down here is howling through the open gateway . . ." Generally in this mode, the didactic strain is not that far away, and similarities with the more unsophisticated narration in early 19th century German and Danish prose are recognizable. This may be felt especially in tales where this mode of narration combines with a very conventional, almost tepid imagery like in **"The Garden of Paradise"** (1839) and **"The Wild Swans"** (1838). But, conversely, the imagery of a tale may be able to dispense of the dangers in this mode as occurs in **"The Emperor's new Suit"** (1837), where one genial strike of allegorical character is capable of totally playing down this dominant narration. When we hear about the cloth whose colours and patterns, "were not only exceptionally beautiful, but the clothes made of their material possessed the wonderful quality of being invisible to any man who was unfit for his office or unpardonably stupid", the focus moves from the narrator to what is told. In some cases, however, Andersen may be able to highlight this authoritative narration and address the reader in a subtle way—activating meta-fictitious or Romantic ironical shifts—as in the opening of **"The Snow Queen"**: "You must attend to the commencement of this story, for when we get to the end we shall know more than we do now about a very wicked hobgoblin . . ."

The omniscient narrator of this type has no restraints as for knowing what the characters think. He may use his inside view with satiric purposes, commenting ironically and in an amusing way on the thinking he renders. But he also discloses a marked tendency for patronizing his characters. He openly castigates the villains and in many tales he cannot do without regularly flavouring the narration with his compassion, often in a very sentimental way, as in **"The Ugly Duckling"** (1844): "the poor little thing did not know where to go, and was quite miserable because he was so ugly and laughed at by the whole farmyard." He may also directly break the narration exclaiming for instance: "It would be very sad, were I to relate all the misery and privations which the poor little duckling endured during the hard winter". Or the numerous exclamations in **"The Fir Tree"** (1845): "How the fir-tree trembled" . . . "oh how they rushed upon it"

Interestingly, this type of narrator interference disappears or is played down when Andersen later again uses the narrative framing device first tried out in **"The Goloshes of Fortune"**. In the frame of **"Soup from a Sausage Skewer"** (1858) a very discreet narrative "we" unites with the reader in the listener's role in relation to what the mice have to tell. In **"The Marsh King's Daughter"** (also 1858) an even more sophisticated sort of frame is set up. The text begins with "The storks relate to their little ones a great many stories", and the narrator of this information exposes himself more as another "we" than seen before:

> We are only acquainted with one of the two longest and oldest stories which the storks relate—it is about Moses, [. . .] Every one knows this story, but not the second; very likely because it is quite an inland story. It has been repeated from mouth to mouth, from one stork-mamma to another, for thousands of years; and each has told it better than the last; and now we mean to tell it better than all.

Here the narrator might seem to show traces of a well-known ostentation, but this is actually not the case as he is going to transfer the narrative voice to stork-papa who relates the story to stork-mama. The explicit narrator-narratee relation that in a number of earlier tales has been performed directly in a quite ostentatious and braggadocio manner, so to say, is, by this framing, transferred to a place inside the fiction and played there with amusing details, whereas the primary narrator takes care of the other parts of the narration with a newly-won discreteness compared with that we meet in earlier texts. There is no doubt about the moral, and we know exactly who the heroes and villains of the tales are, but this emerges as a result of the thematic workings of the text and is not directly communicated by the narrator. Strengthening this trend, the concluding words of the text are not told by the primary narrator; interestingly enough the narrative voice here is placed with the storks who ironically and metafictitiously comment on what has been told by the primary narrator who took over where the stork himself stopped his narration:

> "Now that is a new ending to the story," said stork-papa; "I really never expected it would end in this way, but it seems a very good ending."
>
> "And what will the young ones say to it, I wonder?" said stork-mamma.
>
> "Ah, that is a very important question," replied the stork.

This transfer of narrative voice from the foregrounded I- or we-narrator to first a number of mice in a framed story, later to a stork in an double-voiced narration alternating between a stork and a narrator, whose ultimate reference is, by the way, the stork's tradition of story telling, is no fortuitous detail. In **"The Story of the Wind"** (1859, i.e. the same period) that was cited before the I-narrator initially exposes himself in a very showy way talking insistently to an explicit "you" whose imagination should be roused. Shortly after, however, this effort turns out to be only a primer to what is the really interesting narrative move in this story, namely that the narrative voice is transferred to the wind. The wind is the narrator of this tale. In **"The Bishop of Børglum and his Warriors"** (1861) we find almost exactly the same framing device with a fast transfer of the narration to the wind that is also invoked eventually when the story should be wrapped up: "Hark to the raging of the angry wind, sounding above the rolling sea!" and a little later: "The wind still keeps up mightily . . .".

This distribution of the narrative voice is interesting. It is at odds with the dominant tendency to foreground an explicit I- or we-narrator keeping the word and commenting on the narrated events and persons with short intervals and with no restraints throughout the text. But the wind itself may well help us to detect how the narrative shifts parallel with a set of other changes in Andersen's writings.

If we take an overall view of Andersen's fairy tales, we can observe that from about 1850 the wind as an acting force generally assumes an ever increasing importance, not only in the narration as just shown, but also in the thematic field. It starts in a subtle way in **"Everything in the right Place"** (1853) where the tutor—representing art, faith, and tradition—cuts out of wood a marvellous flute. When he blew it "a storm rose and roared; "Everything in the right place." And with this, the baron, as if carried by the wind, flew out of the hall straight into the shepherd's cottage" etc. Later:

> The flute was heard at the distance of a mile, and strange events took place. A rich banker's family, who were driving in a coach and four, were blown out of it, and could not even find room behind it with their footmen. Two rich farmers who had in our days shot up higher than their own cornfields, were flung into the ditch; it was a dangerous flute.

This fulfilling of justice, and the establishing of the right order of things are called off after its momentary strike. It is only a wishful stunt in this tale. But after this the wind in Andersen's tales returns ever and again as an acting force, and each time as an open symbol of justice, of the right order of things that cannot be found on this earth, only beyond or in the long run of History. Thus, in this later part of his writings the wind competes with God and Eternity as the words representing the ultimate values in the thematic world of Andersen. In **"The Muse of the New Century"** (1861) [not translated] it also represents Future.

It is, of course, a significant detail that God and Eternity in the 1850s and 1860s increasingly are substituted by an anonymous force of nature like the wind in the workings of the text. But this is actually no wonder. His literal religious faith in God was challenged in the period after 1850, as evinced again and again and very expressly in his novelistic writings. The changes observed in theme and imagery parallels these concerns. And if we also include the narrative course of events in the later tales, parallel changes can be seen. The hero protagonist who sweepingly succeeds in the early tales, is more and more often supplanted by a problematic protagonist in the tales of the 50s and 60s, suffering and resigning himself to his fate (e.g. **"The Old Bachelor's Nightcap"** 1858). Concurrently, the obstacles presented by the protagonist's social surroundings are not more mockingly and triumphantly swept away, applauded by the heralding narrator. Instead they tend to present themselves as more or less unmovable hindrances and conditions that may only be dreamt away for a moment like in **"Everything in the right place"**. Or he may appeal to the long run redemption exercised by nature, incarnated in the wind.

Thus, the changes in the narrative technique of the fairy tales that ultimately transfer the voice of the formerly very ostensive narrator to the wind or similar anonymous forces of nature are paralleled by a series of other shifts in the workings of the tales. But following the cue, it may be worthwhile to investigate whether there are further ramifications of the changes in narrative technique mentioned above.

At first sight one might generally be deceived by the fact that the foregrounded, explicit narrator seemingly survives, showing up regularly throughout the tales of the 1850s and 1860s. It is, however, possible to track changes in several respects in the use and shape of this narrator, with the years around 1850 as a turning point. This year the revised version of **"The Goloshes of Fortune"** appears, and it is markedly a technically remodelled story compared to the 1838 version. The narrator himself, as well as the frame with its plot producing characters Fortune and Sorrow, are now both reduced to much more modest roles. The didactic moral in the end has also disappeared.

If we look at **"A Great Grief"** (1853) in the editorial history neighbour to **"Everything in the right place"**, it is once again confirmed that changes are taking place. Again we face the foregrounded narrator that we met many times before in the tales from the 1840s. But you only have to look a little closer to realize that more

strikingly than in the revision of **"The Goloshes of Fortune"** it is a narrator with quite another type of presence and role than he used to have. This very short tale is divided into two parts. But surprisingly they are not narratively connected. The narrator is very much up front in both parts. But instead of tending his usual explanatory and morally summarizing tasks he formerly seemed to love, he now writes in a directly secretive way, as if his purpose is only to tease and puzzle the reader. From the beginning he declares that the first part of the story "might be left out", and he reiterates this declaration at the end of this first part. In the end of the second part he resumes his condescending mockery of the reader saying "whoever does not understand it [this story with its two unconnected parts] may go and purchase a share in the tan-yard from the widow". End of story.

This is quite another narrator and another voice than we knew before. If we perform a meticulous analysis of the theme and the metaphors—in its descriptive parts much more realistic text than we met before in the tales—it is quite possible to connect the two parts and figure out which choice the narrator urges the reader to make himself. But the narrator from the tales of the 1840s who eagerly comments and evaluates what is told and eventually at the end morally summarizes an interpretation of the lesson that should be learned, has disappeared. We still listen to a foregrounded narrator, but he is overly unwilling to interpret the accidental everyday happenings he relates, and the moral is left to the reader to discover. Except for the very presence of the foregrounded narrator on the outer shell of the tale, so to say, it is a 180 degrees about turn in the narrative mode that takes place. One might notice that this story is openly meant for adults and not for children. But it is not that simple to account for the change. We also meet didactic narrators in earlier tales meant for grown ups as well as for children, e.g. **"The Nightingale"** (1842), **"The Ugly Duckling"** (1844) and several others. Conversely, and more importantly, it could be claimed that the self-assured, ostentatiously foregrounded narrator who emphatically communicates his message to his audience does not at all re-emerge after this break around 1850. Superficially he is still alive, but only a little examination tells us that from then he hides by way of a secretive narrative technique.

In **"A Great Grief"** the I-narrator is exposed to an extreme degree. Later on he is modified in different ways, but he never efficiently returns back to the narrator of the 1840s. The new line continues in the same vain directly after **"A Great Grief"** with **"The Goblin and the Huckster"** (1853), a very ironic and subtle story. "I cannot quite give up the huckster, because of the jam" says the goblin in the end, and without being foregrounded in the text at all the narrator just wraps up the story, tartly assenting what the goblin said: "We are like the goblin; we all go to visit the huckster 'because of the jam.'

This sort of moral presented by the narrator continues to occur, but it is a tongue-in-cheek moral expressed in a code calling for interpretation. The narrator receding into the background or remaining in a corner of the text hidden by devious formulations is one version of the transformation of the narrator taking place during these years. We also meet something quite the opposite, namely an expressly foregrounded, but now intra-diegetic narrator far from any other character operating in such a place in Andersen's fictions. **"A Good Temper"** immediately precedes **"A Great Grief,"** and is told by an ostentatiously merry hearse driver who starts the story exclaiming: "From my father I received the best inheritance, namely a "good temper." "And who was my father?" he continues and starts a long monologue discoursing happily, acerbically, and very amusingly on his life in the graveyard, on its inhabitants and their stories, on the death practises of society, the press, etc. Without any interference he concludes the story:

> When the time comes for the history of my life, to be bound by the grave, then they will write upon it as my epitaph—
>
> "The man with a cheerful temper."
> And this is my story.

This is a burlesque. The narrating hearse driver may technically be classified as an unreliable narrator, and as such represents an advanced device for this period of literary history. A thorough analysis of the theme of the text may well decipher what is at stake in this burlesque monologue. But on the level of the narration it is a totally oblique and for the lay reader a deeply puzzling construction. The narrator is fore grounded, but the self-indulgent narrator we met earlier and who made no secret of his unrestrained authority, is far away. He has "pocketed his flute" as the formulations in "Everything in its right place".

Instead, ironies and sardonic interjections flourish lavishly and in all directions. Social satire is prominent, but without a narrator parading his authority. In the 1850s Andersen cannot rewrite an old folk tale like **"Jack the Dullard"** (1855) without flavouring with a number of contemporary satirical hints, and he does not stop even jokes disavowing the tale itself: "this report we have wet from the press of the head clerk and the corporation of printers—but they are not to be depended upon in the least", the story ends. Where no effort to underpin the narrator's authority was missing in the earlier tales, there is now no restraint even to undermine it openly, if it may serve a satirical purpose. The lofty tone re-emerges now and then in some tales (e.g.

"Deilig!"), but only to disappear shortly after, if not, the narrative voice at once takes a sudden leap from the lofty to the sardonic tone.

The loftiness has lost it reassurance, and the unabated authority of the narrator has gone. But the much more oblique narrative mode now at work reveals a narrator with an intensely sharpened capability of seeing and indirectly saying things that should not be seen or said. Irony is tantamount, all-encompassing and excels satirically in stories like **"The Porter's Son"**, **"Our Aunt"** and **"Aunt Toothache"** (all 1866). I said "all-encompassing", but "all-devouring" might be a better term. The change in Andersen's narrative mode around 1850 shuts down a number of positions. But as new subtle and ironic types of narration arise, the lack of restraint is also a steady glide into and around thematic depths not reached before. However, these themes can be addressed in this mode, and Andersen does not step back not even from directly cannibalistic excursions. The anti-authority stance we meet in **"Jack the Dullard"** story disavowing its own credibility returns several times (e.g. **"Ole the Tower-Keeper"** (1859), expands outwardly, so to say, culminating perhaps in the jubilantly absurd and hilarious parody on authority, **"What the Old Man Does Is Always Right"** (1861). Concurrently and conversely the self-scrutinizing excavations into the poet's own mind gains momentum, producing a series of remarkable and strange stories starting with the clever but a little timid formulations of **"The Goblin and the Huckster"**, becoming very personal in **"Soup from a Sausage Skewer"** (1858), **"The Old Batchelor's Night Cap"** (1858) and eventually peaking in the last story, **"Aunt Toothache"**. Thematically as well as for the role of the narrator this conclusive tale is more subtle and enveloped than any tale before, and it is not surprising that it openly refers back to **"The Goblin and the Huckster"** from 1853.

Thus, if we examine more than three decades of storytelling with Andersen, we can observe that beneath a thin surface of stability the narrative technique and the role of the narrator in the fairy tales change remarkably from about 1850, and this change is linked to a set of parallel thematic changes as well as changes in the narrative course of events.

* * *

But these changes are also accompanied by new approaches in other respects, and this is what I am going to focus on now. In his first tales, especially in **"Little Claus and Big Claus"**, Andersen's way of rendering dialogue between characters in fiction, directly as well as indirectly, emerges and shines as original, sophisticated, and lively as never seen before in Danish literature. In the tales from the 1840s the dialogue parts of the texts are still striking and well written but are ostentatiously mixed up with, or interrupted by, recurrent comments emanating from the foregrounded narrator. This is an inherent part of his being foregrounded.

Also, another strain, or rather counter-strain, in the rendering of dialogue runs down in Andersen's tales already in the 1840s. It is remarkable in **"The Shepherdess and the Sweep"** (1845) that dialogue between the protagonists remains mostly uncommented. This unusual behaviour of the narrator may stem from the thematic load of the story. With its marital and sexual connotations it is quite controversial and also unusual in Andersen's writing, especially in this period.

More importantly, however, is a concurrent technical dimension in the field of imagery, namely that Andersen here writes his first great tale based on what is going to be a stable in his fairy tale fiction: prosopopeia of inanimate things. An early beginning in this direction was taken already in **"The Brave Tin Soldier"** (1838) and **"The Top and the Ball"** (1838) and the strain continues in **"The Darning-Needle"** (1846). Thematically it is striking that these early tales presenting inanimate objects as talking characters all deal with sexual and marital matters. But there is a pattern in the design of imagery. The elevated presentation of relations between the sexes takes the shape of animated figures representing human bodies and social roles like **"The Brave Tin Soldier"** and **"The Shepherdess and the Sweep"**. The more debased presentation animates household devices like **"The Top and the Ball"**, and preferably by metonymy, intimate things close to the body, clothing and practical devices connected to its maintenance: **"The Darning-Needle"** and a little later **"The Shirt Collar"** (1848).

Animating things, as it happens here, is a facilitating device for Andersen to give word to phenomena that are difficult to formulate, anathematic, so to say. But as for the narrative technique it is interesting, too, that his "thing"-tales is the place where the narrator most easily withdraws into the background and where, consequently, the unmediated dialogue flourishes. In the first tales of this kind the narrator is still recognizable as a moral judge enveloping the dialogues, but in **"The Shepherdess and the Sweep"** the balance changes. The dialogues between animated objects in the tales of the 1850s present paragons of unmediated and uncommented dialogue, i.e. a narrator on his retreat as in **"The Goblin and the Huckster"**. It may well be claimed that during the 1850s the strain that started in "the thing tales" is allowed to broaden its presence; the disrespectful, even coarse tone in the dialogues was before then a prerogative of these tales, but now it merges more freely with a group of double-bound formulations everywhere, and an even more subtle dialogue can be read widely in the body of stories and tales. Again, the change in the role of the narrator has several ramifications and is part of a larger change in the narrative technique.

The last aspect connected with the abdication of the foregrounded and omnipotent narrator I want to point out is a concurrent intensification of narrative tightness, narrative tempo. In the first fairy tales in the folk tale tradition, i.e. **"The Tinder Box"** and **"Little Claus and Big Claus"** from the 1838 volume, the narration is economical and tight. In the subsequent and more personal tales, the commenting and the moral evaluation of what is told grows remarkably. The authority of the narrator is visible and can be felt everywhere in the text. Consequently the very speed and intensity of the narration is slowed down. The narration never becomes dull, undynamic or boring, but it is not persistently focussed on what happens next or on dialogic exchange. Regularly the lessons that should be learned are summed up. When the foregrounding of the narrator diminishes, a range of new alternative approaches come out. You may see short, almost lyric pieces, where a reticent narrator muses on chosen general subjects or sentimental or melancholic feelings not tied up in any simple conclusion, almost without narrative structure or energy. Fragments and left hand prose experiments also occur. Andersen tries out unpretentious genre studies with local colour (e.g. **"Ib and Little Christina"** (1855)) and does not desist from descending into very conventional prose narration of the mid 19th century type as in **"The Ice Maiden"** (1861), though never without his personal stamp being clearly visible in the writing. In a number of excellent tales, however, the diminished role of the narrator gives way to a narrative tightening up on all levels. Events can be rendered with an almost amazing economy and precision, no long-winded introductions, no "la-la" interludes, but a lot of ellipses—still not harming the understanding, only sharpening it. This economy also works in the dialogues where individualized lines from the characters involved follow closely without explanations and comments like pearls on a string changing now and then from direct discourse into *style indirecte libre*. And finally there are no wordy conclusions with lessons to be learned, just a short laconic cut, a few words telling it all.

This eventually leads to my conclusion which will be about conclusions. I have talked about beginnings, for instance how the narrator abruptly addresses his reader. I have also dwelt on a number of phenomena that are mostly to be found in-between. And of course I have touched on the endings as far as the narrator's lesson-to-be-learned moral is concerned. But a special narrative device often occuring in the endings—but not only there—deserves some attention because it is closely connected with the role of narrator. As mentioned before, it is a striking feature in Andersen's tales that they may often and abruptly leap between different fictitious levels. We saw it in the first version of **"The Goloshes of Fortune"**. It is done with much more adroitness in some of the "thing tales", and I would like to dwell shortly on the most illuminating example namely **"The Shepherdess and the Sweep"**.

> "I wish grandfather was riveted," (. . . .) "Will it cost much, I wonder?"

says the shepherdess after the sweep has explained to her that the broken grandfather figure may be mended.

And then the narrator continues perhaps ironically feigning that her wish was fulfilled because she expressed it; "The family had the Chinaman's back mended, and a strong rivet put through his neck; he looked as good as new, but he could no longer nod his head."

It is two fictitious worlds apart but nonetheless the leaps between them also connect in a most sophisticated way like when the stiff neck of the mended Chinaman in the next clause is set to play a decisive role in the concluding chain of events:

> The chimney-sweep and the little shepherdess looked piteously at the old Chinaman, for they were afraid he might nod [thus preventing their marriage]; but he was not able: besides, it was so tiresome to be always telling strangers he had a rivet in the back of his neck.

> And so the little China people remained together, and were glad of the grandfather's rivet, and continued to love each other till they were broken to pieces.

It looks so simple, the ending, and so does the relationship between the various fictitious levels. But whereas the ending is elegant, the play between the various levels of fiction is much more than that. This will be revealed by looking closer.

In a number of much more unsophisticated, and one might say crude, versions, Andersen in other tales uses leaps, shifts or glides between various fiction and narrative levels to conclude the tales. This is clear in the following passage in **"The Little Elder-Tree Mother"**:

> "I believe you," said the mother; "if one takes two cups of hot elder-tea it is quite natural that one gets into warm countries!" And she covered him up well, so that he might not take cold. "You have slept soundly while I was arguing with the old man whether it was a story or a fairy tale!"

> "And what has become of the little elder-tree mother?" asked the boy.

> "She is in the teapot," said the mother; "and there she may remain."

"The Darning-Needle":

> Crack went the egg-shell, as a wagon passed over it. "Good heavens, how it crushes!" said the darning-needle. "I shall be sick now. I am breaking!" but she did not break, though the wagon went over her as she lay at full length; and there let her lie.

A special version of endings connects two levels of fiction in a sort of metamorphosis and punishment relationship. **"The Shirt Collar"** ends:

> All the rags were made into white paper, and the shirt collar became the very identical piece of paper which we now see, and on which this story is printed. It happened as a punishment to him, for having boasted so shockingly of things which were not true.

Whereas in the early tales this way of wrapping it up may serve as a chance for the narrator to moralize once again, it later seems to serve as an escape, a way for him to get rid of his own authority and any obligation to conclude. In the tale **"The Thistle's Experiences"** a final dialogue between a thistle and the sunbeam runs this way:

> "That's an honourable thought," said the Sunbeam. "You shall also have a good place."

> "In a pot or in a frame?" asked the Thistle.

> "In a story," replied the Sunbeam.

Shifting levels the narrator just adds: "Here it is!" [elided in the translation]. Even more abruptly a tale may end like **"The Candles"**: "Yes, that is the whole story!"

Connected to the endings and the shifts between levels of fiction we find the transformation or metamorphosis figure also found in the later tales. But what a change! Whereas the metamorphosis from rags into white paper in the early tales represents an elevation of a debased material into a clean new shape and a lofty purpose applauded by the narrator, the movement along exactly the same vertical axis in the tales after 1850 takes instead the shape of a degradation; and is at the same time, like other similar tricks, now serving as a distance device freeing the narrator from liability as well as reliability. It starts in the **"The Goblin and the Huckster"** where the printed paper of a poetry book is in the garbage barrel with the huckster who wraps it around cheese etc. It represents all of spiritual worth in this tale and it also functions as its narrative string, but still is only garbage. And similarly it continues all through **"Aunt Toothache",** the last tale, that starts by declaring that this story also stems from the garbage cask. It ends in an even more self-depreciating and self-negating stance fading out with these words: "I wrote down what here has been written. It is not in verse and will never be printed . . ."

This almost ominous way of ending shall not be my way of ending, though. Instead I will conclude by suggesting that you take a closely scrutinizing view at the techniques at play in the final part of **"The Shepherdess and the Sweep",** and try to trace all the shifts between the various levels inside the fiction, the humans, the Chinamen and China women, and finally the narrator. Until the very end of the tale. It is vertiginous. So is the narrative technique of Andersen's tales.

Notes

1. All quotes from Hans Christian Andersen's tales are taken from the English versions available through http://www.hcandersen-homepage.dk/ samlede_eventyr.htm and http:// www.andersen.sdu.dk/vaerk/hersholt/index/html

2. Cf. Propp 1968.

Bibliography

Propp, Vladimir. 1968. *Morphology of the Folktale*, 2nd, rev. ed. Ed. Louis A. Wagner, with a new introduction by Alan Dundes. Austin: U of Texas P. Trans. of *Morfologija skazki*. Leningrad: Academia, 1928.

Jakob Stougaard-Nielsen (essay date summer 2006)

SOURCE: Stougaard-Nielsen, Jakob. "The Idle Spectator. Hans Christian Andersen's *Dryaden* (1868), *Illustreret Tidende,* and the Universal Exposition." *Scandinavian Studies* 78, no. 2 (summer 2006): 129-52.

[*In the following essay, Stougaard-Nielsen examines Andersen's fascination with popular culture and the author's interpretation of nineteenth-century advances in lighting and visual technology as "a potent metaphor for modern urban experience."*]

Hans Christian Andersen was an avid traveller, a true nineteenth-century cosmopolitan, a connoisseur, and fetishist collector of everything new, popular, and spectacular. He took an active part in the new visual fashions of his time, especially as probably the most widely photographed superstar of the nineteenth century. He posed for at least one hundred seventy-five photographs, and his image was reproduced and circulated in daguerreotype, on numerous *cartes de visite* in cabinet photography, and stereoscopic images.

Andersen was always looking for a show at a local panorama or theater to stimulate his hunger for visual entertainment. In September 1867 during his second visit to the Universal Exposition in Paris, Andersen visited the Théâtre Chatelet to see *Cendrillon*. "Det var et Fee-Stykke," he wrote enthusiastically in his diary, "men rettere et See-Stykke, et Caleidoskop med glimrende Farver, et Stereoskop med maleriske Billeder og Grupper. Ilden dryppede ned i Ildspanden, det electriske Lys spillede Helterollen" (*Dagbøger VII,* 345) [It was a fairy play, or rather a visual-play, a kaleidoscope with glimmering colors, a stereoscope with picturesque images and character groups. Fire was dripping into the fire bucket; electric light played the role of the hero]. In his diaries are numerous notes listing his daily visits to the royal theater in Copenhagen, and he meticulously lists the dioramas he visits on his travels. In his diaries of the 1860s, Andersen frequently complains about spending too much money on stereoscopic images, which he, like many other travellers of the century, collected of the sites he visited or famous people he met. Andersen was enthusiastic about visual entertainment, revelled in the celebrity culture of his time, but was also notoriously cheap.[1]

Andersen was a product of the new social structures of the nineteenth century. He engaged the new and fashionable in his letters, diaries, and in his fairy tales where the complex relationship between the old and the new is a constantly recurring theme. He was a modern writer preoccupied with the visual culture and its expressions in its many forms. He sketched landscapes, exotic buildings, and characters to accompany his travel books and was famous for his elaborate paper cuttings, which accompanied his performance as a storyteller. Andersen made extraordinarily elaborate kaleidoscopic picture books for the enjoyment of his best friends' children and was deeply engaged in choosing the right illustrators for his collected works. He was, indeed, preoccupied with the ocular and its illusory technologies such as the microscope or magnifying glass in the tale **"Vanddraaben"** (1847; **"The Drop of Water"**), the uncanny dogs with eyes as large as tea cups, mill wheels, and the round tower in **"Fyrtøiet"** (1835; **"The Tinder Box"**), the tricks that visual perception and self-fashioning plays on adults in **"Keiserens Nye Klæder"** (1837; **"The Emperor's New Clothes"**), and the extension of vision in the haunting tale of **"Skyggen"** (1847; **"The Shadow"**) in which the learned man is careless enough to send his shadow peeking into the house on the other side of the street while he himself hides as a voyeur behind the curtains covering his balcony doors.

Andersen's interest in technology and entertainments was not limited to visual manifestations. He praised modern means of transportation like the comforts and exhilarating speed of his first railway journey in 1841—an event he recollected in the travel book **"En Digters Bazar"** (1842; *A Poet's Bazaar*). Transatlantic air travel on wings of steam forming virtual caravans of air ships bringing young American travellers to Europe is prophesied in the 1852 tale **"Om Aartusinder"** (**"Thousands of Years from Now"**)—eleven years before Jules Verne started publishing his *Voyages Extraordinaires*. Andersen adopted the new technology of electronic telecommunication—the electromagnetic thread under the world sea—as a character in his quaint tale **"Den Store Søslange"** (**"The Great Sea Serpent"**) published in *Illustreret Tidende* in 1871, and the impact of gas lighting on the city is presented as a picture book read within his tale **"Gudfaders Billedbog"** (1868;

"Godfather's Picture Book") published originally in *Illustreret Tidende* with the title: **"Det mærkværdige Aar, da Kjøbenhavn fik Gas istedetfor de Gamle Tranlygter"** [The strange year when Copenhagen got gas lights].

Andersen was not late either in recognizing the popularity and possibilities offered by the wide circulation of the illustrated magazine. It is no coincidence that tales like **"Gudfaders Billedbog"** and **"Den Store Søslange,"** so thoroughly occupied with the new technical wonders of the century, first appeared in *Illustreret Tidende* where the readers expected to find and appreciate a patchwork of diverse subjects such as a fairy tale, a crime story, poems, portraits of foreign emperors, advertisements for various products, and descriptions of new technologies. Andersen published seven tales, a few travel letters, biographies, and many poems in this popular paper beginning with its first issue in 1859. The tale **"To Brødre"** ("Two Brothers") appeared as early as the thirteenth number of that same year just after a portrait of the author—which was featured as a Christmas present to the Danish children—and a short biography recounting the fairy tale of Andersen's life.

Since Andersen published in *Illustreret Tidende,* the paper participated in establishing him as a cultural celebrity of the time and contributed to the ways in which fiction, gossip, news, portraits, and spectacular illustrations could be fused in new ways—a heterogeneous compilation of visual and discursive styles and interests—all of which had an influence on the genesis of *Dryaden. Et Eventyr fra Udstillingstiden i Paris 1867* (1868; *The Dryad: A Tale from the Paris Exposition 1867*).

THE KALEIDOSCOPE, PANORAMA, AND STEREOSCOPE

In many ways, then, Andersen was a writer deeply immersed in the techno-mania of modernity and the visual culture of the nineteenth century. A study of Andersen's work should not miss the importance of the changing aesthetics, technologies, practices, and what Martin Jay has called the "scopic regimes" of the century to Andersen's later work—works dealing with modes of perception and socio-cultural formations in multiple and complex ways.

In one of his first fantasy tales, Andersen played with ocular spectacles and two "devices" for perception, the kaleidoscope and the panorama. In **"Fodreise fra Holmens Canal til Østpynten af Amager i Aarene 1828-1829"** (1829; **"A Journey on Foot"**), the narrator is transported three hundred years into the future where he recognizes a theater, which looks like an immense kaleidoscope. The narrator exclaims that it "viste al Theatereffecten fra det nittende Aarhundrede" (21) [showed

all the theatrical effects of the nineteenth century]. "Dækket rullede op," Andersen writes, "og man saae ind i en uhyre Caleidoskop, der ganske langsomt blev dreiet rundt Klipper med Vandfald, brændende Byer, Skyer med Ildregn, og strandende Skibe, styrtede brogede imellem hinanden" (21) [The curtain went up, and one looked right into an immense kaleidoscope, which slowly turned. Cliffs with a waterfall, burning cities, clouds with rain of fire, and marooned ships plunged indistinguishably together]. The narrator, though, feels the need to escape the oppressive crowds in the theater and finds a staircase leading up into a church tower where he exclaims with relief, "Endeligen kom jeg da heelt op i Kuppelen, og nød nu gjennem den aabne Laage et Panorama, saa skjønt Phantasien kan fremtrylle det. Fra en uhyre Høide stirrede jeg ud over Byen, der laae dybt under mig" (23) [Finally, I reached the dome and could enjoy the panorama through an open gate as wonderful as conjured by fantasy. From great height, I gazed over the city which lay deep beneath me]. This futuristic vision of Andersen's debut fantasy tale portrays the visual entertainment typical of the nineteenth century as kaleidoscopic. But the time traveller from the nineteenth century, in contrast to the immense crowds of the future who speed away on mechanical shoes or fly with steam-powered engines—urban crowd behavior reminiscent of *Dryaden*—needs to escape the chaos of the kaleidoscopic and ascend in order to perceive the totality from a panoramic view point.

The panorama offered the urban public entertainment, distraction, and a cure for the strained eyes, a repossession of stable view points and horizontal vision, according to Martin Zerlang.[2] Visual technologies such as the panorama and later the stereoscope popularized after 1850, protected the city dweller against the loss of place and the loss of control over the viewing body. In the latter part of the century, however, there seemed to be no place from which to see and control the entire city. In Manet's (ironic) painting of the Universal Exposition of 1867, the panoramic belvedere arranged for the visitors does not allow visual control over the city and the exhibition buildings. The view is rendered spatially incoherent. Disparate planes within the panoramic field collide and elude the spectator's control. Jonathan Crary, in his book on vision and modernity in the nineteenth century, *Techniques of the Observer,* finds in this painting a manifestation of the features of stereoscopic imagery, an imagery that fascinates due to "immanent disorder, to the fissures that disrupt its coherence" (126). The stereoscope offered the experience of three dimensional spaces and placed the viewer's body as if in the space of the perceived. If one attempted to grasp the images in a stereoscope, they turned out to be nothing but thin air. What is different about the stereoscope, then, and why it becomes significant for late nineteenth-century visual culture, is the fact that it cancels the space between the perceiver and the perceived. The isolated gaze coincides with the machine, and perception is inescapably understood as fundamentally subjective and mediated. Interesting in the context of this article is also the fact that Manet included this stereoscopic experience in the space of the Universal Exposition in Paris.

Just as Andersen's earliest tale presented a shift between the divergent scopic desires of the kaleidoscope and the panorama, the late tale of *Dryaden,* to which we turn now, will reveal a fundamentally stereoscopic view on modernity.

DRYADEN AND MODERN URBANITY

Dryaden is at first sight a strange hybrid of a classical Andersen fairy tale alluding to both **"Den Lille Havfrue"** (**"The Little Mermaid"**) and **"Grantræet"** (**"The Fir Tree"**) as well as to a travel letter or a journalistic report from the exposition in Paris. The narrator, aloof on his balcony in the center of Paris, recounts the life story of the dryad—a wood nymph. The nymph, nestled in the chestnut tree in its homely Arcadia, yearns for the great city of Paris—a longing stimulated by the gossip of the birds and the reflections of the splendid city she finds illustrated in her picture book of drifting clouds. An old priest warns her about the corruption of the city, but in a great storm, the pleasant Arcadia is obliterated when lightning destroys the old oak tree under which the priest used to tell the children stories from the glorious past of France. Consequently, the dryad's longing increases. She is finally granted her wish to go to see the Exposition in Paris by a luminous figure who foresees that she will be dug up and transported to her new place in the "magical city." The figure also knows that the dryad will wish to leave the confines of her tree to move freely around like the humans. All her wishes will be granted, but her life span will be reduced to only one day in return.

The stock characters and Arcadian setting of the fairy tale are interspersed with descriptions of the many tourists and visitors who daily flock to the "wonder of the world." Guide-book descriptions of the sites to be seen on the exhibition grounds both interrupt and drive the fairy tale plot forward. The two worlds—the fairy tale world and the modern—collide when the dryad inside her tree is re-planted in the middle of Paris on the square beneath the balcony from which the narrator beholds her.

As predicted, the dryad soon grows tired of looking at the same houses, advertisements, balconies, and shops. She desires to see the boulevards and the great wonder of the exhibition, and to do so she must leave her protective shell and move freely like the humans accepting in turn the fact that her life will end with the first rays of the morning sun. Her wish is granted for the second

time, and she leaps up like a gazelle. Like reflections of light in mirrors, she is thrown from site to site. When she comes to rest for a moment, her appearance takes on the shape and clothing of that particular place, a disguise which offers her (almost) complete anonymity. Thus her search for the great "wonder of the world," the Exhibition begins. She drifts around the boulevards, visits the Magdalena church, the sewers under Paris, the magic music garden of the *Mabille,* where the narrator curiously appears to dance with her holding nothing but air in his arms. Finally, she arrives at the Exhibition grounds where she speaks with the curious fish displayed in large aquariums. Her eyes full of desire, she takes in both the outside gardens with the national pavilions and the wonderful halls of the Exhibition building. With a new day approaching, her life slowly ebbs away. A hectic fever and mortal fear overcomes her, the machine driven fountain does not offer her any relief, and in death her thoughts return to her childhood's Arcadia. Her figure dissolves like a soap bubble bursting in a tear falling to the ground. The final tableau of the story shows a withered chestnut flower on the ground trampled on by human feet; and the narrator assures us that it all occurred and was experienced during the time of the Paris Exposition as seen by the many travelers "i vor Tid, i *Eventyrets store vidunderlige Tid*" (90) ["during *our time,* the great, wondrous time of fairy tales" (401)].

The obvious allegory of dangerous erotic desire has been the focus of most commentaries on *Dryaden* in the twentieth century, and the story is easily accommodated within Andersen's anxiety-ridden view of sexual consummation. It is, at the same time, the master plot of more popular tales such as **"Den Lille Havfrue."** I wish to stress, though, that the nature of desire in *Dryaden* is a more complicated matter. Its nature has less to do with Andersen's sexual anxieties than with the scopic desires of modern urban life.

In Walter Benjamin's seminal essay "Der Erzähler," the techniques of mechanical reproduction so pervasive in both the art and science of the early twentieth century condition the haunting experience of the modern subject. Benjamin's portrayal of the modern decline of the storyeller as a result of the new mass media and the disquieting image of the homeless subject conditioned by loss of origins and community are integral to an understanding of the means with which Andersen's *Dryaden* succeeds in portraying the experience of early urban mass culture. Benjamin's "image" of the changes modern media "in our time" impose on the subject will, therefore, be my starting point for discussing the issues of urbanity and visual culture in *Dryaden.*

The time of the true storyteller is coming to an end as the value of experience declines according to Benjamin:

> *Eine Generation, die noch mit der Pferdebahn zur*
> *Schule gefahren war, stand unter freiem Himmel in*

einer Landschaft, in der nichts unverändert geblieben war als die Wolken und unter ihnen, in einem Kraftfeld zerstörender Ströme und Explosionen, der winzige, gebrechliche Menschenkörper.

(439)

(A generation that had gone to school on a horse-drawn streetcar now stood under the open sky in a countryside in which nothing remained unchanged but the clouds, and beneath these clouds, in a field of force of destructive torrents and explosions, was the tiny, fragile human body.

[84])

Mechanical reproduction in modernity exemplified by mechanical warfare and mass media prove to Benjamin that experience has fallen in value. Warfare has technologically overpowered man and physically silenced him; the dissemination of information in the modern sensationalist mass media has played a decisive role in inaugurating this sad state of affairs surrounding true experience and in diminishing the role of the storyteller or the teller of fairy tales in modern times. "Jeder Morgen unterrichtet uns über die Neuigkeiten des Erdkreises. Und doch sind wir an merkwürdigen Geschichten arm" (444) ["Every morning brings us the news of the globe, and yet we are poor in noteworthy stories" (89)], Benjamin writes.

Christine Boyer in *The City of Collective Memory* summarizes Walter Benjamin's definition of the storyteller as "someone who came from afar, a real or imaginary traveller of foreign countries and past traditions who returned with something to say to those who stayed at home or those who lived in the present" (289), and it is as such a storyteller that the narrator of *Dryaden* poses. But storytelling as a spatial art grounded in travel or tradition, following Benjamin, "had been replaced in the nineteenth century by more authoritative and plausible accounts, that is, by the news and by documentary information. Its disappearance was part of the atrophy of experience in the modern world. Storytelling takes over, remembers, and repeats the narrated course of events and thus 'creates the chain of tradition'" (289). By drawing on common experiences, stories integrate these into experiences of a community of listeners; they actually structure the community. But, as Boyer concludes, "Community and experience in modern times were fragmented and to the contrary, information had become directed communication aimed at verifying the pure essence of the thing; it neither transmitted lived experiences nor called on the practice of memory" (289).

The problems of diminished value of experience and the demise of older narratives are tied to their replacement by information and information by sensationalism. The driving force behind this development was the appearance in the nineteenth century of mass news media.

The result of the disappearance of the storyteller is the inevitable fragmentation of experience and community. Benjamin's critique of modernity, which exposes a complex of nostalgia for the past and desire for everything new—as did the critiques of Georg Simmel and Siegfried Kracauer—finds the symptoms of modern homelessness to be connected to fragmentation, "discontinuous experience of time, space and causality as transitory, fleeting and fortuitous or arbitrary" (Frisby 4). The modern experience so defined finds its spatial expression in the urban space that through constant expansion and reorganization as well as through new means of mass transportation becomes a transitory space where subjects, turned into window shoppers, only rest for a while before they move on. The lure of the city becomes the ultimate expression of modernity; as the social theorist Marshall Berman reminds us, "To be modern is to find ourselves in an environment that promises us adventure, power, joy, growth, transformation of ourselves and the world—and, at the same time, that threatens to destroy everything we have, everything we know, everything we are" (15). This definition of the contradictory forces of modern experience is a fitting characterization of the nature of desire in *Dryaden.* The promises of joy, growth, and transformation—the loss of community and a Benjaminian storyteller—along with a fragmented and threatening urban space are all present in Andersen's *Dryaden*: they are all part of "the fairy tale of our time."

The first lines of the tale exclaim jubilantly: "Nu ere vi der! det var en Flugt, en Fart, aldeles uden Trolddom; vi gik med Damp i Fartøi og paa Landevei. *Vor Tid er Eventyrets Tid*" (Andersen, *Eventyr* 5: 71) ["Now we're there! What speed, what haste, without any kind of sorcery; we traveled by steam on ships and along railways. *Our time is the time of fairy tales*" (Nunnaly 381)]. The following description of the urban setting seeks to capture the sense of flow, speed, and chaos awaiting both the travellers to Paris: those coming from around the world as well as the dryad who makes the journey from the familiar community of her countryside home:

Hvilken Vexel! hvilken Flugt! Det var som Husene skøde op af Jorden, flere og flere, tettere og tettere. Skorstenene løftede sig som Blomsterpotter, stillede paa hinanden og Side om Side hen ad Tagene; store Indskrifter med alenlange Bogstaver, malede Skikkelser op ad Veggene fra Grundstykket til Gesimsen skinnede frem.

»Hvor begynder Paris, og naar er jeg derinde?« spurgte Dryaden sig selv. Menneskevrimlen voxede, Tummel og Travlhed tog til, Vogn fulgte Vogn, Gaaende Ridende, og rundt om Boutik ved Boutik, Musik, Sang, Skrig, Tale.

Dryaden i sit Træ var midt inde i Paris.

(78)

(What changes! What speed! The buildings seemed to shoot up from the earth, more and more of them, closer and closer together. The chimneys rose up like flowerpots, stacked on top of each other and side by side along the rooftops. Enormous inscriptions composed of two feet high, and painted shapes that shone brightly, covered the walls from foundation to cornice.

"Where does Paris start, and when will I be there?" the wood nymph asked herself.

The crowds of people swelled, the bustle and commotion grew, carriage followed carriage. There were people on foot and on horseback, and everywhere shop after shop, music, song, shrieks, and conversations. The wood nymph in her tree was in the middle of Paris.

[388])

The dryad and the modern traveller seem to be at ease with the tumult and the crowds. The urban setting does not seem threatening at all as narrated through the naïve eyes of the country bumpkin. The houses shooting up from the earth still resemble trees in the forest and the polluting chimneys are nothing but pleasant flowerpots. Even the advertisements on the walls seem to be pleasantly reminiscent of the clouds illuminated by the city lights and the picture book showing the dryad illustrations of the Exposition. The dryad's naïve vision of the potentially threatening urban scenery mirrors the narrator's optimism in the introductory lines but is constantly confronted with the premonitions of the dryad's inevitable demise in the polluted and crowded city in the reader's imagination.

The dryad is metonymic of the Exposition and as such synonymous with the spectacle witnessed by the narrator from his panoramic view point on the balcony. The Exposition building is described as an immense sunflower on the barren Champ de Mars, where it will bloom for awhile before withering and being blown away to remain only as a fata morgana in the desert. The dryad is described as a flower ready to bloom on the square in the center of Paris and ends her quest for the Exposition as a withering flower trampled on the Champ de Mars. To make things more complicated, the dryad is also a figure for the traveller, i.e. the narrator, who from his balcony sees the tree and identifies with the dryad, who, like him, will find her demise in the polluted air of the city.

The figure of the dryad when finally set loose from her tree to roam the city takes on the traits of a chameleon or a kaleidoscope. She assumes new appearances and clothing depending on the sites she visits and thus escapes the gaze and attention of the crowd. As such a signifier, she is volatile enough to take on almost any signification in the tale. She reflects everything like light bouncing off mirrors in a kaleidoscope but at the same time reflects *on* nothing. She is ephemeral as seen when the young man—a figure for the narrator—dances with her in the *Mabille* and holds nothing but thin air in his arms—a characteristic trait of the stereoscopic experience. This loss of self, of body, and of consistency

might be the nature of a dryad. As a figure in the tale, she reflects the nature of the urban experience: the joy, desire, and anxious search for the spectacular. She also represents the urban experience of transitoriness and loss of home, which her disappearance in the urban machine and the crowd inevitably signify. If the dryad, then, could be said to embody the modern experience, I would suggest that she does so precisely as a modern visual mechanism—like the kaleidoscope—and the essentially kaleidoscopic nature of late nineteenth-century illustrated magazines and World Expositions.

The Universal Exposition 1867

Dryaden is a tale that adopts into its fragmented body the discursive and formal strategies of the new mass media (the illustrated magazine), visual devices (kaleidoscope and panorama), and above all the phantasmagorical nature of the Universal Exposition. Against this background, we can now turn to two visual urban components that offer both structural and thematic material to ***Dryaden***: firstly, the Universal Exposition and the ways ***Dryaden*** adopts its specular design and technology and secondly Andersen's reliance on the education of readers and spectators by the popular illustrated magazines and their reports on the Exposition. Both exhibit kaleidoscopic and stereoscopic ways in which the real was turned into a spectacle and the urban crowd became, as Vanessa Schwartz has it, "a society of spectators" (6). So, how did this "Wonder of the World" reveal itself, the narrator of ***Dryaden*** asks? How may we imagine the Exposition appeared to Andersen and the urban spectators of late nineteenth century?

The Universal Exposition opened in Paris on 1 April 1867, and around seven million visitors saw the exhibition palace on the Champ de Mars. Among the industrial novelties awaiting the public were artificial limbs, a hydraulic elevator, and the rocking chair. The main building on the Champ de Mars was oval with seven concentrically arranged halls, each hosting a particular type of product. The visitor could then choose among a comparative study of products by circling the building or study what one particular country had to offer by moving in and out (see Mattie 20). "Not just an educational performance," Christine Boyer writes, "this exhibition was entertainment as well. Fantasy was inscribed in the space of the fairground as a voyage, and the spectator could choose from many varied itineraries" (262). It was the first time that an exhibition included thematic pavilions placed on the grounds surrounding the main building. These pavilions attracted much attention and presented a veritable amusement park, not unlike the Tivoli Gardens in Copenhagen where exoticism and leisure were obvious qualities. Especially the elevator was flaunted at the 1867 Exhibition taking the visitors from the ground floor to the roof where they could enjoy a panoramic view of the whole Exhibition.

This combination of spectacular illusion and the thrill of documentary realism figured in the panoramic eye was the epitome of rational entertainment at the heart of the great nineteenth-century exhibitions that "turned the industrial world into one immense picture show" (Boyer 257). The showcasing of artifacts and bazaars of "Storheds Nips" (75) ["trinkets of grandeur" (385)] as Andersen calls the souvenirs to be found everywhere, offered the spectator a series of tableaux heterogeneously juxtaposed. Christine Boyer sees this panoramic fantasy world of the Exposition as mimicking the experience of reading an illustrated magazine:

> A ramble through these fairgrounds of the nineteenth century was no different from the visual experience received by turning the pages of an illustrated "Picturesque Voyage," or scanning the random juxtaposition of news columns, illustrations, and advertisements in the popular press. Spectators simply compared one image to another, contrasting the difference between nations and gauging the distance between the past and the present, the so-called developed and the backward.
>
> (257)

The Exposition created an optical space through sequences of tableaux; an environment in which the individual spectator's autonomy was lessened as the subject became subordinated to the objects consumed or admired. The Exposition created a theatrical setting in which the spectator was taught about the new environment of things and as a spectacle in itself, "the exposition enabled the viewer to revel in its make-believe and its myth-making force" (258). The simulated panoramic visions, from the elevator and in the bazaars, took disparate architectural images and modern amusements and "drew them into simultaneous aesthetic expression of architectural unity that the city had already lost" (258). The Exposition building, its exhibited goods, and trinkets functioned as scale-reduction models of the urban experience and became a school for the eye.[3] The overwhelming experience of urban space and swarming crowds were contained in the exposition and made accessible and available for visual appropriation—in stark contrast to the unmanageable metropolis—by adopting well-known visual technologies and media like the panorama, the kaleidoscope, and the illustrated press.

In similar fashion, one might think of Andersen's tale as modeled on the discursive space of the exhibition as well as thematically capturing the experience of the modern visitor to the "immense picture show" (Boyer 257). Before addressing the discursive similarities between the tale, the Exposition, and the visual culture of the nineteenth century, I shall turn to the tale's inception—a search that will be as phantasmagoric as the tale and the exposition themselves.

THE ORIGINS OF *DRYADEN*

According to Andersen's annotations to his collected works, *Dryaden* was initially conceived when he visited

Paris on 13 April 1866. The tale's "exposition," as Philip Hamon would define it—or its narrative frame—recounts a scene that impressed the author during this visit to Paris a year prior to the opening of the Exhibition, which Andersen visited twice during the following year. In his diary of 1866, Andersen writes, "Der kunde skrives et Eventyr om de Træer, deres Længsel efter Verdens Byen, og deres snare Død derinde. Jeg skriver vist et Eventyr derom" (*Dagbøger VII*, 84) [A fairy tale could be written about the trees that long for the city of the world and their certain death therein. I think I shall write a fairy tale about it.]

In the tale, Andersen describes a scene in which the narrator finds himself looking down from his hotel balcony contemplating a tableau that immediately impresses an allegorical meaning on his imagination. On the square below, workers are about to replace an old withered tree with a young chestnut tree. The dead tree lies on the square presumably withered from the polluted city air. Andersen reflects both in the tale and in his diary on the similarity between the longing of the tree for the great city and its inevitable demise and his own troubles with the urban air (*Dagbøger VII*: 336-7). In one singular gesture the tableau below enacts the conflict between the old world and the new, between the loss of innocence and childhood and the longing for the city of the world as well as between its representation "in miniature" in the Exposition (a veritable city within the city) and a desire moving in the opposite direction—a desire to escape the oppressive air of Paris.

The first programmatic lines of the story merge the two worlds in what might seem a paradoxical statement: "Vor Tid er Eventyrets Tid" (71) ["Our time is the time of fairy tales" (381)]. It is among other things this paradoxical construct of the new within the old that offers a highly complex depiction of the modern experience as presented by Andersen in this tale and, as I shall claim, a depiction that draws on both a stock of popular, widely-circulated notions concerning the modern spectacle and the changing modes of "visualizing" the new individual in the urban culture of the nineteenth century.

Above I discussed the ways in which the exposition might be considered a scale model of the urban space—i.e. rendering it available to the panoramic eye—and thereby an education of the spectator with regard to his or her urban experience. In the following, I shall offer some examples of urban experiences that are typical of the time when Andersen was writing and which might have been direct influences on Andersen's choice of subject, and of the kaleidoscopic form of the fairy tale plot mirrored in frenzied descriptions of the urban crowd supplemented by lists of items to be seen at the Exposition.

In an article "Paa Boulevarderne" [On the Boulevards], Andersen's traveling companion to the Universal Exposition, Robert Watt, celebrates the leisurely life experienced in the cafés on the boulevards. "Er Paris den første By i Verden," Watt writes, "saa ere Boulevarderne det første sted i Paris" (364) [If Paris is the first city of the world, then the boulevards are the first places of the city]. From the cafés of the boulevard the colorful Parisian life can be studied, and he recommends that if one only has short time available in Paris, the best illustration of Parisian life is that of the cafés and the boulevards. Especially in the evenings when the fairer sex is in majority, one may learn much from studying them. Watt writes:

> *Der drilles og lees, sees og tales, indbyrdes og med Folk i Strømmen, som ustandseligt rinder forbi. Man kommer ind i Intriguer, seer spændende Indledninger og interessante Opløsninger paa Kjærlighedshistorier, hører Politik, høster Lærdom i Konst og Videnskab, faaer en Mundfuld Skandale og gjør hundrede Opdagelser, blot ved at tilbringe en kølig Aftenstund udenfor en Café paa en af Boulevarderne.*
>
> (364)

(There is much teasing and laughing, looking and speaking, among themselves and with the crowds constantly streaming by. One is invited into intrigues, experiences exciting introductions and interesting resolutions to love stories, one hears about politics, gains knowledge of arts and sciences, a mouthful of scandal, and makes countless discoveries by just spending an afternoon outside a café on the boulevards.)

Life on the boulevards is experienced as the central attraction. It is perceived as a spectacle not unlike the Universal Exposition, which had become the epitome of spectacular display in the nineteenth century's fusing its obsession with industrial progress and romantic intrigue with the urban crowds, spectatorship, and sensuality. The city is to be taken in through the eyes and ears from the comfortable seats of the café, from the front row of the theater of everyday life in the city of spectacles. The eye-witness experience in the cafés resembles the spectacularization of early consumer culture in the grand exhibitions or the Parisian arcades; and the same montage of a fragmented mass of information and impressions from gossip and romance to science, art, and politics is also found within the pages of the medium for the masses, the illustrated magazines such as *Illustreret Tidende* in which Watt's article appeared. The experience of the city of cities, the spectacle of the universal expositions and the new mass medium all share common textual and visual practices that had an impact on all spheres of nineteenth-century art and culture and, most specifically, on Andersen's attempt to capture the new in his conception of the fairy tale nature of our time.

The rise of mass culture and its various accompanying spectacular "genres" had an impact on art in both an abstract and a structural sense. In the case of Andersen

and *Dryaden,* Watt's reports from Paris also had direct influences on the tale. In the same article in which Watt praises Paris as the delightful and magnetic center of the world, whereto everybody should travel at least once, a description of the artificiality of the boulevards also appears. Watt writes about the trees that line the boulevards:

> *Dagligt seer man Arbeidere sysselsatte med at borttage de gamle, sygelige Træer, for at sætte unge og friske istedet. De små Vogne, hvori det frodige, haabefulde Skovens Barn kneiser, medens det føres til sit nye Hjem, hvor dets Livskraft saa snart skal nedbrydes, møder man jævnligt. Der er, som om Pariserlivet hurtigt opbrugte dets Kraft, og snart holder atter Vognen ved det nu henvisnede Træ, for at føre det bort fra den Skjønne By, der har været dets Sotteseng. . . . For den flygtige Iagttager har Boulevarden bestandigt det samme smilende og glimrende Ydre.*
>
> (363)

(Daily one sees workers preoccupied with uprooting the old, sick trees to replace them with the young and fresh. One often meets small wagons on which the fertile and hopeful child of the forest struts as it is taken to its new home where its life force soon will decrease. It is as if Parisian life rapidly used up its powers and soon again the wagon will make a stop by the now withered tree to take it away from the beautiful city which proved to be its deathbed. . . . To the passing observer the boulevard maintains the constant smiling and shining front.)

The passage is illustrated in the magazine with a woodcut depicting the transportation of trees for the beautification of the boulevards on horse-drawn wagons. Watt, like Andersen, is inspired by the obvious symbolism of the young trees meeting their demise in the city, consumed, so to speak, by the passing consumer-observers for whom they are displayed. The trees become symbols for the purely ornamental pleasure for the eyes— the smiling surface veiling the labor, death, and sacrifice behind the urban spectacle and leisurely life.

Though Andersen as editor of and commentator on his collected works poses as the traveler standing on the balcony looking down on the sentimental scene, a scene presumably experienced in 1866 according to his diary but relocated to 1867 in the commentary, we may suspect that Watt's article and its illustration of 1865 had already sown the seeds for his tale about the dryad. As so often in our modern culture of the image, things are never seen for the first time in person but are always mediated by circulated images of newspapers, exhibitions, reproductions, panoramas, and photographs.

During the second half of the nineteenth century, Paris, the Universal Exposition, and Haussmann's boulevards held a magnetic attraction for "cultural tourists" like Watt and Andersen rivalling the obligatory romantic grand tour of Italy. Paris had by the last third of the century become "the European centre of a burgeoning leisure industry" (Schwartz 1). The urban space had conformed to new ways of seeing and perceiving with individuals and crowds participating in and consuming the culture of the metropolis. Paris appeared as a city remodelled by and for the spectacles (Schwartz 90), and the travelers demanded spectacular and curious visual entertainments in order to satisfy their hunger for the modern. Writers and artists were drawn to the spectacles of the metropolis because, according to Philip Hamon, "they [the exposition and the boulevard] allowed the transformation of real places into a series of topoi, literary themes, metaphors, or subjects for newspaper articles" (68)—just as the trees lining the boulevard were transformed into Watt's newspaper article and Andersen's tale. Paris was already "written" for visitors like Andersen—described, fictionalized, and praised in guide books, illustrated magazines, in poems, and novels. Visitors—such as the many writers who would use the city, its darker corners, and illuminated spectacles as back drops for their "modern" novels— were "re-writing, or un-writing the already-written Paris of the novel" (Prendergast 28). For the writer and the tourist, Paris was already "the city of a hundred thousand novels," as Balzac called it and "the capital of the nineteenth century." Although this characterization was already a cliché in the nineteenth century, Christopher Prendergast reminds us that Walter Benjamin meant to evoke Paris as the most visible and obvious topos of "modernity" by foregrounding the complex and unsettling effects developing urban forms of life had on both society and the psyche (Prendergast 5).

The phantasmagoria pervading the experience of the city as spectacle becomes the phantasmagoria of the author's panoramic gaze in **Dryaden.** His original experience of the narrated tableaux is thus also veiled in phantasmagorical images and texts. The disappearance of the author's original experience in the pages of the illustrated press seems to confirm Benjamin's critique of the loss of experience beyond the death of the storyteller. This loss is connected to the rise of popular mass media in the nineteenth century and, we might add, to the circulation of images in illustrated magazines.

ILLUSTRERET TIDENDE AT THE UNIVERSAL EXPOSITION

In 1867, the weekly illustrated magazine, *Illustreret Tidende,* published six reports, three articles, and a novella accompanied by fourteen illustrations from the Universal Exposition. The day prior to the official opening of the Exposition, *Illustreret Tidende* reported that "det længe imødeseete Øieblik, da Telegraphen, så langt dens Næt spænder om Jordkloden, skal forkynde, at Verdensudstillingen er aabnet, nærmer sig nu med stærke skridt" (*Illustreret Tidende* 8/392, 1867: 213) [the long awaited moment is finally drawing nearer

when the telegraph, as far as its web spans the earth, shall proclaim the World Exposition for opened]. This was a spectacle not to be missed by the magazine's readers, and definitely not an opportunity to go unnoticed by the popular press. The obsession with technical novelties characteristic of both the magazine and the industrial exhibitions is signified in the telegraph's role as inaugurator of the exposition. Not the emperor but the symbol for mass communication, modern technology, and the interconnectedness of the world's countries figures prominently in the magazine's techno-mania, a mania that also foregrounds the significance of the news media itself since the telegraphic proclamations materialize most obviously in the illustrated magazine. With all its novelties, curious other-worldly artifacts, nations in open industrial competition, and luxurious ostentation, the exhibition was a treat for any paper that took pride in bringing the very best xylographic pictures to the hungry eyes of its readers. Easily reproduced and accompanied by texts, they appealed to the diverse reading public in the emerging metropolis of Copenhagen.

Much like the ideology behind the expositions, the idea behind the illustrated magazine was the creation of a specific type of urban "interested" reader for whom pictorial reproductions of diverse subjects complemented by stories and news in written form signaled a keeping abreast with the present, being modern and up-to-date with developments in other countries.

In the reports from the Universal Exposition, readers were guided through the exhibit and introduced to interior design as well as the architecture and specific materials of the buildings. Attracting special praise were the new designs in glass and steel made popular by the 1851 London Exposition and its Crystal Palace, a design that opened buildings up to vision by making the interior visible from the exterior.

Readers were shown the more curious highlights of the gigantic salt water aquarium and the national pavilions: the Russian *Isbah* complete with the Czar's horses, the Norwegian exhibition with sculptured folk-types, and a Tunisian castle complete with divans, strong mokka, and sitar music, all shown with full-page illustrations. Other newspapers reported from the Exposition as well, but *Illustreret Tidende*'s purpose was to guide the reader verbally through the illustrations received from Paris:

> *Vi fortsætte idag vor Vandring i og om Udstillingsbygningen i Paris, og skulle ikke trætte læserne med lange Beskrivelser, men derimod hellere ved de Tegninger, der staae til vort Blads Raadighed anskueliggjøre det allerede i forskjellige Correspondancer til Dagbladene Berettede.*

> (*Illustreret Tidende* 8/396, 1867: 247)

(Today we continue our stroll in and around the exhibition building in Paris. We shall not tire our readers with long descriptions, but rather through the drawings made available to us illustrate the stories already recounted in various articles in the daily press.)

First I want to point out the imagined "we" of the article referring to the imagined community of the newspaper's readers corresponding to Andersen's narrative voice in **Dryaden**—"nu ere vi der!" (71) . . . "vi saae det selv" (90) ["now we're there!" (381) . . . "we saw it ourselves" (401)]. Similarly two formulations in the articles characterize the potential traveler to the Exposition. Both depict the late nineteenth-century urban explorer as a highly visual and media-savvy individual, and both have their corollaries in **Dryaden.**

The fourth report on the Exposition in the illustrated magazine describes the *flâneur*, "den ørkesløse Tilskuer" drifting around the exhibition grounds taking in the wonders of the world. It is noted in the article, that this is a much more interesting spectacle than sitting in a theater with eyes wide open in front of a continuously moving panorama. Here, the buildings surely remain in their place, but they are animated by the ever changing mass of people. Involuntarily, the flow carries one away (*Illustreret Tidende* 8/397, 1867). Though the indifference of the spectator to the urban spectacles in the nineteenth century was synonymous with the *flâneur*, the oppressive crowd threatens (or offers) a new way of looking that inhibits the detached and individualized observation of the *flâneur*. For him, the city as spectacle is still readable and knowable in its entirety; it can be mapped through idle strolls in the city, from balconies, church towers, belvederes, or windows. But the observer reporting from the exposition or looking at the illustrations and then reporting on what he imagines he will see revels in the flow of the crowds that in turn are the machines driving the spectacle. This phenomenon of the urban crowds facing the crowds visiting the spectacles of the city resembles the experience of the kaleidoscope: a trick of mirrors that offers pleasure to the eye by seeing the eye observing the changing flow of colors and forms, an eye with no interest in the interior of the objects themselves. A new type of urban spectator arises from the crowds swarming to the spectacle of the city and rendering it unreadable, but not less pleasant. Tom Gunning well formulated this relationship between a second type urban spectator and the kaleidoscope:

> One can find a model for this purely visual delight in a constantly changing spectacle irrelevant to the knowing gaze of the classical *flâneur* modelled in David Brewster's philosophical toy, the kaleidoscope, patented 1817. . . . [T]he kaleidoscope provided a purely visual spectacle, the mechanical complement to the *badaud.*
>
> (31)

In the following article in *Illustreret Tidende*, this second type of urban spectator—the *badaud* or the gawker—whose complementary visual machine is the kaleidoscope, augments the figure of the *flâneur* whose preferred scopic machine is more likely the diorama or the panorama since such visual displays more easily render the urban space legible to the *flâneur*'s gaze. Here, we are introduced to the *badaud* in his most extreme form as window-shopper, as absorbed by the spectacle. The *flâneur* by contrast would remain detached:

> *Veien fører os idag lige fra Jenabroen hen til den Bygning paa Marsmarken, der længe paa Grund af sin Pragt har vinket, nemlig den kejserlige Sommerpavillon, der stadigt samler Nysgjerrige, som med næsen paa Ruderne kaste Blik ind i de aflukkede Værelser.*
>
> (*Illustreret Tidende*, 8/398, 1867: 263)

(Today, we go from the Jena Bridge to the building on the Champ de Mars, which for a long time has beckoned due to its splendor, the Emperor's summer pavilion. Still it attracts curious people, who with their noses pressed against the windows throw long glances into the enclosed spaces of the rooms.)

Martin Jay puts this new character in relation to early mass culture when he, with Fournel and Benjamin, points out that the *flâneur* with his self-possessed observing skills was being replaced by the *badaud*, the mere gaper entirely taken in by what he sees. The individuality of the *badaud* disappears in contrast to that of the *flâneur*. He is absorbed by the outside world, which intoxicates him to the point of forgetting himself. Martin Jay puts this new character in relation to early mass culture when he, with Benjamin, states that the *badaud* becomes "an impersonal creature under the influence of the spectacle which presents itself to him; he is no longer a human being, he is part of the public, of the crowd" (119). Although, this urban "community" of a crowd of gapers is signifying a loss, in Benjamin's nostalgia for the pre-modern, it is, nevertheless, a new "public," a new way of experiencing community and taking possession of the urban space.

In the articles from *Illustreret Tidende*, these urban types are presented side by side as complementary. The "we" of ideal readers to whom the articles address themselves are led through the various illustrations from the exhibition by the guiding voice of the "journalist." They are introduced to the classification of goods in the exhibition and are shown the various itineraries they may follow through the exhibition. The readers are led to identify with the idle spectator who drifts around the exhibition grounds and are taught to stop a while in the Tunisian pavilion and contemplate the cultural differences and particularities; but the readers may also find themselves identifying with the *badaud*, the window shopper, who is entirely absorbed by the sheer phantasmagorical show of light and color, the crowds from whom they are indistinguishable. They therefore turn into objects themselves to be seen. Nineteenth-century travelers and readers expected to encounter Paris as a phantasmagoria, as a consumer item in which there is no longer anything to remind them of how it came into being, as Benjamin's understanding of phantasmagoria suggests.

The urban experience and its metonymic representation in the Exposition were prepared for visual consumption by the illustrated news as the reader of the nineteenth-century magazines was turned into a *flâneur*-reader who navigated the pages of the magazine as he would stroll in the streets of the city. We find that the arabesque richness and the diversity of the magazine's topography mimic the crowding and intensity of experience in the major metropolis as experienced by Watt or Andersen's dryad. Thus the magazine can be said not only to mirror the experience of modern urbanity, but it also serves to indoctrinate the reader into a certain way of looking. To this list of media or modes of urban spectatorship, which seem to indoctrinate the modern reader or at least influence the way in which the urban spectator navigates textual and urban space, we should, as already suggested, include optical machines like the panorama and the kaleidoscope, along with the aesthetic expression of speed, disconnectedness, and illegibility. As the collective focal point at which these technologies of urban perception are both exhibited and constitutive, we find the universal expositions. They are the proving grounds for the meeting of man and technology; they are the ultimate spectacles of modernity, but unlike the spectacles of the city, the exposition offers itself up as a laboratory in which everything is in miniature and therefore comprehensible.

Dryaden, as well, figures as a laboratory of visual strategies adopted by the urban explorer. The tale is not a tale about the Exposition as such, but a tale about the impact of the city and the exposition as spectacle on the about-to-become-modern spectator. The street scenes of the tale as seen through the divergent gazes of the dryad and the narrator are presented in kaleidoscopic fashion. Impressions are jumbled together, and one sight follows another in haste and without rational causality. Stops are made at various locations, but they feature merely as department store windows; they leave no lasting impression on the viewer or the reader since they are mere exhibitions of urban tableaux and products. The Exposition is described both in terms of hear-say and of catalogue entries that follow a strict itinerary from the outer ring of the exposition building—the gallery of machines—to the kaleidoscopic amusement park featuring the national pavilions. The perception characteristic of this urban environment involves two types of spectator analogous to two optical devises capturing the spectacle. The dryad is figured as a *badaud,* the window shopper who tries on different appearances from the "shops" she visits reflecting the city without causality as if caught within a kaleidoscope. The narratorial re-

ports from the Exposition adopts the language of the illustrated magazine and its mix of gossip and panoramic control over the scenes depicted, evokes a certain sense of order in the urban tableaux, and adduces a *flâneur's* knowledge of everything the gaze encounters. These types of spectator—the *badaud* and the *flâneur*—intermingle in *Dryaden* as they do in the articles of *Illustreret Tidende.*

CONCLUSION

I have examined how an urban spectacle like the Universal Exposition was presented to the readers of the illustrated magazine in Denmark and how the experience and exposition of the metropolis were presented as spectacles in a publication, which through visual presentations and verbal guides sought to educate the potential visitors in terms of a specific modern practice of urbanity. My examination focused on the ways in which the magazine explored the relationship between the Exposition itself, the illustrations printed in the magazine, and the travelling spectator. I have shown as well that the magazine not only presupposes certain modern types of spectator, but also plays an active role in the visual education of the modern traveller; following Jonathan Crary's delineation of the observing subject who was "both a product of and at the same time constitutive of modernity" (9).

Furthermore, it is my argument that the characterization of urban spectator types in *Dryaden* is essential to an understanding of the structure of desire in the story. It is, therefore, not a Little-Mermaid story about the longing and erotic desires of the protagonist entering adulthood, but instead a story about the visual, scopophilic desires of the urban crowd engaged in and defining the modern spectacle of the real as communal desire. *Dryaden* and the articles in *Illustreret Tidende* expose what one could call a theatricalization of urban life. The exposition is in both instances described as a participatory theater in which spectators transgress the proscenium arch of the spectacle. The dryad of the story is one of those spectators made a spectacle. She is constantly on display, illuminated by gas lights as in department store windows. We also see her reflecting the sites and crowds as an exposed photographic plate. As such, the narratorial "we," poised above on the balcony, becomes the imagined participant in the urban crowd by proxy. The "we" might as well be reading about the spectacle in the illustrated newspaper or in an illustrated tale.

The specification of the visual typologies of urban spectatorship portrays the desires and anxieties about becoming part of the crowd, an experience which entails surrendering, provisionally, the unmediated and detached gaze of the solid self-contained individual for the mediated and exposed spectacularization of the subject. This experience mediated by the theatricalization and phantasmagoria of the urban space is fundamentally a product of the eye and of the spectator and therefore does not offer a clear demarcation of the border between the outside of the spectacle and the inside of the spectator. This, I shall suggest, is Andersen's reflection of a stereoscopic experience of modernity.

According to Martin Jay, the new modes of seeing and new ways of living in the urban environment were nowhere more widely represented and debated than in the Paris of the nineteenth century (113). It is this constitution of the modern individual through new modes of seeing brought about by visual technologies such as the stereoscope, newspaper illustrations, and new exhibition practices that *Dryaden* reflect. With this emphasis, I wish to restore this tale's importance within Andersen's *oeuvre*, to take it out of the shadow of **"Den Lille Havfrue"** with which it has been unduly compared and judged a weak copy. I wish to show how this tale reflects and engages with popular discourses of modernity and spectatorship recorded in the early mass press and exhibited in the spectacle of the universal exposition as itself a potent metaphor for modern urban experience.

Notes

1. In Andersen's diaries the following notations of stereoscopic images are found: 2 July 1861: "Stereoskop Billed af Byen var ikke at faae alle udsolgte, jeg bladdrede en Masse igjennem." 11 June 1861: "Klokken 6 kaldte jeg paa Jonas der [besteg] Domkirken, jeg gik ud og kjøbte ind, anvendte 10 Frank paa Stereoskop Billeder."

2. "Panoramaet stimulerede den samlede horisontlinie, som ikke var til at få øje på i byen, hvor husrækkerne skyder sig ind foran hinanden. Og det afbillede storbyen som indlejret i naturen, f.eks. omgivet af bjerge eller hav. I virkeligheden tilbød panoramaet sit publikum den dobbeltberoligende oplevelse af, at de stående på udsigtsplatformen kunne holde byen på betryggende afstand, samtidigt med at den reelt ekspanderende og uoverskuelige by her blev sluttet inde i rotundens vinduesløse interiør" (Zerlang, "Det nittende århundrede" 21).

3. See Martin Zerlang's use of the concept of scale-reduction in connection with Universal Expositions in *Bylivets Kunst: København som Metropol og Miniature* (168).

Works Cited

Andersen, Hans Christian. *H. C. Andersens Eventyr.* 7 vols. Copenhagen: Reitzels Forlag, 1963-90.

———. *Fodreise fra Holmens Canal til Østpynten af Amager i Aarene 1828-1829.* København: Det Danske Sprog- og Litteraturselskab, Borgen, 1986.

———. *Hans Christian Andersen Fairy Tales.* Translated by Tiina Nunnaly. London: Penguin, 2005.

———. *H. C. Andersens dagbøger 1-x.* København: Det Danske Sprog- og Litteraturselskab, G. E. C. Gads Forlag, 1971-77.

Benjamin, Walter. "Der Erzähler." *Gesammelte Schriften.* Frankfurt am Main: Suhrkamp, 1972-1989. II.2:438-65.

———. *Illuminations.* Hannah Arendt, ed. New York: Schocken, 1968.

Berman, Marshall. *All That Is Solid Melts into Air: The Experience of Modernity.* New York: Penguin, 1988.

Boyer, M. Christine. *The City of Collective Memory: Its Historical Imagery and Architectural Entertainments.* Cambridge: MIT P, 1994.

Crary, Jonathan. *Techniques of the Observer: On Vision and Modernity in the Nineteenth Century.* Cambridge: MIT P, 1990.

Frisby, David. *Fragments of Modernity: Theories of Modernity in the Work of Simmel, Kracauer and Benjamin.* Cambridge: Polity, 1985.

Gunning, Tom. "From the Kaleidoscope to the X-Ray: Urban Spectatorship, Poe, Benjamin, and Traffic in Souls (1913)." *Wide Angle* 19.4 (1997): 25-61.

Hamon, Philippe. *Expositions: Literature and Architecture in Nineteenth-Century France.* Berkeley: U California P, 1992.

Illustreret Tidende. København: Det Kongelige Bibliotek, 2002. http://www.illustrerettidende.dk/iti_pub/cv/main/Forside.xsql?nnoc=iti_pub (accessed 11 July 2006).

Jay, Martin. *Downcast Eyes: The Denigration of Vision in Twentieth-Century French Thought.* Berkeley: U California P, 1994.

Mattie, Erik. *World's Fairs.* New York: Princeton Architectural P, 1998.

Prendergast, Christopher. *Paris and the Nineteenth Century.* Cambridge: Blackwell, 1992.

Schwartz, Vanessa R. *Spectacular Realities: Early Mass Culture in Fin-de-Siècle Paris.* Berkeley: U California P, 1999.

Watt, Robert. "Billeder fra Paris II: Paa Boulevarderne." *Illustreret Tidende* vol. 6, no. 306 (6 August 1865): 363-4.

Zerlang, Martin. "Det nittende århundredes visuelle kultur—set med danske øjne." *Den Optiske Fordring: Pejlinger i den visuelle kultur omkring Henrik Ibsens forfatterskab.* Ed. Erik Østerud. Aarhus: Aarhus UP, 1997: 14-29.

———. *Bylivets Kultur: København som Metropol og Miniature*. København: Forlaget Spring, 2002.

Julia Briggs (essay date 2006)

SOURCE: Briggs, Julia. "A Liberating Imagination: Andersen in England." *Marvels & Tales* 20, no. 2 (2006): 142, 179-92.

[*In the following essay, Briggs studies Andersen's reception in England and his impact on English authors and literature.*]

"**The Flying Trunk**" is a story about the effects of storytelling, and in this respect it resembles many others that appear among Hans Christian Andersen's 156 or more fairy tales. Like other such tales, it juxtaposes the near and the far, the familiar and the exotic, the domestic and the fantastic. It warns its readers against the dangers of having money, and the very different danger of having dreams. It tells of inheritance, travel, exile, and the sustaining power of the imagination. These were to be vital themes for Andersen throughout his life, reflecting the transition from his romantic roots to a homeless, restless, protomodernist search for the world beyond the self.

"**The Flying Trunk**" ("*Den flyvende Kuffert*" [1839]) begins when a successful merchant dies and leaves a fortune to his son. The unnamed son squanders his fortune, and when there is no more left, he receives a trunk with the instruction to "Pack up." Since he now has nothing left to pack, he climbs inside it and is carried off to the land of the Turks, where the King's daughter falls in love with him. He wins her with a story, and promises to win over her parents, too, but this time he must tell a story that is both instructive and amusing in order to satisfy both her mother and her father. The story he relates is one of Andersen's best kitchen dramas, in which all the domestic utensils compete with one other and with the matches, insisting upon their superior pedigrees and status. The market basket, it is said, is "an out-and-out radical," and is urging the rest of the household to put things straight when the kitchen maid comes in, and everyone freezes: "They all stood still; no one uttered a syllable" (H. Andersen, *Fairy Tales* 1: 198, 201). The maid lights the matches, and they enjoy their brief moment of glory before being burned out. Naturally this story wins the princess for the merchant's son, and their betrothal is celebrated with fireworks, but a spark from one of them sets light to his magic trunk. Without it, he cannot fly back to the palace, where the princess is left grieving for his departure. The merchant's son must now make his living "trudging round the world, telling stories. But they're not so jolly as the one he told about the matches" (204).

"**The Flying Trunk**" records something of where Andersen had come from and something of where he was going, as well as demonstrating the range of voices, devices, and forms of narrative he could command. Jens Andersen has pointed out that the inset story "portrays the Danish critics of the day as fiery little matches that impetuously flare up but go out almost as soon as they're lit." He adds that it was written for actress Fru Heiberg and her family circle, and the various domestic items can be identified with particular members of the family or their friends (270). This story ventriloquizes these items—matches, iron pot, tongs, market basket—so brilliantly and so colloquially that Brian Alderson has recorded eight different English versions of the market basket's speech to the rest of the kitchen (18-20). All of these items would have been familiar to Hans Christian as a child: he would have seen and played with them in the little room at Munkemøllestrëde in Odense, the room that had seemed so "big and rich" to him when he was very small (Bredsdorff 17). It was here his father kept his cobbler's bench, his mother cooked on the stove, and all of them slept. Andersen's father's legacy to him was not a merchant's fortune but a love of poems and stories—an invitation to the life of the imagination that, like the stork or the flying trunk, could carry you over land and sea. Hans Christian's mother's legacy was the everyday world, the immediate, the practical, the domestic—the world of the laundress, and of the shirt collar beneath the iron. Upstairs on the roof she grew herbs and flowers in an old chest: "my mother's sole garden . . . In my story of the '**Snow Queen**' that garden still blooms" (H. Andersen, *Fairy Tale*, 2). "**The Flying Trunk**" may also reveal something of how Andersen saw himself—as a wastrel with no interest in the practical, as a dreamer, an entertainer, a person with moments of brilliance but inclined to blow the advantages they brought.

In the inset story Andersen creates comedy out of the superiority of the matches and their innocently self-destructive social aspirations. In this respect they anticipate later Andersen characters such as the Fir Tree, the Snowman, the absurdly class-conscious ball in "**The Sweethearts, or the Top and the Ball**," and the Darning Needle, while the leather in "**The Old House**" and the snails in "**The Happy Family**" are not only self-destructive but also snobbish, as are the matches in "**The Flying Trunk**" inset. That apparently naïve kitchen tale is, of course, highly sophisticated, and is subtly connected with the rest of the framing story: the King and his Queen can laugh comfortably at the snobbery of the domestic items, no doubt because they themselves are securely placed above the rest of the court. The spark that ignites the flying trunk echoes the kitchen maid setting light to the matches, and so suggests an element of unconscious self-destruction in the merchant's son as well, thus linking the storyteller to the contents of his story.

The narrative complexity of Andersen's stories (and **"The Flying Trunk"** is a typical example) parallels that of his wonderful paper cuts, where one shape is set inside another, and repeated forms ripple through the whole design. Such complexity reflects the seriousness of his literary ambitions, and his intention of writing simultaneously for children and over their heads, in order to produce a new form that retained the immediacy of oral storytelling, while being altogether more consciously constructed and highly wrought. The Danish word he chose for the type of stories he was writing was "*Eventyr*," but this genre had strong links with the märchen, a German Romantic genre adopted by the poets Johann Wolfgang von Goethe and Novalis, and later used by Ludwig Tieck, Adalbert von Chamisso, E. T. A. Hoffmann, and others. The märchen was typically shaped like a folktale and could include allegory, unlikely coincidences, doubles, and other supernatural elements. Though it could include humor, it never lost sight of deeper and more serious purposes, and it drew on the logic of dreams and the unconscious.

Andersen knew German well, as he never knew English (he read Shakespeare, Byron, and Walter Scott in translation), and he was strongly attracted to German Romantic writing. His first publication, *A Walking Tour from the Holmen Canal to the Eastern Point of Amager* (1828), registers the influence of E. T. A. Hoffmann's *A New Year's Eve's Adventure* (1814; see Wullschlager 80-84). It combines local knowledge of Copenhagen and its citizens with a vein of Hoffmanesque fantasy—the near and the far, the familiar and the exotic—for German Romanticism was suffused with a longing for the faraway. Andersen's first travels took him to the Herz Mountains and the Brocken in 1831 (so different from the low-lying landscapes of Denmark). In 1833 he journeyed even further afield, to the south (of which Goethe's Mignon had sung, "Do you know the land where the lemon tree flowers?" ["*Kennst du das Land, wo die Zitronen blühn?*"]), and after Italy to Egypt (where the storks would fly in **"The Marsh King's Daughter"**) and to Turkey (visited by the Flying Trunk). In Andersen's *Poems* (*Digte*) of 1832, he drew a comic, Edward Lear-like self-portrait as a "lanky person,

> His face as pale as that of Werther,
> His nose as mighty as a cannon,
> His eyes are tiny, like green peas.
> He sings a German song with a "*woher?*"
> And longingly stares at the sunset.

> (Bredsdorff 71)

Andersen had found in the märchen a model for his own *Eventyr,* but it was a form that had not yet taken root in England. At an earlier moment in the history of the Romantic movement, William Wordsworth and Samuel Taylor Coleridge had traveled to Germany, climbed the Brocken, and discussed the nature of the sublime. Both were interested in fairy tales and their appeal to the feelings that lay behind or beneath rational thought, but they were primarily poets rather than storytellers, though some characteristics of the märchen can be glimpsed in Coleridge's *Rime of the Ancient Mariner* and his unfinished poem *Christabel.* Near the end of the nineteenth century, George MacDonald began an essay on "The Fantastic Imagination" with a complaint: "That we have no English word corresponding to the German *Mahrchen,* drives us to use the word Fairytale, regardless of the fact that the tale may have nothing to do with any sort of fairy" (1893; MacDonald 5). And, lacking an appropriate name for it, there are few examples of the märchen in English before Andersen, though from the outset, the Scots, always more at home in continental culture, had been more responsive to its possibilities. In stories such as "The Light Princess" (1864), MacDonald had written his own versions of it, and earlier Thomas Carlyle had translated a selection of key examples in his volumes of *German Romance* (1827). Friedrich De la Motte Fouqué's *Undine* (1811, translated by Carlyle) and *Sintram and His Companions* (1815) were widely read and enjoyed by Victorian readers, but there was little English writing on similar lines between the melodrama of the Gothic novel and the fantastic speculations of Thomas de Quincey's dream writings. By contrast, in America during the 1840s, Edgar Allan Poe was exploring the power of the unconscious through a series of fables set in archetypal landscapes, surreal tales of incestuous passion that looked back to stories such as Tieck's "The Fair Eckbert" or "The Runenberg." The failure of the märchen to establish itself on the English literary scene was one of several factors that contributed to the response to Andersen's work in England.

Another factor was the (perhaps inevitable) failure of his early translators to convey the quality of his narrative voice, for Andersen was the writer in whom the colloquial genius of the Danish language was to find its most vigorous expression: "It is true that even the best translations do not do full justice to Andersen's language and style, with its absurdities, its deliberate grammatical inconsistencies and its adherence to the oral rather than the written forms of expression, nor can they always do justice to his fine sense of humour" (Bredsdorff 347; see also Wullschlager 151-52). He created a voice that was at once personal and distinctive, yet also humorous, sophisticated, intimate, and immediate. Even to a reader who knows no Danish, the rhythms and cadences of a speaking voice can be heard behind the opening words of **"The Snow Queen"**: "See saa! nu begynde vi. Naar vi ere ved Enden af Historien, veed vi mere, end vi nu vide, for det var en ond Trold! Det var een af de allervärste, det var 'Dëvelen'! Een dag" (Pedersen 191). Several of Andersen's English admirers from the present day (among them, M. R. James,

Naomi Lewis, and Brian Alderson) have learned Danish from a desire to read what he actually wrote.

Many—perhaps most—of these qualities disappeared beneath the ponderous early translations of Mary Howitt, Charles Boner, Caroline Peachey, and others. Several of them worked from German translations rather than the Danish originals, introducing the occasional howler in the process; for instance, the anonymous *Tales for the Young* (1847) translates **"The Ugly Duckling"** (**"Den grimme Ælling"**) as **"The Little Green Duck"** (Alderson 5). The title of **"The Princess on the Pea"** was usually altered, probably because of the English homonym *pea/pee*, and in the German version the princess slept on three peas, which reduces the joke. If his early translators were aware of Andersen's easy, informal style, they ignored it, replacing it with a stiff, old-fashioned, Sunday-afternoon kind of prose, the voice that can be heard, for example, in Caroline Peachey's version of the Troll's (or ogre's) party in **"The Travelling Companion"**: "He kissed the princess on the forehead, and bade her sit down on the throne beside him. And now the band struck up. Great black grasshoppers played on the jew's harp, and the owl came out with his 'Tu-whit, tu-whoo!' as chief vocalist. It was, in sooth, a ridiculous concert'" (Pedersen 114).

R. P. Keigwin's more modern version of this tale exposes both her pedantry and her misreading of what the owl was actually doing: "He kissed the Princess on her forehead and got her to sit beside him on his gorgeous throne and after that the music began. Great black grasshoppers played on Jews'-harps, and the owl—for want of a drum—beat his own stomach. It was a funny concert" (H. Andersen, *Fairy Tales* 2: 65).

Andersen's Victorian translators ironed out his idiosyncrasies and made his writing more sentimental and moralistic in the process. On his visit to London in 1847, his social awkwardness confirmed the impression that he was a "marvellous child," an impression resulting from too close an identification of the author with his work. One biographer, Jackie Wullschlager, believes that he consciously played up to this persona, and in doing so "helped [to] ensure that the full dimension and scope of his work remained misunderstood and underrated in Britain and America. Had he never visited England, the general perception of him today would be very different" (295). To others, he seemed a sycophant, a traitor to his own class: Mary Russell Mitford described him as "a toad-eater, a hanger-on in great houses . . . [he] uses fame merely as a key to open drawing-room doors, a ladder to climb to high places" (Wullschlager 279). Adverse responses to Andersen often conflate the writer and the man. The late Humphrey Carpenter reflected widespread views when he described the fairy tales as dominated by "self-pity, and the feeling that [Andersen's] true worth had never been appre-

ciated . . . his stories, while incomparably crafted, have a maudlin self-regarding streak that limits their moral applicability." His conclusion—that Andersen's "particular form of introspection does not seem to have struck a chord in the British literary imagination" (4)—like Wullschleger's quoted above, is surprising in view of Andersen's extraordinary popularity in English.

Accusations of solipsism and self-pity, like that of social climbing, are difficult to reconcile with Andersen's frequent—and frequently comic—treatment of these particular traits in his stories. So do these reflect a self-awareness that his critics have been reluctant to concede to him? The Fir Tree, the Darning Needle, the Snowman, and the rest are so obviously gripped by self-pity and ridiculous social aspirations that their author may be mocking himself through them. Yet if Andersen was a solipsist, he was also capable of a rare absorption in the world around him, reflected in his sharp observations of it. In his first memoir, he wrote: "Anyone I have seen and spoken to once, I can later remember their faces clearly, I have their mirror image within me; however, I cannot recall my own features, although God knows I look at myself in the mirror often enough" (Wullschlager 283). His writing reflects a rare, almost Keatsian ability to identify with and re-create from within the thoughts and speech of individuals, but also of animals and even of inanimate objects.

Solipsism and sentimentality, compulsive storytelling, the demystifying vision of the child, the simultaneous mockery of and deference to society—all of these were traits that Andersen shared with Charles Dickens, whose fiction also drew on fairy-tale structures and elements of the grotesque familiar from German Romanticism. Certainly the two men seemed to recognize each other "[a]cross Europe" (as Wullschlager puts it, 287), and Dickens's warm welcome for the Dane at a time when his own star was rising did much to prepare the way and establish Andersen's reputation on his arrival in England in 1847. Andersen's three novels had been translated and published in London two years before— *The Improvisatore* and two others, *Only a Fiddler!* and *O. T. or, Life in Denmark*—in a single volume. Today his novels are never reprinted and are very difficult to find in English versions; but in 1846 his collection of travel writings, *A Poet's Bazaar,* was translated, along with four different editions of the *Eventyr.* Their titles indicate that they were specifically intended for children: Mary Howitt's *Wonderful Stories for Children,* Caroline Peachey's *Danish Fairy Legends and Tales,* Charles Boner's *A Danish Story Book* and *The Nightingale and Other Tales* (Alderson 22-23). In England, from the outset, Andersen was considered "as wholly a children's author, whereas in Denmark and Germany, he was seen as a writer for both adults and children." He criticized Charles Boner for having left out three of his best, as well as his most serious, tales—**"The Fir**

Tree," "The Shadow," and "The Snow Queen" (Wullschlager 291).

The literary status of authors who write for children has always been significantly lower than that of those who write for adults—something Andersen no doubt recognized when he complained to Boner about his selection. Yet there were compensations: by the 1840s publishing for children was well established as a niche market, with fairy tales as a flourishing area within it, yet the field was not yet dominated by any single figure. It provided both a promising environment for a writer with original tales to tell and original ways of telling them. The boundary that demarcated the market for children's books from that for adults provided a degree of protection for its authors at the same time that it created limits and constraints and diminished their literary standing. Despite misinterpretation, and even some antagonism, Andersen's fairy stories, from the moment of their first appearance, seem to have been extraordinarily popular in England. For Brian Alderson, their success was "a portent of the imaginative potential of books for children . . . as the century progressed, editions and translations tumbled from the presses by the thousand, so that **'Hans Andersen's Fairy Tales'** became one of the most widely read children's books in Victorian England" (Alderson 1). With so many cheap versions available, most children were given a copy of Andersen's *Fairy Tales,* if they were given any books at all, often in memorably illustrated editions. They kept them, too. I have my father's copy, given to him on his seventh birthday—an edition illustrated by A. Duncan Carse and published by A. and C. Black in October 1912. It contains a neatly folded newspaper cutting of Andersen's late story **"King, Queen and Knave,"** from when it was first discovered and translated. My father gave me an edition illustrated by Rex Whistler for my fifth birthday, and despite its stiff Victorian translations it is still a prized possession (Alderson discusses Andersen's illustrators [7-17] and provides a bibliography).

Andersen did not see himself as primarily or exclusively a writer for children and saw no reason to protect his readers from cruelty, violence, or horror: the Little Match Girl dies of cold; Karin has her feet chopped off to rid herself of her beloved red shoes; Elisa, in **"The Wild Swans,"** only narrowly escapes being burned to death as a witch; the Little Mermaid sacrifices her tongue and endures silent agonies only to lose her love, and her life as well; the Prince who disguises himself as a Swineherd rejects the Princess in disgust; the Steadfast (or "Staunch" or "Constant") Tin Soldier is thrown on the fire; the merchant's son loses his Princess in **"The Flying Trunk"**; and, worst of all, in Andersen's sinister reworking of Chamisso's *Peter Schlemihl,* the

Shadow marries the Princess amid celebrations, while the poor scholar who formerly owned the Shadow is quietly put to death.

Andersen's world is tough, making few concessions to nursery sensibilities, and some of what is taken for sentimentality may simply be an entirely un-English lack of reticence about strong emotions. How, for example, should we respond to **"The Story of the Mother"** who, when her child dies, pursues Death, determined to get the child back? She sings to the Night, presses the thorny bramble to her breast, weeps out her eyes, and gives away her hair. When she eventually catches up with Death, he shows her two possible futures, one a joy and the other a misery, warning her that only one of them belongs to her child. Unable to guess which is his future, she begs Death to take her child away, despite all she has sacrificed to save him. The story's message—that life is as likely to turn out a curse as a blessing—is as undeniable as it is banal, but the mother's desperate pursuit and its dark outcome never ring false. The story ends with a defeated acceptance of the harsh conditions of life. The Danish scholar Elias Bredsdorff ranked this story with **"The Little Mermaid"** and **"The Snow Queen"** as Andersen's three greatest achievements (316), but twentieth-century selections usually prefer to leave it out.

Terror is often evoked but is sometimes qualified by comedy, as in **"Little Claus and Big Claus,"** Gerda's encounter with the Little Robber Girl, or the riotous parties given by the old Troll in **"The Travelling Companion"** or under **"The Elf Hill"** (A. Duncan Carse memorably illustrated the moment when "The Hell-horse turned quite giddy and had to leave the table"). The sea witch in **"The Little Mermaid"** lives surrounded by hungry polyps, toads, and water snakes—a grotesque domestic touch has her scouring her kettle with a bunch of these creatures. Occasionally Andersen's witches are gratuitously nasty, like those in **"The Wild Swans,"** whom Elisa has to pass in order to reach the nettles she needs to disenchant her brothers. Having thrown off their rags, they sit on a large gravestone and "clawed with their long skinny fingers in the new-made graves, dragged out the corpses, and ate their flesh" (H. Andersen, *Fairy Tales* 2: 154). The wicked stepmother queen in **"The Wild Swans"** is another witch, who has cast a spell on Elisa using three poisonous toads. When Beverley Nichols created the sinister Miss Smith in *The Tree That Sat Down* (1948), he gave her three poisonous toads as her familiars—an example of the way particular details lurked in their readers' memories, only to resurface later in their own writing for children.

What Andersen contributed supremely to English writing for children is, of course, that vein of fantasy and imaginative invention that is often regarded as peculiarly English and that constitutes its peculiar strength—

the tradition that unites writers as different as Roald Dahl and J. K. Rowling, James Barrie and Rudyard Kipling, Kenneth Grahame and A. A. Milne, J. R. R. Tolkien, C. S. Lewis, Alan Garner, and Philip Pullman. The fantasy writing of the märchen had flourished in Germany between 1770 and 1830, reaching Britain through the transitional figure of Andersen rather than through its original authors. Once established, it left its own indelible mark, while remaining largely confined to writing for children. It is impossible to think of the tradition of children's literature without William Makepeace Thackeray's *The Rose and the Ring,* Charles Kingsley's *The Water-Babies,* Lewis Carroll's *Alice* books, or George MacDonald's *The Princess and the Goblin* without Oscar Wilde's *The Happy Prince* or the drily humorous voices of E. Nesbit and Beatrix Potter, yet would any of these have been written as they were without Andersen's liberating intervention? Britain had closed its doors against the disturbing (if occasionally "precious") genre of the märchen; Andersen opened them again from the nursery, and from that point of relative security (as a niche market), he let in fantasy in a wide range of shapes and forms.

It is difficult to quantify Andersen's legacy to the tradition of writing for children in English, in part because it is so pervasive. One aspect of it lies in his direct tone of voice—there is no talking down to young listeners. This quality is conspicuous from the very first story he wrote—**"The Tinder-Box."** After the soldier has fetched the tinderbox from the hollow of the tree, he asks the old witch:

> "What are you going to do with this tinder-box?". . .
>
> "That's no business of yours!" answered the witch. "You've got your money; now just give me my tinder-box!"
>
> "Rubbish!" said the soldier. "Tell me at once what you want to do with it—or I'll have out my sword and cut your head off."
>
> "No," said the witch.
>
> So he cut off her head . . . There she lay!
>
> (H. Andersen, *Fairy Tales* 1: 40)

A degree of easy familiarity characterizes court protocol in **"The Swineherd,"** where the Prince inquires, "I wonder if you've got a job for me here at the Castle," and the Emperor replies, "Ah, well, . . . there are so many who come and ask that. But now, let me see—yes, I want some one to mind the pigs. We've such a lot of pigs." At the end of the story the Emperor smacks the ladies-in-waiting with his slipper and dismisses the Prince/swineherd: "'Out you get!' said the Emperor, for he was furious, and both Princess and swineherd were turned out of his kingdom." Having rejected the spoiled princess, the Prince "went into his kingdom, shut the door and bolted it; but she could stand outside if she cared to" (H. Andersen, *Fairy Tales* 1: 237, 243, 245). This new way of telling fairy tales—as if royal families behaved just like everyone else—appeared in Thackeray's *The Rose and the Ring* (1855), Dickens's *The Magic Fishbone* (in his *Holiday Romance* [1868]), Andrew Lang's "Prince Prigio" stories (1889), and in E. Nesbit's fairy tales written for the *Strand* magazine at the end of the nineteenth century; for example, in Nesbit's "The Book of Beasts," when King Lionel releases the bluebird against his ministers' advice:

> The Chancellor gave the king a good shaking and said[,]
>
> "You're a naughty disobedient little king," and was very angry indeed.
>
> "Well, I'm sorry if I've vexed you," said Lionel—"Come, let's be friends." . . . so he kissed the Prime Minister and they settled down for a nice quiet game of noughts and crosses, while the Chancellor went to add up his accounts.
>
> (Nesbit 12)

By way of indicating something of the pervasive influence of Andersen's imagination, let us take another story, **"Willie Winkie"** (**"Ole Lukøie"** [1841]—literally, "Old Shut-Eyes"), made up of a series of loosely strung episodes that are recalled and echoed in some later fantasy writing in English. Willie Winkie begins by decorating little Hjalmar's room, so that the flowers in their flowerpots shoot up to the ceiling and create an arbor hung with fruits (anticipating the opening of Maurice Sendak's *Where the Wild Things Are* [1963]). On Tuesday evening, Willie Winkie lifts Hjalmar up to a picture of a landscape with a river, and the boy climbs inside the frame and sails down the river in a little silver boat drawn by swans. The idea of climbing into a picture, a delightful experience for Hjalmar, is borrowed and transposed to provide the violent transition to Narnia at the beginning of C. S. Lewis's *The Voyage of the Dawn Treader* (1952). Using pictures as a starting point for stories appealed to Andersen—he also linked a larger group of tales under the title **"A Picture Book without Pictures"** (**"Billedbog uden Billeder,"** also known as **"What the Moon Saw"**). On Saturday, as Willie Winkie begins a story about the stars for Hjalmar, the portrait of his great-grandfather interrupts their conversation: "'I say, look here, Mr. Winkie . . . Thank you for telling the boy these stories, but you mustn't muddle him with wrong ideas. The stars can't be taken down and polished. A star is a globe, the same as the earth is'" (H. Andersen, *Fairy Tales* 1: 228).

In John Masefield's *The Midnight Folk* (1927), Great-Grandpapa Harker's portrait also comes alive, and as in Hjalmar's Tuesday night adventure, the landscape in the painting comes alive, too. Birds sing, clouds fly in the breeze, and "the wind ruffled the skirt of [Great-Grandpapa's] coat, and shook the shrubs behind him. A couple of blue butterflies which had been upon the shrubs for seventy odd years, flew out into the room" (Masefield 48). Masefield also draws on a further episode in **"Willie Winkie"** when he makes Kay Harker grow small and slip into secret passages within the walls and beneath the floorboards with the other household creatures, "The Midnight Folk." On Thursday night a mouse arrives with a wedding invitation for Hjalmar: "'[H]ow am I to get through the tiny mousehole in the floor?' asked Hjalmar." Willie Winkie transforms him with "his magic squirt," and when he has shrunk, he suggests that Hjalmar borrow his tin soldier's clothes for the occasion, on the ground that "it looks so smart to be wearing uniform at a party." Hjalmar climbs into a thimble and is pulled along a passage under the floor to the wedding (H. Andersen, *Fairy Tales* 1: 218-19). This is not, of course, the first story in which a child finds itself magically small—small enough to socialize with mice and keep company with toy soldiers, for Marie in E. T. A. Hoffmann's *Nutcracker and the King of Mice* (1816) had also done so earlier; Hoffmann's story is the source for the *Nutcracker* ballet, as well as contributing to this story. But the combination of "going small" with pictures that come to life is peculiar to Andersen's **"Willie Winkie."**

Going small is a favorite theme in writing for children partly because of the way it collapses the difference between storyteller and listener. Children are fascinated by objects that are proportionate to their size, by dolls and dolls' houses, and by rabbits and mice (given to children to encourage them to develop a sense of responsibility toward something smaller than themselves), while the device allows the adult storyteller to step back into the small world of childhood. As *Gulliver's Travels* so graphically illustrates, relative size is directly connected with empowerment. Interestingly, in this context Andersen's Hjalmar recognizes that though going small may be imaginatively empowering, it brings a counterbalancing loss of dignity: "[H]e had certainly been in very smart society; on the other hand, he had had to put up with no end of shrinking, to make himself small enough to get into a tin soldier's uniform" (H. Andersen, *Fairy Tales* 1: 221).

Paradoxes of size figure largely in what are arguably the greatest of English fantasies for children—*Alice's Adventures in Wonderland* (1865) and *Through the Looking-Glass* (1871). Lewis Carroll's books are so firmly English in idiom—in their obsession with class, manners, and social protocol of all kinds—that it is easy to overlook their debt to the miniature world of **"Thumbelina"**; of talking lizards, crows, and storks; of bizarre social events such as the mouse's wedding in **"Willie Winkie,"** or the engagement party under **"The Elf Hill."** Whatever Carroll borrowed, he made his own, and his cool amusement at conventional morality gives his writing an utterly different tone from Andersen's. Yet his sudden, arbitrary encounters, his vividly ventriloquized creatures, even the conversation of roses and tiger lilies in a magic garden—all point toward the impact that Andersen had on English writing for children, just as his effect can be felt on the fantasy writing of Charles Kingsley, George MacDonald, Frances Browne, Annie Ritchie, and Juliana Ewing. Andersen's inventiveness liberated their imaginations.

At the heart of **"Willie Winkie"** is a celebration of the animating power of imagination, much as it drives **"The Flying Trunk"**—both stories can be read as fables of the power of imagination, as can **"The Goloshes of Fortune," "The Goblin at the Grocer's," "The Marsh King's Daughter,"** and many others. It is the power of imagination that transforms Hjalmar's bedroom into a forest, that brings pictures and their inhabitants to life, and that enables Hjalmar to attend the mouse's wedding. When the great-grandfather's portrait interrupts, Willie Winkie silences him by pointing out his superior age and status. Like Kipling's Puck, he is "an ancient heathen—the Romans and Greeks call me the Dream God." He is, of course, Morpheus. On Sunday night, Hjalmar asks him for stories that Andersen would later write—"about the five peas that lived in a pod, . . . about the darning needle who was so stuck-up"—but instead Willie Winkie shows him his brother Death, and warns him of the need for a good report card, since Death's stories will be beautiful or horrible according to his report. Even the great-grandfather is mollified by this didactic turn: "'Most instructive!" muttered the great-grandfather's portrait. 'It does some good, after all, to express one's opinion'" (H. Andersen, *Fairy Tales* 1: 229, 230, 233).

While Masefield's *The Midnight Folk* includes several echoes of **"Willie Winkie,"** the name of its central character, Kay Harker, recalls **"The Snow Queen"** (**"*Snedronningen*"** [1844]), Andersen's masterpiece that "came out dancing over the paper," according to its author (Wullschlager 243). Francis Spufford, in *I May Be Some Time,* a study of imaginative responses to the North and South Poles, has commented that in this story Andersen "invented a myth: new, but like the oldest myths organised around the most compellingly simple oppositions, between warmth and cold, emotion and reason, the wild and the tame" (139). And as happens with myth, the various elements of this story soon began to reappear in the writings of Andersen's English followers. One of the smaller borrowings was the talking flowers, the rose, tiger lily, daisy, and the rest from the old woman's garden who reappear in *Through the Looking-Glass;* but where Carroll's lily is scornful and combative, Andersen's flowers are thorough-going narcissists. Each one tells a different story about itself, and the narcissus turns out to be the worst of all: "I can see myself, I can see myself! . . . Can't you smell me?" Andersen's old woman had wanted Gerda to stay with her and forget her quest for Kay, so she made all the roses magically sink into the ground in case they should remind Gerda of the roses on her roof garden at home, but she overlooks the roses painted on her hat—"That comes of not having your wits about you!" (H. Andersen, *Fairy Tales* 1: 324, 318).

Christina Rossetti, in the third part of *Speaking Likenesses* (1874), combines elements from **"The Little Match Girl"** and **"The Snow Queen"** as the latter story's heroine, Maggie, struggles through the wood to deliver Christmas parcels but is turned away on the doorstep, without food, warmth, or a glimpse of the Christmas tree, though she is later rewarded by seeing the much brighter and more beautiful lights of the Aurora Borealis. George MacDonald rewrote the figure of the Snow Queen as the beautiful yet mysterious and occasionally threatening figure of North Wind in *At the Back of the North Wind* (1871). MacDonald's most famous disciple, C. S. Lewis, transformed Andersen's icy Queen of reason into the evil White Witch, who, in *The Lion, the Witch, and the Wardrobe* (1950), abducts Edmund and carries him off in her sleigh. Instead of freezing him with a kiss (as the Snow Queen had done), she poisons him with enchanted Turkish delight (a confection that look a little like ice dusted with snow). And one of Lewis's sternest critics, Philip Pullman, unconsciously followed in Lewis's footsteps when he reworked the story of **"The Snow Queen"** in *Northern Lights* (1995; titled *The Golden Compass* in the U.S.), another tale of a small boy who is abducted and carried off to the North by a mysterious woman. In this late twentieth-century version, the Queen's ice palace has become the concentration camp at Bolvangar where sadistic experiments on children's souls are conducted. Gerda, the warmhearted little girl who is loved by everyone she encounters, has become Lyra Silvertongue, and the Snow Queen is transformed into the worldly Mrs. Coulter.

At the heart of Pullman's trilogy is the concept of "dark materials," a phrase taken from John Milton's *Paradise Lost* to describe the formless chaos that Satan must traverse before he can reach earth. As Pullman recognized, it is an apt metaphor for the dark materials of the unconscious from which writers must bring back their travelers' tales. In Andersen's fairy tales, imagination finds wings to traverse the unknown, animating whatever creatures it encounters in the course of that long northern journey. Andersen's example pointed the way for successive generations of children's writers to discover for themselves the comedy and the seriousness, the homeliness and strangeness of fantasy.

Works Cited

Alderson, Brian. *Hans Christian Andersen and His Eventyr in England.* Wormley, Herts: Five Owls Press, 1982.

Andersen, Hans Christian. *The Fairy Tale of My Life: An Autobiography.* Introd. Naomi Lewis. New York: Cooper Square Press, 2000.

———. *Fairy Tales.* Ed. Svend Larsen. Trans. R. P. Keigwin. 3 vols. Odense: Flensted, 1958.

Andersen, Jens. *Hans Christian Andersen: A New Life,* Trans. Tiina Nunnally. New York: Overlook Duckworth, 2005.

Bredsdorff, Elias. *Hans Christian Andersen: The Story of His Life and Work, 1805-1875.* London: Phaidon, 1975.

Carpenter, Humphrey. *Secret Gardens: A Study of the Golden Age of Children's Literature.* Boston: Houghton Mifflin, 1985.

MacDonald, George. *The Complete Fairy Tales.* Ed. U. C. Knoepflmacher. London: Penguin, 1999.

Masefield, John. *The Midnight Folk.* 1927. London: Egmont Books, 2000.

Nesbit, E. "The Book of Beasts." In *The Book of Dragons.* London: Harper and Bros., 1899.

Pedersen, Viggo Hjornager. *Ugly Ducklings? Studies in the English Translations of Hans Christian Andersen's Tales and Stories.* Odense: UP of Southern Denmark, 2004.

Spufford, Francis. *I May Be Some Time: Ice and the English Imagination.* London: Faber and Faber, 1996.

Wullschlager, Jackie. *Hans Christian Andersen: The Life of a Storyteller.* London: Allan Lane, 2000.

Erica Weitzman (essay date December 2007)

SOURCE: Weitzman, Erica. "The World in Pieces: Concepts of Anxiety in H. C. Andersen's 'The Snow Queen'." *MLN* 122, no. 5 (December 2007): 1105-123.

[*In the following essay, Weitzman applies Søren Kierkegaard's conception of anxiety and despair to a reading of Andersen's "The Snow Queen."*]

The rivalry between contemporaries and compatriots Hans Christian Andersen and Søren Kierkegaard is well known. It is documented in Kierkegaard's first published work, *From the Papers of One Still Living,* an extended and harshly critical review of Andersen's novel *Only a Fiddler.* Despite this antagonism, however, and despite a myriad of evident personal, ideological, and stylistic differences, there remains a certain affinity between the fabulist/memoirist/novelist and the philosopher/psychologist/theologian, one that extends far beyond the obvious connection of their common professed Christianity. Setting aside the textual debate between the two writers, we propose here to examine Andersen's celebrated fairy-tale, **"The Snow Queen,"** in light of Kierkegaard's treatment of anxiety and despair in *The Concept of Anxiety* and *The Sickness Unto Death,* respectively. We will also have recourse—however inapplicable it may seem to Andersen's work—to Kierkegaard's *The Concept of Irony* as a work foundational for Kierkegaard's quizzical anti-dialectics of the states of anguish and desire. For anguish and desire, we hope to show, do not exist for Kierkegaard *except* ironically, and at the same time, this irony is the condition of all anguish and desire. And though **"The Snow Queen"** is in many ways a simple and moralistic (if also very strange) tale that in no way partakes of the complexities and perversities of Kierkegaard's thought, at its base there is the same anguish and desire that motivates not only Kierkegaard's preoccupations but also the preoccupations of much post-Kierkegaardian psychology and psychoanalysis.

Ultimately, **"The Snow Queen"** is all too patently an allegory of despair and its overcoming, of the various failures to mourn (the basic definition of melancholy according to Freud), and of the subsequent recoveries. The difference between Kierkegaard and Andersen—regarding the texts in question at least—may lie precisely in this possibility or impossibility of recovery. This may be a factor of genre above all, of allegory versus analysis, and of the function fairy-tales must play explicitly or implicitly in the development of children's consciousness, as opposed to the much more complicated position towards "edification" taken by Kierkegaard. Regardless, the intersection of these texts can serve to reveal not only the profound insightfulness of Andersen's tale but also the extent to which Kierkegaard's critical philosophy is profoundly—and not just incidentally or "merely poetically"—psychological. Nor, in this sense, is it "merely" melancholic. At the cold northern borders of experience, in the white night of the soul, both Kierkegaard and Andersen are engaged in the painful encounter with what it means to be a desiring subject in a fallen world and with what kind of subjectivities may emerge in that encounter's wake.

"The Snow Queen" [**"Snee-Dronningen"**] first existed as a simple ballad-style poem by Andersen about a young girl waiting for her miller-boy lover. Before he can join her, he is abducted by the Snow Queen, who makes him a bed of snow and ice. When the girl, made anxious by her beloved's delay, goes to the mill to search for him, she finds the mill-wheel stopped.[1] The Snow Queen is thus initially a kind of *Erlkönigin* and sexual predator, whose seductions result, it is implied, in the breaking of human bonds—including and especially the consummate break with human bonds (death). The fairy-tale, on the other hand, is written primarily as a cautionary fairy tale for children. (Andersen is almost always didactic, but the opening lines of **"The Snow Queen"**—"Now we are about to begin and you must attend! [*See saa! nu begynde vi*]"[2]—are strikingly pedagogical even for him.) Thus the aspect of sexual seduction and sexual betrayal is more latent, if still powerfully present. "Now I mustn't kiss you any more," the Snow Queen says upon her abduction of Kay, almost but not quite in line with the ballad, "or I should kiss you to death!" (116). But the Snow Queen's seduction is also—and much more overtly—the seduction of absolute knowledge. As the Snow Queen carries Kay off, he tries to impress her with his puerile form of erudition, in one of the strangely comedic but nonetheless telling moments of the story:

> In his eyes she was quite perfect, and he was not a bit afraid of her. He told her that he could do mental arithmetic as far as fractions, and that he knew the number of square miles and the number of inhabitants of the country. She always smiled at him, and he then thought that he surely did not know enough, and he looked up into the wide expanse of heaven, into which they rose higher and higher as she flew with him on a dark cloud, while the storm surged around them, the wind ringing in their ears like well-known old songs.
>
> (116)

The Snow Queen's realm is the realm of frigid mathematical perfection, in which even "The northern lights came and went with such regularity that you could count the seconds between their coming and going" (142). The frozen lake that lies "in the midst of these never-ending snow halls" is "broken up on the surface into a thousand bits, but each piece was so exactly like the others that the whole formed a perfect work of art" (142). This is the apotheosis of the motif of regularity and stasis that runs throughout the tale, beginning with an afflicted Kay's rejection of the summer's rose-bushes—"'How horrid!' he suddenly cried. 'There's a worm in that rose, and that one is quite crooked. After all, they are nasty roses and so are the boxes they are growing in!'" (113)—for the crystalline symmetry of snowflakes.

On a metatextual level, one might also contrast the perfect, iterative sameness of the lake's fragments with the asymmetrical structure of the story that contains them. The seven "stories" that make up **"The Snow Queen"** are indeed anything but identical, neither in size nor in tone nor even in narrative focus. The first story is a kind of preface on the "real demon [*det var 'Dævelen'*]" and his grinning mirror, which is at once the impetus for the entire story and almost entirely forgotten by the end of the second section. The second section introduces Kay and Gerda in their idyllic childhood, and narrates Kay's fall—the piercing of his heart and eye by shards of this mirror—and subsequent abduction by the Snow Queen. The third, fourth, fifth, and sixth story are concerned with Gerda's search for her friend, and take her, in standard fairy-tale style, through a variety of scenarios either perilous or congenial. The final story shifts the scene to Kay and his captivity in the Snow Queen's palace and subsequent rescue. The story is dotted with a number of odd tangents and fantasias, episodes that jar tonally, seemingly irrelevant motifs, and details which are as charming as they are gratuitous. It is, in a word, not classical, as the fairy-tale genre is, in its origins and premises, not classical—hence the genre's interest for a generation of artists and thinkers grown weary of the formalisms of the early Enlightenment. Andersen himself is not subtle about his tale being in many ways a satire of, or slap at, scientism and classicism. On the above-mentioned "perfect work of art" which forms the dead center of the Snow Queen's palace: "The Snow Queen sat in the very middle of it when she sat at home. She then said that she was sitting on 'The Mirror of Reason,' and that it was the best and only one in the world" (142). Kay's final task—the task that will bring him to the point of catatonic breakdown—is to fit together a "Chinese puzzle" made of ice. And his puzzles, the story states,

> were most ingenious, because they were the "Ice Puzzles of Reason." In his eyes they were excellent and of the greatest importance: this was because of the grain of glass still in his eye. He made many patterns forming words, but he never could find the right way to place them for one particular word, a word he was most anxious to make. It was "Eternity" ["*Evigheden*"]. The Snow Queen had said to him that if he could find out this world he should be his own master, and she would give him the whole world and a new pair of skates.

(143)

"If only they would not melt!" (114) Kay exclaims in the second story over the snowflakes he is examining under his microscope. Temporality/finitude is the one persistent flaw in Kay's stricken isolation. The Snow Queen offers the twin promises of imperishability and mastery in what one might call a deadly misunderstanding of the Kantian mathematical sublime: the lure of being able to comprehend that which is "absolutely great" as something sensible rather than supersensible and to bring a cognitive ideality into concrete presence. It may also be seen as a misunderstanding of the Kantian notion of beauty as that which is in accordance with an ideal law, forgetting that this ideal law is only ever valid in relation to its particular manifestations. If

Kant would find a crooked rose no more beautiful than Kay, he would also merely judge it lacking with respect to its ideal form.[3] For Kay, on the other hand, a crooked rose marks the unbridgeable gap between actuality and ideality and, by extension, the intolerable crookedness of all creation.

If the "Mirror of Reason," with its oxymoronically "perfect" pattern of breakage, is "the best and only one in the world," in what relation does it stand to the demons' mirror, shattered in the prelude into fragments and strewn over the world? What, in other words, is the relation of the demons' mirror to the Snow Queen? For there seems to be no necessary connection. The Snow Queen herself is never described as demonic, nor does she grin and grimace, like the mirror of the prelude. A kind of correspondence, the only one in the text, occurs when Gerda prepares to approach the Snow Queen's castle. The Snow Queen's "advance guard" of snowflakes—the crystalline shapes that Kay had once lauded to Gerda for their perfection—now take "the most curious shapes. Some looked like big, horrid porcupines; some like bundles of knotted snakes with their heads sticking out. Others again were like fat little bears with bristling hair, but all were dazzling white and living snowflakes" (141). Nowhere else in the text, however, is the grotesquerie of the demonic and the frigid beauty of the Snow Queen's realm so explicitly allied. That there is a causal connection between Kay's demonic affliction and his abduction by the Snow Queen is made plain—again, the text states that Kay's ability to find importance in the tasks the Snow Queen assigns him is due only to the fragments lodged in his heart and eye— but *why* this should be the case is not clear.

The relationship between the demons' mirror of distortion and the Snow Queen's mirror of sameness thus calls for examination. To do this, we now turn to Kierkegaard's examinations of sin and despair, in *The Concept of Anxiety* and *The Sickness Unto Death* respectively, as well as the work that is in many ways a companion piece to these two, *The Concept of Irony*. Again, **"The Snow Queen"** clearly lacks the dialectical complexity—if not the emotional depth—of Kierkegaard's work; nevertheless, the latter's "psychological expositions for edification and awakening" (the subtitle of *The Sickness Unto Death*) often seem to provide a kind of phenomenological description of what Andersen's fantasy tale evocatively if elliptically narrates.

The devils' mirror is first of all a mirror of mockery, or more precisely, of *irony,* in the sense of "infinite absolute negativity"[4] given by Kierkegaard. In the devils' mirror, "every good and pretty thing reflected in it shrank away to almost nothing. On the other hand, every bad and good-for-nothing thing stood out and looked its worst" (*SQ* 108). Reflected in this mirror, nothing is of value, beauty, or meaning. Moreover, what is displayed in the glass is non-self-identity, or a distortion of self-identity, in an experience that is familiar to anyone who has looked in the curved mirrors at a funhouse. The irony-mirror does not exactly reflect the negation of this identity, however, but "subjectivity's being-for-itself" (*CI* 257): a thoroughly self-involved and self-mirroring apprehension of both self and world in which both lose their reality before the flickerings of a distorted autogenous perception. Kierkegaard distinguishes the concept of irony from that of doubt:

> In doubt, the subject is an eyewitness to a war of conquest in which every phenomenon is destroyed, because the essence must continually lie behind it. In irony, the subject is continually retreating, taking every phenomenon out of its reality in order to save itself— that is, in order to preserve itself in negative independence of everything.
>
> (*CI* 257)

Doubt despairs that it cannot reach the essence through the phenomenon; irony thinks that it has the essence as its own power of negation. And yet the one may also reverse into the other. The demons' mirror presents an image of the real world not only as contingent but also as alien and ugly in its contingency: a kind of instant Sartrean nausea. It is the devils' nihilistic hubris that results in the mirror's shattering, when they attempt "to fly up to heaven with it to mock the angels" (*SQ* 109) and the absolute goodness of the angels causes the mirror to grin, in a kind of affective inversion, so much that it slips from the demons' grasp. The students of the ur-demon's school—"for he kept a school" (108)—fail, then, in unleashing a demonic irony on first philosophy. In this failure, however, their bad irony is dispersed through the human world. Accordingly, the first symptom of Kay's altered, demonic state is *contempt*: he scorns his old pastimes and old playmate, cavils about the grandmother's stories, and viciously mocks the grandmother and eventually "everyone in the street." This wins him not censure, but the approval of the community: "'He will turn out a clever fellow,' said people. . . . He played quite different games now; he seemed to have grown older" (114). Kay no longer communicates; he mimics: he has, in effect, become the incarnation of the mirror's burlesquing grin. Hyperconscious of the world in its inessential particularity—a particularity that evokes only horror and disgust—he comes to exist only in the twinned modes of ridicule and withdrawal.

In his discussion of the "demonic" in *The Concept of Anxiety*, Kierkegaard associates the concepts or states of "the negative," "unfreedom," and "inclosing reserve." "Inclosing reserve" is the unwillingness to communicate, to risk the "disclosure" of language. "Language, the word, is precisely what saves, what saves the individual from the empty abstraction of inclosing reserve"[5]:

but what is this sullenness of the demonic individual, that fears to be broken by language? "Freedom is always *communicierende* (it does no harm even to take into consideration the religious significance of the word); unfreedom becomes more and more inclosed and does not want communication" (*CA* 124). Language is in this sense freedom itself, the possibility for change, communion, interaction, alteration, relation, intercourse (it does no harm even to take into consideration the sexual significance of the word), mutability, uncertainty, limitation, and finitude. To be "anxious about the good" means to be unable to accept freedom, for here freedom is inimical to the ideal. Freedom is infinite possibility, but this means, also and especially, the possibility for arbitrariness and change. The ideal *as* ideal, however, is infinite stasis. When this ideal is conceived of in human terms—when one tries to enact or incarnate in the material world the infinity that is only the property of spirit—what results is death-in-life. One is anxious about the good, i.e., one has no faith that there is a good outside or beyond the actual. Thus the "good," conceived in such a false and solipsistic manner, becomes something private, "inclosing," and abyssal as a hall of mirrors, to be protected at any cost against the dangerous gaze of others.

The more private this vision of the good becomes, however, the more it is emptied out of all meaning and turns into something void and ugly even to the inclosed person. But this ugly ungood has already become the core of the inclosed person's being. One may justly compare the "demoniac" in this stage with melancholia in Freud or the depressive position in Melanie Klein.[6] The melancholic or depressive position emerges in the loss of a desired object whose loss the subject is unable for one reason or another to normalize. In the subject's inability to understand the loss of the object as something independent from his or her own will or person, the desired object is introjected as absence, lack, and badness, "a source of poison and danger inside the subject's body"[7]; this introjected badness then becomes the subject's center and entirety. One might further compare the demoniac's divorce of freedom and the good in Kierkegaard to Klein's notion of "partial objects," or objects which have the freedom, as it were, to be good and bad by turns.[8] Klein's "ambiguity" would then be similar to Kierkegaard's "freedom," in that both represent a certain anguish of becoming. "Faith" or "normalcy" would then be a belief in something above the objects themselves: in other words, while the purely good object may not exist, "goodness," as a category, does. The demoniac and the depressive, however, have confused objects for qualities, instants for time, particular for universal, and damned the latter in each case for the former's failure. Moreover, this failure is experienced as the subject's own failure to reconcile these antimonies, to do away with the terrifying uncertainty of partial objects, at the same time "mak[ing] restitution for all the sadistic attacks [the subject] has launched on the [good/bad] object" ("Psychogenesis," 265). With world and self alike thus consigned to a hell of his or her own making, "from such a demoniac is quite commonly heard a reply that expresses all the horror of this state: Leave me alone in my wretchedness" (*CA* 137).

When against his or her will the demoniac is inevitably forced to relate the world, the language that emerges is a language that refuses all disclosure or genuine communication. Kierkegaard writes that "the demonic is essentially mimical . . . not in the sense of the beautiful but in the sense of the sudden, the abrupt, which life itself often gives opportunity to observe" (*CA* 132). Deprived of seriousness or continuity, disgusted by the incoherency of both the inner and the outer worlds, the demoniac can only speak in empty repetition and imitation, in banalities and parody, in such representation eventually approaching the comic: "When all ethical determinates of evil are excluded, and only metaphysical determinants of emptiness are used, the result is the trivial, which can easily have a comic aspect" (*CA* 133). Lacking any affection for the formerly beloved world around him but not yet exposed to the Snow Queen's cold temptations of the absolute, Kay becomes a gifted mimic. (Indeed, one might call mimicry the very opposite of love, in that both are intensely intimate relations with another being, but the one under the sign of a dead sameness, the other in living difference.) What is key for our purposes here is the relationship between the comic, the empty, and the absolute. Considered ethically, Kierkegaard says, the demonic really must be considered evil, as the sinful refusal of the world in its givenness. Considered ontologically, the demonic is boredom, suddenness, and contentlessness. Considered *aesthetically,* however, the demonic's expression is that of the comic/parodic. The mechanical mimicry of Mephistopheles as described by Kierkegaard is a direct analog to the personal misery and desire for oblivion that the Snow Queen ultimately represents. The relation of the devils' mirror to the Snow Queen's palace is secured in that process by which love of nothing becomes love of Nothing.

Before Kay is pierced by the demons' mirror and thus made vulnerable to the icy charms of the Snow Queen, he catches a glimpse of his future abductor from his window, but here "Her eyes shone like two bright stars, but there was no rest or peace in them" (*SQ* 112). The peace later promised by the Snow Queen is already an illusion and a temptation whose real substance is unrest and an uncanny rather than attractive perfection. The bitter ironizing spirit instilled in Kay by the mirror fragments, however, makes him seek such perfection. When the world is deemed ugly, nothing but the ideal shall suffice. But this ideal can only be conceived as negation, a perpetual *Aufhebung* of the particular that results not in spiritual fulfillment but its empty converse, what

Kierkegaard calls at one point "the form of nothing" (*CA* 134). It is precisely this "form of nothing" that Kay is searching for. In a crucial sentence in *The Sickness Unto Death,* Kierkegaard writes that, "to have a self, to be a self, is the greatest concession made to man, but at the same time it is eternity's demand upon him."[9] Both anxiety and despair, for Kierkegaard, are first of all crises of universal and particular. The universal and the particular exist within each individual absolutely and irreconcilably, as much, one might say, as Father, Son, and Holy Ghost exist within the Christian Trinity at once distinct and indistinguishable—or as the psychical, the physical, and the spiritual exist within each individual (see *CA* 43). The self-conscious human being is the one who is conscious of this impossible tension between the universal, spiritual, and potential aspects of human nature, and the necessity to live out these aspects within earthly, time-bound, particular and actualized existence. The human is bracketed by the only two beings who contained universal and particular in one, that is, Adam and Christ. Temporarily leaving aside the religious dimension of Kierkegaard's thought, we note this tension: "Every individual is essentially interested in the history of all other individuals, and just as essentially as in his own. Perfection in oneself is therefore the perfect participation in the whole" (*CA* 29). But it is not given to any one to actually *be* the whole, to even be more than the individual bounded in time and space that one is, even at the manic extremes of "living poetically." The temptation of despair is above all to refuse this tension: on the one hand, in clinging to particularity, to one's ownness, given reality, or presence; on the other, in taking flight into universality, either the infinity of all possibility (in which one becomes a fantasist, a romantic, or a bad ironist) or—the escape that Kay chooses—the false infinity and "form of nothing" which is formal perfection, idealism, and systematic logic.

Kay's unprotested imprisonment in the Snow Queen's palace is an indirect allegory for the Kierkegaardian modes of despair as lack of finitude (*SD* 163-65) and as lack of necessity (*SD* 168-70). The particular sickens Kay. Among the many words that his ice-pieces make, "Eternity" is the only word that will do. The Chinese puzzle connotes the hubristic desire to achieve the eternal on one's own. The world, shattered into shards, must be put together in its entirety, all at once, with no degrees or half-measures. For the demons' mirror is *also* the fragmentation of the world, and the puzzle is Kay's desperate attempt at effecting its recuperation. Klein's language to describe the depressive position bears an uncanny resemblance at times to Andersen's own imagery. When the infantile ego encounters the explosive power of its own desires, in conflict with the impossibility of completely and always fulfilling those desires, Klein writes, it "finds itself confronted with the psychic reality that its loved objects are in a state of dissolution—in bits":

> there is anxiety how to put the bits together in the right way and at the right time; how to pick out the good bits and do away with the bad ones; how to bring the object to life when it has been put together; and there is the anxiety of being interfered with in this task by bad objects and by one's own hatred, etc.
>
> ("Psychogenesis," 269)

In **"The Snow Queen,"** Kay's neurotic symptoms, so to speak—mocking disappointment in and anger at the world, the quest for knowledge and mathematical certainty, and the imagined perfection of art and beauty—all reveal themselves as substitutes for the one overweening desire: to make the world, shattered into the distorted reflections of the devils' mirror, whole again. But as the ideal is necessarily empty of all content, this attempt to piece together the world brings only the subject's own annihilation: "Kay sat quite alone in all those many miles of empty ice halls. He looked at his bits of ice and thought and thought, till something gave way within him [*saa det knagede i ham*]. He sat so stiff and immovable that one might have thought he was frozen to death" (143). The failure to restore the shattered world—to save the loved departed object, to recuperate the blackened breast, to protect one's desires from one's rage and one's rage from one's desires; or, in a different register, to be redeemed from the stain of original sin—results in paralysis, even a coded suicide. It is not insignificant, moreover, that Kay's "psychic break" occurs just after the Snow Queen has left him for "the warm countries" (143). At the desolate end of the earth, in rooms where "the walls were made of drifted snow, and the windows and doors of the biting winds" (142), the last of Kay's symptoms is finally denied him. Left alone with his impossible and frigid desire to recreate eternity, there is nothing to do but submit to the impossibility of that desire, that is, to submit to impossibility as such: to die.[10] Or else—as Andersen's tale ultimately enacts—to give up on the desire for eternity and the absolute altogether and embrace a living and finite partiality.

In the brief chapter of *Black Sun* entitled "Beauty, the Depressive's Other Realm," Julia Kristeva writes,

> Might the beautiful be the ideal object that never disappoints the libido? Or might the beautiful object appear as the absolute and indestructible restorer of the deserting object? . . . In the place of death and so as not to die of the other's death, I bring forth—or at least I rate highly—an artifice, an ideal, a "beyond" that my psyche produces in order to take up a position outside itself—*ek-stasis*. How beautiful to be able to replace all perishable psychic values.[11]

Beauty, for Kristeva, is one of the possible forms of recuperation or reparation Klein describes: an ideal posited outside the self, in contradistinction from the "object that never disappoints" located *within* the self, i.e., the loss that the subject has initially introjected. The depressive subject falls in love, as it were, with his or her own pain, as the one thing that will not abandon the subject. Kierkegaard expresses the depressive position in precisely these terms:

> In addition to the rest of the numerous circle of my acquaintances, I still have one intimate confidant—my melancholy. In the midst of my joy, in the midst of my work, he beckons to me and calls me aside, even though I remain present in the body. My melancholy is the most faithful mistress I have known; what wonder, then, that I love in return.[12]

(In passing, we note the curious gender switch in this epigram, by which melancholy is able to be the best confidant and the perfect mistress all in one.) External objects may disappear or prove ambiguous, but an introjected suffering may be held onto, controlled, and finally loved as a good and perfect whole. The ideal or the beautiful fulfills a similar role, though it must be located outside, the source not of a melancholic self-destructive repetition but of a melancholic-romantic longing for what *is* but can never truly be achieved, reached, or comprehended in its perfection.

Andersen's tale demonstrates—or at least argues—that the ideality of beauty, while it may be a form of sublimation which saves the subject from real or psychic death, is also *itself* a form of death, of suicide. The question arises: is the positing of the ideal as such a form of creativity, or is it already a denial of life? Andersen's answer seems clear. Gerda, the hero of the story, may be read as the figure who contends with the chaos, joy, and disappointment of the world and of human relations, throwing herself into all sorts of dangers and exposing herself to risk for the sake of friendship and love. Most details of the story support this binary interpretation, that is, the opposition between the chilly and inhuman perfection of the Snow Queen and Gerda's messy, ice-melting warmth (recall that it is Gerda's hot tears that melt the shard in Kay's heart and flush out the one in his eye). The binary is perhaps complicated by the didactic-religious overtones of the tale, which threaten to merely oppose one ideality—albeit an ideality of sentiment, or perhaps community/communion—to another. But it is plain that Andersen at least intends for Gerda to represent a positive, saving alternative to Kay's fallen state—even to the point of compromising the happy ending of the tale. Returning from the Snow Queen's palace, a rescued Kay in tow, Gerda inquires of the little robber girl what has become of some of the characters that helped her on her way:

> "You are a nice fellow to go tramping off!" [the robber girl] said to little Kay. "I should like to know if you deserve to have somebody running to the end of the world for your sake."

But Gerda patted her cheek and asked about the Prince and Princess.

"They are traveling in foreign countries," said the robber girl.

"But the crow?" asked Gerda.

"Oh, the crow is dead," she answered. "The tame sweetheart is a widow and goes about with a bit of black wool tied round her leg. She pities herself bitterly, but it's all nonsense!"

(145)

Gerda naturally belongs much more to the little robber girl's world than to that of the Snow Queen. But it is also undeniable that the robber girl's humorous unconcern for the vicissitudes of life starkly contrasts not only with Kay's former state of frozen melancholic perfectionism but also with Gerda's own failure to mourn. This failure to mourn, of course, is what motivates the story and ultimately saves the day. Nevertheless, from a Freudian as well as a Kierkegaardian perspective, Gerda is every bit as much of a depressive as her lost friend. If Kay shuts himself off from the world in a quest for an imaginary absolute, Gerda, less severely perhaps and with greater subsidiary benefits, abandons the world she knows in quest of the lost friend whom she has made into her reason for existence.[13]

The end of **"The Snow Queen"** is the return of the original stage of innocence, but now after having passed through trials: the trial of anxiety and its overcoming on Kay's part; for Gerda, a less profoundly psychological trial of persistence, risk, and love. Entering the grandmother's house (it is only the very alert reader, incidentally, who will realize that she is the grandmother of Gerda and not Kay), "Everything was just as they had left it. The old clock ticked in the corner, and the hands pointed to the time. As they went through the door into the room, they perceived that they were grown up" (146). The passage through the "cold empty grandeur of the Snow Queen's palace" (146) is what is necessary for a mature life of time-boundedness, meaningful (as opposed to naïve) faith, and domestic heterosexuality. Communion—at once spiritual, social, and sexual—is the antithesis of the cold striving for solitary mastery that is despair. Directly upon Kay's salvation by Gerda from his deafness and isolation:

> He kept tight hold of Gerda, who laughed and cried for joy. Their happiness was so heavenly that even the bits of ice danced for joy around them. And when they settled down, there they lay in just the very position the Snow Queen had told Kay he must find out, if he was to become his own master and have the whole world and a new pair of skates.

(144)

In other words: in their union, Kay and Gerda form the sought-after word "eternity." The puzzle is solved in the breaking of "inclosing reserve" and the sharing of experience within the heterosexual couple. And yet, for all the correspondences with Kierkegaard's investigation of sin, despair, and freedom, Andersen's tale may actually replicate the dialectical or double-bind structure of despair that Kierkegaard describes. While faith appears as the only solution to despair in both the fabulist and the philosopher, Andersen has a more sentimental or at least intersubjective idea of faith. His faith is expressed as love, and especially of love of others in Christ, without which nothing makes sense. "Grandmother sat in God's warm sunshine reading from her Bible": this idyll erases the memory of torment "like a bad dream" (146), restoring order and affect to the world. For Kierkegaard, however, faith is itself the highest irony, a leap into despair, a necessary illusion or precisely the realm in which nothing makes sense. Despair is thus not a stage that must be passed through on one's way to adulthood but rather an interminable task and the precondition for salvation as self-knowledge and understanding of the human condition vis-à-vis God.

Andersen of course provides neither a psychological nor an ontological explanation for Kay's change: the wound is sudden, physical, and literal, at least in its magical force. In this respect, it resembles Kierkegaard's description of anxiety as the product of original sin: one is born into anxiety, *a priori,* as a consequence of one's humanity. Following Kierkegaard, one might say that the shards of mirror that afflict Kay are in fact *not* his fall but rather the first stage in his consciousness of his always-already fallenness and a necessary step towards the final happy resolution of maturity and grace. In any case, the fatality of the desire for absolute knowledge here calls for a return to Kierkegaard's idea of irony. Irony and systematic earnestness—or rather, an earnestness about systematicity—are dialectically linked, not only in Andersen's tale but also in Kierkegaard's thought. An ironic disdain for the actual world allows Kay to fall into the frigid arms of the Snow Queen and her self-reflexive, mathematical rationalism. What Kay is never ironic about, however, is that rationalism itself. The world is a figure of ridicule, for Kay, but the Snow Queen's insoluble puzzles are "excellent and of the greatest importance" (143). In this way, Kay is the fairy-tale antagonist to the figure of Socrates as he figures so prominently in Kierkegaard's writings. His is manifestly *not* the pure nihilism of the Sophists, but it is in many ways even worse, even more despairing, for Kay imagines that he can bridge the gap between the universal and the particular without remainder by his power alone. He does not question but strives for the absolute and the unquestionable. "Let us never forget," Kierkegaard reminds us,

> that the ignorance of Socrates was a kind of godly fear and divine worship, that his ignorance was the Greek rendering of the Jewish perception that the fear of God is the beginning of wisdom. Let us never forget that precisely out of reverence for the Deity he was igno-

rant, that, so far as a pagan could be, he kept watch as a *judge* on the border between God/and man, watching out to see that the deep gulf of qualitative distinction be firmly fixed between them, between God/and man, that God/and man may not in a way, *philosophice, poetice,* etc., coalesce into one. . . . But Christianity teaches that everything Christian exists only for faith; for this reason precisely it wills to be a Socratic, a Godfearing ignorance, which be ignorance defends faith against speculation . . . lest God/and man, still more dreadfully that ever it occurred in paganism, might in a way, *philosphice, poetice,* etc., coalesce into one . . . in the System.

(*CI* 230)

In this sense, it is in fact the *lack* of irony that constitutes the depressive position and the deepest depths of Kierkegaardian despair. Lack of irony—whether towards material and temporal actuality or toward the speculations of the System—is the failure to recognize the intractable rift/connection between "God/and man," the neurotic symptom of failure to properly mourn this rift/connection. Irony, indeed, *is* the mourning of this rift/connection, its constant bringing-to-consciousness. And while Kierkegaard agrees, for once, with Hegel about irony's negating aspect, this is an evil only if it remains as a pure negative, with a posited positive lying somewhere on the other side of the equation. If one accepts Paul Ricoeur's suggestion that the awkward perversities of Kierkegaard's thought constitute a return to Kant, one could say that irony is the rigorous holding to the "as if" *as such.* Hence irony's performative and even showy nature, manifest of course in almost all of Kierkegaard's works. Hence, too, Kierkegaard's dismissal of Andersen, as one who shared many of his beliefs and preoccupations but was too content to state those beliefs dogmatically or allegorically rather than do the hard work of mourning/ironizing that for Kierkegaard was inseparable from them. There are all sorts of ways of fleeing from the analytical necessity of this irony—even, as Peter Fenves notes in his analysis of Kierkegaard's language, the "mastery" of the ironic style itself.[14] To turn faith itself into an ironic stance is perhaps the most positive strategy for remaining within irony's tension: that is, faith is the infinite deferral of that which would *not* be ironic, predicated on an interminable analysis of the existence and the temporality which ineluctably *are* so. Andersen's edifying tale would ostensibly resolve Kay's despair under the sign of conjugal and Christian love. More fundamentally and problematically, it carries out its edification in an act of imaginative projection and an allegorical bid for infinity in contradiction to its own professed moral.[15] For Kierkegaard, on the other hand, there is no edification but the resistance to edification, the turning over and over again of experience as paradoxically and as unavailable to positive categorization as humanly possible.

Despite this crucial divergence of method between Andersen and Kierkegaard, **"The Snow Queen"** may still be read as Andersen's Kierkegaardian attack on speculative dialectics, written as an early warning for children vulnerable to erudition's promises of mastery. But there are also less esoteric ways of interpreting Kay's state in the tale—ways that may even be applied, retroactively as it were, to speculative dialectics and its practitioners. In other words, the affinities between **"The Snow Queen"** and Kierkegaardian critique could *also* be a way to approach speculative dialectics from a psychoanalytic standpoint. The desire to achieve the absolute is *necessarily* a denial of life and its particularity, even as it cannot do without life. The crisis described by Kierkegaard may show up in a variety of forms and psychological states, for as Kierkegaard himself notes in *The Sickness Unto Death,* "despair" does not necessarily mean unhappiness or depression. (Indeed, the automatic conflation of the two is a misunderstanding of despair that he terms "vulgar.") It is at once a disproportionate overvaluing of life, and, often, a disproportionate hatred of it. This may also take the form of an excessive concern for the self, combined with an excessive self-hatred, the source of Freud's claim that the melancholic paradoxically never tires of talking about him or herself, even and especially when abusively.[16] Asceticism and self-disgust (the desire to impose purity by force on the body or the soul, respectively), hypochondria and paranoia (the fear of the impurity or hostility of the world), and personal or social conservatism (the fear of change and an obsessive need for control over time) are but some of the possible pathologies that the search for a *manifest absolute* may turn into.

Again, unlike Freud or Klein, neither Kierkegaard nor Andersen are concerned with discovering the origin of such pathologies: for Kierkegaard in particular, they are simply the human condition, and those who experience neither despair nor anxiety in any of their more pathological manifestations merely experience them latently and thus all the more grievously. As has often been noted, not least by Kierkegaard himself, his philosophy is most of all a phenomenology and a psychology, a personal but not private taxonomy of possible states of existence. In the words of Ricoeur,

> the Kirkegaardian categories of existence could be regarded as a response to problems of practical reason that Kant had rendered insoluble. The categories of existence are to ethics what the categories of objectivity are to natural science. They are the *conditions of possibility of experience*—not the possibility of physical experience, however, but the possibility of the fundamental experience of *the fulfillment of our desire and striving for existence.*[17]

Despair is for Kierkegaard the most extreme experience available of "desire and striving for existence." Indeed, despair is precisely this "desire and striving for existence," in the sense that this desire and this striving are *necessarily* unfulfillable. In the material and actual world, one simply cannot live all possibility; one cannot answer the call of one's own spiritual potentiality. One cannot piece together the fragments of the world. It would appear easier to deny that desire for completion and live contentedly bounded by one's material and temporal particularity, what Kierkegaard calls in *The Sickness Unto Death* the "philistine's" position. But this position, every bit as much as the positing of ideal systems in which the unity of the world is hypothetically achieved, is not an end to despair but merely a flight from it. In order for one not to fall into error and illness, therefore, the fragments must be left as fragments: "Man is a synthesis of the infinite and the finite, of the temporal and the eternal, of freedom and necessity, in short it is a synthesis. A synthesis is a relation between two factors. So regarded, man is not yet a self" (*SD* 146). To eschew the interminable splitting effected by irony and on one's own to constitute oneself as a whole self—or one's world as a whole world—is nothing less than a pathology, the most inauthentic and dangerous of positions. A rigorous, indeed a *relentless* examination of despair is thus the exemplary form of the rigorous examination of experience in general, which is in turn the move that counters both philistinism and fantasism in its refusal to turn away from either the possibility of actuality or the actuality of the possible, from desire and loss in all its forms and the psychic distress that inevitably follows in their wake.

In language reminiscent of Klein (whom he does not reference), Bruno Bettelheim locates the importance of fairy-tales for a child's development in their providing of imaginative projections for psychological forces. "A child," he writes,

> cannot consciously accept that his anger may make him speechless, or that he may wish to destroy those on whom he depends for his existence. To understand this would mean he must accept the fact that his own emotions may so overpower him that he does not have control over them—a very scary thought. The idea that forces may reside within us which are beyond our control is too threatening to be entertained, and not just by a child.[18]

Be that as it may, there is a certain paradoxicality to a fairy-tale which is in many ways about the dangers of projection itself, even if the specific projections narrated are more along the lines of scientism and conceptualism than the free play of the imagination. The strangeness of **"The Snow Queen"** in Andersen's canon may be due to the fact that it is in a certain sense a fairy-tale *against* fairy-tales, in which the parallel longings of Kay and Gerda join to form a troubled eternity of striving for the impossible restoration of a primal broken world. Closer to Kierkegaard than it might seem, Andersen's tale resists its own premises in the demonically ironic refusal to bring its fragments of experience into a unified whole.

Notes

1. See http://www.kb.dk/elib/noder/hcamusik/ snedronningen/index_en.htm for full description and original text.

2. Hans Christian Andersen, "The Snow Queen." In *Andersen's Fairy Tales,* trans. E. V. Lucas and H. B. Paull (New York: Grosset and Dunlap, 1945) 108. [hereafter cited in text as *SQ*]

3. See Immanuel Kant, *Critique of Judgment,* trans. J. H. Bernard (New York: Hafner Press, 1951).

4. Søren Kierkegaard, *The Concept of Irony, with Continual Reference to Socrates,* trans. Howard V. Hong and Edna H. Hong (Princeton: Princeton UP, 1989) 254. [hereafter cited in text as *CI*]

5. Kierkegaard, *The Concept of Anxiety,* trans. Reidar Thomte, (Princeton: Princeton UP, 1980) 124. [hereafter cited in text as *CA*]

6. See Melanie Klein, "Mourning and Its Relation to Manic-Depressive States." In *Love, Guilt, and Reparation: and Other Works 1921-1945* (New York: The Free Press, 1975).

7. Klein, "A Contribution to the Psychogenesis of Manic-Depressive States." In *Love, Guilt, and Reparation: and Other Works 1921-1945* (New York: The Free Press, 1975) 264.

8. Cf. the following passage from Kierkegaard's Journal, from May of 1843, in a passage anticipating the contents of *Fear and Trembling*: "When the child has to be weaned the mother blackens her breast, but her eyes rest just as lovingly upon the child. The child believes it is the breast that has changed, but that the mother is unchanged. . . . This collision is easily resolved, for the breast is only a part of the mother herself. Happy is he who has not experienced more dreadful collisions, who did not need to blacken *himself,* who did not need to go to hell in order to see what the devil looks like, so that he might paint himself accordingly and in that way if possible save another person in that person's God-relationship at least" (quoted in Translator's Introduction, *The Sickness Unto Death* 12). [hereafter cited in text as *SD*]

9. Kierkegaard, *Fear and Trembling* and *The Sickness Unto Death,* trans. Walter Lowrie (Princeton: Princeton UP, 1954) 154.

10. Here we obviously have in mind Freud's thinking on the death drive in *Beyond the Pleasure Principle* as the desire to return to an original or pre-life stasis (Sigmund Freud, *Beyond the Pleasure Principle,* trans. James Strachey [New York: W. W. Norton, 1961] 43, *passim*). Our own line of ar-

gument here leads us to suggest an affinity between Freud's conception of the death drive as a purely regressive mechanism set *against* eros, and the futural/erotic aspects of romanticism and messianism.

11. Julia Kristeva, *Black Sun: Depression and Melancholia,* trans. Leon S. Roudiez (New York: Columbia UP, 1989) 98-99.

12. Kierkegaard, *Either/Or: A Fragment of Life,* trans. Alastair Hannay (London: Penguin, 1992) 16.

13. For better of for worse, in this Andersen's tale agrees with Kierkegaard's schema of "womanly" versus "manly" despair. Man, according to Kierkegaard, despairs of being himself, that is, to achieve his self in its posited infinity; woman, on the other hand, despairs primarily of losing herself. Given that "Woman has neither the selfishly developed conception of the self nor the intellectuality of man," her nature is expressed in "devotion," and her happiness consists in "plung[ing] herself into that to which she devotes herself" (*SD* 184-85 ff.). In short, man's despair is expressed as a (solitary) concern with himself, and as defiance toward a limiting world; woman's despair is manifested in self-sacrifice, even self-abnegation, for (a particular) man. That Kierkegaard gives his more or less unqualified approval to this action of womanly despair, while treating manly despair with a more typical ambivalence or dialectical understanding, is a problem we will not be able to examine here. We do note that Andersen follows the same gendering of desire: Kay rejects interpersonal relationships and instead seeks the abstract absolute (however feminized and personified); Gerda absolutizes interpersonal relationships themselves, but in this second-degree absolutization, becomes heroic rather than enslaved. Furthermore, just as in the concluding lines of Kierkegaard's note, the tensions and complications of this dynamic in Andersen's tale are wiped away in the (mostly) de-sexed relationship to *God*.

14. Peter Fenves, *"Chatter": Language and History in Kierkegaard* (Stanford: Stanford UP, 1993).

15. Here we refer to the vast work on irony, allegory, and figuration that has been done in the past few decades, not least by Paul de Man in his essay "The Rhetoric of Temporality." The dialectics of irony de Man sets up—in which the deferral of absolute meaning marked by allegory and the totalizing negation of absolute meaning in irony constantly turn over and pass through one another in the history of literature—naturally complicate the Andersen/Kierkegaard binary we lay out here, without however removing the tensions of that binary. See Paul de Man, "The Rhetoric of Tempo-

rality," in *Blindness and Insight: Essays in the Rhetoric of Contemporary Criticism* (Minneapolis: University of Minnesota Press, 1983). Similarly, Kristeva's *Black Sun* looks at the process of allegorisis and figuration from a psychoanalytic (as well as a Benjaminian) standpoint, treating allegory as a "hypersign" (99) that negotiates between meaninglessness or fragmentation and the restoration of meaning, a "signifying jubilation over a fundamental, nutritive nonmeaning [which] is nevertheless the very universe of the *possible*" (101).

16. See Sigmund Freud, "Mourning and Melancholia," in *General Psychological Theory* (New York: Simon & Schuster, 1991) 168.

17. Paul Ricoeur, "Philosophy After Kierkegaard," in *Kierkegaard: A Critical Reader,* eds. Jonathan Rée and Jane Chamberlain (Oxford: Blackwell Publishers, 1998) 16-17.

18. Bruno Bettelheim, *The Uses of Enchantment: The Meaning and Importance of Fairy Tales* (New York: Vintage Books, 1989) 30-31.

FURTHER READING

Biographies

Andersen, Jens. *Hans Christian Andersen: A New Life,* translated by Tiina Nunnally. New York: Overlook Duckworth, 2005, 624 p.

Full-length, comprehensive biography of Andersen.

Frank, Diana Crone and Jeffrey Frank. "Hans Christian Andersen's American Dream." *Scandinavian Review* 91, no. 3 (spring 2004): 70-9.

Biographical account of Andersen's personal and professional dealings with the United States.

Criticism

Edgecombe, Rodney Stenning. "An Andersen Letter and *Don Giovanni.*" *Germanic Notes and Reviews* 38, no. 1 (spring 2007): 39-42.

Explores the origins and significance of operatic references in a letter by Andersen.

Eitelgeorge, Janice S. and Nancy A. Anderson. "The Work of Hans Christian Andersen: More than Just Fairy Tales." *Bookbird* 42, no. 3 (July 2004): 37-44.

Examines how Andersen's works depart from the thematic and narrative models of traditional folktales and fairy tales.

Ewers, Hans-Heino. "H. C. Andersen as Seen by Critics of German Children's Literature since the Beginning of the Twentieth Century." *Marvels & Tales* 20, no. 2 (2006): 142, 208-23.

Surveys the widespread critical opinion that Andersen's works are inappropriate for children, and contends that Andersen originated a new type of literature for children that wasn't adopted by later writers until the latter half of the twentieth century.

Frank, Diana Crone and Jeffrey Frank. Introduction to *The Stories of Hans Christian Andersen,* translated by Diana Crone Frank and Jeffrey Frank, pp 1-36. Durham, N.C.: Duke University Press, 2005.

Provides an overview of Andersen's life and works.

Wood, Naomi. "The Ugly Duckling's Legacy: Adulteration, Contemporary Fantasy, and the Dark." *Marvels & Tales* 20, no. 2 (2006): 142, 193-207.

Analyzes how children's fantasy writers have interpreted and adapted Andersen's treatment of such themes as the struggle for individuality and survival amidst tremendous opposition.

Additional coverage of Andersen's life and career is contained in the following sources published by Gale: *Authors and Artists for Young Adults,* **Vol. 57;** *Children's Literature Review,* **Vols. 6, 113;** *DISCovering Authors: British; DISCovering Authors: Canadian; DISCovering Authors Modules: Most-studied Authors* **and** *Popular Fiction and Genres Authors; DISCovering Authors 3.0; European Writers,* **Vol. 6;** *Literature Resource Center; Major Authors and Illustrators for Children and Young Adults,* **Eds. 1, 2;** *Nineteenth-Century Literature Criticism,* **Vols. 7, 79;** *Reference Guide to Short Fiction,* **Ed. 2;** *Reference Guide to World Literature,* **Eds. 2, 3;** *Short Story Criticism,* **Vols. 6, 56;** *Something about the Author,* **Vol. 100;** *Twayne's World Authors; World Literature Criticism; Writers for Children;* **and** *Yesterday's Authors of Books for Children,* **Vol. 1.**

William Beckford
1760-1844

(Also wrote under the pseudonyms Lady Harriet Marlow and Jacquetta Agneta Mariana Jenks) English novelist, satirist, and travel writer.

The following entry presents criticism of Beckford's works from 1988 to 2006. For additional information on Beckford's life and career, see *NCLC,* Volume 16.

INTRODUCTION

Beckford is primarily remembered for his novel *Vathek* (1787), which has been consistently hailed as a seminal contribution to the genre of oriental romance, and less consistently as part of the Gothic tradition. The story of an evil caliph's journey to the underworld in pursuit of forbidden knowledge, *Vathek* is noted for its captivating plot and unique narrative style. Although Beckford also wrote several collections of travel sketches and a number of satirical works, he was chiefly known during his lifetime for *Vathek,* as well as for his fabulous wealth and the rumors surrounding his personal life. Today, Beckford's literary reputation continues to rest almost solely on *Vathek.*

BIOGRAPHICAL INFORMATION

Beckford was born in Fonthill, Wiltshire on October 1, 1760, into one of the richest and most prominent families in England. His father, William Beckford, formerly lord mayor of London, had accumulated great wealth from investments in Jamaican sugar plantations and his mother, Maria Hamilton, was of noble ancestry. As the only child of a late marriage, Beckford was pampered by both parents, but he received a rigorous education in preparation for a political career and could speak French fluently by age four. When he was nine, "England's wealthiest son," as Lord Byron called Beckford, inherited his father's estate. Afterwards, he continued to follow a rigid program of classical studies under the strict guidance of his mother and a succession of tutors. Despite their efforts, an interest in oriental literature, thought to have been brought on by his reading of *The Arabian Nights,* became Beckford's passionate obsession. In 1777, he left with a tutor for Geneva, Switzerland, to complete his education. There Beckford met a number of notable figures, including Voltaire. Geneva is also where Beckford began his first literary work, an

autobiographical narrative entitled *The Long Story* that was never completed and remained unknown until a portion of it was published in 1930 as *The Vision.*

Following his return from Switzerland in 1778, Beckford entered a tumultuous period of his life. While touring England in 1779, he developed what he called a "strange wayward passion" for William Courtenay, the eleven-year-old son of Lord Courtenay of Powderham Castle. Beckford also became romantically involved with Louisa Beckford, the unhappily married wife of one of his cousins. Beckford published his first work in 1780, a burlesque of then-popular sketches of painters' lives entitled *Biographical Memoirs of Extraordinary Painters.* In 1781, Beckford hosted a sumptuous Christmas party that he later credited with directly inspiring his exotic oriental novel, *Vathek.* For three days, Courtenay, Louisa Beckford, and other guests wandered through Beckford's country home surrounded by music, dancers, and theatrical lighting effects. Shortly after this fantastical celebration, Beckford wrote the initial French-language draft of *Vathek* in one sitting, though scholars believe that he revised and expanded the novel many times before its publication. While composing the stories he planned as companion pieces to *Vathek,* Beckford arranged for the Reverend Samuel Henley, an oriental enthusiast and former professor, to translate the entire work into English and add footnotes explaining the oriental allusions. Beckford's completion of the companion stories was, however, hindered by misfortune.

The restless Beckford began a European tour that his family hoped would help solve his emotional problems and prepare him for public life. Though it failed to alleviate his mental anguish, his journey resulted in *Dreams, Waking Thoughts, and Incidents* (1783), an epistolary travel book composed from notes kept during his trip. After this work had been printed, however, Beckford suppressed its distribution and burned all but a few copies; biographers have speculated that his family thought the content of *Dreams, Waking Thoughts, and Incidents* might damage his political prospects or add to rumors circulating about his friendship with Courtenay. At his family's insistence, he married Lady Margaret Gordon in 1783, a match they hoped would quell rumors concerning his homosexuality. In June 1784, the couple's first child was stillborn. Later that same year Beckford was publicly accused of sexual misconduct with Courtenay, and the resulting scandal forced Beckford and his wife to flee to Switzerland, where Margaret Beckford died in childbirth at the age of twenty-four. Throughout these ordeals, Beckford instructed Henley to withhold his English translation of *Vathek* until the companion stories were finished. In a betrayal of trust, however, Henley released an anonymous English translation of *Vathek* in June 1786. Beckford subsequently published a French edition of *Vathek* in order to claim authorship, and the uncompleted episodes remained unpublished until 1912.

For the next ten years, Beckford spent the majority of his time abroad, traveling throughout Switzerland, France, Italy, Spain, and Portugal. In 1796, he returned permanently to England. Ostracized from society, he spent much of the remainder of his life collecting books, paintings, and rare objects of art and building Fonthill Abbey, an extravagant Gothic structure. Beckford grew notorious as the creator of the increasingly popular *Vathek*, which had been reissued numerous times since its initial publication, and as the eccentric owner of Fonthill, where he lived until financial difficulties forced him to sell the estate in 1822 and move to Lansdown Crescent, Bath. Beckford's literary output during this period was scant. In the late 1790s, he wrote two minor novels burlesquing the sentimentalism of contemporary novelists, *Modern Novel Writing; or, The Elegant Enthusiast* (1796) and *Azemia* (1797). In 1834, he published *Italy: With Sketches of Spain and Portugal,* a two-volume work that consists of extensive revision of *Dreams, Waking Thoughts, and Incidents* as the first volume and an account of his journeys through Spain and Portugal as the second. At the age of seventy-four he published his final travel diary, *Recollections of an Excursion to the Monasteries of Alcobaça and Batalha* (1835). After spending his last years in relative seclusion, Beckford died at his residence in Lansdown Crescent on May 2, 1844 at the age of eighty-four.

MAJOR WORKS

Beckford's letters from Rome in June of 1782 suggest that he was still working on *Vathek* about six months after he composed the initial draft. Inspired in part by Beckford's reading about Persia and other parts of the Near East, the novel is an Eastern romance, set in an imagined Arabian or Turkish kingdom. In this work, the caliph Vathek travels to the underworld domain ruled by Eblis, a satanic figure. There, Vathek seeks forbidden wisdom, only to face eternal damnation in the Palace of Subterranean Fire. Beckford based many of his characters upon historical figures and provided a wealth of oriental detail, including descriptions of Eastern costumes, customs, and plant and animal life. He intended to add to this story four episodic tales narrated by sufferers in the Palace of Subterranean Fire.

Apart from *Vathek,* Beckford's works fall loosely into two categories: satirical writings and travel sketches. Of Beckford's satirical writings, *Biographical Memoirs of Extraordinary Painters* has been praised as a witty parody. Written in 1777, this was Beckford's first publication, in which he ridiculed the standard biographies of distinguished painters and set forth his preference for the flamboyant and romantic in art. The book displays a sense of humor seldom found in Beckford's other works as the author discusses with pseudo-solemnity such imaginary worthies as Aldovrandus, Og of Basan, Sucrewasser of Vienna, Watersouchy of Amsterdam, and Blunderbussiana of Venice. Beckford also published works of satire either anonymously or pseudonymously. Beckford's *Modern Novel Writing* pillories the excesses of contemporary popular fiction, from absurd plots and overblown language, to the use of ghosts and the excessive sentimentality of heroines such as Arabella and "the matchless Amelia." In *Azemia,* Beckford presents a stirring and entirely improbable tale of a Turkish girl who is captured by the British Navy and has adventures in England. These novels have been assessed as amusing parodies of the prevailing Gothic and sentimental traditions of eighteenth-century fiction, and their tone recalls the satirical style Beckford employed in *Biographical Memoirs of Extraordinary Painters.* Beckford published both *Modern Novel Writing* and *Azemia* pseudonymously, the former as Lady Harriet Marlow and the latter as Jacquetta Agneta Mariana Jenks. At the time of their publication, Beckford's authorship of the two books was kept a closely guarded secret; only years later, to the writer Samuel Rogers and to his biographer, Cyrus Redding, did he admit that he had written them.

Beckford's travel writings are considered by many to be his best work, marked by an observant eye, felicitous turn of phrase, and a connoisseur's attitude to landscape and history. *Dreams, Waking Thoughts, and Incidents* and *Recollections of an Excursion to the Monasteries of Alcobaça and Batalha* are generally commended for their balanced prose and descriptive artistry. *Recollections* is often considered Beckford's best work other than *Vathek*: it is widely viewed as Beckford's most polished piece of writing, displaying a refined wit and an array of colorful anecdotes that highlight the fictionalization of fact that has been noted as integral to Beckford's oeuvre.

CRITICAL RECEPTION

Though most of Beckford's writings met with favorable receptions and have continued to be praised by scholars, his lasting critical acclaim rests upon *Vathek*. In discussing *Vathek,* critics have focused on its style, autobiographical overtones, and historical significance. Beckford's unusual life and his treatment of aberrant sexual themes, puerile innocence, and domineering mothers have led to a profusion of biographical interpretations of *Vathek,* particularly during the nineteenth and early twentieth centuries. Later twentieth-century commentators, however, have generally avoided biographical critiques, emphasizing instead Beckford's anticipation of the orientalism of such nineteenth-century poets as Lord Byron, Thomas Moore, and Robert Southey. Critics generally note that unlike the works of earlier English authors who employed oriental elements to embellish philosophical musings or to serve moralistic purposes, *Vathek* exhibits a fascination with exoticism for its own sake, with Beckford placing greater emphasis than previous writers upon an accurate depiction of the East. Commentators also point out that in *Vathek* Beckford combined polished Augustan prose with such characteristically Romantic concerns as human aspiration, loss of innocence, and the mysterious, thus reflecting the incipient transition in English literature from Neoclassicism to Romanticism. For its historical significance, as well as its continuing fascination for readers, *Vathek* is regarded as a minor masterpiece, one that has assured Beckford a place in literary history.

PRINCIPAL WORKS

Biographical Memoirs of Extraordinary Painters (satire) 1780

Dreams, Waking Thoughts, and Incidents (travel sketches) 1783

*Vathek (novel) 1787

Modern Novel Writing: or, The Elegant Enthusiast, and Interesting Emotions of Arabella Bloomville [as Lady Harriet Marlow] (novel) 1796

Azemia [as Jacquetta Agneta Mariana Jenks] (novel) 1797

†*Italy: With Sketches of Spain and Portugal.* 2 vols. (travel sketches) 1834

Recollections of an Excursion to the Monasteries of Alcobaça and Batalha (travel sketches) 1835

‡*The Episodes of Vathek* (novel fragment) 1912

#*The Vision, Liber Veritatis* (novel fragment) 1930

*The unauthorized translation of *Vathek* was published as *An Arabian Tale,* 1786.

†The first volume of this work is comprised of a revised version of *Dreams, Waking Thoughts, and Incidents.*

‡Comprises Beckford's original French-language episodes, dated 1783-86, and an English translation of them.

#*The Vision* is part of Beckford's unfinished narrative, known as *The Long Story,* written in 1777.

CRITICISM

Kevin L. Cope (essay date 1988)

SOURCE: Cope, Kevin L. "Moral Travel and the Pursuit of Nothing: *Vathek* and *Siris* as Philosophical Monologue." *Studies in Eighteenth-Century Culture* 18 (1988): 167-86.

[*In the following essay, Cope asserts that Beckford's* Vathek *was informed by George Berkeley's* Siris *in terms of the sense of travel and destination conveyed in the works.*]

> Studious persons also, pent up in narrow holes, breathing bad air, and stooping over their books, are much to be pitied. As they are debarred the free use of air and exercise, this I will venture to recommend as the best succedaneum to both . . . My own sedentary course of life had long since thrown me into an ill habit, attended with many ailments, which rendered my life a burden, and the more so because my pains were exasperated by exercise. But since the use of tar-water, I find, though not such a perfect recovery from my old and rooted illness, yet such a gradual return of health and ease, that I esteem my having taken this medicine the greatest of all temporal blessings, and am convinced that, under Providence, I owe my life to it.
>
> (Berkeley, *Siris,* para. 119)

Two hundred years after the production of his most alarming work, **Vathek,** William Beckford continues to engender an unusual amount of critical consternation. A comprehensive intellect, a brilliant conversationalist, a spoiled prodigy, and a victim of his own ingenuity, Beckford persistently baffles his critics with his perverse desire to deploy his enormous resources on apparently trivial, self-titillating enterprises.[1] Yet the persistent appeal of Beckford's novel, from its writing to this bicentenary occasion, suggests that new, less biographical approaches to the English Caliph might expose the firm foundation beneath his seemingly frivolous productions. Critics have already started to respond. In one provocative study of **Vathek,** for example, Kenneth Graham describes Beckford as the most successfully "metaphysical" of all English fabulists.[2] Taking a cue from Horace Walpole's "Preface" to *The Castle of Otranto,* Beckford so artfully grafts the probable onto the improbable that critics cannot decide whether to accuse him of satirizing or of taking too seriously the oriental tale.[3] James Rieger, likewise, has argued for the legitimacy of seeking moral and stylistic reasons for Beckford's frequent juxtapositions of conflicting modalities, like horror and sarcasm.[4] Beckford's sympathetic critics conclude that Beckford makes a genre out of contradiction; probability and improbability, good and bad, and comic and tragic coinhere completely, throwing readers off balance and producing contradictory interpretations.

The confusion in the evaluation of *Vathek* results partly from, first, a reluctance to distinguish Beckford from his work and, second, from the ensuing assumption that Beckford, as an aesthete, thought and wrote only in a literary context. If startling contrasts and contradictions were his speciality, why, we must ask, should so comprehensive a paradigm be limited to one discipline, even one so large as literature? One need not look far for evidence of Beckford's fascination with the assimilation of the most heterogenous materials. *Vathek* draws explicitly on at least two traditions of diverse ancestry: first, the tradition of travel literature—a tradition perforce dealing with many non-literary concerns—and, second, a longstanding philosophical tradition concerning the analysis of nothingness, a tradition which took a strikingly new and distinctly literary direction in George Berkeley's *Siris*.[5]

From his youth, Beckford indulged a well-known addiction for travel narratives, especially those from the eastern world. Beckford's zeal for the oriental tale, a fictionalized and moralized version of the travel narrative, thus follows from his lifelong interest in writings on travel in general.[6] Enamored of the mystique and paraphernalia as well as the goals of travel, Beckford cultivated an intellectualized travel literature in which the supposititious destination was both everywhere and nowhere in particular. In these explorations of undirected, omnidirected, and philosophical travel, Beckford undertakes an enterprise which would have appealed to another philosopher-travel writer, George Berkeley.[7] In works like his *Analyst,* a critique of the calculus, Berkeley cultivated an intense interest in the problem of nothingness. This interest came to full fruition in his *Siris: A Chain of Philosophical Reflexions and Inquiries,* a work which tries to clear a progressive pathway from an unlikely starting point, tar-water, to an utterly unspecific but nevertheless enticing destination.

It should be said at the outset that a search for a direct line of influence from the elder Berkeley to the wispy young Beckford would lead nowhere. Berkeley, of course, enjoyed a large literary acquaintance, and his work could scarcely have been unknown to the young literary Caliph.[8] The discovery of an "influence" is not, in any case, my task. An analysis of *Siris,* Berkeley's philosophical response to his disappointing trip to America (or, perhaps, "non-trip" to Bermuda), can amplify our understanding of the foundations as well as the conventions of the moralized travel tale, a genre which achieved both prestige and sophistication in the late eighteenth century. An immaterialist approach to *Vathek* can elucidate the philosophical foundation of Beckford's attempt to convert the tale of far-off lands from a mere exotic story into a challenging moral tale. It can explain his provocative program to exalt the

trivial, accidental, and irrelevant and to transform the inconsequential and insignificant into *vehicles* to a destination compounded of both nothingness and meaning.

* * *

When he came to write his tract on tar-water, Berkeley had already established himself as a master of philosophical dialogue. Berkeley had, of course, also published several straightforward essays on philosophical subjects, but in *Siris* he avoids this comparatively impersonal mode. Instead, he presents his work neither as an ordinary tract nor an observed discussion among allegorical characters, but as a mixture of inward colloquy and direct, personal address to a silent reader, as a philosophical or philosophizing monologue. By abjuring dialogue in favor of philosophical monologue, Berkeley signals a re-evaluation of his ideas concerning philosophical *literature.*[9] Consequently, the identification of the genre of his work—"a chain of philosophical reflexions"—becomes the most prominent and memorable part of his title.[10]

This process of reinterpretation is meant to continue indefinitely and in a number of contexts. Berkeley's "chain" never shackles or limits anything, but leads on indefinitely, across huge expanses of ever-expanding philosophical terrain. This travelers' conception of a horizontally and temporally extended chain of philosophical reflections reinterprets the conventional conception of a vertical chain of being which extends from nullity to divinity. Similarly, Berkeley adopts, in his introduction, the classic pose of the travel writer, advising us that he intends to report on useful foreign discoveries. As even the "pilgrims' guides" of the earliest Christian centuries made clear, the travel writer is often—nay, essentially—at odds with himself, for he takes a greater interest in the distractions and useful discoveries of travel than in the destination of his journey. The traveler prefers to view those sights and to reflect on those intelligences which slow down his caravan rather than to plow ahead to the journey's end.[11] Berkeley's opening paragraph re-evaluates these essential tensions, paradoxes, and prejudices of his pose, for he there makes clear that his purpose is not the description of the distractions of tourism at all, not the treatment of the titular subject of his essay, the amazing discovery of tar-water, but instead the arrival at a "reasoning and notional part" which re-evaluates the first, most descriptive part of the volume.[12]

This friction between destination and distraction informs the nature of tar-water itself. At once one of the lowest, most "contemptible" links in the chain of being and also the panacea which all lower medicines only imitate, tar-water seems to reside both within and at the extreme edges of "common" experience (9-10). The only "unctuous" substance which heals rather than harms the trees of the forest (9), tar-water is both a part of this oily "nature" and a highly improved form of it. Similarly, Berkeley defines an organism as an "organized system of tubes" intended to deliver sap to various points (32), as both a thing and a process of transportation. Berkeley's self-styled "Platonism" is a Platonism not of participation but of indication. Every "thing" points and moves toward, as well as partakes of, a remote end. This end, moreover, is not simply an Aristotelian perfection of the object or of the cosmos, but a complex and receding goal that Berkeley never fully defines. By organizing his work as a procession toward an increasingly remote end, Berkeley, ironically, increases the number of distractions to be viewed along the way. He thus praises plants for their ability to *draw* an "endless variety" of "juices" from the "same soil" (31), for their ability to multiply the avenues of approach to a single but complex end, survival, from a single origin, soil. Berkeley clears the way for sentimental novelists, like Sterne, for whom the multiplication of avenues of approach displaces the attainment of an end.

As a result of his emphasis on the achievement of a destination, Berkeley's digressions and side-trips often have an anterior quality to them. His discussions of ancient methods for the preparation of his remedy, for example, inevitably *follow* his presentation of his new and improved procedure (13, 17). In Berkeley's psychological redaction of Aristotle, "the mind, by virtue of her simplicity, conferreth simplicity upon compounded beings" (356). Experience itself stands at the end of a progression from immediately perceived ideas to a destined identity in the mind. Stephen Carr has warned that Berkeley initiates rhetorical digressions in order to show that his conclusions greatly outdistance or even belie his roundabout procedures for obtaining them.[13] A master at conflating technical and mystical discourse, Berkeley often insinuates that divergent routes converge on a single goal—a goal which is itself often paradoxical. To prove that tar-water can cure all diseases, Berkeley must establish that all diseases stand at different points on one vast spectrum, one end of which is defined by his tarry antidote. Tar-water cures erysipelas because it is specific to it; plague differs from erysipelas only in degree; therefore tar-water could cure plague (83). Disease and tar-water are all on one road; both could lead to each other, at least if the progress from disease to tar-water was not, in Berkeley's happy experience, one-way. After a suggestive assertion that the sun exerts a mysterious "influence" on vegetables, Berkeley proffers a shockingly abrupt account of the digestive systems of plants (37-38). The complexities and vulgarities of floral alimentation are re-articulated as the *antecedents* of these solar mysteries. Near the end of *Siris,* after pages of moral rhapsody, this refractory technical language suddenly reappears (296), in a milder form, for similar reasons. To explain the action of tar-water, Berkeley

turns to Homberg's theory of acids (136 ff.), a theory which he openly accounts incorrect. He nevertheless lavishly explicates Homberg's ideas, declaring that "common experience" itself confirms Homberg's mystical conclusions, even though Homberg's route was tortuous and his ideas distracting.[14]

Like most contemporary medical tracts, Berkeley's treatise proceeds anecdotally, from remote report to overheard testimonial (e.g., 2-4). Unlike his less dreamy colleagues, however, Berkeley makes us acutely aware of the *central* role of accidentally acquired information. Taking a grand tour of philosophical history, he *avoids* method, assuming that randomly acquired experience will lead further than will directed study. At each major turn in his argument—from tar to science, from science to philosophy, and from philosophy to theology[15]—he reminds us that he depends only on local advice, on authority, on traditions, and on conjectures and testimonies which have haphazardly come to his attention (125, 360). Anecdotes and maxims encountered in this hit-or-miss way lead less often to definitive conclusions than back into some other anecdote-studded route. After Berkeley completes his rhapsody on fire, for example, he never reveals the mysteries of his turpentinian Eblis. He asks us not to demand the disclosure of some essential fire, but to run through, in a kind of abbreviated narrative sequence, the jobs that fire can do (162; see also 277). The knowable features of a thing, what Locke might call its nominal essence, must be reviewed over time, in a series; the identity of a thing is, potentially, a travel narrative in which particular features of an object are relished one after another. For Berkeley, destinations like the attainment of an identity for an object are novelistic. To appreciate them fully, one must extend them over a long, Cervantian journey from windmill to windmill, from distraction to distraction.

All phenomena, therefore, can serve *both* as sights to be appreciated and vehicles to some other end. Fire may well be the ultimate wonder to behold, but it also discloses a self-contained travelogue. Berkeley dependably tries to convert dead-end distractions into vehicles to some other type of experience.[16] He layers directed journey over wandering travelogue, destination over distraction. The essence of Berkeley's panacea is a potentially inflammatory acid, but the vehicle which disperses its "salutary" effects is an oily, resinous soap, an alkali! (7, 59). Although a stable commodity, tar-water is nevertheless compounded of two opposing acts. While one component of tar-water would burn a hole in everything from stomachs to the mystical foundation of experience, its cooling, balsamic vehicle so extends its destructive fire that, in effect, it becomes constructive. The union of fiery material and quenching vehicle can, together, accomplish anything, for vehicle and agent produce opposite effects! Appropriately, fire itself is presented as the "instrument or medium" (221) by which the Author of Nature works his will, and as the apparel in which "angels, chariots, and such-like phenomena are invested" (186). As *Siris* progresses, moreover, Berkeley turns details into vehicles, then demotes these vehicles back to mere details once he has driven on to the next details, and the process of converting details to vehicles has started again. Tar-water becomes the vehicle for fire, which, once attained, becomes the chariot of God; once Berkeley arrives at God, fire becomes a mere distraction, part of the heavenly paraphernalia, just as tar-water had assumed a secondary position after it had brought Berkeley to fire.

The distractions and destinations which Berkeley traverses and mentions in his philosophical journey are linked together in an alternating pattern. A given digression or distraction may also serve, alternately, as a vehicle to a destination or as a destination itself, but it may not serve as both destination and distraction at the same time. Both fixed and progressive *in turn,* the particular objects and ideas on Berkeley's itinerary combine significance and nullity, final meaning and no meaning. Either vehicles to everything imaginable or mere diverting curiosities, they combine totality with triviality, but admit nothing in between the two. A generalized cure-all rather than an abstraction from all particular medicines, tar-water is "a mixture of things the most heterogenous and even opposite to each other" but is itself only a "subtle substance" yet to be identified (144-47). It can cure *everything* and lacks only the negative side-effects of other drugs (62). Air, likewise, seems to be "an aggregate of the volatile parts of all natural beings" (145). God himself is "all in divers senses" (328), a summation of everything, although no one thing limits him. The particulars which "compose" the divinity never participate in divinity directly, but only as *vehicles to* it. A particular thing is either wholly distinct from or serves as an empty *motion toward* God—as a link at the far end of a chain whose strength is felt but which is never seen.

This emphasis on the conversion of things to vehicles, on the bifurcation of metaphor into diverting tenor and pointing vehicle, never results in a conventionally "neo-Platonic" repudiation of mundane experience. Ironically, the distractions which dot the journey to the top of the chain draw more attention than the elusive destination. Berkeley wants to avoid following his chain back to an Aristotelian first cause; such a *regress,* in admitting regular, systematic connections between events, assumes the presence of the very regulating power whose existence it was to demonstrate (237). Because Berkeley knows, from observing the operation of this system, that the world is a vehicle, a *progression* of causes and effects which always leads to a destination, he can afford to lavish time on distractions. He can tour while he travels. In revising his acrimonious evaluation of Newton, for example, Berkeley declares that light is a primordial material which penetrates and suffuses everything (226). No mere reflection from the junk cluttering the universe, the light involved in every perception assures us that any perception will lead to a desired end, indeed that every distraction implies a destination. Destinations become double negations, distractions from distractions. Berkeley rests assured that casual viewing is not only permissible, but suitably teleological. He takes special delight in experiments in which energy seems to add mass to material (196-97). Although the reduction of moving light to inert mass may seem to move against his overall program for converting things into vehicles, it also demonstrates that the sensible world can literally embody a procession toward totality. Hence Berkeley perforates his text with frequent allusions to poets like Homer (43) in order to interrupt his march to the bogus destination of medical knowledge, even to make medical research itself a distraction. He would show that everything, even his own highly progressive text, embodies a motion toward some still more remote end.

The chain itself is a non-entity which accumulates mass and becomes a sight for intellectual tourists. With its emphasis on the general rather than the abstract, Berkeley's philosophy tends to militate against the use of metaphor. For Berkeley, the "metaphysical" chain really exists, not as a mere conception but as a series of acts. Like the "Language of Nature" (254), the chain is not found, but experienced; it is nothing *but* the sensual manifestation of action (316). The more we talk about and respond to the fiction of the chain, the more it "exists," and, circularly, the more it dominates our *action* on events.[17] Making ideas into things, Berkeley wants to talk something into nothing, to involve his reader in the act of giving measurable meaning to his own metaphors, of making destinations into present, palpable distractions. What could be more startling than Berkeley effectively closing his somewhat eccentric philosophical career with a defense of the ancients (332, 342ff.)? Springing a surprise destination, arriving at Plato's well-known conjectures rather than at a direct, mystical experience of God, Berkeley throws his audience back on the *act* of seeking out a destination. He stops his reader from gawking at the goal of his quest, even if that goal is God, preferring to keep us moving through vehicles rather than arriving at a final end. Twisting Plato's philosophy into an obvious image of his own (335), he presents the end of his travels as the beginning point of his work and of western philosophy in general. Presenting his own work as an awkward mixture of old, incomplete and new, equally incomplete speculations, he distracts the reader back to his journey, to his march toward completion. It cannot be without a touch of humor that Berkeley insinuates that the ancients knew so much that they reflexively practiced his immaterialism (266). Berkeley closes his "chain" in a loop; we return to the beginning of the trip, ready to take the ride once again.[18]

Berkeley's curious essay on tar-water aims less at a particular destination or goal than at the creation of a sense of motion toward a destination. *Siris* suggests that an author can talk the reader toward a destination, whether or not there really is one. Berkeley gives the comically misleading impression that Aristotle anticipates his own thinking (167) in order to suggest that his writing offers not a destination *per se* but a fictional goal for philosophical inquiry. By writing a good deal of *Siris* in the past tense, Berkeley fortifies the suggestion that all philosophical projects both answer questions and *anticipate* something (e.g., 172). With "long poring" over "hoary maxims" (368, 350), over distracting and seemingly directionless anecdotes, Berkeley ends where he began, with curiosities which lead to two conflated but opposed ends, the pitchy translucence of tar-water and the impenetrable radiance of God. "The displeasure of some readers," fears Berkeley, "may perhaps be incurred by surprising them into certain reflections for which they have no curiosity," into "digressions . . . through remote inferences" (350). Shock and surprise, of course, are the stock devices of the travel writer. How much more surprising it is that we should find them to be the principal tools of an author like Berkeley, whose monologue speaks of the journey into and aggrandizement of nothing, and for whom "surprise" can serve as a final goal.

* * *

Long ago, Martha Pike Conant explained that Beckford took a free-wheeling approach to foreign and antique materials. Like Berkeley, Beckford sets out to produce a disordered progress, through literary, philosophical, and archaeological anecdotes, toward *some* but no *one* destination.[19] From the beginning of his story, Caliph Vathek adopts a Berkeleian approach to moralized and fictionalized travel. Vathek moves dependably forward and backward at the same time.[20] When he expands his palace, for example, the new wings serve only to advance his retreat into self-gratification.[21] The more that Vathek runs over the inscriptions on the sabers, the more he recurs to beating his head and biting his nails; the higher he builds his tower, the deeper he sinks toward the "Palace of Subterranean Fire." Such progress as Vathek makes is always associated with a surrender of motive power and a retreat from responsibility. Racing through the letters which flicker across the magical sabers, Vathek lets "giddiness and debility" drag him along. Even a table decked with three hundred dishes can only pull the perennially passive emperor to thirty-two of its selections (7, 12). Similarly, Vathek always tries to quantify infinity, to present an unreachable destination as though it were measurably distant and might be attained by accident, in the course of things, without any direct effort. Vathek knows that his sabers will never run out of letters and that his table will continue to furnish an unending supply of victuals, yet by counting off

words (or culinary dishes) as they appear, he gives the impression that an infinitely remote end could, passively, *be* reached. By trying to measure the mileage to infinity, Vathek ends up pushing his destinations beyond the reach of those powers which would quantify them. He shows precisely, even numerically, how unattainable they are. For Berkeley, the access to any destination was so complicated that every step and every experience led to manifold side-trips. For Vathek, every bit of progress implies an enormous remainder—a remainder which can reduce the voyage itself to a never-ending side trip.

Beckford has a genius for presenting paralysis as though it were progress. Even a strong-willed character like Carathis is *carried* into hell by a demon. Movement is always motionless; characters are pushed, kicked, drawn, or carried, but never self-propelled. Desire itself is hypostasized: Nouranihar is "urged on by an irresistible impulse" toward a suitably indefinite goal, a globe of fire, which she cannot reach but "continued to approach" (69). Beckford commonly reverses the syntactical roles of subjects and objects. Vathek does not gather jasmine, "a handful of jasmine dropped on his face" (62). The active voice depicts a passive process. "Tears insensibly overflowed the cheeks of his audience" (65). So when the mystical ball of the Giaour *draws* Vathek near the gulf of oblivion, an "invisible agency" "arrests" his "progress" (20, 22). Like Beckford's entire book, the Giaour drags Vathek's court to some fiercely sought but nevertheless infinitely receding destination, then terminates the travel before the goal is attained (18-20). So Berkeley draws his reader into a mystical rhapsody only to arrest his spiritual flight with a disappointing technical analysis. The process is repeated on a more local level in the imagery of kicking which animates the scene and which flares up time and again in Vathek's story. Kicking without a specific purpose is effectively arrested by the lack of a definite, reciprocating object to kick.[22] Kicking is the physical counterpart of Vathek's regular address to the deaf void of experience. In both Beckford and Berkeley, the passive actor and the disappointed reader must suspend their quests for a final destination in order to relish distractions. Vathek, for example, discovers that his progress toward his destination is inversely related to the determination with which he seeks it. His "fixed" "resolution" not only deafens him to the suggestion of his guides, but leads him to "determine to cross over the craggy heights" (45), through the worst possible route. In order to travel quickly or smoothly, a traveler must renounce the pursuit of a goal. He must relish and linger in approaches, and must view goals as a means of approaching something else. Goal and approach must somehow—without determined or resolute action by the voyager—exchange roles.

When Berkeley wanted to get to a point, he selected a wrong argument and brutally controverted it until he made it into an inverted vehicle for truth. Beckford, too, practices this rhetoric of inversion and transformation. Vathek interprets his commonplace "thirst" for knowledge literally, spending his days lapping up an infinite supply of spring (or perhaps tar) water (14). Indeed, Vathek invariably assumes that his words will apply to or conjure up those things that they literally represent. He cannot distinguish between monologue or conversation (with all its haphazard metaphors) and reality, nor can he ever quite understand the extent of the distance between verbal vehicles and their tenors. Vathek *is* the pose of the solitary traveler. The Giaour eventually reinterprets the already blatantly conventional metaphor of thirst by presenting Vathek with knowledge, the metaphorical counterpart of his already metaphorical but subsequently literalized "beverage." In a similar instance, Vathek, failing to learn the lesson of his insignificance from his disappointing attempt to build a staircase to the stars, depends on his *perception* of the *comparative* smallness of his subjects to establish the *fact* of his greatness (4). From Pope, Beckford borrows the literary technique of the sequential enumeration of unlike things. A retinue of promised gifts begins with unburnt beards, then progresses to beautiful slaves and finally to apricots (10). One key element in Vathek's character is his inability to form a list which leads up to an adequate or appropriate climax. His reader is forced to reorganize his lists in some meaningful way. Yet any attempt at a reorganization proves to be satiric, cynical, destructive, or simply uninformative. Would it be better to lead up to slaves than apricots? Culminating in the production of loosely defined feelings of incompetence, Vathek's lists dwindle down to distracting but unpleasant sights to behold. Incentives to revision, they lead to a detour back to the beginning. So Vathek gives names to the winds of his palace which suggest eternal gratification—"The Eternal or Unsatiating Banquet," "The Incentive to Pleasure" (20)—but which can only suggest unending repetition of the same act from the same starting point of dissatisfaction, without any progress toward a goal. Because Vathek's attempts to talk his way across the space between language and its referents fails, Beckford's reader is compelled to counteract, correct, and even discard Vathek's jumbled metaphors and to turn them into vehicles for surpassing Vathek's pedantry.

For Vathek and his wicked mother Carathis, moreover, the junk accumulated on the road to Eblis often fits awkwardly with its appointed allegorical meaning. Roaring on toward the underworld, Carathis may not take time to relish anecdotal event after anecdotal event. She has no opportunity to take an interest in the gothic trappery which gives her (and the genre of her story) its literary identity. Her fixation on her destination reduces her literary vehicle itself to a colorful but intolerable distraction. Carathis will not enjoy the accouterments of life in a gothic setting, but instead will try to force the rubble of the gothic tradition to point toward some remote meaning, some unreachable linguistic destination. Like any good gothic novelist, Carathis goes through with the "requisite operations," piling up "phials of serpents' oil, mummies, and bones" and other assorted tools of the gothic trade (32). By creating this utterly indiscriminate mass of spooky paraphernalia, Carathis builds away from the stock meaning of this type of imagery and toward the achievement, through "solemn rites," of some pseudo-religious meaning. Unfortunately, this heap of symbols proves inadequate to the cause. Dissolving in a violent flame, it simply looks, to the inhabitants of Samarah, like a fire. Like gothic imagery generally, it refers to nothing beyond its own effects. Like Berkeley, Carathis would extract new implications from old curiosities, yet her mad pursuit of new meaning only results in the loss of conventional meaning. Descending from gothic genre to a blur of burning junk, she accepts the vehicle but blots out all inadequate—hence all—tenors. So heavy-handed is Carathis's emphasis on vehicles *to* destinations that she usually overshoots her mark. Ending up with a vehicle which has superseded its destination, she ends up with, effectively, no vehicle at all. When Carathis arrives in Eblis, "without regarding in the least the groans of the prophet" (118) or anything else, she continues ripping ahead toward her unknown goal, completely overlooking the very things that she came to see. Hence Beckford's greater sympathy for Vathek, who at least understands that the destination of a journey is a distraction to look and wonder at. Vathek, alas, eventually catches the vehicular fever.

> Nouranihar, enraptured with the scenery of a place which brought back to her remembrance the pleasing solitudes where her infancy had passed, intreated Vathek to stop: but he, suspecting that these oratories might be deemed, by the Giaour, an habitation, commanded his pioneers to level them all.
>
> (101)

As Vathek approaches Eblis, his resolution to progress intensifies, but his capacity for interpretation grows weaker and weaker. Distractions which might delay the wandering Vathek fail to overcome Carathis, who considers even the most lurid scene not a wonder to behold but an opportunity for advancement.

> Carathis was too eager to execute her plan, to stop at the view, charming as it appeared in her eyes. Pondering the advantages that might accrue from her present situation, she said to herself, "So beautiful a cemetery must be haunted by gouls! they never want for intelligence: having heedlessly suffered my stupid guides to expire, I will apply for directions to them; and, as an inducement, will invite them to regale on these fresh corpses.
>
> (91-92)

"She continued her route without interruption" (92). Traveling in dead silence, Carathis insulates herself from even the distraction of conversation (44). Consequently, she covers more terrain than any other character. In the only passage in which the sublime is successfully quantified (and hence trivialized), Beckford makes sure to tell us that Carathis eclipsed precisely eighteen miles. Even in his most frenzied moments Vathek always talks to himself; he at least sustains his monologue (or his dialogue with empty experience). Carathis, moving faster than sound, falls beneath soliloquy and hence fails to move toward any meaningful destination.

Carathis turns distractions into vehicles in order to get to her goal, but Vathek, despite his mother's warnings, relishes the vehicular for its own sake, as a distraction. Vathek's mania for the vehicular, ironically, precludes the possibility of any real progress. So many vehicles jam Vathek's winding pathways that no reader can follow up on all of them. Seemingly evocative events wither away after only a few moments; the narrative paths that they suggested also disappear. Like Berkeley, Beckford quickly demotes vehicles into mere distractions and details, even nothing at all. Often this process of directed decay obstructs the central motivations of the story. The magical sabers, which had pricked Vathek on to his quest in the first place, are altogether "forgotten" by the "confused" Caliph after only a few paragraphs (17). When Vathek creates a blasphemous comedy by tying bearded Imams to rampaging mules, the delight of the show is cut short by an abrupt medical report followed by Vathek's departure (102). Early in the story, Vathek pitches his tent on a precipice between a primeval blackness and a cataract. He amuses himself by conjuring up a few omens, whose "impression was no more than momentary" (21-22). This failure of interpretation leaves him to walk in "hasty strides" around in circles. Unable to communicate, to transport to others the meaning of his conjurations, Vathek, who equates literature with life, also fails to make any physical progress.

Berkeley, too, had found himself suspended between an invisible image of comprehensive fire and the terrible vacuity of his metaphorical vehicles. Berkeleian experience moved between generality and non-entity. Where does Vathek live? "On one side [of his pavilion] a plain of black sand . . . appeared to be unbounded; and, on the other, perpendicular crags, bristled over with those abominable thistles" (50). Vathek stands in an impossible posture between an infinitely vapid horizontal plain and a world of vertical towers which drill into some superhuman void. Delivering a monologue to this wilderness of totality and vacuity, Vathek hears in reply only "the low murmurs of his people" asking "to what purpose have we been brought hither?" (50) Caught in a world of uninterpretable metaphorical vehicles, Vathek

wanders between the implied "purpose" of this scene and the echo, from his people, of his clamorous journeys—an echo which cannot quite reach the traveling Caliph.

Encamped on the brink between total vacuity and incomprehensible, abstract totality, Vathek drifts atop nothingness in its most trivial form. The various voids which confront him seldom prove very interesting. Vathek's insatiable, Faustian curiosity lacks any essential characteristics. Compounded of two opposing parts, it combines the waste products of utterly trivial studies with an abstract yearning for sciences which do not even exist (3). Vathek recognizes either trivial amusements or meaninglessly enormous concepts, but nothing in between.[23] He frustrates in advance the desire for travel *between* experience and interpretation. When Vathek wants to erect his observatory, he allows his tower to build itself; rather than taking an interest in this attempt to bridge the gap between earthly and heavenly knowledge, he pretends that "insensible matter shewed a forwardness to subserve his designs" (4). Through this kind of proclamation, Vathek censors the explanation of interesting causal mechanisms. His observer can only assume that Vathek's world is either magical or inexplicable, but never susceptible of interesting intellectual analysis.

Like tar-water, therefore, Vathek becomes a reluctant intermediate link between non-entity and totality. Like Berkeley, Beckford solidifies the illusion that, in the case of Vathek as in the case of tar-water, progress *toward* a destination occurs automatically, even by accident. Unlike Carathis, who overshoots her goals, Vathek always undershoots his mark. He inevitably (but accidentally) ends up somewhere between his original position and his expected target. Vathek progresses despite himself. Told that a basket of fruit heralds the arrival of a spiritual counselor, Vathek retreats from the social and metaphorical meaning of the gift in order to hit the smorgasbord. Earlier on, in a similar situation, the Giaour's lavish description of Vathek's anticipated procession into Eblis yielded only an interest in infernal mess accommodations (36). But "as he [Vathek] continued to eat, his piety increased" (52), the melons and pomegranates inexorably dragging him into a position between his sensualist impiety and the holiness of the spiritual emissary. So tar-water "insensibly" draws us back to common sense.

When, conversely, Vathek is *intentionally* making progress, he is somehow pulled back before he goes all the way to his goal. As Berkeley truncates his "chain," redirecting us to a distraction before we can achieve the divine vision, so Beckford truncates the many processions which Vathek would make into oblivion. The sacrificed boys are miraculously intercepted before they can finish their parade (97); Vathek himself can only go "wandering on" in Eblis (115), unable to complete his procession for lack of any idea of his final destination. Even after his arrival in Eblis, Vathek continues to delight in speculations concerning its astonishing sights without actually approaching them or assimilating their meaning. But the one sight that Vathek wants to see, the shade of Soliman, only serves to show, in its sublime triviality and teleological austerity, that Vathek's love of the vehicular will, finally, lead him to a destination which will cut short his trip.

Beckford has prepared his reader for such an abrupt conclusion by treating tourism without travel or travel without tourism as miserable in the experience and confused in the conception. Stationary beneath the dome of Fakreddin, the sleeping Vathek relishes a thousand tantalizing distractions.[24] His eunuch Bababalouk, however, completely ignores the cultivation of such "sights" in order to carry out an efficient search for Vathek's missing harem. In punishment for his single-minded pursuit of his goal, Bababalouk is hounded into a Kafkaesque chase through a series of dark tunnels—tunnels which terminate in the languidly motionless center of this dreamy temple, where a nasty joke awaits him (55-58). Similarly, Nouranihar's sublime vision of the Caliph's bed (71) rises during a still sleep. When Nouranihar awakes from the placeless dreams, she stumbles out into a disorienting darkness which leads only back to a sofa. The staircase into Eblis itself dissolves into a dark, unornamented, bottomless pit (108). At its end, beaten out from unrelieved travel, Vathek and Nouranihar can only vent their chagrin over their lack of time to compose themselves for viewing the halls that they had come to see (110). Neither Vathek nor his companion can understand what they behold anyway. All too compliant in releasing the Giaour from his duty as interpreter and guide, they have no option but to gape at the fundamentally inexplicable terrors before them. Although these sights could, perhaps, be explained in an infernal pilgrims' guide, they immediately but mutely show the meaninglessness of the destination to which the Caliph is headed.

Vathek as a whole is organized as a series of processions through increasingly skeletal distractions and toward a destination which surprises us with the profundity of its triviality.[25] The more the attention to distractions, the less the progress toward the goal. The more conscientious the progress, the fewer the distractions, the less definite the goal itself, and the more trivial the pursuit. In the first procession which Vathek organizes, the sacrifice of fifty boys, Vathek never sees the boys reach the end of their journey. Instead, he spends his time watching distracting celebratory games (25-27). The boys who march into the gulf seem to realize nothing about the fate of their respective predecessors; their train is so segmented that they take no account of one another, let alone their destination. Next

Vathek permits his people to march into a mammoth sacrifice atop his tower. Although he sees little purpose to this parade and prefers its pageantry to its proposed destination, he passively permits Carathis to interpret it not as a march into oblivion but as a step toward some magical end. He allows a concern for teleology, but he relishes spectacle, albeit with less intensity than he enjoys feeding boys to the Giaour. The next "procession" of pilgrims approaches Vathek in the interior of his harem, through unornamented "small corridors" which "appeared to terminate in nothing, but nevertheless, led to the cell where the Caliph expected their coming" (40). Near Eblis, Vathek processes through an architecture defined only by the non-talk of negations—"unknown in the records of the earth," characterized by "gloomy watch-towers, whose number could not be counted," "covered by no roof," and built on the decimated bones of those whom his parade tramples (107). Finally, in Eblis, destination and distraction dissolve in a single crepuscular vanishing point.

> Their eyes, growing familiar to the surrounding objects, they extended their view to those at a distance; and discovered rows of columns and arcades, which gradually diminished, till they terminated in a point radiant as the sun, when he darts his last beams athwart the ocean.
>
> (109)

At this point, there is nothing left for Vathek to do other than press on through an "infinity" of distractions, to march through gallery after gallery, and to persuade himself that open-ended tourism and directed journeying are compatible. The climactic ignition of the hearts of the damned results largely from Carathis's refusal to recognize the value of this directed but sightseeing tourism. Rampaging madly through hell, she journeys after mystical knowledge until she overturns one of the Solimans, finding, to her chagrin, that her destination is itself a distraction, an oddity to look at. She simply cannot keep the journey moving further ahead, yet she cannot accept that a destination can be a thing *per se* as well as a thing pursued. Her immolation registers the terrible triviality of any destination which has not been buffered by suggestive distractions or digressive side-trips, by diversions which keep open the process of travel to a goal as well as the approach from symbols to meaning. After their ignition, the three main characters of the story become not only perpetual travelers, unsatisfied seekers doomed to aimless wandering, but also things to look at for future visitors to the underworld. Sights in which convergent, even coinherent vehicles and tenors collapse into a unified nothingness whose meaning is literally clear, Vathek and his friends become walking tourist traps in whom the mania for a destination becomes itself a startling distraction. Having become a thing, Vathek's destination becomes a triviality, a nothing. Vathek would have done better, perhaps, to keep his goal indeterminate, to relish the intermediate steps in his voyage and to read appropriately "terminal" meaning into the distractions along the way. He should never have stopped his travels, for his journeys, unlike those of Carathis, issue in digressive entertainment and chatty instruction. Beckford agrees with Berkeley that any sequel to a chain of reflections should be made not of more accurate studies or goal-directed speculation, but of further soliloquies on tar-water or of further talk about episodes in the life of Vathek—of steps, segments, vehicles, rhetorical addresses, distractions, and other trivialities which suggest an approach to but never quite arrive at their terrifying destinations.

Notes

1. The student of Beckford seldom escapes comments like that of Martha Pike Conant (*The Oriental Tale in England in the Eighteenth Century* [New York: Columbia University Press, 1908; reprinted New York: Octagon Books, 1966], 62), that Vathek deserves only "to live chiefly for the sake of one remarkable scene—the catastrophe in the Hall of Eblis—in which the author, having laid aside the mockery, the coarseness, and the flippancy that reduce the first part of the book to the level of a mere *jeu d'esprit,* shows himself capable of conceiving and depicting an impressive catastrophe."

2. Kenneth Graham, "Beckford's 'Vathek': A Study in Ironic Dissonance," *Criticism* 14 (1972):243-44.

3. See Graham, 246-47, who concludes that Beckford presents Vathek as *both* Promethean hero and as butt of satire. Arguing for the interpretation of *Vathek* as an oriental tale, Robert Gemmet, (*William Beckford* [Boston: Twayne, 1977], 79, 82, 90, 97) explains that Beckford's supposed satire of the ill-starred Caliph results from his concerted attempt to detach the reader from the personality of the lead character. Beckford makes us reflect on the work as a spectacular example of a genre rather than as a sentimental biography of an individual person. Beckford's satire is seldom maintained for long; most of his work is serious and straightforward. Beckford stands alone among the English in producing a genuine, original oriental tale which offers more than a mere translation of a French original or a clumsy presentation of English morals in oriental dress (as in Johnson's *Rasselas* or Goldsmith's *The Citizen of the World*). Brian Fothergill, in *Beckford of Fonthill* (London: Faber & Faber, 1979), 41-42, claims that a satire on an oriental tale would not make much sense in late eighteenth-century England, where the rage for exotic stories never reached as feverish a pitch as it did in France. The comically absurd gusto with which Beckford often reviews the macabre and the perverted, says Boyd Alexander (*England's Wealthiest Son* [London: Centaur, 1962], 69), only registers a popular interest in the "ghoulish" (and in the psychological in general). In favor of the interpretation of *Vathek* as a satire, however, James Folsom, in "Beckford's *Vathek* and the Tradition of Oriental Satire," *Criticism* 6 (1964):69, offers the common-sense insight that Beckford so greatly exaggerates the conventions of the oriental tale that they become ludicrous. Finally, James Rieger, "*Au pied de la lettre*: Stylistic Uncertainty in *Vathek,*" *Criticism* 4 (1962):306, points out that *Vathek* must be taken lightly, for it rests on an amusing anachronism. *Vathek* extrapolates from the "literary chinoiserie" of Montesquieu and his followers and from the taste for oriental settings which gave rise to Johnson's *Rasselas*—both of these tastes having been defunct for twenty years.

4. Rieger, 302-12.

5. There are many examples, from Parmenides to Wittgenstein, of philosophical analyses of nothing and the terms for it (or of analogues of nothing, like folly and deformity). This concern with negations reached a high intensity in the later seventeenth century, when the correspondence semiotics of Locke and others seemed to demand a specific referent for every word. Thus Hobbes declares most general terms vacant; Davenant and Dryden attempt to give meaning to theatrical impossibility; Rochester writes a poem on "Nothing"; Locke tries to render negative terms like "infinity" virtually meaningless; and Berkeley spearheads a vitriolic and unrelenting attack on infinitesimals in the calculus. The analysis of triviality which animates *Siris* thus is the culmination of a long and critically important tradition; *Siris* is more than the work of an aging lunatic.

6. Travel literature always inclines toward the "oriental," for it always includes a fictional element, even if only the repetition of the false fables of the inhabitants of foreign lands. See Percy Adams, *Travel Literature and the Evolution of the Novel* (Lexington, Ky.: University of Kentucky Press, 1983), 72.

7. On the extent of Berkeley's reading in travel writers and on his own practice of the genre, see Adams, 65, 108, 189, 281.

8. On Berkeley's immediate literary acquaintance, especially his regular intercourse with Pope and the Scriblerians, see Marjorie Nicolson and George S. Rousseau, "Bishop Berkeley and Tar Water," in *The Augustan Milieu,* ed. Henry K. Miller, Eric Rothstein, and George S. Rousseau (Oxford: Oxford University Press, 1970), 129-31.

9. Berkeley's decision to move away from dialogue (as practiced in *Hylas and Philonous* and *Alciphron*) as well as from straightforward philosophical essay (as demonstrated in *The Principles of Human Knowledge* and in most of his other works) and toward a kind of dramatic rhapsody, a Shaftesburian monologue, is also philosophically significant. The straightforward essay, unlike rhapsodies or reflections, leaves little room for disputation. Michael Morrisroe, in "Ciceronian, Platonic, and Neo-Classical Dialogues," *Enlightenment Essays* 3 (1973):156, explains that Berkeley's *dialogues* are completely artificial. They permit no Platonic, Ciceronian, or even "Drydenian" doubt concerning which party will win. More proclamation than conversation, they move quickly and purposively to a preconceived conclusion. In contrast, the evocative prose of *Siris* moves slowly, indirectly, and even awkwardly toward its "destination." This freewheeling approach plays against the intellectual teleology implied by the metaphor of a chain which leads inevitably, link by link, to a prescribed goal.

10. Donald Davie, in "Berkeley's Style in *Siris*," *Cambridge Journal* 4 (1951):433 and *passim,* has identified the revivifying of dead metaphors, specifically the "chain of being," as a principal goal of Berkeley's work. The relation between tenor and metaphor becomes reciprocal: while the metaphor makes the work intelligible, the work constantly revises and revives a skeletal metaphor. The tenor of revision throws us back on the vehicle, just as Berkeley's "chain" brings us, eventually, down from heaven and back to tar-water.

11. On the association of travel literature with tourist guidebooks, see Adams, 39. Adams points out, 42, that each journey could spawn several accounts, all from differing points of view (that of the botanist, that of the cartographer, and so forth). Divergence from the main path of the voyage is thus an essential feature of the travel form.

12. See *Siris,* introduction, 31. The text for Berkeley's writings is *The Works of George Berkeley, Bishop of Cloyne,* ed. by A. A. Luce and T. E. Jessop (London: T. Nelson, 1953), vol. 5. Subsequent references, by paragraph number, are incorporated in the text.

13. Stephen Leo Carr, "The Rhetoric of Argument in Berkeley's *Siris*," *University of Toronto Quarterly* 51 (1981):52 and *passim.*

14. This process is repeated on a larger scale with Boerhaave. Boerhaave is used in two opposing ways in two works. In *Alciphron,* Boerhaave's libertine theory that the soul is an oil distilled from the solar light is contemptuously dismissed, along with everything else which Boerhaave has to say. In *Siris,* though, Boerhaave is resurrected as a predecessor of Berkeley in the investigation of the essential fire. He is set up as the founder of a theory with which, Berkeley knew, he would have no sympathy whatsoever. See I. C. Tipton, "The 'Philosopher by Fire,'" in *Berkeley: Critical and Interpretive Essays,* ed. Colin Turbayne (Minneapolis: University of Minnesota Press, 1982), 160-61.

15. On the segmented structure of *Siris,* see Carr, 47-48.

16. Berkeley's thesis that fire animates the world thus never repudiates his *esse est percipi* formula. To explain the present insensibility of this fire, Berkeley tries to hold that its appearance of invisibility means only that we have not yet developed a tool sufficiently powerful to disclose it. This fire would become sensible under improved conditions, like those which the microscope might offer. Invisibility spurs the development of a proper vehicle to visibility. See Tipton, 167-69.

17. As Philip Kohlenberg says, Berkeley's world is best understood "as a cluster of mutually autonomous activities." See his "Bishop Berkeley on Religion and the Church," *Harvard Theological Review* 66 (1973):223.

18. In explaining the apparent contradiction between *Siris* and the rest of Berkeley's work, John Linnell, "Berkeley's *Siris*," *Personalist* 47 (1960):11-12, draws an important distinction between Berkeley's endorsement and his presentation of theories. By presenting but not explicitly endorsing theories, Berkeley implies that they are either wrong or lead to further, clarifying theories. *Siris* is a series of such presentations; hence it leads either to everything, to nothing, or, perhaps, around in circles.

19. Vathek himself, Conant asserts, 69, is "a mere bundle of attributes . . . not a living individual." Yet this is precisely what Beckford desires, for he would force his reader to think of Vathek as a series of characteristics, moods, and behaviors which seem to lead up to but which never produce the expected personality.

20. One felicitous side-effect of Vathek's omnidirectionality is the enormous expansion of what Kenneth Graham calls Beckford's "fictional reality." Taking a wide range of opposites, tackling both the utterly sublime and the absurdly grotesque, moving both forward and backward, Beckford and his Caliph open up a full range of literary territory. They wholeheartedly exceed the "piggish" realism endemic to the novel. See Graham's "Im-

plications of the Grotesque: Beckford's *Vathek* and the Boundaries of Fictional Reality," *Tennessee Studies in Literature* 23 (1978):61-62.

21. See William Beckford, *Vathek,* ed. Roger Lonsdale (London: Oxford University Press, 1970), 1. Subsequent references to *Vathek* are incorporated in the text.

22. Beckford, advises Gemmet, 94-95, is no friend of indefinite mystery. His imagery is always lucid, precise, and couched in a controlled, neo-classical idiom.

23. Folsom, 75, insinuates that Beckford can never present himself as a moralist, for the situations in which his morals would operate are so extreme and the morals themselves so extravagant that no one could seriously apply them to daily life.

24. Beckford was particularly enamored of dome imagery. Domes could create a complete, theatrical, self-enclosed, and aesthetically unchanging world. See Gemmet, 75, and Fothergill, 39.

25. Rieger, 310-12, is at a loss to explain the gradual dissipation, as the story nears its end, of Beckford's characteristic humor. Equally troubling is the introduction of Vathek's sarcastic wit in inappropriate places. Vathek's wit is at once imperialistic and reactive. It requires an object, like a distraction which it crushes with a murderous giggle. As Vathek progresses toward Eblis, the distractions along the way fade into a hazy soft-focus. Eventually, nothing remains to satirize. Meaning, which rises from an intellectual response to the grand distraction of experience, likewise disappears. Thus Graham, in "Beckford's 'Vathek': A Study in Ironic Dissonance" (see note 2), 250, describes *Vathek* as a pilgrimage-romance in which the goal is communion not with heaven but with hell. A quest in which all the stock characters fail to live up to their type roles, *Vathek* presents exploits which are too trivial for the genre invoked. Like Berkeley, Beckford reverses generic expectations: like the chain which leads back to its beginning, *Vathek* recounts a pilgrimage which leads back to the discovery of the inadequacy of the persons making the trip.

Temple J. Maynard (essay date 1990)

SOURCE: Maynard, Temple J. "The Movement Underground and the Escape from Time in Beckford's Fiction." In *Vathek and The Escape from Time: Bicentenary Revaluations,* edited by Kenneth W. Graham, pp. 9-31. New York: AMS Press, 1990.

[*In the following essay, Maynard focuses upon Beckford's treatment of a subterranean world and eluding time in* Vathek.]

One has only to compare the tempo of a novel by Richardson with one by Fielding, or to consider the fluctuating rhythms of a narrative by Defoe, to realize that the perception of time is of major importance in the eighteenth-century novel. The world which the characters inhabit is coloured, indeed characterized, by action and movement in time. The mortal condition is a temporal progression, and man's perception of flux and decay conditions his behaviour throughout his conscious life. Naturally, this perception is reflected in literature, frequently by the depiction of states of existence where the wasting process is less apparent, is retarded, or denied. Of this nature are some myths of a golden age, some aspects of the pastoral scene, some forms of religious prose, and some depictions of paradise. In eighteenth-century England two *genres* particularly rich in the presentation of an altered temporal perception were the oriental and the gothic. In each, the reader is most obviously taken from the real world, and events occur in a temporal stream far different from that of our every day experience. In the work of William Beckford these two *genres* come together, and the result is a sharp disorientation from the normal. In Beckford's early and unfinished tale, **The Vision,**[1] and in both the frame-tale of **Vathek**[2] and in the **Episodes,**[3] the perception of time and place is largely responsible for the intense atmosphere and the curious tensions which are generated.

Because of its publishing history, **Vathek** is commonly read without the **Episodes** that were an integral part of the original conception. The reader is even less likely to compare it with the long story, **The Vision,** though that early work is closely related to **Vathek** in a number of interesting ways. When **Vathek** is read in isolation, the concern with time may seem an insignificant or accidental aspect, while the journey to the underworld may appear as no more than a superficially orientalized analogue of the Christian hell, necessitated by Beckford's apparently conventional moral ending. But when they are examined together, these works reveal a preoccupation with time and mortality. In all of them a perception of the fleeting nature of youth and love is associated with a retreat into enclosed spaces which are frequently subterranean. They thus reiterate an association found in Beckford's letters and rhapsodies from a very early date. But this linking of the descent into subterranean precincts with the indulgence of a forbidden or illicit passion is common in the oriental mode, and a glance at its incidence in that *genre* may further clarify Beckford's intent. Incidentally, similar situations occur in the gothic, though most of the more fully developed examples are subsequent to the publication of **Vathek.**[4] But especially in those oriental tales which came to England *via* France—in Galland's edition of the *Arabian Nights,* in the *Persian Tales* of Petis de la Croix, and in the effusions of T. S. Gueullette such as the *Chinese Tales,* the *Tartarian Tales,* and the *Mogul Tales*[5]—Beckford would have found stories where a descent beneath the surface of the earth was linked with an escape from mundane commitment, the indulgence of forbidden love, or an apparent stay in the flux of time.

In the *Arabian Nights* and the *Persian Tales,* the movement underground opens the way to enchanted realms where the usual constraints of terrestrial existence may be put aside. Gardens of edenic beauty, caves of treasure, fields of flowers, or trees of jewelled fruit attract the sight, while entire subterranean landscapes replete with their own light and water may welcome the intrepid adventurer or seduce the unwary. Such a subterranean garden of jewels, complete with halls of treasure, prefigures untold riches for Aladdin in the *Arabian Nights,*[6] while an underground palace offers a sanctuary of love in the story of the Second Callendar.[7] A complete landscape of this kind occurs in the *Persian Tales*:

> . . . arrived at the Foot of the Mountain . . . I soon perceived a large Opening, the dreadful Darkness of which was no Invitation to enter it . . . I went without Hesitation . . . tho' there was not a glimpse of Light to direct me; I found the Ground was a Descent; and marching still forward for fifteen or twenty Hours, I doubted not but I was descending to the Genies of the Earth. At last the Darkness was dissipated, and I beheld the Light of Day, which I began to think I had lost for ever. The Light led me into a flowery Meadow, the most beautiful I ever saw. The trees in it were loaden with the fairest fruit.[8]

Regions like this abound in the *genre,* and seem to offer security, freedom from responsibility, riches, or a time for love.[9] They can be treacherous, but for a time the wanderer may enjoy the delights that are offered. However, such places belong to the genii, and a mortal is in dangerous company in these realms, as a passage from George Sale's Preliminary Discourse to his edition of the Koran makes clear:

> The *Orientals* pretend that these Genii inhabited the world for many ages before *Adam* was created, under the government of several successive princes, who all bore the name of *Solomon*: but falling at length into an almost general corruption, *Eblis* was sent to drive them into a remote part of the earth there to be confined.[10]

Apparently they were not very securely confined. Throughout the oriental *genre* adventurous men descend to the regions inhabited by the genii, or stumble on their caves and palaces, some of which are near the surface and the habitations of mankind. Some of these genii are well-disposed towards men and are helpful. Others are inherently evil, and always looking for ways to do harm. The trick is to tell which kind of genie one is dealing with. Frequently they extract a severe price for their help or guidance. Nevertheless, the pangs of a hopeless passion may lead a despairing lover to hazard his present life and eternal welfare for a few hours or days of consummation.[11] But there is a sense in these

tales that the asylum or the assistance received from the genii may be worth the price, however fleeting the enjoyment may be. Certainly the protagonists of Beckford's fiction are journeying down paths blazed by earlier travellers. His mages, giaours, afrits, dives and peris are variations of the genii, and can be expected to mislead mankind, even if they are not totally malicious.

The conflict between the consciousness of social responsibility and the desire to escape with a loved one inevitably suggests to Beckford a movement underground. The situation is complex. On the one hand, subterranean precincts seem to promise a secure retreat where one can escape the constraints of society for a time. On the other hand, the spartan rigor of the accommodation in some of the scenes Beckford depicts would seem to represent the price paid for such indulgence. Something must be given up for love. A dream-vision or rhapsody written by Beckford circa 1779, will illustrate the point:

> I seemed stretched in a dreary cave—across which ran several bubbling streams—no termination of the Grot was visible—its roof was lost in obscurity—heaps of cocoa-nuts were piled—to all appearance around me—so immense that whole nations I think could never have consumed them . . . I had not long surveyed this Realm of Darkness and silence before an Angelic Shadow issued suddenly from the depth of the cavern leading in its hand the one I love—he flew to me. I sprang forwards to catch him in my arms. Rest happy said a thrilling voice—no one shall disturb you for ages. The great power—source of all felicity—has abstracted you from both [sic] the multitude of his creatures—as examples of perpetual tenderness—and has alloted this cave—sunk deep in the center of the Earth, for your abode. Those piles of nuts are destined for your nourishment—if ye freely renounce the lustre of the Sun for each other.[12]

A diet consisting entirely of coconuts might occasion the first notable tensions in such a seclusion, but one feels that the bargain would soon seem altogether mistaken. However, just such a retreat recurs in *The Vision,* while variations on the same theme appear in the *Episodes of Vathek.* In another guise the same imagery can be found in Beckford's mature recollections of the notorious Christmas celebration at Fonthill. Reminiscing about this event, Beckford reinvokes the key elements of this topos:

> Immured we were "au pied de la lettre" for three days following—doors and windows so strictly closed that neither common day light nor common place visitors could get in or even peep in—care worn visages were ordered to keep aloof . . . Our société was extremely youthful and lovely to look upon . . . The solid Egyptian Hall looked as if hewn out of a living rock . . . an interminable stair case . . . appeared as deep as the well in the pyramid . . . delightful the straying about this little interior world of exclusive happiness surrounded by lovely beings . . . what absolutely appeared

. . . a Demon Temple deep beneath the earth set apart for tremendous mysteries . . . Whilst the wretched world without lay dark, and bleak, and howling, whilst the storm was raging against our massive walls . . . the very air of summer seemed playing around us . . .[13]

These few phrases, culled from several pages which would support the same interpretation, further illustrate the prevalence of this imagery in Beckford's thought. The exclusion of all save his youthful companions would re-inforce the concept of timelessness which is consistent with such a setting. The word "immured" which begins the preceding quotation, though it may mean "walled up," carries a common connotation of "entombed," a meaning especially fitting in this context.

As has been frequently pointed out, Beckford's sense of oppression, and the need to escape from it, led him early to the oriental tale; the long story, part of which was published by Chapman as *The Vision,* may date from as early as 1777.[14] What is especially notable about it is that the bulk of the action takes place underground. The vast majority of earlier oriental tales are set on or above the surface of the earth. From the first, Beckford's impulses led him to choose for inspiration those stories where the action takes place subterraneously. It is precisely in these stories that the tyranny of time seems most often compromised.

The Vision, as it stands, is patently an unfinished work. Those fragments of its continuation in rough draft which were apparently unknown to Chapman seem never to have been integrated with the rest of the tale.[15] The main body of the material as we have it is comprised of a series of enclosed gardens, caverns, grottoes and valleys through which the main character travels as he ventures further and further into a subterranean realm. Each enclosure takes the narrator further from his mundane past into a subjective and romantically realized inner realm. The reader will speedily recognize the materials from which *Vathek* was later to be cast; even the female figure is similarly named Nouronihar. His journey, and the incidental ordeals he must undergo, both purify him and make him worthy of the love of the Persian maiden. Reunited in the innermost edenic landscape, the young William and his Nouronihar take refuge from the coming season of storms in a cave. Attendant dwarfs roll a huge stone over the entrance that twelve mortals could not shift. All sound fades away. The cave is provisioned, illuminated, and they are alone. The young protagonist declares that he has all he wants: let the storms rage outside, alone with Nouronihar he asks for no more, "No! my fondest wishes never rose to such a measure of happiness!"[16] Surely, the significant fact about *The Vision* is not that it was never finished, but that it does end at just this point. The additional segments were destined never to

be incorporated with this introductory material. In the light of Beckford's later writing, fiction and non-fiction, one may assert that what we are witnessing is not a mere breakdown in the narrative or a failure of inspiration. Rather, the elaborate plans for the continuation were never fully realized, and the fragment ends here, because this is precisely the point at which Beckford needed to arrive.[17] He has his main characters at a point farthest from the real world, where no power on earth can reach them, and where they are permitted to remain by some special dispensation. All the princes in *Vathek* and the *Episodes* seek just such a sanctuary, one which we may presume had a powerful appeal for the author himself.

In the frame-tale of *Vathek* the preoccupation with time and mortality, while not overtly emphasized, is prevalent. Seen in the context of Beckford's other fiction it becomes even more obvious. Time is a major motivating force for Vathek. His hankering for the treasures of the pre-Adamite sultans, and the gems and gold in the palace of subterranean fire, is largely due to his longing for a more lasting influence and power, for the extension of his hegemony through time. The battle within him, such as it is, is fought between the indulgence of immediate sensual pleasure, and an implied promise of release from mortality.

Vathek is already "Ruler of the World," of the Moslem world at least, and within his sphere he possesses almost unlimited power. He can exercise his whims without regard to any retributive action. He has inherited fabulous wealth and can afford to spend lavishly on structures like his palaces and his tower, and the people constantly supply more at his command. How can he desire anything that he doesn't already possess? What is there in the treasures promised by the Giaour more wonderful than what he already has, or could acquire? Can we believe he would give up his considerable wealth and his royal position for a pair of marvelous sabres and their like, or even the carbuncle of Giamschid? He can hardly add significantly to his vast collections nor extend much further his current enjoyment of luxury. No, what Vathek seeks at Istakar is the eternal continuance of his power. His goal is the extension of his influence and his mortal existence through time which he believes could be granted by the associates of the Giaour.

That Vathek wants more from life than other men we already know, hence his addition of the five new wings to the palace of Alkoremi in which each of the senses may be indulged to excess. But it is significant that the collection of rarities from every corner of the earth could not satisfy Vathek himself who was, "of all men . . . the most curious."[18] Vathek's wish, "to know every thing; even sciences that did not exist,"[19] is a clue to his character. He is not content with the lot of mortal man.

But while Mahomet opines that Vathek's tower is built, "from the insolent curiosity of penetrating the secrets of heaven,"[20] what Vathek really seeks in the astrological studies in which he engages on its summit is a favorable prediction of his own future. He seeks to wrest secrets from the stars in order to control his destiny, to avert the effects of time, and to postpone or avoid a personal mortality.

It is the antiquity of Istakar, and the legendary nature of the riches stored up in the halls of Eblis, that wins Vathek's adherence to the quest. In the very name of the treasures of the pre-Adamite sultans there is an inference of longevity that could be coexistent with the creation.[21] Vathek expects to take his place beside the pre-Adamite kings, or even to usurp their position. The Giaour speaks to him of, "the treasures which the stars have promised thee,"[22] and intimates that they will be "conferred" upon him.[23] Vathek is further intrigued by reading in the parchment, "that is the region of wonders: there shalt thou receive the diadem of Gian Ben Gian; the talismans of Soliman; and the treasures of the pre-adamite sultans: there shalt thou be solaced with all kinds of delight."[24] The language is ambiguous, or intentionally misleading, when the Giaour implies the alert corporeal existence and consciousness of the pre-Adamite kings. He tells Vathek, "it is there that Soliman Ben Daoud reposes, surrounded by the talismans that control the world."[25] Repose is unknown in these regions, as all who come there soon learn. But Vathek could hardly avoid accepting this picture, since it is in complete accord with legends of the early sultans, pre-Adamite and post-Adamite, which are prevalent in the oriental *genre,* and which Beckford can suppose both Vathek and his readers will recollect.[26] Carathis also understands the situation in this way. She expects Vathek to reign in the halls of Eblis as, with a notable instance of maternal solicitude, she declares, "either I will perish, or Vathek shall enter the palace of fire. Let me expire in flames, provided he may reign on the throne of Soliman!"[27]

The means of attaining access to the palace of subterranean fire and acquiring these treasures also suggests something of their nature. They are to be won by propitiating the Giaour and the other agents of Eblis with human sacrifice. Vathek expects to ascend the throne of Soliman without a personal demise. It is the shedding of blood, the offering of human lives, that will pay for his release from mortality. The death of his victims will avert his own death. His transference to the underworld is, to that extent, successfully accomplished, though the eternity he has bought is not the expected boon. The fifty children thrust into the chasm, the immolation of countless citizens on the tower, and the burning of the mummies that are themselves representative of a battle fought against death; these are the talismans which Vathek hopes will gain for him an eternity of infernal

dominion. Curiosity enters into his motivation, it is true; greed is not totally divorced from his impulse; but the vital, impelling force lies deeper than that. Vathek seeks in his way, what Gulchenrouz is given in another, the perpetuated enjoyment of a mortal, sensual existence.

The *Episodes of Vathek,* as we have them, are comprised of two complete tales and a portion of a third, though more may have been written.[28] In each, the escape from time or from social constraint is associated with the retreat into enclosed spaces. Ultimately and ironically, as is the case in the frame-tale of *Vathek,* each protagonist seeks sanctuary in the halls of Eblis, mistakenly believing that in those subterranean precincts he can realize his desires. Meanwhile, each character, again like Vathek, tries to ignore or deny the social mores in a series of intermediate retreats into gardens, caverns, or palaces. Each tale conveys a sense of withdrawal, often hasty and ill-considered, from duty and from life. Each story in its own way illustrates an intense and altered perception of time, leading the characters finally and precipitously to the underworld.

In the first Episode, **"The Story of Prince Alasi and the Princess Firouzkah,"** the Prince accepts with reluctance the tasks of a ruler. But as he tells his own tale he emphasizes that he did not abuse his position:

> I fulfilled all my duties exactly, and only from time to time indulged in the delights of solitude. A tent, disposed after the Persian manner, and situated in a dense forest, was the place where I spent these moments of retirement, moments that always seemed to pass too quickly.[29]

But Alasi's exact adherence to duty doesn't survive the arrival of Firouz/Firouzkah, the princess masquerading as a non-existent twin brother, who instantly wins his love. Although he had "already extended beyond its customary term" his indulgence in "seclusion and solitude,"[30] he lingers still longer. After their return to his court, Alasi is content for awhile to see Firouz shine in company, but as he becomes more helplessly under the spell of this self-indulgent figure, this changes. He soon recognizes the "essential badness" of Firouz's heart, but seems powerless to resist the appeal. Alasi comes to share the sentiments of so many of Beckford's characters who would say, as Firouz soon does, "Why are we two not alone in the world?"[31] Thus Alasi's existing impatience with his public responsibilities is augmented. It is in accordance with their desire to be alone together that Firouz induces Alasi to alienate his betrothed, the Princess Rondaba, and embroil the country in war.

The love of Alasi for Firouz is apparently not of the kind that inspires and sustains royal judgment or heroic valor. Inevitably, when Firouz is wounded and subsequently revealed as Firouzkah, Alasi is only too content to be carried off by magic to the subterranean palace of the Mage. Here for a time Alasi and Firouzkah enjoy what each of Beckford's protagonists longs for, the indulgence of passion in a protected subterranean environment. It is enough for Alasi; seeing the enchanted landscape, replete with, "the most beautiful and delicious products of the earth," Alasi exclaims, "what is it to us if we have been carried into Cheheristan itself? The true realms of bliss are in thine arms!"[32] He thus articulates the sentiments of all the lovers in Beckford's fiction. No more self-sufficient stance could be adduced.

But if love is all in all to Alasi and Firouzkah, time is still their enemy. The Mage sanctions and facilitates their union, and Alasi, like Vathek, is enabled to enjoy his love for awhile, indulged in amorous dalliance and magical entertainments by the attentive Firouzkah and the Mage's dives. Almost, they seem already to have escaped temporal constraint. Alasi confesses, "Her assiduous care, her ingenuity of tenderness, made my every moment hurry by in such voluptuous enjoyment that I was in no case to measure the flight of time; and the present had so far obliterated the past that I never once thought of my kingdom."[33] This is the nearest that any of the princes in these tales will attain to freedom from time and mortal care; it most closely approximates the similar situation of the young narrator of *The Vision.* But this is not really a place removed from temporal sway, and the idyl must end. The Mage announces his imminent departure for the palace of subterranean fire, which he describes in terms reminiscent of Vathek's understanding of the place:

> I am expected in the Palace of Subterranean Fire, where I shall bathe in joys untold, and possess treasures passing man's imagination. Ah! why has this moment of supreme felicity been so long delayed? The inexorable hand of death would not then have torn from my side my dear Soudabé, whose charms had never suffered from the ravages of Time! We should then have partaken together of that perfect happiness which neither accident, nor the vicissitudes of life, can ever mar in the place to which I am bound.[34]

The Mage believes, as do others, that time can have no effect there, and that death will have no power. The vocabulary is reminiscent of language usually used to describe heaven, rather than the underworld, and Alasi responds in a similar vein, "where is that divine sojourn in which a happy eternity of mutual love and tenderness may be enjoyed? Let us follow you thither."[35]

Alasi is undismayed when the Mage tells him he must do homage to the infernal powers in order to attain this boon, "I will worship any god you like . . . if he will suffer me to live for ever with Firouzkah, and free from the horrible fear of seeing pale disease or bloody steel threaten her beauteous life."[36] Even the sacrifice of human hair required to propitiate these powers no more

daunts Alasi than the sacrifice of the fifty children to the Giaour had daunted Vathek. He is prepared to behead any number of his faithful subjects in order to collect it. The Mage is himself a deluded victim of the infernal powers, and believes he has won an eternal reward. He exults, "see all these locks of hair that ornament my Hall of Fire—dear evidences that I am about to enter the gates of the only place where lasting joys are to be found."[37] The unscrupulous Firouzkah is likewise convinced, and motivated, like Alasi and the Mage, by her desire for release from mortality, "You will agree, my dear Alasi, that the sacrifice of a whole tribe of crazy wretches who will not accept our belief, is as nothing if we can obtain thereby the supreme felicity of loving each other to all time."[38] Alasi, fearful of losing Firouzkah, is easily persuaded to return to his own country and, by declaring the religion of fire and scalping all who oppose it, to collect such quantities of hair as will win him an eternity of voluptuous indolence with Firouzkah in a fiery afterlife. They put the plan into practice and with the strength of the army to back them collect the necessary hair for the ritual. However, despite their readiness to confront eternity, some doubts remain, and Alasi and Firouzkah linger *en route,* "we could not bring ourselves to finally abandon our present pleasures for those we had been led to anticipate."[39] But the journey to Istakar is finally accomplished, and they burn ten camel-loads of hair in order to gain entrance *via* the ebony portal. Like all the characters who win their way into the halls of Eblis, they are amazed at their reception. They have avoided the uncertainties of a normal span on earth, it is true; but they have gained an eternity, not of seclusion and safety, but of agony and despair.

In the second of the *Episodes of Vathek* the concern with time, though prevalent, is presented somewhat differently in that much of this theme is carried by the interpolated history of Homaiouna who is, by her very nature as a peri, free from mortal considerations. By a curious twist, however, her period of expiation on earth subjects her for a time to some of the inconveniences of human nature, though she is not subject to death. Her history, in which she recounts a series of happenings in the magical country of Ginnistan, augments the reader's perception of what it would mean to be free from the fears of mortality. This awareness is extended in the main narrative of this Episode by Prince Barkiarokh as he makes pretense of a similar magical nature in his wooing of the Princess Gazahidé. Barkiarokh is well aware of the ubiquitous human concern with time and mortality. He wins the hand of his Princess by feigning that through the powerful Jinn, Asfendarmod, whom he claims as his father, he can grant her a stay in the aging process and postpone her death. He falsely reports Asfendarmod as saying, "tell her that, for wedding gift, I allow her to retain, unimpaired, her beauty and her youth, during the hundred years she will live with thee!"[40] It is clear that this promise influences her decision to marry Barkiarokh, because the King, her father, abdicates in favour of Barkiarokh and allows the marriage, saying, "I ask for no greater boon than to see my daughter always fair, young and happy—unless, indeed, you should be willing to add to your favours by prolonging my days so that I may behold the lovely children to be born of your union."[41] No clearer indication could be desired to show the ever-present concern with aging and death in these tales.

The whole course of indulgence and crime in which Barkiarokh engages once he assumes the throne involves a perpetual perception of time in that he lives constantly anticipating the effects of the rod of vengeance wielded by his true wife, the Peri Homaiouna. Otherwise, he continues to live as though he were free from mortal restraints and could do as he wished with impunity. Once he sees his daughter, Leila, however, and conceives his overpoweringly lustful passion for her, he must restrain his appetites, for the first time, until he can get her to some place not subject to the Peri's influence. It is thus that he brings her to Istakar, and the brink of destruction, in the hope of possessing her unmolested in the palace of subterranean fire. What he seeks in that place is freedom to indulge a criminal passion, rather than freedom from mortality. In this way his case differs from those of the other princes, but only at the last. The concern with time has been a constant theme throughout this Episode, and it brings him surely to the palace of subterranean fire.

In the fragment of the third Episode we have a further and more oppressive use of time perception, together with a movement into subterranean enclosures. The twin children, Zulkais and Kalilah, love each other in a fashion more intense than is usual between siblings. Beckford is not here moving far from the common themes of the oriental tale. Critics are inclined to see here a quasi-autobiographical reference to Beckford's illicit affection for his cousin's wife. Such may indeed have been part of the inspiration for the story, but it is not without precedent in the *genre*. In the *Mogul Tales*, for example, the History of Canzade, Princess of Ormuz is based upon an incestuous attachment.[42] The children's father, like Vathek, is subject to, "an inordinate desire to control the future," and sought, "to forestall Providence, and to direct the course of events in despite of the decrees of Heaven."[43] Like Alasi and Firouzkah, the twins seek only to escape from society and enjoy each other's company alone. Although their father seems largely responsible for the intensity of their feelings, since he immersed them in the cabalistic lavers which over-heated their blood, he believes that their passion interferes with his son's education. Therefore, the old Emir decides to separate the twins, and so he arranges for Zulkais to be carried a thirty-day trip up the Nile. Here she is rather encouraged in her passion by the unlikely tutor chosen for her by her father. He confesses to similar feelings for his sister and indicates that Omoultakos, the Jinn of the Great Pyramid, would enter into her feelings, having in his time been similarly disposed towards his own sister. Under these circumstances there is no chance of Zulkais forgetting her love for her brother; instead she is further incited in her feelings. She is easily persuaded to seek a way back to Kalilah by propitiating the infernal powers. Like Alasi and Firouzkah in the first Episode, all she has ever wanted is time to be alone with Kalilah. It is in order to return to the intimacy of their early childhood together that she attempts to contrive their reunion.

Zulkais agrees to undergo the terrifying initiatory ritual. Time and space close in upon her as she prepares for the ordeal. She waits impatiently for night to begin the procedure which she has been led to believe will bring her to her beloved Kalilah. The movement underground is here more than usually sinister, and quite obviously unsafe. She follows her teacher, the Palm-tree Climber, into a narrow passage leading underground, "not more than four feet high, so that I was compelled to walk half doubled up." The scene continues in a claustrophobic journey:

> The air I breathed was damp and stifling. At every step I caught my feet in viscous plants that issued from certain cracks and crevices in the gallery. Through these cracks the feeble light of the moon's rays found an entrance, shedding light every here and there, upon little wells that had been dug to right and left of our path. Through the black waters in these wells I seemed to see reptiles with human faces. I turned away my eyes in horror.[44]

Not for Zulkais the garden landscapes enjoyed by the narrator of *The Vision,* nor the magical settings that soothe Alasi in his erotic interlude with Firouzkah. Here Zulkais has to confront the subterranean landscape in all its horror, and in something like its true colors. It is a mark of the distance Beckford has come that this young girl can still go on, that her courage survives this onslaught and she can seek love in these purlieus. The low, stone-built passage, the foetid air, the feeble light, serve to emphasize the nature of this setting and this quest. This is patently not a journey toward freedom and love, but the road toward death and the desolation of the tomb.

In leaving her, the Climber tells Zulkais to choose between five staircases leading out of a vast subterranean hall, "One only leads to the treasury of Omoultakos. From the others, which go losing themselves in cavernous depths, you would never return. Where they lead you would find nothing but hunger, and the bones of those whom famine has aforetime destroyed."[45] Zulkais is terrified, as she recounts to the princes in the halls of Eblis:

Judge of my terror, you who have heard the ebony portals, which confine us for ever in this place of torment, grind upon their hinges! Indeed I dare to say that my position was, if possible, even more terrible than yours, for I was alone. I fell to the earth at the base of the block of marble.[46]

In a dream-vision Zulkais is inspired, or deluded, by a figure she takes to be her brother, "Suddenly a voice, clear, sweet, insinuating like the voice of Kalilah, flattered my ears . . . 'Allah forbids our union. But Eblis, whom you see here, extends to us his protection. Implore his aid, and follow the path to which he points you.'"[47] Emboldened and determined, Zulkais begins to ascend the stairway upon which the figure of Kalilah seemed to stand; incidentally, not necessarily the one to which Eblis would have pointed her.

> The steps seemed to multiply beneath my feet; but my resolution never faltered and, at last, I reached a chamber, square and immensely spacious, and paved with a marble that was of flesh colour, and marked as with the veins and arteries of the human body. The walls of this place of terror were hidden by huge piles of carpets of a thousand kinds, and a thousand hues, and these moved slowly to and fro, as if painfully stirred by human creatures stifling beneath their weight. All around were arranged black chests, whose steel padlocks seemed encrusted with blood.[48]

As the tale breaks off here, we have no way of knowing what might happen in this strange environment. Does this chamber in some way represent the womb to which Zulkais and Kalilah are striving to return—the only place where the twins were allowed to be alone together? Is it rather another form for the chamber of death? The padlocked chests might stand for coffins in this unpleasant hall. What is clear is that again the quest for freedom from the temporal condition has led to a dead end. Time itself seems slowed as this claustrophobic vignette usurps the reader's attention. The concerns of the real world fall away for Zulkais as she, like Prince Alasi in the first *Episode,* like Vathek in the frame tale, and like the hero of *The Vision,* seek a world of their own choosing divorced from time and place. In these tales, as so often in the oriental *genre,* such a rejection of the real world carries with it a terrible penalty.

Every reader must notice the tensions generated by *Vathek,* tensions noticeable throughout these tales. In part, the fiction is indulged as we witness each character thrill and salivate over the most self-centred longings and desires. At times the author is uncritical of these impulses, and it is really only with the shift of tone towards the end that a moral stance is assumed. Beckford's use of the oriental mode was not merely a fortuitous outcome of early reading in the *genre,* or the influence of Lettice, Cozens, Chambers, and Henley; rather, he found in the oriental tales which were his inspiration a preoccupation with a series of related themes, and a certain uncritical detachment from moral condemnation, which must have had a lasting appeal. To some extent, the apparent moral ending of *Vathek* and the *Episodes* may be conventional. Backford would have been influenced by the decided trend, apparent especially in English oriental tales from Addison to Johnson, used to justify and excuse such ephemeral material. He was obviously conscious, also, of the expectations of his readers, and sought to disarm some of the criticism that the subject matter of his fiction was sure to raise. But the sheer weight of repetition of the theme, as each character seeks to escape from the destructive forces of time and the constraints of society in order to remove with a loved object into a subterranean seclusion, carries with it a certain impetus. There is a nostalgia, noticeable especially in *The Vision* and in the history of the Peri Homaiouna in the second *Episode,* but perceptible also in the other tales, for the plight and longings of each of the protagonists. However evil they may be, their hope for immortality, if not their criminal excess, is allowed in the context of the stories to evoke a sympathetic response. In the fiction of William Beckford no final escape from time is possible for any of his human characters, but in the subterranean fantasies of these tales we are invited to share their longing that such a respite were available to mankind.

Notes

1. *The Vision; Manuscript of a Romance,* ed., Guy Chapman (Cambridge: Cambridge University Press, 1930).

2. *Vathek,* ed., Roger Lonsdale (Oxford: Oxford University Press, 1970).

3. *The Episodes of Vathek,* trans. Sir Frank T. Marzials, ed. Lewis Melville (London: Stephen Swift, 1912).

4. See especially Lewis's *The Monk* and Maturin's *Melmoth the Wanderer.*

5. These tales are far less faithful to the spirit of any Arabic or Persian origina than is the work of Galland in *The Arabian Nights* or of Petis de la Croix in *The Persian Tales* or *The Turkish Tales.*

6. *The Arabian Nights Entertainments,* ed. A. Galland, 6th ed. (London: J. Osborne 1725) IX, 104.

7. *Arabian Nights,* II, 44.

8. *The Thousand and One Days; Persian Tales,* ed. Petis de la Croix, 3 vols., 3 ed. (London: J. Tonson, 1722).

9. See The Story of Prince Cameralzaman in *Arabian Nights,* VI, 115 ff. and The Story of the Great Traveller, Aboulfaouaris, in *Persian Tales,* III, 155 ff.

10. George Sale, *The Koran, Commonly Called The Alcoran of Mohammed . . .* (London: J. Wilcox, 1734) p. 73.

11. The striving for an extension of life, of the years of enjoyment, and the exclusion of apparent danger is a common theme in literature; comparisons may drawn with Faust and with Melmoth. But the forces that grant such privileges aspiring seekers commonly deceive them.

12. Guy Chapman, *Beckford* (New York: Scribners, 1937) p. 57.

13. J. W. Oliver, *The Life of William Beckford* (London: Oxford U. Press, 1932) pp. 89-91.

14. The dating of those sections of the manuscript not published by Chapman may be later. I have not seen the manuscript.

15. The forty-four pages of the rough draft were first printed by André Parreaux in his *William Beckford, Auteur de Vathek: Étude de la Création Littéraire* (Paris: Nizet, 1960), and mentioned by Robert Gemmett in *William Beckford* (Boston: Twaine, 1977) p. 45 ff.

16. *The Vision,* p. 86.

17. It is toward such a seclusion as this that each of the stories seems to hurry its protagonists.

18. *Vathek* p. 2.

19. *Vathek,* p. 3.

20. *Vathek,* p. 4.

21. See George Sale, Preliminary Discourse to his edition of the *Koran* (London, 1734) passim, and John Richardson, *Dissertation on the Languages, Literature, and Manners of the Eastern Nations,* 2nd ed. (Oxford, 1778).

22. *Vathek,* p. 22.

23. *Vathek,* p. 22.

24. *Vathek,* p. 36.

25. *Vathek,* p. 22.

26. See the *Persian Tales,* the *Turkish Tales,* and George Sale, ed. *Koran.*

27. *Vathek,* p. 89.

28. Robert Gemmett cites a reference from the unpublished notebooks of John Mitford to the effect that a Beckford story concerned a prince who, "had carnal connection with his sister, in the center of the great Pyramid;" cited by Robert Gemmett, *William Beckford* (Boston: Twayne, 1977) p. 116. However, this is hardly conclusive evidence. The sentence could merely refer to the material we have, imperfectly recollected.

29. *Episodes of Vathek,* p. 4.

30. *Episodes,* p. 7.

31. *Episodes,* p. 13.

32. *Episodes,* p. 30.

33. *Episodes,* p. 38.

34. *Episodes,* p. 38.

35. *Episodes,* pp. 38-39.

36. *Episodes,* p. 39.

37. *Episodes,* p. 39.

38. *Episodes,* p. 39.

39. *Episodes,* p. 44.

40. *Episodes,* p. 114.

41. *Episodes,* p. 116.

42. See also the story of the First Callendar in the *Arabian Nights.*

43. *Episodes,* p. 165.

44. *Episodes,* p. 205.

45. *Episodes,* p. 206.

46. *Episodes,* p. 206.

47. *Episodes,* p. 206.

48. *Episodes,* pp. 206-207.

John Garrett (essay date October 1992)

SOURCE: Garrett, John. "Ending in Infinity: William Beckford's Arabian Tale." *Eighteenth-Century Fiction* 5, no. 1 (October 1992): 15-34.

[*In the following essay, Garrett delineates* Vathek *as a text that considers the nature of the human soul from both Eastern and Western viewpoints.*]

William Beckford's ***Vathek*** (1786), subtitled ***An Arabian Tale,*** displays an imagination and moral vision deeply penetrated by the perfumes of Arabia and the essence of Islam. Beckford's enthusiasm was not merely simple-minded ecstasy in a falsely perceived "Orient" of "sensuality, promise, terror, sublimity, idyllic pleasure, intense energy," like that which was seized upon and utilized, as Edward Said has shown, by his contemporaries.[1] Although Beckford succumbed to the temptation of projecting his fantasies onto an unknown and unknowable "other" world—a fictional Orient—his

"Arabian" tale also offers evidence of a deeper intuition, in particular a sympathy with Islam (or what he took Islam to be) that lifts Beckford and his narrative beyond the bounds of the traditional English (and Christian) tale. Beckford's East is self-evidently grotesque, without any attempt at historical or geographical veracity. Yet under its wild and extravagant surface Beckford was attempting to introduce a new way of conceiving experience which, while not authentically "Eastern," was not conventionally "Western" either.[2]

Vathek was influenced in its characterization, its description, its philosophy, even its structure, by the practices of the East as Beckford understood them; its consequent lack of conventional guideposts and its unsettling ambience have disconcerted and annoyed critics. The *Monthly Review* (May 1787), for example, adopted a tone of paternalistic rebuke, chastising *Vathek* for its failure to keep within the perimeters of eighteenth-century fiction, remarking that the novel "preserves the peculiar character of the Arabian Tale, which is not only to overstep nature and probability, but even to pass beyond the verge of possibility, and suppose things, which cannot be for a moment conceived."[3] A century later Wilbur Cross, though more enthusiastic about the novel, resorts to terms such as "extravagance," "sarcasm," and "love of grotesque horror" to characterize it,[4] while thirty years after that, Edmund Wilson reduced Beckford's deployment of irony to the need "merely to satisfy a perverse impulse."[5] The inadequacy of these readings is the result of Beckford's overlaying of one cultural topography (English, Christian, known) upon another (Arabic, Islamic, unknown) in order to give himself a new arena, a fresh "orientation," for the exploration of the age-old topic of a man's relationship with his soul. This article will attempt to chart the terrain of *Vathek* from the dual perspective of East and West, which is how Beckford himself viewed it.

* * *

In the course of *Vathek*'s examination of the individual's relation with his or her soul the shadow of the Protestant ethic falls across the novel's pages; the final horror of Vathek's and Nouronihar's separation from God is deeper because it has been self-willed and could have been avoided: "Vathek beheld in the eyes of Nouronihar nothing but rage and vengeance; nor could she discern aught in his, but aversion and despair" (p. 119). The intrusion of Christian eschatology into the hall of Eblis—the Islamic hell—raises the question of whether Beckford intended to merge the two religions. As a proto-orientalist he seems to have subscribed to the conventional wisdom about fundamental disparities between East and West. According to Said, the division between East and West was an artificial boundary drawn by Europeans to mark off their fears of the "other" and to project all the features that their culture could not as-

similate onto a fictional "Orient." Having created this alien entity and assigned territorial limits to it, they then attempted, through the machinery of nineteenth-century colonialism, to penetrate and subdue it to their will.[6] Said analyses the pretensions and perniciousness of this practice, showing that, under the guise of an academic discipline (orientalism), racial inferences about the superiority of one "culture" to another are often assumed. Though he was influenced by the orientalism of his day, Beckford does not privilege "West" above "East"; there are discernible differences between Islam and Christianity which Beckford took serious account of in *Vathek,* while also indicating that neither religion had sufficiently accommodated all the energies and aspirations kindled in the human spirit.

Beckford grounded his novel in historical fact, absorbing from Barthélemy d'Herbelot's *Bibliothèque orientale* (1778) the information that "the grandson of Harun al-Raschid and the ninth Caliph of the Abbasides was Vathek Billah, offspring of Motassem and his Greek wife, Carathis."[7] D'Herbelot's account of the ninth Caliph balances merits and defects; Beckford, however, suppressed most of Vathek's virtues, leaving him an unmitigated villain. His hospitality, for example, is prompted "by motives of curiosity" (p. 5), making self-gratification the basis of his liberality. The Vathek of *Vathek* has no historical authenticity, nor was he intended to have any. Beckford created an autocratic character who jettisons the ballast of his traditions and his religion and thrives by the goodwill of his subjects. Into the waking nightmare of his protagonist's wayward existence—adrift from the influences that would normally have constrained and directed a ruler's actions—Beckford introduced elements from the *Arabian Nights.* The extravagance of Vathek's "uncommonly splendid" caravan (p. 38), for example, emulates the train of "tents, camels, mules, servants, and retainers" that accompanies King Shahzaman to Samarkand;[8] while indecipherable messages and consultations of the astrolabe appear in both works. *Vathek* also resembles its oriental model in its black humour, which frequently exploits the physically infirm—such as the "superb corps of cripples" encountered by the Caliph (p. 61)—as butts for its comic shafts. Both works, ignoring poetic justice, heap afflictions on the backs of those already afflicted.

Beckford, however, modified his inherited material, above all insisting on the moral responsibility of his characters for their deeds. In the *Arabian Nights* wealth falls into the lap of the hero with no deleterious side-effects, as is the case with "Ma'aruf the Cobbler," whose ploughshare becomes snagged on a buried slabstone which opens to reveal "a square vault as large as the city baths containing four separate halls,"[9] each filled with precious stones. His wealth can be enjoyed without a guilty conscience. In *Vathek,* however, the chamber of precious gems has more ambivalent overtones.

The glistering gold may not succour the soul, but may seduce it to corruption. Thus the princess Nouronihar, entering the secret grotto, is "filled . . . with fear" and "sink[s], almost lifeless" despite the delightful appearance of the cave's contents—"appendages of royalty, diadems and feathers of the heron, all sparkling with carbuncles" (pp. 70-71). This vision brings in its train a loss of innocence—"Nouronihar was not altogether so content" after this (p. 82)—which has no parallel in the *Nights*. Once an *ingénu,* always an *ingénu,* in the world of the *Arabian Nights,* probably because the characters are seen as puppets in the hands of fate rather than as persons who are at least partially responsible for their own development or degradation. No trace of Protestant guilt intrudes to mar their full enjoyment of their easily gotten gains.

* * *

Despite his insertion of a Protestant conscience into the matter of the *Arabian Nights,* Beckford was more susceptible to Islamic and Arabian influence than has been generally recognized. Most critics assume that his orientalism was a veneer. But Beckford's Eastern interest went deeper than that of his predecessors and contemporaries, such as Addison, Steele, Johnson, and Goldsmith, all of whom made use of the oriental tale for anglocentric purposes. His understanding of the East—partly instructed, but mainly intuitive—affected the formation of his story in vital ways. Beckford availed himself, in particular, of contrasting attitudes to space and time, introducing alien concepts of boundlessness and timelessness to disconcert his European readers.

One of the claims of orientalists is that oriental structures are open-ended and means-directed whereas occidental structures are finite and end-directed.[10] In the orientalist schemata the inhabitant of the East, unlike his or her Western counterpart, is not conceptually bound to see the purposive framework of every undertaking. It would thus be possible to start making something without worrying about how to conclude it. The *Arabian Nights* are ostensibly tallied at a thousand and one, a number which the mind can only grasp approximately and one that will therefore admit the unobtrusive incorporation of new tales within the original framework: the "one" after the "thousand" may indicate that the series could be expanded indefinitely.

Before *Vathek* was published, Beckford had made provision within its narrative structure for an extension to accommodate other stories, in the manner of the *Arabian Nights.* On Vathek's arrival in the hall of Eblis he meets "four young men, of goodly figure, and a lovely female," all equally damned. One of them invites Vathek to "relate the adventures that have brought you to this fatal place; and we, in return, will acquaint you with ours" (p. 116). These additional "adventures" were originally intended to be incorporated within the text of *Vathek.* "I have gone on sinking my princes to Hell with perseverance," wrote Beckford on 21 March 1785; and sixteen months later, "I would not have him [Vathek] on any account come forth without his companions."[11] But Henley's unauthorized publication of *Vathek* two years later effectively put paid to Beckford's plans to include the additional tales, though he continued to work on them sporadically.

Never published in Beckford's lifetime, the additional anecdotes, translated from Beckford's French by Sir Frank T. Marzials, finally appeared as *The Episodes of Vathek* under the supervision of Lewis Melville in 1912. Their contents have been summarized by Brian Fothergill:

> Each story tells how the narrator has found his way to the halls of Eblis and the subsequent loss of his soul, and in them Beckford explores the various less orthodox aspects of human relationships, including his own unfortunate affair with [William] Courtenay. In [one] story on a pederastic theme propriety is saved in the nick of time when it is discovered that the boy prince Firouz has been a girl all the time, though after the discovery she loses no time in getting back into male dress again.[12]

The ludicrousness of such events contrasts with the macabre horror of the fate suspended over the tellers' heads. Could it be that Beckford was aiming at a multivalence of tone and an encyclopaedic content in the all-inclusive tradition of the Arab *adab* (belles lettres)? His wish to dilate the structure of his novel, to interpolate new narratives just prior to the anticipated climax and delay the end indefinitely, as Shahrazad defers her execution in the *Nights,* suggests plot-weaving after the design of the labyrinth, a favoured Arabic motif.

The corridors of the labyrinth—a seemingly endless intertwining of passages whose centre may never be reached—appear to be without issue; consequently they assume as much significance in themselves as does their "goal." Beckford's design for his Fonthill Abbey residence was obviously based on his belief that oriental structures should be labyrinthine and inconclusive. Looking back on his Fonthill home when he was an old man, he recalled:

> The solid Egyptian Hall looked as if hewn out of a living rock. The line of apartments and apparently endless passages extending from it on either side were all vaulted—an interminable staircase, which when you looked down it, appeared as deep as the well in the pyramid—and when you looked up—was lost in vapour . . . [T]he vastness, the intricacy of this vaulted labyrinth occasioned so bewildering an effect that it became almost impossible for any one to define—at the moment—where he stood, where he had been, or to whither he was wandering. . . . No wonder such scenery inspired the description of the Halls of Eblis.[13]

An orthodox Western design, on the other hand, draws all its lines towards its end, all incidentals being commandeered to serve that purpose. There is no time to stand and stare; all energy is bent and directed to the defined aim. On this basis the vision of **Vathek** is bifocal. As much attention is lavished on the incidental, seemingly irrelevant occurrences of Vathek's expedition as on the end-product of that journey. At certain moments—Vathek's desecration of the sacred "besom" of Mecca (pp. 39-41), the caravan's devastation by "wolves and tigers" (pp. 46-48), Bababalouk's discomfiture in Nouronihar's bath (pp. 58-59), Carathis's ghoulish "supper" of "fresh corpses" (p. 92)—the aim of the journey is entirely lost sight of as the characters devote all their energy and gusto to the task in hand, a task often utterly unconnected to their ultimate goal. At other times Vathek and his mother adopt an inherently teleological attitude, holding an end clearly in view as a justification for all the means used to attain it. Carathis, contemplating human sacrifice to ingratiate herself with the Giaour, affirms "No crimes should be thought too dear for such a reward" (p. 29); and Vathek slaughters with his own hand fifty of "the most beautiful sons" (p. 23) of his chief subjects in order to obtain the golden key to the Palace of Subterranean Fire and "the treasures of Soliman" (p. 46).

The tales-within-a-tale structure of the *Arabian Nights* indicates—as Jerrold Hogle has shown in relationship to Maturin's *Melmoth the Wanderer* (1820)—the lack of a centre; an endless circular pursuit of a meaning that has long since disappeared leaving barely a trace behind. Similarly, the sought-after talismans only reveal "means to other means." No end is in sight. "A desire spawned by crypts and pursued across crypts turns out to be a desire only for more desire."[14] Hogle's point is that Vathek's endeavour to decipher the hieroglyphics of the sabres is a futile attempt to unveil the past and discover a lost meaning. Frustration inevitably follows when an attempt is made to negotiate the labyrinth bearing only its "end" in mind. But in terms of Islamic architecture the very circuitousness of the route, the convolutions of its arabesque curves, may constitute its meaning, by suggesting the infinite magnitude of the unrepresentable God. It is tempting to describe **Vathek** as tinted by Beckford's vision of the East and Islam in its incidentals while adhering to the West and Christianity in its structural plan. But Beckford's interweaving of the two worlds cannot be so simply unravelled.

* * *

Beckford was sensitive to the implications of Islamic architectural design. Above the hall of Eblis are "the vast ruins of Istakhar" which include "gloomy watchtowers, whose number could not be counted . . . covered by no roof" (pp. 106-7); an indication that, though Vathek's earthly quest may now be ended, his spiritual

journey, for which no end is in sight, is just beginning. Every chamber within the "immense" structure of the subterranean palace discloses itself as "without bounds or limit" (pp. 114-15). The sheer monotony of his architectural surroundings reinforces Vathek's awareness of the perpetuity of his punishment. For the Muslim, whose thoughts, directed towards Mecca, go beyond the confines of his place of worship, the horizontality of the mosque's architecture is an aid rather than an obstacle to spiritualization.[15]

The style of the early mosques was open-ended, in order that the edifices could be expanded or contracted in response to demographic changes: "Early Islamic architects did not conceive of the mosque as a complete and enclosed unit like the medieval cathedral; they believed that the mosque should have the potential to be made larger or smaller in the event of changes in a city's population."[16] The mosque, unlike the cathedral, was not intended to be optically absorbed all at once. The vertical spaces contained within the soaring vaults of the Gothic cathedrals were meant to create a sublime effect, a meeting of the earthly and the spiritual for a limited time in a clearly defined area; the horizontal unfolding of the rows of colonnades in the early mosques suggested, on the other hand, timelessness and spaciousness. In the mosque of Cordova, as Titus Burckhardt says, "the limits of space play no role at all; the walls of the prayer-hall disappear beyond a forest of arcades. Their sheer repetition . . . gives an impression of endless extension." Because of the basically open-ended design of the Cordova mosque, it was possible for it to be "steadily enlarged over three centuries without its architectural scheme being altered." Since he was not concerned with expressing a complete belief-system from beginning to end in one simultaneous sweep of apprehension, the mosque-builder was unperturbed if the gaze of the beholder of his work lost itself in "a forest of arcades." Thus "The Arab architect is not afraid of monotony; he will build pillar upon pillar and arcade upon arcade."[17]

For Vathek, whose life has been spent seeking advantage in this world rather than blessing in the next and who has turned his back on Mecca to complete an earthly pilgrimage in the contrary direction, the horizontal perspectives of Eblis's hall, so infinite that he at first thinks himself on "an immeasurable plain," are a constant reprimand. By his wilful disregard of the vertical axis to the Prophet in his "seventh heaven" he has doomed himself to an eternity of pointless wandering, excluded from the sight of God (pp. 109, 3-4).

Vathek's horizontal perspective shows that he shares the Western proclivity for putting bounds around everything, even the unknown. Arab geographers were not hampered by the need to delimit and define *terra incognita*. Al-Idrisi's *Book of Roger* (1154) had as its full title *The Delight of Him Who Desires to Traverse the Horizons*. Arab geography seems to have been eclectic, not driven by a desire to present the whole picture:

> The final synthesis which would have summed up all the geographical work which had been done in Arabic [by twelfth and thirteenth-century geographers, particularly, Al-Idrisi] was never made. . . . [Their] geographical works . . . are extremely useful and meritorious, but remain compilations, made by men of encyclopaedic knowedge indeed, but whose interests were diversified.[18]

That Vathek is a Western rather than an oriental geographer is evident from the mineralogical display in his palace of the senses: "Rarities, collected from every corner of the earth were there found in such profusion as to dazzle and confound, but for the order in which they were arranged" (p. 2). Vathek has classified the earth and its contents and shrunk it to the dimensions of a museum exhibit. Once he begins his expedition, however, the inadequacy of such a reductive approach soon becomes apparent:

> His geographers were ordered to attend him; but, the weather proved so terrible that these poor people exhibited a lamentable appearance: and their maps of the different countries spoiled by the rain, were in a still worse plight than themselves . . . [E]very one was ignorant which way to turn; and Vathek, though well versed in the course of the heavens, no longer knew his situation on earth.

(pp. 44-45)

Vathek's carefully charted course loses its way and its momentum. He has to fall back on the unlettered "guidance of a peasant" to take him across the mountains (p. 45). The remainder of his journey is full of wrong turnings and misadventures, which reveal the hubris and insufficiency of Vathek's approach and show how misguided he is spiritually as well as geographically. He has to be rescued from a desert of "black sand" and "perpendicular crags" by a search party dispatched by the Emir Fakreddin (p. 50); and when he finally arrives at what he believes to be the centre of the earth, Eblis's Palace of Subterranean Fire, he finds only an infertile fount, an invisible cataract. He has been following the wrong charts: terrestrial, deductive, and finite rather than celestial, inductive, and infinite. The occidental approach to geography, inculcated by his Greek mother, is exposed in all its secular shortcoming: "the principles by which Carathis perverted my youth, have been the sole cause of my perdition!" (p. 115).

Vathek, like Marlowe's Dr Faustus, has forsworn his religion for knowledge immortal: "instigated by insatiable curiosity" he "abjure[s]" the Prophet Mohammed (p. 22). Like Faustus, too, he plays practical jokes on devout men, dispatching the mullahs and imams of Schiraz seated backwards on their mules (p. 102). The parallels

with Marlowe's work continue. Nouronihar first appears to Vathek like the spirit of Helen to Faustus, arousing in him the desire for illicit intercourse: "Contrive . . . that I may respire her sweet breath as she bounds panting along these delightful wilds!" (p. 63, cf. Faustus's "Her lips suck forth my soul").[19] Vathek, like Faustus, is exhorted to repent when on the brink of damnation by a figure embodying honest simplicity. The Old Man who tells Faustus to "leave this damned art" (5.1.35) becomes in Beckford a "beneficent Geni[us], assuming . . . the exterior of a shepherd" (p. 103) who admonishes Vathek and advises him to "abandon thy atrocious purpose" (p. 105). In neither work is the warning heeded.

Like Faustus, who aspires to "wall all Germany with brass" (1.1.87), Vathek sins by attempting to put bounds on the boundless, to inscribe a circle round the infinite, to impose Western thought-patterns on Eastern beliefs. Vathek's Hellenistic propensity for rationalization is inherited from his mother Carathis, who "had induced him, being a Greek herself, to adopt the sciences and systems of her country which all good Mussulmans hold in such thorough abhorrence" (p. 8). Through the study of "metaphysics" Faustus hopes to achieve a "dominion" that "Stretcheth as far as doth the mind of man" (1.1.48-60). Vathek wishes "to know every thing; even sciences that did not exist" (p. 3). Hence his frustration when the shifting hieroglyphics on the sabres confront him with something sinuous and ungraspable: an Eastern adumbration that eludes the compartmentalizing impulse of the semi-Western mind. Faustus is similarly balked when he asks Mephostophilis to "reason of divine astrology" and receives no answer that his reductive rationalizing mind can batten on (2.2.34).

* * *

On the face of it, then, *Vathek*'s plot seems strictly in the tradition of Western Christianity. Within the timeless frame of the Arabian setting a highly time-conscious drama—that of Faust—is re-enacted. Where Faustus and Vathek differ most noticeably is in their endings. There is a conclusiveness in the epilogue to Faustus's life ("Cut is the branch . . . Faustus is gone") already foreshadowed earlier in the play by the hero's ironic echoing of Christ's dying words, "*Consummatum est*." All passion spent, his "mangled limbs" are given "due burial" (2.1.74; 5.3.17). Vathek, on the contrary, ends in endlessness, passing directly to "an eternity of unabating anguish" (p. 120) without the transitional stage of death. *Dr Faustus* ends cathartically with the sense that the scholar's career has terminated, violently and definitively. *Vathek* ends with the feeling that the Caliph's lifespan has only just begun. After the interposition of the shepherd-genius, the frivolity of tone that has endured for most of the novel quickly changes into a final sombreness: a contrast that dramatizes the folly of regarding the ephemeral material world as if it possessed the permanence of the spiritual.[20]

It seems, therefore, that, whereas *Dr Faustus* is the typically end-orientated product of Western culture, *Vathek* refuses closure and, by ending in infinity, bears an indelibly Eastern imprint in both its overall organization and its internal parts: it is an early specimen of orientalism.[21] Even without the additional episodes, *Vathek* opens out at the end, resisting the closure common to other works of Western literature. Kindred Gothic novels are no exception to the preference for climactic and finite conclusions. The prototype, Walpole's *Castle of Otranto* (1764), winds up the skeins of its characters' existences and stows them in boxes labelled "death," "marriage," or "convent"; Ann Radcliffe's novels conclude with the mysteries all explained to the satisfaction of the enlightened heroine; the protagonist of Lewis's *The Monk* (1796) meets a Faust-like end, his body smashed beyond the possibility of reconstitution.

The inmates of the hall of Eblis find no such ends. Vathek and his comrades are left with their faculties intact and an infinitude of self-conscious suffering—mental, physical, and spiritual—before them: "All severally plunged themselves into the accursed multitude, there to wander in an eternity of unabating anguish" (pp. 119-20). There is no release from tension, no respite, no finality.

* * *

Other aspects of endlessness, both spatial and temporal, are interwoven into the text of *Vathek.* Repetition to a degree that may appear relentless to Western eyes and ears seems much more acceptable within Islamic culture. Regular observation of the five daily calls to prayer is enjoined on all Muslims, and in the prayer-call itself "each clause is repeated at least once."[22] Beckford shared the orientalist perception of the Islamic tolerance, even nurture, of repetition, but he makes his semi-Westernized caliph impatient of it. Vathek's chief eunuch, Bababalouk, hears the Emir Fakreddin's dwarfs "reading over the Koran" for the "nine hundred and ninety-ninth time in their lives" (p. 56), an exercise which could evidently be continued indefinitely. When they begin "to repeat the Bismillah" to Vathek in person he soon tires of their "officious" practice and, "unable any longer to refrain, exclaimed: 'For the love of Mahomet, my dear Fakreddin, have done! let us proceed to your valley, and enjoy the fruits that Heaven hath vouchsafed you'" (pp. 53-54).

Extravagance, whether in the indulgence of personal appetites or in the hospitality offered to others, is another concept where the differences of Western and Oriental values might disconcert Beckford's readers. Hyperbole suggests boundlessness, infinite. Vathek exhibits an excessive hunger and thirst: "So insatiable was the thirst which tormented him, that his mouth, like a funnel, was always open to receive the various liquors that might be poured into it" (p. 12). He entertains the Giaour with a sitting of thirty-two meals (p. 16). This open-endedness is applicable, however, only to Vathek's physical appetite: his sensual voracity is not repeated in a hunger for anything spiritual. He aspires with his body but not with his soul, so that although the tower he has built surpasses, with exaggerated and dizzying loftiness, the height of the earth's sublimest creations, it is still aimed at horizontal rather than vertical goals: those of this world not the next. Consequently, standing on the pinnacle of his edifice and looking uncharacteristically upwards for a moment, Vathek "saw the stars as high above him as they appeared when he stood on the surface of the earth" (p. 4).

Extravagance may also be found in the way that language is used. Formal greetings in *Vathek* tend to be profuse and prolonged, but one nation's prolixity may be another's politeness. The Arabic sentence, elastic enough to be elongated to a length that would be considered unwieldy in a Western language, is arguably expansive, not only syntactically but semantically, in its invitation to a myriad meanings. "One of the great hallmarks of Islamic culture is its rich and vastly ingenious interpretative energy. . . . Few civilizations have encouraged the arts of verbal interpretation on so wide a scale as Islam."[23] In *Vathek* words refuse to be reduced to single meanings, and Beckford may have been attempting to focus on the function of words, even common ones, as "talismans" to a recasting and revaluing of experience. The unceasing alteration of the characters inscribed at the entrance to the subterranean palace—"characters . . . which possessed the . . . virtue of changing every moment" (p. 107)—reflects the endless "interpretative energy" with which Muslim Arabs approach their written texts: an energy which proceeds from the understanding that, since God contains all, mankind's interpretations unfold in an unlimited labyrinth, and the individual will be just as far from the centre when the enterprise exhausts itself as he or she was on first setting out.

* * *

The final and perhaps most disquieting point of difference between East and West on which Beckford focuses is that of religious belief. Vathek is denied the comfort of a deity whom he can visualize and whose word he can interpret. The kaleidoscopic calligraphy of the sabres conveys a multitude of messages, none of which can be deciphered. It indicates the magnitude of God ("Allah the Mighty, the Praised One; the Sovereign of the heavens and the earth, the Witness of all things"),[24] a multivalency for which there is no simple verbal equivalent. Since Vathek has renounced the faith of which he is the guardian, it is not surprising that the point of the protean characters—visible but ineffable—escapes him. Vathek, obsessed by the Western need to rationalize, insists on a reading that the mind can apprehend. When none is forthcoming, the Caliph's delicate occidentalized mental balance is thrown into disequilibrium, whereupon "the rage of Vathek exceeded all bounds . . . His courtiers and vizirs . . . all united in one vociferation—'The Caliph is gone mad! the Caliph is out of his senses!'" (p. 7).

From the start this episode gives notice of the hopelessness of Vathek's quest for a meaning behind existence. Life's phenomena may offer a glimmer of light to the person who allows for the intangibility of spiritual substance, but they will remain opaque to the one of merely mundane sensibility. Once it dawns on Vathek and Nouronihar that nothing of mental or material value will be yielded to them from their sacrilegious excavations into mankind's physical origin—the "pre-adamite kings" who "lay recumbent" in "funereal gloom" in Eblis's palace (p. 112)—their surging advance is abruptly halted. When Soliman Ben Daoud, keeper of "the talismans that control the world" (p. 22), breaks out of his lethargy sufficiently to address Vathek and his consort, it is not in language which they are willing to hear. They are thence reduced to "wandering" in "apathy," "faltering from this fatal hall; indifferent which way they turned their steps" (pp. 114-15).

Up to this point the Caliph has been described variously as "majestic" (p. 1), "unhappy" (p. 14), "agitated" (p. 64), or "furious" (p. 74), but seldom referred to in disparaging terms. The ambivalence of the narrator's viewpoint intimated by the moral neutrality of his diction is, however, ultimately counteracted by the conventional didacticism of his narrative. Until now the persistence of moral neutrality or even of ambiguity has ensured that the normative intent of the didacticism has been uncertain. Rhetoric did not synchronize with doctrine. But once Vathek nears his final goal the ambiguity of the diction vanishes and the moral purpose becomes clear. At last the narrator's language meshes with his avowed evangelism. "Infatuated mortals! they thus indulged delusive conjecture, unable to fathom the decrees of the Most High!" (p. 103). At the same time the phrase "the Most High" elides the concepts of Allah and the Christian God into the same deity, at the point in the story where Beckford's voice is quite unambiguous. Vathek's contempt for conventional religion is, it now appears plain, not shared by the author's orthodox if undemonstrative Christianity. The novel thus attacks the abuse of religion—particularly what Beckford assumes to be the privileges of the Caliphate and the power accorded the Caliph as Mohammed's "vicegerent" (p. 103)—but not Islam itself, which is shown to encourage the same discipline and devotion as an ideal Christianity and to promote the same purity of heart.

Although Beckford appears at times to blend the two religions, other developments in his story discriminate between them, and it is the Islamic viewpoint that is generally preferred, noticeably in two particulars: the transition from life to death, and the nature of the post-mortal state.

Vathek goes straight to eternal torment without passing through the transitional stage of death, exemplifying the Islamic view that death is a natural event which liberates the spirit from its cadaverous prison. Thus death is not to be feared, being only a kind of journey taking the soul back to God: "Every soul shall taste death, and in the end you shall return to Us."[25] Islam implies a continuity, a natural train of events from birth through life to death followed by eternal life or damnation: "In the life to come a woeful punishment awaits you—or the forgiveness of Allah and His pleasure."[26] The interim between life here and life hereafter is represented by a partition separating the mortal from the immortal condition ("Behind them there shall stand a barrier till the Day of Resurrection"),[27] an interval which in the timeless world of postmortality would be of no duration. At the moment of his translation to the underworld Vathek is confronted by "a vast portal of ebony" which "at once flew open" (pp. 108-9), enabling him to traverse the frontier without a death. *Vathek* displays a predilection for the image of the partition—or *barzakh*—that Ernest Giddey refers to as "gates or portals separating life from eternity, hope from despair and terrestrial light from the fiery darkness of the underworld."[28] This image, with its suggestion of easy passage, is more in sympathy with the Islamic than the Christian attitude to death.

Western thought stresses death as a critical moment, an unnatural punishment for Adam's unnatural sin, interrupting the flow of the individual career ("O Death, thou comest when I had thee least in mind!"),[29] and hence to be deferred at all costs, even by "good" people who might be surer than most of their spiritual salvation. As St Augustine made clear, death is an ordeal that not even the saints can bypass: "This violent sundering of the two elements [soul and body] . . . is without doubt the penalty of all who are born."[30] Christian art and architecture are gathered around the cross or crypt of death, given meaning by Christ's resurrection from the sepulchre into eternal life. Islam, with its guiding tenet that God is in all things, can be more artistically and architecturally diffuse, since God is present not especially in one part but in all corners, however intricate the structure. The absence of the Crucifixion, with the immense symbolic weight of its climax in death, has relieved Islam of the need to focus on death as the end—in both senses—of life.

A profile of postmortal existence is outlined quite graphically in *Vathek*. Here Beckford is again closer to Islam than to Christianity. His vision of paradise is less ethereal and more sensuous than that of most Western eschatologists. Gulchenrouz, who crosses the frontier of death without pain, effort, or even volition, finds himself in a realm of perpetual childhood where many of the comforts are unambiguously physical: "his little friends . . . were all assembled . . . and vied with each other in kissing his serene forehead and beautiful eyelids" (p. 97). This is more akin to the paradise of the Koran, whose denizens "shall be attended by boys graced with eternal youth, who to the beholder's eyes will seem like sprinkled pearls,"[31] than to the more vaguely envisioned afterworld of the Bible.

Moreover, the hell to which Vathek goes resembles the region of the damned depicted in the Koran in clearer and more vivid detail than its counterpart in the Bible. One Koranic reference to the inferno—"They shall wander between fire and water fiercely seething"[32]—is an exact parallel to Vathek's ultimate state in the halls of Eblis, where he and his companions wander between life and death, their hearts burning everlastingly in "unrelenting fire" (p. 114). Though suffering ceaseless pain and contrition, their tears are unable to flow; the perpetual "roar of a cataract visible in part through one of the grated portals" (p. 112) suggests the tantalizing prospect of relief to the doomed reprobate of the Koranic hell, who "will sip, but scarcely swallow." Surah 70 describes in vivid physiognomic detail the self-torment of those who know they are damned: "they shall rush from their graves, like men rallying to a standard, with downcast eyes and countenances distorted with shame."[33] This passage is echoed on Vathek's first arrival in Eblis's kingdom, when he remarks the despondency of his fellow inmates: "They all avoided each other . . . [E]ach wandered at random, unheedful of the rest" (p. 110).

* * *

By his blending of Christian abstraction and Muslim concreteness, particularly in the depiction of the eternal state, Beckford created a novel perspective on the human condition that has continued to disturb his critics, disorientated by his bizarre and apparently random mixture of tones. It may be argued, however, that *Vathek* expands the frontiers of conventional Christian ethics by its imposition of an "oriental" vision on a typically individualistic Western quest. Beckford was not a mere eccentric dabbler in fiction but an innovator who enlarged the boundaries of the novel by "applying the perspectives of the grotesque to it."[34] Walter Allen remarked that this grotesque effect was produced by Beckford's practice of placing before a noun an apparently inappropriate adjective (as in "a *superb* corps of cripples," for example), thereby "disconcerting" the reader's "view of life."[35] Beckford's mixing of Western teleology with "Eastern" open-endedness creates a similar irresolvable discord. A new insight into humanity is displayed and a

judgment of pitiless detachment is made upon it. Moral criteria that diverge from the norm seem to be implied, whereby the naïve self-abnegation of Vathek's adoring subjects emerges as equally culpable with the Caliph's insatiable appetite for self-aggrandizement. The myopic floundering of all characters, good and bad, diminishes them to the stature of dwarfs, as far beneath the stars as Vathek remains after the completion of his skyscraping tower. Beckford thus promulgates a vision of the immense distance between God and his creatures that is Islamic rather than Christian.

Vathek, through the voice of its sardonic narrator, establishes a sense of the futility of all of the Caliph's egregious rebellions against an impersonal and inexorable divine order. The novel expands outwards towards an interminable conclusion: Vathek "became a prey to grief without end," while Gulchenrouz "passed whole ages in undisturbed tranquillity" (p. 120). It has moved effortlessly from a temporal to an eternal sphere of action in a manner both un-Western and un-Christian. By its answering of occidental expectations with "oriental" realizations, *Vathek* succeeds in destabilizing the mental edifices of its readers. Its open-endedness illuminates the limitations of Christian moral constructs, presenting a derisive and desentimentalized vision of human beings—the good are gullible, the wicked monstrous—in the voice of its ironic observer: a tone which echoes that of the Koran in its devaluation of all enterprise that deems itself autonomous ("We moulded man into a most noble image and in the end We shall reduce him to the lowest of the low: except the believers who do good works, for theirs shall be a boundless recompense").[36]

Vathek's journey could be seen not only as an anti-Pilgrim's Progress but also, given the pervasiveness of the East and Islam in the novel, an anti-hegira. The modern Muslim philosopher Ali Shariati has "universalised Mohammed's migration (*hegira*) from Mecca to Medina into the idea of man as 'a choice, a struggle, a constant becoming. He is an infinite migration, a migration within himself, from clay to God; he is a migrant within his own soul.'"[37] Vathek's pilgrimage is in a direction contrary to the true hadj. Descending from his tower to the subterranean palace of Eblis, he journeys from spirit to clay, going literally to the devil and abiding with him for eternity.

Notes

1. Edward Said, *Orientalism* (London: Routledge and Kegan Paul, 1978), pp. 118, 5.

2. The terms "East" and "West" refer, in this article, to a discrimination in Beckford's *Weltanschauung* rather than to any objectively demonstrable bifurcation.

3. Quoted by Roger Lonsdale in his Introduction to William Beckford, *Vathek* (London: Oxford University Press, 1983). References are to this edition.

4. Wilbur L. Cross, *The Development of the English Novel* (London: Macmillan, 1906), p. 103.

5. Edmund Wilson, *The Shores of Light: A Literary Chronicle of the Twenties and Thirties* (London: Allen, 1952), p. 266.

6. *Orientalism,* pp. 39-40, 45-49, 227-30, and *passim.*

7. Kenneth W. Graham, "Beckford's Adaptation of the Oriental Tale in *Vathek,*" *Enlightenment Essays* 5 (1974), 24-25.

8. *Tales from the Thousand and One Nights,* trans. N. J. Dawood, (Harmondsworth: Penguin, 1973), p. 15.

9. *Nights,* p. 393.

10. For instance, see Katharine Slater Gittes, "The *Canterbury Tales* and the Arabic Frame Tradition," *PMLA* 98 (1983), 241-44.

11. See Kenneth W. Graham, "Beckford's Design for *The Episodes*: A History and a Review," *Papers of the Bibliographical Society of America* 71 (1971), 337.

12. Brian Fothergill, "William Beckford, Prince of Amateurs," *Essays by Divers Hands* 38 (1975), 44.

13. Quoted in *Vathek; with the Episodes of Vathek,* ed. Guy Chapman (Cambridge: Constable and Houghton Mifflin, 1929), 2 vols, 1:xiii-xiv. Chapman notes that this "account is a note to a letter to Louisa [Beckford, wife of Beckford's cousin Peter] in Beckford's hand, and made in 1839" (1:xiv, n.). A slightly modified version appears in Chapman's 1937 biography of Beckford, "taken," says the author, "from the original draft written by Beckford on the fly-leaves of a copy of Waagen's *Works of Art and Artists in England* which is now in my possession." *Beckford* (London: Cape, 1937), p. 106 n.

14. Jerrold E. Hogle, "The Restless Labyrinth: Cryptonymy in the Gothic Novel," *Arizona Quarterly* 36 (1980), 351, 350.

15. See Titus Burckhardt, *Art of Islam: Language and Meaning* (London: World of Islam Publishing, 1976), "Every place on earth is directly attached to the Meccan centre" (p. 5).

16. Gittes, 243.

17. Burckhardt, pp. 127, 45.

18. D. M. Dunlop, *Arab Civilization to A.D. 1500* (London: Longman, 1971), p. 171.

19. Christopher Marlowe, *Doctor Faustus,* ed. Roma Gill (London: Ernest Benn, 1965), 5.1.99. References are to this edition, which, like most modern reprints, follows the B-text of the play.

20. Kenneth W. Graham discusses the tonal structure of the novel and the importance of the shepherd-genius episode as a transition point ("*Vathek* in English and French," *Studies in Bibliography: Papers of the Bibliographical Society of America* 28 [1975], 163).

21. Beckford himself made use of the term when writing to Henley before *Vathek*'s publication: "I doubt not [the English text with Henley's annotations] will be received with the honors due to so valuable a morsel of *orientalism*" (*Vathek,* p. xvi).

22. Alfred Guillaume, *Islam* (Harmondsworth: Penguin, 1979), p. 66.

23. Edward Said, *Covering Islam: How the Media and the Experts Determine How We See the Rest of the World* (London: Routledge and Kegan Paul, 1981), pp. 62-63.

24. The Koran, trans. N. J. Dawood (Harmondsworth: Penguin, 1974), "The Constellations" (85.8-9). References are to this edition.

25. The Koran, "The Spider" (29.57).

26. The Koran, "Iron" (57.20).

27. The Koran, "The Believers" (23.100).

28. Ernest Giddey, "Byron and Beckford," *Byron Journal* 6 (1978), 47.

29. *Everyman,* line 119. See *Everyman and Medieval Miracle Plays,* ed. A. C. Cawley (London: Dent, 1977), p. 220.

30. Augustine, *Concerning the City of God against the Pagans,* trans. Henry Bettenson (Harmondsworth: Penguin, 1972), p. 515.

31. The Koran, "Man" (76.15).

32. The Koran, "The Merciful" (55.43).

33. The Koran, "Abraham" (14.17); "The Ladders" (70.43-44).

34. Kenneth W. Graham, "Implications of the Grotesque: Beckford's *Vathek* and the Boundaries of Fictional Reality," *Tennessee Studies in Literature* 23 (1978), 61.

35. Walter Allen, *The English Novel: A Short Critical History* (Harmondsworth: Penguin, 1970), p. 91.

36. The Koran, "The Fig" (95.5-6).

37. Said, *Covering,* p. 63.

Adam Potkay (essay date summer 1993)

SOURCE: Potkay, Adam. "Beckford's Heaven of Boys." *Raritan* 13, no. 1 (summer 1993): 73-86.

[*In the following essay, Potkay studies Beckford's vision of a paradise inhabited solely by adolescent males in* Vathek, *noting how this informed the works of Lord Byron.*]

Lord Bryon's amour with Caroline Lamb has afforded biographers any number of spicy anecdotes, though none perhaps as rich as this:

> One day [in the wake of their affair] she entered his apartment at the Albany, and finding him out, picked up Beckford's **Vathek** from the table and wrote on the first page: "Remember me!" When Byron saw what she had done, in the irritation of the moment he wrote under those words:

> Remember thee! remember thee!
> Till Lethe quench life's burning stream
> Remorse and shame shall cling to thee,
> And haunt thee like a feverish dream!

Leslie Marchand's *Byron: A Portrait* offers this story without remark, a silence that suggests reticence. Louis Crompton, however, observes what's obvious to anyone familiar with William Beckford: the novel in which Caroline Lamb left her *memento amori* was written by a gentleman who, thirty years earlier, had fled England to avoid being prosecuted for pederasty. Since Caroline knew of Byron's own youthful exploits with younger boys, her choice of **Vathek** is certainly intended to point a moral and probably meant to suggest the threat of exposure. But the choice of **Vathek** establishes more than just an ominous parallel between its author's life and Byron's own. With exquisite irony (and not without a deeper pathos), Caroline writes "Remember me!" on the first page of a novel that ends by furiously damning the memory of women and presenting as its ideal a paradise without them, happier far.

However, the irony is apparently lost on Byron. While irony demands distance, Byron's retort suggests that **Vathek** is a tale he is quite uncritically living. The stanza he writes under Caroline's line simply reproduces Vathek's own sentiment at the novel's end. Trapped in the hellish "palace of Eblis," Vathek damns his mother, a woman named Carathis, for his fate: she is, he says, "the sole cause of my perdition," an "execrable woman!" (Vathek merely realizes here what the narrator has known all along, for Carathis is earlier introduced to the reader as being "as wicked as woman could be; which is not saying a little.") As the "remorse" of Byron's stanza "clings" ambiguously to his bitter memory of Caroline and to Caroline's own conscience, so Vathek makes the offending woman share in the pain he feels, summoning his mother to join him in the hell she has putatively made for him.

Vathek relies, in part, on the all-too-familiar logic that when someone must take the blame, *cherchez la femme*. The novel condemns women for inciting men to aspire: Vathek is initially goaded by Carathis to abandon his childlike indolence and go in quest of the treasures of the preadamite sultans in the halls of Eblis; he is later egged on by Nouronihar, a princess he acquires along the way, for whom the promised carbuncle of Giamschid is a sufficient lure away from her sportive playmate, the adolescent boy Gulchenrouz. Carathis and Nouronihar are largely held accountable for "that restless ambition," to quote the novel's penultimate paragraph, "which, aiming at discoveries reserved for beings of a supernatural order, perceives not, through its infatuated pride, that the condition of man upon earth is to be—humble and ignorant." Where ignorance is devoutly to be wished, *all* knowledge becomes forbidden knowledge. The novel concludes, "Thus the Caliph Vathek, for the sake of empty pomp and forbidden power, had sullied himself with a thousand crimes, became a prey to grief without end, and remorse without mitigation: whilst the humble, the despised Gulchenrouz passed whole ages in undisturbed tranquillity, and in the pure happiness of childhood."

As this last sentence makes clear, the moral of **Vathek** is finally neither Faustian lesson nor simple misogynist topos. It involves the more surprising notion that growing up at all—acquiring any kind of knowledge—is inherently damning. Happiness is childhood, or, more specifically, early adolescence, for while Gulchenrouz "has passed his thirteenth year," one suspects he's just barely done so. Gulchenrouz's blessing is never to pass another year, but rather to remain perpetually adolescent, "in nests still higher than the clouds," along with the fifty "handsomest boys" of Persia. Vathek's intention was to have sacrificed these boys to the Giaour, a messenger of Eblis—just as it was Carathis's plan to offer up the "palpitating heart" of Gulchenrouz—but all alike are saved by a deus ex machina, "a good old genius, whose fondness for the company of children, had made it his sole occupation to protect them." Gulchenrouz's entry into the paradise of boys is the novel's one picture of salvation:

> He admitted without fear the congratulations of his little friends, who were all assembled in the nest of the venerable genius, and vied with each other in kissing his serene forehead and beautiful eye-lids.—Remote from the inquietudes of the world; the impertinence of harems, the brutality of eunuchs, and the inconstancy of women; there he found a place truly congenial to the delights of his soul. In this peaceable society his days, months, and years glided on; nor was he less happy than the rest of his companions: for the genius, instead of burthening his pupils with perishable riches, and vain sciences, conferred upon them the boon of perpetual childhood.

Male reciprocity, unlimited mutuality, the communion of kind: these are the attributes of a paradise in which boys placidly reflect one another for all eternity.

And this is the book that Byron kept on his table, referred to in print as a "sublime tale," and reportedly called in conversation "his gospel." His admiration for **Vathek** was early conceived, and long sustained. Beyond any personal sympathy he may have felt for Beckford—whom he dubbed, with dubious tone, "the great Apostle of Paederasty" and "the Martyr of Prejudice"—Byron was first and foremost fascinated with Beckford's novel, which he most fully addressed in a manuscript stanza from *Childe Harold*:

> Unhappy Vathek! in an evil hour
> Gainst Nature's voice seduced to deed accurst,
> Once Fortune's minion, now thou feel'st her Power!
> Wrath's vials on thy lofty head have burst.
> In wit, in genius, as in wealth the first,
> How wondrous bright thy blooming morn arose!
> But thou wert smitted with unhallowed thirst
> Of nameless crime, and thy sad day must close
> To scorn, and solitude unsought—the worst of woes.

As the scandal of Beckford's life has always been better known than the plot of his novel, it seems natural, upon first glancing at Byron's lines, to read "Vathek" as an alias for "Beckford," and the "nameless crime" as a taste for boys. But "Vathek" can be read as more than a mere alias. Indeed, Byron's stanza provides a perfectly lucid commentary on the Caliph's "unhallowed thirst" for untold power and knowledge—a crime always incited, apparently, by mothers and brides. Taken as a reading of the novel, Byron's lines express a marked sympathy with its will to recoil from curious knowledge, from experience itself, and, implicitly, from women. We can well imagine that Byron felt the allure of Beckford's paradise of boys; certainly, this is what Caroline Lamb seems to have imagined. Her "Remember me," whether as plea or threat, warns Byron against denying their liaison, which she might consider a rite of passage, and investing in a puerile fable bound to sour into mere impossibility. Oblivious to admonition, Byron merely conjures his favorite image of the Lethean waters that will wash away all memory of experience, and so allow him to become pristine and inviolable, a boy again.

Of course, as publication history amply attests, Byron's call for Lethe struck a responsive chord in a sizable readership. For all his Childe's talk of alienation, Byron knew that he himself was no island, and he is, perhaps, never less alone than in his puerile longings. The fantasy of being a boy among boys is neither a peculiarity of Byron's biography and Beckford's **Vathek,** nor is it solely an episode in the history of what will come to be called homosexuality. It's a far more pervasive fantasy, and the fact that it is now a thoroughly familiar one— which we are apt to call the "Peter Pan syndrome," and which we have most recently seen glamorized in *Brideshead Revisited's* Sebastian Flyte and his teddy bear— should not should not obsure the fact of its being, at least in literature, an eighteenth-century *invention.*

The desire to be a boy among boys is an utterly novel aspect of the Age of Enlightenment, and one that must be properly distinguished from the pedigreed desire to be a man enjoying boys. Byron's famous stanzas on Don Juan's education show a full awareness of what "Greek Love" entailed, and in a Latin text probably familiar to Byron (if not Juan), Suetonius details Tiberius's entertainments at Capri, which included "training little boys, whom he called his 'minnows,' to chase him while he went swimming and get between his legs to lick and nibble him." Yet for Tiberius, surrounding oneself with boys is altogether opposed to identifying with them. Similarly, paradise contains beautiful boys in the Koran, and pederasty figures more generally in both the Islamic literature and the oriental tales available to Beckford and Byron. In all these cases, however, boys exist for the pleasure of men.

Literature before the eighteenth century doubtless affords examples of boys or young men loath to grow up; that the fair young man of Shakespeare's sonnets should so insistently be told to marry and reproduce indeed implies a certain unwillingness to do so. But the poet of the sonnets doesn't wish that the young man could remain young forever or gravely lament the fact that he cannot. The first poet to do so unequivocally would appear to be Thomas Gray, in "An Ode on a Distant Prospect of Eton College." With Polixenes of *The Winter's Tale*—but without a Hermione to rebuff him maturely— the poet of the Eton Ode longs "to be a boy eternal" alongside other "pretty lordlings," far from the "temptations [that] have since been born to 's."

Gray's poem charts the distance between "a sprightly Race" of schoolboys, blessedly free from self-consciousness or any type of care, and the speaker's own unhappy consciousness of "Misfortune," "the fury Passions," and everything else that distinguishes "Men." Following Gray, poets very often cast longing backward glances at a lost paradise of humble and ignorant boyhood; Byron's *Hours of Idleness* is hardly remarkable for containing a poem entitled "On a Distant View of the Village and School of Harrow on the Hill." What is remarkable is how captivating this genre of recollection became, despite how little it resembles anyone's schooldays. The glamorizing of schoolboys owes something, of course, to the prosaic fact that attending public schools had become a national habit of the well born in England by the mideighteenth century. But this fact alone can hardly explain the adult fantasy of wishing oneself a boy again, especially when, as Gray well knew, public school was not really such a congenial place for budding poets. As Gibbon soberly remarked of Gray's lines, "The poet may gaily describe the short hours of recreation; but he forgets the daily tedious labours of the school, which is approached each morning with anxious and reluctant steps." Moreover, the educational ideal of public school can't account—except ironically—for Gray's influential image of an Eden where "Ignorance is Bliss" and "'Tis Folly to be wise."

Neither can the simple matter of public school segregation adequately explain his image of an Eden without Eve. An almost mythic animus lurks behind a poem in which, if women figure at all, they do so only as the implicit causes of fallen passions such as "pineing Love" and "Jealousy with rankling Tooth." This animus is more clearly displayed in a letter Gray himself would later write to his young student Bonstetten, warning him against the "allurements of painted Women"; it is still more vivid in Johann Müller's engraving of Richard Bentley's "Design" for the Eton Ode (1753). Horace Walpole explained the design: "Boys at their sports, near the chapel of Eton, the god of the Thames sitting by: the passions, misfortunes, and diseases, coming down upon them. On either side, terms representing Jealousy and Madness." Madness is the figure that frames the central scene on the right, a Medusa figure with torch in hand, while Jealousy is the despondent, androgynous figure on the left; the "passions" that descend upon the boys are similarly all feminine forms. In no uncertain terms, women are cast as the enclosing threat to the focal idyll of "boys," who are in turn depicted as duly Hellenized young men. Moreover, Bentley and Müller evoke the homoeroticism merely implicit in Gray's prospect by placing a distinct compositional emphasis on the jutting posteriors of two of the young men, one bathing in, and one stooping beside, the Thames. However, the decidedly homoerotic cast of the Eton poem and design (along with much of Beckford and some of Byron) should not lead us to assume that the paradise of boys was primarily a ghettoized vision in the eighteenth century. Some forty years after Gray composed his Ode, Johnson could disapprove of it on the grounds that it "suggests nothing . . . which every beholder does not equally think and feel."

But by the time that every man shared Gray's tragic vision of boyhood's fragility, Beckford had introduced a strangely compelling comedy in which boyhood need never end. The Eton Ode is an elegy; the fate of Gulchenrouz in *Vathek* is an idyll. Beckford indeed expresses in European letters the same idyll of "never-ending youth" that Johann Winckelmann located at the heart of Greek statuary, in his ground-breaking *History of Ancient Art*. As a neo-Hellenic fantasy of incorruptible adolescence, Gulchenrouz supplies *Vathek* with a counterpoint to the Caliph Vathek, who is irredeemably

damned through growing up. The novel is in effect the first antibildungsroman, ironically poised at the threshold of the nineteenth-century novel of education.

The outset of Beckford's tale provides an allegory of infancy, in which Vathek is comfortably ensconced in his "palaces of the five senses"—an image of oriental sensuality, certainly, but also an illustration of the pancorporal sexuality that precedes the putatively genital-centered sexuality of the adult. In the first third of the novel, Vathek generally acts out the Calvinist conception of the infant as a tyrant of desire. His appetite for food is predominant, and when, in a scene of not untypical grotesqueness, his demands fall upon the (literally) deaf ears of his fifty "mute negresses," he, "having totally forgotten their deafness began to cuff, pinch, and bite them." Kicking is his other common response to frustrated desire, as when a number of his guards are unfortunately found "lying lifeless around him": "In the paroxism of his passion he fell furiously upon the poor carcases, and kicked them till evening without intermission." While servants, quick or dead, are fair game for such abuse, Vathek—here, at one with Beckford—especially relishes kicking, tricking, and treading on venerable elders, eunuchs, and holy men, who are invariably presented as doddering old fools. No briars are about to bind his joys and desires.

Vathek thus starts out as an infantile character, little more than an id, at once ludicrous and, in an iconoclastic way, oddly heroic. Women serve as the agents of his subsequent education. His absurdly wicked mother Carathis, who is first seen putting her son to bed and protecting him from a populace reasonably offended by his various high jinks, ultimately diverts his appetite for food into a more wordly ambition for power and glory. He sets off on his quest for the subterranean palace of Eblis largely at her prompting. But Vathek truly crosses out of infancy only through the heterosexual passion he conceives along the way for the princess Nouronihar. Mistakenly thinking at one point that Nouronihar has died, Vathek significantly loses his appetite, believing it "will not soon be the case" that he will "feel hungry." (The reader has grown so accustomed to Vathek's hunger that the sentence is startling.) It is when Carathis becomes incensed at the dilatoriness of her son's love affair that he first defies, however partially, a maternal authority until then absolute: "Dread lady! you shall be obeyed; but I will not drown Nouronihar. She is sweeter to me than a Myrabolan comfit; and is enamoured of carbuncles; especially that of Giamschid; which hath also been promised to be conferred upon her: she, therefore, shall go along with us; for I intend to repose with her upon the sofas of Soliman: I can sleep no more without her." Vathek remains blissfully ignorant of Nouronihar's real motive in sleeping with him: as the narrator repeatedly tells us, she has more "ardour" for the carbuncle than for "the amorous monarch," whom she manipulates to suit her own ends. Clearly, whether in the hands of Carathis or Nouronihar, Vathek never ceases to be a puppet of women's power and thirst for power. Growing up in *Vathek* means more or less blindly coming under the sway of female ambitions. Vathek's eyes are opened only after his quest has irretrievably damned him; only in the dungeons of Eblis is his own experience explained to him by the preadamite king Soliman Ben Daoud, who similarly "suffered [himself] to be seduced by the love of women, and a curiosity that could not be restrained by sublunary things." The sequence of this sentence is ostensibly causal.

According to the logic of the novel, Carathis, who follows upon Vathek's heels to Eblis, assuredly deserves to be damned, whereas the reader feels a certain illogical regret at Nouronihar's fate, if only because it might have been avoided had she remained Gulchenrouz's playmate. Her own fall proceeds from abandoning the perfect narcissism of their relationship, glowingly described by the narrator: "Nouronihar loved her cousin, more than her own beautiful eyes. Both had the same tastes and amusements; the same long, languishing looks; the same tresses; the same fair complexions; and, when Gulchenrouz appeared in the dress of his cousin, he seemed to be more feminine than even herself." This description of Gulchenrouz's epicene beauty harkens back to Winckelmann's admiration for ancient statues of Hercules, in which "the distinction of sex [is left] almost doubtful, as the beauty of a young man should be." By the same token, Gulchenrouz's casual transvestism may allude to representations of Hercules's sojourn with Omphale. His physical appeal is not at all virile, a point made still clearer in the narrative detail that while he could "draw the bow," he could not "dart the lance." As bowman, he recalls a youthful, puckish Eros, yet Gulchenrouz never has to grow up and "dart the lance"; he is, rather, an Eros eternally without a Psyche. Nouronihar's original ability to mirror her little cousin might have been her salvation, but she comes instead to yearn for Vathek and carbuncles—she becomes, in the novel's terms, a woman. And heterosexuality, in *Vathek,* always leads to hell. Gulchenrouz, by contrast, is transported to a paradise in which he may forever enjoy the pleasure of being a boy passively reflecting other boys. Gibbon deplored Gray's portrayal of "a state of happiness arising only from the want of foresight and reflection," but, in any irony that adheres to the word, the joy of "reflection" is precisely the key to Gray's, and Beckford's, paradise of boys.

Why should this fantasy have become so powerful and pervasive in the later eighteenth century? While any answer must remain broadly speculative, I'll try to taper the breadth of my successive theses. Most generally, the paradise of boys motif contests the ascendent myths of modernity: progressive technological, social, and moral change; a break with the unexamined pieties of the past; "man's emergence," in Kant's phrase, "from his self-imposed non-age." The loneliness of becoming—which, not for Kant alone, means becoming ever more autonomous and responsible—calls forth nostalgia for the comforts of simply being, in the way that adults sometimes think that children simply are. Boys in particular (girls, it seems, are never discussed) are thought to exist without consciousness, without will, undifferentiated from animals, from other boys, from the natural settings in which our fancies invariably place them. While this primitivist vision of boyhood wouldn't have been unrecognizable to Shakespeare, he would have been at least surprised by the urgency with which eighteenth-century authors invoke it. Polixenes recalls his "unfledged days" with merely pleasant grief; he would hardly have sympathized with Gray's grim reluctance to leave boyhood behind, or Beckford's anarchic denial of the need to grow up.

Moreover, even Polixenes—who, as Hermione amusedly notes, implies in passing that wives are "devils"—could scarcely comprehend the bitterness with which later authors blame women for forcing them to grow up. Perhaps the novel emotional demands of what Lawrence Stone calls the ideology of the companionate marriage made (and makes) growing up seem more dreadful than it might otherwise be. Similarly, the attraction of a segregated paradise attests to, even as it rejects, the increasing sexual integration of polite society. Not only did the family circle become a more prominent institution, and the Parisian salon flourish, but the entire eighteenth-century "republic of letters" allowed for a greater accomodation of women, both as audience (Hume, for one, was all but prepared to "resign into their Fair Hands the sovereign Authority over [this] Republic"), and as authority (in the proliferation of popular women novelists, essayists, and letter writers). Traditionally, sexual segregation, attended by varying shades of misogynist sentiment, had been more or less the norm; only in the later eighteenth century does it begin to become a conscious revolt. Beckford and Byron variously rebel against both the rising estimation of women in society, and the concomitant rise of a polite discourse of stylistic and passional restraint, authorized by an ideal of women's natural modesty.

Between Beckford's rebellion and Byron's there lies that portion of Wordsworth which, as Trilling observed, "defends the violence and fearfulness of literature from the 'progressive' ideas of his day." Trilling refers here to book 5 of *The Prelude,* in which lone poetic madness and eschatological vision are preferred over the domestic life of men for whom it is enough "to take in charge / Their wives, their children, and their virgin loves." The same book draws the well-known contrast between the Infant Prodigy, whose self-consciousness has been cultivated according to Maria and Richard Edgeworth's enlightened educational theory, and the Winander Boy, whose heart and mind reflect the dizzying sublimities of nature as passively as nature reflects itself, like "that uncertain heaven, received / Into the bosom of the steady lake." The Infant Prodigy has foresight and reflection, in Gibbon's sense; the Winander Boy simply reflects that which surrounds him. In the elegy that follows upon the recollection of the Winander Boy's early death, Wordsworth unites him with "his mates," "a race of real children" who now all seem to be interred, and all of whom are commemorated for having been in life happily free from volition, "mad at their sports like withered leaves in winds." The Winander Boy is Wordsworth's Gulchenrouz, preserved from the corruptions of thought and experience by abruptly and magically disappearing while still young, and reappearing, if only in the poet's imaginative vision, amidst a veritable paradise of boys.

It is, however, in the broad outlines of Byron's literary career that we may find the Romantics' most thorough engagement with the themes of *Vathek*. Byron early conceived an inclination to glorify his boyhood: his "Distant View of Harrow" begins,

> Ye scenes of my childhood, whose loved recollection
> Embitters the present, compared with the past;
> Where science first dawn'd on the powers of reflection,
> And friendships were form'd, too romantic to last;
> Where fancy yet joys to retrace the resemblance
> Of comrades, in friendship and mischief allied;
> How welcome to me your ne'er fading remembrance,
> Which rests in the bosom, though hope is denied!

In the first stanza the speaker's attitude towards the dawn of science is not unambiguous, and neither is the meaning of *reflection,* which may refer either to cogitation or, in light of the following stanza, the boys' ability romantically to reflect or "resemble" one another. Boyhood attachments are the only memories that Byron is glad are "ne'er fading," and indeed he did much in his life to preserve them, such as always carrying with him a lock of John Edelston's hair. "I certainly love him more than any human being," Byron wrote shortly before leaving Cambridge, "and neither time nor distance have had the least effect on my (in general) changeable disposition."

Yet since most of us, unlike John Edelston, don't die young, the Byronic hero confronts the problem that "The Tree of Knowledge is not that of Life." *Manfred* depicts the damning knowledge—of good and evil, of things seen and unseen, and especially of one's own intolerable isolation—that follows upon a shattered idyll. In the aftermath of his fatal affair with his sister Astarte, Manfred remembers, "She was like me in lineaments; her eyes / Her hair, her features, all, to the very tone / Even of her voice, they said were like mine." We unavoidably see Byron and his sister Augusta reflected

in this passage, but we might just as readily see the unfallen love of Gulchenrouz and Nouronihar. Sexual experience—penetrating the reflective surface—is the unnameable crime that defaces Manfred's paradise with Astarte, and issues (by now expectably) in their deaths.

Yet according to the high Byronic vision, sexual knowledge is as daring as it is damning. Taking a certain pride in feeling himself a damned creature, Byron was apt to satirize a writer such as Keats, who hadn't yet crossed out of adolescence; Byron's letters refer contemptuously to "Johnny Keats's piss a bed poetry," his "Onanism of Poetry." Keats's great odes, however, seem relatively grown up; his fascination with the frozen adolescent figures on a Grecian urn is merely regretful, conventionally Gray-like. *Don Juan* is a far less responsible fantasy of sexual adventures that, magically, do not entail experience. Byron chose for his last and greatest poem a character who, for all his varied episodic adventures, never has to grow up or learn anything. Juan brings to Haidee's island—and even to Gulbeyaz's harem, and Catherine's court—the same un-deflowered innocence he should properly have lost with Julia. Though lent a certain irony, in part, by the poem's more seasoned narrator, the character of Juan still remains perpetually Edenic. He remembers nothing. Byron, not so blessed as this, would die in Greece, in love with an adolescent boy in whom he could no longer see his own reflection.

Adam Roberts and Eric Robertson (essay date summer 1996)

SOURCE: Roberts, Adam and Eric Robertson. "The Giaour's Sabre: A Reading of Beckford's *Vathek*." *Studies in Romanticism* 35, no. 2 (summer 1996): 199-211.

[*In the following essay, Roberts and Robertson offer a detailed literary and linguistic analysis of* Vathek.]

> Behold then in my countenance a strange mixture of pleasure and pain; haste, mark on your tablets that uncertain character.[1]

The Textual Status of *Vathek* is Interestingly Unsettled. It straddles English and French, and although Beckford originally wrote the work in French, which suggests that the English version (rendered by Beckford's literary collaborator, Samuel Henley) is a "translation," with all the associations that word carries with it, the situation is not as simple as it might appear. The usual trajectory of a translation (firstly, composition and publication in original language, secondly, translation and publication in secondary language) does not apply in this case. More importantly, translation itself functions in the novel in ways that reflect the problematizing progress of the work in the real world, to the extent that "translation" can be seen as the organizing principle behind the sort of hermeneutic endeavor a reader of *Vathek* must undertake. It is a text that functions in a state of flux, and that flux operates at the level of the words on the page, as well as at structural, thematic, generic, character and religious levels. The emblem for this textual uncertainty is the magical sword the Giaour brings as one of his gifts for Vathek himself, since it is the message on the sword that prompts the Caliph's doomed search for pre-Adamite treasure and power. The fluid character of the sabre's hieroglyphics mirrors the difficulty in establishing an Ur-text for *Vathek.* This message—the one written on the sword—offers a *mise en abyme* of the novel's own narrative strategy: it promises access to a transcendental signifier, but this is an empty promise. In the final analysis, Vathek is undone by the endlessness of the deferral of the signifier.

It is, in the first place, very difficult to make unambiguous pronouncements about the composition of the text. Certainly, Beckford wrote a version of the book in French, probably in May 1782. Equally certainly, Henley translated a version of the French text during 1783-85, and an English version appeared in print in June 1786. But there are at least two versions of Beckford's composition. In a letter to Cyrus Redding, written fifty years after the event, Beckford claimed:

> I wrote *Vathek* when I was twenty-two years old. I wrote it in one sitting and in French. It cost me three days and two nights of hard labour. I never took my clothes off the whole time. This severe application made me very ill.[2]

This suggests a certain myth of composition—that the work was a spontaneous and inspired whole, thrown off in one session. But copresent with this is a picture of Beckford taking a great deal longer to produce the text. The first mention of the project in his letters appears 25 April 1782, where he says his "Arabian tales" are "going on prodigiously."[3] *Vathek* itself is first mentioned in a letter dated 1 May, and by 29 May 1782 Lady Craven, one of Beckford's intimates, had received a mansucript of the work. Beckford was by this time on the continent, and there was no talk of publishing the version of the book given to Lady Craven. But Beckford did not give up the business of composition; he was involved in (probably) rewriting the original version, and (certainly) composing, in French, a series of episodes relating the lives of some of the damned whom Vathek meets in the Halls of Eblis at the end of the novel. A letter to Henley of January 1783 declares "I go on bravely with the episodes of Vathek"; and from April until the end of June 1785 a series of letters passed between Beckford (at this time in Switzerland) and Henley (in England) that treated the former's work on the episodes and the latter's translation work.[4] Beckford was insistent that publication of the translation should not precede publication of the French version: "The

publication of *Vathek* must be suspended at least another year, I would not have him on any account precede the French edition." When Henley went ahead with publication regardless, Beckford put the matter in the hands of his London agent. Despite his insistence that the text should appear with the episodes or not at all, the publication of two versions of the French text appeared the following year, apparently with Beckford's authority.

The text, then, is not stable. It appeared in French in three main versions (Lausanne 1787, Paris 1787 and a revised edition, published 1815), and then a retranslation into French of Henley's English translation appeared in the 1820s.[5] There were six editions of the English version, although some of these (the so-called "second" edition of 1809, the "fifth" of 1832 and the Bentley's Standard Novels edition of 1834) did not constitute different texts. There were also translations into German (in 1788 three different versions and in 1842) and Dutch (1837) during Beckford's lifetime. The "episodes" were finally published in French in 1909 and in English in 1912, and an edition of the work that incorporated the "episodes" into the narrative appeared (in French) in 1929. The question as to which of these editions is the single, authoritative one is not amenable to straightforward answer, and that fact itself suggests that the traditional model of primary author/authority is particularly problematic in this case.

Indeed, *Vathek* negotiates between three separate languages and linguistic arenas. The Preface of the 1786 English edition suggested that "the original" of the tale had been "collected in the East by a Man of letters" and that the editor had decided "to transcribe, and since to translate it." The Preface even complains of "the difficulty of accommodating our English idioms to the Arabick." There was no Arabic original, of course, a detail Beckford stressed in the Preface to the French edition of 1786, but the fiction of the text is that it transcribes, or records, an oriental tale. Indeed, Henley's notes repeatedly translate Arabic terms ("Caliph," "Houri," "Geni," "Vizir," and so on), often in relation to other languages (Greek, Latin, and Hebrew). In other words, the reader of *Vathek* locates his or her experience with reference to "Arabic," French *and* English, despite the fact that the book open in front of them is (usually) in English, and despite the fact that the author wrote the text in French.

It cannot be argued that Henley's translation was "unauthorized," despite the fact that it was published without Beckford's consent. On the contrary, the detailed interaction of author and translator during the process of translation suggests that the English version was a composite creation. Indeed, Beckford wrote to Henley in 1785 in terms that suggest Henley's work was better, in the sense of being more inspired, than his own:

You make me proud of *Vathek*. The blaze just at present is so overpowering that I can see no faults; but you may depend upon my hunting diligently after them.

Pray send the continuation, I know [not] how it happens; but the original when first born scarce gave me so much rapture as yr translation.

Were I well & in spirits I should run wild amongst my rocks and forests, telling stones, trees & labourers how gloriously you have succeeded. My imagination is again on fire.[6]

There is Beckfordian hyperbole here, of course, but the notion of translation functioning itself as inspiration—"my imagination is again on fire"—points to an interaction of French and English texts, of Beckford and Henley, rather than the traditional model of translation as working secondarily from a primary textual fait accompli.

It is these traditional notions of translation as a hierarchical procedure that are called into question—we might say, using a slightly *démodé* term, deconstructed—here. In the case of *Vathek,* where does authority reside? This is not the same question as "who is the author?" To assert that Beckford is the "author" of *Vathek* does not strain the use of the term, certainly, but such an assertion does not resolve the problems of the text. In order to approach that issue we need to retheorize translation itself as an other than linear progression.

There are, of course, many instances where the relationship between text and translation has been perceived as between greater and lesser. An instance (picked at random) is Henry Chadwick's 1991 translation of Augustine's *Confessions* into English. There is no question that this translation is an excellent piece of work, and provides exemplary access to Augustine's work for the English reader, but it would be difficult to assert that this translation possessed more authority than a Latin version of the same text. This is not because the author somehow mystically "inhabits" the Latin text and not the English—the Latin text is itself a problematic reconstruction from manuscripts that postdate Augustine's life. The issue is not one of absolutes, but of proximity, and in this case a Latin edition is more proximate than an English one. Augustine, naturally, could neither speak nor conceive of English as a language, but the circumstances are not greatly altered if we treat multilingual writers. Beckett's *En Attendant Godot* is a primary text in relation to a secondary *Waiting For Godot,* even though the translator was Beckett himself.[7] The identification of "original" and "posterior" texts inevitably involves the setting up of a mini-hierarchy.[8] Walter Benjamin distinguished between "original" and "translation" in such a way, defining the original as the text that allows itself to be translated and retranslated an indefinite number of times (such as Augustine's *Confessions*), and the translation as the text that does

not allow itself to be translated in turn such as Chadwick's *Augustine's Confessions*.[9] But, clearly, *Vathek* is a text that opposes this distinction. The French text by Beckford was translated into English by Henley, but this latter text was then retranslated back into French by an anonymous editor (1819), as well as translated into German, Dutch and other languages. The English *Vathek* has, to a degree, usurped the status of primary text, and the French *Vathek* has become its own autotranslation. More than this, both English and French texts occupy a theoretically secondary position with respect to a (fictitious) Ur-*Vathek* in Arabic. In this sense it embodies, with a literalism few texts can boast, the aspect of translation identified by George Steiner: "A translation from language A into language B will make tangible the implication of a third, active presence. It will show the lineaments of that 'pure speech' which precedes and underlies both languages."[10] So, the situation of *Vathek* works against hierarchical analysis, in several ways. Henley was considerably older than Beckford, was considered something of an expert on oriental studies, and had been Professor of Moral Philosophy at the William and Mary College, Williamsburg, Virginia, until the outbreak of the American War of Independence. Beckford, at the time of the composition of *Vathek,* was only 22, and had not formally attended a university. This might suggest a certain hierarchy, with Beckford deferring to Henley; but in fact the relationship was shaped by the more powerful vectors of class and money, with the wealthy and aristocratic Beckford the one who received deference. Textually speaking, we might expect the text as first written (in French) to be the one regarded as the original, and the translation as an ancillary document. But the bulk of *Vathek* criticism has concentrated on the English text, and has (for instance) disregarded the "episodes." Certainly, the particular chronology here (translation of work being published before original work) undoes the traditional hierarchy of text-translation.

We might expect to banish these sorts of discussion to the margins of the issue were it not the case that *Vathek* itself is profoundly concerned with questions of authority and translation. The particulars of the appearance of the text, in other words, constitute a sort of elaboration of these internal concerns, rather than an adjunct to them. The authorial insistence that only a text including the episodes could be considered "complete" or "final" is subverted by the fact that Beckford never finished the fourth episode, and that none of the episodes was published during his life. In other words, neither English nor French texts can lay claim to even the fiction of "authority." Both are quite specifically contingent publications; they make explicit that they function as versions of work-in-progress rather than any (hypothetical) finished product.

In this regard, *Vathek* can be seen as typical of, even emblematic of, the age into which it was produced, certainly in the ways that the period is now being interpreted by certain critical schools. As Tilottama Rajan puts it, romanticism represents

> a series of far-reaching shifts in concepts of the location and nature of meaning, the relationship of reader to text, and finally the nature of discourse itself. Corresponding to this shift in literature itself is a shift in romantic aesthetic, from a concern with the text as a finished product that contains its own meaning to a concern with the creative and receptive processes as loci of meaning.[11]

For *Vathek,* these creative and receptive processes are figured primarily in the act of, and concept of, translation itself.

Vathek begins with the Caliph absorbed in the search for sensual gratification, but not yet (apparently) having committed any of the crimes that will ultimately damn him. Indeed his sensuality is reported to us in such a way as to make it difficult for us to disapprove: "nor did he think . . . that it was necessary to make a hell of this world, to injoy Paradise in the next" (2: 1.)[12] Uneasiness sets in when we discover that, with the supernaturally-assisted erection of Vathek's great tower, "his pride arrived at its height" (8: 4); and a retrospective reading would note that the determination the Caliph then makes to become an adept in the mysteries of nature is the single focus of the novel's final moralizing paragraphs:

> Such is, and such should be, the chastisement of blind ambition, that would transgress those bounds which the Creator hath prescribed to human knowledge; and, by aiming at discoveries reserved for pure Intelligence, acquire that infatuated pride, which perceives not the condition appointed to man, is, To be Ignorant and Humble.
>
> (210:120)

In other words, Vathek is condemned not as a murderer, or a tyrant, or as an immoralist, but as an over-reacher. That the Caliph's pride should be promoted in the first instance by his Babel-like "great tower" is itself suggestive. "Babel" figures not merely pride, of course, but also the confusion of languages, and the necessity of translation. The seed of Vathek's doom is planted via his fascination with astrology, and his researches in this field are similarly articulated as a form of translation:

> The inquisitive Prince passed most of his nights on the summit of his tower: till he became an adept in the mysteries of astrology; and imagined that the planets had disclosed to him the most marvellous adventures, which were to be accomplished by an extraordinary personage, from a country altogether unknown.
>
> (8:5)

The issue here is not the accuracy of this act of translation (it precisely anticipates the arrival of the Giaour), but the fact that it is undertaken at all. Beckford's French text is slightly different from this, Henley's translation: there, Vathek "se croi[t] initié dans les mystères astrologiques"—he believes himself to be initiated in the astrological mysteries. Is his belief ill-founded? The French text anticipates the arrival of an extraordinary man ("homme extraordinaire")—the Giaour is a devil, not a man. The English text, specifying an "extraordinary personage" is more to the point. Furthermore the French text (in a phrase simply left out by Henley) suggests that the Giaour will be "le héraut" of his mysterious country. This term is of medieval origin, and according to Henley's own notes means "un officier d'un grade intermédiaire . . . dont les fonctions étaient la transmission des messages, les proclamations solennelles, l'ordonnance des cérémonies" [an officer of intermediate rank . . . whose duties were the transmission of messages, formal declarations, and the order of ceremonies]—a strange description to apply to the Giaour.

The gifts that the Giaour brings with him epitomize most expressively the hermeneutic situation of the text. Each of them is characterized by the fact that they perform their respective tasks without the engagement of human agency. These curiosities "had, besides, their several virtues; described on a parchment fastened to each. There were slippers, which enabled the feet to walk; knives that cut without the motion of a hand; sabres which dealt the blow, at the person they were wished to strike" (9:5). The fact that these attributes are identified by a written message "on a parchment fastened to each" is similarly significant. These artefacts represent the impossible (fantastic, in more than one sense), the text that is entirely self-sufficient, that contains its own meaning and has no need of interpretation (or translation). The very impossibility of this state of affairs is captured in the marvellous nature of these curiosities, but is particularly reinforced by the message on the sabre. "The sabres, especially . . ." we are told, "fixed more than all" the Caliph's attention, "who promised himself to decypher, at his leisure, the uncouth characters engraven on their sides" (9-10:5-6). In French, the "caractères" are "inconnus" rather than "uncouth"—the translator preserving the sound of the word rather better than the sense. Of course, "uncouth" derives from the same root as "inconnu," but by the late eighteenth century its connotations were much the same as today. It is as if the presence of a foreign language is somehow more disruptive in the English text. Vathek tries to translate the message on the sabres himself, "but his reiterated attempts were all of them nugatory" (15:8). On his mother's advice, he advertises for experts to come to his palace and translate the characters, warning that those who fail to give satisfaction will have their beards burnt. Carathis, interestingly, places in low esteem the art of translation ("the knowledge of languages is a trifle, at best; and the accomplishment of none but a pedant" [16:9]). Eventually an old man comes forward to translate the message:

> This venerable personage read the characters with facility; and explained them verbatim, as follows: "We were made where every thing good is made: we are the least of the wonders of a place, where all is wonderful; and deserving the sight of the first Potentate on earth.["]
>
> (19:10-11)

Vathek is pleased ("You translate admirably!") and then interprets, or translates, the rendering himself ("I know to what these marvellous characters allude"). But on asking the old man to translate the sabre's message again the following day ("I cannot hear too often the promise that is made me"), he discovers a different text:

> The old man forthwith put on his green spectacles; but, they instantly dropped from his nose, on perceiving that the characters he had read the day preceding, had given place to others of different import. "What ails you?" asked the Caliph; "and why these symptoms of wonder?"—"Sovereign of the world," replied the old man, "these sabres hold another language to-day, from that they yesterday held."
>
> (20:11)

The old man's comment is ambiguous between "these are different words in the same language as yesterday," and "the words *and* the language are different from yesterday." The ambiguity serves a purpose. Language—specifically, the text that will inspire Vathek to seek out the treasures of the pre-Adamite kings and thereby occasions his doom—is in a state of flux. The French text consistently refers to the writings as "caractères": Henley's "another language" is Beckford's "les caractères de la veille avaient fait place à d'autres." The English text, in other words, suggests a greater change than the French. "Caractères" suggests primarily different letters, "language" different tongues, a reading reinforced by Henley's note to the passage: "In the French King's library is a curious treatise, intitled *Sefat Alaclam*; containing a variety of alphabets, arranged under different heads; such as the *prophetick,* the *mystical,* the *philosophick,* the *magical,* the *talismanick,* & c." (220:—). In other words, in the English text it is suggested that the Giaour's sabre embodies the whole process of language and translation in a fluid state.

The new message ("Woe to the rash mortal who seeks to know that, of which he should remain ignorant; and to undertake that, which surpasseth his power!") displeases the Caliph, and the old man is dismissed. But even without him, it is clear that the language on the sabre changes constantly, which is to say, is in a state of continual flux: "For, thou he could not decypher the characters himself, yet, by constantly poring upon them,

he plainly perceived that they, every day, changed; and, unfortunately, no other candidate offered to explain them" (21:12). The French version lacks the text to support the first ten words of this quotation: the effect, again, is to reinforce the English's text's fascination with the elusiveness of meaning.

The effect of this discovery is remarkable: Vathek suffers "giddiness and debility" after a prolonged attempt to translate the shifting text; when that fails he tries to decipher the stars once more, but fails in this also; "Agitated with so much anxiety, Vathek intirely lost all firmness; a fever seized him and his appetite failed" (22:12). He develops a bizarrely insatiable thirst, such that "his mouth, like a funnel, was always open to receive the various liquors that might be poured into it; and, especially, cold water, which calmed him more than every other." The Caliph is eventually carried to a nearby mountain where he is prostrated on the ground beside a fountain "to lap up the water, of which he could never have enough" (25:14). It is whilst Caliph is in this posture that the Giaour returns; and presenting him with "a phial of red and yellow mixture" tells him to drink. Vathek does so, "and instantaneously found his health restored; his thirst appeased; and his limbs as agile as ever" (26:14-15).

This instant remedy, from the same provenance as the self-walking slippers and the self-cutting knives, provides a supernatural solution to the (in this case, exaggerated) human problem of thirst. Vathek's loss of "firmness" is a kind of *vertige* occasioned by the impossibility of his fixing or determining the thirst is a symptom of this, and the pharmaceutical capabilities of the Giaour's phial exceed the bounds of normal human activity. It is a similarly impossible transcendental signifier, and derives from the same impossible, infinite source.

The Caliph spends the remainder of the novel in search of this impossible realm. He is the architect of an oriental quasi-Babel (the Giaour calls him "Babler" [46:26]), and the great tower figures repeatedly in the novel's design, no matter how far from Samarah he travels. Vathek, and his text, cannot escape the contingent, differential basis of signification (and translation), although he tries. His continual urge to ground or base his power in the transcendental treasures of the pre-Adamite kings—the fact that he seems to have unlimited earthly power notwithstanding—is a form of attempted self-definition. But the conclusion to this quest discovers for Beckford not a palpable ground for the assertion of his "presence," but a realm of suffering that is repeatedly characterized in terms of infinity.[13] The Hall of Eblis is "so spacious and lofty, that, at first, they took it for an immeasurable plain" (191:109); it contains "an infinity of censers" (192:109), and a multitude "that no one could number" that is "incessantly passing" (192-

93:109-10). "An infinity of elders" prostrate themselves before Eblis (194:110), and Vathek and Nouronihar wander from "hall to hall; and gallery to gallery; all without bounds, or limit" (210:115), until, inevitably, their punishment is meted out to them. Their hearts burst into flame and they are condemned to wander "in an eternity of unabating anguish" (210:120). Here the English text reiterates the terms indicative of infinitude to a much greater degree than the French, again reinforcing the proliferation of significance.[14] Eblis himself makes the contradictory promise that indicates the impossibility of their search: in the Halls of Eblis, he announces, "THERE, INSATIABLE AS YOUR CURIOSITY MAY BE, SHALL YOU FIND SUFFICIENT TO GRATIFY IT" (195:111). The aporia dramatizes the hermeneutic dilemma.

We need to return to questions of the theory of translation. It might seem that the texts of **Vathek** (because of their instability, the absence of a primary, authentic "**Vathek**") appropriately enact the elision of "meaning" in the novel itself. But it is equally true that Beckford tried (vainly, as it happened) to resist the ambiguity inherent in this process. As we have seen, he tried to prevent the violation of the chronological order of text-translation, writing to Henley that he would not have "on any account" English version precede French. A similar injunction (equally ignored) seems to have been issued with regard to the names of the protagonists. With respect to proper names, Geoffrey Bennington points out: "A proper name cannot be translated into another language—one would not say that "James" *translates* "Jacques," nor that "Paris" pronounced in the English way *translates* "Paris" pronounced in the French way."[15] At least with "Paris" pronounced the French way we can say that this is how Parisians would name their city, and this fact suggests its authenticity. But with the name "Vathek," since French lacks the 'th' sound English possesses, we have present in the title an interlingual ambiguity that cannot be so easily resolved. Do we pronounce "Vathek" or "Vatek"? Where can we seek for a solution to this problem? Beckford appears to have short-circuited it by scribbling a note on the cover of the manuscript translation: "N.B. If the letter *h* should be found to remain anywhere in the names of *Vatek* or *Caratis*—don't forget to omit it" (quoted in Oliver, 124n). Somebody clearly forgot: but the issue cannot be resolved by an appeal to Beckford anyway. It turns on whether English or French is the source language, and since both languages defer to an imaginary Oriental "original," this in turn develops upon the Persian spelling. But neither the English "Vathek" nor the French "Vat(h)ek" *translates* the name of the Persian king in question: and the text we have before us offers us no guidance on this issue.[16] In the light of this it is perhaps appropriate that the English text seems rather more fascinated with the inherent instability of the reading process than the French.

Bennington and Derrida seek to undo the Benjamin model of translation mentioned above, and replace it with a view of translation as a more complex set of textual interrelations. Translation is not seen as a straightforward "transference of meaning from one language to another": "[translation] is not an exchange of signifieds (we have already warned against this way of putting it) but a passage toward a 'before' or a 'back of' meaning" (173).[17] In *Vathek,* we have the apparent violation of chronological norm, the "translation" occurring *before* the "original"; the "translation," not the "original," the apparent focus of critical activity. And we have a text that plays with notions of the delimitation of translated meaning (and the impossibility of such closure). For Barthes, translation is paradigmatic of the transposition of meaning intrinsic to *all* writing:

> l'écrivain ne peut qu'imiter un geste toujours antérieur, jamais originel; son seul pouvoir est de mêler les écritures, de les contrarier les unes par les autres, de façon à ne jamais prendre appui sur l'une d'elles; voudrait-il s'exprimer, du moins devrait-il savoir même que la 'chose' intérieure qu'il a la prétention de 'traduire', n'est elle-meme qu'un dictionnaire tout composé, dont les mots ne peuvent s'expliquer qu'à travers d'autres mots, et ceci indéfiniment.

> [the writer can only imitate a gesture that is always anterior, never original. His only power is to mix writings, to counter the ones with the others, in such a way as never to rest on any one of them. Did he wish to *express himself,* he ought at least to know that the inner 'thing' he thinks to 'translate' is itself only a ready formed dictionary, its words only explainable through other words, and so on indefinitely.][18]

In this light, the changing characters of the Giaour's sabre may be seen to highlight the displacement inherent in the process of writing and reading. A text, such as the message on the Giaour's sabre (which, in turn, illuminates and occupies the text, **Vathek**) shifts constantly, changing not just *parole* but, it seems, *langue* as well. The suggestion, made explicit in Henley's note, is that different sorts of question require not only different answers, but different languages in which to frame answers: that there are languages devoted to "the *prophetick,* the *mystical,* the *philosophick*" and so on. On this model, Vathek would be seen as operating within the wrong language. Certainly, Allah's last attempt to save the Caliph involves a shepherd speaking simply, lucidly, and conveying to Vathek knowledge of his fate (182-185:103-105). That Vathek is able to simply ignore this warning suggests that he fails to comprehend his own language, misundertakes the process of self-translation inherent in ordinary linguistic comprehension.

The reader of **Vathek** is often faced, as was Robert Kiely, with a sense of confusion, almost fragmentation. This dilemma obtains not just at the level of convention, but of language itself. As with the kicking of the

Giaour, the signified bounces along just ahead of its pursuers, until it disappears into the abyss. Vathek tries to follow, but is prevented by "an invisible agency." He may look into this abyss and see "at the extremity of a vast black chasm" the Giaour "holding in his hand a golden key" that promises to open the door to the Caliph's desires; but when he sacrifices the fifty children demanded by the demon, the abyss merely closes up, and Beckford is no nearer his goal (49:27). As Kiely puts it, the conventions of **Vathek** "do not lead to the exposure of an old lie, or, by implication, to the discovery of a new truth. Like all the highways and byways of Beckford's world, they lead to the abyss."[19] This last term offers a conveniently multi-referential image on which to conclude, one which figures in **Vathek** on a variety of levels; firstly, as in other romantic texts, as the embodiment of romantic irony, the unknowable nature of "meaning," "presence." Moreover, the literal and figurative *mise en abyme* generated by the Giaour's text not only alerts us to the difficulties inherent in literary *translation,* but anticipates more recent observations on the instability of text per se. According to Eco, "la littérature (mais le problème se pose pour tous les arts) *désignerait de façon certaine un objet incertain.*"[20] **Vathek** negotiates between three linguistic arenas, refusing to settle authoritatively in any of them: it enacts as well as relates the dilemmas of translation. As with the mountain-climber in Beckford's *The Long Story* (published as **The Vision** in 1930), who voices the epigraph to this essay, experience is radically ambiguous, pleasure and pain coexist, **Vathek**/*Vat(h)ek* is a text that marks the "uncertain character."

Notes

1. Beckford, *The Vision and Liber Veritatis,* ed., G. Chapman (Cambridge: Cambridge UP, 1930) 9.

2. Quoted in J. W. Oliver, *The Life of William Beckford* (London: Oxford UP; Humphrey Milford, 1932) 94.

3. For this and subsequent references to Beckford's production of *Vathek* see Oliver 98, 100. The "Arabian tales" may have included translations from Persian originals, or other "Contes Arabes," as well as *Vathek.*

4. See Chapman, ed. *Vathek, with the Episodes of Vathek,* 2 vols. (Cambridge: Cambridge UP, 1929) 1: xvi-xviii. See also Kenneth Graham, "*Vathek* in English and French," *Studies in Bibliography* 28 (1975): 153-66.

5. See Roger Lonsdale, ed. *Vathek* (Oxford: Oxford UP, 1983) xxxvii-xxxviii.

6. Alfred Morrison, *Collection of Autograph Letters and Historical Documents,* Second Series 1882-1893 (London, 1893) 1: 193. Quoted in Graham 155.

7. It is a little tricky citing Beckett, because he worked (as Beckford did not) as an autotranslator. For this reason, it is unlikely that *En Attendant Godot* will be translated into English by anyone else, although there have been many English versions of the *Confessions,* and there will probably be many more. But it is not possible to regard the English *Godot* as one-to-one mappings of the French text, without distortion. The French title, for instance, means *Whilst Awaiting Godot*; the English title has different connotations. There are differences of this sort in the body of the text, but this is not to imply that it is an "incorrect" translation, or that, because it is the work of the author at a later date, it represents some form of revision. The relationship is more complex.

8. Graham, for instance, seeks to show that the English *Vathek* is not a translation at all, because "the assumption that [it] is a translation would relegate it to a low position in English letters since scholars are naturally unwilling to study a work not in its original form" (154). It should be clear that the present study does not share Graham's view.

9. See Benjamin, "The Task of the Translator," in *Illuminations,* ed. H. Arendt (New York: Schocken, 1969) 69-82.

10. Steiner, *After Babel: Aspects of Language and Translation,* 2nd ed. (Oxford: Oxford UP, 1992) 67.

11. Rajan, *The Supplement of Reading: Figures of Understanding in Romantic Theory and Practice* (Ithaca: Cornell UP, 1990) 17.

12. The English text of *Vathek* is quoted, unless otherwise stated, from the first English edition, 1786 (reprinted in facsimile, Menston: Scholar P, 1971). For convenience, page references are given in the body of the text, and comprise firstly the page number of the 1786 edition, and secondly the relevant page number from Lonsdale's Oxford edition.

13. John Garrett, "Ending in Infinity: William Beckford's Arabian Tale," *Eighteenth-Century Fiction* 5 (1992): 15-34, points up the open-ended, "infinite" conclusion of *Vathek,* relating this to an argued East-West dichotomy whereby the "West" figures closure and the "East" resists this. ("*Vathek* refuses closure and, by ending in infinity, bears an indelibly Eastern imprint in both its overall organization and its internal parts" [27].)

14. The "immeasurable plain" (191:109) is merely "immense", and the phrases "incessantly" (192:109), "that no one could number" (193:110) and "unabating" (210:120) are absent in Beckford's version.

15. Geoffrey Bennington and Jacques Derrida, *Derridabase/Circumfession,* trans. Bennington (Chicago: U of Chicago P, 1993) 169.

16. We might say, more fancifully, that Beckford's attempt to suppress the 'h' in *Vathek* (though not the 'ck' resonant in his own name Be(ck)ford, despite the fact that at some places in his manuscript the Caliph is named "Vathec") is the attempt to eliminate the 'h', the "Henley" or translator—to consign him to an invisible textual role: and that the resilience of the (h) reflects the unsuppressible priority of the translation.

17. See also Derrida, *Dissemination,* trans. Barbara Johnson (Chicago: U of Chicago P, 1982) 72.

18. Roland Barthes, "La Mort de l'auteur," in Le Bruissement de la langue. Essais critiques IV (Paris: Seuil, "Essais," 1984) 67. Translated by Stephen Heath as "Death of the Author," in *Image Music Text* (London: Fontana, 1977) 146.

19. Kiely, *The Romantic Novel in England* (Cambridge, MA: Harvard UP, 1972) 58-59.

20. Umberto Eco, *L'Œuvre ouverte* (Paris: Editions du Seuil, 1965) 38, n. 2. This text was originally published as *Opera Aperta* (Milan: Bompiani, 1962). [Literature (but the problem is posed for all the arts) *would refer in certain terms to an uncertain object.*] Translated by A. Roberts and E. Robertson. This note is omitted in the published English version, *The Open Work,* trans. Anna Cancogni (London: Hutchinson Radius, 1989).

George E. Haggerty (essay date 1997)

SOURCE: Haggerty, George E. "Beckford's Pæderasty." In *Illicit Sex: Identity Politics in Early Modern Culture,* edited by Thomas DiPiero, pp. 123-42. Athens: University of Georgia Press, 1997.

[*In the following essay, Haggerty examines Beckford's controversial love affair with his young cousin and how the author's conception of "pæderasty" is evidenced in his letters and in* Vathek.]

> What was the exact business, how, when, & by whom, & with whom discovered? Who passive & who active?
>
> —Pembroke Papers

> Beckford is a Professor of Pæderasty
>
> —*Hester Lynch Thrale,* Thraliana

On 27 November 1784, the following notice appeared in the pages of London's *Morning Herald:* "The rumour concerning a *Grammatical mistake of Mr. B——— and the *Hon. Mr. C———,* in regard to the genders, we hope for the honour of Nature originates in *Calumny!*—For, however depraved the being must be, who can propagate such reports without foundation, we must wish such a being exists, in preference to characters, who, regardless of Divine, Natural and Human Law, sink themselves below the lowest class of brutes in the most *preposterous* rites" (Chapman 185). Anyone reading this newspaper report, it seems, would have known that the unnamed gender transgressors were the enormously rich William Beckford and his aristocratic cousin William Courtenay.[1] The occasion for the remarks had come to be known as the Powderham Affair, and private accounts of it had been circulating for some time. Beckford and Courtenay had been caught in compromising circumstances of some kind, and Courtenay's uncle, Lord Loughborough, chief justice of the court of common pleas, was determined to ruin Beckford.[2] The appearance of this announcement, however, set the scandal on new, openly public, terms. These remarks in the *Morning Herald,* which Brian Fothergill suggests were planted by Loughborough, plunged the twenty-five-year-old Beckford into a disgrace that was to haunt him until his death sixty years later. Coming as it does, however, midway between the molly house raids and executions of the 1720s and the Vere Street arrests of 1810, the Beckford scandal offers interesting insight into the history of sexuality and the codification of sexual identities.[3]

This first newspaper account begins to explain this process. It is surely significant that perceived irregularity in gender roles is labeled a "Grammatical Mistake." Grammar, in this reading, becomes the figure of hegemonic control, and it is control exercised most effectively at the level of language. Alain de Lille's twelfth-century *The Complaint of Nature* had made a similar claim: the "Man [who] is made woman . . . both predicate and subject, he becomes likewise of two declensions, he pushes the laws of grammar too far." Gregory W. Bredbeck claims that "De Lille's readers must 'read' sodomy, and hence sodomy becomes a part of who they are as readers. Obviously *The Complaint of Nature* . . . ascribe[s] a subjective potentiality to the rhetoric of homoeroticism" (146-48).[4] By 1784, the naturalization of grammar is such that a "grammatical mistake" of this kind challenges the "honour of Nature." The passage from the *Morning Herald* also ascribes a subjective potentiality, but it does so by means of an inscription that renders subjectivity itself a grammatical impossibility. The "characters" who would be the subjects of this report, its "beings," are here rendered the object of a dependent prepositional phrase. Grammar works, in other words, to marginalize and control that which it finds threatening. But it needs that threat in order to justify, as it were, its exclusionary system. By inscribing gender as a grammatical system without a subject, moreover, this writer suggests ways in which sexuality itself is inscribed. In cultural terms, subjectivity is only possible when a sentence is already passed: this sentence posits a being that could not, should not exist, but that by the very articulation of this "rumour" can and does. Sexual identity, sexuality itself, then, emerges from this cultural attempt to inscribe subjectivity in its own likeness. Beckford's "Grammatical mistake" becomes the sign of sexual difference.

Significantly, the report fails to distinguish between the two "characters" involved. One would imagine that if Beckford alone were the object of the attack, it would emphasize his relation to the much younger William Courtenay (who had reached seventeen by the time of the scandal).[5] If it were not articulated as pæderasty as such, at least some mention of sexual victimization might be expected. But not here: Mr. B. and the Hon. Mr. C. are both involved in "*preposterous* rites": here the language of religion, devotions contrary to nature, gives their activity a status that can render it threatening to social order. For however sunk below the lowest class of brutes, these "*preposterous* rites" threaten, by their inversion of the natural order, the very terms by which a society constructs it own identity. Because "Law" determines what is "Natural," these characters are placed outside of nature. In practical terms, however, nature comes to mean merely polite society. As one writer from Italy asked, "Is Beckford at Fonthill, and is he chassé or still received in company?" (Herbert 274; qtd. in Fothergill 173).

A week later, another popular strain is introduced, and the "scene" of transgression is reinterpreted: "If anything could heighten the detestable scene lately acted in *Wiltshire,* by a pair of fashionable *male lovers,* the ocular demonstration of their infamy, to the young and beautiful wife of one of the monsters, must certainly have effected it (*Morning Herald*; qtd. in Chapman 185).[6] The laws of grammar work similarly here, and not only are the "lovers" relegated again to a prepositional position, but also the scene of their "infamy" is exactly what is not represented. The point of this piece, of course, is to evoke an image of male lovemaking and place it squarely in the public imagination. Margaret Beckford becomes a kind of conduit of voyeuristic pleasure for the reader of the *Morning Herald,* and the "ocular demonstration" that is described invites a range of fantastic recreations of the "detestable scene." More effective, perhaps, than grammar, the visual evocation of the "male lovers" fixes them in all their monstrosity in the imagination of anyone reading this passage. At the same time, however, "a pair of fashionable *male lovers*" is hardly the expression of monstrosity that contemporary accounts of sodomy would lead one to expect. In fact, it articulates the possibility of a male relation in a way that is rare in the eighteenth century, suggesting in its turn of phrase something more like our own configuration of relational possibilities. Of course, it may be possible that the writer, by coining this expression, was

attempting to register horror, but what he or she does register is something like difference—the difference that the description of two men as lovers continues to make today.

Beckford met his cousin William Courtenay at Powderham Castle, the home of Beckford's aristocratic Courtenay relatives, when he was on a tour of England in the summer of 1779. Beckford was eighteen years old and Courtenay eleven. His attachment to the boy quickly became an intense romantic obsession that his closest friends seemed to know about and (perhaps) encourage. To Alexander Cozens, for instance, the drawing master who might himself have introduced young Beckford to exoticized desires, Beckford wrote at Christmas 1779 that he had been walking by moonlight: "I was so charmed with the novelty of the prospect that setting the cold at defiance, I walked to and fro on the platform for several minutes, fancying the fictions of romance realized, and almost imagining myself surrounded by some wondrous misty barrier no *prophane* could penetrate. How I wished for my dear Wm. to share with me this imaginary contentment" (Melville 77). All the elements of Beckford's sexual sensibility are implied in his few remarks to Cozens: the nervous anxiety, almost irritability, the romantic fictions, the imaginative isolation, the mist, the barrier between life and death, and, of course, William. These elements are so worked and reworked over the next five years—some throughout his entire life—that they begin to have an identificatory quality quite unlike that of any simple report of sodomitical behavior.

> My cares have been a little while suspended—for I have been listening these several Evenings to plaintive Sicilian Airs. You can hardly believe what a melancholy has of late possessed me. My ideas of Happiness are at length very simple, for they consist alone in a secure retirement with the one I love. . . . Never could I have believed myself so entirely subdued—by whom you solely are acquainted. I wonder at myself every instant and only wish you was here to be surprized at me—One moment I am for flying into . . . the next . . . my Cheeks glow and I determine to remain immured in my Cell. Is it possible that a few Weeks' absence can have produced such effects—can have rendered me so miserable—Am I not the strangest of Beings?
>
> (Melville 77-78)

The exuberance of youthful infatuation becomes more like misery when emotion gives way to desire. What seems at first a pose—the Sicilian Airs, the melancholy, the "retirement with the one I love"—becomes an almost hysterical torment of frustrated desire. Beckford uses the vocabulary of dis-ease to emphasize the depth of his overheated emotion. The blood rushes to his cheeks in an anatomical redirection that calls to mind the reactions of "female" sensibility. This sensibility combines with the misery of the monkish "Cell" to color potentially "unnatural" desires with an exotic glow that resists the label of criminality. Beckford celebrates his own misery as a way of validating the feelings he has already been forced to question. In doing so, he attempts to defy the cultural conventions that would turn him against himself. This may be the gloomy sensibility of the exoticized man of feeling, but it begins to suggest the makings of a sexual "identity."

As a result of such careful probings of his own sexual makeup, Beckford became for his generation, in Byron's phrase, the "Apostle of Pæderasty," and his novel, **Vathek** (1786), a primer of man-boy love. Hester Lynch Thrale Piozzi announced that she found Beckford's "favourite propensity" in the "luscious descriptions of [the young boy] Gulchenrouz" when she read **Vathek** a few years after publication. She returned to this idea some years later, when complaining of the "luscious fondness" with which Richard Cumberland describes the *"personal Charms"* of the heroes in his novel *Henry* (1795); "The same is to be observed in Vathek," she says, "but then Beckford is a Professor of Pæderasty" (Thrale 2: 799 n. 969). Apostle of Pæderasty and Professor of Pæderasty are close enough—although the difference between a religious and an academic metaphor is hardly negligible; if Mrs Piozzi's comment rings with the astuteness of a cultural critic, then Byron's shimmers with the excitement of a devotee—to suggest that a sexual role was being established for Beckford. This role seems to approximate our own notion of the pæderast. It seems, in other words, that Beckford played a significant role in the popular evocation of a sexual identity distinct from the various sodomitical labels that were current at the time. Beckford's unique blend of erotic desire and almost sickly sensibility makes pæderasty newly available as an explanatory label for male sexuality. Beckford creates his own sexuality in a series of letters that are astonishing in their directness and devastating in their implications. From this material and from the accounts of his life that were circulated in the popular press and in private accounts of his "scandalous" behavior, I hope to show how a sexual identity is articulated and why the public recognition of this articulation is both swift and unequivocal. In his open display of this particular sexual transgression, Beckford threatened to expose the very foundations of culture. The scandal surrounding his pæderasty is culture's response to his "eccentricity." In the language of Beckford's love, however, it is possible to hear a shift in the emphases of male-male desire.[7]

* * *

The *OED* defines *pæderasty* as "unnatural connexion with a boy; sodomy," and it defines *pæderast* as "sodomite." The elision between pæderasty and sodomy, which the *OED* reports and reproduces, is inherent in the translation of the Greek: boy-lover in the original

becomes an "unnatural connexion" or even an activity. But unlike *sodomy* and *sodomite, pæderasty* and *pæderast* imply no activity, natural or unnatural. The words speak of love. Boy-love, if you will. And while this love is often erotic and at times explicitly physical, the term pæderast is not necessarily associated with behavior. It represents a relation that is nonetheless powerful and, some would argue, pervasive in Western culture. Feminist and cultural critics have argued that pæderasty is the structural basis of western civilization and that it goes a long way toward explaining the inherent misogyny of our culture.[8] David Halperin has taught us to understand Greek pæderasty, moreover, not as some cozy classical prelude to "domestic partnership" but rather as a carefully hierarchized system of male relations that both regulated desire and determined sexual positioning (Halperin 20-24, 54-71, and *passim*; also, Dover 16-17, 49-54, 73-109). When Halperin says, for instance, that in Greek terms there is nothing problematical "about a desire on the part of males to obtain sexual pleasure from contact with males—so long as that desire respects the proper phallocentric protocols (which . . . identify 'masculinity' with an insertive sexual role)," the distance from late twentieth-century sexual assumptions is clear. There is little question of seeing classical pæderasty as anything even approximating our own notions of mutual same-sex desire.

Greek love, however, has often been idealized or sentimentalized, and a sentimental reading of the Greeks was implicit in the first articulations of sexual liberation—particularly for male homosexuals—in the late nineteenth century.[9] This emotional understanding of pæderastic love was to a certain extent implicit in the Greek original: platonic love itself involves the idealization that leads to an extravagantly poetic expression of the beauties of the object of desire, the boy, to the extent that the boy himself becomes lost in the effusion of language articulating his attractions.[10]

If this emotional pæderasty existed in early modern England, as a rich range of sources suggests that it did, then by the time of the Restoration, the tendency at least in aristocratic circles was either to condemn it as sodomitical or condone it as no different structurally from other exercises of male privilege, or both.[11] The male libertine, for whom a boy could serve as a sexual partner as readily as a woman, offers a useful example of how this system of simultaneous celebration and censure could work. John Wilmot, Earl of Rochester, has helpfully memorialized this possibility in a number of poems. In a poem about impotence, for instance, the poet insists on his earlier sexual achievements: "The *Dart* of love," he says,

> through ev'ry *Cunt*, reacht ev'ry *Heart*.
> Stiffly resolv'd, twould carelessly invade,

Woman or *Man,* nor ought its fury staid,
Where e're it peirce'd, a *Cunt* it found or made.

("The Imperfect Enjoyment," lines 37-43 [*Poems* 31])

Few would see this as a source for "homosexual" or even homoerotic behavior.[12] What is interesting here, however, is the libertine ability to "make a cunt" in any place of choice. Like Halperin's Greek love, libertine love seems to be more about power than it is about desire. "Cunt-making," after all, is a process of subordination, a process, by the way, that depends on a functioning organ alone. The libertine can take pride in his ability as he takes pride in the position his penis guarantees him. Of course, the anxiety about the ability of that organ to function is an anxiety about the construction of masculinity itself. As the increasingly hysterical tone of the poem suggests, male subjectivity itself is threatened when the penis is flaccid: if it can't make cunts, it might as well become one.

In another poem, "The Disabled *Debauchee,*" an aging rake, in the midst of recounting tales of past conquest, gives in to a moment of nostalgia:

Nor shall our *Love-fits Cloris* be forgot,
When the well-look'd *Link-Boy,* strove t'enjoy,
And the best Kiss, was the deciding *Lot,*
Whether the *Boy* fuck'd you, or I the *Boy.*

(lines 37-40 [*Poems* 99])

Again, the power dynamic seems what is most important here, and we would not want to make any claims about Rochester's "sexuality" on the basis of this kind of remark. And just as "cunt" in the previous passage was not clearly defined by gender, so *"Boy"* in this is not clearly defined by age. *"Boy"* defines social and sexual position more than it represents a sign of crossgenerational desire. But surely that is not surprising when every sexual relation, as these poems suggest, is so rigidly hierarchical as to insist on power relations before any kind of desire can be articulated.[13] This is not even the kind of homosocial bonding that Sedgwick describes so effectively in *Between Men.* This is a sexuality of every "Man" for himself, a libertinism, as Harold Weber argues, that observes "a strict erotic demarcation between the male object of desire and the desiring male subject" (115; see also Trumbach, "The Birth of the Queen").

Pæderasty, then, is not a pretty picture, either in classical Greece or in eighteenth-century England.[14] Throughout the eighteenth century, pæderasty often seems interchangeable with sodomy, even if the former retains its association with boys. The term is less common than sodomy throughout the century, however, and it is not registered in the public imagination as a capital offense, as sodomy is. At times it retains its original meaning, as in Swift's use of the term in *A Tale of a Tub,* and at others it is at least culturally specific, as in specific references to the ancient world in Hume and Gibbon.[15] Whenever the word is used, it is either associated automatically with master-pupil relations in school (as Swift's use suggests), or it is a slightly fancier way of talking about the act of sodomy.[16] What seems clear, however, is that throughout the eighteenth century there was no cult of pæderasty, either in the popular imagination or in fact, as distinct from the sodomitical subcultures that were regularly harassed and persecuted.

The case of William Beckford, however, illustrates the limits of the sodomitical model. The Beckford scandal not only resulted in de facto exile and lifelong ostracism for the talented writer and musician but also a new and different understanding of male-male desire. For all the harm that came to Beckford and his paramour William Courtenay, I would claim that we can discover in this case the originary conception, in Beckford's writing, in the press, and in the popular response to his situation, of a particular kind of male homosexual sensibility. I do not mean that Beckford and Courtenay understood themselves in any way out of keeping with the grotesque way their culture saw them. I do think, however, that Beckford articulated his feelings for Courtenay in such a way that he opened a space, as it were, in which a man could identify his feelings for another male, in terms that suggest the recognition of a sexual identity. The particular combination of intelligence, self-indulgence, narcissism, sensibility, and descriptive power that was Beckford's gives his pæderasty a special place in the history of sexualities. For whatever Beckford is in his own and in the popular imagination, he is not a sodomite. This distinction is more than semantic.

By the time of his twenty-first birthday, in 1781, Beckford had had various emotional attachments with sensitive women within his larger family circle and with adolescent or preadolescent boys both within his family and without. The length he goes to express the emotional intensity of all these affairs suggests that he is making up for their lack of actual physical involvement. What is particularly striking, even at this early stage, is the degree to which his female lovers become a part of his pæderastic enterprise. Again and again throughout these early affairs, Beckford uses a woman to bring him closer to the boy he loves. In letters that I quote below, Charlotte Courtenay, Courtenay's aunt, Louisa, the wife of his cousin Peter Beckford, and the Contessa d'Orsini-Rosenberg each fill this role. Other women seem to have been somehow entangled in his love as well. The impression is one of an emotional bond that included acceptance of his "strange wayward passion."[17] Beckford seems to have needed a female friend to devote herself to him at the same time that she made herself an intermediary with the boy. As Fothergill said about the situation at Powderham, where Charlotte

Courtenay was clearly devoted to Beckford and where Courtenay was quickly capturing his heart: "to be in love with the nephew and not to be unaware of the admiration of the aunt was a situation very much to Beckford's taste" (70). What these letters demonstrate is that this was more than an arrangement of practical or emotional convenience for Beckford: the female figure, like Halperin's Diotoma, is necessary to the erotic attachment to the boy: she allows it, she encourages it, she creates a space through which the man can reach out to the boy.[18]

In one letter, for instance, he writes to Courtenay's Aunt Charlotte, later to become the wife of Beckford's tormentor, Lord Loughborough, asking her to intercede with the boy, who has not responded to his letters:

> Surely he [Courtenay] will never find any other Being so formed by nature for his companion as myself. Of all the human creatures male or female with which I have been acquainted in various countries and at different periods he is the only one that seems to have been cast in my mold.
>
> When I first began to know him the pleasing delusion would often suggest itself of our having been friends in some other existence. You know he was never so happy as when reclined by my side listening to my wild musick or the strange stories which sprang up in my fancy for his amusement. Those were the most delightful hours of my existence.
>
> (Chapman 81-82; see also, Fothergill 98-99)

This letter goes on to tell of shared musical moments and of a friendship on which he depends for life itself. Beckford uses a vocabulary understood as erotic in the eighteenth century: "wild music" and "strange stories" could hardly be considered innocent, nor would the image of the younger and older boy "reclined" together be anything but provocative. Fothergill calls these comments "reckless," but they can only be understood as reckless if Beckford did not mean them actively to imply an intimacy outside of the bounds of social respectability. But he could hardly mean anything else: "How often has my sleep been disturbed by his imaginary cries, how frequently have I seen him approach me, pale and trembling as I lay dozing at Caserta lulled by my dear Lady Hamilton's musick and bathed in tears. . . . If anything could reconcile me to death it twould be the promise of mingling our last breaths together and sharing the same grave" (Fothergill 99). Far from hiding his feelings, or exposing them unwittingly, Beckford seems to threaten the boy's aunt with his own increasingly urgent desire. That he writes this way to a woman who has exposed her own deep feelings for him is more than reckless: it seems on the one hand an elaborate courtship ritual that all his women friends have been subjected to; and it seems on the other an excuse for spelling out the details of his attachment to the boy in heightened emotional detail. The presence of the

woman, in other words, allows Beckford to write out his passion in terms that defy convention and create a new vocabulary for male-male desire at the same time that they mimic conventional sexual transgression. Beckford needs to write about his love because it has been silenced elsewhere, everywhere. Beckford takes the crime not to be mentioned among Christians and gives it all the emotional superstructure of "romantic friendship," and in doing so he liberates himself, as it were, from the silences that surround him.[19]

At the same time, even at this early stage, his "romantic friendship" seems to have taken on a quality that embodies the threat of social opprobrium within it. For all the poetic liberation it embodies, internalized self-hatred seems increasingly to haunt Beckford's pæderasty. Beckford's ever-more perfumed sensibility begins to seem lethal: desire implies death, brings the threat of death, becomes almost a desire for death—as Beckford's culture had taught him all too well. I resist the obvious implication of a Freudian death instinct, here and later, not because I do not see such a function in representations of desire in the eighteenth century but because Beckford's articulation of the attractions of death is never less than conscious.

In a letter to the Contessa d'Orsini-Rosenberg, the wealthy widow who befriended him in Venice and was witness to his emotional attachments to various young men, Beckford writes out the details of his love for Courtenay in a way that confirms the physical expression of their love at the same time that it dramatizes the specific dimensions of his fear:[20]

> From the theater, I take him to my bed. Nature, Virtue, Glory all *disappear*—entirely lost, confused, destroyed. O, heavens, that I could die in these kisses and plunge my soul with his into the happiness or the pain which must never end. Must I live in fear of a moment which must separate us again. Do not be surprised if I desire death with eagerness. Hurry, compose some sweet potion which will put all three of us to sleep, which will close our eyes without anguish, which will steal our souls away and deliver them imperceptively to the flowered fields of some other existence. . . .
>
> Surely there is no hell for me in the other world because I am damned on earth. Do you know of a state more frightening than this which I suffer—spied upon by a thousand Arguses without hearts and without ears, constrained to abandon the unique hope that reconciles me to life, menaced at each instant, accused of the ruin of a being I adore in whom all human affections are concentrated to a point. Such is my present situation, such are the Demons that Destiny has set on my trail.[21]

Beckford, at twenty-two, has effected a link between sensibility and erotic activity that will not be fully realized until the end of the nineteenth century. To say that he is ahead of his time is only to confess that we have not understood the implications of his love for Courtenay. Pæderastic love is not idealized here. Happiness and pain are interchangeable partly because Beckford only finds happiness in pain and partly because he knows that his love brings with it the social condemnation he fears. He asks for death as both a way of preserving their moment of happiness and a way of escaping the torment of a world that persecutes what it does not understand. At the same time, he seems to want to disembody his affection and translate it into a sensuously spiritual realm. The "other existence" that he desires is as much an escape from life, from the implications of the physical, as it is a life away from the spying Arguses. It almost seems as if it would be an escape into life, into a life in which their love would be possible precisely because it would be an impossibility. If this sounds paradoxical, it is no more so than Beckford's desire itself. The "unique hope" that "reconciles [him] to life" is the hope that Courtenay will offer him a way out of this dilemma; but of course that is precisely what Courtenay can never do. That Beckford could imagine that Courtenay could be anything but a victim, either of himself or of his society, is a measure of his delusion. Beckford lives in his emotion, but at the same time, that emotion embodies the fear of desire, the "Demons" that come to torment him from within as well as without. The sympathetic contessa can compose the potion that will effect this transformation because she can sympathize, she can understand, she can give their love a place that exists outside of time and consequently outside of desire as well as fate. It is a place, of course, that Beckford never found.

A little over a year later, he writes to Courtenay in terms that dramatize this complicated emotional stance even more vividly. The boy had scribbled a postscript to a letter written by the ever-devoted Louisa, his cousin Peter's wife, who was by now almost desperate in her love for Beckford. I quote this letter at length because it seems to me to tell the whole story of Beckford's pæderasty:

> I read your letter with a beating heart, my dearest Willy, and kissed it a thousand times. It is needless for me to repeat that I am miserable without you. You know I can scarcely be said to live in your absence. No words can express my feelings when I saw the Afft. lines you wrote in our dear Louisa's letter. At this moment I am ready to cry with joy. Do not forget me my own William. Do not forget the happy hours we have passed together. Your poor Mother loved you not better than I do. At any time I would sacrifice every drop of blood in my veins to do you good, or spare you a moment's misery. I shall never enjoy peace again till I know whether I am to be with you when I return. I am certain your Father is set against us, and will do all in his power as well as your cruel Aunt to keep us asunder; but it will be your fault, if you intirely abandon me. What have we done, Wm., to be treated with such severity! I often dream after a solitary ramble on the dreary plains near Rome, that I am sitting with you in a meadow at Ford on a summer's evening, my arm thrown round your neck. I seem to see the wilds beyond the House and the Cattle winding slowly among them. I even fancy, I hear your voice singing one of the tunes I composed when I was in Devonshire. Whilst thus engaged and giving way to a languid melancholy tenderness, two snakes start from the hedge and twine round us. I see your face turn pale and your limbs tremble. I seem to press you closely in my arms. We both feel the cold writhing of the snakes in our bosoms, both join our lips for the last time and both expire. . . . Louisa can tell you that this is not the first time such horrid dreams have haunted me. If I might interpret my vision, . . . and . . . are the Snakes, who under the appearance of prudence and affection would creep into our bosoms and sting our vitals. Why cannot we be friends in peace? Is there any crime in loving each other as we do? You will hardly be able to read this letter: it is blotted with my tears. My William, my own dear Friend, write to me for God's sake: put all your confidence in Louisa who loves us both.

(Chapman 135-36; dated Rome July 1st, 1782)

This letter exposes the nature of this love affair in dazzling detail. At first, this account heightens the difference that I have articulated between "sodomy" and Beckford's male version of "romantic friendship." Moving, as it does, from the excitement of anticipation ("a beating heart") through misery and lifelessness, to exuberant feelings and tears of joy—all in the first few sentences—the letter comes alive with a high-pitched emotionalism that begins to suggest what Beckford's "pæderasty" has come to mean. A simple "do not forget me" becomes "your poor mother loved you not better than I do"; Courtenay's mother (recently deceased) was Beckford's friend, of course, and Beckford seems quite ready to invoke the female component of his affection even if the female, as in this case, is deceased. A Freudian reading of this attempt to express love for a boy by means of an appeal to his dead mother might suggest that Beckford was rewriting Courtenay's family romance with himself in the maternal position, perfectly reasonable if Beckford's intention was to construct a subjectivity receptive to his "maternal" love. But Beckford also knows that a mother's love can be as brutalizing and devastating as any antagonistic force—his own mother had hardly begun her openly antagonistic campaign against him, nor had her violent affection for her son brought him anything but heartache—and he may have meant the maternal analogy as a threat. Both are implicit in his ready transition from mother to martyr, and his perfunctory willingness to "sacrifice every drop of blood" stops just short of making himself the victim of Courtenay's innocence.

Once Beckford mentions the boy's father, however, undisguised recrimination and threat follow fast upon one another, and the letter quickly turns from a love letter to a death threat. The love itself implies this hideous denouement, the letter suggests, and the boy is made to seem responsible for whatever effect paternal disapproval will finally have—"it will be your fault if you intirely abandon me"—and his pathetic "What have we done"—as if the twelve-year-old could answer that question better than he—smacks either of total innocence or total disingenuousness. What begins then as the tale of music on a summer's evening and is so calculatingly disfigured as a hideous nightmare suggests not just the threat that Beckford is sending to his young cousin but also his own deepest sense of what their affection means. The boys embrace as they are "giving way to a languid melancholy tenderness" only to find that they feel "the cold writhing of the Snakes in our bosoms." Of course, the snakes represent Courtenay's father and his aunt, but they also represent the destructive power of desire to corrupt the pure love that Beckford constantly tries to articulate when talking to the boy. It is as if he is saying that the destruction of their love is present in its very constitution; that he cannot put his arm around the boy without the snakes intruding, winding in their entrails, and finally destroying them. Beckford seems unclear as to whether it is the world outside or the world within that is most destructive.

"Why cannot we be friends in peace? Is there any crime in loving each other as we do?" The answer to Beckford's question is of course both yes and no. There is no crime in their love, or in any other that is as deeply mutual as this seems to have been. But it is a crime to defy cultural dictates in this way, as Beckford knows. By loving the boy as he does, Beckford condemns them both to a life of ignominy and shame. What Beckford has done, however, is subtly to have leveled the criminal accusation at the boy who returns his love. Courtenay is blamed here as blatantly as he will be later on. For after all, Beckford seems to say, he causes the desire that threatens to destroy them both. At Powderham that threat was fulfilled.[22]

When the scandal first broke, Beckford thought of fleeing, but if he did start to leave the country he got no farther than Dover. He sat out the vilification of his name at home in Fonthill. That is what makes the following notice so surprising.

> Mr.——— of ———, & c. & C. is certainly gone post haste to *Italy!*
>
> Master ———, the eldest, indeed the only son of Lord ———, has left Westminster School, and accompanies Mr. ———!
>
> Dr. M——— D——— was the gentleman who was unlucky enough to detect the late nasty flagitious business.
>
> Florence is the place of destination fixed on for the eccentric travellers.
>
> (*Public Advertiser,* 1 December 1784; correction of Chapman 185)

The hints at actual scandal are more suggestive here, and the tone of public outrage has achieved something of its vocabulary of exclusion: the terms, that is, that will keep Beckford out of polite society for sixty years. That such a scandal would place Beckford and Courtenay in Italy is of course no surprise in the eighteenth century. Italy had already been called the "*Mother* and *Nurse* of *Sodomy*" (in *Satan's Harvest Home*) and even Beckford's friend, Sir William Hamilton, received from his nephew the following account of what had happened at Fonthill: "his promised honours will be withheld; he probably will be obliged to vacate his seat, and retire to Italy to make up the loss which Italy has sustained by Lord Tilney's death, unless he aspires to the office of G. Chamberlain to the K[ing] of P[russia]" (Trumbach, *Satan's Harvest Home* 51).[23] Both accounts assume that Beckford has fled, or that he has been sent away ("the destination fixed on for . . ."), and that there are witnesses to a "late nasty flagitious business." Neither assumption is correct, but each remains useful in the years to come. The term "eccentric travellers," however, hints again at a space—however distant from the center—for two such men to occupy. Of course it is a euphemism, but is the very choice that suggests a kind of public recognition even in public censure.[24]

* * *

In the "episodes" of *Vathek,* which were never published in his lifetime, Beckford articulates a tale of pæderasty that is both elegant in its expression and chilling in its implication. In "The Story of Prince Alasi and the Princess Firouzkah," as Brian Fothergill notes, Beckford reworks his portrayal of innocent youth.[25] In this story a young boy, Firouz, becomes the obsession of Prince Alasi and leads him into a nefarious world of desire and recrimination. Notwithstanding an opportune change in the boy's gender—Firouz reveals himself later as the Princess Firouzkah—Beckford's issues are not far from the surface. Fothergill makes an almost too easy connection between Firouz and Courtenay, but it seems fair to say that in the character of Firouz Beckford was looking for ways to explain the failure of his own pæderastic attachments (Fothergill 142). When Firouz first appears Alasi says: "At last . . . Heaven has hearkened to my dearest wish. It has sent me the true heart's-friend I should never have found in my court; it has sent him to me adorned with all the charms of innocence—charms that will be followed, at a maturer age, by those good qualities that make of friendship man's highest blessing." Soon, however, that "innocence" proves to be corrupt and corrupting. Firouz's last act of villainy is his revelation of himself as a woman: no treachery in the story seems greater than this. "What irresistible power compels me to love you," Alasi asks the boy Firouz (Beckford, *Episodes* 5, 13).

Compulsive love of a boy inherently wicked is a not quite fitting epitaph to the affair with William Courte-

nay. Nor was Beckford's love of Courtenay as beneficent as that expressed in this moral tale. Still, the tale is
suggestive. The ideal transition from love-object to
friend that is celebrated in this passage eluded Beckford.[26] Firouz's ability to change gender suggests how
little control one's love can ever exert on another. The
search for a "true heart's-friend" may never be more
than illusory. Beckford found in his own sexuality a
quality that he did not understand, that he did not trust,
and that he knew would destroy him. But he also knew
that this was who he was. He grappled throughout his
life with a sexual instinct that made him a criminal in
his own desire. By acknowledging it in his writing,
however, he gives it an identity, a sexual identity, that
defies "grammatical" convention. With Beckford, the
pæderast becomes a part of speech.

Notes

The Pembroke Papers are quoted in Trumbach, and also
in Fothergill (173). Lord Pembroke was writing to England at the time of the Powderham scandal; interestingly, his knowledge of the situation led him to no conclusions about sexual roles.

1. William Beckford was born in 1760 to one of England's wealthiest families. His father was alderman and lord mayor of London; his mother a strict
Calvinist who did her best, especially after his father died when he was ten years old, to form a
young gentleman who would rise to political
prominence as his father had. Beckford early on
showed tendencies of which his mother disap-
proved: his devotion to music, his fascination with
"oriental" tales, and his love of young boys. William Courtenay, born in 1768, was the son and heir
of the second Viscount Courtenay; the youngest of
thirteen children, and the only boy, he was known
in the family as "Kitty."

2. It is impossible to say what "really" happened at
Powderham. There is little reason to think that
Beckford and Courtenay were exposed in some
dramatic way: Beckford himself protested that he
was innocent of any wrongdoing, and he nursed a
grievance against Loughborough throughout his
entire life. Loughborough may only have had
Beckford's letters to Courtenay. But then, what
more did he need to exercise complete control
over his eccentric victim? For details of the Powderham scandal, see Fothergill 163-75.

3. To prosecute Beckford, Loughborough would have
needed at least an eyewitness, which, in spite of
the lurid accounts that emerged from Powderham,
he seems not to have had; and he would have
needed Courtenay's willingness to hand over letters and to participate in the prosecution. Records
of eighteenth-century sodomy trials, such as they
are, suggest no precedent for prosecuting a person
of Beckford's class or social status. Some of these
trials are reprinted in Trumbach, ed., *Select Trials
at the Sessions-House in the Old Bailey* 2: 362-65,
367-69; and in Trumbach, ed., *Sodomy Trials*; see
also Bray 81-114; and Trumbach, "London's Sodomites."

4. See de Lille, *Complaint of Nature* 3; see also, de
Lille, *Plaint of Nature* 68.

5. Fourteen was the age of consent for males at the
time; see Trumbach, "Sodomitical Assaults" 410.

6. For a similar argument against sodomy, see *Satan's Harvest Home* 50-55.

7. The pæderasty of *Vathek,* obvious to readers such
as Hester Piozzi, is so suffused with the twilight
glow of Beckford's emotion as to defy late
twentieth-century notions of child abuse and victimization. It is centered on the figure of Gulchenrouz, the only central character who escapes damnation in the novel, and he does so by remaining
within "the pure happiness of childhood" in which
love remains unsullied by the promptings of desire. See Haggerty.

8. See, for instance, MacCannell, and Gallop. Mac-
Cannell develops Gallop's argument about the relation between pedagogy and pæderasty from the
time of Plato.

9. As early as 1831, Arthur Hallam wrote his prize-
winning essay on Greek love, which parallels arguments made even earlier by Percy Bysshe Shelley; see Dellamora 16-17, 24-25.

10. For a discussion of the language and imagery of
Greek love, see Dover 39-59.

11. For an instance of Renaissance pæderasty, see
Barnfield.

12. The most complete classification of male-male
sexual possibilities in the eighteenth century is
that found in Rousseau; for Rousseau's account of
Beckford, see 144.

13. It was not only court libertines who felt this way.
Trumbach alludes to the 1761 court martial in
which "Charles Ferret testified that when he was
awakened by the noise of the sexual exertion of
Henry Newton on Thomas Finney's body, '[I] put
my left hand up and got hold of both his stones
fast, the other part was in the body of the boy, I
asked him what he had got there, he said cunt'"
(Trumbach, "Sodomitical Assaults" 415); see also
Gilbert 74-75. Gilbert also explains that, "In spite
of the supposed legal difficulties of proving buggery in the courts, a high percentage of purported
sodomites are convicted and executed. While proof

of penetration rules protected some men on trial for this offense, the navy still managed to hang more than half the men brought to trial for buggery between 1749 and 1806" (86).

14. Pæderasty, of course, was implicit in accounts of male-male erotic attraction that centered on the figure of Ganymede; see, for instance, Saslow; for a discussion of the "cultural translation" of the myth, see Barkin 8, 21-24, 29-36, 56-59. See also Bredbeck 3-23; Bredbeck explains Renaissance distinctions among the terms Ganymede, catamite, and ingle, see 16-18.

15. In *A Tale of a Tub* (1704), Swift mentions that his academy will include a "large *Pederastick* school with *French* and *Italian* masters" (41); see also Gibbon 4: 233. Hume says that "Solon's law forbid pæderasty to slaves, as being an act of too great dignity for such mean persons" (2: 292, n.).

16. Cannon's *Ancient and Modern Pæderasty Investigated* is the text one would wish to turn to in this context, but it is unfortunately lost.

17. Beckford uses this phrase in a reverie written to Courtenay but never sent; see Chapman 55.

18. David Halperin tries to argue the role that femininity might play in the definition of male-male desire, and Kaja Silverman, too, talks about the "place of femininity in male homosexuality." See Halperin 113-51; Silverman 339, also 339-88.

19. On "romantic friendship," Mavor; see also Todd 1-6.

20. Not all of Beckford's women friends were as supportive as these. Beckford's experience in Venice was a source of serious concern to his patroness, Lady Hamilton, wife of Sir William Hamilton, envoy to Naples. Beckford could say to her, typically: "I can venture expressing to you all my wayward thoughts—can murmur—can even weep in your company" (Melville 98; see also, Fothergill 93); her response was clear: "Take courage. You have taken the first steps, continue to resist, and every day you will find the struggle less—the *important* struggle—what is it for? no less than *honour, reputation,* and all that an honest and noble soul holds dear, while infamy, *eternal infamy* (my Soul freezes when I write the word) attends the giving way to the soft alluring of a criminal passion" (qtd. from the *Hamilton Papers,* Chapman 78). It is important to remember that even at the time of the scandal, Beckford's wife was present. It is perhaps because she *was* present that the scandal ever occurred. Perhaps the presence of his wife who supported and loved him and who, if she was like any of the other women to whom he was attached, knew about his devotion to William,

gave him permission, as it were, to pursue the boy during their visit there. Whatever is true, she remained faithful to him till her death a few years later.

21. Written in December 1781, in French; quoted in Alexander 263-66 (my translation).

22. There is ample evidence that Beckford was less charmed with the sixteen-year-old William Courtenay than he had been with the "luscious" youth of twelve or thirteen. He wrote letters complaining of the boy's effeminacy, his interest in fashion, and his lack of attention in matters artistic or musical. After the crisis, Beckford blamed Courtenay for all that occurred.

23. Hamilton quoted in Fothergill 173, from *Hamilton Papers* 1: 95, letter 133; both characters were notorious for sexual "eccentricity."

24. Courtenay may have left Westminster School, but he did not accompany Beckford anywhere, nor were the two ever really close again. He went on to succeed his father as third Viscount Courtenay and later ninth earl of Devon, and himself became notorious as a homosexual who was nearly prosecuted for his behavior. When convinced that a "jury of his peers" would not condone his activities, he "wept like a child and was willingly taken abroad on a vessel . . . and passed there under a false name" (qtd. in Fothergill 178, from *Farington Diary* 6: 273). He died in exile in 1835. Few critics or biographers have shown much interest in the later career of Courtenay, but some have gone so far as to blame him for Beckford's downfall. One biographer, for instance, says that "in apportioning blame it is only fair to Beckford to remember that the life of Courtenay (afterwards Earl of Devon) ended, years after he and Beckford had drifted apart, in shame and moral catastrophe" (Oliver 196 n).

25. On both *Vathek* and "The Story of Prince Alasi and the Princess Firouzkah," see Fothergill 128-34, 142-43.

26. For an account of Beckford's later love affair with Gregorio Franchi, which was uniquely satisfying, see Fothergill 199-200; see also, Norton 221-31.

Works Cited

Alexander, Boyd. *England's Wealthiest Son.* London: Centaur, 1962.

Barkin, Leonard. *Transuming Passion: Ganymede and the Erotics of Humanism.* Stanford: Stanford UP, 1991.

Barnfield, Richard. *The Affectionate Shepheard, Containing the Complaint of Daphnis for the loue of Ganimede.* London, 1594.

Beckford, William. *The Episodes of Vathek.* Trans. Sir Frank T. Marzial. London: Chapman and Dodd, n.d.

———. *Vathek.* 1786. Ed. Roger Lonsdale. Oxford: Oxford UP, 1983.

Bray, Alan. *Homosexuality in Renaissance England.* London: Gay Men's P, 1982.

Bredbeck, Gregory W. *Sodomy and Interpretation: Marlowe to Milton.* Ithaca: Cornell UP, 1991.

Chapman, Guy. *Beckford.* London: Jonathan Cape, 1940.

Dellamora, Richard. *Masculine Desire: The Sexual Politics of Victorian Aestheticism.* Chapel Hill: U of North Carolina P, 1990.

Dover, K. J. *Greek Homosexuality.* Cambridge: Harvard UP, 1978.

Fothergill, Brian. *Beckford at Fonthill.* London: Faber, 1979.

Gallop, Jane. "The Immoral Teachers." *Yale French Studies* 63 (1982): 117-28.

Gibbon, Edward. *The History of the Decline and Fall of the Roman Empire.* Ed. J. B. Bury. 4 vols. London: Methuen, 1900.

Gilbert, Arthur N. "Buggery in the British Navy." *Journal of Social History* 10 (1976): 74-75.

Haggerty, George E. "Literature and Homosexuality in the Later Eighteenth Century: Walpole, Beckford, and Lewis." *Studies in the Novel* 18 (1986): 341-52.

Halperin, David M. "Why Is Diotima a Woman?" *One Hundred Years of Homosexuality and Other Essays on Greek Love.* New York: Routledge, 1990. 113-51.

Herbert, Lord. *Pembroke Papers.* 1780-1794. London, 1950.

Hume, David. *Essays: Moral, Political, and Literary.* Ed. T. H. Green and T. H. Grose. 2 vols. London: Longmans, 1875.

Lille, Alain de. *The Complaint of Nature.* [*De Planctu Naturae,* c. 1165.] Trans. Douglas M. Moffat. New York: H. Holt, 1908.

———. *Plaint of Nature.* Trans. James J. Sheridan. Toronto: Pontifical Institute of Medieval Studies, 1981.

MacCannell, Juliet Flower. "Resistance to Sexual Theory." *Theory/Pedagogy/Politics: Texts for Change.* Ed. Donald Morton and Mas'ud Zavarzadeh. Urbana: U of Illinois P, 1991. 64-89.

Mavor, Elizabeth. *The Ladies of Llangollen.* Harmondsworth: Penguin, 1974.

Melville, Lewis. *The Life and Letters of William Beckford.* London: Heinemann, 1910.

Norton, Rictor. *Mother Clap's Molly House: The Gay Subculture in England 1700-1830.* London: Gay Men's P, 1992.

Oliver, John W. *The Life of William Beckford.* London: Oxford UP, 1932.

Rochester, John Wilmot, earl of. *Poems.* Ed. Keith Walker. Oxford: Basil Blackwell, 1984.

Rousseau, G. S. "The Pursuit of Homosexuality in the Eighteenth Century: 'Utterly Confused Category' and/or Rich Repository?" *'Tis Nature's Fault: Unauthorized Sexuality During the Enlightenment.* Ed. Robert Purks Maccubbin. Cambridge: Cambridge UP, 1987. 132-68.

Saslow, James. *Ganymede in the Renaissance: Homosexuality in Art and Society.* New Haven: Yale UP, 1986.

Sedgwick, Eve Kosofsky. *Between Men: English Literature and Male Homosocial Desire.* New York: Columbia UP, 1985.

Silverman, Kaja. *Male Subjectivity at the Margins.* New York: Routledge, 1992.

Swift, Jonathan. *A Tale of a Tub.* Ed. A. C. Guthkeltch and D. Nichol Smith. 2d ed. Oxford: Clarendon, 1958.

Thrale, Hester Lynch. *Thraliana, The Diary of Mrs. Hester Lynch Thrale (Later Mrs. Piozzi), 1776-1809.* Ed. Katharine C. Balderston. 2d ed. 2 vols. Oxford: Clarendon, 1951.

Todd, Janet. *Women's Friendship in Literature.* New York: Columbia UP, 1980.

Trumbach, Randolph. "The Birth of the Queen: Sodomy and the Emergence of Gender Equality in Modern Culture, 1660-1750." *Hidden from History: Reclaiming the Gay and Lesbian Past.* Ed. Martin Bauml Duberman, Martha Vicinus, and George Chauncey Jr. New York: New American Library, 1989. 129-40.

———. "London's Sodomites: Homosexual Behavior and Western Culture in the Eighteenth Century." *Journal of Social History* 2 (1977): 1-33.

———. ed. *Satan's Harvest Home.* 1749. *Hell Upon Earth and Satan's Harvest Home.* New York: Garland, 1985.

El Habib Benrahhal Serghini (essay date 1998)

SOURCE: Serghini, El Habib Benrahhal. "William Beckford's Symbolic Appropriation of the Oriental Context." In *Oriental Prospects: Western Literature and the Lure of the East,* edited by C. C. Barfoot and Theo D'haen, pp. 43-64. Amsterdam, Netherlands: Rodopi, 1998.

[*In the following essay, Serghini maintains that "Beckford's Orient . . . needs to be understood less as a geographic region of the globe than as a topos whose co-ordinates derive their meaning from that very same sensibility."*]

Elsewhere I have argued that William Beckford's *The Vision* (1777) and *Vathek* (1786) can be seen as instances of the Romantic desire to explore the imagination.[1] In the present essay, I shall attempt to demonstrate that Beckford's Orient too needs to be understood less as a geographic region of the globe than as a topos whose co-ordinates derive their meaning from that very same sensibility. Beckford's aesthetic project to bring the Orient to life, to characterize it, and to depict it to himself and his reader, involved a choice of subject whose inner socio-historical nature was alien to him, and to which he could lend the appearance of reality only by means of the conscientious application of orientalism, that is to say, in an external, decorative and picturesque fashion. The world he draws is full of historically exact costumes and decorations, but its psychology belongs rather to the socio-historical situation of Beckford himself. Specifically, it depends on the representational convention regarding the Orient typical of orientalism as a western discursive system premised on exteriority. Therefore, my concern in this essay is with these representations *as* representations, and not with their "correctness" as presentations of exterior reality. I shall be particularly concerned with the way in which these representations guided Beckford in his vision of the Orient.

In his analysis of *Vathek,* Marcel May has demonstrated the extent to which Beckford's mind was surfeited with traveller's accounts, oriental tales translated or compiled, and oriental lore in general.[2] Evidence of the large number of works behind *Vathek* itself was derived partly from Beckford's hints about his own reading in letters written before 1786, from lists of books in the sale of his Fonthill library in 1823, but mainly from the correspondence with Samuel Henley in the course of 1785-1786, the period during which Henley was engaged in translating *Vathek* into English and in compiling the accompanying notes. Beckford was giving him specific instructions where to turn for illustrations.[3] In answer to Henley's queries Beckford wrote:[4]

> *The Arabian Nights* will furnish some illustrations (particularly as to Ghouls, etc.) but much more may be learnt from d'Herbelot's *Bibliothèque orientale* and Richardson's *Dissertation*.[5]

And:

> The Domes of Shaddukian and Amberabad you will find explained in Richardson. The Cocknos is a bird whose bill is much esteemed in Persia for its beautiful polish, and sometimes used as a spoon; see *Persian Tales,* Hist of the Sorrowful Vizir, and Zelica Begum.

> The butterflies of Cachemire are celebrated in a poem of Memphis!! I slaved at with Zemir, the old Mohammedan, who assisted me in translating W. Montagu's MSS. But they are hardly worth a note.

> . . . you will compose a tolerably long note on the Simorgue. That respectable bird deserves all you can say

of her. Soliman Raad, Soliman Daki (not Dawmin's, for God's Sake) and Soliman surnamed Gian-ben-Gian will furnish ample scope for a display of Oriental conditions.[6]

Besides, Beckford had one great advantage over many of the later contributors to the genre of the oriental tale who sometimes had first-hand experience of the Orient or had good sources of information at their disposal—he had acquired a knowledge of Arabic.[7] Guy Chapman's examinations of the Beckford papers resulted in the revelation of a large number of translations from the *Arabian Nights,* and of E. W. Montagu's manuscripts which Beckford seems to have translated into French as an exercise. Beside the translations, Chapman found manuscripts of at least six tales, many including frame tales in which the author or translator deviated from the original. This led Chapman to remark that only an accomplished oriental scholar could distinguish which of the doubtful tales were original and which translations. The preface which Beckford himself wrote to one of these tales indicates the way most of them were conceived. The preface, as reported by Chapman, runs:

> J'avais commencé à traduire littéralement. Mon maître d'arabe, un vieux musulman natif de la Mecque, me l'avois recommendé comme exercise de langue—j'ai trouvé pourtant la narration si pompeusement ennuieuse que je l'ai jeté de côté—Zemir voulut me brider comme de raison mais ayant pris le mord aux dents, je me suis emporté à grand galop dans les régions de mon imaginations—voici le résultat. . . .[8]

In Beckford's own words, we have here an indication of his trafficking with orientalism; it is a means of erecting fantasies for the reader and himself. If this is so, it is only legitimate to inquire into the purpose of the complete documentation and exhaustive description buttressing *Vathek.* Those travellers who had first-hand experience of the East thought of Beckford's texts as a derivation from an original source rather than as a story made up by an outsider. Byron, for instance, bestowed on Beckford's tale the most lavish praise:

> For correctness of costume, beauty of description, and power of imagination, it far surpasses all European imitations, and bears such marks of originality that those who have visited the East will find some difficulty in believing it to be more than a translation.[9]

Yet Beckford, like Byron, is a secondary, detached figure. Indeed, he is even more detached than Byron because, as the latter knew, Beckford's work was based on library orientalism and its tone of authenticity, however impressive, was mediated through the experience of others. Yet the result for someone like Byron, who himself stood closer to the source than Beckford, is impressive in spite of the fact that the latter's authenticity is second hand, his orientalism parthenogenetic.[10] Byron goes on to argue that Beckford's imagination of the

East is more original, his orientalism more beautiful and exciting than that of anyone else in his time, and, finally, that his work cannot be surpassed for "correctness of costume".

Beckford's correctness in such details was a result of his voracious reading of texts about the East. These he absorbed with avidity and care, as has been pointed out by his biographers and critics. Beckford took the same attitude towards his material that Vathek took towards the world: nothing succeeds like excess; the world is full of objects, tastes and textures, and in order to realize ourselves most fully within the world, we have to make contact with all its minutiae.[11] The result is the creation of a suggestive synthesis, one in which the manner of the telling or the style of presentation become as significant—and evident—a part of the experience of the self as the object itself. His orientalism makes the continuation of such a structure possible by exploiting a suggestive equivalent in which the medium and forms used become part of the truth of the experience communicated. The lushness which characterizes **Vathek** is not simply a matter of countering neo-classical ideas about generality, an aspect for which Beckford was much praised; such profusion is moral as much as textual, the way to understand a state of soul as well as a literary mode. The details and extravagance of **Vathek**'s elaborate contexts are the kind of self-sufficient lushness that was there to be touched by the inner senses as well as to define the qualities of a place.

Such qualities are the result of a synthesis by which the three processes of imagining, experiencing and remembering as the fundamental principles of creative activity find particularly rich and exemplary expression in orientalist literature.[12] In this way, Beckford's orientalism appears as much informed by desire and by mediated observation as by imagination.

As attested by the large number of artists and writers who went to the East, their journeys (whether actual, or imagined or recollected memories) amounted to acts of self-definition. The evidence of such acts prompted Michael Giselman to view the "otherness" of the East which was explored and enjoyed in this way less as an "elsewhere" than a "within".[13] James Thompson takes a somewhat similar stance when he points to the fact that the representations of such travellers can never be neutral since they could not relinquish their own personal and cultural notions. Taking the cases of Gérard de Nerval, Théophile Gautier and Thackeray, Thompson goes as far as to say that despite the distinctive and different tones of such writers, and their first-hand experience of the East, their shared stress on an essentially imaginative component dominated their perception of the Orient.[14] Likewise, Beckford's accounts of the East unfold according to the laws and conventions of the fictional genre. His mediated experience is coloured by the phe-

nomenon of intertextuality: memories of other writers' adventures or imaginings colour and shape his own, just as elements derived from the *Arabian Nights* or from contemporary orientalist texts motivate both thematic and structural developments.

Such derivations do not inform only his oriental texts but are found throughout most of his writing, and especially in his correspondence during his Grand Tour, which bears witness to the complex preparatory work of the imagination. As Beckford travels through Europe, scenes come back to him like a dream of a previous existence, or like one of those forgotten dreams rekindled by the chance discovery of a real object. The accounts of historians and travellers, pictures and engravings compose in the depths of his mind a kind of chimerical geography which satisfies all our expectations of a mirage. Consequently, for the inspired orientalist, the East (like any other distant part of the world) may be conjured up at will and on any occasion:

> I entered the court of the castle, dark and deep, as if hewn out of a rock; surrounded by a vaulted arcade, covered with arabesque ornaments, and supported by pillars as uncouthly carved as those of Persepolis. In the midst appears a marble fount with an image of bronze, that looks quite strange and cabalistic.[15]

Or:

> I was in a dark, remorseless mood, which lasted me till we reached Bree, a shabby decayed town, encompassed by wall and ruined turrets. Having nothing to do, I straggled about them, till night shaded the dreary prospects and gave me an opportunity of imagining them, if I pleased, noble and majestic. . . . I had scarcely begun to mope in tranquillity, before a rapid shower trickled amongst the clusters above me, and forced me to abandon my haunt. Returning in the midst of it to my inn, I hurried to bed, and was soon lulled asleep by the storm. A dream bore me off to Persepolis; and led me, thro' vast subterraneous treasures, to a hall, where Salomon, methought, was holding forth upon their vanity. I was upon the very point of securing a part of this immense wealth, and fancied myself writing down the sage prophet's advice, how to make use of it, when a loud vociferation in the street, and the bell of a neighbouring chapel, dispersed the vision.[16]

Surfeited with oriental lore, the mind composes itineraries that are superimposed upon reality, and it is one of the great disappointments of the tourist to see crumbling one by one before his very eyes the wonderful cities he had created with the rich and unshackled architecture of the imagination.

Thus, from Beckford's point of view, Venice, because of its synthesis of eastern and western racial and cultural types, is perceived as the Babylon of Europe:

> I observed a great number of Orientals amongst the crowd, and heard Turkish and Arabic muttering in every corner. Here the Slavonian dialect predominated;

there some Grecian jargon, almost unintelligible. Had St Mark's Church been the wondrous tower, and its piazza the chief square of the city of Babylon, there could scarcely have been a greater confusion of languages.[17]

As I suggested earlier, the notion of synthesis is central to Beckford's conception of the Orient. The attraction of such places as Italy, Spain or Portugal lay in the fact that they offered a unified plenitude of contrasts and differences inherent in the national or continental hinterlands surrounding them, and were reminiscent of exotic horizons. Literature was conceived by Beckford as operating in a similar way to the great oriental city: its aim was to create an ideal synthesis of the multiple and heterogenous elements which constitute a given culture, a uniting of personal and subjective experience with that recorded by many writers, named or anonymous, from the point of view of history, religion, myth or fantasy. This explains his determination to "have truth to work upon in [his] dreams". Beckford even finds out from others after the event what it is he has missed: this phenomenon, which one might call the paradox of retrospective anticipation, also colours Beckford's oriental texts, and explains the fact that for him no synthesis is ever definitive: cultures, like subjectivities, are inherently mobile, constantly tending towards their own transcendence.

Therefore Beckford's orientalism is never static. Like a poet using rhyme as a point of departure, and as the structural principle of his verse, with similar skill he establishes an aesthetic unity by repeating and harmonizing similar or complementary images, building up in this way a unified impression which is as important to the significance of the text as its content is to meaning, and offering each time a new field for self-projection. Thus, it has been observed that *The Vision* contrasts markedly in atmosphere with *Vathek*. As Fatma M. Moussa has said "Many readers were struck by the atmosphere of luminous wisdom and natural goodness, much in contrast to the sense of evil that hangs over *Vathek*".[18]

André Parreaux does not concur with Moussa's view on account of the fact that the successive additions to *The Vision* not only alter this conception, but also establish a greater similarity between the two works.[19] Yet it seems that Parreaux did not take into consideration the movement of the narrative which animates the two texts and the iconography it determines. Thus in *Vathek* the need for an "elsewhere" is translated as a series of meals: we move in cycles of famine and feast from the first wing of the Palace of the Five Senses, that of Taste or of "*The eternal or unsatiating Banquet*"[20] to the feast set by Nouronihar's father; to the grotesque orgy where Carathis entertains the ghouls; and finally to the ironic banquet in the Halls of Eblis. The significance of Vathek's consuming greed is that to eat one's way

through life is to be existentially incorporative.[21] We may say that Beckford wanted to absorb the Orient in his text, and this figure of appropriation arises physically in the metonymy of eating one's way through the oriental location. In contrast to *Vathek*, the movement of the narrative in *The Vision* is motivated by the need of escapism, since the enclosure in *The Vision* is characterized as the very place of dreams and illusions in which the narrator wants to absorb himself. Here Beckford's fantasy inscribes within itself one of the meanings which the Orient bore for orientalizing Europe—the womb, the origin. In that sense, the movement might be characterized as absorption of the self in the referent.[22]

How can we account for this transformation of tropology? To answer this question we need to turn to historical conjecture and consider such texts against a background of ideological and cultural structures that transcend the peculiarities and susceptibilities of any individual writer.

Edward Said's *Orientalism* suggests the necessity of restoring the specific context and content of such escapism (whether real or imaginary). Said incites us to define, within the network of their ideological and material determinants, the specific contradictions which such texts sought to resolve. For Said, the European formation of an orientalist "idea" and institution depended first of all upon the existence of a power relationship linking West and East in a manner profoundly less innocent than certain literary texts of the period might have suggested. Orientalism, says Said, clarifies how these persistent dreams of escape presuppose the concrete political domination of the territory ideologically invested as the "elsewhere" of romantic imagination. These dreams and these texts inscribe this ascendence. Of course Beckford's texts are hardly reducible to a simple reproduction of the structures of orientalist discourse. He transforms and reworks them, but he cannot obliterate them. For the force of orientalist discourse is not confined to a certain colonialist mentality; it is inscribed in a sociopolitical situation in which Beckford partakes, despite his manifest desire to escape from it, and which also affects the condition of his own texts.[23]

In the perspective defined by Said, since orientalism is a European means of representation, it necessarily figures its referent through the degraded system from which Beckford was trying to escape. Furthermore, this representational system leaves little room for an intrinsic discourse of the Orient itself. Beckford thus seems situated at the intersection of two conflicting representations: an original fantasy project of escape in the Orient, and, at the same time, a textual realization which inscribes clearly conventional, predetermined structures and protocols. The implicit structure of Beckford's fantasy appears as the dream of absorbing himself—almost obliterating himself in this discourse. But the co-ordinate metonymy I referred to earlier as the "absorption of" will gradually alter this paradigm in a significant way, as the procedures of textual representations cause an alien system to intervene in and ultimately to determine its representation. In the context of my argument, such an objectification of the foreignness of the Orient is an act of appropriation and consumption of the oriental referent which involuntarily organizes Beckford's text.

Consequently traces of this twin metonymy tend to surface in Beckford's oscillations between a sentimental, idealized and even religious reverence concerning the cultural system to which he appeals to purge him of his Occident, and a rather methodological exploitation of the same system. The result is that despite Beckford's more enlightened intentions, his orientalism often appears as the text of his own consumption of the Orient. Thus at the age of seventeen, while *The Vision* was in progress, Beckford wrote from Switzerland to Alexander Cozens:

> To receive visits and to return them, to be mightily civil, well-bred, quiet, prettily dressed and smart is to be what your old ladies call in England a charming gentleman. . . . To pay and receive fulsome compliments from the learned, to talk with modesty and precision, to sport an opinion gracefully . . . , to delight in mathematics, logic, geometry and the Rule of Right . . . , to despise poetry and venerable antiquity, murder taste, abhor imagination, detest all the charms of eloquence unless capable of mathematical demonstration, and more than all to be vigorously incredulous, is to gain the reputation of good sense. Such an animal I am sometimes doomed to be! To glory in horses, to know how to knock up and how to cure them, to smell of the stable, swear, talk bawdy, eat roastbeef, drink, speak bad French. . . . Such an animal I am determined not to be.[24]

Such a rhetoric is framed by one structure of difference, that between the discourse of the hated bourgeoisie in England and a discourse which might be labelled the discourse of "everywhere else": a discourse which would remove him from the place where the hegemonic is prevalent, beyond the horizon of restrictions of custom and authority:

> My situation is sad and solitary. I stray disconsolately . . . scarcely knowing which way to bend my steps. I look around and all is a perfect void. Those scenes which were wont to amuse me, delight me no more. My imagination roams to other countries in search of pleasure it no longer finds at home. This evening it has been transported to . . . Tartary. . . . Such delusions as these form my present felicity, without them, I should be the most unhappy of mankind and the persecutions of Franguis would be intolerable. . . . Had I not this power of being transported wheresoever I list . . . I should soon breathe my last. . . .[25]

But Beckford was not only rhapsodical in his praise of the Orient. His intense desire to transcend present diffi-culties and resistances was accompanied by a genuine effort to absorb himself in horizons which were thus passionately projected. Of such efforts Chapman says:

> With a good knowledge of Latin, Greek, Persian, Arabic and Sanskrit, his reading had embraced not only the classical authors, but also the writings of the Romantic movements, which in 1777 had firmly fixed itself on the imagination of Europe. Ossian had captured him, and "My favourite" the melancholy Gray. With these, with Dante and Ariosto, with volumes on Northern mythology, on travels in China, India and Mexico, with the *Arabian Nights* and other Oriental tales . . . he had more than enough. . . .[26]

Later on, Beckford was to tell Cyrus Redding:

> I preferred it [oriental literature] to the classics of Greece and Rome. I began it myself as a relief from the dryness of my other studies. . . . The Latin and Greek were set tasks. The Persian I began of my own accord.[27]

But it is in *The Vision* that this movement of absorption is most characteristic. The subterranean world in which the narrator finds himself inscribes within itself one of the meanings which the Orient bore for orientalizing Europe and is epitomized by the iconography of escapism and repose which stem from a constant reference to places, monuments, terms and mores which were exotic. In this guise, such references stand as the classical product of an antinomic formation—one wants to get away, and the Orient is "away". This accounts for the presence in the body of the narrative of themes, motifs, and details which through their synergy serve to diffuse the sense of an indeterminate Orient.

Besides such catalogues, which serve to "museumize" the Orient, Beckford uses other procedures to evoke and diffuse the idea of the Orient. This specific procedure takes the form of the description and evocation of esoteric traditions and rites, and acts as a mock reality-effect to anchor the narrative within a specific frame, that of arcane rites and specialized knowledge which generate in the reader's mind a referent, and create a sense of meaningfulness to which because of the cultural connotations associated with such referents, the reader does not fail to respond.

Thus, the rite of initiation in *The Vision* seems to have no other function in the narrative apart from evoking the Orient through the montage of particular elements. This procedure is apparent from the description of Moisasour and Nouronihar as the narrator perceives them at the end of a cavern:

> The tallest wore the figure of a majestic sage, his hoary hair bound by a golden fillet inscribed with unknown characters, his beard waving over an ample robe of the deep azure of the colour of the meridian sky and concealing his feet and arms with its folds. . . . The other

. . . a woman who had an imperial mien, a sublime port and a spirit in her opal eyes, a fire which I dare not describe.[28]

Beckford is quick to establish the surface, the milieu of oriental otherness. Using a technique that was to be perfected later on by orientalist painters such as Delacroix, for instance, Beckford dwells on aspects which were as much part of popular orientalism as were images of sensuality and violence. The handling of the figures, particularly the majestic port, the flowing hair and beard, the unknown characters inscribed on the golden fillet are generic conveniences, or conventions currently used at the time to evoke the sublime and majestic gloom of the pseudo-oriental sage, while the cavern itself acts as a stage in which that otherness can realize itself. The mention of gold, "deep azure" and opal as predominant colours, gives the scene a languidness, and a sense of sensuality and repose.

At this level, it must be pointed out that Beckford is doing more than perfecting a segment of popular orientalism. If he is enraptured by those surfaces and things that make a context for the self, he is equally obsessed with the interplay of what we can touch and what we can intuit. This interplay means that the oriental elements in *The Vision* differ in texture and relationship from those in *Vathek*. The surfaces in *The Vision* differ from the cruel, grotesque and dark surfaces of *Vathek* in their relationship to the totality of the world he sees. Though orientalism may be a system of representation, it must also be understood as a mode through which the self authenticates itself, not only by testing itself against otherness but also by rendering the way in which it sees that otherness and seeks to possess it.[29]

It is these qualities and relationships, these doublings of attitude, that Beckford seems to embody in his oriental texts, and it is in this respect that Beckford seems to have been touched most deeply by the otherness of the Orient. The radical form of encounter in *The Vision* links up with his intuitive search for counterparts for the self, and that link makes possible a conception of literary order in which he can, in effect, do anything he wants. *The Vision* never loses its essential order, the essential form that shaped the experience, though the potential is always there as epitomized by the dwarfs' lot. The figures of Moisasour and Nouronihar in their subdued, easy elegance and serenity act as a stage in surrounding and setting off the figure of the narrator, making a central space in which that self-containment can realize itself.

Thus, after the rite of initiation the narrator is conveyed through a set of caverns to view the golden landscape of islands and lakes that are more astonishing to the eye than anything he had previously experienced. Ultimately, this excursion leads him to another meeting with Nouronihar. To avoid an approaching storm, they seek refuge in a cave which turns out to be a sumptuous apartment carved in rock of yellow jasper and lit by a myriad of crystal lamps:

> The pavement was entirely covered with mats of the nicest workmanship, on which some skilful artists had imitated fruits and flowers with so much success that at first sight they could not be distinguished from bunches of real ones. . . . A pile of aromatic wood, neatly cleft, was placed by the side of a cheerful fire, fed with the same fuel and three large baskets heaped with cocoa nuts and all the variety of fruits the valleys produced stood on the other side. The fountain I heard in the dark trickled from a nook in the interior grot and was received in a cavity on the brink of which were placed a variety of clear crystal vases, some empty, others filled with cinnamon and wild roses in full bloom.[30]

As the storm rages in the valley outside, the two delicate beings enjoy the "perfect security" of the cavern. Nouronihar plays melancholic songs on her lute, and then sinks languidly into a carpet of flowers. The sense of repose and self-containment which emanates from both the figures and the space in which they reside sets up a dialectic of the two, an assiduous relation and alternation of figure and context in which each complements the other. This dialectic is the result of a difficult and delicate balance, and that balance is at the centre of Beckford's understanding of orientalism at the time he wrote *The Vision*.

In his study of orientalism in painting, Philip Julian speaks of the association of the East with treasure,[31] and such an association sheds light on Beckford's Orient which for him represented an opulence of both treasure and personality. *The Vision* is essentially an initiation story devoted to the search for self-determination. "Mark well", commands Moisasour, "the true scope of thy initiation. 'Tis the knowledge and government of thyself."[32] The context in which the two protagonists find themselves immersed at the end of the narrative is the logical end-result of the act of absorption initiated at the beginning of the narrative as a consequence of the act of composing the self in its difference. At the end of *The Vision,* Beckford comes to focus with intensity on his work as a representation of a moment of the artist's possession and absorption in that which is quite unlike himself. That consciousness is an answer to the condition of the vagaries of the mind which inaugurates the narrative. It is a correction and a culmination, a rebuttal and a means of survival. Orientalism appears to be not only about the other but about the self, and about the other in its relation to the self.

Since, as I indicated earlier,[33] Chapman's published version of *The Vision* represents only a fragment of a larger work, for knowledge of the additional portions of what was to constitute a longer history and Beckford's original design, we are dependent on the forty-four pages of the rough draft printed by Parreaux, that also enables us to appraise how the work relates to his orientalism.[34] Of particular interest is the part that recounts the life of Nouronihar and her ancestors which is, at the same time, an historico-mythical account of the origins of India. She opens her story by tracing geographical, historical and mythical scenes from India, descriptions which she feels are necessary, since Europeans in general do not understand the eastern countries over which they claim dominion:

> 'Tis true they sail its shores and establish themselves by the mouth of its Rivers, they advance into the maritime province and plunder the less remote possession of the Son of Timur. The desolation of Bengal, of Bashar and Crixa, the cries of oppressed Nations vouch too plainly they are but too well known on the border of these immense Empires, but which of them can boast an expedition into the woods of Pasu or march across the deserts of Mien. Name me a traveller who has penetrated into the interior of Ashem, that can relate the adventures which befell him in Aracanava or that can boast of having drank Regions hidden from European eyes.[35]

As suggested earlier, and as can be perceived through Nouronihar's narrative, orientalism, as a discourse on the East, is imposing itself on what had been conceived as an antidote to domination, forcing its representation upon the text whose function nominally had been to eliminate it. Beckford's text thus registers its contamination by Europe as a systematic and more or less conscious critique of Europe's mode of intervention and domination as voiced by Nouronihar when she points to the fact that European contacts with the East are partial, domineering, and appropriative. One is tempted to say that Beckford allowed European false consciousness to speak within his text in order to mark his own text's difference from it. But the co-ordinate metonymy referred to earlier as "absorption of" makes the text's self-critical potential fall short. Up to now, the text had been unaware of its immersion in the ideological, and traces of this second figure become transparent.

This figure of appropriation arises in the reverence concerning the cultural system to which Beckford appealed as an alternative to his Occident. Beckford's efforts to convince us of the authenticity of his vision, towards authenticating a sense of human presence, towards convincing us that what we see is the actuality of an exotic selfhood, may account at first sight for the richness of his surfaces as evidenced by the explanatory notes which accompany his oriental texts. In fact, such notes, defined by their fragmentary quality, by the possibility of their being extracted from the whole, represent the mode of transaction between East and West. Based on a regime of unequal exchange, such a mode is necessarily appropriative since its object is never the totality of an economic, political or cultural system, but rather a series of detached, reified elements drawn from a given culture, whose value depends upon the conceptual and ideological needs of the determining subject.

Beckford's constant references to d'Herbelot's *Bibliothèque orientale* and other early orientalists is significant in this respect, as Beckford's Orient then begins to construct itself as an almost obsessive series of lists, comparisons, dates and facts, a process that reaches a peak with Henley's notes to *Vathek.* The question to be asked now is how such a signifying and metonymic system of appropriation relates to the ways of the imagination as the main constant of Beckford's project?

The congruence between these two paradigms becomes purposeful if we bear in mind the fact that Beckford's entire literary project can be read as a metaphor of the self in its absolute hunger. *Vathek* brings together the dialectic between self and surfaces (on which the imagination can do its work), and what we have is an assiduous relation, and an alternation of figure and context, in which the presence of each is offered as a counterpart and complement of the other. At this point Beckford's fascination with the Orient goes beyond the enticements of exotic locale and towards a perception of the contours of experience. We may well say that Beckford's fascination is, indeed, a shock of recognition that is forced to acknowledge the extent to which imagination can go in its excesses. The appropriative stance towards the Orient becomes then metonymic of the indiscriminate ways of the imagination in its search for contexts to prey on. This is one of the lessons Beckford learned from his immersion from a very early age in the lushness of the Orient; it helped him to understand that imagination can be a fatal gift, and that the encounter between East and West based on misrepresentation can only produce texts of disenchantment. Beckford sensed much the same kind of thing about the ways of the imagination as Samuel Johnson had done. This is demonstrated by his insistence that he is not completely taken in by what he has created, as we might be tempted to believe were we to judge from the textures of his oriental texts. Beckford handles his store of oriental allusions, names, phrases and imagery so well that other oriental tales of the period pale by comparison. The exotic brilliance of the various scenes is enhanced by constant references to mythology, to religion, to incantations and prayers, etc.—a profusion only paralleled by Vathek's voracious appetite that extends everywhere. However, such profusion, like the system from which it derives, has a built-in principle of hollowness. Vathek is not the prototype of the wise, sagacious, munificent eastern monarch whose personality is derived from the *Arabian Nights.* Vathek, his mother, and the gibbering figures that surround them, are truncated characters. They are gross, and their passions are never quite credible. Of course, such portrayals are made necessary in order to meet the requirements of a literary project. But even from the historical point of view such a figure as Vathek is truncated—a characteristic which a brief examination of the historical tradition from which d'Herbelot's *Bibliothèque orientale* derives might shed some light on.

Writing narrative history in the sixteenth, seventeenth, and even eighteenth centuries was often a matter of retelling a well-known tale whose general contours were fixed and unchanging, bringing it up to date stylistically, and making it more or less compatible with the slowly changing ideas and values of an evolving audience, just as oral storytellers or modern tellers of jokes adapt a fundamentally invariant structure to the expectations and clichés of a varying public. This type of history tended also to write the history not of a dynasty—offering tradition as the legitimation of the reigning monarch—but of an individual prince, distinguished by his charismatic power to rule and by military success impose order. Such a conception of history had remained practically unchanged since the Middle Ages: history was a cycle or collection of stories, not unlike the legends of saints, and bearing little or no relation to other story cycles. Throwing doubts on such traditional stories and chronologies, subjecting all their elements to scrutiny, and opening up the scope of history to include China and America alongside the medieval, classical, and biblical worlds are processes which were to be introduced by the Enlightenment.[36] But again, the other is here identified with the unbounded, the unstructured, the lawless; that is to say with all those primitive, preindividual and almost prehuman forces, blindly productive and destructive at the same time. It is the other of the Romantics that assumes a threatening as well as an alluring aspect. If by virtue of the historian's efforts it seems at times reducible to intelligible order, at other times it looms before him as the terrible, unreadable, unpresentable image of the ultimate irrationality and meaninglessness of existence, his own dreaded Nemesis.

But as Said points out, there is "nothing especially controversial or reprehensible about such domestications of the exotic"; such interactions "take place between all cultures . . . and between all men".[37] However, what remained current about Islam, as exemplified by d'Herbelot from which Beckford drew ample material, is the limited vocabulary and imagery. As far as Islam was concerned, European fear, and occasional respect, was a result of the Muslim world's military, and later its cultural and religious hegemony. During the Dark Ages, contemporary Christian authors showed little interest in the learning and culture of the Muslims. Instead, Islam came to symbolize terror and devastation from hordes of demonic barbarians, an image which prevailed well into the seventeenth century as the "Ottoman peril" appeared as a constant danger to Christian civilization. Many writers have shown how European civilization incorporated that peril into its lore, its great events, figures, virtues, and vices. Christian Europe came to form an "integral and self-sufficient" image of Islam. According to Norman Daniel the function of such image was not so much to represent Islam in itself as to represent it for the medieval Christian:

> The variable tendency to neglect what the Qur'an meant, or what Muslims through it meant, or what Muslims thought or did in any given circumstances, necessarily implies that the Qur'anic and other Islamic doctrine was presented in a form that would convince Christians; and more extravagant forms would stand a chance of acceptance as the distance of the writers and public from the Islamic border increased. It was with very great reluctance that what Muslims said Muslims believed was accepted as what they did believe. There was a Christian picture in which the details (even under the pressure of facts) were abandoned as little as possible, and in which the general outline was never abandoned. There were shades of difference, but only with a common framework. All the corrections that were made in the interests of an increasing accuracy were only a defence of what had newly been realized to be vulnerable, a shoring up of a weakened structure. Christian opinion was an erection which could not be demolished, even to be rebuilt.[38]

The European imagination was nourished extensively from such habits of thoughts which refused to see in the Orient anything but the epitome of debauchery, cruelty, violence, ignorance and a whole battery of assorted treacheries. As Said points out, the repertoire which stands for such imaginary constructs is quite fabulous. The Sphinx, Cleopatra, Eden, Troy, Babylon, Sheba, Astarte and dozens of other images and icons epitomize the larger whole from which they emanate, and "between the Middle Ages and the eighteenth century such major authors as Ariosto, Milton, Marlowe, Tasso, Shakespeare, Cervantes", and others drew on such a "half-imagined, half-known" repertoire in ways that only served to sharpen Europe's ignorance of the Orient. In addition, a great deal of what was considered learned orientalist scholarship in Europe, such as d'Herbelot's work, pressed ideological myths into service under the guise of genuine knowledge of the Orient.[39]

To proceed to an analysis of the ideological or methodological foundations of d'Herbelot's would lead us too far.[40] I shall limit my enquiry to an examination of particular entries which epitomize the way that d'Herbelot, as an orientalist, only confirms a specific conception of the Orient in the reader's eyes; he neither tries nor wants to unsettle already established convictions. What his work does is to represent the Orient more clearly, and with more ample details transforming a free-floating representation of the collective imagination into a rational panorama. Thus, under the entry of Mohammed, d'Herbelot first supplies all of the prophet's given names, then proceeds to confirm Mohammed's ideological and doctrinal value as follows:

> C'est le fameus imposteur Mahomet, Auteur et Fondateur d'une hérésie, qui a pris le nom de religion, que nous appelons Mahométane. Voyez le titre d'Eslam.
>
> Les interprètes de l'alocoran et autres Docteurs de las Loy Musulmane ou Mahométane ont appliqué à ce faux prophète tous les éloges, que les Ariens, Pulitiens ou Paulitianistes et autre Hérétiques ont attribué à Jésus-Christ, en lui otant sa Divinité. . . .[41]

The parameters which d'Herbelot establishes do not serve to locate the prophet within a frame to explain his emergence; rather he is subsumed and located within the frame of a heresy which prevents him from straying elsewhere, and to which the discursive apparatus of a fictional character is assigned, making the apprehension of a generic type immediate and unambiguous. Such apprehension is made possible because "the false prophet is part of a general theatrical representation called *orientale* whose totality is contained in the *Bibliothèque*".[42]

In the same work, under the entry of "Vathek Billah", we come across the same discursive confinement.[43] Not only did Beckford draw amply from d'Herbelot's portrayal, he also made Vathek appear as a grotesque and cruel monarch. Thus, as d'Herbelot reports, Vathek "étoit aussi fort libéral et charitable, ayant grand soin qu'on ne vit jamais aucun mendiant dans ses Etats, de sorte que sous son règne, on n'en vit jamais aucun, ni à la Mecque, ni à Medine".[44] Beckford not only disregarded this aspect, but to meet the requirements of his literary project, he turned into ridicule "the munificence of Fakhreddin, who, as well as attendant grey-beards, dealt about, gratis, plasters and cataplasms to all that applied".[45] The point to be made here is that such representations construct knowledge about the Orient; they construct what Said calls a textual attitude, and this process of conversion is a disciplined one: it is taught, it has its own societies, periodicals, traditions, vocabulary, rhetoric which serve to perpetuate representations building on the earlier ones. How dramatically effective such representations can be is attested by the fact that such critics as Parreaux and others, disregarding the architectonics of Beckford's texts, have no doubt whatsoever about the validity of such representations.[46]

In the context of my argument, Beckford's own built-in principle of irony erases the earlier romantic fantasy of liberation in the Orient. If the oriental texts display such an idealist dream, they are also the place where the fantasy is obliterated. The two metonymic operations which were supposed to have incorporated the foreign into their European representation produced nothing the least bit satisfactory. The trope referred to earlier as "absorption of" with details of authenticity, with intricacies, constitutes the surface through which the West can approach the otherness in the Orient. As Garber says of Byron, the obsession with such intricacies seems to be based on the latter's desire for a true entry, to make certain that what we touch at is genuine in its strangeness. Only by this means, adds Garber, can Byron ensure the authenticity of his vision of the radically other. However, Beckford differs from Byron in the way he manipulates such excess to make a variety of points. Prominent among them is his need to make certain that we understand how he can distance himself from the extravagance of the self. The result is a "satire of excess within a system of excess" as Garber says of Byron.[47] The point about such self-scrutiny is that it becomes metonymic not of an act of consumption, but to prevent a devouring. Such a posture adopted by Beckford epitomizes a more balanced order in which there is indulgence and criticism, compulsion and correction.

Therefore, although the elaborate representations that go into the making of Beckford's oriental texts reveal something of the conventions of orientalism, such representations are also eloquent in telling us of a way of reading the world. Like the other constituents that go into making Beckford's system of artifice, orientalism has permitted the self to show off its glories, but it has also linked the luxuriance of surface with the sad opulence of the condemned soul. Always "in search of inspiring places to fall asleep", the imagination leaps from one context into another. Beckford's orientalism makes possible a continuation of patterns that were already making themselves felt in his work. That Beckford was not totally caught up by the extravagances which storm forth in **Vathek** is evident not only from the ironical posture he takes towards his material, but also by his pronouncements on the matter. Traces of such an attitude may be detected in the implicit reservations he formulated about his own efforts to absorb the exotic reality. This is how he puts the matter to his half-sister as early as 1778:

> Don't fancy, my Dear Sister, I am enraptured with the Orientals themselves. . . . The East must be better known than it is to be sufficiently liked or disliked. If you would form a tolerable judgement upon it not a single relation, not one voyage or volume of travels must be neglected, whether in Portuguese, Spanish or any other language. With this intent I am learning Portuguese. . . .[48]

But such attempts remained sterile, as indeed did all his undertakings during this period. His search for proper contexts for the self appears as a frantic series of attempts—which Beckford was seemingly incapable of abandoning—to transcend perceptions of sterility around him, to seize (if nothing else) at least the representational plenitude of collecting objects observed, of sites explored, of mores experienced. Yet the symbolic appropriation of that reality eluded Beckford systematically, rather like the inscriptions on the Giaour's sword which Vathek could not decipher. Like the failure of the textual paradigm which underlies **Vathek,** it seems that Beckford's imagined trip to the Orient denotes a negativity. Like the system from which it was originally derived, which carries so many objects, so many places, so many misconceptions along, it finds itself exhausted in the face of its own accumulation. That Beckford realized that such a discourse is unsustainable is also evident from the fact that after the writing of the **Episodes,** he turned towards other forms of subversion of the dominant, as epitomized by **Modern Novel Writing, or The Elegant Enthusiast** and **Azemia.**[49] Is this reorientation prompted by Beckford's awareness that the Orient belongs to orientalism, and that any comprehensive vision is fundamentally reductive and conservative, carrying the ideological within it? The lack of open pronouncements on the matter by Beckford himself makes it difficult to form an opinion on the issue. But to do him justice, it should be pointed out that Beckford's oriental tastes were displayed in a more socially acceptable form in his furnishings and collections at Fonthill Abbey which he built between 1796 and 1807 than in **Vathek.**[50]

Notes

1. This present essay is based on part of my unpublished doctoral dissertation, "The Road to Istakhar: a Critical Study of the Text and Context of Williams Beckford's *Vathek* and the *Episodes* 1769-1844", Antwerp University, 1994. Taking the ideology of the power of the creative imagination as conceived by the Romantics as a major premise, my thesis examined William Beckford's work in the light of its textual and contextual constituents. I assimilated Beckford's texts to a specific historical moment in order to examine them in relation to other models of coherence. More specifically I focused on their intertextuality. From this perspective, I attempted to show how orientalism as a system of representation offers a context congenial to a romantic sensibility such as Beckford's. *The Vision* was written when Beckford was only seventeen, but it was never published in his lifetime. Part of the manuscript was discovered by Guy Chapman in 1929, and published under the title of *The Vision and Liber Veritatis,* edited with an Introduction and Notes by Guy Chapman, London, 1930. New material examined by André Parreaux in *William Beckford, Auteur de "Vathek" (1760-1844): Etude de la création littéraire* (Paris, 1960, 97-131), now makes it possible to know more about Beckford's initial project. Also see Robert J. Gemmet, *William Beckford,* Boston: Mass., 1977, 40-52.

2. See Marcel May, *La Jeunesse de William Beckford et la genèse son "Vathek",* Paris, 1928, 260-316.

3. For Beckford's early fascination with the Orient, see Lewis Melville, *The Life and Letters of William Beckford of Fonthill (Author of "Vathek"),* Folcroft, 1970. "A Letter probable to Cozen", written 4 December 1778, shows to what extent Beckford's mind was filled with travellers' accounts of eastern countries even at that early date. The letter headed "Being the full moon" describes a dream Beckford had, sitting on a cushion by the fire, like Orientals, after a long solitary walk: "Meanwhile my thoughts were wandering through into the interior of Africa and dwelt for hours on those countries. I love Strange Tales of Mount Atlas and relations of travellers amused my fancy. One instant, I imagined myself viewing the marble palaces of Ethiopian princes. . . . Some few minutes after, I found myself standing before a thick wood listening to impetuous waterfalls. . . . A tall comely negro wound along the slopes of the hill and without moving his lips made me comprehend I was in Africa on the brink of the Nile beneath the mountains of Amara . . ." (63).

4. The correspondence is published in Melville, but those parts relevant to my argument are to be found in the introduction to *The Episodes of Vathek,* trans. Sir Frank T. Marzials, London, 1912. My references are to this introduction.

5. Marzials, xiv.

6. *Ibid.,* xvii.

7. Cyrus Redding made some observations about Beckford's command of Arabic, although he suspected it was only a smattering of Persian (see Cyrus Redding, *Memoirs of William Beckford, Author of "Vathek",* 2 vols, London, 1859).

8. Guy Chapman, *A Bibliography of William Beckford of Fonthill,* London, 1930, 93.

9. For Byron's relationship to Beckford, see Gemmett, 137-42.

10. See May, 269-326, and also Frederik Garber, *Self, Text, and Romantic Irony: The Example of Byron,* Princeton: NJ, 1988, 69-101.

11. I am indebted to Garber for this suggestion concerning Beckford and Byron's orientalism.

12. David Scott and James Thompson present a thorough study of this aspect in *The East Imagined, Experienced, Remembered: Orientalist Nineteenth-Century Painting,* Dublin, National Gallery of Ireland, 1988.

13. Michael Giselman, *Imagined Cities of the East,* Oxford, 1986, 11.

14. See Scott and Thompson, 18-35.

15. William Beckford, *The Travel Diaries of William Beckford of Fonthill,* ed. with a Memoir and Notes by Guy Chapman, Cambridge, 1928, 162.

16. *Ibid.,* 30.

17. *Ibid.,* 91.

18. Fatma M. Moussa, "A Monument to the Author of *Vathek*", *Etudes Anglaises,* XV (1962), 138-47.

19. Parreaux, 106-108.

20. William Beckford, *Vathek,* ed. Roger Lonsdale, Oxford, 1970, 2.

21. For a thorough analysis of this aspect, see Alan Liu, "Towards a Theory of Common Sense: Beckford's *Vathek* and Johnson's *Rasselas*", *Texas Studies in Literature and Language,* 26 (1984), 183-217.

22. Concerning this double movement, I am indebted to ch. 5 of Richard Terdiman's *Discourse/Counter Discourse: The Theory and Practice of Symbolic Resistance in Nineteenth Century France,* Ithaca: NY and London, 1985.

23. The biographical reasons behind Beckford's need to substitute other scenes and occupations for an England resolutely middle-class, self-absorbed, yet uncertain of its self-sufficiency, is well documented by most of his biographers. For a convenient synopsis, see Gemmett, 29-39.

24. Melville, 31.

25. *Ibid.,* 82-83.

26. *The Vision and Liber Veritatis,* xiii. It is highly improbable that Beckford had any knowledge of Sanskrit in 1777. He had probably read Anquetil Du Perron, and Abraham Roger's account of the Hindu in Picart's *Religious Ceremonies* (see Fatma M. Moussa, "Beckford, *Vathek* and the Oriental Tale", in *William Beckford of Fonthill, 1760-1844: Bicentenary Essays,* Port Washington, 1972).

27. Redding, II, 243.

28. *The Vision and Liber Veritatis,* 15.

29. For this particular aspect of orientalism, see Garber, 69-101.

30. *The Vision and Liber Veritatis,* 85.

31. Philip Julian, *Orientalism,* Oxford, 1977, 84.

32. *The Vision and Liber Veritatis,* 66.

33. See n. 1.

34. See Parreaux, 99-101.

35. Quoted in Parreaux, 102-103.

36. See Lionel Gossman, "History as Decipherment: Romantic Historiography and the Discovery of the Other", *New Literary History,* 18 (1986), 23-27.

37. Edward W. Said, *Orientalism* (1978), Penguin edn, 1985, 60.

38. Norman Daniel, *Islam and the West: The Making of an Image,* Edinburgh, 1973, 252 and 259-60 (quoted in *Orientalism,* 60-61); see also Dorothy Metlitzki, *The Matter of Araby in Medieval England,* New Haven: Conn., 1977.

39. *Orientalism,* 63.

40. Such a perspective is provided by Said, especially in chapter 1 of *Orientalism.*

41. Barthélemy d'Herbelot, *Bibliothèque orientale ou dictionnaire universel contenant tout ce qui fait connaître les peuples de l'Orient,* The Hague, 1777, II, 648. Note the derogatory term "Mahométane" to refer to Islam. For similar terms used within the compass of such discourse, see Norman Daniel, *Heroes and Saracens: An Interpretation of the Chansons de Geste,* Edinburgh, 1984.

42. *Orientalism,* 66.

43. D'Herbelot, II, 902-903.

44. *Ibid.,* II, 911.

45. *Vathek,* 61.

46. See, for instance, Parreaux, 319-25.

47. Garber, 77.

48. Quoted in John W. Oliver, *The Life of William Beckford,* London, 1932, 23.

49. Beckford published these two works, respectively under the pseudonyms of Lady Harriet Marlow and J. A. M. Jenks, in 1796 and 1797.

50. See "Beckford and Islam", *Connoisseur,* 191 (1976), 250-53.

Diego Saglia (essay date April 2002)

SOURCE: Saglia, Diego. "William Beckford's 'Sparks of Orientalism' and the Material-Discursive Orient of British Romanticism." *Textual Practice* 16, no. 1 (April 2002): 75-92.

[*In the following essay, Saglia views* Vathek *within the context of both eighteenth- and nineteenth-century European appropriation of Eastern culture.*]

Between the late eighteenth and early nineteenth centuries the orient is a proliferating presence in British literature, as well as in the visual and decorative arts, architecture, manufacture, political and economic discourse, and countless other disciplines and areas of knowledge. An integral component of Romantic-period culture in Britain, the imaginary of the orient is rooted in figures and objects circulating in European culture since classical times. However, from the late sixteenth century, Britain was increasingly exposed to the East through a growing network of diplomatic, commercial and political links, beginning from the initial, tentative contacts between Elizabethan England and the Ottoman Empire, and climaxing in the conquest of ever larger portions of the Indian subcontinent from the mid-eighteenth century onwards. At the same time, the popularization of Eastern images, narratives and objects in British culture takes place in the context of successive waves of fashions, from eighteenth-century *turquerie* and *chinoiserie,* through the Indian and Spanish-Moorish manias of the Romantic era, and the late nineteenth-century craze for all things Japanese. An uninterruptedly present and active element in British culture, and one crucially related to Britain's expansion in the wider world, between the eighteenth and nineteenth centuries the orientalist dimension gradually develops from earlier manifestations into an intersection of texts and objects which is increasingly pervasive, visible and accessible within British culture.

As an area of consumption and production—the assemblage, demolition and reconstitution of otherness—the oriental undergoes important transformations in Romantic-period culture and, perhaps most conspicuously, in literary discourse where this shift emerges in the transition from 'pseudo-oriental' eighteenth-century textuality to the more accurate, archaeologically documented works of Romantic literature, a development parallel to the contemporaneous popularization of the orient in the form of objects, spectacles and narratives.[1] Placed between eighteenth-century culture and the Romantic era, William Beckford's orientalist texts, especially his romance *The History of Caliph Vathek* (1786), are fundamental loci for an investigation of such shifts. Indeed, thanks to its voluminous annotations, *Vathek* illustrates that, besides the persistence of eighteenth-century exoticisms, Romantic uses of the East are distinguished by an increased representational accuracy and a growing materiality of the orient within an overarching 'consumer orientalism'.[2] The East is more and more readily available in a metropolitan space which sees a burgeoning consumption of the oriental in the shape of products, objects, visual experiences and literary texts. This distinctive convergence of material and discursive artefacts is related to what John E. Wills defines as the contemporary concurrence of European consumption, Asian production and the growing exports of oriental commodities 'for which there was a steadily broadening market at stable or falling prices' during the long eighteenth century.[3]

In the mid-eighteenth century Malachy Postlethwayt's influential *Universal Dictionary of Trade and Commerce* (1751-55) describes the East India trade as based on 'an exchange of the most valuable merchandizes in the world', which he then lists in a catalogue of marvels or *mirabilia Indiae* such as 'China ware, of the finest kinds', 'diamonds from the mines in Golconda', 'the fine silk of Georgia and Guylan', 'ivory, imported from Mocca or Melinda, and the coast of Zanzibar', 'rich Persian silks, rich Turkey carpets', 'Persian wines, Armenian brandies, Arabian coffee, raisins, almonds from Ispahan'.[4] The aura of precious, talismanic inaccessibility bestowed by Postlethwayt's account slowly fades out, and is replaced by more generally available oriental products and wares between the end of the eighteenth and the first decades of the nineteenth century. Carefully examined by economic and cultural historians, this ever-widening 'consumer orientalism' may provide new and useful insights into Romantic-period orientalism as a continuum of texts and objects increasingly present in the metropolitan British dimension, and directly relevant to the Romantic intersection of fictions of the East and encounters with a material, 'real' orient.[5] As Edward Said suggests in *Orientalism,* the East designates both a discourse and 'an integral part of European *material* civilization and culture', a statement seemingly attuned to more recent debates on the hybrid or transitive structure of orientalist contacts.[6] Focusing on a marginal but highly significant instance of the Romantic fascination with the East, this article aims to throw light on orientalism as both narrative and object, and as a fraught moment of cultural interweaving of the material into the discursive.

In the context of a popularization of Eastern consumer items—be they products or texts—the privileged aesthete William Beckford may seem more aligned with eighteenth-century patterns of aristocratic consumption than to the progressive diffusion of orientalism in early nineteenth-century Britain. Yet, although Beckford was 'England's wealthiest son', as Byron hailed him in the first canto of *Childe Harold's Pilgrimage* (1812), his heavily fictionalized autobiographical texts open up suggestive and emblematic vistas into the overlapping of material and discursive, written and experienced orients within the literature and culture of the Romantic era. The sole heir to a fortune based on extensive plantations in the West Indies, Beckford was a connoisseur, a collector, a traveller, the 'builder' of Fonthill Abbey, and an author of novels, romances, short stories and autobiographical writings. Although operating in a cultural environment still indebted to eighteenth-century patterns of privilege and patronage, Beckford interpreted and gave shape to some of the central issues in Romantic-period culture, especially through his creation of the 'fantastical' Gothic mansion at Fonthill and through *Vathek*'s combination of the eighteenth-century moralizing oriental tale with orientalist scholarship and narrative elements from the Gothic novel. Indeed, the cultural significance of his Eastern romance lies also in its promotion of a literary orientalism heavily dependent on the figures, images and situations of the tradition of the *Arabian Nights' Entertainments,* yet steeped in the factual knowledge about the East that Western scholars had been accumulating since the seventeenth century. *Vathek* exerted a lasting influence on early nineteenth-century literary orientalism, especially on Byron who, in the notes to his poem *The Giaour* (1813), paid homage to Beckford's masterpiece, observing that 'for correctness of costume, beauty of description, and power of imagination, it far surpasses all European imitations' of Eastern narratives.[7]

In 1787 the author of *Vathek* undertakes a journey to the south of Europe, following the 1784 scandal caused by rumours that he and the 16-year-old William Courtenay had been entertaining a homosexual relationship, and after the death of his wife Margaret in 1786, the same year in which the English translation of *Vathek,* originally composed in French, appeared. The journey of 1787 takes Beckford to stay first in Portugal, and then in Spain. And, in the Iberian Peninsula the imaginary, textual East of *Vathek* unexpectedly comes up against the signs, objects and human figures of an 'authentic', material orient. Even if Beckford's stay in these countries at the margin of the Grand Tour is only a brief one, his arrival in the Iberian Peninsula, a traditional geocultural bridge between European culture and Islam, brings him into contact with and exposes him to a hybrid and distinctly orientalized cultural geography.

The exiled aesthete's desire to find the orient in the West typifies his initial approach to Portugal, since, on his arrival, Beckford writes in his journal: 'From what I learn from every person, Lisbon abounded more than any city in Europe with precious Japan ware and Indian curiosities.'[8] Beckford's orientalist desire is caught between the (imperial) past of Portugal and his own (archaeological) present, and his expectations are not dissatisfied as he contributes to the actualization of his imagined orient, by this token confirming orientalism as a nexus of consumption and production of the East. Indeed, the archive of fragments scattered in the multiple narrative levels of *Vathek* first begins to materialize in Portugal where Beckford decorates the large central room in the Quinta of Ramalhão (to the south of Sintra) in the popular Turkish-tent style, an example of which, decorated with sofas in silk and velvet, had also featured on the ground floor of his paternal Fonthill Splendens.[9] Ramalhão, which Beckford rents on his arrival without having inspected it first, turns out to be a cold and rather inhospitable residence. The process of decorating it is lengthy and elaborate, and in his journal Beckford accurately records the progressive metamorphosis of the interior until 'the lantern-like apartment hung round with curtains of beautiful English chintz,

and furnished with ample sofas, begins to look like the tent of an *omrah* [a Muslim grandee]' (*J,* p. 165) and a perfect instance of 'oriental scenery' (*J,* p. 165). Eventually transformed 'into a magnificent tent' (*J,* p. 185), the lantern room is described as a display of decorative luxuries, containing 'drapery falling in ample folds over the large sofas and glasses' and '[f]our tripod stands of burnished gold, supporting lustres of brilliant glass half concealed by chintz curtains' (*J,* p. 185). In this miniature materialization of a mythical orient, Beckford acts as its single and most fascinated spectator, 'fancying [himself] admitted by enchantment into a series of magic saloons' (*J,* p. 192), a character in his own realization of a fantasy in the style of the *Arabian Nights.* Beckford's desire, consumption and production of the East is already firmly located in a network of texts and objects which are readable not only in terms of Jean Baudrillard's definition of consumption as a 'displaced expression of desire', but also through his concept of 'sign-value', that hybrid dimension in which 'the commodity is immediately produced as a sign, as sign value, and where signs (culture) are produced as commodities'.[10]

Fictional suggestions and material objects start to intersect in Beckford's Iberian experience. No longer relegated to a purely mythical dimension, the discursive orient now takes shape in Beckford's domestic space as a combination of artefacts and narrative traces set in a specific social and cultural environment. In a later conversation with Cyrus Redding, Beckford censured this environment, describing 'the [Portuguese] nobility and ecclesiastics' as 'an indolent, luxurious race'; a race, however, in whose sumptuous lifestyle he actively participated.[11] During his stay in Lisbon, his friend the wealthy and powerful Marquis of Marialva treats him to a luxurious dinner, the opulence of which is approvingly listed by the author: 'Not less than fifty servants were in waiting; and, exclusive of half a dozen wax torches, which were borne in state before the company, not less than a hundred of different sizes were lighted up in the rooms, intermingled with silver braziery, and casolettes giving out pleasant perfumes.'[12] Later, the profusion and abundance characterizing Beckford's social activities in Portugal are further expanded in his accounts of gold-bedecked religious processions, suppers and entertainments, musical and operatic evenings, and sensual enjoyments which culminate in the architectural, artistic and culinary pleasures afforded by his 'state visit' to the palace-convent of Mafra.[13]

The Portuguese interlude offers a foretaste of the combination of material and discursive orientalism which takes actual shape in Madrid, where Beckford arrives on 12 December 1787 and stays until June 1788. This is one of the most carefree periods of his exile, yet also one generally overlooked by his biographers.[14] It is in the Spanish capital, while driving in his carriage near the Prado, that Beckford perceives a group of figures dressed in oriental attire: 'Upon entering the large court of the Palace . . . I spied some venerable figures in caftans and turbans leaning against a doorway' (*J*, p. 290). Intrigued by the unexpected sight of the orient, Beckford turns to his friend and chaperon José de Rojas:

> 'Who are those picturesque animals?' said I to our conductor. 'Is it lawful to approach them?' 'As often as you please to,' answered Rojas. 'They belong to the Turkish Ambassador, who is lodged with all his train at the Buen Retiro. If you have a mind we will go upstairs and examine the whole menagerie.'

In this transcription of his first encounter with the orient *in propria persona,* the exiled orientalist records his excitement and curiosity, while at the same time setting in train a series of mechanisms of definition that slowly overcome the 'self and other' confrontation apparent from this first contact. It is interesting that Beckford should not 'name' the other geoculturally, but rather approach this still undefined oriental spectacle through allusion ('some venerable figures') and metaphor ('those picturesque animals', 'menagerie'). His language thus inhabits the gap between self and other, functioning both as a signal of ethnic and cultural barriers and as a vehicle of desire. Without cataloguing or encoding oriental difference, Beckford's allusive language conjures proverbial images of Eastern wisdom harking back to the eighteenth-century oriental tale (as in 'venerable', later repeated in 'venerable Mussulman', *J*, p. 302), as well as conveying a form of exotic animality and sensuality capable of capturing the Western gaze and, as in 'picturesque', conforming to its visual conventions. In this first sighting of the other, language approaches the 'real' East and evokes it by the transfiguring and fictionalizing devices of the oriental tale or imagery akin to Philippe de Loutherbourg's picturesque oriental phantasmagorias, such as those commissioned for Beckford's birthday celebrations at Fonthill Splendens for the Christmas season of 1781.[15] The immediacy of reality and the conventions of fiction are locked within the overarching frame of an autobiographical account which is itself moulded out of insistent fictional reinventions both in the unpublished journal and in its re-elaborated version as *Sketches of Spain and Portugal,* published in 1834.[16] The line between the 'real' and the fictional is visibly blurred in a nexus of texts which are pervaded by 'Lies, compressions, erasures and second thoughts'.[17]

In this light, the transfiguration of the oriental characters into a 'menagerie' of 'picturesque animals' is not just an attempt to separate self and other and reduce the orient to complete difference. Rather, the semantic field of animality seems to be invoked both as a kind of facetious ethological language and in order to convey a hypnotic, enigmatic spectacle. The Western observer's desire further transpires from Beckford's doubt about

the legitimacy of contact with such people: the question 'Is it lawful to approach them?' draws a line of separation which his desire for the oriental other brings him to cross during the narrative of his unfolding relation with the materialized East.[18] The gap between self and other is here the space where an initial intention to keep his distance from the orientals, shrouding them in metaphor and allusion, turns into a desire to approach them and access what, to adapt Mary Louise Pratt's term, is the 'contact zone' where East and West superimpose.[19] Tellingly, the critical moment of Beckford's crossing over into the 'real' orient is problematized through the fictional and fictitious barrier of 'legitimacy' which, although eventually crossed, never entirely disappears, since the author's approach to the East is constantly mediated by the presence of an interpreter.[20]

From the very first approach, actual and imaginary orients intersect in a nexus of reality and fiction, legality, desire and visual attraction, all encapsulated in Beckford's observation 'I have still sufficient sparks of Orientalism about me to catch fire at such a sight' (*J*, p. 290) which, in the later re-elaboration of *Sketches of Spain and Portugal,* is retrospectively formulated as: 'My sparks of orientalism instantly burst into a flame at such a sight' (*S*, p. 200). The other is a privileged space for the play of the self's desire, or, in Christian Jacob's apposite definition, 'un espace de projection privilégié pour les désirs, les aspirations, la mémoire affective, la mémoire culturelle du sujet'.[21] Unable to resist its fascinations, Beckford impatiently rushes to discover the East for himself ('I cleared four steps at a leap, to the great delight of his whiskered Excellency's pages and attendants', *J*, p. 291), hastening to make the acquaintance of His Excellency Ahmed Vassif Effendi, the Turkish ambassador in Madrid, whose appearance on the stage of Beckford's Spanish spectacle eventually provides a directly physical manifestation of the orient:

> Never was I more delighted than upon entering a stately saloon, spread with the richest carpets and perfumed with the fragrance of wood of aloes. In a corner of the apartment sat the Ambassador, wrapped up in a pelisse 'of the most precious sables', playing with a light cane he held in his hand, and every now and then passing it under the noses of some tall slaves who were standing in a row before him.

Beckford's fascinated gaze wanders around the apartment, busily collecting material signs of the East as an objective dimension transplanted in a European capital. Later, added references to 'Bagdad, the tomb of Zobeida, the vestiges of the Dhar al Khalifat, or the palace of the Abbasides' (*S*, p. 202) confirm that the fictional orient of the *Arabian Nights* is never too far removed from Beckford's material orientalism, directing his architectural, spatial and objective evaluations of the personally experienced East.[22] Lingering on the vast dimensions of the room, his description records a sumptuous procession of ornaments, scents, attire and the row of slaves, themselves objects in the decorative scheme of Vassif's space. Reified into a spectacle of precious things, this 'real' orient harks back to the displays of fictional Eastern opulence in **Vathek** that, as Andrew Elfenbein has perceptively remarked, foreground luxury consumption and luxury collecting while rejecting late eighteenth-century discriminations between good and bad luxury, such as David Hume's or Adam Smith's, and aligning the text with a 'laissez-faire consumerism' in which 'the base and selfish dispositions despised by Smith have become the law of the land'.[23] The land of Vathek's doomed adventures yet also the East of Beckford's Spain. Aptly, the Madrid encounter with Ahmed Vassif and his oriental court opens through a visual collecting of luxuries, not least the row of objectified slaves, that distinctive self-making practice that enabled Beckford to foreground his own uniqueness and gain distinction in a hostile social environment by celebrating 'the product of the genius of consumption, in which all the traits of genius belonged to consumers, not producers'.[24]

In addition to the list of luxurious objects, the scene presents the enigmatic 'power game' which the ambassador plays by passing his stick 'under the noses of some tall slaves who were standing in a row before him'. One of the symbols of Ahmed Vassif's authority, the stick reveals an orient centred on an all-powerful male figure, situated within a geography of forbidden places such as royal palaces and harems. In other words, the enigmatic game links Ahmed Vassif to traditional and stereotypical figurations of oriental despotism and the attendant political-cultural system of Eastern tyranny demonized by Enlightenment thought. The 1834 rewriting thus depicts Vassif as a man 'of considerable talent, deeply skilled in Turkish literature', 'rich, munificent, and nobly born', 'gracious in his address', yet 'not without something like a spark of despotism in a corner of his eye' (**S,** p. 202). The repository of a whole series of oriental topoi, the ambassador, during one of Beckford's later visits, appears 'seated in pomp under the canopy of a huge embroidered State bed that looked like the pavilion of Darius in an opera dance' (**J,** p. 299), a vignette compounding the figure of the eighteenth-century operatic Turk with intimations of oriental opulence and indolence.[25] Stereotypes of Eastern sloth and luxury then emerge in the processional scene in Beckford's journal entry for 1 January 1788 when, on entering Ahmed Vassif's apartment, he finds the foreign dignitary seated 'in all his glory surrounded by twenty or thirty of his attendants in their most splendid dress, giving audience to the Tripolitan Ambassador' (**J,** p. 308). The symbolic positioning of the oriental characters in this scene unveils the social balance in the Eastern enclave of the Ottoman ambassador. Similarly, the repeated scenes of parades, pageants and processions set off the ambassador's static figure, sitting or lying at the centre of a moving, revolving or simply encircling *tableau vivant* of Eastern luxury. From the contrast between the pivotal, static figure of the Turkish dignitary and the surrounding entourage there emerges a confirmation of the oriental's inbred 'supineness and indolence' (**J,** p. 299), as well as an interpretation of the Eastern dimension as a power structure centripetally keyed to the figure of the tyrant and an economy of desire intriguingly described by Alain Grosrichard's study of the sexual and visual structure of Asiatic despotism: 'Objet d'amour et cause de désir, le regard du despote cache et désigne le gouffre où tout ce qui, dans l'Empire, vaut comme objet de jouissance vient s'engloutir, corps et biens.'[26]

This amply layered construction of the exotic other is further complicated by the narrator's progressive moves of integration into, and mimesis of, the orient and its manners, starting from his introduction to Ahmed Vassif, when Beckford records his own readiness to 'make [his] salaam to the Ambassador' (**J,** p. 291) and express 'the respect [he] had always conceived for the Sublime Porte' (**J,** p. 291). In the material-discursive continuum of Beckford's 'real' orient, however, integration also implies finding one's own place within the catalogue of precious objects and the economy of movement and stillness regulating the Ottoman ambassador's world. This additional process of integration begins immediately after Beckford has presented himself to Ahmed Vassif: 'As soon as I had taken my seat in a ponderous fauteuil of figured velvet, coffee was brought in cups of most beautiful china with gold enamelled saucers' (**J,** p. 291). The consumption of coffee in the precious and luxuriously decorated cups develops the processional features already remarked in Beckford's orient while furthering his desire to cross over into the orient—as in the opening question 'Is it lawful to approach them?' (**J,** p. 290)—and find his own niche in the other space of the Turkish East of Madrid. Nevertheless, his desire for effortless, spontaneous integration comes up against a very material obstacle. The coffee is too bitter for the narrator who, despite his love for all things oriental, brings himself to swallow it only with great difficulty: 'Notwithstanding my predilection for the east and its customs, I could hardly get down this beverage, it was so thick and bitter' (**J,** p. 291). The sparks of orientalism are unexpectedly, and ironically, dampened through an observation that, although little more than an aside, once again evokes the dividing line which Beckford and his writing must negotiate in their contact with the orient.

Nonetheless, even the irony which Beckford levels at his own literal consumption of the East does not interrupt or neutralize the desire to consume, possess and appropriate the other, as well as its obverse: his own desire to be included in the orient.[27] His account therefore repeatedly throws into relief the approval bestowed on him by Ahmed Vassif and his motley entourage—'all his whiskered suite are enchanted whenever I make my appearance' (*J*, p. 299)—and his own continuous mimesis of the orient through observations punctuating his Madrid days, such as 'I shall have the megrims for want of exercise, like my friend Ahmed Vassif, if I don't alter my way of life' (*J*, p. 302) or 'I was seated on the carpet like an Oriental' (*J*, p. 309). From a textual point of view, the process of integration develops through the metaphoric rhetoric already encountered during Beckford's first approximation to the oriental other, when the mysterious figures in the Buen Retiro Palace are metaphorically described as 'picturesque animals' and a 'menagerie' (*J*, p. 290). In addition, the language of integration features the metonymic catalogue of a reified East, an East made up of lists of precious objects such as the carpet on which Beckford sits, as well as the simile more overtly and directly linking self and orient. Indeed, the double-edged dynamics of cultural assimilation is intimated in 'like an oriental', which evidences the successful appropriation of the other into the space of the Western observer. At the same time, however, this comparison hints at the inclusion of the Western narrating subject and culture into the modes of the other, as set out in Beckford's proud announcement, on 1 January 1788, that Ahmed Vassif 'has hopes of alluring me to Constantinople' (*J*, p. 309).

The boundary between subject and object, East and West, becomes a zone of co-presence in which possessor and possessed actively influence each other in ways that echo the creative potential implicit in Beckford's 'projective collecting', based on the 'displacement of a passive collection of objects by an intense, aesthetically charged, collecting act' so that 'formed, shaped, and above all aesthetically interesting constructions . . . evolve, improve, and please, with or without assistance from their inventor'.[28] The oscillation between activity and passivity reflects how the observed and desired orient, by turns, gazes at and desires Beckford, and how subject and object invert any expected hierarchy within a structure based on firmly entrenched social differences.

Beckford's pivotal position remains unchallenged, as his narrative confirms through the remark: 'What is there in me to attract the affections of these infidels at first sight, I cannot imagine' (*J*, p. 309). This self-congratulation is further expanded in the later *Sketches of Spain and Portugal* as part of a more radical process of self-fashioning, the construction of a cosmopolitan, feeling and discerning persona at the centre of a web of exquisite fantasies. But the narrator's self as fulcrum is not a Western prerogative, for this role is prefigured by Ahmed Vassif's dominant position in his own centripetal oriental economy. In effect, despite the insistently central Western self, and the fact that Beckford's text draws upon a complex Western tradition of writing and

consuming the orient, his account hinges on the ambivalences of assimilation, the alternative directions which the act of 'making similar' may take, and thus deploys a variety of mechanisms of exchange that regulate the traffic between East and West, capturing Beckford and his 'picturesque animals' in nets of reciprocal desire and mutual consumption.

A crucial role in this structure of exchange is played by the currents of attraction between Beckford, the ambassador and his circle of male associates. In the journal's narrative Ahmed Vassif is the first to appear attracted to the narrator, a situation rendered by Beckford through the physiological language of sentimentalism: 'The Ambassador kept poring upon my countenance and appeared much delighted with the effect his music seemed to have upon it' (*J*, p. 291). Endowing the Turk, much as in the literature of sentiment, with the ability to record the physical traces of inner feelings, Beckford evokes a scene of homosocial intimacy which seems to prefigure Byron's encounter with Ali Pacha of Albania in 1809. During his unusual Grand Tour to the Iberian Peninsula, Greece and Constantinople, Byron stops in this westernmost Ottoman province and goes to pay his respects to the local ruler at his palace in Tepelene. Ali receives him 'in a large room paved with marble, a fountain . . . playing in the centre' and 'surrounded by scarlet Ottomans', and in his letters the highly impressed young aristocrat records the elderly ruler's affectionate familiarity towards him:

> He said he was certain I was a man of birth because I had small ears, curling hair, & little white hands, and expressed himself pleased with my appearance & garb. . . . He treated me like a child, sending me almonds & sugared sherbet, fruit & sweetmeats 20 times a day.—He begged me to visit him often, and at night when he was more at leisure.[29]

Byron's visit to Ali Pacha and Beckford's relationship with Ahmed Vassif are very similar episodes of seduction of a young British male by an older oriental man, although Beckford's episode acquires different resonances from its geographical embedding of the East within the West and the overarching principle of a superimposition, co-presence and exchange between the two cultural dimensions.[30] Later, through another ambiguous appropriation of the language of feeling, Beckford announces: 'I have quite won [the ambassador's] heart by these attentions and he will miss me when I depart' (*J*, p. 299). This interweaving of cross-cultural desires is then further complicated by Beckford's meeting with yet another one of those 'fair youths' whose presence punctuates his life and his transcriptions of it. Indeed, at Ahmed Vassif's he makes the acquaintance of Mohammed, the young brother of the ambassador of the Berber state of Tripoli, a 'child' whom he describes as a personification of *Vathek*'s Gulchenrouz, turning this sentimental encounter into a further episode in his orientalist exchange:

There is a languid tenderness in his eyes, a softness in the contour of his face, a bewitching in his smile that enchanted me . . . I was seated on the carpet like an Oriental, to the great delight of Ahmed Vassif . . . but still more to that of little Mohammed, who kept whispering to me with a tone of voice that went to my soul, and pressing my hands with inconceivable tenderness. I thought myself in a dream—nay, I still think myself so, and expect to wake . . . Mohammed and I continued drinking each other's looks, to use the phraseology of Hafiz, with such avidity that we forgot how the time passed.

(*J,* p. 309)

As an important player in an economy of exchanges within the contact zone of East and West, Beckford centres on himself the homosocial climate and homosexual desire pervading his direct contact with the orient in Madrid. Ahmed Vassif's 'delight' in Beckford is thus added on to little Mohammed's passion for the narrator, who transmutes into the focal point (and repository) of different trajectories of desire. In the above passage, attraction is once more conveyed by a traditionally 'sentimentalist' amorous diction, oscillating between the sensual (the eyes) and the ineffable (the soul). In addition, the text visibly combines sensual or sexual desire as a self-identifying dimension—evidenced by the insistent first-person tone of the passage—with the desire for cultural otherness represented by Beckford's adoption of oriental manners ('I was seated on the carpet') and language ('the phraseology of Hafiz'). Unlike in **Vathek,** however, here the author shows no interest in representing the harem, the *locus classicus* of the orient as imagined by the West. The narrative, by contrast, lingers on Vassif's male 'favourites', 'tall, handsome slaves' (*S,* p. 201) and 'good-looking Georgian pages' (*S,* p. 202) as the most immediate circle in the centripetal economy and structure of the ambassador's orient. Beckford is invited by Vassif to sit at the very centre of this sexual-social structure on 'a well-cushioned divan . . . prepared for [the ambassador's] lollification' (*S,* p. 238). Ambivalently, while representing yet another aspect of the desire linking Beckford and the East, the homosocial and homosexual tenor of the exchange reinforces the author's location as a central figure in an emblematic interweaving of fictional and real oriental spaces.[31]

The instability of the subject-object hierarchy is further reinforced by the fact that consumption literally plays a relevant part in this 'sentimental' exchange. In the economy of reciprocal desire established by the text, Beckford consumes and enjoys the luxuries surrounding Ahmed Vassif while, in return, he offers the Eastern potentate the brioches prepared by his own personal pastry cook and of which the Turk is extremely fond: 'Every morning I have the pleasure of supplying the Grand Signior's representative with rolls and *brioches* baked at home for my breakfast. I have quite won his heart by

these attentions and he will miss me when I depart' (*J,* p. 299). In his later re-elaboration of this anecdote in **Sketches of Spain and Portugal,** Beckford adds: 'this very day he [Ahmed Vassif] came himself in one of the king's lumbering state coaches, with some of his special favourites, to thank me for these piping hot attentions' (*S,* p. 235). On 12 January the ambassador returns the favour: 'Ahmed Vassif sent me his favourite slave Taker with a magnificent present of wood of aloes, amber and odour of roses; by this token of regard I conclude that I am in high favour' (*J,* p. 313).

Such mutual gifts and courtesies unveil a structure of exchanges between East and West—coffee, precious cups, brioches, precious exotic presents—which delimits an intercultural relationship based on reciprocal assimilation. Simultaneously, the structure of reciprocity in this exchange points to a strategy of self-identification—as in the reference to 'one of the king's lumbering state coaches'—intimating Beckford's desire to be formally recognized, received and fêted by the Spanish institutions, and thus amounting to a post facto (fiction of) integration through the mediating presence of the Ottoman ambassador. Beckford's already mentioned inclusion in the upper echelons of the Lisbon aristocracy, with its conspicuous consumption of luxury and culture, is thus reprised within the more complex intercultural domain of the exchange in Ahmed Vassif's oriental space. In this fashion, the benefits of the traffic between East and West are also reaped by the narrating self who may fictionally transmute into a socially accepted individual rather than an exile whom the British ministers in Iberia—Robert Walpole at Lisbon and Robert Liston in Madrid—did not officially introduce to the local courts because of the scandal attached to his name. As if aiming to remedy such an exclusion, in the 1834 rewriting of his already highly inventive journal, Beckford's masterful self-referential narration positions his version of events in Madrid within a network of looks, desires and objects, of which he is one of the focal points, his own centrality based on the exchange with the oriental dimension of Ahmed Vassif.

The longing for self-definition in Beckford's account therefore intertwines with his desire for and ambivalent assimilation of the orient. The position and status of the self are guaranteed by those of the other, something which, throughout the Spanish-oriental interlude, is reinforced by a language of sensual pleasure—looking, gazing, smoking, lolling on soft cushions—predicated on the narrator's awareness of occupying the highest position in the social hierarchy of the Ottoman enclave. If in the public sphere of Madrid Beckford is deprived of the social recognition he feels he deserves, by contrast, inside the social network centred on Ahmed Vassif, Beckford places himself in a crucially pivotal position thanks to his intimate friendship with the ambassador and, more visibly, through the repeated invocation of an entourage of slaves and servants signifying the social distinctions in the Turkish orient. Beckford's account indeed obsessively records the presence of these figures around Vassif's person: 'his whiskered Excellency's pages and attendants' (*J*, p. 291), 'His attendants were standing silently around' (*J*, p. 299), 'all his whiskered suite' (*J*, p. 299), '[he was] surrounded by twenty or thirty of his attendants in their most splendid dress' (*J*, p. 308), 'Walked in the Retiro with Ahmed Vassif, whose slaves were romping' (*J*, p. 311), an ambiguous remark about 'Ahmed Vassif in the midst with his chicks all round him' (*J*, pp. 312-13), '[the ambassador's] principal favourites were mounted on Spanish prancers almost hid by enormous Turkish trappings' (*J*, p. 315), and 'Ahmed's messes were cooked by his own slaves' (*J*, p. 315). Ahmed Vassif is the central figure in a social structure that Beckford is invited to share: 'Ahmed Vassif made me sit by him the whole night in state and form' (*J*, p. 307). In this actualization of Grosrichard's scheme of an oriental domain centred on the despot, hierarchy is not exclusive or excluding, but rather an inclusively reassuring structure in which Beckford is (vicariously) the fulcrum of a social space sanctioned on the basis of a two-way exchange shot through with mutual desire and forms of reciprocal consumption.

Beckford's direct encounter with the orient in the winter of 1787 fuses cultural phantasms from the eighteenth-century oriental tale and the *Arabian Nights* tradition to a material orient presented as authentic in the repeated depictions of the Asiatic luxury surrounding Ahmed Vassif, the 'actual' embodiment of *Vathek*'s luxury. If, on the one hand, his autobiographical account aims at recording the immediacy of his contact with the East, on the other, it discloses the manifold fictionality of the 'real' orient, for the dimension of the Ottoman ambassador, itself the reproduction of an original space, is *de facto* transposed into the West, and also because the 'real' is inescapably filtered through Beckford's fictional and discursive approach. The ubiquitous opulence and the procession of choice objects—cushions, sofas, curtains, slaves, musical instruments, porcelain and vases—are both present to Beckford in Madrid in the winter of 1787 and recollected and reinvented in the different phases of composition of his diary and *Sketches of Spain and Portugal.*

The vacillation between real and fictional affects every aspect of the contact between East and West, and Beckford's fortuitous and dazzling meeting with the orient in the transitional space of Spain throws into relief some fundamental features of the orientalist imaginary of British Romantic culture, most visibly the orient's gradual transformation into a real object, a place to be visited and experienced, and one whose artefacts become more and more widely present and available in British culture. Beckford's contact with Ahmed Vassif

may thus be taken as a symbolic instance of this transition from the bookish to the experiential, from the mythical to the objective. This conclusion, however, reductively delimits the Romantic period as the zone of contact between British culture and an unmediated orient, so that any examination of Romantic orientalism would then amount to an assessment of the accuracy of its representation. Conversely, Beckford's account confirms the inescapable discursivity of the 'real' East, the hybrid nature of an orient already overwritten with tales and interpretations and not immune to the fictions of desire. Vassif's material and referential orient is filtered through an archive of acquired images which enable Beckford's approach to and appropriation of it within a scheme of exchange issuing in a further kind of hybridity through the Western subject's inclusion into the ambivalent dimension of assimilation.

Beckford's account usefully points out the overlapping of East and West in the culture of the Romantic period and the structure of reciprocal intercourse and exchange regulating their contact. As seen above, the assimilation of the East does not imply its domestication and naturalization, for the orient itself assimilates the narrating Western subject within a network of mutually supportive desires that flow in both directions. Calling Ahmed Vassif 'my dearly beloved Mahomet' (*J*, p. 299), Beckford assimilates the other into the cultural categories of the narrating culture, yet the Mahometan also plays a fundamental function in the self-defining orientalist panorama depicted in Beckford's accounts. If, following Célestin Roger's definition, exoticism is based on a tension between home and other rather than a relinquishing of either, Beckford's text may indeed be seen as 'negotiating subjective and discursive positions *between* Home and the exotic rather than being incorporated into one or the other' in that scheme of cultural intersection which Roger resonantly calls a 'triangular trade'.[32]

Beckford's emblematic experiences in the orient of 'Turkish Madrid' evidence how one of the most influential Romantic orientalist authors, the creator of an eminently textual orient, finally confronts his visions and reconstructs them in writing through a fascinating combination of fact and fiction. An intriguing expansion of the seminal orient of *Vathek,* the fragmented narrative of his direct contact with the East in Madrid may be read as a blueprint map of emblematic features and issues in Romantic orientalist figuration, especially the distinctively problematic overlap of materiality and a fictional, mythical orient. The macroscopic instances of desire for (and of) difference in Beckford's account disclose the less obvious aspects of the intercourse between a narrated East and a narrating West. That the narrative subject is ready to be consumed by the East as an object of visual, sensual or even (implicit) sexual desire, may indeed signal the mixture of attraction and angst pervading the economy of desire and consumption instigated by a subject who finds himself objectified within Ahmed Vassif's domain. Beckford's tale can therefore be read biographically as a narrative investment, the gains of which may be the satisfaction of a desire to be accepted and the exorcizing of solitude or exclusion. The narrative of the Madrid orient would then be yet another instance of that spectacularization of selfhood proper to Beckford's writings, buildings and collections. But, from a wider cultural perspective, the depiction and dramatization of the Turkish enclave in Madrid—Beckford's own 'menagerie' and seraglio—defines orientalism as a material and discursive zone of overlapping of East and West, a space delimited by the increasing availability and growing consumption of orientalist artefacts, and the dimension where two cultures coincide within intricate economies of desire and exchange that suspend hierarchies and the identification of any 'legitimate' divide between subject and object, orient and occident.

Notes

1. On the shift from eighteenth-century to Romantic orientalism as marked by an increase in the direct knowledge of the East, see e.g. Wallace Cable Brown, 'The popularity of English travel books about the Near East, 1775-1825', *Philological Quarterly,* 15 (1936), pp. 70-80; Nigel Leask, *British Romantic Writers and the East* (Cambridge: Cambridge University Press, 1992), pp. 18-20; Mohammed Sharafuddin, *Islam and Romantic Orientalism* (London and New York: I. B. Tauris, 1994), pp. xiii-xxxv; C. C. Barfoot, 'English Romantic poets and the "free-floating orient"', in C. C. Barfoot and Theo D'haen (eds) *Oriental Prospects: Western Literature and the Lure of the East* (Amsterdam: Rodopi, 1998), pp. 65-96.

2. On the pivotal role of *Vathek* in the transition from eighteenth-century to Romantic-period orientalist fiction, see Mohammed Sharafuddin, *Islam and Romantic Orientalism,* pp. xxxi-v; and, also on the accurate representation of exotic objects and luxuries in *Vathek*'s text and notes, see Nigel Leask, '"Wandering through Eblis": absorption and containment in Romantic exoticism', in Tim Fulford and Peter J. Kitson (eds) *Romanticism and Colonialism: Writing and Empire, 1780-1830* (Cambridge: Cambridge University Press, 1998), pp. 180-1.

3. John E. Wills, Jr., 'European consumption and Asian production in the seventeenth and eighteenth centuries', in John Brewer and Roy Porter (eds) *Consumption and the World of Goods* (New York and London: Routledge, 1993), p. 133.

4. Malachy Postlethwayt, *The Universal Dictionary of Trade and Commerce,* 2 vols (London: John and Paul Knachton, 1751-55), Vol. I, p. 694.

5. Besides John E. Wills, Jr., 'European consumption and Asian production', see also Maxine Berg, 'New commodities, luxuries and their consumers in eighteenth-century England', in Maxine Berg and Helen Clifford (eds) *Consumers and Luxury: Consumer Culture in Europe 1650-1850* (Manchester: Manchester University Press, 1999), pp. 63-85; Beverly Lemire, *Fashion's Favourite: The Cotton Trade and the Consumer in Britain, 1660-1800* (Oxford: Oxford University Press, 1991); and, about the intersections between material and discursive orientalism, see John M. MacKenzie, *Orientalism: History, Theory and the Arts* (Manchester: Manchester University Press, 1995); and John Sweetman, *The Oriental Obsession: Islamic Inspiration in British and Americal Art and Architecture 1500-1920* (Cambridge: Cambridge University Press, 1988).

6. Edward W. Said, *Orientalism* (London: Penguin, 1991), p. 2. For a recent, stimulating discussion (and questioning) of the now widely accepted principle of 'hybridity', see Antony Easthope, 'Bhabha, hybridity and identity', *Textual Practice,* 12 (1998), pp. 341-8.

7. Lord Byron, *The Complete Poetical Works,* ed. Jerome J. McGann, 7 vols (Oxford: Clarendon Press, 1980-93), Vol. III, p. 423.

8. *The Journal of William Beckford in Portugal and Spain 1787-1788,* ed. Boyd Alexander (London: Rupert Hart-Davies, 1954), p. 112 (henceforth *J*).

9. On the Turkish fashion in eighteenth-century Britain, see Sweetman, *The Oriental Obession,* pp. 44-72.

10. In *La société de consommation* (1970) Baudrillard defines consumption as 'the metaphoric or displaced expression of desire, and the production of a code of social values through the use of differentiating signs': Jean Baudrillard, *Selected Writings,* ed. Mark Poster (Cambridge: Polity Press, 1988), p. 46.

11. Cyrus Redding, *Memoirs of William Beckford of Fonthill, Author of 'Vathek',* 2 vols (London: Charles J. Skeet, 1859), Vol. I, p. 283.

12. Ibid., Vol. I, p. 296.

13. Beckford's Gothic-style house at Monserrate (or quinta of 'Montserrat'), where he lived during his later journey to Portugal in 1793, attracted the attention of his contemporaries who, most visibly in Byron's *Childe Harold* I, turned it into an important location of Beckford's investments in exotic luxury. See Redding, *Memoirs of William Beckford of Fonthill,* Vol. I, pp. 278-80. On Beckford's sojourns in Portugal, see André Parreaux, *Le Por-*

tugal dans l'oeuvre de William Beckford (Paris: Les Belles Lettres, 1930); Magdi Wahba, 'Beckford, Portugal and "childish error"', in Fatma Moussa Mahmoud (ed.) *William Beckford of Fonthill 1760-1844: Bicentenary Essays* (Port Washington and London: Kennikat Press, 1960), pp. 51-62; and Boyd Alexander, *England's Wealthiest Son: A Study of William Beckford* (London: Centaur Press, 1962), pp. 125-38.

14. Timothy Mowl, *William Beckford: Composing for Mozart* (London: John Murray, 1998), p. 193.

15. On the multiple relevance of this episode see Nigel Leask, '"Wandering through Eblis"', pp. 165-88.

16. The present reading of Beckford's encounter with the East in Madrid in 1787 draws on the journal he kept during his journey and which was published only in 1954 by Boyd Alexander as *The Journal of William Beckford in Portugal and Spain 1787-1788*. Although it is often a very direct piece of personal writing, Beckford, however, modified and edited it at different stages during the following years. In addition, this discussion draws on the letters Beckford published in 1834, together with a reworked version of *Dreams, Waking Thoughts and Incidents* (1783), as *Italy; with Sketches of Spain and Portugal,* contained in Guy Chapman (ed.) *The Travel-Diaries of William Beckford of Fonthill,* 2 vols (Cambridge: Constable, Houghton-Mifflin, 1928), Vol. II (henceforth *S*).

17. Mowl, *William Beckford,* p. 145.

18. In *On Longing,* Susan Stewart starts her investigation of the cultural categories of the miniature, the gigantic, the souvenir and the collection by way of an important reflection on desire and narration, and the premiss that 'Narrative is seen . . . as a structure of desire, a structure that both invents and distances its object and thereby inscribes again and again the gap between signifier and signified that is the place of generation for the symbolic.' *On Longing* (Durham and London: Duke University Press, 1993), p. ix.

19. Mary Louise Pratt, *Imperial Eyes: Travel-Writing and Transculturation* (London and New York: Routledge, 1992), p. 6.

20. During the first meeting, the Turkish ambassador's 'interpreter explained my nation' (*J,* p. 291); then on 23 December, 'My friend Ahmed Vassif stalked in with his Turkish interpreter, who is much more to my liking than Mr Timon' (*J,* p. 302); during a musical evening, an 'Armenian interpreter' explains to Beckford the meaning of an oriental 'doleful ditty' (*J,* p. 306); and the interpreter Timoni, whom Beckford disliked, reappears on 14 January on the occasion of a trip out of town (*J,* p. 315). Interestingly, the mediating function of the interpreter occasionally fails during the exchange between East and West as, for instance, during Beckford's first meeting with Ahmed Vassif: 'when I added a few quotations from some of his favourite authors, particularly Mesihi, he became so flowingly communicative, that a shrewd dapper Greek, called Timoni, who acted as his most confidential interpreter, could hardly keep pace with him' (*S,* p. 202).

21. *L'Empire des cartes: approche théorique de la cartographie à travers l'Histoire* (Paris: Albin Michel, 1992), p. 16.

22. On the eighteenth-century orientalist fashion as centred on 'an idealized world of consumerist delights' and an expression of aristocratic conspicuous consumption, see Marilyn Butler, 'Orientalism', in *The Penguin History of Literature,* Vol. 5: The *Romantic Period,* ed. David B. Pirie (London: Penguin, 1994), p. 396. Romantic-period conceptions of luxury as an interface between the material and the transcendental are examined by Timothy Morton in *The Poetics of Spice: Romantic Consumerism and the Exotic* (Cambridge: Cambridge University Press, 2000).

23. Andrew Elfenbein, *Romantic Genius: The Prehistory of a Homosexual Role* (New York: Columbia University Press, 1999), pp. 43, 42.

24. Ibid., p. 49; see also Susan Stewart's observations on collecting as an activity that 'serves both to give integrity to the self and at the same time to overload the self with signification', in *On Longing,* p. 163.

25. On eighteenth-century operatic Turks see W. Daniel Wilson, 'Turks on the eighteenth-century operatic stage and European political, military, and cultural history', *Eighteenth-Century Life,* 2 (1985), pp. 79-92; and Eve R. Meyer, 'Turquerie and eighteenth-century music', *Eighteenth-Century Studies,* 7 (1973-74), pp. 474-88.

26. Alain Grosrichard, *Structure du sérail: la fiction du despotisme asiatique dans l'Occident classique* (Paris: Seuil, 1979), p. 90 (English translation: *The Structure of the Seraglio,* trans Liz Heron (London: Verso, 1997)).

27. In Baudrillard's *La Société de consommation,* consumption is a subjective process defined as 'primarily organized as a discourse to oneself, and [with] a tendency to play itself out, with its gratifications and deceptions, in this minimal exchange' (*Selected Writings,* p. 54). A similar perspective, albeit from an overtly sociological and cultural-

historical standpoint, characterizes Colin Campbell's *The Romantic Ethic and the Spirit of Modern Consumerism* (Oxford: Blackwell, 1987).

28. Kevin L. Cope, 'Beckford and the emerging consciousness: projective collecting and the aesthetic dynamics of acquisition', *Studies in Voltaire and the Eighteenth Century,* 305 (1992), pp. 1815, 1818.

29. Letter of 12 November 1809 to his mother, in Leslie A. Marchand (ed.) *Byron's Letters and Journals,* 13 vols (London: Murray, 1973-94), Vol. I, pp. 227-8.

30. On Byron's experience at Ali Pacha's court, see Cecil Y. Lang, 'Narcissus jilted: Byron, *Don Juan,* and the biographical imperative', in Jerome J. McGann (ed.) *Historical Studies and Literary Criticism* (Madison: The Wisconsin University Press, 1985), pp. 143-79.

31. In Beckford's account the only trace of a divide comparable to that of the harem is a curtain hiding a group of unseen musicians: 'music like flutes and dulcimers, accompanied by a sort of tabor, issued from behind a curtain which separated us from another apartment' (*J,* p. 291). Female figures are visibly absent from the oriental enclave ruled by Ahmed Vassif, the only ones described being a group of ladies ridiculed as 'a bevy of young tits dressed out in a fantastic, blowzy style' (*S,* p. 238) and vainly trying to catch the potentate's attention.

32. Roger Célestin, *From Cannibals to Radicals: Figures and Limits of Exoticism* (Minneapolis and London: Minnesota University Press, 1996), p. 23. In particular, Célestin considers the exotic as delimited by 'the tension between the gravitational pull of Home, the Same, the familiar, the dominant, and the individual subject's dissident desire for another place, an outside—an outside that simultaneously embodies desire and destabilizes the desiring subject' (p. 4).

R. B. Gill (essay date January 2003)

SOURCE: Gill, R. B. "The Author in the Novel: Creating Beckford in *Vathek.*" *Eighteenth-Century Fiction* 15, no. 2 (January 2003): 241-54.

[*In the following essay, Gill focuses upon the limitations of various autobiographical and psychological interpretations of* Vathek.]

According to David Hume, "The mind is a kind of theatre where several perceptions successively make their appearance; pass, re-pass, glide away, and mingle in an infinite variety of postures and situations."[1] Hume's well-known account of personal identity aptly describes William Beckford—petulant heir to great wealth, a member of Parliament, connoisseur, architectural dilettante, fugitive from sexual scandal, and author of *Vathek,* one of the most enjoyable and intriguing of the eighteenth-century Oriental tales. Across the pages of *Vathek* and, indeed, of Beckford's whole life pass and mingle the successive actors of his disjointed identity.

Hume's caution to the reader is especially relevant in Beckford's case: "the comparison with theatre must not mislead us. They are the successive perceptions only, that constitute the mind; nor have we the most distant notion of the place, where these scenes are represented, or of the materials, of which it is compos'd." The spectators of Beckford's life and the readers of his tale have wished to know the materials of which his inner self was composed in order to explain his theatrics, but they have never agreed on what they found. And Beckford himself, complaining of the mask he wore, yet intent on preserving a gentlemanly image, a man unwillingly hastened by his family and his wealth from one performance to the next, seems never to have found that inner being with which he could be at peace. The result is that there are many Beckfords, some he himself created and many created by his various critics.

But these created selves are, to use Hume's terms for personal identity, "merely verbal" (p. 262). These verbal Beckfords are plots without a story, the texts he and we write in lieu of an anchoring identity. The problem in Beckford's case lies not so much in this textuality as in our desire (and his) to find the originating self of that text. The ambiguities surrounding Beckford prompt a search for biographical explanations. Yet Beckford's personae within *Vathek* and his life are clearly created ones, even though they are offered as biographical fact. In this respect, Beckford's presence in the novel is typical of other authorial personae, artistic creations that paradoxically function properly only when taken as factual biography. But when that paradox tempts critics into the impossible task of locating the true self of the author, they find only what Hume notes is a mysterious and inexplicable fiction. *Vathek* is a clear case of a novel especially in need of a biographical centre to resolve its ambiguities.[2] Not finding that centre or authorial identity, critics (and Beckford himself) have created a number of identities to satisfy their own perceptions of the needs of the novel.

* * *

A straightforward Oriental tale whose quick narrative and polished style cover no depths of complex psychological characterization, *Vathek* would not seem to offer special problems of interpretation. Yet critical views of this novel vary widely. It has been seen as both Gothic and non-Gothic, satiric and non-satiric, realistic and fantastic, neo-classic and romantic, socially conventional and anti-bourgeois, metaphysical and message-less, as well as both unified and split in its sensibility. *Vathek* has been valued for its "correctness of costume," criticized for its elaborate explanatory notes, and, notably, regarded as moral, immoral, amoral, and "anti-moral."[3]

The diverse critical opinions arise in part from the intriguing mixture of opposites in Beckford's style. Whether we consider it Oriental or Gothic or whatever, *Vathek* is essentially the sort of fabular parable that the eighteenth-century reader enjoyed. It is thus outside the realistic mainstream that has come to represent for us the novel's most characteristic mode of addressing moral issues. And yet, on its surface at least, it is an explicitly moral parable. Consequently, there is difficulty for us, as there was for Beckford's contemporaries, in reconciling the fabular, Eastern exoticism of *Vathek* with its moral elements. Further, we cannot say of *Vathek,* as we can of *Candide* and *Rasselas,* that its imaginative centre lies in the moral message, for our interest in the perverse actions of the characters frequently jars with the conventional morals, particularly the closing moral that "the condition of man upon earth is to be—humble and ignorant."

There is an additional mixing of opposites in the self-conscious playfulness of Beckford's style. Like Sterne, Beckford watches himself write and is intrigued by the possibilities of expressing himself in guises—now moral, now perverse, now coy, now sublime. He cannot resist indulging himself momentarily in some ludicrous or incongruous aspect of his material. The storks, for instance, that join the morning prayers of Nouronihar and Gulchenrouz by the lake are a poke at the solemnity of religious greybeards, but their incongruity as members of the worshipping congregation is so striking that it distracts attention from the narrative, an indulgence we enjoy as part of a highly self-referential style. Beckford is not willing to suppress these moments of self-conscious fun; *Vathek* smiles at its sardonic incongruities from the first paragraph to its closing moralisms.

Beckford uses authorial self-consciousness in the text of *Vathek* to remove himself from his occult material and thus to preserve, or create, an aura of sophistication and control. Here is no romantic subordination or merging of author with his outré creation, as we find in the works of Poe. Rather, *Vathek* is an eighteenth-century amalgam of Pope's proud epic notes in the *Dunciad* (a similarity Beckford recognized) and Sterne's sophisticated and intensely self-aware metafiction. Beckford wants us to observe him laughing at his subject, manipulating it: a gentleman engaged with compromising material but, nevertheless, in thorough control of it and able to smile knowingly at his own folly. In this mixture of opposites, *Vathek,* like many other neoclassical works, has a civilized sophistication that acknowledges its own role-playing.

In fact, Beckford cared greatly about the image of himself created in *Vathek.* In this respect the novel is a literary counterpart of Fonthill, the Gothic abbey on which he later lavished his efforts and money. On occasion he claimed, somewhat misleadingly, to have written the novel in several days in a fit of inspiration, and he romanticized about the "most extravagant intensity" of the Christmas celebration at Fonthill that formed part of the inspiration of the novel. Beckford's letters reveal that he was very much aware of the effect of his image on others—and that he enjoyed the thought. *Vathek* is "the only production of mine which I am not ashamed of" he wrote to Samuel Henley; and in a different letter he spoke of the "honours" with which he expected *Vathek* to be received. To another correspondent he wrote of "ma vanité" of the Caliph, and in the journal of his stay in Portugal he noted that he was "extremely impatient" to receive "the last monthly reviews in which I expect to read a critique on *Vathek.*" Cyrus Redding, his first biographer, recalled, "To abuse *Vathek* he deemed a personal insult. His pride took the alarm and he could scarcely restrain his anger, so fierce when aroused, though evanescent."[4]

The references in his letters to shame, honour, and pride reveal his characteristic concern with the relationship between his work and his reputation. Biographers often note the changes that Beckford made in his papers and letters in order that they appear most advantageous. Contemporaries of Beckford such as Mrs Thrale, William Hazlitt, and Byron understood the degree to which public appearance was involved in Beckford's effects and enjoyed the scandal that attended his reputation. A continuing motif in the Portuguese journal, written shortly after publication of *Vathek,* is Beckford's awareness that others are watching his carefully contrived self-image: "I hear there is no conversation in Lisbon but of my poetry." "My reputation as a devotee spreads prodigiously." Although he notes, "I am sick of forming the chief subject of conversation at all the card tables," he also takes care to record the surprise with which "the whole herd of precentors, priests, musicians and fencing masters" listen to his playing and singing. Again, "my singing, playing and capering subdues every Portuguese that approaches me." In preparation for a trip to a convent, he writes, "I am furbishing up a string of highly polished saintly speeches for the occasion." And later, "for flippery in crossing myself and goosishness in poking out my head I will turn my back to no one." Beckford, then, works carefully to create a persona; he attentively watches people react to that image; and he self-consciously distances himself from his creation through self-abnegating humour with such references as "flippery," "goosishness," and "capering."[5]

It is true that he grew restive with his public self. In one entry, after worrying about a possible scrape with a "young friend," he continues with the complaint often quoted by critics, "How tired I am of keeping a mask on my countenance. How tight it sticks—it makes me sore." Significantly, he immediately follows this complaint with self-conscious observation upon it: "There's a metaphor for you. I have all the fancies and levity of a child."[6] The ingredients of Beckford's dilemma are here—the concern with image, the restiveness, and the recurrent self-consciousness that flickers over his thoughts and actions. He does not remove his mask but worries, instead, about getting into a scrape. For all the restiveness, the image of himself that Beckford contrived to project was exterior: he was concerned with his public reputation, with the appurtenances of a gentlemanly and leisured class, with his adeptness in Oriental matters, and with the skill of his style and of the "magnificence" with which *Vathek* concludes.

Yet that exterior image has never seemed sufficient or trustworthy, a circumstance that accounts for the central critical dilemma of *Vathek.* The novel's puzzling mixture of opposites invites the reader to seek an inner author, the "real" Beckford accessible through psychological examination. Behind the varying judgments of Beckford's novel lie critical assessments of his inner person. There are explanations that he was impotent, homosexual, bisexual, dominated by a Calvinist mother, grieving for his dead wife, a leisurely country gentleman, bitter, mad, vile, sadistic, a "barely socialized psychopath," and so on.[7] Without question, the novel is a document in Beckford's life, as biographically relevant as, say, his construction of Fonthill. Nor is Beckford the type of artist whose work rises self-contained and impersonal above its historical contingencies. *Vathek* is a minor novel, interesting in itself certainly, but also of legitimate interest as a record of the tastes of its author and age.

Nevertheless, for all the care and intelligence expended on it, the search for the inner, unifying Beckford has not been successful. Mme de Staël, to whom Beckford had given a copy of his travelogue *Dreams, Waking Thoughts and Incidents,* wrote to him, "You dream when you have nothing to describe. Imagination, which invents or represents objects, has never been given more freedom." Likewise, André Parreaux has noted that seeing "le vrai visage" of Beckford behind his mask is a matter of great difficulty. V. S. Pritchett claimed that "everything Beckford writes is suspect, for truth and fiction are hard to separate in this incessantly revising and play-acting autobiographer."[8] And that is the dilemma. The search for the interior Beckford seems a necessary step to reconciling the opposites in his life and work, but that search cannot lead us past the contrived and public mask it was Beckford's fate to wear.

* * *

For both practical and theoretical reasons, the inner Beckford cannot be found. First, it is important to bear in mind the well-known dangers of moving back and forth between biography and art. One need not be unduly afraid of the Intentional Fallacy or of its reverse, biography based on interpretation of the artist's works, to recognize the difficulties and dangers and, therefore, the need of great caution. Is Fielding the compassionate observer of the ambiguities of mercy in *Tom Jones* or the sterner remembrancer of justice in *Amelia*? And to what extent can we move from his actual experience as magistrate of the Bow Street police court to the more sombre judicial tone of that later novel?

But no matter how receptive we are to the intermingling of biography and art, we must allow for the great practical difficulties that interfere with our understanding of the relevant facts of Beckford's life. Beckford was born to a public family with the expectation and the means of creating and protecting an appropriate public image. There is evidence that the suppression of *Dreams, Waking Thoughts and Incidents* came as a result of family fears that its injudicious subjectivity might endanger a public career. "Neither Orlando nor Brandimart," he wrote of the matter, "were ever more tormented by Daemons and Spectres in an enchanted Castle than Wm. Bd. in his own Hall by his nearest relations."[9]

His marriage to Lady Margaret Gordon again seems the result of a family strategy, as was his short stay in Parliament. Lady Hamilton's vivid letter to Beckford in 1780 attempting to dissuade him from a scandalous liaison in Venice stresses the public image that Beckford's relations valued above all. What is the struggle against temptation for, she asks. "No less than *honor, reputation* and all that an honest and noble Soul holds most dear, while Infamy, eternal infamy (my soul freezes while I write the word), attends the giving way to the soft alluring of a criminal passion."[10] For most of his life Beckford seems to have resented and struggled against these impositions on his private self, but he did not throw them off. The private Beckford remained cloistered. Unlike Byron, Parreaux notes, Beckford would not play the role of outcast but tried to maintain the fiction of having a privileged place in the society of his time.[11] In fact, much of the pathos of Beckford's life results from the disparity between his compromised reputation and his expectations of an aristocratic, privileged position. Beckford chose an unhappy role to play, but the important point here is that he chose the public and proper role urged on him by his family.

Beckford's sexuality has been a key concern of critics looking for the inner explanation of *Vathek*'s opposites. In 1785 Beckford left England temporarily in the wake of a scandal over his relationship with the young William Courtenay. The opprobrium remaining from this incident together with continuing rumours plagued him throughout his life. But our understanding of this matter is enormously complicated by the practical difficulties of determining the facts, by the different theoretical models used to explain the facts, by the limitations of any sort of psychological explanation, and by the divergent uses that critics make of their conclusions even when they agree on the facts. We know that Beckford was married with two daughters, that his wife maintained her faith in him, and that he grieved her death. What lies behind the protective public face must be surmised. Beckford's letters and papers contain helpful information, but, as noted, they were revised in places with the intention of portraying a desirable image; they are often oblique, and, as Boyd Alexander observes, Beckford "dramatises and exaggerates his moods and feelings." Beckford himself lamented in his *Journal,* "I have more profligacy of tongue than of character and often do my utmost to make myself appear worse than I am in reality."[12]

Further, even where the facts seem clear, there is the theoretical difficulty of knowing how to interpret them. What do we want to say—that he was homosexual, bisexual, merely self-indulgent without a strongly marked sexual orientation? Do we want to psychoanalyse him as a case of "narcissistic paederasty"? This last diagnosis is informative, a perceptive use of psychological criticism to explain the tensions in Beckford's style, but at bottom it illustrates the limitations of attempts to explain what lurks behind the scenes of the mind. Its diagnosis, "narcissistic paederasty,"[13] is not defined precisely enough for use as the key to a complex man's very difficult personality. It includes childishness as well as child-love; it is metaphorical ("a self-devouring child wishing to rape his own image"); and it is governed by the need to find a psychological unity beneath the behavioural data. Like so many explanations of sexuality, it is an imposition of a unifying concept on separate facets of behaviour. This interpretation, then, leaves us in the biographical dilemma. It is meaningful precisely because it creates a unifying matrix for separate and heterogeneous elements in Beckford's actions. As we have seen, we need interpretation imposed on the discrete items of Beckford's life in order to understand them in relationship with each other. Yet, equally clearly, there is no justification for believing that whatever interpretation we may impose is historically verifiable truth.

What indeed does it mean to "understand" the sources of a person's acts and ideas? One's actions stem from the intricate causal network that is one's whole being;

therefore, no explanation can be complete. Any attempt at explanation must be an abstraction, a grouping or a simplification of a myriad causes. It represents the critic's decision about where to draw the line between significance and insignificance. And that decision must necessarily be personal and subjective. What shall we make, for instance, of an opinion that *Vathek* may embody Beckford's complex reaction to his "possessive and autocratic mother"?[14] Again, I find the suggestion reasonable but am not certain that any array of biographical facts, no matter how extensive, would persuade another reader less convinced of the importance of parental influence than I am. What then of his equally dominating father, Alderman Beckford, twice Lord Mayor of London, robust heterosexual and extrovert, who seems to have been both amused and impatient with the whims of his wilful child? Do our own explanatory models hold that fathers are not as influential as mothers?[15] Or do we see a malign conjunction in their mutual influences? The point, of course, is that each of us will delineate the boundaries between significance and insignificance in different ways, ways owing as much to our explanatory models of child development as to objectively demonstrable facts about William Beckford.

Critics whose thinking is determined by one explanatory model will regard another as lacking in the requisite rigour of method and verifiability. Many types of explanations have only practical justification and, therefore, offer no *a priori* reasons why their results may not be duplicated by another type of explanation. Thus, psychoanalysis may in practice accomplish in contemporary society what advice from village elders or purification rituals accomplished in other ages. Because these explanatory models enable a person better to function in his or her environment and a critic to unite disparate facts under a common hypothesis, we value them highly. A model or system of beliefs with explanatory powers will come to seem self-evident, its underlying assumptions justified by the results they produce. In Beckford's case, some sort of sexual hypothesis may unite his behaviour patterns with the ambivalent closing moral of *Vathek* and with what we know of human behaviour from our own experiences and studies. These are significant results. They may lead us to accept the critic's interpretation, but they leave unanswered such questions as whether we understand Beckford's behaviour patterns as they really were and whether the psychological aspects of the hypothesis (for instance, "narcissistic paederasty") are empirically verifiable concepts.

Further, even satisfying explanations leave undetermined the extent to which the critic's own interpretations are mediated by personal and social codes.[16] The subtleties of George Haggerty's account of Beckford's search for a "true heart's friend"[17] are an advance over earlier stereotypes or what he calls "essentialist" categorizations, but his views so clearly originate in a personal thesis concerning "love" that one accepts them with the same caution necessary in reading Timothy Mowl's more commonsensical portrait of Beckford as robust bisexual horseman. The openness with which we now discuss sexual behaviour allows honest explorations, but falls easy prey to the temptations of biographical creation, which it is the purpose of this paper to delineate. Sex is far too interesting a matter to approach dispassionately. Self-congratulation on exposing the equivocations of past critics, the wrinkled pleasure of rehearsing Beckford's perfervid letters, and the rivalries of competing models of Beckford's desires all increase the risks that personal zest rather than objectivity accounts for our explanations.

What in the end are the truth-value and the verification procedure of a claim that Beckford died "at the age of eighty-four—unrepentant, unreformed, and immature"?[18] I choose this remark because it comes from a respected critic of Beckford; it is both adroit and compelling. Yet its virtues are dexterity of statement (entirely a verbal virtue) and ability to bring a number of biographical strands into a single formulation (a literary and logical virtue). Neat summation is appealing in a linear, logical mode such as biography, but life itself is confused, contradictory, and illogical. What counts as a literary virtue may be in fact a liability in the search for truth. As we have seen, such a claim has its own sort of meaningfulness, but we who understand ourselves only with difficulty may remain sceptical of the biographer's ability to reduce another human's inner being to clear patterns.[19]

Hume's point was similar and adds to the theoretical obstacles we face in finding a "real" Beckford. Although we have a great "propension . . . to imagine something unknown and mysterious, connecting the parts" of our personal identity, that mysterious something is a feigned support and centre rather than a "true" entity. We know only the perceptions of others and ourselves rather than their causes. Instead of the "nice and subtle questions concerning personal identity [which] can never possibly be decided," Hume notes that the mind "gives rise to some fiction or imaginary principle of union." Our personal identity is a "grammatical" matter, a syntax of the self created from discrete parts (pp. 254, 262-63).

Hume's scepticism springs from philosophical analysis and properly concerns the existence of personal identity rather than its characteristics, which I claim Beckford and his critics are searching for. Back of Hume's analysis, however, lies an English—and especially an eighteenth-century English—emphasis on the social bases of personality, the self as acted role. As Lord Chesterfield writes (notoriously but not atypically) to his son, "Manner is all, in everything; it is by manner only that you can please, and consequently rise."[20] And in his account of himself, Hume stresses his own man-

ners and sociability: "I was a man of mild dispositions, of command of temper, of an open, social, and cheerful humour. . . . Even my love of literary fame, my ruling passion, never soured my temper."[21] An eighteenth-century gentleman might well doubt the inner self, for the class and the age place their interests in mannerly, social roles. For Hume, Chesterfield, and Beckford, one's identity was created, a composed grammar or syntax of the self rather than a deep structure.

We can return now to Beckford with some sympathy and understanding for his lot, that of replacing personal identity with a public face. In *Vathek* we have a work whose mixture of opposites seems to demand an author's personality to give it unity. Yet the very prominent personality that Beckford interjects into *Vathek* stands aloof from his material, for Beckford is eager that we see him laughing and manipulating the diverse attitudes of *Vathek* without being compromised by naïve commitment to them. That public, mannered Beckford is all we have—but not all we need if we are to depart satisfied with a unified impression of *Vathek*. And so we create for Beckford an inner, unifying personality, *aware now that it is our own creation*. We do for the novel what Beckford did for it: we write an imaginatively embellished biography of the Caliph of Fonthill just as he wrote of *Vathek* Billah, ninth Caliph of the Abassides.[22]

We end up with creations—an aristocratic Beckford defying middle-class morality in *Vathek*, or an infantile, sexually insecure Beckford projecting his interests on the novel, or a "nervous, self-conscious, shoulder-shrugging" littérateur, or even the impersonal artist whose work "might not be due so much to [his] own neuroses as to certain conventions" within an artistic tradition.[23] Our Beckford may or may not be the "true" Beckford, but this construction renders the novel more meaningful. Where conflicting opposites have deconstructed author and novel, the interpretive critic has reconstructed them. Thus, we find the many different Beckfords in the critical literature. To some extent these critics are creating their own selves in the person of Beckford, shaping the work so it will pass through the network of their own adaptive and defensive strategies, as Norman Holland has put it. To some extent, no doubt, their work is a more literary attempt to supply an orderly grammar of logical relationships to their perceptions of *Vathek*.[24]

In each of these cases lies the reality, now often noted in biographical as well as critical studies, that every subject is changed by the discourse that embodies it. William Epstein has observed that "the decline of faith in the unmediated, ontological status of 'events'" must influence all but the most unexamined approaches to biography.[25] Any Beckford that we (and he) perceive is a product of the interpretive codes that govern our cognitive being. What sort of man lies behind or transcends these codes is, as Hume would put it, a "nice and subtile question" (p. 262). For, indeed, whether we take our cue from Hume or Derrida, the absolute origin of perception is inseparable from the activity that records it. Whether we look at the issue practically, theoretically, or (to use eighteenth-century terms) in the clear light of reason, the Beckford we find is a creation of cultural and interpretive codes. The insights of Enlightenment English empiricism, the twists of postmodern criticism, and the reticence of polite and experienced observers of human nature can go no further than the public Beckford.

There is no alternative to accepting the dilemma of the desirability and impossibility of biographical interpretation. A critic must put together a unified interpretation of the data, knowing all along that interpreted data is meaningful creation rather than fact independent of its expression. That is the dilemma of all biography; Beckford's case only makes it especially clear. In the end, we come to something very close to Hume's sceptical reflections on personal identity. We (and Beckford himself) know the "successive perceptions" (p. 253) of the novel and the life but lack the most distant notion of their underlying causes or, for that matter, of their basic unity. Yet we see Beckford struggling unsuccessfully to find himself and critics struggling to create narratives to bind together their perceptions. The effort in each case must be unsuccessful, but, paradoxically, it is also understandable and necessary.

Notes

1. David Hume, *A Treatise of Human Nature,* ed. L. A. Selby-Bigg (Oxford: Oxford University Press, 1965), p. 253. References are to this edition.

2. Roger Lonsdale writes: the "difficulty of attaching any clear meaning or satiric purpose to *Vathek* has also tended to force its readers back on the author itself for enlightenment." See introduction, William Beckford, *Vathek* (Oxford: World's Classics, 1983), p. viii.

3. Summaries of critical reactions can be found in Lonsdale, pp. xix-xxii; Dan J. McNutt, *The Eighteenth-Century Gothic Novel: An Annotated Bibliography of Criticism and Selected Texts* (New York: Garland, 1985), pp. 265-310; and Brian Fothergill, *Beckford of Fonthill* (London: Faber and Faber, 1978), pp. 128-35.

4. Fothergill, p. 134. See also Lonsdale, pp. x-xiv; and *The Journal of William Beckford in Portugal and Spain 1787-1788,* ed. Boyd Alexander (New York: John Day, 1955), p. 139.

5. Beckford, *Journal,* pp. 38, 41, 44, 76, 86, 92, and 225. For discussion of Beckford's revisions and

his reputation, see Guy Chapman, *Beckford* (New York: Scribner's, 1937), p. 323; Timothy Mowl, *William Beckford: Composing for Mozart* (London: John Murray, 1998), passim; James Lees-Milne, *William Beckford* (Montclair, NJ: Allanheld, Osmun, 1979), p. 107; and McNutt, pp. 288, 301-4.

6. Beckford, *Journal,* p. 41. See also André Parreaux, *William Beckford: Auteur de "Vathek"* (Paris: Nizet, 1960), p. 76.

7. See John T. Farrell, "A Reinterpretation of the Major Literary Works of William Beckford," *Dissertation Abstracts* 45 (1984), 1758A (University of Delaware); George E. Haggerty, *Men in Love: Masculinity and Sexuality in the Eighteenth Century* (New York: Columbia University Press, 1999), pp. 136-51; and Mowl, p. 111.

8. Mme de Staël is quoted in William Beckford, *Dreams, Waking Thoughts and Incidents,* ed. Robert J. Gemmett (Rutherford, NJ: Fairleigh Dickinson University Press, 1971), p. 26; Parreaux, p. 78; V. S. Pritchett, "Vile Body," *New Statesman* 63 (1962), 265-66.

9. Chapman, p. 168.

10. Beckford, *Dreams, Waking Thoughts and Incidents,* pp. 16-17.

11. Parreaux, p. 77.

12. Quoted in Boyd Alexander, *Life at Fonthill, 1807-1822* (London: Rupert Hart Davies, 1957), p. 26.

13. See Magdi Wahba, "Beckford, Portugal and 'Childish Error,'" *William Beckford of Fonthill, 1760-1844: Bicentary Essays,* ed. Fatma Moussa Mahmoud (Port Washington, NY: Kennikat, 1960), p. 58.

14. Lonsdale, introduction to *Vathek,* p. viii.

15. For differing ideas of parental influence, see Lonsdale, introduction to *Vathek,* p. viii; and Mowl, p. 31.

16. For discussions of limitations imposed by "conceptual paradigms" and hypotheses, see David E. Swalm, "Locating Belief in Biography," *Biography* 3 (1980), 23; and Ira Bruce Nadel, *Biography: Fiction, Fact and Form* (New York: St Martin's Press, 1984), pp. 10, 209.

17. Haggerty, p. 151.

18. Alexander, p. 15.

19. See Noel Chabani Manganyi, "Psychobiography and the Truth of the Subject," *Biography* 6 (1983), 44-45, 50.

20. Earl of Chesterfield, *Letters to His Son by the Earl of Chesterfield* (Washington: M. Walter Dunne, 1901), 2:395.

21. Ernest Campbell Mossner, "My Own Life," *The Life of David Hume* (Austin: University of Texas Press, 1954), p. 615.

22. See Kenneth W. Graham, "Implications of the Grotesque: Beckford's *Vathek* and the Boundaries of Fictional Reality," *Tennessee Studies in Literature* 23 (1978), 64.

23. James Henry Rieger, "Au Pied de la Lettre: Stylistic Uncertainty in *Vathek*," *Criticism* 4 (1962), 310; James K. Folsom, "Beckford's *Vathek* and the Tradition of Oriental Satire," *Criticism* 6 (1964), 53.

24. Norman Holland, "Unity Identity Text Self," *PMLA* 90 (1975), 816-17; Peter Nagourney, "The Basic Assumptions of Literary Biography," *Biography* 1 (1978), 93.

25. William Epstein, *Recognizing Biography* (Philadelphia: University of Pennsylvania Press, 1987), p. 36.

Robert J. Gemmett (essay date September 2004)

SOURCE: Gemmett, Robert J. "William Beckford's Authorship of *Modern Novel Writing* and *Azemia*." *Papers of the Bibliographical Society of America* 98, no. 3 (September 2004): 313-25.

[*In the following essay, Gemmett outlines the history of two pseudonymously published novels written by Beckford.*]

In 1796 William Beckford published *Modern Novel Writing, or the Elegant Enthusiast; and Interesting Emotions of Arabella Bloomville. A Rhapsodical Romance; Interspersed with Poetry* under the pseudonym of Lady Harriet Marlow.[1] This volume was followed almost immediately in 1797 by *Azemia: A Descriptive and Sentimental Novel. Interspersed with Pieces of Poetry* under the name of Jacquetta Agneta Mariana Jenks. Beckford linked the two volumes together as companion works by dedicating *Azemia* to "The Right Honourable Lady Harriet Marlow." Reminiscent of the satiric style of his first published book, *Biographical Memoirs of Extraordinary Painters* (1780), both books were designed in part to ridicule the sentimental and sensational novels of the day, particularly the productions of William Lane's Minerva Press. Elizabeth Hervey, Beckford's half-sister, is usually identified as the principal object of attack for her works in the sentimental vein, particularly *Melissa and Marcia* (1788) and *Louisa* (1790). It is clear that Beckford was also thinking of the more general proliferation of sentimental and Gothic novels in the 1780s and 1790s, particularly if they were authored by women. Towards the end

of *Azemia,* he mentions the authors parodied, including Fanny Burney, Ann Radcliffe, Sophia Lee, Charlotte Smith, Helen Maria Williams, Elizabeth Inchbald, Elizabeth Gunning, and Maria Robinson. In 1821 he revealed how he felt about their works. "It might be as well," he wrote, "if instead of weaving historical romances the super-literary ladies of the present period would pass a little more of their time at cross stitch and yabble stitch. We should gain some pretty chair and screen covers and lose little by not being tempted to pore over the mazes of their interminable scribbleations."[2]

In *Modern Novel Writing* Beckford manages to highlight almost all of the flagrant excesses of the fashionable novelists of the day. Instead of a carefully articulated plot, for example, he presents the reader with a patchwork of incidents—poorly constructed and crowded with irrelevant detail. As in the novels he parodies, the characters tend to appear and disappear without purpose or meaning. Bombast replaces natural speech for the purpose of giving expression to the false sentiment and overstrained emotions that pervade the book. An exquisite type of poetry, which is scattered throughout the novel, is also in keeping with the conventions of the sentimental school:

> Love is a soft, involuntary flame,
>   Beyond the pow'r of language to express;
> That throws resistless magic o'er the frame,
>   And leads to boundless pleasure or distress.[3]

There is a painfully familiar heroine, Arabella Bloomville, who can swoon in the face of indecency. Lord Mahogany, the pursuing villain, is an exaggerated version of Samuel Richardson's Lovelace who ultimately expires while giving a speech. The hero, Henry Lambert, with his bright hazel eyes, a nose "inclined to the Grecian" and a complexion "fair as alabaster," is the stylized Man of Feeling. Henry's problem is also not without precedent: he finds it impossible to propose marriage to Arabella because of her exalted rank. But the deterrent is removed before long, and the two lovers are allowed to unite in marriage to live happily ever after as "Lord and Lady Laughable." By employing these stock characteristics, Beckford demonstrates the flaws of sentimental fiction.

Both books have other targets in view, however, in that they devote considerable space to political satire directed against the Tory Party and its leader William Pitt. Interspersed among the nonsense in *Modern Novel Writing* are moments of lucidity given over to attacking the British government's policy of war against France that had been raging since 1793. A case in point is Lord Mahogany's speech in the throes of his final illness. Amidst his incoherent ravings, he reveals his deep guilt for supporting the war in the House of Lords: "I might have given my vote for peace! but O! 'twas war, war,

war! how they bleed! thousands, ten thousands dead! such a waste of murder! . . . O! this cursed war—I voted for it—how it burns my brain. . . . O! conscience, conscience! . . . alas! the war is mine. . . . Bottle up the war in a corn-field, and put my vote in hell" (2:39, 42, 44, 48). In another section, Beckford satirizes Pitt's government for such repressive measures as the Treasonable and Seditious Practices Act and Seditious Meetings Act of 1795, which aimed at frustrating the legitimate complaints of the people:

> Then the people assembled in great multitudes to complain, and petitioned their oppressors to grant them some relief, but they found none, their just remonstrances were deemed seditious and treasonable, and the men who had thus seized the reigns of authority, published an order forbidding all persons to assemble, or even to murmur. . . .

(2:100-1)

These acts, when carried into execution, ensured a "dead silence throughout the nation." Order and tranquillity were restored, but England had now become, as Beckford characterizes it, "THE ISLAND OF MUM" (2:101).

Azemia expands the political satire of *Modern Novel Writing* in its continuing attack on anti-democratic policies and practices. Once again, William Pitt is in Beckford's line of fire. In a mock ode he castigates the Prime Minister:

> All he does is grand and daring,
>   All he says is right and fit;
> Never let us then be sparing
>   In the praise of Mister Pitt.
> Who, like him, can prate down reason,
>   Who so well on taxes hit?
> Who detect a plot of treason
>   Half so well as Mister Pitt?

(2:12)

. . . . .

> He the multitude is humbling,
>   Britons that doth well befit:
> Swinish crowds, who minds your grumbling?
>   Bow the knee to Mister Pitt.
> Tho' abroad our men are dying,
>   Why should he his projects quit?
> What are orphans, widows, crying,
>   To our steady Mister Pitt?

(2:14)

Inflation, repressive legislation, rising debt, decline of the farmer, mistreatment of the poor, and the apathy of the rich are also objects of Beckford's concern in this book. These liberal views were unusual for a member of the English landowner class in 1797 and seem more appropriate for William Godwin than Beckford. But the Whig tradition of Beckford's father had some measure of influence on him, while the personal tragedies he

suffered in the 1780s, and his ostracism from English society over a public scandal involving accusations of a homosexual affair, help also to explain his unorthodox political opinions at this time and his need to retaliate against various forms of authority.

It was also in 1797 that Beckford took it upon himself—in what might be viewed as a bizarre and audacious act—to broker a peace treaty between France and England operating completely outside the normal channels of diplomacy.[4] Working through a personal agent in Paris and taking advantage of high-level connections in Paris, Beckford actually submitted the preliminary terms of an agreement, acceptable to the French, to officials of the British government. He might have been successful had it not been for Pitt's reluctance to allow Beckford, who was still considered to be a pariah in British society, to play such a role. In the end, Pitt declined to be associated with this initiative, but it must have rankled with the Prime Minister to know that Beckford had more support from the French than did Britain's ambassador Lord Malmesbury, who at this time was unsuccessful in his own negotiations to win a peace.

The early reviews of both books did not suspect that Beckford was the author. Under the cloak of anonymity, he was free to vent his spleen against some of the literary and political extravagances of his day without fear of reprisal. In the case of *Modern Novel Writing,* reviewers readily recognized that Lady Harriet Marlow was an assumed name. The *Monthly Review* provided a footnote to its review observing from internal evidence that "the writer is really of the masculine gender." They claimed the name had been "sounded in our ears" but did not believe that they had the authority to "report the whisper."[5] The *Critical Review* ventured to ascribe "this whimsical performance" to the "pen of a gentleman well known for his poetical compositions" but provided no further identification.[6] By January 1797 the *British Critic* and the *Monthly Magazine and British Register* identified the whispered name as that of Robert Merry.[7] In its review of *Azemia,* the *Critical Review* went further by noting that "this performance is written upon the plan of *Modern Novel Writing*" and that "miss J. A. M. Jenks is of the same sex with lady Harriet Marlow, *alias,* Robert Merry, esq."[8]

While Merry was considered a sentimental versifier who published under the name "Della Crusca," he had also become known by this time for his vigorously pro-French and anti-Pitt views, which may explain why he was identified as the author. The misattribution may also have something to do with the strong criticism of William Gifford in *Modern Novel Writing.* Gifford, the Tory satirist and editor of the *Anti-Jacobin Weekly,* was well known for his scathing condemnation of Merry's rhapsodic poetry in *Baviad* (1791) and *Maeviad* (1793). The assault on Gifford in these two books may have been viewed by contemporaries as Merry's method of seeking revenge. Ironically, the reviewers failed to see Merry himself as an object of attack in the thrusts against the sentimentality of Della Cruscan verse in *Azemia.*

Curiously, no information exists as to the composition history of either book. There is a possible allusion to these satirical works in a letter Beckford wrote to his bookseller George Clarke in 1832, in which he asserted: "If ever the world discovers the key of certain anonymous publications, it will find I have not been idle. All things considered, it had better not goad me to publish. Many would wince if I did."[9] Beckford also seems to be making a sly reference to his authorship of *Modern Novel Writing* in a hand-written note he left behind in his personal copy of this book now at the Beinecke Library at Yale, which reads: "W. B. Presentation copy from the divine authoress."[10] Other evidence for identifying Beckford as the author of these burlesques, in fact, has rested on the testimony of the poets Thomas Moore and Samuel Rogers and that of Beckford's first biographer Cyrus Redding. After a three-day visit to Fonthill in 1817, Rogers recorded that Beckford read him two unpublished "episodes to Vathek" and then noted that "Beckford is the author of two burlesque novels,—*Azemia* and *The Elegant Enthusiast.* I have a copy of the former, which he presented to me."[11] Rogers was the source of Moore's own recorded statement in his personal journal indicating that he and Rogers "talked of Beckford's two mock novels, Azemia & the Elegant Enthusiast." Moore goes on to describe a scene in *Modern Novel Writing* where "the Heroine writes a Song, which she sings at a Masquerade, & which produces such an effect that my Lord Mahogany, in the character of a Mile-stone, bursts into tears." He then adds: "It is in *Azemia* that all the heroes & heroines are killed at the conclusion by a supper of stewed Lampreys."[12] While the former incident does occur in *Modern Novel Writing,* the catastrophe involving "stewed Lampresy" is nowhere to be found in either novel. There is a similar incident that takes place in *Modern Novel Writing* involving the deaths of a number of people owing to a copper stew-pan in which some celery had been cooked. Moore's confusion here reveals that while he learned from Rogers of Beckford's authorship, he probably never read the books himself.

Cyrus Redding, who met Beckford during the period of time he was serving as editor of the *Bath Guardian* (1834-5) and then later became his biographer with access to Beckford's personal papers, was, as in the case of Rogers, another important source of attribution. Redding provides information about Beckford's intent in writing these novels. In his biography, he explained that though Beckford praised Hervey's *Louisa,* he found it to be reflective of the bad taste of the time as promoted by the "Minerva press in Leadenhall Street."[13] As he wrote: "It is no doubt a singular and degrading thing in literature, that it should have become, in the department of novel writing, and continue to be, as changeable in its fashion as the cut of the ladies' dresses, or the fashionable music. In the period of the Leadenhall Street reign, of which the present generation [in 1859] can know little, just as in those days which succeeded it down to this hour, the style, mode of thinking, and sentimentality in novels, underwent continual mutations. A comparison of the novels of Mary Robinson, or Charlotte Smith, Ann Radcliff, and Monk Lewis, with those which succeeded by Scott, would explain the differences, and still more those of the present hour, set in comparison with them."[14] According to Redding, it was Beckford's sense that the growing taste for this undisciplined and extravagant style of writing was corrupting the standards of good literature. Regarding the basis for the political satire that runs through both novels, Redding explained that while Beckford supported Whig principles in the tradition of his father, Pitt demonstrated in office "how cheaply he held the principles of his father," who was the Earl of Chatham, the prominent Whig Prime Minister of the mid-eighteenth century.

While evidence for the attribution of authorship for these two novels has rested on Rogers, Moore, and Redding and Beckford's own tantalizing allusions to it, there exists some additional support from contemporary writers that has not hitherto been reported. The first is an article in *The Ladies' Monthly Museum* in 1824. This magazine was running a biographical series devoted to "eccentric characters" and included Beckford as one of them in their February issue of that year. Beckford was enjoying a great deal of attention in the press during this time largely because of Fonthill Abbey and the two major sales which drew thousands of visitors to the estate in 1822 and 1823. The anonymous writer of this biography explains that while the creation of Beckford's Fonthill and his subsequent "Saxon tower" at Lansdown Crescent, Bath were the primary reasons for his inclusion in the gallery of eccentrics, he had also distinguished himself in the field of literature with the publication of *Vathek.* The writer then went on to note that there were other publications attributed to his authorship that "though less known, are hardly less distinguished, for the traits of talent which they display, and the peculiar satirical turn of mind which uniformly seems to actuate the author." The article mentions *Biographical Memoirs of Extraordinary Painters* and then *Modern Novel Writing* and *Azemia.* "Both these latter publications," the author wrote, "were intended as satires on the sentimental style of novel writing; a species of composition once very popular, but now deservedly fallen into contempt."[15]

Another unreported source for identifying Beckford as the author of these two novels is John Mitford, editor of the *Gentleman's Magazine,* 1834-50, and of the works of Thomas Gray, John Milton, and other poets. Mitford had a high regard for Beckford as a writer and publicly praised his literary talents in major reviews of *Italy; with Sketches of Spain and Portugal* and *Recollections of an Excursion to the Monasteries of Alcobaça and Batalha* in the *Gentleman's Magazine.*[16] In Mitford's unpublished recollections written in 1844, consisting of anecdotes on leading figures of his time, he reveals having seen a "Novel written by 'Beckford,' called Azemia," and that he once owned *Modern Novel Writing,* which he describes as "a Novel of Beckford's, in which the Party take Salts at Night, & write Sonnets in the Morning. Ld Mahogany sheds tears & is turnd into a Milestone, and the whole die of a dish of Lampreys stewd in a Copper Sauce Pan."[17] Mitford comes up with the true copper pot in his account, but the inclusion of the fanciful Lamphrey stew indicates that his source of information was Moore since he repeats the poet's flawed description.

One of the most reliable sources for establishing Beckford as the author of these two burlesques, not hitherto fully noted, is John Britton, a leading publicist of the Gothic revival movement in England and author of one of the descriptive accounts of Fonthill Abbey. Britton was impressed to the point of intimidation with Beckford's intellectual capabilities and range of knowledge. He told Beckford in 1835 that when he first met him in 1799, he was "astonished and terrified" by his "splendours & powers."[18] Britton often made it a point to discover the names of the authors of anonymous books and articles that appeared in the press. In the unpublished correspondence between Beckford and Britton at the Bodleian Library, Britton makes some significant remarks about *Azemia* wherein he appears to be attempting to confirm Beckford's authorship. Near the end of a letter to Beckford in November 1823, Britton writes that he was impressed with the book: "We have lately caught the fair 'Azemia' and have derived much risibility over some of its burlesques. It contains some truly original & *striking* pages. Its author seems to have read every thing & knows every thing. I hope *she* has produced other works for the benefit of readers." Beckford's response exists in draft form, but he plays along with Britton's coyness: "Upon the subject of the fair Author of Azemia. . . . I am as ignorant as yourself whether she has produced or is likely to produce any other works for inst[ruction] or amuse[ment]."[19] Finally, in Britton's letter to Beckford of 27 November 1823, he adds a postscript in which he says that Sampson Low, the publisher of *Azemia,* told him that Charlotte Smith was the author, to which Britton responds: "I will not believe it, tho' the Compositor & even the Devil himself swore to it."[20] In the sale of his books at Southgate's in June 1832, Britton makes it clear that he ultimately believed Beckford was the author by listing his personal copy of *Azemia* as Beckford's work.[21]

Beckford was able to keep his authorship of these two novels a secret for over twenty years before he divulged the truth to Samuel Rogers and then confirmed it later with Britton and Cyrus Redding. It was necessary, perhaps, to do so in view of the risks one had to face at this time for publicly criticizing the government and its leaders. Again, it has been suggested that these writings were borne out of Beckford's own feelings of social and political isolation and that they reveal a "bitterness and disillusion of his life on the threshold of middle-age, despite a surface veneer of parody and ridicule."[22] There may be some truth to this statement, but, beneath the surface of *Modern Novel Writing* and *Azemia,* there is a display of incisive social criticism that contributes to their historical and political importance and that calls for a renewed critical assessment of these neglected works. In Beckford's mind the form of sentimentalism promoted by such writers as Samuel Richardson, Henry Fielding, and Laurence Sterne had now become the province of second- and third-rate novelists. Furthermore, these new sentimental novels were being aided near the end of the century by the proliferation of circulating libraries. Beckford feared that by making such inferior literary works available, the circulating libraries were fostering a taste for them. Particularly troublesome to him was that the sentimental view of reality seemed an absurd defense against the harsh realities of war, poverty, and political oppression in the 1790s. Sensibility carried to such extremes seemed grotesquely escapist at a time when more realism and common sense were needed. And it is on this point that the political and sentimental satire of these two novels converge and achieve a coherent thematic relationship. For Beckford, circulating-library novels of the sentimental strain provided a vision of life that was equivalent to the political schemes of Pitt's government—both were equally irrational and irresponsible in view of the serious social and political challenges that England was facing at this time.

Notes

1. Arthur Freeman has discovered an unrecorded copy of *Modern Novel Writing* with the dedication leaf in volume 1 dated "Sept. 21st, 1795," which he believes is the first issue pointing to a possible publication date of 1795 rather than 1796. See "William Beckford's *Modern Novel Writing,* 1795-6: Two Issues, 'Three States,'" *Book Collector* 41 (Spring 1992): 69-73. Freeman does not address problems posed by internal and external evidence that work against the possibility of publication prior to 1796. For example, there are a number of references in *Modern Novel Writing* to the Treasonable and Seditious Practices and Seditious Meetings Acts, which were not passed until 18 December 1795. In at least three of these references, Beckford addresses these repressive measures in the past tense, that is, as having already

been enacted (2:101, 124, 219). For example, in the "Humble Address to the Doers of that Excellent and Impartial Review, called *The British Critic*," which appears at the end of the novel, he writes ironically: "I perfectly approve of the two restraining bills which have lately passed into laws" (see note 3 for source information). It is also worth noting that all of the recorded initial reviews of *Modern Novel Writing* identify 1796 as the publishing date. Finally, Cyrus Redding, Beckford's first biographer, indicated that both "burlesque novels were written at Fonthill before the decease of his mother in 1798" (*Memoirs of William Beckford of Fonthill,* vol. 2 [London: Charles Skeet, 1859], 223). But it is known that Beckford had not been in residence at Fonthill since November 1793, when he left for an extended stay in Portugal. He did not return to England until 20 June 1796, once again making 1795 an unlikely publishing date. See *The Times,* 30 June 1796, p. 3.

2. Howard Gotlieb, ed., *William Beckford of Fonthill Writer: Traveller, Collector, Caliph, 1760-1844* (New Haven: Yale Univ. Library, 1960), 64.

3. *Modern Novel Writing (1796) and Azemia (1797),* intro. Herman Mittle Levy, Jr. (Gainsville: Scholars' Facsimiles, 1970), 1:41. All references hereafter to both books are to this facsimile edition and are incorporated in the text. The most comprehensive discussion of these novels to date is Deborah Griebel's unpublished dissertation, "A Critical Edition of William Beckford's *Modern Novel Writing* and *Azemia*," University of Toronto, 1984.

4. For details on Beckford's adventure in diplomacy, see Lewis Melville, *The Life and Letters of William Beckford of Fonthill* (New York: Duffield, 1910), 185-212.

5. *Monthly Review,* n. s., 20 (August 1796): 477.

6. *Critical Review,* n. s., 18 (December 1796): 472.

7. *British Critic* 9 (January 1797): 76; *Monthly Magazine and British Register* 3 (January 1797): 47.

8. *Critical Review,* n. s., 20 (August 1797): 470.

9. *The Consummate Collector: William Beckford's Letters to His Bookseller,* ed. Robert J. Gemmett (Norwich: Michael Russell, 2000), 157.

10. Gotlieb, 35.

11. *Recollections of the Table-Talk of Samuel Rogers* (New York: Appleton, 1856), 215. Rogers's copy of *Azemia* showed up in the Christie and Manson sale of his books in 1856 as lot 1737. Deborah Griebel has located it in the rare book library of UCLA, bearing the inscription "S. Rogers, Esqr." in the first volume (Griebel, vi).

12. *The Journal of Thomas Moore,* ed. Wilfred Dowden, vol. 1 (Newark: Univ. of Delaware Press, 1983), 70.

13. Redding, 2:161.

14. Ibid., 161-2.

15. "Biography of Eccentric Characters. William Beckford," *The Ladies' Monthly Museum* 19 (February 1824): 71. How this writer obtained this information is not possible to determine since the identity of the author is not known and even the name of the editor of the journal for this year remains a mystery.

16. *Gentleman's Magazine,* n. s., 2 (August, September 1834): 115-21, 234-41.

17. John Hodgkin's transcription of Mitford's notes on Beckford from British Museum Add. MSS. 32.567. For Hodgkin's notes, see Bodleian Library, MS. Eng. Misc., e. 198, fol. 36.

18. ALS, 13 July 1835, Bodleian Library, MS. Beckford, c. 27, fols. 32-3.

19. Bodleian Library, MS. Beckford, c. 27, fols. 18-20.

20. Ibid., fols. 22-3. Guy Chapman cites this passage but omits mention of Britton's earlier statements about *Azemia.* See *A Bibliography of William Beckford of Fonthill,* ed. Guy Chapman and John Hodgkin (London: Constable, 1930), 47.

21. Lot 376 of the sale: "Jenks' (J. A. M.) Azemia, a Novel, by W. Beckford, 2 vol. 1798" [second edition].

22. Brian Fothergill, *Beckford of Fonthill* (London: Faber and Faber, 1979), 244.

Jeffrey Cass (essay date 2006)

SOURCE: Cass, Jeffrey. "Homoerotics and Orientalism in William Beckford's *Vathek*: Liberalism and the Problem of Pederasty." In *Interrogating Orientalism: Contextual Approaches and Pedagogical Practices,* edited by Diane Long Hoeveler and Jeffrey Cass, pp. 107-20. Columbus: Ohio State University Press, 2006.

[*In the following essay, Cass discusses the ironies that become apparent when considering various modern, post-Colonial, and liberal critical analyses of* Vathek.]

The postcolonial perspective forces us to rethink the profound limitations of a consensual and collusive "liberal" sense of cultural community. It insists that cultural and political identity are constructed through a process of alterity. Questions of race and cultural difference overlay issues of sexuality and gender and overdetermine the social alliances of class and democratic socialism. The time for "assimilating" minorities to holistic and organic notions of cultural value has dramatically passed.

(251)—Homi Bhabha, *The Location of Culture*

Bhabha's challenging remarks (1994) about the intersections of postcolonial theory and sexuality have resulted in some notable studies about the "alterity" of the sexual other. Hawley's *Postcolonial, Queer* (2001), Patton and Sanchez-Eppler's *Queer Diasporas* (2000), and Jan Campbell's *Arguing with the Phallus: Feminist, Queer and Postcolonial Theory* (2000) begin to address the "questions" Bhabha raises in his "postcolonial perspective" by demonstrating how the "liberal sense of cultural community" has largely failed to achieve its intended end—constructing and maintaining a communitarian ideology that emphasizes unity among disparate groups and de-emphasizes their differences. Far from achieving a homegrown, heterogeneous, yet harmonious group of subalterns who subscribe to what Bhabha identifies as "the holistic and organic notions of cultural values" and then joyfully merge into the collective, this heterosexist utopianism ironically illustrates the unconscious dread and discomfort many "liberals" feel with the actual lives and histories of marginalized groups. Accepting "alternative lifestyles" into the "cultural community"—giving GLBT citizens a place at the table— becomes such a leavening outcome that the queer body (and its interpretive sites) actually disappears into the larger body politic. "Alternative lifestyle" becomes a polite characterization, a periphrasis for a life whose true sexual realities and activities are alien and off-putting and disturbingly different, even for Rainbow Coalition liberals. After all, in common parlance, *deviation* from social and cultural norms all too easily slips into *deviance*. Analogously, for queer theorists who appropriate a postcolonial critique, conventional representational strategies are frustrating precisely because they result from "liberal" attempts at wide-ranging inclusiveness and cultural assimilation. Rather than affirming and celebrating "queerness," the very differences that distinguish "alternative" sexualities in the first place, these strategies have contributed to the erasure of queer desire and difference, awarding them an undifferentiated place within the harmonious universe of human desire.

Not coincidentally, the postcolonial critique of liberalism coincides with its equally cogent critique of Saidian Orientalism, for sexual deviance also underwrites the stereotypical expectations evoked by the "Oriental Other." As many readers of *Orientalism* have noted, because colonial discourse was so powerful, the Orient remains forever fixed, static, and inert, rather than, as

Ania Loomba remarks in her book *Colonialism/ Postcolonialism,* relationally dependent (178). She writes: "Colonial identities—on both sides of the divide—are unstable, agonized, and in constant flux" (178). Of course, in a Saidian context, colonial sexual identity emerges from a form of stereotyping. Orientalist texts, in this view, reify the sensuality and exoticism of the female body, which never changes position or shifts its focus back to the colonizer because it is always the object of imperial desire. Likewise, Western expectations of the Oriental text also inscribe a version of the homosexual man, but the beauty of the male body is feminized, open to secret queer inspection, but never explicitly the object of desire. The relationship between effeminacy and beauty also suggests close ties to camp, particularly in dress, because its exaggerated otherness is permitted and even expected in the public display of the Orientalized male body.[1] Unfortunately, Orientalizing the homosexual male in this fashion still underscores an essentialist view of sexual identity. Such desire may indeed be transgressive, but the breaking of sexual taboo is well within the logics of Saidian Orientalism; in fact, it is "embedded within a myth of reciprocity" (158). According to this "myth," sexual relations between the colonizer and the colonized are "reciprocal," comprising a "transaction" to which both parties agree. These relations are necessary to the development of social and cultural harmony though, as Loomba also claims, "colonial sexual encounters, both heterosexual and homosexual, often exploited inequities of class, age, gender, race, and power" (158). Orientalism tends to minimize the force of these "inequities" by naturalizing—making them appear eternal and timeless and standing in place. By contrast, Sánchez-Eppler and Patton suggest in *Queer Diasporas,* "Sexuality is not only not essence, not timeless, it is also not fixed in place; sexuality is on the move" (2). They make this argument in order to emphasize that sexual identity (as is the case with race, gender, and class) is not essential, though typical Orientalized representations of sexuality might so indicate, nor is it "a succession of strategic moves" (4). Sexual identity is, in fact, a "cluster of claims to self that appear and transmogrify in and of place" (4), largely confirming Loomba's arguments about the "flux" of colonial sexual identities and undercutting Said's views about the hegemony of the West and the powerlessness of the East within Orientalist representations.

While Sánchez-Eppler and Patton transform sexual identity into something presently active rather than eternally passive, precisely the positioning of the Saidian Oriental Other, whether female or male, a postcolonial critique of arch-Orientalist texts such as William Beckford's **Vathek** actually makes "deviant" sexual practice visible and conventional readings of homoerotic representations quaint and perhaps even homophobic.

Whether on the supportive liberal Left or the discrimi-natory conservative Right, both sets of readers wish that the reality of queer sexual practices would simply go away. *Vathek* becomes an interesting test case for "liberal" ideology because the author's biography, which hints darkly at a subterranean sexuality that lies beneath his heterosexual cover story (Beckford was married and had a daughter), so easily fuses with the persistently Orientalized sexualities contained in the novel. For *Vathek* admirers, uneasiness about the novel derives from the conflation of homosexuality and ped-erasty, a connection most liberals go to great lengths to avoid because the social and political anger (rightly) vented against child molestation can all too easily spill over into antigay sentiment. Called "the great Apostle of Paederasty" by Byron (Eisler, 176-77), Beckford be-comes a problematic author to engage openly, for he uses the novel's hyper-Orientalism to disguise, displace, and diffuse his scandalous life, which includes a per-haps chaste affair with thirteen-year-old William Courte-nay and a whole bevy of boy servants whom he spies on from his tower at Fonthill. One is even tempted to say that Beckford's fascination with Orientalist tropes (and much of his knowledge is authentic, coming di-rectly from sources in the French; Beckford originally even composes *Vathek* in French) is the source of his corruption. Even more outrageously, however, and this is the real source of critical unease, Beckford enjoys his corruption, which, as we shall see, he coyly embeds in the narrative.

And a sampling of critical opinion over the last sixty years reveals an entrenched desire to cleanse Beckford from a squeamish form of sexuality by burying its de-tails within the larger (and acceptable) spectrum of hu-man desire. Eagleton writes that "it is characteristic of liberalism to find names and definitions restrictive" (*Illusions,* 68), and so critics of Beckford, asserting his rightful place in the literary canon, but not wishing to outline his (or any other) "alternative" sexual practice too definitely, tend to make Beckford's pederasty van-ish while permitting traces of Beckford's homosexuality to survive. As Fuery and Mansfield claim in their book, "[T]he cultural real contains elements that much of the social order refuses to acknowledge as being part of its systems" (34). Representatives of a profession prone to attack by cultural conservatives, Beckford's academic critics, as Foucault might suggest in *Discipline and Punish,* attempt to manage Beckford's "body" so that they do not appear to approve of or tacitly support any specific behaviors or actions. And because Beckford has so ably contrived arch-Orientalist landscapes in which "deviant" desire can safely inhabit and even invisibly flourish (with the collusive help of his "liberal" critics), Beckford neatly avoids the messiness of his pederasty. Many of his critics divert attention away from Beck-ford's pederastic practices and direct the focus toward

his presumed psychosexual guilt for homosexuality. A dirty old man becomes a tragic closet case. Thus, sev-eral critics assume the podium of heterosexist moraliz-ing in order to create a cleaner, more sexually hygienic Beckford. They often emphasize the Orientalized "sen-suous desires" and the "intoxicating joys" in *Vathek* while at the same time projecting Vathek's ultimate doom on Beckford's psychic life. In other words, the (straight) caliph atones for the (queer) author's crimes, confirming moral judgment against Vathek while dissi-pating moral outrage against Beckford. Though not alone in this version of Vathek's relationship to Beck-ford, Mohammed Sharafuddin, one of the most impor-tant recent critics of Romantic Orientalism, succinctly summarizes this interpretation of Beckford's novel: "*Vathek* is part of [Beckford's] inner world. It is a pro-jection of an amoral, secret life into the public domain; it gives the rein for the first time to what could well be called the outlawed self" (1).[2]

One of the most insightful of Beckford's critics, Adam Potkay, rightly identifies the novel's emphasis on "male reciprocity, unlimited mutuality, [and] the communion of kind" as forming the basis for the "heaven of boys" that concludes the novel. Yet Potkay sees this pubescent homosociety as faintly misogynistic. Potkay drolly sums up his argument: "*Vathek* relies, in part, on the all-too-familiar logic that when someone must take the blame, *cherchez la femme*" (297). Moreover, he argues, "the at-traction of a segregated paradise [at the end of the novel] attests to, even as it rejects, the increasing sexual integration of polite society" (303-4). While Beckford's novel does indeed reflect the anxiety of British society toward its altered sexual landscapes, this reading of *Vathek* neatly sidesteps the issue of Beckford's trafficking-ing in homosexual pleasure and loudly ignores his com-placent and smug consumerism. Closer to the mark than other critics of the novel, therefore, is Diego Sa-glia who observes that for Beckford, the East "is more and more readily available in a metropolitan space which sees a burgeoning consumption of the oriental in the shape of products, objects, visual experiences and literary texts" (76). In the end, most critics prefer to avoid Beckford's hoggish and shameless appetites, re-ducing his bothersome *jouissance* to safe and pious epi-thets.

Though not intentional, the more seriously critics take Vathek's fate as a reification of Beckford's "tormented soul," the more glaringly they misread the exuberance of both Beckford's novel and its homoerotic imagin-ings. An implicit judgment of high moral seriousness underlies such persnickety, sermonizing critical strate-gies, but such strategies also raise the red flag of homo-sexual panic, thereby illustrating what Eve Kosofsky Sedgewick refers to as the "Gothic unspeakable" of the Romantic period (95), that public abhorrence of aristocratic representations of homoerotic desire (pederastic desire even more) that might actually "wash through" and infect the "middle classes" (95). If Beckford really does have all those pederastic dreams (or occasional homosexual couplings, and with boys), then the conclusion to his novel represents his justifiable fear of divine "retribution," the worried resolution to the psychic conflicts inherent in all lustful deviates, the understandable anxiety at the activities of sexual predators. And if Beckford, the married proprietor of Fonthill and father of two, actually enjoys his fantasies and occasional homosexual couplings, then, at the very least, he should make no overt displays of desire or love of pleasure that lead the unsuspecting public back to his indiscretions. Although Beckford outrageously indulges in hyperbole when he describes Vathek's fickleness and fecklessness, as well as his uncontrollable appetites and terrifying gothic eye, critics eagerly see an opening that moves the reader away from pederastic desire and toward psychosexual guilt, thus pushing the suggestion that Beckford self-identifies with or can be linked to a psychologically impaired and morally damaged Vathek. In so doing, these critics posit a strange bricolage, for readers must refashion the homosexually combustible, real-life Beckford into the heterosexually conflicted but doomed, fictional Vathek. This process advances a moral whitewash, but it does have the advantage of preserving a liberal commitment to homosexual desire without also having to connect that desire to a discomfiting pederasty.

R. B. Gill makes much the same point in his essay "The Author in the Novel: Creating Beckford in *Vathek.*" He interrogates the performativity of Beckford's public image, postulating that the apparent contradiction between Beckford's public and private personae produces "many Beckfords, some he himself created and many created by his various critics" (242). Gill continues: "*Vathek* is a clear case of a novel especially in need of a biographical centre to resolve its ambiguities" (242). Yet Beckford ultimately thwarts the resolution of the novel's "ambiguities," the tantalizing journey of critical ambition provoked by the novel's dazzling exoticism and the novelist's equally exotic biography. Beckford thus hides in open sight his unrestrained glee at creating a queer fantasy under the noses of an audience that simultaneously embraces puritanical sexual mores yet indulges in imaginative "alternative" sexual practices. "Beckford is eager," Gill writes, "that we see him laughing and manipulating the diverse attitudes of Vathek without being compromised by naïve commitment to them" (253).

Readings of *Vathek* that stress the moralistic connections between Beckford's and Vathek's character and actions are, of course, not entirely inaccurate, for one cannot say that Beckford does not at all resemble Vathek. Like Vathek, he is whimsical in his interests, fanciful in his desires, and extravagant in their planning and execution. And like Vathek, Beckford (from a very early age) has the financial resources to be as whimsical, fanciful, and extravagant as he imagines. Finally, and perhaps most tellingly, like Vathek, Beckford can generally afford to resist public disapproval (or at least separate himself from it). Despite a publicly sullied heterosexual reputation, Beckford manages for almost eighty-five years to live the luscious "Oriental" life he is able to purchase, eluding his constrictive, draining family; jealous enemies; sycophantic hangers-on; and titillated, pseudo-ardent admirers (such as Byron). Forcing Beckford to emerge as an author who perceives he is a moral reprobate confirms a critical view that takes Beckford's psychosexual guilt seriously. But if one decouples the seriousness of the novel's ending with Beckford's more playful attitudes toward his title character, the critical field shifts away from inescapable homosexual tragedy and tilts instead toward homoerotic farce. As Malcolm Jack indicates, *Vathek* "shows distinct touches of humour in its . . . bathetic contrast between drama and absurdity" (xxii). Properly contextualized, the "bathetic" mordancy of the novel lies in humorously pitching the caliph from his own heterosexual pedestal, puncturing the traditional sexual norms he represents by lampooning him as a petulant "Mama's boy" who knows nothing of sacrifice, courage, or self-denial, but only omnivorous self-gratification.

In the final analysis, even Byron's Sardanapalus, who spontaneously transforms himself from feminized Oriental despot to glorious and masculine warrior, is more convincing as a serious character than Vathek because, at the last, love and honor form the basis of Sardanapalus's commitment to his country, Byron's last-ditch effort at genuine dramatic pathos. The bathos of Beckford's Orientalized protagonist stems, in part, from Vathek's utter inability to maintain a single idea, to conform to a single standard of predictable public behavior, reasonable or not. In effect, Beckford deliberately exaggerates Vathek's despotism, making him more despotic than other despots in eighteenth-century Oriental tales, precisely because he cannot master or control his appetites at all; he fails to subsume them under any sort of overarching plan of action that he himself conceives.

In a very real sense, Vathek is a boy expected to rule in an adult world, a very dangerous and intelligent boy who dresses up as a caliph and who cannot possibly meet the social, political, and cultural obligations expected of him. As a religious leader, for example, Vathek fails to listen to or abide by any orthodox sentiments. Though Vathek has a "predilection for theological controversy" (3), he nonetheless ruthlessly persecutes those who contest his heterodoxy, imprisoning them "to cool their blood" (5). His desire to build his own tower that imitates Nimrod so inflames the ire of Mahomet that the Prophet curiously commands his own servants, the "genii," to assist Vathek in its completion in order to see how far Vathek will go in his impieties. But Vathek is no mere dark servant for Eblis, the Islamic equivalent of Lucifer, for Vathek undermines the gravity of his own moral blasphemy. Since he does not appreciate fully his own "irreligious conduct" (4), we cannot regard his inflated, exaggerated desire to enter Eblis's dark kingdom as a serious threat to traditional cultural norms. At best, Vathek parodies a satanic figure, pathetically oblivious to the consequences of his and his mother's caprices or to the damage that his violent rage may cause to his reputation. After the Indian (not yet identified as the Giaour) escapes from Vathek's prison, he kills the guards. Infuriated, Vathek kicks their dead carcasses "till evening without intermission" (7), convincing his subjects he has gone mad. After an old man can only translate the runes on Vathek's magical sabers for one day because the runes themselves change daily, Vathek mercifully orders that only half his beard be burnt. When "reverend Moullahs" bring Vathek a besom (broom) that had been used "to sweep the sacred Cahaba" (39), Vathek takes the besom and brushes away cobwebs from the ceiling as if it were a common cleaning implement, causing two Moslem clerics to die "on the spot" (41). Finally, never truly her adult equal, Vathek says nothing admonitory to Carathis. Ferreting out the hiding place of Gulchenrouz, his mother conspires with her evil camel Alboufaki, uses her necromantic powers to resurrect ghouls, steals mummies from catacombs to supply herself with magical rhinoceros horns and oil of venomous serpents, and ritualistically slaughters Vathek's loyal subjects as fiery oblations to the Giaour. Yet Vathek remains aloof from her actions, even as he grows ever more dependent on her powerful magic and on her brilliant public relations.

Although Islamic bees loyal to Allah on one occasion attempt to sting Vathek for his brutal treatment of clerics, no subject ever reproves his decadence or attacks his overindulgence. So committed is he to see the banquet halls and riches of the Underworld that he even lapses into the homoerotic to seal his relationship to the Giaour. For example, during a bout with a virulent form of dipsomania, the Indian/Giaour cures him with a draught that finally quenches his thirst. His health restored, Vathek "leap[s] upon the neck of the frightful Indian, and kiss[es] his horrid mouth and hollow cheeks, as though they had been the coral lips and the lilies and the roses of his most beautiful wives" (15). This amazingly unsexy kiss confirms their unholy union, their unbreakable bond. When Vathek treats the Giaour to a lover's kiss, however, he unwittingly makes a lover's promise. Soon after Vathek makes his journey onto the plains outside Samarah, the Indian reveals himself as

the Giaour, gives Vathek a glimpse of the Palace of Subterranean Fire, and demands the blood sacrifice of fifty sons as a "libation" he must drink ("Where are they?—Where are they?—perceivest not how my mouth waters?" 26), suggesting perhaps that Vathek's previously insatiable thirst was actually a symptom of the Giaour's authority over Vathek.

To cure the Giaour's thirst, Vathek proposes a contest for fifty of the "handsomest" boys among his subjects, and the proud parents celebrate the Caliph's sudden generosity:

> The lovely innocents destined for the sacrifice, added not a little to the hilarity of the scene. They approached the plain full of sportiveness, some coursing butterflies, others culling flowers, or picking up the shiny little pebbles that attracted their notice. At intervals they nimbly started from each other for the sake of being caught again, and mutually imparting a thousand caresses.
>
> (25)

The "cavalcade" of boys, not yet weaned from the feminized ways of the harem and of inconstant women, "sport" with one another and, despite the fact they are contesting for the caliph's favor, impart affection to one another. Blissfully unaware that Vathek intends to sacrifice them to the Giaour by throwing them into a chasm that magically appears behind Vathek, the boys in turn approach Vathek one by one, unable to see the danger ahead of them. In a horrifying striptease, Vathek "undresses himself by degrees" (27), taking off items of clothing and jewelry as prizes for the youthful combatants:

> To the first, I will give my diamond bracelet; to the second, my collar of emeralds; to the third, my aigret of rubies; to the fourth, my girdle of topazes; and to the rest, each a part of my dress, even down to my slippers.
>
> (26)

As each child comes forward, Vathek tempts each one with a piece of his ensemble and then "pushes" the unsuspecting boy into the "gulph" and the waiting mouth of the Giaour (27). While Vathek feels compassion for the boys, appreciating their "beauty" even as the Giaour salivates over his victims, Vathek does not intuit his homoerotic connection with the Giaour, not even when he himself becomes ravenously hungry after the sacrifice of the boys, eating everything he can find. In fact, Vathek's stripping itself is a mirage. The more clothing and valuable baubles Vathek removes from his body, the less one discerns his body or true motivations. As with the Giaour, physical proximity and intimacy breed blindness and ignorance. Nakedness becomes a metaphor for secrecy, kissing a metonymy for suspicion and deceit.

In addition, the Giaour's presumed pedophagia literally incarnates a typical form of Orientalized discourse that "constructs the Orient as a passive, childlike entity that can be lover and abused, shaped and contained, managed and consumed" (Sardar, 6). Of this passage, Alan Richardson aptly concludes: "Beckford's private sexual fantasies cannot be disentangled from the cultural fantasy of a supine, infantile, inviting East" (10). But fantasy and consumption are separate realities—an "inviting East" is not the same as an "abused, shaped and contained, managed and consumed" Orient. *Vathek* certainly parodies the Caliph's overindulgence and hyperconsumption, but that parodic representation does not necessarily entail feelings of pederastic guilt. Indeed, it is dangerous to equate Vathek's use of young boys for his infernal purposes and Beckford's exuberance for boys for his domestic ones. Beckford's almost giddy desire for prepubescent males may not amount to a sexual practice; instead, Beckford's pederasty—occluded within Orientalized landscapes—may actually become a scarcely concealed sexual politics that, in the end, is almost too unbearable to contemplate, for it challenges both heteronormative and homonormative categories of acceptable sexual expression.

Indeed, Beckford revels in his outrageousness, basks in his defiance of social norms and expectations. He writes: ". . . I am determined to enjoy my dreams, my phantasies and all my singularities, however discordant to the worldlings around . . ." (quoted in Richardson, 8). That determination helps to explain why Eblis, the Giaour's residence of Orientalized evil, remains so "discordant" to Beckford's "wordling" critics and why those same critics attempt to align the shape of the narrative with their own moralist expectations. While Vathek's travails within the halls of Eblis ultimately do result in the proper punishment of all in service to the Giaour, a predictable conclusion for all literary works of the period that employ satanic tropes, the end matter of Beckford's novel does not presuppose that Beckford feels he is in personal moral jeopardy or that he identifies at all with the justice of its conclusions. In fact, the Eblis scenes in *Vathek* principally serve to reinforce the self-indulgence that drives his Orientalism. In effect, Eblis constitutes a revenge fantasy that challenges the basis of British heterosexist politics in the late eighteenth and early nineteenth centuries. From Beckford's perspective, it is a politics that demands his social and cultural expulsion for his own deviance while refusing to examine its own ideological inconsistencies and sexual foibles.

Familiar with both Christian and Islamic traditions, Beckford cleverly transforms Milton's Satan into the Giaour, Milton's Pandaemonium into Eblis. But whereas Milton emphasizes both the internal agony of Hell's dominion ("The mind is its own place, and itself / Can make a heaven of hell, a hell of heaven," [*Paradise Lost*; henceforth *PL*] 1.254-55) and the internal relief of spiritual redemption (". . . but shalt possess / A paradise within thee, happier far," *PL* 12.586-87), Beckford delightedly gloats over the horrifying physical torments of the (heterosexual) damned and glosses over the internal spiritual agony that must ensue when a soul is utterly separated from the divine. Beckford also parodies perhaps the most famous religious trope of Milton and seventeenth-century metaphysical poetry, the flaming heart. Beckford appropriates the flaming heart by literally rendering the passion and desire that kindle spiritual desire and Orientalizing it through one of the most famous exponents of sexual excess, Soliman ben Daoud. No longer Solomonic in wisdom and judiciousness, Soliman displays his allegiance to the Koranic, not the biblical, traditions. He had been able to conjure genii and other spirits—that was his divine gift or talent, which, like Vathek, he squanders in the service of licentiousness ("I forsook the holy city, and commanded the Genii to rear the stupendous palace of Istakar. . . . There, for a while, I enjoyed myself in the zenith of glory and pleasure," 113). Soliman's belief that his punishment is merely purgatorial underscores the scope of his torment. He deludes himself into hoping that the "cataract" will eventually cease flowing and his enflamed heart will be extinguished. Vathek and Nouronihar immediately recognize not only the horrific nature of his physical torment, but that it will eventually engulf them as well, making valueless the genii's offer of riches, banquets, and honors. More importantly, however, once the hellish flames do engulf their hearts, Beckford stresses their physical revulsion for one another (". . . all testified their horror for each other by the most ghastly convulsions," 119). Even in Milton's Hell, Satan and the rebel angels can, in some measure, still take pleasure in their physical presence and physical transformations, which helps explain Milton's catalog of demons marching into the Hall of Pandaemonium, as well as Satan's ability to morph into a beautiful angel, the illusion of which only Ithuriel's spear can break. In Beckford's novel, Eblis becomes the imagined place of torment for his deluded tormentors, where the trappings of socially validated and culturally embraced heterosexual passion reveals itself for what it is—sexual colonialism—comprised of vacuous preaching, empty moralizing, vain consumption, and gratuitous threats to achieve worldly mastery and authority.

Interestingly, however, Beckford gives the last word in his novel not to Vathek, but to Vathek's pubescent, hyperfeminized rival, Gulchenrouz (and by extension the "good old genius" who miraculously saves him from Vathek and Carathis, as well as the fifty boys from the bloodlust of the Giaour). Beckford gleefully concludes that the "humble, the despised Gulchenrouz passed whole ages in undisturbed tranquility, and in the pure happiness of childhood" (120). Or, to paraphrase Adam Potkay, Gulchenrouz forever dwells in boy heaven. The pouty boy-consort to Princess Nouronihar escapes Vathek's vindictive whimsy and Carathis's obsession with diabolic power, but not to take his rightful and manly place as head of a kingdom and an arranged marriage. Rather, Gulchenrouz's happy fate is to consort "undisturbed" with other boy-men who may now frolic and play with Gulchenrouz, free of the very adult privileges and responsibilities that should have normally attended them. And the "good old genius" brings the boys to Roc nests "higher than the clouds" (97), where he himself "fixes" his own "abode," "in a . . . nest more capacious than the rest" (97). In the campiest (and, from the Islamic perspective, the most blasphemous) passage in the novel, Allah himself and the Prophet inscribe their names on waving streamers, flashing like lightning and guarding these pederastic but "inviolable asylums" against any magical intrusions from afrits, zombies, or Carathis's potent incantations. For his part, Gulchenrouz receives the accolades of all the boys who "vie[. . .] with each other in kissing his serene forehead and beautiful eye-lids" (97). Beckford continues: "Remote from the inquietudes of the world; the impertinence of harems, the brutality of eunuchs, and the inconstancy of women; there [Gulchenrouz] found a place truly congenial to the delights of *his* soul" (97; emphasis added). For the first time in the novel, Gulchenrouz is free to act as he wishes, and not as the result of the dubious plans of Fakreddin, the faithlessness of Nouronihar, the untrammeled and dark desires of Carathis, or Vathek's unabated search for absolute power. The "good old genius" ironically saves the other boys *from* the fires of Hell by taking them away from Vathek as he is about to make them a blood sacrifice to the Giaour. In addition, however, the "genius" removes the endangered boys from the burden and duty of propagation. They no longer have to endure a harem's "inconstant" women, nor must they face the sexual uselessness of castrated men. In carving out a niche among the Roc nests for his charges, the "good old genius" has firmly established a pederastic oasis among the clouds, a pleasant and eternal homosociety that need never confront the social and cultural exigencies of conventionally Orientalized manhood. In fact, the homoerotics of this boy heaven, its innocent attractiveness (though perhaps it might appear sinister from our contemporary perspective), lies in the boys never becoming fully sexualized, "for the genius, instead of burthening his pupils with perishable and vain sciences, conferred upon them the boon of perpetual childhood" (98). In the words of Adam Potkay, the novel is an antibildungsroman, with Beckford's boy heaven becoming "an allegory of infancy" that always and everywhere preempts the unavoidable dissatisfactions that come with adult maturity, in particular sexual segregation and propriety (301).

Diego Saglia points to Beckford's heaven of boys as an Orientalist simulacrum, in which "actual and imaginary orients intersect in a nexus of reality and fiction, legality, desire and visual attraction, [are] all encapsulated in Beckford's observation 'I have still sparks of Orientalism about me to catch fire at such a sight'" (80). But this simulacrum exhibits slippage even as it feigns representational and moral fixity. Beckford uses this simulacrum to construct his Orientalized queerness, a refuge for his homoerotic desire (and submerged pederasty). Beckford's readership accepts his outrageous campiness because camp often underlies the Gothic, as it does in the works of Matthew Lewis, Ann Radcliffe, or Charlotte Dacre, and because the Gothic is ultimately a conservative genre, often confirming a culture's ethological underpinnings even as it appears to explode them. Beckford can, therefore, easily hide his homoerotics—his "sparks of Orientalism"—in plain sight because he aligns the fate of his title character with the conventions and expectations of most eighteenth- and nineteenth-century literary figures who truck with the sexually satanic. In other words, despite the resemblances between Vathek and Beckford, it would be a mistake to equate them. The man who in his letters salaciously refers to his boy servants by wicked epithets—"Pale Ambrose," "Cadaverous Nicobuse," "Miss Long," "Miss Butterfly," "Countess Pox," or "Mr. Prudent Well-Sealed Up" (Norton, 2)—can hardly be said to rue his homoerotic/pederastic passions or truly identify with Vathek's doom. After his return to England from an exile originally urged by a family terrified of scandal (but perhaps equally upset that they would receive no peerage), Beckford, though married and a father, still aspires to the status of the "good old genius" in the novel of his youth. Dwelling within the panoptic fortress of Fonthill and free from prying scrutiny, Beckford magnanimously reviews his Orientalized estates, at the head of women whose fear of public exposure and ridicule makes them ultimately complicit with his psychosexual proclivities, and in charge of a large group of boy servants who incarnate his fictional male harem. In a very real sense, Beckford's own guiltless and shameless terrestrial paradise is, mutatis mutandis, the "heaven of boys" in *Vathek.*

Robert Mack may be right when he suggests that "Homosexual writers are at home in the oriental tale . . . it is a place to be free of the restrictions of the mundane realism tied to the demands of the market-place and the goings on of 'real' society" (xvii). But *Vathek* is no mere escapist fantasy that briefly distracts the reader from the exigencies of the world and its commercial realities. Nor is its Orientalism the exuberant screen through which Beckford secretes his tragic sexual identity; or, as El Habib Benrahhal Serghini likens it, "Beckford's orientalism has permitted the self to show off its glories, but it has also linked the luxuriance of surface with the sad opulence of the condemned soul" (63). Rather, Beckford's Orientalist tale not only reifies the moralistic expectations inherent to much eighteenth- and nineteenth-century Oriental literature, it also cheerfully undermines them by refusing to acknowledge sexual perversion, licentiousness, or personal embarrassment of any kind. That Beckford may have embraced his own pederastic desires makes him challenging to critics who wish to recontextualize him within a more manageable heterosexist ideology. They then can more readily pass comfortable (and comforting) moral judgments, and critics frequently do so because the "chilling" (to use Haggerty's word) homoerotics of Beckford's writing makes many heterosexual readers uneasy, calling into question any encoded prescriptions about sexuality or the identity politics of the social and cultural status quo. Beckford's Orientalist homoerotics perhaps even threaten the legitimacy of such readers to pass these judgments. In the end, however, the novel may just as easily make gay readers queasy because it shamelessly conflates pederasty and homosexuality, an absolute distinction that activists have recently gone to great lengths to make in order to establish, to the extent possible, a mainstream sexual politics that permits gay men a place at the table (to use Bruce Bawer's clichéd phrase). Long gone are the pre-AIDS, sexual outlawry of John Rechy; the shocking yet titillating fetishism of leather queens; and the winking presence of NAMBLA (North American Man-Boy Love Association) in gay pride parades. Now "queers" find themselves in the astonishing position of recommending lifestyle changes to hapless heterosexual men, of making them over, of transforming them into better and improved versions of their own masculinity. As a result, being mainstreamed means rejecting any kind of separation, especially a sexual separation that promises or justifies pedophilic play within the fantastic landscapes that Beckford conjures. Being mainstreamed signifies normalization, a jettisoning of the closeted but fanciful ghettoes contained by Orientalized discourse. Heterosexual and homosexual readers of *Vathek* thus find themselves ironically bound and committed to an ideology that uncovers Beckford's presumed psychosexual guilt within the text, for without this shame, Beckford's heaven of boys becomes the panicked, postmodern hell of liberals.

Notes

1. Adrienne McLean makes this case in her essay "The Thousand Ways There Are to Move: Camp and Oriental Dance in the Hollywood Musicals of Jack Cole." McLean cites the important work of Michael Moon, who also makes use of Said's *Orientalism,* in order to argue that despite the campy flamboyancy of Orientalist representations, Orientalism is homophobic because it fixes homosexuality within a heterosexist system, rendering it powerless within such a dominant paradigm. In his work "Flaming Closets," Moon connects the subjugating practices of Orientalism to racist sexual fantasies in which "masters" can freely couple with "the dominated bodies of others" (58).

2. In an unwittingly amusing application of Freudian theory, Brian Fothergill writes that Beckford's trip to Switzerland had quite failed to instill "manly attributes" (62). Indeed, Fothergill melodramatically continues, "Even worse was happening . . . in the city where Calvin's shadow seemed to offer so little protection against the temptations of the world and the flesh if not of the very Devil himself; for by the shores of the lake of Geneva [Beckford's mother's] son found himself involved in a romantic entanglement with another youth" (62). For Fothergill, the problem is not that Beckford had a homosexual dalliance but that "the intensity of his responses to any stimulation of the senses, be it personal or artistic in origin," never diminishes. Beckford assigns too much emotional meaning "to what was in reality no more than an adolescent infatuation" (63). The tragedy of being eternally stuck in a homosexual phase also occurs to Robert Gemmett as well, for in his description of Beckford's relationship to Courtenay, Gemmett reluctantly affirms the hermeneutic circle between Beckford's life and his book: "It is the frustration of this great effort in the Kingdom of Eblis that provides the best image of Beckford, the artist-voluptuary, who, subjected inexorably to the furies of time and reason, must witness a failure of imagination and the ultimate collapse of his palace of art" (117). Even much more recent readings of *Vathek* rely on the absolute identity between Beckford's psychology and *Vathek*'s retributive fate. Sounding much like Ernest Bernbaum, Marilyn Gaull writes, "But just as the ending, a conventional one of symbolic retribution, conflicted with the novel itself, so Beckford's conventional side—the one who would marry the loyal and agreeable Lady Margaret Gordon, serve in Parliament, and father two daughters who were devoted to him—seemed constantly in conflict with the *deviate*" (234-35; emphasis added). In "Beckford's Paederasty," George E. Haggerty more explicitly ties Beckford's life with the horrifying end of *Vathek* in Eblis: "[Beckford] grappled throughout his life with a sexual instinct that made him a criminal in his own desire" (137). Eric Meyer views *Vathek* in postcolonial terms, whereby Beckford embodies the colonized East and the imperial West: "The structure of narrative in *Vathek* . . . closely approximates Teresa de Lauretis's Oedipal paradigm, although with a more obviously politically overdetermined subtext: the Orient becomes

a feminized passive object that is subject to male desire . . ." (668). Vathek becomes, in this view, the Orientalist penetrator who is himself penetrated or "subject to male desire."

FURTHER READING

Biographies

Cope, Kevin L. "Beckford and the Emerging Consciousness: Projective Collecting and the Aesthetic Dynamics of Acquisition." *Studies on Voltaire and the Eighteenth Century* 305 (1992): 1815-19.

Studies the nature of Beckford's literary collecting.

James, Jamie. "The Caliph of Fonthill." *American Scholar* 72, no. 1 (January 2003): 67-79.

Offers a biographical account of Beckford as a book collector.

Criticism

Davies, Damian Walford and Laurent Châtel. "'A Mad Hornet': Beckford's Riposte to Hazlitt." *European Romantic Review* 10, no. 4 (October 1999): 452-79.

Examines Beckford's reaction and responses to William Hazlitt's censure of his art collection at his estate, Fonthill Abbey.

Haggerty, George E. "Literature and Homosexuality in the Late Eighteenth Century: Walpole, Beckford, and Lewis." *Studies in the Novel* 18, no. 4 (winter 1986): 341-52.

A comparative study that focuses on recurring homosexual themes in the works of Beckford, Horace Walpole, and Matthew Gregory Lewis.

Additional coverage of Beckford's life and career is contained in the following sources published by Gale: *British Writers,* **Vol. 3;** *Dictionary of Literary Biography,* **Vols. 39, 213;** *Gothic Literature: A Gale Critical Companion*; *Literary Movements for Students,* **Vol. 1;** *Literature Resource Center*; *Nineteenth-Century Literature Criticism,* **Vol. 16;** *St. James Guide to Horror, Ghost and Gothic Writers*; **and** *Supernatural Fiction Writers.*

Elizabeth Cleghorn Gaskell
1810-1865

(Born Elizabeth Cleghorn Stevenson; also wrote under the pseudonym Cotton Mather Mills, Esquire) English novelist, biographer, novella, sketch, and short story writer, poet, and essayist.

The following entry presents criticism of Gaskell's works from 2000 to 2007. For criticism of Gaskell's career prior to 2000, see *NCLC,* Volumes 5 and 70; for discussion of the novel *Cranford* (1853), see *NCLC,* Volume 97; and for discussion of the novel *Mary Barton: A Tale of Manchester Life* (1848), see *NCLC,* Volume 137.

INTRODUCTION

A figure of the "golden age" of nineteenth-century English literature, Gaskell is best known for her novels of social reform and psychological realism, such as *Ruth* (1853) and *North and South* (1855). Her treatment of topics ranging from prostitution to conflict between manufacturers and workers both captured the public imagination and caused a great deal of controversy and has attracted the attention of modern-day critics interested in issues of authorship and social responsibility. Gaskell's refined and compassionate portrayals of her central characters—often young, unmarried women who suffer misfortune—and her skillful use of detail have established an enduring popularity for and interest in her work.

BIOGRAPHICAL INFORMATION

Born in London in 1810, Gaskell was the daughter of an occasional minister of the Unitarian Church in England. When Gaskell was a year old her mother died, and she was sent to live with her maternal aunt in rural Cheshire, where she attended a school for girls. Educated in fine arts and languages, Gaskell began to read extensively, particularly novels, developing a lifelong love for books. In 1831, she traveled to Newcastle, Edinburgh, and Manchester to visit prominent Unitarian ministers. In Manchester, she met William Gaskell, a young Unitarian clergyman; they were married in 1832 and lived in Manchester. She gave birth to seven children; four daughters survived infancy, and Gaskell stayed close to all of them throughout her life. Gaskell wrote diaries and some poems and stories in the early

years of her marriage, but starting in the mid-1840s, she devoted increasing time and effort to writing. Her first novel, *Mary Barton* (1848) reflected Gaskell's concern for the plight of families, and particularly of women, facing the rapid industrialization of England. After the popular success of *Mary Barton,* Gaskell produced numerous short stories and novels during the remaining years of her life. Because William Gaskell was a professor of history and literature at Manchester New College, the family was relatively affluent, which helped support Gaskell's charitable endeavors and extensive travel in Europe; in addition, she earned a considerable independent income from her successful literary career. She developed and sustained friendships with many prominent contemporaries, such as George Eliot, Harriet Martineau, Charlotte Brontë, and Florence Nightingale. Gaskell published many of her short stories and serialized novels in *Household Words,* a popular journal edited by Charles Dickens. Although Gaskell published *Mary Barton* and many of her other works anonymously, her identity as an author soon became widely known, and she became a literary celebrity. She was known in Manchester to be a gracious hostess but nevertheless remained a very private person, who clearly struggled to reconcile the demands of private and public life, as do many of her central characters. In the mid-1850s, Gaskell was asked by the Reverend Patrick Brontë to write a biography of his daughter Charlotte, the renowned novelist and friend of Gaskell who had recently died. This work was published in 1857 as *The Life of Charlotte Brontë,* which many critics accused of taking an overly sympathetic and sentimental attitude toward its subject and thus misrepresenting her. Disappointed at this criticism, Gaskell returned to writing fiction. She died suddenly in 1865, leaving her last novel, *Wives and Daughters* (1866), unfinished.

MAJOR WORKS

Gaskell's novels and stories are often characterized as simultaneously industrial and domestic, promoting social reform by focusing on deeply personal conflicts and injustices in a variety of settings. *Mary Barton* and *North and South* directly confront the turbulent industrial economy of Manchester, where Gaskell lived. The story "Lois the Witch" (1859) explores the baleful consequences of religious intolerance and repression of women and girls through a fictional retelling of the witch trials of Salem, Massachusetts, in 1692. Even works such as *Cranford* (1853) and *My Lady Ludlow* (1858), which seem intended to evoke nostalgia for the placid English countryside of a previous generation, can be seen as dramatizing individuals' responses to the gradual supplanting of the traditional agricultural economy by urban-based industrial capitalism. Throughout her literary career, Gaskell was preoccupied with the role and status of women, specifically of women before marriage. She depicts characters who struggle against rigid social roles in an often irrational world, such as the title characters of *Ruth* and *Sylvia's Lovers* (1863). True to her Unitarian faith, Gaskell believed that individuals should strive to accept their moral responsibilities and live according to rational principles; yet she also recognized how public opinion, economic desperation, and misfortune could easily overwhelm people. Her novels thus reflect a tension between the operations of freedom and destiny. Gaskell also sought to question the legitimacy of established authority: in her fiction, the characters with the most political or social power are often the least trustworthy, and despised and powerless figures such as single women, servants, and the poor are the central or more sympathetic characters. Gaskell firmly advocated that Christian love and charity, leading to mutual sympathy between individuals and classes, were the only true means of relieving poverty and injustice and resolving Britain's deep-rooted social conflicts—not laws or political activism—and she sought to show in her industrial novels how this might be accomplished in the world. Her writing also reveals an ear highly attuned to dialect and natural conversation. Gaskell was a prolific and dedicated letter writer, and her letters contain both personal communications and valuable comments upon her own writing and other works of literature.

CRITICAL RECEPTION

In her own lifetime, Gaskell's novels and stories were both remarkably popular and widely praised by critics and other authors, though some reviewers and readers attacked her sympathetic portrayals of "fallen women," the improvident poor, and striking workers. Curiously, despite the controversy that had surrounded many of her works upon publication, Gaskell later developed a reputation as a conventionally pious Christian and typically maternal Victorian woman; both admirers and detractors judged her literary work as if it were a straightforward expression of an imagined personality, focusing their attention on *Cranford,* her most outwardly pastoral and nostalgic novel, as well as on her role as biographer of Charlotte Brontë. Starting in the 1950s and 1960s, critical interest in Gaskell's literary career reawakened, as commentators rediscovered an author responsive to the social turmoil, political conflicts, and intellectual currents of her day. Marxist critics praised the dramatization of class conflict in her narratives even

as they often deplored her hostility to labor unions and her insistence on individual contact and friendship rather than collective action as the key to alleviating the misery of the working class. Feminist scholars aiming to revive the reputations of neglected female writers of the past turned their attention to Gaskell, lauding her depictions of morally complex women chafing against restrictive female roles and hypocritical standards of sexual morality, although faulting the tendency of her heroines to seek personal fulfillment through marriage. The publication of *The Letters of Mrs. Gaskell* in 1966 also did much to stimulate renewed interest in Gaskell's life and writing. Critical studies, biographies, and reprintings of Gaskell's works proliferated in the following decades.

Critical attention on Gaskell has endured. Many scholars' work continues to address Gaskell's distinctive treatment of working-class characters. A number of recent critics, including Mary Elizabeth Hotz, Natalka Freeland, and Elizabeth Starr, emphasize how Gaskell made her portrayals of these characters more positive than those of other contemporary writers and social reformers and made it clear that conventional middle-class understandings of the nature and causes of poverty were inadequate. Commentators Susan E. Colón and Julie Nash discern in Gaskell's works hints of the breakdown of the old aristocratic order, providing new professional opportunities for ambitious women and working-class persons. Critic Melissa Schaub, however, regards Gaskell's appeal for mutual sympathy between classes as exerting a particularly "chilling" form of control over the working class, maintaining that encouraging members to practice such self-discipline not only denies their autonomy but paralyzes them from taking action to demand their rights to better living and working conditions. Critic Peter Gardner complements Schaub's analysis by showing how Gaskell, drawing upon Thomas Carlyle's social theories, metaphorically equates broken relationships within families in *Mary Barton* and other works with broken relationships within the British nation, which she idealized as a family consisting of benevolent patriarchs and obedient servants, wives, and children.

Critics continue to explore the consequences of Gaskell's conflict between her desire to remain a private individual, and her perhaps even stronger sense of duty to express her ideas to the public. Critic Linda H. Peterson surmises that Gaskell also had herself in mind in her description of Charlotte Brontë in *The Life of Charlotte Brontë* as having had two distinct identities, "as Currer Bell, the author" and "as Charlotte Brontë, the woman." Starr assesses Gaskell's novels as representing the author's struggles to position herself as a professional writer within the expanding industrial economy of England. Novels such as *Mary Barton* and *North and South* present characters who seek ways in which to intervene and help resolve social conflicts, suggesting that novelists such as Gaskell could use their literary talent to serve society. Peterson shows how Gaskell, in her biography of Brontë, edited her subject's correspondence so that it would appear that she was more concerned with artistic expression than with money and business arrangements with her publishers. Gaskell herself was well acquainted with these matters, even if she, like Brontë, initially shied away from publicly acknowledging her authorship. In spite of her own ambivalence toward professional authorship, Gaskell openly acknowledged how money and other economic exchanges mold individuals' identities and relationships; many of her novels, for example, include characters—typically women—who chronically hoard, or misinterpret the value of, money, objects, and property. Commentator Freeland interprets the behavior of these characters as embodying isolation from or resistance to modern capitalism, with its tendency to commodify all possessions and even women's own bodies. Freeland analyzes *Ruth* as demonstrating that society's treatment of women as a form of property owned by men closely links the supposedly separate spheres of the home and the marketplace, thus making marriage scarcely distinguishable from prostitution. A related, burgeoning area of Gaskell criticism considers the author's relationships with magazines and publishers and their influence on the creation and reception of her works. Critic Jerome Meckier discusses how in *North and South* Gaskell parodied Charles Dickens's notorious technique of delaying the resolution of plot elements to build suspense, in part to attack Dickens's attitude toward poverty and social reform as too negative, as well as to wittily pay him back for compelling her to hasten the novel's ending in its original serialization in *Household Words*.

PRINCIPAL WORKS

*Life in Manchester. 2 vols. [as Cotton Mather Mills, Esquire] (short stories) 1848

Mary Barton: A Tale of Manchester Life. 2 vols. [published anonymously] (novel) 1848

†Cranford [published anonymously] (novel) 1853

Ruth. 3 vols. [published anonymously] (novel) 1853

Lizzie Leigh and Other Tales [published anonymously] (short stories) 1855

North and South. 2 vols. [published anonymously] (novel) 1855

The Life of Charlotte Brontë (biography) 1857

My Lady Ludlow (novella) 1858

Round the Sofa. 2 vols. (short stories) 1859

Right at Last and Other Tales (short stories) 1860

‡Lois the Witch and Other Tales (short stories) 1861

Cousin Phillis: A Tale (novella) 1863

Sylvia's Lovers. 3 vols. (novel) 1863

The Gray Woman and Other Tales (short stories) 1865

#Wives and Daughters: An Every-Day Story (unfinished novel) 1866

The Works of Mrs. Gaskell. 11 vols. (novels, novellas, short stories, poetry, essays, sketches, and biography) 1906-19

The Letters of Mrs. Gaskell [edited by John Chapple] (letters) 1966

Further Letters of Mrs. Gaskell [edited by Chapple and Alan Shelston] (letters) 2000

*Contains the short stories "Libbie Marsh's Three Eras," "The Sexton's Hero," and "Christmas Storms and Sunshine."

†This work was originally published as a series of sketches in the journal *Household Words* in 1851-53. A complete edition was published in 1853.

‡The title story in this collection was first published in the journal *All the Year Round* in October, 1859.

#This work was originally published in serial form in the *Cornhill Magazine* from August 1864 to January 1866. A complete two-volume edition was published in 1866.

CRITICISM

Mary Elizabeth Hotz (essay date summer 2000)

SOURCE: Hotz, Mary Elizabeth. "'Taught by Death What Life Should Be': Elizabeth Gaskell's Representation of Death in *North and South*." *Studies in the Novel* 32, no. 2 (summer 2000): 165-84.

[*In the following essay, Hotz studies Gaskell's social and moral perspective on death, labor relations, and individual rights and responsibilities.*]

Literature in the nineteenth century was a discourse in which the representation of death was enormously popular. One need only remember that Dickens's *The Old Curiosity Shop* (1840-1841), in which we read about little Nell's death, sold 100,000 copies on its first appearance.[1] Elizabeth Gaskell also wrote about death just at the moment when the burial reform debate reached its height in mid-nineteenth-century England.[2] In *North and South* (1854-1855),[3] Gaskell assuages the threat of death proposed by contemporary burial reform discourse—especially as Edwin Chadwick, Secretary to the New Poor Law Commission from 1834-1842 and Commissioner for the Board of Health from 1848-1852, framed and articulated the debate.[4] Gaskell advocated a very different sort of interaction among labor relations, death and domesticity that she believed would transform mid-Victorian society, especially when effected through the agency of women.

I

To better understand how Gaskell negotiates this relationship between classes and individuals within them and how exactly this relationship intersects with her representation of death in **North and South,** we first need to consider her relationship to Manchester Unitarianism and to Chadwick's proposals for burial reform legislation. In particular, Gaskell's belief in the Christian impulse to ameliorate social evil not only underwrites her novel but differs significantly from Edwin Chadwick's idea that only national mechanisms can solve social problems. The version of Unitarianism Elizabeth Gaskell and her husband, William, espoused was essentially optimistic.[5] They believed in a God who is merciful and trusted in the innate goodness of human nature, even though human actions might become warped by material, emotional or spiritual deprivation. According to Jenny Uglow, "it was against social evil, not original sin or the works of the devil, that the Gaskells took their stand. If such evil was humanly created, it must, they felt, be open to human remedy through practical measures and through the power of the Word to awaken conscience and modify behavior."[6] Given this belief in the merciful nature of God and the power of human beings to counteract evil in the world, Unitarians rejected the concept of everlasting punishment in favor of a future afterlife where there is discipline for the soul, where even the guiltiest may be redeemed and the stained spirit may be cleansed by fire. Reconciliation with God occurs through Christ, who offers a system of ethics on which everyday morality should be based. Charity toward others becomes the outward mark of the true Christian. Within the world of **North and South,** then, as Michael Wheeler suggests, "images of hell on earth are consistent with a Unitarian theology that denies everlasting punishment, and with a Unitarian tradition of visiting the poor, getting to know them individually, trying to improve their appalling lot in the slums of industrial cities."[7]

The Unitarian espousal of freedom, reason, tolerance and an essentially optimistic outlook on life and the afterlife motivated small Unitarian communities like the Cross Street Chapel congregation in Manchester to contribute to social progress.[8] For example, Unitarians advocated parliamentary reform from the turn of the century. The Anti-Corn Law League was initiated and supported by Manchester Unitarians like Robert Hyde Greg, elected MP for Manchester in 1839, and the most aggressive agitator against the Corn Laws. Further, the Municipal Reform Act enabled Unitarians to participate more fully in local government. Thomas Potter, a warehouse owner and member of the Cross Street Chapel, headed the movement for Manchester to become a corporation, which occurred in 1838.[9]

In addition to parliamentary reform, Manchester Unitarians became involved in sanitary reform as well, since they discounted a belief in divine retribution which absolved society of any responsibilities in times of epidemics. Rather, they stressed that such conditions were caused by the filth and overcrowding in the cities. For example, James P. Kay, a Unitarian doctor who took the post of medical officer at the New Ardwick and Ancoats dispensary—particularly afflicted sections of Manchester—engaged in sanitary reform work. In 1832 he published the highly influential *The Moral and Physical Condition of the Working Classes Employed in the Cotton Manufacturers of Manchester,* which was underwritten by the assumption that since epidemics were aggravated by men, they could also be eradicated, or at least ameliorated, by human endeavors. This attitude led Kay, along with the brothers Samuel and William Rathbone Greg and Benjamin Haywood, to found the Manchester Statistical Society in 1833, a society designed to gather information that would eventually engender reform. All four men were connected with the Cross Street Chapel and were well-known to the Gaskells, as were Edwin Chadwick and Thomas Southwood Smith, who succeeded Chadwick at the Board of Health.[10]

These ideals of service played a dominant role in Unitarian thinking. Unitarians became champions of the oppressed, advocates for education, religious tolerance and women's rights. But, as Donald Stone so succinctly states, "accompanying this reformist strain was an impulse that favored economic individualism, that saw in the industrialists—many of whom were Unitarians—a power and a right deriving from natural law that was not to be interfered with."[11] A look at the composition of the Cross Street Chapel will confirm Stone's assessment, for Cross Street was where the bourgeois of Manchester worshiped. Valentine Cunningham claims that "the trustees and members were the millocracy, the benefactors, the leaders of Manchester society: corn millers, silk manufacturers, calico painters, patent-reed makers, engineers, bankers and barristers; founders of hospitals, libraries, educational institutions, charitable funds and missions to the poor."[12] The congregation, needless to say, did not take kindly to criticism of the laissez-faire economy. Promoting an ideal of individualism rather than equality, the ethic of the free market as well as the Gospel, Unitarian MPs spoke vehemently against government intervention in factory hours and conditions.[13]

Elizabeth Gaskell participated in a religion that espoused the responsibilities of the individual on behalf of local society: Unitarian chapels were full of proponents of contemporary political economy and model self-employers who believed, essentially, that self-help was the key to reform and that the government should not intervene in the "natural" rhythms of the market economy, especially with regard to free trade and tariff reform. Yet she could see for herself that all was not well with the liberal-bourgeois-dissenting millocracy. It failed to feed, clothe, and house adequately the poor of Manchester in the 1840s. In other words, Gaskell faced two contending groups: Unitarian political economists in concert with model employers versus distressed employees. Specifically, Gaskell, through representations of death, negotiates these pressures by depicting in **North and South** individuals acting according to the spirit of Christ rather than to the rules of the state as the regulating law between the middle and working classes. For example, Gaskell moves away from what I perceive as Chadwickean proposals for impersonal state legislation and toward a voluntary cooperation among individuals within a local rather than a national context in **North and South.** The informed Thornton suggests that "intercourse" between the classes "is the very breath of life" (p. 432). He articulates an "evolution of understanding" one another based on common interests "which invariably makes people find means and ways of seeing each other, and becoming acquainted with each others' characters and persons, and even tricks of temper and modes of speech. We should understand each other."

The Unitarian rejection of everlasting punishment emphasized, in earthly life, the need for social progress advanced by individual initiative. This emphasis accounts, in part, for the fact that Gaskell, in representing death, articulated specific cultural attitudes about sociopolitical life in mid-nineteenth-century England. But Gaskell's strategy of relying on the individual Christian impulse to ameliorate the living conditions of the poor differs significantly from Chadwick's idea that only national mechanisms can solve their problems. Gaskell's emphasis on the individual addresses distinctions in the assignation of power by the middle class at a time when it was solidifying its own enfranchisement and defining itself in relation to national bureaucratic structures. In the texts by Gaskell and Chadwick, the status of the working-class corpse and the representation of peoples' reactions to it form different and conflicting strategies for middle-class survival and power over the working class. In *The Supplementary Report,* Chadwick, by depicting the working-class corpse as an agent of contagious disease and a lag on economic productivity, implies a need for separating, confining, and ultimately neutralizing its threat to survivors through sanitary measures. Such a construct serves to define the middle class as survivors—as opposed to the sick and dead poor— and justifies state apparatuses to police the working-class corpse and the family and community to which it belonged. The state evacuates the meaning of death and displaces the function of family and community by the efficient removal of the corpse from the home by an officer of the state and by the replacement of communal rituals with standardized procedures for burial. Both the corpse and the survivors in the working-class community become nuisances to be contained and controlled by centralized measures that limited what the working-

class people could do for themselves. In effect, Chadwick limits their power of association and seeks to depoliticize even as he secularizes their activity by removing any possibility for reflection on the causes of death among the poor because he believed that the social order depended upon what Herbert Marcuse has described as the working class's "unfreedom, toil, hard work and resignation in the face of death."[14] To secure this social stability, then, only the middle class had the power to assign meaning to the working-class experience of death. The effect of Chadwick's strategy, I believe, was to deny the existence of unique local communities and to define people according to their labor functions.

Gaskell, while very much concerned with the same social conditions that preoccupied Chadwick, considers the working-class corpse to be an opportunity for the masters to understand the motivations of men. The corpse becomes an occasion to fathom the causes of death among the poor, to seek remedies for their cure, and to affirm local kinship networks and communities as entities that negotiate class collaboration. Thus, the corpse draws a community of mourners from all ranks and provides an instance in which individuals may be transformed to act in the best interests of society. Gaskell neutralizes the threat of the working-class death by arguing for its transformative potential to improve life for everyone. Individual contact with death engenders an understanding of the human condition that transcends class boundaries and provokes action to improve that human condition so threatened by England's industrialization. Only by standing in the presence of working-class death, represented by the corpse and the activities of the mourners, will the middle class be able to protect its interests through the collaboration—not conflict—with the working class. But Gaskell's emphasis on the individual's ethical behavior also depoliticizes—as did Chadwick's—the working class by qualifying or removing the possibility for collective political or economic associations which might emerge as a result of death or reflection on the particular causes of death.

These two different and conflicting approaches to the problem of death and burial turn out to be a problem about the poor, how the middle class will relate to them, and how they will be allowed to relate to themselves. From Chadwick's perspective, given the enormous scale of the public health problem—which, he claims, the working-class corpse embodies—individual efforts could never be enough; only centralized measures could solve the problem. From Gaskell's point of view, since the state can only be counted on to protect laissez-faire liberalism, the middle-class individual must attend to the needs of society. It is the middle-class individual, especially the individual female, who must not only sustain a balance of interests between the two classes but render the economy more productive. Through her characterization of Margaret Hale, Gaskell seeks to reconstitute the working-class connection between life and death to produce meaningful social reform at home. In particular, Margaret intervenes in the strike scene to argue for a more comprehensive, public role for middle-class women in Victorian society and to stand in the place of working-class bodies—those bodies, both dead and alive, which have become such problems to Gaskell's middle-class readers. According to Gaskell, this kind of heroine transforms the economy and bridges the gap between England's "two nations." However, as we will see, Margaret's relationship to power is quite ambivalent. She produces social reform by identifying with the working class but without sacrificing her position in the social formation.

II

The distinction between the public world of politics and market activity and the private world of domestic activity, morality and emotion became ever more crucial in mid-Victorian England.[15] But these divisions were by no means fixed, although increasingly they were solidified in rules for social interaction. Over time, separation between the public and the private widened; it had become, by 1850, identified with gender. As Davidoff and Hall argue, "a masculine penumbra surrounded that which was defined as public while women were increasingly engulfed by the private realm, bounded by physical, social and psychic partitions."[16] Men, because of their privileged status, could move easily between both realms; women, however, were increasingly confined to the private.

But none of these divisions were so set as not to be open to contestation and negotiation. In this mercurial space, Gaskell wrote **North and South** to suggest that feminine identity is as much determined by public political action as by private, interior moral development. She strikes an essential balance between the two forces by focusing her attention on the responses and rituals surrounding death because it was a crucial site where women's restriction to the private could be affirmed. While large funerals were increasingly used to demonstrate public status, records show that women had begun to stay away from funeral and burial services because it was becoming unacceptable for daughters or widows to display their grief in public. Instead, the more genteel woman moved away from a potentially undifferentiated public gathered for a funeral and was drawn toward a more private experience of emotion in her own home.[17]

However, Gaskell believed that women's identity depends upon the renegotiation of traditional concepts and exercises of authority, and that her capacity for reflection should lead her to an ever-widening idea of her

traffic in the world beyond the front door of the home. For Margaret to fulfill her obligations to reform society, she must learn to appreciate the continuity between life and death and reject certain religious and social structures which seek to confine women to restricting domestic roles.

In the first several chapters of the novel, narrow definitions of the home (as Mr. Hale and his position in the patriarchal order of the Church defined it) and Margaret's place in it begin to fall away for the heroine: "The one staid foundation of her home, her idea of her beloved father seemed reeling and rocking. What could she say? What was to be done?" (p. 34). Mr. Hale's decision to leave the Church forces her into action. She must make arrangements for the family's move to Milton, pack the furniture and locate decent housing in their new city. As the authority of the father breaks down in the face of his own uncertainty and inability to live beyond his initial decision, Margaret faces the challenge of developing her own authority to act in the world. This empowerment depends upon her relinquishing the sleepy life in London, rejecting Mr. Lennox, who, in Margaret's dream, falls from a tree to his death as he tries to reach for Margaret's bonnet (symbol of a conventional life as a Victorian woman), and exercising her capacity to read and interpret her new surroundings in Milton. Mr. Hale asks that she think of his situation in terms of the early martyrs, for "the early martyrs suffered for the truth" (p. 35). The early martyrs also crossed conventional boundaries, walked into the desert alone there to shape prophetic roles for Christians in the future. But, Gaskell suggests, Margaret must walk the same path. Gaskell deploys the analogy with some precision here as she qualifies Mr. Hale's theoretical self-sacrifice. She, too, must step outside the home and into the public arena, though she will need time and space to reflect on the world before her first. This move to contemplation, and the developing capacity to integrate risk in one's life, serves to shape the prophetic role women are to have in society.

A limited sense of continuity between mother and daughter determines the prophetic role Gaskell envisions for women because the strength of the heroine is conditioned in large measure by her capacity to be influenced by her mother as well as her ability to do what her mother could not do.[18] Margaret must reject her mother's shallow attraction to the accouterments of wealth and status in favor of reflection and action in the world "outdoors," in the world of Milton's industrial economy. Margaret's behavior toward her dying mother must be considered in broader terms than conventional domestic ones which posit the heroine as primary caretaker and nurturer. Each contact with death propels Margaret into the grimy world of Milton-Northern where she begins to take notice of the loiterers in the street, her first recognition that the economic depression affected not just a faceless mass of people but individuals. Moreover, Gaskell defines a middle-class woman's domestic activities as work and equates that work to men's work in the mill. Describing to her father her experience at Thornton's party, Margaret admits she "'felt like a great hypocrite to-night, sitting there in my white silk gown, with my idle hands before me, when I remembered all the good, thorough, house-work they had done to-day. They took me for a fine lady, I'm sure'" (p. 167). The experience with her dying mother forces Margaret to become "a hand" herself as she must stand in the kitchen and do the ironing, and provides the opportunity for her to wake up to the working world of Milton and move outside of herself, taking notice of the consequences of economic depression.

But Gaskell qualifies this move by suggesting that a woman's position in the world also demands reflection upon its exigencies. Underwriting Gaskell's vision of a woman's place in the world is her Unitarian belief that action in the world is necessarily informed by Gospel values clarified by contemplation. Death provides occasions for this contemplation. In facing the deaths of her mother, her working-class friend Bessy, her father, and finally her guardian, Margaret learns what her mother could not learn—the need to adapt to constantly changing environments and, therefore, the need to enter into a dynamic tension between prayer and action. In a thoughtful moment at the end of the novel, Margaret realizes "she had learnt that not only to will, but also to pray, was a necessary condition in the truly heroic" (p. 412). Gaskell argues that women bring particular strength and stability to a society under stress at mid-century because their contribution consists of the power to discern the proper course of action amid deep change and to act from the strength of that discernment, not by rigid adherence to inflexible, gendered cultural precepts.

This dynamic between action and reflection, as Gaskell articulates it first in her description of Mrs. Hale's funeral and Margaret's participation in it, also shares the terms but revises the conclusions of Edwin Chadwick's attempts to articulate relations of gender, class and power over the space of the grave. First, Margaret insists, over her father's objections, that she attend the funeral with him because his closest friend, Mr. Bell, could not come. To her father's objection that women do not generally go to funerals, Margaret responds: "'No: because they can't control themselves. Women of our class don't go, because they have no power over their emotions, and yet are ashamed of showing them. Poor women go, and don't care if they are seen overwhelmed with grief'" (pp. 266-67). This quotation suggests that emotionality is coded both as lower class and female. That is, self-control is valued especially by middle-class men and is a power attributed both by and to them in a greater degree than to working-class men or women of any class. Margaret marks her desire to

embrace the value of self-control for herself, thus identifying herself with the middle classes and with masculine power. By contrast, Mr. Hale cannot control his emotions in this situation, thus femininizing himself, but not presumably calling his class location into question.

Gaskell is careful to portray the positive effects of a middle-class woman's entry into the public territory of Mrs. Hale's burial site. Also attending the funeral is Nicholas Higgins, the working-class man whose daughter Margaret has befriended:

> Margaret's fortitude nearly gave way as Dixon, with a slight motion of her hand, directed her notice to Nicholas Higgins and his daughter, standing a little aloof, but deeply attentive to the ceremonial. Nicholas wore his usual fustian clothes, but had a bit of black stuff sewn round his hat—a mark of mourning which he had never shown to his daughter Bessy's memory.
>
> (p. 269)

Higgins's "mark of mourning," which is a decidedly middle-class practice at this point in nineteenth-century England, differentiates him from the working class and suggests his adoption of middle-class values and sensibility. The gesture indicates Margaret's capacity to influence members of the working class as she leaves her home to seek contact with them.

Gaskell fashions a middle-class woman able eventually to influence the local economy through her marriage to the industrialist Thornton, but only after she has developed her courage through exposure to the dying. Margaret's experience of caring for the dying Bessy and her dying mother prepares her to intervene in the strike at Thornton's mill, Marlborough. Margaret shuttles between her aristocratic mother and Bessy, who represents a deferential order in which the working classes pay tribute to the upper classes in return for personal care and benevolence. But Margaret becomes increasingly aware of a new industrial order represented by the strike. Neither her mother's retreat to an older aristocratic past nor Bessy's deference can meet the demands of the present industrial crisis. The unbending attitudes of masters like Thornton are equally ineffective. Instead, Gaskell argues, a woman like Margaret must intervene in the cycle of violence between masters and men because she sees what Thornton cannot see and her mother and Bessy do not have the will to change: the face of Boucher "with starving children at home . . . and enraged beyond measure at discovering that Irish men were to be brought into rob [his] little ones of bread" (p. 177).

In the novel's juxtaposition of Margaret with Bessy, Gaskell unsettles, through the depiction of feminine influence and action, conventional redemptive paradigms available to the poor, namely apocalyptic solutions to specifically temporal problems. Margaret's zeal for reform provides a striking contrast to Bessy, who has no strength or spirit for life because she cannot adjust to the demands of the work situation. She tells Margaret she "'began to work in a carding-room soon after, and the fluff got into [her] lungs and poisoned [her]'" (p. 102). Certainly I think Gaskell means to portray Bessy's hardship in an effort to disclose what measures are necessary to improve working conditions, in much the same way she did in **Mary Barton.** But here she is also interested in the way that Bessy's piety—her emotional anticipation of relief in the afterlife—may keep her from struggling against these hardships. Bessy dies not only because she cannot manage the work physically, but because she cannot understand the problems in the industrial economy or find their solutions in human terms. Similarly, in **Mary Barton,** even though John understood the dynamic of market capitalism and its oppressive effect on laborers, he could only see violence as the solution to the problem. Not surprisingly, then, he too died while Mr. Carson lived to improve employment conditions for workers. In both instances, Gaskell seeks to apply the spiritual benefits of contact with the dead, which the working class had traditionally reaped, to the preoccupying problems of the middle-class temporal and material world of industrial England.

North and South offers Margaret and Higgins as models who together form the solution for a new industrial order. They also reject Bessy's tendency to rely upon religion to provide consolation in another world for the social problems of this one. From their perspective, this kind of continuity between life and death is excessive and ineffective. Bessy's desire, which is characterized as weariness, is to move to some place Edenic: "the land of Beulah"; the country with trees; the south of England where there are no strikes. Bessy longs to die, especially at times when her father speaks of the need to strike: "'What he says at times make me long to die more than ever, for I want to know so many things, and am so tossed about wi' wonder'" (p. 91). Nicholas resists Bessy's apocalyptic solutions by arguing that the answers to industrial problems are to be found in this world, not the next. "'Hoo's so full of th' life to come, hoo cannot think of th' present'" (p. 132). Further, Higgins claims northerners—except Bessy, who longs to retreat to the south to avoid the strike and have peace and quiet at any price—have "too much blood" to stand the injustice imposed by the masters. To Margaret's assertion that southerners have too much sense to strike, Higgins claims "'they've too little spirit'" (p. 133).

Margaret, on the other hand, responds to Bessy from a religious model that emphasizes society's improvement through practical human solutions. To Bessy's allusions to the Book of Revelation, Margaret replies: "'Don't dwell so much on the prophecies, but read the clearer parts of the Bible'" (p. 137). Rejecting Bessy's philoso-

phy of death as an escape, for she "shrank from death herself, with all the clinging to life so natural to the young and healthy" (p. 89), Margaret presses her to dwell on aspects of life on this earth: "'Don't let us talk of what fancies come into your head when you are feverish. I would rather hear something about what you used to do when you were well'" (p. 102). For Margaret and Higgins, social evil, since humanly created, must be open to human remedy through practical measures and the power of the Gospel to modify behavior—which means that social evil must first of all be seen and assessed by a middle-class woman.

Gaskell takes up the representation of death, where the rituals surrounding it were being plotted and codified according to gender, to suggest that contact with it strengthens a woman's resolve to spur social reform. The effect of Margaret's experience with Bessy is a positive one, one I claim impels her to intervene in the strike. She feels her intensified interest in the crowded narrow streets "by the simple fact of her having learnt to care for a dweller in them" (p. 99), and she feels stronger for having visited Bessy, for having heard how much Bessy has had to bear through the years. After Bessy dies, her corpse provides Margaret with yet another opportunity to develop her courage: Mary Higgins, Bessy's sister, asks Margaret if she would like to view Bessy, a gesture of respect for the departed that the Hale servant Dixon must interpret for Margaret. Initially, Margaret rejects the idea but immediately changes her mind. "'No . . . I will go' . . . and for fear of her own cowardice, she went away, in order to take from herself any chance of changing her determination" (p. 217). Margaret's initial fear of the corpse indicates the middle-class preference for avoiding contact with the dead body and curtailing social interactions in its presence. Her decision to offer this mark of respect affirms her other actions that will further the social union and rejuvenation Gaskell envisions for England. As Margaret's courage to act in the social sphere increases, so do other people's willingness to relinquish their power to her. In anticipation of Nicholas's adoption of a middle-class practice at Mrs. Hale's funeral, he acquiesces to Margaret's power over him when she suggests that he come to her house to visit with Mr. Hale and to keep him from drinking. "Margaret felt that he acknowledged her power" (p. 220). Bessy, too, acknowledges Margaret's power over her. As Dixon reports to Margaret about Bessy, "'It seems, the young woman who died had a fancy for being buried in something of yours'" (p. 216).

Gaskell attempts to found social power in women—or justify it—on the personal ties they establish through their treatment of others, a duty which emerges directly from the New Testament, as Bessy's allusion to the crucifixion of Christ reveals. By asking for a bit of Margaret's clothing, Bessy reveals how much Margaret has earned her authority over Bessy, even to her grave. Despite Bessy's belief that "'[s]ome's pre-elected to sumptuous feasts, and purple and fine linen, . . . [o]thers toil and moil all their lives long'" (p. 150), she protested to Margaret that "'if yo' ask me to cool yo'r tongue wi' th' tip of my finger, I'll come across the great gulf to yo' just for th' thought o' what you've been to me here.'" Bessy perceives Margaret as a savior and compels her to reach across the class divide. But Gaskell alludes to this defining moment in the New Testament to suggest that a middle-class woman's experience with the dying poor, based as it is on personal relationship, not only earns their loyalty, but creates in such women the responsibility to act for reform.

Deeply ambivalent about violent trade union activity and working-class dismissal of the self-help philosophy, Gaskell concludes that female authority is critical to resuscitating the self-help philosophy in the working-class home. The Boucher suicide episode, which occurs after the strike scene, serves to endorse Gaskell's belief in the necessary exercise of female authority. John Boucher commits suicide by lying face down in a shallow, dye-filled stream after being unable to find work because of his violent participation in union activity. The chapter in which we read of the body's discovery is entitled "Union Not Always Strength" to suggest Gaskell's anxiety about groups of male laborers engaged in trade union activity as opposed to her support of local community. Higgins had just complained to Margaret and her father that "'we had public opinion on our side, till he and his sort began rioting and breaking laws'" (p. 293). By pointing out that Boucher's violent behavior stemmed from being forced into the union by Higgins, "'driving him into the Union against his will—without his heart going with it. You've made him what he is!'" (p. 294), Margaret questions the coercive nature of union activity. By contrast, Gaskell suggests, individual middle-class influence breeds more responsible communal activity. Margaret's regular visits to the Higgins's home, where her influence has been appreciated by Nicholas, Bessy, and Mary, foster Higgins's sense of responsibility to the Boucher family, whose dire circumstances motivate him to seek work. "'I set him off o' th' road, and so I mun answer for him'" (p. 305). Eventually, the evidence that he believes in self-help persuades Margaret to use her influence to bring together Thornton and Higgins.

But Margaret seems significantly unsuccessful with Mrs. Boucher, not only because of the nature of Boucher's union activity, but because of Margaret's necessary rejection of those who do not subscribe to the self-help philosophy—particularly as it applies in the working-class home—and the sense of reciprocity that her understanding of personal obligation demands. Margaret describes the Boucher household in middle-class stereotypic terms about the poor: the children are "ill-ordered"

and the house "looked as if [it] had been untouched for days by any effort at cleanliness" (p. 295). Even though Margaret had some experience with the dead and dying among the working class, here she seems particularly eager to escape from the house. When a neighbor woman arrives to help with the arrangements for the funeral, Margaret feels great relief, thinking "that it would be better, perhaps, to set an example of clearing the house, which was filled with *idle,* if sympathising gazers" (p. 297; my emphasis). Finally, Mrs. Boucher's reaction to her husband's suicide proves unacceptable to Margaret and Mr. Hale: "Still it was unsatisfactory to see how completely her thoughts were turned upon herself and her own position, and this selfishness extended even to her relations with her children, whom she considered as incumbrances, even in the very midst of her somewhat animal affection for them" (p. 300). Denied the luxury of considering her own desperate state as a result of her husband's shameful death, Mrs. Boucher resembles an animal barely deserving Margaret's attention. Even as Mr. Hale tries to rouse Mrs. Boucher into some sympathy for her husband and what he might have felt at the moment of his death, Mrs. Boucher looked upon all—the masters, the union, the children—as one great army of personal enemies "whose fault it was that she was now a helpless widow" (p. 301). Margaret, for her part, "had heard enough of this unreasonableness."

In contrast to Gaskell's description of the Davenports in **Mary Barton,** where a visit to their home in times of death prompts John Barton and Mr. Wilson to act for the sake of the working-class community, a visit to the Bouchers only reinforces the notion that those poor people who refuse influence from the middle class are bitterly resented by them. Nonetheless, the scene must have been reassuring to middle-class readers because Margaret gains the perspective proper to her station and gendered position in life. Gaskell places Margaret in the home of very poor and marginal people to show just how in need they are of local middle-class influence and just how hopeless they have become by rejecting it. But, as we will see in the next section, Gaskell also insists that Margaret's process of individuation depends upon her ability to cross conventional domestic boundaries in order to solve class conflict through direct participation in the industrial world.

III

When, in the strike scene, Margaret positions herself between the laborers and Thornton, Gaskell suggests that a woman's sympathy for others marks her development and compels her to redefine herself bodily, rejecting the conventional Victorian placement of women only in the home. Gaskell restructures women's identity by depicting Margaret's "intense sympathy" (p. 175) for the workers and her use of bodily power to enter the public arena and contribute to new definitions of class relations. When she first arrives at Thornton's home, she is instructed to remain indoors and shut down the windows. She cannot remain inside for long, as her mother and Bessy must, but begins to move outdoors. The first indication of this movement occurs when she "threw the window wide open," "tore off her bonnet and bent forward to hear" the exchange between Thornton and the workers below (pp. 177, 178). Her initial excursion into the public arena is to draw attention to the difference she sees in others. She pleads with Thornton to treat the strikers like human beings, not the "demoniac mob" that yells "fiendlike noises," as Thornton characterizes them (pp. 176, 177). Finally, she rushed downstairs, "lifted the great iron bar with an imperious force—had thrown the door open wide—and was there, in the face of that angry sea of men . . . [standing] between them and their enemy" (p. 178).

The struggle for position in mediating class relations manifests itself here in a very physical way: "Mr. Thornton stood a little on one side; he had moved away from behind her, as if jealous of anything that should come between him and danger" (p. 178). Margaret speaks first, although she must hold her arms out until she recovers her breath. She argues against the use of violence but fails to pacify the workers. With Thornton's refusal to back down on the use of Irish scabs, the "storm broke" and Margaret, sensing an attack on Thornton, "threw her arms around him and she made her body a shield from the fierce people beyond" (p. 179). Thornton insists this arena is no place for a woman, but Margaret claims otherwise. Her move outdoors and her position between the strikers and Thornton suggest that she believes herself to be empowered to influence shifting labor relations, a position that has been anticipated by Margaret's growing consciousness of the world of Milton. The scene further suggests that Margaret associates power with her body, an intriguing move because she has just been shuttling between her dying mother and the consumptive Bessy. Both Mrs. Hale and Bessy have not only taught Margaret to become aware of her external surroundings, but they have taught her, by default, that the body instantiates the lineaments of power and gender.

Barbara Leah Harman argues that Margaret "overestimates her power as maiden to deflect assault," for as the narrator remarks, "if she thought her sex would be a protection . . . she was wrong."[19] In one respect, Gaskell's description of Margaret, once pummeled with a stone, as "one dead," "cold," "look[ing] like a corpse," underscores Harman's point that Margaret overestimated her power and failed (pp. 179, 181, 183). To rehearse Harman's argument for a moment, even as Margaret enters the outdoor world, her capacity to act in the public sphere as a woman is limited, which would explain her figurative death. She fails to break up the riot

with the rhetoric of political economy, but she succeeds by becoming a woman assaulted. Even though she had done woman's work, recognizing Thornton's unfairness and the mob's potential to do violence to him, she fails ultimately because she falls into the Victorian gendered position which figures women as victims, nearly lifeless and passive. Along these lines, then, the strike scene suggests that a woman's appearance in the public sphere is complicated by the notion that these scenes cannot be represented without becoming even more complicated by sexuality. By figuring Margaret as dead and a passive object of Thornton's affection in a context in which she has been removed from competition with him, Gaskell circumscribes Margaret's power to influence economy. She cannot achieve success by direct intervention but must wait for the more conventional avenue of marriage.

But another turn of the kaleidoscope brings into view a startling emphasis on the thanatological and the possibility that Margaret's "failure" to influence the economy may be considered more successful than Harman admits. Since the scene devolves into Margaret's symbolic death, Gaskell contests in explicit terms a key principle of political economy instantiated by representations of death: the division of the world into public and private spheres. Unlike Mr. and Mrs. Hale, Bessy, and John Boucher, Margaret is only figured as dead so that she can associate herself with working-class interests without losing her position in the social formation. This move allows her to sympathize with the workers, escape the confines of the purely domestic, and cross its boundaries to effect social change. Margaret's deathlike disposition provokes Thornton's spontaneous expression of love for her and anticipates not only the conventional marriage, but a renewed industrial economy as well. Now, according to Gaskell, women's "work" means using one's own body as a means to enter the public and political arena. As Margaret remarks to Thornton, hers was not "a personal act between you and me," but an act natural to her womanly instinct: "'It was only a natural instinct; any woman would have done just the same. We all feel the sanctity of our sex as a high privilege when we see danger'" (pp. 195, 194). Because Margaret rejects the act as personal, she makes it a political one of class and gender action.

Gaskell extends the reach of Margaret's political action and deepens her personal authority when she has Margaret flatly deny to the policeman, an official regulator of working-class bodies, her presence at the railway station the night of Leonard's death. He has threatened to reveal her brother's presence in England to the authorities who have unjustly condemned him for supporting his men in a mutiny against a tyrannical captain. Gaskell figures the consequences of Margaret's actions as deathly, just as she did in the strike scene. When the policeman left the house, "she went into the study, paused—tottered forward—paused again—swayed for an instant where she stood, and fell prone on the floor in a *dead* swoon" (p. 275; my emphasis). She lay still, "white as death," and when she awoke she could not remember the details "which had thrown her into such deadly fright" (pp. 276, 277). In fact, Dixon observes that she is "'more dead than alive'" (p. 281). At first glance it would appear again that the consequences of stepping outside the defined limits of influence—the domestic sphere for the mid-Victorian woman—leads to an experience of death and degradation. Indeed, Margaret's faith in conventional rules for the exercise of authority has given way (p. 276).

But Gaskell's strategy here resembles her work in the strike scene. Borrowing from thanatological discourse, Gaskell again associates Margaret with death and recalcitrance, which connects her to those corpses provoking the mid-Victorian power struggle between the middle and working classes. And indeed, her lie "to save the son" (p. 284) leaves her dependent upon Thornton and ultimately opens the way for their psychological and economic reconciliation to take place, a reconciliation that has practical benefits for the working class. Further, it is no accident that as Margaret recovers from her grief over the loss of her innocence in the strike scene, her father's health worsens: "And almost in proportion to her re-establishment in health, was her father's relapse into his abstracted musing upon the wife he had lost, and the past era in his life that was closed to him for ever" (p. 289). Margaret's lie and recovery from the shock of it strengthen her capacity to claim her own authority. Gaskell's description of her as if dead reinforces the idea that Gaskell understood the debate raging at mid-century but with a singular twist that serves, in part, to undermine Chadwick: real working-class corpses were pivots for social and economic debate; but figurative, middle-class corpses became links to working-class interests without sacrificing the power invested in them as members of the middle class.

Gaskell's depiction of Margaret's metaphoric death is significant because it has class implications. When Gaskell envisions workers gathering at Thornton's mill and the Irish scabs cowering in a small room at the head of a back flight of stairs, she imagines them as material, embodied creatures and "amenable to aggregation," as individuals personally known to her, yet nonetheless as a group of particular persons rather than the inchoate mass or mob.[20] At the same time, however, Gaskell conceptualizes Margaret Hale as an active participant in the process of redefining social relations. In the strike, improved social relations depend upon her sympathy and oneness with the working class and, paradoxically, their being clearly different from her. For working-class conditions to improve along with the industrial health of the nation, workers have to be treated differently by being known at work and at home by middle-class persons who will actively gather that knowledge. Margaret's figurative's death satisfies this necessary paradox because Gaskell depicts Margaret momentarily as a body like those of the working-class crowd for whom she has just pleaded to Thornton. Still, her figurative death at their hands clearly distinguishes her from the crowd, eventually reinforcing her growing sense of her social responsibilities as a middle-class individual, not as part of the working-class crowd.

Gaskell draws on the discourse of death to construct a version of individuation that seems both to affirm and subvert gender and class positions. Even as she depicts Margaret's transgressions of gender and class lines to enter Milton's industrial complex, Gaskell seems unable to relinquish the concept that a woman must enact some obedience to authority. In one sense, Margaret seems to fulfill the messianic potential Bessy perceived in her: a woman crucified for her public infringements. She secures a woman's position of influence in the public arena by foregrounding individual human qualities in the industrial context, seemingly diminishing the importance of class and gender to effect social change. But Gaskell writes the novel to solve a problem framed by class and gender. Gaskell asks the most challenging question for middle-class women of her time: "[H]ow much was to be utterly merged in obedience to authority, and how much might be set apart for freedom in working" (p. 416).

The problem—how much to be merged with authority and how much to be set apart—Gaskell again wrestles with in thanatological terms in the last sections of the novel. When Margaret's father dies Gaskell describes her, not as a corpse as in previous moments when she confronts traditional authority and her own position in it, but as "an altar-tomb, and she the stone statue on it" (p. 354) because she is so devastated by the death of the father and the end of patriarchal influence. Her father's death throws Margaret into a struggle between her aunt Shaw's desire to restore her to the aristocratic Beresford family of her mother and her guardian Mr. Bell's desire to underwrite her in a life of private charity at Oxford. The death of Mr. Hale turns Margaret into an object; in the first instance, the text represents her as a monument, a tribute to history and the power of lineage so obviously suggested by the Beresford line. In the second instance, Mr. Bell claims that Margaret, with no personal authority (outside of his influence), should accept his help to avoid becoming an accouterment in the Shaw household and retreat to a different kind of private life.

However, Gaskell prepares us for Margaret's resistance to the passivity, objectification and "obedience to authority" of both choices in a way that emphasizes her particular association of death with the necessary power to resist confining Victorian ideologies. Before Margaret leaves Milton, she requests from the Higginses a memento of Bessy's, which Mary Higgins supplies by giving Bessy's drinking cup to Margaret. The cup, reminiscent of Christ's acceptance of his ultimate mission in the garden at Gethsemane, serves to remind Margaret of her own capacity to work, which means she must cross the divide separating the private domestic sphere from the public political one, and resist the temptation to "become sleepily deadened into forgetfulness of anything beyond the life which was lapping her round with luxury" (p. 373). Choosing the Beresford line, the ambition to sleep in luxury, means death in this novel, death to women and to the progress of society. To resist this choice Margaret must face change squarely in her former home, the village of Helstone, geographic symbol of England's former rural order. She observes in her promenades and conversations with Helstone residents that "here and there old trees had been felled"; decaying cottages had disappeared as had roots of trees where she talked with Mr. Lennox; the old man and inhabitant of the ruinous cottage had died; and even the language system had changed—the indefinite article had become the absolute adjective (pp. 387, 388, 394). While Margaret grieves over these changes "like old friends" (p. 388), she prepares herself to confess her lie to Mr. Bell. She stands poised between her former life, dying before her eyes, and her commitment to an unpredictable future. In this moment she feels "a sense of change, of individual nothingness, of perplexity and disappointment" (p. 400). The disillusionment, begun so intensely with her father's death, comes to fruition at Helstone. The emptiness she feels, while painful, allows room for the present time to live in her. Because of her shifts in perspective, Margaret recognizes the need for perpetual change: "'now this, now that—now disappointed and peevish because all is not exactly as [she] had pictured it, and now suddenly discovering that the reality is far more beautiful than [she] had imagined it'" (p. 401).

The death of Mr. Bell, the last of the six characters to die in the novel, brings Margaret to the moment of self-understanding: "Now that she was afresh taught by death what life should be . . . she prayed that she might have strength to speak and act the truth for evermore" (p. 412), not as maid and Lady Bountiful living in Oxford, as Mr. Bell once suggested to Mr. Hale, but as a woman who struggles for her place of influence in England's economy. She resolves to take her life into her own hands, to answer for herself and to negotiate with Thornton her position somewhere between "obedience to authority" and "freedom in working."

IV

Elizabeth Gaskell's careful attention to death and burial as it was and could be—the participation of a kinship network, the Unitarian framework to initiate collaboration, as well as the powerful effect death has on the de-

velopment of a woman's identity—are used to imagine the positive and powerful experiences in middle- and working-class individuals. In calling attention to these realities, however, she makes her own middle-class desires to reform class relations that much more visible. Gaskell's middle-class appropriations of working-class practices and beliefs concerning death become effective links to working-class interests without the middle class relinquishing the power invested in them by virtue of their being members of the middle class.

Nonetheless, because of Gaskell's investment in discussions of political economy, class relations and death as a woman, author and resident of Manchester, she was not limited by a narrow bureaucratic perspective. Instead, she was able to relate the facts, which saturate a report like Chadwick's, to the experiences of differentiated individuals of both the working and middle classes. In doing so, she reverses the emphasis, so as to give value and dignity to the lives of the poor and to suggest that a powerful machine like England's economy may be successfully operated by the hands of concerned working-class and middle-class men and women.

Notes

1. W. L. G. James, "The Portrayal of Death and 'Substance of Life': Aspects of the Modern Reader's Response to 'Victorianism,'" in *Reading the Victorian Novel: Detail Into Form*, ed. Ian Gregor (New York: Barnes and Noble, 1980), p. 227.

2. Death was no stranger to Elizabeth Gaskell. Her brother, John Stevenson, mysteriously vanished at sea on a voyage to India in 1828; her mother died when she was eleven months old; she gave birth to a stillborn child in 1833; and her son, Willie, died of scarlet fever in 1845.

3. Elizabeth Gaskell, *North and South* (Oxford Univ. Press, 1973). Hereafter cited parenthetically in the text.

4. To answer mid-Victorian society's growing concern about overcrowded churchyards and cemeteries in urban areas, Edwin Chadwick wrote *A Supplementary Report on the Results of a Special Inquiry into the Practice of Interment in Towns* (London: W. Clowes and Sons, 1843). The report consists of statistical tables, diagrams of mortuary houses, numerous eyewitness accounts and scientific theories concerning the dangers of miasma, and administrative recommendations for burial reform. Chadwick calls for the speedy removal of the corpse from the home, a ban on all intramural interments, both in churchyards and privately operated cemeteries, and the creation of national cemeteries managed by qualified personnel appointed by the state. For a more detailed analysis of Chadwick's report, see Mary Elizabeth Hotz,

"Down Among the Dead: Edwin Chadwick's Burial Reform Discourse in Mid-Nineteenth-Century England," *Victorian Literature and Culture,* forthcoming.

5. Elizabeth Gaskell's husband, William, was a Unitarian minister at the Cross Street Chapel in Manchester from 1828 until his death in 1884. According to Monica Fryckstedt, *Elizabeth Gaskell's Mary Barton and Ruth: A Challenge to Christian England* (Stockholm: Uppsala, 1982), pp. 64-65, there were two wings of Unitarianism active at mid-century. The liberal wing, led by James Martineau and others, contended that the seat of authority lies in reason, a test even Scripture must submit to. The conservative wing, which included Elizabeth and William Gaskell and John Robberds at the Cross Street Chapel, Joseph Ashton at the Brook Street Chapel in Knutsford and William Turner, whom Elizabeth visited at Newcastle as a young woman, believed that authority is derived from Scripture rather than reason.

6. Jenny Uglow, *Elizabeth Gaskell: A Habit of Stories* (New York: Farrar, Straus, Giroux, 1993), p. 73.

7. Michael Wheeler, "Elizabeth Gaskell and Unitarianism," *Gaskell Society Journal* 6 (1992): 32, 34.

8. Raymond V. Holt, *The Unitarian Contribution to Social Progress in England* (London: George Allen and Unwin, Ltd., 1938), p. 277.

9. Fryckstedt, p. 67.

10. Uglow, p. 89. In fact, Ross D. Waller, ed., "Letters Addressed to Mrs. Gaskell by Celebrated Contemporaries Now in the Possession of the John Rylands Library," *Bulletin of the John Rylands Library* 19 (1935): 165, shows that Edwin Chadwick corresponded with Elizabeth Gaskell on October 3, 1851. Chadwick offered to show the Swedish novelist, Fredricka Bremer, new model houses in London. Included with the letter was a copy of a recent report on the origin and spread of cholera.

11. Donald Stone, *The Romantic Impulse in Victorian Fiction* (Cambridge, Massachusetts: Harvard Univ. Press, 1980), p. 40.

12. Valentine Cunningham, *Everywhere Spoken Against: Dissent in the Victorian Novel* (Oxford: The Clarendon Press, 1975), p. 132.

13. Uglow, p. 75; Cunningham, pp. 133-34.

14. Herbert Marcuse, "The Ideology of Death," in *The Meaning of Death,* ed. Herman Feifel (New York: The McGraw-Hill Book Company, Inc., 1959), p. 74.

15. I am indebted to Lenore Davidoff and Catherine Hall, *Family Fortunes: Men and Women of the English Middle Class, 1780-1850* (Chicago: Univ. of Chicago Press, 1987), pp. 32-34, 319, 419-49, for their discussions of what constituted the public and the private at mid-century.

16. Ibid., p. 319.

17. Ibid., pp. 408-09. To recall the Ogdens from *Mary Barton,* neither the widow nor the daughters attended Mr. Ogden's funeral or burial.

18. Deanna L. Davis, "Feminist Critics and Literary Mothers: Daughters Reading Elizabeth Gaskell," *Signs* 17 (1992): 507-32, contends that "the complicated interrelatedness of motherhood and daughterhood have shaped the way feminist critics analyze both the mother/daughter relationship and Gaskell's presentation of feminine nurturance" (p. 509).

19. See Barbara Leah Harman, "In Promiscuous Company: Female Public Appearance in Elizabeth Gaskell's *North and South,*" *Victorian Studies* 31 (1988): 367.

20. Mary Poovey, *Making a Social Body: British Cultural Formation, 1830-1864* (Chicago: Univ. of Chicago Press, 1995), pp. 32-37, delineates this paradox and its relation to abstract space in Adam Smith's *Wealth of Nations.* I find her analysis of Smith's work particularly helpful to my own analysis of Margaret's position in the strike scene and the paradox of her metaphorical death.

Marie E. Warmbold (essay date summer 2000)

SOURCE: Warmbold, Marie E. "Elizabeth Gaskell in *Cornhill* Country." *Victorian Periodicals Review* 33, no. 2 (summer 2000): 138-49.

[*In the following essay, Warmbold examines the works Gaskell contributed to* Cornhill Magazine, *comparing them to works contributed by Anthony Trollope to the same magazine.*]

Elizabeth Gaskell set what would be her last novel, **Wives and Daughters,** which was serialized in the *Cornhill Magazine,* in "the little straggling town" of Hollingford, located in a shire of the English countryside, before the passage of the 1832 Reform Bill, probably to appeal to the *Cornhill's* audience following the stunning example of Anthony Trollope's Barsetshire. The *Cornhill's* audience wanted to be entertained, not exhorted, and they were both nostalgic for the "good old days" of idyllic English country life, which included lords and their shires, and desirous of believing that society could both progress and retain tradition. In his most successful *Cornhill* serials, *Framley Parsonage* and *The Small House At Allington,* Trollope gave them what they wanted. Gaskell, a savvy and gifted periodical writer, did the same, but with some differences. Although Trollope's novels contain a wider cross-section of English society, from the poor curate Mr. Crawley to the Duke of Omnium, from the political parties of the Grants and the Gods to city clerk Johnny Eames, Gaskell focuses on the daughter of the local doctor in a small country town and her growth towards young womanhood. While Trollope's narrator often addresses the reader directly, pointing out his characters and their flaws, as well as apostrophizing on various topics, Gaskell, focusing on Molly Gibson, and to a lesser extent, her stepsister, uses her most self-effacing narrator. Trollope encourages readers to laugh at the follies of his characters. Gaskell, however, focuses solely on building empathy towards her characters, who experience the difficulties and discomfort of unavoidable change.

I

The Cornhill Magazine aimed at the cosmopolitan gentleman, who may have had to earn his money in the city but enjoyed thinking of himself as a country gentleman, and his family. A review of the serial novels published within the magazine's first four years shows that the successful ones catered to this audience.

Cornhill's first editor, W. M. Thackeray, wrote to would-be contributors advising them of the magazine's desire for literature of the highest possible quality. George Smith, the proprietor, desired novels to be descriptive of contemporary English life, society and manners, especially on English rural and provincial life.

Smith commissioned Trollope's *Framley Parsonage,* a story set in the English provinces and involving the clergy. In his *Autobiography* Trollope described the novel:

> The story was thoroughly English. There was a little fox-hunting and a little tuft-hunting, some Christian virtue and some Christian cant. There was no heroism and no villainy. There was much Church, but more love-making.
>
> (106)

The cover of the magazine was also in this mode. It had a black sketch on orange ground, and the sketch showed a ploughman, sower, reaper, and thresher representing the seasons of the year (Huxley 96). It was English country life at its most nostalgic, showing apparently contented workers close to Nature and Nature's abundance.

The first issue of the *Cornhill,* January 1860, began with the first three chapters of *Framley Parsonage.* The first chapter's Latin title: "*Omnes Omnia Bona Dicere*"

translates as "Woe to you when all men speak well of you" (Luke 6:26). The use of a Latin phrase in itself assumes a well-educated audience.[1] And the characters—Mark Robarts and Lord Lufton—are well-educated men who attended Harrow and Oxford together.

The country town, Framley in Barsetshire, the scene of Trollope's earlier successful novels, is described in terms of its politics: "[it is] as true blue a county as any in England. There have been backslidings even here, it is true; but then, in what country have there not been such backslidings? Where, in these pinchbeck days, can we hope to find *the old agricultural virtue in all its purity?*" (*Cornhill* 1:10; emphasis added).

Here are fitting elements for this first issue of *Cornhill*: a humorous conflict in a rural county, involving members of the peerage: Lady and Lord Lufton, the Duke of Omnium, clergy: Mark Robarts, whose living Lady Lufton secured in her parish, and less important local politicians. Trollope's "thoroughly English" story with "no heroism and no villainy" promised comfortable realism. Mark Robarts, the main character, is neither a heaven's cherub nor a fallen devil's spirit. He is a man of manners: his fortune "consisting rather in the highly respectable manner in which he lived, than in any wonderful career of collegiate success" and "the excellence of his general conduct" made his father and family proud (1:2). In other words, he is a type of man that many of the magazine's male readers would identify with.

In addition to Trollope's serial, the article that most sets the tone of this first issue—and subsequent ones—is the first *Roundabout Paper* by Thackeray, "On a Lazy Idle Boy," which closes the issue. The lazy boy is in the country town of Chur: "What a quiet, kind, quaint, pleasant, pretty old town! Has it been asleep these hundred and hundreds of years. [. . .] Time was when there must have been life and bustle and commerce here" (1:125). The young boy is completely engrossed in reading a book, so much so that the narrator conjectures he will never learn his lessons or be on time for supper. "No; it was a NOVEL that you were reading, you lazy, not very clean, good-for-nothing, sensible boy!" (126). Thackeray then compares novels to sweets: everybody likes them, so merchants must supply them, but if you "eat" too many, you will be sick of them. Therefore, *Cornhill* will strive to provide readers with facts as well as fiction. He then lists the credentials and areas of expertise of the articles' authors. But even the imagined setting of Thackeray's editorial essay has a nostalgic feel: a small country town where time seems to have stopped, and where there are no apparent social problems or concerns.

Among the many readers of this first issue of *Cornhill* was Elizabeth Gaskell, who had left Chapman and Hall, her first publisher, and gone to Smith, Elder at the urging of Charlotte Brontë. Gaskell's *The Life of Charlotte Brontë* and *Sylvia's Lovers* were published by Smith, Elder, and Gaskell and Smith had become good friends, exchanging many letters. In a letter to George Smith in late December 1859,[2] she gives her reactions to the first issue: "I extremely like and admire Framley Parsonage,—& the Idle Boy. [. . .] I like Lovel the Widower, only (perhaps because I am stupid,) it is a little confusing on account of its discursiveness [. . .]" (GL 451a). Three months later, in March 1860, she is even more enthusiastic: "I wish Mr. Trollope would go on writing Framley Parsonage for ever. I don't see any reason why it should ever come to an end, and *every one I know is always dreading the last number*. I hope he will make the jilting of Griselda a long while a-doing" (GL 456; emphasis added).

Gaskell found the works closest to the *Cornhill* themes to be the best, and in recognizing the appeal and popularity of Trollope's serial, she followed Trollope's lead. In November 1863, Gaskell's first serial for the magazine[3], **"Cousin Phillis,"** begins; the lead serial is by Trollope—*The Small House At Allington*. Allington is a small country town with Christopher Dale, Esq. living there as squire. In the Small House at Allington lives the Widow Dale, only a Dale by marriage. The fortunes and romances of her two daughters, Lilian (Lily) and Isabella (Bell) provide the focus for the novel, as the fortunes of Molly Gibson and, to a lesser degree, her step-sister Cynthia, are followed in *Wives and Daughters,* which commences in August 1864, four months after Trollope's novel ended.

In the January 1864 issue after Part Three of "Cousin Phillis" is "Yorkshire," a travel piece describing rural England:

> In some of the most secluded parts there are people living who have never been farther than the nearest market town, and many who have never in their lives beheld a railway engine, and are more than content to receive their letters as often as once in the fortnight. [. . .] The women are, according to the old Saxon custom, kept in a certain subjection, and this is in some places so far carried out that they wait upon the men at meals, and do not eat until their masters are served.
>
> (9:96)

The emphasis is on a place where time seems to have stopped, where progress has not yet come. There is a sense of yearning for these places, and even the backward way of treating women is passed over with barely a murmur: "Nevertheless, these dalesmen are a fine, well-grown race, hospitable to strangers, shrewd and honest (except in the matters of horse-dealing). [. . .]"

In this issue, the other fiction is "Margaret Denzil's History" (chapters vii-ix), by Fredrick Greenwood. "Margaret Denzil" is about a prodigal son in France

who impoverishes his family through gambling and giving money to another, recalling Mark Robarts' problems with money and signing notes for payment.

"Cousin Phillis" recalls the country motif. Phillis Holman, the heroine, lives on Hope Farm with her parents, and her father is both farmer and minister. Hope Farm is located in Heathbridge, a small country town, near Hornby, where a small branch line of the railroad is being built. Paul Manning, Phillis' cousin, suggests to his boss, Holdsworth, the engineer of the new line, who is weakened by a low fever, that he recuperate at Hope Farm. During this stay and subsequent visits, love begins to grow between Phillis and Holdsworth.

Phillis, dressed in a pinafore more befitting a child than a young woman of seventeen, is described by Holdsworth as being in a state of "high tranquility" and "pure innocence." "She lives in such seclusion, almost like the sleeping beauty" (9:58).

But the agents of Progress, the railroad and Holdsworth, have disturbed the peaceful idyll, and Gaskell seems to be asking, is it wise to remain so locked in the past? In this long short story, and later in *Wives and Daughters,* Gaskell shows scenes in the past, or in a peaceful place seemingly untouched by the modern world, but she does not indulge the audience's nostalgia completely. Life evolves. In the fourth and final part of **"Cousin Phillis,"** Phillis's tranquility is forever lost. Her love for Holdsworth remains steadfast, but he, relocated to Canada, has married a Canadian beauty. Phillis suffers a long, wasting illness and is never the same; her physical and spiritual bloom is gone forever. In his article "The Education of Cousin Phillis," Philip Rogers argues that "the shame-sickness of her breakdown is [. . .] as much a product of her male education as of her loss of Holdsworth" (28). Yet he notes at the end that Gaskell does give her the will to live, but Phillis is not permitted "to free herself [fully] from regressive nostalgia for the dependence of the 'old days'" (50). Those who remain in the past pay a dear price, for change is inevitable.

Other novelists' contributions did not fit the *Cornhill* as well. They lacked a recognizable English setting and/or appealing characters and story.

Trollope's novels, set in the fictitious county of Barsetshire, fit nicely with the *Cornhill* emphasis on rural and provincial life. But his *The Struggles of Brown, Jones, and Robinson* (August 1861-March 1862), an urban satire on trade and advertising, did not do well. The typical middle-class gentleman reader of the magazine certainly didn't want his family to spend leisure time reading a satire about work. A very negative notice in the *Westminster Review* criticized: "Mr. Trollope's satire is as coarse as the people whom he describes [. . .] It is wasting time to say another word upon this miserable production" (*Trollope: The Critical Heritage* 138-9).

Thackeray's initial contribution, a six-part story, *Lovel the Widower,* "did not quite 'hit the public'" (Ray 303). And his next, *The Adventures of Philip* (January 1861-August 1862), Walter Bagehot concluded in the *Spectator* of August 9, 1862, was a failure in terms of plot and probably did not interest most readers (*Critical Heritage* 307).

Harriet Beecher Stowe's *Agnes of Sorrento* appeared simultaneously as a serial in the *Atlantic Monthly* in the United States and in the *Cornhill Magazine* (May 1861-May 1862) in England. The story, set in Florence in the time of Savonarola with an angelic, innocent young heroine, lacked the intensive research on the period that George Eliot would do for *Romola* for *Cornhill* (July 1862-August 1863). The *Atlantic* editor "grimaced" when he published it in his magazine, and "if the story did not discredit the *Atlantic* it was as poor a piece of fiction as that magazine ever printed in its early years under a celebrated name" (Wilson 464). The ultra-Catholic imagery surely did not suit the *Cornhill* audience either.

After neither *The Struggles of Brown, Jones and Robinson,* nor *The Adventures of Philip,* nor *Agnes of Sorrento*—all running simultaneously—had attracted a popular following, Smith offered George Eliot £10,000 for *Romola* because he needed a successful new serial. A serial novel by Eliot, the most respected woman novelist, would lend prestige, be intelligent and well-written. Her usual publisher, Blackwood, wrote to an employee of his magazine: "it was doubtful in my mind how far it would bear being given in fragments in the Magazine *and certainly it would not suit the readers of the Cornhill*" (Haight 359; emphasis added). Her friend Trollope, after reading the beginning part, cautioned wisely, "Do not fire too much over the heads of your readers. You have to write to tens of thousands, and not to single thousands" (qtd. in Brown xxxvii). Indeed, the novel's "instructive antiquarianism" sometimes quite "drowns the novelist" (Brown xlv). As the *Westminster Review* pointed out, "the general novel-reader is impatient at such details" (Brown xlvi). And Trollope's perception proved to be accurate, for *Romola* did not increase the sale of the magazine, and, as a result, Trollope's novel *The Small House At Allington* began in the third month of *Romola*'s serialization and assumed the opening position after its run.

Elizabeth Gaskell's desire "in acquiring a public voice" (Schor 5) led her to follow the best model she observed: the popular reception of Trollope's serials and how well they fit the magazine. In shaping **Wives and Daughters**

along similar lines, she takes a Trollopean theme, however, in a different direction.

II

Gaskell scholar J. G. Sharps said of **Wives and Daughters**: "There is a Trollopean fidelity about the novel" (477). For example the scene between Squire Hamley and Preston, the Cumnor's land agent, demonstrates "Mrs. Gaskell's Trollopean Englishness" (481). This discussion between members of different classes is the first and only time her characters included members of the aristocracy,[4] the Cumnors and the venerable but poor Hamleys, an indication of Trollope's influence.

Smith had told Trollope he "wanted a English tale, on English life, with a clerical flavour. On these orders [Trollope says] I went to work, and framed what I suppose I must call the plot of *Framley Parsonage*" (*Autobiography* 106). Smith obviously was hoping Trollope would repeat the success of *Barchester Towers.* And Trollope had aimed for verisimilitude, for he wrote about that novel and its characters: "The bishop and Mrs. Proudie were very real to me, as were also the troubles of the archdeacon and the loves of Mr. Slope" (*Autobiography* 78). The archdeacon, Mrs. Proudie, and Dr. Arabin reappear in *Framley Parsonage.* So Trollope wrote again about English life, about a vicar who is somewhat too beholden to the lady who secures his living, and who gets himself in trouble. The narrator obligingly underlines the moral failings.

In Chapter IV, "A Matter of Conscience," Mark Robarts, seeking to advance himself, becomes associated with the crowd at Chaldicotes and the followers of the Duke of Omnium, whom Lady Lufton believes are evil. Trollope's narrator emphasizes the reality of the situation:

> It is no doubt very wrong to long after a naughty thing. But nevertheless we all do. [. . .] And ambition is a great vice. [. . .] But then, how many of us are there who are not ambitious in this vicious manner? And there is nothing viler than the desire to know great people—people of great rank, I should say; nothing worse than the hunting of titles and worshipping of wealth. [. . .] And I trust that the fact of his being a clergyman will not be allowed to press against him unfairly. Clergymen are subject to the same passions as other men; and so far as I can see, give way to them, in one line or another, almost as frequently.
>
> (1:150)

The poor, but upright curate Mr. Crawley cautions him in Chapter XV: "Mr. Robarts, men say that your present mode of life is one that is not befitting a soldier in Christ's army" (1:535). When Robarts' goods and furniture are about to be repossessed near the end of the novel because of bills and notes he signed for Mr. Sowerby, Lord Lufton comes to his rescue, causing Robarts to shed tears of relief and remorse. However, the narrator softens the lesson: "That Mr. Sowerby had been a rogue, I cannot deny. [. . .] But, for all that, in spite of his acknowledged roguery, Lord Lufton was too hard upon him in his judgement. There was yet within him [Sowerby] the means of repentance, could a *locus penitentiae* have been supplied to him" (3:357). Trollope's novels often serve as social guides showing how to avoid problems through right behavior and following suitable models.

But there is more to Trollope's social canvas. The election of the Lord Petty Bag, Harold Smith, the parties of the Grants and the Gods [supposedly the Tories and the Whigs] and the power of the *Jupiter* [the *Times*] to make and unmake political candidates provide wonderful comic moments. Trollope doles out lessons and levity for his readers.

While Trollope emphasizes the moral and the social, Gaskell blends the close interconnections of people in a small town, and how even the smallest thing can affect someone else. She focuses simply on the childhood to early womanhood of Molly Gibson; the opening scenes show Molly awaiting the trip to the Towers, the annual event held by Lady Cumnor to honor those who helped out in the local school she had set up. The characters are shown only as they are involved in the life of the heroine. Gaskell's narrator is less direct than Trollope's:

> They expected to be submitted to, and obeyed; the simple worship of the townspeople was accepted by the earl and countess as a right; [. . .] But, yielded all that obeisance, they did a good deal for the town, and were generally condescending, and often thoughtful and kind in their treatment of their vassals.
>
> (10:131)

By a perceptive choice of words: "worship," "obeisance," "condescending," and especially "vassal"—a feudal term which means one who receives protection in return for homage and allegiance—the picture is sketched. There is no need for apostrophes about backslidings and the "old agricultural virtue," or Lady Lufton's thoughts in defense of hunting while she is speaking to the morally righteous Mr. Crawley (1:532-3).

Gaskell's choice of heroine is also significant in two other ways. As Gaskell notes, the story begins "before the passing of the Reform Bill" and "Five-and-forty years ago, children's pleasures in a country town were very simple" (10:130). Angus Easson observes, "Gaskell is more concerned with a sense of a past world" (WD n.1 689), beginning in 1822, with the main action from early summer 1827 to early autumn 1830 (WD 689 n.2). Thus she was writing about a period that many *Cornhill* readers would remember from their childhood or their parents' childhood. In doing so, she created a

singular effect: not only would her readers feel the longing for the security and peace of "the good old days" but also feel the shock of difference between the then and the now. "For the reader in the mid-1860s, that world of only forty years ago must have seemed strangely remote and separate, so much had happened to transform society in such a short time" (Easson, "Introduction" xiv). Molly Gibson grows up in a changing world as her readers did. *The Small House At Allington* tells the story of Lily and Bell Dale as already grown up and eligible for marriage, a familiar romantic plot line. Part of the problems Molly faces result from her budding young womanhood. When one of Dr. Gibson's students becomes infatuated with her, Dr. Gibson starts to search for a new wife and mother, with disastrous results for both himself and Molly. An unpleasant stepmother becomes part of the pain of growing up.

The problems and moral issues Molly confronts are sketched finely, without a long running commentary on them. Molly's biggest problems arise through her father's second marriage to a woman who is not of his caliber, and through the stepsister she gains. While Trollope goes into great detail on Crosbie's mistaken marriage to Lady Alexandrina, we only intuit Dr. Gibson's error through little comments here and there. For example, when he finds out his wife was eavesdropping on a conversation about Osborne Hamley's health and has used the information for her daughter's advantage: "Mr. Gibson did not answer—did not look at her. His face was very pale, and both forehead and lips were contracted. [. . .] 'Well! I suppose as one brews one must bake?'" (12:16).

Cynthia, following her mother's influence, creates difficulties for Molly in two ways. First, Molly loves Roger Hamley, who reaches an understanding with Cynthia about a future marriage. But Cynthia already had an understanding with Mr. Preston, the Cumnor's land agent, to whom she wrote incriminating letters. Molly is seen twice with him, returning the letters, resulting in town gossip. "Scandal sleeps in the summer, comparatively speaking. Its nature is the reverse of that of the dormouse. [. . .] But when evenings grew short, and people gathered round the fires, and put their feet in a circle—not on the fenders, that was not allowed—then was the time for confidential conversation!" (12:388).

While the Trollopean narrator addresses the reader and uses rhetorical questions to make his moral point, the only comments here are from Gaskell's characters. Mrs. Goodenough, an old lady of the town who has known Molly for years, comes close to the truth: "All as ever I said was that I was surprised at it in Molly Gibson; and that I'd ha' thought it was liker that pretty minx of a Cynthia as they call her; indeed at one time I was ready to swear as it was her Mr. Preston was after" (12:392). Lord Cumnor, however, refers to a report from his old land-agent Sheepshanks as fact: "He says there's a great deal of gossip going on about him [Preston] and Gibson's daughter. They've been caught meeting in the park, and corresponding, and all that kind of thing that is likely to end in a marriage." Lady Harriet first responds: "I shall be very sorry. [. . .] I always liked that girl; and I can't bear papa's model land-agent" (12:410) and later deliberately walks Molly around the town, and thus by association, rescues her good character. The gossip circulating among all the various classes gives the real feeling of a small town near the beginning of the nineteenth century more effectively than a narrator's commentary.

And going off on amusing tangents on political topics or discussing the moral failings or the follies of his characters is one of the trademarks of the Trollopean narrator. Nathaniel Hawthorne created a famous metaphor about Trollope's verisimilitude: It was as if "some giant had hewn a great lump out of the earth and put it under a glass case, with all its inhabitants going about their daily business, and not suspecting that they were being made a show of" (*Critical Heritage* 110). Trollope relished this quote and thought it expressed the aim of his novels perfectly. However, James Kincaid, in his Trollope study, while continuing the Hawthorne metaphor, asks: "Why is it we are so very much aware of the giant, the difficulties he has with the hewing, and the shape and form of the glass case?" (*The Novels of Anthony Trollope* 4).

Henry James, meanwhile, describes Gaskell's narration in *Wives and Daughters* in the following terms: "the gentle skill with which the reader is slowly involved in the tissue of the story; [. . .] the lightness of touch, which, while he stands all unsuspicious of literary artifice, [. . .] the admirable, inaudible, invisible exercise of creative power" (*Critical Heritage* 463). Gaskell developed in this last novel her most self-effacing narrator-for which she earned much critical praise-no doubt because of increasing literary skill but certainly out of reaction to Trollope's genial but intrusive narrator who talks "man-to-man." Both writers aimed for realism, but the reader is less aware of artistic distance in Gaskell. The reader almost feels there is no rhetorical "glass case" as opposed to having his/her nose pushed against it.

That Gaskell refined what she learned from Trollope can be seen in her use of the word "hobbledehoy." When John Eames is introduced at the beginning of the fourth chapter of *The Small House At Allington,* Trollope makes it very clear that this shy and awkward young man is a "hobbledehoy" (6:552). The narrator then goes on to discuss the nature of hobbledehoys for four paragraphs, and for the rest of the novel Eames is identified with this tag, and the reader is never allowed to forget it. At the end when Eames finally becomes a

man, the narrator apologizes: "I feel that I have been in fault in giving such prominence to a hobbledehoy" (9:457).

Gaskell uses the word once simply to describe Roger's thoughts when he first meets Molly:

> He certainly did not seem to care much what impression he made upon his mother's visitor. He was at that age when young men admire a formed beauty more than a face with any amount of future capability of loveliness, and when they are morbidly conscious of the difficulty of finding subjects of conversation in talking to girls in a state of female *hobbledehoyhood.*

> (10:394; emphasis added)

The passage continues, showing both Roger's and Molly's inner impressions of each other at this time. The use of the word here is deft, since it portrays the feelings of a young man, and young men would more likely know the term as a taunt to another clumsy or stupid youth, usually male, and at the time it is how he thinks of Molly. It is also ironic, since Roger is considered by both his parents as "clumsy and heavily built" (10:360), and Molly herself thinks of him as "heavy-looking, clumsy" (10:394) in the passage immediately preceding the above quotation. Gaskell's use of this most Trollopean word indicates she most likely had seen and read it in *The Small House At Allington* serial in *Cornhill,* and how she adapts Trollope. She uses the word to reflect the feelings of the characters, not to label them.

But it is Gaskell's character of Roger Hamley, the scientist, that marks her biggest change from Trollope. Neither *Framley Parsonage* nor *The Small House At Allington* reveals any interest in science or scientists. However, scientific articles in *Cornhill,* such as George Henry Lewes' "Studies of Animal Life" (Jan. 1860-June 1860), discussed Darwin's new evolutionary theory. Gaskell had met Darwin several times and was related to him through marriage. When Gaskell wrote to George Smith on May 3, 1864, she outlined the basic plot of *Wives and Daughters* and described the character of Roger Hamley (then called Roger Newton) as working in natural history, and going around the world as a naturalist—like Charles Darwin (GL 550). Although Gaskell did not live to finish it, there is little doubt that Molly will marry the man of science, "the new man." Indeed, in the last chapter Gaskell wrote, Roger reaches an understanding with Dr. Gibson, Molly's father, before he goes off on his voyage to Africa to collect more scientific specimens. The new couple would probably live in London, as Roger is a scientist, a man of the world, who would perhaps "become professor at some great scientific institution" (13:12). Thus, the novel moves from the nostalgic world of a small town many years ago into a glimpse of the future, and the novel, "far from offering a picture of cozy retrospection and statics, is vividly conscious of (though not insistent upon) evolutionary activity" (Easson, "Introduction" xvi). Darwin's evolutionary ideas could be connected to progress, but they also caused great anxiety because they lacked a moral and divine basis. There is great sorrow in the "old stock" Hamley family, when the refined, handsome but delicate Osborne turns out a failure and dies, and Mrs. Hamley, originally plucked from London society, cannot cope with the Hollingford environment, and she also dies. Change is not always comfortable. But it is common-sense—and also moral—Roger, most like his father, who succeeds and survives.

Trollope's novels of current times fit the yearnings for the past of the *Cornhill* audience by going back to the roots of the pastoral. "The conservative bias we note in these chronicles [the Barsetshire series . . .] is not really different from the defensive quality exhibited by the traditional pastoral in its need to protect itself from the great force of cosmopolitan, sophisticated values" (Kincaid 92-93). The politics of *Framley Parsonage* and the influence of the media, as well as the busy railroad station where Eames assaults Crosbie are very timely, almost too timely, but the "conservative bias" keeps this progress in check. Indeed, "readers go to Trollope for many reasons; no doubt, some perfectly credible if not central—for consolation rooted in nostalgia" (Wright 9). Both of Trollope's novels end with the married couples and most of the other characters of the novel in the pastoral world of the landed aristocracy. Lady Lufton's values still hold primary at the end of *Framley Parsonage*; Lord Lufton and Lucy will spend part of their time at Framley Court where Lady Lufton continues to rule. Mrs. Dale and Lily will still live in the small house on Squire Dale's property in *The Small House*. Both Sowerby and Crosbie get their come-uppance; Johnny Eames grows up. Nobody dies.

Roger Hamley, the younger son of the Squire of Hamley and an old aristocratic family, is a scientist, the "new man," and he and Molly will likely live a more cosmopolitan life. Unlike Trollope's characters, they will not remain in the pastoral world; they will not stay in small Hollingford, still dominated by the aristocratic Cumnors.

Cornhill Magazine gave Trollope the opportunity "to prove his power of gauging public taste" (P. D. Edwards, "Introduction" n.p.). Gaskell, already seasoned with serial audiences from *Household Words,* received the chance to write for a different audience in a less demanding format: monthly deadlines, as opposed to weekly. Both writers skillfully brought their readers back to "simpler" times, but only Gaskell also brings them forward. For Gaskell was not retreating to or "thirsting [. . .] after a lost Arcadia" (Gerin 280). She worked within the narrative conventions of the country novel, only to subvert them for her own purposes, showing a changing world moving forward to a future enriched by scientific knowledge.

Notes

1. The 1989 Oxford University Press edition of *Framley Parsonage* gives the translation and the source in page 583 of the Notes. *Cornhill* does neither. Apparently today's audience is not as well educated as the *Cornhill*'s was assumed to be.

2. Although the first issue of *Cornhill* was dated January 1860, it was on sale before Christmas.

3. A short story, "Curious If True," did appear in the February 1860 issue.

4. See W. A. Craik: "[The Cumnors] embody a higher society than Elizabeth Gaskell has hitherto dealt with" (204) or Arthur Pollard (226).

Works Cited

Bagehot, Walter. "Review of *Philip* in the *Spectator.*" *Thackeray: The Critical Heritage.* Ed. Geoffrey Tillotson and Donald Hawes. New York: Barnes and Noble, 1968. 305-314.

Brown, Andrew. Introduction. *Romola.* By George Eliot. Oxford: Clarendon Press, 1993. xi-lxxii.

Chapple, J. A. V., and Arthur Pollard, eds. *The Letters of Mrs. Gaskell.* Manchester: Manchester UP, 1966. [Abbreviated as *GL.*]

Craik, W. A. *Elizabeth Gaskell and the English Provincial Novel.* London: Methuen and Co., 1975.

Easson, Angus. Introduction. *Wives and Daughters.* By Elizabeth Gaskell. New York: Oxford UP, 1987. ix-xxiv. [Abbreviated as *WD.*]

Edwards, P. D. Introduction. *Framley Parsonage.* By Anthony Trollope. NewYork: Oxford UP, 1989. n. pag.

Gaskell, Elizabeth. "Cousin Phillis." *Cornhill Magazine* 8 (Nov. 1863)–9 (Feb. 1864).

———. *Wives and Daughters.* New York: Oxford UP, 1987.

———. *Wives and Daughters.Cornhill Magazine* 10 (Aug. 1864)–13 (Jan. 1866).

Gerin, Winifred. *Elizabeth Gaskell.* Oxford: Clarendon Press, 1976.

Haight, Gordon S. *George Eliot: A Biography.* New York: Oxford UP, 1968.

Huxley, Leonard. *The House of Smith Elder.* London: William Clowes and Sons, Ltd., 1923.

Kincaid, James. *The Novels of Anthony Trollope.* Oxford: The Clarendon Press, 1977.

Pollard, Arthur. *Mrs. Gaskell: Novelist and Biographer.* Cambridge: Harvard UP, 1966.

Ray, Gordon N. *Thackeray: The Age of Wisdom.* Vol II of 2 vols. New York: McGraw Hill, 1958.

Rogers, Philip. "The Education of Cousin Phillis." *Nineteenth Century Literature* 50 (1995): 27-50.

Schor, Hilary M. *Scheherezade in the Marketplace.* New York: Oxford UP, 1992.

Sharps, John Geoffrey. *Mrs. Gaskell's Observation and Invention.* Sussex: Linden Press, 1970.

Smalley, Donald, ed. *Trollope: The Critical Heritage.* New York: Barnes and Noble, 1969.

Thackeray, William. "Roundabout Papers—No. I On a Lazy Idle Boy." *Cornhill Magazine*1 (1860):124-128.

Trollope, Anthony. *An Illustrated Autobiography.* Wolfeboro, N.H.: Alan Sutton, 1989.

———. *Framley Parsonage.* New York: Oxford UP, 1989.

———. *Framley Parsonage. Cornhill Magazine* 1 (Jan. 1860)–3 (April 1861).

———. *The Small House At Allington. Cornhill Magazine* 6 (Sept. 1862)–9 (April 1864).

Wilson, Forrest. *Crusader in Crinoline: The Life of Harriet Beecher Stowe.* Westport, Conn.: Greenwood Press, 1972.

Wright, Andrew. *Anthony Trollope: Dream and Art.* Chicago: U of Chicago P, 1983.

Elizabeth Starr (essay date winter 2002)

SOURCE: Starr, Elizabeth. "'A Great Engine for Good': The Industry of Fiction in Elizabeth Gaskell's *Mary Barton* and *North and South*." *Studies in the Novel* 34, no. 4 (winter 2002): 385-402.

[*In the following essay, Starr studies the emphasis upon industrial settings and reform themes in* Mary Barton *and* North and South.]

Written in an age that evaded mundane representations of both women's and literary work, Elizabeth Gaskell's social-problem novels express discomfort with commercial and competitive enterprises. By the end of *Mary Barton,* the novel's most public and commercial woman—the prostitute Esther—lies buried in an unmarked grave with the hapless John Barton; in the middle-class home of the Hales in *North and South,* work and payment for services rendered often go unmentioned. Yet Gaskell's fiction also embraces commerce and conflict. As factory workers confront their employers and would-be lovers argue and debate, *Mary Barton* (1848) and *North and South* (1855) place narrators, heroines, and authors firmly at the center of urban industry and social struggle.[1] Despite the novels' frequent maneuvers and omissions—and in some respects through them—*Mary Barton* and *North and South* insistently write fiction onto the industrial landscape. Most notably, by refusing to contain fiction-writing within the figure of the fallen woman or the (albeit unconventional) middle-class ingénue, Gaskell's novels demonstrate an effort to present authorship as a legitimate part of the often aggressive, contentious world of public streets and factories.

Recognizing Gaskell's efforts to find a place for her fictional work in the midst of urban commerce and industry is one way in which contemporary readers can make sense of this writer's struggle to negotiate her public persona and her private integrity. As her novels embody fiction in the social world, they enable Gaskell to make sense of her own incorporation within a literary profession. The significance of reading Gaskell's social-problem novels in this light, then, is two-fold: while the novels suggest that fiction can materially intervene in the conflicts they represent, changing public life and commercial relations because they figure themselves as part of this world, they also require readers and critics to reconsider popular conceptions of a reassuringly domestic, self-effacing, and properly maternal Elizabeth Gaskell. As her correspondence attests, for Gaskell, authorship was both rewarding and discomfiting work. Relishing her first major literary accomplishment after the publication of *Mary Barton,* Gaskell issues an authorial missive to her publisher:

> I find every one here has most convincing proofs that the authorship of Mary Barton should be attributed to a Mrs Wheeler, nèe Miss Stone, and authoress of some book called the 'Cotton Lord'. I am only afraid lest you also should be convinced and transact that part of the business which yet remains unaccomplished with her. I do assure you that I am the author, and so remain
>
> Yours very truly,
>
> E. C. Gaskell[2]

In this letter, Gaskell enthusiastically engages in the "business" of literature. Teasing out the relationship between authorship and commerce, Gaskell assures John Chapman of her willingness to "transact."

Yet as Gaskell was emphatically aware, at the time she was putting her name into print, publicity was largely incommensurate with Victorian womanhood. Gaskell recoiled from the threat such publicity posed to her privacy and integrity as speculation over the initially anonymous *Mary Barton* increased:

> Hitherto the whole affair of publication has been one of extreme annoyance to me, from the impertinent and unjustifiable curiosity of people, who have tried to force

me either into an absolute denial, or an acknowledgment of what they must have seen the writer wished to keep concealed.

(Elizabeth Gaskell to Edward Chapman, 5 December
1848, letter 33, 64)

While these two excerpts can hardly do justice to the complex range of Gaskell's response to authorship as expressed in letters to friends, publishers, admirers and detractors, they distinctly illustrate the conflicted feelings that accompanied her ascension to public notice. This epistolary combination of assurance and reserve plays itself out in the particularly conspicuous publicity of authorial work in Gaskell's social-problem fiction. As Gaskell confronts personal and cultural anxieties surrounding women, labor, and popular fiction, *Mary Barton* and *North and South* present literary work as a means of mediating—and embracing—these conflicts.

Gaskell scholarship frequently notes the specter of inappropriate female publicity in these novels, lurking with the prostitute Esther in *Mary Barton* and circulating beneath rumors about Margaret in *North and South*.[3] This critical attention, however, rarely extends to the novels' internal responses to the danger inappropriate publicity poses to female agency and mobility. As Gaskell's social-problem novels embody literary work, they defend their position as a productive and corrective form of urban industry. In *Mary Barton,* Gaskell's narrator counters the seemingly inevitable translation of feminine publicity into fallenness. As improved printing methods and widespread literacy created larger, paying audiences for fiction, popular novels carried the stigma of debased labor—writing could be viewed as a form of prostitution.[4] As *Mary Barton* takes readers on a sympathetic tour of working-class life, recounting the events leading up to and following the murder of Henry Carson, a mill-owner's son, the novel acknowledges and responds to the censure facing women who walk and work on the streets. By delineating and then severing ties between the prostitute and the woman writer,[5] Gaskell frames her sympathetic representation of the fallen woman Esther with determination not to share her fate.

In *North and South,* Gaskell models fiction's capacity for enabling communication between classes. Like the narrator of *Mary Barton, North and South*'s protagonist Margaret Hale is wary of the consequences of being seen in public. Yet as the increasingly street-savvy heroine encourages a local mill-owner to sympathize with the living and working conditions of his employees, she illustrates narrative's ability to shape social relationships. In both novels, telling stories and constructing coherent accounts of potentially bewildering urban settings and conflicts become prominent and integral parts of the plot. As these stories and accounts surface in various forms—gossip, anecdote, conversation, argument—Gaskell's fiction draws attention to the construction of narrative as a social act. Encouraging readers to see connections between the mundane, varied narratives that circulate on the streets and in the homes of her novels with her own authorship, Gaskell demonstrates her investment in the messy, contentious, and public process of storytelling. Yet like Gaskell's first social-problem novel, *North and South* also emphasizes authorial skill and composure in the midst of urban anxiety and discord, arguing for the inclusion of literary work in labor conflicts. Reading the internal struggles in this novel as evidence of authorial frustration, too often Gaskell's readers focus only on this surface tension: "Written at a moment when working-class women were beginning to accede to the demands of the ideology of domesticity and written by a woman author who was struggling herself toward a sense of 'freedom in working' and of her market value as an author, *North and South* registers in its plot and characterization powerful tensions that lead to silence" (Stevenson 80). Such readings fail to account for either Gaskell's own persistent and prolific engagement in a literary profession or her faith in her own narrative work as a means of mediating, rather than avoiding, social conflict.

Gaskell's intent to present social commentary in *Mary Barton* is clear both in her correspondence with Edward Chapman[6] and in the novel's preface written at his suggestion. As it portrays the movement of a woman writer from private domesticity to public intervention, Gaskell's preface unsettles these conventional boundaries. Initially, the unknown author compounds the anonymity of not putting her name on the title page by indicating that the novel was conceived as a personal, therapeutic occupation. Impressing this privacy on readers, she refuses to disclose the reason why she would need to be thus occupied: "Three years ago I became anxious (from circumstances that need not be fully alluded to) to employ myself in writing a work of fiction." Yet despite her appropriate feminine reserve and self-effacement—"I know nothing of Political Economy, or the theories of trade" (xxvi)—the preface does not, of course, limit itself to domestic matters. The author clearly recognizes the political importance of her work: "whatever public effort can do in the way of legislation, or private effort in the way of merciful deeds, or helpless love in the way of widow's mites, should be done, and that speedily" (xxxvi). Calling her readers to collective and individual action, she identifies herself as an authority on the basis of her familiarity with the working classes and her understanding of the measures that should be taken to help them.

Enacting the preface's implicit connection of private lives and social issues, women frequently move between domestic and public spaces in the pages of *Mary Barton*. Mary's presence in the streets and the courtroom are, perhaps, the most obvious examples of this as she desperately searches an unfamiliar city for Jem Wilson's alibi and them becomes the center of attention in a sensational murder trial. Mary also exemplifies the hazards of public appearance for women. Falling insensible in chapter 32 as a result of the trauma of her experiences, she is quickly relegated to the domestic sphere (first in Manchester, then Canada), where she remains for the rest of the novel.

Like women who publish, women who walk the streets are always vulnerable—subject to speculation and injury. The streets of *Mary Barton* are not grim places in and of themselves—they are used as means of traveling to and from workplaces, homes, and friends, and are often the site of friendly meetings—but they pose particular challenges to women. There are, the narrator notes, appropriate times and reasons to be in public, and pedestrians who exceed these, "all those whose duty, or whose want, or whose errors, caused them to be abroad in the streets of Manchester" (274), face particular scrutiny. Female characters are always particularly subject to speculation, and as a result, "duty," "want," and "errors" prove to be slippery categories. While this slipperiness allows Esther to temporarily disguise herself as a decent working-class wife, it also underlies John Barton's equation of factory girls with loose women and the suspicion Mary faces as she attempts to locate Will Wilson in Liverpool. In *Mary Barton,* this uneasiness extends to any woman in public, including the narrator herself.

The speculation that accompanies women's work and publicity is clearly perilous for a narrator whose mobility is the source of her authority. Like the implied author of the preface, the narrator of *Mary Barton* speaks with a personal voice and argues for the public import of her novel, repeatedly drawing attention to the skillful navigation of the complex settings and cultural codes that literary work requires. Presenting herself as guide, Gaskell's narrator confidently directs readers through the "many half-finished streets, all so like one another, that you might have easily been bewildered and lost your way" (11-12). Footnotes explaining the dialect used by characters and referencing examples of working-class culture also emphasize this narrating persona's facility at moving between regions and communities: "Do you know 'The Oldham Weaver'? Not unless you are Lancashire born and bred, for it is a complete Lancashire ditty. I will copy it for you" (37). Drawing attention to her familiarity with both urban and rural settings, these asides serve as the basis for her authority.

Rather than shying away from the consequences of public exposure, Gaskell's narrator firmly establishes herself in the midst of the characters and streets she represents. Admittedly, as an omniscient narrator, she doesn't share the physical limitations of the average pedestrian:

she is able to move freely in and out of public and private spaces, to convey events from bedrooms as well as from courtrooms, and to know, in most cases, what is going on in the minds of her characters as well as to speak with authority on wider public and social issues. This narrator, however, makes a point of locating herself in the story, stressing her familiarity with characters and places, and establishing her presence in Manchester while the events she describes took place.[7]

While the novel remains uneasy about female publicity, then, Gaskell's text is invested in its narrator's public knowledge and mobility. This conflict shapes the relationship between the narrator and the prostitute. As the narrator reveals that, for Esther, fallenness is not the outcome of her preference for finery and public flirtation (as John Barton maintains) but of the pressing need, in the face of her child's suffering, to work, she sympathetically presents Esther as her contemporary; when readers initially see Esther on the streets, she is occupied with plot rather than prostitution. Esther's first impulse after her return to Manchester is to locate and construct the stories of her friends' and family's lives: "I used to watch about the court where John lived, for many and many a night, and gather all I could about them from the neighbors' talk . . . I put this and that together, and followed one and listened to the other" (190). Esther gets her bearings by making a coherent narrative; here, and throughout *Mary Barton,* Esther's activity sounds strikingly like the authorial work of navigating streets, plot, and character.

As *Mary Barton* progresses, the narrating persona and the prostitute, both mothers suffering from the death of a child, share experiences and operate under similar restraints. The narrator's revelation of her own loss comes late in the novel, as friends keep vigil with the unconscious Alice. Describing Alice's dreams, the narrator digresses: "that land whose scenes are unspeakable terrors, are hidden mysteries, are priceless treasures to one alone,—that land where alone I may see, while yet I tarry here, the sweet looks of my dear child" (316). This interruption, often read as an insertion of Gaskell's private tragedy, echoes Esther's dream in which her mother, sister, and child circle her bed (192). Esther's child, the evidence of her fallenness and the impetus for her tainted profession, serves as a powerful tie between prostitute, narrator, and, once Gaskell's identity became known, the author herself.

The fact that the author's identity *wasn't* known with the initial publication of *Mary Barton* heightens the association of the narrator with the prostitute. In another interruption of the novel, the narrator makes a telling disclosure in the courtroom at Jem's trial: "I was not there myself; but one who was, told me . . ." The narrator takes this bold step into the text of *Mary Barton* at the height of the trial as Mary is placed on the witness stand. This scene is fraught with the perils of public exposure, as Mary, a spectacle for a sensation-hungry audience, collapses under the doubled stress of having to disclose personal secrets in public while battling to keep her knowledge of her father's guilt secret. The culmination of this charged scene is the successful result of Mary's earlier foray into public, as her inquiries in the streets of Liverpool secure the entrance of a witness who saves Jem (381). In the face of so many intersections of the personal and the public, it is a significant point for the narrator to make her own presence, or lack thereof, explicit. Yet this admission does not only clarify the fact that the narrator was *not* present at Jem's trial; it also situates her as a figure who is capable of being present (and who therefore must bring attention to her absence). Though this passage, coming directly after a mild condemnation of the unladylike characteristic of coming to a trial to gape at someone else's tragedy, can be read as an indication that the narrator is too reputable to be present at such an unladylike event (though she's not too ladylike to hear about it afterwards), this disclosure also identifies the narrator with Esther, who both has informants and, since she can't bear to be seen in the light of day, would be equally unable to appear at the trial. In this admission, *Mary Barton* draws attention to how the pressure not to be seen has equal effect on the respectable woman and the remorseful prostitute.

These connections between narrator and prostitute themselves speak to a profound anxiety about the public circulation of women. Yet the significance of this association in Gaskell's novel is the effect of Esther's fallenness on her discursive work. While Esther benefits from a freedom of movement and a ring of sources that allow her to collect information, the narrator is also careful to point out Esther's profound difficulties passing on this information: "To whom shall the outcast prostitute tell her tale . . . Hers is the leper-sin, and all stand aloof dreading to be counted unclean" (185). As the source of Esther's authority undermines the use she would make of it, she is separated from her audience. While the narrator may sympathize with these limitations, she goes to some length to demonstrate that she doesn't share them. Certainly, Esther's attempts to gather bits and pieces of information, "greedily listening to every word of the passers-by, and loitering near each group of talkers, anxious to scrape together every morsel of information, or conjecture, or suspicion," do not compare favorably with the narrator's repeated references to the depth and breadth of her own understanding and knowledge of the streets of Manchester. Esther's information-collecting is "without any definite purpose" (277); "The time was past when there was much wisdom or consistency in her projects" (278). At the points when Esther's work most resembles her own, the narrator takes care to emphasize the damage done to denigrated narratives and narrators.

While Gaskell's text attempts to gather sympathy for Esther, then, it also requires the removal of the inappropriately commercial and public woman. The novel ultimately severs connections between Gaskell's authorship and Esther's debased labor, asserting the skill and value of its own narrative work. Esther herself overestimates her responsibility for the events that unfold around her. When, for example, she believes that she has led Jem to murder Henry Carson, readers know that she has only helped to instigate an argument that places suspicion on him. Her influence is mitigated both by her own sense that her actions are determined by outside forces ("The black curse of Heaven rested on all her doings"), and the narrator's sympathetic emphasis of her "Poor diseased mind!" (277). Absent from the point of her covert meeting with Mary in chapter 21, Esther's reappearance in the last chapter emphasizes her irreversible decline. As Jem searches the streets, Esther surfaces only in a series of external layers: references to her clothing, her street name, and a description of her as "nought but skin and bone" (461). When Esther finally shows up on the Barton doorstep, she melts into "a heap of white or light-colored clothes . . . the poor crushed Butterfly" (462). The narration of Esther's last days thereby physically enacts the evacuation of her ominous presence.

With the threat of Esther and Mary's publicity resolved, the novel can focus readers' attention on the results of its characters' circulation on the streets. The industrialist Mr. Carson's transformation is motivated by the fact that he has been physically present in the homes of his workers, and therefore can more clearly understand the extent of their distress: "Mr. Carson had been accustomed to poverty; not the grinding squalid misery he had remarked in every part of John Barton's house, and which contrasted strangely with the pompous sumptuousness of the room in which he now sat" (436). By extension, the novel indicates that readers who have witnessed these scenes should be moved to similar sympathetic action.[8]

The removal of tainted street authority also frees the narrator to emphasize her own knowledge of the streets. In this way, both by identifying with and distinguishing herself from Esther, the narrator in *Mary Barton* counters negative portrayals of female public authority; *Mary Barton* is as much a portrayal of Gaskell's determination to legitimate literary work as it is a portrayal of her sympathy for the working classes. Always sensitive to the material consequences of reputation for women—as this reputation shaped every aspect of their life and labor within communities—Gaskell defends this valuable literary work against the violence done to women who appear in public. This defense entails its own act of (albeit sympathetic) literary violence—the removal of a character whose presence threatens the integrity of her own public mobility, an aggressive legitimization of female authorship and public authority that was crucial for Gaskell's own standing within Victorian ideologies of gender, work, and respectability. This complex reaction to Esther—garnering sympathy for her position and questioning others' overly simplistic assessments of her fall while yet rejecting the problems she poses—is part of the novel's efforts to place itself within (and to help resolve) urban social conflict. Yet focusing, as Patsy Stoneman does, only on the removal of female characters (with the notable exception of the singer Margaret, a fellow artist) from *Mary Barton,* mothers, and Gaskell's own literary motherhood, seemingly get drowned out in a flood of fictional and fiction-writing fathers (85).[9] This is not the case when we recognize the significant female presence—Gaskell's implied author/narrator—who effectively secures her position as a public authority. Gaskell's next industrial social-problem novel attests to the centrality of this authority as her characters again hit the streets in order to demonstrate the social value of narratives that can transcend boundaries between classes and separate spheres.

Gaskell's correspondence during the composition of *North and South* shows evidence of absorbing and sometimes frustrating literary work. In a letter to Emily Shaen, she narrates the process of working through disjointed characterizations and ideas and organizing them into the plot of a novel:

> when they've quarrelled [sic], silently, after the lie and she knows she loves him, and he is trying not to love her; and Frederick is gone back to Spain and Mrs Hale is dead and Mr Bell has come to stay with the Hales, and Mr Thornton ought to be developing himself—and Mr Hale ought to die—and if I could get over this next piece I could swim through the London life beautifully into the sunset glory of the last scene. But hitherto Thornton is good; and I'm afraid of a touch marring him; and I want to keep his character consistent with itself, and large and strong and tender, and *yet a master.* That's my next puzzle. I am enough on not to hurry; and yet I don't know if waiting and thinking will bring any new ideas about him.
>
> (27 October 1854, letter 217, 321)

Despite her concerns about how the project will develop, this is an assured voice describing work in terms of a logical progression of tasks. This letter, written in October of 1854 at the height of her editorial struggles with Charles Dickens over the serial publication of *North and South* in *Household Words,* shows Gaskell's sense of authorial assurance at a point at which this assurance is widely held to have been at an ebb.[10] Other letters written during the composition and publication of *North and South* testify to this struggle. In a letter to Anna Jameson, the author's description of the circumstances under which she was forced to write is direct and antagonistic:

> though I had the plot and characters in my head long ago, I have often been in despair about the working of them out; because of course, in this way of publishing it, I had to write pretty hard without waiting for the happy leisure hours. And then 20 numbers was, I found my allowance; instead of the too scant 22 . . . Every page was grudged me, just at last, when I did certainly infringe all the bounds & limits they set me as to quantity.
>
> (January 1855, letter 225, 328)

In the opening pages of the two-volume edition of *North and South,* the author's note also draws attention to this frustrating lack of control, this time in diplomatic terms: "Although these conditions were made as light as they well could be, the author found it impossible to develop the story in the manner originally intended, and, more especially, was compelled to hurry on events with an improbable rapidity towards the close" (5).

Despite this apology, the opening pages of *North and South* echo the preface to *Mary Barton* as Gaskell reasserts authorial competence. The note quickly proceeds from an acknowledgment of the extent to which the text was shaped (and marred) "by the requirements of a weekly publication," to an assertion that emphasizes her modifications: "In some degree to remedy this obvious defect, various short passages have been inserted, and several new chapters added" (5). While the preface to *Mary Barton* is careful to acquaint readers with the author's ability to maintain her private identity while intervening in complex social and political issues, this opening proves her ability to reclaim the integrity of a text that has been subjected to the commercial constraints of serialization.

By emphasizing the author's renewed control over the plot, this opening note sets in motion an emphasis on the valuable work of constructing and revising narrative that informs the novel's thematic content. *North and South* extends the emphasis of the narrator's presence in *Mary Barton,* providing a concrete model of the implications of and possibilities for women's literary work. Like *Mary Barton,* then, *North and South* concerns itself with complex social issues in order to emphasize its own literary intervention in these issues.[11] In *Mary Barton,* the narrator defends her efficacious narration by distinguishing it from the commercial and determining associations of fallenness. *North and South* demonstrates how the protagonist Margaret Hale is able to defend herself from similar threats as she intervenes in social conflicts. In *North and South,* I will argue, this work takes two forms. First, as Margaret struggles to redirect misleading accounts of her behavior, she practices a form of self-representation that echoes Gaskell's efforts in her novels and correspondence to shape her public image. Second, as Margaret models the process by which the novel attempts to mobilize corrective storytelling[12] in the service of reconciliation between classes, she modifies the false perceptions held by workers and mill-owners alike. In both cases, *North and South* represents the challenges Gaskell associated with her commercially successful social-problem fiction.

Though the first readers of the anonymously-authored *Mary Barton* couldn't be completely certain who was walking the streets, by the time of its serial publication, *North and South* was readily identified with an established literary reputation. While in accordance with convention in *Household Words,* installments did not include a byline, they did proclaim with each section, "By the Author of *Mary Barton,*" who was then widely known to be Elizabeth Gaskell. By linking this novel with the earlier text, *Household Words* both highlights the commercial nature of these installments (as Dickens was hoping to capitalize off of Gaskell's popularity to sell magazines), and links the two works of social fiction even before they were linked as a genre.

The two novels were certainly connected for Gaskell. Working through a frustrating and exhausting series of deadlines, she was composing a novel that would respond to reviewers' critiques and her own reservations about *Mary Barton.* Reading the two novels against each other immediately marks the differences in their treatment of similar problems. Aside from the obvious shift in point of view, in which the later novel is focalized largely through the genteel middle-class Hale family and industrial, newly middle-class Thorntons, *North and South* is often considered the more conventional text. One of the explanations for this novel's less dramatic effect has to do with the comparatively unintrusive presence of its narrating guide (D'Albertis 63; Schor 122). Unlike the narrator of *Mary Barton,* the narrator of *North and South* makes no overt reference to either her direct participation in or knowledge of events. Yet while an extradiegetic-homodiegetic narrator in *Mary Barton* gives way to a heterodiegetic narrator in *North and South,* the authoritative voice still definitely resides in and manages the text; by the end of the novel, the effects of influential narratives are palpable and significant.

While Margaret Hale is the primary focalizer in *North and South*—the novel opens with Margaret contemplating her sleeping cousin and continues to filter events through her point of view—the narrator does not directly identify herself with her protagonist.[13] As the narrator works to distinguish Margaret from her relatives throughout the first chapter, she makes her own discriminating authorial presence known. Certainly by contrasting Margaret's thoughtful behavior with unflattering assessments of her relatives, the narrator lends authority to Margaret's person and values, and the narrator's physical descriptions of her as "the tall stately girl of eighteen" do little to qualify this (10). Yet at the point where the narrator most emphatically denies any family resemblance between Margaret and the rest of her aunt's household, she makes a perceptive shift. As Margaret obligingly models her cousin's Indian shawls for guests, the narrator quietly steps in by making the observation no one else in the room is qualified to make:

"No one thought about it; but Margaret's tall, finely made figure . . . set off the long beautiful folds of the gorgeous shawls that would have half-smothered Edith" (11). As the narrator encourages readers to identify with Margaret, then, she also encourages them to recognize a source of authority that exceeds hers. Significantly, it is by noting the limitations of the information and impressions the reader receives—"the *fragments* of conversation" (emphasis added 8)—that the narrative initially establishes its sympathetic, but incomplete, connection with Margaret. As Margaret's initial lack of *savoir faire* compares unfavorably to the streetwise narrator, the novel sets the stage for the development of her narrative skills. Rather than standing in for the narrator or implied author's concerns, she is used as a means of working through these concerns.

The Hales set up residence in the industrial town of Milton-Northern for the very reason that it will prove foreign to them, in the words of Margaret's father, "'Because I know no one there, and no one knows Helstone, or can ever talk to me about it'" (38). In Milton-Northern, the Hales are an anomaly, and much of the novel draws attention to the conflict of social codes that results from the clash of the industrial wealth and influence of the Thorntons and the cultural capital of the relatively impoverished Hales. Once in Milton-Northern, the Hales discover that they are outside their realm of influence, and they are able to secure adequate living quarters only with the help and direction of Mr. Hale's student and employer, John Thornton.

Thornton's confusion about what to do with Margaret sets in motion the first of several relationships in which she will play a transformative role. While the Hales may not have the status, in the eyes of their landlord, to rate new, tasteful wallpaper, Margaret makes John Thornton reassess his initial impression of the family: "Mr. Thornton had thought the house in Crampton was really just the thing; but now that he saw Margaret, with her superb ways of moving and looking, he began to feel ashamed of having imagined that it would do very well for the Hales" (63). As John and Margaret develop a relationship based on mutual admiration and conflict, the novel's romance plot leads to a reworking of worker/industrialist relations.[14]

Margaret's uncertain status in Milton-Northern is reminiscent of the anxiety about female authority in *Mary Barton*; once again, this anxiety surfaces in terms of women's presence on the streets. As Margaret walks the public streets, however, she's less likely to have her class-status or occupation misinterpreted. Instead, when she is swept up in the crowds of workers going to and from factories, it is the very legibility of her position that initiates "loud laughs and jests" among working-class pedestrians, "particularly aimed at all those who appeared to be above them in rank or station." Inexperience is the only real threat, and the narrator is quick to qualify Margaret's distress with her own street-savvy: "the very out-spokenness marked their innocence of any intention to hurt her delicacy, as she would have perceived if she had been less frightened by the disorderly tumult" (72). Margaret's growing navigational competence will later serve as adequate protection from more legitimately grim streets. As she observes "unusual loiterers . . . men with their hands in their pockets sauntering along; loud-laughing and loud-spoken girls clustered together, apparently excited to high spirits, and a boisterous independence of temper and behavior," she's able to avoid the indignity of "the discredible minority . . . commenting pretty freely on each passer-by" by redirecting her steps to the home of Nicholas and Bessy Higgins, working-class friends (131). Like the narrator of *Mary Barton,* Margaret's integrity ultimately remains intact because of her ability to navigate.

Being in public is a less daunting enterprise for Margaret (and for an established author), and streets continue to function as a site for Gaskell's social-problem fiction to model literary work. In *North and South,* city streets serve as a backdrop for Margaret's developing social skills as she is forced to reassess her rural assumptions about appropriate forms of sympathetic engagement. Early in her introduction to Milton-Northern, Margaret's acquaintance with factory-worker Nicholas Higgins and his daughter Bessy unsettles her initial, automatic recourse to paternalistic benevolence: "at Helstone it would have been an understood thing, after the inquiries she had made, that she intended to come and call upon any poor neighbor whose name and habitation she had asked for." Yet, as "[i]t seemed all at once to take the shape of an impertinence on her part; she read this meaning too in the man's eyes" (74), she is forced to reconsider the implications of her assumptions. As the influence of Margaret's experiences on the street spread, her changing relationship with the Higginses shapes her exchanges with John Thornton over questions of the proper relationship between managerial and working classes.

Margaret's most dramatic intervention in the social debates of the novel is indisputably her impulsive decision to stand as a shield between a mob of desperate workers and the resolute John Thornton. Yet what makes this scene dramatic is not only its portrayal of Margaret as the object of scrutiny "in face of that angry sea of men" (176),[15] but its resonance, as the novel emphasizes the many different versions of the scene that circulate after the fact. While the strike scene itself is contained in chapter 22, significantly titled "A Blow and Its Consequences," the narrative consequences are palpable for the next three chapters. The fact that the novel goes to such lengths to dramatize these various interpretations signifies the extent to which, in this novel, events don't exist apart from the narrative accounts of them. As Margaret sorts through both her own and other versions of the confrontation, she exemplifies a determination to shape and alter perceptions that parallels the work Gaskell imagined for authorship.

Immediately following her dramatic intervention, Margaret indignantly rejects misleading descriptions of the scene. Before she has fully recovered consciousness from her blow, she encounters the first version, a statement which is already weighted with the apparent authority of a first-person point of view: "Sarah, you see, was in the best place for seeing, being at the right-hand window; and she says, and said at the very time too, that she saw Miss Hale with her arms about master's neck, hugging him before all the people" (181). The story quickly passes from Fanny Thornton to her mother, and while both claim skepticism at first, ultimately the very existence of this account carries enough explanatory force that both sister and mother become convinced of Margaret's designs on John Thornton. Margaret leaves the Thornton home shaken, and is only able to recover by reassuring herself of the authority of her own point of view: "She looked up, and a noble peace seemed to descend and calm her face" (189). Margaret then pits her version of events against the prevailing account as she first responds to John Thornton by pointing out his misinterpretation—"'you seem to have imagined, that I was not merely guided by womanly instinct, but . . . that I was prompted by some particular feeling for you'" (193)—and then counters Bessy's more overtly flawed report: "'they do say, that Boucher threw a stone at Thornton's sister, that welly killed her'" (198). At this point in the novel, it is not simply the threatening consequences of a woman's presence in public that are at issue, but the representations of this presence. While, as Deborah Nord argues, it is true that Margaret suffers at the hands of these dangerously influential narratives (174), she's also able to muster her own representational power with a counter narrative that more fairly dignifies her position.

Ultimately, the public circulation of narrative proves to be the most powerful force of the novel. Margaret's initial encounter with the Higginses on the street starts a chain of events that eventually leads to a successful, if contentious, model of mutual respect between industrialist and worker. John Thornton and Margaret Hale's relationship coalesces around a series of exchanges that sets the process of change in motion. In the midst of these discussions, Margaret presents an argument that draws attention to the value of narrative skill. As she tells the story of a wealthy man who refuses to educate his son "'in order to save him from temptation and error,'" and argues against the corresponding practice of treating workers as inferiors, Margaret encourages her listeners to note not only that the child of her story grows up morally bankrupt, but also that he lacks the means of caring for himself: "'He could not even use words effectively enough to be a successful beggar.'" In this rhetorical move, Margaret both asserts and models narrative power, power that can be used as a tool for survival, and, as John Thornton acknowledges, as "a weapon against me" (121).

These rhetorical exchanges between Thornton and Margaret are transformative not only as each gradually grows to respect the other, but also as they foster another crucial and contentious exchange in the novel: that between Thornton and Higgins. In an echo of Margaret's appeal to Thornton to "'Go down and face them like a man. . . . Speak to your workmen as if they were human beings'" (175), Margaret first visualizes and then brings about the friendship between industrialist and worker: "'If he and Mr Thornton would speak out together as man to man—if Higgins would forget that Mr Thornton was a master, and speak to him as he does to us—and if Mr Thornton would be patient enough to listen to him with his human heart, not with his master's ears'" (302). While Higgins and Thornton's relationship begins with an antagonistic meeting, Margaret's influence has a profound material result. Like Mr. Carson in *Mary Barton,* who only truly understands the depth of his workers' poverty when he sees the inside of John Barton's home, Thornton's visits to Higgins lead him to see the "'greasy cinder of meat, as first set me a-thinking.'" As Thornton describes it, his resulting plan is fostered through direct rhetorical conflict:

> "So I spoke to my friend—or my enemy—the man I told you of—and he found fault with every detail of my plan; and in consequence I laid it aside . . . when suddenly this Higgins came to me and graciously signified his approval of a scheme so nearly the same as mine, that I might fairly have claimed it. . . . I was a little 'riled,' I confess."
>
> (353)

The discord of this relationship, rather than being erased by the founding of a cooperative dining room, in which Thornton and the workers institute a self-supporting system for supplying food at cost, actually fosters healthy conflict as workers and industrialist regularly disagree over shared meals.

As the narrator calmly asserts, it is this kind of active, interpersonal struggle which enables real progress: "Once brought face to face, man to man, with an individual of the masses around him, and (take notice) out of the character of master and workman, in the first instance, they had each begun to recognize that 'we have all of us one human heart'" (409). While, as Thornton himself admits, this model does not guarantee the end of all conflict, even in the more directly hostile form of future strikes, these exchanges do result in informative

and curative discourse: "Besides this improvement of feeling, both Mr Thornton and his workmen found out their ignorance as to positive matters of fact, known heretofore to one side, but not to the other" (410). What the combination of antagonistic, conflicting points of view ultimately results in, then, is something more closely resembling a full, accurate picture.

As Hilary Schor deftly notes, literature, conceptualized conventionally and narrowly, does not enact much change in this novel.[16] Mr. Hale's initial attempts to impart "literature, or high mental cultivation" (69) to John Thornton fall by the wayside, fulfilling the implied critique in Margaret's first response to her father's new vocation: "'What in the world do manufacturers want with the classics, or literature, or the accomplishments of gentlemen?'" (40). Yet rather than reading this failure merely in terms of a general dismissal or frustration with the limited power of literature to effect real influence or change, it is important to recognize what Mr. Hale's tutelage is replaced with. If Thornton falls off in his studies, "he came very seldom. . . . Mr Hale was disappointed in his pupil's lukewarmness about Greek literature, which had but a short time ago so great an interest for him" (331), it is because Thornton is instead spending his evenings with the Higginses. Rather than evidence of the failure of literature, Thornton's shift in alliances actually emphasizes the success of a specific literary enterprise, notably that of *Mary Barton* and *North and South,* to bring readers into contact with the antagonistic narratives of different classes in an effort to transform these differences into direct, meaningful relationships. Rather than positing literature's inability to intervene in real world issues, then, *North and South* leads to a reassessment of what "the literary" is and what it can do.

In a letter to Lady Kay-Shuttlesworth after the publication of *Mary Barton,* Gaskell's response to her friend's critiques prefigures the conclusion of *North and South*:

> "You say 'I think there are good mill-owners; I think the factory system might be made a great engine for good'; and in this no one can more earnestly and heartily agree with you than I do. I can not imagine a nobler scope for a thoughtful energetic man, desirous of doing good to his kind, than that presented to his powers as the master of a factory."
>
> (16 July 1850, letter 72A, 119)

In 1850, Gaskell's suggestion of this premise was accompanied by a disclaimer that she was not qualified (either by experience or gender) to write the novel that should follow *Mary Barton*: "It would require a wise man, practical and full of experience, øne/ able to calculate consequences, to choose out the best among the many systems which are being tried by the benevolent mill-owners" (letter 72A, 120). By 1853, however,

Gaskell envisioned this "'great engine for good'" within her fiction. Writing a novel that attempted to address working-class unrest from the point of view of the male, middle-class industrialist as well as the working classes, Gaskell took up the task she claims appropriate for "a wise man, practical and full of experience." As the project of writing social-problem novels moved Gaskell into conventionally male spheres of experience and expertise, she illustrated the revisionist potential of literature by asserting its connection to social and economic relations. Foregrounding her own labor against the background of labor conflicts and illustrating how her presence fostered solutions to these conflicts, Gaskell addressed any uneasiness she may have felt about appearing before readers in print by providing repeated assurances of the public value of her work.

Notes

1. Even before the publication of *Mary Barton,* Gaskell's early work employed urban settings and social themes. "Sketches Among the Poor," written with her husband William Gaskell and published in *Blackwood's Magazine* in 1837, narrates the decline and death of a transplanted country-girl near the end of her life who occupies a "dark house" on "gloomy streets" and longs to return to her rural childhood home. In "Libbie Marsh's Three Eras," published under a pseudonym in *Howitt's Journal* in 1847, Gaskell sets her short story about working-class characters in industrial Manchester.

2. Elizabeth Gaskell to Edward Chapman, 3 November 1848, letter 31 of *The Letters of Mrs. Gaskell.* Chapple and Pollard 63. All future references to Gaskell's correspondance are to this source.

3. See especially Schor; Nord 157-60; D'Albertis; and Harman 351-74.

4. Also see Gallagher, "George Eliot and Daniel Deronda," 39-62.

5. Anderson's claim that "discourses on prostitutes and representations of fallen women register Victorian culture's most extreme threats to cherished notions of private selfhood and autonomous self-control" (47) is particularly resonant for Gaskell at points in her career in which she was working to establish and maintain control over her own authorial persona. See also D'Albertis.

6. Gaskell writes: "I am, (above every other consideration,) desirous that it should be *read*; and if you think there would be a better chance of a large circulation by deferring it's [sic] appearance, of course I defer to your superior knowledge, only repeating my own belief that the tale would bear directly upon the present circumstances." From Elizabeth Gaskell to Edward Chapman, 13 April 1848, letter 24, 56.

7. See Warhol's discussion of the "engaging narrator" in *Mary Barton.* Also see Lanser's influential combination of narratological and feminist analysis.

8. Anderson argues that Esther stands in as a generic representative of melodrama in a novel that instead means to function as social realism. In this reading, Esther, as a melodramatic figure, poses a threat to the novel's attempt to incite sympathetic, active response on the part of readers (112-26).

9. Stoneman's reading of *Mary Barton* culminates in the novel's emphasis on fatherhood as a means of addressing class differences as well as Gaskell's authorship. For Stoneman, fatherhood underlies the resolution of class conflict in the novel, and Mary's distress in having to deal with her own father's secret is the dilemma that drives Mary out of the story into a silent, marginalized motherhood. Yet while the end of the novel does entail the marginalization of its title character, I contend that the significant presence in the text is not Mary, but the narrator: a female, literary voice which not only works to prove its control in the text, but also clearly finds a place for itself throughout the novel.

10. See Hughes and Lund. Stevenson focuses on Gaskell's struggle during this period, arguing that the portrayal of uncertainty about the power and merit of women's speech within the novel itself is a strong indication both of Gaskell's frustrations with what proved to be her most alienating project, "the work most clearly produced under severe time restraints and subject to direct market pressure" (70), and of Gaskell's more general ambivalence about women's work (80).

11. Though this reading of *North and South* is indebted to Gallagher's attention to the self-consciousness of *North and South* in *The Industrial Reformation,* I take issue with her assertion that the novel enacts a pervasive critique of its own realist project. According to Gallagher, "*North and South* is partly a book about metonymy because it is a book about the difficulty of interpreting the surfaces of reality, of finding the meaning of objects, words, and actions" (179). While I agree that the novel does address this difficulty, my reading falls more into line with that of Rosemarie Bodenheimer as she argues: "Revising paternalistic images of government, views of the working class, and the separate women's sphere, Gaskell's narrative is itself an enactment of the experimental social activity it recommends, for it takes us through a general break down of traditional ways of thinking about society and into the confusion generated by the process of working toward new ones" (55). More specifically, I contend

that Gaskell presents an argument for the valuable work of social change through encounters with influential narratives.

12. See also Anderson's compelling reading of the ending of *North and South* as a model of "the Habermasian communicative ideal" in action (233): "Gaskell thereby articulates a model of communicative practice aimed not merely at mutual understanding but at social transformation, and mediated not only by rational discourse but by a sympathetic, continually renewed, nonreified recognition of the other" (140).

13. Critical treatments of the novel often make this direct connection between Margaret and the implied (or actual) author. According to Nord, "Her [Margaret's] experiences act as a mirror of Gaskell's own" (173). Gallagher, in *Industrial Reformation,* also makes this connection between the implied author and Margaret, the "implied author . . . establishing her narrative vantage point in this heroine's mind" (171). By so completely connecting Margaret's point of view with that of the implied author, however, Gallagher's emphasis falls on Margaret's own frustrations and limitations. As I will argue, it's the narrator's *use* of Margaret that lends coherence to Margaret's and the novel's narrative projects.

14. This reading of Margaret and John's relationship as a model of, rather than a distraction from, the political plot of the novel differs from that of Gallagher: "When the class conflict becomes unresolvable without extreme violence, the plot turns into a love story" (106). For another reading of distracting romance plots, see Yeazell.

15. Harman notes the heightened tension surrounding Margaret's actions in this scene, connecting it to a more general concern for women who allow themselves to be seen and heard: "illicit sexuality in *North and South* is just another name for female publicity" (371). This reading nicely connects the narrator's concerns about Margaret with *Mary Barton*'s narratorial concern with Mary and Esther. While Harman argues that Gaskell ultimately reconciles herself to this connection, however, I argue that Gaskell responds to the threat of publicity with a faith in the woman writer's ability to shape her public image. While, unlike Nord, I agree with Harman that both Margaret and the implied author find room for themselves *as* public figures in the novel, I maintain that she finds this position through an avocation of literary work rather than (as Harman suggests) celebratory, if also treacherous, female public appearance.

16. According to Schor: "the novel is deeply skeptical about solutions per se, and specifically, about fiction itself as a solution; *North and South* raises its own criticism of the Condition-of-England Novel it is usually assumed to be, and of the myth of the all-knowing author, who proposes, disposes, and resolves the differences between 'the Two Nations'" (121).

Works Cited

Anderson, Amanda. *Tainted Souls and Painted Faces: The Rhetoric of Fallenness in Victorian Culture.* Ithaca: Cornell UP, 1993.

Bodenheimer, Rosemarie. *The Politics of Story in Victorian Social Fiction.* Ithaca: Cornell UP, 1988.

D'Albertis, Dierdre. *Dissembling Fictions: Elizabeth Gaskell and the Victorian Social Text.* New York: St. Martin's Press, 1997.

Gallagher, Catherine. "George Eliot and Daniel Deronda: The Prostitute and the Jewish Question." *Sex, Politics, and Science in the Nineteenth-Century Novel: Selected Papers from the English Institute, 1983-84.* Ed. Ruth Bernard Yeazell. Baltimore: Johns Hopkins UP, 1986. 39-62.

———. *The Industrial Reformation of English Fiction: Social Discourse and Narrative Form.* Chicago: U of Chicago P, 1985.

Gaskell, Elizabeth. *The Letters of Mrs. Gaskell.* Ed. J. A. V. Chapple and Arthur Pollard. Cambridge: Harvard UP, 1967.

———. *Mary Barton: A Tale of Manchester Life.* 1848. Oxford: Oxford UP-World's Classics, 1987.

———. *North and South.* 1855. Harmondsworth: Penguin, 1995.

Harman, Barbara Leah. "In Promiscuous Company: Female Public Appearance in Elizabeth Gaskell's *North and South.*" *Victorian Studies* 31.3 (1988): 351-74.

Hughes, Linda and Michael Lund. "Textual/Sexual Pleasure and Serial Publication." *Literature in the Marketplace: Nineteenth-century British Publishing and Reading Practices.* Ed. John O. Jordan and Robert L. Patten. Cambridge: Cambridge UP, 1995. 165-94.

Lanser, Susan Sniader. *Fictions of Authority: Women Writers and Narrative Voice.* Ithaca: Cornell UP, 1992.

Nord, Deborah Epstein. *Walking the Victorian Streets: Women, Representation, and the City.* Ithaca: Cornell UP, 1995.

Schor, Hilary M. *Scheherezade in the Marketplace: Elizabeth Gaskell and the Victorian Novel.* Oxford: Oxford UP, 1992.

Stevenson, Catherine Barnes. "'What Must Not Be Said': *North and South* and the Problem of Women's Work." *Victorian Literature and Culture* 19 (1991): 67-84.

Stoneman, Patsy. *Elizabeth Gaskell*. Bloomington: Indiana UP, 1987.

Warhol, Robyn. "Toward a Theory of the Engaging Narrator: Earnest Interventions in Gaskell, Stowe, and Eliot." *PMLA* 101:5 (1986): 811-18.

Yeazell, Ruth Bernard. "Why Political Novels Have Heroines: *Sybil, Mary Barton*, and *Felix Holt*." *Novel: A Forum on Fiction* 18.2 (1985): 126-44.

Natalka Freeland (essay date autumn 2002)

SOURCE: Freeland, Natalka. "The Politics of Dirt in *Mary Barton* and *Ruth*." *Studies in English Literature, 1500-1900* 42, no. 4 (autumn 2002): 799-818.

[*In the following essay, Freeland illustrates how Gaskell uses the issue of sanitation to inform her broader appeals for social reform in her novels* Mary Barton *and* Ruth.]

Social problem fiction is defined by its dirtiness: transgressively graphic accounts of filth and waste herald a novel's entry into the Condition of England debate. Early examples of the genre spell out the polemical importance of filth, as in the preface to *Oliver Twist* (1837-38), where Charles Dickens insists that portraying "miserable reality" entails focusing on "the squalid . . . dirtiest paths of life."[1] Contemporary critics have confirmed the equation of social problems and dirt: Louis Cazamian, for instance, asserts that Elizabeth Gaskell's *Mary Barton* lays down irrefutable concrete evidence for thinking intervention to be necessary . . . *There is no scene in any novel of the time* which more powerfully evokes the conditions of social distress than that in which Barton and Wilson go to the aid of their comrade Davenport's family . . . We are shown a street littered with filth and ashes . . . The broken windowpanes are stuffed with rags, and a fetid smell almost overpowers the visitors as they enter."[2] The sanitary conditions *Mary Barton* (1848) describes are undeniably deplorable; but since the novel also details much worse effects of industrial poverty, including prostitution, drug addiction, starvation, and murder, we should question the emphasis placed by novelists and critics alike on mere dirt. Often invoked as a definitive social problem novel, *Mary Barton* is a particularly fruitful place to start this investigation: while Gaskell's novel appears to conform to generic expectations in its lurid representation of filthy slums, in the course of the narrative this filth acquires surprisingly positive connotations. As we shall see, the suggestion that dirt may not be the most pressing social problem radically revises the project of the industrial novel. Along with Condition of England fiction more generally, Gaskell's novels have routinely been criticized for accurately identifying real social problems but then retreating to imaginary, romanticized resolutions. In particular, these novels supposedly celebrate a middle-class ideal of domesticity (signaled by cleanliness and its moral corollary, decency).[3] Yet critics have failed to perceive that instead of endorsing these imaginary solutions, Gaskell's novels systematically expose their inadequacy by demonstrating that the terms in which middle-class observers formulated social problems elided the reality of working-class experience. Gaskell's transvaluation of dirt forecloses the possibility that social problems can be reduced to sanitary problems; her description of middle-class housekeeping further registers the inefficacy of cleanliness as a guarantor of moral authority. Finally, *Ruth* (1853) proposes an analogy between the ideologies of sanitation and domestic morality (as embodied in female sexual purity), revealing that projects aiming to clean up both dirty streets and dirty women distract attention from the social problems they ostensibly address.

Mary Barton's descriptions of filth and refuse *are* shockingly explicit:

> [Berry Street] was unpaved; and down the middle a gutter forced its way, every now and then forming pools in the holes with which the street abounded. Never was the old Edinburgh cry of 'Gardez l'eau!' more necessary than in this street. As they passed, women from their doors tossed household scraps of *every* description into the gutter; they ran into the next pool, which overflowed and stagnated. Heaps of ashes were the stepping-stones, on which the passer-by, who cared in the least for cleanliness, took care not to put his foot. Our friends were not dainty, but even they picked their way.[4]

Although passages such as this one rely on a middle-class readership's prurient interest in the squalid living conditions of its social inferiors, Gaskell explicitly rejects this middle-class perspective.[5] Oddly downplaying the disgust that it works so hard to elicit, the novel maintains that George Wilson and John Barton, who would otherwise incite sympathy and reforming zeal, are not particularly troubled by their dirty surroundings. The most immediate effect of filtering this appalling account of Berry Street through the consciousness of men "inured to such things" (p. 66) is of course to call attention to the excessive filth that makes even them pick their way with care and later almost faint from the stench. As a narrative strategy, though, this denial of daintiness appears puzzling: Gaskell strengthens the impact of this particular passage at the cost of undercutting the larger indictment of urban filth. If "[o]ur friends" are characterized by their comfortable familiarity with dirt, the narrative cannot simply equate cleanliness with godliness. More importantly, if Gaskell's working-class protagonists are "not dainty," their revolting living conditions can hardly matter. Here

Gaskell comes dangerously close to the popular claim that conditions in the slums did not constitute the crisis that benevolent observers might have supposed, since long exposure to unsanitary surroundings could actually result in immunity to disease: even an article intended to mobilize popular support for improved sewers acknowledged that "as Niger fever does not destroy negroes, so it would appear that men can become, in some degree, acclimatised, even to the emanations from corrupt animal matter. The man who has spent all his life in a foul court, acquires a constitution adapted by the beneficent operations of nature to that external condition of his life."[6]

This ambivalence in the representation of dirt uncovers a code conflict in the social problem novel: on the one hand, the explicit purpose of these novels is as much to deplore as to describe the filthy Condition of England; on the other hand, novels such as *Mary Barton* aim to reconcile the conventions of sentimental fiction, in which a domestic angel always presides over a suitably clean house, with the harsher realities of working-class life.[7] This dual agenda is most evident when the novel's focus shifts from outdoor dirt to filthy interiors. After passing through the street dirty enough to disturb even them, Barton and Wilson arrive at the Davenports': "a door . . . led into a back cellar, with a grating instead of a window, down which dropped the moisture from pigsties, and worse abominations. It was not paved; the floor was one mass of bad smelling mud. It had never been used, for there was not an article of furniture in it; nor could a human being, much less a pig, have lived there many days" (p. 71). This passage's power lies in the contrast between the Davenports' filthy dwelling and the stereotypical domestic haven. Living in a pigsty, the Davenports could be considered pigs; here their degradation is so complete that they have *lower* standards for cleanliness than a pig could tolerate. But this comment is tellingly couched in terms that generalize the Davenports' condition: according to Gaskell's narrator, all people, not just this impoverished family, can stand more dirt than the proverbially filthy swine. By universalizing human dirtiness, Gaskell effaces the moral connotations that descriptions such as this one generally carry. Even the shocking magnitude of filth helps to clear the Davenports of any charges of bad housekeeping, since it would obviously be impossible to clean this cellar, into which, in a particularly unpleasant reversal, "the stagnant, filthy moisture of the street oozed up" (p. 67).[8]

Mary Barton thus dramatizes the incongruity of applying a middle-class model of domesticity to the real conditions of the urban poor. Just as the Davenports cannot prevent the filth of the street from seeping into their home, none of the novel's working-class characters can escape the social problems this dirt metonymically represents. Indeed, social conditions violate the sanctity of

the home in many ways that are less literal than the Davenports' oozing floor. *Mary Barton* thus insists that the failure of working-class homes to conform to middle-class ideals—and, in particular, the dirtiness that middle-class observers found so troubling—is a direct result of the industrial economy. Jane Wilson describes how factory work creates domestic disorder: "I had been in a factory sin' five years old a'most, and I knew nought about cleaning, or cooking, let alone washing and such-like work . . . I could reckon up . . . nine men I know, as has been driven to th' public-house by having wives as worked in factories . . . letting their house go all dirty, and their fires all out; and that was a place as was tempting for a husband to stay in, was it? He soon finds out gin-shops, where all is clean and bright" (pp. 138-9). More directly, when the Barton household becomes "dingy," the narrator explains that this was simply because, with John Barton out of work, "money was . . . wanted to purchase soap and brushes" (p. 134).[9]

By demonstrating how impossible it would be for its working-class characters to create tidy domestic havens, the narrative intimates that the "great unwashed" remain dirty because of circumstances beyond their control. This may seem so self-evident that it hardly needs Gaskell's defensive repetitions, except of course that many Victorians considered the omnipresent coincidence of filth and poverty evidence that the poor chose to be dirty. Thus, Edwin Chadwick complains that sanitary progress is an uphill battle because the poor value their dirt as their only property: "When it is necessary to wash [paupers entering the work-house] on their admission, they usually manifest an extreme repugnance to the process. Their common feeling was expressed by one of them when he declared that he considered it 'equal to robbing him of a great coat which he had had for some years.'"[10] Similarly, George Sims, who published his survey of the slums of *Horrible London* (1889) with the avowed intention of "enlist[ing] the sympathies of a class not generally given to the study of 'low life,'" maintains that the dirtiness of the poor is not only voluntary but also innate: "The people I refer to are dirty and foul and vicious, as tigers are fierce and vindictive and cruel, because it is part of their nature. Take from them their dirt tomorrow, and put them in clean rooms amid wholesome surroundings, and what would be the result?—the dirty people would not be improved, but the clean rooms would be dirtied."[11] Other chroniclers of poverty, such as Arthur Morrison, ascribe such sentiments to working-class characters themselves: "As to washing, [Dicky Perrott] was never especially fond of it . . . and anything savouring of moderate cleanliness was resented in the Jago as an assumption of superiority."[12]

With the connections between dirt and poverty so well established, Gaskell's shocking descriptions of the living conditions of the poor could hardly have shocked anyone: after all, *Mary Barton* appeared eleven years after *Oliver Twist*, six years after Chadwick's *Report on the Sanitary Condition of the Labouring Population of Gt. Britain* (1842), and well into the sanitary reform movement.[13] Gaskell asserts, however, that these conditions have never been adequately described, and that the poor "only wanted a Dante to record their sufferings" (p. 96). Apparently, the narrator shares John Barton's faith that "surely, in a Christian land, [the distress of the poor] was not known even so feebly as words could tell it, or the more happy and fortunate would have thronged with their sympathy and their aid" (p. 96). But when *Mary Barton*'s Chartists adopt this explanation, the narrative implies that they may be deluded: "They could not believe that government knew of their misery: they rather chose to think it possible that men could voluntarily assume the office of legislators for a nation who were ignorant of its real state . . . the idea that their misery had still to be revealed in all its depths, and that then some remedy would be found, soothed their aching hearts, and kept down their rising fury" (p. 97). Once again, the novel's presentation of its social commentary through the consciousness of its working-class characters creates an epistemological impasse: the indirection here makes it almost impossible to determine whether the narrator herself believes in the ignorance that gives the novel its *raison d'être*.[14]

Yet, despite the narrator's ambivalent suggestion that social problem fiction may need only to alert its readers to the dreadful conditions of working-class life, *Mary Barton* leaves no doubt that "the more happy and more fortunate" are all too well aware of the dirtiness of the poor, and that in fact they rely on a predictable association of poverty and filth for disciplinary as well as philanthropic ends. Wealthy Harry Carson presumes he can gauge Jem Wilson's personal stature by his cleanliness: "He looked at Jem from head to foot, a black, grimy mechanic, in dirty fustian clothes, strongly built, and awakward (according to the dancing master); then he glanced at himself, and recalled the reflection he had so lately quitted in his bedroom. It was impossible. No woman with eyes could choose the one when the other wooed. It was Hyperion to a Satyr" (p. 207).[15] Harry's mistaken assumption that he can casually dismiss and insult such a filthy rival sparks the brawl for which Jem is arrested. This arrest shows that the police share, or even exceed, Carson's prejudice against dirt: while the industrialist reads Jem's dirtiness as a sign of his irrelevance, the police interpret his appearance as evidence of his guilt. Although Harry strikes first, a nearby police officer restrains Jem instead, apparently because he presupposes that the dirty laborer is the more likely criminal. The agencies of authority that equate filth, poverty, and crime then exploit this equation so as to police the working class.[16] After inferring Jem's guilt from his dirtiness, the police mobilize dirt as a synecdoche for

poverty in order to infiltrate the working-class community to gather evidence against Jem: "When Mrs. Wilson caught a glimpse of the intruder [a disguised policeman] through the stair-rails, she at once saw he was a stranger, a working man, it might be a fellow-labourer with her son, for his dress was grimy enough for the supposition" (p. 260). If grime alone makes a convincing working-class disguise, the conjunction of dirt and poverty, which Gaskell's narrator proposes to uncover, must be at best an open secret.

Jem's arrest and prosecution further demonstrate how readily the metonymic relation between poverty and dirt could be translated into a metaphoric association of poverty and vice. When observing the coincidence of dirt and crime, sanitarians such as Chadwick had blamed filthy surroundings for moral turpitude. Chadwick contends, with evident dismay, that "much of rebellion, of moral depravity and of crime has its root in physical disorder and depravity . . . The fever nests and seats of physical depravity are also the seats of moral depravity, disorder and crime with which the police have the most to do."[17] *Mary Barton* reveals, however, that social agencies such as the police, in presuming this causality, make dirt not simply an antecedent of crime but also a means of conjecturing motives, gathering evidence, and assigning guilt. Here it is the operation of the judicial system, not the etiology of infectious disease and physical decay invoked by Chadwick, which makes Jem's dirtiness the source of his putative guilt.

But *Mary Barton*'s references to indirect connections between dirt and policing understate the case: the Victorians made dirtiness itself a crime. While Gaskell mentions refuse in the street as a source of disgust, she fails to add that in mid-nineteenth-century Manchester convictions for *crimes* such as "emptying chamber utensils in the street" were "fairly numerous."[18] Since the fines for such violations were a greater source of apprehension to most working-class families than mere dirt, sanitary awareness among the poor was above all a fear of the authorities, who were entitled to confiscate and burn any furniture, clothes, and bedding that they deemed a public health threat.[19] Indeed, soap and the police were often compared as ways of addressing the threat posed by the poor: a notorious soap advertisement depicts a policeman holding up his lantern to illuminate a signboard extoling the soap's virtues, implying, as Peter Stallybrass and Allon White have discerned, that "the policeman and soap are analogous: they penetrate the dark, public realm with its disease and danger so as to secure the domestic realm . . . from contamination."[20] Moreover, the medical officers enlisted by the Poor Law, suggestively known as the "medical police," were liable to reverse Chadwick's observation that dirt and disease led to vice and to assert, conversely, that disease was no more than the external sign and consequence of moral corruption: "I am no preacher," wrote the Medical Officer of Health for Bermondsey, "but I do not hesitate to declare that hereditary diseases of the body are almost always, if not invariably, the consequence of sin, or departure from God's natural laws."[21]

In the context of the prevailing rhetoric, bolstered by the authority of the medical profession as well as the police, Gaskell's dissociation of dirt and vice was genuinely radical. In *Mary Barton,* the subplot concerning Mary's aunt Esther recasts the relation between dirt and vice as a choice between opposites. As a prostitute, Esther habitually dresses in gaudy "finery," yet wishes she could permanently exchange her attire for the "suit of outer clothes, befitting the wife of a working man," that she briefly borrows from a pawnshop (p. 278). This working-class outfit is "dirty and rather worn to be sure, but [it] had a sort of sanctity to the eyes of the street-walker, as being the appropriate garb of that happy class to which she could never, never more belong" (p. 278). Rather than signifying innate criminality or moral degeneration, dirt is the expected accessory of respectable, working-class domesticity. Given the choice between dirt and sin, it is clear which alternative Esther, with the wisdom of experience, would prefer. After revisiting the Bartons' unwelcoming and poverty-stricken home, she laments that "she must leave the old dwelling-place, whose very walls, and flags, dingy and sordid as they were, had a charm for her. Must leave the abode of poverty, for the more terrible abodes of vice" (p. 284).

When Mary goes out to work, she faces a decision parallel to Esther's choice between suits of clothes representing vice and dirt. Since her father does not approve of factory work for girls (because it prevents them from learning to clean and keep house), Mary's options are limited to entering domestic service or being apprenticed to a dressmaker. Gaskell spells out the moral stakes involved in this decision. On the one hand, saintly Alice Wilson describes "the pleasure o' helping others" that makes domestic service "as happy . . . as could be; almost as happy as . . . [being] at home" (p. 34). On the other hand, even fallen Esther disapproves of dressmaking, because "it's a bad life for a girl to be out late at night in the streets, and after many an hour of weary work, they're ready to follow after any novelty that makes a little change" (p. 190).[22] When Mary chooses the dubious alternative of dressmaking, the narrative immediately ascribes her dangerous mistake to a misplaced affinity for cleanliness: "she had early determined that her beauty should make her a lady . . . the rank to which she firmly believed her lost Aunt Esther had arrived. Now, while a servant must often drudge and be dirty . . . a dressmaker's apprentice must (or so Mary thought) be always dressed with a certain regard to appearance; must never soil her hands, and need never redden or dirty her face with hard labour" (p. 27). After choosing dressmaking on the basis of little more than her desire to avoid dirt during her working hours, Mary falls into a risky flirtation with her social superior, Harry Carson, largely because his company allows her to escape in the evenings from her "dingy and comfortless" home: "If he had known what Mary's home was, he would not have been so much convinced of his increasing influence over her, by her being more and more ready to linger with him in the sweet summer air. For when she returned for the night her father was often out, and the house wanted the cheerful look it had had in those days when money was never wanted to purchase soap" (p. 134).

In both Mary's and Esther's stories, then, the novel presents a surprising opposition, in lieu of the typical equation, between filth and poverty on the one hand and vice on the other—concluding, of course, that dirt is the lesser of these two evils. Even more importantly, by specifying that it was the desire to be clean that led Mary into a perilous position in the first place, *Mary Barton* makes cleanliness itself appear morally suspect, while Esther's association of dinginess and squalor with virtue confirms that dirt here is not simply preferable to vice, but is in fact actively desirable. The contrast between dirtily industrious labor and affected cleanliness recurs in the conflict between Jem and Harry Carson: "Jem put his black, working, right hand upon [Harry's] arm to detain him. The haughty young man shook it off, and with his glove pretended to brush away the sooty contamination that might be left upon his light greatcoat sleeve" (p. 208).[23]

Even when cleanliness is not directly associated with affectation or vice, Gaskell questions its exaggerated importance by insisting that it is simply not worth the effort. Consider the case of *Mary Barton*'s Alice, a washerwoman who is so unequivocally associated with cleaning that, as she lies on her deathbed, her friends remember her principally as "so rare and clean all her life long" (p. 253). Although her cellar room is, predictably, "the perfection of cleanliness" (p. 15), it is hardly an appealing home. On the contrary, her constant cleaning makes Alice's room comfortless and unpleasant: "the floor was bricked, and scrupulously clean, although so damp that it seemed as if the last washing would never dry up" (p. 15). The Thornton residence in Gaskell's *North and South* (1854-55) provides more detailed and unmistakable evidence that excessive cleanliness can destroy domestic comfort:

> It seemed as though no one had been in [the drawing-room] since the day when the furniture was bagged up with as much care as if the house was to be overwhelmed with lava, and discovered a thousand years hence . . . [T]he pattern on the carpet represented bunches of flowers on a light ground, but it was carefully covered up in the centre by a linen drugget, glazed

and colourless . . . [E]ach chair and sofa had its own particular veil of netting, or knitting. Great alabaster groups occupied every flat surface, safe from dust under their glass shades. In the middle of the room . . . [there was a] bagged up chandelier . . . Everything reflected light, nothing absorbed it. The whole room had a painfully spotted, spangled, speckled look about it, which impressed Margaret so unpleasantly that she was hardly conscious of the peculiar cleanliness required to keep everything so white and pure in such an atmosphere, or of the trouble that must be willingly expended to secure that effect of icy, snowy discomfort. Wherever she looked there was evidence of care and labour, but not care and labour to procure ease, to help on habits of tranquil home employment; solely to ornament, and then to preserve ornament from dirt or destruction.[24]

By contrast, the casually mentioned homey disorder in the Barton household—where the unwashed tea things are left piled up when everyone is too tired to clean them—makes occasional lapses from perfect tidiness appear eminently desirable.

If the inordinate actions taken to guard against "dirt or destruction" can render a home colorless, painful, and unpleasant, they are also, ultimately, unavailing. In *Ruth,* even when people such as the Bensons succeed in removing all traces of visible dirt, they cannot keep their home, their reputations, or indeed themselves in the state of spiritual purity this physical tidiness is supposed merely to represent. Leonore Davidoff and Catherine Hall have observed that the equation of physical and moral cleanliness was often interpreted particularly literally where women were concerned. They note, for example, that "The experience of conversion was often described as a process of cleansing and purification from the pollutions of the world" and that "The concept of purity had taken on a special resonance for women partly because of fears associated with the polluting powers of sexuality."[25] Yet the Bensons' oft-noted cleanliness fails to keep out the "contamination" (p. 349) that Ruth brings into their home, and which spreads from her even to the morally upright Mr. Benson, who agrees to lie on her behalf.[26] Their maid Sally, a compulsive cleaner, voices the strongest objections to Ruth, comparing her to dirt-spreading vermin: "a baby in the house!" she exclaims, as she begins to suspect that the story of Ruth's widowhood is a fabrication, "Nay, then my time's come, and I'll pack up and begone. I never could abide them things. I'd sooner have rats in the house" (p. 138). Gaskell's rejection of the arbitrary link between material and moral purity is evidenced not only by Sally's housekeeping, which provides no protection against immorality, but also by Ruth herself, a fallen woman who is nonetheless a model of middle-class cleanliness: remarkably "nice and tidy" (p. 230), Ruth impresses her adopted family by "washing the breakfast things . . . in so quiet and orderly a manner, that neither Miss Benson nor Sally, both particular

enough, had any of their little fancies or prejudices annoyed" (p. 148).

Only the unsympathetic characters in the novel continue to mistake moral for material dirtiness. When pharisaical Mr. Bradshaw learns about Ruth's sinful past, he produces a catalogue of synonyms equating sexual transgression with actual filth: he denounces the "corruption," "defilement," and "impurity" which the "stained" and "contaminated" governess has covertly introduced into his pristine household (pp. 338-40). Mr. Bradshaw consequently throws Ruth into the street as unceremoniously as the women in *Mary Barton* toss out the garbage, as though moral housekeeping could be as straightforward as expelling and ignoring any sources of contamination (p. 341). Bradshaw's vocabulary here echoes the popular homologies between dirty streets and streetwalkers: the *Lancet,* for example, argued that "Sooner or later the public authorities must investigate [the common prostitute's] condition with as much care as they are about to do the cesspools, and the other collections of refuse left in the slums of our large cities. The period cannot be far distant, when all engaged in the sanatory condition of our population must become aware of the physical contamination arising from the neglect in which prostitutes are at present allowed to remain; and then it is we may look for amendment."[27] But in Bradshaw's rhetoric the slippage between moral and physical defilement obfuscates rather than uncovers any causal links between them by making material conditions no more than *metaphors* for spiritual purity. If *Mary Barton* maintained that the urban poor could not possibly live up to a middle-class ideal equating decency with cleanliness, here we see that this ideal itself functions as a cover, which figuratively acknowledges, so as to practically erase, real social conditions, while blaming the victims of those very conditions. Just as middle-class observers concluded that working-class homes and neighborhoods were filthy because the poor liked to be dirty, Bradshaw's description of Ruth as impure implies that her fall was caused by an individual failure of self-regulation, and so apparently not by social conditions at all. Ruth's economic problems then appear to issue from her personal moral failure: she cannot find work to support herself because she is an unwed mother, and so by definition an immoral woman. But the novel's explicit providential plotting is undercut by its actual narrative sequence: long before Ruth's fall *resulted in* her social problems it *resulted from* them, since she succumbed to her seducer only because she was already jobless, friendless, and broke. Economic determinism precedes and ultimately supersedes personal redemption: if Ruth's hardships and dilemmas stem from her social position as a "redundant" woman, then any attempt to address her situation in personal, psychological, or moral terms is manifestly inadequate.[28] Underneath its story of a fallen woman's sin and atonement, *Ruth* thus debunks the ideal of domesticated female sexual purity as a solution to social problems by recalling that sexual morality itself is firmly rooted in the economic system which it promises to repair.

Gaskell's critique of middle-class housekeeping is therefore continuous with her transvaluation of working-class dirt: *Ruth* reinforces *Mary Barton*'s suggestion that cleanliness is a suspiciously misdirected response to social problems. Considering that neither literal housekeeping nor the measures Mr. Bradshaw takes to guard against figurative "impurity" and "defilement" seem to be effective, Sally's constant scrubbing appears difficult to justify. Sally spends the climactic scenes of the novel, during which Ruth admits her dirty secret, doing her usual housework. In the midst of the crisis, Mr. Benson surprisingly discovers her "as busy as ever about her cleaning"; even when he begins to hint at the magnitude of the situation, she simply continues "scouring in no very good temper" (p. 353). This reaction to the disaster precipitated by Ruth's sexual sins is not, however, nearly as remarkable as Sally's similar response to the mention of fully lawful and sanctioned sexuality. Although Sally longs to receive a marriage proposal, her reaction the one time she is asked is anything but welcoming. When Jeremiah Dickson proposes, she "all at once . . . couldn't abide the chap" (p. 168). Even before developing this sudden antipathy, Sally provides a clue to her feelings for Jeremiah by deliberately sullying his coat, "and a pretty brushing he'd have," she guesses, "to get it off again" (p. 167). She then unintentionally rejects his offer because, although she is, as ever, cleaning when he asks for her hand, she considers it literally too dirty to give to him without washing it first (pp. 167-8).

If the prospect of marriage is less important to Sally than her housekeeping duties, this admittedly unusual assignment of priorities pales in comparison to the near blasphemy with which she allows cleaning to supplant her religious duties as well. Initially believing that Dickson is on his knees to pray with her, not to ask for her hand, Sally is annoyed at the prospect of religion coming in the way of her housework: "forgive me! but I thought why couldn't the fellow go in and pray wi' Master Thurstan, as had always a calm spirit ready for prayer, instead o' me, who had my dresser to scour, let alone an apron to iron" (p. 167). Reluctantly deciding to pray if necessary, Sally is even then prepared with a plan to keep clean during these impromptu devotions: "The Methodees are terrible hands at unexpected prayers when one least looks for 'em . . . I'd been caught once or twice unawares, so this time I thought I'd be up to it, and I moved a dry duster wherever I went, to kneel upon in case he began when I were in a wet place" (p. 166). This incident illustrates a larger pattern, in which cleaning takes the place of religion for Sally, who believes that "there's a right and a wrong

way of setting about everything—and to my thinking, the right way is to take a thing up heartily, if it is only making a bed. Why! dear ah me, making a bed may be done after a Christian fashion, I take it, or else what's to become of such as me in heaven, who've had little enough time on earth for clapping ourselves down on our knees for set prayers?" (pp. 174-5).

Sally's comic story is recast as a sentimental tragedy with much the same moral in Faith Benson's refusal of her own suitor on the grounds that she too should continue to keep house for her brother. In each of these instances, marriageable women reject matrimony in favor of their duties as housekeepers; but of course the same emphasis on running an efficient and, especially, clean, household informs the role of Victorian women *within* marriage as well. It is easy to see why women, expected to give up all other pursuits and pleasures to devote themselves to an untenable ideal of cleanliness, could become obsessive as a result. As Robert Roberts observes, in an account of late-Victorian Lancashire that recalls both the Thornton and Benson residences:

> Women wore their lives away washing clothes in heavy, iron-hooped tubs, scrubbing wood and stone, polishing furniture and fire-irons. There were housewives who finally lost real interest in anything save dirt removing. Almost every working hour of the week they devoted to cleanliness and re-cleaning the same objects so that their family, drilled into slavish tidiness, could sit in state, newspaper covers removed, for a few hours each Sunday evening. On Monday the purification began all over again. Two of these compulsives left us for the "lunatic asylum," one of them, I remember vividly, passing with a man in uniform through a group of us watching children to a van, still washing her hands like a poor Lady Macbeth.[29]

While she may not quite attain the status of a Lady Macbeth, Sally evidently allows her domestic duties to become a compulsion until, when she pipe-clays Jeremiah Dickson's coat, her cleaning itself becomes a kind of dirt.

Novels such as *Mary Barton* and *Ruth* thus reveal that a misplaced obsession with cleanliness, and the entire domestic ideology it underwrites, are at best irrelevant in the face of larger social problems. Despite the good intentions of sanitary reformers, the solutions that predominated in mid-Victorian discussions of the Condition of England simply ignored the economic realities of poverty, "as [one] who should make domestic rules for the pretty behaviour of children without caring to know that those children had been kept for days without food" (*Mary Barton*, p. 97). In her preface to *Mary Barton*, Gaskell announces that she "know[s] nothing of Political Economy, or the theories of trade" (p. xxxvi). Critics have been quick to take her at her word, deriding social problem fiction's supposed retreat from real (political and economic) conditions to novelistic (personal, emotional, and domestic) fantasies. But while novels such as **Mary Barton** and **Ruth** stop short of providing programmatic economic solutions to the problems they identify, they compellingly argue for the necessity of such solutions, precisely by establishing the inadequacy of any idealized, sentimental resolutions. When a character such as Jane Wilson proposes to address social problems by translating shortcomings in government policy into failures of private housekeeping, she appears laughably naïve and misguided: "I say it's Prince Albert as ought to be asked how he'd like his missis to be from home when he comes in, tired and worn, and wanting some one to cheer him; and maybe, her to come in by and by, just as tired and down in th' mouth; and how he'd like for her never to be at home to see to th' cleaning of his house . . . I'd be bound, prince as he is, if his missis served him so, he'd be off to a gin-palace, or summut o' that kind. So why can't they make a law again poor folks' wives working in factories?" (**Mary Barton,** p. 140). The joke here is, of course, that the details of domestic management in the royal house have no impact whatsoever on the social ills that are Mrs. Wilson's real concern. The incongruity of imagining the queen staying home to clean her own house further uncovers a deep ambivalence about cleaning: although ostensibly virtuous, it is also implicitly demeaning.[30] Gaskell thus recasts the external problems besetting the domestic sphere, like the dirt and vice that seem to enter the home from the street, as contradictions within a middle-class domestic ideology. The politics of cleanliness proposed by Jane Wilson, like the religion of cleanliness practiced by Sally, is exposed as both an overreaction to superficial dirt and a failure to address its underlying causes. No amount of housekeeping can resolve the crises or rebalance the inequities of industrial economics; despite the tidy sentimental endings of novels such as **Mary Barton** and **Ruth,** domestic solutions resolutely leave their social problems as messy as ever.

Notes

1. Charles Dickens, *The Adventures of Oliver Twist,* Oxford Illustrated Dickens (Oxford: Oxford Univ. Press, 1949; rprt. 1991), p. xv.

2. Louis Cazamian, *The Social Novel in England, 1830-1850: Dickens, Disraeli, Mrs. Gaskell, Kingsley,* trans. Martin Fido (London: Routledge and Kegan Paul, 1973), pp. 220-1, emphasis added.

3. Many critics have noticed that novels such as *Mary Barton* seem to retreat from social and industrial problems to individual, domestic solutions. Raymond Williams's seminal analysis of *Mary Barton* praises the early chapters for conveying "the characteristic response of a generation to the new and crushing experience of industrial-

ism," but decries the novel's subsequent descent into "the familiar and orthodox plot of the Victorian novel of sentiment" (*Culture and Society, 1780-1950* [1958; rprt. New York: Columbia Univ. Press, 1983], pp. 88-9). More generally, John Lucas ascribes "the flaws inherent in the genre of the social-problem novel" to "the novelists' failure to deal really honestly with the social experiences their novels are intended to portray"; he refers, in particular, to the ending of *Mary Barton,* where the main characters "are given a purely fortuitous, and individual, release from a context which had been shown to be so inescapable" ("Mrs. Gaskell and Brotherhood," in *Tradition and Tolerance in Nineteenth-Century Fiction: Critical Essays on Some English and American Novels,* ed. David Howard, John Lucas, and John Goode [London: Routledge and Kegan Paul, 1966], pp. 141-205, 141, 174). Similarly, Igor Webb argues that novels such as this one invoke "the structure of courtship" to solve social problems as "a protective means to cope with the shock of a violent mass" (*From Custom to Capital: The English Novel and the Industrial Revolution* [Ithaca: Cornell Univ. Press, 1981], p. 192). Also see Mary Poovey, *Making a Social Body: British Cultural Formation, 1830-1864* (Chicago: Univ. Chicago Press, 1995), pp. 143-54. By contrast, Hilary Schor traces the multiple crossings of the novel's double plot, compellingly concluding that "they constitute at once a critique of the myth of a separate, domestic, private sphere (and of the woman's static place within it) and an interesting examination of what might seem conventional plotting, of the heroine's role within that plot" (*Scheherezade in the Marketplace: Elizabeth Gaskell and the Victorian Novel* [Oxford: Oxford Univ. Press, 1992], p. 21). Also see Rosemarie Bodenheimer's *The Politics of Story in Victorian Social Fiction* (Ithaca: Cornell Univ. Press, 1988), which argues that industrial novels' focus on heroines, who were ostensibly "exempted by [their] sex from obedience to the 'natural' laws of supply and demand that . . . regulated the marketplace" (p. 17), allowed them to challenge the premises of political economy.

4. Elizabeth Gaskell, *Mary Barton: A Tale of Manchester Life* (Oxford: Oxford Univ. Press, 1987), p. 66. Further references will appear parenthetically in the text by page numbers.

5. In *The Fallen Angel: Chastity, Class, and Women's Reading, 1835-1880* (Bowling Green: Bowling Green Univ. Press, 1981), Sally Mitchell stresses that Gaskell's novels would reach an almost exclusively "ordinary, middle class" (p. 40) audience, despite the comments of contemporaries such as Charlotte Brontë, who seemed to believe that these novels were intended to "restore hope

and energy" to downtrodden or criminal working-class readers (Elizabeth Gaskell, *The Life of Charlotte Brontë* [London: Dent, 1971], p. 358; qtd. in Mitchell, p. 40).

6. [Henry Morley], "A Foe under Foot," *Household Words* 6, 142 (11 December 1852): 289-92, 290. As I argue below, Gaskell in fact develops a surprisingly positive connotation to this symbiotic dirtiness. Victorian autobiographer Stephen Reynolds later makes a similar claim for the evolutionary advantage of not being "dainty": "just as the habit of aiding nature by eating predigested food is bad, so too rigid a habit, too great a need of cleanliness is a positive disadvantage in the struggle for existence . . . It is good to be clean, but it is better to be able to be dirty" (*A Poor Man's House* [1909; rprt. London: London Magazine Editions, 1980], pp. 92-3).

7. Lucas has suggested that this duality is inherent in the social problem genre, which manifests "first, the desire to dispel ignorance; second, to promote sympathy" (p. 145). Meanwhile, Catherine Gallagher has called attention to the various subgenres invoked, and rejected, by *Mary Barton,* and has suggested that this generic ambivalence can be traced to divisions within the English Unitarianism of the 1840s and 1850s, and its split between advocates of a "Religion of Causality," which circumscribed moral issues with material and therefore economic determinism, and proponents of an emerging "Religion of Conscience," which emphasized free will and thus personal moral responsibility (*The Industrial Reformation of English Fiction, 1832—1867* [Chicago: Univ. of Chicago Press, 1988], pp. 63-5).

8. Frederick Engels similarly insists that the extreme dirtiness of the Mancunian poor shows that it is simply not possible for them to keep clean: "There are not even adequate facilities for satisfying the most natural daily needs. There are so few privies that they are either filled up every day or are too far away from those who need to use them . . . Pumps and piped water are to be found only in the better-class districts of the town. Indeed no one can blame these helots of modern civilisation if their homes are no cleaner than the occasional pigsties which are a feature of these slums" (*The Condition of the Working Class in England in 1844,* trans. W. O. Henderson and W. H. Chaloner [1845; rprt. Oxford: Basil Blackwell, 1971], p. 62). Also see Léon Faucher, *Études sur l'Angleterre,* 2 vols. (Brussels: Wouters, 1845), 1:218.

9. In his richly detailed and convincing account of Victorian sanitation, Anthony Wohl provides evidence that this would have been literally true for many working-class families on a regular basis, as well as during periods of unemployment. He notes, for example, that "in some working-class budgets as much was spent on soap and washing materials as on fuel, or tea and milk" (*Endangered Lives: Public Health in Victorian Britain* [Cambridge MA: Harvard Univ. Press, 1983], p. 65). *Mary Barton*'s emphasis on working-class families' inability to live up to a standard of bourgeois domesticity echoes numerous working-class Victorian autobiographies. David Vincent cites, for instance, a cabinetmaker named Henry Price: "The Merry Homes of England Around their fires by night. Some one has sung about them. But they could not have known much about them. The vast majority of them in the Towns and Cities Have no room to be merry in" (Henry Edward Price, "Diary" MS Autobiography [written 1904], qtd. in David Vincent, *Bread, Knowledge and Freedom: A Study of Nineteenth-Century Working-Class Autobiography* [London: Europa Publications, 1981], p. 55). A similar complaint appears in Henry Mayhew's "Home is Home, Be It Never So Homely" (in *Meliora, or Better Times to Come: Being the Contributions of Many Men Touching the Present State and Prospects of Society,* ed. Viscount Ingestre [London: John W. Parker and Son, 1852], 1:258-80; see esp. 263-4).

10. Edwin Chadwick, *Report on the Sanitary Condition of the Labouring Population of Gt. Britain* (1842; rprt. Edinburgh: Edinburgh Univ. Press, 1965), p. 316.

11. George Sims, *How the Poor Live and Horrible London* (1889; rprt. New York: Garland Publishing, 1984), p. 115.

12. Arthur Morrison, *A Child of the Jago* (1896; rprt. Woodbridge, Suffolk: Boydell, 1982), p. 63. The pervasiveness of the attitude Morrison shares with Chadwick and Sims is reflected in the responses of many of Gaskell's early readers, who objected to her characterization of the working class as *victims* of social problems, arguing, for example, that John Barton's poverty was caused by his improvidence: see W[illiam] E[llis and Mary Turner Ellis], "*Mary Barton,*" *Westminster and Foreign Quarterly Review* 51 (April 1849): 48-63, 49 and [W. R. Greg], "*Mary Barton,*" *Edinburgh Review* 89 (April 1849): 402-35, 414.

13. Other novelists had already followed Dickens's lead: Frances Trollope's *Michael Armstrong, the Factory Boy* and Charlotte Elizabeth Tonna's *Helen Fleetwood* appeared in 1839-40; Benjamin Disraeli's *Coningsby; or, The New Generation* appeared in 1844 and *Sybil; or, The Two Nations* in 1846.

14. The critics have echoed this confusion. For example, Kathleen Tillotson first claims that Gaskell
"was not a discoverer, but was writing of what
had long been sadly familiar"; later she says that
the opening chapters of *Mary Barton* "needed to
be slow, because of the novelty of the material;
they needed also to be reassuring" (*Novels of the
Eighteen-Forties* [Oxford: Clarendon Press, 1954],
pp. 208, 214). Also see Coral Lansbury, *Elizabeth
Gaskell* (Boston: Twayne Publishers, 1984), pp.
14-7. Even some early reviewers were puzzled by
Gaskell's assertion that she was voicing unknown
experiences and sentiments: after noting that *Sybil*
had already made these disclosures, the critic for
the *British Quarterly Review* adds, "The idea of
calling the factory population of Manchester a
dumb people, is rather diverting. They have always seemed to us by no means chary of expressing what they think and feel, and that too in no
very timid or measured manner" ("*Mary Barton*,"
British Quarterly Review 9 [February 1849]: 117-
36, 121).

15. The mutually reinforcing links between hygiene
and hierarchy with which a newly prominent
middle class consolidated its social power have
often been remarked. As Leonore Davidoff and
Catherine Hall have observed, "At a time when
the middle rank were using soap for laundry, many
labourers' families still used urine. Given their resources, the gap in [personal hygiene] between the
habits of the poor and the moderately well off was
widening" (*Family Fortunes: Men and Women of
the English Middle Class, 1780-1850* [Chicago:
Univ. of Chicago Press, 1987], p. 383). Reynolds
in fact called cleanliness "our greatest class symbol," adding that there was "a greater social gulf
fixed between the man who takes his morning tub
and him who does not, than between the man of
wealth or family and him who has neither . . . At
the bottom of our social ladder is a dirty shirt; at
the top is fixed not laurels, but a tub!" (pp. 88-9).

16. Gaskell's account of the disciplinary uses of dirt
thus confirms anthropologist Mary Douglas's reading of pollution as a category not only defined by
social structures, but also definitive of them: drawing on Lord Chesterfield's classic definition of dirt
as matter out of place, Douglas argues both that
"Where there is dirt there is system. Dirt is the
by-product of a systematic ordering and classification of matter, in so far as ordering involves rejecting inappropriate elements," and that "ideas
about separating, purifying, demarcating and pun-
ishing transgressions have as their main function
to impose system on an inherently untidy experience" (*Purity and Danger: An Analysis of the Concepts of Pollution and Taboo* [1966; rprt. New
York: Routledge, 1984], pp. 36, 4). Also see

Michael Thompson, *Rubbish Theory: The Cre-
ation and Destruction of Value* (Oxford: Oxford
Univ. Press, 1979); Terence McLaughlin, *Dirt: A
Social History as Seen through the Uses and
Abuses of Dirt* (New York: Stein and Day, 1971);
and Stephen Greenblatt, "Filthy Rites," *Dædalus:
Journal of the American Academy of Arts and Sci-
ences* 111, 3 (Summer 1982): 1-16.

17. Edwin Chadwick, *Transactions of the Sanitary Institute of Great Britain* (1874), p. 274; qtd. in
Wohl, p. 7. Engels also argued that much of a
poor man's vicious behavior—particularly dissipation and "brutish intoxication"—could be attributed to "his degraded condition, combined with
his dirty habits and his abject poverty" (p. 106).

18. Arthur Redford, *The History of Local Government
in Manchester,* 3 vols. (London: Longmans Green,
1939), 1:147; qtd. in Wohl, p. 92.

19. Wohl, p. 70.

20. Peter Stallybrass and Allon White, *The Politics
and Poetics of Transgression* (Ithaca: Cornell
Univ. Press, 1986), p. 134. John Simon, one of the
foremost Victorian sanitary reformers, insisted that
dirtiness should be subject to criminal as well as
civil prosecution; he went so far as to claim that
sanitary violations were on a par with murder
(*English Sanitary Institutions: Reviewed in the
Course of Their Development, and in Some of
Their Political and Social Relations* [London: Cas-
sell and Co., 1890], pp. 469-71).

21. Dr. Challice, *How People Hasten Death! Plain
Words for Plain Folks* (pamphlet, n.d.), qtd. in
Wohl, p. 67.

22. This opposition is, of course, purely arbitrary:
Mayhew, for instance, describes maidservants as
particularly immoral and likely to turn to prostitution (*London Labor and the London Poor,* 4 vols.
[New York: Dover Publications, 1968], 2:257).
That there is no moral distinction between Mary's
alternatives underscores the real difference between these two jobs, which is, as Mary recognizes, that maidservants have to get dirty.

23. This is not just a case of Gaskell's greater sympathy with laborers than with the manufacturers who
are their "masters"—when, in a later novel,
Gaskell sympathizes with the masters, they are the
ones represented as virtuously dirty. Recall Margaret Hale's first meeting with Mr. Thornton in
North and South, where he appears to be "not
quite a gentleman," largely because of his "not
over-brushed, nor over-polished" appearance after
walking through the dirty streets of smoky and industrial Milton-Northern (*North and South* [Har-
mondsworth: Penguin, 1986], pp. 102, 100). Mar-

garet's early reactions to Mr. Thornton hint at the middle-class disgust aroused even by the honest dirt of labor. Here we can also see Gaskell's distance from Dickens, whose heroes (with the exception of *Bleak House*'s melodramatic Jo) are notoriously clean. Dickens's unrealistic insistence on the cleanliness of his "good" characters is brought into particularly sharp focus by Harland Nelson's juxtaposition of certain passages in *Our Mutual Friend* with the ones in Mayhew's *London Labour and the London Poor* that may have served as models for them. As Nelson observes, this comparison turns up a salient difference: Dickens makes his old woman, Betty Higden, a laundress while Mayhew's is a pure finder. Dickens would not "risk making her an object of disgust: the Deserving Poor, to his readers, would have to be not only honest and self-reliant but clean" ("Dickens's *Our Mutual Friend* and Henry Mayhew's *London Labour and the London Poor*," *NCF* 20, 3 [Dec. 1965]: 207-22, 216).

24. *North and South*, p. 158.

25. Davidoff and Hall, p. 90.

26. Gaskell, *Ruth* (Oxford: Oxford Univ. Press, 1985), p. 349. Further references will appear parenthetically in the text by page numbers. Judith Walkowitz suggests that many of the programs designed to combat working-class immorality stem from this fear that fallen women will pass their apparently infectious contamination on to the members of the respectable households in which they live (*Prostitution and Victorian Society: Women, Class, and the State* [Cambridge: Cambridge Univ. Press, 1982], pp. 48-65, 243-5).

27. *Lancet* (21 November 1846), p. 569; qtd. in David Trotter, *Circulation: Defoe, Dickens, and the Economies of the Novel* (Houndmills: Macmillan, 1988), p. 75.

28. W. R. Greg, who later called attention to the problem of female socioeconomic redundancy ("Why Are Women Redundant?" *National Review* 14 [April 1862]: 434-60), cites *Mary Barton* in his discussion of "Prostitution" (*Westminster Review* 53 [1850]: 448-506, 454). As Sally Mitchell observes, Gaskell in turn borrowed Greg's terms of analysis for *Ruth*.

29. Robert Roberts, *The Classic Slum: Salford Life in the First Quarter of the Century* (Manchester: Manchester Univ. Press, 1971), p. 21; qtd. in Wohl, p. 65.

30. On the cultural anxieties about the act of cleaning, see Michael Hiley, *Victorian Working Women: Portraits From Life* (Boston: David R. Godine, 1979); Bruce Robbins, *The Servant's Hand: En-*

glish Fiction from Below (New York: Columbia Univ. Press, 1986); and, on the case of Hannah Cullwick, Anne McClintock, *Imperial Leather: Race, Gender, and Sexuality in the Colonial Conquest* (New York: Routledge, 1995), pp. 132-80. Also recall Charlotte Yonge's *The Three Brides* (London: MacMillan, 1876), which ambivalently suggests that sanitary reform may not be a proper subject for ladies.

Natalka Freeland (essay date spring 2003)

SOURCE: Freeland, Natalka. "*Ruth*'s Perverse Economies: Women, Hoarding, and Expenditure." *ELH* 70, no. 1 (spring 2003): 197-221.

[*In the following essay, Freeland explores Gaskell's parallels between women and property, and labor markets and marriage in* Ruth.]

A minor domestic scene in Elizabeth Gaskell's ***Ruth*** juxtaposes two different standards of value:

> After dusting the looking-glass, [Faith] suddenly stopped in her operation, and after a close inspection of herself, startled Sally by this speech:
>
> "Sally! I'm looking a great deal older than I used to do!"
>
> Sally, who was busy dilating on the increased price of flour, considered this remark of Miss Benson's as strangely irrelevant to the matter in hand, and only noticed it by a
>
> "To be sure! I suppose we all on us do. But two and fourpence a dozen is too much to make us pay for it."
>
> Miss Benson went on with her inspection of herself, and Sally with her economical projects.
>
> "Sally!" said Miss Benson, "my hair is nearly white. The last time I looked it was only pepper-and-salt."[1]

No reader is likely to believe that these parallel conversations are "irrelevant" to one another, especially once Gaskell underscores the connection by having Faith respond to Sally's comments about flour by comparing herself to "pepper-and-salt." But if scenes such as this one openly announce the commodification of women that other Victorian novels strive to disguise, they also uncover a conflict between the sexual and market economies. Unlike flour, whose price increases with scarcity, these old maids are gradually depreciating—recapitulating, in slow motion, Ruth's precipitous "fall" in market value. The unexpected parallel in the sexual marketability of these elderly virgins and the prematurely "corrupted" teenager reveals that neither removing oneself from nor participating in sexual exchange successfully navigates this volatile market. In fact, these alternatives—corresponding to hoarding on the one hand and promiscuous expenditure on the other—test the limits of a market economy, laying bare its faultlines and internal contradictions.[2]

Of course, the description of women as a form of property was a timeworn trope, but it assumed particular urgency amidst the fluctuating markets and political unrest of the early nineteenth century. Protofeminists joined labor activists in borrowing the language of abolition to protest the social structures which enacted this commodification by confining "one half the human race" to domestic "slavery."[3] Friedrich Engels echoed this rhetoric, and codified the relationship between the sexual and market economies, by providing a mechanism—the private ownership of property and industrial production—for the enslavement of women:

> Household management . . . became a *private service*; the wife became the head servant, excluded from all participation in social production. . . . The modern individual family is founded on the open or concealed domestic slavery of the wife, and modern society is a mass composed of these individual families as its molecules.[4]

This description makes the marriage and commodity markets appear perfectly complementary, implying that the traffic in women which is enabled by capitalist production and exchange is also strictly analogous to other property transactions: in Karl Marx's metonymy, women are one of the many kinds of property a bourgeois can own ("*Marriage* . . . is incontestably a form of exclusive private *property*"); in Engels's metaphor, household dynamics replicate industrial production ("within the family he is the bourgeois, and the wife represents the proletariat").[5] Modern critics have endorsed this analogy: Mary Poovey has recently contended that a wife's ability to *represent* her husband's private property stabilizes the market economy by compensating for "the alienation of market relations" which the (male) worker experiences outside the home, where he himself becomes an object when he sells his labor-power.[6]

Surprisingly, then, both Victorian celebrations of the separate spheres, and nineteenth- and twentieth-century condemnations of them, consistently maintain that a sheltered home and a bustling marketplace reinforce one another.[7] On the surface, *Ruth*'s cautionary tale appears to provide further evidence for this familiar assertion: when Ruth transgresses against the rules of one sphere, she is punished in the other as well. Yet if the complicity of the domestic and market economies creates the vicious circle which forms the novel's plot—Ruth loses her job because of her "improper" conduct; she is seduced because she is helpless without the means and position provided by a job; she is again fired when her sexual history becomes public—this intimate connection allows Ruth's sexual transgressions to become

a critique of the market economy as a whole, while the novel's gestures towards alternative economies also destabilize its domestic ideology. Ruth's most profound transgression is thus not her violation of Victorian purity codes—as Sally Mitchell has noted, the Victorians were all too familiar with the social phenomenon of the fallen woman, and with her literary representative, the fallen woman novel. Yet the publication of *Ruth* caused a disproportionate scandal: two of Gaskell's friends even burnt their copies to demonstrate how "*very* bad" they thought it.[8] This reaction initially appears puzzling, since Gaskell's novel is in many ways less overtly shocking than its predecessors: after her initial fall, Ruth remains uncharacteristically chaste, neither cementing her moral depravity by descending into prostitution nor redeeming it by marrying. But the novel's careful quarantine of its heroine's tainted sexuality ironically enables a more fundamental disruption of Victorian social standards. If Ruth's fall violates Victorian sexual mores, her compensatory rejection of both money and an offer of marriage from her seducer compounds her transgression by flouting the rules of commodity capitalism as well. By refusing to become either a prostitute or a wife (which, as many Victorian feminists noted, were simply two configurations of the same transaction), Ruth breaks down the categories which kept the sexual and market economies working in tandem.[9] More radical than having sex outside of marriage, Ruth has sex outside of the cash nexus: in this novel which lays bare women's status as private property, the heroine will not be bought and sold. Ruth's resistance to exchange links her to the spinsters in the Benson household, and the economy of hoarding that dominates it in the later sections of the novel. Meanwhile, her excessive productivity (of an illegitimate child, whom she declines to transfer to his father's legitimating possession) corresponds to the various forms of extravagant expenditure that equally threaten the novelistic economy.

Ruth's unorthodox refusal to be commodified is mirrored in the novel's most conventional subplot: when Jemima Bradshaw rejects the analogy between marriage and the marketplace, she almost derails the novel's courtship plot altogether. Taking refuge in the sentimental logic of her mother's novels, she repudiates the commercial ethics motivating her father to try to transfer her to his business partner "as a sort of stock in trade" (228). Commodification, in her eyes, is tantamount to objectification, prompting Jemima's protests that her future husband is shopping for a wife "just as you would do for a carpet" (224). Despite the narrator's claim that this description is an "exaggeration of all her father had said" (223), British law would have confirmed Jemima's sense that she had an actual property value for her father much as she later would for her husband: husbands could collect monetary damages for "criminal conversation"; so too, the *Law Review* clarified in 1854 (the year after *Ruth*'s publication), "if the father loses the benefit or profit of his daughter's services through the act of her seducer, his right to damages accrues, and a jury is directed to award him compensation for the consequential injury he has sustained."[10] Mr. Bradshaw himself makes perfectly clear that his daughter's economic terminology is neither overstated nor merely figurative. He intends, literally, to profit from Jemima's marriage, which he views almost exclusively in the light of a financial transaction:

> The fitness of the thing had long ago struck him; her father's partner—so the fortune he meant to give her might continue in the business; a man of such steadiness of character, and such a capital eye for a desirable speculation as Mr Farquhar . . . a house ready-furnished . . . no near relations . . . [to] add to the household expenses—in short, what could be more suitable in every way? Mr Bradshaw respected the very self-restraint he thought he saw in Mr Farquhar's demeanour, attributing it to a wise desire to wait until trade should be rather more slack, and the man of business more at leisure to become the lover. (216-17)

If Bradshaw respects Farquhar's self-restraint, it is correspondingly Jemima's feminine modesty which he expects to close the deal. Indeed, he lectures her, explaining that to do "credit" to her exemplary "moral and religious training," she should curb the expression of her opinions, and moderate the opinions themselves, so as to avoid "going into a passion" (222). These paternal injunctions, commonplace as they may appear, begin to indicate the contradictions under which Jemima is laboring. Bradshaw's desire to cash in on his daughter's virtue makes that virtue itself appear economically motivated and therefore suspect; Jemima's modesty at once establishes her value on the marriage market and necessitates her exclusion from it.[11] Further, this paradoxical definition of feminine purity is matched by contradictory standards for masculine middle-class virtue. In *Family Fortunes,* Leonore Davidoff and Catherine Hall argue that men's reputations in the business world were as fragile—and as crucial—as female modesty: women needed spotless reputations to get husbands; men needed spotless reputations to get credit.[12] Jemima can thus attack Farquhar for his attempts to gain "credit" in the business world by suggesting that they rely on the same hypocrisy that her father exerts on her behalf in the marriage market: "'Oh, Mr Farquhar!' said she, suddenly changing to a sort of upbraiding tone of voice. . . . '[Y]ou are good because it adds to your business credit—you talk in that high strain because it sounds well, and is respectable'" (223-24). She expresses her own dilemma in nearly identical terms: "So! I am to behave well, not because it is right—not because it is right—but to show off before Mr Farquhar" (223).

If marrying a modest wife and then maintaining her in leisure was a key step in a middle-class man's efforts to

establish financial credit, Jemima's refusal to display modesty in order to win a husband who will display her uncovers the circularity of middle-class discourses of both feminine and masculine virtue. Her modest rejection of a solvent suitor reveals that, instead of reinforcing one another, the ideal of feminine purity and the language of exchange create a paradoxical system in which women are simultaneously central to the market economy and, by definition, excluded from it. Although Victorian feminists described women as domestic slaves, they drew the line at actual purchase: in her *Brief Summary in Plain Language of the Most Important Laws Concerning Women,* Barbara Leigh Smith Bodichon famously informed readers that at least the literal traffic in women, exemplified by "the belief that a man can rid himself of his wife by going through the farce of a sale," violated every standard of law and decency.[13] Jemima extends this argument, explaining her paralyzed inability to participate in the marriage market by describing herself not just as inalienable property, but as capitalism's impossible object—a commodity without a price. When her father explains the "pecuniary point of view" which would make her marriage to Farquhar "most fortunate" for him, she rhetorically asks, "were those the terms upon which her rich woman's heart was to be given?" (221). Still describing herself as property, and even as portable property, Jemima repeats Ruth's transgressive escape from the strictures of exchange: unwilling to sell herself at any price, she insists that she is worth so much that she can only be given away. As I discuss more fully below, here two apparently opposite kinds of anti-economic activity—refusal to circulate (hoarding) and circulation without payment (pure expenditure)—begin to appear suspiciously close.

Since the logic of exchange, as much as the ideology of female purity, mandates that Jemima can only give herself away once, she spends most of the novel resisting its nuptial teleology.[14] In this economy centered around hoarding, a woman's sexual purity, preserved as carefully as a miser's wealth, at once defines the standard of value and remains suspended in a kind of unproductive and noncirculating uselessness. This is not Thorstein Veblen's usefully useless conspicuous leisure, in which a woman's withdrawal from the marketplace serves (necessarily, in a credit economy) as one of the signs of her husband's or father's solvency—any more than a miser's hoarded treasure is equivalent to a capitalist's productively invested wealth.[15] Most Victorian discussions of hoarding confuse these two types of saving; even Frederick Merryweather's frankly critical *Lives and Anecdotes of Misers* employs a Smilesian rhetoric praising thrift, maintaining that "the propensity to acquire is natural to the human mind, and when it is manifested by a prudent frugality, is one of the greatest moral blessings of life."[16] Thomas Malthus, however, recognized the fundamental difference: "No political economist of the present day can by saving mean mere hoarding. . . . [Real saving involves an] application of what is saved" to maintain labor."[17] For Malthus, genuine saving requires an escape-valve for expenditure, which is segregated from the work of accumulation: a separate class of spenders—landowners, aristocrats, clergy—waste what industrialists earn. Of course, most critics have identified *women* as the main constituents of this spending class, which, in Malthus's terms, works to "keep separate the passion for expenditure and the passion for accumulation."[18]

Jemima, however, proposes a different division of labor, between economic agents and their *objects*: so long as she is to be bought and sold "like a carpet," her reduction to the status of property should be complete. In a reversal of Bodichon's rhetoric, Jemima finally

> even wished that they might not go through the form of pretending to try to gain her consent to the marriage, if it involved all this premeditated action and speech-making. . . . She felt as if she would rather be bought openly, like an Oriental daughter, where no one is degraded in their own eyes by being parties to such a contract.
>
> (240-41)

Here, the woman's commodification resolves not her husband's alienation, but her own: Jemima's oriental projection provides a foil to the self-division governing English courtship plots, in which the buying and selling which determine a young woman's social worth have to be conducted under the veil of what Ruth Bernard Yeazell has dubbed a "fiction of modesty."[19] As Yeazell observes, the division between the heroine who is marketed and the modest girl who isn't aware of the transaction may (temporarily) disable courtship, but it enables plot: once the heroine becomes self-conscious, her transfer to a husband and her story come to a simultaneous end. Thus, after spending the novel reviling the marriage market, Jemima is saved from spinsterhood by an eleventh-hour husband *ex machina* and immediately becomes an almost insignificant, and conspicuously absent, footnote to *Ruth*'s main narrative.

The potential value which accrues to Jemima's purity is realized when she marries, but the peculiar proposition that female chastity has an inherent value, even outside of the system of exchanges between fathers and husbands, is reinforced by the situation of the elderly virgins in the Benson household. Although Gaskell is usually quite explicit about economic details, the novel is deliberately vague in its implication that the mere fact that Faith and Sally have scrupulously avoided any contact with the sexual marketplace somehow gives them a positive economic value. Without describing the process that makes this possible, both spinsters identify their failure to marry as altruistic, explaining that they

are sacrificing themselves to care for Mr. Benson. Yet, since neither of them works outside of the home, and Sally is paid for the work which she does in the home, it is difficult to understand how they serve as an addition to, rather than a drain on, the household finances, except insofar as their chastity constitutes a socially bankable possession. Historians of Victorian sexuality such as Steven Marcus and Fraser Harrison have called attention to a rhetorical slippage which facilitates this conflation of chastity and property:

> the body is regarded as a productive system with only a limited amount of material at its disposal. And the model on which the notion of sems is formed is clearly that of money. Thus a common Victorian euphemism for orgasm was "to spend" and a man who indulged in excessive sexual activities could be said to face "ruin. . . . [H]e goes bankrupt and is sold up . . . like the head of a company who has invested wildly in shares."

Hence, "celibate and capitalist alike resolutely fought off the desire to spend."[20] Moreover, within this bodily economy (in contrast to the market economy), women were supposed to be natural savers: as Jill Conway recalls, "[Scottish biologist Patrick] Geddes was convinced that sex differences should be viewed as arising from a basic difference in cell metabolism. . . . At the level of the cell, maleness was characterized by the tendency to dissipate energy, femaleness, by the capacity to store or build up energy."[21]

Despite its apparently organic underpinnings, the sexual economy in *Ruth* quickly devolves into pure wish fulfillment, blatantly incapable of resolving real economic problems. *Ruth*'s publication coincided with an overabundance of unmarried women like Faith and Sally, and contemporary observers recognized that they were the source of a financial crisis rather than an economic asset. Even before W. R. Greg's "Why are Women Redundant?" (1862) quantified the problem of women for whom there were, statistically, no husbands available, social observers such as Henry Mayhew and Léon Faucher drew attention to the limited economic prospects for unmarried women. Both Mayhew and Faucher further attribute the number of "fallen women" to the problem of female redundancy, intimating that prostitution might be the sole means of support for these otherwise economically helpless women.[22] This argument underscores the sheer illogic of Gaskell's economic structure, in which the spinsters are an asset, but Ruth—who, unlike Sally and Faith, earns wages which she contributes to the family budget—is a financial burden. Despite all of her plans to make herself "useful" (367), Ruth is invariably described in terms which make clear that she has a negative value in the household economy. Her polluting presence is such a drain on the domestic resources that the narrator holds her responsible for the shabby condition of the Benson home: "Then as to the house. It was not one where the sitting-rooms are refurnished every two or three years; not now, even (since Ruth came to share their living) a place where, as an article grew shabby or worn, a new one was purchased. The furniture looked poor, and the carpets almost threadbare" (207). In this passage metonymy slips into metaphor, and the worn-out look of the Benson furniture recalls that Ruth is useless because she too is used goods. A causal justification for this comparison is provided only long after the fact, when Mr. Bradshaw fires Ruth on account of her sexual history and, finding it impossible to get other work, she becomes even more of "a burden and an expense" (386).

If the novel's equation of moral and material value thus makes a sexually tainted Ruth more of a liability than the elderly spinsters in the Benson household—by preventing her from earning an income or even, mysteriously, when she is earning an income—Ruth has to repair her economic status from within the realm of sexual exchange. By holding herself aloof from sexual circulation, Ruth is remarkably successful in her effort to restore the social credit which she lost by being overcirculated. The modesty of her demeanor during the years in which she lives in Eccleston under false pretenses impresses everyone, including her rival Jemima, who understands that this withdrawal from the system of sexual exchange actually compensates for and erases Ruth's earlier transgression:

> I watched her, and I watched her with my wild-beast eyes. If I had seen one paltering with duty—if I had witnessed one flickering shadow of untruth in word or action—if, more than all things, my woman's instinct had ever been conscious of the faintest speck of impurity in thought, or word, or look, my old hate would have flamed out with the flame of hell! My contempt would have turned to loathing disgust, instead of my being full of pity, and the stirrings of new-awakened love, and most true respect.
>
> (339)

Ruth's chaste behavior wins Farquhar's as well as Jemima's admiration. By avoiding sexual exchange she almost qualifies to re-enter it: although Ruth's history is discovered before he actually proposes, Farquhar was undoubtedly planning to make her an offer, prompted by "her shy reserve, and her quiet daily walk within the lines of duty, [which] were much in accordance with Mr Farquhar's notion of what a wife should be" (241).

The history which prevents Farquhar from proposing to Ruth does not, however, completely annihilate her marital prospects, since Donne himself offers to marry her when he discovers that she will not become his mistress again. Like Farquhar, Donne is impressed by Ruth's "reserve"—her retreat from sexual circulation—which he meets with a determination to "bid a higher price" (302) and marry her. This phrase at once confirms that

Ruth's "price" rises the more she declines to be bought, and exhibits Donne's absolute failure to understand the permutations of this sexual economy. For what is at stake here is not a simple question of supply and demand. Rather, when, like Jemima, Ruth resists selling her "rich woman's heart" for any amount of money, her value changes not in degree but in kind. Ruth becomes an entirely different commodity, a marriageable woman, which means that she will reject Donne's offers, whatever they are—his "bid," which he makes precisely because he realizes that Ruth cannot be bought, is inherently self-defeating.[23] The only way that a redeemed Ruth can prove her virtue is to refuse to circulate sexually, even within the legally and morally sanctioned confines of marriage; to emerge as the heroine of the novel, Ruth cannot marry either Farquhar or Donne. By the end of the novel, then, Ruth has become simultaneously marriageable and unable to marry, or in fact marriageable precisely because she will not marry.

Of course, this effectively puts Ruth in much the same position as the one occupied by Jemima, whose cash value depends, as her father explained, on her modest withdrawal from sexual circulation—and who therefore, in what is overtly a marriage *market,* incongruously becomes the most valuable kind of commodity because she cannot enter into exchange. In one sense, this parallel provides the novel with a kind of structural unity: the women in **Ruth** systematically deconstruct the entire repertoire of social roles—spinster, prostitute, wife—that connect the sexual and market economies. Yet the similarity between the two heroines is unexpected: in terms of their sexual value, Jemima and Ruth should represent opposite extremes, a pure treasure and damaged goods. Instead, they are explicitly and consistently portrayed as doubles, in ways prefigured by the novel's assignment of the lead role, which should go to the chaste young lady involved in a courtship plot, to Ruth.[24] While each woman negotiates the increasingly untenable distinctions between being a valuable commodity (a marriageable woman) and a valueless redundancy (a commodity which cannot be circulated or exchanged), this reminder of their similarity further breaks down the barriers separating the plot and the subplot, the modest girl and the fallen woman, the valuable and the useless.[25]

This peculiar doubling sharpens the novel's critique of the market economy, which (as critics of capitalism noted from the outset) both relies on and causes a general obliteration of difference to facilitate the universal interconvertibility of goods and labor. Albert Hirschman adds that the cash nexus collapses formerly opposed "passions" (such as the desire for power, ambition, or lust) into a generalized economy of "interests" (encapsulated in the desire for money).[26] This homogenization of desire in the marketplace underscores the importance of a separate domestic sphere, ostensibly governed by a model of individuality and difference. The ideology of romantic love, in particular, rests on the premise that each person is importantly unique—as opposed, most directly, to prostitution, which presumes that, within certain limited parameters, everyone's desires are the same: not one ideal woman, but any woman, can satisfy those desires. This conflict between the reduction of all desire to comparable sameness and individuation is central to almost every nineteenth-century novel plot: realist fiction may create and valorize the interiority which allows for difference, but its gnomic premises and conclusions reincorporate that difference into comfortably general maxims. From Jane Austen's "truth universally acknowledged" to Wilkie Collins's universalizing description of an object of desire ("Think of *her*, as you thought of the first woman who quickened the pulses *within you* that the rest of her sex had no art to stir"), love plots in nineteenth-century novels repeatedly concede that the logic of sameness and exchangeability permeates the romantic as well as the economic sphere.[27] ***Ruth*** once again departs from the pattern only by making it explicit: when Farquhar alternately wishes to marry two women with virtually opposite personalities (whatever structural similarities the novel establishes between them), Jemima's refusal to be commodified becomes a rejection of the application of the principle of exchange to her personal life, and with it of the analogy between sexual and market economies on which Victorian courtship plots—and middle-class courtships—relied.

Even more surprisingly, the novel extends this disruption of the principles of identity and exchange to financial transactions as well. In a properly functioning economy, money should of course be the measure of sameness, and nothing more: in Georg Simmel's formulation of a standard economic doctrine, "money becomes the absolutely commensurate expression and equivalent of all values"; "it rises to abstract heights way above the whole broad diversity of objects; it becomes the centre in which the most opposed, the most estranged and the most distant things find their common denominator." But, as Simmel also notes, money thereby acquires a disproportionate value, in which it appears not as a means to an end, but as an end itself: "Never has an object that owes its value exclusively to its quality as a means, to its convertibility into more definite values, so thoroughly and unreservedly developed into a psychological value absolute, into a completely engrossing final purpose."[28] ***Ruth*** most clearly illustrates this elevation of means to ends through Sally's nonsensical financial arrangements, which reveal that the anti-economic logic Jemima applies to her marital prospects does not alleviate the tensions of the marketplace so much as reproduce them. For eighteen years, Sally saves most of the salary which Mr. Benson insists on giving her, although he can barely afford it, only to return the combined amount to him, as his own, at the end of that time. Her unexpected gift astonishes Mr. Benson, prompting him to ask where the money has come from. Sally's answer is almost a tautology: "'Come from!' she replied. 'Where does all money come from, but the Bank, to be sure'" (379). Sally's literalism calls attention to the gap between the actual and material origins of money, between wealth and its signs. In Mr. Benson's case, this gap is significant: he responds to Sally's circular and uninformative reply by announcing that he has no money in the bank. Nonetheless, when Sally returns her unspent income, he also refuses to use it, proposing that, just as she has held onto it for him, he will now store it for her.

The absurdity of this situation is emphasized by Mr. Benson's effort to find a safe and profitable way to take care of Sally's tiny nest egg, which appears superfluous considering that no one seems to intend ever to spend this money. "I'll take care of it for you with the greatest pleasure," he tells Sally, before confirming the unproductiveness of her savings, "Still, you know, banks allow interest" (380). Sally takes even stricter precautions to ensure the security of this carefully, albeit pointlessly, saved hoard: after withdrawing all forty-two pounds in sovereigns, "for fear of fire," she bizarrely advises Mr. Benson to protect the money from her: "Lock it up safe, out o' the way," she warns Mr. Benson, "Dunnot go and leave it about to tempt folks. I'll not answer for myself if money's left about. I may be cribbing a sovereign" (379).[29]

Evidently, Sally's and Mr. Benson's reciprocal generosity is a reciprocal fiction. When returning the money, Sally maintains that it has been Mr. Benson's all along—which is to say that she only pretended, from the outset and continuously for eighteen years, not to have rejected her pay-raise: "It's your own," she assures Mr. Benson, "It's not mine. It always was yours. Now you're not going to fret me by saying you think it mine" (380). Similarly, while "Mr Benson had been too much gratified and touched, by her unconditional gift of all she had in the world, to reject it" (380), this is exactly what he does, although he continues to humor Sally, much as she humored him: "but he only held it in his hands as a deposit until he could find a safe investment befitting so small a sum" (380-81). Sally's hoarding calls into question the economic norms to which it is contrasted by reversing the hypostatization which usually obscures the meaning of money: for Sally and Mr. Benson, her sovereigns are not so many material objects, nor even markers of abstract and exchangeable value, but rather the concrete signs of their relationship. By repersonalizing this money—and with it the labor-relation it represents—Sally's hoarding becomes not simply an aberration within a commodity culture, much less an exaggeration of its principles, but instead a fundamental disruption of the reification on which capitalist exchange depends.

Sally violates the logic of economics by arresting the cycle of exchange, unmasking money as a symbol rather than a material reality; she then similarly defamiliarizes language (in this case, language about money) when she orders her will. The uselessness of this document is overdetermined: it bequeaths money to Mr. Benson which, as we have seen, Sally need not have taken in the first place if she planned to hoard and then return it; moreover, since she does return the money, the will is ultimately meaningless. Sally herself recognizes this, and has Leonard build a frame for what she tacitly acknowledges is a purely ornamental object. But the most telling way in which Sally's will is, like her saved income, a pure symbol divorced from its purported use value is in the actual language which it employs. Assuming that the purpose of language is to communicate, Sally not only accepts a will which is too obscure to be of any use to her, she demands it. When she hears the first draft of the will, she is distinctly unimpressed:

> And would you belie' me, he read it out as if it were as clear a business as your giving me that thimble—no more ado, though it were thirty pound! I could understand it mysel'—that were no law for me. I wanted summat to consider about, and for th' meaning to be wrapped up as I wrap up my best gown.

(194-95)

Although Sally seems to be speaking about the value of both her property (which is worth more than a thimble) and the meaning of the law which will protect it (which she would treat as carefully as her most precious possessions), the real question here is the value of the language of the document itself. Determined to fill her testament with words which she cannot read, pronounce, or understand—with words which are, as far as she is concerned, empty signs—Sally takes the drastic measure of paying an extra sixpence for every difficult word which is "not to be caught up as a person runs" (195). Numerous economic theorists have remarked on the distinct congruity between the roles of money and language as sign systems: "as a visible object, money is the substance that embodies abstract economic value, in a similar fashion to the sound of words which is an acoustic-physiological occurrence but has significance for us only through the representation that it bears or symbolizes."[30] In Sally's abstruse will, language, like sexuality and money elsewhere in the novel, registers the persistence of alternative values, outside of the logic of exchangeability and usefulness.[31]

While Sally carefully saves her wages to bequeath them back to her employer, the household suffers for lack of basic necessities. By this point, the Bensons' budget has become so strained that, in an additionally ironic twist, they are reduced to making furnishings out of scraps of refuse:

> Few events broke the monotony of their lives, and those events were of a depressing kind. They consisted in Ruth's futile endeavors to obtain some employment, however humble . . . [and] in the final and unmendable wearing-out of the parlour carpet, which there was no spare money to replace, and so they cheerfully supplied its want by a large hearth-rug that Ruth made out of ends of list.

(377)

Even under these circumstances, Sally's money is of course not touched; more importantly, the recycling in this scene, and throughout *Ruth,* is itself a kind of hoarding, extending Sally's refusal to spend any of her money to a range of other objects.[32] Simmel's analysis is again revealing; he explains that it is a mistake to interpret this hyperbole of conservation as an endorsement of the values of the cash nexus:

> It is very characteristic of the mastery that money has attained over the general way of thinking that we are accustomed to designating a series of phenomena as avarice—in the sense of greed for money—which in reality are its exact opposite. Such phenomena are manifested in people who use a burned-out match again, who carefully tear off empty letter pages, who don't throw away a piece of string and who spend a lot of time in searching for every lost pin. . . . In many cases, it is not the fraction of a penny that the thrifty person is concerned to save; often they have no consideration for the money by which the object itself could be easily replaced, but instead merely value the object itself. In this category belong peculiar, but not altogether rare, people who give away a hundred marks without hesitation, but give away a sheet of paper from their writing desk, or something similar, only with true self-conquest.[33]

Simmel's account almost exactly reproduces Gaskell's description of the peculiar conjunction of hoarding and expenditure in *Cranford,* which was being serialized as *Ruth* came out. In Cranford, everyone considers something or other too precious ever to be used, something whose "little unnecessary waste" seems worse than "spending shillings or pounds on some real extravagance." The narrator herself collects string and rubber rings, supposedly because she cannot stand to see them wasted. In effect, though, her manic collecting is scarcely distinguishable from sheer wastefulness:

> String is my foible. My pockets get full of little hanks of it, picked up and twisted together, ready for uses that never come. I am seriously annoyed if any one cuts the string of a parcel, instead of patiently and faithfully undoing it fold by fold. How people can bring themselves to use India-rubber rings, which are a sort of deification of string, as lightly as they do, I cannot imagine. To me an India-rubber ring is a precious treasure. I have one which is not new; one that I picked up off the floor, nearly six years ago. I have really tried to use it; but my heart failed me, and I could not commit the extravagance.[34]

Surprisingly, both Simmel's and Gaskell's descriptions link the notions of irrational hoarding and extravagance: the economic rebel spends as well as saves. In *Cran-*

ford, expenditure outside of the strict boundaries of use and exchange acquires a moral connotation. When a store clerk rejects a poor farmer's banknote because it is "little better than waste paper" now that the bank has failed, Miss Matty exchanges the note for sovereigns of her own. Although she admits that she cannot account for her feeling that because she was a shareholder in the bank she would "rather exchange [her] gold for the note," it is surely a feeling that the reader is meant to respect.[35]

Even when such delicate questions of responsibility are not involved, Gaskell endorses a certain amount of pure wastefulness. Notably, in **Mary Barton** Gaskell is much less critical than most middle-class authors of industrial fiction about the high rate of expenditure in working-class families during periods of economic prosperity.[36] The comfortable furnishings and the comparatively abundant though not lavish fare of the Bartons' "tea party," with which **Mary Barton** begins, are depicted as necessary contributions to the domestic comfort and tranquillity of this scene. Although the party is an "extravagance" which will cause later scarcities, it proceeds with the narrator's full support and approbation.[37] In **Ruth,** the same attitude is expressed as a general moral homily. When the Bensons prepare cakes and tea for Jemima, and her father forbids her to eat them because he feels that the Bensons are too poor for this unnecessary expense, the narrator explains that

> Sally could have told of the self-denial when no one was by . . . practiced without thinking even to themselves that it was either a sacrifice or a virtue, in order to enable them to help those who were in need, or even to gratify Miss Benson's kind, old-fashioned feelings on such occasions as the present, when a stranger came to the house. Her homely, affectionate pleasure in making others comfortable, might have shown that such little extravagances were not waste, but a good work; and were not to be gauged by the standard of money spending.
>
> (182)

Almost seamlessly, this passage implies that because extravagance requires sacrifice it is also a virtue, and that domestic wastefulness in the interest of entertaining well-off guests somehow has essentially the same status as charities given to those in need. Above all, it suggests that wastefulness is really a kind of usefulness, since rightly viewed it qualifies as another "good work."

Gaskell's proto-Bataillean celebration of expenditure complements the economy of hoarding exemplified by the strict removal of women (defined as markers of value) from the system of exchange.[38] Just as Ruth will not put a price on herself, she willfully disregards the material value of other objects (even of money), performing a kind of passive expenditure by turning down the gifts which are offered to her throughout the novel.

Her lack of interest in money is an important component of the novel's scrupulous effort to distance Ruth's story from any of the polluting connotations of prostitution. Yet the novel exaggerates this attitude until it is almost incomprehensible by making Ruth treat everything with financial value as though it were entirely worthless. Mr. Benson alone understands the unmercenary attitude behind Ruth's strange wish to receive valueless gifts. "I understand what you mean," he assures her,

> It is a delight to have gifts made to you by those whom you esteem and love, because then such gifts are merely to be considered as fringes to the garment—as inconsiderable additions to the mighty treasure of their affection, adding a grace, *but no additional value,* to what before was precious . . . but you feel it to be different when there is no regard for the giver to idealize the gift—when it simply takes its stand among your property *as so much money's value.*
>
> (157, my emphases)

As a result of this aversion to gifts with "so much money's value," Ruth regularly returns the expensive presents which Mr. Bradshaw sends her. In particular, she sends back the dress with which he tries to buy her moral influence on Jemima: "With the fragrance of Ruth's sweetness lingering about her, Jemima was her best self during the next half hour. Mr Bradshaw was more and more pleased, and raised the price of the silk, which he was going to give Ruth, sixpence a yard during the time" (236). Although Ruth will not allow a cash value to be affixed to her expression of friendship, Bradshaw's offer reveals just how fine the line dividing the separate spheres, insulating the emotional from the economic, has become. Donne's attempts to buy Ruth at auction make the point even more clearly, though he too is eventually forced to realize that she "despise[s]" money (300). His mother, meanwhile, cannot understand Ruth's rejection of the usual forms of property and value: when she is asked to help Ruth, Mrs. Bellingham twice tries to offer her a fifty-pound note instead of more personal assistance. What Ruth thinks of this offer is aptly demonstrated by the fact that, even though she is penniless, pregnant, and alone, she leaves "the banknote lying quite promiscuous, like wastepaper, on the floor" (107). Violating a central rule of the exchange economy—that money is impersonal, with no origins or emotional value attached to it: *pecunia non olet*—Ruth recognizes that Mrs. Bellingham's money is *dirty,* and returns it so as to "wash [her] hands of these Bellinghams" (127).

Ruth's extravagance also recalls the medical discourse which conflated sexual and financial "saving"; Dr. Charles Mercier articulated the corollary equation, explaining the sequence of events issuing from women's unchastity:

> they exhibit other forms of vice, showing that generally, their capacity of unrestraint is undeveloped. They are usually drunkards; they are always spendthrift . . .

they are thoroughly immoral. . . . It is not that the moral impulse towards lust is greater in them than in most women, but the restraint of modesty is less. Incapable of continuous industry, they are yet under the necessity of making a livelihood, and in the absence of restraint of modesty, they turn to that occupation in which a livelihood can be made without industry.[39]

In Mercier's account, prostitution resolves the paradox of the fallen woman's perverse economy: she spends irresponsibly, but does not produce. This formula also defines her sexual economy since the fallen woman either fails to reproduce or has an illegitimate child, a social and economic liability rather than an asset: even the sympathetic doctor describes Ruth's child as "all plague and no profit" (309). In one of the novel's most shocking reversals, however, Ruth and Mr. Benson overturn this assessment of Leonard's economic value. Mr. Benson opposes the general belief that Leonard is a "disgrace" or a "badge of [Ruth's] shame," and rather sees him as "God's messenger to lead [Ruth] back to Him" (118). Ruth, who refused to commodify her sexuality by accepting either Donne's money or his offer of marriage, even more clearly transgresses the boundaries between legitimate and illegitimate production when she describes Leonard as "her one treasure" (209). As Bradshaw recognizes, here Ruth not only disregards the established standards of value, she more troublingly founds an alternate value system which mimics the legitimate economy. Bradshaw objects to Leonard because he constitutes a kind of forgery, an illicit copy whose authorship is not acknowledged, and which has a *negative* value, since it has the potential to deflate and contaminate the authentic goods it counterfeits. Voicing a common view of illegitimacy, Bradshaw insists that Leonard is too "stained and marked with sin from . . . birth" to "associate with [his] own innocent children," and goes so far as to conclude that "the best thing that could happen to him would be for him to be lost to all sense of shame, dead to all knowledge of guilt" (340). The success of Ruth's efforts to create an alternative system of value is confirmed when the doctor offers to accept her son as his apprentice, not despite Leonard's illegitimacy but because of it—since, as we then discover, the doctor himself is illegitimate.[40]

Gaskell's employment of the popularly recognized homologies between a forged document and an illegitimate child to characterize Leonard becomes even more pointed when Bradshaw's son—the "innocent" he tried to protect from Leonard's contamination—becomes a forger. Richard's crime completes the novel's overturn of standard economic proprieties: Ruth treats valuables as though they are worthless; he circulates worthless paper as a valuable commodity. While the episodes describing these events may seem to be a nearly unmotivated and inappropriately melodramatic subplot, in fact Richard's forgery in many ways echoes Ruth's story. She too circulates and gains admission where she does

not belong by assuming a false name and acting under false pretenses; Bradshaw expels her from his family and from his home, as he does Richard, when he discovers the deceit.[41] *Ruth* thus begins with an act of unlicensed sexuality and ends with an unauthorized commercial transaction. These violations—resulting in illegitimacy on the one hand and forgery and fraud on the other—challenge the usual structures of sexual and economic exchange. More radically, they also point out the contradictions already embedded within these structures. Throughout *Ruth*, value is defined not by exchange but by its conspicuous absence: this hoarding economy reverses the hypostatization which makes money and women endlessly exchangeable. Meanwhile, extravagant expenditure reinvests value in a world of objects which is at once concrete and sublime: *Cranford*'s "deification of string" becomes *Ruth*'s substitution of "the mighty treasure of . . . affection" for unidealized gifts with "so much money's value." By the end of *Ruth*, "the standard of money spending" recedes into the background as the redeemed heroine prepares to "take her wages" (447) in the spiritualized form of God's ultimate reward. If Georg Lukács described the novel as "the epic of a world that has been abandoned by God," Simmel maintains that *money* fills this void, providing a new measure of all things, a new origin, means, and end to impose on the chaos of experience.[42] By disrupting the economy of equivalence and its teleology of exchange, *Ruth*'s apparently orthodox conclusion reveals a challenge to the apotheosis of Mammon and the strict narrative logic which it imposes: in the end, you can't take it with you.

Notes

1. Elizabeth Gaskell, *Ruth* (1853) (Oxford: Oxford Univ. Press, 1985), 205-6. Hereafter cited parenthetically by page number.

2. My argument draws on Jeff Nunokawa's perceptive account of the infiltration of the language and values of the marketplace into the domestic realm: "The nineteenth-century novel . . . observes the saving distance between home and marketplace only in its breach. The novel's celebration of domesticity as a sanctuary from the vicissitudes of the cash nexus is everywhere spoiled; everywhere the shades of the countinghouse fall upon the home" (*The Afterlife of Property: Domestic Security and the Victorian Novel* [Princeton: Princeton Univ. Press, 1994], 4).

3. See, for instance, William Thompson's 1825 comparison of women and slaves in his *Appeal of One Half the Human Race, Women, Against the Pretensions of the Other Half, Men, to Retain them in Political, and Thence in Civil and Domestic, Slavery* (New York: Source Book Press, 1970). Thompson argued that female "slavery" could only

be ended by radically reforming the competitive basis of the capitalist economy, as well as by giving women full political rights (196-209).

4. Friedrich Engels, *The Origin of the Family, Private Property and the State* (1884), trans. Alec West and Eleanor Burke Leacock (New York: International Publishers, 1972), 137.

5. Karl Marx, "Private Property and Communism," in *Early Writings* (1844), trans. T. B. Bottomore (New York, McGraw-Hill, 1963), 153; Engels, *Origins of the Family,* 137. Susan Kent discusses the commercial language which Victorian women employed to describe the interpenetration of market forces in the domestic sphere in *Sex and Suffrage in Britain, 1860-1914* (Princeton: Princeton Univ. Press, 1987), 85.

6. Mary Poovey, *Uneven Developments: The Ideological Work of Gender in Mid-Victorian England* (Chicago: Univ. of Chicago Press, 1988), 77.

7. Ruskin was of course the most famous proponent of this position: "We are foolish, and without excuse foolish, in speaking of the 'superiority' of one sex to the other, as if they could be compared in similar things. Each has what the other has not: each completes the other, and is completed by the other: they are in nothing alike, and the happiness and perfection of both depends on each asking and receiving from the other what the other only can give" (Ruskin, *Sesame and Lilies: Three Lectures* [1865] [London: George Allen and Co., 1900], 107). Barbara Caine, however, has noted that many Victorian feminists also supported the notion of separate spheres:

> Quite large numbers of . . . feminists tended rather to stress their own acceptance of the full extent and importance of sexual difference, and to put forward their own ideas about the unique contributions which women could make to society, in a framework very similar to that of Victorian domestic ideology—the frame of mind which is so often seen as the one against which they were protesting. The point for them, of course, was that domestic ideology, with its emphasis on the importance of the domestic sphere and of women's dominant role within it, was the only language in the nineteenth century which offered the basis for asserting the sexual differences between men and women, not in terms of women's inadequacy, but rather in terms of their distinctive merits and virtues.
>
> (*English Feminism, 1780-1980* [Oxford: Oxford Univ. Press, 1997], 114)

8. Sally Mitchell, *The Fallen Angel: Chastity, Class and Women's Reading, 1835-1880* (Bowling Green, OH: Bowling Green Univ. Press, 1981), 40-41. For the book-burning incident, see *The Letters of Mrs Gaskell,* ed. J. A. V. Chapple and Arthur Pollard (Manchester: Manchester Univ. Press, 1966), 226.

9. Ruth's refusal to accept money for sex is all the more surprising given that, according to popular definitions, she already was a prostitute: *London Labour and the London Poor,* for instance, had classified *all* fallen women as prostitutes, on the assumption that even those who were not hired piecemeal were simply "kept" on a longer term (Henry Mayhew, *London Labor and the London Poor,* 4 vols. [1861-1862; reprint, New York: Dover Publications, 1968], 4:213). In the century following Mary Wollstonecraft's discussion of marriage as an institution in which women are "legally prostituted" (in *A Vindication of the Rights of Woman* [1792] [Harmondsworth: Penguin, 1983], 151), the equation of marriage and prostitution became practically ubiquitous. An influential expression of this metaphor which is nearly contemporary with *Ruth* appears in George Drysdale's *Elements of Social Science* (London: E. Truelove, 1854): "Marriage . . . is in short the instrument, in numberless cases, of making the man a tyrant and the wife a slave . . . we see matches every day in which . . . the wish to obtain the social advantages and protection of marriage, is the real motive which influences the woman. Such marriages are in reality cases of *legalized prostitution*" (357). Also see Frances Power Cobbe's response to W. R. Greg's "Why are Women Redundant?", "What Shall We Do with Our Old Maids?" *Fraser's Magazine* (November 1862): and John Stuart Mill, *The Subjection of Women* (1869), chap. 2.

10. "The Laws Relating to Women," quoted in Poovey, *Uneven Developments,* 224 n. 32.

11. George Watt identifies the same double bind in the heroine's predicament, noting that it is Ruth's appropriately feminine passivity—not far removed from the modesty for which Jemima is praised—that sets her up for a fall (*The Fallen Woman in Nineteenth Century Fiction* [Totowa: Barnes and Noble, 1984]).

12. Leonore Davidoff and Catherine Hall, *Family Fortunes: Men and Women of the English Middle Class, 1780-1850* (Chicago: Univ. of Chicago Press, 1991), 207-22, 272-315.

13. Barbara Leigh Smith Bodichon, *Brief Summary in Plain Language of the Most Important Laws Concerning Women* (1854), quoted in Nunokawa, 5.

14. Following Walter Benn Michaels, Nunokawa argues that nineteenth-century narratives describe the eventual alienation of property as not only

possible but inevitable. See Michaels, *The Gold Standard and the Logic of Naturalism* (Berkeley: Univ. of California Press, 1987), and Nunokawa.

15. For Thorstein Veblen, conspicuous leisure precedes conspicuous consumption as a sign of middle-class wealth (*The Theory of the Leisure Class* [1899] [Boston: Houghton Mifflin, 1973], 41-80). As I argue later, in its alternation between hoarding and excessive expenditure, *Ruth* uncovers an analogous structural similarity, not between conspicuous leisure and conspicuous consumption (both of which enable the economy of exchange) but between women's refusal to enter the marriage market and the economy of the gift (both of which destabilize market dynamics).

16. Frederick Merryweather, *Lives and Anecdotes of Misers; or, the Passion of Avarice Displayed* (London: Simpkin, Marshall, 1850), 35.

17. Thomas Malthus, *Principles of Political Economy*, 2nd ed. (London, 1836), 38-39, quoted in Karl Marx, *Capital*, vol. 1, trans. Ben Fowkes (1867; New York, Vintage, 1977), 735. For Marx, this confusion is not merely a mistake, but a mystification, part of capital's erasure of its own history by way of the "abstinence theory," according to which "all the conditions necessary for the labour process are now converted into acts of abstinence on the part of the capitalist. If the corn is not all eaten, but in part also sown—abstinence of the capitalist. If the wine gets time to mature—abstinence of the capitalist" (*Capital*, 744-45).

18. Malthus, *Principles of Political Economy*, quoted in Marx, *Capital*, 743.

19. See Ruth Bernard Yeazell, *Fictions of Modesty: Women and Courtship in the English Novel* (Chicago: Univ. of Chicago Press, 1991). Yeazell's discussion of the paradoxes and contradictions of female modesty includes an analysis of John Cleland's *Fanny Hill*, whose story coyly deemphasizes the economic component of sexual exchange, even when the context is prostitution (112-13).

20. Steven Marcus, *The Other Victorians: A Study of Sexuality and Pornography in Mid-Nineteenth-Century England* (New York: Basic Books, 1964), 21-22, 26, 22; Fraser Harrison, *The Dark Angel: Aspects of Victorian Sexuality* (London: Sheldon, 1977), 20-21.

21. Jill Conway, "Stereotypes of Femininity in a Theory of Sexual Evolution," in *Suffer and be Still: Women in the Victorian Age*, ed. Martha Vicinus (Bloomington: Indiana Univ. Press, 1973), 144. See Patrick Geddes and J. Arthur Thomson, *The Evolution of Sex* (London: W. Scott, 1889).

22. Greg, "Why Are Women Redundant?" *National Review* 14 (1862): 434-60; Mayhew, *London Labour*, 2:213; Léon Faucher, *Études sur l'Angleterre* (Brussels: Wouters, 1845), 1:202. Also see Greg's "Prostitution" (*Westminster Review* 53 [July 1850]: 238-68), which cites Gaskell's earlier novel *Mary Barton*; Mitchell notes that Gaskell drew on Greg's terms of analysis for *Ruth*. Engels and other Victorian critics argued that if economic pressures contributed to prostitution, so did the structure of monogamous marriage, with its emphasis on female chastity. Engels concluded that patriarchal monogamy, like capitalism, would ultimately collapse as a result of its own internal contradictions: "We are now approaching a social revolution in which the economic foundations of monogamy as they have existed hitherto will disappear just as surely as those of its complement—prostitution. Monogamy arose from the concentration of considerable wealth in the hands of a single individual—a man—and from the need to bequeath this wealth to the children of that man and of no other. . . . By transforming the greater portion, at any rate, of permanent, heritable wealth—the means of production—into social property, the coming social revolution will reduce to a minimum all this anxiety about bequeathing and inheriting" (*Origins of the Family*, 138-39).

23. As Hilary Schor observes, the morally corrupt characters in *Ruth* attempt to fix prices in order to sidestep the more difficult (and interminable) work of evaluation: "the question of 'price' is really one of interpretation, of how to move between seeing and valuing, and specifically, how to evaluate once the stable, female object seems to shift, to resist your valuation. Putting a price on everything, of course, saves one from having to decide the value of individual souls and individual actions . . . But for Gaskell, morality is never absolutely fixed" (*Scheherezade in the Marketplace: Elizabeth Gaskell and the Victorian Novel* [Oxford: Oxford Univ. Press, 1992], 70). Schor's valuable analysis of the novel's ambivalent creation of Ruth as an aesthetic object provides another way of accounting for the heroine's ability to transcend the cash nexus.

24. The forms in which the doubling of Ruth and Jemima is revealed are various: Ruth takes over Jemima's role in the Bradshaw household, acting as a surrogate older sister to the young girls; Farquhar, and then Donne, are mentioned as possible husbands of both women; both even try on the same bonnet, in the scene which ends with the revelation of Ruth's secret. The contrast to Gaskell's own "Lizzie Leigh" (1850) and *Mary Barton* recalls that even in social problem fiction, sexual deviants are generally confined to the mar-

gins of the text, where they serve as reflections of and foils to the modest heroine's plot. For a discussion of the heroine's role in social problem fiction, see Yeazell, "Why Political Novels Have Heroines: *Sybil, Mary Barton,* and *Felix Holt,*" *Novel* 18 (1985): 126-44. On the doubling of Jemima and Ruth, see Felicia Bonaparte, *The Gypsy-Bachelor of Manchester: The Life of Mrs. Gaskell's Demon* (Charlottesville: Univ. Press of Virginia, 1992), 124-25.

25. In *Elizabeth Gaskell and the English Provincial Novel* (London: Methuen, 1975), W. A. Craik suggests that the lack of distinction between the main plot and the subplots in Gaskell's novels is part of a pattern in which she "reveals the significance of the apparently minor" (15).

26. Albert Hirschman, *The Passions and the Interests: Political Arguments for Capitalism Before its Triumph* (Princeton: Princeton Univ. Press, 1977). Nunokawa reads (sexual) difference back into this homogenized economy: "if the desire for the commodity resembles an undeniable sexual attraction, it is unlike any that accords with our own Balkanized erotic sensibilities. The passion for money transcends any local distinctions of desire. . . . While the appeal of an erotic object is confined to a particular sector of desire, the urge to exchange is assumed to be universal. . . . But sometimes the power of capital shrinks to the confines of particular sexualities" (17).

27. Paradigmatically, Hartright claims to differentiate Laura from other women only to collapse all loved women back into a general sameness. To get a "clear" image of Laura, the (heterosexual male) reader can substitute his own love-object for Hartright's portrait: "Think of *her,* as you thought of the first woman who quickened the pulses *within you* that the rest of her sex had no art to stir. . . . Let her voice speak the music that you once loved best. . . . Let her footstep . . . be like that other footstep" (1860) (Wilkie Collins, *The Woman In White* [Oxford: Oxford Univ. Press, 1980], 42, my emphases).

28. Georg Simmel, *The Philosophy of Money,* trans. Tom Bottomore and David Frisby (London: Routledge & Kegan Paul, 1978), 236, 232.

29. As we have seen, the refusal of Jemima, Faith, and Sally to become the commodified carriers of exchange value violates the logic of a sexual marketplace classically premised on "*the virginal woman['s] . . . pure exchange value.* She is nothing but the possibility, the place, the sign of relations among men. In and of herself, she does not exist: she is a simple envelope veiling what is really at stake in social exchange" (Luce Irigaray, *This Sex Which is Not One* [1977], trans. Catherine Porter with Carolyn Burke [Ithaca: Cornell Univ. Press, 1985], 186). By recuperating money from the abstract realm of exchange to the material world of petty burglary and fire, Sally violates an economic logic which functions within precisely the same parameters: "A coin has stamped upon its body that it is to serve as a means of exchange and not as an object of use. . . . Its physical matter has visibly become a mere carrier of its social function. A coin, therefore, is a thing which conforms to the postulates of the exchange abstraction" (Alfred Sohn-Rethel, *Intellectual and Manual Labour: A Critique of Epistemology* [1970], trans. Martin Sohn-Rethel [London: Macmillan, 1978], 59).

30. Simmel, 120.

31. In tracing some of the similarities between money and words, both of which have value and meaning only if they are circulated, I am drawing in part on Mark Shell's *Money, Language and Thought: Literary and Philosophical Economies from the Medieval to the Modern Era* (Baltimore: The Johns Hopkins Univ. Press, 1982). I disagree, however, with Shell's premise that money or language functions the most straightforwardly when there is the least distance between the sign and its referent, as in the case of coins: "During its historical metamorphosis from commodity (a lump of gold) to coin (a commodity impressed with the stamp of the state) to paper money (a mere impression), *solid* metal undergoes and participates in culturally and philosophically subversive changes. The widespread use of coins, which are both symbols and commodities, may precipitate some conceptual misunderstanding of the relationship between signs and things, but it does not encourage its users to believe that symbol and commodity, or word and concept, are entirely separable. . . . Paper money, on the other hand, does appear to be a symbol entirely disassociated from the commodity it symbolizes" (105). On the contrary, Sally's insistence on withdrawing her money in coins goes hand in hand with the deliberate uselessness of her will. In each case, the function of the money or language as a sign collapses because of the absolute identity of the sign and the referent: Sally's money, never being spent, will remain money, but will thus remain only a marker of value, without fulfilling its function; similarly, all that the incomprehensible "law-word[s]" (195) in her will ultimately mean is that it is a will.

32. There are several important instances of recycling, invariably portrayed positively, in the novel. Signaling the possibility of her own redemption, Ruth

makes Leonard's baby clothes out of her dresses (159), and then begins sewing clothes for the poor out of "every article of spare or worn-out clothing . . . [in] a variety of strange materials" which Miss Benson can "rummag[e] up" (160). Other forms of recycling initially appear less desirable: it hardly seems encouraging, for instance, that Ruth's first encounter with Mr. Bellingham consists of his giving her a used flower "that someone had left on the table" (16). We soon learn, though, that the flower is still "perfect" and "pure" (18) after this change of hands, providing an early hope that Ruth's fall will not be irrecuperable. Finally, after the tragedy of Ruth's public exposure, the heroine's genuine redemption and the novel's dénouement begin when Farquhar offers the increasingly socially ostracized and impoverished Bensons the use of his newspapers when he has finished reading them: "Will you allow me to send you over my *Times*?," he asks, "I have generally done with it before twelve o'clock, and after that it is really waste-paper in my house. You will oblige me by making use of it" (371). Of course, this reference to waste-paper is only to show that Farquhar believes that the paper need *not* be wasted, as long as it can be re-used.

33. Simmel, 246.

34. Gaskell, *Cranford* (1851-1853) (Harmondsworth: Penguin, 1976), 83.

35. Gaskell, *Cranford,* 176, 177.

36. In fact, many of Gaskell's early critics objected to her representation of the poor, insisting that John Barton forfeits his claim to pity by his improvidence (see W[illiam] E[llis and Mary Turner Ellis], "*Mary Barton,*" *Westminster and Foreign Quarterly Review* 51 [April 1849]: 49; and [Greg], "*Mary Barton,*" *Edinburgh Review* 89 [April 1849]: 414).

37. Elizabeth Gaskell, *Mary Barton: A Tale of Manchester Life* (1848) (Oxford: Oxford Univ. Press, 1987), 22. Not surprisingly, Engels voiced a similar endorsement of working-class expenditure: "To save is unavailing, for at the utmost [the worker] cannot save more than suffices to sustain life for a short period of time, while if he falls out of work, it is for no brief period. To accumulate lasting property for himself is impossible. . . . What better thing can he do, then, when he gets high wages, than live well upon them? The English bourgeoisie is violently scandalized at the extravagant living of the workers when wages are high; yet it is not only very natural but very sensible of them to enjoy life when they can, instead of laying up treasures which are of no lasting use to them, and which in the end moth and rust (i.e.,

the bourgeoisie) get possession of" (*The Condition of the Working Class in England* [1845], trans. Florence Kelley-Wischnewetsky [Oxford: Oxford Univ. Press, 1993], 127-28).

38. Georges Bataille argues, in contrast to Marcel Mauss's model (in "*Essai Sur le Don, Forme Archaïque de l'Échange,*" *Année Sociologique,* 1925), of gifts as covert acts of equal exchange, for a "principle of loss . . . of unconditional expenditure . . . contrary . . . to the economic principle of balanced accounts (expenditure regularly compensated for by acquisition)." In Bataille's analysis, this expenditure constitutes a rejection of bourgeois ideology, accomplished by exaggerating its inherent contradictions: "In trying to maintain sterility in regard to expenditure, in conformity with a reasoning that balances *accounts,* bourgeois society has only managed to develop a universal meanness. Human life only rediscovers agitation on the scale of irreducible needs through the efforts of those who push the consequences of current rationalist conceptions as far as they will go"; "in the most universal way, isolated or in groups, men find themselves constantly engaged in processes of expenditure. Variations in form do not in any way alter the fundamental characteristics of these processes, whose principle is loss. . . . Connected to the losses that are realized in this way . . . is the creation of unproductive values" (Bataille, "The Notion of Expenditure," in *Visions of Excess: Selected Writings, 1927-1939,* trans. Allan Stoekl [Minneapolis: Univ. of Minnesota Press, 1985], 118, 125, 128).

39. Dr. Charles Mercier, "Vice, Crime, and Insanity," quoted in Peter T. Cominos. "Innocent Femina Sensualis in Unconscious Conflict," in *Suffer and he Still,* 167.

40. As John Vernon suggests, "we fear the counterfeit, and rightly so, not because it scandalously disrespects reality—indeed, counterfeiters so *respect* reality as to pay it the highest homage, imitation—but because it creates uncertainty, ambiguity" (*Money and Fiction: Literary Realism in the Nineteenth and Early Twentieth Centuries* [Ithaca: Cornell Univ. Press, 1984], 201).

41. As various critics have observed, this contrast between hypocrisy and romantic turbulence in a morally strict household and the domestic tranquility of a woman with a checkered past is reworked in Charles Dickens's *Hard Times:* see, for instance, Craik, 72; Rosemarie Bodenheimer, *The Politics of Story in Victorian Social Fiction* (Ithaca: Cornell Univ. Press, 1988), 162; and Coral Lansbury, *Elizabeth Gaskell* (Boston: Twayne, 1984), 32. Like Dickens, Gaskell uses this contrast to underscore the causal link between this domestic unrest

and an internally fractured market ideology: if Richard's economic crimes have their immediate cause in his father's excessively strict morality, that very strictness is itself, as we have seen, an attempt to establish a fixed point of reference within the circular logic of the sexual and literal marketplaces.

42. Georg Lukács, *The Theory of the Novel: A Historico-Philosophical Essay on the Forms of Great Epic Literature,* trans. Anna Bostock (Cambridge: MIT Press, 1971), 88; Simmel, 236-37.

Allan C. Christensen (essay date 2003)

SOURCE: Christensen, Allan C. "'Ruth . . . Sick for Home': The Keatsian Imagination in the Novel of Elizabeth Gaskell." In *Configuring Romanticism,* edited by Theo D'haen, Peter Liebregts, and Wim Tigges, pp. 105-22. New York: Rodopi, 2003.

[*In the following essay, Christensen outlines how the title character in Gaskell's* Ruth *is informed by John Keats' Ruth in "Ode to a Nightingale."*]

Among the Romantic poets, Wordsworth holds a particular fascination for Elizabeth Gaskell. Margaret Homans thus discusses Gaskell's pleasure, described in a letter of 1836, as she composes in a *"fit place"*—"a field gay with bright spring flowers . . . & with lambs"—an essay on Wordsworth now lost.[1] In Homans' interesting analysis Gaskell is further absorbed at this point in the delight of sharing with her infant daughter Marianne "the nonsymbolic language of infancy".[2] Yet a tension exists between the joy of that direct, non-symbolic communication and the need to write about Wordsworthian joy in a more literary or symbolic language. Gaskell experiences the same tension that she must discern in Wordsworth's own treatment of the "Babe" and the animals—the "blessed Creatures"—of the "Immortality" ode. In his self-conscious need to speak a literate language, the poet feels alienated from "the call / Ye to each other make". For Homans the alienation is also typically that of the woman writer, who will not be heard unless she adopts a male language, foreign to her instinctive nature.

As well as in Wordsworth, however, Gaskell finds representations of the alienation typical of women in Keats, whose influence operates most tellingly in her conception of the protagonist's plight in **Ruth.** At the beginning of her story, that protagonist seems even obviously—although the fact has not received critical attention—to derive from the Ruth of the "Ode to a Nightingale".[3] In the ode the bird's voice reaches "Ruth, when, sick for home, / She stood in tears amid the alien

corn".[4] In the first chapter of the novel too the heroine stands lost in homesick tears: "Ruth pressed her hot forehead against the cold glass, and strained her aching eyes in gazing out on the lovely sky of a winter's night. . . . [Her] eyes filled with tears, and she stood quite still, dreaming of the days that were gone." At "the large old window" she is herself like a bird: "[she] pressed against it as a bird presses against the bars of its cage. She put back the blind, and gazed into the quiet moonlight night" (I).[5] Recollection of such nights in childhood quickly brings her mother to mind: "'Oh! at home,'" she tells the companion that is concerned by her tears, "'I have many a time run up the lane all the way to the mill, just to see the icicles hang on the great wheel, and when I was once out, I could hardly find in my heart to come in, even to mother, sitting by the fire;—even to mother'" (I). Besides the wintry memories, her thoughts fly back to the blossoming seasons at home, and here the night of May described in Stanza V of Keats's ode becomes relevant:

> I cannot see what flowers are at my feet,
> 　　Nor what soft incense hangs upon the boughs,
> But, in embalmèd darkness, guess each sweet
> 　　Wherewith the seasonable month endows
> The grass, the thicket, and the fruit-tree wild—
> 　　White hawthorn, and the pastoral eglantine;
> 　　　Fast fading violets covered up in leaves;
> 　　　　And mid-May's eldest child,
> The coming musk-rose, full of dewy wine,
> 　　The murmurous haunt of flies on summer eves.

In Gaskell's story the flowers that "conjured up visions of other sister-flowers that grew, and blossomed, and withered away in her early home" are those painted on the wall opposite the window. Where is the heavy odours enable the poet of the ode to imagine the invisible flowers, the visible aspect of the painted flowers in Ruth's room permits one to imagine their odours: "on [the] panels were painted . . . the most lovely wreaths of flowers, profuse and luxuriant beyond description, and so real-looking, that you could almost fancy you smelt their fragrance, and heard the south wind go softly rustling in and out among the crimson roses—the branches of purple and white lilac—the floating golden-tressed laburnum boughs". And the catalogue continues, to conclude as in Keats with summer and the odour of musk: "crowning all, came gorgeous summer with the sweet musk-roses, and the rich-coloured flowers of June and July" (I).

Opposite this garden that mocks the lost paradise of childhood, the window through which Ruth gazes so ardently resembles Keats's "magic casements, opening on the foam / Of perilous seas, in faery lands forlorn". Another window in Ruth's house is, moreover, strikingly similar to that in another poem by Keats, "The Eve of St Agnes". Madeline, the heroine of this poem, experiences the perilous "faery" lure as she climbs the stairs to her bedroom and kneels before the famous "triple-arched" Gothic casement. Intricate tracery decorates the window, which, features "a shielded scutcheon" of royalty dating from an earlier period. Shining through the magnificent stained glass, the moonlight transfigures Madeline, throwing "warm gules" on her breast, "rose-bloom" on her hands, "soft amethyst" on her silver cross and "a glory, like a saint" upon her hair. The house inhabited by poor Ruth too contains, as a remnant of a more splendid epoch, "a grand carved oaken staircase, lighted by a window of stained glass, storied all over with armorial bearings". Here we have our first view of Ruth: "up such a stair—past such a window (through which the moonlight fell on her with a glory of many colours)—Ruth Hilton passed wearily one January night, now many years ago" (I).[6]

The bitter cold, moonlit night of January may even fall close to the festivity of St Agnes, on the twentieth of the month, for other details as well connect Gaskell's Ruth with Keats's heroine. Shortly after this night there is a ball which Ruth, like Madeline, observes dreamily from the sidelines: "it was enough to gaze and dream of the happy smoothness of the lives in which such music, and such profusion of flowers, of jewels, elegance of every description, and beauty of all shapes and hues, were everyday things". Like Madeline she will also dream that night of the man of her destiny, although unlike Madeline she has seen him first at the ball. In her waking life, his courtship will begin the next day and will lead to an invitation, like Porphyro's to Madeline, to flee far away.[7]

Suggesting the ambiguity of the imagination, the fairy land beyond the magic casements possesses two aspects in Keats's poems. It is first the region ruled by the "Queen-Moon", whose female energy fills the Nightingale with such happiness and whose light immortalises Madeline. The vision, "so free from mortal taint", will lift Porphyro too into the dimension of immortality:

> Beyond a mortal man impassioned far
> At these voluptuous accents, he arose,
> Ethereal, flushed, and like a throbbing star
> Seen mid the sapphire heaven's deep repose;
> Into her dream he melted, as the rose
> Blendeth its odour with the violet—
> Solution sweet. . .

The imaginative dream, just as in the "Ode to a Nightingale", can effectuate an unseasonable blending of the odours of violet and rose. But at this point the second aspect of the region beyond the casement asserts itself: "Meantime the frost-wind blows / Like Love's alarum pattering the sharp sleet / Against the window-panes; St Agnes' moon hath set". In daring to escape into that now darkened region the lovers must brave the "perilous seas", which may nevertheless be less perilous than they appear: "'Hark! 'tis an elfin-storm from faery land, / Of haggard seeming, but a boon indeed.'"

Gaskell too indicates the duality of this region of imagination—but, as I have suggested, with particular reference to the female condition. In its first aspect it is the female paradise in which mother and daughter dwell in blissful communication before the imposition of what Lacan calls "the Law of the Father".[8] As is usual with paradises, Ruth has never actually existed there but has constructed (or "conjure[d] up") in her retrospective imagination what has been lost. With anguished nostalgia she recalls its features chiefly at night when the other girls with whom she shares a bedroom are sleeping:

> She watched and waited till one by one dropped off to sleep, and then she buried her face in the pillow, and shook with sobbing grief; and then she paused to conjure up, with fond luxuriance, every recollection of the happy days, so little valued in their uneventful peace while they lasted, so passionately regretted when once gone for ever; to remember every look and word of the dear mother, and to moan afresh over the change caused by her death.
>
> (III)

In her dreams she encounters her dear mother, but these dreams offer no consolation because the mother mysteriously abandons her: "'I thought I saw mamma by the side of the bed, coming, as she used to do, to see if I were asleep and comfortable'", Ruth tells the concerned Jenny, who has awakened the sobbing sleeper, "'and when I tried to take hold of her, she went away and left me alone—I don't know where'" (I). The mother has possibly betrayed her daughter by leaving her so early in life. Failing in particular to warn Ruth about the perils posed by men, she has left her in vulnerable ignorance. And yet, as the narrator speculates, perhaps no parent can warn a daughter in adequate words of the peril:

> [Ruth] was too young when her mother died to have received any cautions or words of advice respecting *the* subject of a woman's life—if, indeed, wise parents ever directly speak of what, in its depth and power, cannot be put into words—which is a brooding spirit with no definite form or shape that men should know it, but which is there, and present before we have recognized its existence.
>
> (III)

The second aspect of Ruth's imaginary paradise involves precisely the brooding male presence, which is not initially perceived as a danger. In contrast to the paradise of the past with her mother, this vision refers to a future of improbable bliss. The "young and elegant" gentleman that she has seen at the ball, where he has offered her a camellia, enters her dream, introducing there too a floral element (as Porphyro had done in melting with the blended odours of violet and rose into Madeline's dream): "He presented flower after flower to her in that baseless morning dream, which was all too quickly ended." His arrival in her fairy land serves to occupy the void left there by the disappearance of the dear mother: "The night before she had seen her dead mother in her sleep, and she wakened, weeping. And now she dreamed of Mr Bellingham, and smiled" (II).

The imagination of the inexperienced Ruth enables her to perceive Bellingham less as supplanting her mother than as repairing the maternal loss and possibly leading her back to the original paradise. Suggesting Keats's "deceiving elf", Bellingham ingratiates himself with Ruth by encouraging this deception. His courtship culminates in the long-desired excursion to Milham Grange, the now neglected house of her childhood that still, "as a whole, gave a full and complete idea of a 'Home'". It is, to be sure, a ruined paradise: "They went silently through the untrimmed garden, full of the pale-coloured flowers of spring. A spider had spread her web over the front door. The sight of this conveyed a sense of desolation to Ruth's heart." Yet for a moment, when they enter her mother's favourite room, she can fancy that the past has been restored:

> Ruth stood gazing into the room, seeing nothing of what was present. She saw a vision of former days—an evening in the days of her childhood; her father sitting in the "master's corner" near the fire, sedately smoking his pipe, while he dreamily watched his wife and child; her mother reading to her, as she sat on a little stool at her feet. It was gone—all gone into the land of shadows; but for the moment it seemed so present in the old room, that Ruth believed her actual life to be the dream.
>
> (IV)

When tears soon enough signal an imminent awakening—"To toll me back", in the Keatsian phrase, "to my sole self"—or to Ruth's "actual life"—Bellingham averts the threatening intrusion of reality. He invites her into another corner of her "land of shadows": "'Come away; I cannot have you stay here, full of painful associations as these rooms must be. Come'—raising her with gentle violence—'show me your little garden you have often told me about. Near the window of this very room, is it not?'" Poised between conflicting emotions—a "melancholy . . . which was infinitely charming" and a "sunny happiness"—Ruth obeys him, proceeding "on her way, all unconscious of the dark phantoms of the future that were gathering around her". Later that evening her employer Mrs Mason will believe that she has already fallen and will expel her from the sewing establishment. Lost in a spectral territory of imagination—between the "land of shadows" of her past and "the dark phantoms of the future"—Ruth has no figure to impose some reality principle. Bellingham urges her literally homeless condition upon her as a reason to accept his invitation to fly away with him: "'My darling, I cannot leave you here without a home . . . so

friendless, so homeless—it is impossible. You must come with me, love, and trust to me.'" The narrator urges upon us readers too a reflection upon the helplessness of a child cut off from the home and the mother of her imagination: "Remember how young, and innocent, and motherless she was!". To Bellingham's importunate pleading—"'Will you not come with me? Do you not love me enough to trust me?'"—she must at last respond with "'Yes'; the fatal word of which she so little imagined the infinite consequences".

Her answer evidently echoes that of Keats's Madeline when, pleading for "trust", Porphyro promises to take her to "a home [I have] for thee": she "hurried at his words, beset with fears", and "like phantoms" they "fled away into the storm". Whether they reach "home" remains unknown, but Ruth's trusting imagination does virtually restore her to the home of childhood. Through another window are wafted, at an inn that evening, the scents of her mother's garden. In the terms of Keats, she is able "in embalmèd darkness, [to] guess each sweet":

> [Ruth] opened the window, and leant out into the still, sweet, evening air. The bush of sweetbrier, underneath the window, scented the place, and the delicious fragrance reminded her of her old home. I think scents affect and quicken the memory more than either sights or sounds; for Ruth had instantly before her eyes the little garden beneath the window of her mother's room, with the old man leaning on his stick, watching her, just as he had done, not three hours before, on that very afternoon.
>
> (IV)

Ruth asks Bellingham then to take her back in fact to that garden and to the protection of that old man—Thomas, the family servant during her childhood. But of course Bellingham has other intentions and conducts her instead to London and thereafter to Wales, where we next meet them. There she continues to exist happily for a time with her seducer in a setting, often perceived through a window, that resembles a paradise. In their inn Ruth sits most characteristically "in the window-seat of their parlour" and observes from there the beautiful spectacles of nature: "she saw the swift fleeting showers . . . ; she watched the purple darkness on the heathery mountain side, and then the pale golden gleam which succeeded. There was no change or alteration of nature that had not its own peculiar beauty" (V). Beneath the window, once again, there also flourishes a garden: "The garden lay close under the house; a bright spot enough by day; for in that soil, whatever was planted grew and blossomed in spite of neglect. The white roses glimmered out in the dusk all the night through; the red were lost in shadow" (VII).

In a significant episode Ruth and her lover descend into a thickly wooded hollow while a heron rising from a pool in the centre soars "up into the very sky itself". As mirrored in the pool, that sky appears "clear and dark, a blue which looked as if a black void lay behind". The pool contains water-lilies that Bellingham gathers for the delighted Ruth. Arranging them in her hair, he has her admire her own beauty in the mirroring pond. With the blue sky behind her, the halo of the lilies upon her head, and the glow of her face—"flushed into a brilliancy of colour which resembled that of a rose in June"—she reminds us again of Keats's Madeline before the stained glass. Yet the dimension of the "black void" beyond her transfigured self and the allusion to Narcissus hint at the dangerous lure of an imagined beauty (VI).

Bellingham's fever and the arrival of his mother to interrupt the lovers' idyll will soon make Ruth aware that her paradise has been an illusion or what is sometimes called a "vision": "Poor Ruth!", remarks the narrator, "her faith was only building up vain castles in the air; they towered up into heaven, it is true, but, after all, they were but visions" (VII). The "vision", it appears, is little better than the "waking dream" to which in Keats's ode it is an alternative. During the night when her lover's illness approaches its crisis, Ruth is herself compared to a "vision" as she looks through the window:

> She rose with as little noise as if she were a vision, and crept to the open window. . . . Out beyond, under the calm sky, veiled with a mist rather than with a cloud, rose the high, dark outlines of the mountains, shutting in that village as if it lay in a nest. They stood, like giants, solemnly watching for the end of Earth and Time. Here and there a black round shadow reminded Ruth of some "Cwm," or hollow, where she and her lover had rambled in sun and in gladness. She then thought the land enchanted into everlasting brightness and happiness; she fancied, then, that into a region so lovely no bale or woe could enter, but would be charmed away and disappear before the sight of the glorious guardian mountains. Now she knew the truth, that earth has no barrier which avails against agony. It comes lightning-like down from heaven, into the mountain house and the town garret; into the palace and into the cottage.
>
> (VII)

In her enchanted view her lover has guarded, like one of the mountainous "giants", the maternal "nest", but a new "truth" exposes the impotence of his stalwart guardianship. In the enchanted landscape, however, she has already encountered another guardian whose role requires examination. The day before the excursion with Bellingham to the pool of the water-lilies, a solitary stroll has led her to another setting that involves dangerous water and flowers. While attempting to cross on stepping stones a rapidly flowing, high stream, she hears "a voice offering help". The voice belongs to what she first takes to be a dwarf and then recognises as a hunchback, whose kindly hand she accepts. During the ensuing conversation, he tells her an odd story about

the fox-gloves swaying in the breeze around them. For it is apparently not the wind that makes them "'bend and sway so gracefully'": "'the Welsh tell you'", he informs Ruth, "'that this flower is sacred to the fairies, and that it has the power of recognising them, and all spiritual beings who pass by, and that it bows in deference to them as they waft along'" (V). While thus introducing her to a Welsh fairy-land, this strange man seems himself a fairy creature, whom Bellingham will compare that evening to the dwarf Riquet-with-the-Tuft in the fairy tales of Perrault. It is also interesting that when Ruth sees him for the second time it will be through a window. In this case she is standing outside while he observes from inside the scene of her being insulted by the boy in the street: "As she turned, she saw the mild sad face of the deformed gentleman, who was sitting at the open window above the shop; he looked sadder and graver than ever; and his eyes met her glance with an expression of deep sorrow" (VI). Whereas Bellingham has deceived Ruth and lured her towards "the foam / Of perilous seas", this other inhabitant of fairy land pities her and seeks to help her to pass safely over the waters.

The nature of the opposition emerges clearly when Bellingham abandons Ruth and she desires passionately to die. He has not restored her, as seemed the original promise, to something like the paradise of her existence with her mother. But at this crisis it is the hunchback Benson that brings back to her a new yearning recollection of that mother. In this, their third, encounter he finds her by the roadside, "crouched up like some hunted creature, with a wild, scared look of despair, which almost made her lovely face seem fierce". When he murmurs, "'Oh, my God! for Christ's sake, pity her!'", it appears "as if [his words] struck some chord in her heart, and she were listening to its echo": "His pitiful look, or his words, reminded her of the childish days when she knelt at her mother's knee, and she was only conscious of a straining, longing desire to recall it all." His voice, echoing in her heart, continues nevertheless to compete with the voice coming from the "mountain stream, the dashing sound of whose waters had been tempting her . . . to seek forgetfulness in the deep pool into which they fell" (VIII). The conflict between the two voices is at last resolved when "the still small voice whispered [through him], and he spake": "'In your mother's name, whether she be dead or alive, I command you to stay here until I am able to speak to you'". He is sure from her reaction then that she will not now drift away, in the Keatsian phrase, to "easeful death": "'I know you will not go—you could not—for her sake. You will not, will you?'" (IX).

"'No'", she whispers, in contrast to the "'Yes!' the fatal word", uttered to Bellingham. But not even Benson is able to restore her to the imagined paradise of childhood. In not dying, she must henceforth live outside of any paradise: "then there was a great blank in her heart. She had given up her chance. She was calm, in the utter absence of all hope" (IX). As the Ruth of Keats's ode has intuited too, all "faery lands [are] forlorn".

Although he has first appeared within the fairy setting, allied there with the recollected mother, Benson may perform mainly the role of the rescuer of Ruth from the fairy spell. He releases her from the fascination of Bellingham and conducts her out of the dangerous regions. For many years afterwards Ruth lives a seemingly placid, disciplined existence in his house while her imagination lies dormant. In another possible allusion to the cult of St Agnes, the shearing of the often lamb-like heroine's beautiful, abundant hair may identify her as Keats's Madeline shorn of illusions. For while still "hoodwinked with faery fancy", Madeline's mind had entertained images only of "St Agnes and her lambs *un-shorn* [my emphasis] / And all the bliss to be before to-morrow morn". Besides truncating blissful imagination, the shearing has sometimes suggested a sexual mutilation, with the result that Ruth now possesses no sexual nature at all.[9] The hostile spying of Jemima later on thus discerns no trace in her of erotic awareness.

Yet the recurrence of the familiar motifs indicates that her imagination is not entirely dormant. Unable to sleep during her first night in the home of Benson, "many a time did she rise, and go to the long casement window, and look abroad . . . to the far-away hilly line of the horizon, lying calm under the bright moonshine".[10] And on the next day "a purer ether, a diviner air, which she was breathing in now, than what she had been accustomed to for long months" makes her recall "the gentle, blessed mother, who had made her childhood's home holy ground" (XIII). The day after that, recollections of the wilder landscape of Wales haunt her too with a poignance that makes her doubt the reality of the present setting. While sewing, she finds

> an opportunity of retreating into the haunts of memory; and soon the work fell from her hands, and her eyes were fixed on the little garden beyond, but she did not see its flowers or its walls; she saw the mountains which girdled Llan-dhu, and saw the sun rise from behind their iron outline, just as it had done—how long ago? was it months or was it years?—since she had watched the night through, crouched up at his door. Which was the dream and which the reality? that distant life, or this? His moans rang more clearly in her ears than the buzzing of the conversation between Mrs Bradshaw and Miss Benson.
>
> (XIV)

Indeed Benson has led her not into "reality" but into still another site of imagination, where she must enact, as the widowed Mrs Denbigh, the fictional identity constructed for her. With nostalgia for other voices, scents and settings, she remains the homesick Ruth, who char-acteristically "fell into trains of reverie, and mournful regretful recollections which rendered her languid and tearful". Her reconciliation to present circumstances then occurs insofar as the motifs of the window and garden, hitherto associated with the past, can now be referred to her new identity: "The peacefulness of the time, the window open into the little garden, the scents that came stealing in, and the clear summer heaven above, made the time be remembered as a happy festival by Ruth". Even here the happiness associated with the window and garden emerges mainly in the retrospective dimension. But Ruth comes at least to prize this garden for its own sake rather than as a reminder of one that has been lost. As time passes, she measures the changes in her life largely in terms of what happens here. No longer a field of "alien corn", this garden is viewed as if it had always been her frame of reference:

> It was now nearly a year since she came to the Benson's [sic]; it seemed like yesterday, and yet as if a lifetime had gone between. The flowers were budding now, that were all in bloom when she came down, on the first autumnal morning, into the sunny parlour. The yellow jessamine, that was then a tender plant, had now taken firm root in the soil, and was sending out strong shoots; the wallflowers, which Miss Benson had sown on the wall a day or two after her arrival, were scenting the air with their fragrant flowers. Ruth knew every plant now; it seemed as though she had always lived here, and always known the inhabitants of the house.
>
> (XVIII)

For another six or seven years Ruth registers the passing of the seasons in that garden, and as the plants grow, her own roots reach ever deeper into the soil. The apparently serene resignation that she achieves in what the world considers her chaste widowhood contrasts with the increasing turbulence of the sexual yearnings that Ruth discerns in her friend and alter ego Jemima.[11] From her position of strength she wishes indeed to help the latter: "It was time that some one should come to still the storm in Jemima's turbulent heart, which was daily and hourly knowing less and less of peace" (XX). Yet Ruth's own peace is not after all so secure, and one day the treacherous "voice . . . heard / In ancient days by emperor and clown" will again find "a path / Through the sad heart of Ruth". She is on the beach of Abermouth, but again on the shore of the "perilous seas" too, when its sound dissolves the realities of her more recent existence:

> The sands heaved and trembled beneath Ruth. The figures near her vanished into strange nothingness; the sounds of their voices were as distant sounds in a dream, while the echo of one voice thrilled through and through. . . . That voice! No! if name, and face, and figure, were all changed, that voice was the same which had touched her girlish heart, which had spoken most tender words of love, which had won and wrecked her,

and which she had last heard in the low mutterings of fever. . . . It seemed . . . as if the steadfast rocks receded—as if time stood still.

(XXIII)

Struggling not to collapse, she leads the little girls for whom she is caring away, into a field of Keatsian scents "where wild thyme and heather were now throwing out their sweets to the soft night air". Then she wanders into the atmosphere of another poem by Keats, that in which we find the knight-at-arms, after his enchantment by the Belle Dame, "palely loitering"—"So haggard and so woe-begone"—his "brow, / With anguish moist and fever-dew". (In the form of Porphyro's song, "an ancient ditty . . . / In Provence called, 'La belle dame sans mercy'", the bewitching sound has also intruded into Madeline's dream.) The little girls look in frightened wonder at Ruth: "So pale, so haggard, so wild and wandering a look, the girls had never seen on human countenance before" (XXIII). The voice that she has heard again belongs, she knows, to "'a bad man'", but even under the new name of Donne he maintains his power over her: "'oh! pitiful God, I love him; I cannot forget—I cannot!'" She must once more brave Porphyro's "'elfin-storm from faery land, / Of haggard seeming, but a boon indeed'"—the storm that pelts its sleet against the high casement. That night a storm, which does indeed rage outside Ruth's window, strikes her too as a possible boon:

> She threw her body half out of the window into the cold night air. The wind was rising, and came in great gusts. The rain beat down on her. It did her good. A still, calm night would not have soothed her as this did. The wild tattered clouds, hurrying past the moon, gave her a foolish kind of pleasure that almost made her smile a vacant smile. The blast-driven rain came on her again, and drenched her hair through and through. The words "stormy wind fulfilling his word" came into her mind.

(XXIII)[12]

The phrase from the Psalms indicates some hope for a divine intervention, like the rescue that Benson had effectuated in Wales. With its violence the storm may purge the undesired passion. Yet she is not after all saved, for her new life proves insufficiently rooted in the soil of the Bensons' garden: "Those wild autumnal storms had torn aside the quiet flowers and herbage that had gathered over the wreck of her early life, and shown her that all deeds, however hidden, and long passed by, have their eternal consequences." Knowing that sooner or later the original spell cast upon her must fulfil its doom, "she turned sick and faint whenever Mr Donne's name was casually mentioned" (XXV).

The sickness, which resembles the nympholepsy of Keats's knight-at-arms, has long lain latent in Ruth. It eventually finds its reflection in the outbreak in town of pestilential typhus, compared both to "the blaze of a fire which had long smouldered" and to a reptile: "there came creeping, creeping, in hidden, slimy courses, the terrible fever—the fever which is never utterly banished". With a sense of destiny, Ruth goes for what may be the final time "into the old familiar garden and gathered a nosegay of the last lingering autumn flowers—a few roses and the like"—and then on to the fever ward (XXXIII). She does not contract the fever from her ministrations as nurse in that ward but, more appropriately, from Bellingham-Donne, whom she insists upon nursing privately. In his delirium, while recognising the girl that he had seduced so many years before, he wonders, "'Where are the water-lilies? Where are the lilies in her hair?'" (XXXV). Instead of a relationship of love, however, in which, as in their first meeting and in her first dream of him, he has offered her flowers, their relationship is now one of contagion. He conveys to her, literally, the sickness that has always been metaphorically implicit in the appeals to her girlish imagination.

Now explicitly sick, the imagination of Ruth becomes "a sweet, childlike insanity within" that brings back, to ring in her dying ears, the musical voices that have haunted her life (XXXV). These include the sounds of Wales associated with Bellingham. For on her last night at the Welsh inn, we have been told, "she wandered from window to window" to memorise all the precious sights and sounds: "The sound of running waters she heard that quiet evening, was in her ears as she lay on her death-bed; so well had she learnt their tune" (XII). In her delirium she hears another singing voice too. Through the sickness, Bellingham has after all restored her to her mother, as she had originally hoped that he would do. The attendants at her death-bed hear a childish version of the Nightingale's "high requiem" as "the self-same song" reaches a Ruth whose homesickness is no longer sad. She is listening and responding to her mother as they sing together in "the nonsymbolic language of infancy":

> They had never heard her sing; indeed the simple art which her mother had taught her, had died, with her early joyousness, at that dear mother's death. But now she sang continually, very soft and low. She went from one childish ditty to another without let or pause, keeping a strange sort of time with her pretty fingers, as they closed and unclosed themselves upon the counterpane. She never looked at anyone with the slightest glimpse of memory or intelligence in her face; no, not even at Leonard.

(XXXV)[13]

In the musical reunion with her mother, she abandons Leonard, her own child: "'Mother! mother! mother!'", he cries, "'You have not left me alone! You will not leave me alone! You are not dead! Mother! Mother!'" (XXXV). She bequeaths him her homesick condition at the same age, twelve years, at which she has lost her own mother. More than the story of an illicit love affair and its consequences, the novel has concerned that primary anguish deriving from the mother's absence. If all desire springs from a lack, like the "great blank in [Ruth's] heart", then the story of erotic desire and seduction is a secondary manifestation of the more basic phenomenon. "We are severed from the mother's body", in Terry Eagleton's reductive description: "We will spend all our lives hunting for it."[14] In part the fault is that of the mothers themselves, who desert their children or otherwise betray the maternal identity. In Mrs Mason and Mrs Bellingham **Ruth** thus portrays maternal figures that treacherously impose upon their charges the father's law and language.

Gaskell lost her mother when she was barely a year old, Wordsworth his when he was eight and Keats his when he was fourteen. The mother's absence may function as a ghostly subtext in many of their works and, among the poems of Keats, particularly in "The Eve of St Agnes". While Madeline evidently possesses a father—"That night the Baron dreamt of many a woe"—she has no mother, but only the timorous old Angela and St Agnes herself. And they betray her into the power of the seducer that promises to restore her to paradise. Such a reading is suggested, at least, by analogy with what happens in Gaskell's **Ruth.** Whereas the Keatsian motifs have contributed their coherence to Gaskell's exploration of the ways of imagination, her own story leads in return to intuitions about the hidden dynamics of Keats's poetry.

Notes

1. J. A. V. Chapple & Arthur Pollard, eds, *The Letters of Mrs Gaskell,* Manchester & New York, 1997, 7. The editors describe Gaskell's project as an imitation of Wordsworth, but she refers to writing "my first chapr of W".

2. Margaret Homans, *Bearing the Word: Language and Female Experience in Nineteenth-Century Women's Writing,* Chicago & London, 1986, 33.

3. Besides the Ruth of the Old Testament, the protagonist of Wordsworth's "Ruth" has often been seen as a source for Gaskell's heroine. Rosemarie Bodenheimer, *The Politics of Story in Victorian Fiction,* Ithaca & London, 1988, 153-158, thus discusses with respect to Wordsworth's poetry the pastoral aspects of the first nine chapters of Gaskell's novel, involving the "conflation of nature and individual psychology". Hilary M. Schor, *Scheherezade in the Marketplace: Elizabeth Gaskell and the Victorian Novel,* New York & Oxford, 1992, similarly considers *Ruth* to be Gaskell's "most Wordsworthian novel" but believes that the heroine's "name is taken not only

from Wordsworth's abandoned Ruth but from a similar poem in Crabbe's *Tales of the Hall*" (50, 54).

4. Citations of Keats are from John Keats, *The Complete Poems* (3rd edn), ed. John Barnard, Penguin, 1988.

5. References in text are to chapters of Elizabeth Gaskell, *Ruth,* ed. Alan Shelston, Oxford & New York, 1985. The comparison of the heroine in this passage to the bird pressing against the bars of its cage also recalls Shelley's apostrophe of the heroine of his *Epipsychidion* as "my adored Nightingale": "Poor captive bird! who, from thy narrow cage, / Pourest such music" . . . "who dost for ever / Beat thine unfeeling bars with vain endeavour" (ll. 5-14).

6. Angus Easson, *Elizabeth Gaskell,* London, Boston & Henley, 1979, 115, finds that the scene of Ruth at the stained-glass window "invokes echoes of Keats's Madeline, on whose breast the moonlight threw 'warm gules', or more complexly of Shelley's dome of many coloured glass". Jenny Uglow, *Elizabeth Gaskell: A Habit of Stories,* London & Boston, 1993, 327, also quotes the phrase referring to "the moonlight" and "a glow of many colours" and remarks that Ruth is here "a Romantic figure, reminiscent of Keats or Shelley". But Uglow does not point out the specific echoing of the situation in "The Eve of St Agnes". Nina Auerbach, *Woman and the Demon: The Life of a Victorian Myth,* Cambridge, MA & London, 1982, 170, suggests the "consecrating" effect of "the moon through the window", making Ruth's later fall "devoid of sexuality and will".

7. Ruth's dream, like Madeline's, thus recalls Keats's famous observation of 1817 to Benjamin Bailey: "The Imagination may be compared to Adam's dream—he awoke and found it truth"; *The Letters of John Keats,* ed. Hyder Edward Rollins, Cambridge, MA, 1958, Vol. 1, 185.

8. Homans, 5-7, discusses with reference to Lacan how the father comes to interrupt or silence the originally blissful mother—daughter communication.

9. Felicia Bonaparte, *The Gypsy-Bachelor of Manchester: The Life of Mrs Gaskell's Demon,* Charlottesville & London, 1992, 122, points out the parallel between the earlier episode of crowning and this scene, which figures the "desexing of [a] fertility goddess". Jill L. Matus, *Unstable Bodies: Victorian Representations of Sexuality and Maternity,* Manchester & New York, 1995, 117-119, similarly associates "luxuriant hair with a luxuriant sexuality" and suggests that Ruth ex-

presses no regret for her shorn hair because she has no sexual awareness.

10. Commenting on this "casement window", Angus Easson, "Noah's Arks and Birds' Nests: Domestic Space in *Ruth*", in *Elizabeth Gaskell: Text and Context,* eds Francesco Marroni & Alan Shelston, Pescara, 1999, 102, finds that "casements for Gaskell have very positive associations of the right order of established things", But I believe that all of her windows can imply openings into dangerous dimensions too.

11. Bonaparte, 123, observes that the apparent "death of [Ruth's] demon engenders a dæmonic double in Jemima".

12. A victim of her passionate jealousy of Ruth, Jemima suffers during a stormy, moonlit night three chapters later (XXVI) at another window "that looked into the garden": "She opened the window, to let the cool night air blow in on her hot cheeks. The clouds were hurrying over the moon's face in a tempestuous and unstable manner, making all things seem unreal. . . . She laid her head on her arms, which rested on the window-sill, and grew dizzy with the sick weary notion that the earth was wandering lawless and aimless through the heavens, where all seemed one tossed and whirling wrack of clouds".

13. Francesco Marroni, *La fabbrica nella valle: Saggio sulla narrativa di Elizabeth Gaskell,* Bari, 1987, 59, also reads this scene as possessing "the warmth of a maternal embrace . . . the (re)conquest of an idyllic dimension—that probably never existed" (my translation).

14. Homans, 8, cites Eagleton. Marianne Hirsch, *The Mother/Daughter Plot: Narrative, Psychoanalysis, Feminism,* Bloomington & Indianapolis, 1989, 52, remarks that "psychoanalysis identifies the place of the mother as the very absence which lies at the point of linguistic origin".

Alyson J. Kiesel (essay date winter 2004)

SOURCE: Kiesel, Alyson J. "Meaning and Misinterpretation in *Cranford*." *ELH* 71, no. 4 (winter 2004): 1001-17.

[*In the following essay, Kiesel explores Gaskell's means of expressing meaning in her novel,* Cranford, *noting in particular the author's treatment of writing, trauma, and colonialism.*]

> They looking back, all th' Eastern side beheld
> Of Paradise, so late thir happie seat,
> Wav'd over by that flaming Brand, the Gate
> With dreadful faces throng'd and fierie Armes:
> Som natural tears they drop'd, but wip'd them soon;
> The World was all before them, where to choose
> Thir place of rest, and Providence thir guide:
> They hand in hand with wandring steps and slow,
> Through Eden took thir solitarie way.

—John Milton, *Paradise Lost*

"Molly!" said he, "I did not think all this would happen." He looked into her face for comfort—her poor face, all wild and white; for neither she nor my father had dared to acknowledge—much less act upon—the terror that was in their hearts, lest Peter should have made away with himself. My father saw no conscious look in his wife's hot, dreary eyes, and he missed the sympathy that she had always been ready to give him—strong man as he was; and at the dumb despair in her face, his tears began to flow. But when she saw this, a gentle sorrow came over her countenance, and she said, "Dearest John! don't cry; come with me, and we'll find him," almost as cheerfully as if she knew where he was. And she took my father's great hand in her little soft one, and led him along, the tears dropping, as he walked on that same unceasing, weary walk, from room to room, through house and garden.

—Elizabeth Gaskell, *Cranford*[1]

About one third of the way through Elizabeth Gaskell's *Cranford,* Miss Matilda Jenkyns (hereafter, Miss Matty) rereads and then burns a number of family letters, keeping only a particularly affecting one that her brother, Peter, sent to her mother. This letter and the questions it inspires from the narrator, Mary Smith, elicit from Miss Matty the surprising story of Peter's departure from Cranford. Until this moment in the novel, Peter had been mentioned twice. The first mention also occurs in the context of an old family letter (his birth announcement). After reading the letter, Mary remarks: "It seemed curious that I should never have heard of this brother before; but I concluded that he had died young; or else surely his name would have been alluded to by his sisters" (46). The second time, following a harrowing story from Miss Matty's girlhood describing their fear of French invasion, Mary announces with a merely cosmetic attempt at temporal transition and without apparent surprise at the correction to her initial assumption: "Peter Marmaduke Arley Jenkyns ('poor Peter!' as Miss Matty began to call him) was at school at Shrewsbury by this time" (48). After a brief description of Peter's letters from school (including the one Miss Matty saves), the chapter "Old Letters" ends, and the story of "Poor Peter" begins.

This chapter (from which the second excerpted quote above is taken) is focalized almost entirely through Miss Matty's point of view (the only chapter in *Cranford* that doesn't privilege Mary's viewpoint) with Mary's questions appearing only periodically to frame and lead the are of the story. As we soon learn, the young, mischievous Peter enjoyed playing practical jokes; on two occasions, he dressed in women's cloth-ing in attempts to fool first his father and then the townspeople. Posing as a female admirer of his father's sermons, Peter succeeded the first time presumably be-cause his father was blinded by vanity. But the second time, Peter impersonated his older sister, Deborah; and in addition to wearing her clothes, he fashioned a "little baby" out of a pillow (52). Promenading about the fam-ily garden with her (scandalously secret, thus assumed illegitimate) ersatz baby, this drag version of Deborah drew a sizeable crowd of spectators until Mr. Jenkyns recognized his son, stripped the women's clothing from him, and flogged him before the gathered throng. After the flogging, Peter bid farewell to his mother and disap-peared, leaving Cranford bereft, and his parents, as I've tried to suggest by the opening quotes, fallen.

For this story, Gaskell allows Miss Matty's normally hesitant, ladylike fluttering to expand into the soaring, romantic, and deeply engaging prose of the excerpted passage. Remembering the desperate scene seems to el-evate Miss Matty's style and permits her to access (at least in imagination) the internal states of her forlorn and long-dead parents. Miss Matty describes a Cranford that existed long before the one Mary Smith records. In fact, the story of Peter is really one of origin—it's the violent rupture of his parting that seals Cranford off from the rest of the world and locks it in a timeless, changeless, Eden of "Amazons" (1). After Peter leaves, Mrs. Jenkyns sickens and dies, and a guilt-ridden, femi-nized version of her husband soon follows. The day her mother dies, Deborah vows never to marry because it would mean abandoning her father, and, as we learn obliquely, she compels Miss Matty to do the same. These two characters and the ways in which their broth-er's loss teaches them to read the world create both Cranford and *Cranford.*

At the start of the novel Cranford appears aligned with Eden: one of the primary duties of its citizens is to tend the many gardens and defend them from meddling young boys and inquisitive geese. Because of this im-plicit parallel, Mary's narrative promises to tell of an-other fall—this time into modernity. In this short, de-ceptively tranquil novel, Gaskell portrays the intricate codes and interpretive systems that this new Eden re-quires while simultaneously chronicling the story of its transformation/corruption. In *Scheherezade in the Mar-ketplace,* Hilary M. Schor describes this phenomenon in terms of Gaskell's other works: "*Cranford* is most of-ten praised for its own quality of loving nostalgia, but what it in fact registers is panic about change; it is be-ing written in the face of its own demolition, in the face of social changes that novels like *Mary Barton* and *Ruth* address more directly."[2] Through its inescapable penetration by men, industrial and financial capitalism, technology, and alien imports, Cranford approaches a second fall so dire that only the miraculous, messianic

return of Peter can redeem it. In this essay, I examine Cranford's peculiar modes of signification, consider the ways in which Gaskell often couples moments of read-ing (in all its forms) with thematic trauma, and suggest a relationship between these aspects of her project and her strange but conspicuous representations of colonial conquest.[3]

As I've implied, Gaskell takes the seemingly banal ma-terials of village life and makes something intriguing out of them—so, too, do the ladies of Cranford. Mary notes early on:

> I had often occasion to notice the use that was made of fragments and small opportunities in Cranford; the rose-leaves that were gathered ere they fell, to make into a pot-pourri for some one who had no garden; the little bundles of lavender-flowers sent to strew the drawers of some town-dweller, or to burn in the chamber of some invalid. Things that many would despise, and ac-tions which it seemed scarcely worth while to perform, were all attended to in Cranford.
>
> (15)

The Cranfordians notice the details of fabrics, food, voices, and scents and impute to them significances so arcane as to require translation by Mary Smith. Such precise (and, in Cranford, often literal) attention to "fragments and small opportunities" yields alternately tragic and comic results.

Peter's flight, which I've characterized as a kind of foundational myth that institutes Cranford's construal of meaning, occurs when his father's gaze pierces the ma-terial appearance of his disguise. Mr. Jenkyns's ability to unmask the true identity (that is, the true meaning) beneath surfaces makes his subsequent violence pos-sible and differs sharply from the way in which Miss Matty recounts the incidents of Peter's cross-dressing. When describing Peter dressed as the woman interested in Mr. Jenkyns's sermons, Miss Matty has difficulty getting her pronouns to tally:

> Peter said he was awfully frightened himself when he saw how my father took it all in, and even offered to copy out all his Napoleon Bounaparte sermons for her—him, I mean, no, her, for Peter was a lady then. . . . As it was, he was none so glad of it, for my father kept him hard at work copying out all those twelve Bounaparte sermons for the lady—that was for Peter himself, you know. He was the lady.
>
> (51)

For the adult Miss Matty, Peter's prank temporarily makes him a woman; a change in clothes results in a corresponding change in gender. This reading of the situation, which insists upon taking appearances at face value and resists plumbing hidden depths as "close read-ing" might, is an example of the kind of reliance upon surfaces that I see determining the production of mean-ing in post-fall Cranford.

Early in the novel (though in terms of its overarching chronology, long after Peter's departure) another tragic incident takes place in a way that would seem to reinforce this aversion toward "close reading." Captain Brown, a recently arrived masculine presence in the functionally feminine Cranford, is crushed by an equally recently arrived train with which he was associated. Begrudgingly adored by the town, the Captain dies trying to save a child; but the story of his death carries an added dimension. Narrated by a series of servants and townspeople, the Captain's death is described thus:

> The Captain was a-reading some new book as he was deep-in, a-waiting for the down-train; and there was a little lass as wanted to come to its mammy, and gave its sister the slip, and came toddling across the line. And he looked up sudden at the sound of the train coming, and seed the child, and he darted on the line and cotehed it up, and his foot slipped, and the train came over him in no time.
>
> (16)

Though we might read the train and the inhuman, indifferent progress it symbolizes as more to blame than the book, Deborah Jenkyns disagrees. Toward the end of chapter 2, the plot skips ahead many years. The Captain's younger daughter, Jessic, has married and left Cranford, and her daughter, Flora, sits reading by the side of an invalid and faltering Deborah. Mary Smith records her last conversation with Deborah as follows:

> "Ah!" said Miss Jenkyns, "you find me changed, my dear, I can't see as I used to do. If Flora were not here to read to me, I hardly know how I should get through the day. Did you ever read the 'Rambler?' It's a wonderful book—wonderful! And the most improving reading for Flora"—(which I dare say it would have been, if she could have read half the words without spelling, and could have understood the meaning of a third)— "better than that strange old book, with the queer name, poor Captain Brown was killed for reading."
>
> (22)

Of course, Deborah's understanding of the Captain's death is her own; her criticism of the Captain's reading arises more from her dislike of Charles Dickens than from the manner in which the Captain reads him (that is, "deep-in"). But, as Mary's parenthetical remark hints, for anyone other than Deborah in Cranford, reading Samuel Johnson amounts to reading unintelligible nonsense (Miss Matty understands so little that she conflates Johnson's poetry with Alfred Tennyson's "Locksley Hall"). One reads Johnson for the impressive sound and size of the words, whereas reading Dickens provides access to meaningful content. But more than any other character in the novel, Deborah represents a rigid adherence to the set of rituals and etiquette that defines the process of meaning production in Cranford. Long after her sister's death, Miss Matty continues to judge her own actions and make decisions according to Deborah's presumed wishes. As Mary Smith notes: "[Deborah's] rules were made more stringent than ever, because the framer of them was gone where there could be no appeal" (26). Deborah's words, then—that he was "killed for reading"—are significant insofar as they represent the pattern of propriety in Cranford.

For outside observers, by contrast, this refusal to read "deep-in" can easily result in comedy. In chapter 9, "Signor Brunoni," an eponymous magician brings his show to the town and delights the ladies with his "pretty broken English" and incomprehensible magic (83). In the chapter that immediately follows, "Panic" (ironically so named in that its purpose is chiefly comic and it foreshadows the true panic of the novel, the collapse of Miss Matty's bank), Mary admits that the town felt Signor Brunoni might be connected to some recent robberies since, as Mary paraphrases Mrs. Forrester,

> [W]e must believe that the robbers were strangers—if strangers, why not foreigners?—if foreigners, who so likely as the French? Signor Brunoni spoke broken English like a Frenchman, and, though he wore a turban like a Turk, Mrs. Forrester had seen a print of Madame de Staël with a turban on, and another of Mr. Denon in just such a dress as that in which the conjuror had made his appearance; showing clearly that the French, as well as the Turks, wore turbans: there could be no doubt Signor Brunoni was a Frenchman—a French spy, come to discover the weak and undefended places of England.
>
> (90)

This passage would be amusing enough with its flawed logic, conflation of the turban with the idea of foreignness, and willingness to believe that a man named Signor Brunoni came from France (rather than Italy); but only when, in the next chapter, the Signor's wife reveals that his given name is Samuel Brown and that he is English by birth does the full force of its comedy take effect.

Similarly, in chapter 1, Captain Brown teases Miss Betty Barker by sarcastically advising her to dress her bald cow in gray flannel (the cow lost its hair in an accident so is unable to keep warm). Miss Betty Barker takes him at his word and makes a suit for the shivering creature. Following her description of this incident, Mary Smith remarks: "Do you ever see cows dressed in grey flannel in London?" (5). This moment of gentle humor (and others like it) immediately establishes oppositional relationships between meaning for women and meaning for men, meaning for Cranford and meaning for London, and meaning for Miss Betty Barker and meaning for the reader (with whom Mary Smith is momentarily aligned).[4] With one fell rhetorical question, Gaskell posits an imaginary, perfectly complementary audience for her tale: it is masculine, city-dwelling, and modern—and because its members comprehend the ostensibly more sophisticated systems of meaning that obtain in London, they can chuckle in unison at Cranford's misreading Brunoni or the Captain. Actually, Gaskell begins referencing her model listener even earlier in the novel and with the identical gesture. On page 2, Mary Smith relates a typically Cranfordian anecdote in which a woman continues using a red silk umbrella long after cotton umbrellas became the fashion for Londoners. In the midst of this vignette, she asks, "Have you any red silk umbrellas in London?"

What does it mean that Cranford's mode of meaning-making is deliberately contrasted with that of London's? On the one hand, London might represent a kind of normative model to which Cranford can never attain; but on the other, London might operate with a set of hermeneutic principles that run parallel to Cranford's without ever intersecting them. In a tour de force of materialist description, Mary Smith makes clear that the peculiar overvaluing of small things and surfaces she's chronicling is not necessarily unique to Cranford. She describes a pair of such "individual small economies," accordingly:

> An old gentleman of my acquaintance, who took the intelligence of the failure of a Joint-Stock Bank, in which some of his money was invested, with stoical mildness, worried his family all through a long summer's day because one of them had torn (instead of cutting) out the written leaves of his now useless bankbook; of course all the corresponding pages at the other end came out as well; and this little unnecessary waste of paper (his private economy) chafed him more than all the loss of his money. . . . I am not above owning that I have this human weakness myself. String is my foible. . . . How people can bring themselves to use Indian-rubber rings, which are a sort of deification of string, as lightly as they do, I cannot imagine.
>
> (40-41)[5]

Attachments to paper, string, rubber bands (and, later, butter and Miss Matty's personal economy, candles) defy London's conventional standard of worth (of "economy"). Indeed, the Cranfordians' whimsical impulses toward thrift reveal a lack of any universal exchange value, and, in clinging to their unaccountable predilections, these villagers charmingly resist the easy installation of capitalism. This tendency to bestow or extract meaning where it might not exist for others seems at the center of Gaskell's undertaking. As *Cranford* makes plain, material traces (and the manner in which people interpret them) are at once clues to overcoming and emblems of the barriers between individuals, between cultures. Obviously, valorizing surfaces and material objects in this way can occlude certain contents (as in the Captain's joke, Brunoni's nationality, Johnson's prose, or the fact that a boy in his sister's dress is still a boy); but, like the personal economies, Cranford's readings of surfaces also create a breadth of meanings that do not resonate for those outside its gates.

It's this breadth of meaning that Mary Smith's narrative aims to recuperate in order to preserve. *Cranford*'s first lines famously detail its unique qualities and delineate a border between it and Drumble, the more developed city to the north where Mary's family lives:

> In the first place, Cranford is in possession of the Amazons; all the holders of houses, above a certain rent, are women. If a married couple come to settle in the town, somehow the gentleman disappears; he is either fairly frightened to death by being the only man in the Cranford evening parties, or he is accounted for by being with his regiment, his ship, or closely engaged in business all the week in the great neighbouring commercial town of Drumble, distant only twenty miles on a railroad. In short, whatever does become of the gentlemen, they are not at Cranford. What could they do if they were there?
>
> (1)

Most striking in this opening paragraph is the way in which Gaskell demands that we first see Cranford in terms of its difference, its exoticism. "This is not England (or at least London)," the text seems to shout. Instead, Gaskell presents a truly separate island—one populated by a different race, by (as we are told explicitly, if humorously) a race of Amazons.

But if we're to see Cranford as an idyllic, innocent island of natives (the image of Eden works here as well), how should we make sense of the fact that this innocent realm is forever altered by the end of the novel? Aren't we also forced to recognize in its eventual penetration by men, technology, capitalism, and foreign trade an enactment of some darker purpose? I'd like to propose that the transformation of Cranford might be read in three ways. First, it stages England's self-maiming through the uneven advance of industrial and financial capitalism (in a manner more oblique than that of *Mary Barton,* but nonetheless evident). Second, the extreme anxiety the citizens of Cranford betray in the face of all sorts of literal and figurative imports dramatizes a paranoia about contamination (or counter-colonization) through the inexorable return of the colonial Other.[6] Third, by figuring a part of older England as being invaded by a newer England (or even by France), Gaskell represents the reality of colonial violence as turned inward. In this third, oddly inverted image of colonialism, Cranford might stand in for any English colony, and the pangs its (Cranford's) inhabitants endure throughout the narrative (or to which they succumb) might stand in for those of any colonized subject. This third possibility seems to make sense of the fact that Brunoni is English, the robbers are English, and the joint-stock bank and Deborah are both English. Any threat—imagined (Brunoni) or real (bank failure)—has never been foreign but always utterly English. Just as the novel cannot explicitly name Deborah its "villain" (despite her responsibility for Miss Matty's failed love affair and failed investment), so must it suppress England's role in imperial brutality by relocating the event within England proper—with London (via the buffer of Drumble) as colonizer and Cranford as colony.

I want to focus on this third option for a moment, and look more closely at the effort Gaskell makes to defamiliarize Cranford. As Schor helpfully observes, Mary Smith's narrative voice often sounds like that of an "anthropologist" or "ethnographer" who "visit[s] an alien culture and watch[es] it 'make meaning.'" She continues, comparing Gaskell and Mary's strategies for illuminating unfamiliar systems of signification to those outlined by Clifford Geertz in *The Interpretation of Culture*:

> Critics have assumed, simplistically, that Gaskell was only describing from *within* the village life she missed, but the other terms with which we might describe her project are those of Clifford Geertz. Gaskell is writing what he calls a "thick description," one that "tri[es] to rescue the 'said' of [social] discourse from its perishing occasions and fix it in perusable terms."[7]

Mary's own need of "thick description" appears in chapter 1 when Miss Matty explains to her the Cranford etiquette regarding the "rules and regulations for visiting and calls":

> "It is the third day; I dare say your mamma has told you, my dear, never to let more than three days elapse between receiving a call and returning it; and also, that you are never to stay longer than a quarter of an hour."

> "But am I to look at my watch? How am I to find out when a quarter of an hour is passed?"

> "You must keep thinking about the time, my dear, and not allow yourself to forget it in conversation."

> As everybody had this rule in their minds, whether they received or paid a call, of course no absorbing subject was ever spoken about. We kept ourselves to short sentences of small talk, and were punctual to our time.

(2-3)

Again, the ladies of Cranford seem to prefer communicating their good will through an adherence to proper forms rather than by trying to share or receive any compliments that approach content. To a London observer without the benefit of Miss Matty's tutorial, these calls might appear typical, but Mary's somewhat indeterminate allegiances allow her to make more sense, more meaning of the "perishing occasions" these precisely timed, content-free visits epitomize.

The kind of "deep interpretation" required to decipher such "thick description" tends always to reveal the essential constructedness of all rules, codes, and meanings. Schor makes this point with reference to the (London) codes that the comedy of Cranford's trendless taste reveals:

> But *all* such codes begin to seem arbitrary. They are codes only because they are agreed on; no one in Cranford is out-of-date, because all the out-of-date fashions are accepted as *à la mode*. . . . If the systems that the Amazons follow so religiously seem absurd to us, then so, too, must the codes of the outside world.[8]

The ladies of Cranford, content with London's cast-offs, dance a hand-me-down parody of English fashion. In celebrating the final days of their ignorant bliss (before turbans replace beribboned caps), Gaskell's relentless translation uncovers the living, visible proof of England's all too fragile hegemony and the sort of persistently undermining threat to imperial dominance that might precipitate such a nightmare version of colonization.

Without her ideal audience, Gaskell would lose the gap that produces humor. But it's within the space temporarily occupied by laughter (at Miss Betty Barker for her innocence, Mary Smith for her string fetish, or any of the ladies for their willing appropriation of past seasons' fashions) that a kind of colonial, self/Other confrontation occurs. Even as Londoners chuckle at Cranford's naïveté and misunderstandings, so must they risk becoming the butt of one of Cranford's jokes. As Homi Bhabha writes in "Signs Taken for Wonders," a colonial difference "is the effect of uncertainty that afflicts the discourse of power, an uncertainty that estranges the familiar symbol of English 'national' authority and emerges from its colonial appropriation as the sign of its difference."[9] Cranford's proffered mode of reading (that is, of reading surfaces) leads necessarily to misreadings whenever outsiders struggle to comprehend insiders (and vice versa). If we continue to imagine Cranford as a placeholder for any English colony, then the kinds of violence that attend certain moments in the plot seem to make more sense. On the one hand, characters like the Captain and Mr. Holbrook seem to be eliminated by the narrative's desire to preserve an uninterrupted version of Cranford (their deaths fulfill Mary's somewhat sinister opening pronouncement that if men come to Cranford, they "somehow disappear" [1]). But in the midst of this fading instinct for static self-preservation, the vast and mighty array of imperialism awakes; and, ascending with it, the inescapable desire for narrative progress and resolution triumphs. Mary Smith occupies a unique position between these worlds and seems to pass as a kind of covert hybrid from one to the next.[10]

In order to read and write Cranford, Mary must allow herself to become part of it. She must make sense of and learn to use its speech patterns and opaque modes of meaning-making. As Schor puts it,

> Because [Gaskell] is telling a story of people already outdated, she needs a narrator who can move from one world to another, without the implied superiority of an

omniscient narrator. She needs a narrator detached enough not to take Cranford's "elegant economics" too seriously, but enough of an insider to translate such customs for the uninitiate. Her narrator must understand the business, masculine world of Drumble but have a sense of what Cranford holds that that bustling town lacks.[11]

In Mary, Gaskell creates the perfect answer to these variable needs. Mary navigates between worlds with infinite flexibility and, as I've mentioned, without calling attention to her plural loyalties. At one point in the novel Mary decides to break with Cranfordian precedent in order to eat a plate of peas (since she was given only a two-pronged fork, she must proceed against custom and use her knife). Whereas the other ladies refuse to break with their rigid etiquette, Mary observes her male host's technique, eats the peas, and declares: "I saw, I imitated, I survived!" (33). In addition to this kind of adaptability, Mary constructs little identity for herself prior to that of her narrative voice—even withholding her full name until Peter gives it to her in the last chapters. She rarely portrays herself as participating in the action (sometimes she even fails to reply to another character's direct questions). She tries literally to bring nothing new to Cranford. In fact, when Miss Matty requests that she purchase her a green turban, Mary refuses ("[I was] most particularly anxious to prevent her from disfiguring her small gentle mousey face with a Great Saracen's-head turban" [81]) and brings a proper Cranfordian cap instead. In contrast to Mary's noninterference, other characters (often the very ones who die) try to incorporate something new into the space of Cranford: Captain Brown brings masculinity, the railroad, plain speech, and Dickens; Mr. Holbrook brings masculinity, the threat of marriage, Tennyson, and France; and Deborah brings Johnson and (her ill-fated) capitalist investment. In fact, the only novelty Mary agrees to introduce (or reintroduce) is Peter.

The moments of traumatic confrontation with misinterpretation and disconnection that suffuse *Cranford* require that Mary span, return to, circle, rewrite, and reincorporate the past before it can resurface as history, at which point it would be transformed into a readable narrative of (albeit elliptically) causal connection. In this fictional history, Mary's frequent use of qualifying language ("probably," "as if," "seemed," "I cannot say," "I dare say," "perhaps," "I think," "I don't know") might be read as a hedging, narratorial humility that diverges from and attempts to relieve some of the scientific bravado affected in her earlier anthropological pose. But it should also be regarded as a sign of her subtle and permanently self-aware maneuvering between the positions of insider and outsider. I see this facility as particularly discernible in her repetition of words like "somehow" (as in, "I could see, that somehow or other the Captain was a favourite with all the ladies present" [7]) and "evidently" (as in, "Miss Jenkyns was evidently very

much alarmed; and the first part of her letters was often written in pretty intelligible English" [48]).

With the word "somehow," the narrator emphasizes her own inability to observe and interpret (often, as in the quoted example, because the agent whose action Mary tries to describe is, like the Captain, not originally from Cranford). With the word "evidently" she attempts to overstep the untranslatable with rhetoric—we're meant to trust her instinct though she may not provide details. *Cranford* is consummately attuned to the fact that what can stand as evidence varies between narrator and reader, between colonist and colonized, between self and Other. These words and phrases of acknowledged ambiguity—of the impossibility of transparent transmission—use strategic sleight-of-hand to balance the incommensurable.

The narrative also disguises processes of incomprehensible (either for Mary or for the reader) development as repetition. Peter Brooks states in *Reading for the Plot: Design and Intention in Narrative*:

> An event gains meaning by its repetition, which is both the recall of an earlier moment and a variation of it: the concept of repetition hovers ambiguously between the idea of reproduction and that of change, forward and backward movement. . . . Repetitions create a *return* in the text, a doubling back. We cannot say whether this return is a return *to* or a return *of*: for instance, a return to origins or a return of the repressed. Repetition through this ambiguity appears to suspend temporal process, or rather, to subject it to an indeterminate shuttling or oscillation that binds different moments together as a middle that might turn forward or back. This inescapable middle is suggestive of the demonic: repetition and return are perverse and difficult, interrupting simple movement forward.[12]

It's exactly this "simple movement forward" that eludes *Cranford.* Until Miss Matty's financial distress (which is contemporary with Mary's narration) requires that Mary take action and summon Peter, Cranford and *Cranford* stay suspended in a virtually timeless recuperation of past events. The whole narrative consists of a series of these returns and repetitions—sometimes brought about by letters, or recalled after noticing a certain facial expression. When first introducing the Captain, Mary says, "I never shall forget the dismay felt when a certain Captain Brown came to live at Cranford, and openly spoke about his being poor—not in a whisper to an intimate friend, the doors and windows being previously closed; but, in the public street!" Within the space of a paragraph, Mary repeats four variations of this comment about the Captain's lack of shame regarding his circumstances. Toward the end of the passage (before the final iteration of Cranford's perception that the Captain is vulgar), Mary must revert to "somehow" to describe the Captain's apparent integration: "Yet somehow, Captain Brown made himself respected in

Cranford." It's as if the paragraph tries to rehearse the process of acceptance (which also dramatizes the reorganization of the trauma of his "invasion") but cannot reproduce anything resembling a linear development and so must provide the illusion of progress by replacing it with repetition (4).

The one letter in the text that accomplishes a forward movement of plot cannot be reproduced or excerpted—it seems to walk too delicate a line. We're not allowed to see the magic words that can accomplish such perfect contact with one and only one reader. This letter, Mary's masterpiece of textual hybridity, appears only in her enigmatic description of it: "That night, after Miss Matty went to bed, I treacherously lighted the candle again, and sat down in the drawing-room to compose a letter to the Aga Jenkyns—a letter which should affect him, if he were Peter, and yet seem a mere statement of dry facts if he were a stranger" (127). The splendidly conclusive ending that this letter achieves marks a final bridge between the initial trauma of Peter's departure and the contemporary plight of Cranford.

The letter, in fact, replicates and repairs that first, failed act of "passing," Peter's transvestism. When he dresses in Deborah's clothing, Peter transgresses the boundaries of both gender and decorum, but his transgressions disrupt only insofar as his father (and only his father) manages to read beyond the camouflage. It's the recognition of these other falls (into femininity and indecorum) that generates the fundamental break with Mr. Jenkyns's mode of analysis. But "somehow" Mary, at least, seems to have learned from this incident; her letter can cross into unknown colonial territories, speak to a single stranger (a man), and be heard by him alone—it can transgress largely unnoticed and without collateral consequences. She contrives a style of discourse that cloaks her naked meaning in an (almost) impenetrable garment of "dry facts." The letter does just what Peter's cross-dressing did but with one revision: it bequeaths revelation to only its intended audience.

Without that initial, traumatic catalyst, *Cranford* could not have been written; but without the current (in terms of Mary) crisis of encroaching modernity, it could not have continued. For *Cranford,* it seems to be a precondition of narratability that a traumatic disruption occur. Without traumatic ruptures in the supple skin of village life, no story would be possible. Any of the anecdotes contained within *Cranford* has its root in the traumatic stimulation of an outside influence (a man, a train, a marriage, a visitor, a new novel, a bank). Brooks gives a useful reading of this phenomenon and its relation to Freud's vision of the pleasure principle:

> As a dynamic-energetic model of narrative plot, *Beyond the Pleasure Principle* gives an image of how the nonnarratable existence is stimulated into the condition of narratability, to enter a state of deviance and detour (ambition, quest, the pose of a mask) in which it is maintained for a certain time, through an at least minimally complex extravagance, before returning to the quiescence of the nonnarratable.[13]

The ladies' collective misreading of the Brunoni/robbery connection and the various hauntings that attend the text (Miss Matty has a recurring dream of a phantom child, the ladies tell gruesome ghost stories in the heat of the entirely imagined "panic") all seem to derive from an absent and longed-for external stimulation that Peter's homecoming puts to rest. Just as Peter the boy tries to excite gossip and create events that will encourage conversation (Miss Matty remarks: "He used to say, the old ladies in the town wanted something to talk about" [51]), so does the grown Peter (the "Aga Jenkyns") draw Cranford into the infinitely narratable miracle of his return—scattering his tall tales of the Orient to those starving for stories—though this time leaving the reader with satisfaction as a merely temporary antidote for desire.

I'd like to return for a moment to a sentence Mr. Jenkyns speaks in reference to the terrible upshot of his flogging Peter. Looking to his wife for sympathy, he laments, "I did not think all this would happen." This comment is particularly poignant coming from a man who trained his daughters to monitor their expectations in double-entry diaries, the design and intent of which Miss Matty describes to Mary:

> "[O]n one side we were to put down in the morning what we thought would be the course and events of the coming day, and at night we were to put down on the other side what really had happened. It would be to some people rather a sad way of telling their lives"—(a tear dropped upon my hand at these words)—"I don't mean that mine has been sad, only so very different to what I expected."
>
> (107)

This sad difference, this ache of not knowing, seems in some ways equivalent to the gulf between quiescence and stimulation, between the self and the Other, between perception and consciousness. It's within the space of such gaps that writing and life and *Cranford* take place. If any of these blanks could be at once overcome, then a second Eden might really be a possibility—but it would be a silent one.

Notes

I would like to thank Mary Poovey for her patient guidance and encouragement during the writing and revision of this essay. Her help and insights have been invaluable.

1. Elizabeth Gaskell, *Cranford* (Oxford, New York: Oxford Univ. Press, 1998), 54-55. All references

to this text are hereafter cited parenthetically by page number.

2. Hilary M. Schor, *Scheherezade in the Marketplace: Elizabeth Gaskell and the Victorian Novel* (New York: Oxford Univ. Press, 1992), 85.

3. For the purposes of this essay, I use the definition of trauma that Sigmund Freud articulates in *Beyond the Pleasure Principle,* trans. and ed. James Strachey (New York: Norton, 1961). He writes, "We describe as 'traumatic' any excitations from outside which are powerful enough to break through the protective shield. It seems to me that the concept of trauma necessarily implies a connection of this kind with a breach in an otherwise efficacious barrier against stimuli" (33).

4. Mary Smith explicitly invokes a distinction between masculine and feminine interpretation when she cites the latter's ability to assess the cost of Miss Jessie Brown's wardrobe in relation to that of her sister's: "[A]ny female observer might detect a slight difference in the attire if the two sisters—that of Miss Jessie being about two pounds per annum more expensive than Miss Brown's" (6). But, as I'll explore later, even when Gaskell codes this kind of interpretation as gendered, she complicates the gap between women's writing/reading and men's writing/reading by employing a female narrator capable of what Schor labels more "mixed responses" (Schor, 104).

5. This seemingly benign example assumes additional import when read in light of the fact that a joint-stock bank's failure precipitates Miss Matty's financial ruin. Having invested her fortune according to Deborah's wishes, Matty loses all (as opposed to "some") of her savings and is forced to sell most of her belongings, rent out her home, and convert her parlor (the symbolic last bastion of Cranford's pre-industrial oasis) into a tea shop.

6. Gaskell carefully itemizes a range of colonial commodities and the often anxious associations they engender. Turbans (both Brunoni's and one that Miss Matty wants but never receives), green tea (which Miss Matty fears to be unwholesome), sugar (the high price of which endangers the ladies' annual batches of preserves), and the white "India shawl" Peter sends home (which arrives too late to be anything but his mother's shroud) all seem to suggest a troubling double valence—simultaneously alluring and threatening (58). Of course, Brunoni (or the idea of Brunoni) might constitute a similarly dual significance. In addition, India and France are both represented as potentially lethal but nevertheless seductive. All but one of Samuel Brown's children die in India (yet it's also the site of Peter's offstage financial suc-

cess and maturation into the resolutely masculine "Aga Jenkyns"), and Miss Matty's girlhood sweetheart, Mr. Holbrook, dies soon after (and in Cranford's mind, because of) a gleefully anticipated trip to Paris.

7. Schor, 86.

8. Schor, 111-12. For Schor, the arbitrariness of signs and sign systems in Cranford becomes a feminist critique of the ways in which "literary signs—mere affairs of the alphabet—shape the individual perception, mediate experience for us, limit the ways we read and hence write our own lives" (112). Schor argues that Gaskell and Mary carve out a place for female literary authority from within the overwhelmingly masculine discourse of authorship. My argument extends in a different direction and considers how such arbitrary codes also gesture toward the imperfections of imperial control.

9. Homi K. Bhabha, "Signs Taken for Wonders: Questions of Ambivalence and Authority under a Tree outside Delhi, May 1817," in *The Location of Culture* (London and New York: Routledge, 1994), 113.

10. Bhabha writes: "Hybridity is a problematic of colonial representation and individuation that reverses the effects of the colonialist disavowal, so that other 'denied' knowledges enter upon the dominant discourse and estrange the basis of its authority—its rules of recognition" (114). Gaskell, her narrative, and narrator seem to accomplish exactly this kind of reversal.

11. Schor, 114.

12. Peter Brooks, *Reading for the Plot: Design and Intention in Narrative* (New York: Alfred A. Knopf, 1984), 99-100.

13. Brooks, 108.

Joellen Masters (essay date winter 2004)

SOURCE: Masters, Joellen. "'Nothing More' and 'Nothing Definite': First Wives in Elizabeth Gaskell's *Wives and Daughters* (1866)." *Journal of Narrative Theory* 34, no. 1 (winter 2004): 1-26.

[*In the following essay, Masters centers on the significance of the primacy of first wives in Gaskell's novel* Wives and Daughters.]

Early in *Wives and Daughters,* Hamley, the aging country squire, makes a private assessment of Molly Gibson, the novel's heroine:

"That's a nice girl of Gibson's," quoth [Squire Hamley] to himself. "But what a tight hold the wench got of the notion of his marrying again! . . . To think of her never having thought of the chance of a stepmother. To be sure; a step-mother to a girl is a different thing to a second wife to a man!"

(Gaskell 74)[1]

The Squire's statement anticipates the novel's critical heritage: in its "tight hold" on certain subjects, like mothers and step-mothers, the scholarship has neglected a stringent examination of the key role first wives play in Gaskell's *Wives and Daughters.*[2] Certainly the book explores the ironies concealed in the Squire's remark— Molly Gibson will struggle with the inadequate attentions of a superficial stepmother; her father's remarriage will prove less than satisfactory to both husband and wife; and Squire Hamley himself will lose his beloved spouse. Implicit in the Squire's comment is the first wife's primacy, the place she holds in Hamley's understanding of familial security and, more particularly, of male need. As a personal reflection, the Squire's remark acknowledges that his own sense of self depends on the first wife's presence. A second wife would be a "different thing" to and for a man. Indeed, as this essay will discuss, when Mrs. Hamley dies, the novel shows that the Squire's carefully constructed world of a patriarchal and landed regimen must allow for a different one to begin.

Hamley's comparison also alludes to the paradox the first wife becomes in *Wives and Daughters.* As a criterion, the social the first wife represents exists only as an absented form; in the epigraph's example she "is" because the Squire omits her from his actual statement. However, linguistic exclusion does not disempower the first wife. Rather, her absence often affords her a place of remarkable centrality—in the characters' imaginations, in plot development, and in narrative structure. *Wives and Daugthers* is not the first time Gaskell works with replacements for a dead wife. *Mary Barton* (1848), for instance, immediately readies the young heroine to step into the domestic role her mother, the elder Mary Barton vacates when she dies in Chapter Three. In *North and South* (1854-1855) Margaret Hale, an efficient manager of household affairs, moral support to her father's trials, nursemaid to her invalid mother's sensitivities, plays the role of "wife" before the real Mrs. Hale dies, and eventually she becomes a "second" Margaret Thornton when she marries at the end. With these two novels, daughters replace dead wives; however, in *Wives and Daughters* Gaskell takes another approach to the problem of the dead wife, reaching for something different in her own fictional families as well as in the novel's focus itself. Gaskell assigns the first wife in *Wives and Daughters* an unusual authority. She may be already dead (as with Mary Pearson Gibson), or she may be ill, dying, and ultimately dead (as with Mrs. Hamley), but she is always present. Her constancy often signals, sometimes even creates, a confused clash of perspectives. At times the first wife frustrates the novel's progress since the text itself seems undecided about whether to keep her or not, whether to let her rest peacefully or to resurrect her.

This resulting ambivalence endows the first wife with the unexpected power to unsettle and disrupt the chronological unfolding of the novel's story of remarriage and its theme of an evolutionary growth within the family unit. In concentrating my energies on Gaskell's first wives I myself add a "different thing" to the existing scholarship's focus on the domestic, on female subjectivity, and on the woman author. Despite the narrator's and the characters' needs to memorialize the middle-class Victorian angel in the house, Gaskell does not give them a peaceful time with the image. First wives in *Wives and Daughters* create a variety of disturbances that only begin to be stabilized toward the novel's conclusion when the author introduces a new and foreign model, "French, Catholic, servant" (495). In forcibly writing her way into the story as she does, Aimee, Osborne Hamley's wife, makes a two-fold impact that trumps the power of those wives before her. Aimee suggests an edgier and confident authorial energy that seeks a departure from the nineteenth-century novel's focus on a familial harmony dependent on the construct of the middle-class domestic angel. Aimee first effectively lays to rest the wandering spirits of first wives in *Wives and Daughters* and thus resolves the formal and narrative troubles they posed with their restless interferences with the text. Second, in turning the genre away from an illusory central stability the Victorian novel sought to preserve, the "second" Mrs. Hamley lays the ground for the powerfully fractured irresolution in stories about marriage later novelists would explore.

"NOTHING MORE": THE FIRST MRS. GIBSON

In Chapter Three, Gaskell introduces, describes, and then eliminates Mr. Gibson's first wife in a paragraph depiction that predates the action of the novel. Despite its brevity, the character sketch efficiently establishes the first Mrs. Gibson as a specific class and gender type intrinsic to the culture's domestic ideology. This first wife was the "orphan grand-niece" of the town's aging physician and

the woman-contemning old bachelor, became thankful for the cheerful presence of the pretty, bonny Mary Preston, who was good and sensible and nothing more. She formed a close friendship with the daughters of the vicar, Mr. Browning, and Mr. Gibson found time to be intimate with all three. Hollingford speculated much on which young lady would become Mrs. Gibson, and was rather sorry when the talk about possibilities, and the gossip about probabilities with regard to the handsome young surgeon's marriage, ended in the most natural manner in the world, by his marrying his predecessor's niece.

(31)

Of "nothing more" I will say much later, but here I want to highlight the novel's practicality in constructing the first wife's image, an effect especially noticeable in the limited and plain physical description the text provides. She was a "cheerful presence" for those to whom she ministers; she was "pretty and bonny." In this narrative postmortem, Gaskell sets up what will become one comparison between the former and the latter Mrs. Gibsons: Mary Preston, "good and sensible" and the languid Hyacinth, vain, manipulative, and extravagant. Establishing Mary Preston as part of the history of the Gibson household, and of the Hollingsford village community, anchors the novel via a character who, despite her modest first appearance, functions as a constant reminder of a past which many seem loath to leave.

Frequent references to Mary Preston expose the novel's reluctance, even inability, to dismiss the image of the angel of the house. She seems a permanent fixture, secure in the Hollingford social world before and after her marriage, elevated to iconic status after her death. Gaskell retains that female presence in curious ways that, as I will show, affect the novel's development. Mary Preston's memory haunts Hollingford residents, in particular, the Browning sisters, as many moments demonstrate. Miss Phoebe justifies her thrilling (albeit mistaken) hope that Gibson will propose to her with the thought that "she would feel bound to accept him, for poor dear Mary's sake" (144). Her sister later confides her fears about Molly's future to Gibson and claims that "you ought to know; for though you're married again, I can't forget you were dear Mary's husband once upon a time; and Molly's her child" (513). When gossip about Molly and Mr. Preston, Cynthia's suitor, reaches them, the sisters' concern is that "it would be a bad match for Mary Preston's daughter" (444), as marriage to the land agent would be a crass gesture toward a middle-class respectability. In the most triumphant display of loyalty for the departed wife Phoebe Browning compliments Gibson, saying

> "All men are not—like you, Mr. Gibson—faithful to the memory of their first love." Mr. Gibson winced. Jeannie was his first love; but her name had never been breathed in Hollingford. His wife—good, sensible, and beloved as she had been—was not his second; no, nor his third love.
>
> (143)

For the two spinsters, Mary Preston carries hagiographic appeal and they assume others to be as devoted in their nostalgia for the dead woman. Thus, although Gaskell's gentle humor with Phoebe Browning turns on how the first wife's image easily conceals misinterpretations of a character's intentions—her own, Gibson's—the author, at the same time, presents the first wife as a standard for fidelity, an ideal that often links daughter, husband, and female friends in a tight bond.

This narrative allegiance to the first wife's primacy shapes an underlying thematic force, so that, despite her brief appearance in *Wives and Daughters,* Mary Preston lives in the text. Invoked again and again, the first wife illustrates the pattern for a desirable feminine mode that Gaskell locates in women's emotions, like the Brownings' sentimental chastisements. As added emphasis, Gaskell allows this first wife's influence a mildly inherent and instinctual quality. Stoneman has argued that, like Wollstonecraft, Gaskell believes that the role of a "good" mother is not a role a woman came by naturally (199), and many have noted that Gaskell's title excludes "mothers" from its categories of female socialization. In debating a woman's natural maternal tendencies *Wives and Daughters* uses Mary Preston for a gentle argument against it even while behavior associated with the first wife's "good" nature lives on through her daughter. The first wife's image represents mother love; she symbolizes a tactile female sympathy domestic ideology framed as an essential and biologically driven way of being as we see when Molly comforts her step-sister Cynthia by stroking the girl's hand, "a mode of caressing that had come down to her from her mother." However, the narrator's vested conviction in this physical inheritance slides into an analytic uncertainty when she admits another's view: "whether as an hereditary instinct, or as a lingering remembrance of the tender way of the dead woman, Mr. Gibson often wondered within himself when he observed it" (328). The novel needs to idealize the first wife and the place she occupies as a reminder of a more desirable past located in an evocative symbol of femininity. Mary Preston's ghost inspires an unspoken female bond, here handed down through gestures of selfless comfort. Although Gibson's observation raises the question of woman's natural versus socialized behavior, he remains outside this particular and female realm; he is "within himself" and not part of a gendered central place carefully enshrined within the text.

And yet, while *Wives and Daughters* establishes Mary Preston as an ideal and thus seems to affirm the domestic angel's vitality, the novel also wrestles to move on from a history and attitudes about class, about gender and about genre the first wife represents. For all the times when Gaskell uses Mary Preston as the wifely ideal, she also, often simultaneously, counters that notion with an alternate view. For instance, in the scene when he is asked to recall his own youthful ardors, Gibson thinks not of his first wife but of another woman completely outside the story in *Wives and Daughters*: "'poor Jeannie was not so old, and how I did love her!'

(Mrs. Gibson's name was Mary, so he must have been referring to someone else.)" (49). The narrator's own observation comically underscores how negligible the first wife actually may be for some. Rather than living in sainthood as she does for those like the Browning sisters, Mary Preston moves farther and farther down Gibson's hierarchy of romantic importance. She is not only not his first, but also not the second nor even the third. In this narratorial indiscretion Gaskell suggests the differences in audience interpretations of the marriage plot. Gaskell casts a cool eye on the rationale for Gibson's second marriage: he wants a mother for Molly. Rather than stressing spousal fidelity, the first wife's death reinforces Gibson as a man of reason, distanced from the world of feeling, and Hollingford gossips about the degree of his sorrow, measuring it by the "narrowness of his crape hat-band" (32). The spinster sisters want the romance of a love story (and an old story at that) rather than the realities of a marriage between a widowed governess and a country doctor. Gibson may harbor thoughts of old loves but in deciding to remarry, he chooses a woman from a social class less secure than that of his first wife and opts for the contractual arrangement that could make his home a site for constructive familial energy.

Furthermore, while the novel situates a particularly female manner in the idealized first wife, it often suggests its own hesitancy regarding an inherent connection that would link all women. When the narrator and Gibson wonder about Molly's physical tenderness toward her stepsister, Gaskell compares these affectionate moments of women's physical touch with several when Hyacinth holds Molly's hand. Earlier the girl sits in silent rebellion when Hyacinth, recently betrothed to Mr. Gibson, "fondled her hand" as Lady Cumnor questions Molly about her education and background, a line of interrogation that irritates and frustrates Molly.[3] The more the girl chafes under the investigation, the more Hyacinth fondles, holding "her hand more perseveringly than ever, hoping thus to express a sufficient amount of sympathy to prevent her from saying anything so injudicious" (132). Hyacinth's caress is not a gesture of selfless comfort; it silences Molly and "[irritates] her nerves" and she eventually breaks the touch.

Hyacinth's grasp of Molly's hand cannot replace or imitate the first wife's maternal affection; however, rather than trying to be the mother she is not, Hyacinth roots her intentions in the practical approach this middle-aged bride-to-be takes in her life. Holding Molly's hand makes a pretty display of a love Hyacinth does not ultimately feel. As a woman who has been dependent on the kindness of her social betters, Hyacinth knows the importance in adapting to Lady Cumnor's manner. She understands she must often play a part not natural to her own inclinations. Hyacinth's gesture—not quite parody but still emptied of maternal emotive force—conceals her clear sense of the value in Lady Cumnor's good will and how to curry that kind of favor. Her knowledge is a wisdom gleaned from the vicissitudes associated with her unstable class status, a wisdom that Molly, tied to the middle-class ideal the first wife represents, rejects. Hyacinth's play-acting reveals an arbitrariness and adaptability to roles deemed natural to a particular type of female gender. By showing how the pretty image cloaks economic motivations crucial to individual well-being, even survival, Gaskell includes her readers in the actual mechanics that form and sustain that gendered image.

Nancy Armstrong has argued that the discursive construction of an ideal middle-class female stressed a self-command that would, in turn, foster a well-regulated domestic sphere with a woman at its center (80-86; 95). As a novel of domestic life, *Wives and Daughters* does not refute Armstrong's assessment of the domestic angel's place in the nineteenth-century novel, but Gaskell's text steadily questions whether the image deserves such a long-lived centrality. After Hyacinth and Gibson marry, Gaskell explores with even greater relish Hyacinth's energetic command, developing it into a battle waged on the domestic front. When Hyacinth announces her plans to redecorate Molly's bedroom, to make it "look quite a different place" (182), Molly protests since it was her "own mamma's before she was married" (183). Hyacinth's will for the newfangled overrides Molly's wish to dwell in a room at one time occupied by the girl who would become the first Mrs. Gibson. Granted, we may sympathize with Molly but Hyacinth's words rightly challenge the dead first wife's power and authorize Hyacinth's intrusion into this home. It is the home Hyacinth now controls, not one in which she merely works as she had in the past as either a governess or as a house guest invited to distract and entertain her hosts.

Redecoration symbolizes not solely the rights of a new wife—why shouldn't this second Mrs. Gibson redo her home?—but also the healthy, even evolutionary soundness in change. Hyacinth is, as Elizabeth Langland has claimed, "socially productive rather than destructive."[4] She expresses her right to redecorate in a direct and confident tone. As she says to Molly: "'It's very much to your credit that you should have such feelings, I'm sure. But don't you think sentiment may be carried too far? Why we should have no new furniture at all, and should have to put up with worm-eaten horrors" (183). The Brownings' idolatry steadily resurrects "Mary Preston," but perhaps that "sentiment may be carried too far." Is Mary Preston," after all, "nothing more" than an empty form, a phrase for a gender type and a social and literary past the novel questions? Gaskell regularly reintroduces the idealized image in her story so that the narrator's complacent use of "nothing more" seems somewhat counterfeit, its finality as a pronouncement not quite conclusive since the "nothing more" that is Mary Preston seems to signal a perverse longevity in the first wife's utility. The first Mrs. Gibson may remain "bonny . . . good and sensible" in memory, but because she disturbs the action, she pulls the characters back into the past to stagnate there. And while perhaps not exactly like the "worm-eaten horrors" of Gothic convention, this power nevertheless undermines the novel's focus on the present and the future. As Armstrong notes, the ideal domestic woman reflects a "peculiar combination of invisibility and vigilance"; she is capable of "disappearing into the woodwork to watch over the household" (80). Gaskell, however, critiques the ideal and its function in the nineteenth-century novel: Mary Preston's vigilant efforts to control what had been her home and her story produce visible discord.

Wives and Daughters regularly undermines the symbolic legitimacy in the self-sacrificing first wife and seeks, instead, a more earthly and reasonable substitute. As appealing a memory as it can be, it is one that offers ambivalent securities. For an audience like the Brownings, loyalty to the image must be strictly maintained; however, for those like Hyacinth and Gibson, intent on progress, the insistent connection to a cultural ideal is an irritant, an anxiety, a platitude that can leave one wincing with embarrassment and even impatience. Gaskell loosens the ties her characters and her audience may have to a singular female perfection by developing other types driven by other, and viable, ways of being. Hyacinth longs for an escape from the drudgery of teaching and the dangers of an insecure financial future. Marrying Gibson saves her from slipping further down the class scale, brings her into the novel's domestic focus, and, as a result, revises the role of class for the narrative. Hyacinth challenges the legitimacy of that old story of middle-class marital stability and domestic closure. Inured to earning her own living, Hyacinth approaches marriage and motherhood like the jobs they are, and she performs them with an eye for future opportunities. She is a new force in the Gibson home and in the story, "sensible" in a way the ghostly Mary Preston could not be.

As a result, the novel regularly unsettles the characters' and the culture's need to sentimentalize the first wife. Mary Preston's thumbnail biography and the abbreviated statement of her death relegate the first wife to the realm of the matter-of-fact to articulate the paradoxical role the first wife plays in the novel. As noted above, the narrator's observation that she was "good and sensible, and nothing more" seems to assign the first wife a limited space in the text. Her death—"poor Mrs. Gibson it was that died of consumption, four or five years after her marriage"—reinforces that the trope may be easily discarded, carried out of the story by the convenience of another nineteenth-century literary conven-

tion.[5] Gaskell shows authorial ease with the cultural and aesthetic materials of her time: she can simultaneously invoke and eliminate the angel of the house. The characters in *Wives and Daughters* try to anchor themselves with a ready-made figure from their own history only to have the text resist the image as a concrete truth.

Judith Butler's influential contributions to 1990's poststructuralist thought on writing and historical veracity note the emptiness, the "nothing more" that lies beneath ideologically determined types like an essential female nature.[6] Her point that feminism's error is in believing there to be "some existing identity understood through the category of women" (3) glosses Gaskell's ironized investment in the first wife. The novel is, after all, entitled *Wives and Daughters,* and yet the narrative's presentation of several different wives and daughters rests on its yearning for one specific kind. Gaskell's novel raises the question that there may not be an essential female self that "[awaits] representation in or by the law" and that language fashions a "nonhistorical" identity, since representation itself continues the illusions of a fixed female nature outside social and cultural markers (Butler 5). To emphasize what could be regarded as an optimistic belief in an ideal first wife who lives outside the narrative's chronological plotting, the novel clings to that figure so that while Gaskell may question the limits in categories like "wives," the critique she offers in her novel is an often unwilling or indecisive one, even as she herself begins to explore new authorial ground.

In *Wives and Daughters,* the "nothing more" of the first wife paradoxically signifies "something" as she, to draw on Butler's terminology, troubles the text. Despite her position as dead wife, Mary Preston exercises a subtle ability to stall the narrative's progress forward. Characters' references to her throw the story back to a time before, an historical past existing prior to the actual events in *Wives and Daughters.* In her rare linguistic appearances, the first Mrs. Gibson stays always "Mary Preston" and the label names the discursive identity and connotes the secure class position she held before becoming Gibson's first wife. Gaskell argues for a female self that cannot stand outside the socialized identities culture and language bestow upon her, a case particularly evident in her depiction of Hyacinth whose surname suffers an unrelenting mobility.[7] She is first the widow Fitzpatrick, next the second Mrs. Gibson, but always, for Lady Cumnor, the governess Clare, a titular fate that causes her embarrassment as that last name repeatedly equates her with a socioeconomic status and a female employment nineteenth-century novels and social discourse explored with such anxious frequency.[8] Mary Preston's constant reminder lives outside the narrative's parameters and suggests the feminist failings Butler, and Gaskell, in her scrutiny of domestic ideology, notes. While she may seem an essential female type, the first wife is also the nothing beneath representational practices. By destabilizing the narrative as she does, Mary Preston undermines the nurturing attributes associated with her "good and sensible" self, the Victorian angel of the house. She reveals a textual struggle with accepted cultural clichés that form part of the novel's generic formula and that also, for Gaskell, expose the genre's own need to enliven its internal energies. This textual ambivalence—should the novel keep her or not?—and its argument about a gendered literary trope the first wife represents find a special embodiment in the other first wife in *Wives and Daughters,* Mrs. Hamley.

"NOTHING DEFINITE": THE GHOST OF HAMLEY HALL

Mrs. Hamley's fragile, poetic femininity develops the domestic angel icon Gaskell outlines with Mary Preston's sensible immortality. Whereas the latter's spectral presence turns on the contradictory "nothing more" she is in the narrative, Mrs. Hamley's influence—pervasive, alternately soothing and unsettling—finds its root in "nothing definite" (43). Indeed, ambiguity and vagueness characterize most everything about Mrs. Hamley, and the text, from the start, locates the origins of this first wife's power in the inexplicable.

The narrator associates desirable feminine traits— "gentle and sentimental; tender and good" (43)—with Mrs. Hamley in keeping with the idealized domesticating influence men like Squire Hamley—rough and ill-educated, but naturally good—require. However, despite the amicability of this partnership, the Hamley union itself is "one of those perplexing marriages of which one cannot understand the reasons" (42). Mrs. Hamley was a "delicate fine London lady" (42) and, unlike her husband, "had considerable literary taste" (43); the narrator claims "yet they were very happy, though possibly Mrs. Hamley would not have sunk into the condition of a chronic invalid, if her husband had cared a little more for her various tastes or allowed her the companionship of those who did" (43). The narrator cannot really say what makes the Hamley marriage and the Hamleys "happy," cannot describe what determines a companionate union. The Hamley marriage eludes full articulation, evinced by the narrator's rather contradictory syntax: "yet" and "though" quickly revise any clear position each conjunction could record about the Hamley marriage. The novel's ambivalent description of the marriage highlights the first wife's role in the novel—she is there and also not there; she represents a key cultural icon but also an unhealthy continuation of the image. Squire Hamley, we learn, "loved his wife all the more dearly for her sacrifices for him; but, deprived of all her strong interests, she sank into ill-health; nothing definite; only she never was well" (43). Self-sacrifice characterizes this type beloved by Victorian

culture (and adored by many in *Wives and Daughters*)—Mary Preston is consumed by disease in the very paragraph that applauds her perfection; Mrs. Hamley falls into a chronic invalidism. However, just as Mary Preston's "nothing more" does not limit her power in the story, Mrs. Hamley's soft vagueness does not "invalidate" her own narrative control. Rather, "nothing definite" allows this first wife an often vivid and pronounced weight in the text's design.

Mrs. Hamley's languid figure is the "ruling spirit" (246) of Hamley Hall and her rooms enclose her in the heart of this domestic and ancestral world. Miriam Bailin has argued for the primacy of the sickroom in the Victorian literary imagination, and Mrs. Hamley's chambers anchor the movements of the characters, providing a place to which they come and go and that provides a fixed and secure location. Mrs. Hamley may be a chronic invalid, but her housekeeping talents show a superlative efficiency as she issues her "directions to the servants, down to the most minute particulars . . . from her sitting-room, or from the sofa on which she lay." Like Mary Preston, she portrays the gender type central to domestic ideology and central to the genre itself; however, unlike the novel's other first wife, Mrs. Hamley is a far more visible figure, a more assertive creator and manager of the domestic terrain. Her "pleasant influence" teaches servants and sons, and in an image and language that Woolf, in 1927, surely takes up in her depiction of the Ramsay marriage, [her husband] "became at peace with himself when in her presence, just as a child is at ease when with some one who is both firm and gentle" (247).[9]

But while her "darkened room" often seems a place of quiet retreat, entering it removes characters from the world of animated daily life and naturally progressive time, particularly for Molly often called to Hamley Hall to be Mrs. Hamley's companion and nurse and who finds there a soothing escape from her own troubling new home. Temporally and spatially separate from the vitality of Hollingford society, the first wife dwells in a shadowy world, decorated with crayon portraits of her younger self and her sons, and filled with the poetry and sentimental literature she loves. Mrs. Hamley dies over an extended period of narrative time, but Gaskell pushes her actual death to the perimeter of narrative description. "At length," the narrator notes, "the end came." Mrs. Hamley leaves "her place in this world" and "her place knew her no more" (219).[10] However, just as her quarantine in her rooms at Hamley Hall gave her a base for domestic and narrative control, once deceased she continues to regularly direct the characters' thoughts and actions. Like the first Mrs. Gibson, Mrs. Hamley becomes a touchstone for many—the butler, for instance, complains about how "things is a deal changed since poor miss went" (256); Osborne and his father quarrel about the depths of "loyalty to her memory"

(253) in their daily routines. Her passing also marks the plot's chronology as, for instance, we discover that an argument between Osborne and his father takes place "on an evening in the March succeeding Mrs. Hamley's death" (251); Molly will explain she learned of Osborne's secret marriage in a conversation she overheard "at the time of Mrs. Hamley's last illness" (558).

Mrs. Hamley's death coincides with many of the estate's sudden and potential economic insecurities, and her dominance, so integral to sustaining a certain way of life associated with rank and privilege, from beyond the grave also affects the authority of her husband's family. Mrs. Hamley remains a symbol of moral decency for her grief-stricken husband, a powerful "nothing definite" for the Squire, but she also retains her image as the real manager of the estate's many affairs. Unlike the Squire, who fumbles for words when trying to say what "she" would have done or thought in situations that leave him in such a quandary that he cannot even work on the jumbled mathematics of the estate's accounts (256-257),[11] Mrs. Hamley, "quiet and passive as [she] had always been in appearance" (246), had commanded the Hamley business affairs. She upheld the patriarchal control of the ancestral Hall; she protected her husband's family name, underscoring the social heft wielded by old blood and old money. The Squire's stiff-necked pride conceals his sense of his own failings—he is "deficient in manners, and in education" (251), and, consequently, timid in society. The first wife had softened his rough qualities and had encouraged his involvement with work subsidized by Government loans that would improve the estate grounds. After her death, the Squire

> grew indifferent to it himself, and cared no more to go out on his stout roan cob, and sit square on his seat, watching the labourers on the marshy land all overgrown with rushes; speaking to them from time to time in their own strong nervous country dialect.
>
> (248)

Poetic yet also practical, docile yet also determined Mrs. Hamley's keen ability to maintain and improve the Hamley family home included her knack at bolstering the Squire's male authority. Without her his sense of ancestral duty, his fluency in his workers' peculiear language, his physical prestige, his "squareness," if you will, diminishes. Mrs. Hamley's absence provokes a subtle erasure of male identity, an emasculation that affects even the Estate's animals. One of the horses, as the carriage is "no longer needed after madam's death," is also, now, too old for more taxing work. Like the Squire who drifts without the central force of his wife, the horse, suitably named "Conqueror," has been "turned out to grass" (250).

Gaskell shows that the ideal female image mourned by so many conceals a strength and will that haunts and disables the characters and the plot as she seeks to pull them all back to her earlier command. Whether dying or dead, the Victorian domestic angel, an ailing figure in *Wives and Daughters,* poses a rigorous counter energy to much in the story. Rather than nurturing an orderly flow to the narrative, Mrs. Hamley's "ghost" confuses and stalls the novel. She creates what seems a willed and willful interference with the text. Her illness breaks into the story of Mr. Gibson's new marriage and new domesticity, underscoring the class implications in the union. When the new Mrs. Gibson takes up her role as wife and stepmother, Mrs. Hamley indirectly challenges this authority. Squire Hamley's call on "The Bride at Home" is solely to take Molly back to his sick wife. As selfish as the narrator may ask us to understand Hyacinth's plans are for her stepdaughter and that prevent Molly from going to Hamley Hall, her insistence that Molly "visit people" (186) that night creates a symbolic conflict between the world of a weakened past and that of a rigorous present. The novel's ambivalence about the first wife—her utility, suitability, force—surrenders to the necessity in the "new" that Gaskell locates here in Gibson's second wife. Hyacinth's victory over Mrs. Hamley's request keeps Molly in the world of lively social engagement and away from a fading world of privilege. Molly may dislike the vanities in this life around her, but the narrative infuses the superficialities of a newly feminine everyday that now controls what had been Mary Preston's territory with vivid liveliness so that the quotidian compete with the dying and historical past represented by the first wife:

> Day after day the course of these small frivolities was broken in upon by the news Mr. Gibson brought of Mrs. Hamley's nearer approach to death. Molly—very often sitting by Cynthia and surrounded by ribbon, and wire, and net,—heard the bulletins like the toll of a funeral bell at a marriage feast.
>
> (218)

As evocative an image the first wife may be, Gaskell writes a strong critique of the feminine ideal and its function in the period's fiction. Mary Preston and Mrs. Hamley adequately portray the role, affirming what the culture and Gaskell's audience would recognize about this female type. However, the novel's dead first wives enact a macabre abuse of the reincarnated image's authority, taking self-command beyond what any conduct book would advocate, refusing to give up the ghost completely or to melt into Armstrong's "woodwork" of the text. Mrs. Hamley, before and after her death, continually seeks to bring us all back to a scented and dim chamber Gibson had feared for his growing girl. In scenes like those discussed above, the first wife often succeeds in destabilizing the beginning of "new" stories, but, as the novel eventually demonstrates, her victory is a temporary one. Unable to venture beyond the estate's gardens and its world of entitlement, and unable to live through the entirety of *Wives and Daugh-*

ters, this first wife, reading and writing on her sofa, dressed in her soft gowns, suggests the hypnotic as well as eviscerated utility in literary motifs. The invalid first wife, ensconced in her sickroom, enshrined in characters' memories, enclosed by narrative form shows the self-contained, almost rarified quality of a literary convention that, in Gaskell's hands, must eventually clear a way for the new.

AIMEE: THE "UNSPEAKABLE" MRS. HAMLEY

Osborne Hamley's "mysterious wife" (233) is not quite a literal second Mrs. Hamley, as she does not wed the widower Squire but his son, Osbourne. In highlighting the novel's efforts with the first wife trope, Aimee writes another tale that foregrounds Gaskell's creative energies to reach beyond many of her own representations of dead wives and wife substitutes. Like Hyacinth, Aimee has supported herself as a governess/nursemaid, and, like Hyacinth, she makes her way into a domestic setting that is, because of her social rank, technically not her legitimate territory. Aimee's trespass, like Hyacinth's, suggests something new about the role class may play in the domestic narratives of the late nineteenth-century novel.

While the first Mrs. Hamley's frail and elegant corporeality exerts tremendous power in the text, Aimee's character lives, at first, entirely in the realm of writing. She is, almost always, a figure imagined and imaginary, and her own writerly efforts to make herself known, although proof to an independent and autonomous identity, at first only add to the characters' fanciful perceptions of her. Aimee makes her initial surprise appearance in a letter to Osborne. This textual intrusion, which occurs during the slow spelling of Mrs. Hamley's death, shows what will become the novel's struggles to accommodate both a first wife, whose refusal to leave the action destabilizes narrative movement, and a second, whose demands for invitation and acknowledgement inspire a counter energy. The discovery of Aimee in letter form intrigues Molly as she tries to envision "what unspeakable elegant beauty had [Osborne] chosen for his wife" (211). The written word, proof of a new Mrs. Hamley, also stimulates Molly to create an imaged ideal but one that only repeats the outline of Mrs. Hamley's "elegant" and well-bred figure. Similarly, Osborne's sonnet series, which he hopes could provide his secret wife with financial support, suspends Aimee in the sphere of the linguistic. These poems may chronicle "an autobiographical passage in his life" (259), but they also reflect how writing transforms a "real" woman into a cultural icon as the titles move from those like "To Aimee, Walking with a Little Child" (the first in the series) to "Aimee's Confession" or "Aimee's Despair." In choosing a poetic form borne from a man's love for an unattainable object of desire, Osborne shapes Aimee as a purely textual being; Aimee's gendered perfection

exists only because poetry's discursive "regulated process of repetition" creates her (Butler 145). The final sonnet legitimizes Aimee as "the" wife and the course of the poetry reflects a desirable end stage in a girl's social maturity. To be a wife, and a particular type of wife, is of primary importance in Gaskell's novel. To be capable of writing in a new way about "The Wife" is even more significant. Through Osborne's feeble attempts at poetry Gaskell critiques the shoddy and sentimental commercial output that help circulate trite images through the cultural imagination and that successfully elide class and class struggle from the province of representation. However, Gaskell's talents as a commercial writer lie in her ability to write "outside" the very conventions she herself must use.[12] Osborne's last poem, "The Wife," reflects domestic ideology's standards and norms; Gaskell's title for this fictitious sonnet foreshadows how her novel will cede the "first" Mrs. Hamley's centrality to a new literary construct whose vigor seems rooted in the class and national differences other characters find so disturbing or wish to ignore.

Like a series of genre paintings, Osborne's poetry fixes Aimee in a clear pattern of female perfection—she is silent, passive, and distant. Aimee's own writing, her letters, however, resists such a portrayal and such a static role. Margaret Homans's scrutiny of women and language in *Wives and Daughters* examines the crucial part Gaskell assigns to Molly the "bearer" and interpreter of so many others' words, but my interests here lie with the autonomy the act of writing actually provides Aimee. Ultimately, letter-writing, more than letter-reading, in *Wives and Daughters* shapes how the book itself, in burying first wives, turns toward newer, more novel ways of writing. If the first Mrs. Hamley still lives in the spectral core of the narrative action, that core cannot support the psychic and domestic structures it once defended. Her absence frustrates and weakens characters that feel powerless to act without her, unable themselves, as this essay's opening quotation has suggested, to move on. "No letter will reach her now" (265), the Squire thinks, just as Osborne's wish that his mother were alive to help with his marriage keeps the younger man locked in a similar condition of befuddled passivity. However, both the Squire's and Osborne's difficulty with change expose the text's irony: that the novel *will* move on, that *Wives and Daughters,* ultimately, cannot and will not keep both Mrs. Hamleys. Thus, although the silent and dead first wife weakens and confuses the desire for progress, when confronted by the second Mrs. Hamley, the first cannot continue her enthrallment of the text. Indeed, Gaskell's concentration on Aimee's writing gives the new wife and the novel the means to move safely away from the first wife's command. The letters Molly dutifully writes to Osborne's wife do not reach the young woman because Aimee, independent of any summons, has left her place on the story's perimeter, her unidentified "farmhouse lodgings" in Winchester (304), and begun her movement toward Hamley Hall.

With Aimee's letters Gaskell certainly suggests language's precious fragility and particularly the language any writer may use for the private and epistolary mode. There seems, at first, something so elusive about Aimee that her letters cannot "bear translating into English" (303); we wonder how this delicate textual phantom can compete with that of the first Mrs. Hamley. However, Aimee's letters point to far more complicated notions about reading and writing that underpin the novel's use of first wives. As Aimee moves from her marginal to a more primary place, the characters struggle with their symbolic idolatry of the first wife. The challenge in translating Aimee's letters points to something crucial that *Wives and Daughters* notes with the "new" model, the "new" story, the "new" wife that has yet to find a form for complete articulation. When Molly, for instance, tells the Squire all she knows of Aimee, her voice, at first, sounds "high and unnatural" (558). Gaskell shows the discomfort readers can experience with the "new" or the "novel" since literary form itself is vulnerable to alteration or foreign influence, but she herself is intrigued by the possibilities, possibilities she had toyed with in *North and South* with Dolores, Frederick Hale's Spanish wife. "It seems strange to think," Margaret Hale says in that novel, "that what gives us the most hope for the future should be called Dolores" (Chap. 10). A decade later, Gaskell works again on a future dependent on a continental outsider.

Aimee's metamorphosis from strictly textual representation (her letters, Osbourne's poetry) into a textuality intended to reproduce the real (Gaskell's character) exposes the struggles and vacillations an author may have with literary traditions. Aimee's forced entry into the story enlivens the text and wrests the narrative away from the first wife's control. Reading Aimee's letters aloud in the "darkened living room," Molly and the Squire are roused from their cloistered pursuits: "Suddenly through this quiet, there came a ring at the front-door bell that sounded, and went on sounding, through the house, pulled by an ignorant, vigorous hand" (572). Gaskell provides the first wife's replacement with a healthy will—she is "vigorous" and unstoppable and her determination to enter her predecessor's home keeps on "sounding." Aimee's entry challenges Mrs. Hamley's ordered world of class privilege. Her refusal to stop would seem a rebuke to those like the Cumnors who

> expected to be submitted to, and obeyed; the simple worship of the townspeople was accepted by the earl and countess as a right; and they would have stood still in amazement, and with a horrid memory of the French

sans-culottes who were the bugbears of their youth, had any inhabitant of Hollingford ventured to set his will or opinions in opposition to those of the earl.

(7)

However, unlike the angry French female associated with politcal revolution, and characterized by Dickens's Madame Defarge in 1859, Gaskell's *citoyenne* who makes her way across the Channel and into the house of British history brings a gentle reform of domestic life. Like a more modestly garbed version of the allegorical figure in Delacroix's *Liberty Leading the People,* painted in 1830, the historical time in which Gaskell locates her action, Aimee emancipates the Hamley household and the domestic narrative from what has become an unhealthy rule.[13]

With *Wives and Daughters* Gaskell shows the emptiness in the nineteenth-century novel's necessary convention of the domestic angel. The "great sad event' of Mrs. Hamley's death is there to "fill [the] mind" (319) so that as Aimee, the second and "vigorous" Mrs. Hamley steps into that vacated place, Gaskell revives one of the novel's central *tableaux* to underscore the first wives' diseased control and to question the healthiness of the trope this essay has argued about. When Aimee faints and falls ill, overwhelmed by the news of Osborne's death, Gaskell allows the dead first wife, that "fine London lady" (42), one more effort to retain her place as the necessary void at the text's center. Indeed, the effect entering the first wife's place has on Aimee assumes contagious proportions for even Molly, who resumes her role as nurse to this second Mrs. Hamley, realizes that "she felt unaccountably weary; that her head ached heavily, and that she was aware of a sluggishness of thought which it required a painful effort to overcome" (580). Gibson's early fears that the "life in Mrs. Hamley's heated and scented room would not be good for the girl" (45) have proven true. Characters idolize Mary Preston and long for Mrs. Hamley but these wives, dead and dying, point to the disease in a narrative form that simultaneously tries in the "most natural manner in the world" (31) to evolve, to discover new strategies for survival.[14]

If the first wife, the Victorian angel in Gaskell's novel reveals pestilent energies at the heart of the form, what antidote does the writer prescribe? This essay has argued that Gaskell proposes a story that could differ from the one promoted by the feminine ideal so dear to nineteenth-century domestic fiction and borne from notions about class and gender that very fiction continued to endorse. In her discussion of *Wives and Daughters,* Coral Lansbury has said that "class can only function when everyone knows his proper place" (*Gaskell* 42). Gaskell's second wives refuse to stay in place, even ask us to question the propriety about that place since the novel demonstrates that the way outsider second wives maneuver class fluidity can produce an outcome that is healthy for all. Gaskell places the responsibility for this type of new story, for now, in her little foreign wife, a "genuine working woman with practical skills" (Stoneman 199). She is the peripheral heroine who rejects the Hamley tradition, the Hamley home, the Squire's life to choose her own new one. In bringing the second Mrs. Hamley in from the margins, Gaskell confronts the tradition of the first wife. When she returns Aimee to a spot about "ten minutes' walk from the Hall so that she and [and her son] may easily go backwards and forwards as often as they like" (641), Gaskell valorizes a new family structure and gives this new wife a complex mobility the first-wife trope could never beat. In this way, Gaskell's second Mrs. Hamley sets her "will" and "opposition" to authority—social and narrative—even more than the second Mrs. Gibson had. By abandoning that central position within an outmoded domesticity, the morbid place at the heart of the text, Aimee paradoxically fills it up: the first Mrs. Hamley disappears and is heard from no more.

In 1931 Virgina Woolf would claim that "killing the Angel in the House was part of the occupation of a woman writer" (238); only by quelling that Victorian feminine ideal could Woolf work as she wished. Nearly seventy years earlier Gaskell recognizes the powerful artillery in her own inkpot and begins the metaphoric attack on the novelistic image her future countrywoman would take up for her own survival. *Wives and Daughters'* concentration on the angelic first wife's centrality to novelistic design and stability questions the motif's endurance and its power to maintain the form's own domestic harmony. Turning from that ideal, Gaskell's novel sets its sights elsewhere and looks away from the mid-century's affectionate belief in historical permanence and predictable time and toward new modes as yet questioned and questionable, foreshadowed yet unknown, toward a novel, perhaps, in which the first wife is something more than an unattainable ideal or an outworn convenience.

Gaskell's sudden death in November 1865 left *Wives and Daughters* a text always in progress. The *Cornhill* editor reassured readers that "we know that Roger Hamley will marry Molly, and that is what we are most concerned with" (648). But what remain the novel's final pages leave us with a very different image and one that Margaret Homans has criticized as the author's rejection of a female literary tradition and her capitulation to a patriarchal one (273-276). However, I think that Gaskell suggests quite "a different thing" (74). Molly and her stepmother look from the window as Roger Hamley rides away. Mrs. Gibson

> took out her watch and held it up, tapping it with her forefinger, and occupying the very center of the window. Molly could only peep here and there, dodging

now up, now down, now on this side, now on that, of the perpetually-moving arms . . . at length he went away, slowly, slowly, and often looking back, in spite of the tapped watch. Mrs. Gibson at last retreated, and Molly quietly moved into her place. . .

(645)

Molly's animated movements, and the eager gaze she directs toward Roger's retreating figure, turn the novel away from the past and into a distant future. Not yet a wife, Molly peeps and dodges on the borders of that pivotal role and even when she "quietly" moves to the window's center, Gaskell refuses to grant that place its former legitimacy: "how sweet," Molly thinks, "is—friendship!" (645). In turning away from the center, in burying the first wives who had constructed and maintained that place, *Wives and Daughters* anticipates new narrative forms, and (perhaps) new first wives, whom the novel, in 1865, trusts will come in time.

Notes

1. All quotations from *Wives and Daughters* will appear parenthetically in the text.

2. Coral Lansbury's and Elizabeth Langland's discussions on social class, historical change, and female autonomy in the domestic sphere have been particularly useful for my essay. In-text references to Lansbury will be abbreviated in the following manner: *Social Crisis* for *Elizabeth Gaskell: The Novel of Social Crisis* and *Gaskell* for *Elizabeth Gaskell*.

   Other contributions cover an impressive scope, ranging from female socialization and female subjectivity, to the conflicts between sentimental and scientific discourse, to Gaskell's own growth as a novelist. On the topic of women's education and socialization, Stoneman makes rich use of contemporary conduct books as well as Wollestonecraft's *A Vindication of the Rights of Woman*, arguing that Gaskell shows that learning to be a good mother requires a certain amount of independent action and thought. Foster notes that while *Wives and Daughters* certainly questions marriage and women's subjectivity, the novel demonstrates greater acceptance of women's social roles, reflecting Gaskell's own marital happiness. d'Albertis explores Gaskell's concern with a Darwinian system of selection and classification that underpins the novel's social argument. Studies of Gaskell's growth as a writer include those by Homans, Bonaparte, Billington, and Uglow's biography. Hughes and Lund discuss the influence serial publishing had on *Wives and Daughters* and Gaskell's assertion of a female authorial voice within the form.

3. Terence Wright has listed the many ways handholding in the novel shows intimacy, domination, and independence.

4. In her compelling and detailed argument, Langland reads Hyacinth as the force that reshapes the foundering Gibson household into one that not only runs smoothly and efficiently, but that allows for social advancement and opportunity. It is Langland's contention, and one with which I agree, that the second Mrs. Gibson's energetic command of the household's domestic and social economies creates a progressive and healthy movement away from a stagnant past and into an active future. See 132-147. Felicia Bonaparte emphasizes the subtleties in Hyacinth's characterization. Like the other women in Gaskell's story, Hyacinth must conform to certain social rules and standards and is often injured by the very roles she must assume (65-66).

5. In her discussion of *Ruth,* Hilary Schor claims that Gaskell's decision to let her fallen and redeemed heroine die from typhus reflects the author's acquiescence to her readers' tastes (71-75). In her well-known 1852 letter to Gaskell, Charlotte Bronte bemoaned this turn to convention that forces the audience to "shut up the book weeping" (letter 570).

6. In a previous article, I have discussed Butler's "nothing" and female gender in George Moore's 1885 novel *A Mummer's Wife.*

7. In a cogent discussion, Homans has made a similar point, reinforcing Hyacinth as a "shifting signifier" in the text, able to elude, in particular, the role of "mother" (263-265).

8. The extensive attention to this topic is best represented in scholarship by Wanda Fraiken Neff, M. Jeanne Peterson, Nancy Armstrong, Mary Poovey, and Helena Michie.

9. Mrs. Ramsay's unspoken love for her husband, her steady "strength flaring up," relieves him in his crisis of self-doubt: "filled with her words, like a child who drops off satisfied, he said, at last, looking at her with humble gratitude, restored, renewed, that he would take a turn; he would watch the children playing cricket" (Woolf 38).

10. Critics have noted Gaskell's reworking of her 1850 novella *The Moorland Cottage* as an influence on *Wives and Daughters* (Bonaparte 24, 72-74; Uglow 255-256). The novella's Mrs. Buxton, a delicate invalid who dresses in soft muslin gowns and robes, provides the heroine Maggie with a gently feminine maternal influence. In a way then, Mrs. Buxton is a "first-wife" for Mrs. Hamley even down to her own death that Gaskell portrays within the space of a one-sentence paragraph.

11. As if taking up the elliptical fate Gaskell awards the Victorian angel of the house, Virginia Woolf will push Mrs. Ramsay, the female center of *To the Lighthouse,* into a matter-of-fact bracketed note to her sudden death and her grieving husband's groping confusion.

12. Stoneman has discussed how Osborne's debt to Wordsworth cannot, as much as he would like, make Aimee another "Lucy" (198-199). Hughes and Lund emphasize that point as well in their discussion of how Osbourne's "Aimee" poems emphasize Gaskell's understanding of herself as an author and the profession of writing (28). Homans makes a more extended analysis of Gaskell's intertextual use of "A Slumber Did My Spirit Seal" (260-262).

13. Delacroix's painting experienced a highly unstable period of exhibition from its initial display in the 1831 Salon, to reinstatement at the Luxembourg in 1861, and then its installment at the Louvre in 1874. See Barthelemy 128-133. It is more than probable that Gaskell knew of Delacroix's painting as she made frequent trips to France and actually composed much of *Wives and Daughters* during an extended stay in the country. As Uglow notes, Gaskell adored France, its people and the culture, and her letters, as well as the series "French Life" she wrote for *Fraser's* in 1864, testify to this enthusiasm.

14. Gaskell, who described Darwin as a cousin, had met the scientist in 1851 (Unsworth 47). See also Uglow for these family connections and for the intense interest a book like *On the Origin of Species* provided Gaskell in the spring of 1860. Both Schor and d'Albertis discuss the novel's Darwinian emphasis on kinship, heredity, and knowledge in the context of authorship and gender. For other scholarly works on Darwin's influence on the Victorian novel see Beer and Levine.

Works Cited

Armstrong, Nancy. *Desire and Domestic Fiction: A Political History of the Novel.* New York and Oxford: Oxford UP, 1987.

Barthelemy, Jobert. *Delacroix.* Princeton, N.J.: Princeton UP, 1997.

Beer, Gillian. *Darwin's Plots: Evolutionary Narrative in Darwin, George Eliot, and Nineteenth-Century Fiction.* 1983. Cambridge and New York: Cambridge UP, 2000.

Bailin, Miriam. *The Sickroom in Victorian Fiction: The Art of Being Ill.* Cambridge: Cambridge UP, 1994.

Billington, Josie. "Watching a Writer Write: Manuscript Revisions in Mrs. Gaskell's *Wives and Daughters* and Why They Matter." *Real Voices: On Reading.* Ed. Philip Davis. New York: St. Martin's P, 1997. 224-235.

Bonaparte, Felicia. *The Gypsy-Bachelor of Manchester: The Life of Mrs. Gaskell's Demon.* Charlottesville and London: UP of Virginia, 1992.

Butler, Judith. *Gender Trouble: Feminism and the Subversion of Identity.* 1990. New York and London: Routledge P, 1999.

Chapple, John and Alan Shelston, eds. *Further Letters of Mrs. Gaskell.* Manchester and New York: Manchester UP, 2000.

————. *The Letters of Mrs. Gaskell.* Cambridge, Mass.: Harvard UP, 1967.

d'Albertis, Deirdre. *Dissembling Fictions: Elizabeth Gaskell and the Victorian Social Text.* New York: St. Martin's P, 1997.

Foster, Shirley. *Victorian Women's Fiction: Marriage, Freedom and the Individual.* Totowa, N.J.: Barnes & Noble Books, 1985.

Gaskell, Elizabeth. *Mary Barton.* Intro. Stephen Gill. 1848. Harmondsworth and New York: Penguin Books, 1970.

————. *North and South.* Intro. Pam Morris. 1854-1855. Harmondsworth and New York: Penguin Classics, 2001.

————. *Wives and Daughters.* 1866. Ed. Pam. Morris. New York and London: Penguin, 1996.

Homans, Margaret. *Bearing the Word: Language and Female Experience in Nineteenth-Century Women's Writing.* Chicago and London: U of Chicago P, 1986.

Hughes, Linda K., and Michael Lund. *Victorian Publishing and Mrs. Gaskell's Work.* Charlottesville and London: UP of Virginia, 1999.

Langland, Elizabeth. *Nobody's Angels: Middle-Class Women and Domestic Ideology in Victorian Culture.* Ithaca and London: Cornell UP, 1995.

————. *Elizabeth Gaskell.* Boston: Twayne, 1984.]

Lansbury, Coral. *Elizabeth Gaskell: The Novel of Social Crisis.* New York: Barnes and Noble Books, 1975.

Levine, George. *Darwin and the Novelists: Patterns of Science in Victorian Fiction.* Cambridge, Mass. and London: Harvard UP, 1988.

Masters, Joellen. "'A Great Part to Play': Gender, Genre, and Literary Fame in George Moore's *A Mummer's Wife.*" *Victorian Literature and Culture* 29 (2001): 285-301.

Michie, Helena. *The Flesh Made Word: Female Figures and Women's Bodies.* New York and Oxford: Oxford UP, 1987.

Neff, Wanda Fraiken. *Victorian Working Women: An Historical and Literary Study of Women in British Industries and Professions, 1832-1850.* New York: AMS P, 1966.

Peterson, M. Jeanne. "The Victorian Governess: Status Incongruence in Family and Society." *Suffer and Be Still: Women in the Victorian Age.* Ed. Martha Vicinus. Bloomington and Indianapolis: Indiana UP, 1972. 3-19.

Poovey, Mary. "The Anathematized Race: The Governess and *Jane Eyre.*" *Uneven Developments: The Ideological Work of Gender in Mid-Victorian England.* Chicago: Chicago UP, 1988. 126-163.

Schor, Hilary M. *Scheherezade in the Marketplace: Elizabeth Gaskell and the Victorian Novel.* New York and Oxford: Oxford UP, 1992.

Shorter, Clement. *The Brontes: Life and Letters.* New York: Haskell House, 1969.

Stoneman, Patsy. *Elizabeth Gaskell.* Bloomington and Indianapolis: Indiana UP, 1987.

Uglow, Jenny. *Elizabeth Gaskell: A Habit of Stories.* New York: Farrar, Straus Giroux, 1993.

Unsworth, Anna. "Some Social Themes in *Wives and Daughters.* 1. Education, Science, and Heredity." *Gaskell Society Journal* 4 (1990): 40-51.

Woolf, Virginia. "Professions for Women." *The Death of the Moth and Other Essays.* New York: Harcourt Brace Jovanovich, 1942. 235-242.

————. *To the Lighthouse.* 1927. Intro. Eudora Welty. San Diego, New York, and London: Harcourt Brace Jovanovich, 1981.

Wright, Terence. *Elizabeth Gaskell: "We are not angels": Realism, Gender, Values.* London: Macmillan P, 1995.

Melissa Schaub (essay date fall 2004)

SOURCE: Schaub, Melissa. "Sympathy and Discipline in *Mary Barton.*" *Victorian Newsletter,* no. 106 (fall 2004): 15-20.

[*In the following essay, Schaub studies Gaskell's treatment of sympathy in* Mary Barton, *illustrating how the author's call for sympathy even for those who are responsible for one's suffering is a powerful means of keeping the poor and disenfranchised under control.*]

Sympathy is dangerous. This insight, so counterintuitive to most everyday applications of the word, has become more and more commonplace in scholarly investigations of its history. For nineteenth-century readers, sympathy—the ability to feel another's pain as one's own—posed the danger of loss of control in the sympathizer, brought on by excess of feeling. Another danger is that recently pointed out by Audrey Jaffe in *Scenes of Sympathy,* that sympathy can cause great discomfort to the sympathizer as it forces upon her the "fear of falling" (18) to the level of the object of sympathy. Sympathy poses yet another danger to the sympathizer, as yet uninvestigated. Though most scholarly studies of the political role of sympathy (especially in industrial novels), including Jaffe's, focus on sympathizers in superior positions, not every sympathetic transaction involves a privileged professional coming to a greater understanding of a member of the underclass. In Elizabeth Gaskell's *Mary Barton* (1848), sympathy flows just as frequently from the workers to the masters. This sort of sympathy contains an entirely different danger—that it will paralyze victims by making them morally unable to take action against their own victimization. Gaskell deploys sympathy in exactly this way, using it as a tool to discipline both the workers in her novels and the workers who read her novels.

Of course, this sinister view of sympathy is a bit out of step with mainstream notions. The eighteenth century idea that sympathy is the root of morality, and is desirable in itself as a feature of a mature character, is still the dominant view in modern culture. And the idea that sympathy has political value because of its power to transform one's views of people unlike oneself, introduced in the eighteenth-century and a truism for nineteenth-century industrial novelists like Gaskell, is still the most popular view even for Americans who have never heard of Gaskell or of factory novels. In *Mary Barton,* Gaskell presents sympathy as the solution to the violence caused by mistrust between classes. If workers and owners could simply come into one-on-one contact and be enabled to understand each other's problems, as they do in the famous reconciliation between John Barton and the mill-owner whose son he has murdered, the violent dislocations of industrialization could be avoided or at least ameliorated. That theory of the power of sympathy is still operative today. One Thanksgiving my local newspaper ran a holiday-themed column by the editor, who had changed his attitude toward homelessness after a homeless man cared selflessly for his dying dog (a victim of a hit and run) until he could find it. Michael Marshall, the editor, reaches the crisis of his story specifically with a vision of the homeless man's discomfort: He took off his coat . . . and covered Pepper. He stayed next to her, stroking her and talking to her, probably shivering himself, until well after sunrise." The exercise of the sympathetic imagination in feeling the homeless man's chills inspires in him this insight: "There have been times in my life when I have not had much patience for homeless people. I remember once calmly explaining to a couple of panhandlers that, given my mortgage and other financial encumbranches, their net worth was far greater than my own. 'So how about y'all giving me some of your spare change.' But I will never look at those folks in the same light, not after this." Elizabeth Gaskell would have been very pleased by Michael Mar-

shall's conversion experience, which so exactly brings to life her theory. So, in a different way, would Audrey Jaffe, who uses the modern American's tortured anxiety over meeting the gazes of homeless persons as the paradigmatic example of the discomfort of sympathy. Marshall's last sentence illustrates her contention that it is specifically "the act of looking . . . [that] fills the spectator with the anxiety of bodily contagion, the fear of inhabiting the beggar's place" (Jaffe 5). Marshall's story illustrates my theory just as well. The homeless man, after all, showed just as much sympathy as Michael Marshall, and as far as one can learn from the editor's account, he got nothing from it.

Gaskell's more positive view of sympathy as a means of checking the excesses of the upper classes—changing one's views of homelessness or of the Hands—is certainly the dominant mode of industrial fiction. Scenes of suffering, with which the reader is meant to sympathize, abound in factory novels. Description of the physical misery of working-class characters is a standard means by which such authors produce a desire for political reform. That "the response to the suffering body" (Sanders 317) is the moral mechanism of condition of England novels has been a commonplace in modern study of the genre.[1] *Mary Barton,* while it gets most of its emotional force from this same mechanism, complicates it, and these complications create the ideological fissures that allow one to glimpse the more ominous possibilities of sympathy. Gaskell uses suffering for political effect, but she is not interested only in physical pain, placing just as much emphasis on the wounded emotions of her characters. Even when she does describe more standard physical suffering such as cold or hunger, she erases the bodies of the workers who suffer, the reality of their anguish being expressed as discourse (their words, and the words of other characters) rather than as somatic description. Finally, she allows sympathy to flow in both directions: from workers to masters as well as the reverse. The effects produced by the disappearance of workers' bodies from particular scenes in the novel, and by the greater emphasis on the workers' own powers of sympathetic emotion, force us to revise our understanding of the role of sympathy in Victorian culture.

Sympathy has had a complex history since Adam Smith first made it the keystone of *The Theory of Moral Sentiments* (1759). The Romantics, who were suspicious of the cult of sensibility, saw the depiction of pain as a dangerously double-edged sword that could be made to support any political position (Bruhm 20-5). Later Victorian writers' medicalized vision of female bodies and the body politic created alarm over the effects sympathy might have on hysteria and crowds (Vrettos 83). Throughout the nineteenth century, sympathy was acknowledged to have great but dangerous imaginative power, which though desirable had always to be accompanied by stringent attempts at management and control, often through distancing the reader from the very scenes of pain which the author had just gone to such effort to describe.[2] Bodiliness itself had an equally ambiguous value. The unique individuality conferred by the experience of ineffable pain or by the imaginative experience of feeling another's pain could detach one from the larger social body (Bailin 29), and yet paradoxically also make one better able to exist within that social body by melting the boundaries between inside and outside yet preserving individuality at the same time (Bruhm 19). The body, in short, was capable either of eroding the discipline necessary to an industrial society, or of preserving it.

The most powerful and yet most dangerous component of bodily sympathy was the melding of the points of view of reader and character. Though that melding was necessary to produce the political energy desired by industrial writers, it also had a potential drawback. Athena Vrettos argues in *Somatic Fictions* that by the 1860s Victorians feared that "to view suffering was potentially to collapse the rational boundaries between imagination and reality and to reliquish the power of self-control" (86). But *Mary Barton* does not display precisely the same anxieties about sympathy and bodily suffering that modern critics have discerned in the periods that bracket it. Gaskell does not treat sympathy as a dangerous tool to be handled carefully; rather, she depicts her scenes of suffering even more intensely, to provide even more sympathetic engagement than would otherwise be the case. However, while her novel abounds in the kind of realistic verisimilar description that is found in other industrial fiction, the materiality of her description is usually reserved for settings and events. The actual feelings of the workers are not described physically. Even hunger and dirt are translated out of the bodily realm and into the verbal and emotional realm, so that the sympathizing character has to divine the suffers' feelings by translating their words into emotions and hence into sensations. The sensations, however, are rarely described, and Gaskell lays the most emphasis on the speaking, thinking, and feeling part of the process—on the cognitive bridge between two people that sympathy represents, not on the sensations that result from crossing that bridge. This emphasis on the immaterial force of sympathy is what allows her to depict it as a source of discipline for the poor workers who feel it. John Barton's greatest flaw, according to the narrator, is irrationality. The narrator describes his rage at the masters and his decision to join a trade union as the result of diseased thoughts, and even implies that opium might have influenced his decision making (198). Without education, his outrage over suffering results only in his "wild" (199) decision to be a Chartist. At this stage of his career the narrator compares Barton to Frankenstein's monster, a being without a soul or the "inner means of happiness" (199). But the cognitive nature of

sympathy—its existence as a process of translation of the signs of emotion (especially words) in others into a feeling in oneself—requires the exercise of rationality, and that makes it, in Gaskell's model, a tool of self-discipline. John Barton's growth in sympathy is a growth in rationality denied him by his lack of education. *Mary Barton* thus argues that sympathy will increase self-control rather than dangerously eroding it (as many nineteenth-century writers feared), but Gaskell achieves this effect by de-emphasizing the physicality of suffering and highlighting instead its emotional force.

The displacement of the body into discourse or representation is a key element of Audrey Jaffe's theory of sympathy as well. She defines sympathy as an imagined relation, in which the sympathizer does not identify with the sufferer, but rather puts herself in the sufferer's place, representing the sensations as being her own. This process of imaginative representation necessarily "do[es] away with bodies" (13) and emphasizes the mental processes of the sympathizer, as I have described. But Jaffe's theory cannot wholly account for the absence of bodies from this particular novel. She argues that sympathy usually produces a "swerve toward the visual" (3) in Victorian fiction because it is a specular relation (one sympathizes with a sufferer one looks at). Gaskell, however, represents her scenes of sympathy as often through words and sounds as through the visual. This difference, I think, is a symptom of the larger difference in theories of class structure that separates Jaffe's model from mine. For Jaffe, sympathy produces anxiety in middle-class characters and readers who fear that their own identity (or place) is vulnerable to being exchanged with the place of the lower-class object of their sympathy. The middle-class character's position on a continuum of three classes is essential to this transaction, since it is the possibility of going either up or down that produces anxiety. Industrial novels, however, generally represent England as a dual-class system: "two nations" or Masters and Hands. Perhaps for this reason the sympathizing characters in these novels do not display the anxiety about identity that Jaffe finds fundamental, but are, rather, stabilized in their identities by their experience of sympathy. Ultimately, the anxiety of sympathy, according to Jaffe, "threatens the desired stability and presumed naturalness of middle-class identity" (19), and as a result, by the end of the century sympathy leads to a type of modern identity politics subversive of liberal capitalist ideals (22-3). In industrial novels, however, the very different class structure produces a correspondingly different structure of feeling, one that lends itself to the circulation and consolidation of power in the two-term system of labor and capital.[3]

In fact, bodily suffering without sympathy frequently has the effect of stabilizing identities and social norms in early Victorian writing.[4] Authors and activists of the

1830s and 40s used intensely physical descriptions of poverty, filth, and disease as evidence in political works on the reform of the urban industrial environment. The metaphor of the "body politic" dominates such discussions, from debate over the Factory Acts to theories of labor value[5] to Edwin Chadwick's seminal work on sanitary reform. In *Nerves and Narratives,* Peter Logan argues that Chadwick's descriptions of disease-producing filth are meant as a spur for middle-class readers to impose their values (derived from their greater physical sensitivity to bad smells) on the poor, through inspection and surveillance (157-63). Chadwick does not seek to produce sympathy through his descriptions, merely a desire in the reader to promote governmental reform. Suffering here is not a means to sympathy, but a metaphor used for essentially bloodless purposes (deriving the state of the nation from the physical state of the People). Some industrial novels fit this model as well—for example, Disraeli's *Sybil,* which relies as much on its narrator's ironically distanced voice as it does on ethnographically detailed descriptions of working-class characters' pain. Gaskell's novel, however, does not, even though she uses passages from Chadwick's *Sanitary Report* in **Mary Barton.**

Gaskell's novel does, however, share one major feature with Chadwick's writing—the desire to control the poor. For Chadwick the control must come, in the traditional manner, from above (sanitary inspectors forcing discipline on the masses). For Gaskell, the control will come from within the workers themselves, ultimately a far more chilling vision. In **Mary Barton,** the working-class characters whose pain is represented in their own voices are denied power and political reality because of the nature of those voices. Gaskell uses the pain-wracked language of her suffering workers to create sympathy not only between reader and character but also, and primarily, between working-class characters. It is in modeling sympathy for the working classes that Gaskell's book functions disciplinarily, as sympathy for the suffering of others becomes the force that will prevent workers from rioting and will teach them self-command as members of an emerging modern body politic.

In generating this sympathy, Gaskell controls point of view delicately in order to avoid collapsing the distinction between imagination and reality (the outcome so feared by her contemporaries). Instead, as Mary Poovey explains in *Making a Social Body,* Gaskell produces sympathy and identification paradoxically enough by emphasizing the separation of points of view between character and reader (145). Poovey illustrates her point with the visit to the Davenports' cellar apartment, by far the most-quoted scene in the novel and one often cited as the paradigmatic example of how industrial authors use physical description to create sympathy: "After the account I have given of the state of the street, no one can be surprised that on going into the cellar inhabited by Davenport, the smell was so fetid as almost to knock the two men down. Quickly recovering themselves, as those inured to such things do, they began to penetrate the thick darkness of the place" (Gaskell 66-7). Peter Logan points out that this scene echoes many in Chadwick's report in which middle-class observers enter a filthy tenement and are overcome by the smell of it because of their superior sensibility. Both Logan and Poovey emphasize the separation Gaskell creates between the middle-class narrator/reader and the lower-class characters through her use of pronouns and her declaration that the men are "inured" to squalor (whereas, presumably, the readers are not). I, however, would argue that Gaskell's description, while indeed enforcing separation, also emphasizes the degree to which the working men hate filth as much as the reader can—the fact that they are almost knocked down stands out far more than their subsequent recovery. Logan argues that the upper and middle classes saw the lower classes as susceptible to disease precisely because they were not sensitive enough to mind living in filth, and that this is why a government bureaucracy of surveillance was necessary, but at least in this instance Gaskell is not trying to support Chadwick's dehumanization of workers. She is, instead, modeling in her working characters the kind of sympathy for suffering that readers are expected to learn. By acknowledging both the separation between classes and points of views and the similarities between them, she models sympathy for readers of all classes, including other workers, and her particular method of doing so transforms sympathy into exactly the tool of discipline that the less-sophisticated Chadwick envisions as sanitary inspection.

The sympathy Gaskell creates for the Davenports comes from physical description, but the setting receives far more attention than the human bodies within it. The Davenports' feelings of hunger or pain are not described directly from their point of view by the narrator, but instead we are given indirect, largely verbal, evidence: the children cry out for food, Mrs. Davenport faints in hunger, and Mr. Davenport (ill of typhus) can only express himself through "screams and shrieks of agonized anxiety" (68). This early in the novel, John Barton pays little attention to Ben Davenport's voice, preferring to focus on the physical tasks of relief available to him, such as lifting Mrs. Davenport's head off the bare floor. Eventually the voice forces itself on the men's attention, as both Barton and Wilson are required to restrain Davenport from hurting himself during a fit of "mad agony" in which he yells and swears deliriously (72). Barton is described as surprised by the cursing, through his inexperience with delirium. But as the concept of sympathy evolves throughout the novel, the voice of pain takes on more and more importance, and Barton's experience with it increases.

The pattern established in the Davenports' cellar, in which we are told about "agony" through the abstract word but given illustration of it only through the victim's voice and not a direct description of the pain from his or her point of view, deepens as John Barton's character evolves throughout the novel. Barton's speech at the union meeting that condemns Harry Carson to execution is an important stage in this process. The younger Carson's doom is sealed not only because the workers discover a derisive cartoon he has drawn of their delegation during talks over a strike, but also because of their sense of guilty sympathy with the woes of a fellow worker. The transformation of the workers' rage into violence is accomplished by Barton's description of his visit to the sickbed of an Irish "knobstick" whom one of the union members had injured with vitriol during the strike. The man's pitiable state caused Barton to sympathize with him, and resolve to give up future violence against their fellow working-class victims. This emotional transaction—the conversion of animosity to amicability through the medium of sympathy for another's pain—is the paradigmatic moment of industrial fiction. John Barton has not yet achieved perfectly disciplined sympathy, however. At this point his new positive feeling for a former enemy merely adds fuel to his rage against the owners: "'I've thought we han all on us been more like cowards in attacking the poor like ourselves; them as has none to help, but mun choose between vitriol and starvation. I say we're more cowardly in doing that than in leaving them alone. No! what I would do is this. Have at the masters!'" (223). Barton clearly still has some evolution to do, as his rage has not yet been dissipated, merely redirected. But the power of sympathy to refine and control the otherwise formless rage of the workers is an essential element of Gaskell's theory.

As with the Davenports, the depiction of the injured Irishman focuses on his disordered speech. His ravings specifically draw Barton's sympathy, as the audible sign of his pain. Though Barton begins by saying "'bless your life, none on us would ever throw vitriol again (at least at a knobstick) if they could see the sight I saw today'" (222) he goes on to admit that the man's face was bandaged and so he really couldn't see anything. The evidence of the man's pain turns out to be his "moans," and while Barton tries to initiate somatic sympathy by squeezing the man's hand, the response he gets is verbal: "'when I axed his wife's name he shrieked out 'Mary, Mary, shall I never see you again? Mary, my darling, they've made me blind because I wanted to work for you and our own baby; oh, Mary, Mary!' Then the nurse came, and said he were raving, and that I had made him worse'" (222). This speech succeeds in producing the sympathy for knobsticks that Barton wants—when he breaks off his story, his listeners ask him with "anxious voices" whether he ever found out where the wife lived. Barton is forced to admit that he could not, because the Irishman "'went on talking to her, till his words cut my heart like a knife'" (222). Throughout Barton's account and the use he makes of it in persuading the workers to violence, the most salient feature of the Irishman's invalid state is not his pain but his voice, crying out incoherently.

Barton's use of the Irishman's incoherent and pained voice exactly echoes Gaskell's description of her own project in writing the novel in the Preface, in which she will "give some utterance to the agony" of "this dumb people" (xxxvi). The transformation of mute or unintelligible pain into language for political purpose is a basic goal of industrial fiction. But as Pamela Corpron Parker points out, the control of the language in which pain is expressed is a vexed issue in Gaskell's novel, the suffering worker often vying with the author for power over the language (321-2); and as Hilary Schor argues, Gaskell's desire to valorize maternal care as a model for political relations too frequently results in reducing the suffering workers to "infants" who have to "move back, almost beyond language" (35) in order to be able to generate sympathy.[6] The reassertion of control over language requires the narrator to lay more emphasis on the nature of tortured speech than on suffering bodies. This evaporation of workers into the language of pain, beginning with the Davenports and culminating in the knobstick, paradoxically blunts the impact of Gaskell's ostensible project, transferring agency not to the sufferer who utters words, but to the non-suffering observer who interprets them.[7] When that observer refuses to interpret, language has no power for the victim. When Barton's sister-in-law Esther, now a prostitute, comes to him with incoherent warnings about his daughter Mary, Barton is too impatient to make sense of her words, misunderstanding her as referring to his dead wife rather than his daughter. When she tries to speak to him she is out of breath, and even "put her hand to her side, and caught her breath with evident pain" (143), but the sight of her so enrages Barton because he blames Esther for his wife's death that he ignores these obvious bodily symptoms and her broken speech as well. After he throws her aside, a policeman takes her into custody under suspicion of drunkenness, and the warden of the prison spends the rest of the night listening to her "half-delirious wails and moanings" (145). He attributes them to intoxication, but readers are told what she is saying, and while her speech is heated, it is perfectly understandable. In this case, male interpreters wilfully fail to interpret her speech. Because sympathy is so thoroughly a linguistic and rational act in **Mary Barton,** there is no room for Esther to create sympathy if observers will not make the effort to meet her halfway.[8] But the encounter with the knobstick seems to have changed Barton's attitude toward irrational speech permanently. Ironically, he displays "beautiful patience" in gathering "fragments of meaning from . . . half-spoken words" (233) to figure out how to take a lost little boy home—on his way to commit the murder. Barton is willing to invest imaginative energy in one victim and not another; in either case the power rests with him, the potential sympathizer.

Ultimately, however, Gaskell strips agency away from sympathizers as well. Sympathy is the ability to imagine another's pain and thus interpret it correctly, but in the end it is not a means of increasing the power of the one who possesses it, instead becoming an impetus to self-control and a conduit by which power flows outward into the surrounding society that imposes restraint and has created the conditions causing pain in the first place. When applied widely enough, sympathy can flow not only downward, but upward as well. Barton's final stage of evolution away from monstrosity and toward disciplined individuality is to be able to sympathize with the more fortunate as well as the less fortunate. Gaskell is not content for Barton to learn sympathy only for other workers; for sympathy to be a completely successful political force it must exist between workers and owners as well. This type of sympathy dominates the ending of the novel, in the final reconciliation between Barton and Carson. Significantly, however, while both men in the end learn a lesson of sympathy for the suffering of others, the narrative emphasis is laid on Barton's realization of the suffering he has caused Carson by killing his son. When Carson at last expresses in words the pain he has felt, Barton realizes that "[r]ich and poor, masters and men, were then brothers in the deep suffering of the heart; for was not this the very anguish he had felt for little Tom in years so long gone by, that they seemed like another life!" (431). This realization of common emotion produces in Barton a desire to speak words of comfort, and the "blasting thought" that his guilt deprives him of "the right to bind up his brother's wounds" (431) is the blow that finally crushes him and produces the repentant death-bed speech that seals his claim to pathetic heroism.

In this speech Barton claims that the most irritating factor that led to his Chartism and union activity was the owners' lack of sympathy for the workers, and this assertion is echoed later by Job Legh in his and Jem Wilson's final visit to Mr. Carson. Job claims that "what we all feel sharpest is the want of inclination to try and help . . . even if they could find no help, and at the end of all could only say, 'Poor fellows, our hearts are sore for ye; we've done all we could, and can't find a cure,'—we'd bear up like men through bad times'" (456). Apparently all the workers really require is the belief "that men are caring for their sorrows" (456) to satisfy them. Here at last the narrator finally addresses the need for owners to feel sympathy for workers. And yet until this point in the novel, the descriptions of the poverty and suffering of the workers had focused on material details: the dank and fetid basement of the Davenports, the starving children on all sides, the con-

stant deaths from illness and want. In the end, where a solution is finally offered, those sufferings are translated from the physical to the emotional realm: they become "sorrows" rather than pains. This transformation structurally parallels the transformation of physical suffering into speech that had caused sympathy in Barton earlier in the novel. Both movements result in the idea that the owning classes of England can purchase security from a workers' revolution very cheaply, merely through attempting to *feel* rather than to *do* anything.[9] The workers' consciousness of those sympathetic feelings will produce a gratitude that leads to self-discipline and a resolution to suffer in silence, and their own sympathies for the emotional trials of owners (whom they have learned are as human as themselves) will reinforce their submission.

The success of the program of sympathy between classes leading to self-discipline in the workers is forecast by an incident the elder Carson witnesses at the end of the novel. A working-class boy accidentally knocks a wealthy child down to the pavement, giving her a bloody nose; her nurse threatens to take him to a policeman, but the girl forgives the boy instead, kissing and making up. A passerby is convinced that "That lad will mind, and be more gentle for the time to come, I'll be bound, thanks to that little lady" (435). The repressive authority of the policeman is to be replaced in the boy's mind by the ideological authority of the little girl, an internalized image of the consequences of violence that will cause him to discipline himself, obviating any need for the state to do so. Frankenstein's monster will discover anger management. And, of course, it is the realization of the expedient power of sympathy in this scene that motivates Carson to go home and read his Bible rather than call the police on Barton, which in turn leads him ultimately to forgiveness and sympathy. This scene, and not Carson's embrace of the dying Barton, is the one most truly emblematic of Gaskell's vision of the future relations between classes.

My reading of **Mary Barton** runs counter to more than one strain of criticism about the novel. Though Marxists have sometimes criticized Gaskell for not going far enough to emphasize the sufferings of the workers and foment class revolution, most critics have defended her, describing the novel's ability to transform English class relations for the better through forcing upper- and middle-class readers to confront the realities of working-class life and change their treatment of workers accordingly—exactly the way Michael Marshall, the editor, promises to treat homeless people differently in the future. Thomas Recchio's description of the "self reformation" (17) **Mary Barton** requires of readers exemplifies this tendency to ascribe "resistant power" and "disruptive and humanizing energies" (10) to Gaskell's fiction. Both this article and many of the books on industrial fiction that take a similar tack emphasize the power of sympathy to transform the behavior of the owners and the presumably similar readers.[10] As Hilary Schor puts it: "Having read these lives, like Mr Carson, we cannot turn away" (43). Schor, like most critics, equates the reader with the owner—"we" are more like Mr. Carson than like John Barton. My reading, however, has focused on the effect sympathy has on the workers, duplicating the emphasis of the novel—almost all the examples of sympathy operating in the novel involve working-class characters exclusively. They model the effect imaginative identification with others has on one's personality and political behavior, and that effect is considerably more sinister than readings focusing solely on Carson's reconciliation with John Barton convey. What Gaskell chooses to emphasize in the end is not the softened behavior of factory owners, but sympathy's power to avert a violent revolution of the workers. John Barton's tortured repentance and the incident with the little girl are far more vividly described than any reformations in factory owners' behavior. The bare statement that Carson's own lesson of sympathy has resulted in "[m]any of the improvements now in practice in the system of employment in Manchester" (458) is too perfunctory and vague to have any real impact. Sympathy, no matter how positive a force it might be in exposing the plight of those who suffer, becomes a vector of social control, because its cumulative effect in the novel is to prevent the outraged workers from taking action, whether against rival workers or against their employers' children. Thus sympathy paradoxically dissipates agency rather than enabling it.

Gaskell's treatment of working-class suffering in this novel reflects the emerging discourses of power and discipline in the period. According to Mary Poovey, "disciplinary individualism" (expressing freedom through voluntary compliance with the law) was the established vision of the social body by the 1860s (22). Gaskell is clearly part of this emergent discourse. Her vision of industrial relations is more optimistic than those of her contemporaries, Disraeli and Dickens, one of whom forecasts violent riots and burning castles, and the other of whom concludes famously that it's all nothing but a "muddle." But Gaskell's more optimistic faith in the lower classes' moral progress paradoxically produces the more chilling vision. She truly seems to expect sympathy to enable the factory workers to internalize their class position, creating an inner policeman to take the place of the outer one. At least Disraeli's factory workers get to keep their gin palace, and Dickens's will always have the circus. Gaskell's workers have nothing to look forward to but self-imposed orderliness in the colonies (where Jem and Mary emigrate), voluntarily avoiding the personal space of rich little girls.

Notes

1. For a recent survey of the vast body of secondary literature on the sentimentalist discourse of sym-

pathy in relation to industrial fiction, see Mary Lenard's *Preaching Pity.*

2. See Steven Bruhm's discussion of Wordsworth's revisions of his early poetry, which make the body less immediate and more processed (44-58), or Lawrence Rothfield's description of the narrative voice in realist novels as resembling a doctor's "repression of the impulse toward identification with the patient, a silencing of one's sympathy" (85).

3. Jaffe, like other critics, also tends to assume that only middle-class Victorians read novels. Since Gaskell cut her authorial teeth writing short fiction for *Howitt's Journal,* a "working-class weekly" (Schor 24) it seems unsafe to assume that this particular author was writing only for her peers. The possibly different experience of a worker—or an aristocrat, for that matter—who is forced to feel sympathy is a lacuna in most critical considerations both of sympathy and of the Victorian novel.

4. Both Miriam Bailin and Athena Vrettos argue that scenes of pain and physical illness in later Victorian fiction act as metaphors for emotional and cultural issues, and that by transposing those issues onto the body, novelists can assert control over them (Vrettos 3) and reconfirm a "stable, unified self" (Bailin 6). On the other hand, Bailin points out that the sickroom itself is often the scene of the suspension of "institutional and internalized" discipline (21), and the overall unifying effect of the novel is achieved despite this relaxation of discipline. Gaskell rarely provides even this temporary relaxation, however. Figures of ideological control such as nurses and police officers are present in most of the scenes of sympathy I shall discuss.

5. See Catherine Gallagher on Malthus and Mayhew in The *Making of the Modern Body.*

6. Schor's argument about maternal care develops a common thread in feminist criticism that sees Gaskell's politics being encoded primarily in gender rather than class. Feminists who want to defend Gaskell from the Marxist charge that the romance and domestic plots distract from the class politics have generally argued that in fact those plots enact a progressive gender politics that cannot be separated from class; sympathy and emotion in general are key to this very popular line of argument. Patsy Stoneman argues that the male working-class characters illustrate a Carol Gilligan-esque "female ethic" (71) through their sympathetic and nurturing behavior, and other feminist critics have taken up this line of argument to depict Gaskell's vision of sympathy as a

truly radical force rather than as wishful thinking or a compromise. Such readings, however, ignore the more negative effects of sympathy I am trying to elucidate here. See, for example, the note below about Esther's "surveillance" of her niece.

7. My theory here runs counter to Elaine Scarry's in *The Body in Pain,* which begins with the assertion that "[p]hysical pain has no voice" (3) and that the pre-linguistic state induced by suffering is a key element in the work of torturers, who must destroy or subvert the prisoner's voice, which is "the locus of power" (51). She argues that the expression of pain in linguistic form is the first step toward re-empowerment for victims (12), and she valorizes the transformational power of human creativity in language, since metaphor is the most basic tool for expressing pain. Scarry's theory has merit but is not as universal in its application as she clearly wishes to make it. I am not the first to make this claim; Lucy Bending describes the transfer of agency from sufferer to interpreter as a potentially negative effect of Scarry's emphasis on the ineffability of pain (114-5).

8. I have focused here only on Esther's role as a victim of insufficient sympathy. Hilary Schor provides an interesting counterpoint in her discussion of Esther as a detective and narrator, whose "surveillance" of her niece Mary transforms that activity from an "official" action to one of "affection" (31)—a movement Schor sees as key to the novel's politics of gender, which valorizes all-seeing mother-love as a solution to the crisis of class. Of course, one person's all-seeing love is another person's panopticon.

9. Of course Gaskell most earnestly believed that true sympathetic feeling would have inevitably produced alleviating action in the physical realm, but this belief requires assumptions that a cynical reader might very well not share. The promise that her program of sympathy will avert revolution is made fairly overt by her reference in the Preface to "the events which have so recently occurred among a similar class on the Continent" (xxxvi)—the revolutions of 1848.

10. Mary Lenard provides another recent example of this standard reading of the religious conversion of the elder Carson at John Barton's deathbed (120-6). Indeed, she argues (as many critics do) that "Carson's literary conversion experience [reading the Bible] is probably the most important moment in the entire novel" and that "Gaskell invites her readers to put themselves in the place of Carson" (126). It is worth noting that Lenard designates Carson as middle-class (in order to align him with the presumably middle-class reader). But as I have already argued, industrial fiction depicts a two-class world, and within an industrial town, Carson is not in the "middle" of anything. Thus one might question how far a truly bourgeois reader would identify with him. Though Lisa Surridge falls into this same habit as well, describing Carson as middle-class, her otherwise perceptive analysis of the contrasting masculinities of workers and owners leads her to a different conclusion: "In a novel which locates manly nurturance firmly in the working class, the final scene of Carson embracing the dying Barton simply does not ring true" (341).

Works Cited

Bailin, Miriam. *The Sickroom in Victorian Fiction: The Art of Being Ill.* Cambridge: Cambridge UP, 1994.

Bending, Lucy. *The Representation of Bodily Pain in Late Nineteenth-Century English Culture.* Oxford: Clarendon P, 2000.

Bruhm, Steven. *Gothic Bodies: The Politics of Pain in Romantic Fiction.* Philadelphia: U Pennsylvania P, 1994.

Gallagher, Catherine. "The Body Versus the Social Body in the Works of Thomas Malthus and Henry Mayhew." *The Making of the Modern Body: Sexuality and Society in the Nineteenth Century.* Ed. Catherine Gallagher and Thomas Laqueur. Berkeley: U of California P, 1987. 83-106.

Gaskell, Elizabeth. *Mary Barton.* 1848. Ed. Edgar Wright. Oxford: World's Classics-Oxford UP, 1987.

Jaffe, Audrey. *Scenes of Sympathy: Identity and Representation in Victorian Fiction.* Ithaca: Cornell UP, 2000.

Lenard, Mary. *Preaching Pity: Dickens, Gaskell, and Sentimentalism in Victorian Culture.* New York: Peter Lang, 1999.

Logan, Peter Melville. *Nerves and Narratives: A Cultural History of Hysteria in Nineteenth-Century British Prose.* Berkeley: U of California P, 1997.

Marshall, Michael. "Give thanks for a homeless guy who helped a dog die right." Editorial. Mobile *Register* (24 November 2002: 3D).

Parker, Pamela Corpron. "Fictional Philanthropy in Elizabeth Gaskell's *Mary Barton* and *North and South.*" *Victorian Literature and Culture* 25 (1997): 321-31.

Poovey, Mary. *Making a Social Body: British Cultural Formation, 1830-1864.* Chicago: U of Chicago P, 1995.

Recchio, Thomas E. "A Monstrous Reading of *Mary Barton*: Fiction as 'Communitas.'" *College Literature* 23 (1996): 2-22.

Rothfield, Lawrence. *Vital Signs: Medical Realism in Nineteenth-Century Fiction.* Princeton: Princeton UP, 1992.

Sanders, Mike. "Manufacturing Accident: Industrialism and the Worker's Body in Early Victorian Fiction." *Victorian Literature and Culture* 28 (2000): 313-29.

Scarry, Elaine. *The Body in Pain: The Making and Unmaking of the World.* Oxford: Oxford UP, 1985.

Schor, Hilary. *Scheherezade in the Marketplace: Elizabeth Gaskell and the Victorian Novel.* Oxford: Oxford UP, 1992.

Stoneman, Patsy. *Elizabeth Gaskell.* Bloomington: Indiana UP, 1987.

Surridge, Lisa. "Working-Class Maculinities in *Mary Barton.*" *Victorian Literature and Culture* 28 (2000): 331-43.

Vrettos, Athena. *Somatic Fictions: Imagining Illness in Victorian Culture.* Stanford: Stanford UP, 1995.

Stefanie Markovits (essay date March 2005)

SOURCE: Markovits, Stefanie. "*North and South*, East and West: Elizabeth Gaskell, the Crimean War, and the Condition of England." *Nineteenth-Century Literature* 59, no. 4 (March 2005): 463-93.

[*In the following essay, Markovits offers a reading of Gaskell's* North and South *within the context of the Crimean War.*]

In the middle of the nineteenth century, Britain entered into a full-fledged war for the first time in forty years, as the great historical foes Britain and France stood shoulder-to-shoulder against Russia in defense of Turkey and a land-route to the East in the Crimean War (1854-56). Such novel events might have been expected to generate a slew of novelistic responses, especially as the subject of the unprecedented public uproar at the mismanagement of the war (enough to topple a government) was added to the usual heady mix of military heroics. Henry Clifford, a bored army officer who was reading Charles Dickens's *Hard Times* (1854) from his position in the Crimea, wrote of its author: "I wish he could sit, with my pen and paper, and write a book, 'Hard Times' in the Crimea. . . . Only just what is passing in front of the door of my comfortable little tent would give him plenty of matter."[1] But Clifford's wish was not fulfilled; in fact, relatively few novelists engaged with the events of the war directly, and Dickens himself (for all his involvement in the conflict through his work with the Administrative Reform Association) limited his novelistic response to the portrayal of the bureaucratic bungling associated with the Crimea in the Circumlocution Office of *Little Dorrit* (1855-57).[2] Indeed, for all the oriental glamour of its location, the Crimean War captured the imagination of

novelists at home in a decidedly domestic fashion. One of the best-known novels of the war years deals not so much with questions of East and West as with those of North and South. Nevertheless, while overt signs of the war may be absent from Elizabeth Gaskell's work of that title, I want to argue that her book can be read fruitfully in the context of the Crimean conflict.

Gaskell was preoccupied with thoughts of the war throughout the writing of **North and South** (1854-55). Her concern was heightened by the fact that she wrote much of the novel from Lea Hurst, the Nightingale family home. As Jenny Uglow notes, the famous accounts in *The Times* on 9, 10, and 13 October 1854 of the desperate conditions in the English camps were published during Gaskell's first days at Lea Hurst; almost immediately, Florence Nightingale began organizing her departure for the East (she left on 21 October).[3] While the Nightingale family was in London helping Florence to prepare, Elizabeth Gaskell sat in their house, concocting her own story of a young woman's heroism. Her letters of the period are full of references to the war, in particular to the working-class reaction to the war effort. She describes to Dickens how "Some fine-spinners in a mill at Bolton, earning their 36 shillings a week, threw up their work and enlisted last week, on hearing of the sufferings in the Crimea, for they said they could neither sleep nor eat for thinking how the soldiers there wanted help."[4] And to Parthenope Nightingale, she writes: "Babies ad libitum are being christened Florence here; poor little factory babies, whose grimed stunted parents brighten up at the name, although you'd think their lives & thoughts were bound up in fluffy mills. But it's the old story 'for we have all of us one human heart', & these poor unromantic fellows are made, somehow, of the same stuff as *her* heroes of the East, who turned their faces to the wall, & cried at her illness."[5] In **North and South** Gaskell used the same quotation (from Wordsworth) to suggest the possibility for reconciliation in the war between masters and men.[6] And the conflation of her "unromantic" workers with the "heroes of the East" suggests that her novel can be read as an attempt to add some Crimean romance to a conflict closer to home. A letter from Parthenope Nightingale to Gaskell, discussing the success of local efforts to raise money to support Florence's activities in the Crimea, bolsters this conflation. Parthenope begins by proclaiming: "Truly 'North and South' have mingled their good thoughts in this. I believe much charity to our neighbours and love of God is brought forth by the war." But her words easily lead her down a different path: "By the bye, I must say what a deal of wisdom there seems to me in 'N. & S.'"[7]

John Peck argues that **North and South** provides an example of the army in its domestic capacity of maintaining civil order at home. As Peck describes it, "the army is called in [during the strike at Thornton's mill], as at

Peterloo, to suppress political unrest." Indeed, he claims more broadly that "in a period when most people all but ignore the army, [Condition-of-England] works actively consider its role."[8] But while this statement may apply with truth to earlier works in the category, such as *Shirley* (1849) or even *Hard Times* (which was published in Dickens's periodical *Household Words* in 1854, right before *North and South* began serialization there), it seems far-fetched to claim a lack of interest in the army during wartime. Nevertheless, while the riot scene in *North and South* is punctuated by Mrs. Thornton's question, "When can the soldiers be here?" (p. 175), it turns out that the answer to her demand is not until "five minutes too late to make this vanquished crowd feel the power of authority and order" (p. 180). Instead, Margaret's act of feminine heroics (albeit accompanied by Thornton's manly reprimand, expressed in a tone that Peck sees as inflected with "the traditional qualities of military leadership" [*War, the Army, and Victorian Literature,* p. 97]) serves to diffuse the anger of the mob. But to read "the thread of dark-red blood" (*North and South,* p. 179) that trickles down Margaret's face in the climactic riot scene of the novel as a replacement for the "thin red line" made famous as a symbol of heroism at Balaclava is to recognize the Crimean War as a part of the condition of England.[9] In what follows I do not propose reading *North and South* as an allegory of the war; rather, I want to suggest that considering the novel in the context of the war and of Gaskell's involvement with Florence Nightingale helps both to historicize the book more precisely and to illuminate the moment.

* * *

While Gaskell's novel contains no overt mention of the Crimean War, contemporary readers understood it as a product of the war years. A reviewer in the *Athenæum* declared: "We imagine that this year of war will produce few better tales than 'North and South.'"[10] Moreover, Thomas Ballantyne noted in an article in *Blackwood's* titled "Lancashire Strikes" (in which he cites Gaskell's novel as evidence in his argument against unions) that the Preston Strike that Gaskell bases her story upon coincided with the onset of the war: "The Preston Strike of 1853 began a few months after Russia had crossed the Pruth."[11] So it might be argued that the Crimean War had an unspoken effect on the plot of *North and South* by virtue of its effect on trade. As Ballantyne explains, "The period chosen by the Preston operatives for their trial of strength with the masters was very unfortunate" because, in addition to the usual problems following a deficient harvest, "the Eastern question, which had hitherto seemed likely to end in a peaceful solution, assumed all at once a more complicated and unsatisfactory aspect" ("Lancashire Strikes," p. 52).

In his essay Ballantyne asserts: "although [the strike] lasted about half a year, the public mind was too much occupied with Vienna negotiations and the impending war to pay much attention to a mere quarrel between a few thousands of work-people and their employers" ("Lancashire Strikes," p. 52). And Arthur Hugh Clough (an acquaintance of both Gaskell and the Nightingales, and perhaps an influence on her portrait of Mr. Hale) wrote in a letter at the start of 1855: "our literature at present is the War Column in the Newspaper."[12] While Gaskell's own letters of the war years contain repeated reference to the newspapers of the day (and in particular to *The Times*),[13] it is possible to read Gaskell's novel as both redressing and supporting this point. The redress lies in her telling a tale that depends heavily on those supposedly unnoticed stories in the papers about the Preston strike.[14] But we can see some support for Clough's statement in the manner in which Gaskell transforms the newspaper stories—in the signs of *The Times* found in her novel. We can, in fact, consider the book as a kind of offshoot of journalism.

Journalism was by far the most prominent literary form of the day. The hunger for news actually led to the repeal of a newspaper stamp act that allowed for a proliferation of inexpensive dailies. The Russophobe diplomat David Urquhart lamented in his 1856 tract *The Effect of the Misuse of Familiar Words on the Character of Men and the Fate of Nations* that "heretofore the people had 'leaders' whom at least they knew; now they have columns of anonymous type."[15] Similarly, Thomas Carlyle notoriously blamed the "war" on the "Editors."[16] The relatively few novels that actually portray the Crimean War often evince nervousness at having to compete with the overwhelming popularity of journalistic accounts from the East, especially Russell's famous dispatches from the Crimea written for *The Times*. In Henry Kingsley's *Ravenshoe* (1862), the narrator says: "I could [describe Sebastopol] capitally by buying a copy of Mr. Russell's "War." . . . But I think you will agree with me that it is better left alone. One hardly likes to come into the field in that line after Russell."[17]

Conversely, according to John Peck, who has pointed to similarities between Russell's prose descriptions and those of Dickens, Crimean War journalism is overwhelmingly novelistic in its methodology. Peck contrasts Russell's dispatches to traditional war writing, which is based on epic conventions: "What Russell offers is a largely static plot, where the fighting is almost incidental; what is of interest is what he sees in the details behind the fighting. And essentially, in the manner of a realistic novelist, what Russell sees is a social problem" (*War, the Army, and Victorian Literature,* p. 30). This comment places Russell's writings in the context of a "social novel" that contains a non-incidental episode of fighting (and an obscure but relevant epic backdrop: in *North and South* Thornton first employs Mr. Hale to read Homer with him, and the question of the use-value of his reading enters the novel when the modern-day conflict of the strike rears its head).[18] But if Russell's dispatches are novelistic, then Gaskell's novel is journalistic: in *North and South* Gaskell seems to be melding journalism to the novel through her fictionalization of a variety of newspaper and other nonfiction accounts. More specifically, she transforms journalism by participating in the development of a new form: what will come to be called the "human interest" story.

The term "human interest" appears at a crucial juncture in Gaskell's novel, in a scene that generates both the title for the novel and one of its central methods of resolution: the idea that class division can be healed through contact between individuals. It is in this scene that Margaret first comes to feel some concern for Milton through her encounter with Higgins and his family. Higgins comments on Margaret's being from Hampshire: "That's beyond London, I reckon? And I come fro' Burnley-ways, and forty miles to th' North. And yet, yo see, North and South has both met and made kind o' friends in this big smoky place" (*North and South*, p. 73). And the narrator tells us: "Milton became a brighter place to Margaret. It was not the long, bleak sunny days of spring, nor yet was it that time was reconciling her to the town of her habitation. It was that in it she had found a human interest" (p. 74). The earliest use of the phrase "human interest" in the *Oxford English Dictionary* is from 1824—from Byron, describing his attempt to make his angels humanly sympathetic. Actually, a broader search brings up older examples; nevertheless, the phrase's popularity seems to have blossomed in the Romantic period.[19] The second *OED* example, from Dickens in 1860, has attached a commercial element to the expression (it is from his serial *All the Year Round*): "Figuratively speaking, I travel for the house of Human Interest Brothers." But by the twentieth century, every one of the examples listed by the *OED* is linked explicitly to the journalistic idea of the human-interest story, a story that melds reportorial fact with Romantic emotion—and perhaps best exemplified by those tales of heroic suffering that we endure during every Olympics broadcast to ensure that even those with an utter lack of interest in sports will have reason to watch.[20] This evolution of the phrase is already implicit in Gaskell's use of it: we can think of the novel *North and South* as a human-interest-story version of the journalistic reports both in the newspapers and in works like Gaskell's friend James Phillips Kay-Shuttleworth's *The Moral and Physical Condition of the Working Classes Employed in the Cotton Manufacture in Manchester* (1832). And this form owes something to the Crimean background to the tale, to the pull of journalism in the period.

* * *

Of course, the kind of journalism of most immediate relevance to *North and South* is found in its method of publication; the novel first appeared serialized in Dickens's *Household Words*. Again, considering this fact can help us to contextualize the novel in terms of the Crimean War. Cynthia Dereli has argued that "the editorial policy of *Household Words* . . . , under Dickens's editorship, was to concentrate on the issues of concern at home, instead of jumping on the war bandwagon."[21] Actually, Dickens seems to have recognized that it was becoming harder and harder to distinguish between concerns at home and concerns abroad. As consecutive installments of *North and South* appeared in the journal, more and more of the surrounding articles and poems reflected the political realities of the war in the East. Stories gave sociological insights into the cultures of the combatant nations, such as a piece on "Devil Worshippers" (a sect of peaceful "Mohammedans" who are persecuted by their forced conscription into the Turkish Army) and an article entitled "At Home with the Russians." There were discussions of military dress ("Mars a la Mode") and of artillery ("Field Service").[22] These articles showed how "telescopic philanthropy" toward the Turks should not blind readers to more proximate problems. For example, an article entitled "The Home Office" offered "a plain account of the manner in which the government business of this country is transacted," reflecting the burgeoning concern with the administrative flaws revealed by the war effort.[23] Another article, "A Home Question," begins with this declaration:

> In the war that we now wage with Russia, should it be ended in another year or two, we shall scarcely have lost upon all the fields of Alma, and before all the Sebastopols, in all the campaigns, as many of our fellow-countrymen as cholera has slain DURING THE PAST FEW WEEKS in London. Even to our troops in the East, Pestilence has proved incomparably more destructive than the redoubts and batteries of any mortal foe.[24]

The article describes the "battle" being waged by working men for their health and argues that typhus is "a more deadly enemy than any Czar" (p. 294).

In addition to such articles, the volume of *Household Words* in which *North and South* came out contains a series of poems about the Crimean War that immediately preceded installments of Gaskell's novel in the journal's layout. For example, "The Moral of This Year" (which precedes the tenth portion of *North and South*) also compares the enemy abroad to disease, the enemy at home:

> But white-robed peace droops down and dies, as from
> a self-trod shore
> Comes o'er the land, like flash of brand, the gathering
> din of war;
> Where sword to sword, and hand to hand, in brother-
> hood advance
> The warriors of England, the chivalry of France!

> And whilst with peaceful scythe we cut the poppy-
>   bannered grain;
> Whilst crimson War *his* harvest reaps on the sad battle-
>   plain;
> Comes yet another enemy, with pain, and ruth, and
>   blight,
> To mow another harvest-field—to wage a darker fight!
> A Giant-King, a dread disease, with poison in his
>   breath. . . .[25]

Once again, the Condition-of-England question is entwined with the Eastern Question. Such thematic overlap is of course especially understandable given the fact that disease prevailed on the battlefront as well as on the home front.[26]

Many of the war poems in *Household Words* were written by Gaskell's acquaintance (and Queen Victoria's favorite poet) Adelaide Anne Procter.[27] Procter's poem "Waiting" comes before the seventh installment of *North and South*.[28] A typical tale of female patience (the basic premise can be compared to that in Tennyson's "Mariana" [1830]), the poem records a working-class woman's conversation with a "Lady" in which she explains why she dwells at the seashore instead of passing a life of "rest and ease" "beside the castle, / Shadowed by our ancient trees!" ("Waiting," p. 204). As we shall see, the dangerous temptations of ease in a time of war were registered by Gaskell as well, and would culminate in Margaret's reflections during her seaside holiday. In "Waiting" the war remains in the background, something to be inferred rather than stated. But the inference is supported by a later Procter poem, "The Lesson of the War," in which a "breathless," feminized nation "waits, and listens / For every eastern breeze / That bears upon its bloody wings / News from beyond the seas."[29] Joseph Bristow points to how this poem describes a seemingly passive female figure, representative of England, actually taking an active stance in calling on her "children" to do their "duty."[30] Gaskell places Margaret in a comparable position in the riot scene, when she calls on Thornton to "go down and face" his men (*North and South*, p. 177).

Moreover, both of Procter's poems express a commonplace theme of the war literature in theorizing how the conflict might unite a nation that had been divided by class distinctions.[31] As an article entitled "Peace and War" in the Tory and pro-war *Blackwood*'s put it, "war . . . makes us feel we are countrymen, brothers, friends, and neighbours, all of us (not Quakers only), while peace sets us all together by the ears like hounds in an ill-regulated kennel."[32] In "Waiting" the conversation between the speakers promises a form of unity, although one that rests largely on a kind of paternalism (or rather, maternalism), as the "Lady" tries to take care of the cottage-woman. But in "The Lesson of the War" concord comes from the recognition of a more lateral relationship both of brotherhood in arms and also, more

strikingly, of what could be called a "motherhood in arms" implied in the (albeit, in this poem, masculinized) shared home-front experience of the war. As though joining the three classes of *North and South* (represented in Gaskell's novel by London, Helstone, and Milton), Procter records the fact that "The rich man who reposes / In his ancestral shade, / The peasant at his ploughshare, / The worker at his trade" are all the "children" of mother England:

> The rulers of the nation,
>   The poor ones at their gate,
> With the same eager wonder
>   The same great news await!
> The poor man's stay and comfort,
>   The rich man's joy and pride,
> Upon the bleak Crimean shore
>   Are fighting side by side.
>
>   ("The Lesson of the War," p. 12)

Another poem by Procter, "The Two Spirits" (which appeared ahead of the twentieth installment of *North and South*), also couches a discussion of the war in terms that resonate in Gaskell's novel.[33] The spirit of the past and the spirit of the present, represented by mother figures, debate the claims of their soldier-sons to glory. The voice of the past is resolute in the conviction of the value of glory; the voice of the present is more muted, more sorrowful, more desiring of peace—and also more insistent on the cause being one of right. Like *North and South*, the poem negotiates a conversation between old and new forms of heroism. It also hints at a discussion of the value of pacifism and the notion of a just war.

* * *

The idea of the just war was central to the pro-war faction at the onset of the Crimean War. The term had gained some currency with a recent translation by Professor William Whewell of Hugo Grotius's 1625 treatise on the topic.[34] Arthur Hugh Clough, for example, somewhat dryly commented to Charles Eliot Norton in February 1854: "Well, here we are going to war—and really people after their long and dreary commercial period seem quite glad; the feeling of the war being just, of course, is a great thing."[35] As here, the idea of the just war was often combined with the claim that the forty-year peace or "Pax Britannica" had been no such thing after all—that it had merely disguised an ongoing civil war in the land, a battle between rich and poor, the blame for which could be laid at least in part at the feet of industrial progress and the uncaring commercial ethos with which it was associated.

Such a "civil war" is the topic of *North and South*; the connection is underwritten by the hints of the English Civil War that permeate the novel.[36] The Crimean context to these overlapping ideas can be seen more clearly, though, in Tennyson's *Maud*, where a state of "Civil war" at home leads the speaker to embrace the war: "It is better to fight for the good than to rail at the ill; / I have felt with my native land, I am one with my kind."[37] In her letters Gaskell suggests (albeit in a comic register) a slightly more alarming version of the connection between civil and foreign wars—the idea that the lack of soldiers on the home front would precipitate an uprising. In 1854 she wrote: "I bade farewell to a Capn Campbell, bound for the East, last week—he told me there [was] [w]ould/not [be] a soldier left in Manchester on Saturday last; whereupon somebody observed that we were on the verge of a precipice! I don't know what they meant; but don't be surprized if you hear of a rising of the weavers, headed by a modern Boadicea."[38] But she also suggests that the war can produce an unprecedented feeling of national unity, as in her quotation of Wordsworth's claim that "We have all of us one human heart," mentioned above.

In *Maud* Tennyson's speaker rants at the "Quaker" who is unable to see the difference between "lawful and lawless war" (*Maud*, p. 581; Part II, ll. 330, 332). Gaskell's attitudes toward the Peace Society—the Quaker pacifist group founded in 1816 but coming to prominence at the onset of the Crimean War (against which the Society actively campaigned)—are rather more complex. Two references to the Peace Society in **North and South** constitute the novel's most obvious nod toward the war being fought in the East. In the first instance Edith writes from Corfu, asking Margaret and her mother to visit her there. But she adds that she does not ask Mr. Hale, "because, I dare say, he disapproves of war, and soldiers, and bands of music; at least I know that many Dissenters are members of the Peace Society" (**North and South**, p. 235). Later, Mr. Bell comments that Margaret has been changed by her time in the North: "Her residence in Milton has quite corrupted her. She's a democrat, a red republican, a member of the Peace Society, a socialist—" (p. 330).

Included in the list of Dissenters with involvement in the Peace Society were the Gaskells themselves. As Andrew Sanders has pointed out, Gaskell told Florence Nightingale that she and her husband lived "in the very midst of what was once called the peace party" in Manchester.[39] But it would be a mistake to see Gaskell as a straightforward advocate for peace in the novel. The comments in her letters about the war tend to focus on the soldiers' heroism, not on the justice or injustice of their cause. But her attitudes toward the violence of the workers at home are sympathetic (even if not condoning), and her discussion of the conflict between a morality of "rights" upheld by the men and one of "duties" that should be the province of the masters shows that issues of justice are central to her conception of class struggle.[40] Moreover, Higgins himself invokes a military parallel when describing his "cause

o'justice": "I just look forward to the chance of dying at my post sooner than yield. That's what folk call fine and honourable in a soldier, and why not in a poor weaver-chap?" When Margaret objects that the soldier dies not for himself but "in the cause of the Nation," Higgins makes it quite clear that with his family and the families of others dependent upon him, his battle is "just as much in the cause of others as yon soldier" (**North and South**, p. 134).

In fact, while she clearly prefers a peaceful outcome to the crisis, Gaskell recognizes that the absence of war is not equivalent to the presence of peace. Late in the novel the narrator describes Margaret's reflections on her cosseted London life: "She was getting surfeited of the eventless ease in which no struggle or endeavour was required. She was afraid lest she should even become sleepily deadened into forgetfulness of anything beyond the life which was lapping her round with luxury. There might be toilers and moilers there in London, but she never saw them" (p. 373). Indeed, the chapter containing these reflections is entitled "Ease Not Peace"—a title that would have been translated during the war years as a reference to the ongoing civil war that had until recently been obscured by the Pax Britannica.

Yet it would also have come to the attention of Gaskell's readership at a time when (as Tennyson puts it) a "blood-red" war had "blossom[ed]" (*Maud*, p. 584; Part III, l. 53). Tennyson's macabre phrase conflates the garden imagery of the domestic love story in his poem with the martial tones of the foreign conflict. But in **North and South** the transfer of the war to the home front is accompanied by a nostalgic sanitizing (given contemporary events) of military life, which seems to be all ease and, if not peace, certainly not war. Edith's description of her life in Corfu as being one of "war, and soldiers, and bands of music" dramatically de-emphasizes the first term in her list. It makes Corfu seem like an island out of a romance (it has been identified as the utopian Skheria, home of the Phaiakians in *The Odyssey*). But, in reality, during the war Captain Lennox's regiment would have been engaged in supplying the troops in the Crimea with goods; several regiments in Corfu were even sent to the front. The lead editorial in *The Times* of 27 November 1854 actually suggests Corfu as a possible way-station for holding large numbers of British reserves.[41] Gaskell's novel obscures all such marks of the Crimean conflict.

In truth, Gaskell's descriptions of army life owe more to the old-fashioned notions of an aristocratic military than to the military as it would come to be perceived during the Crimean War. For many years (ever since the end of the Napoleonic Wars), British soldiers had been identified with dandified dress rather than daring deeds; as a character says of the young hero in Thackeray's

The Newcomes (which appeared in installments from October 1853 to August 1855), "I think I should send him into the army, that's the best place for him—there's the least to do, and the handsomest clothes to wear."[42] But as the war progressed and news came home from the front, perceptions of soldiers were changing. Gaskell herself implies the shift in attitudes toward the military in her comments in her December 1858 letter to Nightingale about her involvement in the Peace Party, when she adds that before the war that party "spoke lightly of, if not positively sneered at" the army.[43] After the war, such sneers were no longer possible. One of the greatest of shifts was that from a conception of the military centered upon the aristocratic-officer class to one centered upon the heroism and suffering of the common soldier.[44]

Gaskell's repeated interest in her letters in showing the workers' sympathy for the soldiers in the East supports her recognition of the changing opinions about the military. It also suggests that in depicting the sufferings of the men in her novel—and in using language for them that implicitly compares their suffering to that of the men in the Crimea—she may well have been taking advantage of the shifts in perception occasioned by the war. *North and South* proposes a domestic "hot-pot" solution to the conflict between masters and men (that is, the establishment of a dining hall for the workers, which Thornton occasionally visits in order to converse with his men). But a parallel with the war experience appears in Thornton's insistence on leaving the men their independence: "If they had not asked me, I would no more have intruded on them than I'd have gone to the mess at the barracks without invitation" (*North and South,* p. 362). Indeed, Gaskell appears to consider the visits as a kind of peaceful (albeit ludicrously optimistic) substitute for the leveling effects of the battlefield; as Mr. Bell notes, "Nothing like the act of eating for equalising men. Dying is nothing to it" (p. 362). Still, the thrust of Gaskell's military analogy is typically ambivalent. While she uses it to garner support for the suffering of her army of workers, her decision to romanticize military life abroad no doubt also owes much to her desire to emphasize the harsh realities of the war at home.

* * *

If Captain Lennox and Corfu provide one version of military life in the novel, then Frederick Hale provides another. Andrew Sanders has argued (in the context of a broader discussion of the role of political liberalism in the novel) that "Frederick's stand against military oppression, his moral uprightness and his resistance to injustice were . . . singularly apposite to readers caught up in the progress of the War in the Crimea" ("Crisis of Liberalism," p. 47). These qualities might also have resonated with the contemporary discussion of just wars. Still, like Captain Lennox, Frederick is described in un-

realistic and outmoded terms. In many ways, he serves as a double for Margaret. But his rebellion is the stuff of romance (as is evidenced by Gaskell's chapter epigraphs from Byron), whereas Margaret's is implicated in the modern world of the strike. And Catholicism—to which Frederick converts—stands for the ways of the past, just as Margaret's turn to industry represents the future.

One quality the siblings do share is their capacity for passion: Frederick's mouth gives Margaret "such an idea of latent passion, that it almost made her afraid" (*North and South,* p. 247), and her own passionate nature is something that Gaskell must also negotiate. Gaskell's novel aligns sexual passion with social conflict, as the "reckless" passion of the mob in the riot scene suggests (p. 178), beginning with a phallic breaching of the gates of the mill and ending with the symbolic rape of Margaret. Indeed, Bessy, Higgins, Thornton, Frederick, the mob, and, above all, Margaret herself must learn the appropriate balance between a life of passion and one of self-control—both key terms in the novel, and both key elements also of military life, where the passion required to steel oneself to battle must be controlled by a willingness to submit to military authority.

And ultimately, for all of Gaskell's pacifism, *North and South* seems to argue that one of the problems with peace is that it can inhibit a productive passion. In her discussion of passion, Gaskell once again seems to be tapping into a contemporary war-based discourse about the healthy benefits of conflict. The term "Muscular Christianity" was coined in response to Charles Kingsley's *Two Years Ago,* set during the war years, and the war also appears in the great "Ode to Fighting" in Thomas Hughes's *Tom Brown's Schooldays* (1857), a core text of the Muscular-Christian movement: "I am dead against crying peace when there is no peace, and isn't meant to be."[45] The speaker of *Maud* initially proposes a life of "passionless peace" as a substitute for lost happiness (*Maud,* p. 532; Part I, l. 151), but soon discovers his need for both passion and war. Late in *North and South* Margaret shows her awareness of the benefits of conflict in her appreciation for Edith's boy's "stormy passions":

> Margaret almost liked him better in these manifestations of character than in his good blue-sashed moods. She would carry him off into a room, where they two alone battled it out; she with a firm power which subdued him into peace, while every sudden charm and wile she possessed, was exerted on the side of right, until he would rub his little hot and tear-smeared face all over hers, kissing and caressing till he often fell asleep in her arms or on her shoulder.
>
> (p. 405)

The language of the war pervades the passage, from the allusion to the blue ribbon of a knight of the garter to the mentions of battle, peace, and right. Of course, this encounter stands in for the novel's primary "antagonistic friendship" (p. 239): that between Margaret and Thornton. And if the resolution of the conflict between these two represents in turn the resolution of a larger class conflict and the resolution of North and South and of past and present, then it can also be read in terms of the broader discussion during the war years of the merits of passionate, violent struggle.

For all that conflict has always been at the heart of romance (one need think no further than Beatrice and Benedick or Darcy and Lizzy to recognize this), this form of struggle struck Gaskell's contemporaries as something new. In her review of *North and South* in an article in *Blackwood's,* Margaret Oliphant complains of the "desperate, bitter quarrel out of which love is to come." "Shall all our love-stories be squabbles after this?" she protests; "Shall we have nothing but encounters of arms between the knight and the lady—bitter personal altercations, and mutual defiance?"[46] Oliphant traces this trend to the influence of *Jane Eyre* (1847), but she couches it in terms of the current war: "Talk of a balance of power which may be adjusted by taking a Crimea, or fighting a dozen battles—here is a battle which must always be going forward." She describes how the modern heroine, a "new Bellona," "rushes into the field, makes desperate sorties out of her Sebastopol . . . , and finally permits herself to be ignominiously captured." Of *North and South* itself Oliphant adds, "There is one consolation: Have we not in these favoured realms a Peace Society?" (p. 558). Oliphant's comments suggest that debates about the relative merits of war and peace are being played out in both military and sexual registers, and with some overlapping effects.

If the idea of passion can be understood in both martial and romantic contexts, then so can the idea of honor. Richard Lovelace's "To Lucasta, Going to the Warres" (1649) describes iconic competing notions of honor, not only martial and romantic but also masculine and feminine. Feminine honor is held safe in the nunnery of Lucasta's "chaste breast" while masculine honor lies in the glory to be achieved through bravery in war.[47] During the riot in *North and South,* Margaret calls on Thornton to display something like military bravery: "If you have any courage or noble quality in you, go out and speak to them, man to man" (p. 177). But the issue of Thornton's masculine "honor" in this scene is soon supplanted by the issue of Margaret's "truth" in regard to the lie that she tells to her protect her brother. Still, while it is easy to read the strange emphasis on this lie in terms of Gaskell's attempts to navigate the rocky terrain of Margaret's sexual desire (the lie acts as a decoy, drawing our attention away from the more difficult question of Margaret's passion as it is manifested in the symbolic deflowering of the riot scene), the choice of "truthfulness" as the virtue in question can be read not only in a sexual or military register but also in a commercial one, as some comments by Margaret as she thinks about her lie suggest:

> Her cheeks burnt as she recollected how proudly she had implied an objection to trade . . . , because it too often led to the deceit of passing off inferior for superior goods, in the one branch; of assuming credit for wealth and resources not possessed, in the other. She remembered Mr. Thornton's look of calm disdain, as in few words he gave her to understand that, in the great scheme of commerce, all dishonourable ways of acting were sure to prove injurious in the long run. . . . She remembered—she, then strong in her own untempted truth—asking him, if he did not think that buying in the cheapest and selling in the dearest market proved some want of the transparent justice which is so intimately connected with the idea of truth: and she had used the word chivalric—and her father had corrected her with the higher word, Christian. . . .
>
> (pp. 302-3)

North and South does much of its arguing by shifting between registers—by arguing, for example, that Frederick's mutiny, Mr. Hale's crisis of doubt, and the workers' strike all represent analogous forms of rebellion. In this passage, something similar seems to be happening to the idea of honor or truth.

Alexander Welsh has noted that truth became a particularly important virtue in the nineteenth century in part because of the strain on religious belief; indeed, Mr. Hale's decision to leave the Church rests on his unwillingness to tell a lie. Frederick's transgression against military honor seems, in contrast (like so much of his story), to be outmoded—or open to redescription as an honorable deed, "an heroic protection of the weak" (*North and South,* p. 259). But Welsh points out: "The new sociology confirmed that increased truthfulness was one of the important differences between an 'industrial' and a 'military' society. W. E. H. Lecky ventured that 'industrial veracity' was the *only* positive contribution of the growth of manufactures to morals."[48] This opinion was not held universally: in *Maud* the aristocratic speaker sees commercialism as a threat to truth ("When only the ledger lives, and when only not all men lie" [p. 521; Part I, l. 35]). But Gaskell's substitution of commercial for military honor in *North and South* was no doubt made easier by the increasingly managerial attitude held toward the ongoing war effort. On 31 October 1854 *The Times* announced: "War has become an affair of science and machinery, of accumulated capital, and skilful combination."[49] By 1 March 1855 that organ of popular opinion was lamenting how "this great commercial and mechanical country is governed by an official body comparatively ignorant of commerce and the mechanical arts."[50] Austen Henry Layard asked Commons on 24 July 1854, "Why does not the government allow some great firm to contract for carrying on the war?"[51] In such a climate, the idea of honor would naturally comprise both military and industrial senses, allowing the novel's much-contested title of "gentleman" to be expanded from its aristocratic and soldierly definition to include the honorable bourgeois industrialist.[52] And Gaskell adds feminine honor to this mix, thereby letting her heroine enter the fray not only bodily but also intellectually.

Still, the shift in the hero's honor from a military to a commercial register does threaten to undermine his masculinity, as is made clear in the pivotal riot scene, when Margaret demands that Thornton "face" his workers "like a man." We can also link the new philosophy of conflict (for which the Crimean War was responsible) to a burgeoning interest in the idea of masculinity, as manifested in the tenets of Muscular Christianity. Gaskell recorded in a letter that she was worried about Thornton's manliness: "I want to keep his character consistent with itself, and large and strong and tender, and *yet a master.*"[53] But an equally difficult problem—and one that can also be read in the context of shifting gender roles during the war years—arose in negotiating Margaret's womanliness. Part of the reason that Gaskell had trouble making Thornton masterful arose from the fact that she had made her heroine so strong.

The novel begins with a rather gentle vision of womanhood in Edith: "If Titania had ever been dressed in white muslin and blue ribbons, and had fallen asleep on a crimson damask sofa in a back drawing-room, Edith might have been taken for her" (*North and South,* p. 5). Yet Gaskell soon supplants Edith's kittenish and placid Titania—woman as fairy queen—with a representative of a different kind of queenliness in Margaret (and versions of this label keep reappearing).[54] The change is already indicated in her heroine's dress in the opening scene of the book (and this novel, set in part in the mills of Lancashire, is always sensitive to the meanings of cloth); Edith's muslin and ribbon are replaced by the Indian shawl that Margaret models for her aunt, "the usual garb of a princess" (p. 9), but also a significant symbol of empire. As it happens, this is how the shawl strikes Thornton in their first meeting, when he takes note of "a large Indian shawl, which hung about her in long heavy folds, and which she wore as an empress wears her drapery" (p. 62). The effect undermines—even unmans—him: "Mr. Thornton was in habits of authority himself, but she seemed to assume some kind of rule over him at once" (p. 62).

Margaret's looks belong to the figure of Britannia, not fairy queen but warrior queen (recall Oliphant's Bellona), who would appear so often in the cartoons and drawings of the day as a representative of the motherland at war: "the short curled upper lip, the round, massive up-turned chin, the manner of carrying her head, her movements, full of a soft feminine defiance, always gave strangers the impression of haughtiness" (*North and South,* p. 62).[55] Contemporary critics may have mocked her description—the repeated mention of the haughtily curved lip and "flexile throat" (*North and South,* p. 63)—but they must have done so in part because of its obviousness; it would be like giving the heroine of a novel written during World War II the polka-dotted headscarf and bulging bicep of Rosie the Riveter.[56] Britannia attained unprecedented iconic significance during the period of the Crimean War in part because of the conjunction of two influential icons of authoritative womanhood: Queen Victoria and Florence Nightingale. Actually, these two figures were often conflated: Nightingale herself was frequently represented as a queen.[57]

Of course, as critics have argued, both Nightingale and Victoria provided acceptable models of womanhood because of the ambivalence of their roles. Mary Poovey notes how Queen Victoria "was compared less frequently to a patriarchal commander than to a loving mother" ("A Housewifely Woman," p. 171). She also describes the "two faces" of the "mythic" Nightingale, domestic and military: "One was obviously allied with the normative definition of the middle-class woman . . . ; it was the image of the English Sister of Charity, the self-denying caretaker—a mother, a saint, or even a female Christ. . . . The second face of Florence Nightingale bore a greater likeness to a politician or a soldier than a gentle mother; it was the image of the tough-minded administrator who 'encountered opposition' but persevered" (p. 168). Similarly, depictions of Britannia in the pages of *Punch* during the war portrayed her alternately as woman-warrior and almost Christ-like mother-figure, as Joseph Bristow (who would add Tennyson's Maud to the list of female icons of nationhood of the times) has argued.[58]

Cynthia Dereli has suggested that poets and journalists of the war period transformed Nightingale, who would seemingly have been breaking gender barriers, into a symbol of national unity by occluding the "problematic aspects" of her role and bringing to the foreground "the acceptable role of carer," which was "reinforced through religious imagery" ("Gender Issues," p. 75). Dereli's analysis contrasts with the ways in which Gaskell relies on the "problematic aspects" of Margaret's role to make her argument. Poovey astutely observes that the fact that the two models of womanhood she identifies "converged in Florence Nightingale suggests that the military narrative was always at least compatible with—if not implicit in—the domestic narrative"; in female sexuality, "the domestic ideal always contained an aggressive component" ("A Housewifely Woman," pp. 169, 170). To Gaskell, trying to create a figure of female heroism in a novel in which the political Condition-of-England plot and the private courtship plot were so interdependent (Margaret's *Bildung* is to represent that of the nation as a whole), such ambiguities and overlaps would have been particularly welcome.

The compatibility between military and domestic models of womanhood appears forcefully in the riot scene of *North and South*. When Margaret describes her act of throwing her body in front of Thornton to shield him from the mob as "a woman's work" (*North and South*, p. 191), she is suggesting that her position was one of what Poovey calls "self-denying caretaker." And Margaret's suffering, even her pietà-like position in Thornton's arms after she faints away (complete with the stigmata of her wound) could in fact be seen to turn her into a female Christ, like Nightingale. But if Gaskell recognized Nightingale's Christ-like ability to sacrifice herself to her cause, then she also saw her soldierliness, comparing her to an archetypal female soldier, Joan of Arc.[59] Margaret's position in front of the mob, attempting (albeit with little success) to command them, might also remind us of Bodicea, the Anglo-Saxon warrior queen who had appeared in Gaskell's summer 1854 letter to Eliza Fox as a possible savior for the workers: "don't be surprized if you hear of a rising of the weavers, headed by a modern Boadicea." In another letter Gaskell describes how the workers see Nightingale as "*their* heroine";[60] in *North and South* Margaret seeks to assume, more modestly, a similar role.

Still, Margaret's authority stands as a central issue in the novel. While her looks may suggest that she rules over her domain, her experiences highlight the degree to which she is restrained by her position: as daughter, as sister, as middle-class woman. After the death of Margaret's parents and Margaret's achievement of financial independence through Mr. Bell's bequest, Gaskell records how "she tried to settle that most difficult problem for women, how much was to be utterly merged in obedience to authority, and how much might be set apart for freedom in working" (*North and South*, p. 416). While the real Nightingale struggled with this very question for years,[61] Gaskell, in her October 1854 letter to Catherine Winkworth, shows a Florence Nightingale who was never troubled by such matters, whose "clinging to one object" appears to belong to "a creature of another race so high & mighty & angelic, doing things by impulse—or some divine inspiration & not by effort & struggle of will" (*Letters*, p. 307). In a January 1855 letter to Winkworth, Gaskell responds to Charlotte Brontë's opinion of her novel, explicitly contrasting such saintliness with her own heroine's more human virtue: "I'm glad [Brontë] likes 'North and South'. I did not think Margaret *was so over* good. What would Miss B. say to Florence Nightingale? I can't imagine!"[62] Margaret is not so good, because she is less icon and more person; we see her from the inside in a way in which you never see an icon, which remains resolutely two-dimensional. This is what makes Margaret the heroine of a novel; Nightingale (at least as Gaskell sees her) would have required an epic to contain her.

But Gaskell's admiration for Florence Nightingale is mixed with a degree of suspicion.[63] Jenny Uglow argues that Gaskell was both "intrigued and appalled" by Nightingale's "self-isolation," and (as Gaskell's letters indicate) by her ability to annihilate any private feelings for individuals in her broader concerns for the race. Uglow also notes that the figure of Nightingale may have stood behind Margaret's musings toward the end of *North and South*, after her visit to a changed Helstone: "If I were a Roman Catholic and could deaden my heart, stun it with some great blow, I might become a nun. But I should pine after my kind; no, not my kind, for love for my species could never fill my heart to the utter exclusion of love for individuals" (*North and South*, p. 400).[64] Gaskell actually implies that there is something "unwomanly" in this attitude when, in her 27 October 1854 letter to Emily Shaen, she singles out for objection Nightingale's belief that children are better off in a "well-managed crèche" than with their mothers (*Letters*, p. 320). Ultimately, according to Uglow, Gaskell's suspicions win out: "Although Gaskell described Nightingale's tireless efforts in the Crimea as 'a visible march to heaven', and warmly supported her work in future years, the whole of her own fiction—and especially *North and South*—opposes the route that Florence had chosen, the subordination of relationships to causes and of people to ideas" (*Elizabeth Gaskell*, pp. 364, 365). As though to declare her allegiances, Gaskell echoes Arnold's "Dover Beach" on Margaret's seaside holiday, as she describes her heroine "gazing intently on the waves as they chafed with perpetual motion against the pebbly shore" (*North and South*, p. 414). Arnold's poem is a response to a world that has been taken over by an invisible but all-encompassing battle ("Where ignorant armies clash by night"), in which the only safety lies in the bonds between individuals: "Ah love, let us be true / To one another!"[65] Margaret spends significant portions of the novel serving as nurse to her mother and to Bessy, who sees her in a dream as a saintly figure, "drest in shining raiment," with her "hair blown off from [her] brow, and going out like rays round [her] forehead" (*North and South*, p. 149)—an iconography one might associate with Nightingale. But unlike Nightingale, Margaret nurses only those individuals in whom she has a specific "human interest."[66]

Nevertheless, in Gaskell's novel individual relationships can both foster and stand in for larger causes; the effectiveness of the comic ending of the book depends upon its ability to signify a larger bond than that between one man and one woman. And her marriage does not turn Margaret into an Edith-like wife and mother; one can imagine her more along the lines of the officers' wives whom Gaskell describes in one of her more curious mentions of the Crimean War in her letters (in a complete non sequitur between comments about her need for more postage stamps and some gossip about a quarrel): "Lady Errol, Mrs Daubeny, & Mrs Galton the 3 officer's [sic] wives who are with the Camp in the Crimea, dress as Vivandieres & wash their husbands' shirts, cook [each other's] their/ dinners & c, & say 'they never were so happy in their lives.'"[67] Moreover, like Jane Eyre, Margaret retains some of her independence by making her husband a dependent—in this case a financial one, as is appropriate to this industrial battle-queen.[68] But to recognize in Margaret Hale a home-front counterpart to those officers' wives, if not, indeed, to Florence Nightingale herself—to see her as a kind of "Britannia of the market-place" (to steal and misuse an epithet from Henry James)—is to recognize that the Eastern Question can provide us with a novel angle on the problems and solutions that Gaskell addresses in ***North and South.***

* * *

A question remains, to which I have no definite answer: if ***North and South*** is indeed so saturated with the culture of the Crimean War, then why do so few traces of the war appear in the novel? One need not be conversant with the developments in critical theory of the last half-century to recognize that a literary work necessarily contains much that is "unsaid," and a variety of unspoken cultural forces are at play here, as I have suggested in my discussions of the journalistic underpinnings to the novel and Margaret's heroism. But I would hesitate to argue that the absence of the war is proof of Gaskell's subconscious preoccupation with it. After all, in her letters she demonstrates a preoccupation that was relatively conscious. In part, I am sure that such traces of the war as are there would have been more readily apparent both to Gaskell herself and to her contemporary audience than they are to us; I have argued that this would have been true of Gaskell's references to the Peace Societies and to the distinction that she makes between ease and peace, to name but two examples.

Yet there may be something more to the occlusion of the war in the novel. If I am right in claiming that Gaskell wishes (either consciously or not) to draw on support garnered by the Crimean War for her characters—for the sufferings of the workers, for Thornton's managerial skills, and, more ambivalently, for Margaret's strength—then she is engaging in a delicate balancing act. Earlier I suggested that Gaskell's treatment of the workers takes advantage of the growing sympathy felt for private (i.e., lower-class) soldiers in the Crimea. While some hints are needed to form the connection (as in those provided by the military metaphors she uses), too explicit a comparison would have caused her readers to divert their attention from the workers to the far more "fashionable" cause of the soldiers in the East. In this case, the optimal effect on the reader would perhaps be a subconscious one, balanced out by a mask-

ing of the device in the otherwise romanticized version of military life that Gaskell provides. All of this is, of course, impossible to prove. But to expand the analogical possibilities of a novel that does so much of its arguing through analogy seems an appropriate move, and one that expands the horizon of interpretive possibility both for the novel and for the period.

Notes

1. Clifford, 16 December 1854 letter, quoted in Alan Palmer, *The Banner of Battle: The Story of the Crimean War* (New York: St. Martin's Press, 1987), p. 172.

2. For a relatively complete list of novels that treat the Crimean War explicitly, see Anna Belle Laughbaum, *Some English Novels (1855-1917) that Deal with the Crimean War: An Abstract of a Thesis* (Urbana: Univ. of Illinois, 1948). Foremost among the "war" novelists are the Kingsley brothers, Charles and Henry, although my comments on their works below should indicate that they shared in Gaskell's tendency to transpose the Crimean experience onto more familiar ground.

3. See Uglow, *Elizabeth Gaskell: A Habit of Stories* (London: Faber and Faber, 1993), pp. 363-64. Like many others, Uglow attributes these accounts to William Howard Russell, though they were actually written by the newspaper's editor, John Delane, and Thomas Chenery (see Palmer, *Banner of Battle,* pp. 136-37).

4. Elizabeth Gaskell, letter to? Charles Dickens,? 17 December 1854, in *The Letters of Mrs Gaskell,* ed. J. A. V. Chapple and Arthur Pollard (Cambridge, Mass.: Harvard Univ. Press, 1967), p. 324. Hereafter referred to as *Letters.*

5. Elizabeth Gaskell, letter to Parthenope Nightingale, 21 July 1855, in *Letters,* p. 359. Florence had taken ill with Crimean fever.

6. "Once brought face to face, man to man, with an individual of the masses around him, and (take notice) out of the character of master and workman, in the first instance, they [Thornton and Higgins] had each begun to recognise that 'we have all of us one human heart'" (Elizabeth Gaskell, *North and South,* ed. Angus Easson [New York: Oxford Univ. Press, 1973], p. 419). Further references to *North and South* are to this edition and appear in the text.

7. Parthenope Nightingale, letter to Elizabeth Gaskell, no date, quoted in Elizabeth Haldane, *Mrs. Gaskell and Her Friends* (London: Hodder and Stoughton, 1930), p. 105. In "A Crisis of Liberalism in *North and South,*" *Gaskell Society Journal,* 10 (1996), Andrew Sanders discusses this passage in the context of its claims for liberalism (see p. 48).

8. John Peck, *War, the Army, and Victorian Literature* (New York: St. Martin's, 1998), p. 94.

9. William Howard Russell used the term "thin red streak" (soon transformed into the famous "thin red line") to designate the 93d Highlanders as they charged into battle. See William Howard Russell, *Russell's Despatches from the Crimea, 1854-1856,* ed. Nicolas Bentley (New York: Hill and Wang, 1966), p. 123.

10. [Henry Fothergill Chorley], rev. of *North and South,* by Elizabeth Gaskell, *Athenæum,* 7 April 1855, p. 403.

11. [Thomas Ballantyne], "Lancashire Strikes," *Blackwood's Edinburgh Magazine,* 79 (1856), 52.

12. Arthur Hugh Clough, letter to F. J. Child, 31 January 1855, in *The Correspondence of Arthur Hugh Clough,* ed. Frederick L. Mulhauser, 2 vols. (Oxford: Clarendon Press, 1957), II, 497.

13. See Gaskell, *Letters,* pp. 300, 321, 324, 326.

14. See H. I. Dutton and J. E. King, *"Ten Per Cent and No Surrender": The Preston Strike, 1853-1854* (Cambridge: Cambridge Univ. Press, 1981), esp. pp. 198-201.

15. David Urquhart, *The Effect of the Misuse of Familiar Words on the Character of Men and the Fate of Nations* (London: Trübner and Co., 1856), p. 279.

16. Carlyle's blame of the "Editors" appears frequently in his letters and journals—see, for example, his 20 October 1854 letter to Lady Ashburton (in *The Collected Letters of Thomas and Jane Welsh Carlyle,* ed. Kenneth J. Fielding, et al., 30 vols. to date [Durham, N.C.: Duke Univ. Press, 1970-], XXIX, 175). In a 22 March 1855 letter to James Carlyle, Carlyle puts the word *war* into scare quotes, as though to suggest that the conflict does not deserve the heroic name (see *Collected Letters,* XXIX, 275). The comments of both Urquhart and Carlyle resonate forcefully in today's political climate.

17. Henry Kingsley, *Ravenshoe,* ed. William H. Scheuerle (Lincoln: Univ. of Nebraska Press, 1967), p. 350.

18. See *North and South,* pp. 113 and 334, for example.

19. A *Literature Online* keyword search for the phrase "human interest" generated examples in works by Samuel Taylor Coleridge, Percy Bysshe Shelley, Helen Maria Williams, and William Wordsworth, and in a review by Charles Kingsley discussing the poetry of John Keats, among others (see <http:lion.chadwyck.com/gotoSearchTexts.do?initialise=All>).

20. The Romantic roots of the genre are nicely caught in a poem by Samuel Hoffenstein, "Mr. William Wordsworth Covers a Human Interest Story for a Tabloid Newspaper" (a parody of Wordsworth's "We Are Seven" [1798]), in Hoffenstein, *A Treasury of Humorous Verse* (New York: Liveright, 1946), pp. 161-64.

21. Dereli, "Gender Issues and the Crimean War: Creating Roles for Women?" in *Gender Roles and Sexuality in Victorian Literature,* ed. Christopher Parker (Aldershot, Hants: Scolar Press, 1995), p. 74.

22. See [Eliza Lynn], "Devil Worshippers," *Household Words,* 10, (1854), 57-61; [Henry Morley], "At Home with the Russians," *Household Words,* 10 (1855), 533-38; [George A. Sala], "Mars a la Mode," *Household Words,* 10 (1854), 193-96; and [Anon.], "Field Service," *Household Words,* 10 (1854), 339-44. Authorial attributions for *Household Words* are taken from Ann Lohrli, comp., *Household Words: A Weekly Journal, 1850—1859, Conducted by Charles Dickens* (Toronto: Univ. of Toronto Press, 1973).

23. [Anon.], "The Home Office," *Household Words,* 10 (1854), 270.

24. [Henry Morley], "A Home Question," *Household Words,* 10 (1854), 292.

25. [Edwin C. Smales], "The Moral of This Year," *Household Words,* 10 (1854), 276.

26. In Charles Kingsley's second take on a war novel, *Two Years Ago* (1857) (after the propagandistic *Westward Ho!* of 1855, translatable into *Eastward Ho!* and distributed to the troops in the East), the Crimea serves as a field of honor to which characters must go to prove their worth. Yet we see nothing of what happens there, and the heroism of soldiers is replaced by that of doctors and nurses fighting against the cholera, not in Scutari but on the Cornish Coast: the events of the war have been transposed onto native ground. For a discussion of *Westward Ho!* as a war novel, see Peck, *War, the Army, and Victorian Literature,* pp. 41-47. Kingsley, Gaskell's *"hero"* (see Elizabeth Gaskell, letter to Eliza Fox, 26 November 1849, in *Letters,* p. 90), had come to prominence writing the Condition-of-England novel *Alton Locke* (1850).

27. See Joseph Bristow, "Nation, Class, and Gender: Tennyson's *Maud* and War," *Genders,* no. 9 (1990), 94. Procter had stayed with the Gaskells in 1851 (see Uglow, *Elizabeth Gaskell,* p. 369).

28. See [Adelaide Anne Procter], "Waiting," *Household Words,* 10 (1854), 204-5.

29. [Adelaide Anne Procter], "The Lesson of the War," *Household Words,* 11 (1855), 12.

30. See Bristow, "Nation, Class, and Gender," p. 107. For "Waiting" as a war poem, see Dereli, "Gender Issues," p. 74.

31. For a typical description of such division as registered in the Condition-of-England novel, see Benjamin Disraeli, *Sybil, or The Two Nations* (1844-45). Disraeli wrote of the widening gap between "two nations," rich and poor, "between whom there is no intercourse and no sympathy; who are as ignorant of each other's habits, thoughts, and feelings, as if they were dwellers in different zones, or inhabitants of different planets; who are formed by a different breeding, are fed by a different food, are ordered by different manners, and are not governed by the same laws" (Disraeli, *Sybil, or The Two Nations,* ed. Sheila M. Smith [New York: Oxford Univ. Press, 1981], pp. 65-66).

32. [G. C. Swayne], "Peace and War: A Dialogue," *Blackwood's Edinburgh Magazine,* 76 (1854), 595. For a discussion of this article in the context of *Maud,* see Bristow, "Nation, Class, and Gender," p. 97.

33. See [Adelaide Anne Procter], "The Two Spirits," *Household Words,* 10 (1855), 516-17.

34. See *Grotius on the Rights of War and Peace: An Abridged Translation,* trans. William Whewell (Cambridge: Univ. Press, 1853).

35. Clough, letter to C. E. Norton, 28 February 1854, in *Correspondence,* II, 476.

36. See for example "down with the Rump" (*North and South,* p. 45), as well as Thornton's comment that "Cromwell would have made a capital mill-owner, Miss Hale" (p. 123). For a brief discussion of the role of the English Civil War in the novel, see Robin Gilmour, *The Victorian Period: The Intellectual and Cultural Context of English Literature, 1830-1890* (London and New York: Longman, 1993), p. 52. Ballantyne, whose article on Lancashire Strikes includes a discussion of *North and South,* also refers to "the civil war between labour and capital" ("Lancashire Strikes," p. 54).

37. Alfred Tennyson, *Maud: A Monodrama,* in *The Poems of Tennyson in Three Volumes, Second Edition, Incorporating the Trinity College Manuscripts,* ed. Christopher Ricks (Berkeley and Los Angeles: Univ. of California Press, 1987), II, 521 (Part I, l. 27); and II, 584 (Part III, ll. 57-58). All further references are to this edition and are included in the text by page, part, and line number. For the connection between Tennyson's poem and the Crimean War, both at home and abroad, see Bristow, "Nation, Gender, and Class"; as Bristow argues: "Put simply, a war abroad should rightly make for peace at home" (p. 96). For more on the idea of civil war in the period and in *Maud,* see Chris R. Vanden Bossche, "Realism versus Romance: The War of Cultural Codes in Tennyson's *Maud,*" *Victorian Poetry,* 24 (1986), 74.

38. Elizabeth Gaskell, letter to?Eliza Fox,?Summer 1854, in *Letters,* p. 302. Gaskell continues by reverting to an external threat: "I am thinking of fastening Will's scythe to *one* of the wheels of the poney carriage and defending my country if the Russians do land at Liverpool."

39. Elizabeth Gaskell, unpublished letter to Florence Nightingale, 31 December 1858 (Brotherton Library, Univ. of Leeds); quoted in Sanders, "Crisis of Liberalism," p. 47.

40. See *North and South,* pp. 117-18. See also Sally Shuttleworth's comments in her introduction to the Oxford World's Classics edition of *North and South,* ed. Angus Easson (New York: Oxford Univ. Press, 1998), p. xix.

41. See editorial, London *Times,* 27 November 1854, p. 6.

42. William Makepeace Thackeray, *The Newcomes: Memoirs of a Most Respectable Family,* ed. Peter L. Shillingsburg (Ann Arbor: Univ. of Michigan Press, 1996), p. 79.

43. Gaskell, quoted in Sanders, "Crisis of Liberalism," p. 47.

44. In *The Army and Society, 1815-1914* (London and New York: Longman, 1980), Edward M. Spiers discusses this shift in attitudes. In *Realism and Politics in Victorian Art of the Crimean War* (Ann Arbor: UMI Research Press, 1984), Matthew Paul Lalumia shows how the shift manifested itself in visual art. For a reading of the shift in terms of the novel, see John R. Reed, "Soldier Boy: Forming Masculinity in *Adam Bede,*" *Studies in the Novel,* 33 (2001), 268-84.

45. Thomas Hughes, *Tom Brown's Schooldays* (London: Epsworth Press, n.d.), p. 278 (Part 2, chapter 5).

46. [Margaret Oliphant], "Modern Novelists—Great and Small," *Blackwood's Edinburgh Magazine,* 77 (1855), 559, 560. In her famous article on "Sensation Novels," *Blackwood's Edinburgh Magazine,* 91 (1862), 564-84, Oliphant would recognize the Crimean War as one of the contributing factors in the development of the new genre. This argument can already be found in the review from 1855. Oliphant acknowledges the "strange change" that

"has passed upon the thoughts of this peace-loving nation. What piece of abstract literature, though its writer were laureated poet or throned philosopher, would not be put aside to-day for the simple letter of some poor private from the fated seat of war?" She continues by describing the perpetual need for "Something new!" that drives Wilkie Collins to produce for his readers a "sensation" ("Modern Novelists," p. 566).

47. Richard Lovelace, "To Lucasta, Going to the Warres," in *The Poems of Richard Lovelace,* ed. C. H. Wilkinson (Oxford: Clarendon Press, 1930), p. 18, l. 3.

48. Alexander Welsh, *The City of Dickens* (Oxford: Clarendon Press, 1971), p. 167. The phrase "industrial veracity" comes from Lecky's *History of European Morals,* first published in 1869. Welsh also sees a connection between the emphasis placed on truthfulness in the period and the prominence of chivalric motifs, as in the previously quoted passage. He mentions Thackeray's assertion in *The Four Georges* (1855-56) of the prerogative of the gentleman "through evil or good to maintain truth always" (*City of Dickens,* p. 167). In the middle of the nineteenth century, such gentlemanliness is often figured through the metaphor of chivalry—the true knight, the chevalier gallant, *sans peur et sans reproche.* But Margaret's mention of chivalry also places her within the context of the war literature. Critics have understated the role of the Crimean War in reanimating the ideal of chivalry, after its deflation following the disastrous Eglinton tournament in 1839. We find chivalry everywhere in the poems, prose, and paintings of the war years: Frederick Watts's first chivalric paintings were from sketches done in a war-crazed Paris in the winter of 1855-56, and William Holman Hunt, another great user of chivalric conventions in his paintings, visited the Crimea on his way back from Palestine just before the Armistice. Tennyson, who used chivalric motifs in both "The Charge of the Light Brigade" (1854) and *Maud,* began his first four *Idylls* in 1855; chivalry is also central in both *Westward Ho!* and *Two Years Ago.*

49. Editorial, London *Times,* 31 October 1854, p. 6.

50. Editorial, London *Times,* 1 March 1855, p. 8.

51. See Michael Cotsell, "Politics and Peeling Frescoes: Layard of Nineveh and *Little Dorrit,*" *Dickens Studies Annual,* 15 (1986), 188.

52. See, for example, *North and South,* chap. 20, "Men and Gentlemen" (pp. 157-65).

53. Elizabeth Gaskell, letter to Emily Shaen, 27 October 1854, in *Letters,* p. 321.

54. See *North and South,* pp. 23, 77, 123.

55. For some examples of illustrations of Britannia in the period, see "Britannia Taking Care of the Soldiers' Children," *Punch,* 26 (1854), 85; "Right against Wrong," *Punch,* 26 (1854), 143; "England's War Vigil," *Punch,* 26 (1854), 185; and "Britannia Takes the Widows and Orphans of the Brave under her Protection," *Punch,* 27 (1854), 161. See also Bristow, "Nation, Gender, and Class," pp. 100, 101.

56. See, for example, the unsigned review of *North and South* in the *Examiner,* 21 April 1855, pp. 244-45: "We fancy her now and then a little too 'superb' in the description. We have too much of her 'curled upper lip,' of the 'lovely haughty curve' of her face, and of her 'round white flexile throat.'" Of course, these descriptions of Margaret (and the critics' responses to them) also alert the reader to her sensuality; Oliphant's objections respond mainly to this feature and make Margaret seem a little too much like a Pre-Raphaelite beauty: "Margaret has glorious black hair, in which the pomegranate blossoms glow like a flame; she has exquisite full lips . . . ; she is altogether a splendid and princely personage" ("Modern Novelists," pp. 559-60).

57. See Mary Poovey, "A Housewifely Woman: The Social Construction of Florence Nightingale," in her *Uneven Developments: The Ideological Work of Gender in Mid-Victorian England* (Chicago: Univ. of Chicago Press, 1988), p. 171.

58. See Bristow, "Nation, Class, and Gender," pp. 99-102. The "two faces" of Nightingale are captured nicely in a phrase from a poem in *Punch,* where she is called "Mercy's Amazon" ([Anon.], "A Nightingale in the Camp," *Punch,* 28 [1855], 229).

59. See Elizabeth Gaskell, letter to Catherine Winkworth, 11 to 14 October 1854, in *Letters,* p. 307.

60. Elizabeth Gaskell, letter to Parthenope Nightingale, 18 January 1856, in *Letters,* p. 382.

61. See Cecil Woodham-Smith, *Florence Nightingale, 1820-1910* (London: McGraw-Hill, 1951), esp. pp. 23-73.

62. Elizabeth Gaskell, letter to Catherine Winkworth, 1 January 1855, in *Letters,* p. 327.

63. Nightingale's admiration for Gaskell's novel seems to have been more straightforward. In a letter from the Crimea she asks to be sent a "whole Edition" copy of *North and South* (which she had already read in *Household Words*), calling it "a good Novel" for the hospital Reading Room (Florence Nightingale, letter to Charles Holt Bracebridge and Selina Bracebridge, 7 August 1855,

in *Florence Nightingale: Letters from the Crimea, 1854-1856,* ed. Sue M. Goldie [Manchester: Mandolin, 1997], p. 144).

64. See Uglow, *Elizabeth Gaskell,* p. 364. Uglow attributes the connection to Nightingale's earlier attractions to Catholicism, but because of the importance of the French Sisters of Mercy in the war, Catholicism and nursing were generally conflated in the popular imagination.

65. Matthew Arnold, "Dover Beach," in *The Poems of Matthew Arnold,* ed. Kenneth Allott, Second Edition ed. Miriam Allott (London and New York: Longman, 1979), pp. 257, 256. Although "Dover Beach" was not published until 1867, it was most likely written sometime in 1851. For an argument in favor of the echo, see Angus Easson's note to p. 414 in the 1998 Oxford World's Classics edition of *North and South,* pp. 451-52.

66. Similarly, when Higgins defends the justice of his cause, he argues that unlike a soldier who fights for the abstract cause of nation, he is fighting to keep alive those he knows and loves. See *North and South,* p. 134.

67. Elizabeth Gaskell, letter to Marianne Gaskell, ?13 October 1854, in *Letters,* p. 311.

68. In Elizabeth Barrett Browning's conclusion to *Aurora Leigh* (1856), the hero is blinded before he can be joined with the heroine. Like Gaskell's work, Barrett Browning's epic novel-in-verse tackles the interplay of issues of "heroinism" and the Condition-of-England novel during the war years. Her opinions of Nightingale were suggestively different, though: "Every man is on his knees before ladies carrying lint, calling them 'angelic she's,' whereas, if they stir an inch as thinkers or artists from the beaten line . . . , the very same men would curse the impudence of the very same women and stop there. . . . I do not consider the best use to which we can put a gifted and accomplished woman is to *make her a hospital nurse*" (Elizabeth Barrett Browning, letter to Anna Jameson, 24 February 1855, in *The Letters of Elizabeth Barrett Browning,* ed. Frederic G. Kenyon, 2 vols. [New York: Macmillan, 1897], II, 189). It is tempting to draw connections between these writers' views of Nightingale and their choices of genre.

Peter Gardner (essay date 2005)

SOURCE: Gardner, Peter. "The Seductive Politics of *Mary Barton.*" *Victorians Institute Journal* 33 (2005): 45-67.

[*In the following essay, Gardner views* Mary Barton *as a melodrama in relation to Thomas Carlyle's* Past and Present *in order to illuminate Gaskell's "adroit handling of Carlylean melodrama to enable her political strategies of class."*]

> The present splendid brotherhood of fiction-writers in England, whose graphic and eloquent pages have issued to the world more political and social truths than have been uttered by all the professional politicians, publicists and moralists put together, have described every section of the middle class [. . . .] And how have Dickens and Thackeray, Miss Brontë and Mrs. Gaskell painted them? As full of presumption, affectation, petty tyranny and ignorance [. . .] "they are servile to those above, and tyrannical to those beneath them."
>
> Karl Marx, *New-York Tribune,* 1 August 1854

Thomas Carlyle had published *Past and Present* five years before Elizabeth Gaskell set five of his lines on the title page of **Mary Barton** (1848), simultaneously ironizing her first effort and obliquely referring to the aesthetics underpinning her "Long-ear of a fictitious Biography." This essay will attempt to reconnect **Mary Barton** to Carlylean aesthetics by focusing on the question of melodrama in **Mary Barton.** Through positioning Gaskell's unnamed union delegate from London and the elder Mr. Carson within the Carlylean melodrama of *Past and Present,* I hope to demonstrate that **Mary Barton** is a melodrama fraught with the dangers of seduction for both the male and female characters.[1]

Reading **Mary Barton** as melodrama allows the highly political valence of the novel and its relationship to Carlyle's solution to the Condition-of-England question to be recovered. There is, I contend, a double seduction plot in the novel. Sexual seduction, similar to the Esther subplot of seduction, abandonment and prostitution, threatens Mary Barton, while the political seduction of Chartism and trade unionism is the danger for John Barton. In the course of making this argument, I also hope to demonstrate that Gaskell's use of melodrama in **Mary Barton** is not the failing of an inexperienced writer but an adroit handling of Carlylean melodrama to enable her political strategies of class.

As the title of *Past and Present* (1843) suggests, antithesis is the rhetorical strategy used by Carlyle to melodramatize trade unionism and Chartism. Positive moral values are ascribed to an organic medieval past, and negative ones to a *laissez-faire* present, in his appeal for enlightened despotism. The paternalistic upper classes happily rule the childlike lower classes of Carlyle's idyllic feudal society. Peace and prosperity, he claims, depend on defending the social hierarchy established by God, which the "last two centuries of Atheistic Government" have left "very ominously, shuddering, reeling, and let us hope trying to recoil, on the cliff's edge!" (149). That precipice is Chartism and trade unionism. *Past and Present* pits aristocracy against democracy as an irreconcilable clash between order and chaos, good and evil, the basic topos of melodrama.[2]

John Holloway discloses how "Carlyle rings many changes, but the guiding principle is simply that there are contrasting extremes and nothing whatever between them" (34). The core of melodramatic poetics is this logic of the excluded middle, found throughout *Past and Present* with "the wise [. . .] and [. . .] jackasses," "just and unjust," "true and false," "work and sham-work," "genuine speech and jargon," and a "Heavenly thing and an Infernal" on the first two pages of the fourth chapter alone (28-29). The Carlylean melodrama of *Past and Present* posits, as Peter Brooks explains, "a world subsumed by an underlying manichaeism, and the narrative creates the excitement of its drama by putting us in touch with the conflict of good and evil played out under the surface of things" (4). It is there to be seen, Carlyle says, were a cleric to

> take the old spectacles off his nose, and looking up discover, almost in contact with him, what the *real* Satanas, and soul devouring *Devil,* now is! Original Sin and such like are bad enough, I doubt not: but distilled Gin, dark ignorance, Stupidity, dark Corn-Law, Bastille and Company, what are they! *Will* he discover our new real Satan, whom he has to fight; or go on droning through his old nose-spectacles about the old extinct Satans; and never see the real one, till he *feel* him at his own throat and ours? That is a question for the world!
>
> (242)

God and Mammon, soulless industrialists, idle aristocrats, imprisoned workers and sham-heroes usher the reader into the dichotomized Industrial Revolution of *Past and Present,* exposing what Peter Brooks aptly dubs the "moral occult" lurking behind the people and the events of the day (4-5).

A distinctive feature of Carlyle's use of the melodramatic mode in *Past and Present* is his metaphor of the society as a family, inverting the more common metaphor of melodramatic narratives that ordinarily represent society through the synecdoche of the family. Carlyle first constructs his fictitious Britain as an extended family by rejecting a mechanistic conception of society where "God's Laws are become a Greatest-Happiness Principle, a Parliamentary Expediency: the Heavens overarch us only as an Astronomical Time-keeper; a butt for Herschel-telescopes to shoot science at" (139). Then, resorting to the bloodline of Teutonic Anglo-Saxonism for his family of aristocrats, mill owners and workers, the mechanical is replaced by an organic model where "we are all bound together, for mutual good or else for mutual misery, as living nerves in the same body" (282). The "Saxon" bloodline of *Past and Present* recasts economic relations as familial ones, revealing the secret and unsuspected kinship of English and Scottish workers and industrialists through Carlyle's Teutonic "voix du sang," and excluding the Irish whom E. P. Thompson estimates as almost one-third of the working population of Manchester (429).

Carlyle's aristocrats fail to govern; his manufacturers have forgotten the paternalistic ideals of feudal Britain; a "workhouse Bastille" holds his "Saxon children" prisoners (7, 213). These discarded familial relations become Carlyle's critique of industrial capitalism within the codes of patriarchal deference hierarchies, while the working class and the upper classes perform the melodramatic mode throughout *Past and Present* as neglected children and heedless parents. "The melodramatic mode," Hadley cogently contends, "insists that social relationships must be described and judged in terms of the public yet familial relationships and codes of behavior characteristic of patriarchal status hierarchies" (125).

Imploring the aristocracy, industrialists and the working classes to recognize their membership in the national family was an old solution to the new social, political and economic problems of the day. In 1833 Peter Gaskell cited an even earlier work fretting over the ill effects of "no common bond [. . .] existing between [the manufacturer] and his labourers" (72). He goes on to say that workers detested their employers' families and received harsh treatment from them. The social distance created by the "want of sympathy and proper intercourse between the master manufacturer and those employed by him, is one very powerful cause which tends to keep down their moral habits and physical condition" (170-171). Correlating the decay of "distinctions of rank" to that of the family, he concludes, exactly as Carlyle was to do nine years later, as long as the family remains in disarray "no nostrums of political economy, no extension of political rights, ever can or ever will make [industrial workers] a happy, respectable, or contented race of men" (20-67).

Not only is Carlyle's analysis an unexceptional one, so is his solution of reinforcing deference hierarchies. Arguing from the fictional Gurth in *Ivanhoe,* he deduces that "man is forever the 'born thrall' of certain men, born master of certain other men, born equal of certain others, let him acknowledge the fact or not" (249). The choice of Sir Walter Scott is a telling one. Working-class publications, Thomas Paul Murphy notes, anathematized the Tory writer's novels for depicting the common people "as a cringing, fawning, creeping, half-crazed vermin, executing the despotic will of their masters without compunction" (355).

Since democracy only "means despair of finding any Heroes to govern you" (214), Carlyle calls for an autocratic hero to set foot upon the stage. Melodrama, with its focus on the heroic individual, lends itself readily to the triumph of his benevolent despot over collective action. There is no need for sweeping reforms but for a spiritually regenerated individual, a hero in Carlylean terms. For the hero is the character who defeats evil and preserves innocence in melodrama, and that hero is identified by Carlyle as the strong and virtuous man who complies with divine will by imposing order in the universe. "Mights [. . .] do in the long-run, and forever will in this just Universe in the long-run, mean Rights" (191).

Doing what God commands leaves no room for the doubt or inner conflict that characterizes the tragic hero. Man is divided in tragedy, Robert Bechtold Heilman points out, but "in melodrama, his troubles, though they may reflect some weakness or inadequacy, do not arise from the urgency of unreconciled impulses" (79). The Carlylean hero is a model of wholeness; for the "difference between a good man and a bad man was as yet felt to be, what it forever is, an immeasurable one" (245). This is a reflection of the polarization of good and evil in the melodramatized universe; it is a poetics with unquestioning faith in antithetical values. Whoever shares this melodramatic vision of uncompromising conflict between good and evil can, in the words of James L. Smith, "enjoy triumph without considering its cost to others, despair without seeking for alternative courses, and protest without seeking the bases for our own moral integrity" (10).

While any melodramatic hero must defeat evil and restore order, to the Carlylean hero falls the specific task of reunifying the imagined family of employers and employed by subduing the "mutinous" workers. In short, this hero saves the working class from itself.

> You do not allow a palpable madman to leap over precipices; you violate his liberty, you that are wise; and keep him, were it in strait-waist-coats, away from the precipices! Every stupid, every cowardly and foolish man is but a less palpable madman: his true liberty were that a wiser man, that any and every wiser man, could by brass collars, or in whatever milder or sharper way, lay hold of him when he was going wrong, and order and compel him to go a little righter. O if thou art really my *Senior*, Seigneur, my *Elder*, Presbyter or Priest,—if thou art in very deed my *Wiser*, may a beneficent instinct lead and impel thee to 'conquer' me, to command me! If thou know better than I what is good and right, I conjure thee in the name of God, force me to do it; were it by never such brass collars, whips and handcuffs, leave me not to walk over precipices!
>
> (*Past* 212)

The rhetorical masterstroke of appealing to the titles of the upper classes transforms a lunatic into the entire working class. The pathetic call for help masks the violent content of Carlyle's answer to labor unrest and political agitation; liberty is the disease and despotism is the cure. *Past and Present* leads the reader from the loathsome sight of British workers held prisoners in a "workhouse Bastille" at the opening of the book, toward the paradoxically congenial sight of British workers in brass collars and handcuffs before the end of the

book.[3] While the brass collars refer to the one worn by the bondsman Gurth, the image of chained workers would be familiar to anyone acquainted with chattel slavery.

Although Carlyle upbraids the upper classes for having abandoned the paternalistic virtues of feudal England, the real villains of *Past and Present* are the "quacks, sham-heroes [. . . .] They are the one bane of the world. Once clear the world of them, it ceases to be a Devil's-world" (31). Insisting on the familial responsibility of the stronger protecting the weaker, Carlyle posits sham-heroes as the external evil threatening innocence in his melodramatized Manchester. *Past and Present* thus conforms to Brooks's typical melodramatic telos concerned with "reforming of the old society of innocence, which has now driven out the threat to its existence and reaffirmed its values" (32). The metonyms of light and darkness are manipulated throughout the essay, derisively coalescing the quacks and sham-heroes into the trope of the "gaslighted Histrios" (219), becoming a signifier of cant and the darkness of ignorance and evil. The "gaslighted Histrios" include the trade unionists and Chartists accused of fomenting "French Revolutions, Chartisms [and] Manchester Insurrections" (40).

Equating Chartists with French revolutionaries is not mere bombast. The Chartist *Northern Star,* the newspaper to which Fredrick Engels contributed and which John Barton reads in **Mary Barton,** describes a skirmish between the police and a procession of Chartists who were parading with banners, one of which was topped with "the cap of liberty," a symbol of the French Revolution (82-83).[4] The middle and upper classes would have been even more apprehensive had they known how another newspaper, *The Charter,* appropriated the melodramatic mode. Here, an editorial proclaims that the "battle is now to be fought between democracy and aristocracy. These are the two contending powers of light and darkness, the result of whose conflict will determine whether the third estate of this realm is to be subject to the domination of the second." To Carlyle's admirers, such as Elizabeth Gaskell, the more than three million John Bartons who petitioned for the People's Charter, joined trade unions and took part in strikes were the victims of the rabble-rousing "gaslighted Histrios" who were luring them to the brink of mob rule.[5]

Chartism and trade unionism are often relegated to the background of **Mary Barton.** Catherine Gallagher is not alone in deciding that "John Barton's [. . .] story, with its unresolved contradictions, tends to fade into the background" (77). While Benjamin Disraeli places his barbarous Chartist "Liberator" center stage in *Sybil, or the Two Nations,* the Chartists and trade unionists are on page after page of **Mary Barton,** yet nearly invisible at the same time. Gaskell focuses on Mary Barton's dread of the nightmarish hands and arms of the off-stage villains invading the domestic space of the novel.

> Strange faces of pale men, with dark glaring eyes, peered into the inner darkness, and seemed desirous to ascertain if her father was at home. Or, a hand and arm (the body hidden) was put within the door, and beckoned him away. He always went[. . .]
>
> They were all desperate members of Trades' Unions, ready for anything; made ready by want.
>
> (118)

Dismembering the union creates a faceless and nameless evil, but developing the character of Mary Barton's potential seducer renders his villainy less menacing. Henry Carson is represented as a "vain" "masculine flirt" (203) who is less a villain than a man imbued with the monetary values of a market economy who decides that "at any price he must have her, only that he would obtain her as cheaply as he could" (135). Young Carson is deprived of the thoroughgoing wickedness required of melodramatic villainy. The narrator's comment, "He was passionately in love," substantiates the earnestness of his offer of marriage to Mary Barton. He is ready to "get a licence to-morrow morning—nay, to-night, and I'll marry you in defiance of all the world, rather than give you up" (137). In all likelihood a similar promise persuaded Esther, Mary's aunt, to run off with a military officer and, after he deserted her, to turn to prostitution and drunkenness (161).

Amanda Anderson discerningly parallels Esther's seduction and alcoholism not only to the Mary Barton and Henry Carson plot, but also to John Barton's radical politics and drug addiction (125). Politics and opium push John Barton toward "incipient madness" until he becomes Carlyle's madman who is ready to plunge over the precipice (*Mary Barton* 169). Anderson further demonstrates that the correspondence between Esther and John Barton "disempowers John Barton partly by bringing him closer and closer to the prostitute," rendering both "monomaniacal" as well as "oddly collapsed and deflated figures" before the "'two wanderers' are buried together at the end of the novel." Despite arguing that Esther "provides a key to the intersection of Gaskell's social and aesthetic concerns as an industrial novelist," Anderson surprisingly excludes John Barton from her rhetoric of fallenness. Rather than include him, as does this analysis, Anderson insists that "*Mary Barton* develops as the gradual convergence and then final splitting of two competing plot lines, Mary Barton's romance plot and John Barton's political tragedy," and that fallenness in the novel is "gender-marked" (112, 126).

Patsy Stoneman offers an alternative to the apparent impasse between romance and politics, persuasively arguing that *Mary Barton* needs its seemingly irrelevant sub-plots to critique the aggressive, middle-class male confrontational politics of the narrative. Seeing the novel as a contest between the working-class ethic of nurturing and cooperation and the middle-class one of authority and ownership, Stoneman notes that

> [a]lthough class struggle is most clearly seen in public confrontations, the family is the mechanism which reproduces class attitudes, and parent-child relationships as worked out in the 'extraneous' sections of the novel, demonstrate how the personal becomes political. If we approach the novel through the ethics of the family, therefore, we do not detract from its value as an exploration of class relations, but instead of seeing it as an 'industrial novel' flawed by political naïvety and superfluous sub-plots, we can see it as an attempt to understand the interaction of class and gender. In particular, its opposed class-based images of fatherhood prompt us to rethink the political concept of 'paternalism.'
>
> (70)

Her valuable insight raises two issues. The first is, if class relations are performed within the novel as metaphorical parent-child relationships, arguably *Mary Barton* can be read as melodrama, since, as Hadley points out, "the melodramatic mode insists that social relations must be described and judged in terms of the public yet familial relationships and codes of behavior characteristic of patriarchal status hierarchies" (125). The second issue arises when Stoneman calls attention to John Barton's nurturing to point out that his son's death by starvation incites him to desperate political action (71), just as Esther's dying daughter drives her to prostitution, as Anderson notes (118). Stoneman is attentive to the explicit criticism in the work directed at "Carson for not extending the same sort of care to his workers that they show to one another," but devotes less discussion to Barton's paternal failings which compromise his nurturing working-class ethic (71-72). If, as I argue, the narrative strategy of paternalism in the novel conforms to the public and familial patriarchal status hierarchies of Carlylean melodrama, Stoneman's thesis will be complicated by the inclusion of melodramatic poetics and her analysis of fatherhood in *Mary Barton* extended.

While present-day readers might gloss a dysfunctional parent as an individual or social problem, few would consider it a political one. This assumption is challenged by Alexis de Tocqueville's assertion that in "aristocracies society is, in truth, only concerned with the father. It only controls the sons through the father; it rules him, and he rules them." Aristocratic authority, he asserts, "never addresses the whole of the governed directly. Men are linked one to the other and confine themselves to controlling the next on the chain. The rest follows. This applies to the family as well as to all associations with a leader" (586). Thomas Carlyle hallows this patriarchal chain in *Chartism*. "Parents, teachers, superiors, leaders, these all creatures recognise as deserving obedience. Recognised or not recognised, a man *has* his superiors, a regular hierarchy above him; extending up, degree above degree, to heaven itself and God the maker, who made his world not for anarchy but for rule and order" (218).

Esther is the first to break this patriarchal chain in **Mary Barton,** by moving into lodgings. Despite his wife being "more like a mother to her" or his prediction that Esther will eventually become a streetwalker, Esther leaves her family with John Barton's approval. Granted the posited economy of caring working-class fathers in the novel, the logical expectation is for Barton to be as much of a father to Esther as his wife is a mother. The void created by not defining Barton's relation to Esther in a paternal simile constitutes a tacit criticism. Barton interrupts his account of Esther's disappearance to begin a passionate denunciation of the indifference of the rich to the poor. George Wilson, who is "tenderly carrying a baby in arms," responds with "all that may be very true, but what I want to know now is about Esther" (8-11). Anderson argues this abrupt break not only reintroduces the immediate question of Esther but also "reflects a desire to shift from the oppressively 'true' presentation of class inequity to a romantic 'story'" (115). In the familial terms of the melodramatic mode, a nurturing father insisting Barton stop speaking in the language of class and speak in that of family constitutes further silent censure that class is of greater importance to Barton than his sister-in-law.

Barton's abdication of paternal responsibility toward Esther as his surrogate daughter is once more suggested in Chapter 10 by his refusal to hear her warning about Carson's seduction of Mary, about which he is unaware. His action of thrusting Esther aside and walking away parallels not only Henry Carson curtly breaking off "all communication" with the union delegation (183), but also how parliament "so cruelly refused to hear" the Chartists (102). Stoneman notes that only in this Esther episode does Barton behave as a middle-class man, which she finds appropriate because Esther, in her view, has joined the "do-nothing" class (78). That Barton identifies Esther as a bedraggled prostitute to be shaken off before recognizing her makes this construal less convincing, whereas framing all three refusals to listen within the disregarded patriarchal status hierarchies of the melodramatic mode corroborates and extends Stoneman's understanding of the novel's critique of paternity.

This reading suggests the deaths of Esther's daughter and Barton's son recover significance within the neglected patriarchal status hierarchies of Carlyle's melodramatized industrial revolution. **Mary Barton** translates indifference and abandonment into economic terms in each instance. In Esther's case, her daughter's upper-class father pays her fifty pounds before abandoning them (161). This substitution of paternal responsibility

with Carlyle's "cash nexus" corresponds to Carson's neglect of any relationship with his workers beyond paying their wages.[6] John Barton's "improvidence" (24), and Esther's admitted ignorance of the value of money, represents these working-class parents as economic children in the harsh world of *laissez-faire* enterprise (161). Therefore, while Anderson and Stoneman relevantly draw attention to the abandonment of Esther, and her daughter's subsequent death as driving Esther to prostitution, and John Barton's son starving to death as transforming John Barton from a nurturing father into a murderous maniac, it is worth underlining the implicit economic critique embedded in the narration of each event. Recognizing the children's deaths as a consequence of discarded paternal values, expressed as cash payment, sets both as much within the public, familial relationships of the melodramatic mode as inside the personal motivations of the realistic tradition. Anderson's view that Esther is a key to Gaskell's social and aesthetic concerns and Stoneman's contention that adversarial politics in the novel are directly correlated to "thwarted parental love" profit by the inclusion of Carson as a metaphorical father (52).

The novel represents John Barton as a child needing parental supervision by constructing the trope of the childlike worker. The narrator invests her words with a claim to privileged knowledge: "I know what is the truth in such matters: [. . .] I wish to impress what the workman feels and thinks [. . . .] with child-like improvidence, good times will often dissipate his grumbling" (24). Gaskell applies this trope of the worker-as-child to Barton as an analepsis. With "child-like improvidence" Barton's home at the beginning of the novel is crowded with furniture and bric-a-brac which "(setting all taste but that of a child's aside) gave a richness of colouring to [. . .] the room" (15). When Barton is selected as a Chartist delegate he feels a "childish delight of seeing London" (86). Barton describes himself as a child after returning from his unsuccessful attempt to present the People's Charter to parliament; "I were like a child, I forgot a' my errand in looking about me" (101).

The breakdown of patriarchal authority continues in the narrative with Barton's failure to supervise his daughter. After her mother's death "Mary took her own way, [. . .] her father was chairman at many a Trades' Union meeting; a friend of delegates, and ambitious of being a delegate himself; a Chartist, and ready to do anything for his order" (25). The use of the word "order" may be a syllepsis, signifying not only a social class but also a religious order, with an implied critique that radical politics substitute for religion. The critique is explicit when applied to "order" as class; neglecting his paternal responsibilities is the price of John Barton's class consciousness.

As Esther's disappearance in the opening chapter suggests, Barton is represented as more interested in his class than his family. This leaves Mary vulnerable to Carson's son. The narrator explicitly rebukes Barton's delinquency by telling the reader that if young Carson "had known what Mary's home was, he would not have been so much convinced of his increasing influence over her [. . . .] For when she returned for the night her father was often out" (116-17). When Mary is asked where her father is she answers, "I guess he's at his Union! he's there most evenings" (155). His paternal negligence corresponds to his employer's repudiation of his paternal obligations to his workers: "I don't pretend to know the names of the men I employ; that I leave to the overlooker" (70). The elder Carson has ignored Carlyle's charge in *Past and Present* for the "millocracy" to imitate the feudal baron and "have men round him who in heart loved him; whose life he watched over with rigour yet with love." John Barton is left to become a Chartist and a Communist, because Carson has failed to join Barton to him in "sonhood" as Carlyle entreats manufacturers to do (270-271).

John Barton's confrontational politics clash with Job Legh's nurturing paternalism in the counter tale of Legh's journey to London to bring his orphaned grandchild to Manchester (102-110). Legh's sentimental account finally pushes aside that of John Barton's journey to London as a Chartist delegate and dominates the chapter. In the terms of the novel, Legh's successful shouldering of the individual responsibilities of his link in the patriarchal chain, and his dislike of the union (197), obliquely censure not only Barton's displacing familial duties with collective action—the narrator describes the Chartist petition to parliament as "cherished as a darling child by many a one"—but also Carson's *laissez-faire* management of his workers (85). The breakdown of the patriarchal chain is thus a consecution in *Mary Barton.* Barton's paternal failing of supplanting Mary by the People's Charter refers to the elder Carson's unwillingness to be a patriarch to his employees. Carson fails to rule Barton as surely as Barton fails to rule his daughter. Neither John Barton nor Mary Barton is taught to distinguish right from wrong. Barton's deathbed confession to Carson that since no one tried to "teach me right from wrong [. . .] I've been sore puzzled here" (364), echoes the words of Carlyle's madman: "If thou know better than I what is good and right, I conjure thee in the name of God, force me to do it." Nicholas Higgins makes the same accusation in Gaskell's later *North and South* (1855): "If I'm going wrong when I think I'm going right, it's their sin, who ha' left me where I am, in my ignorance" (154).

Not only have middle-class Carson and working-class John Barton failed to guide those under them, but Anglican and Dissenting clerics are also missing in the "Sooty Hell of mutiny and savagery" of Gaskell's Manchester (*Past and Present* 294). The narrator states that no clergy are permitted to enter the working class homes in *Mary Barton* because the "indigence and sufferings of the operatives induced a suspicion in the minds of many of them, that their legislators, their magistrates, their employers, and even the ministers of religion, were, in general, their oppressors and enemies; and were in league for their prostration and enthralment" (85).

Although Gaskell's working class seem to be more sinning than sinned against, the dearth of clergymen in *Mary Barton* is a fictional version of Carlyle's argument that the working class has no contact with the two vital elements of society, the "Aristocracy and Priesthood, a Governing Class and a Teaching Class" (241). Gaskell enlarges upon this estrangement when discussing the privations of industrial workers from 1839 to 1841. The authorial intrusion reframes economics and politics as extended family relations. "The most deplorable and enduring evil [. . . .] was this feeling of alienation between the different classes of society [. . . .] Their vindictive feelings exhibited themselves in rabid politics" (85). Carlyle's melodramatic poetics, with its familial conception of society, connects Barton's failure to protect his naïve daughter from Henry Carson's temptations to the elder Carson's failure to protect his uneducated worker from "rabid politics." Carson's paternal failure, colluding with that of Barton's, unwittingly abets his son's illicit courtship of Mary Barton and simultaneously allows John Barton to be seduced by "sham-heroes." Young Carson's attempted seduction in this reading becomes one of the variations on the theme of seduction.

The double-seduction narrative strategy locates sexual anxiety in the workplace and streets. Gaskell does this by coupling sex and money as a metonym for Esther's streetwalking through the mercenary lewdness of Sally Leadbitter, Carson's intermediary in Mary's workshop, whose "willingness was strengthened by sundry halfsovereigns" (90). The chaste love of Jem Wilson for Mary Barton in the domestic spaces of the novel is differentiated from Esther's streetwalking and the lascivious attentions of Henry Carson in the public spaces of the novel. Consequently, Esther's prostitution and young Carson's attentions shift sexuality to the streets and workplace until Mary "loathed the idea of meeting Sally Leadbitter at her daily work," and fears being "constantly being waylaid as she went home," since Carson "might come up some cross street when she had just congratulated herself on evading him for that day" (140).

The danger of seduction in the streets and workplaces associates Henry Carson's failed seduction of Mary to the successful seduction of her father, first by the siren of Chartism, leading John Barton to wander the London streets, and later, at a union meeting, by a Carlylean villain, one of the "gaslighted Histrios" damned in *Past and Present*. The villain of this reading of *Mary Barton* is the unnamed trade-union representative from London. The novel replicates Carlyle's formula of gaslight, theatricality, cant and villainy as the "gentleman from London" enters the room where "[u]nshaded gas flared down on the lean and unwashed artisans [. . . .] He looked so self-conscious, so far from earnest, among the group of eager, fierce, absorbed men, among whom he now stood. He might have been [. . .] an unsuccessful actor [. . .] The impression he would have given you would have been unfavourable" (185). The engaging narrator's use of "you" establishes the union representative as the Other in a far less ambiguous manner than Mary's seducer.

The villain begins his seduction of the union delegates by treating them to "pipes and liquor" until they are "ready to listen to him with approbation. He felt it; and rising like a great orator, with his right arm outstretched, his left in the breast of his waistcoat, he began to declaim, with a forced theatrical voice." After arousing their passions with bombast, dictating a plan of action and giving "real, clinking, blinking, golden sovereigns" to the union delegates, the anonymous gentleman from London forsakes them forever (186). Gaskell eroticizes the body politic with her deceitful outsider who is from neither the same class nor town; he seduces the men with alcohol, persuades them to take an immoral course of action and then abandons them after giving money, just as Esther's seducer does. Skillfully adapting a typical melodramatic pattern of seduction, abandonment and repentance to the politics of Carlylean melodrama, Gaskell fits the classist rhetoric of *Past and Present* to a class-based seduction plot.

It is not only Gaskell who casts a trade unionist as a villain. Charles Dickens later uses the same trope in *Hard Times* (1854), his novel dedicated to Thomas Carlyle. Here the union leader, "the orator" Slackbridge, another of Carlyle's "gaslighted Histrios," is literally "roaring at the top of his voice under a flaring gaslight, clenching his fists, knitting his brows, setting his teeth and pounding with his arms" (182). Not only are the gas-lit villains the same, but labor disturbances in both of these Carlylean melodramas are represented as the failure of employers to assume their patriarchal responsibilities to their workers (*HT* 194), ending, in *Hard Times,* with Stephen Blackpool's death, after Slackbridge ostracizes and separates him from his family of workers.

Sending the other exile of the novel, "the villainous whelp," Thomas Gradgrind, "to North or South America, or any distant part of the world" (376), illustrates Carlyle's proposal to deport malcontents, thinly disguised as emigration, in *Past and Present* (263-4), a solution that had also been offered as the means of resolving the racial and class issues of slavery. Gaskell, on the contrary, ends her novel by sending Mary and Jem Wilson to Canada. The pastoral ending of *Mary Barton* requires separating the lovers from their community, a tacit admission that the economic and social problems posed by the novel cannot be resolved by reunifying the fictive family of employers and employed (392-393).

Although *Hard Times* and *Mary Barton* avoid the macabre trappings of the union initiation in *Sybil, Or The Two Nations,* with its black drapery, skeleton, sword and battle-axe, the novels draw the same parallel between unions, family dissolution and death. The patriarchal void in *Mary Barton* is filled by the union becoming John Barton's shadow family, and leading him to madness and death. Esther's seduction begins with her leaving Barton's home, is followed by the death of her child and finally ends with prostitution, alcoholism, prison and death. Barton's seduction by "rabid politics" makes him neglect his paternal duty to his daughter, takes him out of his home, and drives him to opium addiction, the murder of Henry Carson and death.

Barton is not the only casualty of the shadow family. Another union member is "like one crazy," as Barton later becomes, when union activism separates him from his family by sending him to prison "for throwing vitriol in a knob-stick's face" (188). Rather than being a family of love and fertility the shadow family created by the union is one of hatred and death. While planning to murder Carson's son the union members agree with the orator's rhetoric "I could kill [my stepson] if he took part wi' the masters" (186). While patriarchal family relationships are based on reciprocal deference, each member of the trade union's shadow family is "suspicious of his neighbour; each dreaded the treachery of another" (190).

Reconnecting *Mary Barton* to Thomas Carlyle's rhetoric reveals both villain and victim, but Carlylean melodrama requires the god-inspired hero to reunify the family of employers and employed. In *Past and Present* Carlyle not only entreats the upper classes to "pray for a soul; struggle, as with life and death energy, to get back thy soul! [. . .] by *Working*" (230), but also urges them "to believe in God, that so Chartism might abate, and the Manchester Operatives be got to spin peaceably!" (224). These words inform the narrator's comment regarding the elder Carson's gospel reading: "All night long, the Archangel combated with the Demon" (370). The elder Carson's Old Testament thirst for vengeance for the murder of his son yields to New Testament forgiveness when Carson reads the gospel "with all the interest of a little child. He began at the beginning, and read on almost greedily, understanding for the first time the full meaning of the story" (370). Applying the child trope to Carson allows his forgiveness to be seen as realizing his filial duties to God and his paternal duties to his workers in Carlyle's divine patriarchal chain. The chapter title and Carson's prayer at Barton's death, "Forgive us our trespasses as we forgive them that trespass against us," indict the paternal failings of both fathers. Hadley's "public yet familial relationships" of melodrama are articulated in the language of Carlylean melodrama.

The adoption of Carlyle's metaphor to enable the public performance of these paternal relationships suggests that *Mary Barton* be included among melodramatic representations of society told through narratives of familial dissolution and reunification. This reading complicates Stoneman's reading of "*Mary Barton* as a novel about fatherhood—a relationship rather than a person" by including the metaphorical parent and child social relations of the melodramatic mode (83). Opposing nurturing and authoritarian paternity as ethical systems rather than as class markers, Gaskell uses Carlyle's melodrama to further her narrative strategies of class and simultaneously to subvert Carlyle's despotic solution, by illustrating the inadequacy of authoritarian patriarchy.[7]

The elder Carson becomes the divinely-inspired Carlylean hero of the novel, dedicating his life to work as worship. Behind the heavenly victory still lingers Carlyle's ethical imperative to subjugate the working class and to bind the worker-children to the industrialists in "sonhood," a notion difficult to reconcile with Gaskell's Unitarian precept of mature, rational adults who are responsible for their own conduct (Stoneman 56). Although the narrator describes her heroic manufacturer as "stern," "hard" and "cold," she hastens to assure the reader that "the wish that lay nearest to his heart was that [. . .] complete confidence and love, might exist between masters and men; [. . .] to have them bound to their employers by the ties of respect and affection, not by mere money bargains alone" (387-388). Although Stoneman states that Gaskell's "work as a whole does constitute a challenge to patriarchy itself, which confers on one set of people the right to command, and other the other the duty to obey," she nevertheless acknowledges the "optimistic paternalism of *Mary Barton*" (53-57). The juxtaposition of the authoritarian "stern," "hard" and "cold," against the nurturing "confidence and love" and "respect and affection," hints at the anxiety with which Gaskell negotiates Carlyle's answer to the problem, even as she appropriates his language.

Carlyle had published his "Occasional Discourse on the Nigger Question" the year after *Mary Barton,* and *North and South* unblushingly rejects Carlyle's increasingly strident despotism when Margaret Hale replies, "Cromwell is no hero of mine" to Thornton's assertion that Thomas Carlyle's hero would have been "a capital mill-owner" (123). Thornton's respect for his workers by the end of the novel is engendered by talking and listening to them, the teaching and learning across classes which structures *North and South,* but is thwarted in *Mary Barton.* He rephrases Carlyle when he says his "only wish is to have the opportunity of cultivating some intercourse with the hands beyond the mere 'cash nexus.'" Although he does not believe that this will prevent strikes, "they may render strikes not the bitter, venomous sources of hatred they have hitherto been. A more hopeful man might imagine that a closer and more genial intercourse between classes might do away with strikes. But I am not a hopeful man" (420-421). Pessimistic economic reality questions the cautious, optimistic paternalism of *Mary Barton,* and the hero changes from the stern patriarch of Gaskell's first novel to a cooperative paternalist. Through Margaret Hale's mediating meaningful exchanges between master and men, by the end of *North and South* Thornton becomes a master who "obeyed the men's orders" concerning the worker's collective dining-room (353). This minor business matter may be difficult to appreciate adequately when viewed as versimiltude, but recovers meaning when set in the fictionality of Stoneman's cooperative, nurturing males.

North and South achieves the transformation of Thornton by first constructing, and then dismantling, the mill owner as one of the warlike manufacturers Carlyle calls on to convert the working class from a disorderly mob into "a firm regimented mass, with real captains over them" (*Past* 272). Carlyle's military metaphor is constructed around Thornton by a series of metonymies that liken him to a ship's captain when he is in Margaret's gaze. As he tells Margaret "Yes; the fools will have a strike [. . . .] They think trade is flourishing as it was last year. We see the storm on the horizon and draw in our sails. But because we don't explain our reasons, they won't believe we're acting reasonably" (117).

The narrator again introduces military metonymies in developing the trope of Thornton as a Carlylean captain of industry. When Margaret overhears him discussing preparations for the strike "the short clear answers Mr Thornton gave, [. . .] came steady and firm as the boom of a distant minute gun" (163). The metaphor reaches full development when "the unseen maddened crowd" of strikers "made battering-rams of their bodies" to attack Thornton's home (172). Thornton arrives "a little flushed, but his eyes gleaming, as in answer to the trumpet call of danger [. . .] that made him a noble, if not a handsome man" (173). Margaret's wound, the arrival of soldiers and Boucher's death evacuate the military metaphor and its armed conflict, as does Barton's murder of Henry Carson in *Mary Barton.*

Gaskell evades the full endorsement of Carlyle's authoritarian patriarchy in subtler ways in *Mary Barton.* The most important to this study are the positive representations of working-class women and caring fathers.

Patricia E. Johnson notes that the modest, although happy and boisterous, factory girls who possess "an acuteness and intelligence of countenance" in the opening chapter "contradict[s] the inflammatory accusations made in parliamentary debates and press coverage, indicating Gaskell's desire to, at least partially, refute them" (28). The members of this group are identified as "most of them factory girls," but the young men in the scene are neither specified as factory workers nor characterized as the women are in *Mary Barton* (6-7). This gender strategy acquires significance when contrasted to the opposite one used in *North and South* where the strikers are represented as "hundreds of infuriated men and reckless boys" and women are excluded (176).[8] Similarly, Mary Barton's shift from the object of Carson's seduction to the subject of her own and Jem Wilson's rescue confirms gender expectations of women as the carriers of positive cultural values, and contradicts those expectations by forcing Mary Barton to articulate those values in the public, and therefore masculine, world of the docks and the courtroom and having men articulate them in the domestic, feminine, world of the family.

Friedrich Engels's *The Condition of the Working Class in England* provides a glimpse of how the caring fathers and respectable female operatives in *Mary Barton* oppose the dominant ideology. Engels's vision of working-class fathers claims that if "the family is not wholly dissolved by the employment of the wife [it is] turned upside down. The wife supports the family, the husband sits at home, tends the children, sweeps the room and cooks [. . . .] It is easy to imagine to imagine the wrath aroused among the working men by this reversal of all relations within the family [. . .] which unsexes the man and takes from the woman all womanliness" (154-155). Engels's account of domestic difficulties also invalidates Carlyle's rhapsody of the factory in *Chartism*: "Manchester, with its cotton-fuzz, its smoke and dust, its tumult and contentious squalor [is as] sublime as a Niagara, or more so. Cotton-spinning is the clothing of the naked in its result; the triumph of man over matter in its means" (211). Carlyle can do no less than sing the praises of a system that is doing God's work by transforming chaos into order, but would presumably be embarrassed to celebrate the breakdown of patriarchal relations and social chaos.

Perhaps this is why the world of *Past and Present* is a male one. Dispirited men sit in front of workhouses; energetic men are cast as warriors, buccaneers, mutineers, and captains of industry as well as monks and abbots who battle the enemies of God. Men are wise kings, silent heroes or crazed workers, playing an active role on nearly every page. In so doing *Past and Present* ignores the women who E. P. Thompson calculates as making up more than fifty percent of adult workers in Manchester (308). Females so rarely appear in *Past and*

Present that Carlyle paradoxically validates a central tenet of the New Poor Law that he attacks; as Hadley observes, the single male laborer is the primary economic and social unit of Carlyle's fictive industrial family (91).

Stoneman faults Gaskell's aesthetic solution of using men to ventriloquize the female ethos of cooperation and nurturing (85-86). When evaluated from the viewpoint of Carlylean melodrama, however, Gaskell's solution is a multifaceted critique of patriarchal authority, including Carlyle himself. Using Carlylean imaginative argument, *Mary Barton* discredits Carlyle's paradigm of power, control and dominance and negotiates an alternative criterion of nurturing and cooperation that, in this reading, does not define class lines but cuts across them. Until Carson is delineated as exercising stern patriarchal authority over his metaphorical children, the novel imagines a champion of domestic values reuniting the family of workers and employers.

Mary Barton simultaneously draws on and subverts Carlylean melodramatic poetics to define the problem and to propose an ambiguous answer to the Condition-of-England question. Adapting Carlylean melodrama, characters and the rhetorical style of repetitions-with-variations, Gaskell uses a double seduction plot to narrate her tale of the dissolution and reunification of Carlyle's family of workers.[9] As in *Past and Present,* a "gaslighted Histrio" is her villain, an alienated madman is her victim and her hero rejects the "cash-nexus." From the pastoral opening to the pastoral closing, Mary's race against the clock, the temporary triumph of evil and the climatic trial in which virtue is restored, *Mary Barton* is an ingeniously wrought Carlylean melodrama and not merely a realistic novel with extraneous melodramatic episodes (Brooks 31). Melodrama, with its focus on the heroic individual, is the genre best suited to her tale of familial dissolution and final reunification by a Carlylean hero.

A plausible resolution of the formal question of the melodramatic structure of the novel is one advantage of reconnecting *Mary Barton* to Carlyle's rhetoric of a rebellious working class sundered from the upper classes. Another, perhaps more significant one, is a critical perspective from which to study Carlyle's problematic dichotomy of the ungoverned working class and the ungoverning upper classes, and Gaskell's intricate negotiation of the political implications of paternalism, which has attracted less critical interest than other aspects of the novel. From this perspective, the cooperative action of Chartism and trade unionism in Gaskell's highly political melodrama are not relegated to the background, but are once more at its center.

Notes

I am grateful to Carole Bebe Tarantelli, M. Giulia Fabi, Andrew H. Miller, Thomas Mills, Portia Prebys, Abe

Ravitz, Susan Warner and the anonymous referees of the *Victorians Institute Journal* for their valuable advice and suggestions. My thanks are also due to the staffs of the New York Public Library and the library of the Fondazione Lelio e Lisli Basso in Rome for their assistance.

1. The wide-ranging critical discussion of melodrama in *Mary Barton* has moved from deploring it as a lapse to analyzing and theorizing the perceived tension between the romance and political plots. Catherine Gallagher's influential explication maintains that Gaskell juxtaposes tragedy, melodrama and a working-class domestic tale as a critical exploration of conventional ways of interpreting reality. Gallagher argues the exploration reveals "that melodrama is a mere conventional distortion, a genre inappropriate to modern reality" (75). Other critics of particular interest to this essay include Thomas E. Recchio, who claims that there are no villains in *Mary Barton* (16); Dierdre D'Albertis, who discerns Carlyle's influence in Gaskell's *Life of Charlotte Brontë* (39), but argues that *Mary Barton* fuses melodrama and social realism, with Esther's story competing with realistic representation (58) and Amanda Anderson, who construes Esther as "a *real* melodramatic character" constituting "the conflation of romantic melodrama and the real." Through Esther, Anderson interrogates Catherine Gallagher's reading "that a melodramatic reading is wrong and a political reading is right," and that "the novel demonstrates that melodrama is false and class conflict is real" (115). Although Patricia E. Johnson similarly locates the tension between melodrama and realism in Esther, she wonders: "Anderson provocatively describes Esther's character as 'a ghost from another genre,' but one might question precisely what that genre is. At first glance an apparition out of a romantic melodrama who finds herself on the streets of an industrial novel, Esther also haunts the text like a ghost out of some parliamentary blue book" (29). Finally, I am indebted throughout to Patsy Stoneman's fine discussion of parent-child relations in *Mary Barton.*

2. Elaine Hadley illustrates how narratives of family dissolution and reunification, together with personifications of good and evil, are not only to be found in the nineteenth-century theater but in a number of literary and non-literary texts as well (3).

3. A distinctive feature of Carlyle's rhetoric is the illogical. "He emphasizes that he has answers to ultimate questions; that his answers offer themselves to imagination rather than logic" (Holloway 4).

4. *Northern Star* 17 Aug 1839: 3.

5. Gaskell was undoubtedly thinking of Thomas Carlyle when writing her first novel. Not only is there the quotation by Carlyle on the title page but the narrator also refers to his *Sartor Resartus* on page 182 of the text. The admiration was mutual; Gaskell prized Carlyle's letter complimenting *Mary Barton (Letters* 68).

6. Carlyle's early admirers also included Karl Marx and Friedrich Engels, whose censure of "no other nexus between man and man than naked self-interest, than callous 'cash payment'" in *The Communist Manifesto* (5) rephrases Carlyle's, "Cash-payment is not the sole nexus of man with man," found first in *Chartism* (195) and repeated in *Past and Present* (187).

7. John Tosh, in "Masculinities in an Industrializing Society: Britain, 1800-1914," studies the social discourse of the period. Significantly, Tosh argues that "it would be a mistake to confine the analysis of nineteenth-century masculinity to a class perspective. In recent years there has been a greater emphasis on masculinity as a marker whose meaning in some ways transcended distinctions of class" (336).

8. The political ramifications of representing the savage mob as masculine cannot be ignored. Allan Pinkerton, who began his illustrious career as a strike breaker in Britain, recounts that in England and Scotland "women, in almost every instance after the strike is inaugurated, seem the most savage in preventing the breaking of the strike by the employment of 'nobs' [sic] as 'scabs' are called there, and in both inciting and participating in riots. [. . .] these women who had been waiting out of sight, and who, with clubs, stones, bits of iron and other hastily improvised weapons, would pounce upon the "bobbies" and the "nobs' [. . .]" (20-21). Newspaper reports of nineteenth-century labor unrest corroborate the involvement of women in strikes. Some examples are the women in the illustrations of July 16, 1842 article in the *London Illustrated News* on the Manchester riots, while the text uses the gender-neutral "mob" and "persons" (232-233). The *London Illustrated News* continues this practice in its coverage of the 1853 Preston strike, fictionalized in *North and South* and *Hard Times.* The November 12 edition, for example, uses "hands" and "operatives" in the text while placing three women in the foreground of the illustration (404). The *Manchester Guardian* of August 27, 1842 reports that among the disturbances caused by "a dense mob" at a silk mill, it "was found necessary to take one female into custody for throwing stones at the constables," much like the sharp pebble that strikes Margaret (n.pag.). Yet the narrator of *North and*

South insists that "[. . .] it is always the savage lads, with their love of cruel excitement, who head the riot—reckless to what bloodshed it may lead" (177).

9. Richard D. Altick's introduction to *Past and Present*, xii.

Works Cited

Anderson, Amanda. *Tainted Souls and Painted Faces: The Rhetoric of Fallenness in Victorian Culture.* Ithaca: Cornell UP, 1993.

Brooks, Peter. *The Melodramatic Imagination: Balzac, Henry James, Melodrama, and the Mode of Excess.* New Haven: Yale UP, 1995.

Carlyle, Thomas. *Past and Present.* Ed. Richard D. Altick. New York: New York UP, 1965.

———. "Chartism" in *Thomas Carlyle: Selected Writings.* Ed. Alan Shelston. London, Penguin, 1986.

"Country Riots." *Illustrated London News.* 16 July 1842: 225-236.

D'Albertis, Deirdre. *Dissembling Fictions: Elizabeth Gaskell and the Victorian Social Text.* New York: St. Martin's. 1997.

"Democracy or aristocracy—which?" *Charter* 16 June 1839: 1.

de Tocqueville, Alexis. *Democracy in America.* Trans. George Lawrence. Ed. J. P. Mayer. New York: Harper Perennial, 1988.

Dickens, Charles. *Hard Times.* Oxford: Oxford UP, 1989.

Engels, Friedrich. *The Condition of the Working Class in England.* Ed. David McLellan. Oxford: Oxford UP, 1993.

Gallagher, Catherine. *The Industrial Reformation of English Fiction: Social Discourse and Narrative Form 1832-1867.* Chicago: U of Chicago P. 1985.

Gaskell, Elizabeth. *Mary Barton.* London: Penguin, 1996.

———. *North and South.* London: Penguin, 1994.

———. *The Letters of Mrs. Gaskell.* Ed. J. A. V. Chapple and Arthur Pollard. Cambridge: Harvard UP, 1967.

Gaskell, Peter. *The Manufacturing Population of England* [. . .]. (1833) New York: Arno, 1972.

Hadley, Elaine. *Melodramatic Tactics: Theatricalized Dissent in the English Market-place 1800-1885.* Stanford: Stanford UP, 1995.

Heilman, Robert Bechtold. *Tragedy and Melodrama: Varieties of Experience.* Seattle: U of Washington P, 1968.

Holloway, John. *The Victorian Sage: Studies in Argument.* London: Archon, 1953.

Johnson, Particia E. *Hidden Hands: Working-Class Women and Victorian Social-Problem Fiction.* Athens, Ohio: Ohio UP, 2001.

"Manchester. The National Holiday-Disturbances—Attack of the New Police on the People—Two Policemen Stabbed-Examination and Committal of the Leaders." *Northern Star* 17 Aug 1839: 3.

Marx, Karl and Friedrich Engels. *The Communist Manifesto.* Ed. David McLellan. Oxford UP, 1998.

"More Rioting." *The Guardian* [Manchester] 27 Aug 1842.

Murphy, Thomas Paul. "'Imagination Flaps Its Sportive Wings': Views of Fiction in British Working-Class Periodicals, 1816-1858." *Victorian Studies* 32 (1989): 339-363.

Pinkerton, Allan. *Strikers, Communists, Tramps and Detectives.* New York: Carleton, 1878.

Recchio, Thomas E. "'A Monstrous Reading of Mary Barton: Fiction as 'Communitas'." *College Literature* 23:3 (1996): 2-22.

"Sketches of Strikes and Riots in the Cotton Districts." *Illustrated London News* 12 Nov. 1853: 403-404.

Smith, James L. *Melodrama.* London: Methuen, 1973.

Stoneman, Patsy. *Elizabeth Gaskell.* Bloomington: Indiana UP, 1987.

Thompson, E. P. *The Making of the English Working Class.* New York: Vintage, 1966.

Tosh, John. "Masculinities in an Industrializing Society: Britain, 1800-1914." *Journal of British Studies* 44 (2005): 330-342.

Deborah Wynne (essay date 2005)

SOURCE: Wynne, Deborah. "Hysteria Repeating Itself: Elizabeth Gaskell's *Lois the Witch.*" *Women's Writing* 12, no. 1 (2005): 85-97.

[*In the following essay, Wynne analyzes how Gaskell rejects the notion that hysteria is a natural state for women, and offers an alternative viewpoint on gender, politics, and history in* Lois the Witch.]

Elizabeth Gaskell's novella **Lois the Witch,** a fictional account of the Salem witch trials of 1692, was first published in Charles Dickens's newly established magazine *All the Year Round* in 1859. It appeared within a particularly rich environment, positioned alongside three climactic instalments of Dickens's historical novel *A Tale of Two Cities,* which depicted Darnay's trial and the resurrection of Dr Manette's "forgotten" letter.[1] Dickens's and Gaskell's representations of violent historical events were supported in *All The Year Round* by non-fiction features covering a range of historical subjects, including "Hysteria and Devotion", an overview of the effects of religious unrest from the Middle Ages to the nineteenth century, and "Subterranean Switzerland", on archaeological evidence suggesting that ritual human sacrifices once took place in Europe.[2] A regular series called "Drift" had for several months kept *All The Year Round*'s readers focused on history. Written by "Matthew Mole", who burrowed through archives to retrieve "debris, *disjecta membra,* or salvage" from the past, "Drift" asserted the importance of these fragments of history as "significant, symbolical, speaking unmistakably of the race, clime and circumstance whence the scattered morsels came".[3]

Gaskell's novella was, then, originally presented to an audience whose attention had for some months been turned towards history as an important and exciting arena for study and entertainment. For Gaskell, history was a useful territory for the writer of fiction. Although her reputation had been built around her social-problem novels representing contemporary urban life, *Mary Barton* (1848) and *North and South* (1855), she regularly turned towards historical subjects in her short stories as her 1858 collection *My Lady Ludlow* attests.[4] *Lois the Witch* is unlike much of Gaskell's historical fiction, however, in that an actual event from history is represented. It is also one of the most unremittingly bleak of her stories, closing as it does with the teenage heroine's execution before a hostile crowd. *All The Year Round*'s readers, once they had read of Lois's violent death, encountered a few weeks later the execution of Sydney Carton in *A Tale of Two Cities.* However, while Carton's action embodies the idea of heroic self-sacrifice, Gaskell's heroine faces a pointless death, merely bewildered by the accusations of witchcraft which led to her trial.[5] In *Lois the Witch* history is presented not as a repository of heroic actions, but as a warning against human cruelty and stupidity.

This article examines Gaskell's engagement with history in order to reveal the ways in which she used the past as a comment on women's lives in mid-Victorian Britain. The witchcraft panic in Salem offered Gaskell an opportunity to examine the issues surrounding female hysteria, representing it less as a condition of women's biology (a prevalent view among many contemporary medical theorists) and more as a desperate response to repressive political and domestic regimes.[6] Indeed, in some respects Gaskell anticipated Freud and later feminist revisions of the "hysterical woman".[7]

Writing at a time when history was usually explored by male historians in terms of the epic past of nation states, she also anticipated the work of modern feminist historians. As both Hilary M. Schor and Christine L. Krueger have suggested, Gaskell's historical fiction brings to light the submerged histories of women as she sets out to rewrite "official" versions of the past.[8] Although she relied heavily for the background to *Lois* [Lois the Witch] on Charles Upham's 1831 book *Lectures on Witchcraft, Comprising a History of the Delusions in Salem in 1692* (even lifting the occasional passage verbatim), Gaskell's focus is not on specific "facts", but an imaginative recreation of the conditions which engendered this hysterical outburst and its distorting effects upon the female community.[9] *Lois the Witch,* despite its historical subject matter, is also a text intimately bound up with the contexts of its publication as a magazine story and the social events of the late 1850s, and before turning to the novella itself, I will consider the significance of these contexts in relation to Gaskell's role as a writer of historical fiction.

Gaskell's representation of girls unleashing destructive social forces in seventeenth-century Salem appeared quite literally alongside Dickens's images of violent female revolutionaries in *All The Year Round.* This was very topical, for the theme of violent women in history surfaced in many periodicals in the late 1850s.[10] There are a number of possible reasons for this. Firstly, feminist agitation for property rights and full citizenship was gaining momentum during this period, which no doubt suggested to many Victorians the possibility of the emergence of new gender identities.[11] Secondly, the passive heroine of Victorian literature was gradually making way for more startling representations of femininity, as indicated by the emergence of the transgressive heroines of the sensation novel (both Ellen Wood and Mary Braddon were shortly to publish their bestsellers *East Lynne* and *Lady Audley's Secret*).[12] However, there was an even more topical factor which may have influenced the choice of violent women in history as a fictional subject: the Ulster religious revivals, a phenomenon which dominated the news in 1859. These revivals foregrounded the dramatic actions of Ulster women in public meetings, their violent displays of religious awakening sending shock waves throughout Britain.[13] The Irish revivalists, most of them working-class Presbyterian women, took part in spontaneous open-air prayer meetings, which frequently lasted late into the night. Seized by a sense of spiritual conviction, the women fell into convulsions, suffering from a range of hysterical symptoms, from paralysis and temporary blindness to uncontrollable weeping and shouting. Many claimed to experience visions which allowed them direct access to God and asserted their rights as "chosen" disciples to usurp the authority of the clergy. Significantly, the Victorian press compared the scenes in the north of Ireland to both the Salem witchcraft panic of

1692 and the behaviour of women in revolutionary France.[14] In the light of the Ulster revivals, then, Dickens's images of the female revolutionaries of France and Gaskell's depiction of the hysterical girls of Salem may have appeared highly relevant to contemporary readers.

Gaskell's account of religious panic in seventeenth-century Salem, when read in the light of the overreactions in the press to the women of Ulster, appears to be addressing a contemporary social "problem" in the way that *Mary Barton* and *North and South* addressed the problem of class conflict in Victorian industrial relations. However, it would be inaccurate to suggest that Gaskell was making a crude link between Salem in 1692 and Ulster in 1859 in *Lois the Witch*; instead, she used her story to contribute to contemporary debates about women and the public sphere.[15] Original readers of her novella were invited to consider the effects of the events in both Salem and Ulster, which centred on the unruly behaviour of young women who, hitherto excluded from power, had found socially destructive ways of gaining it. Reading *Lois the Witch* alongside accounts of the Irish revivals and nineteenth-century discourses surrounding the disruptive, hysterical woman highlights Gaskell's emphasis on the relationship between politics and the social and psychological lives of women.

The very notion of religious revivalism offered a link for Victorian readers between the events in Ireland and seventeenth-century New England, for the term "revival", signifying a spiritual awakening, was coined by the Puritan theologian Cotton Mather. He was widely believed to be the perpetrator of the witchcraft scare in Salem in 1692, which resulted in the execution of 19 people, one of whom was a five-year-old child.[16] Gaskell (rather inexplicably, considering Mather's reputation for religious intolerance) chose his name as the basis of her pseudonym "Cotton Mather Mills" when she first began to publish her work in the late 1840s in *Howitt's Journal*.[17] Mather also features as a character in *Lois the Witch*; indeed, one of his speeches is quoted verbatim. Years after the Salem events Mather wrote a medical account of female hysteria in which he appeared to revise his belief in the demonic possession of the Salem women, finally admitting that factors other than supernatural ones lay behind the social panic of the times.[18] However, Gaskell, although she is also careful to dispel the idea of supernatural agency, goes further than Mather in representing the social panic of Salem as the result of a political upheaval acting upon an ignorant and oppressed female population.

Gaskell's linkage of hysteria and politics was, of course, not entirely new. Throughout the nineteenth century, a period which witnessed a burgeoning interest in the science of psychology, there was a strong belief among many medical theorists that female hysterical symptoms inevitably emerged at times of political unrest.[19] In 1835 James Cowles Prichard published his *Treatise on Insanity and Other Disorders Affecting the Mind* where he described the female hysteric as a woman who, when sane, may be "modest and circumspect", but who is transformed by hysteria into someone who is "violent and abrupt in her manners, loquacious, impetuous, talks loudly and abusively against her relations and guardians . . . Sometimes she uses indecent expressions, and betrays without reserve unbecoming feelings and trains of thought."[20] Female hysteria was thus read as a sign of a decline into the social and political chaos that heralds the breakdown of traditional orders. The fact that hysteria manifested itself as a series of signs based on bodily performances also put its authenticity as a disease into question, and both Gaskell and the commentators on the Irish revivals presumed that hysterical symptoms were consciously deployed by women to serve their own ends.[21] However, Gaskell saw the threat posed by the hysteric not in terms of a breakdown of traditional femininity, but as a breakdown of the female community itself. In other words, in Gaskell's view the destruction unleashed by the hysterical woman, while constituting a challenge to authority, ultimately led to women turning against other women.

One of the dominant images of the French Revolution for many Victorians was of disruptive women violently engaging in politics (an image Dickens exploits to the full in *A Tale of Two Cities*). Similarly, the prevailing image of the Irish revivals was of hysterical women drawing attention to themselves in public places and disrupting the smooth running of the factories and mills in which they worked. While the revivals were generally interpreted in the British press as a harbinger of political "trouble" in Ireland (the Ulster women being seen as a signal of the onset of a revolutionary moment in Irish history), the local press tended to be sceptical about working-class women's claims to be suffering the torments of a violent spiritual awakening. The *Londonderry Standard,* for example, suggested that for female revivalists, "clairvoyant laziness became a better paying occupation than honest labour".[22] The idea of "laziness" was also suggested in a *Belfast Newsletter* report of a mill in Ballymena, where several women were seized with violent convulsions one morning and within an hour nearly 30 other women were prostrated and the mill was forced to close.[23] In the visions the women claimed to experience they saw themselves seated on thrones in beautiful gowns, and able to speak and read fluently and with authority.[24] This ability on the part of the lowest paid workers to bring the local economy to a halt, wielding power by means of the ambiguous yet irrefutable language of religious conversion, contained for many eyewitnesses of the revivals more than a flavour of political unrest.

While recent historians of the revivals in Ulster fully recognise the social and political causes underpinning revivalism, many Victorian commentators glossed over these, preferring to interpret the phenomenon in terms of a superstitious throwback to the Dark Ages, a sign of primitive irrationality and proof that history has a habit of repeating itself.[25] The focus of this irrationality was the figure of the hysterical woman, who allowed herself to forget her feminine social role, publicly succumbing to uncontrollable emotions. In *Lois the Witch* Gaskell represents the Salem girls' hysterical symptoms as being consciously deployed to delude and undermine the authorities. Her focus on the social causes for hysteria was often in sharp contrast to articles on revivalism which appeared in the press. The *New Monthly Magazine,* for example, stated that, "The recent revivals in Ireland appear to indicate that religion is subjected to certain crises among us which return with all the regularity of the trade winds", as though hysteria was "natural", like the weather, and bound to reappear sooner or later.[26] This article then focused on medieval Europe, describing how in 1587 a woman "possessed" by spirits challenged the clergy in a "masculine and unusual voice", a reminder to readers of how the working-class women of Ulster had spoken out in public, endowing themselves with the authority of the clergy.[27] The *Saturday Review* quoted one female participant's assessment of the mood at revival meetings as feeling as though trapped in "a house on fire with the doors shut".[28] This mood is evident in *Lois the Witch,* where the English heroine Lois Barclay is fatally trapped within a community aflame with hatred and anger.

Images of unruly women provided the dramatic energy for both Gaskell's and Dickens's fiction, and these images were further echoed in 1859 in *All the Year Round.* Shortly after the serialisation of *Lois the Witch,* and before *A Tale of Two Cities* had finished its run, there was a discussion of "revivalism" in France during the eighteenth century entitled "A 'Revival' Under Louis the Fifteenth". The anonymous author emphasised the parallels between Paris and Ulster, seeing the French outbreak as "singularly similar to those of the exhibitions which have recently taken place among ourselves, that, though the modern term 'Revival' had not been invented, they are at once recognised as belonging to the same category".[29] The French "revival" centred on a group of working-class women called "Convulsionnaires", who underwent public torture in order to "save their souls".[30] Their torments allowed them certain powers, such as loudly insulting the aristocrats who came to watch their displays. This image of working women entering the public sphere (albeit in bizarre circumstances) and assuming an authority hitherto denied them was an image which dominated the press at the time of the Ulster revivals. Journalists invited readers to consider the new phenomenon in the light of previous outbreaks of religious intensity, an alarming sign of history repeating

itself.[31] Yet, as Gaskell shows in *Lois,* women's unregulated attempts to wield power in public more often ended in self-harm, or harm to other women, than constituted an effective challenge to male authority.

The history of women and hysteria was, then, thoroughly charted in *All The Year Round,* not only in *Lois,* but also in articles and in Dickens's *A Tale of Two Cities* with his depiction of Madame Defarge and her fellow female revolutionaries. However, although *All The Year Round*'s historical fiction and journalism in 1859 focused on the revengeful behaviour of oppressed women, the various authors differed in their interpretations. As I have indicated, most journalists made the link between revivalism and outbreaks of religious turmoil in the past simply on the basis that these events were characterised by the hysterical displays of young women, suggesting that women historically had been prone to hysteria because of their weak bodies and minds. Dickens simply evades the issue of women and hysteria by creating a division between the "natural" violence and emotional displays of the French working-class women and the perfect control of his middle-class anglicised heroine Lucie Manette. Gaskell, however, is unusual among Victorian writers in not only asking the question, "What makes women act hysterically?", but in also attempting to address it. In *Lois the Witch* she analyses hysteria by considering a range of issues, from the effects of the limiting roles traditionally offered to women, to the formation and reformation of power relationships at times of crisis, highlighting the ways in which communities create and maintain boundaries, and emphasising the social effects of exclusion and conformity.

Lois the Witch shows how a restrictive community based on puritanical values engenders an outbreak of hysteria, which has fatal results. It concerns the story of Lois Barclay from Warwickshire who, on the death of her parents, seeks her surviving relatives in New England. Shortly after her arrival in Salem, her uncle dies and she has no choice but to remain with his uncongenial wife Grace Hickson and her cousins. Each of these cousins is damaged in some way by the repressions imposed upon them by family and community. The eldest daughter Faith is depressive and her sexual attraction to a young minister results in a morbid introspection. Her younger sister, the overindulged and malevolent Prudence, eventually brings about Lois's death, while her mentally ill brother Manasseh suffers from tormented visions of Lois as his bride and, unable to comprehend his feelings of sexual attraction, makes insistent and deranged proposals of marriage. When the witch scare breaks out, Lois, perceived by the female Hicksons as a disruptive force in the household, is accused of witchcraft. The novella ends with Lois's execution followed by the arrival of her grief-stricken lover from England.

Gaskell suggests that women forced to live within an oppressive society, denied a public role or voice, turn their energies inwards, and the image of inwardness is used repeatedly throughout *Lois* to signify mental illness. The political turmoil in Salem as "one by one the patriarchs . . . had rapidly followed each other to the grave" leaves the community isolated, "left to prey upon itself", engendering "diseases of the imagination".[32] Gaskell's achievement with *Lois the Witch* is to expose the instability of power structures and the ways in which the powerful can at times be threatened by the powerless. She traces the links between hysteria (seen as a morbid psychological state) and repressive social regimes, emphasising the female hysteric's tendency towards display and performance. For Gaskell, hysteria is a strategy which has traditionally been used by women to engage in a power struggle, a way of resisting and wielding power. By focusing upon the historical contexts of the idea of demonic possession, Gaskell indicates the deeply rational origins for the apparent irrationality of the female hysteric. For her, hysteria is always a symptom of a social problem.

In *Lois* the social problems of Salem are made clear: the rigidity of the Puritan ideology leads to a psychologically unhealthy community, and this morbidity is exhibited most strongly in the less powerful members of the community, particularly women and children. The novella opens with a reference to the religious intensity and political turmoil of New England when the newly arrived heroine is informed by the captain of her ship that the people of New England are "rare chaps for praying; down on their knees at every turn of their life".[33] During this period the Puritan settlers were engaged in conflicts with both the British and the French, and Lois's arrival in Salem also coincides with a generational conflict between the older Puritans and younger members of the community who seek social change. The deaths of its patriarchs within a short space of time has left Salem particularly vulnerable, creating a "division in the religious body" which produces a marked effect upon the female body as the fear of witches rises into a full-blown panic.[34] Gaskell describes how: "Here and there girls, women uttering strange cries . . . were centres of a group of agitated friends."[35] Yet she is careful to delineate the rational basis for these apparently irrational outbursts through her character Prudence, that "evil child", whose calculations as to how she can gain attention indicate the ways in which the powerless can seize power at a time of social instability.[36] When she sees her friends writhing in convulsions, Prudence wonders, "how long I might wriggle before great and godly folk would take so much notice of me?"—an experiment which she later tries when she accuses Lois of bewitching her.[37] As Gaskell's narrator states, "every one must see what immense and terrible power was abroad for revenge".[38]

Lois Barclay, as an outsider, is particularly vulnerable. She appears at first to be a representative of conservative British values, the daughter of a clergyman, an outspoken upholder of "Church and State".[39] The Hickson family, on the other hand, appear to be vulnerable radicals, fighting for their independence and facing the dangers of maintaining a settlement in a hostile and alien territory. Yet Lois, even as a child, is aware of the tenuousness of her social position when she witnesses the drowning of a "witch" in her home village of Barford. The witch vents her anger against the clergyman's collusion with her oppressors by cursing his daughter and apparently prophesying her execution as a witch when she shouts, "parson's wench . . . none shall save thee when thou art brought up for a witch".[40] However, the witch's prophesy is best read as a comment on the dangers of social exclusion, a warning against the powerful social forces that fear difference and nonconformity. Lois's early identification with the Barford "witch" (after witnessing the drowning she repeatedly dreams that *she* is submerged in the pond) indicates the vulnerability of all women, their social position usually being tenuously determined by their relationship to fathers or husbands. Once her father is dead, Lois has been cut adrift from society, inhabiting a space on the margins of the community outside male control and protection. This point is further stressed when Gaskell ironically comments on the condemnation of Hota, Salem's first "witch", "she was an Indian, a heathen, whose life would be no great loss to the community", suggesting the idea of the "redundancy" of women who lack the status conferred by stable family connections.[41]

However, while highlighting women's vulnerability through the story of Lois's fall from sheltered clergyman's daughter to executed witch, Gaskell is also concerned with exploring the ways in which difference engenders fear and hatred, hence the demonisation of Salem's outsiders: the Native American servants, the girl from England, elderly women, and young men intent on social reform. Being safely accommodated within a community, as Lois is as the parson's daughter, may be only a temporary state, for the shifting of power, the accidents of death and ageing, the loss of social position and money can lead to the safe becoming unsafe, the powerful becoming vulnerable.

The tenuousness of women's position in society is emphasised by Gaskell's linkage of the body politic and the female body, as though disease in the former leads to disease in the latter. Gaskell's comment on the "great division in the religious body" in Salem is immediately followed by the image of the self-divided Faith Hickson, unable to control her restless body as she lies in bed, disturbing Lois's sleep with the "convulsive motions of her limbs".[42] Gaskell makes it clear that this is the outward sign of her repressed feelings for Mr Nolan, the young reforming clergyman who has been hounded out of Salem by the patriarchal authorities. Faith's restlessness spreads through the female community. Her mother Grace is seen "rocking her body backwards and forwards, and praying to herself", while Pastor Tappau's daughters fall into convulsions, "their howlings like the wild beasts of the field".[43] When the Salem elders die and the status quo disintegrates, Gaskell illustrates the ways in which all that has been hidden and suppressed is exposed to view. The Hickson family, staunch representatives of Salem's Puritan values, falls apart with the political changes as the "distortions" of the family members are publicly exposed. Prudence's malevolence is highlighted when she calculatedly falls into convulsions and accuses Lois of witchcraft as a perverted act of revenge. She is described as a "distorted child", and this not only suggests the physical contortions of her body, but also indicates her already "distorted" mind.[44] Gaskell suggests that the distortions within Salem were already a problem *before* the witchcraft panic broke out. When Grace, returning with the news that Satan is abroad, takes measures (that is, placing straw across the door sill) to prevent his entering her house, Prudence says, "'But if he be already entered in . . . may not that make it difficult for him to depart?' Her mother, taking no notice of her question, went on rocking herself, and praying."[45] The knowing Prudence is aware that the "evil" (which, Gaskell suggests, is the result of repression, tyranny, and intolerance) is already within.

The social oppression which characterises the Puritan community is matched by an unhealthy sexual repression. Faith is not the only member of the Hickson family tormented by unfulfilled sexual longings. Manasseh Hickson's troubled visions, symptomatic of his insanity, are also publicly exposed at this time of crisis. His crazed pursuit of Lois as his wife hints at his "distorted" sexuality, a point reinforced by a suggestion of incest when Gaskell states that before Lois arrived Manasseh was tormented by the presence of his own sister Faith.[46] Salem is represented by Gaskell as a site of hysteria and distortion, a prisonlike structure from which few can escape, and Lois's entrapment and execution as a witch serve as examples of the fatal consequences of repression and social tyranny. The fact that Lois is condemned to death because of the accusations of hysterical girls revenging themselves on those they view as oppressors indicates the isolation and separation of women in the community, another example of diseased inwardness, which characterises this text. As Gaskell suggests, however, their rebellion is useless as, once the crisis is over, the status quo is reinstated and hysteria is exposed as an ineffective political tool. For her, the figure of the witch is symptomatic of any outsider, which is why all of those accused of witchcraft in *Lois the Witch,* as well as those who exhibit signs of possession, are those on the margins of the community.

Lois offered *All The Year Round*'s readers a stark warning from history on the dangers of hysteria. It is highly probable that the perceived excesses of revivalism in Ulster made such a warning seem necessary. The dangers of marginality, emphasised so forcefully in *Lois,* were rarely addressed in accounts of the Ulster revivals, where working-class women's engagement in disturbing public displays of religious emotion was usually read simplistically as the result of women's weak natures.[47] However, virtually all of the female revivalists were working-class women who were denied a public voice, ill-paid, and exploited, and extreme action within a public arena clearly gained them the attention they would not have otherwise received. Some commentators suggested that Ulster's poverty and isolation from the cultural and political centre of Britain were contributing factors to the revival frenzy, as though British neglect may have forced the community to turn in on itself. The revivals eventually spread to Scotland, Wales, and Cornwall, the Celtic margins of Britain which had long been associated with social, cultural, and economic neglect as well as religious excess.[48] Gaskell, a Unitarian wary of the dangers of religious intolerance and social exclusion, may have seen parallels between the explosions of female hysteria in the isolated communities of seventeenth-century Salem and the impoverished towns and villages of nineteenth-century Ireland, and believed that in order to prevent history/hysteria repeating itself, she needed to dramatically represent the social causes of female discontent.

Notes

1. *Lois the Witch* appeared in *All The Year Round* (vol. 1) in three instalments on 8, 15, and 22 October 1859. *A Tale of Two Cities* was serialised between April and November in the same year.

2. "Hysteria and Devotion", *All The Year Round,* 1 (5 November 1859), pp. 31-35 and "Subterranean Switzerland", which appeared in the same issue, pp. 25-31.

3. The first instalment of "Drift" appeared in *All The Year Round,* 1 (18 June 1859), p. 183. All quotations are from this issue.

4. The stories in *My Lady Ludlow* are set during the eighteenth century, as is Gaskell's 1863 novel *Sylvia's Lovers,* which was actually begun in 1859. Gaskell also wrote historical articles for Dickens's magazine, such as her account of the history of the French Cagots, "An Accursed Race", *Household Words,* 12 (25 August 1855), pp. 73-80.

5. Despite these differences, however, the moment in *Lois the Witch* when Lois comforts a fellow prisoner as they are led to their deaths anticipates the

episode in *A Tale of Two Cities* where Carton comforts the seamstress as they face execution at the guillotine.

6. See Helen Small (1996) *Love's Madness: Medicine, the Novel and Female Insanity, 1800-1865* (Oxford: Clarendon Press), p. 109.

7. See Linda Ruth Williams (1995) *Critical Desire: Psychoanalysis and the Literary Subject* (London & New York: Edward Arnold) for an interesting chapter linking Freud's theories with Gaskell's representation of hysteria in *Cousin Phillis* (1865).

8. See Hilary M. Schor (1992) *Scheherazade in the Marketplace: Elizabeth Gaskell and the Victorian Novel* (New York & Oxford: Oxford University Press), pp. 98, 153-168, and Christine L. Krueger "The 'Female Paternalist' as Historian: Elizabeth Gaskell's *My Lady Ludlow*", in Linda M. Shires (ed.) (1992) *Rewriting the Victorians: Theory, History and the Politics of Gender* (New York & London: Routledge), p. 166.

9. See John G. Sharps (1970) *Mrs Gaskell's Observation and Invention: A Study of Her Non-biographic Works* (Sussex: Linden Press), pp. 315-324 for details of Gaskell's historical sources for *Lois the Witch*.

10. See, for example, "The Irish Revivals", *Saturday Review*, 8 (3 September 1859), pp. 285-286; *Daily News* (19 September 1859); *The Times* (8 October 1859); "Hysteria and Devotion", *All The Year Round*, 1 (5 November 1859), pp. 31-35; "Antecedents of Revivalism", *Saturday Review*, 8 (3 December 1859), pp. 669-670; "Medieval Demonology", *New Monthly Magazine*, 1 (January 1860), pp. 100-107; and "The Revivals of 1859", *Macmillan's Magazine*, 1 (March 1860), pp. 363-373.

11. See Lee Holcombe (1983) *Wives and Property: Reform of the Married Women's Property Law in Nineteenth-century England* (Buffalo: University of Toronto Press) and Mary Lyndon Shanley (1989) *Feminism, Marriage and the Law in Victorian England* (Princeton: Princeton University Press) for discussions of the feminist movement during the mid-Victorian period.

12. *East Lynne* was first published serially from 1860 to 1861, while *Lady Audley's Secret* first appeared in 1861. For a discussion of the transgressive, often violent, heroines of the sensation novel, see Deborah Wynne (2001) *The Sensation Novel and the Victorian Family Magazine* (Basingstoke & New York: Palgrave).

13. See "The Irish Revivals", p. 286.

14. See "Antecedents of Revivalism", pp. 669-670.

15. For general discussions of these debates, see Holcombe, *Wives and Property*, and Shanley, *Feminism, Marriage and the Law in Victorian England*.

16. For a discussion of Mather's role in the events in Salem, see Ilza Veith (1965) *Hysteria: The History of a Disease* (Chicago & London: University of Chicago Press), p. 71.

17. See Winifred Gérin (1976) *Elizabeth Gaskell: A Biography* (Oxford: Clarendon Press), p. 76.

18. Cotton Mather's *The Wonders of the Invisible World, An Account of the Tryals of Several Witches Lately Executed in New England* was published in 1693. See Veith, *Hysteria*, p. 71.

19. See Small, *Love's Madness*, pp. 105-112.

20. Quoted in Scott Dransfield (1999) "History, Hysteria, and the Revolutionary Subject in Thomas Carlyle's *French Revolution*", *Prose Studies*, 22:3, p. 60.

21. For a discussion of women and hysteria in the nineteenth century which considers issues of performance, see Elaine Showalter (1985) *The Female Malady: Women, Madness, and English Culture, 1830-1980* (London: Virago).

22. *Londonderry Standard* (15 September 1859), p. 2, quoted in Janice Holmes (1994) "The 'World Turned Upside Down': Women in the Ulster Revival of 1859", in *Coming into the Light: The Work, Politics and Religion of Women in Ulster, 1840-1940*, ed. Janice Holmes & Diane Urquhart (Belfast: Queen's University of Belfast Press), p. 143.

23. *Belfast Newsletter* (25 May 1859), p. 3, quoted in Holmes, "The 'World Turned Upside Down'", p. 134.

24. Ibid., p. 136.

25. See in particular "Antecedents of Revivalism", pp. 669-670. Recent feminist historians' accounts of the revivals include Holmes & Urquhart, *Coming into the Light* and David Hempton & Myrtle Hill (1992) *Evangelical Protestantism in Ulster Society, 1740-1890* (London: Routledge). One nineteenth-century work which did consider women's participation in the Irish revivals as politically motivated was John Chapman (1860) *Christian Revivals: Their History and Natural History* (London: n.p.).

26. "Medieval Demonology", p. 100.

27. Ibid., p. 102.

28. Quoted in "The Irish Revivals", p. 286.

29. "A 'Revival' Under Louis the Fifteenth", *All The Year Round*, 1 (19 November 1859), p. 82.

30. Ibid., p. 86.

31. See "The Irish Revivals", "Antecedents of Revivalism", "Medieval Demonology", and "Hysteria and Devotion" for discussions of history repeating itself.

32. Elizabeth Gaskell (2000) *Lois the Witch, Gothic Tales,* ed. Laura Kranzler (London: Penguin), pp. 181, 172, 171.

33. Ibid., p. 143.

34. Ibid., p. 163.

35. Ibid., p. 207.

36. Ibid.

37. Ibid., p. 190.

38. Ibid., p. 186.

39. Ibid., p. 158.

40. Ibid., p. 150.

41. Ibid., p. 192.

42. Ibid., pp. 163, 164.

43. Ibid., pp. 182, 182-183.

44. Ibid., p. 204.

45. Ibid., p. 183.

46. Ibid., p. 195.

47. See in particular "Hysteria and Devotion" and "Antecedents of Revivalism" for contemporary views of women and religious hysteria.

48. Tennyson's reference to "the blind hysterics of the Celt" in *In Memoriam* (Section CIX, l. 16) is just one of many nineteenth-century literary allusions to the supposed emotional instability of people in Celtic regions.

Natalie Kapetanios Meir (essay date spring 2006)

SOURCE: Meir, Natalie Kapetanios. "'Household Forms and Ceremonies': Narrating Routines in Elizabeth Gaskell's *Cranford.*" *Studies in the Novel* 38, no. 1 (spring 2006): 1-14.

[*In the following essay, Meir argues that "the sketches that make up* Cranford *are organized by a means of the ongoing theme of eating rituals, and its plot is focused primarily on characters struggling with social conventions."*]

Critics discussing Elizabeth Gaskell's *Cranford* (1851-53) frequently situate it in relation to other genres of writing. In fact, owing in part to *Cranford*'s original composition, a series of sketches published in rather irregular increments in *Household Words,* and in part to its unique emphasis on daily life, critics often question whether *Cranford* is even a novel.[1] While some have argued that *Cranford* is lacking formal unity, Tim Dolin argues that the novel does have a particular structure,

though it is "organized like a collection of anecdotes, printed on cards and bundled together" (193). In this essay, I also pay special attention to the generic exigencies of *Cranford* by considering it with respect to another genre, the social instruction handbook. Yet in doing so, I argue that, paradoxically, a set of concerns usually associated with the handbook lends *Cranford* a novelistic structure; *Cranford* can thus be seen as a novel by virtue of its functional and methodological overlap with works on dining manners. For I suggest that the sketches that make up *Cranford* are organized by means of the ongoing theme of eating rituals, and its plot is focused primarily on characters struggling with social conventions.[2]

Noticing the predominance of the rituals of gentility as one of the novel's main themes, a number of critics have regarded the novel as defiant of conventions and handbooks alike. Hilary Schor, for instance, suggests that *Cranford* ridicules the rigid "codification of experience" (296) associated with handbooks. Elsewhere, Margaret Tarratt argues that Gaskell examines the implications of social codes on women's lives; the novel's basic message, according to Tarratt, is that the individual has an "occasional need to question authority and in certain cases to defy convention" (163). *Cranford* does certainly lend itself to the types of arguments that both Schor and Tarratt make. For Gaskell satirizes the extent to which the most minute behaviors of her fictional town are regulated by established codes, and she consistently unmasks the comical contradictions involved in maintaining the fiction of gentility.[3]

For the most part, however, when critics suggest that the novel questions conventions they refer to thematic representations of characters struggling with shared models for social behavior. While Eileen Gillooly examines the subtleties of how the narrator's use of humor challenges the authority of Cranford's "strict code of gentility" and Schor offers a complex reading of Gaskell's experimentation with different narrative styles as she provides a "guide-book" to Cranford life (303), critics have not often made explicit connections between issues of etiquette and issues of narrative. Nancy Armstrong's *Desire and Domestic Fiction,* an analysis of the ways in which novels and conduct books perform the regulatory function of conveying domestic ideology, is one work whose generic scope is similar to my own. Yet, whereas Armstrong discusses how literary and nonliterary texts share a sociopolitical function, I am particularly interested in linking the two genres through a set of specific narrative operations that codify social behavior.[4] I want to suggest that considering the ways in which Gaskell narrates conventions can lead to a unique perspective on the novel's relationship to questions of manners. Rather than focus on Gaskell's thematic critiques of conventions, then, I consider how her ideas are intertwined with her narrative methods. My use of the word "conventions" (rather than the term "manners") captures my dual interest in narrative and social practices, as well as my consideration of the concept of the convention as a novelistic device. I argue that while Gaskell is clearly trying to develop a humorous critique of the moral and social value of etiquette, the narrative techniques that she employs complicate, and indeed undermine, this satiric commentary.

By engaging with concepts from narratology, I situate Gaskell's narrative techniques with respect to those that tend to recur in social instruction handbooks of the mid-to-late nineteenth century.[5] In doing so, I suggest that although novels may provide similar content as handbooks, they both mimic and implicitly raise questions about handbooks' methodology.[6] For unlike handbooks, which present conventions as finished products apart from individual experience and agency, Victorian novels' narrative methods can provide insight into the ways in which social practices are codified. My argument works in two ways. First, I argue that Gaskell examines how dining conventions are generated, circulated, and sustained. Using questions about these conventions as the basis of plot, Gaskell consistently narrates the process by which idiosyncratic dining preferences become shared paradigms.[7] Second, I consider, in turn, how Gaskell conveys the notion that such conventions are routine. I argue that even as Gaskell may question the origin and importance of certain social graces, the narrative devices that she uses produce the effect that these behaviors are ever-present and enduring.

> "The bread was cut to the imaginary pattern of excellence that existed in Miss Matty's mind."
>
> Mary Smith,
>
> *Cranford*

Cranford does not contain a book that the women of Cranford consult for their dinner parties and visiting calls. Instead, at times the novel itself resembles a handbook.[8] Since Gaskell begins in *medias res,* with Cranford's inhabitants secure in their value system, she elaborates the women's code of conduct by means of the narrator, Mary Smith, an outsider who is a regular visitor to the town. As Schor explains, Gaskell "needs a narrator detached enough not to take Cranford's 'elegant economies' too seriously, but enough of an insider to interpret such customs to the uninitiated" (299).[9] On the one hand, this narrative position of insider-outsider poises Mary to possess reliable knowledge regarding the social intricacies of Cranford while, at the same time, questioning their logic and function. On the other hand, this narrative persona contributes to the novel's narrative complexity surrounding conventions. Gillooly argues that although as a character Mary is "disembodied" (117), or difficult to locate, Mary's narrative persona shapes the narrative structure such that there is a repetition of "linguistic clusters" and associations filtered through Mary's perspective (131). Like Gillooly, I also want to emphasize Mary's important narrative role. I argue that her narrative style not only provides instruction in the town's system of etiquette but also, and more important, in how social practices are codified through repetition. For as Gaskell captures the town's rhythms, routines, and rules in Mary's descriptions of Cranford daily life, she employs a narrative mode that is similar to one that the numerous etiquette books, household manuals, and how-to handbooks that were published in the mid-to-late nineteenth century use in their codification of social experience.

We would now call this technique "iterative narrative," a mode of description that creates the impression that a certain narrative event is customary. As Mieke Bal explains, iterative "scenes frequently present an event in extenso as an example of a whole series of such events" (105). In other words, iterative narratives are characterized by their ability to imply that a single description is representative of a larger pattern of behavior. In a handbook, a description of the conventions for hosting a formal dinner would be an iterative narrative, for what is narrated once ostensibly describes a routine occurrence. In a novel, a dinner ritual that presumably takes place every Sunday but is narrated once in detail would also be iterative. Although both novels and handbooks convey routine behaviors, handbooks are particularly prone to iterative narrative in that their descriptions have as their very purpose articulating the customary ways of comporting oneself in the social world.

Yet, like a handbook, Gaskell's novel is also especially prone to iterative narrative. On the very first page of the serialized version of *Cranford,* in Mary's narration of the unwritten code for behavior in the town of Cranford, Gaskell provides the following iterative description. In doing so, she illuminates how behaviors become routine in the town of Cranford through recurrent dialogue: "Then there were rules and regulations for visiting and calls; and they were announced to any young people, who might be staying in the town, with all the solemnity with which the old Manx laws were read once a year on the Tinwald Mount" (2). In this remark, Gaskell suggests that the "rules and regulations" are perennial, passed down from one generation to the next. Since the rules are conveyed on an individual basis by means of dialogue, it may seem as if they are merely personal advice. After all, the rules are not "announced" all at once but rather when appropriate, that is, when a situation arises for which the Cranfordians have established a precedent that the visitor should be aware of.

Mary provides an example:

"Our friends have sent to inquire how you are after your journey to-night, my dear . . . [T]hey will give you some rest to-morrow, but the next day, I have no doubt, they will call; so be at liberty after twelve;-from twelve to three are our calling-hours."

(2)

Gaskell's use of dialogue, a basic narrative device, creates an effect that is similar to a handbook's narratives of conventions. Although this quotation may resemble friendly conversation, it is not attached to an individual person or scenario. Rather, it seems to be floating and timeless. This example's lack of a specific social context and confident assertion of what tends to happen in this social event are in keeping with the kind of iterative description that might be found in a handbook.

For while narratological definitions of dialogue suggest that it represents an oral exchange as it was uttered, here dialogue does not capture a particular speech.[10] Instead, it conveys a series of speeches, a customary type of speech, or a pattern of speech. The anonymous speaker in this example begins by describing a particular social situation: a visitor has arrived in town. Next, she informs the visitor of the protocol: one day of rest followed by a visit. By the end of the quotation, the speaker articulates the "regulation" behind her advice: "from twelve to three are our calling-hours." As the anonymous speaker's phrase, "I have no doubt," implies, the social activity of paying visits has been regularized in Cranford such that there is no element of surprise. The speaker, in turn, renders this social situation predictable for the visitor and for the reader. Mary's narration of the "rules and regulations" of Cranford transforms the novel into the very handbook the women of Cranford lack. It simultaneously provides the reader with an introduction to Cranford's social codes and a lesson in how they are disseminated.

I do not wish to imply, however, that the fictional world Gaskell creates is simply a pretext for elaborating social conventions for readers seeking instruction in propriety. To the extent that handbooks prescribe rules for visiting irrespective of a specific social context, *Cranford* functions differently. Not only does Gaskell people Cranford with idiosyncratic characters who have histories and long-standing relationships but also, and more important, she consistently tests conventions and examines their implications in her characters' lives. For example, whereas on the subject of the appropriate length of a visit the nineteenth-century household guide author Mrs. Beeton simply states, "These visits should be short, a stay of from fifteen to twenty minutes being quite sufficient" (10), Mary takes the advice a step further. After narrating one of the town's guidelines for visiting-"'you must keep thinking about the time, my dear, and not allow yourself to forget it in conversation'" (2)-she explains: "As everybody had this rule in their minds,

whether they received or paid a call, of course no absorbing subject was ever spoken about. We kept ourselves to short sentences of small talk, and were punctual to our time" (2-3). While this example may seem to imply that the women of Cranford are automatons who blindly follow precedent, they are extremely self-conscious about sustaining their code of social conduct.

The women of Cranford maintain their system of propriety through patterns of behavior and speech, which replicate the patterns in the novel's narrative structure. Mary explains one of the reasons for these patterns' continued existence: the collective "rules and regulations" for domestic rituals promise moral stability in the absence of economic security.

It was considered "vulgar" (a tremendous word in Cranford) to give anything expensive, in the way of eatable or drinkable, at the evening entertainments. Wafer bread-and-butter and sponge-biscuits were all that the Honourable Mrs. Jamieson gave; and she was sister-in-law to the late Earl of Glenmire, although she did practise such "elegant economy."

(3)

In referring to "the Hounourable Mrs. Jamieson" as the paradigmatic hostess, this passage suggests that the unwritten conventions for behavior circulate from the upper classes to the lower classes. In the absence of capital, the women of Cranford develop a manner of entertaining guests that seems "natural" and "elegant" to them. They do so primarily by fixating on certain foods as symbols of gentility and propriety. This process involves altering common meanings: re-signifying economical food such as "wafer bread-and-butter and sponge-biscuits" as elegant.

Gaskell makes this idea apparent when Mary describes the term "elegant economy" both as a social practice and as a part of the lexicon: "'Elegant economy!' How naturally one falls back into the phraseology of Cranford! There, economy was always 'elegant,' and money-spending always 'vulgar and ostentatious'" (3-4). The words "naturally" and "always" suggest that a routine is in place, one involving the kind of iteration that I am suggesting is part and parcel of a handbook's methodology. I want to emphasize, however, that this routine is a narrative one, just as it is in a handbook. The difference, of course, is that while in a handbook this narrative pattern is textual here it is oral: the habitual pairing of "economy" and "elegant" in the ladies' conversation assists them in pretending to believe that conserving their resources is a sign of sophistication. Throughout the novel, Gaskell implies that the process of maintaining social conventions requires a routine of collective dissembling through shared language and interpretation.

This iteration is not, however, without its challenges. *Cranford* is a novel and not simply a handbook to the extent that the rules for social behavior are constantly on the verge of being broken. For suspense, a novelistic device, depends upon an element of unpredictability. Chapter One, then, not only provides the town's rules and demonstrates their enactment but also presents a challenge to them in the character of Captain Brown.[11] Thus Gaskell introduces deviance as a theme in chapters that are nevertheless distinctly ritualized. As in the example of Chapter One, nearly every chapter proposes a theory of dining and visiting decorum that is subsequently put to the test, often when an outsider-usually a man or a person of another social class-enters town. While the novel is intently focused on the rituals of Cranford life, it also contains a series of unique social scenarios, or singulative narratives, that challenge the women's adherence to routine. In contrast to an iterative narrative, which describes what presumably occurs on a regular basis, a singulative narrative refers to a unique narrative event. A description of a particular dining event that took place on a single occasion and is presented once in detail would be singulative; or, as Mieke Bal succinctly explains, "one event, one presentation" (113). In each chapter, Gaskell tests the limits of the principles that the women of Cranford have tacitly agreed upon through singulative examples. For example, Chapter Three centers on the question: when Major Jenkyns comes to visit, will Matty know how to host a male guest? Chapter Four: when the ladies visit Mr. Holbrook, whose manners will they follow, his or theirs? Chapter Eight: when Lady Glenmire arrives, will the ladies be invited to visit Miss Jamieson's home? Chapter Ten: when robbers enter town, should the ladies still attend Mrs. Forrester's anniversary tea?

The very fact that questions of etiquette can become crises-the basis of plot-not only highlights the extraordinary meanings the rituals hold as symbols of morality and class but also emphasizes the rituals themselves. In narrative terms, on the occasions when Gaskell employs such singulative narratives as the ones above, she often does so in the context of the rituals she has elaborated through iterative narrative. In *Narrative Discourse,* Genette explains a subtlety of the way in which iterative and singulative narrative can work together that helps explain the way in which these plot events that challenge the ladies' rituals function in the novel: "through the play of *once*'s, *one day*'s, etc., the singulative itself is to some extent *integrated* into the iterative, compelled to serve and illustrate it, positively or negatively, either by respecting its code or by transgressing it, which is another way of manifesting it" (140). According to Genette, deviance does not necessarily undermine a novel's overall effect of routinization. Rather, as Genette's explanation clarifies, it can help contribute to it by highlighting the routine from which it departs.

For example, when Mrs. Forrester's maid nearly puts her tea party in crisis by revealing the household's limited means, the event nonetheless serves as an opportunity for Mary to emphasize the standard tea party ritual. After providing the iterative statement-"We none of us spoke of money, because that subject savoured of commerce and trade, and though some might be poor, we were all aristocratic"—Mary provides the following singulative narrative as evidence:

> When Mrs. Forrester, for instance, gave a party in her baby-house of a dwelling, and the little maiden disturbed the ladies on the sofa by a request that she might get the tea-tray out from underneath, every one took this novel proceeding as the most natural thing in the world; and talked on about household forms and ceremonies, as if we all believed that our hostess had a regular servants' hall, second table, with housekeeper and steward; instead of the one little charity-school maiden, whose short ruddy arms could never have been strong enough to carry the tray up-stairs, if she had not been assisted in private by her mistress, who now sat in state, pretending not to know what cakes were sent up; though she knew, and we knew, and she knew that we knew, and we knew that she knew that we knew, she had been busy all the morning making tea-bread and sponge-cakes.

(3)

This example demonstrates how a deviant event, or "novel proceeding," can nevertheless be seen as "the most natural thing in the world." It is highly significant that the women of Cranford often discuss social practices even and especially when they are participating in social events. The fact that "household forms and ceremonies" serve as the basis of the women's conversation while a household ceremony takes place not only emphasizes the orality and repetition involved in sustaining Cranford's system of etiquette. It also suggests that by turning to "forms and ceremonies" as "subjects of conversation," particularly in times of social crisis, the ladies regularly provide alternative presentations of events that emphasize the convention they would like to believe in.[12] In other words, as I am arguing, their language ensures that unprecedented events nonetheless exemplify their routine.

These routines dominate in Cranford even if there is brazen evidence to contradict their logic. The phrase, "she knew, and we knew, and she knew that we knew, and we knew that she knew that we knew," highlights the disparity between what the women know and the story they tell. To the extent that the conventions are devoid of "natural" meanings in and of themselves and require conversation to support them, Gaskell suggests that in order for a behavior to acquire symbolic social significance, consensus is required. Complicit in the act of maintaining the fiction of gentility, the others know the truth behind Mrs. Forrester's performance because they share the same set of dissembling behaviors.

"And after dinner, how am I to know when to get up, and leave him to his wine? Deborah would have done it so well."

Miss Matty,

Cranford

While throughout *Cranford* Gaskell represents habits of behavior and speech as contributing to the maintenance of conventions, she also examines how practices proceed from being idiosyncratic to routine or, in narrative terms, from singulative to iterative. She figures the "imaginary pattern of excellence," the shared code of living that shapes life in Cranford, as emanating from individuals' preferences, most often Deborah Jenkyns's. While Miss Jenkyns's role as arbiter of propriety accounts for much of the novel's humor, her character also serves an important narrative function in that she enables Gaskell to explore further where conventions originate and how they endure. One particularly good example of Miss Jenkyns's dual comic and narrative role is her repeated interference with others' eating preferences. Mary describes one instance when Miss Jenkyns imposes her notions of proper diet upon another: "she brought Miss Jessie up a basin of delicately-made arrowroot, and stood over her like a dragoon until the last spoonful was finished: then she disappeared" (20). In this example, Miss Jenkyns physically hovers over Miss Jessie. Yet, Gaskell's point is that she stands "like a dragoon" even when she has "disappeared." Though her physical presence may be fleeting, Miss Jenkyns is a lasting presence that exerts a palpable influence over others' behaviors. Miss Jenkyns is only alive in the present moment of the narrative in the first two chapters, but her influence can be seen throughout the remaining fourteen.

Gaskell implies the extent to which individual eating behavior is informed by others in the following iterative narrative about a ritualistic way of eating oranges. Put another way, this example focuses upon the routinization of an eccentric dining practice:

> When oranges came in, a curious proceeding was gone through. Miss Jenkyns did not like to cut the fruit; for, as she observed, the juice all ran out nobody knew where; sucking (only I think she used some more recondite word) was in fact the only way of enjoying oranges; but then there was the unpleasant association with a ceremony frequently gone through by little babies; and so, after dessert, in orange season, Miss Jenkyns and Miss Matty used to rise up, possess themselves each of an orange in silence, and withdraw to the privacy of their own rooms, to indulge in sucking oranges.
>
> (26)

In this example, Gaskell examines how what could be considered public behavior—eating an orange at the dinner table—is relegated to the private realm, the bed-room, as a direct result of the interference of Miss Jenkyns. The word "curious proceeding" implies the bizarre and indeed humorous way in which ritual resignifies the meaning of individual behavior. On the one hand, Miss Jenkyns's regulations turn a dinner table act into a bedroom act. On the other hand, it is the very possibility of the dinner table act being read as a bodily act that creates a situation in which Miss Jenkyns would need to regulate it.

This passage is a mini-narrative of how a ritual comes into being, including its rationale, its potential problems, and its solution. First, as Mary reports, Miss Jenkyns notices a possible disconnection between social decorum and orange-eating. The wayward juice and the unintended "sucking" associations are unsuited for the dining room and thus become channeled toward an even more private domain within the private. In dramatizing the synchronous nature of the two women's actions ("Miss Jenkyns and Miss Matty used to rise up"), Gaskell brings the reader full circle to the point at which an arbitrary convention has become second nature. It is important to note, however, that this narrative is marked by a gap: Gaskell does not narrate the specific process by which Miss Jenkyns was able to turn a personal preference into a dining convention. She simply states the preference ("Miss Jenkyns did not like to cut the fruit") and the result ("and so"). Rather than narrate this nonnarratable aspect of sociality, Gaskell moves on to narrate yet another subtlety of convention-making: the conventions sometimes predominate in the absence of a model more visibly than in its presence.

The private sucking ritual continues after Miss Jenkyns's death, as do most of her other laughable regulations. James Mulvihill explains that the Cranford ladies' habits endure because they have greater moral significance. He theorizes the subtle changes in the meaning of the word "economy" over the course of the nineteenth century—from referring to a private household system to a large-scale system of production—and suggests that Gaskell conceptualizes economy in the earlier sense in which the moral and the material would be yoked (342). Thus, even and especially when the Jenkyns women lose their money as a result of a bad speculation, their routines prevail. A narrative-based explanation for the way in which particular social behaviors endure in the novel would be that the narrative patterns mimic the patterns of the ladies' routines; as the striking repetition of the words "always," "constantly," and "used to" suggests, by representing the perpetuation of social conventions regardless of whether they are viable, *Cranford* draws attention to the iteration involved in sociality.

Mary explains how "Miss Jenkyns's rules were made more stringent than ever" (26) after her death in the following example. This passage is doubly iterative in that both the opening statement and the iterative narrative, or "instance," that Mary provides are suggestive of a repetitive behavior:

> Many a domestic rule and regulation had been a subject of plaintive whispered murmur to me, during Miss Jenkyns's life; but now that she was gone, I do not think that even I, who was a favourite, durst have suggested an alternation. To give an instance: we constantly adhered to the forms which were observed, at meal times, in "my father, the Rector's house." Accordingly, we had always wine and dessert; but the decanters were only filled when there was a party; and what remained was seldom touched, though we had two wine glasses apiece every day after dinner, until the next festive occasion arrived; when the state of the remainder wine was examined into, in a family council.
>
> (25)

One of the appeals of perpetuating her sister's practices and ideals is that it is a means by which Miss Matty can assert her family identity; Matty is a Jenkyns to the extent that she "observes" the "forms" that her sister preserved from her father's time.[13] As the words "constantly" and "always" imply, custom offers reliability to one's daily life even when death alters one's surroundings. In and of itself, reliable behavior is not necessarily meaningful, however. Although Matty and Mary go through the routine of a family dinner, it is what Gillooly would call an "empty ritual" (122), as symbolized by the empty wine glasses. In the end, the automatic nature of custom empties it of significance, for Matty does not continue Miss Jenkyns's rituals because she has a preference for them but because she does not know what else to do.

Matty is so reliant upon her sister's mode of comporting herself that crisis ensues when an unexpected behavior arises for which she does not know her sister's routine.

> "Oh! how must I manage?" asked she, helplessly. "If Deborah had been alive, she would have known what to do with a gentleman visitor. Must I put razors in his dressing-room? Dear! dear! and I've got none. Deborah would have had them. . . . And after dinner, how am I to know when to get up, and leave him to his wine? Deborah would have done it so well."
>
> (27)

Matty's repetition of Deborah's name after each problem suggests an anxious return to Deborah as a repository of etiquette and implies a weakness of individual authority. Matty is unable to proceed without a formal paradigm for each social behavior. It is as if the missing piece of her sister's social code—how to comport oneself around men—manifests itself as a void in Matty's imagination. Mary helps Matty avert this crisis by devising a step-by-step process for managing the guests. Singulative moments such as this one do not simply demonstrate the perils of excessive reliance on routine. Rather, they enable Gaskell to narrate the social process by which a new routine is created.

Another example of how new routines are created owing to a distinctive social event occurs at a dinner at Mr. Holbrook's house. Gaskell narrates a difference between Matty's and Mary's reliance on convention by means of a singulative narrative that describes their dining comportment.

> When the ducks and green peas came, we looked at each other in dismay; we had only two-pronged, black-handled forks. . . . What were we to do? Miss Matty picked up her peas, one by one, on the point of the prongs. . . . Miss Pole sighed over her delicate young peas as she left them on her plate untasted; for they would drop between the prongs. I looked at my host: the peas were going wholesale into his capacious mouth, shoveled up by his large round-ended knife. I saw, I imitated, I survived! My friends, in spite of my precedent, could not muster up courage enough to do an ungenteel thing; and, if Mr. Holbrook had not been so heartily hungry, he would probably have seen that the good peas went away almost untasted.
>
> (33)

In a sense, the conflict of table manners in this scene elucidates the extent to which social routines can appear to be unbreakable codes. In Genette's terms, this scene demonstrates that "transgressing" the code can be "another way of manifesting it" (140). Yet by asking, "What were we to do?," Mary's narrative involves the reader in this crisis of table manners and asks him or her to participate in a possible solution. This passage can also inspire the innocent reader to ask the question, how do *I* eat peas?, as the more knowing reader laughs at the inside joke and understands the nonnarrated complexities of just how mortified Miss Matty and Miss Pole might feel.

Although Mary's use of the pronoun "we" connotes a collective experience, the passage includes three different responses, ranging from semi-resourceful (Matty) to paralyzed (Miss Pole) to courageous (Mary). Whereas Matty is "helpless" without Deborah, Mary is willing to act according to what makes sense to her, even if she commits what some would consider a faux pas. As an outsider to Cranford, Mary is more resilient than the others, and hence able to shift her behavior to suit different social scenarios. The repetition of the pronoun "I," particularly in the final declaration "I survived," is in marked contrast to Matty's habitual repetition of the name "Deborah." For it suggests that one can create a new narrative of table manners. Mary's exclamation, "I saw, I imitated, I survived!", is a testimony that etiquette can change as long as one reconsiders one's social assumptions, such as the automatic pairing together of the label "ungenteel" with the practice of eating with one's knife.

In Mary's case, this challenge to an established dining habit suggests that unique social scenarios require re-evaluations of one's ideas about gentility. Nevertheless, it is important to emphasize that Mary does not invent the idea of eating peas with a knife. Rather, she does so after observing her host's behavior and deciding that, under the circumstances, his way is best. Ultimately, then, the tension between the two different perspectives on conventions in this scene—Mary's willingness to change her manners and the older women's inability to—points to two different forms of repetition. While Mary's decision to mimic Mr. Holbrook conveys an impromptu type of repetition and Matty and Miss Pole's adherence to their own codes suggests a repetition rooted in fixity, the two competing models nonetheless demonstrate how the social process of sustaining conventions is grounded in repetition.

Gaskell demonstrates that concepts that people assume to be moral truths are ideas, creations of tacit social agreements that, when repeated, take on the appearance of truth. Although rituals may not have absolute referents and may be products of a shared social process, they are nonetheless meaningful signs in Gaskell's narrative. When Mary describes Mrs. Forrester's decision to bequeath her "receipt" for "bread-jelly" to Miss Matty after her death (104), she captures the salient nature of social routines both in the town and the novel. Building on Dolin's suggestion that Cranford's "most valuable currency is language, and 'happenings' become important only in their exchangeable form, as stories" (200), I want to suggest that eating rituals have currency in **Cranford**.[14] In addition to being the means by which the ladies of Cranford express their class position, eating routines bear an important relationship to the stories they exchange; these routines engender narrative, not only by means of the introduction of suspense, the basis of plot, but also in more literal ways. An example of this idea occurs when a borrowed cookery book serves as a pretext for Miss Pole to acquire knowledge about one of the novel's biggest scandals, whether Lady Glenmire is going to marry Mr. Hoggins. While dining rituals provide a social opportunity for exchanging stories, in this example a dining-related object plays a structural role in the revelation of a story. As such, dining rituals can be seen to have narrative import both for the inhabitants of Cranford and for the novel itself, much as the repetitive nature of the social conventions the ladies embrace has an analogue in the narrative methods used to convey them.

As I have shown, on the one hand, through the narrator's perspective of insider-outsider Gaskell queries the extent to which repetition is involved in sustaining the town's rituals. On the other hand, the repetition that organizes the novel generates the rhythm of routine, as does the frequent use of iterative narrative. Furthermore, even when Gaskell's narrator presents singulative narratives, or idiosyncratic stories regarding deviance from the town's social routines, such moments can work in the service of iterative narrative. For such stories often function to highlight the persistence of those very routines that are momentarily in peril. Thus, although Mary's narration may suggest that Cranford's social practices are financially untenable or morally ridiculous, a premium is put on maintaining the ritual-either through thematic elements or, more interesting, at the level of narrative effects. This insight suggests that the narrative devices of novels can perpetuate the very concept that they question. Yet, this perpetuation of conventions occurs in another sense as well, for Gaskell figures codification as exciting by repeatedly using it as the basis of plot. In Gaskell's hands, questions related to manners such as "what fork will she use?" take on the urgency of the most sensational material. Ironically, the very fact that such issues are routine within Gaskell's narrative also highlights the notion that the conventions themselves are persistently in question.

Notes

1. For a discussion of the form of *Cranford* and its original publication in *Household Words,* see Huett. For further discussion of *Cranford*'s unique narrative structure, see Croskery, Gillooly, Schor, and Miller.

2. Miller also notes the importance of daily routines to the novel's structure. He suggests that the cyclical, or repetitive, structure "has eluded the appreciation of critics accustomed to considering linear stories" (93).

3. For more on this issue, see Watson, who suggests that the novel offers a "persistent criticism of snobbishness" (xix). See also Dolin, who writes that *Cranford* is "a caricature of (comfortable middle-class female) everyday life in Victorian England" (195).

4. The difference in the interpretive frame that Armstrong and I use lies, first and foremost, in Armstrong's espousal of a Foucauldian perspective. Borrowing the Foucauldian idea that discourse constructs ideology, Armstrong argues that the conduct book and the domestic novel constitute the notion of the household as a distinctly "feminine space." According to Armstrong, this ideal of the household not only takes hold in the subjectivity of readers (providing them with ideas about sexuality), but it also provides a form of regulation of individual identities and spaces that works in the service of a larger political agenda (such as capitalism).

5. For further discussion of how iterative narrative works in nineteenth-century social instruction handbooks, see Meir. For a theoretical discussion

of iterative narrative as well as on a contrasting mode, singulative narrative, see Prince and Genette, especially Chapter Three.

6. While I regard *Cranford* as a narrative that shares features with handbooks and novels—both in terms of content and narrative devices—I am aware of the problems that arise from making narrative features conform to contemporary definitions that act as norms. Thus, I embrace a more flexible understanding of how genres are "formed of several networks of partial resemblances" that overlap (Schaeffer 175). For further discussion of this conception of genre, see Schaeffer. For further discussion of Gaskell's use of traditional narrative forms in innovative ways, see Hughes and Lund.

7. Tarratt also notes that the novel investigates the genesis of the town's idiosyncratic habits and rightly attributes many of the town's practices to Miss Jenkyns (154). However, our approaches are distinct given that I focus upon how these habits are constituted and perpetuated through particular narrative devices.

8. In his discussion of American school editions of *Cranford* in the early twentieth-century, Recchio also suggests that the novel "serves as a kind of conduct book" (607).

9. Other critics have noted that Mary's status as visiting outsider provides her with the ability to offer a unique perspective on the town. See Gillooly, Dolin, Mulvihill, and Watson.

10. For example, Prince explains dialogue as follows: "The representation (dramatic in type) of an oral exchange involving two or more characters. In dialogue, the characters' speeches are presented as they (supposedly) were uttered" (20).

11. Other critics have discussed Captain Brown's challenge to Cranford's "strict code of gentility." See Gillooly 124 and Huett 42.

12. In her discussion of this scene, Gillooly makes a similar point by focusing instead on the women's silence. She argues that the "restricted" nature of the women's discourse is an attempt to avoid the "stark character of reality" (123). Mulvihill also discusses the Cranfordians' habit of "turning a blind eye to the arrangements necessary to maintain social amenities" (344).

13. See Gillooly for further discussion of the relationship between social codes and patriarchal law in the novel.

14. Mulvihill plays upon the double meaning of the word "store" to suggest that the ladies of Cranford manage anecdotes in much the same way that they might conserve provisions. In doing so, he begins to imply an important relationship between food and narrative as objects in the private economy of the novel.

Works Cited

Armstrong, Nancy. *Desire and Domestic Fiction: A Political History of the Novel.* New York: Oxford UP, 1987.

Bal, Mieke. *Narratology: Introduction to the Theory of Narrative.* 2nd ed. Toronto: U of Toronto P, 1997.

Beeton, Isabella. *Beeton's Book of Household Management.* London: S. O. Beeton, 1861. Facsim. ed. London: Jonathan Cape, 1968.

Croskery, Margaret Case. "Mothers without Children, Unity without Plot: *Cranford*'s Radical Charm." *Nineteenth-Century Literature* 52 (1997): 198-220.

Dolin, Tim. "*Cranford* and the Victorian Collection." *Victorian Studies* 36 (1993): 179-206.

Gaskell, Elizabeth. *Cranford.* (1851-53). Ed. Elizabeth Porges Watson. New York: Oxford UP, 1998.

Genette, Gerard. *Narrative Discourse: An Essay in Method.* Trans. Jane Lewin. Ithaca, NY: Cornell UP, 1980.

Gillooly, Eileen. "Humor as Daughterly Defense in *Cranford.*" *The Victorian Comic Spirit: New Perspectives.* Ed. Jennifer A. Wagner-Lawlor. Aldershot, England: Ashgate, 2000. 115-40.

Huett, Lorna. "Commodity and Collectivity: *Cranford* in the Context of *Household Words.*" *Gaskell Society Journal* 17 (2003): 34-49.

Hughes, Linda and Michael Lund. *Victorian Publishing and Mrs. Gaskell's Work.* Charlottesville: UP of Virginia, 1999.

Meir, Natalie Kapetanios. "'A fashionable dinner is arranged as follows': Victorian Dining Taxonomies." *Victorian Literature and Culture* 33 (2005). 133-48.

Miller, Andrew. "The Fragments and Small Opportunities of *Cranford.*" *Novels Behind Glass: Commodity Culture and Victorian Narrative.* Ed. Andrew Miller. New York: Cambridge UP, 1995. 91-118.

Mulvihill, James. "Economies of Living in Mrs. Gaskell's *Cranford.*" *Nineteenth-Century Literature* 50 (1995): 337-66.

Prince, Gerald. *A Dictionary of Narratology.* Lincoln, NE: U of Nebraska P, 1987.

Recchio, Thomas. "'Charming and Sane': School Editions of *Cranford* in America, 1905-1914." *Victorian Studies* 45 (2003): 597-623.

Schaeffer, Jean-Marie. "Literary Genres and Textual Genericity." *The Future of Literary Theory*. Ed. Ralph Cohen. New York: Routledge, 1989. 167-87.

Schor, Hilary. "Affairs of the Alphabet: Reading, Writing and Narrating in *Cranford*." *Novel* 22 (1989): 288-304.

Tarratt, Margaret. "*Cranford* and the Strict Code of Gentility." *Essays in Criticism* 18 (1968): 152-63.

Watson, Elizabeth Porges. Introduction. *Cranford*. By Elizabeth Gaskell. New York: Oxford UP, 1998.

Susan E. Colón (essay date October 2006)

SOURCE: Colón, Susan E. "Professional Frontiers in Elizabeth Gaskell's *My Lady Ludlow*." *Women's Writing* 13, no. 3 (October 2006): 475-94.

[*In the following essay, Colón describes how Gaskell anticipates feminist notions of the empowering aspects of professional pursuits for women through her support for the rising power of the professional—versus aristocratic—society in* My Lady Ludlow.]

After more than a century in which Elizabeth Gaskell was taken for an uncomplicated celebrant of conservative ideology, it has now become a commonplace in Gaskell gender studies to find that the author's work is subversive of patriarchal orthodoxies.[1] Gaskell's class politics have been more contested, with most but not all critics continuing to see her class politics as essentially conservative.[2] Neither debate has much invoked the 1858 novel *My Lady Ludlow.* Besides the peculiar character of Miss Galindo, a meddling but kindly spinster who works as a clerk for a short time, the novel has apparently offered but little illumination for critics working on class and gender issues. Set at the eponymous countess's ancestral seat of Hanbury during the Regency, *My Lady Ludlow* has at times an idyllic feel that makes it seem an unlikely place to look for progressive political views. Moreover, the long inset narrative told by Lady Ludlow, decrying the excesses of the French Reign of Terror, seems to establish the book's conservative, if not reactionary, outlook.[3]

The novel's gently nostalgic depiction of the waning of aristocratic power is self-evident and frequently remarked upon[4], but what has not been adequately recognized is the shape of the specific class structure which comes to replace the aristocracy, and the relationship of that class structure to both the gender and class orthodoxies of Gaskell's time. I argue that the novel represents a shift from traditional aristocratic hegemony to that of a professional meritocracy, while at the same time challenging the assumption of middle-class male superiority that the new meritocracy tended to privilege. The aristocratic ideal of Lady Ludlow, according to which birth is absolute and essential, gives way to the meritocratic and inclusive professional ideal of the vicar Mr Gray and the land agent Captain James. According to Gaskell's formulation of this ideal, prejudices against women, the working class and those of illegitimate birth are discredited and dismissed. Thus, Gaskell's text demonstrates the potential for inclusiveness in the professional ideal, which she represents as open, even to groups formerly marginalized by gender and birth status.

What I call professional logic or rationality is the fundamental notion that mental skills are a form of capital—a scarce resource that can command a "rent" in the strict Ricardian sense of the word.[5] Thus, capital is not only to be found in land, in the means of manufacture and in financial assets, but also within the heads of trained individuals. Professionals themselves would naturally have it that this human capital is the nation's most valuable asset. The professional ideal is the belief that leadership in all the social domains is best held and exercised by a class of people who are trained in specialized and esoteric expertise, who are meritocratically selected, and who are motivated not by monetary gain but by their intrinsic desire to serve the public by holding to the highest standards of their guild.[6] Professional logic has several easily recognizable corollaries; three are of special significance in *My Lady Ludlow.* First, an individual's standing at birth is of no lasting consequence; merit alone, defined in terms of both mental and moral qualities, should be the sole determinant of an individual's professional success. Second, increasing the human capital of an individual or of an entire class by means of education is a good investment for society. To fail to educate an intelligent person is to waste potentially valuable human capital. Third, the holders of human capital must be autonomous agents, acting according to their trained judgment and internalized ethical code, and holding such considerations above traditional notions of social rank.

This professional logic prevails in the contest between Lady Ludlow's traditionalism and the emergent order represented by the novel's professionals. Given Gaskell's own position in the professional class, it is perhaps no surprise to find that she subscribes to this set of ideals. What is remarkable, however, is that she takes this logic to the subversive conclusion that a true meritocracy should be blind to considerations of birth and gender. Hence the triumph of professional rationality, as played out in the book, is accompanied by the expansion of the professional class to accommodate women, workers and the illegitimately born. Gaskell's warmly nostalgic novel subtly draws on professional assumptions to make progressive claims for gender and class egalitarianism in the public sphere.

Moreover, Gaskell's republication of the novel in *Round the Sofa* (1859), in which she sets *My Lady Ludlow* and a few short stories within a fictional frame, brings the professional transformation of society described in the novel into the reader's present. This frame, which concerns a young woman who hears and transcribes the text of *My Lady Ludlow* from an elderly friend, shows the contemporaneous application of the professional logic that unfolds in the main story. It makes clear that in this novel, the first significant fiction Gaskell wrote after finishing *The Life of Charlotte Brontë* (1857), the relationship of women to esoteric and remunerative labor, particularly authorship, is very much on Gaskell's agenda.

This article will first analyse Lady Ludlow and her changing relationships with professionals in order to illuminate the role that professional logic plays in the social transformations of the novel. Closer study of the characters of Miss Galindo and Harry Gregson, a laboring boy, will then illuminate the interplay of work, class and gender that gives this account of professional hegemony its particularly progressive turn. Finally, I will explore the parallels between the frame story and the characters and events in the main story in order to illuminate the book's embedded commentary about women's progress in the mid-Victorian professional economy.

I

To understand the social transformations wrought by the professionals, it is first necessary to understand the a-priori aristocratic status quo upon which they work. That status quo is personified by Lady Ludlow. Reigning with unquestioned supremacy over Hanbury in 1811, Lady Ludlow embodies the aristocratic ideal of paternalistic grandeur based on heredity. Already old, Lady Ludlow has lost her husband and eight of her nine children by the time the narrator Margaret Dawson goes to live with her. Certain that class is essence, Lady Ludlow seeks to save shabby-genteel women like Margaret from slipping to a station lower than that to which their birth and breeding entitle them; she is equally vigilant to prevent any low-born individuals from raising their social position. The poor must not be taught to read, she believes, because education will make them prone to challenge their social superiors. Those whose birth is not sanctioned by marriage are even less privileged: the illegitimately born must not be recognized, because they "had no legal right to exist at all".[7] Margaret recalls: "My Lady Ludlow could not endure any mention of illegitimate children. It was a principle of hers that society ought to ignore them" (194). Lady Ludlow's fixation on class and birth, interestingly enough, translates into a singular disregard for mere wealth or poverty, or for gender, as we will see.

Lady Ludlow's aristocratic notions are represented by Margaret in a usually reverent tone that only occasionally approaches gentle satire. One such moment occurs when Lady Ludlow urges on Margaret that the ability to perceive certain scents is hereditary in the aristocracy. Naturally, she feels, the pure blood of the aristocratic class engenders a keenness of sense unheard of among the masses, just as is the case with pure-bred bloodhounds. It may be significant that the smell she urges Margaret to perceive by way of proving Margaret's slight proportion of noble blood is the autumnal scent of decaying strawberry leaves. Lady Ludlow can pick out this fragrance on the evening breeze, but she is slow to realize the decay of the aristocracy itself, perhaps symbolized by the leaves that make up a ducal coronet.

For all that Lady Ludlow's notions occasionally border on the ridiculous, even in Margaret's eyes, Margaret ensures that the reader's picture of Lady Ludlow is one of almost unmitigated good. In her abundant charity to the needy, her perfect hospitality to high and low, and her unselfish dignity, Lady Ludlow earns and keeps the goodwill of all the inhabitants of her little village.[8] The common folk adore her for her hereditary associations combined with her gracious mien. Miss Galindo tells the countess:

> Your ancestors have lived here time out of mind, and have owned the land on which their forefathers have lived ever since there were forefathers. You yourself were born amongst them, and have been like a little queen to them ever since, I might say, and they've never known your ladyship do anything but what was kind and gentle.
>
> (162)

Lady Ludlow maintains the spectacle of aristocratic grandeur and reserve somehow without hauteur; she sincerely regards that spectacle as the duty of her station, which she fulfills with personal humility. Margaret observes that:

> [. . .] great as was my lady's liking and approval of respect, nay, even reverence, being paid to her as a person of quality—a sort of tribute to her Order, which she had no individual right to remit, or, indeed, not to exact—yet she, being personally simple, sincere, and holding herself in low esteem, could not endure anything like [. . .] servility.
>
> (160)

Lady Ludlow represents, in short, the idealized premodern aristocracy, offered with only a shade of irony.

At the beginning of the novel, Lady Ludlow holds the status of patroness in relation to the professionals around her, particularly the vicar and the land agent. The clergyman Mr Mountford had been appointed because he "had won his lordship's [the late Lord Ludlow's] favour by his excellent horsemanship" (22), not, be it noted, for any particular competence or zeal in his professional tasks. Indeed, his role as parish priest seems secondary to his position as a country gentleman: the dominant interests of his life are those of the palate and the stable. Mr Mountford is generous in aid to the poor but keeps his distance from them as much as possible, with the result that, according to his successor, the inhabitants of Hanbury are as woefully ignorant of Christian teaching as they are of worldly instruction. Lady Ludlow does not scruple to command Mr Mountford, even in the performance of his clerical duties. On Sundays when she is not disposed to hear a sermon, the countess routinely announces: "I will not trouble you for a discourse this morning" (20). Mr Mountford always complies without murmuring, apparently without concern for the spiritual edification of the other parishioners. In traditional Hanbury, both countess and parson tacitly understand that the clergyman is at the service of—and takes all his cues from—his patroness. As long as she is pleased, he considers he has no further duty to perform for the parish.

Lady Ludlow's land steward Mr Horner behaves toward his mistress in a similarly old-fashioned way. Mr Horner, almost as old as Lady Ludlow and thoroughly imbued with a feudal view of class relations, regards himself essentially as an upper servant, whose task it is to carry out Lady Ludlow's orders about the estate. Lady Ludlow manages many of her own affairs about her land and her tenantry, usually basing her decisions on the "hereditary sense of right and wrong between landlord and tenant" (175), which is frequently at a variance with "mere worldly and business calculations" (153). She manages the estate the same way it was done in her father's time, considering that continuity with the old ways is more valuable than newfangled improvements. The result is that the land is badly mismanaged: crops are not rotated, fertilizer is not used, rents are not always collected and the land produces well below capacity. The mortgage taken out years ago to fund improvements to Lord Ludlow's estates in Scotland drains Hanbury's resources yet cannot be repaid. Mr Horner, however, was once a clerk to a London attorney, and he brings to Hanbury an early whiff of the professional ideal. Like Mr Mountford's successor Mr Gray, Mr Horner deplores the ignorance of the estate workers, as we shall see shortly.

Thus, the opening picture of Hanbury is only superficially wholesome. The idyllic stability of the hereditary estate masks actual instability and weakness born of the poor use of resources, both human and real. The successors to Mr Mountford and Mr Horner bring to their tasks a professional ethos that collides with Lady Ludlow's sense of hereditary privilege. However, those collisions issue decisively in the good of the community, as the founding of a ragged school and the implementation of modern farming methods revitalize the sinking estate.

Mr Gray, the new vicar, belongs to the new order of professional, zealous and diligent clergy. He is committed to his religious duty to the exclusion of all considerations of rank. He single-mindedly, humbly and courageously works towards the spiritual regeneration of the parishioners, especially the poor and even the extraparochial squatters. His evangelical leanings are seen in his willingness to pray in parishioners' homes, his encouragement of Bible reading, and especially in his desire to found a "Sabbath school" for poor children.[9] When Lady Ludlow tries to silence Mr Gray's sermon on Sabbath schools, as she had routinely silenced Mr Mountford's sermons in the past, he ignores her and preaches his sermon anyway. On another occasion the clergyman tells his lady that "he was bound to remember that he was under the bishop's authority, not under [Lady Ludlow's]" (59). In other words, Mr Gray's professional hierarchy is pre-eminent over his social hierarchy.

Although Mr Gray defers to Lady Ludlow on matters not touching his duty, he does not hesitate to incur her displeasure if necessary in following his professional judgment. Their first confrontation occurs when Mr Gray pleads with Lady Ludlow to intervene in the wrongful imprisonment of an innocent man—a man, however, with a criminal record. Lady Ludlow refuses, using her characteristic assumptions of class essentialism to regard the gentlemen's agreement of the magistrates as more important than the actual fact of guilt or innocence of the accused. She tells Mr Gray:

> I may wonder whether a young man of your age and position has any right to assume that he is a better judge than one with the experience which I have naturally gained at my time of life, and in the station I hold.
>
> (33)

Mr Gray's position is equally in character:

> [. . .] it may be my duty to speak to my parishioners on many subjects on which they do not agree with me. [. . .] If I, madam, am not to shrink from telling what I believe to be the truth to the poor and lowly, no more am I to hold my peace in the presence of the rich and titled.
>
> (33)

In Mr Gray's mind, the demands of professional duty pre-empt considerations of age and status.

The most serious disagreement between the conscientious clergyman and the arch-traditionalist, though, concerns the school Mr Gray desires to found for the benefit of poor children. Lady Ludlow is convinced that teaching the lower orders to read and write is the first step toward a peasants' revolution. She repeats the classic formulation of the paternalistic aristocracy: education "unfits the lower orders for their duties, the duties to which they are called by God; of submission to those placed in authority over them" (149). Lady Ludlow sees a direct chain of causality from popular literacy to regicide.[10]

Both Mr Gray and Mr Horner resist in different ways and for different reasons Lady Ludlow's reactionary views on education. Dismayed at the spiritual degeneration of the laborers' children, Mr Gray hopes that basic literacy education will train the children to higher thoughts and thereby facilitate their receptivity to spiritual instruction as well. For his part, Mr Horner keenly regrets the waste of human resources under the current practice of keeping the estate workers ignorant. Earnestly and faithfully desirous of his lady's prosperity, Mr Horner

> [. . .] wanted to make every man useful and active in this world, and to direct as much activity and usefulness as possible to the improvement of the Hanbury estates. [. . .] Mr Horner [. . .] hoped for a day-school at some future time, to train up intelligent labourers for working on the estate.
>
> (52-53)

Since this aim is impossible given Lady Ludlow's decided opposition, Mr Horner contents himself with identifying the cleverest boy he can find among the local poor and teaching him to read, "with a view to making use of him as a kind of foreman in process of time" (53). This boy, the son of none other than the ne'er-do-well poacher Job Gregson, becomes deeply attached to his reserved master. Mr Horner's small experiment in embourgeoisement is aborted, as we will see shortly, but it indicates his partial adherence to professional meritocratic logic.

As Mr Mountford was replaced by a clergyman with a professional mentality, so Mr Horner is replaced after his death with a steward who takes a professional approach to the management of the countess's estate. Captain James is chosen for the post because of a past connection with Lady Ludlow's dead son, who was once in the navy. When Mr Smithson, the family solicitor, protests that a sailor cannot manage land, Lady Ludlow's perseverance testifies to her belief that hereditary connections are more important than mere expertise.

From that inauspicious beginning, however, Captain James proves to be, like Mr Gray, an adherent to a professional paradigm. He seeks specialized training, acts autonomously and disregards traditional class boundaries. He intends to "set to in good earnest and study

agriculture, and see how he could remedy the state of things" (197). Not content, like Lady Ludlow, to do things the way they have always been done, Captain James experiments ambitiously, fails and then experiments again more cautiously. In performing his experimental reforms, he seeks advice from the neighboring (successful) farmer, who is, to Lady Ludlow's horror, a Baptist who purchased the estate with the proceeds of his successful bakery in Birmingham. Lady Ludlow delicately protests Captain James's management innovations, but Captain James has none of Mr Horner's deep-grained deference. Rather, "he would judge in all things for himself. [. . .] [H]e spoke as if he were responsible for the good management of the whole and must, consequently, be allowed full liberty of action" (196). In short, Captain James operates like a professional: he expects autonomy and seeks expertise regardless of the respectability of the source. His marriage to Mr Brooke's daughter completes Captain James's acceptance of the new professional class mobility. Lady Ludlow declares it "impossible" that Captain James should pay court to a Dissenting tradesman's daughter, but the young Captain has no prejudices against the family's religious opinions or their background in trade (200).

By the time Margaret Dawson prepares to leave Hanbury, a mere four years after her arrival, the professional ideals of Mr Gray and Captain James have wrought a transformation in the village. The human resources of the parish are being utilized to good effect because of the dismantlement of the aristocratic rationality in the face of the rationality of expertise. As a result of the new school house, "the children were hushed up in school, and better behaved out of it, too" (211). As a result of the improvements in land management, "there were no more lounging young men to form a group at the cross roads, at a time of the day when young men ought to be at work" (211). Traditional class barriers are eroding, and expertise has come to be valued more than birth status. Captain James has married the Baptist baker's daughter, signaling the weakening of the traditional barriers between trade and land, Church of England and Dissent. Mr Gray has married Bessy, the illegitimate daughter of a former lover of Miss Galindo, in another remarkable subversion of Lady Ludlow's social norms. Hanbury is still dominated by the countess's great house, and she still sets the tone for local social life. But her social tone must necessarily follow that taken by the professionals around her. She cannot refuse to countenance the Baptist baker's daughter or the illegitimate girl once they are married to the professionals whom she respects and on whom she depends. In receiving Mrs James and Mrs Gray, Lady Ludlow again "mak[es] the best of a bad job" as she did when she insisted that the girls at Mr Gray's school learn spinning and knitting before they are taught to read (199). In the case of the social recognition of these hitherto unrecognizable persons, making the best of a bad job means turning her irresistible and inimitable social grace toward the welcome of even the gauche professional wives. In the account of a tea that closes Miss Galindo's final letter, Lady Ludlow shames her supercilious servants not only by accepting Bessy and the overawed wives of the nearby clergy, but also by covering up the breaches of etiquette of Mrs James, the daughter of the Baptist baker from Birmingham.

In *My Lady Ludlow,* the replacement of aristocratic ideals with professional ideals is presented as the irresistible and natural outcome of usually mild conflict. Lady Ludlow is finally a gracious loser. When appeals to her age and position no longer command the same reflexive deference from the professionals around her as they did with an earlier generation of professionals, Lady Ludlow does exactly as she does when a dispute arises about the burial place of her last son: she "withdrew from the discussion, before it degenerated into an unseemly contest" (169). She retains her privileged social position, her undiminished grandeur, by giving up her benevolent autocracy and sharing the real power of the society with professionals who expect her to defer to their expertise rather than expecting to defer to her hereditary social position.[11]

II

There is perhaps little that is remarkable about Gaskell's positive portrayal of rural England's transition from a landed or aristocratic social order to a professional one. What is remarkable, however, is the relative elasticity of the professional constructs with regard to class and gender. In *My Lady Ludlow,* the shift toward professional social hegemony occurs simultaneously with the expansion of access to the increasingly powerful professional class. At the same time as Mr Gray and Captain James are redefining the relationship of their professions to the aristocracy, the working class and women are redefining their relationships to the professional class. In the characters of Harry Gregson and Miss Galindo, Gaskell experiments with the boundaries of professional expertise and the power which accompanies that expertise. In a subtly symmetrical narrative device, Gaskell subverts separately the class-based prejudices of the aristocrat and the gender-based prejudices of the traditional professional, leaving the reader to connect the dots of an inclusive ethos of work exemplified in Mr Gray.

Harry Gregson and Miss Galindo indirectly interact in the novel with respect to the position of clerkship: Mr Horner intends to train Harry to be his clerk, but is soon constrained to have Miss Galindo as his clerk instead. In the last third of the century, clerkships became the means by which working-class men and middle-class women gained their first large-scale access to white-collar work. For working-class men, the putative meritocracy manifested by the competitive examination of the Civil Service motivated the ambitious and intelligent to "cram", in hopes of winning entrance to a respectable career. No such movement was visible in the 1810s, when this story is set, but clerkship would suggest an association with the aspiring lower middle class for Gaskell's 1858 *Household Words* audience. For middle-class women, the proliferation of the telegraph and the typewriter from the 1870s on opened clerical careers for women in significant numbers. It thus appears that Gaskell is using her plot to suggest presciently how barriers to professional status can be undermined by competent members of traditionally marginalized groups.

In plotting the story so that Harry initially is trained as a clerk because his patron is ambitious for him to be a professional, Gaskell recreates the progress of a class of intelligent but low-born men into professional circles. Harry Gregson represents in the novel the meritocratic recruitment of the working class into the professional class. As the "brightest and sharpest" of the farm lads, Harry is specially chosen by Mr Horner to learn the basic skills of reading, writing and arithmetic (53). Mr Horner admits to his lady that he wants to train Harry as his clerk, but Margaret suspects that Mr Horner retains other, "almost unconscious" aspirations for his beloved assistant: "that Harry might be trained so as to be first his clerk, and next his assistant, and finally his successor in his stewardship to the Hanbury estates" (154). In other words, Mr Horner intends to advance Harry through various stages of promotion until he attains a securely professional position. This project runs aground when Harry innocently reads an unsealed message from Mr Horner to Lady Ludlow. Harry cannot understand Lady Ludlow's dismayed reaction: "You must never try to read any letters that are not directed to you, even if they be open before you" (58).

This transmission of literacy skills apart from the code of honor governing their use is precisely calculated to bring out all Lady Ludlow's horror at the dangers of indiscriminate education. When the possibility of Harry's serving as a clerk is mentioned, Lady Ludlow declares that "the son of a poacher and vagabond", not raised with what she calls the "instinct" of honor, is not capable of holding a position of trust (128). In Lady Ludlow's mind, trustworthiness, like every personal attribute, is hereditary and essential. No working-class boy, certainly not the son of a criminal, can acquire "instincts" necessary to trustworthiness; consequently, the powerful skills of literacy must be withheld from his ilk.

Lady Ludlow's assessment of Harry's education proves to be the wrong one, of course. After crippling himself in a fall, Harry "will never be able to earn his livelihood in any active way" (163). He must either be a pauper on the parish or what our age might call a "mental worker"; thus, his literacy prevents the waste of his life. Initially inspired by the prospect of being schoolmaster, and then presumably fired by Mr Gray's example, Harry uses his legacy from Mr Horner to go to university. Harry becomes vicar of Hanbury following Mr Gray's early death. Lady Ludlow's belief that low birth is a permanent bar to professional trustworthiness is thereby invalidated.

It is not Lady Ludlow, but Mr Horner who objects to the employment of Miss Galindo, a spinster who lives off the production of her genteel needlework. The bleak economic situation of the "surplus" unmarried woman—unable to earn money without compromising her middle-class position—is illustrated in Miss Galindo's very limited means of support. Her only marketable skills are her literacy and her needlework. At one point in youth she contemplated writing a novel, but following elaborate preparations, she confessed she had "nothing to say" (137). Failing that, Miss Galindo relies on her needle for sustenance. The direct sale of the productions of her needle would, of course, be an unforgivable transgression against her gentility, so she participates in an elaborate system by which the "ornamental" and "useful" productions of "ladies of little or no fortune" are sold indirectly and anonymously through a repository created by a committee of wealthy ladies and managed by a "decayed gentlewoman" (130).

In Lady Ludlow's eyes, Miss Galindo is qualified as a clerk in a way Harry Gregson can never be:

> Miss Galindo was by birth and breeding a lady of the strictest honour, and would, if possible, forget the substance of any letters that passed through her hands; at any rate, no one would ever hear of them again from her.
>
> (133)

In other words, Miss Galindo's birth status obviates her gender to an extent. This tendency has been seen before in Lady Ludlow. When she demands that the magistrate Mr Lathom release Job Gregson on bail in defiance of the law disallowing bail for theft, she dismisses his objection cavalierly: "Bah! Who makes laws? Such as I, in the House of Lords—such as you, in the House of Commons" (38). By including herself among those who make laws in the House of Lords, she apparently unconsciously negates gender in her assertion of class authority.[12]

Whereas Lady Ludlow's class prejudices lead her to scorn Harry as a clerk while overlooking Miss Galindo's gender, Mr Horner's gender prejudices make him antipathetic to Miss Galindo as a clerk. Miss Galindo is an eccentric; even Margaret says: "To tell the truth, I was rather afraid of Miss Galindo's tongue, for I never knew what she would say next" (140). As the village scold, Miss Galindo makes frequent visits to poor cottages; these visits are alternately missions of genuine mercy and investigations of private extravagances. She always keeps a servant who is really a charity case: her servants are blind, deaf, hunchbacked or epileptic, and she takes care of them more than they do her.[13] Despite her eccentricity, Miss Galindo is a perfectly good clerk. Well aware of Mr Horner's prejudice against using a female clerk, she tries to ease his discomfort by performing her job as well as a man: "I try to make him forget I'm a woman; I do everything as ship-shape as a masculine man-clerk" (143). When he continues to be nonplussed, she tries assuming male manners: "I have stuck my pen behind my ear; I have made him a bow instead of a curtsey; I have whistled [. . .] I have said 'Confound it!' and 'Zounds!'" (143-44). In spite of all her efforts, Mr Horner cannot overlook her gender, with the result that, according to Miss Galindo, "I am not half the use I might be" (144). Mr Horner's usual desire to maximize human resources for Lady Ludlow's benefit here runs aground on his gender prejudices.

Only after Mr Horner's death is Miss Galindo known to be the proficient person she is. Miss Galindo knows that Mr Smithson, the London solicitor, assumes that this unusual clerk is a whim of the countess: "It was a form to be gone through to please my lady [. . .]. It was keeping a woman out of harm's way, at any rate, to let her fancy herself useful" (173). She gets the better of him, however, by her undeniable competence:

> He believed that a woman could not write straight lines, and that she required a man to tell her that two and two made four. I was not above ruling my books, and I had Cocker a little more at my fingers' ends than he had.
>
> (173-74)

Her competence extends not only to the content of her work but also her manner and bearing as a worker. As she tells Margaret:

> [M]y greatest triumph was holding my tongue. He would have thought nothing of my books, or my sums, or my black silk gown, if I had spoken unasked. [. . .] I have been so curt, so abrupt, so abominably dull, that I'll answer for it he thinks me worthy to be a man.
>
> (174)

The power to control her speech is related, as is her "strictest honour", to her class background: "But, odd as Miss Galindo was in general, she could be as well-bred a lady as any one when she chose" (132). This characterization is emphasized by repetition: "But Miss Galindo was both a lady and a spirited, sensible woman, and she could put aside her self-indulgence in eccentricity of speech and manner whenever she chose" (173). In other words, specifically because she is a "lady", Miss Galindo can pass as a professional man. At the same time, Miss Galindo's refusal of pay for her work illustrates the difficulty she experiences in participating in the norms of traditionally masculine professional logic. Though her work is worthy of financial reward, she cannot bring herself to accept it, insisting that her primary motive of gratitude necessarily excludes pecuniary gain.

Gaskell's handling of the clerkship subplot finally undermines both gender and class prejudices. Harry Gregson, dismissed in disgrace from the apprenticeship of clerkship, grows up to be the parish rector. Miss Galindo's outcome is less triumphant: she returns to her eccentric mode of life as village scold, supported only by her needlework, but not before vindicating herself before Mr Smithson as a thoroughly good professional worker. Mr Horner's and Mr Smithson's suspicion of the female clerk is gently castigated as surely as Lady Ludlow's horror at the young vagabond clerk. Yet the working-class man's access to professional status is attained in the generation following Mr Gray's reforms, while that of the woman is only prefigured.

The only character in the novel completely without prejudices, Mr Gray, is finally its hero. Mr Gray's acceptance of the professional ideal is totally unselfconscious and is bound up with his admirable religious and humanitarian zeal. In striving to advance the spiritual good of his parishioners, he unknowingly does them more material good than had been done in generations of aristocratic paternalism. In urging Lady Ludlow's acceptance of professional rationality, Mr Gray, together with his professional allies, succeeds in transforming the character of the village in ways that not only benefit but also empower the villagers. As we have seen, Mr Gray gets Lady Ludlow's permission to found the school where the poor children are educated, but that is not his only significant contribution to the village. Before that, it is he who saves Harry Gregson's life at risk of his own—Mr Gray suffers a stroke in the process of rescuing Harry, who was trapped in a quarry with a broken thigh. The vagabond poacher Job Gregson, softened and redeemed by Mr Gray's love and care for his son, reforms into a model citizen and becomes gamekeeper under Captain James. Finally, Mr Gray's lack of prejudice is seen in his hiring of the illegitimate Bessy as schoolmistress, thereby admitting her to a sort of professional legitimacy.

In all these examples, Mr Gray's generous and self-effacing labors enable and empower the productive labor of others, especially the most marginalized members of the society. The labor of these hitherto excluded workers then enables the productive labor of still others: Job Gregson oversees the building of the school, with his youngest ragamuffin son mixing the mortar; and Bessy teaches the girls of the village to sew and

read, thereby equipping them for more genteel labor than they could otherwise have performed. The novel thus affirms that the efficient and productive use of human resources requires setting aside both class and gender prejudices, and that this process results in the common social good. The meritocratic ideal valorized in Mr Gray becomes the means to demolish barriers against women's professional employment and against working-class social advancement. This demolition is good for everyone, even Lady Ludlow, because the more complete use of the estate's human resources causes the standard of living and the prosperity of the estate to rise across the board.

III

The potential for professionalism to open doors for women is broached but then tabled in *My Lady Ludlow* by Miss Galindo's capable but only temporary and unremunerated performance in white-collar work. This plot element receives closure, however, in **Round the Sofa.** Shirley Foster has suggested that "the retrospective setting of 'My Lady Ludlow' tends to point the reader away from contemporary application of its unorthodoxy".[14] However, the Miss Greatorex plot, thin as it is, brings the social progress of Margaret Dawson's youth into the reader's present.[15] Most critics have ignored the frame in **Round the Sofa,** regarding it as irrelevant to the text of **My Lady Ludlow.** When they have commented on it, they have usually treated it as a mere throwaway, a clumsy and mercenary effort to re-market a book that was overshadowed in *Household Words* by Dickens publicizing his marriage difficulties.[16] This frame, however, contains important echoes of the main story, which provide clues for the reader to perceive the contemporary continuity—and advancement—of the social transformations described in **My Lady Ludlow.** Miss Greatorex, the first-person narrator of the frame, benefits from an apprenticeship in writing that converts the amateur storytelling of her older friends into a professional and implicitly remunerative skill. Two years after Gaskell completed **The Life of Charlotte Brontë,** the conclusion to the frame of **My Lady Ludlow** points toward a picture of the woman professional novelist, like Brontë and Gaskell herself.[17]

Miss Greatorex is away from her parents receiving medical treatment in Scotland from Mr Dawson, the brother of Margaret Dawson, who is now a crippled old maid (in spite of her spinsterhood, she claims the courtesy title "Mrs Dawson"). When the doctor invites Miss Greatorex and her governess, Miss Duncan, to join him and his sister for their weekly "at-home" evenings, Miss Greatorex is positioned to hear Mrs Dawson's narration of her relations with Lady Ludlow. At the suggestion of her governess, Miss Greatorex transcribes the story each Tuesday morning as a "good exercise [. . .] both in memory and composition" (216).[18] This transition from an oral to a written paradigm is reminiscent of Harry Gregson's acquisition of literacy skills, by which he effected his rise from laborer to parson. Similarly, Miss Greatorex's shift from the amateur, drawing-room narrations she hears to the book she writes encapsulates the difference between a Miss Galindo and a Mrs Gaskell.

This frame implicitly poses questions about the difference the professionalization of society makes to women. How do the events and shifts related in *My Lady Ludlow* affect the position and opportunities for Miss Greatorex? The answer will be evident when we consider the parallels and the differences between the world of Margaret Dawson and that of Miss Greatorex. We should begin by noting that Miss Greatorex is an analogue of the young Margaret Dawson. The young women's feelings, apprehensions and impressions correspond almost exactly, and many physical details of their environments match up as well. Both girls are shy and overawed by the grandeur of the people they encounter while away from their families in late adolescence (5, 13-15). Both Hanbury Hall and the Dawsons' home are old-fashioned and grandly impressive (5, 15). Both homes are richly decorated with china jars filled with potpourri, and even have matching Indian wallpaper patterns (5-6, 45-46).[19] Mrs Dawson and Lady Ludlow even resemble each other: both elderly ladies have beautiful smooth skin and wear white satin ribbons on their heads (5, 15-16). Lady Ludlow and Mrs Dawson both dine on a roll or biscuit and milk while serving their guests more elegant fare (6, 18). Like Margaret Dawson, Miss Greatorex is one of numerous children of parents who are "not rich" (1). Like both Margaret Dawson and Harry Gregson, she is physically infirm. Since a young invalid woman's chances of marriage were exceedingly slim, Miss Greatorex may well be required to earn a living eventually.

Yet the differences between the young women's situations are telling as well. Whereas the young Margaret enters a house filled with the riches and collections of aristocratic lineage, Miss Greatorex enters a house filled with artifacts of the wealth "Mr Dawson had acquired [. . .] in his profession" (5). Whereas Margaret's activity at Lady Ludlow's house consists almost entirely of needlework, Miss Greatorex is expected to use her time in Scotland "to combine lessons with the excellent Edinburgh masters, with the medicines and exercises needed for [her] indisposition" (1). When Margaret is lamed at Hanbury, she is treated only by the local general practitioner and by Miss Medlicott's "homeopathic" remedies (28), not for lack of means but simply because no other options are considered. Miss Greatorex, however, is sent away to the best physician who can be found, an expert with a national reputation. These details show Miss Greatorex inhabits a world in which the professional order—ushered in by the progressive Mr

Gray and Captain James—carries the day. In a sense, professionals are the new aristocrats, as Mr and Mrs Dawson have, in a manner, replaced Lord and Lady Ludlow to Miss Greatorex. The questions of Miss Greatorex's life, then, are whether the professional order will allow any room for her (as the aristocratic order did for Lady Ludlow), and whether the quasi-professional women of a previous generation will make any difference for her. Will Miss Galindo's pioneering incursion into the professions smooth Miss Greatorex's way to use her mental capacity to be productive in spite of her physical infirmity, as Harry Gregson had done a generation before? Will Lady Ludlow's assertion of gender-neutral competence blaze a trail Miss Greatorex can follow?

When Miss Duncan instructs Miss Greatorex to use no small portion of her school hours to write out Mrs Dawson's story, Miss Greatorex seems to undergo an apprenticeship in narrative writing. Her mistresses are not just Miss Duncan and Margaret Dawson, but also Lady Ludlow and Miss Galindo, who share the role of narrator with Margaret Dawson. Like Gaskell herself did, Miss Greatorex writes her tale in weekly "installments" the morning after she hears each portion of the tale. Given that Miss Duncan asks Miss Greatorex to write each week's installment as a "good exercise [. . .] both in memory and composition", it appears that Miss Greatorex is being trained in the writing of fiction (216). Following this exercise, it is unlikely that Miss Greatorex would ever replicate the experience of Miss Galindo when she attempted to write a novel: "it ended in my having nothing to say, when I sat down to write" (137). Miss Galindo had fine handwriting and abundant paper and pens, but she lacked something to say. She experienced a gap between literacy and literary production. This gap is puzzling given Miss Galindo's colorful life and her flair for anecdote, frequently on display before Margaret. What Miss Galindo lacked was the mental training, the training in memory, to turn her impromptu anecdotal flourish into coherent and extended narrative. This is exactly what Miss Greatorex acquires by her opportunity not only to hear but also to transcribe from memory the nested stories of Mrs Dawson.

Unlike Miss Galindo, who received no guidance on how to make her way in the world as a single woman, Miss Greatorex is surrounded by women who facilitate her transition from an oral, amateur paradigm of storytelling to a literate and literary professional paradigm, such as Gaskell herself put to good professional use. Felicia Bonaparte has observed:

> What clerking is for Miss Galindo, writing was for Elizabeth Gaskell. The images in which she thinks of women working in her fiction are those in which she thinks of herself as the writer of her books.[20]

This link between Miss Galindo's clerking and Mrs Gaskell's writing is made visible by Miss Greatorex, who transfers the oral stories of her foremothers into a literary product. The result of Miss Greatorex's memory and composition skills is a marketable commodity: "and thus it came to pass that I have the manuscript of 'My Lady Ludlow' now lying by me" (216). Reading these words in a printed book, the reader knows that that manuscript has since been transmuted into a volume which he or she has paid money to read.

My Lady Ludlow, therefore, does more than tell the story of Miss Galindo's creative and competent strategies for situating herself in an emergent social order dominated by professionals. Gaskell's plot, as I have shown, represents simultaneously a shift in power structures towards professionalism *and* an enlargement and reconfiguration of the professional class by means of meritocratic recruitment among women and the working class. Taken together with its frame, however, it also suggests a continued scenario of professional progress for women, one that carries forward into Gaskell's own time. The failed novelist becomes a clerk who is a pioneer for female white-collar workers; two generations later, the young middle-class woman is trained, by both aural and clerkly practices, in the marketable craft of storytelling. **My Lady Ludlow** ends, not with the death of the countess nor yet with the circle around the sofa, but with the finished manuscript "now lying by" Miss Greatorex, whose "memory and composition" skills have been honed by its production (257). It ends, then, with the female writer poised to take the oral narratives of her female community and render them as literary products which not only challenge the hegemony of linear male narrative but also constitute her claim to professional status in her own right.

Notes

1. For a few examples, see Patsy Stoneman, *Elizabeth Gaskell* (Bloomington: Indiana UP, 1987); Felicia Bonaparte, *The Gypsy-Bachelor of Manchester: The Life of Mrs Gaskell's Demon* (Charlottesville: UP of Virginia, 1992) and Shirley Foster, *Elizabeth Gaskell: A Literary Life* (New York: Palgrave Macmillan, 2002).

2. See John Lucas, *The Literature of Change* (Brighton: Harvester, 1977) 1-33; Raymond Williams, *Culture and Society, 1780-1950* (New York: Columbia UP, 1983) 87-92 and Melissa Schaub, "Sympathy and Discipline in *Mary Barton*," *Victorian Newsletter* 106 (2004): 15-20.

3. Recent critical commentary on the text has focused largely on rehabilitating it against charges of narrative clumsiness lodged in early assessments. In *Mrs Gaskell's Observation and Invention: A Study of Her Non-Biographic Works* (Arundel: Linden Press, 1970), John Sharps is very critical of what he perceives to be the struc-tural flaws and disorganization of the novel: "The chief and most obvious structural fault is the long digression, told by Lady Ludlow for the flimsiest of reasons, which occupies nearly a third of the work. This tale within a tale is a story of Revolutionary France, and has every appearance of having been included solely to draw out the weekly numbers" (276). In *Mrs Gaskell: Novelist and Biographer* (Cambridge, MA: Harvard UP, 1966), Arthur Pollard similarly complains of the novel's haphazard structure: "*My Lady Ludlow* would not suffer for the excision of the whole of the Créquy incident in revolutionary Paris" (178). Since then, others have sought to establish grounds for renewed interest in the largely neglected novel, most of them while conceding its structural flaws. See Terence Wright, *Elizabeth Gaskell "We Are Not Angels": Realism, Gender, Values* (New York: St. Martin's Press, 1995). Feminist studies of the book include Aina Rubenius, *The Woman Question in Mrs Gaskell's Life and Works* (Uppsala: English Institute, U of Uppsala, 1950); Ruth McDowell Cook, "Women's Work as Paradigm for Autonomy in Gaskell's *My Lady Ludlow*," *Gaskell Society Journal* 11 (1997): 68-76 and Shirley Foster, *Elizabeth Gaskell: A Literary Life* (New York: Palgrave Macmillan, 2002). Edgar Wright and Elizabeth Leaver have used the revolution/evolution contrast to uncover a narrative rationale for the secondary plot. See Edgar Wright, "*My Lady Ludlow*: Forms of Social Change and Forms of Fiction," *Gaskell Society Journal* 3 (1989) and Elizabeth Leaver, "What Will this World Come To? Old Ways and Education in Elizabeth Gaskell's *My Lady Ludlow*," *Gaskell Society Journal* 10 (1996). In "The 'Female Paternalist' as Historian: Elizabeth Gaskell's *My Lady Ludlow*," *Rewriting the Victorians: Theory, History and the Politics of Gender,* ed. Linda Shires (New York: Routledge, 1992), Christine Krueger finds that the text's representation of a "female paternalist" uses heterogeneous narrators and narratives to "examine the narratives' varied genealogies and to multiply the forms of resistance to hegemonic historical discourse" (166). My own reading will suggest a thematic intention for the nested stories, especially the much-deplored de Créquy narrative, which comprise the book; namely, I will show that the stories told by Lady Ludlow and Miss Galindo, and later renarrated by Margaret Dawson to Miss Greatorex, comprise a pre-professional variety of female storytelling that informs Miss Greatorex's presumed arrival at professional status. Thus, while the de Créquy narrative is not an explicit part of my argument, I do see its inclusion in the text as germane to Gaskell's commentary on women and professionalism.

4. Sharps finds that the book's "historical interest" partly compensates for what he calls its clumsy structure (284). Edgar Wright observes that Gaskell "reveal[s] by illustration how the transition to changed social attitudes is achieved over a period of time, while recollection and explanation extend the time presented" (37). In *Elizabeth Gaskell* (London: Routledge, 1979), Angus Easson offers a conventional assessment of the novel's "clash between the old aristocratic ways of Lady Ludlow and the new evangelicalism of the clergyman Mr Gray" (214). In *Elizabeth Gaskell: A Habit of Stories* (New York: Farrar, 1993), Jenny Uglow observes that within the novel's span "[w]e recognize a fundamental change—in [Lady Ludlow] and in the society. Nothing, and everything, has happened" (470).

5. Harold Perkin, *The Rise of Professional Society: England since 1880* (London: Routledge, 1989) 7.

6. See Harold Perkin, *Origins of Modern English Society* (London: Routledge, 1969) 218-70 for the classic formulation of the professional ideal, as well as the other class ideals. See also Perkin's explanation of the genealogy of the class ideals, including the influence of utilitarianism on the professional ideal.

7. Elizabeth Gaskell, *My Lady Ludlow and Other Tales, The Works of Mrs Gaskell,* vol. 5 (1858; London: Smith, Elder & Co., 1906) 196. Subsequent citations from this text are given parenthetically.

8. See Terence Wright on the "gracious accommodating love which my lady stands for" (124).

9. In *Origins of Modern English Society,* Perkin calls evangelicalism an "effort to professionalize the clergy" (362).

10. One overeducated young girl is dismissed with the injunction to "beware of French principles, which had led the French to cut off their king's and queen's heads" (20).

11. Daniel Duman describes this phenomenon in historical terms: "The patron-professional relationship of the eighteenth century, in which the professional practitioner was dependent upon aristocratic custom, was replaced by a client-professional relationship. Demand for professional services increased and the clientele became more and more socially diversified; consequently professional men were freed from the domination of a small, wealthy, and homogeneous group of patrons." Daniel Duman, "The Creation and Diffusion of a Professional Ideology in Nineteenth Century England," *Sociological Review* 27 (1977): 115.

12. This attitude is explained by the fact that she has been a long-time widow, and more so by the fact that she was her father's only child and he consequently "had given her a training which was thought unusual in those days" (208).

13. Probably because of this eccentricity Miss Galindo has been dismissed by some critics as an unsavory portrait of a working woman. See Patricia Beer, *Reader, I Married Him: A Study of the Women Characters of Jane Austen, Charlotte Brontë, Elizabeth Gaskell and George Eliot* (London: Macmillan, 1974) 170. Other critics have been more laudatory of Miss Galindo; most notably, Ruth McDowell Cook's "Women's Work" has emphasized the nurturing ethic that pervades her work and the sturdy autonomy that gives her the power to resist not only the male work culture but also the failing aristocratic code of Lady Ludlow. In a similar vein, Shirley Foster has said that Miss Galindo and Lady Ludlow both model autonomous work: "With both these women, Gaskell shows us that she has faith, albeit cautious faith, in the capacities of female independence." See Shirley Foster, *Victorian Women's Fiction: Marriage, Freedom, and the Individual* (Totowa: Barnes and Noble, 1985) 166. Among those who share this more optimistic assessment of Miss Galindo are Rubenius 126-28; Françoise Basch, *Relative Creatures: Victorian Women in Society and the Novel* (New York: Schocken, 1974) 179-80; Uglow 471-72 and Wright, *Elizabeth Gaskell* 123. Christine Krueger privileges Miss Galindo's role as "the recording angel, the historian of everyday life" (179).

14. Foster, *Victorian Women's Fiction* 166.

15. Krueger takes the frame seriously as part of Gaskell's project "to show how women might use and discard a variety of literary forms to represent their experience, and write their histories" (171). She notes the similarity of Margaret Dawson and Miss Greatorex: both experience an infirmity which "figures forth the simultaneously abnormal and privileged position of the female author and her intimate relationships with her audience of sororal sufferers" (172).

16. See Winifred Gérin, *Elizabeth Gaskell: A Biography* (Oxford: Clarendon, 1976) 206 and Wright, *"My Lady Ludlow"* 29-30. Of course, Gaskell's undisguised financial motive in this republication, which Gérin documents, by no means excludes the possibility that Gaskell also used the opportunity of republication to say something in the frame that she wanted said. Gaskell's own position as a thoroughly professional novelist admits of simultaneous "mercenary" and artistic aims for her productions.

17. *My Lady Ludlow* (1858) began serialization just over one year after the publication of *The Life of Charlotte Brontë* (1857); the frame was first included in *Round the Sofa* (1859), which appeared the year after the serialized form of the novel.

18. Foster argues that *My Lady Ludlow* "not only resists the formal shaping of history as 'story' but also seems to represent a feminine mode of writing, expressing a Kristevan female cyclical temporality" (*Elizabeth Gaskell* 90). Similarly, Krueger finds that the narrative form in *My Lady Ludlow* "suggest[s] the diversity of female desire and practice in the production of historical narrative" (180).

19. The similarity in the wallpaper pattern is pointed out in Sharps (311).

20. Bonaparte 222.

Jerome Meckier (essay date December 2006)

SOURCE: Meckier, Jerome. "Parodic Prolongation in *North and South*: Elizabeth Gaskell Revaluates Dickens's Suspenseful Delays." *Dickens Quarterly* 23, no. 4 (December 2006): 217-28.

[*In the following essay, Meckier maintains that in* North and South *Gaskell "utilizes her mutiny and strike episodes to dispute [Charles] Dickens's low estimate of walk-outs and to determine their ethical parameters."*]

"'Loyalty and obedience to wisdom and justice are fine,'" Margaret Hale tells her mother, "'but it is still finer to defy arbitrary power, unjustly and cruelly used'" (154; ch. 14). This speech occurs in "The Mutiny" chapter of *North and South,* seven chapters before the riveting strike episodes at Mr. Thornton's manufactory.[1] Margaret staunchly defends her brother's conduct toward the tyrannical Captain Reid. The seemingly extraneous subplot involving Lieutenant Hale's insubordination—"pure plot-spinning" in one commentator's opinion (Wright 144-46)—deserves its place: Elizabeth Gaskell spells out the rules for rebellion that John Boucher violates but that Dickens allegedly does not know.[2]

Like Nicholas Nickleby pummeling Squeers, Frederick Hale acted as a champion of the badly used when he revolted against a bully. Captain Reid's authority, while at sea, could be checked by no other means. Mutiny is justifiable because it takes place far from Manchester. On shore, in an industrial setting, extreme situations of the kind Frederick faced seldom materialize, unless a bogus mutineer like Boucher interferes with his union's efforts and instigates strike into riot. The existence of groups like the union, Gaskell maintains, makes individual revolt unnecessary. Just as Frederick is not Boucher, Thornton is hardly Captain Reid.

Josiah Bounderby, however, invites the kind of abuse Frederick expended on his commander. Dickens, Gaskell complains, presents the domination of Bounderby over Stephen Blackpool crudely, as if it were Squeers abusing Smike over again. When Bounderby accuses "'that fellow Slackbridge'" of "'stirring up the people to mutiny'" (112; bk. 2, ch. 5), his calumniation of the labor organizer may have confirmed Gaskell's intention to write contrasting chapters on *mutiny* and *strike.* Her point is that Dickens, like Bounderby, cannot tell one from the other. Gaskell utilizes her mutiny and strike episodes to dispute Dickens's low estimate of walk-outs and to determine their ethical parameters. In her opinion, Blackpool is as wrong not to go along with the union as Boucher is to hurl a stone at Thornton. Neither is entitled to act singlehandedly the way Lieutenant Hale must.

Frederick appears in Milton-Northern only briefly to visit his dying mother. He little realizes that his short stay will result in an additional death: that of a tipsy railroad porter eager to claim the reward for apprehending a fugitive. Margaret assists Frederick to escape from Leonards at the Outwood station, then denies involvement. Leonards dies from the injuries of a fall suffered in his scuffle with Frederick. Aiding and abetting Frederick, Miss Hale almost loses all chance with Mr. Thornton, who sees her with Frederick and mistakes brother for lover.

During the uprising of the strikers at Marlborough Mills, Margaret shields Thornton from their wrath. Her heroic embrace gives the beleaguered industrialist the notion that she cares for him, although she rejects his marriage offer. Events at the train station convince Thornton that Margaret cares about someone else when, actually, he has become uppermost in her regard. His glimpse of her with a strange man in chapter 32 and the lie she tells to facilitate her brother's escape—an apparent impropriety compounded by a palpable falsehood—are not explained to everyone's satisfaction for twenty chapters. The riot and Frederick's close call become related incidents that intertwine the novel's love story with its economic themes. Beginning with these scenes, Gaskell prolongs endlessly the misunderstandings that keep Thornton and Miss Hale apart.[3] In a novel assiduously affirming conciliation, she postpones, by every conceivable means, the most desirable association of all.

Immediate rapprochement could have occurred as early as chapter 33 (the next chapter), when Thornton inquires for Miss Hale upon hearing of her mother's death. But for "some reason or other," Dixon, the maid, never mentions Thornton's visit: "It might have been mere chance, but so it was that Margaret never heard that he [Thornton] had attended her mother's funeral" (340; ch. 33). "Mere chance" or for "some reason or other"—Gaskell's insouciant use of missed opportunities seems designed to belittle the power of Destiny, a staple of the melodramatic serial.

Although Margaret has "stained her whiteness" with an untruth (351; ch. 35)—her failing is made to sound like sexual indiscretion—Thornton does her a favor. Ironically, it prevents instant exoneration. In Chapter 35, only five chapters since he encountered her with Frederick, he asks the police-inspector not to conduct a public inquest into Leonards's death; it would have revealed Margaret's complicity and the identity of her alleged suitor.

In chapter 38, Mrs. Thornton tries to straighten things out. Fulfilling her promise to Mrs. Hale to act as a second mother to Margaret, she asks for "the circumstances . . . that, if explained, may take off from the seeming impropriety'" (393; ch. 38) of trysting with a gentleman at the railway station. But Margaret, "an offended princess," declines to justify herself. Gaskell reduces Fate's obstinacy to a young heroine's haughtiness.

Talking with Mr. Hale and Mr. Bell in chapter 40, Thornton interrupts their request for Margaret's opinion of printed calicoes. "'Is Miss Hale so remarkable for truth?'" he blurts out "bitterly" (415). Unfortunately, Margaret does not dispute this veiled accusation. Thornton's misapprehensions are allowed to continue. In the same chapter, Bell asks Hale if he has noticed an attraction between his daughter and Thornton and is told the idea is absurd. Later, Hale questions Margaret, who confesses that Thornton once proposed to her. Before her father can intervene, he dies during a visit to Mr. Bell.

Returning to Milton from Oxford to arrange Hale's funeral, Bell meets Thornton on the train (ch. 41). He misleads the manufacturer into believing that Margaret, now alone in the world, will marry Henry Lennox (433; ch. 41). Because Bell dislikes "'those Lennoxes!'" he refers to Henry, a clever young barrister, as "'that brother!'" He means brother to Captain Lennox, allegedly "'a fool,'" not to Margaret's Aunt Shaw and certainly not to Margaret, although it is her brother that Thornton needs to be told about.

In chapter 42, Bell tells Thornton about Frederick, whose name the industrialist claims he has "'never heard before'" (443). Bell says he mentioned Frederick when the Hales "'first came to Milton.'" Finally on the scent, Thornton asks if Frederick was in England at the time he saw "'a young man walking with Miss Hale'" (443). Bell replies that Frederick "'never'" comes to England and that it must have been "'young Lennox.'" "'I once fancied that you had a little tenderness for Margaret,'" teases Bell. Although Thornton is disconcerted by such "pertinacious questioning," he forces himself to undergo "no change of countenance," thereby denying Bell a tell-tale sign.

Not until chapter 44 does Bell, now also something of a detective, discover from Margaret that Frederick was indeed recently in England to see his mother. "'Frederick in England!'" Bell exclaims, "you never told me that!'" (462). Regrettably, Margaret fails to learn that Bell denied Frederick's presence to Mr. Thornton. Bell recalls being asked "'not many weeks ago'" if her brother "'had not been over then,'" but cannot remember by whom. "'Oh! I recollect!'" he says after thinking hard for several moments, but "did not say the name" (463; ch. 44).

Although Margaret burns to know if it was Thornton, she "could not ask the question of Mr Bell, much as she longed to do so" (463). Ironically, she obeys convention by not showing unlady-like curiosity, despite having violated decorum at the railway station. On a visit to Helstone with Mr. Bell (chapter 46), Margaret finally unburdens herself. Bell now has all the facts and promises to explain her conduct to Thornton in hopes of removing the "shadow of impropriety" (486; ch. 46) under which she has been living in the mill-owner's eyes.

This never happens because in chapter 48 Bell is "seized with an apoplectic fit" (500) and carried off. Several times in the previous chapter, Bell postpones his trip to Milton and so never discusses with Thornton Margaret's indiscretion. Her resolve—"she must be patient. Sooner or later the mists would be cleared away" (492; ch. 47)—may be read as tongue-in-cheek advice to the reader, whose patience Gaskell deliberately exhausts.

Finally, in chapter 50, Higgins asks Mr. Thornton for news of Miss Hale and, quite by accident, informs his master that it was her brother with whom he saw her. Had Margaret not prompted an alliance between unionist and manufacturer, the mix-up might never have ended. Before she intercedes, Thornton and Higgins scarcely speak to each other.

Eighteen chapters after coming upon Margaret with Frederick, Thornton finally knows the truth. Consequently, when Margaret asks Lennox to come to her assistance (chapter 51), the reader need not share the lawyer's belief that she is "learning to depend upon him" (526; ch. 51) or fear that she might reconsider his suit. Instead, she seeks legal advice on how to loan Thornton enough of her legacy from Mr. Bell to keep the mills running. Her financial proposal and Thornton's proposal of marriage fill up the concluding chapter.

On several occasions between chapters 32 and 52, Thornton almost renews his courtship. In chapter 39, for example, the master has just hired Higgins but neglects to capitalize on Margaret's approval. "'I see we are nothing to each other'" (407), he declares, ending discussion before it starts. Margaret, too, develops a defeatist attitude. In chapter 49, she concludes that she has "no possible way of explaining" herself to Thornton "save the one she had lost by Mr Bell's death. She must submit, like many another, to be misunderstood" (514; ch. 50). Ironically, matters improve from this point: Thornton learns about Frederick from Higgins in the next chapter, eight pages later.

Gaskell permitted Dickens to divide her manuscript into weekly installments but baulked at shortening the concluding episodes.[4] Before releasing the hardcover version, she added two chapters and expanded three others to obtain the elbow room that *Household Words* had denied her: "Three chapters were expanded and two entirely new added," so that chapters 44, 45, and 46 became chapters 47-51 (Easson 246, n.2).[5] She also took the opportunity to get even with Dickens for his editorial interference by ridiculing the popular novelist's stock in trade: allegedly unrealistic delays that artificially increase suspense.

Parodic prolongation was already under way in chapter 32, before Dickens compelled Gaskell to hasten toward resolution. He blamed a decline in sales on what he called her "wearisome" novel (Page 33). But Dickens may have been offended by the anti-Dickensian way *North and South* goes on, not by elongation per se.

Credible when met singly, obstacles in the way of union between Margaret and Thornton escalate into a parody of Dickens if totaled. The last twenty chapters of *North and South,* the novel as modified for the hardcover edition, tantalize the reader while expertly parodying the delaying tactics that Dickens invented to promote the sales of his weekly serials: *The Old Curiosity Shop* (1840-41), for example, and, just prior to Gaskell's novel, *Hard Times* in *Household Words.*

Dickens kept readers on edge for nine weeks before supplying final news of Little Nell (Meckier 1972, 199). Her death, heavily foreshadowed in No. 35 (28 November 1840, chapters 54-55), does not actually happen until over two months of weekly installments later in No. 44 for 30 January 1841. In *Hard Times,* Stephen Blackpool's departure from Coketown coincides with the robbery of Mr. Bounderby's bank. Then Dickens made readers ponder the power-loom weaver's whereabouts through six weekly installments (17 June to 5 August 1854).

To increase suspense, Dickens interweaves three delays in *Hard Times*: the identity of the "Old Woman" (who is she?), the Louisa Gradgrind-Josiah Bounderby-James Harthouse triangle (will she fall?), and the disappearance of Stephen Blackpool (where is he?). The Old Woman is seen first in installment 6 (bk. 1, ch. 2). Having been fired in installment 11, Blackpool departs in installment 12 (bk. 2: ch. 6), the same weekly number

in which the Old Woman reappears, calling herself "Mrs. Pegler." Harthouse arrives in installment 9 (bk. 2: ch. 1). Althoug Louisa starts down Mrs. Sparsit's symbolic "Staircase" in installment 15 (bk. 2: ch. 10) and descends "Lower and Lower" in installment 16 (bk. 2: ch. 12), she is saved from infidelity when Sissy Jupe routs Harthouse in installment 17 (bk. 3: ch. 2). The rout occurs over two installments, that is, three and four chapters respectively, before the collapse of Bounderby's myth of himself as a self-made man and Blackpool's fatal fall into "the Old Hell Shaft." Mrs. Pegler identifies herself as Bounderby's self-sacrificing mother in Book 3, chapter 5; Sissy and Rachael stumble upon Stephen, lying at the bottom of an abandoned mine, in Book 3, chapter 6.

To exacerbate the delay created by intervals between weekly installments, Dickens multiplies the anxieties that time's passage causes within them. Having written Stephen to come back and clear himself of the bank robbery, Rachael predicts his return "'in two days'"; instead, four go by (185, 188; bk. 3, ch. 4). After messengers are sent to the "working colony," Stephen's last-known address, all expect his capture "next day" (188). But two more days pass, Stephen having "decamped" for Coketown upon receiving Rachael's letter. In sum, at least eight days, possibly as long as a week and a half, pass in chapters 4 and 5 of Book 3 (installment 18) while Coketown awaits Stephen. Chapter 5 begins and ends with the same persistent question: "Where was the man, and why did he not come back?" (188, 194; bk. 3, chs. 4, 5).

In the enlarged hardcover version of *North and South,* Thornton does not correct the mistake he made in chapter 32 until chapter 50; he reaches an understanding with Margaret two chapters later. So twenty chapters keep Thornton and Margaret at odds, compared to seventeen between Nell's decline and expiration once chapter numbers were introduced for the hardback edition. The striking difference is the number of deaths: only Nell perishes in the final chapters of *The Old Curiosity Shop,* but death claims Mrs. Hale, Leonards, Mr. Hale, and Mr. Bell before Thornton can renew his marriage proposal. Surely no laughing matter, the Oxford don's "apoplectic fit" (500; ch. 48) becomes almost comical as the last in a crescendo. Deriding the Dickens who withheld news of Little Nell and concealed Blackpool's whereabouts, Gaskell dooms nearly everyone with information vital to the improvement of Margaret's marriage prospects.

North and South teased Dickens's admirers three times over. 1. Will the police-inspector hold an inquiry into Leonards's death? Ironically he would be doing Thornton a favor by pursuing the matter. 2. Can Mr. Hale survive his wife long enough to settle his daughter's affair of the heart? 3. Will Mr. Bell survive Mr. Hale long enough to act *in loco parentis*? The answer is "no" each time.

Rachael wonders repeatedly why Blackpool does not return to Coketown. Similarly, Margaret asks herself over and over why Mr. Bell does not go "to Milton" (492; ch. 47). Her "strange undefined longing" for him to undeceive Thornton about Frederick gives rise to concerns for the Oxford don's health. Once Margaret fears that Bell "could not be well" (492), Dickensians surely sensed what would happen next.

One doubts that Wilkie Collins ever uttered the sensational novelist's shibboleth: "make 'em laugh; make 'em cry; make 'em wait" (Davis 75). Still, this three-pronged battle-cry accurately sums up the Victorian serialist's creed. But Gaskell takes the crying out of delay. In both *The Old Curiosity Shop* and *Hard Times,* the reader, after agonizing for weeks, is reduced to tears when misfortune strikes. Anxiety in **North and South** serves to make eventual relief much sweeter. Gaskell revises the Dickensian delay from a time of dread to a feeling of expectancy.

Hughes and Lund downplay the extraordinary "number of obstacles" that "prevent" the "union" of Hale and Thornton "until the final page." This plot strand, they argue, is "a familiar one": "the erotic plot that characterizes romance fiction." Thanks to waiting, anticipating, and postponing in the romance plot and in serials generally, the format is inherently erotic (157-58). Less enthralled, an early reviewer objected to the confusion stemming from the "flat lie" that Margaret "is made to tell in order to secure the escape of her brother." It "is gratuitous, painful—staggering as an incident, and without useful result as a lesson," fumed Henry Fothergill Chorley (*Athenaneum* 403). Actually, neither eroticism nor gratuitousness applies. A fundamental philosophical disagreement with Dickens's world view motivated Gaskell's parodic revaluation of suspenseful delays in serials such as *Hard Times.* Teleology is at issue in *North and South,* not just methodology. For both Gaskell and Dickens, technique strives to reveal life's purpose and design.

Book 3 of *Hard Times* ends with a flurry of comedowns and failures: Harthouse put to flight, the breakup of the Louisa Gradgrind-Josiah Bounderby marriage, after which a sort of spinsterhood awaits Mr. Gradgrind's daughter. The disclosure that Mrs. Pegler is Bounderby's mother deflates the myth of the self-made man, exploding laissez-faire economics, a cornerstone of Utilitarianism, along with it. Although Blackpool will be proven innocent, he is mortally injured when found and will not be reunited with friends for long. Tom, Mr. Gradgrind's son, who is the actual bank robber, is captured by Bitzer, Mr. Gradgrind's star pupil.

In *North and South,* by contrast, delay is prelude to agreement. Gaskell offers the prospect of new and richer life for both halves of England once Margaret's essential blamelessness has been reestablished. Which sort of world should one aspire to live in, Gaskell asked readers of *Household Words,* one that reaches marital accord between Mr. Thornton and Miss Hale (North and South) and establishes friendly relations between master and man (Thornton and Higgins)—or one that inflicts disaster on Blackpool and brings disappointment for Rachael, frustration for Louisa, exile for Tom? Gaskell urged Dickens's subscribers to heed the novelist capable of delivering positive occurrences; they should ignore her less sanguine rival, who could only produce let-downs and calamities.

Gaskell read *Hard Times* while composing **North and South**; her editor-publisher had portions of her manuscript in hand while his anti-industrial novel was still appearing. Dickens often seems to be refuting the novel that Mrs. Gaskell was writing in response to his. In redoing each other, each claimed to be substituting realism for unreality—Gaskell by rendering industrialism less gloomy, Dickens by blackening his contributor's settings and themes. In short, a case of mutual recrimination.[6] Dickens suggests that **North and South** is wish fulfillment, unlike his hard-nosed critique of the negative impact that factory conditions were having on interpersonal relationships. In Gaskell's view, satirists such as Dickens, an outsider in Preston and Manchester, paint the life process much bleaker than it is.

Dickens stalls to disguise his shortage of solutions, Gaskell insinuates. Instead of demanding answers, readers are fooled into relishing the painful pleasure of protracted delays. Ending these, Gaskell objected, becomes the equivalent of, if not a substitute for, ameliorating society's problems. Through the last twenty chapters of **North and South,** Gaskell showed believers in Dickens's suspenseful serials how easily she could manufacture suspense. She derived all of the benefits that Dickens reaped from making readers wait, yet she strove to cancel this stratagem once for all by aggravating a rival's delaying tactics for purposes of her own.

Misunderstandings, missed opportunities, and failures to communicate—all abound in chapters 32 through 52—are not *bona fide* delays. Ultimately, **North and South** turns delay against itself, dismissing the very idea as an ontological impossibility. Dickens's addiction to it, Gaskell complained, is responsible for much of his popularity, whereas his misuse of suspense ought to exclude him from the ranks of social realists.

Two paradoxes operate simultaneously. 1. Gaskell laughs at Dickens without eschewing the suspense that parodying his supposedly phony delays can create; her parodic revision of the suspenseful delay insidiously resembles the tactic being discredited. 2. Gaskell argues that delay—life temporarily suspended—is an illusion. *North and South* redoes such suspension as continual process: strictly speaking, Gaskell argues, the realization of life's designs is never on hold, no matter how long until resolution arrives or how slowly answers take shape.

In Gaskell's opinion, prolonged delays in Victorian serials misrepresent the way life works. Even apparent setbacks in *North and South* can be viewed positively as attempts to move forward, Gaskell suggests. Temporary disappointments serve to facilitate subsequent efforts. Mr. Hale's death, for example, empowers Bell to intervene; his fatal fit leaves it up to Higgins to enlighten Thornton. A third agent finally succeeds where the first two failed. Gaskell may be said to emphasize the determination of the life process to clear up a misunderstanding, not the number of unsuccessful tries before it does so.

Admittedly, Blackpool is eventually found, Bounderby finally disgraced. Yet these are recoveries on life's part and ought not to be confused with moral or social progress. Dickens's world is self-policing, Gaskell concedes, but never self-perfecting. At the end of *Hard Times,* the attitude of factory owners like Bounderby has not improved an iota, nor has the lot of their employees from whom they remain estranged.

"'Th' world is in a confusion,'" Higgins observes (382; ch. 37), his outburst designed to soften Blackpool's oft-repeated complaint that it is "'a muddle, and that's aw'" (54; bk. 1, ch. 10). Confusion for Gaskell is a state of mind, muddle one of matter. The first can be cleared up; the second means that the human condition remains a perennially hard time. Gaskell substitutes "confusion" for "muddle." The eventual betrothal of Miss Hale to Mr. Thornton illustrates the clarification process that Blackpool is wrong to despair of.

Delay in Dickens is not always delay either. The day of reckoning inexorably approaches, even if it seems unavoidable only in retrospect. Be it Mrs. Pegler's manifestation of her true identity, Krook's spontaneous combustion, or the French Revolution—sudden disclosure or major upheaval seldom occurs without warning. Even Nell's death, which punishes society for its inhospitability to goodness, has its harbinger when the little scholar, the heroine's alter ego, dies in the fifteenth installment.

The question arises: which deserves to be called life's basic rhythm? Which subsumes the other—clarification of confusions or cathartic catastrophe? Gaskell invites readers to trust in gradual improvement, an idea that George Eliot subsequently embraces even more confidently; *Hard Times* asks them to rely on periodic admonishment.

Given diametrically opposed perceptions of life's tempo, its patterns and pace, Dickens and Gaskell were doomed to remain at loggerheads. Unlike Thornton and Miss Hale or North and South, they could not reconcile, a blow, in effect, to Gaskell's philosophy. She and Dickens were bound to write different kinds of novel forever. Not surprisingly, he preferred serials composed of "self-sufficient units with powerful conclusions" (Hughes/Lund 153) because he believed they imitate real life, in which matters inevitably come to a head. She believed in unfolding, not compression, expansion over contraction, an asymmetrical continuity of ameliorations instead of clear-cut stages culminating in a resounding climax.

Dickens was not deterred by Gaskell's disdain for the suspenseful delays in *Hard Times*. In *Great Expectations* he created the consummate delay by postponing Magwitch's return until installment 24, chapter 39 (11 May 1861). After Pip's last sight of the recaptured convict being "taken up the side" of "the prison-ship" in chapter five, one must wait to confirm the identity of the hero's secret benefactor for thirty-four chapters, twenty weekly installments, roughly five and a half months. With exactly two-thirds of *Great Expectations* in print, Magwitch's reappearance marks the final installment of the novel's "Second Stage."

The understanding eventually reached by Gaskell's lovers validates her contention that worthwhile unions are not only possible but inevitable, whether between men and women or managers and workers. Appearances to the contrary, her serial demonstrates, life inches toward connection. Awareness of our mutual dependency, greater understanding between individuals and classes— such is "'the very breath of life,'" an enlightened Thornton instructs Mr. Colthurst (525; ch. 51). Despite Dickens's ability to make the reader hold his breath, this elixir is absent from his serials, Gaskell charged.

Union for Margaret Hale and Mr. Thornton spells victory for the life force, which Gaskell's serial pattern wishes to serve. Already on everyone's mind five years before Darwin published *The Origin of Species,* this strong, evolutionary drive is subtler than anything in *Hard Times*. Providence can only set things right drastically at appointed times; the life force, Gaskell points out, runs deeper than sectional rivalries, bad feelings between classes, or misunderstandings between men and women.

Regardless of the several deaths listed earlier, characters fittest for survival "live and thrive" in *North and South*; the long-awaited union of Hale and Thornton entails "a fusion of their strengths" (Martin 98, 105). Offspring from this "fusion," one imagines, will be hybrids for the future, as capable as they are compassionate, hence ample compensation for a childless Louisa and superior to "Sissy's happy children," who seem generic (222; bk. 3, ch. 9).

"The experience of writing a serialized novel for Charles Dickens was disappointing, frustrating, and aggravating for Gaskell," as one of her recent interpreters overstates (Schor 140). It may also have been exhilarating; although she had lost the contest within Dickens's periodical, she could reverse the outcome in hardcovers by expanding her final chapters. Granted, *North and South* was unsuited "by its very nature" to "the form of serialization followed in *Household Words*" (Hopkins 143); nevertheless, it was capable of parodying that form, as Dickens may have realized belatedly. Thus he threatened to apply the scissors to Gaskell's final installments if she failed to conclude expediently.

To supporters Gaskell wrote disparagingly of *North and South* as it appears in *Household Words*:

> at last the story is huddled and hurried up, especially in the rapidity with which the sudden death of Mr Bell, succeeds to the sudden death of Mr Hale. But what could I do? Every page was grudged me . . . Just at the very last I was compelled to desperate compression . . . I can not insert small pieces here and there—I feel as if I must throw myself back a certain distance in the story, and re-write it from there; retaining all the present incidents, but filling up intervals of time etc. etc.

(quoted in Schor 141-42)

For once nearly as histrionic as Dickens, Gaskell makes it sound as if the editor stood over her desk, compressing her physically along with her manuscript. She pleaded for each additional page as if it were a starving person's last morsel. In effect, Dickens did everything Gaskell accuses him of and more. He was trying not just to change the way she wrote but also to alter the way she saw the world.

"Huddled," "hurried," "rapidity," "sudden" (used twice), "compression"—these are obscenities for Gaskell. None of them applies to the dispelling of Mr. Thornton's misconception of Miss Hale, Gaskell refused to repair her story with inserts, a passage added "here and there" the way Dickens expanded his own serials on those rare occasions when he produced insufficient copy to fill up the space allotted. She had to readjust her story's overall speed, slowing things down by "filling up intervals of time" between "the present incidents" until the novel moved along at a rate she felt matched life's. In the final version, Mr. Hale dies in chapter 40, Mr. Bell in chapter 48, Gaskell's revision of a suddenness in her serial turns out to be an anti-sensational delay.

North and South needs nearly two hundred pages to rectify mistakes introduced in chapter 32 when Thornton sees Margaret with Frederick. Mocking while mimicking, Gaskell parodies suspenseful delay as a cardinal instance of Dickensian hyperbole. Dickens, she implies, exaggerates delays the way his novels magnify society's ills. Through parodic prolongation, Gaskell defied the arbitrary power that her editor-publisher had exercised when he shortened the denouement of her serial while darkening her view of the industrial situation in his. Seemingly interminable misapprehension caused by events in the strike and mutiny chapters constitutes a sort of mutiny on Gaskell's part. Her parody struck back at a tyrannical London-based editor who was protecting his penchant for sensational serials.

Notes

1. Chapter 14 is titled "The Mutiny." In chapter 22, "A Blow and its Consequences," a "sharp pebble" grazes Margaret's "forehead and cheek" when she protects Thornton from the strikers' fury (235).

2. Material from this essay originally formed part of chapter three of *Hidden Rivalries in Victorian Fiction*; only a few paragraphs survived into the printed text. See pp. 55-57.

3. Ironically, chapters 24 and 25, in which Thornton decides to propose to Margaret and is rebuffed, are titled "Mistakes" and, prematurely, "Mistakes Cleared Up." Chapter 32 is appropriately titled "Mischances."

4. At Dickens's request, Gaskell changed her title from *Margaret Hale* to *North and South,* a good decision one feels (see Vann 64-71). But Gaskell could be uncooperative as well as compliant. Having sent "too large a batch" of manuscript, she urged Dickens to "shorten it as you think best" (letter quoted in Schor 141). However, when she agreed to do a "condensation," she would sometimes return proofs unaltered (Easson 88).

5. According to J. Don Vann, Gaskell rewrote chapter 44 and added chapters 45, 46, 47, 48, and 50 (see *Victorian Novels* 79). Also see Dorothy Collin, 67-93. In her "Note on the Text" for the Penguin edition, she states that "the concluding chapter of the twenty-first part published in *Household Words* (chapter 44) was expanded to form chapters 44 to 48" (27).

6. See chapter 3 of Meckier (1987), titled "Mutual Recrimination: *Hard Times, North and South.*"

Works Cited

Chorley, Henry Fothergill. Unsigned review of *North and South,* the *Athenaeum,* 7 April 1855, p. 403. In Angus Easson, Ed. *Elizabeth Gaskell: The Critical Heritage.* London: Routledge, 1991.

Collin, Dorothy. "The Composition of Mrs. Gaskell's *North and South.*" *Bulletin of the Rylands Library,* 54 (1971): 67-93.

Davis, Earle. *The Flint and the Flame: The Artistry of Charles Dickens.* Columbia: U of Missouri P, 1963.

Dickens, Charles. *Great Expectations.* Ed. Edgar Rosenberg. New York: Norton, 1999.

———. *Hard Times.* Eds. George Ford and Sylvère Monod. New York: Norton, 1990.

———. *The Old Curiosity Shop.* Ed. Paul Schlicke. London: J. M. Dent, 1995.

Easson, Angus. *Elizabeth Gaskell.* London: Routledge and Kegan Paul, 1979.

Gaskell, Elizabeth. *North and South.* Ed. Dorothy Collin. Harmondsworth: Penguin, 1970.

Hopkins, A. B. *Elizabeth Gaskell: Her Life and Work.* London: John Lehmann, 1952.

Hughes, Linda K. and Michael Lund. "Textual/sexual pleasure and serial publication." *Literature and the Marketplace: Nineteenth-century British publishing and reading practices.* Eds. John O. Jordan and Robert L. Patten. Cambridge: Cambridge UP, 1995. Pp. 143-64.

Martin, Carol A. "Gaskell, Darwin, and *North and South.*" *Studies in the Novel,* 15 (1983): 91-107.

Meckier, Jerome. *Hidden Rivalries in Victorian Fiction: Dickens, Realism, and Revaluation.* Lexington: UP of Kentucky, 1987.

———. "Suspense in *The Old Curiosity Shop*: Dickens' Contrapuntal Artistry." *The Journal of Narrative Technique,* 2 (1972): 199-207.

Page, Norman. *A Dickens Companion.* London: Macmillan, 1984.

Schor, Hilary M. *Scheherezade in the Marketplace: Elizabeth Gaskell and the Victorian Novel.* New York: OUP, 1992.

Vann, J. Don. "Dickens, Charles Lever, and Mrs. Gaskell." *Victorian Periodicals Review,* 22 (1989): 64-71.

———. *Victorian Novels in Serial.* New York: MLA, 1985.

Wright, Edgar. *Mrs. Gaskell: The Basis for Reassessment.* Oxford: OUP, 1965.

Joanne Wilkes (essay date summer 2007)

SOURCE: Wilkes, Joanne. "'Have at the Masters'?: Literary Allusions in Elizabeth Gaskell's *Mary Barton.*" *Studies in the Novel* 39, no. 2 (summer 2007): 147-60.

[*In the following essay, Wilkes delineates how Gaskell traces the Lancashire dialect of her working-class characters in* Mary Barton *to works by such esteemed English authors as William Shakespeare, Edmund Spenser, and Geoffrey Chaucer.*]

When Elizabeth Gaskell published her first novel, **Mary Barton,** in 1848, she gave it the subtitle, **A Tale of Manchester Life,** and announced in her preface that the book's aim was to "give some utterance to the agony which from time to time convulses [the] dumb people" of Manchester (7).[1] An important aspect of this giving utterance was the use of the Lancashire dialect for the speech of her working-class characters. This was something with which Gaskell took particular care, as is evident from the corrections and changes she made to the successive editions of the novel that she oversaw: the dialect had to be authentic. But while she ventriloquized to her readers speech that was, the preface implies, foreign to them, she also showed that, rather than being some kind of corruption of southern, educated English, the Lancashire dialect incorporated words and turns of phrase that had been used by admired, even canonical authors of earlier centuries. So when, in chapter 2, "two rude lads" cry out "Polly Barton's getten a sweetheart" (18), a footnote traces the usage of "getten" back to Chaucer's *Canterbury Tales.* When Alice Wilson tells Mary Barton and Margaret Jennings that the news of her mother's death had made her cry "many a night at after" (33), the footnote cites a line where the protagonist of Shakespeare's *Richard III* uses the phrase "at after." Other authors deployed in this way include John Wycliffe, Ben Jonson, Edmund Spenser, William Langland and John Skelton. Moreover, the last edition overseen by Gaskell—the 5th of 1854—had appended to it two lectures on the Lancashire dialect that her husband William had given in that year. They reflected the pair's concern to demonstrate in detail that Lancashire vocabulary and grammatical forms had their roots in the very origins of the language and that many of them could be found in the works of respected authors.

Highlighting the connections between Lancashire dialect forms and authors likely to be respected by her middle- and upper-class readers was, then, a relatively straightforward means for Gaskell of giving her working-class characters an idiomatic language while linking this language to her readers' frame of reference in a way that invested it with dignity. By contrast, as has long been recognized, using the role of the narrator's voice to bridge the gap between working-class characters and readers of other classes—to interpret the experience of the former for the latter—is much more problematic. In particular, the narrative commentary on John Barton's thoughts and motives is given to heavy-handed disclaiming of any endorsement of his perspective. So when Barton pawns his better coat and best handkerchief to buy food for the destitute Davenports and feels "bitter hatred" toward the apparently happy people in the streets plus resentment of the "well-filled, well-lighted shops," the narrator points to the suffering that may be concealed behind people's carefree appearance and declares that Barton's heart was "touched by sin" (57-58). A later analysis of Barton's feelings towards the masters (see ch. 15) becomes confused, as Catherine Gallagher has demonstrated, in that Barton's political radicalism is "presented both as proof that he is incapable of making moral choices and as an emblem of his moral responsibility." The narrator compares the "actions of the uneducated" to those of a monster without a soul or "a knowledge of the difference between good and evil," but offers John Barton's ideas, despite their "wild and visionary" nature, as evidence that he does actually possess a soul (Gallagher 73-75).

Marjorie Stone has portrayed this narrative instability more positively, interpreting the text as a "polyphony [of] multiple voices," both of varying narrative voices and working-class voices, which combine to "subvert the hegemony of middle-class discourse that empowers [Gaskell] to speak" (175-77).[2] Stone also notes the novel's plethora of mottos and literary and religious allusions, which, she contends, convey the virtues of the novel's working-class characters and, conversely, the deficiencies of its middle-class representatives. Insofar as they bear on the working-class characters, the allusions fulfill a function similar to the notes and lectures that link working-class Lancashire dialect to well-known literary figures. They thus sometimes work against the novel's overt disavowals of the workers' grievances.

The novel's epigraphs and literary and religious allusions are numerous, as Stone observes. This fact is also evident in the editorial annotations to the various modern editions of *Mary Barton*,[3] so my focus here is not on identifying hitherto-unrecognized allusions. Rather, I am concerned to show, how a number of "high-culture" literary allusions are geared to dignify the feelings and experiences of the working-class characters in the eyes of middle- and upper-class readers. The major part of the article then goes on to draw out the significance of two important clusters of allusions that relate, firstly, to the Barton/Carson class-conflict plot, and secondly, to the ambivalent figure of John Barton's sister-in-law, the prostitute Esther.

The cluster of allusions bearing on the class-conflict plot is mainly Shakespearean, and it is linked specifically to the masters-characters of the same class as the readers implied by Gaskell's preface. The allusions thus invite those readers to ask themselves how far they share the masters' perspectives; one allusion, moreover, has a crucial bearing on the development of events. While the narrative commentary at times disavows sympathy with the workers', and especially with John Barton's, attitudes, this cluster of allusions conveys a very negative impression of the masters' attitudes; in so doing, it questions the adequacy of readers' own responses to the workers' suffering and grievances.

The novel links Esther with John Barton, not simply because of their familial relationship: John talks of Es-

ther's sudden disappearance in the novel's first conversation, the two share the experience of a child dying from illness aggravated by malnutrition, and they finally rest in the same grave. In John's case, the cluster of allusions relating to the class-conflict plot steers reader sympathy toward him, against the grain of some of the overt narrative commentary. In Esther's case, by contrast, the narrative commentary represents her primarily as a victim while the textual allusions relating to her convey a more contradictory picture. Although she has been subject to circumstances beyond her control, and her own sense of guilt is overstrained, some of the allusions associated with her seem to endorse her feelings of sinfulness. This ambiguity, I will argue, contributes to an impression that, unlike John Barton, Esther is marginal to the novel, while at the same time, paradoxically, she gestures beyond it.

It is important to note that the novel represents the cultural frames of reference of the working classes and the higher classes both inside and outside the novel as very different from each other. There is no evidence that the working-class characters themselves have access to the texts of Shakespeare and other literary figures whom Gaskell evokes in connection with them. (The exception here is the poetry of Robert Burns.) This is despite the fact that, as Jonathan Rose has shown, some members of the working classes of the period would have been familiar with canonical authors (Rose 166-85). The key problem, as Gaskell identifies it in her preface, is one of communication across classes, and the contrasts she creates between the cultural frames of reference of the different classes reinforce this message.

Thus working-class characters engage with poems written by and about working-class people—Joseph Lees's "The Oldham Weaver" (35-36) and Samuel Bamford's "God Help the Poor" (96-97)—while John Barton reads the Chartist newspaper *The Northern Star* (73). These texts are all obviously concerned with the plight of working people, and, significantly, do not involve any expense when money is at a premium (Barton borrows rather than buys his newspaper). Job Legh, it is true, attains a kind of expertise more common among men of higher classes (38-39)—but this is in entomology rather than literature.

The text that the working-class characters know best, however, is without doubt the Bible. Although none of them have any contact with church or clergy, they are familiar enough with the Bible to quote from it fairly unselfconsciously. So Jane Wilson, unable to believe that a policeman has induced her to incriminate her son Jem for the murder of Harry Carson, declares that doing so "would be like seething a kid in its mother's milk; and that th' Bible forbids" (218; Exod. 23:19; Deut. 14:21), while Mary thinks of the hospitable Mrs. Sturgis, who gave her house-room in Liverpool when she was unprovided for, in terms of Christ's words to the virtuous: "I was a stranger and you took me in" (261; Matt. 25:35). Even John Barton, who comes to perceive life as a struggle to the death between workers and masters, does so via a Biblical frame of reference; he constantly grapples with the meaning of the parable of Dives and Lazarus (Luke 16:19-26). The masters, on the other hand, do not pay heed to the Bible, a circumstance that becomes significant in the final interviews between Barton and the elder Carson.

In general, the novel's allusions to "high-culture" texts and contexts evoke literary and cultural contexts to which the working-class characters themselves have no access but that highlight to readers of other classes how the qualities, feelings, and experiences of working-class people can be worthy of sympathy, respect, or admiration-not to mention worth recording in fiction. In chapter 6, for example, the "self-denial, among rude, coarse men" when their families experience extreme poverty is said to be "akin to that of Sir Philip Sidney's most glorious deed"—an allusion to the celebrated Renaissance writer and aristocrat who, when fatally wounded on the battlefield of Zutphen, supposedly passed a cup of water to another wounded soldier, declaring, "Thy necessity is yet greater than mine" (54). Later, the sufferings of the working-classes are said to be worthy of Dante's pen, with the implication that a writer who can evoke sinners' sufferings in hell could be at least equally eloquent about the largely undeserved trials of the contemporary urban poor (75).

On a more individual level, working-class characters' emotional bonds are also invested with more seriousness for readers of other classes by being linked to texts familiar to the latter. This is particularly the case with the central pair of lovers, Jem Wilson and Mary Barton. Jem's resolve to risk proposing to Mary is described as his determination to "put his fortune to the touch, to win or lose it all" (110), evoking a well-known love poem by James Graham, Marquis of Montrose (1612-1650). Jem has earlier been credited with "the sure instinct of love, by which almost his body thought" (73), an echo of John Donne's "Of the Progresse of the Soule: The Second Anniversarie" ("That one might also say, her body thought," line 246). Mary is soon afterwards linked to the same poem in the reference to the flushing of her cheeks in sleep as the movement of her "eloquent blood" (95, Donne 1. 244). Later, her desperate waiting to see Jem again (after mistakenly declining his proposal of marriage) is expressed by an allusion to Tennyson's Mariana awaiting her betrothed:

> "Why comes he not," she said,
> "I am aweary, aweary,
> I would that I were dead."[4]

(134)

Mary and Jem do not meet again until the trial scene, but she has been determined to prove his innocence of murder, and her "high, resolved purpose of right-doing" is compared to the lion that guided Una through the wilderness in the first book of Spenser's *Faerie Queene*. The narrator says of Mary's ordeal as the trial approaches,

> she had so struggled and triumphed (though a sadly-bleeding victor at heart) over herself these last two days, had so concealed agony, and hidden her inward woe and bewilderment, that she began to take confidence, and to have faith in her own powers of meeting any one with a passably fair show, whatever might be rending her life beneath the cloak of her deception.

(226)

Readers would have picked up here the allusion to the famous story from Plutarch of the Spartan boy who stole a fox cub, concealed it under his cloak, and was prepared to suffer clawing and biting, even death, to escape detection. Then, when the strain of all she has had to do brings Mary near death, one epigraph to chapter 33 in which this state is described (277) is part of the lament for Imogen in Shakespeare's *Cymbeline*:

> Fear no more the heat o' th' sun,
>   Nor the furious winter's rages;
> Thou thy worldly task hast done,
>   Home art gone and ta'en thy wages.

(IV.ii.259-62)

Because *Cymbeline* loomed larger in the Shakespearean canon in the nineteenth century than it does now, these famous lines are likely to have evoked their original context for Victorian readers, and thus would have linked Mary with a much-admired heroine; moreover, as well as highlighting the extent of Mary's ordeal, the lines hint that, like Imogen's, it will not have a fatal outcome.

Mary herself does not know any Shakespeare, let alone any Spenser or Plutarch. That privilege is reserved for her would-be lover, Harry Carson, and is evidently the result of his father's wealth, which has also allowed him to live the life of an idle young man of fashion. On Harry's first appearance in the novel, "lazily" eating a copious and well-prepared breakfast, he is introduced thus:

> The son was strikingly handsome, and knew it. His dress was neat and well-appointed, and his manners far more gentlemanly than his father's. He was the only son, and his sisters were proud of him; his father and mother were proud of him: he could not set up his judgment against theirs; he was proud of himself.

(62)

For Harry, appearance is the main criterion for judging both others and himself. As a result, although his education enables him to draw on his knowledge of Shakespeare, he does so just as "lazily" as he eats his breakfast—he reads Shakespeare in a simplistic and self-aggrandizing way. So when Harry is accosted by Jem and suspects Jem of being a rival for Mary's love, he revels in his own superiority in appearance and class, perceiving Jem only as "a black, grimy mechanic, in dirty fustian clothes, strongly built, and awkward." Hence he concludes that no woman could choose Jem in preference to himself, bolstering his self-esteem by evoking *Hamlet*: "It was Hyperion to a Satyr" (150). In the play, this is how Hamlet compares his mother's first husband, old Hamlet, to her second, his brother Claudius (I.ii.139-40)—but the prince's emphasis is less on the difference in physical appearance than on old Hamlet's protectiveness of his wife: "so loving to my mother / That he might not beteem the winds of heaven / Visit her face too roughly!" (I.ii. 140-42). Harry is fixated on the physical contrast between himself and Jem; but the novel as a whole makes it clear that, in his sexually predatory attitude towards Mary, it is Harry who is the "Satyr" while Jem is the "Hyperion." Later, in the aftermath of Jem's trial and Mary's physical collapse, Jem is actually said to protect Mary from "every wind of heaven" (295). As if to emphasize even more strongly Harry's misreading of Shakespeare and of the true nature of the contrast between him and Jem, the novel has Jem, just before the showdown with Harry, console himself over his inferior outward appearance by invoking a poet and poem familiar to him, Robert Burns's "For A' That, And A' That": "a man's a man for a' that, for a' that, and twice as much as a' that" (149). Slightly later, the narrator points out that Harry had forgotten that "The man's a man for a' that" (150). That is, the egalitarian spirit of Burns's poetry (which was known to readers of all classes) should have been recalled by Harry as well as by Jem.

The next chapter (16), which presents the confrontation between masters and workers and the workers' response thereto, focuses partly on the interpretation by the masters of Shakespeare's *I Henry IV*. Again, the key figure is Harry Carson who is the most intemperate and unsympathetic of this caste, but the take on Shakespeare of the masters as a group is important as well.

I Henry IV is associated with Harry from his first appearance in the novel. During the breakfast mentioned earlier, it emerges that Harry had spent half-a-crown on a bunch of lilies, but he had refused to give them to his youngest sister Amy. She challenges him to deny this, with "Answer me that, Master Hal": he picks up an allusion here to the scene in the play in which Prince Hal challenges Falstaff to tell more of his and his comrades' supposed trouncing of a large number of men during the robbery at Gadshill. Harry replies in the role of Falstaff, looking vexed and embarrassed, "Not on compulsion" (63; *I Henry IV,* II.iv.240). This exchange thus evokes for the reader Harry's pursuit of Mary (the re-

cipient of the lillies) and hints that the pursuit is as dubious as Falstaff's clandestine activities.

The first evocation of *I Henry IV* in chapter 16 concerns the reaction of the masters to the Trades Union delegates who have come to negotiate with them over the strike. Because of the delegates' dire poverty, their garments are old, ragged, and tattered; but the narrator points out that these rags "yet clothed men of parts and of power." Some of the masters, however, are said to be offended at the men's appearance, "rather affronted at such a ragged detachment coming between the wind and their nobility" (154). That this response reflects a superficial judgment on these masters' part is evident to the readers who register the allusion: the comment echoes Hotspur's description of a foppish lord (I.iii.132-44), who, when soldiers carry past him the corpses of those slain in battle, berates them for bringing "a slovenly unhandsome corpse / Betwixt the wind and his nobility" (I.iii.143-44). Shakespeare's lines valorize the hard work of fighting over the finicky sensitivities of self-important bystanders just as the novel valorizes the kinds of talent that surface in the working classes despite all the obstacles they face.

The last and most significant allusion to *I Henry IV* implicates Harry Carson in particular and the masters in general. Although Harry is the most obdurate of the masters in standing out against the delegates' demands, what eventually catalyzes their decision to murder him after the failure of negotiations is less his obduracy than his ridicule of their appearance. At the sight of the delegates, Harry had-reacting in a way that obviously recalls his response to Jem Wilson—"taken out his silver pencil, and had drawn an admirable caricature [of them—] lank, ragged, dispirited, and famine stricken." Then he had written underneath it "a hasty quotation from the fat knight's well-known speech in Henry IV" (156). This would be from the scene in *I Henry IV* in which Falstaff cynically describes the men he has recruited as his detachment for the forthcoming battle:

> . . . now my whole charge consists of ensigns, corporals, lieutenants, gentlemen of companies-slaves as ragged as Lazarus in the painted cloth, where the glutton's dogs licked his sores . . . you would think that I had a hundred and fifty tattered prodigals lately come from swine-keeping, from eating draff and husks. . . . No eye hath seen such scarecrows. . . . There's not a shirt and a half in all my company; and the half-shirt is two napkins tacked together and thrown over the shoulders like a herald's coat without sleeves. . . .
>
> (IV.iii.23-45)

The caricature is passed on to other masters, "who all smiled and nodded their heads" (156).

Harry's caricature with accompanying quotation, and the masters' reaction to this, clearly underline their misprision of what the workers' appearance really betokens: the ability and determination to struggle to fight poverty and near-starvation. The masters' incapacity to "read" the workers correctly is illustrated by their superficial understanding of Shakespeare. For in the play, both Falstaff's condition (as a "fat knight" amid half-starved men) and his treatment of his quasi-employees reflect badly on him rather than on them. He is in fact a kind of profiteering employer who has exploited the recruiting exercise for financial gain. Falstaff has commandeered the poverty-stricken who have no choice—much as the masters in the novel have made "knobsticks" of desperate, unemployed men from outside Manchester—while the more prosperous have bribed him to avoid being pressed.

While the delegates are deciding how to respond to the masters' ultimatum, one of them retrieves Harry's sketch from the fire. When the men look at it more closely, they recognize that it is a caricature of them. It is this awareness that brings on the powerful words from John Barton that in turn precipitate the murder. John is incensed by what seems to him the masters' callous indifference to the suffering of the workers and their families:

> It makes me more than sad, it makes my heart burn within me, to see that folk can make a jest of striving men; of chaps who comed to ask for a bit o' fire for th' old granny, as shivers i' th' cold; for a bit o' bedding, and some warm clothing to the poor wife who lies in labour on th' damp flags; and for victuals for the childer, whose little voices are getting too faint and weak to cry aloud wi' hunger. . . .
>
> (158)

The workers are not aware of Harry's self-satisfied appropriation of Shakespeare: there is no evidence that the quotation is still visible on the charred caricature or that the workers would recognize it if it were. The references to *Hamlet* and to *I Henry IV* are there for the middle- and upper-class readers who share the education of Harry and the other masters and who are therefore challenged to interpret the quotations in a different way than they do—in a way that highlights the deficiencies of the masters' perceptions. The allusion to Falstaff's speech about his recruits, moreover, obliges readers to align themselves with the masters in identifying the quotation: as mentioned, the text refers to "the fat knight's well-known speech in Henry IV," but the speech itself is not actually given. Just as the masters can recognize the speech from what Harry writes, the readers are assumed to have the education needed to recall the speech without any of its words being cited. The readers, then, draw on the background that they share with the masters, but are encouraged to reject the masters' viewpoint and to gain some understanding of the feelings of John Barton and his fellows. These feelings are also articulated at length in Barton's characteristic Lancashire dialect. Gaskell's deployment of the

Shakespeare quotations and of Barton's speech is thus in keeping with the emphasis of the preface to the novel, which is less on finding economic ways of alleviating class divisions than on alerting the middle- and upper-class readers to the widespread belief among the poor that the masters and their class are indifferent to their sufferings.

In the lead-up to the murder, then, although the narrative voice has disclaimed endorsement of John Barton's grievances against the masters, the text's Shakespearean references—not to mention its giving space to a long excursus from Barton on the pervasiveness of suffering among the poor—have the effect of giving some credibility to these grievances. But after John and the delegate resolve upon murder, as has often been argued, its full implications are not followed through.[5] Readers lose access to John Barton's consciousness, and the focus of the text moves squarely onto Mary and her friends' efforts to arrange the alibi that will acquit the falsely-accused Jem Wilson, and to the concomitant resolution of the Mary-Jem love-plot.

When John Barton's murder of Harry Carson again comes to the fore near the end of the novel, it is very much as an individual deed; the text itself ignores the fact that, although John's speech was the catalyst for the decision to murder Harry, his being the actual murderer was a matter of chance. The delegates drew pieces of paper in the time-honoured way of groups' choosing individual agents to carry out collective decisions, and John happened to draw the marked piece. The text also mobilizes again the idea that Barton's heart was "touched by sin": just as he had not registered any underlying distress beneath the apparently carefree people visiting the well-filled shops, so had he not grasped that in killing Harry, he was depriving a father of his only son. John Barton is therefore guilty of a failure of perception just as the masters were, and this comes home to him when he confronts John Carson as an individual: he confesses, "I did not know what I was doing . . . God knows I didn't" (303).[6]

John Barton's declaration, "I did not know what I was doing" eventually triggers an act of forgiveness on the part of John Carson, but it is an act that first demonstrates Carson's own failure of understanding—not through a misinterpretation of a text but through a failure to identify one. John Barton echoes Christ's words on the cross about those who have put Him to death: "Father, forgive them; for they know not what they do" (Luke 23:34). Carson repudiates him; but on witnessing an incident in the street in which a little girl urges clemency for the boy who had inadvertently knocked her down, claiming, *"he did not know what he was doing"* (305), Carson recognizes the echo of Christ's words in both her words and John Barton's. On returning home, he opens up his fine but largely unread family Bible, and after studying Luke's Gospel, he is induced to forgive his son's assassin just before Barton expires. This episode also points up the fact that Carson, for all his prosperity and hence access to the written word, has neglected his Bible, whereas in the novel as a whole, the working-class characters, despite their limited education, frequently quote from or echo this text.

Readers have generally found the confrontation and then reconciliation between John Carson and John Barton unconvincing. The deployment of the Biblical citation is clumsy and strained (especially in the interlude of the little girl), and Carson has not been portrayed as a man who would easily forgive. It is a case of a Biblical allusion's being made to do too much work, being made to drive the plot. There is also a strong sense that something complex is being noticeably simplified. Whereas the chapters preceding the murder might confuse readers on account of the text's competing discourses, as I have illustrated, the reconciliation scene is reductive. It both makes of John Barton an ignorant and now penitent sinner, and, as Gallagher has argued in relation to the Biblical citation, it "points to narrative as the instrument of God's providence without having to sort out the tangle of its own narrative threads" (87). Barton's grievances and their causes, plus his role as the agent of a group rather than as an individual, drop from sight. He ends up in an unmarked grave whose only words, a line from a Psalm about God's forgiveness, emphasize his identity as a sinner: "For he will not always chide, neither will he keep his anger for ever" (324; Ps. 103:9).

When John Barton is buried, it is together with his sister-in-law Esther: the pair are termed "these two wanderers" (324). The very first conversation in the novel, between John Barton and George Wilson, concerns Esther's mysterious disappearance from her lodgings. Throughout the text, John and Esther are linked, but this pattern ultimately serves to highlight that Gaskell found it easier to give some coherence to his story than to hers.[7] Again, the novel's use of textual allusions is illuminating here.

The only scene between John and Esther that is dramatized (rather than recalled) occurs when she approaches him in the street to warn him about what she perceives as the danger to Mary in Harry Carson's attentions. John spurns his sister-in-law here—she has become the streetwalker he had predicted she would be, and he has long blamed his beloved wife's death on Esther's unexplained disappearance. But the literary allusions in the chapter (10) create implicit connections between them. John perceives Esther by "the darkness visible of that badly-lighted street" (107): the words "darkness visible," by evoking Milton's description of Hell in *Paradise Lost* (Book 1, 1.63), underline both Esther's outcast state and the way John and the other starving members of the working classes have come to view their lives. (Just before his encounter with Esther, John is said to be near-dependent on opium on account of his habitual depression.) Moreover, an allusion to Shakespeare's *King Lear* reinforces the readers' sense of John and Esther's being fellow-sufferers. Esther's flimsy clothes make her "all unfit to meet the pelting of that pitiless storm" recalling Lear's words in the storm scene on the heath about the "[p]oor naked wretches" who are unable to "bide the pelting of this pitiless storm" (III.iv,38-39)—people whose suffering the king realizes he had ignored when he had the capacity to alleviate it. Like the evocations of *I Henry IV* already discussed, this allusion hints at the insensitivity of those with money and power to the ordeals faced by the less fortunate.

These literary allusions, then, convey to Gaskell's readers that, despite John's hostility to his sister-in-law, the similarities between the pair are more salient than their differences. John's hostility here is in fact short-lived: on his return home, "his conscience smote him with harshness" (109), and he tries for some time to find Esther again—thwarted only by not realizing that she has been imprisoned for a month for vagrancy and drunkenness. Later, too, in John's speech to his fellow-delegates about the heartlessness of the rich toward the poor, the reference to the storm in *King Lear,* connected earlier with Esther, is echoed for the readers when John says, "We donnot want their grand houses, we want a roof to cover us from the rain, and the snow, and the storm" (158).

Esther can also be aligned with John in that both have been deeply affected by the death of a child from disease rendered fatal by malnutrition. Just as Esther desperately turned to prostitution in a doomed attempt to save her daughter, John had contemplated stealing in order to nourish his dying son Tom. In both cases, the deaths are associated with the callousness of those of a higher class: Esther's former lover, an army officer, ignores her letters pleading for help while John, unemployed and unable to feed his son, sees his former employer's wife emerge from a shop laden with food.

Esther's story, however, never takes on the wider resonances that John Barton's eventually gains. Her experience can be interpreted as one specifically female—which is how both she and John Barton interpret it: a grim warning against the dangers posed by the blandishments of socially superior wooers for good-looking and self-confident young working women like Mary. Yet in context, Esther's potential role as an example to Mary is diminished in relevance because Mary finally has no need for warning or protection: she has been able to see through Harry's falseness unaided. The implication seems to be, rather, that a young woman like Mary who, unlike the country-born Esther, has lived all her life in Manchester is clear-sighted enough both to look after herself and to recognize the value of an honest working-class man as a husband.

The narrative and its commentary depict Esther mainly as a victim and sufferer: she has only taken to prostitution in a bid to save her daughter and has kept it up because her despair over her child's death has driven her to drink. Moreover, her homelessness and near-destitution are regularly emphasized. Despite all this, she remains concerned for the welfare of her family and former friends, though she is hampered in her efforts to aid them by her outcast condition. She is clearly the victim of a man, too, and this faithless army-officer lover is a man of the implied readers' own class. Yet some of the literary allusions deployed in the novel's treatment of Esther create ambiguity as to whether she is to be read primarily as victim or as sinner.

When Esther tells her story to Jem, she feels cut off by her sinful life from ever seeing her dead daughter again: "I've done that since, which separates us as far asunder as heaven and hell can be." Her feeling is exacerbated when she recalls the line from the Sermon on the Mount—"Blessed are the pure in heart, for they shall see God" (137-38; Matt. 5:8)—and she thus rejects Jem's offer of help. Her self-hatred becomes even worse when her discovery of the gun-wadding with Jem's writing on it convinces her that her own intervention with Jem had induced him to murder Harry, so she concludes that "[t]he black curse of Heaven rested on all her doings, were they for good or evil" (197). The narrator's immediate comment implies that Esther is mistaken here since she is not in her right mind, and it stresses also, in its echo of the Bible, Esther's solitary, neglected state. That is, the narrator's outburst, "Poor, diseased mind! and there were none to minister to thee!" (197), recalls Christ's words that ministering to anyone "an hungred, or athirst, or a stranger, or naked, or sick, or in prison" (Matt. 25:44-45) means ministering to Christ—thus highlighting that no one offers Esther Christian charity.

But Esther is associated in the text with evildoers as well: the comment just quoted evokes the sleep-walking of the tormented Lady Macbeth, of whom Macbeth asks the Doctor, "Canst thou not minister to a mind diseased" (V.iii.42). Esther believes that her conduct has inadvertently led to murder: Lady Macbeth's has of course deliberately encouraged it. Furthermore, when Esther seeks out Mary to show her the gun-wadding, she feels "as if some holy spell would prevent her . . . from crossing the threshold of that home of her early innocence" (199). The narrator thus alludes to "unholy Lady Geraldine['s]" being prevented from entering Christabel's house—a reference to the mysterious villainess of Coleridge's "Christabel"—despite the fact that Esther's intervention here actually gives Mary es-

sential information. An earlier evocation of a Coleridge poem has already associated Esther by implication with a literary sinner; when in her interview with Jem, Esther gains his attention by invoking Mary: "The spell of her name was as potent as that of the mariner's glittering eye. 'He listened like a three-year child'" (136). Esther is thus linked with Coleridge's famously guilt-ridden Ancient Mariner. The novel may often stress Esther's pitiful state, yet the evocations of Lady Macbeth, Lady Geraldine, and the Ancient Mariner give her an aura of guilt. Moreover, for none of these figures is the sinfulness associated with prostitution or extra-marital sex: it is as if, while overtly excusing what contemporary readers might have construed as sinful in Esther's conduct, the text at another level accepts their supposed assumption that she is indeed a wrongdoer.

For all the reductiveness of the reconciliation scene between Barton and Carson, the wider ramifications of John Barton's story are ultimately recuperated in some measure, which is not the case with Esther. The novel's penultimate chapter is devoted to a discussion involving John Carson, Job Legh, and Jem Wilson over industrial relations in which Job elucidates for Carson Barton's beliefs about inter-class relations. In addition, Barton's life is credited with progressive consequences in that Carson, after coming to understand his former enemy's viewpoint, resolves to foster confidence, understanding, and even love between masters and men. Barton is finally a man whose life has some lasting public significance. On the personal level, he is also in a sense reincarnated in his daughter's first child, whom she and Jem name Johnnie. But when Esther dies, it is without anyone, not even the narrator, reflecting on the personal or public legacy of her life.

The novel, then, not only has Esther die, but strives to empty her story of meaning by not following through with the implications of her ambiguous presentation. Something oddly similar transpires with a very different character, the pious Alice Wilson, as regards her religious beliefs. Alice has coped with the occasional joys and more numerous disappointments of her life by accepting that everything that has happened to her has been due to God's will, and according to His plan for her. But she falls fatally ill and lapses into her second childhood just at the point when, with the arrest of her nephew Jem for murder, her family and friends are about to face their most difficult ordeal. Thus Alice's simple faith is never tested by this experience, and the issues it raises are hence partly occluded so that her lapse becomes the text's. The pious virgin Alice must die because the Providential schema that has made her life meaningful to her cannot easily be sustained under the pressure of the narrative's events (although the novel tries to resuscitate it in the Barton/Carson reconciliation scene); the prostitute Esther must die because the meaning of her life cannot be defined.

In Esther's case, nonetheless, killing her off and stripping her life of overt significance, while at the same time leaving readers with an ambiguous image on account of the allusions associated with her, risks giving her an afterlife in readers' minds. Not only in readers' minds, either: in her next full-length novel, **Ruth,** Gaskell was to move the figure of the fallen woman, who haunts the margins of **Mary Barton,** to the role of protagonist. Yet the ambivalence of this figure, inscribed as it was in the culture Gaskell and her readers shared, continued to be telling.

Notes

1. All quotations from the novel will be from the text found in volume 5 of *The Works of Elizabeth Gaskell,* which is based on the 5th (1854) edition, the last one revised and corrected by Gaskell.

2. Coral Lansbury argues that the narrator's voice in *Mary Barton* tends to "engage in false pleading" because it reflects "her version of the average middle-class reader of her day," rather than "her own taste and feeling" (9).

3. Editions I found helpful in preparing my own for Pickering & Chatto (London 2005) include, in date order, Edgar Wright's OUP (Oxford 1987), Angus Easson's Ryburn (Halifax 1993), MacDonald Daly's Penguin (London 1996), and Jennifer Foster's Broadview (Peterborough, Ontario 2000).

4. Slightly misquoted: the original reads, "'He cometh not,' / She said, 'I am aweary, aweary, / I would that I were dead.'"

5. The novel's change of emphasis and direction from about halfway through has generated a rich critical tradition. Mid-twentieth-century critics like Raymond Williams and John Goode saw Gaskell as retreating from the implications of the workers' grievances that she has articulated into violence and a resolution presented very much in individualistic terms (Williams 87-91, Lucas 141-206). More recent critics have explored the question in terms of the intractability of the issues that Gaskell was dealing with, the religious and economic doctrines available to her, her mixing of genres, and gender roles as they bear on both the novel and herself as a woman writer. I am especially indebted to the studies by Bodenheimer, Gallagher, Yeazell, Krueger, Harsh, Guy, and D'Albertis.

6. The similarity between Barton's and Carson's surnames would be no accident; when Carson belatedly looks at his Bible (305), we learn that he and Barton have the same Christian name.

7. Esther's role has been discussed in detail by Krueger (176-85), who finds her portrayal in the novel an extended comment on patriarchal misreadings of women. I do not think it possesses this kind of consistency. More convincing is Starr's argument that the narrator both identifies with and distinguishes herself from Esther because of Gaskell's concern over being, as a female novelist, a kind of "public woman" (390).

Works Cited

Bodenheimer, Rosemarie. "Private Grief and Public Acts in *Mary Barton.*" *Dickens Studies Annual* 9 (1981): 195-216.

D'Albertis, Deirdre. *Dissembling Fictions: Elizabeth Gaskell and the Victorian Social Text.* New York: St Martin's, 1997.

Donne, John. "Of the Progresse of the Soule: The Second Anniversarie." *Poetical Works.* Ed. Herbert J. C. Grierson. Oxford: Oxford UP, 1971. 234.

Gallagher, Catherine. *The Industrial Reformation of English Fiction: Social Discourse and Narrative Form, 1832-1867.* Chicago: U of Chicago P, 1985.

Gaskell, Elizabeth. *Mary Barton; A Tale of Manchester Life.* 1848. Ed. Joanne Wilkes. *The Works of Elizabeth Gaskell.* Vol. 5. London: Pickering & Chatto, 2005.

Guy, Josephine M. *The Victorian Social-Problem Novel: The Market, the Individual and Communal Life.* Houndmills: Macmillan, 1996.

Harsh, Constance D. *Subversive Heroines: Feminist Resolutions of Social Crisis in the Condition-of-England Novel.* Ann Arbor: U of Michigan P, 1994.

Krueger, Christine L. *The Reader's Repentance: Women Preachers, Women Writers, and Nineteenth-Century Social Discourse.* Chicago: U of Chicago P, 1992.

Lansbury, Coral. *Elizabeth Gaskell: The Novel of Social Crisis.* London: Elek, 1975.

Lucas, John. "Mrs. Gaskell and Brotherhood." *Tradition and Tolerance in Nineteenth-Century Fiction: Critical Essays on Some English and American Novels.* Ed. David Howard, John Lucas, and John Goode. London: Routledge & Kegan Paul, 1966. 141-206.

Rose, Jonathan. *The Intellectual Life of the British Working Classes.* New Haven, CT: Yale UP, 2001.

Shakespeare, William. *Cymbeline.* In *Complete Works.* Ed. Stanley Wells and Gary Taylor. Oxford: Clarendon P, 1986. 1301.

———. *Hamlet. Complete Works.* 740.

———. *I Henry IV. Complete Works.* 514, 522, 533.

———. *King Lear. Complete Works.* 1082.

———. *Macbeth. Complete Works.* 1124.

Starr, Elizabeth. "'A great engine for good': The Industry of Fiction in Elizabeth Gaskell's *Mary Barton* and *North and South*." *Studies in the Novel* 34.4 (2002): 385-402.

Stone, Marjorie. "Bakhtinian Polyphony in *Mary Barton*: Class, Gender, and the Textual Voice." *Dickens Studies Annual* 20 (1991): 175-200.

Williams, Raymond. *Culture and Society, 1780-1950.* London: Chatto & Windus, 1958.

Yeazell, Ruth Bernard. "Why Political Novels Have Heroines: *Sybil, Mary Barton,* and *Felix Holt*." *Novel* 18.2 (1985): 126-44.

Linda H. Peterson (essay date autumn 2007)

SOURCE: Peterson, Linda H. "Triangulation, Desire, and Discontent in *The Life of Charlotte Brontë*." *Studies in English Literature, 1500-1900* 47, no. 4 (autumn 2007): 901-20.

[*In the following essay, Peterson illustrates how Gaskell's* The Life of Charlotte Brontë *explores not only Brontë's biography, but the nature of the relationship between Gaskell, Brontë, and Harriet Martineau, as well as the role of the woman writer in society in general.*]

Most, if not all, critical analyses of Elizabeth Gaskell's *Life of Charlotte Brontë* (1857) discuss the parallels between the two novelists and the personal stake that Gaskell held in her biography of a fellow woman writer. It is, after all, a commonplace to speak of a biographer's investment in her subject.[1] Yet accounts of this particular biographer-subject relationship vary enormously—from the benign to the malignant, from "a friendship of tremendous warmth and attachment" to "self-aggrandizement and misrepresentation," even "treason."[2] At one end of the spectrum, Angus Easson suggests that the goal of the *Life* [Life of Charlotte Brontë] was "above all to do justice to Charlotte Brontë."[3] In the middle, Linda K. Hughes and Michael Lund note that the *Life* was "a form of benign self-advertisement," that Gaskell's presentation of "the brilliant but pure Brontë vouches for the worth of [her] own writing" at a moment in her own career when she came under fire for the subject matter of *Ruth* (1853).[4] More skeptical or hostile analyses of the *Life,* such as those by Deirdre d'Albertis or Juliet Barker, acknowledge the connections between the two writers—their mutual interest in women, factory workers, and social reform; their identification with northern concerns such as manufacturing and industry; and their embrace of a "parallel currents" model of authorship, with the "woman" and the "author" as fulfilling two different, if

important, roles. Yet, despite the mutual interests, such skeptical critics treat the biography as "book-making on the remains of the dead" and Gaskell as ultimately "subordinat[ing] the other woman," even selling her subject out.[5]

This essay reconsiders the Gaskell-Brontë relationship—and explores the reasons for the sharp divergence of critical views—by returning to their first encounter in the Lake District in July 1850 at Briery Close, the summer residence of Sir James and Lady Janet Kay-Shuttleworth. It treats the writerly dyad as a triad or, more properly, a triangle, by focusing on their attempt, during that first visit, to pay a call on Harriet Martineau, another famous woman writer living nearby at the Knoll, Ambleside. In so doing, I explore the role that Martineau played in the Gaskell-Brontë relationship and highlight an important agenda that illumines Gaskell's presentation of her subject in the *Life*: the creation of a community of women authors based in the north of England; operating in the geographical triangle of Manchester, Haworth, and the Lake District; and fulfilling the role that William Wordsworth had proposed at the end of *The Prelude* (1850): that of serving as "joint labourers in the Work . . . / Of [Man's] deliverance."[6] I thus view the *Life* as concerned with representations of the mid-Victorian woman writer as much as with the biography of a single author and treat Martineau's role as pivotal in this project.

TRIANGULATION: MARTINEAU AS OBJECT OF DESIRE

Triangles, as René Girard has taught us, are formations that allow the members to express bonds of identification and attraction, even as they may hide feelings of jealousy, envy, and rivalry. Two male characters competing for a female heroine express competition, antagonism, and difference, yet this triangle also expresses mediated desire and reveals the essential function of a second male in erotic attraction; in Girard's words, "In the birth of desire, the third person is always present."[7] As Eve Kosofsky Sedgwick further suggests, triangular desire accounts for homosocial bonding between men and the continuity of patriarchal power; more generally, the triangle can be used as a "sensitive register . . . for making graphically intelligible the play of desire and identification by which individuals negotiate with their societies for empowerment."[8] Two members of a triangle may thus express both bonding and competition, attraction and repulsion, and this ambivalent response, fundamental to triangular relationships, often reveals itself when issues of social power arise. Although the triangle in *The Life of Charlotte Brontë* involves three literary women rather than a romantic heterosexual triangle, the ambivalent nature of the Gaskell-Brontë relationship expresses itself most clearly, I believe, through a triangulation that involves their relationship with Martineau, and it erupts over issues of the woman writer's literary authority and social status.

In reading this writerly triangle, however, we must be historically cognizant of the values that Victorians invested in *sororal* relationships, as the Gaskell-Brontë-Martineau relationship presented itself. As Diane M. Chambers has argued in "Triangular Desire and the Sororal Bond: The 'Deceased Wife's Sister Bill,'" Victorians considered the relationship between sisters, both ideal and real, to be a "bond that would transcend other earthly relationships"; "no one else . . . not parents, children, or even a husband, could provide the same kind of support, comfort, and love that a sister could."[9] This cultural belief in sororal unity, in women's supportive relationships with each other, helps explain Gaskell's unremittingly positive representation of her friendship with Brontë—even as our modern skepticism about such Victorian beliefs helps account for recent critical analyses that deconstruct this representation.

Brontë instigated, intentionally or not, a triangular relationship when she wrote to both Gaskell and Martineau on 17 November 1849. With her letter to Martineau, she presented a copy of *Shirley* (1849) "in acknowledgment of the pleasure and profit she [sic] he has derived from her works. When C. B. first read 'Deerbrook' he tasted a new and keen pleasure, and experienced a genuine benefit."[10] With her letter to Gaskell, Brontë did not include a copy of her new novel, for Gaskell had already read *Shirley* and posted a letter of praise to "Currer Bell" via the publisher, George Smith; rather, in the letter of 17 November 1849 to Gaskell, Brontë responded in order to "acknowledge its kind, generous sympathy with all her heart."[11] The difference between the letters signifies the different status of the women writers. Martineau was the eldest by virtually a generation, the most famous, and the most well-established woman author of her day, having written professionally since the 1820s and made her fame with the *Illustrations of Political Economy* (1823-24), including "A Manchester Strike" (1832); in 1850, she was writing regularly for the radical *Westminster Review*, Charles Dickens's *Household Words,* and the London *Daily News.* Gaskell, like Brontë, was a relative newcomer to literary life, having published **Mary Barton: A Tale of Manchester Life** in 1848, a year before receiving Brontë's letter. Key to both letters, however, is a role that Brontë hoped the two women might play: replacements for her dead sister, Emily. To W. S. Williams, her editor and advisor at Smith, Elder, Brontë also wrote on 17 November 1849: "In Mrs. Gaskell's nature—it mournfully pleases me to fancy a remote affinity to my Sister Emily—in Miss Martineau's mind I have always felt the same."[12] The Brontë-Gaskell-Martineau triangle was established, then, as a substitute for that of Acton, Currer, and Ellis Bell—with the elements of attraction and competition already embedded in the sororal and authorial relationships, with Martineau occupying the place of dominant writer, yet with Brontë seeking for an "Emily" in Gaskell or Martineau or both.

When Gaskell and Brontë were introduced in the Lake District the following summer, they expressed their attraction. After the visit, Brontë wrote to her friend Ellen Nussey: "fortunately there was Mrs. Gaskell . . . who came to the Briery the day after me—I was truly glad of her companionship. She is a woman of the most genuine talent—of cheerful, pleasing and cordial manners and—I believe—of a kind and good heart."[13] Gaskell similarly wrote to Charlotte Froude: "I never heard of so hard, and dreary a life . . . She is truth itself—and of a very noble sterling nature,—which has never been called out by anything kind or genial."[14] Before the visit, however, the two women writers had expressed anxiety about their likely competition in the literary marketplace. As Brontë was preparing *Shirley* for publication, she wrote on 1 February 1849 to her editor at Smith, Elder about Gaskell's first novel, released in October 1848: "In reading 'Mary Barton'—(a clever though painful tale) I was a little dismayed to find myself in some measure anticipated both in subject and incident."[15] Gaskell, too, worried about *Shirley* and wrote of it with mixed response: "I think I told you that I disliked a good deal in the plot of Shirley, but the expression of her own thoughts in it is so true and brave, that I greatly admire her."[16]

Gaskell's distinction between the writer and the work is one technique she invokes for overcoming literary rivalry and emphasizing cooperation among women writers. Another technique deployed in the **Life** is more basic: in this case, for example, Gaskell simply omits Brontë's 1849 letter to Smith, Elder expressing competition and selects instead a letter of 12 January 1853 showing cooperation, when Brontë requests a slight delay in the publication of *Villette* so that Gaskell's **Ruth** will not be overshadowed: "Mr. Smith proposes, accordingly, to defer the publication of my book till the 24th inst.; he says that will give 'Ruth' the start in the papers daily and weekly, and also will leave free to her all the February magazines."[17] In the **Life,** sisterly cooperation, rather than competition, is set as the norm.

Yet in the **Life,** as in real life, Gaskell had to negotiate significant differences between herself and her subject that emerge in Brontë's letters and that, as her primary source, Gaskell necessarily relied upon for constructing the biography: religious (Brontë was Anglican, Gaskell Unitarian), ethnic (Brontë was Irish, Gaskell English and Scots), and social (Brontë was single, by training a governess; Gaskell married with four children, the wife of a Unitarian minister). Initially in the **Life,** the most significant contrast is geographical, the difference between Manchester and Haworth, between civilized urban life and the remoteness and wildness of the Yorkshire moors that "explain" the traces of "coarseness" in the Brontës' novels and must be overcome in order to incorporate Charlotte Brontë into a community of exemplary women authors. The *Life* famously begins with a journey to the Haworth Parsonage—away from the city, out through barren country, up the steep main street of Haworth to an isolated parsonage—a place in stark contrast to Gaskell's new home in Plymouth Grove, easily reached by train yet deliciously away from the city's black smoke. This geographical difference will be overcome by a mutual domesticity—a prominent feature of the *Life* that begins with the visit to Martineau and continues with an exchange of visits between Plymouth Grove and Haworth Parsonage: Brontë visiting Gaskell in Manchester in June 1851, April 1853, and May 1854 and Gaskell visiting Haworth in September 1853.

The call on Martineau was meant, I suggest, to consolidate the writers' friendship, to allow the two younger women to pay tribute to an older, well-established woman author, and thus to ally themselves with a tradition of serious women's writing for social good and political reform. This pilgrimage to an older woman writer's house is a *topos* in the memoirs of Victorian women writers; in the *Life* it specifically functions to reinforce the exemplary domesticity of all three women and the high literary goals that they share. Martineau had the reputation of being a writer committed to the social good—"a character," to quote her contemporary John Morley, "of many large thoughts and much generous purpose."[18] Brontë echoes this view in her letter of 17 November 1849: "'Deerbrook' ranks with the writings that have really done him [Currer Bell] good, added to his stock of ideas, and rectified his view of life."[19] Visiting Martineau would, then, confirm the two younger women's literary friendship and further Gaskell's project of creating a regional community of women writers dedicated to addressing social problems and their amelioration.

Martineau's home, the Knoll, fit the need for both literary achievement and exemplary domesticity, as it had been self-designed and built from the profits of her didactic fiction, including the *Illustrations of Political Economy,* the American travelogues *Society in America* (1837) and *Retrospect of Western Travel* (1838), and the novel *Deerbrook* (1839). The Knoll was within walking distance of Wordsworth's house, Rydal Mount, and the Arnold family home, Fox How, and shared their literary aura. Indeed, in her *Autobiography* (written 1855, published 1877) Martineau underscores the encouragement of Wordsworth and the Arnolds to build the Knoll near them in the Lake District, and she records their active participation in its construction—saying that "Mrs. Arnold consulted the Wordsworths: and they all came to exhort me to try to get the nook." Wordsworth even plants two young oaks "for a commemorative occa-

sion."[20] The Knoll therefore represents literary ground blessed by the poet laureate and suitable for a meeting of "joint labourers" in literature's work for the improvement of humankind; it symbolizes the successful career of a woman writer and the incorporation of women into the English literary tradition.

Thus, whereas d'Albertis sees Gaskell striking "a Faustian bargain" by using gendered domesticity ultimately "to dissociate herself from the other woman," I see Gaskell as using domestic space—including Martineau's The Knoll in Ambleside and her own home at Plymouth Grove—to enact a myth of association and bring into being an important sorority of writers identified with the north of England, committed to the Wordsworthian goal of "plain living and high thinking."[21] In Joanne Shattock's terms, this move involves finding a substitute for the usual sites of literary affiliation of male authors, who attended university together, met at London Clubs, or joined the Royal Literary Fund and attended its public dinners.[22] Women writers needed an equivalent space and found it, perhaps inevitably, in their homes. In Pierre Bourdieu's terms, Martineau's depiction of the Knoll in her *Autobiography* and Gaskell's use of this home in the *Life,* as well as her own house at Plymouth Grove and the Brontë parsonage at Haworth, is a gesture of "consecration," a move to establish symbolic criteria of lasting value in that the women writers are shown not merely writing for pleasure or for money but are demonstrating the high ideals associated with literary domestic space.[23]

As it turned out, Gaskell and Brontë were unable to visit Martineau during their 1850 meeting in the Lake District. Ironically, as Brontë noted in her letter to Nussey: "Miss Martineau was from home—she always leaves her house at Ambleside during the Lake Season to avoid the constant influx of visitors to which she would otherwise be subject."[24] While this failure to meet may seem to signal a failure to consolidate the literary triangle, in fact Martineau's absence may have been enabling, even serendipitous. As Erica Hateley explains, elaborating the Girard-Sedgwick theory of triangulation, "the object [of desire] will always be passivised"; it does not matter whether the desired object is present or absent.[25] Indeed, we might say that Martineau's absence—her physical distance from the two other women writers—allowed them to consolidate their friendship as one of attraction and cooperation. Once she became an active member, their relationship became more competitive.

TRIANGULATION: COMPETITION OVER THE REPRESENTATION OF BRONTË

If introducing Martineau into the Gaskell-Brontë dyad helped to consolidate a writerly community, it also introduced some discontents. Individually, Gaskell and

Brontë had met Martineau the year before their encounter in the Lake District, and the accounts of these earlier meetings reveal an element of competition already infiltrating a triangle meant for bonding. Gaskell met Martineau in London in November 1849 after her novel *Mary Barton* created a literary sensation and made her a "literary lion" for the season. (Gaskell's earliest reference to Martineau appears in a letter to Eliza Fox of 26 November 1849, but we learn little of this meeting other than the fact that "Miss Martineau and I spoke about you [Eliza Fox], a l'envoie l'une de l'autre.")[26] Brontë met Martineau a month later in December 1849, after the publication of *Shirley* took her to London for a visit to George Smith, her publisher. When Brontë learned that Martineau was staying around the corner with cousins, Richard and Lucy Martineau, she wrote a brief note, asking if she might call—and did so for tea on Sunday, 9 December 1849. The *Life* recounts this initial meeting between Brontë and Martineau—a wonderful anecdote with suspense as to the sex of "Currer Bell" and the appearance of a tall man right at the time of Brontë's expected visit (2:135). Nonetheless, Gaskell gives priority to her *own* first encounter with Brontë; in the table of contents in the *Life* it is singled out with the heading "the biographer's impressions of Miss Brontë" (2:vi), whereas the other encounter is noted as "Miss Brontë's . . . estimate of her hostess" (2:vii). If in my first analysis of triangulation Martineau was the object of desire, in this version desire has shifted, and the two other members of the triangle—Gaskell and Martineau—compete for priority with Brontë.

Martineau's account of "Currer Bell," which circulated via letter in London, Birmingham, and Manchester circles and was revised for her *Autobiography,* focuses on the author as "the smallest creature I had ever seen" and on Brontë's desire "to consult me about certain strictures of the reviewers which she did not understand, and had every desire to profit by."[27] In the *Life,* Gaskell turns this into an impression of a "young-looking lady, almost child-like in stature" who "with intuitive recognition" walks straight to Miss Martineau "with the free-masonry of good feeling and gentle breeding" (2:135). That is, Martineau presents Brontë as a younger writer consulting an older, more experienced one on matters of literary decorum, whereas Gaskell emphasizes Brontë's inherent gentility and the "freemasonry" of one author intuitively recognizing another. Gaskell here pursues a complex agenda: the project of "doing justice to Brontë by demonstrating her "gentle breeding" and of constructing a recognizable community of women writers joined by shared talent and taste.

As various critics have noted, a primary motivation for writing the *Life* was clearing Brontë's name of charges of coarseness and unfemininity. Initially, it was Nussey who, after her friend's death, urged Brontë's widower,

the Reverend Arthur Nicholls, to authorize a biography in order to refute errors in fact and judgment that were circulating in the obituaries. Most irritating to Nussey was an article in *Sharpe's London Magazine* for June 1855, "A Few Words about 'Jane Eyre,'" that "hurt and pained" her in its "tissue of malign falsehoods."[28] Published anonymously, the article revived many of the rumors about Currer Bell that had circulated at the publication of *Jane Eyre* and included suggestions of impropriety and coarseness based on the character of Mr. Rochester, who used "real wicked oaths, like a bold, bad, live man" and on the 1848 *Quarterly* speculation that the novel was written by a "strange man" or, if by a woman, by someone who had "long forfeited the society of her own sex."[29] This revival of old wounds led Nussey to urge "a just and honourable defence,"[30] which could be best mounted, she believed, by the novelist Mrs. Gaskell. Nussey pledged her support in terms of her personal testimony and her cache of letters—an offer of great importance to Gaskell, who similarly wished, as she had told George Smith upon hearing of Brontë's death, to "publish what I know of her, and make the world (if I am but strong enough in expression,) honour the woman as much as they have admired the writer."[31]

The role of *Sharpe's London Magazine* in creating the Brontë myth has been amply discussed in Brontë scholarship, including Gaskell's own role, witting or unwitting, in supplying some of the false facts, via a letter to Catherine Winkworth, that the *Sharpe's* author drew on. But equally pertinent to the need for a "just and honorable defence" was the obituary that Martineau had published in the London *Daily News* in April 1855. Martineau had privately chastised Brontë for making the heroines of her novels overly and obsessively concerned with romantic love. She repeated this criticism (albeit less stringently) in the obituary: "Though passion occupies too prominent a place in her pictures of Life, though women have to complain that she represents Love as the whole and sole concern of their lives . . . it is a true social blessing that we have had a female writer who has discountenanced sentimentalism and feeble egotism with such practical force as is apparent in the works of 'Currer Bell.'"[32] In writing the *Life,* Gaskell seeks to diminish the view that Brontë, like her heroines, was obsessed with love. She systematically does so by minimizing the romantic aspect of the correspondence between Brontë and Nussey—excising phrases or sentences from the letters that reveal an interest in courtship and love (e.g., "We write of little else but love and marriage" in a letter of 15 May 1840) and omitting anecdotes of social life that involve flirtation or erotic playfulness (e.g., in a letter of 3 March 1841 when Brontë asks Nussey whether she has received a valentine "from our bonny-faced friend the curate of Haworth," a man she had a year earlier dubbed "Miss Celia Amelia," a nickname Gaskell carefully omits by emending the letter to read "Mr. W. delivered a noble, eloquent, High-Church, Apostolical-Succession discourse").[33] At one point, Gaskell even responds to Martineau directly (or indirectly, in that the obituary was anonymous). In her account of the proposal of marriage from James Taylor of Smith, Elder, Gaskell refutes the assumption that "some are apt to imagine, from the extraordinary power with which she represented the passion of love in her novels, that she herself was easily susceptible of it" (2:206).[34] Gaskell cites Brontë's testimony to Nussey of 9 April 1851 that "each moment he came near me, and that I could see his eyes fastened on me, my veins ran ice" (2:207). Not passion as in Martineau's obituary, but ice in Gaskell's treatment.

Such treatment reveals the competition embedded in the triangle, with Gaskell contesting Martineau about the character of Brontë and vying for control over their mutual friend. Yet Gaskell is motivated not only by competition but also by her desire to "bond" with Brontë and, in so doing, create a community of exemplary women writers. In order to enact this desire, Gaskell must confirm Brontë's purity so that she can confirm intimacy, so that she can finally write in the penultimate chapter of the *Life*: "We were so happy together; we were so full of interest in each other's subjects" (2:300). The goal of bonding is consonant with the strategies of representing a specific kind of Victorian woman writer.

Gaskell's community of women writers is a gendered version of Isaac D'Israeli's conception of an international fraternity of authors joined by "genius" and rising above the common run of hacks.[35] Whereas D'Israeli concerns himself exclusively with male authors and collects anecdotes of their early traits of genius, Gaskell emphasizes both literary genius and domestic exemplarity in her model and provides examples of both in her depictions of women's authorship. In the most famous passage of the biography, Gaskell describes Brontë's life, and by extension that of other women writers, as one with "two parallel currents": "her life as Currer Bell, the author; her life as Charlotte Brontë, the woman." Gaskell suggests that there are "separate duties belonging to each character—not opposing each other; not impossible, but difficult to be reconciled" (2:49). Speaking for herself as much as for her subject, Gaskell reconciles these "separate duties" through a rewriting of the New Testament parable of the talents. The gifted writer who possesses such talents "must not shrink from the extra responsibility . . . must not hide her gift in a napkin; it was meant for the use and service of others" (2:50). "Duty" and "service," then, are crucial to Gaskell's understanding of authorship in terms of the domestic and literary aspects of the woman writer's experience. These aspects merge in the visits the women authors pay one another.

The combination of the literary and domestic begins in volume 2, chapter 7 of the *Life* with "the biographer's impressions of Miss Brontë" at their first meeting in the Lake District. As Gaskell shapes this episode, it focuses on intellectual exchange (the two women discuss John Ruskin, John Newman, Wordsworth, Alfred Tennyson, et al.), demonstrates a Wordsworthian appreciation of natural scenery (evident in Brontë, if absent in the reformer Sir James Kay-Shuttleworth, who is their host), and involves an inclusion of Brontë and Gaskell in the domestic circle at the Knoll (or potential inclusion, in that Martineau is actually absent). This combination continues in the exchange of visits described in later chapters: Brontë's three visits to Gaskell in June 1851, April 1853, and May 1854 and Gaskell's visit to Haworth in September 1853. In all accounts of these visits, there is domestic intimacy and literary exchange. For example, in the visit to Plymouth Grove in April 1853, Gaskell includes intimate domestic details (Brontë's emotional response to Scottish ballads sung in the drawing room, the "trying headaches" brought on by a "nervous dread of encountering strangers," and the revelation of the superstitious gloom that ghost stories produce), yet Gaskell also emphasizes the spirited literary exchange that occurs when Brontë is roused to defend William Makepeace Thackeray's lecture on Henry Fielding (2:289-91). Similarly, in Gaskell's visit to Haworth Parsonage the following September, the *Life* records the "exquisitely clean" space, the orderly domestic routine, and the "harmony" of the "country parsonage," along with the books "which tell of her [Brontë's] individual pursuits and tastes" and the conversations the two women authors had about their literary works and methods of composition (2:297, 298, 301-2).

If the *Life* shows the two younger women authors consolidating their literary friendship within domestic space, it also reveals, probably unintentionally, the discord that arises when the Knoll comes into the triangle. Soon after the 1850 meeting of Gaskell and Brontë in the Lake District, Martineau invited the latter to spend a week at Christmastime at the Knoll. In recounting this episode, Gaskell predictably emphasizes literary and domestic exemplarity, quoting Brontë's letters to Nussey about Martineau's domestic routine and her praise of "the manner in which she [Martineau] combines the highest mental culture with the nicest discharge of feminine duties" (2:200). One extract ends: "Miss Martineau I relish inexpressibly" (2:199). Nonetheless, when the *Life* appeared in 1857, Martineau objected to the account and insisted that Gaskell add a qualifying footnote to the third edition. Under contention were two sentences from Brontë's letter to Nussey: "I rise at my own hour, breakfast alone (she is up at five, takes a cold bath, and a walk by starlight, and has finished breakfast and got to her work by seven o'clock). I pass the morning in the drawing-room—she, in her study"

(2:198). The correction Martineau sent to Gaskell, inserted in brackets in the third edition, reads as follows: "I must insert a correction of this mistake as to Miss Martineau's hours; the fact being that Miss Martineau rose at six, and went to work at half-past eight, breakfasting separately from her visitor,—as she says in a letter with which she has favoured me, 'it was my practice to come and speak to C. B. when she sat down to breakfast, and *before* I went to work.'"[36] Why should it matter whether Martineau rose at five or six in the morning or whether she greeted Brontë at breakfast or went straight to work at seven? To modern readers, these seem like insignificant details, but to Victorians, the apparent breach of domestic politeness—in going straight to work and failing to greet a guest—was significant. Martineau cared about her reputation as a domestic manager enough to insist on a "correction," even though Brontë's letter had the facts right.[37]

So, too, Martineau cared about her literary reputation enough to insist on other corrections in the third edition—most notably that she had not lost any friends as a result of copublishing *The Letters on the Laws of Man's Nature and Development* (1851) with Henry Atkinson.[38] The Atkinson letters, as they were known, approached human existence in a purely "scientific" way, without reference to a divine being, and were treated by reviewers as an avowal of materialism and *de facto* atheism (though the authors did not use the latter term); indeed, Brontë's letter of 11 February 1851, quoted in the *Life,* states: "It is the first exposition of avowed atheism and materialism I have ever read; the first unequivocal declaration of disbelief in the existence of a God or a future life I have ever seen" (2:203-4). Gaskell knew that Brontë's friends had urged her to break with the "atheistic" Martineau and knew, too, that Brontë found the rejection of an afterlife repugnant, a "hopeless blank" (2:204). Yet Gaskell insists in the *Life* that Brontë remained true to her literary friendship and deplored "the contemptuous tone in which this work was spoken of by many critics"—a treatment that takes sisterly unity to an extreme (2:204). Even so, Martineau sought to preserve her prestige as a literary figure, to dismiss the note of pity in Gaskell's account, and to discount the suggestion that it cost friends a great deal to stand by her after the scandalous Atkinson letters appeared. So, in deference, Gaskell modified the chapter in the third edition, omitting the most contested phrase: that the publication of the book "was but one error—the gravity of which she admitted—in the conduct of a person who had, all her life long, been striving, by deep thought and noble words, to serve her kind" (2:205).

Underlying this disagreement between Gaskell and Martineau was a contest over who best knew and understood their mutual friend, Charlotte Brontë. Intentionally or not, Gaskell had used extracts from Brontë's letters, and thus "plotted" the *Life,* to show a waning of friendship with Martineau after 1851 and a correspondent waxing of her own friendship with her subject. Martineau may legitimately have resented this plot in that her friendship with Brontë remained strong throughout 1851-52, during which period Brontë encouraged Martineau to write a new novel, *Oliver Weld,* and acted as go-between with George Smith of Smith, Elder. Indeed, even after the appearance of the "atheistic" Atkinson letters and the awkward rejection of *Oliver Weld* by Smith, Brontë planned an 1852 Christmas visit to Martineau at the Knoll—one deferred (then abandoned) because Nussey exerted pressure for a longer visit at Brookroyd in the company of their former teacher, Margaret Wooler.[39] Perhaps Martineau thought that the two single women authors—she and Brontë—had more in common with each other than with the married, motherly Gaskell and that their literary friendship was based on a stronger foundation of mutual personal and professional interest.

Whatever the truth, the Martineau-Brontë side of the triangle never fully materialized, and after Brontë's death the contest between Martineau and Gaskell, the two remaining members, became stronger, as revealed in the dispute that arose after the publication of the *Life.* If Gaskell agreed to insert some of the corrections Martineau sent, as well as an account of Brontë's "personal experiment" with mesmerism at the Knoll, Gaskell also shored up her own position by adding further personal correspondence. To the penultimate chapter of the third edition, Gaskell added two personal letters—neither necessary to the plot, but both extending invitations to visit Haworth: "Ever since I was at Manchester, I have been anticipating your visit" (1 June 1853). "Come to Haworth as soon as you can: the heath is in bloom now: I have waited and watched for its purple signal as the forerunner of your coming" (31 August 1853). These letters, in their generous welcome and lyrical anticipatory joy, place Gaskell, the biographer, in the place of supreme intimacy, fully bonded with her subject.

THREE LITERARY FRIENDS AND THE CONSTRUCTION OF THE VICTORIAN WOMAN WRITER

What Gaskell's *Life* leaves unresolved is whether the community of literary women she envisions in northern England is a group of *professional* women writers or whether she means to eschew the label "professional" as a lesser status (in Bourdieu's terms, applicable to the "field of large-scale cultural production" rather than a designation of high or canonical status).[40] To return to the famous passage of the *Life:* Gaskell depicts Brontë as a woman with a divided existence, with "two parallel currents": "her life as Currer Bell, the author; her life as Charlotte Brontë, the woman" (2:49). In volume 1, Gaskell concentrates on the "quiet regular duties of the daughter, the wife, or the mother" as she presents her subject; in volume 2, she turns to the responsibilities of the gifted writer who, "possessing such talents," "must not hide her gift in a napkin" but labor "for the use and service of others." This sequence is not unlike the one Gaskell proposed to an unknown young woman aspiring to authorship: she advised the woman to attend to her children and husband first and wait for later years when "you will write ten times as good a novel as you could do now, just because you will have gone through so much more of the interests of a wife and a mother."[41]

Does this dichotomy pit the domestic against the professional, or are they simply separate "currents"? And, once again, does the dichotomy pit Gaskell against Martineau in competition over Brontë and the representation of the Victorian woman writer? Martineau certainly constructed her career in professional terms. In a letter to her mother, published in the "Memorials" volume of her *Autobiography,* she requests that, with the success of the *Illustrations of Political Economy,* she be henceforth treated as a "citizen of the world" and a "professional *son.*"[42] More broadly, Martineau's life writing traces her professional progress as "a solitary young authoress, who has had no pioneer in her literary path," and revels in charting the steady accumulation of her earnings, noting that she "earned altogether by my books somewhere about ten thousand pounds."[43] Gaskell is less willing than Martineau to invoke the term "professional" or to present the professional aspects of Brontë's career in the *Life.* From recent work by Carol A. Bock on the Brontës' entry into authorship, we know that Brontë was more "professionalized" than the *Life* acknowledges—that she carefully studied the *Fraser's* articles of the 1830s on authorship; compared books of verse on matters of paper, typeface, and layout; bought *The Author's Printing and Publishing Assistant* (1839) to inform herself before publishing the *Poems* (1846) by Acton, Currer, and Ellis Bell; and exchanged letters with George Smith, her publisher, and Williams, his reader, on matters of copyright and royalty.[44] Yet at various points in the *Life,* Gaskell excludes portions of Brontë's letters that deal with publishers' terms, contracts for manuscripts, and other practical aspects of midcentury authorship. These omissions may be as small as the amount of a bank draft sent by her publisher (£100) or as significant as the exclusion of letters that she and Brontë exchanged about the differences between working for Chapman and Hall (Gaskell's publisher) and Smith, Elder (Brontë's).[45]

It is unclear whether Gaskell avoids the mid-nineteenth-century discourse of professionalism because she felt it inappropriate for the "proper lady" (to adopt Mary Poovey's phrase), because she felt Brontë's character might be injured by it, or because she felt it might lower the status of the Victorian woman writer.[46] After all, reviewers had criticized *Jane Eyre,* along with *Wuth-*

ering Heights, as "coarse" and "unfeminine," and they might have found further ammunition in a construction of Brontë's authorial self as "professional" and thus implicitly "masculine." Perhaps, too, Gaskell recognized in Brontë's letters an association of authorship with Romantic claims of genius, inspiration, and self-expression rather than with mid-Victorian interests in professional status and author's royalties. In constructing a model of Brontë's authorial self that emphasized literary inspiration and eschewed financial negotiations, Gaskell was no doubt representing her own authorial self as well. Whatever the motivation, the *Life* projects a different view of the woman author from that presented in Martineau's *Autobiography.* Gaskell minimizes the professional aspects of Brontë's career, excludes financial details when she extracts from Brontë's letters, and shows her subject as much more interested in ideas than in profits. This strategy might not be a betrayal of Brontë as an amateur but instead an attempt to distinguish between the more professionalized, commercialized London literary scene and the more high-minded intellectual exchange of the northern writers.

In the Gaskell-Martineau competition over Brontë, there was also a competition between books of women's life writing. In 1855, the year Brontë died, Martineau received a diagnosis of a "mortal disease" and, as an act of social "duty," began writing her *Autobiography.*[47] She wrote furiously for six months, finishing the text in the summer of 1855 and instructing Smith, Elder—now the publisher of all three women authors—to print and store the *Autobiography* for release after her death. Martineau expected to die soon and, given how quickly she wrote and how much research she knew Gaskell had to complete, she surely expected her personal memoir to precede Gaskell's *Life* into the literary marketplace and thereby to establish a professional model of women's authorship. But, in one of life's ironies, Martineau lived on (until December 1876), and *The Life of Charlotte Brontë* (published in March 1857) claimed its place as the preeminent work of Victorian women's biography, remaining in print until this day while Martineau's *Autobiography* went out of print soon after its 1877 release.[48] Small wonder, then, that Martineau requested "corrections" in Gaskell's *Life* about her own mode of domesticity and approach to authorship.

Yet the friendship between Gaskell and Martineau continued, despite the dispute over details in *The Life of Charlotte Brontë* and the submerged differences between their models of women's authorship. One impetus to re-bonding was the insertion of Nicholls, Brontë's widower, into the absent place in the triangle. In 1857, Nicholls took up correspondence with both women over details in the *Life,* engaging in "a warlike correspondence" with Martineau and then "accusing me [Gaskell] of stating quite falsely that I told Miss Martineau that he had destroyed all his wife's papers."[49] Gaskell and

Martineau joined forces against this common enemy. But a stronger motive for re-bonding was the appearance of a new, pseudonymous woman writer on the literary scene: George Eliot. One of the final recorded letters between Gaskell and Martineau, written late in October 1859, a few months before Gaskell's death, begins: "And after all one gets into a desponding state of mind about writing at all, after 'Adam Bede', and 'Janet's Repentence' choose (as the Lanchashire people say,) whoever wrote them."[50] Gaskell despairs not only because George Eliot's fictions are so good but also because she "would rather they had not been written by Miss Evans," whose public character would not bear close scrutiny. "Oh *how* I wish Miss Evans had never seen Mr Lewes," she laments.[51] As Gaskell must have understood, the combination of exemplary domestic life *and* female authorship that both she and Martineau had championed and that they had, in different ways, intended to represent in their memoirs would be set aside for a new kind of woman writer—one willing to risk social censure for that bugaboo "Love," yet one also demonstrating supreme literary genius and achieving great fame.[52]

Notes

1. A seminal study of this relationship is Gabriele Helms's "The Coincidence of Biography and Autobiography: Elizabeth Gaskell's *The Life of Charlotte Brontë*," *Biography* 18, 4 (Fall 1995): 339-59. Helms explores "the creation of the biographer-persona as a core device in biographical texts" that allows a biography also to "be read as an autobiographical work about this persona" (p. 339). See also Maria H. Frawley's useful discussion of Gaskell as a "participant-observer" working in an ethnographic tradition, in "Elizabeth Gaskell's Ethnographic Imagination in *The Life of Charlotte Brontë*," *Biography* 21, 2 (Spring 1998): 175-94.

2. Arthur Pollard, *Mrs Gaskell: Novelist and Biographer* (Cambridge MA: Harvard Univ. Press, 1965), pp. 139-71, 139; Deirdre d'Albertis, "Bookmaking out of the Remains of the Dead," *VS* 39, 1 (Autumn 1995): 1-31, 17; and Juliet Barker, *The Brontës* (New York: St. Martin's, 1994), pp. 777-808, 777.

3. Angus Easson, *Elizabeth Gaskell* (London: Routledge and Kegan Paul, 1979), pp. 126-58, 150.

4. Linda K. Hughes and Michael Lund, *Victorian Publishing and Mrs. Gaskell's Work* (Charlottesville and London: Univ. Press of Virginia, 1999), p. 142.

5. d'Albertis, pp. 1, 2; Barker, pp. 777-808. The phrase "bookmaking out of the remains of the dead" originates with William Blackwood, whose periodical, *Blackwood's Edinburgh Magazine,* objected to the biographizing of famous authors.

6. William Wordsworth, *The Prelude,* in *Poetical Works,* ed. Thomas Hutchinson, rev. Ernest de Selincourt (Oxford: Oxford Univ. Press, 1969), XIV, 441, 443, p. 588.

7. René Girard, *Deceit, Desire, and the Novel: Self and Other in Literary Structure,* trans. Yvonne Freccero (Baltimore: Johns Hopkins Univ. Press, 1976), p. 21.

8. Eve Kosofsky Sedgwick, *Between Men: English Literature and Male Homosocial Desire* (New York: Columbia Univ. Press, 1985), p. 27. Sedgwick argues that "in any male-dominated society, there is a special relationship between male homosocial (*including* homosexual) desire and the structures for maintaining and transmitting patriarchal power" (p. 25).

9. Diane M. Chambers, "Triangular Desire and the Sororal Bond: The 'Deceased Wife's Sister Bill,'" *Mosaic* 29, 1 (March 1996): 19-36, 24.

10. Charlotte Brontë to Harriet Martineau, [Haworth], [?17 November 1849], in *The Letters of Charlotte Brontë, with a Selection of Letters by Family and Friends,* ed. Margaret Smith, 3 vols. (Oxford: Clarendon Press, 1995-2004), 2:287-8, 287. Subsequent quotations from Brontë's letters will be from this edition, hereafter cited in the notes as *Brontë Letters,* except when Gaskell's version in the *Life* is used for comparison. Brontë's reference to "C. B." is to Currer Bell, Brontë's pseudonym. Emily and Anne wrote under the pseudonyms Ellis Bell and Acton Bell, respectively.

11. Brontë to Gaskell, [Haworth], 17 November 1849, in *Brontë Letters,* 2:288-9, 288.

12. Brontë to W. S. Williams, [Haworth], [?17 November 1849], in *Brontë Letters,* 2:286-7.

13. Brontë to Ellen Nussey, Haworth, 26 August 1850, in *Brontë Letters,* 2:450-3, 450.

14. Gaskell to Charlotte Froude, [c. 25 August 1850], in *The Letters of Mrs. Gaskell,* ed. J. A. V. Chapple and Arthur Pollard (Manchester: Manchester Univ. Press, 1966), pp. 128-9, 128. Subsequent quotations from Gaskell's letters will be from this edition, hereafter cited in the notes as *Gaskell Letters.*

15. Brontë to Williams, [Haworth], 1 February 1849, in *Brontë Letters,* 2:174-5, 174.

16. Gaskell to Lady Kay-Shuttleworth, Knutsford, 14 May [1850], in *Gaskell Letters,* pp. 115-8, 116.

17. Gaskell, *The Life of Charlotte Brontë,* 2 vols. (London: Smith, Elder, 1857), 2:276-7, quoting (and slightly adapting) Brontë to Gaskell, [Lon-

don], 12 January 1853, in *Brontë Letters,* 3:104-5. Unless otherwise noted, subsequent quotations from the *Life* will be to the first edition and cited parenthetically in the text by volume and page number.

18. J[ohn] M[orley], "Harriet Martineau," *Macmillan's Magazine* 36 (May 1877): 47-60, 60.

19. Brontë to Martineau, [Haworth], [?17 November 1849], in *Brontë Letters,* 2:287-8, 288.

20. Martineau, *Autobiography,* 3 vols. (London: Smith, Elder, 1877), 2:227, 234.

21. d'Albertis, p. 19. The Wordsworthian phrase "plain living and high thinking" comes from the sonnet "Written in London, September, 1802," line 11 in *Poetical Works,* p. 244.

22. On the substitutes women found for the common literary affiliations of male authors, see Joanne Shattock, "Victorian Women as Writers and Readers of (Auto)biography," in *Mortal Pages, Literary Lives: Studies in Nineteenth-Century Autobiography,* ed. Vincent Newey and Philip Shaw (Aldershot, Hants: Scolar Press, 1996), pp. 140-52.

23. See Pierre Bourdieu, "The Field of Instances of Reproduction and Consecration," in *The Field of Cultural Production: Essays on Art and Literature,* ed. Randal Johnson (New York: Columbia Univ. Press, 1993), pp. 120-5, 120.

24. Brontë to Nussey, Haworth, 26 August 1850, in *Brontë Letters,* 2:450-3, 450.

25. Erica Hateley, "Erotic Triangles in Amis and Barnes," www.eng.fju.edu.tw.

26. Gaskell to Eliza Fox, 26 November 1849, in *Gaskell Letters,* pp. 89-93, 92. Gaskell may have met Martineau earlier through James, Harriet's brother, a Unitarian minister in Liverpool who in the 1840s served as Professor of Mental and Moral Philosophy at Manchester New College, where William Gaskell was active. Yet because Martineau was ill, on her sickbed in Tynemouth, from 1840 to 1845, an earlier meeting is unlikely, particularly since Harriet and James Martineau became estranged during the later 1840s. See Valerie Sanders, "Harriet Martineau and Elizabeth Gaskell," *GSJ* 16 (2002): 64-75, for an overview of their friendship and mutual acquaintants within Unitarian circles.

27. Martineau, *Autobiography,* 2:326.

28. Nussey to Arthur Bell Nicholls, 6 June 1855, qtd. in *Brontë Letters,* 1:27.

29. Margaret Smith, editor of the *Brontë Letters,* speculates that the article was written by Frank Smedley, a novelist and former editor of *Sharpe's* (see *Brontë Letters,* 1:27n1); Smedley was perhaps also an acquaintance of Catherine Winkworth, from whom he may have heard tales about Currer Bell deriving from the letter that Gaskell wrote to Winkworth on 25 August 1850, after first meeting Brontë at the Kay-Shuttleworths. For a thorough discussion of Gaskell's role in this unfortunate transmission, see Hughes and Lund, pp. 124-40. All phrases but the penultimate one come from "A Few Words about 'Jane Eyre,'" *Sharpe's London Magazine,* 6 n.s. (June 1855): 339-42. The hurtful expression "who has . . . long forfeited the society of her own sex" is Elizabeth Rigby's in an unsigned review in *The Quarterly Review* 84 (December 1848): 153-85, 176, which the reviewer for *Sharpe's* elsewhere paraphrases.

30. Nussey to Arthur Bell Nicholls, 6 June 1855, *Brontë Letters,* 1:27.

31. Gaskell to Smith, Plymouth Grove, 31 May [1855], in *Gaskell Letters,* p. 345.

32. Martineau, "Charlotte Brontë ('Currer Bell')," rprt. in *Biographical Sketches* (London: Macmillan, 1869), pp. 44-50, 46.

33. Cf. Brontë to Nussey, [Haworth], [15 May 1840], in *Brontë Letters,* 1:217-8; Brontë to Nussey, [Upperwood House, Rawdon], [?3 March 1841], in *Brontë Letters,* 1:246-8, 247; Brontë to Nussey, [Haworth], [?7 April 1840], in *Brontë Letters,* 1:213-6, 214 and Gaskell, *Life,* 1:215-6.

34. See Barker, pp. 669-71, for an account of this third proposal, including Patrick Brontë's sense that an engagement with a deferral of marriage for five years while Taylor went to India would be a good arrangement.

35. Isaac Disraeli, *An Essay on the Manners and Genius of the Literary Character,* ed. B[enjamin] Disraeli (1795; London: Frederick Warne, 1840).

36. Gaskell, *The Life of Charlotte Brontë,* 3d edn., 2:199. These variants and others that Martineau requested are recorded in a new scholarly edition of *The Complete Works of Elizabeth Gaskell,* ed. Joanne Shattock, 10 vols. (London: Pickering & Chatto, 2005-06); see *The Life of Charlotte Brontë,* ed. Linda H. Peterson, 8:511-3.

37. Despite Martineau's correction of Brontë's facts, the same routine was described by Crabb Robinson: "She rose at six . . . walked out by moonlight, bathed and finished breakfast by half past seven, then went to work at her writing until two" (R. K. Webb, *Harriet Martineau: A Radical Victorian,* Kings-wood Books on Social History [New York: Columbia Univ. Press; London: Heinemann, 1960], p. 257).

38. Martineau also insisted that she had resisted Brontë's repeated requests to mesmerize her and did so only when refusal became impossible. In this detail, Martineau was protecting against potential criticism that she had used domestic intimacy to enforce her philosophical and medical beliefs on a guest.

39. See Barker, who suggests that Margaret Wooler "joined Ellen in arguing that it was quite wrong of Charlotte to go to the house of a self-declared atheist. Under their combined pressure, she gave way" (pp. 707-10, 709). It is equally likely, however, that Brontë's anxiety over Smith's silence about the manuscript of *Villette* and her projected trip to London to settle the matter caused her to abandon the holiday visit to Martineau; see Brontë to Smith, Brookroyd, 1 December 1852 and 6 December 1852, in *Brontë Letters,* 3:87-9.

40. Bourdieu, p. 120.

41. Gaskell to unknown, Eastborne, Sussex, 25 September [?1862], *Gaskell Letters,* pp. 693-6, 695.

42. Martineau, "Memorials," ed. Maria Weston Chapman, vol. 3 of *Autobiography,* p. 91. The letter to Mrs. Martineau is dated 8 July 1833. See also Martineau to Lord Brougham, Norwich, 10 October 1832, in *The Collected Letters of Harriet Martineau,* ed. Deborah Anna Logan, 5 vols. (London: Pickering and Chatto, 2007), 1: 153-4, 154; Martineau to Richard H. Horne, Tynemouth, 4 June [1844], 2:308-12, 311.

43. Martineau, *Autobiography,* 1:268.

44. Carol A. Bock, "Authorship, the Brontë's, and *Fraser's Magazine*: 'Coming Forward' as an Author in Early Victorian England," *VLC* 29, 2 (September 2001): 241-66.

45. The amount of payment is omitted from Brontë to Smith, [Haworth], 10 December 1847, in *Brontë Letters,* 1:570, quoted in *Life,* 2:34; see also Brontë to Smith, Brookroyd, 6 December 1852, in *Brontë Letters,* 3:88, quoted in *Life,* 2:271, which omits financial dealings; for a letter about publishers, see Gaskell to John Forster, Plymouth Grove, 3 May 1853, included in *Brontë Letters,* 3:159-61.

46. Mary Poovey, *The Proper Lady and the Woman Writer: Ideology as Style in the Works of Mary Wollstonecraft, Mary Shelley, and Jane Austen* (Chicago and London: Univ. of Chicago Press, 1984).

47. Martineau, *Autobiography,* 1:2, 1.

48. Since its 1877 publication, there have been only two editions of Martineau's *Autobiography,* one a facsimile of the original, ed. Gaby Weiner (London: Virago, 1983), the second with annotations, ed. Linda H. Peterson (Petersborough, Ontario: Broadview Press, 2007).

49. See Gaskell to Smith, Plymouth Grove, 26 November [1857] and Gaskell to Maria Martineau, Plymouth Grove, 24 November [1857], in *Gaskell Letters,* pp. 482-3.

50. Gaskell to ?Harriet Martineau, [?late October 1859], pp. 903-4 and Gaskell to Martineau, [29 October 1859], pp. 583-6, in *Gaskell Letters*; see also the letter addressed to Maria Martineau, Whitby, 4 November [1859], pp. 904-5, which continues the discussion of "Miss Evans" as the writer behind the pseudonym "George Eliot."

51. Gaskell to Martineau, 42 P- Grove, [29 October 1859], *Gaskell Letters,* pp. 583-6, 586.

52. As Gaskell acknowledged in her correspondence with Martineau, George Eliot's fiction challenged her assumptions about the quality of a woman's writing and the integrity of her character: "I would rather they had not been written by Miss Evans, it is true; but justice should be done to all; & after all the writing such a book should raise her in every one's opinion, because no dramatic power would, I think enable her to think & say such *noble* things, unless her own character—perhaps somewhere hidden away from our sight at present,—has such possibilities of greatness & goodness in it" (Gaskell to ?Harriet Martineau, [? late October 1859], in *Gaskell Letters,* p. 903).

Julie Nash (essay date 2007)

SOURCE: Nash, Julie. "'Submitting to Fate': Servants in Gaskell's Domestic Fiction." In *Servants and Paternalism in the Works of Maria Edgeworth and Elizabeth Gaskell*, pp. 53-74. Aldershot, England: Ashgate, 2007.

[*In the following essay, Nash maintains that Gaskell uses servants in her novels to illustrate the challenges inherent in changing social roles and norms within a domestic setting and as a means of commenting indirectly on the issues within a greater social context.*]

> Have as many and as large and varied interests as you can; but do not again give a decided opinion on a subject on which you can at present know nothing.
>
> Elizabeth Gaskell to her daughter

Like her literary predecessor Maria Edgeworth, who publicly denied having an interest in politics even while she actively discussed and debated political issues, Elizabeth Gaskell was wary of coming across as too opinionated. It may be surprising that Elizabeth Gaskell, the controversial author of the industrial novels *Mary Barton* and *North and South,* advised her own daughter to refrain from any active discussion of politics and economics while she was a young woman away at school. The author whose writings stirred national debates about political and economic reform admonished Marianne Gaskell to hold her tongue:

> Seriously dear, you must not be a *partizan* in politics or in anything else,—you must have a "reason for the faith that is in you",—and not in three weeks suppose you can know enough to form an opinion about measures of state. That is one reason why so many people dislike that women should meddle with politics; they say it is a subject requiring long, patient study of many branches of science; and a logical training which few women have had,—that women are apt to take up a thing without being able to state their reasons clearly, and yet on that insufficient knowledge they take a more violent and bigoted stand than thoughtful *men* dare to do.
>
> (1. 148)

In essence, Gaskell advised her daughter to keep her political views to herself rather than have them dismissed or criticized by "so many people." She would know. As the "radical" author of *Mary Barton* and *North and South,* she had often faced accusations that her analysis of class conflict was based on insufficient knowledge of economic and political matters. Perhaps to disarm her critics, the author claimed to know "nothing of political economy," and she clearly wished to shield her bright, well-educated daughter from the censure of popular opinion.

Gaskell's advice to Marianne echoes that Lady Davenant in Maria Edgeworth's final novel *Helen,* who tells her protegé that "Female influence must, will, and ought to exist on political subjects as on all others; but this influence should always be domestic, not public— the customs of society have so ruled it" (254). In both cases, the authors do not claim that women are incapable of speaking intelligently on political issues, but that "many people" and "the customs of society" are uncomfortable with the idea of "violent and bigoted" women setting their views up against those of "thoughtful men." As we will see in the following chapters, both Edgeworth and Gaskell did speak out directly about national and political issues, but even when they wrote about more private experiences—family, marriage, and household management—their political fingerprints are everywhere. Referring specifically to *Mary Barton,* Patsy Stoneman notes a trend that applies to all of Gaskell's novels: "Although class struggle is most clearly seen in public confrontations, the family is the mechanism which reproduces class attitudes" (70). Like Edgeworth, Gaskell critiques the potential abuses within the paternalistic family model, revealing the parallel weaknesses in society at large and prescribing ways to accommodate change by breaking down class barriers in the home and in the world.

Mrs Gaskell, the wife, mother, and hostess, and Elizabeth Gaskell, the author of controversial political novels, do not comprise a "split personality" as critic Felicia Bonaparte contends. All of Gaskell's works depict characters struggling with new sources of authority and power in a changing society. Some do so in the larger economic arena of factory life; others do so in a smaller domestic setting. Like Edgeworth, Gaskell uses servant characters strategically in her novels of English domestic life, even more so than she does in those works that are more overtly political. Servant characters enable Gaskell to render the home as effective a setting as the factory for examining the tensions produced by changing social roles. Servants in these works function both as witnesses to and (often unwilling) agents of these changes. Far from being child-like dependents, these servant characters are an intricate part of Gaskell's plan for revising the definitions of family and the roles of family members. Each of the novels and short stories covered in this chapter—**"The Manchester Marriage,"** *Cranford, Ruth,* and *Sylvia's Lovers*—depict individuals struggling in their private lives, and each of them exposes the traditional family and social structures as inadequate remedies for the characters' struggles. These works expose the self-destructive tyrannies and hypocrisies of individuals who bring about their own downfall and who are slowly bringing about a change in the rigidly hierarchical social system that had defined people for generations. In each of these works, it is a servant, rather than the powerful paternal figure who "rescues" a fallen family by serving as a surrogate parent, suggesting the necessity for a more fluid society with less rigidly defined roles.

Ironically, the connections between the public and private dominions were becoming increasingly clear in the Victorian age just as the cultural zeitgeist emphasized the importance of keeping these spheres separate. While authors such as Coventry Patmore and John Ruskin were glorifying the Victorian home as a haven from the horrors of the working world, Victorian housewives were under increasing pressure to run their homes like factories, with regularized timetables and distinct duties. One advice manual suggests the following simple but daunting rules for making every house "a well-ordered one . . . : 1. Do everything in its proper time. 2. Put everything to its proper use. 3. Put everything to its proper place" (Logan 28). As Thad Logan notes: "A rigid domestic schedule has its counterpart, of course, in the increasing regularization of time in the industrial and commercial spheres" (28). Despite the attractive notion that the world of the home was defined apart from that of the business sector, the two worlds resembled one another more than ever. Even in Gaskell's industrial novels, the two worlds interact and influence one another. As Chapter 5 [of *Servants and Paternalism*] demonstrates, and as critic Constance D. Harsh points out: "Gaskell's *Mary Barton,* like *North and*

South, establishes domestic life as the fundamental reality upon which all else is built" (27).

Elizabeth Langland's study on Victorian middle-class women further deconstructs the notion of separate realms of home and business:

> Running the middle-class household, which by definition became "middle-class" in its possession of at least one servant, was an exercise in class management, a process both inscribed and exposed in the Victorian novel. Although the nineteenth-century novel presented the household as a moral haven secure from economic and political storms, alongside this figuration one may discern another process at work, the active management of class power.
>
> (14)

In her domestic novels, those which focus primarily on the private lives of individual characters, Gaskell exemplifies Langland's notion that: "It was in the home, with its select, few workers, each under the surveillance of another in a rigid hierarchic chain, that the moral dimensions of class could be most fully and effectively articulated and enforced" (14). For Gaskell, as for Maria Edgeworth, many of the same problems were confronted in the public and private arenas, problems that could better be addressed by embracing inevitable changes in class relations.

Gaskell's motherly advice to her daughter to avoid controversial topics may not surprise some readers who know the novelist primarily through her reputation as the charming "Mrs Gaskell," the proper Unitarian minister's wife who managed to squeeze her literary career in between the more conventional and time-consuming demands of motherhood and marriage. Felicia Bonaparte points out that: "While many other women novelists escaped, at least in bare essentials, becoming models of 'femininity,' Gaskell appears to have been the epitome of the ideal Victorian woman. . . . Except for the fact that she wrote fiction, Gaskell seems thus to have lived, in Coventry Patmore's now infamous words, the life of 'the angel in the house'" (1-2). Of course, Elizabeth Gaskell did write fiction, and she was a far cry from the Victorian ideal of the passive, self-sacrificing domestic angel. But her conventional domestic situation enabled her to critique the values of her culture from a safe and respectable vantage point. As an amiable minister's wife, she could turn her critical eye toward the despotism within the Victorian home and family while still maintaining her non-threatening reputation, and appearing not to be "meddling in politics" when she was doing just that.

Another way Gaskell was able to play it safe was to write in a genre that was not particularly threatening. Gaskell's supernatural stories, in particular, explore guilty secrets and forbidden passions more directly than her longer, more conventional works. With the exception of **"Lois the Witch,"** Gaskell's supernatural tales are domestic dramas—stories of women, children, and servants terrorized in their own homes. The villains are almost invariably comprised of those who should be society's protectors: fathers, husbands, aristocrats, judges. Vanessa Dickerson, author of *Victorian Ghosts in the Noontide: Women Writers and the Supernatural,* suggests that Gaskell felt freer to criticize these powerful figures while writing within this genre:

> [The ghost story] was not a literature scrutinized and judged with the same strictness and wariness as were realistic works. . . . Even though the nineteenth-century ghost story had its base in realism, its very nature, of course, was to treat the absent, the transcendent, and the unreal. Part of the reason that the ghost story was not subjected to the same rigorous scrutiny as were historical and realistic texts is that it tended to take the form of the short story, not a particularly significant genre at the time.
>
> (110)

Thus Gaskell could address the same issues of illegitimacy, sexual jealousy, and class oppression in her supernatural tales as she would do in some of her more controversial novels without fear of public condemnation. Jenny Uglow writes in her introduction to her edited collection of Gaskell's **"Strange Tales,"** "Under the guise of pure fun, Gaskell could be far more outspoken . . . than in her 'serious novels,' where she had to brace herself for controversy" (ix). Uglow also points out that Gaskell's tales of the uncanny have something else in common: they prominently feature loving, competent servant characters who take charge. These heroic domestics, according to Uglow, "offer counter-images of triumph and rescue which carried their own political and feminist message: the old nurse, with her brave protective love, is typical of another aspect of Gaskell's writing, her admiration and respect for servants, so often wise and stronger than their supposed 'betters'" (ix).

"The Old Nurse's Story" is a classic example of Gaskell's depiction of servants in a multiplicity of roles. Just as Maria Edgeworth's novels feature servant characters who are honest and dishonest, strong and weak, selfish and giving, so does Gaskell's fiction present servants in a similarly diverse light. Like Edgeworth's, Gaskell's servants all have names, personalities, and agency. The "old nurse" of the story's title is the narrator Hester, who tells a story of being haunted during her younger days when she was nurse and lady's maid to her former mistress, Rosamond. Hester is loving and honest, but Gaskell does not depict her as perfect. Though a servant, she is highly conscious of her own social status: when Hester learns that she and her mistress may be moving to a grand hall, she declares: "I was well pleased that all the folks in the Dale should stare and admire, when they heard I was going to be a young lady's maid at my Lord Furnivall's at Furnivall Manor" (2-3). Arriving with the orphaned Miss Rosamond at Furnivall Hall, Hester joins a group of servants whose relationships are hierarchically ordered, as was typical in Victorian homes, with upper servants keeping their social distance from those below them. At one point, hearing strange noises, Hester seeks an explanation from the housekeeper Dorothy and her husband James, but is met with only silence. She then turns to Bessy the kitchen maid, "though I had always held my head rather above her, as I was evened to James and Dorothy, and she was little better than their servant" (9).

Hester's pride at her relatively high-ranking position within the lower ranks in her household is a minor character flaw, but one Gaskell includes for a reason. Social pride is literally at the root of all evil in this story, and when we see that even Hester is capable of it, we see how pervasive it is. Hester eventually learns the history of the household, which had once been ruthlessly presided over by the now-dead Lord Furnivall and his two beautiful daughters: "The old lord was eaten up with pride. Such a proud man was never seen or heard of; and his daughters were like him. No one was good enough to wed them, although they had choice enough" (18). When Lord Furnivall learns that his eldest daughter has secretly married and had a child with a foreign musician, he turns them both out into a snowstorm, killing the child and driving the mother insane. The mysterious sounds Hester hears years later are the ghosts of this proud family, and the cries of the dead child, trying to lure Rosamond into the storm. Hester is the only member of the household able to protect Rosamond from this danger: "I held her tight with all my strength; with a set will, I held her. If I had died, my hands would have grasped her still, I was so resolved in my mind" (23). Hester's courage and generosity contrasts both with the old Lord's cruelty and pride and that of his aristocratic younger daughter who stood silently by as her sister and niece were banished many years before. This story illustrates that pride may be a normal human flaw—even Hester is guilty of it—but it can be particularly dangerous in the hands of the wealthy and powerful.

The work that has been most influential in fostering the reputation of the charming and angelic "Mrs Gaskell" is *Cranford,* first published serially from 1851-53 in Dickens' literary magazine *Household Words.* Written nearly simultaneously with *Ruth, Cranford* is in some ways the antithesis of that controversial tale of illegitimacy and redemption. Gaskell's contemporary critics and those who wrote during the century after her death almost universally found *Cranford* to be "delightful" and "delicate" (Dickens), "exquisite" (John Forster), and of course, "charming" (A. B. Hopkins). Each of these

words of praise, while welcomed by Gaskell herself, has done the author and her novel a disservice. To be charming means to be enjoyed and to be smiled over, but the word connotes a lack of depth or complexity. As Margaret Case Croskery writes, "[B]y dubbing *Cranford* 'charming' early critics dispensed with the necessity for explaining how it is that *Cranford* delights. Since charm dissolves under scrutiny, charming works and charming women neither deserve nor reward critical attention. In fact, they are best appreciated without it" (200). In some respects, the fictional village of Cranford, which Gaskell based on her childhood home of Knutsford, *is* a charming little town populated by charming characters, but the novel is also a serious investigation of a dying social system and the sometimes comic, often tragic, human consequences faced by those who cling too tightly to the old ways.

Gaskell set *Cranford* in the 1830s and 1840s, allowing her to investigate the tension between her perceptions of the more orderly domestic world of the late eighteenth and early nineteenth century (which, as we've seen in Edgeworth's novels, was not really so stable) and what Gaskell saw as the dynamic, energetic newly-emerging Victorian era. As Borislav Knezevic notes, "The railroad is already at Cranford in the first chapter, and there are cotton mills in Drumble. Thus, the Cranford ideology we are introduced to is one already in dialogue with the social effects of industrial capitalism" (413). A literary argument between the proper spinster Miss Jenkyns and the outspoken Captain Brown serves as a metaphor for the conflict of values which is at the heart of *Cranford.* Deborah Jenkyns embodies the values of the ruling class of the late eighteenth century. She is unyielding in her views, and wedded to the past, a character who resembles Maria Edgeworth's General Clarendon from *Helen* in her distrust of change. Captain Brown, on the other hand, represents the changes facing Victorian England. He has made his career in the railroads, a symbol of movement and change, and is ignorant of the social hierarchy that defines the rest of the inhabitants of Cranford. Gaskell makes Captain Brown an avid reader of her own favorite author and friend, Charles Dickens. He reads scenes from *Pickwick Papers* out loud, evoking the ready laughter of his friends. Deborah Jenkyns, however, finds Dickens' literary ascendancy appalling; she calls him vulgar, and recommends Samuel Johnson's *Rasselas* as a better model of letters. When Captain Brown informs Miss Jenkyns that he "should be very sorry for [Dickens] to exchange his style for such pompous writing" (48), the resentment he engenders simmers unabated until his death: "Miss Jenkyns felt this [critique of Johnson] as a personal affront, in a way of which the captain had not dreamed" (19). In his "Introduction" to the Penguin edition of *Cranford,* Peter Keating comments on this important, if comical, exchange:

Captain Brown may not appreciate the full significance of the revolution he is advocating, but Mrs Gaskell certainly did. She makes it clear in this exchange and later that Miss Jenkyns is merely mouthing opinions handed down . . . [with] a mind closed to anything going on in the world around her. Captain Brown not only has more knowledge of Dr Johnson than Miss Jenkyns, he possesses the warmth and immediacy of character required to recognize the startling originality of a young writer.

(19)

Keating's use of the term "revolution" is not overstated. Gaskell rightly recognized that men like Captain Brown would do for society what writers like Dickens were doing for literature. In contrast to most of the Cranford gentility, who have "difficulty making ends meet," but go to great lengths to conceal their poverty, Captain Brown bellows to anyone who will listen that that he is too poor "to take a particular house" (42). The captain's unpretentious manner and his connection to the railroads, as well as his colloquial taste in literature, make him a classic representative of the changes facing Cranford, as well as the rest of English society.

In the "new" society, dominated by characters like Captain Brown, the role of servants is less clear than it might have been a generation before. Their job description essentially remains the same, of course, but their relations with their employers become unsettled as the proper relationship between master and employee is debated throughout England. In an 1868 essay, the "progressive" proto-feminist Frances Power Cobb addressed some of the common middle-class anxieties about the changing nature of domestic service and the general sense that some of the "better" representatives of the lower classes were leaving service for work in industry. Just as liberals such as John Stuart Mill argued that the private lives of factory workers did not concern their employers, Cobb argued that the relationship between masters and mistresses and their servants must shift from one of paternal interest to a strict "contract of service" with "no moral element" to it if the service industry was to survive. Cobb admits that such a clear boundary is nearly impossible to draw:

A contract to do the service of the employer at his direction is one thing; submission to orders having nothing to do with his service, but regulating the private and family affairs of the servant, is quite another. Here is the difficulty of the case, for some regulations of the servants' habits may be indispensable to the comfort of the master and the order of his household. At this moment, the point where such regulations should stop is naturally a matter of dispute, for the old theory of service, wherein the patriarchal idea was predominant, has left behind it customs and notions wholly foreign to the new theory wherein contract is all in all. . . . The transition, then, is troublesome.

(124)

"Troublesome" might be an understatement. As I point out in Chapter 5 [of *Servants and Paternalism*], in **Mary Barton** and **North and South,** Gaskell argues that industry should adopt a system in which the relationship between employee and employer closely resembles the one between servant and master. In "Household Service," Cobb argues for the opposite: that servants and their employers conduct themselves according to the *laissez-faire* model of industry. Her argument never completely caught on, mostly due to the nature of domestic service. Household servants, living and working intimately with their masters and mistresses, inevitably took on a hybrid role of family member/employee. Still, Cobb's essay suggests that both masters and servants were seeking a new way to define their relations at the same time that industry leaders were calling social paternalism into question. Cobb tells nostalgic members of the middle-class to brace themselves for a new era, like it or not:

In the first place, employers must strive to eradicate from their minds the whole patriarchal idea of service. It may have been beautiful, it may have been happier than any other, but it is past and gone, and the sooner we bury it the better. A servant is not now or henceforth a retainer, a dependant, a menial who, in receiving from his master food and wages, becomes his temporary property—somewhat between a child and a slave—to be ordered in all things concerning, or not concerning, the master's service. . . . No obedience beyond the contract can be required of him; nor, on the other hand (and this is very needful to mark), has the servant any claims against the master beyond his stipulated contract of food and wages.

(132)

Such a relationship between servant and mistress would have appalled Gaskell, whose only son died in the arms of his nurse, and who maintained close relationships with many servants long after they left her employment. Like Cobb, Gaskell recognized the tyrannies inherent in the social paternalist system, but her solution was not to give servants greater "freedom" away from the family, but to bring servants closer to their masters and mistresses as equals.

In **Cranford,** which takes place at the beginning of this time of transition, "the subject of servants was a standing grievance" (64), according to the novel's narrator, Mary Smith. Because of the genteel poverty of the residents of Cranford, mistress and maid live and work in close proximity, but both happily perpetuate the myth that a wide gulf separates the two classes. In one example, Mary Smith describes a dinner party given by Mrs Forrester "in a baby house of a dwelling." Her guests:

talked on about household forms and ceremonies, as if we all believed that our hostess had a regular servants' hall, second table, with housekeeper and steward, instead of the one little charity-school maiden, whose short ruddy arms could never have been strong enough to carry the tray up-stairs, if she had not been assisted in private by her mistress, who now sat in state, pretending not to know what cakes were sent up, though she knew, and we knew, and she knew we knew, and we knew that she knew we knew, she had been busy all morning making tea-bread and sponge cakes.

(41)

Gaskell treats this class hypocrisy gently. A household with any servant, however humble, can still claim to be part of the gentry. As Thad Logan notes, "[I]t is by now clear how profoundly the bourgeois way of life was grounded in the availability and relative tractability of servants. The presence of a servant or servants was not only of enormous symbolic value in asserting a family's claim to middle-class status, but it was also crucial in maintaining the exacting standards of housekeeping that had developed by mid-century" (29). Often the servant's work is performed alongside her mistress, a fact that was less important than the status the servant's presence confers. Gaskell makes it clear by the novel's early chapters that this system cannot survive for long. The servants are willing enough to play their deferential role, but the fact that they conspire to maintain false appearances indicates that there is more social equality between the two classes than anyone will openly admit. These servants are not incidental to the happenings in Cranford; they make things happen, and everyone knows it.

Gaskell was a passionate advocate of close interaction between social classes, and in *Cranford,* she creates intense personal bonds between servants and mistresses, bonds that eventually dissolve the class distinctions almost entirely. Gaskell believed that such intimacy served both classes well. In short piece entitled "French Life," the narrator comments on the French practice of living in close proximity with one's servants:

> [T]here is the moral advantage of uniting mistress and maid in a more complete family bond. I remember a very charming young married lady, who had been brought by her husband from the country to share his home in Ashley Buildings, Victoria Street, saying that, if they had to live in the depths of a London kitchen, she should not have tried bringing them out of their primitive country homes; as it was, she could have them under her own eye without any appearance of watching them; and, besides this, she could hear of their joys and sorrows and, by taking an interest in their interests, induce them to care for hers. French people appear to me to live in this pleasant kind of familiarity with their servants—familiarity which does not breed contempt, in spite of proverbs.

(609)

Here, Gaskell expresses genuine enthusiasm for the mixing of classes, but also ambivalence about servants' trustworthiness, a need to "have them under [one's]

own eye" as one would with children. This ambivalence is similar to Edgeworth's uncertain depiction of *Belinda*'s Marriott, a servant whose interest in her mistress is suspect until she can prove her fidelity. Both authors prefer a solution in which "mistress and maid" are united "in a more complete family bond," but both introduce barriers that make such a bond difficult. Edgeworth dignifies Marriott's character and gives her a voice and agency, but she keeps Marriott in her place as a loyal dependent. Gaskell, on the other hand, ultimately places Cranford's servant class on more equal footing with their mistresses.

In the opening chapters, Miss Matty's servant Martha is the type of country girl to whom Gaskell refers in "French Life." Mary Smith believes that Martha needs to be kept "under her own eye" when she first begins her work as a servant. Like Captain Brown, Martha is "blunt and plain-spoken to a fault; otherwise she was a brisk, well-meaning, but very ignorant girl" (67). Gaskell's initial portrayal of Martha is that of a comic fumbler straight out of the long literary tradition of incompetent servants. Before entertaining some relatives of Miss Matty's, Mary Smith instructs Martha "in the art of waiting, in which it must be owned she was terribly deficient" (67). Mary worries that too many instructions will "muddle the poor girl's mind," and Gaskell describes the maid as standing "open-mouthed" and "sadly fluttered" (68) as she listens to her job description. This depiction of a comically stupid servant character is unusual in Gaskell, and it should not come as a surprise to find that Gaskell soon remedies Martha's incompetence, replacing that quality with generosity and wisdom.

Although hardly a reader of Dickens, Martha resembles Captain Brown in that she represents some of the changes facing Cranford and she lacks the hypocrisy that keeps the community socially segregated. Gaskell had originally intended to write only one episode of *Cranford,* and the opening chapters that feature Captain Brown can stand alone as a short story. Gaskell later told John Ruskin that she "never meant to write more, so killed Capt Brown very much against my will" (Uglow 283). With the iconoclastic Captain out of the story, Gaskell had to find other ways to represent the possibilities of social change. She introduces the servant character of Martha soon after Captain Brown's death, creating in Martha the embodiment of Gaskell's ideal new Victorian society.

Although Martha may be an uncouth country girl, she represents the future while the Miss Jenkynses represent the past. Many years before, the young Miss Matty had rejected a marriage offer from Mr Holbrook, a local farmer. She had reluctantly submitted to her sister's and father's objections to the match on the grounds of Holbrook's inferior social status. According to Gaskell, these sacrifices to social rank are helping to tear down the very hierarchy that they are designed to preserve. Miss Matty is a victim of the aristocratic ideals that meant so much to her sister and her father. Meeting Mr Holbrook as a middle-aged woman, Miss Matty tries to suppress her intense feelings by thinking about the romantic life of her maid. She projects her own thwarted desires for romance and love onto Martha. After visiting Mr Holbrook's house, Miss Matty is "pleased and fluttered," but "gradually absorb[s her sentiments] into a distressing wonder as to whether Martha had broken her word, and seized on the opportunity of her mistress's absence to have a 'follower'" (77).

"Having a follower" may seem like an innocent enough transgression, but the townspeople of Cranford are practically obsessed with preventing their maids from becoming romantically involved. The narrator Mary Smith tells the reader that: "if gentlemen were scarce, and almost unheard of in the 'genteel society' of Cranford, they or their counterparts—handsome young men—abounded in the lower classes. The pretty neat servant-maids had their choice of desirable 'followers'" (64). Despite (or because of) the romantic odds in the maids' favor, their mistresses generally forbade involvement, as was often the policy in Victorian households. Frances Power Cobb might have been referring to the residents of Cranford when she advised people to cease regulating the private lives of their domestic help: Martha's only complaint about working for Miss Matty is her rule forbidding followers.

Although Miss Matty expends a considerable amount of energy trying to prevent her servants from having followers, she reconsiders her restrictions as she confronts the many lonely and irretrievable years spent away from the man she once loved. On the day of Holbrook's death, she tells Martha that henceforth followers will be permitted, provided they are respectable: "'God forbid!' said she, in a low voice, 'that I should grieve any young hearts.'" After Martha eagerly informs her that she already has a would-be suitor: "Miss Matty was startled, [but] she submitted to Fate and Love" (82). Miss Matty recognizes that in preventing Martha from becoming romantically involved, she is perpetuating the tyrannical social system that sentenced her to an isolated life. In drawing this parallel between a maid and her mistress, Gaskell realigns Miss Matty with the servant class against the values of her own class. Miss Matty identifies with her young servant more than with the sister and father who determined her fate; she places the happiness of an "inferior" above the necessity of maintaining the longstanding regulations that govern domestic life in Cranford. In "submitting to Fate," Miss Matty surrenders to the inevitable changes facing her community and acknowledges the failure of the existing class system to ensure the greater good. Gaskell makes it clear that the gentry cannot continue to function as a romantic police force, if they are going to continue to function at all.

Unlike the spinsters who dominate social life in Cranford, Martha marries and has a child, bringing a new generation into the village. Martha's relationship with Miss Matty deepens as the novel progresses, and Martha's character evolves until there exists no sign of the comical country girl whose serving skills Mary Smith had so lamented. When Miss Matty later learns that she is financially ruined, Gaskell irreversibly blurs the line between mistress and maid. As Miss Matty increasingly assumes the role of the helpless child, Martha's strength increases. She devises a plan that enables her to "save" her mistress. When Mary Smith begs the servant to "Listen to reason," Martha retorts: "Reason always means what some one else has got to say. Now I think what I've got to say is good enough reason; but, reason or not, I'll say it and stick to it" (155). Martha's ability to stand up for her ideas and insist on the "reasonableness" of her own plan indicates that she is emerging from the shadows of dependency and into a new role within the family. Martha and her suitor Jem agree to marry and take in Miss Matty as a lodger. Within a year, Miss Matty has tentatively entered the commercial sector and opened a tea shop, and she and Martha live like family members, with Miss Matty helping care for Martha's daughter Mathilda, and Martha presiding like a matriarch over a pieced-together family which includes her sister, husband, daughter, Miss Matty herself, and Miss Matty's brother Peter, returned from India. In this new "family," bonds of care trump bonds of kinship, and the family servant has become the new family matriarch.

Toward the novel's end, Mary Smith concludes, "As for Cranford in general, it was going on much as usual." Yet just the opposite is true. Granted, some townspeople such as the rigid Mrs Jamieson and her imposing servant Mr Mulliner refuse to "submit to Fate and Love" like the rest of the town. They stubbornly draw their shades as if in mourning to protest the marriage of Lady Glenmire to a social inferior, and they isolate themselves from those of whom they disapprove. But the rest of Cranford adapts remarkably well. In this comedy, Gaskell celebrates social change and the breakdown of class distinctions while still retaining a distinct affection for the old-fashioned ways of Miss Matty who remains bewildered, though happy, through all the changes. Gaskell ends the novel by praising "Miss Matty's love of peace and kindliness," claiming that: "We all love Miss Matty, and I somehow think we are all of us better when she is near us" (218). Yet Gaskell is hardly advocating a return to the more traditional values that Miss Matty's generation represents. As Peter Keating writes, "By . . . gradually revealing the deep sadness of Miss Matty's life, we see a society which for all its charm is narrow, exclusive, indifferent to the world outside its own boundaries, and, because of this, often unconsciously cruel" (24). We can admire Miss Matty's love of peace and kindliness, but Gaskell also points out that these qualities are present in people of all social classes, specifically the servant class whose resourcefulness and energy will revive and ultimately dominate communities like Cranford. The caring and mutual dependence implicit in social paternalism are still present in Cranford's new community, but Gaskell rejects the philosophy's emphasis on an *ordered* society, specifically one dominated by a male authority figure. In fact, no individual roles are predetermined. People step up to help one another when needed, and the new arrangement works because everybody helps according to their talents.

Although Gaskell's novel is a stinging critique of the despotism inherent in a strictly hierarchical society and a fervent call for change, *Cranford* never earned Gaskell the type of criticism she feared for her daughter: that of being too political. In fact, the novel helped ensure Gaskell's reputation as a charming lady of letters. In contrast, *Ruth,* written during the same period, threatened to have the opposite effect. The story of Ruth's sexual fall, her love for her illegitimate child, and her moral redemption through self-sacrifice shocked some members of Victorian society and called into question Mrs Gaskell's reputation as a writer of charming tales. Whereas *Cranford* merely hints at the effects of repressed sexuality on maid and mistress alike, *Ruth* holds a magnifying glass over the sexual nature of women, the predatory potential in upper-class men, and the hypocrisy of "respectable" society that condemns the first while turning a blind eye on the second. As in all of her works, Gaskell uses a private matter to shed light on the public issues of the abuses and proper uses of power. Yet many of her readers found themselves more concerned about the private matter: ironically, many were shocked by Gaskell's "forgiveness" of Ruth's sexual fall, but were less bothered by her scathing portrayal of Mr Bradshaw, the town's tyrannical patriarch who condemns Ruth and terrifies his own wife and children. Mr Bradshaw embodies Gaskell's most glaring critique of social paternalism. He is the most wealthy and influential member of his community, and as such he believes his duty is to care for and protect both his own family and the community at large. Yet the way he lives out these aims is antithetical to Gaskell's ideal of caring: he beats his children, and terrifies his wife into meek submission. When he believes that Ruth is a virtuous widow, he offers her a position as governess to his children, and like a good paternalist, he also extends his patronage to her son and encourages her friendship with his daughter. Yet when he discovers the truth about her past, he uses the power that had once aided her to shame her and drive her out of his house. He is so resistant to the idea of Ruth's reformation and reintegration into respectable society, that he

scoffs when Thurston Benson reminds him of God's call to forgiveness: "The world has decided how such women are to be treated: and, you may depend upon it, there is so much practical wisdom in the world that its way of acting is right in the long run, and that no one can fly in its face with impunity" (351). Nowhere in Gaskell's *oeuvre* do we find such a pitiless figure, one who would put the world's laws before God's in the name of protecting society. The "practical wisdom" that Bradshaw praises enables him to maintain his power over his family and community while ensuring that no one is able to threaten that power from below. Here again, Gaskell depicts the traditional patriarchal family, the model upon which social paternalism is based, to be the worst possible form of protection for those in need. Bradshaw's own son is a criminal, his daughter is consumed with anger, and his wife is ineffective and childlike.

Mr Bradshaw's absolutism, rather than Ruth's sexual transgression, was the primary target of Gaskell's social critique, but the novel was controversial for other reasons. Gaskell compared herself to the martyr "St. Sebastian tied to a tree to be shot with arrows" (l. 221) in describing the hostile reception of *Ruth. The Literary Gazette* lamented Gaskell's "loss of reputation" and the *Christian Observer* balked at *Ruth*'s message that "a woman who has violated the laws of purity is entitled to occupy precisely the same position in society as one who has never thus offended" (Uglow 338). Gaskell was so upset by the animosity awakened by *Ruth* that she was seriously ill for five weeks. Although *Ruth* had many defenders—including the Brownings, Charlotte Brontë, and Charles Dickens—Gaskell's morals would always be suspect by some. She wrote: "I knew all this before; but I was determined to speak my mind out about it; only how I shrink with more pain than I can tell you from what people are saying, though I would do every jot of it over again tomorrow" (l. 220).

As in *Cranford,* Gaskell argues for social change in *Ruth,* and creates a servant character, Sally, to demonstrate the possibilities for change and to help "rescue" Ruth. Although Faith and Thurston Benson take Ruth in and give her shelter and a place in society, it is their "nattered" maid Sally who becomes a mother figure to her and helps her grow into a woman. Like Martha, Sally becomes the voice of reason and generosity when the novel's other characters lose their solid footing. Like Martha's, Sally's role in the Benson household changes as the novel progresses, shifting from domestic servant to family member. In many ways, she resembles another one of Gaskell's servants, *North and South*'s Dixon: she has lived with the Benson family since Faith and Thurston were children and she loves the two of them devotedly. Like Dixon, she is old-fashioned, quick-tempered, and capable of inspiring terror in her master and mistress. Ruth notices that Sally's comments are uttered "quite in the tone of an equal, if not a superior" (137). Sally begins the novel in open conflict with the heroine, and the story of their relationship is one of the most important told in ***Ruth*** because it is the story of how even the most prejudiced members of society can open their minds to the idea of redemption. Sally's potential for change provides a model for the rest of society, most notably for Mr Bradshaw.

Though Sally lives out her life on the bottom of the social hierarchy while Mr Bradshaw looks down from his place at the top, the two share a rather conservative belief in the "practical wisdom" of the world to dictate right and wrong. On the surface, Sally's wisdom is that of the acquiescent subject who accepts her servitude as her divinely ordained place. Sally tells Ruth that:

> there's a right way and a wrong way of setting about everything—and to my thinking, the right way is to take a thing up heartily, if it is only making a bed. Why! dear ah me, making a bed may be done after a Christian fashion, I take it, or else what's to come of such as me in heaven, who've had little enough time on earth for clapping ourselves down on our knees for set prayers.
>
> (174)

She goes on to tell Ruth that Mrs Benson had once told her "your station is a servant, and it is as honourable as a king's, if you look at it right; you are to help and serve others in one way, just as a king is to help others in another" (174-5). Like many of Gaskell's servants, such as ***North and South***'s Dixon, Sally is an unwilling agent of change. She wishes no more than Mr Bradshaw himself to overturn the hierarchical structure of social arrangements under which they both live or to alter the traditions and beliefs that have defined her.

However, though she accepts her position on the social ladder, Sally is no meek dependent. Even before the Bensons return to their home with the pregnant Ruth, their thoughts are focused on how they will manage Sally who would certainly "go distraught" (125) at the thought of an unmarried mother and her baby in the house. It is clear from the early chapters of the novel that Sally will be a character to be reckoned with. Though the Bensons tell Sally that Ruth is a widow, the servant quickly sees through the lie and tests Ruth by cutting her long hair. Symbolically pruning away at Ruth's sexuality, Sally roughly chops off the curls of the "broken-spirited" girl, but finds herself surprised at Ruth's submissiveness: "I thought we should ha' had some crying—I did. They're pretty curls enough; you've not been so bad to let them be cut off neither. You see, Master Thurston is no wiser than a babby in some things; and Miss Faith just lets him have his own way; so it's all left to me to keep him out of scrapes" (145-6). Her rigid morality resembles that of Mr Bradshaw: both characters have a strong sense of moral "duty" to protect those in their charge, and both characters will resort to intimidation and cruelty to maintain the status quo. Yet until the novel's final chapters, Mr Bradshaw remains incapable of change while Sally's character gradually comes to accept Thurston Benson's view that "[it is] time to change some of our ways of thinking and acting" (351).

Sally's distrust toward Ruth begins to change when Ruth becomes a mother, and Sally witnesses Ruth's repentance for her sexual transgression. Ironically, only Sally, Ruth's harshest critic, can bring Ruth out of her self-pity and depression following the birth of her son:

> Sally took [the baby] briskly from his mother's arms; Ruth looked up in grave surprise, for in truth she had forgotten Sally's presence, and the suddenness of the motion startled her.
>
> "My bonny boy! are they letting the salt tears drop on thy sweet face before thou'rt weaned! Little somebody knows how to be a mother—I could make a better myself. . . . Thou'rt not fit to have a babby, and so I've said many a time. I've a great mind to buy thee a doll, and take thy babby myself."
>
> (174)

Sally's harsh words do for Ruth what the Bensons' care and kindness cannot. In claiming that she would make a better mother herself, Sally challenges Ruth to grow into her own place as a mother. From this moment on, it is Sally—not Faith or Thurston—who assumes the role of Ruth's and her son Leonard's surrogate parent. When Leonard is taunted about his mother's past, Sally once again symbolically "nurses" the boy: "[H]e used to come back, and run trembling to Sally, who would hush him to her breast with many a rough-spoken word of pity and sympathy" (373). The scene in which Sally scolds Ruth for feeling sorry for herself is a turning point for Ruth's character, in which she transforms into an adult woman responsible for her own life and that of her son: "Henceforward Ruth nursed her boy with a vigour and cheerfulness that were reflected back from him" (177).

As the novel progresses, Sally's position as the moral center solidifies. Like Cranford's Martha, she insists on speaking "reason" regardless of whether her ideas contradict more conventional views of morality. In one instance, she prevents Thurston Benson from whipping Leonard as a punishment for lying. Reminding him that the family is deceptively passing Ruth off to the community as a widow instead of as an unwed mother, Sally states harshly, "I think it's for them without sin to throw stones at a poor child, and cut up good laburnum branches to whip him. I only do as my betters do when I call Leonard's mother Mrs—" (204). Reminded of his own hypocrisy, Thurston Benson puts down the switch like an obedient child.

During the course of the novel, the social distinctions between the family and their servant are eclipsed by the stronger ties of caring and mutual dependence, as in *Cranford.* As the characters grow older, they begin to eat together in the kitchen, Sally's domain:

> [T]hey all sat together in the kitchen in the evenings; but the kitchen, with the well-scoured dresser, the shining saucepans, the well-blacked grate and whitened hearth, and the warmth which seemed to rise up from the very flags, and ruddily cheer the most distant corners appeared a very cozy and charming setting; and besides, it appeared but right that Sally, in her old age, should have the companionship of those with whom she had lived in love and faithfulness for many years.

(381)

Gaskell uses humble kitchen items—pots and pans, grate, dresser, and hearth—to symbolize the Victorian ideal of domestic private sanctuary. As in *Cranford,* this "family" has been created through ties of care and faithfulness: a brother and sister, an old servant, a young mother and her child. Notably absent in this familial tableaux is a patriarch. In fact, the novel's only example of a father as family leader is Mr Bradshaw, who had failed to love and support his own family. Barbara Z. Thaden points out that "While many critics have seen this novel as a plea for greater sympathy with fallen women, Gaskell is also making the point that mothers do not need fathers to help raise their children" (62). What they do need, Gaskell implies, is a servant. Strikingly, in her representation of this ideal family image, Gaskell chooses to move the Benson family into the kitchen, rather than have the group gather in the parlour. Thad Logan's study on *The Victorian Parlour* demonstrates that the parlour, in both Victorian literature and life, was "the center of the home and the most important room in the house" (23). It was depicted in literature and in art as the heart of domestic life, where families gathered in their most private moments. The parlour was one of the few rooms in the Victorian home from which servants were generally excluded, and it was considered the place where public cares were cast aside to seek refuge in the privacy of domestic life. Yet in Gaskell's redefinition of the familial ideal, the servant's territory—the kitchen—is the site where the concept of home and family is played out. Through Sally, Gaskell has demonstrated the need for a number of changes, changes in the way society is structured, and changes in the way human beings define morality. The climax in *Ruth* depicts a confrontation between Ruth's seducer and Sally following the heroine's death. More than any other character in the novel, Sally embodies Gaskell's vision for Christian forgiveness, an ethical conversion that is both complex and difficult.

In her story **"The Manchester Marriage,"** Gaskell depicts another servant whose relationship with her family is complicated and unusual. Unlike many of Gaskell's servant characters, Norah is not a rural family retainer, but a Manchester woman whose relationship with her mistress is more socially equal than that of Sally and the Bensons, or any of Edgeworth's English servants. Gaskell introduces Norah as "the only bridesmaid" at Alice Openshaw's first wedding. As the story opens, Norah appears to be yet another one-dimensional self-sacrificing dependent. She foregoes her position with Alice's in-laws to stay with Alice, she devotes her life to helping care for Alice's deformed child, and at first she accepts matters obediently when Alice's second husband dismisses her for her old-fashioned child-caring methods. It is not until about mid-way through the story that we see that the relationship between Norah and her new master will become the most complex relationship in the story. Although they live passably well together, "Norah and Mr Openshaw were not on the most thoroughly cordial terms, neither of them appreciating the other's best qualities" (13), Gaskell writes, demonstrating the essential equality of these two characters. One is a successful businessman and the other a long-term servant, but they each have "best qualities" and they are equally prejudiced against one another.

As in *Ruth,* the climax of **"The Manchester Marriage"** involves a confrontation between a servant and a man from her mistress's past. Alice's first husband, Frank, believed lost at sea, returns one night when her mistress and master are out. Contrary to our expectations, neither Alice nor Mr Openshaw confront Frank at any point in the story. The story's dilemma does not center upon how Alice and her two husbands will resolve their impossible situation, as one might expect. Norah quickly sends Frank away in order to protect her mistress from the knowledge that her first husband is alive: "Norah had no time for pity. Tomorrow she would be as compassionate as her heart prompted. At length she guided him downstairs, and shut the outer door, and bolted it—as if by bolts to keep out facts" (18). In bolting the door against one master, she lets in the other, Mr Openshaw, the only person to whom she confides. After learning of Frank's suicide, Mr Openshaw and Norah collude to keep Frank's return and death a secret. Together they share a burden that will connect them for the rest of their lives and one that puts them on the same footing. As Mr Openshaw says, "'I go with a dreadful secret on my mind. I shall never speak of it again, after these days are over. I know you will not either.' He shook hands with her, and they never named the subject again, the one to the other" (29). Thanks to his servant's decisiveness and her trustworthiness, the practical businessman Mr Openshaw was "from that time forth, curiously changed" (30). As a representative of the new wealthy class of businessmen, Gaskell suggests, Mr Openshaw must not revert to the old feudal relations between employer and employee. Their secret is sealed with a handshake and gesture of mutual respect.

Gaskell's 1861 novella, *The Grey Woman,* features an even more stinging indictment of patriarchal power and its failure to protect the vulnerable. Gaskell sets this gothic tale in Europe prior to the French Revolution, a time in which the paternalist social order still governed human relations, a time in which, ideally, daughters and wives were owed protection from their fathers and husbands in return for obedience. Instead, Gaskell describes a world in which women must protect themselves from powerful and dangerous men. The story's narrator, Anna, is forced to marry a man who makes her uncomfortable because she discovers, too late, that she has permitted his attentions and people consider them to be betrothed. When Anna tells her father she does not wish to get married, he refuses to listen. It was as if, says Anna, "no one had any right over me but my future husband" (200). As a newlywed who is afraid of her husband and most of the servants in his household, Anna becomes close to her maid, Amante, who assumes the role of her mistress's protector and friend:

> Perhaps one of the reasons that made me take pleasure and comfort in Amante's society was, that whereas I was afraid of everybody (I do not think I was half as much afraid of things as persons), Amante feared no one. She would quietly beard Lefebvre [her husband's servant], and he respected her all the more for it . . . And with all her shrewdness to others, she had quite tender ways with me.

(206)

Despite their differences of position, maid and mistress relate to one another as equals. The narrator tells Amante about her loneliness and her unhappy marriage, and, importantly, Gaskell notes that "Amante listened with interest, and in return told me some of the events and sorrows in her own life" (208). While it is not entirely unusual in literature for a servant to be the confidant of her mistress (as we saw in Edgeworth's *Belinda,* for example), this mutual exchange of confidences is rare and marks this relationship as unusually close even within Gaskell's *oeuvre.*

Anna and Amande eventually discover that Anna's charming but controlling husband is in fact a thief and a murderer, and Amante plans their escape from the castle. Like the Hester in **"The Old Nurse's Story,"** Amante becomes her mistress's savior, bravely confronting danger and risking her own life with the practical competence that characterizes so many of Gaskell's servant characters: "She gave me direction—short condensed directions, without reasons—just as you do to a child; and like a child, I obeyed her . . . For me, I saw nothing but her, and I dared not let my eyes wander from her for a minute" (221). The mistress of the castle has been reduced to an obedient child as her servant gives orders and leads her out of the home that had become her prison.

While this escape marks a dramatic reversal of traditional hierarchical roles, it is only the beginning. Amante and Anna remain safe from Anna's murderous husband by posing as husband and wife, with Amante in the masculine role. Amante had already assumed the social position of husband and protector when she helped Anna escape; all that was left was for her was to look the part:

> She looked into every box and chest during the man's absence at this mill; and finding in one box an old suit of man's clothes, which had probably belonged to the miller's absent son, she put them on to see if they would fit her; and, when she found that they did, she cut her own hair to the shortness of a man's, made me clip her black eyebrows as close as though they had been shaved, and by cutting up old corks into pieces such as would go into her cheeks, she altered both the shape of her face and her voice to a degree I should not have believed possible.
>
> All this time I lay like one stunned; my body resting, and renewing its strength, but I myself in an almost idiotic state—else surely I could not have taken the stupid interest which I remember I did in all Amante's energetic preparations for disguise. I absolutely recollect at once the feeling of a smile coming over my face as some new exercise of her cleverness proved a success.

(229)

Anna and Amante recast their roles of mistress and servant and become instead wife and husband, suggesting that both relationships are socially constructed rather than "natural." Having been victimized by the men who should have protected them, the two women create their own family, based on the paternalist ideal, but with a twist: Amante becomes the strong husband that Anna clearly wants, one who uses "his" strength to nurture and lead, not to frighten and brutalize. While Amante is undoubtedly the stronger of the two characters, the two women have a clear mutual bond that does not depend on hierarchical status. Anna notes that Amante's manner of speaking to her changes, "breaking out of her respectful formality into the way of talking more natural to those who had shared and escaped from common dangers, more natural, too, where the speaker was conscious of a power of protection which the other did not possess" (242).

Aside from the fact of Amante's sex, the two settle into a fairly conventional married life. Amante suggests that the two move to Frankfurt with Anna's soon-to-be-born child, where, "We will still be husband and wife; we will take a small lodging, and you should housekeep and live indoors. I, as the rougher and the more alert, will continue my father's trade, and seek work at the tailor's shops" (242). Their "married" life together consists of caring for Anna's child, working to support themselves, and trying to stay safe. Although fear for their safety is always present, neither character expresses any wish to revert to previous positions with regard to gender or class. The "man" of the house is a female servant, and neither Gaskell nor her narrator seem to find that detail all that remarkable. Although the novella ends with Amante's murder and Anna's (bigamist) marriage to a male doctor, that relatively conventional ending does not change the story's premise that social (and gender) roles are better determined by aptitude and inclination than by birth.

In *Sylvia's Lovers,* Gaskell once again weaves together the public, political world and the domestic, private world of struggling people, and she once again depicts a servant who emerges as the novel's source of strength, wisdom, and moral leadership. The historical novel, which takes place in the 1790's during the first phase of the Napoleonic wars, is rarely grouped with Gaskell's public "condition of England" novels or her more private domestic works. Even Gaskell's contemporary critics were unsure how to label this work. An anonymous critic in the *Saturday Review* of 4 April 1863 admitted that, "we can scarcely say in what class we should rank *Sylvia's Lovers* or to what other novel we should liken it." The novel takes place in a coastal Yorkshire whaling town, Monkshaven, and focuses on the character of Sylvia Robson, daughter of a farmer and former whaler, and her passionate love for the whaling specksioneer Charley Kinraid, who is kidnapped for naval service by one of England's notorious press-gangs. More recent critics have agreed with the *Saturday Review* writer in finding it difficult to link this novel to Gaskell's other works. Felicia Bonaparte writes that "[p]olitical and economic matters are central concerns in two of her novels [*Mary Barton* and *North and South*], and in the rest, as in her stories, they turn up in peripheral ways" (136). Words like "pastoral," "non-political," "non-controversial," and "non-engaged with social criticism" (Stoneman 139) have all been used in conjunction with the work, and it is true that the exotic setting does give *Sylvia's Lovers* a feeling of distance and Romanticism which the realism of her industrial novels do not share. Yet Nancy Henry's assessment of the novel—as "a tragic narrative of unforeseen encroachments of national events on individual lives" (Introduction xxiv)—stresses many of the same issues that Gaskell explores in all of her novels. Henry points out the connection that Gaskell draws between the press-gangs, which trapped men into service "for the good of the nation," and the character of Philip Hepburn, who traps Sylvia into marrying him for her own protection: "*Sylvia's Lovers* suggests that, in both political and domestic relationships, the line between paternalism and tyranny is easily crossed . . . Obscure people like Sylvia are marginal to the making of political decisions and the fighting of national battles, but Gaskell represents their experiences as central to English history" (xxvi).

The same *Saturday Review* critic who was unsure how to classify *Sylvia's Lovers* did have the insight to take note of the Robsons' farm servant, Kester, whom the critic identified as one of three "careful studies" in the work. Since then, astonishingly little has been written about this important character who "was almost like one of the family" and who regards Sylvia "with loving, faithful admiration" (44). Yet in *Sylvia's Lovers,* perhaps more than in any other full-length novel by Gaskell or her contemporaries, the relationship between the protagonist and a servant character is arguably the central relationship in the novel; in some ways Kester is Sylvia's true "lover," if not in a physical sense, then in the sense that he is the only man to remain faithful to her throughout her life.

In the novel's early chapters, "good old Kester" (45) is yet another a relatively one-dimensional character, yet another dutiful subject. He is happy enough working for the family, and is satisfied with the occasional privilege of basking in the light of Sylvia's bright presence, gazing at his young mistress with "mooney eyes" (45). In the novel's seaside town of Monkshaven, Gaskell tells us that "the distinction between class and class [was] less apparent" (9) than in other parts of England. As a result, the fact that Kester is merely a servant is less of an issue to the characters of *Sylvia's Lovers* than it is in Gaskell's novels in which maintaining social status and respectability are central concerns. Kester, it is true, looks up to his master's family and dutifully accepts his servile position, but the social distance between the Robson family and their farm-hand is relatively slight. After Sylvia's father Daniel is arrested during the press-gang riots, Kester asks Bell Robson if he may sleep in the house to be closer to the family. She replies, "God bless thee, my man; come in and lay thee down on t' settle, and I'll cover thee up wi' my cloak as hangs behind t' door. We're not many on us that love him, an' we'll be all on us under one roof, an' niver a stone wall of a lock betwist us" (249). Bell and Kester are united by their shared love for Daniel, and that bond is enough to bridge the social distance between them. Yet by morning, Kester has left his makeshift bed, so that "none knew of [his sleeping there] besides Bell" (249). Even in Monkshaven, people may try to keep up the appearance of class distinctions, but the classes are drawn to one another for comfort more freely than in Gaskell's other works.

Throughout Sylvia's courtship with Charley Kinraid, her father's execution, her disastrous marriage to Philip Hepburn, and her life as a mother, Kester is her only consistent confidant and friend. He assumes a paternal role after her own father's death, and there is no other character in the novel who offers her an honest unconditional relationship: Charley's trustworthiness is later called into question, and her marriage with Philip is based on a lie. As a man in his fifties, Kester is old enough to be Sylvia's father and their relationship most resembles that of a father and daughter, but there is an underlying element of sexual attraction in his response to her that complicates their relationship. Although there is no possibility of a romantic storyline between the two characters, Gaskell strengthens the attachment between Kester and Sylvia by demonstrating that Kester is bound to Sylvia by more than merely dutiful ties. Though he had approved of Sylvia's relationship with Charley, he comes to resent Philip's overtures to Sylvia out of "hot jealousy" (276). He upbraids Sylvia for courting Philip "'when her feyther's in prison' . . . with a consciousness as he uttered these last words that he was cruel and unjust and going too far" (276). Kester's jealousy increases after Daniel's execution as he watches Sylvia and her mother return from the hanging accompanied by Philip:

> Kester . . . went quickly out through the back-kitchen into the farm-yard, not staying to greet them, as he had meant to do; and yet it was dull-sighted of him not to have perceived that whatever might be the relations between Philip and Sylvia, he was sure to have accompanied them home; for alas! he was the only male protector of their blood remaining in the world. Poor Kester, who would fain have taken that office upon himself, chose to esteem himself cast off, and went heavily about the farm-yard, knowing that he ought to go in and bid such poor welcome as he had to offer, yet feeling too much to show himself before Philip.
>
> (286)

Kester's real fear is that Philip will ostracize him from the Robson family. During Daniel Robson's arrest and incarceration, we have seen that Kester had earned himself a place by the fire, "under the same roof" as the rest of the family. In stating his desire to be "the only male protector of their blood remaining in the world," Kester implies his desire to do what most of Gaskell's servants do—assume the role of family guardian. It is not until later, after Philip has shown his inability to perform that function that Kester will have his wish. Gaskell first demonstrates the failure of traditional marriage to "save" Sylvia before she allows the servant character to intercede.

Kester's warm feelings for Sylvia are not unrequited; far from being an invisible farm-hand, Kester is an object of Sylvia's intense speculation and concern. Despite her own financial and emotional distractions, Sylvia immediately notices that Kester has not stayed to welcome the family home and, understanding him well, she knows why: "She knew by some sort of intuition that if Philip accompanied them home . . . the old servant and friend of the family would absent himself; and so she slipped away at the first possible moment to go in search of him" (286). Like her mother had done before her, Sylvia takes Kester into the house and re-establishes him as a family member.

The relationship between Sylvia and Kester evolves throughout the novel, and Gaskell relates numerous conversations between them in which both characters express their views honestly. Sylvia hides her doubts about her future husband from her mother and from Philip himself, but she confides in Kester that she is only planning to marry him because "he's been so good to us in a' this time o' trouble and heavy grief, and he'll keep mother in comfort all t' rest of her days. . . . [but] I've niver forgotten Charley; I think on him, I see him ivery night drowned at t' bottom o' t' sea" (293). Kester is the novel's only character to suspect that Philip is lying about Charley's fate, reminding Sylvia that Philip was the source of that information: "An who told thee so sure and certain as he were drowned?," he asks, adding perceptively, "He might ha' been carried off by t' press-gang as well as other men" (292). His words are clearly out of line for a family servant, but Kester goes on to give Sylvia a final warning: "Sylvie . . . dunnot go and marry a man as thou's noane taken wi', and another as is most like for t' be dead, but who mebbe, is alive, havin' a pull on thy heart" (293). Though she does not take his advice, Sylvia clearly values his insight.

After Sylvia marries Philip, she moves away from the farm and into the town, but she continues to see Kester regularly. Despite an initial "estrangement caused by their new positions" (310), Sylvia continues to rely on Kester's friendship and the two resume their confidences. Sylvia seeks Kester out as soon as she learns that Philip had lied to her about Charley, revealing to him the story of her husband's deceit and disappearance. As time goes on, and she struggles to raise her daughter alone, Gaskell tells us that, "The only person who seemed to have pity on her was Kester" who came to see her "from time to time" (377). By the end of the novel, he continues to be charmed in her presence: "As the earliest friend she had, and also as one who knew the real secrets of her life, Sylvia always gave him the warm welcome, the cordial words, and the sweet looks in which the old man delighted" (423). Once again, Gaskell has exposed the traditional patriarchal family structure as inadequate at best and despotic at worst, and once again, she has placed a servant character in the role of the protector and parent in a redefined version of kinship.

As in *Cranford* and *Ruth,* the servant character is also the embodiment of the possibility for change and redemption. Throughout the novel, Kester treats Philip as his rival and enemy. He had sought to prevent Philip's marriage to Sylvia and vowed that "that chap has a deal to answer for" (361) when he learned of Philip's deceit. Yet in the novel's final scenes, Kester becomes a model of forgiveness. As Philip lies dying after saving their daughter from a drowning accident, Kester goes to Sylvia and tells her that Philip needs her "if iver a husband needed a wife" (441). Witnessing the reunion between the two, Kester "was sobbing bitterly; but she not at all" (449). At the climax of her long novel, Gaskell goes out of her way to detail the emotions of the family servant along with the novel's heroine, giving the reaction of each equal weight.

Like Gaskell's other servants, Kester had been the voice of wisdom throughout *Sylvia's Lovers,* and Gaskell gives him the last word. The final passage of the novel takes place years later, after Sylvia has died and her daughter has married and moved away to America. Two women relate the now legendary story of Sylvia and Philip Hepburn. At the end of the story, one woman adds, almost as an afterthought: "I knew an old man when I was a girl . . . as could niver abide to hear t' wife blamed. He would say nothing again' th' husband; he used to say as it were not fit for men to be judging; that she had had her sore trial, as well as Hepburn hisself" (450-1). That old man, of course, is Kester, and it is he who provides the final interpretation of her story. Like *Cranford*'s Martha, he rejects the notion that "reason always means what other people have to say," and provides his own views, "reason or not."

Given the clear pattern of criticism that Gaskell leveled at the traditional family led by a firm patriarch, and the paternalist social structure that was based upon that familial model, it is ironic that "Mrs Gaskell" should be remembered as a paragon of domestic womanhood. And there is no question that Gaskell embraced her domestic side: "I am always glad and thankful that I am a wife and mother and that I am so happy in the performance of those clear and defined duties," (l. 118) she wrote in a letter. That she derived satisfaction from both motherhood and her relationship with her husband is somewhat remarkable given that so many memorable women writers have been single or at least free from the dangers and demands of childbirth and childrearing. Biographer Winifred Gerin describes Gaskell at her writing, suddenly "called off yet once again by her busy household aides to settle some domestic problem, and resume, without perceptible strain, the role of housewife as she had just assumed that of author. No one can say which was her truer element" (303). Yet Gaskell did not exactly find her roles as wife and mother to be "clear and defined," just as she felt that the duties of her characters were mutable and evolving. Like her characters, she was ambivalent about her assigned position in life. Ironically, given the importance that some critics have placed on her publishing as "*Mrs* Gaskell," the author never used her husband's first name when referring to herself. Chafing at the idea of being "Mrs William Gaskell," she always signed her letters "Elizabeth Gaskell" after her marriage, accusing women who did not use their own "proper name" as indulging in "a silly piece of bride-like affectation" (Uglow 77).

A "silly affectation" might also have been Gaskell's opinion of those who cling too tightly to their social positions and worldviews. In *Cranford, Ruth,* and *Sylvia's Lovers,* Gaskell does not address the kind of overtly political topics of *Mary Barton* and *North and South,* but instead keeps to the advice which she gave her daughter Marianne: not to "meddle" in politics, but keep to more private matters of relationships and family, matters to which many felt the proper minister's wife was more suited. But the private world did not and could not exist apart from the worlds of power and commerce, and Gaskell's comments on the private lives of her characters were at once comments on these political and economic issues. For her, there was no better way to drive home a critique of despotic authority while holding up an ideal of caring than to foreground servants as saviors of the family.

Bibliography

Bonaparte, Felicia. *The Gypsy Bachelor of Manchester: The Life of Mrs Gaskell's Demon.* Charlottesville and London: The University Press of Virginia, 1992.

Chapple, J. A. V. and Arthur Pollards, eds. *The Letters of Mrs Gaskell.* Cambridge, MA: Harvard University Press, 1967.

Cobb, Frances Power. "Household Service." 1868. *Working Conditions in the Victorian Age: Debates on the Issue from Nineteenth-Century Critical Journals.* Ed. John Saville. UK: Gregg International Publishers Limited, 1973.

Dickerson, Vanessa. *Victorian Ghosts in the Noontide: Women Writers and the Supernatural.* Columbia and London: University of Missouri Press, 1996.

Edgeworth, Maria. *Belinda.* 1801. Intro. Eva Figes. London: Pandora Press, 1986.

Edgeworth, Maria. *Helen.* 1834. New York: Pandora Press, 1987.

Gaskell, Elizabeth. *Cranford/Cousin Phyllis.* 1851. Ed. Peter Keating. New York: Penguin Books, 1976.

———. *The Manchester Marriage and Other Stories.* Gloucestershire, UK: Alan Sutton Publishing, 1985.

———. *Mary Barton.* 1848. Jennifer Foster, ed. Ontario, Canada: Broadview Press, 2000.

———. "The Old Nurse's Story." 1852. Jenny Uglow, ed. *Curious, If True: Strange Tales by Mrs Gaskell.* 1-25.

———. *North and South.* 1855. Dorothy Collin, ed. New York: Penguin, 1970.

———. *Ruth.* 1853. Ed. Alan Shelston. Oxford and New York: Oxford University Press, 1985.

———. *Sylvia's Lovers.* 1863. Ed. Nancy Henry. London: Everyman, 1997.

Gerin, Winifred. *Elizabeth Gaskell: A Biography.* Oxford: Clarendon Press, 1976.

Knezevic, Borislav. "'An Ethnography of the Provincial' The Social Geography of Gentility in Elizabeth Gaskell's *Cranford.*" *Victorian Studies* 41:3 (1998): 405-26.

Langland, Elizabeth. *Nobody's Angels: Middle-Class Women and Domestic Ideology.* Ithaca and London: Cornell University Press, 1995.

Logan, Thad. *The Victorian Parlour.* Cambridge: Cambridge University Press, 2001.

Stoneman, Patsy. *Elizabeth Gaskell.* Bloomington and Indianapolis: Indiana University Press, 1987.

[Thaden, Barbara Z. *The Maternal Voice in Victorian Fiction: Rewriting the Patriarchal Family.* New York: Garland, 1997.]

Uglow, Jenny. *Elizabeth Gaskell: A Habit of Stories.* New York: Farrar Straus Giroux, 1993.

FURTHER READING

Criticism

Ellison, David. "Glazed Expression: *Mary Barton,* Ghosts and Glass." *Studies in the Novel* 36, no. 4 (January 2004): 484-508.
> Discusses Gaskell's treatment of the invisibility of the poor in *Mary Barton.*

Hamilton, Susan. "Ten Years of Gaskell Criticism." *Dickens Studies Annual* 31 (2002): 397-414.
> Surveys critical analyses of Gaskell's work during the 1990s, through 2002, emphasizing the feminist appraisals of the author and her status as a member of the literary canon.

Lee, Julia Sun-Joo. "The Return of the 'Unnative': The Transnational Politics of Elizabeth Gaskell's *North and South.*" *Nineteenth-Century Literature* 61, no. 4 (March 2007): 449-78.
> Asserts that the much-debated section treating mutiny in *North and South* places the themes treated in the novel within an international, rather than strictly national, context.

Lesjak, Carolyn. "Authenticity and the Geography of Empire: Reading Gaskell and Emecheta." *Studies in the Literary Imagination* 35, no. 2 (October 2002): 123-46.
> "[A]n attempt to take seriously Edward Said's challenge, in *Culture and Imperialism,* to read imperial history contrapuntally," in Gaskell's *Mary Barton* and Buchi Emecheta's *The Joys of Motherhood.*

——. "'How Deep Might Be the Romance': Representing Work and the Working Class in Elizabeth Gaskell's *Mary Barton.*" In *Working Fictions: A Genealogy of the Victorian Novel,* pp. 29-61. Durham, N.C.: Duke University Press, 2006.
> Focuses on Gaskell's courageous support for labor reform and the rights of the working class in *Mary Barton.*

Palmer, Sean. "Macaulay's Revolution: New Historicism, the Working Classes, and Elizabeth Gaskell's *North and South.*" *Nineteenth-Century Prose* 33, no. 2 (October 2006): 197-224.
> Notes the influence of Thomas Babington Macauley's views on Gaskell's treatment of the working class in her industrial novels.

Recchio, Thomas. "'Charming and Sane': School Editions of *Cranford* in America, 1905-1914." *Victorian Studies* 45, no. 4 (summer 2003): 597-623.
> Explores the reasons behind the widespread use of *Cranford* in American schools at the beginning of the twentieth century.

Webb, Igor. "Reading *Mary Barton.*" *Literary Imagination* 7, no. 1 (January 2005): 43-65.
> Translated by Roger Shattuck. Studies *Mary Barton* within the context of "reading the past."

How to Use This Index

The main references

> **Calvino, Italo**
> 1923-1985 .... CLC 5, 8, 11, 22, 33, 39,
> 73; SSC 3, 48

list all author entries in the following Gale Literary Criticism series:

AAL = *Asian American Literature*
BG = *The Beat Generation: A Gale Critical Companion*
BLC = *Black Literature Criticism*
BLCS = *Black Literature Criticism Supplement*
CLC = *Contemporary Literary Criticism*
CLR = *Children's Literature Review*
CMLC = *Classical and Medieval Literature Criticism*
DC = *Drama Criticism*
FL = *Feminism in Literature: A Gale Critical Companion*
GL = *Gothic Literature: A Gale Critical Companion*
HLC = *Hispanic Literature Criticism*
HLCS = *Hispanic Literature Criticism Supplement*
HR = *Harlem Renaissance: A Gale Critical Companion*
LC = *Literature Criticism from 1400 to 1800*
NCLC = *Nineteenth-Century Literature Criticism*
NNAL = *Native North American Literature*
PC = *Poetry Criticism*
SSC = *Short Story Criticism*
TCLC = *Twentieth-Century Literary Criticism*
WLC = *World Literature Criticism, 1500 to the Present*
WLCS = *World Literature Criticism Supplement*

The cross-references

> See also CA 85-88, 116; CANR 23, 61;
> DAM NOV; DLB 196; EW 13; MTCW 1, 2;
> RGSF 2; RGWL 2; SFW 4; SSFS 12

list all author entries in the following Gale biographical and literary sources:

AAYA = *Authors & Artists for Young Adults*
AFAW = *African American Writers*
AFW = *African Writers*
AITN = *Authors in the News*
AMW = *American Writers*
AMWR = *American Writers Retrospective Supplement*
AMWS = *American Writers Supplement*
ANW = *American Nature Writers*
AW = *Ancient Writers*
BEST = *Bestsellers*
BPFB = *Beacham's Encyclopedia of Popular Fiction: Biography and Resources*
BRW = *British Writers*
BRWS = *British Writers Supplement*
BW = *Black Writers*
BYA = *Beacham's Guide to Literature for Young Adults*
CA = *Contemporary Authors*
CAAS = *Contemporary Authors Autobiography Series*
CABS = *Contemporary Authors Bibliographical Series*
CAD = *Contemporary American Dramatists*
CANR = *Contemporary Authors New Revision Series*
CAP = *Contemporary Authors Permanent Series*
CBD = *Contemporary British Dramatists*
CCA = *Contemporary Canadian Authors*
CD = *Contemporary Dramatists*
CDALB = *Concise Dictionary of American Literary Biography*

CDALBS = *Concise Dictionary of American Literary Biography Supplement*
CDBLB = *Concise Dictionary of British Literary Biography*
CMW = *St. James Guide to Crime & Mystery Writers*
CN = *Contemporary Novelists*
CP = *Contemporary Poets*
CPW = *Contemporary Popular Writers*
CSW = *Contemporary Southern Writers*
CWD = *Contemporary Women Dramatists*
CWP = *Contemporary Women Poets*
CWRI = *St. James Guide to Children's Writers*
CWW = *Contemporary World Writers*
DA = *DISCovering Authors*
DA3 = *DISCovering Authors 3.0*
DAB = *DISCovering Authors: British Edition*
DAC = *DISCovering Authors: Canadian Edition*
DAM = *DISCovering Authors: Modules*
   DRAM: *Dramatists Module;* **MST:** *Most-studied Authors Module;*
   MULT: *Multicultural Authors Module;* **NOV:** *Novelists Module;*
   POET: *Poets Module;* **POP:** *Popular Fiction and Genre Authors Module*
DFS = *Drama for Students*
DLB = *Dictionary of Literary Biography*
DLBD = *Dictionary of Literary Biography Documentary Series*
DLBY = *Dictionary of Literary Biography Yearbook*
DNFS = *Literature of Developing Nations for Students*
EFS = *Epics for Students*
EW = *European Writers*
EWL = *Encyclopedia of World Literature in the 20th Century*
EXPN = *Exploring Novels*
EXPP = *Exploring Poetry*
EXPS = *Exploring Short Stories*
FANT = *St. James Guide to Fantasy Writers*
FW = *Feminist Writers*
GFL = *Guide to French Literature,* Beginnings to 1789, 1798 to the Present
GLL = *Gay and Lesbian Literature*
HGG = *St. James Guide to Horror, Ghost & Gothic Writers*
HW = *Hispanic Writers*
IDFW = *International Dictionary of Films and Filmmakers: Writers and Production Artists*
IDTP = *International Dictionary of Theatre: Playwrights*
LAIT = *Literature and Its Times*
LAW = *Latin American Writers*
JRDA = *Junior DISCovering Authors*
MAICYA = *Major Authors and Illustrators for Children and Young Adults*
MAICYAS = *Major Authors and Illustrators for Children and Young Adults Supplement*
MAWW = *Modern American Women Writers*
MJW = *Modern Japanese Writers*
MTCW = *Major 20th-Century Writers*
NCFS = *Nonfiction Classics for Students*
NFS = *Novels for Students*
PAB = *Poets: American and British*
PFS = *Poetry for Students*
RGAL = *Reference Guide to American Literature*
RGEL = *Reference Guide to English Literature*
RGSF = *Reference Guide to Short Fiction*
RGWL = *Reference Guide to World Literature*
RHW = *Twentieth-Century Romance and Historical Writers*
SAAS = *Something about the Author Autobiography Series*
SATA = *Something about the Author*
SFW = *St. James Guide to Science Fiction Writers*
SSFS = *Short Stories for Students*
TCWW = *Twentieth-Century Western Writers*
WLIT = *World Literature and Its Times*
WP = *World Poets*
YABC = *Yesterday's Authors of Books for Children*
YAW = *St. James Guide to Young Adult Writers*

Literary Criticism Series
Cumulative Author Index

Appelfeld, Aharon 1932- ... **CLC 23, 47; SSC 42**
See also CA 112; 133; CANR 86, 160; CWW 2; DLB 299; EWL 3; RGHL; RGSF 2; WLIT 6

Appelfeld, Aron
See Appelfeld, Aharon

Apple, Max (Isaac) 1941- .... **CLC 9, 33; SSC 50**
See also AMWS 17; CA 81-84; CANR 19, 54; DLB 130

Appleman, Philip (Dean) 1926- .... **CLC 51**
See also CA 13-16R; CAAS 18; CANR 6, 29, 56

Appleton, Lawrence
See Lovecraft, H. P.

Apteryx
See Eliot, T(homas) S(tearns)

Apuleius, (Lucius Madaurensis) c. 125-c. 164 .... **CMLC 1, 84**
See also AW 2; CDWLB 1; DLB 211; RGWL 2, 3; SUFW; WLIT 8

Aquin, Hubert 1929-1977 .... **CLC 15**
See also CA 105; DLB 53; EWL 3

Aquinas, Thomas 1224(?)-1274 ..... **CMLC 33**
See also DLB 115; EW 1; TWA

Aragon, Louis 1897-1982 .... **CLC 3, 22; TCLC 123**
See also CA 69-72; 108; CANR 28, 71; DAM NOV, POET; DLB 72, 258; EW 11; EWL 3; GFL 1789 to the Present; GLL 2; LMFS 2; MTCW 1, 2; RGWL 2, 3

Arany, Janos 1817-1882 .... **NCLC 34**

Aranyos, Kakay 1847-1910
See Mikszath, Kalman

Aratus of Soli c. 315B.C.-c. 240B.C. .... **CMLC 64**
See also DLB 176

Arbuthnot, John 1667-1735 .... **LC 1**
See also DLB 101

Archer, Herbert Winslow
See Mencken, H(enry) L(ouis)

Archer, Jeffrey 1940- .... **CLC 28**
See also AAYA 16; BEST 89:3; BPFB 1; CA 77-80; CANR 22, 52, 95, 136; CPW; DA3; DAM POP; INT CANR-22; MTFW 2005

Archer, Jeffrey Howard
See Archer, Jeffrey

Archer, Jules 1915- .... **CLC 12**
See also CA 9-12R; CANR 6, 69; SAAS 5; SATA 4, 85

Archer, Lee
See Ellison, Harlan

Archilochus c. 7th cent. B.C.- .... **CMLC 44**
See also DLB 176

Ard, William
See Jakes, John

Arden, John 1930- .... **CLC 6, 13, 15**
See also BRWS 2; CA 13-16R; CAAS 4; CANR 31, 65, 67, 124; CBD; CD 5, 6; DAM DRAM; DFS 9; DLB 13, 245; EWL 3; MTCW 1

Arenas, Reinaldo 1943-1990 .. **CLC 41; HLC 1; TCLC 191**
See also CA 124; 128; 133; CANR 73, 106; DAM MULT; DLB 145; EWL 3; GLL 2; HW 1; LAW; LAWS 1; MTCW 2; MTFW 2005; RGSF 2; RGWL 3; WLIT 1

Arendt, Hannah 1906-1975 .... **CLC 66, 98; TCLC 193**
See also CA 17-20R; 61-64; CANR 26, 60, 172; DLB 242; MTCW 1, 2

Aretino, Pietro 1492-1556 .... **LC 12, 165**
See also RGWL 2, 3

Arghezi, Tudor
See Theodorescu, Ion N.

Arguedas, Jose Maria 1911-1969 .... **CLC 10, 18; HLCS 1; TCLC 147**
See also CA 89-92; CANR 73; DLB 113; EWL 3; HW 1; LAW; RGWL 2, 3; WLIT 1

Argueta, Manlio 1936- .... **CLC 31**
See also CA 131; CANR 73; CWW 2; DLB 145; EWL 3; HW 1; RGWL 3

Arias, Ron 1941- .... **HLC 1**
See also CA 131; CANR 81, 136; DAM MULT; DLB 82; HW 1, 2; MTCW 2; MTFW 2005

Ariosto, Lodovico
See Ariosto, Ludovico

Ariosto, Ludovico 1474-1533 ... **LC 6, 87; PC 42**
See also EW 2; RGWL 2, 3; WLIT 7

Aristides
See Epstein, Joseph

Aristophanes 450B.C.-385B.C. .... **CMLC 4, 51; DC 2; WLCS**
See also AW 1; CDWLB 1; DA; DA3; DAB; DAC; DAM DRAM, MST; DFS 10; DLB 176; LMFS 1; RGWL 2, 3; TWA; WLIT 8

Aristotle 384B.C.-322B.C. .... **CMLC 31; WLCS**
See also AW 1; CDWLB 1; DA; DA3; DAB; DAC; DAM MST; DLB 176; RGWL 2, 3; TWA; WLIT 8

Arlt, Roberto (Godofredo Christophersen) 1900-1942 .... **HLC 1; TCLC 29**
See also CA 123; 131; CANR 67; DAM MULT; DLB 305; EWL 3; HW 1, 2; IDTP; LAW

Armah, Ayi Kwei 1939- . **BLC 1:1, 2:1; CLC 5, 33, 136**
See also AFW; BRWS 10; BW 1; CA 61-64; CANR 21, 64; CDWLB 3; CN 1, 2, 3, 4, 5, 6, 7; DAM MULT, POET; DLB 117; EWL 3; MTCW 1; WLIT 2

Armatrading, Joan 1950- .... **CLC 17**
See also CA 114; 186

Armin, Robert 1568(?)-1615(?) .... **LC 120**

Armitage, Frank
See Carpenter, John (Howard)

Armstrong, Jeannette (C.) 1948- .... **NNAL**
See also CA 149; CCA 1; CN 6, 7; DAC; DLB 334; SATA 102

Arnette, Robert
See Silverberg, Robert

Arnim, Achim von (Ludwig Joachim von Arnim) 1781-1831 .. **NCLC 5, 159; SSC 29**
See also DLB 90

Arnim, Bettina von 1785-1859 ...... **NCLC 38, 123**
See also DLB 90; RGWL 2, 3

Arnold, Matthew 1822-1888 ..... **NCLC 6, 29, 89, 126; PC 5, 94; WLC 1**
See also BRW 5; CDBLB 1832-1890; DA; DAB; DAC; DAM MST, POET; DLB 32, 57; EXPP; PAB; PFS 2; TEA; WP

Arnold, Thomas 1795-1842 .... **NCLC 18**
See also DLB 55

Arnow, Harriette (Louisa) Simpson 1908-1986 ...... **CLC 2, 7, 18; TCLC 196**
See also BPFB 1; CA 9-12R; 118; CANR 14; CN 2, 3, 4; DLB 6; FW; MTCW 1, 2; RHW; SATA 42; SATA-Obit 47

Arouet, Francois-Marie
See Voltaire

Arp, Hans
See Arp, Jean

Arp, Jean 1887-1966 .... **CLC 5; TCLC 115**
See also CA 81-84; 25-28R; CANR 42, 77; EW 10

Arrabal
See Arrabal, Fernando

Arrabal (Teran), Fernando
See Arrabal, Fernando

Arrabal, Fernando 1932- ... **CLC 2, 9, 18, 58**
See also CA 9-12R; CANR 15; CWW 2; DLB 321; EWL 3; LMFS 2

Arreola, Juan Jose 1918-2001 .... **CLC 147; HLC 1; SSC 38**
See also CA 113; 131; 200; CANR 81; CWW 2; DAM MULT; DLB 113; DNFS 2; EWL 3; HW 1, 2; LAW; RGSF 2

Arrian c. 89(?)-c. 155(?) .... **CMLC 43**
See also DLB 176

Arrick, Fran
See Angell, Judie

Arrley, Richmond
See Delany, Samuel R., Jr.

Artaud, Antonin (Marie Joseph) 1896-1948 .... **DC 14; TCLC 3, 36**
See also CA 104; 149; DA3; DAM DRAM; DFS 22; DLB 258, 321; EW 11; EWL 3; GFL 1789 to the Present; MTCW 2; MTFW 2005; RGWL 2, 3

Arthur, Ruth M(abel) 1905-1979 ..... **CLC 12**
See also CA 9-12R; 85-88; CANR 4; CWRI 5; SATA 7, 26

Artsybashev, Mikhail (Petrovich) 1878-1927 .... **TCLC 31**
See also CA 170; DLB 295

Arundel, Honor (Morfydd) 1919-1973 .... **CLC 17**
See also CA 21-22; 41-44R; CAP 2; CLR 35; CWRI 5; SATA 4; SATA-Obit 24

Arzner, Dorothy 1900-1979 .... **CLC 98**

Asch, Sholem 1880-1957 .... **TCLC 3**
See also CA 105; DLB 333; EWL 3; GLL 2; RGHL

Ascham, Roger 1516(?)-1568 .... **LC 101**
See also DLB 236

Ash, Shalom
See Asch, Sholem

Ashbery, John 1927- ... **CLC 2, 3, 4, 6, 9, 13, 15, 25, 41, 77, 125, 221; PC 26**
See also AMWS 3; CA 5-8R; CANR 9, 37, 66, 102, 132, 170; CP 1, 2, 3, 4, 5, 6, 7; DA3; DAM POET; DLB 5, 165; DLBY 1981; EWL 3; GLL 1; INT CANR-9; MAL 5; MTCW 1, 2; MTFW 2005; PAB; PFS 11, 28; RGAL 4; TCLE 1:1; WP

Ashbery, John Lawrence
See Ashbery, John

Ashbridge, Elizabeth 1713-1755 .... **LC 147**
See also DLB 200

Ashdown, Clifford
See Freeman, R(ichard) Austin

Ashe, Gordon
See Creasey, John

Ashton-Warner, Sylvia (Constance) 1908-1984 .... **CLC 19**
See also CA 69-72; 112; CANR 29; CN 1, 2, 3; MTCW 1, 2

Asimov, Isaac 1920-1992 ..... **CLC 1, 3, 9, 19, 26, 76, 92**
See also AAYA 13; BEST 90:2; BPFB 1; BYA 4, 6, 7, 9; CA 1-4R; 137; CANR 2, 19, 36, 60, 125; CLR 12, 79; CMW 4; CN 1, 2, 3, 4, 5; CPW; DA3; DAM POP; DLB 8; DLBY 1992; INT CANR-19; JRDA; LAIT 5; LMFS 2; MAICYA 1, 2; MAL 5; MTCW 1, 2; MTFW 2005; NFS 29; RGAL 4; SATA 1, 26, 74; SCFW 1, 2; SFW 4; SSFS 17; TUS; YAW

Askew, Anne 1521(?)-1546 .... **LC 81**
See also DLB 136

Assis, Joaquim Maria Machado de
See Machado de Assis, Joaquim Maria

Astell, Mary 1666-1731 .... **LC 68**
See also DLB 252, 336; FW

Bacon, Francis 1561-1626 ..... **LC 18, 32, 131**
See also BRW 1; CDBLB Before 1660;
DLB 151, 236, 252; RGEL 2; TEA
Bacon, Roger 1214(?)-1294 ... **CMLC 14, 108**
See also DLB 115
Bacovia, George 1881-1957 .... **TCLC 24**
See also CA 123; 189; CDWLB 4; DLB
220; EWL 3
Badanes, Jerome 1937-1995 .... **CLC 59**
See also CA 234
Bage, Robert 1728-1801 .... **NCLC 182**
See also DLB 39; RGEL 2
Bagehot, Walter 1826-1877 .... **NCLC 10**
See also DLB 55
Bagnold, Enid 1889-1981 .... **CLC 25**
See also AAYA 75; BYA 2; CA 5-8R; 103;
CANR 5, 40; CBD; CN 2; CWD; CWRI
5; DAM DRAM; DLB 13, 160, 191, 245;
FW; MAICYA 1, 2; RGEL 2; SATA 1, 25
Bagritsky, Eduard
See Dzyubin, Eduard Georgievich
Bagritsky, Edvard
See Dzyubin, Eduard Georgievich
Bagrjana, Elisaveta
See Belcheva, Elisaveta Lyubomirova
Bagryana, Elisaveta
See Belcheva, Elisaveta Lyubomirova
Bailey, Paul 1937- .... **CLC 45**
See also CA 21-24R; CANR 16, 62, 124;
CN 1, 2, 3, 4, 5, 6, 7; DLB 14, 271; GLL
2
Baillie, Joanna 1762-1851 ...... **NCLC 71, 151**
See also DLB 93, 344; GL 2; RGEL 2
Bainbridge, Beryl 1934- ...... **CLC 4, 5, 8, 10,
14, 18, 22, 62, 130**
See also BRWS 6; CA 21-24R; CANR 24,
55, 75, 88, 128; CN 2, 3, 4, 5, 6, 7; DAM
NOV; DLB 14, 231; EWL 3; MTCW 1,
2; MTFW 2005
Baker, Carlos (Heard)
1909-1987 .... **TCLC 119**
See also CA 5-8R; 122; CANR 3, 63; DLB
103
Baker, Elliott 1922-2007 .... **CLC 8**
See also CA 45-48; 257; CANR 2, 63; CN
1, 2, 3, 4, 5, 6, 7
Baker, Elliott Joseph
See Baker, Elliott
Baker, Jean H.
See Russell, George William
Baker, Nicholson 1957- .... **CLC 61, 165**
See also AMWS 13; CA 135; CANR 63,
120, 138; CN 6; CPW; DA3; DAM POP;
DLB 227; MTFW 2005
Baker, Ray Stannard 1870-1946 .... **TCLC 47**
See also CA 118; DLB 345
Baker, Russell 1925- .... **CLC 31**
See also BEST 89:4; CA 57-60; CANR 11,
41, 59, 137; MTCW 1, 2; MTFW 2005
Bakhtin, M.
See Bakhtin, Mikhail Mikhailovich
Bakhtin, M. M.
See Bakhtin, Mikhail Mikhailovich
Bakhtin, Mikhail
See Bakhtin, Mikhail Mikhailovich
Bakhtin, Mikhail Mikhailovich
1895-1975 .... **CLC 83; TCLC 160**
See also CA 128; 113; DLB 242; EWL 3
Bakshi, Ralph 1938(?)- .... **CLC 26**
See also CA 112; 138; IDFW 3
Bakunin, Mikhail (Alexandrovich)
1814-1876 .... **NCLC 25, 58**
See also DLB 277
Bal, Mieke (Maria Gertrudis)
1946- .... **CLC 252**
See also CA 156; CANR 99

Baldwin, James 1924-1987 ...... **BLC 1:1, 2:1;
CLC 1, 2, 3, 4, 5, 8, 13, 15, 17, 42, 50,
67, 90, 127; DC 1; SSC 10, 33, 98;
WLC 1**
See also AAYA 4, 34; AFAW 1, 2; AMWR
2; AMWS 1; BPFB 1; BW 1; CA 1-4R;
124; CABS 1; CAD; CANR 3, 24;
CDALB 1941-1968; CN 1, 2, 3, 4; CPW;
DA; DA3; DAB; DAC; DAM MST,
MULT, NOV, POP; DFS 11, 15; DLB 2,
7, 33, 249, 278; DLBY 1987; EWL 3;
EXPS; LAIT 5; MAL 5; MTCW 1, 2;
MTFW 2005; NCFS 4; NFS 4; RGAL 4;
RGSF 2; SATA 9; SATA-Obit 54; SSFS
2, 18; TUS
Baldwin, William c. 1515-1563 .... **LC 113**
See also DLB 132
Bale, John 1495-1563 .... **LC 62**
See also DLB 132; RGEL 2; TEA
Ball, Hugo 1886-1927 .... **TCLC 104**
Ballard, J.G. 1930-2009 ..... **CLC 3, 6, 14, 36,
137; SSC 1, 53**
See also AAYA 3, 52; BRWS 5; CA 5-8R;
CANR 15, 39, 65, 107, 133; CN 1, 2, 3,
4, 5, 6, 7; DA3; DAM NOV, POP; DLB
14, 207, 261, 319; EWL 3; HGG; MTCW
1, 2; MTFW 2005; NFS 8; RGEL 2;
RGSF 2; SATA 93; SCFW 1, 2; SFW 4
Balmont, Konstantin (Dmitriyevich)
1867-1943 .... **TCLC 11**
See also CA 109; 155; DLB 295; EWL 3
Baltausis, Vincas 1847-1910
See Mikszath, Kalman
Balzac, Guez de (?)-
See Balzac, Jean-Louis Guez de
Balzac, Honore de 1799-1850 ... **NCLC 5, 35,
53, 153; SSC 5, 59, 102; WLC 1**
See also DA; DA3; DAB; DAC; DAM
MST, NOV; DLB 119; EW 5; GFL 1789
to the Present; LMFS 1; RGSF 2; RGWL
2, 3; SSFS 10; SUFW; TWA
Balzac, Jean-Louis Guez de
1597-1654 .... **LC 162**
See also DLB 268; GFL Beginnings to 1789
Bambara, Toni Cade 1939-1995 ... **BLC 1:1,
2:1; CLC 19, 88; SSC 35, 107; TCLC
116; WLCS**
See also AAYA 5, 49; AFAW 2; AMWS 11;
BW 2, 3; BYA 12, 14; CA 29-32R; 150;
CANR 24, 49, 81; CDALBS; DA; DA3;
DAC; DAM MST, MULT; DLB 38, 218;
EXPS; MAL 5; MTCW 1, 2; MTFW
2005; RGAL 4; RGSF 2; SATA 112; SSFS
4, 7, 12, 21
Bamdad, A.
See Shamlu, Ahmad
Bamdad, Alef
See Shamlu, Ahmad
Banat, D. R.
See Bradbury, Ray
Bancroft, Laura
See Baum, L(yman) Frank
Banim, John 1798-1842 .... **NCLC 13**
See also DLB 116, 158, 159; RGEL 2
Banim, Michael 1796-1874 .... **NCLC 13**
See also DLB 158, 159
Banjo, The
See Paterson, A(ndrew) B(arton)
Banks, Iain 1954- .... **CLC 34**
See also BRWS 11; CA 123; 128; CANR
61, 106, 180; DLB 194, 261; EWL 3;
HGG; INT CA-128; MTFW 2005; SFW 4
Banks, Iain M.
See Banks, Iain
Banks, Iain Menzies
See Banks, Iain
Banks, Lynne Reid
See Reid Banks, Lynne

Banks, Russell 1940- . **CLC 37, 72, 187; SSC
42**
See also AAYA 45; AMWS 5; CA 65-68;
CAAS 15; CANR 19, 52, 73, 118; CN 4,
5, 6, 7; DLB 130, 278; EWL 3; MAL 5;
MTCW 2; MTFW 2005; NFS 13
Banks, Russell Earl
See Banks, Russell
Banville, John 1945- .... **CLC 46, 118, 224**
See also CA 117; 128; CANR 104, 150,
176; CN 4, 5, 6, 7; DLB 14, 271, 326;
INT CA-128
Banville, Theodore (Faullain) de
1832-1891 .... **NCLC 9**
See also DLB 217; GFL 1789 to the Present
Baraka, Amiri 1934- .. **BLC 1:1, 2:1; CLC 1,
2, 3, 5, 10, 14, 33, 115, 213; DC 6; PC
4; WLCS**
See also AAYA 63; AFAW 1, 2; AMWS 2;
BW 2, 3; CA 21-24R; CABS 3; CAD;
CANR 27, 38, 61, 133, 172; CD 3, 5, 6;
CDALB 1941-1968; CN 1, 2; CP 1, 2, 3,
4, 5, 6, 7; CPW; DA; DA3; DAC; DAM
MST, MULT, POET, POP; DFS 3, 11, 16;
DLB 5, 7, 16, 38; DLBD 8; EWL 3; MAL
5; MTCW 1, 2; MTFW 2005; PFS 9;
RGAL 4; TCLE 1:1; TUS; WP
Baratynsky, Evgenii Abramovich
1800-1844 .... **NCLC 103**
See also DLB 205
Barbauld, Anna Laetitia
1743-1825 .... **NCLC 50, 185**
See also DLB 107, 109, 142, 158, 336;
RGEL 2
Barbellion, W. N. P.
See Cummings, Bruce F(rederick)
Barber, Benjamin R. 1939- .... **CLC 141**
See also CA 29-32R; CANR 12, 32, 64, 119
Barbera, Jack (Vincent) 1945- .... **CLC 44**
See also CA 110; CANR 45
Barbey d'Aurevilly, Jules-Amedee
1808-1889 .... **NCLC 1, 213; SSC 17**
See also DLB 119; GFL 1789 to the Present
Barbour, John c. 1316-1395 .... **CMLC 33**
See also DLB 146
Barbusse, Henri 1873-1935 .... **TCLC 5**
See also CA 105; 154; DLB 65; EWL 3;
RGWL 2, 3
Barclay, Alexander c. 1475-1552 .... **LC 109**
See also DLB 132
Barclay, Bill
See Moorcock, Michael
Barclay, William Ewert
See Moorcock, Michael
Barea, Arturo 1897-1957 .... **TCLC 14**
See also CA 111; 201
Barfoot, Joan 1946- .... **CLC 18**
See also CA 105; CANR 141, 179
Barham, Richard Harris
1788-1845 .... **NCLC 77**
See also DLB 159
Baring, Maurice 1874-1945 .... **TCLC 8**
See also CA 105; 168; DLB 34; HGG
Baring-Gould, Sabine 1834-1924 ... **TCLC 88**
See also DLB 156, 190
Barker, Clive 1952- .... **CLC 52, 205; SSC 53**
See also AAYA 10, 54; BEST 90:3; BPFB
1; CA 121; 129; CANR 71, 111, 133, 187;
CPW; DA3; DAM POP; DLB 261; HGG;
INT CA-129; MTCW 1, 2; MTFW 2005;
SUFW 2
Barker, George Granville
1913-1991 .... **CLC 8, 48; PC 77**
See also CA 9-12R; 135; CANR 7, 38; CP
1, 2, 3, 4, 5; DAM POET; DLB 20; EWL
3; MTCW 1
Barker, Harley Granville
See Granville-Barker, Harley

Blake, William 1757-1827 . **NCLC 13, 37, 57, 127, 173, 190, 201; PC 12, 63; WLC 1**
See also AAYA 47; BRW 3; BRWR 1; CD-BLB 1789-1832; CLR 52; DA; DA3; DAB; DAC; DAM MST, POET; DLB 93, 163; EXPP; LATS 1:1; LMFS 1; MAI-CYA 1, 2; PAB; PFS 2, 12, 24; SATA 30; TEA; WCH; WLIT 3; WP

Blanchot, Maurice 1907-2003 .... **CLC 135**
See also CA 117; 144; 213; CANR 138; DLB 72, 296; EWL 3

Blasco Ibanez, Vicente 1867-1928 . **TCLC 12**
See also BPFB 1; CA 110; 131; CANR 81; DA3; DAM NOV; DLB 322; EW 8; EWL 3; HW 1, 2; MTCW 1

Blatty, William Peter 1928- .... **CLC 2**
See also CA 5-8R; CANR 9, 124; DAM POP; HGG

Bleeck, Oliver
See Thomas, Ross (Elmore)

Bleecker, Ann Eliza 1752-1783 .... **LC 161**
See also DLB 200

Blessing, Lee (Knowlton) 1949- .... **CLC 54**
See also CA 236; CAD; CD 5, 6; DFS 23, 26

Blight, Rose
See Greer, Germaine

Blind, Mathilde 1841-1896 .... **NCLC 202**
See also DLB 199

Blish, James (Benjamin) 1921-1975 . **CLC 14**
See also BPFB 1; CA 1-4R; 57-60; CANR 3; CN 2; DLB 8; MTCW 1; SATA 66; SCFW 1, 2; SFW 4

Bliss, Frederick
See Card, Orson Scott

Bliss, Gillian
See Paton Walsh, Jill

Bliss, Reginald
See Wells, H(erbert) G(eorge)

Blixen, Karen (Christentze Dinesen)
1885-1962 ... **CLC 10, 29, 95; SSC 7, 75**
See also CA 25-28; CANR 22, 50; CAP 2; DA3; DLB 214; EW 10; EWL 3; EXPS; FW; GL 2; HGG; LAIT 3; LMFS 1; MTCW 1; NCFS 2; NFS 9; RGSF 2; RGWL 2, 3; SATA 44; SSFS 3, 6, 13; WLIT 2

Bloch, Robert (Albert) 1917-1994 .... **CLC 33**
See also AAYA 29; CA 5-8R, 179; 146; CAAE 179; CAAS 20; CANR 5, 78; DA3; DLB 44; HGG; INT CANR-5; MTCW 2; SATA 12; SATA-Obit 82; SFW 4; SUFW 1, 2

Blok, Alexander (Alexandrovich)
1880-1921 .... **PC 21; TCLC 5**
See also CA 104; 183; DLB 295; EW 9; EWL 3; LMFS 2; RGWL 2, 3

Blom, Jan
See Breytenbach, Breyten

Bloom, Harold 1930- .... **CLC 24, 103, 221**
See also CA 13-16R; CANR 39, 75, 92, 133, 181; DLB 67; EWL 3; MTCW 2; MTFW 2005; RGAL 4

Bloomfield, Aurelius
See Bourne, Randolph S(illiman)

Bloomfield, Robert 1766-1823 ..... **NCLC 145**
See also DLB 93

Blount, Roy, Jr. 1941- .... **CLC 38**
See also CA 53-56; CANR 10, 28, 61, 125, 176; CSW; INT CANR-28; MTCW 1, 2; MTFW 2005

Blount, Roy Alton
See Blount, Roy, Jr.

Blowsnake, Sam 1875-(?) .... **NNAL**

Bloy, Leon 1846-1917 .... **TCLC 22**
See also CA 121; 183; DLB 123; GFL 1789 to the Present

Blue Cloud, Peter (Aroniawenrate)
1933- .... **NNAL**
See also CA 117; CANR 40; DAM MULT; DLB 342

Bluggage, Oranthy
See Alcott, Louisa May

Blume, Judy 1938- .... **CLC 12, 30**
See also AAYA 3, 26; BYA 1, 8, 12; CA 29-32R; CANR 13, 37, 66, 124, 186; CLR 2, 15, 69; CPW; DA3; DAM NOV, POP; DLB 52; JRDA; MAICYA 1, 2; MAIC-YAS 1; MTCW 1, 2; MTFW 2005; NFS 24; SATA 2, 31, 79, 142, 195; WYA; YAW

Blume, Judy Sussman
See Blume, Judy

Blunden, Edmund (Charles)
1896-1974 .... **CLC 2, 56; PC 66**
See also BRW 6; BRWS 11; CA 17-18; 45-48; CANR 54; CAP 2; CP 1, 2; DLB 20, 100, 155; MTCW 1; PAB

Bly, Robert (Elwood) 1926- .... **CLC 1, 2, 5, 10, 15, 38, 128; PC 39**
See also AMWS 4; CA 5-8R; CANR 41, 73, 125; CP 1, 2, 3, 4, 5, 6, 7; DA3; DAM POET; DLB 5, 342; EWL 3; MAL 5; MTCW 1, 2; MTFW 2005; PFS 6, 17; RGAL 4

Boas, Franz 1858-1942 .... **TCLC 56**
See also CA 115; 181

Bobette
See Simenon, Georges (Jacques Christian)

Boccaccio, Giovanni 1313-1375 ... **CMLC 13, 57; SSC 10, 87**
See also EW 2; RGSF 2; RGWL 2, 3; TWA; WLIT 7

Bochco, Steven 1943- .... **CLC 35**
See also AAYA 11, 71; CA 124; 138

Bode, Sigmund
See O'Doherty, Brian

Bodel, Jean 1167(?)-1210 .... **CMLC 28**

Bodenheim, Maxwell 1892-1954 .... **TCLC 44**
See also CA 110; 187; DLB 9, 45; MAL 5; RGAL 4

Bodenheimer, Maxwell
See Bodenheim, Maxwell

Bodker, Cecil 1927-
See Bodker, Cecil

Bodker, Cecil 1927- .... **CLC 21**
See also CA 73-76; CANR 13, 44, 111; CLR 23; MAICYA 1, 2; SATA 14, 133

Boell, Heinrich (Theodor)
1917-1985 ..... **CLC 2, 3, 6, 9, 11, 15, 27, 32, 72; SSC 23; TCLC 185; WLC 1**
See also BPFB 1; CA 21-24R; 116; CANR 24; CDWLB 2; DA; DA3; DAB; DAC; DAM MST, NOV; DLB 69, 329; DLBY 1985; EW 13; EWL 3; MTCW 1, 2; MTFW 2005; RGHL; RGSF 2; RGWL 2, 3; SSFS 20; TWA

Boerne, Alfred
See Doeblin, Alfred

Boethius c. 480-c. 524 .... **CMLC 15**
See also DLB 115; RGWL 2, 3; WLIT 8

Boff, Leonardo (Genezio Darci)
1938- .... **CLC 70; HLC 1**
See also CA 150; DAM MULT; HW 2

Bogan, Louise 1897-1970 .... **CLC 4, 39, 46, 93; PC 12**
See also AMWS 3; CA 73-76; 25-28R; CANR 33, 82; CP 1; DAM POET; DLB 45, 169; EWL 3; MAL 5; MBL; MTCW 1, 2; PFS 21; RGAL 4

Bogarde, Dirk
See Van Den Bogarde, Derek Jules Gaspard Ulric Niven

Bogat, Shatan
See Kacew, Romain

Bogomolny, Robert L(ee) 1938- .... **SSC 41; TCLC 11**
See Tsushima, Shuji
See also CA 121, 164; DLB 182; EWL 3; MJW; RGSF 2; RGWL 2, 3; TWA

Bogosian, Eric 1953- .... **CLC 45, 141**
See also CA 138; CAD; CANR 102, 148; CD 5, 6; DLB 341

Bograd, Larry 1953- .... **CLC 35**
See also CA 93-96; CANR 57; SAAS 21; SATA 33, 89; WYA

Boiardo, Matteo Maria 1441-1494 .... **LC 6**

Boileau-Despreaux, Nicolas
1636-1711 .... **LC 3, 164**
See also DLB 268; EW 3; GFL Beginnings to 1789; RGWL 2, 3

Boissard, Maurice
See Leautaud, Paul

Bojer, Johan 1872-1959 .... **TCLC 64**
See also CA 189; EWL 3

Bok, Edward W(illiam)
1863-1930 .... **TCLC 101**
See also CA 217; DLB 91; DLBD 16

Boker, George Henry 1823-1890 . **NCLC 125**
See also RGAL 4

Boland, Eavan 1944- ... **CLC 40, 67, 113; PC 58**
See also BRWS 5; CA 143, 207; CAAE 207; CANR 61, 180; CP 1, 6, 7; CWP; DAM POET; DLB 40; FW; MTCW 2; MTFW 2005; PFS 12, 22

Boland, Eavan Aisling
See Boland, Eavan

Boll, Heinrich (Theodor)
See Boell, Heinrich (Theodor)

Bolt, Lee
See Faust, Frederick (Schiller)

Bolt, Robert (Oxton) 1924-1995 ...... **CLC 14; TCLC 175**
See also CA 17-20R; 147; CANR 35, 67; CBD; DAM DRAM; DFS 2; DLB 13, 233; EWL 3; LAIT 1; MTCW 1

Bombal, Maria Luisa 1910-1980 .... **HLCS 1; SSC 37**
See also CA 127; CANR 72; EWL 3; HW 1; LAW; RGSF 2

Bombet, Louis-Alexandre-Cesar
See Stendhal

Bomkauf
See Kaufman, Bob (Garnell)

Bonaventura .... **NCLC 35**
See also DLB 90

Bonaventure 1217(?)-1274 .... **CMLC 79**
See also DLB 115; LMFS 1

Bond, Edward 1934- .... **CLC 4, 6, 13, 23**
See also AAYA 50; BRWS 1; CA 25-28R; CANR 38, 67, 106; CBD; CD 5, 6; DAM DRAM; DFS 3, 8; DLB 13, 310; EWL 3; MTCW 1

Bonham, Frank 1914-1989 .... **CLC 12**
See also AAYA 1, 70; BYA 1, 3; CA 9-12R; CANR 4, 36; JRDA; MAICYA 1, 2; SAAS 3; SATA 1, 49; SATA-Obit 62; TCWW 1, 2; YAW

Bonnefoy, Yves 1923- . **CLC 9, 15, 58; PC 58**
See also CA 85-88; CANR 33, 75, 97, 136; CWW 2; DAM MST, POET; DLB 258; EWL 3; GFL 1789 to the Present; MTCW 1, 2; MTFW 2005

Bonner, Marita
See Occomy, Marita (Odette) Bonner

Bonnin, Gertrude 1876-1938 .... **NNAL**
See also CA 150; DAM MULT; DLB 175

Bontemps, Arna(ud Wendell)
1902-1973 ..... **BLC 1:1; CLC 1, 18; HR 1:2**
See also BW 1; CA 1-4R; 41-44R; CANR 4, 35; CLR 6; CP 1; CWRI 5; DA3; DAM MULT, NOV, POET; DLB 48, 51; JRDA; MAICYA 1, 2; MAL 5; MTCW 1, 2; SATA 2, 44; SATA-Obit 24; WCH; WP

Boot, William
See Stoppard, Tom
Booth, Irwin
See Hoch, Edward D.
Booth, Martin 1944-2004 .... **CLC 13**
See also CA 93-96, 188; 223; CAAE 188; CAAS 2; CANR 92; CP 1, 2, 3, 4
Booth, Philip 1925-2007 .... **CLC 23**
See also CA 5-8R; 262; CANR 5, 88; CP 1, 2, 3, 4, 5, 6, 7; DLBY 1982
Booth, Philip Edmund
See Booth, Philip
Booth, Wayne C. 1921-2005 .... **CLC 24**
See also CA 1-4R; 244; CAAS 5; CANR 3, 43, 117; DLB 67
Booth, Wayne Clayson
See Booth, Wayne C.
Borchert, Wolfgang 1921-1947 .... **TCLC 5**
See also CA 104; 188; DLB 69, 124; EWL 3
Borel, Petrus 1809-1859 .... **NCLC 41**
See also DLB 119; GFL 1789 to the Present
Borges, Jorge Luis 1899-1986 ... **CLC 1, 2, 3, 4, 6, 8, 9, 10, 13, 19, 44, 48, 83; HLC 1; PC 22, 32; SSC 4, 41, 100; TCLC 109; WLC 1**
See also AAYA 26; BPFB 1; CA 21-24R; CANR 19, 33, 75, 105, 133; CDWLB 3; DA; DA3; DAB; DAC; DAM MST, MULT; DLB 113, 283; DLBY 1986; DNFS 1, 2; EWL 3; HW 1, 2; LAW; LMFS 2; MSW; MTCW 1, 2; MTFW 2005; PFS 27; RGHL; RGSF 2; RGWL 2, 3; SFW 4; SSFS 17; TWA; WLIT 1
Borne, Ludwig 1786-1837 .... **NCLC 193**
See also DLB 90
Borowski, Tadeusz 1922-1951 .... **SSC 48; TCLC 9**
See also CA 106; 154; CDWLB 4; DLB 215; EWL 3; RGHL; RGSF 2; RGWL 3; SSFS 13
Borrow, George (Henry)
1803-1881 .... **NCLC 9**
See also BRWS 12; DLB 21, 55, 166
Bosch (Gavino), Juan 1909-2001 ..... **HLCS 1**
See also CA 151; 204; DAM MST, MULT; DLB 145; HW 1, 2
Bosman, Herman Charles
1905-1951 .... **TCLC 49**
See also CA 160; DLB 225; RGSF 2
Bosschere, Jean de 1878(?)-1953 ... **TCLC 19**
See also CA 115; 186
Boswell, James 1740-1795 ... **LC 4, 50; WLC 1**
See also BRW 3; CDBLB 1660-1789; DA; DAB; DAC; DAM MST; DLB 104, 142; TEA; WLIT 3
Boto, Eza
See Biyidi, Alexandre
Bottomley, Gordon 1874-1948 ..... **TCLC 107**
See also CA 120; 192; DLB 10
Bottoms, David 1949- .... **CLC 53**
See also CA 105; CANR 22; CSW; DLB 120; DLBY 1983
Boucicault, Dion 1820-1890 .... **NCLC 41**
See also DLB 344
Boucolon, Maryse
See Conde, Maryse
Bourcicault, Dion
See Boucicault, Dion
Bourdieu, Pierre 1930-2002 .... **CLC 198**
See also CA 130; 204
Bourget, Paul (Charles Joseph)
1852-1935 .... **TCLC 12**
See also CA 107; 196; DLB 123; GFL 1789 to the Present

Bourjaily, Vance (Nye) 1922- .... **CLC 8, 62**
See also CA 1-4R; CAAS 1; CANR 2, 72; CN 1, 2, 3, 4, 5, 6, 7; DLB 2, 143; MAL 5
Bourne, Randolph S(illiman)
1886-1918 .... **TCLC 16**
See also AMW; CA 117; 155; DLB 63; MAL 5
Boursiquot, Dionysius
See Boucicault, Dion
Bova, Ben 1932- .... **CLC 45**
See also AAYA 16; CA 5-8R; CAAS 18; CANR 11, 56, 94, 111, 157; CLR 3, 96; DLBY 1981; INT CANR-11; MAICYA 1, 2; MTCW 1; SATA 6, 68, 133; SFW 4
Bova, Benjamin William
See Bova, Ben
Bowen, Elizabeth (Dorothea Cole)
1899-1973 . **CLC 1, 3, 6, 11, 15, 22, 118; SSC 3, 28, 66; TCLC 148**
See also BRWS 2; CA 17-18; 41-44R; CANR 35, 105; CAP 2; CDBLB 1945-1960; CN 1; DA3; DAM NOV; DLB 15, 162; EWL 3; EXPS; FW; HGG; MTCW 1, 2; MTFW 2005; NFS 13; RGSF 2; SSFS 5, 22; SUFW 1; TEA; WLIT 4
Bowering, George 1935- .... **CLC 15, 47**
See also CA 21-24R; CAAS 16; CANR 10; CN 7; CP 1, 2, 3, 4, 5, 6, 7; DLB 53
Bowering, Marilyn R(uthe) 1949- .... **CLC 32**
See also CA 101; CANR 49; CP 4, 5, 6, 7; CWP; DLB 334
Bowers, Edgar 1924-2000 .... **CLC 9**
See also CA 5-8R; 188; CANR 24; CP 1, 2, 3, 4, 5, 6, 7; CSW; DLB 5
Bowers, Mrs. J. Milton 1842-1914
See Bierce, Ambrose (Gwinett)
Bowie, David
See Jones, David Robert
Bowles, Jane (Sydney) 1917-1973 ..... **CLC 3, 68**
See also CA 19-20; 41-44R; CAP 2; CN 1; EWL 3; MAL 5
Bowles, Jane Auer
See Bowles, Jane (Sydney)
Bowles, Paul 1910-1999 ..... **CLC 1, 2, 19, 53; SSC 3, 98; TCLC 209**
See also AMWS 4; CA 1-4R; 186; CAAS 1; CANR 1, 19, 50, 75; CN 1, 2, 3, 4, 5, 6; DA3; DLB 5, 6, 218; EWL 3; MAL 5; MTCW 1, 2; MTFW 2005; RGAL 4; SSFS 17
Bowles, William Lisle 1762-1850 . **NCLC 103**
See also DLB 93
Box, Edgar
See Vidal, Gore
Boyd, James 1888-1944 .... **TCLC 115**
See also CA 186; DLB 9; DLBD 16; RGAL 4; RHW
Boyd, Nancy
See Millay, Edna St. Vincent
Boyd, Thomas (Alexander)
1898-1935 .... **TCLC 111**
See also CA 111; 183; DLB 9; DLBD 16, 316
Boyd, William 1952- .... **CLC 28, 53, 70**
See also CA 114; 120; CANR 51, 71, 131, 174; CN 4, 5, 6, 7; DLB 231
Boyesen, Hjalmar Hjorth
1848-1895 .... **NCLC 135**
See also DLB 12, 71; DLBD 13; RGAL 4
Boyle, Kay 1902-1992 .... **CLC 1, 5, 19, 58, 121; SSC 5, 102**
See also CA 13-16R; 140; CAAS 1; CANR 29, 61, 110; CN 1, 2, 3, 4, 5; CP 1, 2, 3, 4, 5; DLB 4, 9, 48, 86; DLBY 1993; EWL 3; MAL 5; MTCW 1, 2; MTFW 2005; RGAL 4; RGSF 2; SSFS 10, 13, 14

Boyle, Mark
See Kienzle, William X.
Boyle, Patrick 1905-1982 .... **CLC 19**
See also CA 127
Boyle, T. C.
See Boyle, T. Coraghessan
Boyle, T. Coraghessan 1948- ..... **CLC 36, 55, 90; SSC 16**
See also AAYA 47; AMWS 8; BEST 90:4; BPFB 1; CA 120; CANR 44, 76, 89, 132; CN 6, 7; CPW; DA3; DAM POP; DLB 218, 278; DLBY 1986; EWL 3; MAL 5; MTCW 2; MTFW 2005; SSFS 13, 19
Boz
See Dickens, Charles (John Huffam)
Brackenridge, Hugh Henry
1748-1816 .... **NCLC 7**
See also DLB 11, 37; RGAL 4
Bradbury, Edward P.
See Moorcock, Michael
Bradbury, Malcolm (Stanley)
1932-2000 .... **CLC 32, 61**
See also CA 1-4R; CANR 1, 33, 91, 98, 137; CN 1, 2, 3, 4, 5, 6, 7; CP 1; DA3; DAM NOV; DLB 14, 207; EWL 3; MTCW 1, 2; MTFW 2005
Bradbury, Ray 1920- ... **CLC 1, 3, 10, 15, 42, 98, 235; SSC 29, 53; WLC 1**
See also AAYA 15; AITN 1, 2; AMWS 4; BPFB 1; BYA 4, 5, 11; CA 1-4R; CANR 2, 30, 75, 125, 186; CDALB 1968-1988; CN 1, 2, 3, 4, 5, 6, 7; CPW; DA; DA3; DAB; DAC; DAM MST, NOV, POP; DLB 2, 8; EXPN; EXPS; LAIT 3, 5; LATS 1:2; LMFS 2; MAL 5; MTCW 1, 2; MTFW 2005; NFS 1, 22, 29; RGAL 4; RGSF 2; SATA 11, 64, 123; SCFW 1, 2; SFW 4; SSFS 1, 20; SUFW 1, 2; TUS; YAW
Bradbury, Ray Douglas
See Bradbury, Ray
Braddon, Mary Elizabeth
1837-1915 .... **TCLC 111**
See also BRWS 8; CA 108; 179; CMW 4; DLB 18, 70, 156; HGG
Bradfield, Scott 1955- .... **SSC 65**
See also CA 147; CANR 90; HGG; SUFW 2
Bradfield, Scott Michael
See Bradfield, Scott
Bradford, Gamaliel 1863-1932 .... **TCLC 36**
See also CA 160; DLB 17
Bradford, William 1590-1657 .... **LC 64**
See also DLB 24, 30; RGAL 4
Bradley, David, Jr. 1950- ...... **BLC 1:1; CLC 23, 118**
See also BW 1, 3; CA 104; CANR 26, 81; CN 4, 5, 6, 7; DAM MULT; DLB 33
Bradley, David Henry, Jr.
See Bradley, David, Jr.
Bradley, John Ed 1958- .... **CLC 55**
See also CA 139; CANR 99; CN 6, 7; CSW
Bradley, John Edmund, Jr.
See Bradley, John Ed
Bradley, Marion Zimmer
1930-1999 .... **CLC 30**
See also AAYA 40; BPFB 1; CA 57-60; 185; CAAS 10; CANR 7, 31, 51, 75, 107; CPW; DA3; DAM POP; DLB 8; FANT; FW; GLL 1; MTCW 1, 2; MTFW 2005; SATA 90, 139; SATA-Obit 116; SFW 4; SUFW 2; YAW
Bradshaw, John 1933- .... **CLC 70**
See also CA 138; CANR 61
Bradstreet, Anne 1612(?)-1672 .... **LC 4, 30, 130; PC 10**
See also AMWS 1; CDALB 1640-1865; DA; DA3; DAC; DAM MST, POET; DLB 24; EXPP; FW; PFS 6; RGAL 4; TUS; WP

Brontes
See Bronte, Anne; Bronte, (Patrick) Branwell; Bronte, Charlotte; Bronte, Emily (Jane)

Brooke, Frances 1724-1789 .... **LC 6, 48**
See also DLB 39, 99

Brooke, Henry 1703(?)-1783 .... **LC 1**
See also DLB 39

Brooke, Rupert (Chawner)
1887-1915 .. **PC 24; TCLC 2, 7; WLC 1**
See also BRWS 3; CA 104; 132; CANR 61; CDBLB 1914-1945; DA; DAB; DAC; DAM MST, POET; DLB 19, 216; EXPP; GLL 2; MTCW 1, 2; MTFW 2005; PFS 7; TEA

Brooke-Haven, P.
See Wodehouse, P(elham) G(renville)

Brooke-Rose, Christine 1923(?)- ..... **CLC 40, 184**
See also BRWS 4; CA 13-16R; CANR 58, 118, 183; CN 1, 2, 3, 4, 5, 6, 7; DLB 14, 231; EWL 3; SFW 4

Brookner, Anita 1928- . **CLC 32, 34, 51, 136, 237**
See also BRWS 4; CA 114; 120; CANR 37, 56, 87, 130; CN 4, 5, 6, 7; CPW; DA3; DAB; DAM POP; DLB 194, 326; DLBY 1987; EWL 3; MTCW 1, 2; MTFW 2005; NFS 23; TEA

Brooks, Cleanth 1906-1994 . **CLC 24, 86, 110**
See also AMWS 14; CA 17-20R; 145; CANR 33, 35; CSW; DLB 63; DLBY 1994; EWL 3; INT CANR-35; MAL 5; MTCW 1, 2; MTFW 2005

Brooks, George
See Baum, L(yman) Frank

Brooks, Gwendolyn 1917-2000 .... **BLC 1:1, 2:1; CLC 1, 2, 4, 5, 15, 49, 125; PC 7; WLC 1**
See also AAYA 20; AFAW 1, 2; AITN 1; AMWS 3; BW 2, 3; CA 1-4R; 190; CANR 1, 27, 52, 75, 132; CDALB 1941-1968; CLR 27; CP 1, 2, 3, 4, 5, 6, 7; CWP; DA; DA3; DAC; DAM MST, MULT, POET; DLB 5, 76, 165; EWL 3; EXPP; FL 1:5; MAL 5; MBL; MTCW 1, 2; MTFW 2005; PFS 1, 2, 4, 6; RGAL 4; SATA 6; SATA-Obit 123; TUS; WP

Brooks, Mel 1926-
See Kaminsky, Melvin
See also CA 65-68; CANR 16; DFS 21

Brooks, Peter 1938- .... **CLC 34**
See also CA 45-48; CANR 1, 107, 182

Brooks, Peter Preston
See Brooks, Peter

Brooks, Van Wyck 1886-1963 .... **CLC 29**
See also AMW; CA 1-4R; CANR 6; DLB 45, 63, 103; MAL 5; TUS

Brophy, Brigid (Antonia)
1929-1995 .... **CLC 6, 11, 29, 105**
See also CA 5-8R; 149; CAAS 4; CANR 25, 53; CBD; CN 1, 2, 3, 4, 5, 6; CWD; DA3; DLB 14, 271; EWL 3; MTCW 1, 2

Brosman, Catharine Savage 1934- ..... **CLC 9**
See also CA 61-64; CANR 21, 46, 149

Brossard, Nicole 1943- .... **CLC 115, 169; PC 80**
See also CA 122; CAAS 16; CANR 140; CCA 1; CWP; CWW 2; DLB 53; EWL 3; FW; GLL 2; RGWL 3

Brother Antoninus
See Everson, William (Oliver)

Brothers Grimm
See Grimm, Jacob Ludwig Karl; Grimm, Wilhelm Karl

The Brothers Quay
See Quay, Stephen; Quay, Timothy

Broughton, T(homas) Alan 1936- ..... **CLC 19**
See also CA 45-48; CANR 2, 23, 48, 111

Broumas, Olga 1949- .... **CLC 10, 73**
See also CA 85-88; CANR 20, 69, 110; CP 5, 6, 7; CWP; GLL 2

Broun, Heywood 1888-1939 .... **TCLC 104**
See also DLB 29, 171

Brown, Alan 1950- .... **CLC 99**
See also CA 156

Brown, Charles Brockden
1771-1810 .... **NCLC 22, 74, 122**
See also AMWS 1; CDALB 1640-1865; DLB 37, 59, 73; FW; GL 2; HGG; LMFS 1; RGAL 4; TUS

Brown, Christy 1932-1981 .... **CLC 63**
See also BYA 13; CA 105; 104; CANR 72; DLB 14

Brown, Claude 1937-2002 ..... **BLC 1:1; CLC 30**
See also AAYA 7; BW 1, 3; CA 73-76; 205; CANR 81; DAM MULT

Brown, Dan 1964- .... **CLC 209**
See also AAYA 55; CA 217; MTFW 2005

Brown, Dee 1908-2002 .... **CLC 18, 47**
See also AAYA 30; CA 13-16R; CAAS 6; CANR 11, 45, 60, 150; CPW; CSW; DA3; DAM POP; DLBY 1980; LAIT 2; MTCW 1, 2; MTFW 2005; NCFS 5; SATA 5, 110; SATA-Obit 141; TCWW 1, 2

Brown, Dee Alexander
See Brown, Dee

Brown, George
See Wertmueller, Lina

Brown, George Douglas
1869-1902 .... **TCLC 28**
See also CA 162; RGEL 2

Brown, George Mackay 1921-1996 ... **CLC 5, 48, 100**
See also BRWS 6; CA 21-24R; 151; CAAS 6; CANR 12, 37, 67; CN 1, 2, 3, 4, 5, 6; CP 1, 2, 3, 4, 5, 6; DLB 14, 27, 139, 271; MTCW 1; RGSF 2; SATA 35

Brown, James Willie
See Komunyakaa, Yusef

Brown, James Willie, Jr.
See Komunyakaa, Yusef

Brown, Larry 1951-2004 .... **CLC 73**
See also CA 130; 134; 233; CANR 117, 145; CSW; DLB 234; INT CA-134

Brown, Moses
See Barrett, William (Christopher)

Brown, Rita Mae 1944- .... **CLC 18, 43, 79, 259**
See also BPFB 1; CA 45-48; CANR 2, 11, 35, 62, 95, 138, 183; CN 5, 6, 7; CPW; CSW; DA3; DAM NOV, POP; FW; INT CANR-11; MAL 5; MTCW 1, 2; MTFW 2005; NFS 9; RGAL 4; TUS

Brown, Roderick (Langmere) Haig-
See Haig-Brown, Roderick (Langmere)

Brown, Rosellen 1939- .... **CLC 32, 170**
See also CA 77-80; CAAS 10; CANR 14, 44, 98; CN 6, 7

Brown, Sterling Allen 1901-1989 ...... **BLC 1; CLC 1, 23, 59; HR 1:2; PC 55**
See also AFAW 1, 2; BW 1, 3; CA 85-88; 127; CANR 26; CP 3, 4; DA3; DAM MULT, POET; DLB 48, 51, 63; MAL 5; MTCW 1, 2; MTFW 2005; RGAL 4; WP

Brown, Will
See Ainsworth, William Harrison

Brown, William Hill 1765-1793 .... **LC 93**
See also DLB 37

Brown, William Larry
See Brown, Larry

Brown, William Wells 1815-1884 ... **BLC 1:1; DC 1; NCLC 2, 89**
See also DAM MULT; DLB 3, 50, 183, 248; RGAL 4

Browne, Clyde Jackson
See Browne, Jackson

Browne, Jackson 1948(?)- .... **CLC 21**
See also CA 120

Browne, Sir Thomas 1605-1682 .... **LC 111**
See also BRW 2; DLB 151

Browning, Robert 1812-1889 . **NCLC 19, 79; PC 2, 61, 97; WLCS**
See also BRW 4; BRWC 2; BRWR 2; CDBLB 1832-1890; CLR 97; DA; DA3; DAB; DAC; DAM MST, POET; DLB 32, 163; EXPP; LATS 1:1; PAB; PFS 1, 15; RGEL 2; TEA; WLIT 4; WP; YABC 1

Browning, Tod 1882-1962 .... **CLC 16**
See also CA 141; 117

Brownmiller, Susan 1935- .... **CLC 159**
See also CA 103; CANR 35, 75, 137; DAM NOV; FW; MTCW 1, 2; MTFW 2005

Brownson, Orestes Augustus
1803-1876 .... **NCLC 50**
See also DLB 1, 59, 73, 243

Bruccoli, Matthew J. 1931-2008 .... **CLC 34**
See also CA 9-12R; 274; CANR 7, 87; DLB 103

Bruccoli, Matthew Joseph
See Bruccoli, Matthew J.

Bruce, Lenny
See Schneider, Leonard Alfred

Bruchac, Joseph 1942- .... **NNAL**
See also AAYA 19; CA 33-36R, 256; CAAE 256; CANR 13, 47, 75, 94, 137, 161; CLR 46; CWRI 5; DAM MULT; DLB 342; JRDA; MAICYA 2; MAICYAS 1; MTCW 2; MTFW 2005; SATA 42, 89, 131, 176; SATA-Essay 176

Bruin, John
See Brutus, Dennis

Brulard, Henri
See Stendhal

Brulls, Christian
See Simenon, Georges (Jacques Christian)

Brunetto Latini c. 1220-1294 .... **CMLC 73**

Brunner, John (Kilian Houston)
1934-1995 .... **CLC 8, 10**
See also CA 1-4R; 149; CAAS 8; CANR 2, 37; CPW; DAM POP; DLB 261; MTCW 1, 2; SCFW 1, 2; SFW 4

Bruno, Giordano 1548-1600 .... **LC 27, 167**
See also RGWL 2, 3

Brutus, Dennis 1924- ...... **BLC 1:1; CLC 43; PC 24**
See also AFW; BW 2, 3; CA 49-52; CAAS 14; CANR 2, 27, 42, 81; CDWLB 3; CP 1, 2, 3, 4, 5, 6, 7; DAM MULT, POET; DLB 117, 225; EWL 3

Bryan, C(ourtlandt) D(ixon) B(arnes)
1936- .... **CLC 29**
See also CA 73-76; CANR 13, 68; DLB 185; INT CANR-13

Bryan, Michael
See Moore, Brian

Bryan, William Jennings
1860-1925 .... **TCLC 99**
See also DLB 303

Bryant, William Cullen 1794-1878 . **NCLC 6, 46; PC 20**
See also AMWS 1; CDALB 1640-1865; DA; DAB; DAC; DAM MST, POET; DLB 3, 43, 59, 189, 250; EXPP; PAB; PFS 30; RGAL 4; TUS

Bryusov, Valery Yakovlevich
1873-1924 .... **TCLC 10**
See also CA 107; 155; EWL 3; SFW 4

Buchan, John 1875-1940 .... **TCLC 41**
See also CA 108; 145; CMW 4; DAB; DAM POP; DLB 34, 70, 156; HGG; MSW; MTCW 2; RGEL 2; RHW; YABC 2

Casal, Julian del 1863-1893 .... **NCLC 131**
See also DLB 283; LAW

Casanova, Giacomo
See Casanova de Seingalt, Giovanni Jacopo

Casanova, Giovanni Giacomo
See Casanova de Seingalt, Giovanni Jacopo

Casanova de Seingalt, Giovanni Jacopo
1725-1798 .... **LC 13, 151**
See also WLIT 7

Casares, Adolfo Bioy
See Bioy Casares, Adolfo

Casas, Bartolome de las 1474-1566
See Las Casas, Bartolome de

Case, John
See Hougan, Carolyn

Casely-Hayford, J(oseph) E(phraim)
1866-1903 .... **BLC 1:1; TCLC 24**
See also BW 2; CA 123; 152; DAM MULT

Casey, John (Dudley) 1939- .... **CLC 59**
See also BEST 90:2; CA 69-72; CANR 23,
100

Casey, Michael 1947- .... **CLC 2**
See also CA 65-68; CANR 109; CP 2, 3;
DLB 5

Casey, Patrick
See Thurman, Wallace (Henry)

Casey, Warren (Peter) 1935-1988 .... **CLC 12**
See also CA 101; 127; INT CA-101

Casona, Alejandro
See Alvarez, Alejandro Rodriguez

Cassavetes, John 1929-1989 .... **CLC 20**
See also CA 85-88; 127; CANR 82

Cassian, Nina 1924- .... **PC 17**
See also CWP; CWW 2

Cassill, R(onald) V(erlin)
1919-2002 .... **CLC 4, 23**
See also CA 9-12R; 208; CAAS 1; CANR
7, 45; CN 1, 2, 3, 4, 5, 6, 7; DLB 6, 218;
DLBY 2002

Cassiodorus, Flavius Magnus c. 490(?)-c.
583(?) .... **CMLC 43**

Cassirer, Ernst 1874-1945 .... **TCLC 61**
See also CA 157

Cassity, (Allen) Turner 1929- .... **CLC 6, 42**
See also CA 17-20R, 223; CAAE 223;
CAAS 8; CANR 11; CSW; DLB 105

Cassius Dio c. 155-c. 229 .... **CMLC 99**
See also DLB 176

Castaneda, Carlos (Cesar Aranha)
1931(?)-1998 .... **CLC 12, 119**
See also CA 25-28R; CANR 32, 66, 105;
DNFS 1; HW 1; MTCW 1

Castedo, Elena 1937- .... **CLC 65**
See also CA 132

Castedo-Ellerman, Elena
See Castedo, Elena

Castellanos, Rosario 1925-1974 .... **CLC 66;
HLC 1; SSC 39, 68**
See also CA 131; 53-56; CANR 58; CD-
WLB 3; DAM MULT; DLB 113, 290;
EWL 3; FW; HW 1; LAW; MTCW 2;
MTFW 2005; RGSF 2; RGWL 2, 3

Castelvetro, Lodovico 1505-1571 .... **LC 12**

Castiglione, Baldassare 1478-1529 ..... **LC 12,
165**
See also EW 2; LMFS 1; RGWL 2, 3;
WLIT 7

Castiglione, Baldesar
See Castiglione, Baldassare

Castillo, Ana 1953- .... **CLC 151**
See also AAYA 42; CA 131; CANR 51, 86,
128, 172; CWP; DLB 122, 227; DNFS 2;
FW; HW 1; LLW; PFS 21

Castillo, Ana Hernandez Del
See Castillo, Ana

Castle, Robert
See Hamilton, Edmond

Castro (Ruz), Fidel 1926(?)- .... **HLC 1**
See also CA 110; 129; CANR 81; DAM
MULT; HW 2

Castro, Guillen de 1569-1631 .... **LC 19**

Castro, Rosalia de 1837-1885 ... **NCLC 3, 78;
PC 41**
See also DAM MULT

Castro Alves, Antonio de
1847-1871 .... **NCLC 205**
See also DLB 307; LAW

Cather, Willa (Sibert) 1873-1947 . **SSC 2, 50,
114; TCLC 1, 11, 31, 99, 132, 152;
WLC 1**
See also AAYA 24; AMW; AMWC 1;
AMWR 1; BPFB 1; CA 104; 128; CDALB
1865-1917; CLR 98; DA; DA3; DAB;
DAC; DAM MST, NOV; DLB 9, 54, 78,
256; DLBD 1; EWL 3; EXPN; EXPS; FL
1:5; LAIT 3; LATS 1:1; MAL 5; MBL;
MTCW 1, 2; MTFW 2005; NFS 2, 19;
RGAL 4; RGSF 2; RHW; SATA 30; SSFS
2, 7, 16, 27; TCWW 1, 2; TUS

Catherine II
See Catherine the Great

Catherine, Saint 1347-1380 .... **CMLC 27**

Catherine the Great 1729-1796 .... **LC 69**
See also DLB 150

Cato, Marcus Porcius
234B.C.-149B.C. .... **CMLC 21**
See also DLB 211

Cato, Marcus Porcius, the Elder
See Cato, Marcus Porcius

Cato the Elder
See Cato, Marcus Porcius

Catton, (Charles) Bruce 1899-1978 . **CLC 35**
See also AITN 1; CA 5-8R; 81-84; CANR
7, 74; DLB 17; MTCW 2; MTFW 2005;
SATA 2; SATA-Obit 24

Catullus c. 84B.C.-54B.C. .... **CMLC 18**
See also AW 2; CDWLB 1; DLB 211;
RGWL 2, 3; WLIT 8

Cauldwell, Frank
See King, Francis (Henry)

Caunitz, William J. 1933-1996 .... **CLC 34**
See also BEST 89:3; CA 125; 130; 152;
CANR 73; INT CA-130

Causley, Charles (Stanley)
1917-2003 .... **CLC 7**
See also CA 9-12R; 223; CANR 5, 35, 94;
CLR 30; CP 1, 2, 3, 4, 5; CWRI 5; DLB
27; MTCW 1; SATA 3, 66; SATA-Obit
149

Caute, (John) David 1936- .... **CLC 29**
See also CA 1-4R; CAAS 4; CANR 1, 33,
64, 120; CBD; CD 5, 6; CN 1, 2, 3, 4, 5,
6, 7; DAM NOV; DLB 14, 231

Cavafy, C. P.
See Kavafis, Konstantinos Petrou

Cavafy, Constantine Peter
See Kavafis, Konstantinos Petrou

Cavalcanti, Guido c. 1250-c.
1300 .... **CMLC 54**
See also RGWL 2, 3; WLIT 7

Cavallo, Evelyn
See Spark, Muriel

Cavanna, Betty
See Harrison, Elizabeth (Allen) Cavanna

Cavanna, Elizabeth
See Harrison, Elizabeth (Allen) Cavanna

Cavanna, Elizabeth Allen
See Harrison, Elizabeth (Allen) Cavanna

Cavendish, Margaret Lucas
1623-1673 .... **LC 30, 132**
See also DLB 131, 252, 281; RGEL 2

Caxton, William 1421(?)-1491(?) .... **LC 17**
See also DLB 170

Cayer, D. M.
See Duffy, Maureen (Patricia)

Cayrol, Jean 1911-2005 .... **CLC 11**
See also CA 89-92; 236; DLB 83; EWL 3

Cela (y Trulock), Camilo Jose
See Cela, Camilo Jose

Cela, Camilo Jose 1916-2002 .... **CLC 4, 13,
59, 122; HLC 1; SSC 71**
See also BEST 90:2; CA 21-24R; 206;
CAAS 10; CANR 21, 32, 76, 139; CWW
2; DAM MULT; DLB 322; DLBY 1989;
EW 13; EWL 3; HW 1; MTCW 1, 2;
MTFW 2005; RGSF 2; RGWL 2, 3

Celan, Paul
See Antschel, Paul

Celine, Louis-Ferdinand
See Destouches, Louis-Ferdinand

Cellini, Benvenuto 1500-1571 .... **LC 7**
See also WLIT 7

Cendrars, Blaise
See Sauser-Hall, Frederic

Centlivre, Susanna 1669(?)-1723 .... **DC 25;
LC 65**
See also DLB 84; RGEL 2

Cernuda (y Bidon), Luis
1902-1963 .... **CLC 54; PC 62**
See also CA 131; 89-92; DAM POET; DLB
134; EWL 3; GLL 1; HW 1; RGWL 2, 3

Cervantes, Lorna Dee 1954- ..... **HLCS 1; PC
35**
See also CA 131; CANR 80; CP 7; CWP;
DLB 82; EXPP; HW 1; LLW; PFS 30

Cervantes (Saavedra), Miguel de
1547-1616 .... **HLCS; LC 6, 23, 93; SSC
12, 108; WLC 1**
See also AAYA 56; BYA 1, 14; DA; DAB;
DAC; DAM MST, NOV; EW 2; LAIT 1;
LATS 1:1; LMFS 1; NFS 8; RGSF 2;
RGWL 2, 3; TWA

Cesaire, Aime
See Cesaire, Aime

Cesaire, Aime 1913-2008 .... **BLC 1:1; CLC
19, 32, 112; DC 22; PC 25**
See also BW 2, 3; CA 65-68; 271; CANR
24, 43, 81; CWW 2; DA3; DAM MULT,
POET; DLB 321; EWL 3; GFL 1789 to
the Present; MTCW 1, 2; MTFW 2005;
WP

Cesaire, Aime Fernand
See Cesaire, Aime

Chaadaev, Petr Iakovlevich
1794-1856 .... **NCLC 197**
See also DLB 198

Chabon, Michael 1963- ... **CLC 55, 149, 265;
SSC 59**
See also AAYA 45; AMWS 11; CA 139;
CANR 57, 96, 127, 138; DLB 278; MAL
5; MTFW 2005; NFS 25; SATA 145

Chabrol, Claude 1930- .... **CLC 16**
See also CA 110

Chairil Anwar
See Anwar, Chairil

Challans, Mary 1905-1983 ...... **CLC 3, 11, 17**
See also BPFB 3; BYA 2; CA 81-84; 111;
CANR 74; CN 1, 2, 3; DA3; DLBY 1983;
EWL 3; GLL 1; LAIT 1; MTCW 2;
MTFW 2005; RGEL 2; RHW; SATA 23;
SATA-Obit 36; TEA

Challis, George
See Faust, Frederick (Schiller)

Chambers, Aidan 1934- .... **CLC 35**
See also AAYA 27; CA 25-28R; CANR 12,
31, 58, 116; JRDA; MAICYA 1, 2; SAAS
12; SATA 1, 69, 108, 171; WYA; YAW

Chambers, James .... **CLC 21**
See also CA 124; 199

Chambers, Jessie
See Lawrence, D(avid) H(erbert Richards)

Child, Mrs.
See Child, Lydia Maria

Child, Philip 1898-1978 .... **CLC 19, 68**
See also CA 13-14; CAP 1; CP 1; DLB 68;
RHW; SATA 47

Childers, (Robert) Erskine
1870-1922 .... **TCLC 65**
See also CA 113; 153; DLB 70

Childress, Alice 1920-1994 .... **BLC 1:1; CLC
12, 15, 86, 96; DC 4; TCLC 116**
See also AAYA 8; BW 2, 3; BYA 2; CA 45-
48; 146; CAD; CANR 3, 27, 50, 74; CLR
14; CWD; DA3; DAM DRAM, MULT,
NOV; DFS 2, 8, 14, 26; DLB 7, 38, 249;
JRDA; LAIT 5; MAICYA 1, 2; MAIC-
YAS 1; MAL 5; MTCW 1, 2; MTFW
2005; RGAL 4; SATA 7, 48, 81; TUS;
WYA; YAW

Chin, Frank (Chew, Jr.) 1940- .... **AAL; CLC
135; DC 7**
See also CA 33-36R; CAD; CANR 71; CD
5, 6; DAM MULT; DLB 206, 312; LAIT
5; RGAL 4

Chin, Marilyn (Mei Ling) 1955- .... **PC 40**
See also CA 129; CANR 70, 113; CWP;
DLB 312; PFS 28

Chislett, (Margaret) Anne 1943- ...... **CLC 34**
See also CA 151

Chitty, Thomas Willes 1926- .... **CLC 6, 11**
See also CA 5-8R; CN 1, 2, 3, 4, 5, 6; EWL
3

Chivers, Thomas Holley
1809-1858 .... **NCLC 49**
See also DLB 3, 248; RGAL 4

Chlamyda, Jehudil
See Peshkov, Alexei Maximovich

Ch'o, Chou
See Shu-Jen, Chou

Choi, Susan 1969- .... **CLC 119**
See also CA 223; CANR 188

Chomette, Rene Lucien 1898-1981 .. **CLC 20**
See also CA 103

Chomsky, Avram Noam
See Chomsky, Noam

Chomsky, Noam 1928- .... **CLC 132**
See also CA 17-20R; CANR 28, 62, 110,
132, 179; DA3; DLB 246; MTCW 1, 2;
MTFW 2005

Chona, Maria 1845(?)-1936 .... **NNAL**
See also CA 144

Chopin, Kate
See Chopin, Katherine

Chopin, Katherine 1851-1904 .... **SSC 8, 68,
110; TCLC 127; WLCS**
See also AAYA 33; AMWR 2; BYA 11, 15;
CA 104; 122; CDALB 1865-1917; DA3;
DAB; DAC; DAM MST, NOV; DLB 12,
78; EXPN; EXPS; FL 1:3; FW; LAIT 3;
MAL 5; MBL; NFS 3; RGAL 4; RGSF 2;
SSFS 2, 13, 17, 26; TUS

Chretien de Troyes c. 12th cent. - . **CMLC 10**
See also DLB 208; EW 1; RGWL 2, 3;
TWA

Christie
See Ichikawa, Kon

Christie, Agatha (Mary Clarissa)
1890-1976 .. **CLC 1, 6, 8, 12, 39, 48, 110**
See also AAYA 9; AITN 1, 2; BPFB 1;
BRWS 2; CA 17-20R; 61-64; CANR 10,
37, 108; CBD; CDBLB 1914-1945; CMW
4; CN 1, 2; CPW; CWD; DA3; DAB;
DAC; DAM NOV; DFS 2; DLB 13, 77,
245; MSW; MTCW 1, 2; MTFW 2005;
NFS 8; RGEL 2; RHW; SATA 36; TEA;
YAW

Christie, Ann Philippa
See Pearce, Philippa

Christie, Philippa
See Pearce, Philippa

Christine de Pisan
See Christine de Pizan

Christine de Pizan 1365(?)-1431(?) ...... **LC 9,
130; PC 68**
See also DLB 208; FL 1:1; FW; RGWL 2,
3

Chuang-Tzu c. 369B.C.-c.
286B.C. .... **CMLC 57**

Chubb, Elmer
See Masters, Edgar Lee

Chulkov, Mikhail Dmitrievich
1743-1792 .... **LC 2**
See also DLB 150

Churchill, Caryl 1938- .... **CLC 31, 55, 157;
DC 5**
See also BRWS 4; CA 102; CANR 22, 46,
108; CBD; CD 5, 6; CWD; DFS 25; DLB
13, 310; EWL 3; FW; MTCW 1; RGEL 2

Churchill, Charles 1731-1764 .... **LC 3**
See also DLB 109; RGEL 2

Churchill, Chick
See Churchill, Caryl

Churchill, Sir Winston (Leonard Spencer)
1874-1965 .... **TCLC 113**
See also BRW 6; CA 97-100; CDBLB
1890-1914; DA3; DLB 100, 329; DLBD
16; LAIT 4; MTCW 1, 2

Chute, Carolyn 1947- .... **CLC 39**
See also CA 123; CANR 135; CN 7

Ciardi, John (Anthony) 1916-1986 . **CLC 10,
40, 44, 129; PC 69**
See also CA 5-8R; 118; CAAS 2; CANR 5,
33; CLR 19; CP 1, 2, 3, 4; CWRI 5; DAM
POET; DLB 5; DLBY 1986; INT
CANR-5; MAICYA 1, 2; MAL 5; MTCW
1, 2; MTFW 2005; RGAL 4; SAAS 26;
SATA 1, 65; SATA-Obit 46

Cibber, Colley 1671-1757 .... **LC 66**
See also DLB 84; RGEL 2

Cicero, Marcus Tullius
106B.C.-43B.C. .... **CMLC 3, 81**
See also AW 1; CDWLB 1; DLB 211;
RGWL 2, 3; WLIT 8

Cimino, Michael 1943- .... **CLC 16**
See also CA 105

Cioran, E(mil) M. 1911-1995 .... **CLC 64**
See also CA 25-28R; 149; CANR 91; DLB
220; EWL 3

Circus, Anthony
See Hoch, Edward D.

Cisneros, Sandra 1954- .... **CLC 69, 118, 193;
HLC 1; PC 52; SSC 32, 72**
See also AAYA 9, 53; AMWS 7; CA 131;
CANR 64, 118; CLR 123; CN 7; CWP;
DA3; DAM MULT; DLB 122, 152; EWL
3; EXPN; FL 1:5; FW; HW 1, 2; LAIT 5;
LATS 1:2; LLW; MAICYA 2; MAL 5;
MTCW 2; MTFW 2005; NFS 2; PFS 19;
RGAL 4; RGSF 2; SSFS 3, 13, 27; WLIT
1; YAW

Cixous, Helene 1937- .... **CLC 92, 253**
See also CA 126; CANR 55, 123; CWW 2;
DLB 83, 242; EWL 3; FL 1:5; FW; GLL
2; MTCW 1, 2; MTFW 2005; TWA

Clair, Rene
See Chomette, Rene Lucien

Clampitt, Amy 1920-1994 .... **CLC 32; PC 19**
See also AMWS 9; CA 110; 146; CANR
29, 79; CP 4, 5; DLB 105; MAL 5; PFS
27

Clancy, Thomas L., Jr. 1947- ... **CLC 45, 112**
See also AAYA 9, 51; BEST 89:1, 90:1;
BPFB 1; BYA 10, 11; CA 125; 131;
CANR 62, 105, 132; CMW 4; CPW;
DA3; DAM NOV, POP; DLB 227; INT
CA-131; MTCW 1, 2; MTFW 2005

Clancy, Tom
See Clancy, Thomas L., Jr.

Clare, John 1793-1864 .. **NCLC 9, 86; PC 23**
See also BRWS 11; DAB; DAM POET;
DLB 55, 96; RGEL 2

Clarin
See Alas (y Urena), Leopoldo (Enrique
Garcia)

Clark, Al C.
See Goines, Donald

Clark, Brian (Robert)
See Clark, (Robert) Brian

Clark, (Robert) Brian 1932- .... **CLC 29**
See also CA 41-44R; CANR 67; CBD; CD
5, 6

Clark, Curt
See Westlake, Donald E.

Clark, Eleanor 1913-1996 .... **CLC 5, 19**
See also CA 9-12R; 151; CANR 41; CN 1,
2, 3, 4, 5, 6; DLB 6

Clark, J. P.
See Clark Bekederemo, J.P.

Clark, John Pepper
See Clark Bekederemo, J.P.
See also AFW; CD 5; CP 1, 2, 3, 4, 5, 6, 7;
RGEL 2

Clark, Kenneth (Mackenzie)
1903-1983 .... **TCLC 147**
See also CA 93-96; 109; CANR 36; MTCW
1, 2; MTFW 2005

Clark, M. R.
See Clark, Mavis Thorpe

Clark, Mavis Thorpe 1909-1999 ...... **CLC 12**
See also CA 57-60; CANR 8, 37, 107; CLR
30; CWRI 5; MAICYA 1, 2; SAAS 5;
SATA 8, 74

Clark, Walter Van Tilburg
1909-1971 .... **CLC 28**
See also CA 9-12R; 33-36R; CANR 63,
113; CN 1; DLB 9, 206; LAIT 5; MAL 5;
RGAL 4; SATA 8; TCWW 1, 2

Clark Bekederemo, J.P. 1935- .... **BLC 1:1;
CLC 38; DC 5**
See Clark, John Pepper
See also AAYA 79; BW 1; CA 65-68;
CANR 16, 72; CD 6; CDWLB 3; DAM
DRAM, MULT; DFS 13; DLB 117; EWL
3; MTCW 2; MTFW 2005

Clarke, Arthur
See Clarke, Arthur C.

Clarke, Arthur C. 1917-2008 .. **CLC 1, 4, 13,
18, 35, 136; SSC 3**
See also AAYA 4, 33; BPFB 1; BYA 13;
CA 1-4R; 270; CANR 2, 28, 55, 74, 130;
CLR 119; CN 1, 2, 3, 4, 5, 6, 7; CPW;
DA3; DAM POP; DLB 261; JRDA; LAIT
5; MAICYA 1, 2; MTCW 1, 2; MTFW
2005; SATA 13, 70, 115; SATA-Obit 191;
SCFW 1, 2; SFW 4; SSFS 4, 18; TCLE
1:1; YAW

Clarke, Arthur Charles
See Clarke, Arthur C.

Clarke, Austin 1896-1974 .... **CLC 6, 9**
See also CA 29-32; 49-52; CAP 2; CP 1, 2;
DAM POET; DLB 10, 20; EWL 3; RGEL
2

Clarke, Austin C. 1934- .... **BLC 1:1; CLC 8,
53; SSC 45, 116**
See also BW 1; CA 25-28R; CAAS 16;
CANR 14, 32, 68, 140; CN 1, 2, 3, 4, 5,
6, 7; DAC; DAM MULT; DLB 53, 125;
DNFS 2; MTCW 2; MTFW 2005; RGSF
2

Clarke, Gillian 1937- .... **CLC 61**
See also CA 106; CP 3, 4, 5, 6, 7; CWP;
DLB 40

Clarke, Marcus (Andrew Hislop)
1846-1881 .... **NCLC 19; SSC 94**
See also DLB 230; RGEL 2; RGSF 2

Clarke, Shirley 1925-1997 .... **CLC 16**
See also CA 189

Clash, The
See Headon, (Nicky) Topper; Jones, Mick; Simonon, Paul; Strummer, Joe

Claudel, Paul (Louis Charles Marie)
1868-1955 .... TCLC 2, 10
See also CA 104; 165; DLB 192, 258, 321; EW 8; EWL 3; GFL 1789 to the Present; RGWL 2, 3; TWA

Claudian 370(?)-404(?) .... CMLC 46
See also RGWL 2, 3

Claudius, Matthias 1740-1815 .... NCLC 75
See also DLB 97

Clavell, James 1925-1994 .... CLC 6, 25, 87
See also BPFB 1; CA 25-28R; 146; CANR 26, 48; CN 5; CPW; DA3; DAM NOV, POP; MTCW 1, 2; MTFW 2005; NFS 10; RHW

Clayman, Gregory .... CLC 65

Cleage, Pearl 1948- .... DC 32
See also BW 2; CA 41-44R; CANR 27, 148, 177; DFS 14, 16; DLB 228; NFS 17

Cleage, Pearl Michelle
See Cleage, Pearl

Cleaver, (Leroy) Eldridge
1935-1998 .... BLC 1:1; CLC 30, 119
See also BW 1, 3; CA 21-24R; 167; CANR 16, 75; DA3; DAM MULT; MTCW 2; YAW

Cleese, John (Marwood) 1939- .... CLC 21
See also CA 112; 116; CANR 35; MTCW 1

Cleishbotham, Jebediah
See Scott, Sir Walter

Cleland, John 1710-1789 .... LC 2, 48
See also DLB 39; RGEL 2

Clemens, Samuel Langhorne
See Twain, Mark

Clement of Alexandria
150(?)-215(?) .... CMLC 41

Cleophil
See Congreve, William

Clerihew, E.
See Bentley, E(dmund) C(lerihew)

Clerk, N. W.
See Lewis, C.S.

Cleveland, John 1613-1658 .... LC 106
See also DLB 126; RGEL 2

Cliff, Jimmy
See Chambers, James

Cliff, Michelle 1946- .... BLCS; CLC 120
See also BW 2; CA 116; CANR 39, 72; CD-WLB 3; DLB 157; FW; GLL 2

Clifford, Lady Anne 1590-1676 .... LC 76
See also DLB 151

Clifton, Lucille 1936- ..... BLC 1:1, 2:1; CLC 19, 66, 162; PC 17
See also AFAW 2; BW 2, 3; CA 49-52; CANR 2, 24, 42, 76, 97, 138; CLR 5; CP 2, 3, 4, 5, 6, 7; CSW; CWP; CWRI 5; DA3; DAM MULT, POET; DLB 5, 41; EXPP; MAICYA 1, 2; MTCW 1, 2; MTFW 2005; PFS 1, 14, 29; SATA 20, 69, 128; WP

Clinton, Dirk
See Silverberg, Robert

Clough, Arthur Hugh 1819-1861 .. NCLC 27, 163
See also BRW 5; DLB 32; RGEL 2

Clutha, Janet Paterson Frame
See Frame, Janet

Clyne, Terence
See Blatty, William Peter

Cobalt, Martin
See Mayne, William (James Carter)

Cobb, Irvin S(hrewsbury)
1876-1944 .... TCLC 77
See also CA 175; DLB 11, 25, 86

Cobbett, William 1763-1835 .... NCLC 49
See also DLB 43, 107, 158; RGEL 2

Coben, Harlan 1962- .... CLC 269
See also CA 164; CANR 162

Coburn, D(onald) L(ee) 1938- .... CLC 10
See also CA 89-92; DFS 23

Cocteau, Jean 1889-1963 ... CLC 1, 8, 15, 16, 43; DC 17; TCLC 119; WLC 2
See also AAYA 74; CA 25-28; CANR 40; CAP 2; DA; DA3; DAB; DAC; DAM DRAM, MST, NOV; DFS 24; DLB 65, 258, 321; EW 10; EWL 3; GFL 1789 to the Present; MTCW 1, 2; RGWL 2, 3; TWA

Cocteau, Jean Maurice Eugene Clement
See Cocteau, Jean

Codrescu, Andrei 1946- .... CLC 46, 121
See also CA 33-36R; CAAS 19; CANR 13, 34, 53, 76, 125; CN 7; DA3; DAM POET; MAL 5; MTCW 2; MTFW 2005

Coe, Max
See Bourne, Randolph S(illiman)

Coe, Tucker
See Westlake, Donald E.

Coelho, Paulo 1947- .... CLC 258
See also CA 152; CANR 80, 93, 155; NFS 29

Coen, Ethan 1957- .... CLC 108, 267
See also AAYA 54; CA 126; CANR 85

Coen, Joel 1954- .... CLC 108, 267
See also AAYA 54; CA 126; CANR 119

The Coen Brothers
See Coen, Ethan; Coen, Joel

Coetzee, J.M. 1940- ...... CLC 23, 33, 66, 117, 161, 162
See also AAYA 37; AFW; BRWS 6; CA 77-80; CANR 41, 54, 74, 114, 133, 180; CN 4, 5, 6, 7; DA3; DAM NOV; DLB 225, 326, 329; EWL 3; LMFS 2; MTCW 1, 2; MTFW 2005; NFS 21; WLIT 2; WWE 1

Coetzee, John Maxwell
See Coetzee, J.M.

Coffey, Brian
See Koontz, Dean R.

Coffin, Robert P(eter) Tristram
1892-1955 .... TCLC 95
See also CA 123; 169; DLB 45

Cohan, George M. 1878-1942 .... TCLC 60
See also CA 157; DLB 249; RGAL 4

Cohan, George Michael
See Cohan, George M.

Cohen, Arthur A(llen) 1928-1986 ...... CLC 7, 31
See also CA 1-4R; 120; CANR 1, 17, 42; DLB 28; RGHL

Cohen, Leonard 1934- .... CLC 3, 38, 260
See also CA 21-24R; CANR 14, 69; CN 1, 2, 3, 4, 5, 6; CP 1, 2, 3, 4, 5, 6, 7; DAC; DAM MST; DLB 53; EWL 3; MTCW 1

Cohen, Leonard Norman
See Cohen, Leonard

Cohen, Matt(hew) 1942-1999 .... CLC 19
See also CA 61-64; 187; CAAS 18; CANR 40; CN 1, 2, 3, 4, 5, 6; DAC; DLB 53

Cohen-Solal, Annie 1948- .... CLC 50
See also CA 239

Colegate, Isabel 1931- .... CLC 36
See also CA 17-20R; CANR 8, 22, 74; CN 4, 5, 6, 7; DLB 14, 231; INT CANR-22; MTCW 1

Coleman, Emmett
See Reed, Ishmael

Coleridge, Hartley 1796-1849 .... NCLC 90
See also DLB 96

Coleridge, M. E.
See Coleridge, Mary E(lizabeth)

Coleridge, Mary E(lizabeth)
1861-1907 .... TCLC 73
See also CA 116; 166; DLB 19, 98

Coleridge, Samuel Taylor
1772-1834 ..... NCLC 9, 54, 99, 111, 177, 197; PC 11, 39, 67; WLC 2
See also AAYA 66; BRW 4; BRWR 2; BYA 4; CDBLB 1789-1832; DA; DA3; DAB; DAC; DAM MST, POET; DLB 93, 107; EXPP; LATS 1:1; PAB; PFS 4, 5; RGEL 2; TEA; WLIT 3; WP

Coleridge, Sara 1802-1852 .... NCLC 31
See also DLB 199

Coles, Don 1928- .... CLC 46
See also CA 115; CANR 38; CP 5, 6, 7

Coles, Robert (Martin) 1929- .... CLC 108
See also CA 45-48; CANR 3, 32, 66, 70, 135; INT CANR-32; SATA 23

Colette, (Sidonie-Gabrielle)
1873-1954 .. SSC 10, 93; TCLC 1, 5, 16
See also CA 104; 131; DA3; DAM NOV; DLB 65; EW 9; EWL 3; GFL 1789 to the Present; GLL 1; MTCW 1, 2; MTFW 2005; RGWL 2, 3; TWA

Collett, (Jacobine) Camilla (Wergeland)
1813-1895 .... NCLC 22

Collier, Christopher 1930- .... CLC 30
See also AAYA 13; BYA 2; CA 33-36R; CANR 13, 33, 102; CLR 126; JRDA; MAICYA 1, 2; SATA 16, 70; WYA; YAW 1

Collier, James Lincoln 1928- .... CLC 30
See also AAYA 13; BYA 2; CA 9-12R; CANR 4, 33, 60, 102; CLR 3, 126; DAM POP; JRDA; MAICYA 1, 2; SAAS 21; SATA 8, 70, 166; WYA; YAW 1

Collier, Jeremy 1650-1726 .... LC 6, 157
See also DLB 336

Collier, John 1901-1980 . SSC 19; TCLC 127
See also CA 65-68; 97-100; CANR 10; CN 1, 2; DLB 77, 255; FANT; SUFW 1

Collier, Mary 1690-1762 .... LC 86
See also DLB 95

Collingwood, R(obin) G(eorge)
1889(?)-1943 .... TCLC 67
See also CA 117; 155; DLB 262

Collins, Billy 1941- .... PC 68
See also AAYA 64; CA 151; CANR 92; CP 7; MTFW 2005; PFS 18

Collins, Hunt
See Hunter, Evan

Collins, Linda 1931- .... CLC 44
See also CA 125

Collins, Merle 1950- .... BLC 2:1
See also BW 3; CA 175; DLB 157

Collins, Tom
See Furphy, Joseph

Collins, (William) Wilkie
1824-1889 .... NCLC 1, 18, 93; SSC 93
See also BRWS 6; CDBLB 1832-1890; CMW 4; DLB 18, 70, 159; GL 2; MSW; RGEL 2; RGSF 2; SUFW 1; WLIT 4

Collins, William 1721-1759 ...... LC 4, 40; PC 72
See also BRW 3; DAM POET; DLB 109; RGEL 2

Collodi, Carlo
See Lorenzini, Carlo

Colman, George
See Glassco, John

Colman, George, the Elder
1732-1794 .... LC 98
See also RGEL 2

Colonna, Vittoria 1492-1547 .... LC 71
See also RGWL 2, 3

Colt, Winchester Remington
See Hubbard, L. Ron

Colter, Cyrus J. 1910-2002 .... CLC 58
See also BW 1; CA 65-68; 205; CANR 10, 66; CN 2, 3, 4, 5, 6; DLB 33

Colton, James
See Hansen, Joseph

Colum, Padraic 1881-1972 .... **CLC 28**
 See also BYA 4; CA 73-76; 33-36R; CANR
 35; CLR 36; CP 1; CWRI 5; DLB 19;
 MAICYA 1, 2; MTCW 1; RGEL 2; SATA
 15; WCH

Colvin, James
 See Moorcock, Michael

Colwin, Laurie (E.) 1944-1992 .... **CLC 5, 13,
23, 84**
 See also CA 89-92; 139; CANR 20, 46;
 DLB 218; DLBY 1980; MTCW 1

Comfort, Alex(ander) 1920-2000 .... **CLC 7**
 See also CA 1-4R; 190; CANR 1, 45; CN
 1, 2, 3, 4; CP 1, 2, 3, 4, 5, 6, 7; DAM
 POP; MTCW 2

Comfort, Montgomery
 See Campbell, Ramsey

Compton-Burnett, I(vy)
 1892(?)-1969 .... **CLC 1, 3, 10, 15, 34;
TCLC 180**
 See also BRW 7; CA 1-4R; 25-28R; CANR
 4; DAM NOV; DLB 36; EWL 3; MTCW
 1, 2; RGEL 2

Comstock, Anthony 1844-1915 ...... **TCLC 13**
 See also CA 110; 169

Comte, Auguste 1798-1857 .... **NCLC 54**

Conan Doyle, Arthur
 See Doyle, Sir Arthur Conan

Conde (Abellan), Carmen
 1901-1996 .... **HLCS 1**
 See also CA 177; CWW 2; DLB 108; EWL
 3; HW 2

Conde, Maryse 1937- .... **BLC 2:1; BLCS;
CLC 52, 92, 247**
 See also BW 2, 3; CA 110, 190; CAAE 190;
 CANR 30, 53, 76, 171; CWW 2; DAM
 MULT; EWL 3; MTCW 2; MTFW 2005

Condillac, Etienne Bonnot de
 1714-1780 .... **LC 26**
 See also DLB 313

Condon, Richard 1915-1996 ...... **CLC 4, 6, 8,
10, 45, 100**
 See also BEST 90:3; BPFB 1; CA 1-4R;
 151; CAAS 1; CANR 2, 23, 164; CMW
 4; CN 1, 2, 3, 4, 5, 6; DAM NOV; INT
 CANR-23; MAL 5; MTCW 1, 2

Condon, Richard Thomas
 See Condon, Richard

Condorcet
 See Condorcet, marquis de Marie-Jean-
 Antoine-Nicolas Caritat

**Condorcet, marquis de
Marie-Jean-Antoine-Nicolas Caritat**
 1743-1794 .... **LC 104**
 See also DLB 313; GFL Beginnings to 1789

Confucius 551B.C.-479B.C. .... **CMLC 19, 65;
WLCS**
 See also DA; DA3; DAB; DAC; DAM
 MST

Congreve, William 1670-1729 ... **DC 2; LC 5,
21; WLC 2**
 See also BRW 2; CDBLB 1660-1789; DA;
 DAB; DAC; DAM DRAM, MST, POET;
 DFS 15; DLB 39, 84; RGEL 2; WLIT 3

Conley, Robert J. 1940- .... **NNAL**
 See also CA 41-44R; CANR 15, 34, 45, 96,
 186; DAM MULT; TCWW 2

Connell, Evan S., Jr. 1924- .... **CLC 4, 6, 45**
 See also AAYA 7; AMWS 14; CA 1-4R;
 CAAS 2; CANR 2, 39, 76, 97, 140; CN
 1, 2, 3, 4, 5, 6; DAM NOV; DLB 2, 335;
 DLBY 1981; MAL 5; MTCW 1, 2;
 MTFW 2005

Connelly, Marc(us Cook) 1890-1980 . **CLC 7**
 See also CA 85-88; 102; CAD; CANR 30;
 DFS 12; DLB 7; DLBY 1980; MAL 5;
 RGAL 4; SATA-Obit 25

Connolly, Paul
 See Wicker, Tom

Connor, Ralph
 See Gordon, Charles William

Conrad, Joseph 1857-1924 ..... **SSC 9, 67, 69,
71; TCLC 1, 6, 13, 25, 43, 57; WLC 2**
 See also AAYA 26; BPFB 1; BRW 6;
 BRWC 1; BRWR 2; BYA 2; CA 104; 131;
 CANR 60; CDBLB 1890-1914; DA; DA3;
 DAB; DAC; DAM MST, NOV; DLB 10,
 34, 98, 156; EWL 3; EXPN; EXPS; LAIT
 2; LATS 1:1; LMFS 1; MTCW 1, 2;
 MTFW 2005; NFS 2, 16; RGEL 2; RGSF
 2; SATA 27; SSFS 1, 12; TEA; WLIT 4

Conrad, Robert Arnold
 See Hart, Moss

Conroy, Pat 1945- .... **CLC 30, 74**
 See also AAYA 8, 52; AITN 1; BPFB 1;
 CA 85-88; CANR 24, 53, 129; CN 7;
 CPW; CSW; DA3; DAM NOV, POP;
 DLB 6; LAIT 5; MAL 5; MTCW 1, 2;
 MTFW 2005

Constant (de Rebecque), (Henri) Benjamin
 1767-1830 .... **NCLC 6, 182**
 See also DLB 119; EW 4; GFL 1789 to the
 Present

Conway, Jill K. 1934- .... **CLC 152**
 See also CA 130; CANR 94

Conway, Jill Kathryn Ker
 See Conway, Jill K.

Conybeare, Charles Augustus
 See Eliot, T(homas) S(tearns)

Cook, Michael 1933-1994 .... **CLC 58**
 See also CA 93-96; CANR 68; DLB 53

Cook, Robin 1940- .... **CLC 14**
 See also AAYA 32; BEST 90:2; BPFB 1;
 CA 108; 111; CANR 41, 90, 109, 181;
 CPW; DA3; DAM POP; HGG; INT CA-
 111

Cook, Roy
 See Silverberg, Robert

Cooke, Elizabeth 1948- .... **CLC 55**
 See also CA 129

Cooke, John Esten 1830-1886 .... **NCLC 5**
 See also DLB 3, 248; RGAL 4

Cooke, John Estes
 See Baum, L(yman) Frank

Cooke, M. E.
 See Creasey, John

Cooke, Margaret
 See Creasey, John

Cooke, Rose Terry 1827-1892 ...... **NCLC 110**
 See also DLB 12, 74

Cook-Lynn, Elizabeth 1930- .... **CLC 93;
NNAL**
 See also CA 133; DAM MULT; DLB 175

Cooney, Ray .... **CLC 62**
 See also CBD

Cooper, Anthony Ashley 1671-1713 .. **LC 107**
 See also DLB 101, 336

Cooper, Dennis 1953- .... **CLC 203**
 See also CA 133; CANR 72, 86; GLL 1;
 HGG

Cooper, Douglas 1960- .... **CLC 86**

Cooper, Henry St. John
 See Creasey, John

Cooper, J. California (?)- .... **CLC 56**
 See also AAYA 12; BW 1; CA 125; CANR
 55; DAM MULT; DLB 212

Cooper, James Fenimore
 1789-1851 .... **NCLC 1, 27, 54, 203**
 See also AAYA 22; AMW; BPFB 1;
 CDALB 1640-1865; CLR 105; DA3;
 DLB 3, 183, 250, 254; LAIT 1; NFS 25;
 RGAL 4; SATA 19; TUS; WCH

Cooper, Susan Fenimore
 1813-1894 .... **NCLC 129**
 See also ANW; DLB 239, 254

Coover, Robert 1932- .. **CLC 3, 7, 15, 32, 46,
87, 161; SSC 15, 101**
 See also AMWS 5; BPFB 1; CA 45-48;
 CANR 3, 37, 58, 115; CN 1, 2, 3, 4, 5, 6,
 7; DAM NOV; DLB 2, 227; DLBY 1981;
 EWL 3; MAL 5; MTCW 1, 2; MTFW
 2005; RGAL 4; RGSF 2

Copeland, Stewart (Armstrong)
 1952- .... **CLC 26**

Copernicus, Nicolaus 1473-1543 .... **LC 45**

Coppard, A(lfred) E(dgar)
 1878-1957 .... **SSC 21; TCLC 5**
 See also BRWS 8; CA 114; 167; DLB 162;
 EWL 3; HGG; RGEL 2; RGSF 2; SUFW
 1; YABC 1

Coppee, Francois 1842-1908 .... **TCLC 25**
 See also CA 170; DLB 217

Coppola, Francis Ford 1939- ... **CLC 16, 126**
 See also AAYA 39; CA 77-80; CANR 40,
 78; DLB 44

Copway, George 1818-1869 .... **NNAL**
 See also DAM MULT; DLB 175, 183

Corbiere, Tristan 1845-1875 .... **NCLC 43**
 See also DLB 217; GFL 1789 to the Present

Corcoran, Barbara (Asenath)
 1911- .... **CLC 17**
 See also AAYA 14; CA 21-24R, 191; CAAE
 191; CAAS 2; CANR 11, 28, 48; CLR
 50; DLB 52; JRDA; MAICYA 2; MAIC-
 YAS 1; RHW; SAAS 20; SATA 3, 77;
 SATA-Essay 125

Cordelier, Maurice
 See Giraudoux, Jean(-Hippolyte)

Cordier, Gilbert
 See Scherer, Jean-Marie Maurice

Corelli, Marie
 See Mackay, Mary

Corinna c. 225B.C.-c. 305B.C. ...... **CMLC 72**

Corman, Cid 1924-2004 .... **CLC 9**
 See also CA 85-88; 225; CAAS 2; CANR
 44; CP 1, 2, 3, 4, 5, 6, 7; DAM POET;
 DLB 5, 193

Corman, Sidney
 See Corman, Cid

Cormier, Robert 1925-2000 .... **CLC 12, 30**
 See also AAYA 3, 19; BYA 1, 2, 6, 8, 9;
 CA 1-4R; CANR 5, 23, 76, 93; CDALB
 1968-1988; CLR 12, 55; DA; DAB; DAC;
 DAM MST, NOV; DLB 52; EXPN; INT
 CANR-23; JRDA; LAIT 5; MAICYA 1,
 2; MTCW 1, 2; MTFW 2005; NFS 2, 18;
 SATA 10, 45, 83; SATA-Obit 122; WYA;
 YAW

Corn, Alfred (DeWitt III) 1943- .... **CLC 33**
 See also CA 179; CAAE 179; CAAS 25;
 CANR 44; CP 3, 4, 5, 6, 7; CSW; DLB
 120, 282; DLBY 1980

Corneille, Pierre 1606-1684 .. **DC 21; LC 28,
135**
 See also DAB; DAM MST; DFS 21; DLB
 268; EW 3; GFL Beginnings to 1789;
 RGWL 2, 3; TWA

Cornwell, David
 See le Carre, John

Cornwell, David John Moore
 See le Carre, John

Cornwell, Patricia 1956- .... **CLC 155**
 See also AAYA 16, 56; BPFB 1; CA 134;
 CANR 53, 131; CMW 4; CPW; CSW;
 DAM POP; DLB 306; MSW; MTCW 2;
 MTFW 2005

Cornwell, Patricia Daniels
 See Cornwell, Patricia

Cornwell, Smith
 See Smith, David (Jeddie)

Crommelynck, Fernand 1885-1970 .. **CLC 75**
See also CA 189; 89-92; EWL 3

Cromwell, Oliver 1599-1658 .... **LC 43**

Cronenberg, David 1943- .... **CLC 143**
See also CA 138; CCA 1

Cronin, A(rchibald) J(oseph)
1896-1981 .... **CLC 32**
See also BPFB 1; CA 1-4R; 102; CANR 5;
CN 2; DLB 191; SATA 47; SATA-Obit 25

Cross, Amanda
See Heilbrun, Carolyn G(old)

Crothers, Rachel 1878-1958 .... **TCLC 19**
See also CA 113; 194; CAD; CWD; DLB
7, 266; RGAL 4

Croves, Hal
See Traven, B.

Crow Dog, Mary (?)- .... **CLC 93; NNAL**
See also CA 154

Crowfield, Christopher
See Stowe, Harriet (Elizabeth) Beecher

Crowley, Aleister
See Crowley, Edward Alexander

Crowley, Edward Alexander
1875-1947 .... **TCLC 7**
See also CA 104; GLL 1; HGG

Crowley, John 1942- .... **CLC 57**
See also AAYA 57; BPFB 1; CA 61-64;
CANR 43, 98, 138, 177; DLBY 1982;
FANT; MTFW 2005; SATA 65, 140; SFW
4; SUFW 2

Crowne, John 1641-1712 .... **LC 104**
See also DLB 80; RGEL 2

Crud
See Crumb, R.

Crumarums
See Crumb, R.

Crumb, R. 1943- .... **CLC 17**
See also CA 106; CANR 107, 150

Crumb, Robert
See Crumb, R.

Crumbum
See Crumb, R.

Crumski
See Crumb, R.

Crum the Bum
See Crumb, R.

Crunk
See Crumb, R.

Crustt
See Crumb, R.

Crutchfield, Les
See Trumbo, Dalton

Cruz, Victor Hernandez 1949- ... **HLC 1; PC
37**
See also BW 2; CA 65-68, 271; CAAE 271;
CAAS 17; CANR 14, 32, 74, 132; CP 1,
2, 3, 4, 5, 6, 7; DAM MULT, POET; DLB
41; DNFS 1; EXPP; HW 1; LLW;
MTCW 2; MTFW 2005; PFS 16; WP

Cryer, Gretchen (Kiger) 1935- .... **CLC 21**
See also CA 114; 123

Csath, Geza
See Brenner, Jozef

Cudlip, David R(ockwell) 1933- .... **CLC 34**
See also CA 177

Cullen, Countee 1903-1946 ..... **BLC 1:1; HR
1:2; PC 20; TCLC 4, 37, 220; WLCS**
See also AAYA 78; AFAW 2; AMWS 4; BW
1; CA 108; 124; CDALB 1917-1929; DA;
DA3; DAC; DAM MST, MULT, POET;
DLB 4, 48, 51; EWL 3; EXPP; LMFS 2;
MAL 5; MTCW 1, 2; MTFW 2005; PFS
3; RGAL 4; SATA 18; WP

Culleton, Beatrice 1949- .... **NNAL**
See also CA 120; CANR 83; DAC

Culver, Timothy J.
See Westlake, Donald E.

Culver, Timothy J.
See Westlake, Donald E.

Cum, R.
See Crumb, R.

Cumberland, Richard
1732-1811 .... **NCLC 167**
See also DLB 89; RGEL 2

Cummings, Bruce F(rederick)
1889-1919 .... **TCLC 24**
See also CA 123

Cummings, E(dward) E(stlin)
1894-1962 .. **CLC 1, 3, 8, 12, 15, 68; PC
5; TCLC 137; WLC 2**
See also AAYA 41; AMW; CA 73-76;
CANR 31; CDALB 1929-1941; DA;
DA3; DAB; DAC; DAM MST, POET;
DLB 4, 48; EWL 3; EXPP; MAL 5;
MTCW 1, 2; MTFW 2005; PAB; PFS 1,
3, 12, 13, 19, 30; RGAL 4; TUS; WP

Cummins, Maria Susanna
1827-1866 .... **NCLC 139**
See also DLB 42; YABC 1

Cunha, Euclides (Rodrigues Pimenta) da
1866-1909 .... **TCLC 24**
See also CA 123; 219; DLB 307; LAW;
WLIT 1

Cunningham, E. V.
See Fast, Howard

Cunningham, J. Morgan
See Westlake, Donald E.

Cunningham, J(ames) V(incent)
1911-1985 .... **CLC 3, 31; PC 92**
See also CA 1-4R; 115; CANR 1, 72; CP 1,
2, 3, 4; DLB 5

Cunningham, Julia (Woolfolk)
1916- .... **CLC 12**
See also CA 9-12R; CANR 4, 19, 36; CWRI
5; JRDA; MAICYA 1, 2; SAAS 2; SATA
1, 26, 132

Cunningham, Michael 1952- .... **CLC 34, 243**
See also AMWS 15; CA 136; CANR 96,
160; CN 7; DLB 292; GLL 2; MTFW
2005; NFS 23

Cunninghame Graham, R. B.
See Cunninghame Graham, Robert
(Gallnigad) Bontine

**Cunninghame Graham, Robert (Gallnigad)
Bontine** 1852-1936 .... **TCLC 19**
See also CA 119; 184; DLB 98, 135, 174;
RGEL 2; RGSF 2

Curnow, (Thomas) Allen (Monro)
1911-2001 .... **PC 48**
See also CA 69-72; 202; CANR 48, 99; CP
1, 2, 3, 4, 5, 6, 7; EWL 3; RGEL 2

Currie, Ellen 19(?)- .... **CLC 44**

Curtin, Philip
See Lowndes, Marie Adelaide (Belloc)

Curtin, Phillip
See Lowndes, Marie Adelaide (Belloc)

Curtis, Price
See Ellison, Harlan

Cusanus, Nicolaus 1401-1464
See Nicholas of Cusa

Cutrate, Joe
See Spiegelman, Art

Cynewulf c. 770- .... **CMLC 23**
See also DLB 146; RGEL 2

Cyrano de Bergerac, Savinien de
1619-1655 .... **LC 65**
See also DLB 268; GFL Beginnings to
1789; RGWL 2, 3

Cyril of Alexandria c. 375-c. 430 . **CMLC 59**

Czaczkes, Shmuel Yosef Halevi
See Agnon, S.Y.

Dabrowska, Maria (Szumska)
1889-1965 .... **CLC 15**
See also CA 106; CDWLB 4; DLB 215;
EWL 3

Dabydeen, David 1955- .... **CLC 34**
See also BW 1; CA 125; CANR 56, 92; CN
6, 7; CP 5, 6, 7; DLB 347

Dacey, Philip 1939- .... **CLC 51**
See also CA 37-40R, 231; CAAE 231;
CAAS 17; CANR 14, 32, 64; CP 4, 5, 6,
7; DLB 105

Dacre, Charlotte c. 1772-1825(?) . **NCLC 151**

Dafydd ap Gwilym c. 1320-c. 1380 ..... **PC 56**

Dagerman, Stig (Halvard)
1923-1954 .... **TCLC 17**
See also CA 117; 155; DLB 259; EWL 3

D'Aguiar, Fred 1960- ..... **BLC 2:1; CLC 145**
See also CA 148; CANR 83, 101; CN 7;
CP 5, 6, 7; DLB 157; EWL 3

Dahl, Roald 1916-1990 ...... **CLC 1, 6, 18, 79;
TCLC 173**
See also AAYA 15; BPFB 1; BRWS 4; BYA
5; CA 1-4R; 133; CANR 6, 32, 37, 62;
CLR 1, 7, 41, 111; CN 1, 2, 3, 4; CPW;
DA3; DAB; DAC; DAM MST, NOV,
POP; DLB 139, 255; HGG; JRDA; MAI-
CYA 1, 2; MTCW 1, 2; MTFW 2005;
RGSF 2; SATA 1, 26, 73; SATA-Obit 65;
SSFS 4; TEA; YAW

Dahlberg, Edward 1900-1977 . **CLC 1, 7, 14;
TCLC 208**
See also CA 9-12R; 69-72; CANR 31, 62;
CN 1, 2; DLB 48; MAL 5; MTCW 1;
RGAL 4

Daitch, Susan 1954- .... **CLC 103**
See also CA 161

Dale, Colin
See Lawrence, T(homas) E(dward)

Dale, George E.
See Asimov, Isaac

d'Alembert, Jean Le Rond
1717-1783 .... **LC 126**

Dalton, Roque 1935-1975(?) ..... **HLCS 1; PC
36**
See also CA 176; DLB 283; HW 2

Daly, Elizabeth 1878-1967 .... **CLC 52**
See also CA 23-24; 25-28R; CANR 60;
CAP 2; CMW 4

Daly, Mary 1928- .... **CLC 173**
See also CA 25-28R; CANR 30, 62, 166;
FW; GLL 1; MTCW 1

Daly, Maureen 1921-2006 .... **CLC 17**
See also AAYA 5, 58; BYA 6; CA 253;
CANR 37, 83, 108; CLR 96; JRDA; MAI-
CYA 1, 2; SAAS 1; SATA 2, 129; SATA-
Obit 176; WYA; YAW

Damas, Leon-Gontran 1912-1978 ... **CLC 84;
TCLC 204**
See also BW 1; CA 125; 73-76; EWL 3

Dana, Richard Henry Sr.
1787-1879 .... **NCLC 53**

Dangarembga, Tsitsi 1959- .... **BLC 2:1**
See also BW 3; CA 163; NFS 28; WLIT 2

Daniel, Samuel 1562(?)-1619 .... **LC 24**
See also DLB 62; RGEL 2

Daniels, Brett
See Adler, Renata

Dannay, Frederic 1905-1982 .... **CLC 3, 11**
See also BPFB 3; CA 1-4R; 107; CANR 1,
39; CMW 4; DAM POP; DLB 137; MSW;
MTCW 1; RGAL 4

D'Annunzio, Gabriele 1863-1938 ... **TCLC 6,
40, 215**
See also CA 104; 155; EW 8; EWL 3;
RGWL 2, 3; TWA; WLIT 7

Danois, N. le
See Gourmont, Remy(-Marie-Charles) de

Dante 1265-1321 .... **CMLC 3, 18, 39, 70; PC
21; WLCS**
See also DA; DA3; DAB; DAC; DAM
MST, POET; EFS 1; EW 1; LAIT 1;
RGWL 2, 3; TWA; WLIT 7; WP

Deighton, Leonard Cyril 1929- ..... **CLC 4, 7, 22, 46**
See also AAYA 57, 6; BEST 89:2; BPFB 1; CA 9-12R; CANR 19, 33, 68; CDBLB 1960- Present; CMW 4; CN 1, 2, 3, 4, 5, 6, 7; CPW; DA3; DAM NOV, POP; DLB 87; MTCW 1, 2; MTFW 2005

Dekker, Thomas 1572(?)-1632 ..... **DC 12; LC 22, 159**
See also CDBLB Before 1660; DAM DRAM; DLB 62, 172; LMFS 1; RGEL 2

de Laclos, Pierre Ambroise Franois
See Laclos, Pierre-Ambroise Francois

Delacroix, (Ferdinand-Victor-)Eugene 1798-1863 .... **NCLC 133**
See also EW 5

Delafield, E. M.
See Dashwood, Edmee Elizabeth Monica de la Pasture

de la Mare, Walter (John) 1873-1956 ..... **PC 77; SSC 14; TCLC 4, 53; WLC 2**
See also CA 163; CDBLB 1914-1945; CLR 23; CWRI 5; DA3; DAB; DAC; DAM MST, POET; DLB 19, 153, 162, 255, 284; EWL 3; EXPP; HGG; MAICYA 1, 2; MTCW 2; MTFW 2005; RGEL 2; RGSF 2; SATA 16; SUFW 1; TEA; WCH

de Lamartine, Alphonse (Marie Louis Prat)
See Lamartine, Alphonse (Marie Louis Prat) de

Delaney, Franey
See O'Hara, John (Henry)

Delaney, Shelagh 1939- .... **CLC 29**
See also CA 17-20R; CANR 30, 67; CBD; CD 5, 6; CDBLB 1960 to Present; CWD; DAM DRAM; DFS 7; DLB 13; MTCW 1

Delany, Martin Robison 1812-1885 .... **NCLC 93**
See also DLB 50; RGAL 4

Delany, Mary (Granville Pendarves) 1700-1788 .... **LC 12**

Delany, Samuel R., Jr. 1942- .... **BLC 1:1; CLC 8, 14, 38, 141**
See also AAYA 24; AFAW 2; BPFB 1; BW 2, 3; CA 81-84; CANR 27, 43, 116, 172; CN 2, 3, 4, 5, 6, 7; DAM MULT; DLB 8, 33; FANT; MAL 5; MTCW 1, 2; RGAL 4; SATA 92; SCFW 1, 2; SFW 4; SUFW 2

Delany, Samuel Ray
See Delany, Samuel R., Jr.

de la Parra, (Ana) Teresa (Sonojo) 1890(?)-1936 .... **HLCS 2; TCLC 185**
See also CA 178; HW 2; LAW

Delaporte, Theophile
See Green, Julien (Hartridge)

De La Ramee, Marie Louise 1839-1908 .... **TCLC 43**
See also CA 204; DLB 18, 156; RGEL 2; SATA 20

de la Roche, Mazo 1879-1961 .... **CLC 14**
See also CA 85-88; CANR 30; DLB 68; RGEL 2; RHW; SATA 64

De La Salle, Innocent
See Hartmann, Sadakichi

de Laureamont, Comte
See Lautreamont

Delbanco, Nicholas 1942- ..... **CLC 6, 13, 167**
See also CA 17-20R, 189; CAAE 189; CAAS 2; CANR 29, 55, 116, 150; CN 7; DLB 6, 234

Delbanco, Nicholas Franklin
See Delbanco, Nicholas

del Castillo, Michel 1933- .... **CLC 38**
See also CA 109; CANR 77

Deledda, Grazia (Cosima) 1875(?)-1936 .... **TCLC 23**
See also CA 123; 205; DLB 264, 329; EWL 3; RGWL 2, 3; WLIT 7

Deleuze, Gilles 1925-1995 .... **TCLC 116**
See also DLB 296

Delgado, Abelardo (Lalo) B(arrientos) 1930-2004 .... **HLC 1**
See also CA 131; 230; CAAS 15; CANR 90; DAM MST, MULT; DLB 82; HW 1, 2

Delibes, Miguel
See Delibes Setien, Miguel

Delibes Setien, Miguel 1920- .... **CLC 8, 18**
See also CA 45-48; CANR 1, 32; CWW 2; DLB 322; EWL 3; HW 1; MTCW 1

DeLillo, Don 1936- ..... **CLC 8, 10, 13, 27, 39, 54, 76, 143, 210, 213**
See also AMWC 2; AMWS 6; BEST 89:1; BPFB 1; CA 81-84; CANR 21, 76, 92, 133, 173; CN 3, 4, 5, 6, 7; CPW; DA3; DAM NOV, POP; DLB 6, 173; EWL 3; MAL 5; MTCW 1, 2; MTFW 2005; NFS 28; RGAL 4; TUS

de Lisser, H. G.
See De Lisser, H(erbert) G(eorge)

De Lisser, H(erbert) G(eorge) 1878-1944 .... **TCLC 12**
See also BW 2; CA 109; 152; DLB 117

Deloire, Pierre
See Peguy, Charles (Pierre)

Deloney, Thomas 1543(?)-1600 .... **LC 41; PC 79**
See also DLB 167; RGEL 2

Deloria, Ella (Cara) 1889-1971(?) ..... **NNAL**
See also CA 152; DAM MULT; DLB 175

Deloria, Vine, Jr. 1933-2005 .... **CLC 21, 122; NNAL**
See also CA 53-56; 245; CANR 5, 20, 48, 98; DAM MULT; DLB 175; MTCW 1; SATA 21; SATA-Obit 171

Deloria, Vine Victor, Jr.
See Deloria, Vine, Jr.

del Valle-Inclan, Ramon (Maria)
See Valle-Inclan, Ramon (Maria) del

Del Vecchio, John M(ichael) 1947- .. **CLC 29**
See also CA 110; DLBD 9

de Man, Paul (Adolph Michel) 1919-1983 .... **CLC 55**
See also CA 128; 111; CANR 61; DLB 67; MTCW 1, 2

de Mandiargues, Andre Pieyre
See Pieyre de Mandiargues, Andre

DeMarinis, Rick 1934- .... **CLC 54**
See also CA 57-60, 184; CAAE 184; CAAS 24; CANR 9, 25, 50, 160; DLB 218; TCWW 2

de Maupassant, (Henri Rene Albert) Guy
See Maupassant, (Henri Rene Albert) Guy de

Dembry, R. Emmet
See Murfree, Mary Noailles

Demby, William 1922- ...... **BLC 1:1; CLC 53**
See also BW 1, 3; CA 81-84; CANR 81; DAM MULT; DLB 33

de Menton, Francisco
See Chin, Frank (Chew, Jr.)

Demetrius of Phalerum c. 307B.C.- .... **CMLC 34**

Demijohn, Thom
See Disch, Thomas M.

De Mille, James 1833-1880 .... **NCLC 123**
See also DLB 99, 251

Democritus c. 460B.C.-c. 370B.C. . **CMLC 47**

de Montaigne, Michel (Eyquem)
See Montaigne, Michel (Eyquem) de

de Montherlant, Henry (Milon)
See Montherlant, Henry (Milon) de

Demosthenes 384B.C.-322B.C. ...... **CMLC 13**
See also AW 1; DLB 176; RGWL 2, 3; WLIT 8

de Musset, (Louis Charles) Alfred
See Musset, Alfred de

de Natale, Francine
See Malzberg, Barry N(athaniel)

de Navarre, Marguerite 1492-1549 .... **LC 61, 167; SSC 85**
See also DLB 327; GFL Beginnings to 1789; RGWL 2, 3

Denby, Edwin (Orr) 1903-1983 .... **CLC 48**
See also CA 138; 110; CP 1

de Nerval, Gerard
See Nerval, Gerard de

Denham, John 1615-1669 .... **LC 73**
See also DLB 58, 126; RGEL 2

Denis, Julio
See Cortazar, Julio

Denmark, Harrison
See Zelazny, Roger

Dennis, John 1658-1734 .... **LC 11, 154**
See also DLB 101; RGEL 2

Dennis, Nigel (Forbes) 1912-1989 ...... **CLC 8**
See also CA 25-28R; 129; CN 1, 2, 3, 4; DLB 13, 15, 233; EWL 3; MTCW 1

Dent, Lester 1904-1959 .... **TCLC 72**
See also CA 112; 161; CMW 4; DLB 306; SFW 4

Dentinger, Stephen
See Hoch, Edward D.

De Palma, Brian 1940- .... **CLC 20, 247**
See also CA 109

De Palma, Brian Russell
See De Palma, Brian

de Pizan, Christine
See Christine de Pizan

De Quincey, Thomas 1785-1859 ..... **NCLC 4, 87, 198**
See also BRW 4; CDBLB 1789-1832; DLB 110, 144; RGEL 2

De Ray, Jill
See Moore, Alan

Deren, Eleanora 1908(?)-1961 .. **CLC 16, 102**
See also CA 192; 111

Deren, Maya
See Deren, Eleanora

Derleth, August (William) 1909-1971 .... **CLC 31**
See also BPFB 1; BYA 9, 10; CA 1-4R; 29-32R; CANR 4; CMW 4; CN 1; DLB 9; DLBD 17; HGG; SATA 5; SUFW 1

Der Nister 1884-1950 .... **TCLC 56**
See also DLB 333; EWL 3

de Routisie, Albert
See Aragon, Louis

Derrida, Jacques 1930-2004 ...... **CLC 24, 87, 225**
See also CA 124; 127; 232; CANR 76, 98, 133; DLB 242; EWL 3; LMFS 2; MTCW 2; TWA

Derry Down Derry
See Lear, Edward

Dersonnes, Jacques
See Simenon, Georges (Jacques Christian)

Der Stricker c. 1190-c. 1250 .... **CMLC 75**
See also DLB 138

Desai, Anita 1937- . **CLC 19, 37, 97, 175, 271**
See also BRWS 5; CA 81-84; CANR 33, 53, 95, 133; CN 1, 2, 3, 4, 5, 6, 7; CWRI 5; DA3; DAB; DAM NOV; DLB 271, 323; DNFS 2; EWL 3; FW; MTCW 1, 2; MTFW 2005; SATA 63, 126

Desai, Kiran 1971- .... **CLC 119**
See also BYA 16; CA 171; CANR 127; NFS 28

de Saint-Luc, Jean
See Glassco, John

EWL 3; LAIT 3; MAL 5; MTCW 1, 2; MTFW 2005; NFS 6; RGAL 4; RGHL; RHW; SSFS 27; TCLE 1:1; TCWW 1, 2; TUS

Dodgson, Charles Lutwidge
  See Carroll, Lewis

Dodsley, Robert 1703-1764 .... **LC 97**
  See also DLB 95; RGEL 2

Dodson, Owen (Vincent)
  1914-1983 .... **BLC 1:1; CLC 79**
  See also BW 1; CA 65-68; 110; CANR 24; DAM MULT; DLB 76

Doeblin, Alfred 1878-1957 .... **TCLC 13**
  See also CA 110; 141; CDWLB 2; DLB 66; EWL 3; RGWL 2, 3

Doerr, Harriet 1910-2002 .... **CLC 34**
  See also CA 117; 122; 213; CANR 47; INT CA-122; LATS 1:2

Domecq, H(onorio) Bustos
  See Bioy Casares, Adolfo; Borges, Jorge Luis

Domini, Rey
  See Lorde, Audre

Dominic, R. B.
  See Hennissart, Martha

Dominique
  See Proust, (Valentin-Louis-George-Eugene) Marcel

Don, A
  See Stephen, Sir Leslie

Donaldson, Stephen R. 1947- ... **CLC 46, 138**
  See also AAYA 36; BPFB 1; CA 89-92; CANR 13, 55, 99; CPW; DAM POP; FANT; INT CANR-13; SATA 121; SFW 4; SUFW 1, 2

Donleavy, J(ames) P(atrick) 1926- .... **CLC 1, 4, 6, 10, 45**
  See also AITN 2; BPFB 1; CA 9-12R; CANR 24, 49, 62, 80, 124; CBD; CD 5, 6; CN 1, 2, 3, 4, 5, 6, 7; DLB 6, 173; INT CANR-24; MAL 5; MTCW 1, 2; MTFW 2005; RGAL 4

Donnadieu, Marguerite
  See Duras, Marguerite

Donne, John 1572-1631 ... **LC 10, 24, 91; PC 1, 43; WLC 2**
  See also AAYA 67; BRW 1; BRWC 1; BRWR 2; CDBLB Before 1660; DA; DAB; DAC; DAM MST, POET; DLB 121, 151; EXPP; PAB; PFS 2, 11; RGEL 3; TEA; WLIT 3; WP

Donnell, David 1939(?)- .... **CLC 34**
  See also CA 197

Donoghue, Denis 1928- .... **CLC 209**
  See also CA 17-20R; CANR 16, 102

Donoghue, Emma 1969- .... **CLC 239**
  See also CA 155; CANR 103, 152; DLB 267; GLL 2; SATA 101

Donoghue, P.S.
  See Hunt, E. Howard

Donoso (Yanez), Jose 1924-1996 ... **CLC 4, 8, 11, 32, 99; HLC 1; SSC 34; TCLC 133**
  See also CA 81-84; 155; CANR 32, 73; CDWLB 3; CWW 2; DAM MULT; DLB 113; EWL 3; HW 1, 2; LAW; LAWS 1; MTCW 1, 2; MTFW 2005; RGSF 2; WLIT 1

Donovan, John 1928-1992 .... **CLC 35**
  See also AAYA 20; CA 97-100; 137; CLR 3; MAICYA 1, 2; SATA 72; SATA-Brief 29; YAW

Don Roberto
  See Cunninghame Graham, Robert (Gallnigad) Bontine

Doolittle, Hilda 1886-1961 . **CLC 3, 8, 14, 31, 34, 73; PC 5; WLC 3**
  See also AAYA 66; AMWS 1; CA 97-100; CANR 35, 131; DA; DAC; DAM MST, POET; DLB 4, 45; EWL 3; FL 1:5; FW; GLL 1; LMFS 2; MAL 5; MBL; MTCW 1, 2; MTFW 2005; PFS 6, 28; RGAL 4

Doppo
  See Kunikida Doppo

Doppo, Kunikida
  See Kunikida Doppo

Dorfman, Ariel 1942- .... **CLC 48, 77, 189; HLC 1**
  See also CA 124; 130; CANR 67, 70, 135; CWW 2; DAM MULT; DFS 4; EWL 3; HW 1, 2; INT CA-130; WLIT 1

Dorn, Edward (Merton)
  1929-1999 .... **CLC 10, 18**
  See also CA 93-96; 187; CANR 42, 79; CP 1, 2, 3, 4, 5, 6, 7; DLB 5; INT CA-93-96; WP

Dor-Ner, Zvi .... **CLC 70**

Dorris, Michael 1945-1997 .... **CLC 109; NNAL**
  See also AAYA 20; BEST 90:1; BYA 12; CA 102; 157; CANR 19, 46, 75; CLR 58; DA3; DAM MULT, NOV; DLB 175; LAIT 5; MTCW 2; MTFW 2005; NFS 3; RGAL 4; SATA 75; SATA-Obit 94; TCWW 2; YAW

Dorris, Michael A.
  See Dorris, Michael

Dorsan, Luc
  See Simenon, Georges (Jacques Christian)

Dorsange, Jean
  See Simenon, Georges (Jacques Christian)

Dorset
  See Sackville, Thomas

Dos Passos, John (Roderigo)
  1896-1970 ... **CLC 1, 4, 8, 11, 15, 25, 34, 82; WLC 2**
  See also AMW; BPFB 1; CA 1-4R; 29-32R; CANR 3; CDALB 1929-1941; DA; DA3; DAB; DAC; DAM MST, NOV; DLB 4, 9, 274, 316; DLBD 1, 15; DLBY 1996; EWL 3; MAL 5; MTCW 1, 2; MTFW 2005; NFS 14; RGAL 4; TUS

Dossage, Jean
  See Simenon, Georges (Jacques Christian)

Dostoevsky, Fedor Mikhailovich
  1821-1881 .. **NCLC 2, 7, 21, 33, 43, 119, 167, 202; SSC 2, 33, 44; WLC 2**
  See also AAYA 40; DA; DA3; DAB; DAC; DAM MST, NOV; DLB 238; EW 7; EXPN; LATS 1:1; LMFS 1, 2; NFS 28; RGSF 2; RGWL 2, 3; SSFS 8; TWA

Dostoevsky, Fyodor
  See Dostoevsky, Fedor Mikhailovich

Doty, Mark 1953(?)- .... **CLC 176; PC 53**
  See also AMWS 11; CA 161, 183; CAAE 183; CANR 110, 173; CP 7; PFS 28

Doty, Mark A.
  See Doty, Mark

Doty, Mark Alan
  See Doty, Mark

Doty, M.R.
  See Doty, Mark

Doughty, Charles M(ontagu)
  1843-1926 .... **TCLC 27**
  See also CA 115; 178; DLB 19, 57, 174

Douglas, Ellen 1921- .... **CLC 73**
  See also CA 115; CANR 41, 83; CN 5, 6, 7; CSW; DLB 292

Douglas, Gavin 1475(?)-1522 .... **LC 20**
  See also DLB 132; RGEL 2

Douglas, George
  See Brown, George Douglas

Douglas, Keith (Castellain)
  1920-1944 .... **TCLC 40**
  See also BRW 7; CA 160; DLB 27; EWL 3; PAB; RGEL 2

Douglas, Leonard
  See Bradbury, Ray

Douglas, Michael
  See Crichton, Michael

Douglas, Michael
  See Crichton, Michael

Douglas, (George) Norman
  1868-1952 .... **TCLC 68**
  See also BRW 6; CA 119; 157; DLB 34, 195; RGEL 2

Douglas, William
  See Brown, George Douglas

Douglass, Frederick 1817(?)-1895 .. **BLC 1:1; NCLC 7, 55, 141; WLC 2**
  See also AAYA 48; AFAW 1, 2; AMWC 1; AMWS 3; CDALB 1640-1865; DA; DA3; DAC; DAM MST, MULT; DLB 1, 43, 50, 79, 243; FW; LAIT 2; NCFS 2; RGAL 4; SATA 29

Dourado, (Waldomiro Freitas) Autran
  1926- .... **CLC 23, 60**
  See also CA 25-28R; 179; CANR 34, 81; DLB 145, 307; HW 2

Dourado, Waldomiro Freitas Autran
  See Dourado, (Waldomiro Freitas) Autran

Dove, Rita 1952- . **BLC 2:1; BLCS; CLC 50, 81; PC 6**
  See also AAYA 46; AMWS 4; BW 2; CA 109; CAAS 19; CANR 27, 42, 68, 76, 97, 132; CDALBS; CP 5, 6, 7; CSW; CWP; DA3; DAM MULT, POET; DLB 120; EWL 3; EXPP; MAL 5; MTCW 2; MTFW 2005; PFS 1, 15; RGAL 4

Dove, Rita Frances
  See Dove, Rita

Doveglion
  See Villa, Jose Garcia

Dowell, Coleman 1925-1985 .... **CLC 60**
  See also CA 25-28R; 117; CANR 10; DLB 130; GLL 2

Downing, Major Jack
  See Smith, Seba

Dowson, Ernest (Christopher)
  1867-1900 .... **TCLC 4**
  See also CA 105; 150; DLB 19, 135; RGEL 2

Doyle, A. Conan
  See Doyle, Sir Arthur Conan

Doyle, Sir Arthur Conan
  1859-1930 ..... **SSC 12, 83, 95; TCLC 7; WLC 2**
  See also AAYA 14; BPFB 1; BRWS 2; BYA 4, 5, 11; CA 104; 122; CANR 131; CD-BLB 1890-1914; CLR 106; CMW 4; DA; DA3; DAB; DAC; DAM MST, NOV; DLB 18, 70, 156, 178; EXPS; HGG; LAIT 2; MSW; MTCW 1, 2; MTFW 2005; NFS 28; RGEL 2; RGSF 2; RHW; SATA 24; SCFW 1, 2; SFW 4; SSFS 2; TEA; WCH; WLIT 4; WYA; YAW

Doyle, Conan
  See Doyle, Sir Arthur Conan

Doyle, John
  See Graves, Robert

Doyle, Roddy 1958- .... **CLC 81, 178**
  See also AAYA 14; BRWS 5; CA 143; CANR 73, 128, 168; CN 6, 7; DA3; DLB 194, 326; MTCW 2; MTFW 2005

Doyle, Sir A. Conan
  See Doyle, Sir Arthur Conan

Dr. A
  See Asimov, Isaac; Silverstein, Alvin; Silverstein, Virginia B(arbara Opshelor)

Drabble, Margaret 1939- ...... **CLC 2, 3, 5, 8, 10, 22, 53, 129**
  See also BRWS 4; CA 13-16R; CANR 18, 35, 63, 112, 131, 174; CDBLB 1960 to Present; CN 1, 2, 3, 4, 5, 6, 7; CPW; DA3; DAB; DAC; DAM MST, NOV, POP; DLB 14, 155, 231; EWL 3; FW; MTCW 1, 2; MTFW 2005; RGEL 2; SATA 48; TEA

Drakulic, Slavenka 1949- .... **CLC 173**
  See also CA 144; CANR 92

Engelhardt, Frederick
    See Hubbard, L. Ron
Engels, Friedrich 1820-1895 .. **NCLC 85, 114**
    See also DLB 129; LATS 1:1
Enquist, Per Olov 1934- .... **CLC 257**
    See also CA 109; 193; CANR 155; CWW
    2; DLB 257; EWL 3
Enright, D(ennis) J(oseph)
    1920-2002 .... **CLC 4, 8, 31; PC 93**
    See also CA 1-4R; 211; CANR 1, 42, 83;
    CN 1, 2; CP 1, 2, 3, 4, 5, 6, 7; DLB 27;
    EWL 3; SATA 25; SATA-Obit 140
Ensler, Eve 1953- .... **CLC 212**
    See also CA 172; CANR 126, 163; DFS 23
Enzensberger, Hans Magnus
    1929- .... **CLC 43; PC 28**
    See also CA 116; 119; CANR 103; CWW
    2; EWL 3
Ephron, Nora 1941- .... **CLC 17, 31**
    See also AAYA 35; AITN 2; CA 65-68;
    CANR 12, 39, 83, 161; DFS 22
Epicurus 341B.C.-270B.C. .... **CMLC 21**
    See also DLB 176
Epinay, Louise d' 1726-1783 .... **LC 138**
    See also DLB 313
Epsilon
    See Betjeman, John
Epstein, Daniel Mark 1948- .... **CLC 7**
    See also CA 49-52; CANR 2, 53, 90
Epstein, Jacob 1956- .... **CLC 19**
    See also CA 114
Epstein, Jean 1897-1953 .... **TCLC 92**
Epstein, Joseph 1937- .... **CLC 39, 204**
    See also AMWS 14; CA 112; 119; CANR
    50, 65, 117, 164
Epstein, Leslie 1938- .... **CLC 27**
    See also AMWS 12; CA 73-76, 215; CAAE
    215; CAAS 12; CANR 23, 69, 162; DLB
    299; RGHL
Equiano, Olaudah 1745(?)-1797 ..... **BLC 1:2;**
    LC 16, 143
    See also AFAW 1, 2; CDWLB 3; DAM
    MULT; DLB 37, 50; WLIT 2
Erasmus, Desiderius 1469(?)-1536 ..... **LC 16,**
    93
    See also DLB 136; EW 2; LMFS 1; RGWL
    2, 3; TWA
Erdman, Paul E. 1932-2007 .... **CLC 25**
    See also AITN 1; CA 61-64; 259; CANR
    13, 43, 84
Erdman, Paul Emil
    See Erdman, Paul E.
Erdrich, Karen Louise
    See Erdrich, Louise
Erdrich, Louise 1954- .... **CLC 39, 54, 120,**
    176; NNAL; PC 52; SSC 121
    See also AAYA 10, 47; AMWS 4; BEST
    89:1; BPFB 1; CA 114; CANR 41, 62,
    118, 138; CDALBS; CN 5, 6, 7; CP 6, 7;
    CPW; CWP; DA3; DAM MULT, NOV,
    POP; DLB 152, 175, 206; EWL 3; EXPP;
    FL 1:5; LAIT 5; LATS 1:2; MAL 5;
    MTCW 1, 2; MTFW 2005; NFS 5; PFS
    14; RGAL 4; SATA 94, 141; SSFS 14,
    22; TCWW 2
Erenburg, Ilya (Grigoryevich)
    See Ehrenburg, Ilya (Grigoryevich)
    See also DLB 272
Erickson, Stephen Michael
    See Erickson, Steve
Erickson, Steve 1950- .... **CLC 64**
    See also CA 129; CANR 60, 68, 136;
    MTFW 2005; SFW 4; SUFW 2
Erickson, Walter
    See Fast, Howard
Ericson, Walter
    See Fast, Howard
Eriksson, Buntel
    See Bergman, Ingmar

Eriugena, John Scottus c.
    810-877 .... **CMLC 65**
    See also DLB 115
Ernaux, Annie 1940- .... **CLC 88, 184**
    See also CA 147; CANR 93; MTFW 2005;
    NCFS 3, 5
Erskine, John 1879-1951 .... **TCLC 84**
    See also CA 112; 159; DLB 9, 102; FANT
Erwin, Will
    See Eisner, Will
Eschenbach, Wolfram von
    See von Eschenbach, Wolfram
Eseki, Bruno
    See Mphahlele, Es'kia
Esekie, Bruno
    See Mphahlele, Es'kia
Esenin, S.A.
    See Esenin, Sergei
Esenin, Sergei 1895-1925 .... **TCLC 4**
    See also CA 104; EWL 3; RGWL 2, 3
Esenin, Sergei Aleksandrovich
    See Esenin, Sergei
Eshleman, Clayton 1935- .... **CLC 7**
    See also CA 33-36R, 212; CAAE 212;
    CAAS 6; CANR 93; CP 1, 2, 3, 4, 5, 6,
    7; DLB 5
Espada, Martin 1957- .... **PC 74**
    See also CA 159; CANR 80; CP 7; EXPP;
    LLW; MAL 5; PFS 13, 16
Espriella, Don Manuel Alvarez
    See Southey, Robert
Espriu, Salvador 1913-1985 .... **CLC 9**
    See also CA 154; 115; DLB 134; EWL 3
Espronceda, Jose de 1808-1842 ..... **NCLC 39**
Esquivel, Laura 1950(?)- .. **CLC 141; HLCS**
    1
    See also AAYA 29; CA 143; CANR 68, 113,
    161; DA3; DNFS 2; LAIT 3; LMFS 2;
    MTCW 2; MTFW 2005; NFS 5; WLIT 1
Esse, James
    See Stephens, James
Esterbrook, Tom
    See Hubbard, L. Ron
Esterhazy, Peter 1950- .... **CLC 251**
    See also CA 140; CANR 137; CDWLB 4;
    CWW 2; DLB 232; EWL 3; RGWL 3
Estleman, Loren D. 1952- .... **CLC 48**
    See also AAYA 27; CA 85-88; CANR 27,
    74, 139, 177; CMW 4; CPW; DA3; DAM
    NOV, POP; DLB 226; INT CANR-27;
    MTCW 1, 2; MTFW 2005; TCWW 1, 2
Etherege, Sir George 1636-1692 . **DC 23; LC**
    78
    See also BRW 2; DAM DRAM; DLB 80;
    PAB; RGEL 2
Euclid 306B.C.-283B.C. .... **CMLC 25**
Eugenides, Jeffrey 1960- .... **CLC 81, 212**
    See also AAYA 51; CA 144; CANR 120;
    MTFW 2005; NFS 24
Euripides c. 484B.C.-406B.C. .... **CMLC 23,**
    51; DC 4; WLCS
    See also AW 1; CDWLB 1; DA; DA3;
    DAB; DAC; DAM DRAM, MST; DFS 1,
    4, 6, 25; DLB 176; LAIT 1; LMFS 1;
    RGWL 2, 3; WLIT 8
Eusebius c. 263-c. 339 .... **CMLC 103**
Evan, Evin
    See Faust, Frederick (Schiller)
Evans, Caradoc 1878-1945 ... **SSC 43; TCLC**
    85
    See also DLB 162
Evans, Evan
    See Faust, Frederick (Schiller)
Evans, Marian
    See Eliot, George
Evans, Mary Ann
    See Eliot, George

Evarts, Esther
    See Benson, Sally
Evelyn, John 1620-1706 .... **LC 144**
    See also BRW 2; RGEL 2
Everett, Percival 1956- .... **CLC 57**
    See Everett, Percival L.
    See also AMWS 18; BW 2; CA 129; CANR
    94, 134, 179; CN 7; MTFW 2005
Everett, Percival L.
    See Everett, Percival
    See also CSW
Everson, R(onald) G(ilmour)
    1903-1992 .... **CLC 27**
    See also CA 17-20R; CP 1, 2, 3, 4; DLB 88
Everson, William (Oliver)
    1912-1994 .... **CLC 1, 5, 14**
    See also BG 1:2; CA 9-12R; 145; CANR
    20; CP 1; DLB 5, 16, 212; MTCW 1
Evtushenko, Evgenii Aleksandrovich
    See Yevtushenko, Yevgeny (Alexandrovich)
Ewart, Gavin (Buchanan)
    1916-1995 .... **CLC 13, 46**
    See also BRWS 7; CA 89-92; 150; CANR
    17, 46; CP 1, 2, 3, 4, 5, 6; DLB 40;
    MTCW 1
Ewers, Hanns Heinz 1871-1943 ..... **TCLC 12**
    See also CA 109; 149
Ewing, Frederick R.
    See Sturgeon, Theodore (Hamilton)
Exley, Frederick (Earl) 1929-1992 .... **CLC 6,**
    11
    See also AITN 2; BPFB 1; CA 81-84; 138;
    CANR 117; DLB 143; DLBY 1981
Eynhardt, Guillermo
    See Quiroga, Horacio (Sylvestre)
Ezekiel, Nissim (Moses) 1924-2004 .. **CLC 61**
    See also CA 61-64; 223; CP 1, 2, 3, 4, 5, 6,
    7; DLB 323; EWL 3
Ezekiel, Tish O'Dowd 1943- .... **CLC 34**
    See also CA 129
Fadeev, Aleksandr Aleksandrovich
    See Bulgya, Alexander Alexandrovich
Fadeev, Alexandr Alexandrovich
    See Bulgya, Alexander Alexandrovich
Fadeyev, A.
    See Bulgya, Alexander Alexandrovich
Fadeyev, Alexander
    See Bulgya, Alexander Alexandrovich
Fagen, Donald 1948- .... **CLC 26**
Fainzil'berg, Il'ia Arnol'dovich
    See Fainzilberg, Ilya Arnoldovich
Fainzilberg, Ilya Arnoldovich
    1897-1937 .... **TCLC 21**
    See also CA 120; 165; DLB 272; EWL 3
Fair, Ronald L. 1932- .... **CLC 18**
    See also BW 1; CA 69-72; CANR 25; DLB
    33
Fairbairn, Roger
    See Carr, John Dickson
Fairbairns, Zoe (Ann) 1948- .... **CLC 32**
    See also CA 103; CANR 21, 85; CN 4, 5,
    6, 7
Fairfield, Flora
    See Alcott, Louisa May
Falco, Gian
    See Papini, Giovanni
Falconer, James
    See Kirkup, James
Falconer, Kenneth
    See Kornbluth, C(yril) M.
Falkland, Samuel
    See Heijermans, Herman
Fallaci, Oriana 1930-2006 .... **CLC 11, 110**
    See also CA 77-80; 253; CANR 15, 58, 134;
    FW; MTCW 1
Faludi, Susan 1959- .... **CLC 140**
    See also CA 138; CANR 126; FW; MTCW
    2; MTFW 2005; NCFS 3

Faludy, George 1913- .... **CLC 42**
See also CA 21-24R

Faludy, Gyoergy
See Faludy, George

Fanon, Frantz 1925-1961 ...... **BLC 1:2; CLC 74; TCLC 188**
See also BW 1; CA 116; 89-92; DAM MULT; DLB 296; LMFS 2; WLIT 2

Fanshawe, Ann 1625-1680 .... **LC 11**

Fante, John (Thomas) 1911-1983 .... **CLC 60; SSC 65**
See also AMWS 11; CA 69-72; 109; CANR 23, 104; DLB 130; DLBY 1983

Farah, Nuruddin 1945- .. **BLC 1:2, 2:2; CLC 53, 137**
See also AFW; BW 2, 3; CA 106; CANR 81, 148; CDWLB 3; CN 4, 5, 6, 7; DAM MULT; DLB 125; EWL 3; WLIT 2

Fardusi
See Ferdowsi, Abu'l Qasem

Fargue, Leon-Paul 1876(?)-1947 .... **TCLC 11**
See also CA 109; CANR 107; DLB 258; EWL 3

Farigoule, Louis
See Romains, Jules

Farina, Richard 1936(?)-1966 .... **CLC 9**
See also CA 81-84; 25-28R

Farley, Walter (Lorimer)
1915-1989 .... **CLC 17**
See also AAYA 58; BYA 14; CA 17-20R; CANR 8, 29, 84; DLB 22; JRDA; MAICYA 1, 2; SATA 2, 43, 132; YAW

Farmer, Philip Jose 1918-2009 ..... **CLC 1, 19**
See also AAYA 28; BPFB 1; CA 1-4R; CANR 4, 35, 111; DLB 8; MTCW 1; SATA 93; SCFW 1, 2; SFW 4

Farquhar, George 1677-1707 .... **LC 21**
See also BRW 2; DAM DRAM; DLB 84; RGEL 2

Farrell, J(ames) G(ordon)
1935-1979 .... **CLC 6**
See also CA 73-76; 89-92; CANR 36; CN 1, 2; DLB 14, 271, 326; MTCW 1; RGEL 2; RHW; WLIT 4

Farrell, James T(homas) 1904-1979 . **CLC 1, 4, 8, 11, 66; SSC 28**
See also AMW; BPFB 1; CA 5-8R; 89-92; CANR 9, 61; CN 1, 2; DLB 4, 9, 86; DLBD 2; EWL 3; MAL 5; MTCW 1, 2; MTFW 2005; RGAL 4

Farrell, M. J.
See Keane, Mary Nesta (Skrine)

Farrell, Warren (Thomas) 1943- ...... **CLC 70**
See also CA 146; CANR 120

Farren, Richard J.
See Betjeman, John

Farren, Richard M.
See Betjeman, John

Fassbinder, Rainer Werner
1946-1982 .... **CLC 20**
See also CA 93-96; 106; CANR 31

Fast, Howard 1914-2003 .... **CLC 23, 131**
See also AAYA 16; BPFB 1; CA 1-4R, 181; 214; CAAE 181; CAAS 18; CANR 1, 33, 54, 75, 98, 140; CMW 4; CN 1, 2, 3, 4, 5, 6, 7; CPW; DAM NOV; DLB 9; INT CANR-33; LATS 1:1; MAL 5; MTCW 2; MTFW 2005; RHW; SATA 7; SATA-Essay 107; TCWW 1, 2; YAW

Faulcon, Robert
See Holdstock, Robert

Faulkner, William (Cuthbert)
1897-1962 .... **CLC 1, 3, 6, 8, 9, 11, 14, 18, 28, 52, 68; SSC 1, 35, 42, 92, 97; TCLC 141; WLC 2**
See also AAYA 7; AMW; AMWR 1; BPFB 1; BYA 5, 15; CA 81-84; CANR 33; CDALB 1929-1941; DA; DA3; DAB; DAC; DAM MST, NOV; DLB 9, 11, 44,

102, 316, 330; DLBD 2; DLBY 1986, 1997; EWL 3; EXPN; EXPS; GL 2; LAIT 2; LATS 1:1; LMFS 2; MAL 5; MTCW 1, 2; MTFW 2005; NFS 4, 8, 13, 24; RGAL 4; RGSF 2; SSFS 2, 5, 6, 12, 27; TUS

Fauset, Jessie Redmon
1882(?)-1961 ...... **BLC 1:2; CLC 19, 54; HR 1:2**
See also AFAW 2; BW 1; CA 109; CANR 83; DAM MULT; DLB 51; FW; LMFS 2; MAL 5; MBL

Faust, Frederick (Schiller)
1892-1944 .... **TCLC 49**
See also BPFB 1; CA 108; 152; CANR 143; DAM POP; DLB 256; TCWW 1, 2; TUS

Faust, Irvin 1924- .... **CLC 8**
See also CA 33-36R; CANR 28, 67; CN 1, 2, 3, 4, 5, 6, 7; DLB 2, 28, 218, 278; DLBY 1980

Fawkes, Guy
See Benchley, Robert (Charles)

Fearing, Kenneth (Flexner)
1902-1961 .... **CLC 51**
See also CA 93-96; CANR 59; CMW 4; DLB 9; MAL 5; RGAL 4

Fecamps, Elise
See Creasey, John

Federman, Raymond 1928- .... **CLC 6, 47**
See also CA 17-20R, 208; CAAE 208; CAAS 8; CANR 10, 43, 83, 108; CN 3, 4, 5, 6; DLBY 1980

Federspiel, J.F. 1931-2007 .... **CLC 42**
See also CA 146; 257

Federspiel, Juerg F.
See Federspiel, J.F.

Federspiel, Jurg F.
See Federspiel, J.F.

Feiffer, Jules 1929- .... **CLC 2, 8, 64**
See also AAYA 3, 62; CA 17-20R; CAD; CANR 30, 59, 129, 161; CD 5, 6; DAM DRAM; DLB 7, 44; INT CANR-30; MTCW 1; SATA 8, 61, 111, 157

Feiffer, Jules Ralph
See Feiffer, Jules

Feige, Hermann Albert Otto Maximilian
See Traven, B.

Fei-Kan, Li
See Jin, Ba

Feinberg, David B. 1956-1994 .... **CLC 59**
See also CA 135; 147

Feinstein, Elaine 1930- .... **CLC 36**
See also CA 69-72; CAAS 1; CANR 31, 68, 121, 162; CN 3, 4, 5, 6, 7; CP 2, 3, 4, 5, 6, 7; CWP; DLB 14, 40; MTCW 1

Feke, Gilbert David .... **CLC 65**

Feldman, Irving (Mordecai) 1928- ..... **CLC 7**
See also CA 1-4R; CANR 1; CP 1, 2, 3, 4, 5, 6, 7; DLB 169; TCLE 1:1

Felix-Tchicaya, Gerald
See Tchicaya, Gerald Felix

Fellini, Federico 1920-1993 .... **CLC 16, 85**
See also CA 65-68; 143; CANR 33

Felltham, Owen 1602(?)-1668 .... **LC 92**
See also DLB 126, 151

Felsen, Henry Gregor 1916-1995 ..... **CLC 17**
See also CA 1-4R; 180; CANR 1; SAAS 2; SATA 1

Felski, Rita .... **CLC 65**

Fenelon, Francois de Pons de Salignac de la Mothe- 1651-1715 .... **LC 134**
See also DLB 268; EW 3; GFL Beginnings to 1789

Fenno, Jack
See Calisher, Hortense

Fenollosa, Ernest (Francisco)
1853-1908 .... **TCLC 91**

Fenton, James 1949- .... **CLC 32, 209**
See also CA 102; CANR 108, 160; CP 2, 3, 4, 5, 6, 7; DLB 40; PFS 11

Fenton, James Martin
See Fenton, James

Ferber, Edna 1887-1968 .... **CLC 18, 93**
See also AITN 1; CA 5-8R; 25-28R; CANR 68, 105; DLB 9, 28, 86, 266; MAL 5; MTCW 1, 2; MTFW 2005; RGAL 4; RHW; SATA 7; TCWW 1, 2

Ferdousi
See Ferdowsi, Abu'l Qasem

Ferdovsi
See Ferdowsi, Abu'l Qasem

Ferdowsi
See Ferdowsi, Abu'l Qasem

Ferdowsi, Abolghasem Mansour
See Ferdowsi, Abu'l Qasem

Ferdowsi, Abolqasem
See Ferdowsi, Abu'l Qasem

Ferdowsi, Abol-Qasem
See Ferdowsi, Abu'l Qasem

Ferdowsi, Abu'l Qasem
940-1020(?) .... **CMLC 43**
See also CA 276; RGWL 2, 3; WLIT 6

Ferdowsi, A.M.
See Ferdowsi, Abu'l Qasem

Ferdowsi, Hakim Abolghasem
See Ferdowsi, Abu'l Qasem

Ferguson, Helen
See Kavan, Anna

Ferguson, Niall 1964- .... **CLC 134, 250**
See also CA 190; CANR 154

Ferguson, Niall Campbell
See Ferguson, Niall

Ferguson, Samuel 1810-1886 .... **NCLC 33**
See also DLB 32; RGEL 2

Fergusson, Robert 1750-1774 .... **LC 29**
See also DLB 109; RGEL 2

Ferling, Lawrence
See Ferlinghetti, Lawrence

Ferlinghetti, Lawrence 1919(?)- .... **CLC 2, 6, 10, 27, 111; PC 1**
See also AAYA 74; BG 1:2; CA 5-8R; CAD; CANR 3, 41, 73, 125, 172; CDALB 1941-1968; CP 1, 2, 3, 4, 5, 6, 7; DA3; DAM POET; DLB 5, 16; MAL 5; MTCW 1, 2; MTFW 2005; PFS 28; RGAL 4; WP

Ferlinghetti, Lawrence Monsanto
See Ferlinghetti, Lawrence

Fern, Fanny
See Parton, Sara Payson Willis

Fernandez, Vicente Garcia Huidobro
See Huidobro Fernandez, Vicente Garcia

Fernandez-Armesto, Felipe .... **CLC 70**
See also CA 142; CANR 93, 153, 189

Fernandez-Armesto, Felipe Fermin Ricardo
1950-
See Fernandez-Armesto, Felipe

Fernandez de Lizardi, Jose Joaquin
See Lizardi, Jose Joaquin Fernandez de

Ferre, Rosario 1938- ...... **CLC 139; HLCS 1; SSC 36, 106**
See also CA 131; CANR 55, 81, 134; CWW 2; DLB 145; EWL 3; HW 1, 2; LAWS 1; MTCW 2; MTFW 2005; WLIT 1

Ferrer, Gabriel (Francisco Victor) Miro
See Miro (Ferrer), Gabriel (Francisco Victor)

Ferrier, Susan (Edmonstone)
1782-1854 .... **NCLC 8**
See also DLB 116; RGEL 2

Ferrigno, Robert 1947- .... **CLC 65**
See also CA 140; CANR 125, 161

Ferron, Jacques 1921-1985 .... **CLC 94**
See also CA 117; 129; CCA 1; DAC; DLB 60; EWL 3

Feuchtwanger, Lion 1884-1958 .... **TCLC 3**
 See also CA 104; 187; DLB 66; EWL 3;
 RGHL

Feuerbach, Ludwig 1804-1872 ..... **NCLC 139**
 See also DLB 133

Feuillet, Octave 1821-1890 .... **NCLC 45**
 See also DLB 192

Feydeau, Georges (Leon Jules Marie)
 1862-1921 .... **TCLC 22**
 See also CA 113; 152; CANR 84; DAM
 DRAM; DLB 192; EWL 3; GFL 1789 to
 the Present; RGWL 2, 3

Fichte, Johann Gottlieb
 1762-1814 .... **NCLC 62**
 See also DLB 90

Ficino, Marsilio 1433-1499 .... **LC 12, 152**
 See also LMFS 1

Fiedeler, Hans
 See Doeblin, Alfred

Fiedler, Leslie A(aron) 1917-2003 ..... **CLC 4,
 13, 24**
 See also AMWS 13; CA 9-12R; 212; CANR
 7, 63; CN 1, 2, 3, 4, 5, 6; DLB 28, 67;
 EWL 3; MAL 5; MTCW 1, 2; RGAL 4;
 TUS

Field, Andrew 1938- .... **CLC 44**
 See also CA 97-100; CANR 25

Field, Eugene 1850-1895 .... **NCLC 3**
 See also DLB 23, 42, 140; DLBD 13; MAI-
 CYA 1, 2; RGAL 4; SATA 16

Field, Gans T.
 See Wellman, Manly Wade

Field, Michael 1915-1971 .... **TCLC 43**
 See also CA 29-32R

Fielding, Helen 1958- .... **CLC 146, 217**
 See also AAYA 65; CA 172; CANR 127;
 DLB 231; MTFW 2005

Fielding, Henry 1707-1754 .... **LC 1, 46, 85,
 151, 154; WLC 2**
 See also BRW 3; BRWR 1; CDBLB 1660-
 1789; DA; DA3; DAB; DAC; DAM
 DRAM, MST, NOV; DLB 39, 84, 101;
 NFS 18; RGEL 2; TEA; WLIT 3

Fielding, Sarah 1710-1768 .... **LC 1, 44**
 See also DLB 39; RGEL 2; TEA

Fields, W. C. 1880-1946 .... **TCLC 80**
 See also DLB 44

Fierstein, Harvey (Forbes) 1954- ..... **CLC 33**
 See also CA 123; 129; CAD; CD 5, 6;
 CPW; DA3; DAM DRAM, POP; DFS 6;
 DLB 266; GLL; MAL 5

Figes, Eva 1932- .... **CLC 31**
 See also CA 53-56; CANR 4, 44, 83; CN 2,
 3, 4, 5, 6, 7; DLB 14, 271; FW; RGHL

Filippo, Eduardo de
 See de Filippo, Eduardo

Finch, Anne 1661-1720 ..... **LC 3, 137; PC 21**
 See also BRWS 9; DLB 95; PFS 30

Finch, Robert (Duer Claydon)
 1900-1995 .... **CLC 18**
 See also CA 57-60; CANR 9, 24, 49; CP 1,
 2, 3, 4, 5, 6; DLB 88

Findley, Timothy (Irving Frederick)
 1930-2002 .... **CLC 27, 102**
 See also CA 25-28R; 206; CANR 12, 42,
 69, 109; CCA 1; CN 4, 5, 6, 7; DAC;
 DAM MST; DLB 53; FANT; RHW

Fink, William
 See Mencken, H(enry) L(ouis)

Firbank, Louis 1942- .... **CLC 21**
 See also CA 117

Firbank, (Arthur Annesley) Ronald
 1886-1926 .... **TCLC 1**
 See also BRWS 2; CA 104; 177; DLB 36;
 EWL 3; RGEL 2

Firdaosi
 See Ferdowsi, Abu'l Qasem

Firdausi
 See Ferdowsi, Abu'l Qasem

Firdavsi, Abulqosimi
 See Ferdowsi, Abu'l Qasem

Firdavsii, Abulqosim
 See Ferdowsi, Abu'l Qasem

Firdawsi, Abu al-Qasim
 See Ferdowsi, Abu'l Qasem

Firdosi
 See Ferdowsi, Abu'l Qasem

Firdousi
 See Ferdowsi, Abu'l Qasem

Firdousi, Abu'l-Qasim
 See Ferdowsi, Abu'l Qasem

Firdovsi, A.
 See Ferdowsi, Abu'l Qasem

Firdovsi, Abulgasim
 See Ferdowsi, Abu'l Qasem

Firdusi
 See Ferdowsi, Abu'l Qasem

Fish, Stanley
 See Fish, Stanley Eugene

Fish, Stanley E.
 See Fish, Stanley Eugene

Fish, Stanley Eugene 1938- .... **CLC 142**
 See also CA 112; 132; CANR 90; DLB 67

Fisher, Dorothy (Frances) Canfield
 1879-1958 .... **TCLC 87**
 See also CA 114; 136; CANR 80; CLR 71;
 CWRI 5; DLB 9, 102, 284; MAICYA 1,
 2; MAL 5; YABC 1

Fisher, M(ary) F(rances) K(ennedy)
 1908-1992 .... **CLC 76, 87**
 See also AMWS 17; CA 77-80; 138; CANR
 44; MTCW 2

Fisher, Roy 1930- .... **CLC 25**
 See also CA 81-84; CAAS 10; CANR 16;
 CP 1, 2, 3, 4, 5, 6, 7; DLB 40

Fisher, Rudolph 1897-1934 ...... **BLC 1:2; HR
 1:2; SSC 25; TCLC 11**
 See also BW 1, 3; CA 107; 124; CANR 80;
 DAM MULT; DLB 51, 102

Fisher, Vardis (Alvero) 1895-1968 .... **CLC 7;
 TCLC 140**
 See also CA 5-8R; 25-28R; CANR 68; DLB
 9, 206; MAL 5; RGAL 4; TCWW 1, 2

Fiske, Tarleton
 See Bloch, Robert (Albert)

Fitch, Clarke
 See Sinclair, Upton

Fitch, John IV
 See Cormier, Robert

Fitzgerald, Captain Hugh
 See Baum, L(yman) Frank

FitzGerald, Edward 1809-1883 ...... **NCLC 9,
 153; PC 79**
 See also BRW 4; DLB 32; RGEL 2

Fitzgerald, F(rancis) Scott (Key)
 1896-1940 ... **SSC 6, 31, 75; TCLC 1, 6,
 14, 28, 55, 157; WLC 2**
 See also AAYA 24; AITN 1; AMW; AMWC
 2; AMWR 1; BPFB 1; CA 110; 123;
 CDALB 1917-1929; DA; DA3; DAB;
 DAC; DAM MST, NOV; DLB 4, 9, 86,
 219, 273; DLBD 1, 15, 16; DLBY 1981,
 1996; EWL 3; EXPN; EXPS; LAIT 3;
 MAL 5; MTCW 1, 2; MTFW 2005; NFS
 2, 19, 20; RGAL 4; RGSF 2; SSFS 4, 15,
 21, 25; TUS

Fitzgerald, Penelope 1916-2000 . **CLC 19, 51,
 61, 143**
 See also BRWS 5; CA 85-88; 190; CAAS
 10; CANR 56, 86, 131; CN 3, 4, 5, 6, 7;
 DLB 14, 194, 326; EWL 3; MTCW 2;
 MTFW 2005

Fitzgerald, Robert (Stuart)
 1910-1985 .... **CLC 39**
 See also CA 1-4R; 114; CANR 1; CP 1, 2,
 3, 4; DLBY 1980; MAL 5

FitzGerald, Robert D(avid)
 1902-1987 .... **CLC 19**
 See also CA 17-20R; CP 1, 2, 3, 4; DLB
 260; RGEL 2

Fitzgerald, Zelda (Sayre)
 1900-1948 .... **TCLC 52**
 See also AMWS 9; CA 117; 126; DLBY
 1984

Flanagan, Thomas (James Bonner)
 1923-2002 .... **CLC 25, 52**
 See also CA 108; 206; CANR 55; CN 3, 4,
 5, 6, 7; DLBY 1980; INT CA-108; MTCW
 1; RHW; TCLE 1:1

Flaubert, Gustave 1821-1880 .... **NCLC 2, 10,
 19, 62, 66, 135, 179, 185; SSC 11, 60;
 WLC 2**
 See also DA; DA3; DAB; DAC; DAM
 MST, NOV; DLB 119, 301; EW 7; EXPS;
 GFL 1789 to the Present; LAIT 2; LMFS
 1; NFS 14; RGSF 2; RGWL 2, 3; SSFS
 6; TWA

Flavius Josephus
 See Josephus, Flavius

Flecker, Herman Elroy
 See Flecker, (Herman) James Elroy

Flecker, (Herman) James Elroy
 1884-1915 .... **TCLC 43**
 See also CA 109; 150; DLB 10, 19; RGEL
 2

Fleming, Ian 1908-1964 ... **CLC 3, 30; TCLC
 193**
 See also AAYA 26; BPFB 1; BRWS 14; CA
 5-8R; CANR 59; CDBLB 1945-1960;
 CMW 4; CPW; DA3; DAM POP; DLB
 87, 201; MSW; MTCW 1, 2; MTFW
 2005; RGEL 2; SATA 9; TEA; YAW

Fleming, Ian Lancaster
 See Fleming, Ian

Fleming, Thomas 1927- .... **CLC 37**
 See also CA 5-8R; CANR 10, 102, 155;
 INT CANR-10; SATA 8

Fleming, Thomas James
 See Fleming, Thomas

Fletcher, John 1579-1625 . **DC 6; LC 33, 151**
 See also BRW 2; CDBLB Before 1660;
 DLB 58; RGEL 2; TEA

Fletcher, John Gould 1886-1950 .... **TCLC 35**
 See also CA 107; 167; DLB 4, 45; LMFS
 2; MAL 5; RGAL 4

Fleur, Paul
 See Pohl, Frederik

Flieg, Helmut
 See Heym, Stefan

Floogglebuckle, Al
 See Spiegelman, Art

Flying Officer X
 See Bates, H(erbert) E(rnest)

Fo, Dario 1926- .... **CLC 32, 109, 227; DC 10**
 See also CA 116; 128; CANR 68, 114, 134,
 164; CWW 2; DA3; DAM DRAM; DFS
 23; DLB 330; DLBY 1997; EWL 3;
 MTCW 1, 2; MTFW 2005; WLIT 7

Foden, Giles 1967- .... **CLC 231**
 See also CA 240; DLB 267; NFS 15

Fogarty, Jonathan Titulescu Esq.
 See Farrell, James T(homas)

Follett, Ken 1949- .... **CLC 18**
 See also AAYA 6, 50; BEST 89:4; BPFB 1;
 CA 81-84; CANR 13, 33, 54, 102, 156;
 CMW 4; CPW; DA3; DAM NOV, POP;
 DLB 87; DLBY 1981; INT CANR-33;
 MTCW 1

Follett, Kenneth Martin
 See Follett, Ken

Fondane, Benjamin 1898-1944 ..... **TCLC 159**

Fontane, Theodor 1819-1898 . **NCLC 26, 163**
 See also CDWLB 2; DLB 129; EW 6;
 RGWL 2, 3; TWA

Fonte, Moderata 1555-1592 .... **LC 118**

Fraser, Antonia 1932- .... **CLC 32, 107**
See also AAYA 57; CA 85-88; CANR 44, 65, 119, 164; CMW; DLB 276; MTCW 1, 2; MTFW 2005; SATA-Brief 32

Fraser, George MacDonald 1925-2008 .... **CLC 7**
See also AAYA 48; CA 45-48, 180; 268; CAAE 180; CANR 2, 48, 74; MTCW 2; RHW

Fraser, Sylvia 1935- .... **CLC 64**
See also CA 45-48; CANR 1, 16, 60; CCA 1

Frater Perdurabo
See Crowley, Edward Alexander

Frayn, Michael 1933- .... **CLC 3, 7, 31, 47, 176; DC 27**
See also AAYA 69; BRWC 2; BRWS 7; CA 5-8R; CANR 30, 69, 114, 133, 166; CBD; CD 5, 6; CN 1, 2, 3, 4, 5, 6, 7; DAM DRAM, NOV; DFS 22; DLB 13, 14, 194, 245; FANT; MTCW 1, 2; MTFW 2005; SFW 4

Fraze, Candida (Merrill) 1945- .... **CLC 50**
See also CA 126

Frazer, Andrew
See Marlowe, Stephen

Frazer, J(ames) G(eorge) 1854-1941 .... **TCLC 32**
See also BRWS 3; CA 118; NCFS 5

Frazer, Robert Caine
See Creasey, John

Frazer, Sir James George
See Frazer, J(ames) G(eorge)

Frazier, Charles 1950- .... **CLC 109, 224**
See also AAYA 34; CA 161; CANR 126, 170; CSW; DLB 292; MTFW 2005; NFS 25

Frazier, Charles R.
See Frazier, Charles

Frazier, Charles Robinson
See Frazier, Charles

Frazier, Ian 1951- .... **CLC 46**
See also CA 130; CANR 54, 93

Frederic, Harold 1856-1898 ... **NCLC 10, 175**
See also AMW; DLB 12, 23; DLBD 13; MAL 5; NFS 22; RGAL 4

Frederick, John
See Faust, Frederick (Schiller)

Frederick the Great 1712-1786 .... **LC 14**

Fredro, Aleksander 1793-1876 .... **NCLC 8**

Freeling, Nicolas 1927-2003 .... **CLC 38**
See also CA 49-52; 218; CAAS 12; CANR 1, 17, 50, 84; CMW 4; CN 1, 2, 3, 4, 5, 6; DLB 87

Freeman, Douglas Southall 1886-1953 .... **TCLC 11**
See also CA 109; 195; DLB 17; DLBD 17

Freeman, Judith 1946- .... **CLC 55**
See also CA 148; CANR 120, 179; DLB 256

Freeman, Mary E(leanor) Wilkins 1852-1930 .... **SSC 1, 47, 113; TCLC 9**
See also CA 106; 177; DLB 12, 78, 221; EXPS; FW; HGG; MBL; RGAL 4; RGSF 2; SSFS 4, 8, 26; SUFW 1; TUS

Freeman, R(ichard) Austin 1862-1943 .... **TCLC 21**
See also CA 113; CANR 84; CMW 4; DLB 70

French, Albert 1943- .... **CLC 86**
See also BW 3; CA 167

French, Antonia
See Kureishi, Hanif

French, Marilyn 1929- .. **CLC 10, 18, 60, 177**
See also BPFB 1; CA 69-72; CANR 3, 31, 134, 163; CN 5, 6, 7; CPW; DAM DRAM, NOV, POP; FL 1:5; FW; INT CANR-31; MTCW 1, 2; MTFW 2005

French, Paul
See Asimov, Isaac

Freneau, Philip Morin 1752-1832 .. **NCLC 1, 111**
See also AMWS 2; DLB 37, 43; RGAL 4

Freud, Sigmund 1856-1939 .... **TCLC 52**
See also CA 115; 133; CANR 69; DLB 296; EW 8; EWL 3; LATS 1:1; MTCW 1, 2; MTFW 2005; NCFS 3; TWA

Freytag, Gustav 1816-1895 .... **NCLC 109**
See also DLB 129

Friedan, Betty 1921-2006 .... **CLC 74**
See also CA 65-68; 248; CANR 18, 45, 74; DLB 246; FW; MTCW 1, 2; MTFW 2005; NCFS 5

Friedan, Betty Naomi
See Friedan, Betty

Friedlander, Saul 1932- .... **CLC 90**
See also CA 117; 130; CANR 72; RGHL

Friedman, B(ernard) H(arper) 1926- .... **CLC 7**
See also CA 1-4R; CANR 3, 48

Friedman, Bruce Jay 1930- ...... **CLC 3, 5, 56**
See also CA 9-12R; CAD; CANR 25, 52, 101; CD 5, 6; CN 1, 2, 3, 4, 5, 6, 7; DLB 2, 28, 244; INT CANR-25; MAL 5; SSFS 18

Friel, Brian 1929- .. **CLC 5, 42, 59, 115, 253; DC 8; SSC 76**
See also BRWS 5; CA 21-24R; CANR 33, 69, 131; CBD; CD 5, 6; DFS 11; DLB 13, 319; EWL 3; MTCW 1; RGEL 2; TEA

Friis-Baastad, Babbis Ellinor 1921-1970 .... **CLC 12**
See also CA 17-20R; 134; SATA 7

Frisch, Max 1911-1991 ...... **CLC 3, 9, 14, 18, 32, 44; TCLC 121**
See also CA 85-88; 134; CANR 32, 74; CD-WLB 2; DAM DRAM, NOV; DFS 25; DLB 69, 124; EW 13; EWL 3; MTCW 1, 2; MTFW 2005; RGHL; RGWL 2, 3

Fromentin, Eugene (Samuel Auguste) 1820-1876 .... **NCLC 10, 125**
See also DLB 123; GFL 1789 to the Present

Frost, Frederick
See Faust, Frederick (Schiller)

Frost, Robert 1874-1963 . **CLC 1, 3, 4, 9, 10, 13, 15, 26, 34, 44; PC 1, 39, 71; WLC 2**
See also AAYA 21; AMW; AMWR 1; CA 89-92; CANR 33; CDALB 1917-1929; CLR 67; DA; DA3; DAB; DAC; DAM MST, POET; DLB 54, 284, 342; DLBD 7; EWL 3; EXPP; MAL 5; MTCW 1, 2; MTFW 2005; PAB; PFS 1, 2, 3, 4, 5, 6, 7, 10, 13; RGAL 4; SATA 14; TUS; WP; WYA

Frost, Robert Lee
See Frost, Robert

Froude, James Anthony 1818-1894 .... **NCLC 43**
See also DLB 18, 57, 144

Froy, Herald
See Waterhouse, Keith (Spencer)

Fry, Christopher 1907-2005 ... **CLC 2, 10, 14**
See also BRWS 3; CA 17-20R; 240; CAAS 23; CANR 9, 30, 74, 132; CBD; CD 5, 6; CP 1, 2, 3, 4, 5, 6, 7; DAM DRAM; DLB 13; EWL 3; MTCW 1, 2; MTFW 2005; RGEL 2; SATA 66; TEA

Frye, (Herman) Northrop 1912-1991 .... **CLC 24, 70; TCLC 165**
See also CA 5-8R; 133; CANR 8, 37; DLB 67, 68, 246; EWL 3; MTCW 1, 2; MTFW 2005; RGAL 4; TWA

Fuchs, Daniel 1909-1993 .... **CLC 8, 22**
See also CA 81-84; 142; CAAS 5; CANR 40; CN 1, 2, 3, 4, 5; DLB 9, 26, 28; DLBY 1993; MAL 5

Fuchs, Daniel 1934- .... **CLC 34**
See also CA 37-40R; CANR 14, 48

Fuentes, Carlos 1928- .. **CLC 3, 8, 10, 13, 22, 41, 60, 113; HLC 1; SSC 24; WLC 2**
See also AAYA 4, 45; AITN 2; BPFB 1; CA 69-72; CANR 10, 32, 68, 104, 138; CDWLB 3; CWW 2; DA; DA3; DAB; DAC; DAM MST, MULT, NOV; DLB 113; DNFS 2; EWL 3; HW 1, 2; LAIT 3; LATS 1:2; LAW; LAWS 1; LMFS 2; MTCW 1, 2; MTFW 2005; NFS 8; RGSF 2; RGWL 2, 3; TWA; WLIT 1

Fuentes, Gregorio Lopez y
See Lopez y Fuentes, Gregorio

Fuertes, Gloria 1918-1998 .... **PC 27**
See also CA 178, 180; DLB 108; HW 2; SATA 115

Fugard, (Harold) Athol 1932- . **CLC 5, 9, 14, 25, 40, 80, 211; DC 3**
See also AAYA 17; AFW; CA 85-88; CANR 32, 54, 118; CD 5, 6; DAM DRAM; DFS 3, 6, 10, 24; DLB 225; DNFS 1, 2; EWL 3; LATS 1:2; MTCW 1; MTFW 2005; RGEL 2; WLIT 2

Fugard, Sheila 1932- .... **CLC 48**
See also CA 125

Fujiwara no Teika 1162-1241 .... **CMLC 73**
See also DLB 203

Fukuyama, Francis 1952- .... **CLC 131**
See also CA 140; CANR 72, 125, 170

Fuller, Charles (H.), (Jr.) 1939- ..... **BLC 1:2; CLC 25; DC 1**
See also BW 2; CA 108; 112; CAD; CANR 87; CD 5, 6; DAM DRAM, MULT; DFS 8; DLB 38, 266; EWL 3; INT CA-112; MAL 5; MTCW 1

Fuller, Henry Blake 1857-1929 .... **TCLC 103**
See also CA 108; 177; DLB 12; RGAL 4

Fuller, John (Leopold) 1937- .... **CLC 62**
See also CA 21-24R; CANR 9, 44; CP 1, 2, 3, 4, 5, 6, 7; DLB 40

Fuller, Margaret
See Ossoli, Sarah Margaret (Fuller)

Fuller, Roy (Broadbent) 1912-1991 ... **CLC 4, 28**
See also BRWS 7; CA 5-8R; 135; CAAS 10; CANR 53, 83; CN 1, 2, 3, 4, 5; CP 1, 2, 3, 4, 5; CWRI 5; DLB 15, 20; EWL 3; RGEL 2; SATA 87

Fuller, Sarah Margaret
See Ossoli, Sarah Margaret (Fuller)

Fuller, Thomas 1608-1661 .... **LC 111**
See also DLB 151

Fulton, Alice 1952- .... **CLC 52**
See also CA 116; CANR 57, 88; CP 5, 6, 7; CWP; DLB 193; PFS 25

Furey, Michael
See Ward, Arthur Henry Sarsfield

Furphy, Joseph 1843-1912 .... **TCLC 25**
See also CA 163; DLB 230; EWL 3; RGEL 2

Furst, Alan 1941- .... **CLC 255**
See also CA 69-72; CANR 12, 34, 59, 102, 159; DLBY 01

Fuson, Robert H(enderson) 1927- .... **CLC 70**
See also CA 89-92; CANR 103

Fussell, Paul 1924- .... **CLC 74**
See also BEST 90:1; CA 17-20R; CANR 8, 21, 35, 69, 135; INT CANR-21; MTCW 1, 2; MTFW 2005

Futabatei, Shimei 1864-1909 .... **TCLC 44**
See also CA 162; DLB 180; EWL 3; MJW

Futabatei Shimei
See Futabatei, Shimei

Futrelle, Jacques 1875-1912 .... **TCLC 19**
See also CA 113; 155; CMW 4

GAB
See Russell, George William

Garth, Will
See Hamilton, Edmond; Kuttner, Henry

Garvey, Marcus (Moziah, Jr.)
1887-1940 ..... **BLC 1:2; HR 1:2; TCLC 41**
See also BW 1; CA 120; 124; CANR 79; DAM MULT; DLB 345

Gary, Romain
See Kacew, Romain

Gascar, Pierre
See Fournier, Pierre

Gascoigne, George 1539-1577 .... **LC 108**
See also DLB 136; RGEL 2

Gascoyne, David (Emery)
1916-2001 .... **CLC 45**
See also CA 65-68; 200; CANR 10, 28, 54; CP 1, 2, 3, 4, 5, 6, 7; DLB 20; MTCW 1; RGEL 2

Gaskell, Elizabeth Cleghorn
1810-1865 .... **NCLC 5, 70, 97, 137, 214; SSC 25, 97**
See also BRW 5; CDBLB 1832-1890; DAB; DAM MST; DLB 21, 144, 159; RGEL 2; RGSF 2; TEA

Gass, William H. 1924- . **CLC 1, 2, 8, 11, 15, 39, 132; SSC 12**
See also AMWS 6; CA 17-20R; CANR 30, 71, 100; CN 1, 2, 3, 4, 5, 6, 7; DLB 2, 227; EWL 3; MAL 5; MTCW 1, 2; MTFW 2005; RGAL 4

Gassendi, Pierre 1592-1655 .... **LC 54**
See also GFL Beginnings to 1789

Gasset, Jose Ortega y
See Ortega y Gasset, Jose

Gates, Henry Louis, Jr. 1950- ... **BLCS; CLC 65**
See also BW 2, 3; CA 109; CANR 25, 53, 75, 125; CSW; DA3; DAM MULT; DLB 67; EWL 3; MAL 5; MTCW 2; MTFW 2005; RGAL 4

Gatos, Stephanie
See Katz, Steve

Gautier, Theophile 1811-1872 .. **NCLC 1, 59; PC 18; SSC 20**
See also DAM POET; DLB 119; EW 6; GFL 1789 to the Present; RGWL 2, 3; SUFW; TWA

Gautreaux, Tim 1947- .... **CLC 270**
See also CA 187; CSW; DLB 292

Gay, John 1685-1732 .... **LC 49**
See also BRW 3; DAM DRAM; DLB 84, 95; RGEL 2; WLIT 3

Gay, Oliver
See Gogarty, Oliver St. John

Gay, Peter 1923- .... **CLC 158**
See also CA 13-16R; CANR 18, 41, 77, 147; INT CANR-18; RGHL

Gay, Peter Jack
See Gay, Peter

Gaye, Marvin (Pentz, Jr.)
1939-1984 .... **CLC 26**
See also CA 195; 112

Gebler, Carlo 1954- .... **CLC 39**
See also CA 119; 133; CANR 96, 186; DLB 271

Gebler, Carlo Ernest
See Gebler, Carlo

Gee, Maggie 1948- .... **CLC 57**
See also CA 130; CANR 125; CN 4, 5, 6, 7; DLB 207; MTFW 2005

Gee, Maurice 1931- .... **CLC 29**
See also AAYA 42; CA 97-100; CANR 67, 123; CLR 56; CN 2, 3, 4, 5, 6, 7; CWRI 5; EWL 3; MAICYA 2; RGSF 2; SATA 46, 101

Gee, Maurice Gough
See Gee, Maurice

Geiogamah, Hanay 1945- .... **NNAL**
See also CA 153; DAM MULT; DLB 175

Gelbart, Larry
See Gelbart, Larry (Simon)

Gelbart, Larry (Simon) 1928- .... **CLC 21, 61**
See also CA 73-76; CAD; CANR 45, 94; CD 5, 6

Gelber, Jack 1932-2003 ...... **CLC 1, 6, 14, 79**
See also CA 1-4R; 216; CAD; CANR 2; DLB 7, 228; MAL 5

Gellhorn, Martha (Ellis)
1908-1998 .... **CLC 14, 60**
See also CA 77-80; 164; CANR 44; CN 1, 2, 3, 4, 5, 6 7; DLBY 1982, 1998

Genet, Jean 1910-1986 .. **CLC 1, 2, 5, 10, 14, 44, 46; DC 25; TCLC 128**
See also CA 13-16R; CANR 18; DA3; DAM DRAM; DFS 10; DLB 72, 321; DLBY 1986; EW 13; EWL 3; GFL 1789 to the Present; GLL 1; LMFS 2; MTCW 1, 2; MTFW 2005; RGWL 2, 3; TWA

Genlis, Stephanie-Felicite Ducrest
1746-1830 .... **NCLC 166**
See also DLB 313

Gent, Peter 1942- .... **CLC 29**
See also AITN 1; CA 89-92; DLBY 1982

Gentile, Giovanni 1875-1944 .... **TCLC 96**
See also CA 119

Geoffrey of Monmouth c.
1100-1155 .... **CMLC 44**
See also DLB 146; TEA

George, Jean
See George, Jean Craighead

George, Jean Craighead 1919- .... **CLC 35**
See also AAYA 8, 69; BYA 2, 4; CA 5-8R; CANR 25; CLR 1, 80, 136; DLB 52; JRDA; MAICYA 1, 2; SATA 2, 68, 124, 170; WYA; YAW

George, Stefan (Anton) 1868-1933 . **TCLC 2, 14**
See also CA 104; 193; EW 8; EWL 3

Georges, Georges Martin
See Simenon, Georges (Jacques Christian)

Gerald of Wales c. 1146-c. 1223 ... **CMLC 60**

Gerhardi, William Alexander
See Gerhardie, William Alexander

Gerhardie, William Alexander
1895-1977 .... **CLC 5**
See also CA 25-28R; 73-76; CANR 18; CN 1, 2; DLB 36; RGEL 2

Gerome
See Thibault, Jacques Anatole Francois

Gerson, Jean 1363-1429 .... **LC 77**
See also DLB 208

Gersonides 1288-1344 .... **CMLC 49**
See also DLB 115

Gerstler, Amy 1956- .... **CLC 70**
See also CA 146; CANR 99

Gertler, T. .... **CLC 34**
See also CA 116; 121

Gertrude of Helfta c. 1256-c.
1301 .... **CMLC 105**

Gertsen, Aleksandr Ivanovich
See Herzen, Aleksandr Ivanovich

Ghalib
See Ghalib, Asadullah Khan

Ghalib, Asadullah Khan
1797-1869 .... **NCLC 39, 78**
See also DAM POET; RGWL 2, 3

Ghelderode, Michel de 1898-1962 ..... **CLC 6, 11; DC 15; TCLC 187**
See also CA 85-88; CANR 40, 77; DAM DRAM; DLB 321; EW 11; EWL 3; TWA

Ghiselin, Brewster 1903-2001 .... **CLC 23**
See also CA 13-16R; CAAS 10; CANR 13; CP 1, 2, 3, 4, 5, 6, 7

Ghose, Aurabinda 1872-1950 .... **TCLC 63**
See also CA 163; EWL 3

Ghose, Aurobindo
See Ghose, Aurabinda

Ghose, Zulfikar 1935- .... **CLC 42, 200**
See also CA 65-68; CANR 67; CN 1, 2, 3, 4, 5, 6, 7; CP 1, 2, 3, 4, 5, 6, 7; DLB 323; EWL 3

Ghosh, Amitav 1956- .... **CLC 44, 153**
See also CA 147; CANR 80, 158; CN 6, 7; DLB 323; WWE 1

Giacosa, Giuseppe 1847-1906 .... **TCLC 7**
See also CA 104

Gibb, Lee
See Waterhouse, Keith (Spencer)

Gibbon, Edward 1737-1794 .... **LC 97**
See also BRW 3; DLB 104, 336; RGEL 2

Gibbon, Lewis Grassic
See Mitchell, James Leslie

Gibbons, Kaye 1960- .... **CLC 50, 88, 145**
See also AAYA 34; AMWS 10; CA 151; CANR 75, 127; CN 7; CSW; DA3; DAM POP; DLB 292; MTCW 2; MTFW 2005; NFS 3; RGAL 4; SATA 117

Gibran, Kahlil 1883-1931 ..... **PC 9; TCLC 1, 9, 205**
See also CA 104; 150; DA3; DAM POET, POP; DLB 346; EWL 3; MTCW 2; WLIT 6

Gibran, Khalil
See Gibran, Kahlil

Gibson, Mel 1956- .... **CLC 215**

Gibson, William 1914-2008 .... **CLC 23**
See also CA 9-12R; 279; CAD; CANR 9, 42, 75, 125; CD 5, 6; DA; DAB; DAC; DAM DRAM, MST; DFS 2; DLB 7; LAIT 2; MAL 5; MTCW 2; MTFW 2005; SATA 66; SATA-Obit 199; YAW

Gibson, William 1948- .... **CLC 39, 63, 186, 192; SSC 52**
See also AAYA 12, 59; AMWS 16; BPFB 2; CA 126; 133; CANR 52, 90, 106, 172; CN 6, 7; CPW; DA3; DAM POP; DLB 251; MTCW 2; MTFW 2005; SCFW 2; SFW 4; SSFS 26

Gibson, William Ford
See Gibson, William

Gide, Andre (Paul Guillaume)
1869-1951 ...... **SSC 13; TCLC 5, 12, 36, 177; WLC 3**
See also CA 104; 124; DA; DA3; DAB; DAC; DAM MST, NOV; DLB 65, 321, 330; EW 8; EWL 3; GFL 1789 to the Present; MTCW 1, 2; MTFW 2005; NFS 21; RGSF 2; RGWL 2, 3; TWA

Gifford, Barry 1946- .... **CLC 34**
See also CA 65-68; CANR 9, 30, 40, 90, 180

Gifford, Barry Colby
See Gifford, Barry

Gilbert, Frank
See De Voto, Bernard (Augustine)

Gilbert, W(illiam) S(chwenck)
1836-1911 .... **TCLC 3**
See also CA 104; 173; DAM DRAM, POET; DLB 344; RGEL 2; SATA 36

Gilbert of Poitiers c. 1085-1154 .... **CMLC 85**

Gilbreth, Frank B(unker), Jr.
1911-2001 .... **CLC 17**
See also CA 9-12R; SATA 2

Gilchrist, Ellen (Louise) 1935- .. **CLC 34, 48, 143, 264; SSC 14, 63**
See also BPFB 2; CA 113; 116; CANR 41, 61, 104; CN 4, 5, 6, 7; CPW; CSW; DAM POP; DLB 130; EWL 3; EXPS; MTCW 1, 2; MTFW 2005; RGAL 4; RGSF 2; SSFS 9

Gildas fl. 6th cent. - .... **CMLC 99**

Giles, Molly 1942- .... **CLC 39**
See also CA 126; CANR 98

Gill, Eric
See Gill, (Arthur) Eric (Rowton Peter Joseph)

Goldemberg, Isaac 1945- .... **CLC 52**
See also CA 69-72; CAAS 12; CANR 11, 32; EWL 3; HW 1; WLIT 1

Golding, Arthur 1536-1606 .... **LC 101**
See also DLB 136

Golding, William 1911-1993 . **CLC 1, 2, 3, 8, 10, 17, 27, 58, 81; WLC 3**
See also AAYA 5, 44; BPFB 2; BRWR 1; BRWS 1; BYA 2; CA 5-8R; 141; CANR 13, 33, 54; CD 5; CDBLB 1945-1960; CLR 94, 130; CN 1, 2, 3, 4; DA; DA3; DAB; DAC; DAM MST, NOV; DLB 15, 100, 255, 326, 330; EWL 3; EXPN; HGG; LAIT 4; MTCW 1, 2; MTFW 2005; NFS 2; RGEL 2; RHW; SFW 4; TEA; WLIT 4; YAW

Golding, William Gerald
See Golding, William

Goldman, Emma 1869-1940 .... **TCLC 13**
See also CA 110; 150; DLB 221; FW; RGAL 4; TUS

Goldman, Francisco 1954- .... **CLC 76**
See also CA 162; CANR 185

Goldman, William 1931- .... **CLC 1, 48**
See also BPFB 2; CA 9-12R; CANR 29, 69, 106; CN 1, 2, 3, 4, 5, 6, 7; DLB 44; FANT; IDFW 3, 4

Goldman, William W.
See Goldman, William

Goldmann, Lucien 1913-1970 .... **CLC 24**
See also CA 25-28; CAP 2

Goldoni, Carlo 1707-1793 .... **LC 4, 152**
See also DAM DRAM; EW 4; RGWL 2, 3; WLIT 7

Goldsberry, Steven 1949- .... **CLC 34**
See also CA 131

Goldsmith, Oliver 1730(?)-1774 .... **DC 8; LC 2, 48, 122; PC 77; WLC 3**
See also BRW 3; CDBLB 1660-1789; DA; DAB; DAC; DAM DRAM, MST, NOV, POET; DFS 1; DLB 39, 89, 104, 109, 142, 336; IDTP; RGEL 2; SATA 26; TEA; WLIT 3

Goldsmith, Peter
See Priestley, J(ohn) B(oynton)

Goldstein, Rebecca 1950- .... **CLC 239**
See also CA 144; CANR 99, 165; TCLE 1:1

Goldstein, Rebecca Newberger
See Goldstein, Rebecca

Gombrowicz, Witold 1904-1969 .... **CLC 4, 7, 11, 49**
See also CA 19-20; 25-28R; CANR 105; CAP 2; CDWLB 4; DAM DRAM; DLB 215; EW 12; EWL 3; RGWL 2, 3; TWA

Gomez de Avellaneda, Gertrudis 1814-1873 .... **NCLC 111**
See also LAW

Gomez de la Serna, Ramon 1888-1963 .... **CLC 9**
See also CA 153; 116; CANR 79; EWL 3; HW 1, 2

Goncharov, Ivan Alexandrovich 1812-1891 .... **NCLC 1, 63**
See also DLB 238; EW 6; RGWL 2, 3

Goncourt, Edmond (Louis Antoine Huot) de 1822-1896 .... **NCLC 7**
See also DLB 123; EW 7; GFL 1789 to the Present; RGWL 2, 3

Goncourt, Jules (Alfred Huot) de 1830-1870 .... **NCLC 7**
See also DLB 123; EW 7; GFL 1789 to the Present; RGWL 2, 3

Gongora (y Argote), Luis de 1561-1627 .... **LC 72**
See also RGWL 2, 3

Gontier, Fernande 19(?)- .... **CLC 50**

Gonzalez Martinez, Enrique
See Gonzalez Martinez, Enrique

Gonzalez Martinez, Enrique 1871-1952 .... **TCLC 72**
See also CA 166; CANR 81; DLB 290; EWL 3; HW 1, 2

Goodison, Lorna 1947- .... **BLC 2:2; PC 36**
See also CA 142; CANR 88, 189; CP 5, 6, 7; CWP; DLB 157; EWL 3; PFS 25

Goodman, Allegra 1967- .... **CLC 241**
See also CA 204; CANR 162; DLB 244

Goodman, Paul 1911-1972 ..... **CLC 1, 2, 4, 7**
See also CA 19-20; 37-40R; CAD; CANR 34; CAP 2; CN 1; DLB 130, 246; MAL 5; MTCW 1; RGAL 4

Goodweather, Hartley
See King, Thomas

GoodWeather, Hartley
See King, Thomas

Googe, Barnabe 1540-1594 .... **LC 94**
See also DLB 132; RGEL 2

Gordimer, Nadine 1923- ...... **CLC 3, 5, 7, 10, 18, 33, 51, 70, 123, 160, 161, 263; SSC 17, 80; WLCS**
See also AAYA 39; AFW; BRWS 2; CA 5-8R; CANR 3, 28, 56, 88, 131; CN 1, 2, 3, 4, 5, 6, 7; DA; DA3; DAB; DAC; DAM MST, NOV; DLB 225, 326, 330; EWL 3; EXPS; INT CANR-28; LATS 1:2; MTCW 1, 2; MTFW 2005; NFS 4; RGEL 2; RGSF 2; SSFS 2, 14, 19; TWA; WLIT 2; YAW

Gordon, Adam Lindsay 1833-1870 .... **NCLC 21**
See also DLB 230

Gordon, Caroline 1895-1981 . **CLC 6, 13, 29, 83; SSC 15**
See also AMW; CA 11-12; 103; CANR 36; CAP 1; CN 1, 2; DLB 4, 9, 102; DLBD 17; DLBY 1981; EWL 3; MAL 5; MTCW 1, 2; MTFW 2005; RGAL 4; RGSF 2

Gordon, Charles William 1860-1937 .... **TCLC 31**
See also CA 109; DLB 92; TCWW 1, 2

Gordon, Mary 1949- .. **CLC 13, 22, 128, 216; SSC 59**
See also AMWS 4; BPFB 2; CA 102; CANR 44, 92, 154, 179; CN 4, 5, 6, 7; DLB 6; DLBY 1981; FW; INT CA-102; MAL 5; MTCW 1

Gordon, Mary Catherine
See Gordon, Mary

Gordon, N. J.
See Bosman, Herman Charles

Gordon, Sol 1923- .... **CLC 26**
See also CA 53-56; CANR 4; SATA 11

Gordone, Charles 1925-1995 .... **BLC 2:2; CLC 1, 4; DC 8**
See also BW 1, 3; CA 93-96; 180; 150; CAAE 180; CAD; CANR 55; DAM DRAM; DLB 7; INT CA-93-96; MTCW 1

Gore, Catherine 1800-1861 .... **NCLC 65**
See also DLB 116, 344; RGEL 2

Gorenko, Anna Andreevna
See Akhmatova, Anna

Gor'kii, Maksim
See Peshkov, Alexei Maximovich

Gorky, Maxim
See Peshkov, Alexei Maximovich

Goryan, Sirak
See Saroyan, William

Gosse, Edmund (William) 1849-1928 .... **TCLC 28**
See also CA 117; DLB 57, 144, 184; RGEL 2

Gotlieb, Phyllis (Fay Bloom) 1926- .. **CLC 18**
See also CA 13-16R; CANR 7, 135; CN 7; CP 1, 2, 3, 4; DLB 88, 251; SFW 4

Gottesman, S. D.
See Kornbluth, C(yril) M.; Pohl, Frederik

Gottfried von Strassburg fl. c. 1170-1215 .... **CMLC 10, 96**
See also CDWLB 2; DLB 138; EW 1; RGWL 2, 3

Gotthelf, Jeremias 1797-1854 .... **NCLC 117**
See also DLB 133; RGWL 2, 3

Gottschalk, Laura Riding
See Jackson, Laura (Riding)

Gould, Lois 1932(?)-2002 .... **CLC 4, 10**
See also CA 77-80; 208; CANR 29; MTCW 1

Gould, Stephen Jay 1941-2002 .... **CLC 163**
See also AAYA 26; BEST 90:2; CA 77-80; 205; CANR 10, 27, 56, 75, 125; CPW; INT CANR-27; MTCW 1, 2; MTFW 2005

Gourmont, Remy(-Marie-Charles) de 1858-1915 .... **TCLC 17**
See also CA 109; 150; GFL 1789 to the Present; MTCW 2

Gournay, Marie le Jars de
See de Gournay, Marie le Jars

Govier, Katherine 1948- .... **CLC 51**
See also CA 101; CANR 18, 40, 128; CCA 1

Gower, John c. 1330-1408 .... **LC 76; PC 59**
See also BRW 1; DLB 146; RGEL 2

Goyen, (Charles) William 1915-1983 .... **CLC 5, 8, 14, 40**
See also AITN 2; CA 5-8R; 110; CANR 6, 71; CN 1, 2, 3; DLB 2, 218; DLBY 1983; EWL 3; INT CANR-6; MAL 5

Goytisolo, Juan 1931- .... **CLC 5, 10, 23, 133; HLC 1**
See also CA 85-88; CANR 32, 61, 131, 182; CWW 2; DAM MULT; DLB 322; EWL 3; GLL 2; HW 1, 2; MTCW 1, 2; MTFW 2005

Gozzano, Guido 1883-1916 .... **PC 10**
See also CA 154; DLB 114; EWL 3

Gozzi, (Conte) Carlo 1720-1806 .... **NCLC 23**

Grabbe, Christian Dietrich 1801-1836 .... **NCLC 2**
See also DLB 133; RGWL 2, 3

Grace, Patricia Frances 1937- .... **CLC 56**
See also CA 176; CANR 118; CN 4, 5, 6, 7; EWL 3; RGSF 2

Gracian, Baltasar 1601-1658 .... **LC 15, 160**

Gracian y Morales, Baltasar
See Gracian, Baltasar

Gracq, Julien 1910-2007 ..... **CLC 11, 48, 259**
See also CA 122; 126; 267; CANR 141; CWW 2; DLB 83; GFL 1789 to the present

Grade, Chaim 1910-1982 .... **CLC 10**
See also CA 93-96; 107; DLB 333; EWL 3; RGHL

Grade, Khayim
See Grade, Chaim

Graduate of Oxford, A
See Ruskin, John

Grafton, Garth
See Duncan, Sara Jeannette

Grafton, Sue 1940- .... **CLC 163**
See also AAYA 11, 49; BEST 90:3; CA 108; CANR 31, 55, 111, 134; CMW 4; CPW; CSW; DA3; DAM POP; DLB 226; FW; MSW; MTFW 2005

Graham, John
See Phillips, David Graham

Graham, Jorie 1950- .... **CLC 48, 118; PC 59**
See also AAYA 67; CA 111; CANR 63, 118; CP 4, 5, 6, 7; CWP; DLB 120; EWL 3; MTFW 2005; PFS 10, 17; TCLE 1:1

Graham, R(obert) B(ontine) Cunninghame
See Cunninghame Graham, Robert (Gallnigad) Bontine

Graham, Robert
See Haldeman, Joe

Griffin, Gerald 1803-1840 .... **NCLC 7**
See also DLB 159; RGEL 2

Griffin, John Howard 1920-1980 ..... **CLC 68**
See also AITN 1; CA 1-4R; 101; CANR 2

Griffin, Peter 1942- .... **CLC 39**
See also CA 136

Griffith, David Lewelyn Wark
See Griffith, D.W.

Griffith, D.W. 1875(?)-1948 .... **TCLC 68**
See also AAYA 78; CA 119; 150; CANR 80

Griffith, Lawrence
See Griffith, D.W.

Griffiths, Trevor 1935- .... **CLC 13, 52**
See also CA 97-100; CANR 45; CBD; CD
5, 6; DLB 13, 245

Griggs, Sutton (Elbert)
1872-1930 .... **TCLC 77**
See also CA 123; 186; DLB 50

Grigson, Geoffrey (Edward Harvey)
1905-1985 .... **CLC 7, 39**
See also CA 25-28R; 118; CANR 20, 33;
CP 1, 2, 3, 4; DLB 27; MTCW 1, 2

Grile, Dod
See Bierce, Ambrose (Gwinett)

Grillparzer, Franz 1791-1872 .... **DC 14;**
NCLC 1, 102; SSC 37
See also CDWLB 2; DLB 133; EW 5;
RGWL 2, 3; TWA

Grimble, Reverend Charles James
See Eliot, T(homas) S(tearns)

Grimke, Angelina (Emily) Weld
1880-1958 .... **HR 1:2**
See also BW 1; CA 124; DAM POET; DLB
50, 54; FW

Grimke, Charlotte L(ottie) Forten
1837(?)-1914 .... **BLC 1:2; TCLC 16**
See also BW 1; CA 117; 124; DAM MULT,
POET; DLB 50, 239

Grimm, Jacob Ludwig Karl
1785-1863 .... **NCLC 3, 77; SSC 36, 88**
See also CLR 112; DLB 90; MAICYA 1, 2;
RGSF 2; RGWL 2, 3; SATA 22; WCH

Grimm, Wilhelm Karl 1786-1859 .. **NCLC 3,**
77; SSC 36
See also CDWLB 2; CLR 112; DLB 90;
MAICYA 1, 2; RGSF 2; RGWL 2, 3;
SATA 22; WCH

Grimm and Grim
See Grimm, Jacob Ludwig Karl; Grimm,
Wilhelm Karl

Grimm Brothers
See Grimm, Jacob Ludwig Karl; Grimm,
Wilhelm Karl

Grimmelshausen, Hans Jakob Christoffel
von
See Grimmelshausen, Johann Jakob Christoffel von

Grimmelshausen, Johann Jakob Christoffel
von 1621-1676 .... **LC 6**
See also CDWLB 2; DLB 168; RGWL 2, 3

Grindel, Eugene 1895-1952 .... **PC 38; TCLC**
7, 41
See also CA 104; 193; EWL 3; GFL 1789
to the Present; LMFS 2; RGWL 2, 3

Grisham, John 1955- .... **CLC 84, 273**
See also AAYA 14, 47; BPFB 2; CA 138;
CANR 47, 69, 114, 133; CMW 4; CN 6,
7; CPW; CSW; DA3; DAM POP; MSW;
MTCW 2; MTFW 2005

Grosseteste, Robert 1175(?)-1253 . **CMLC 62**
See also DLB 115

Grossman, David 1954- .... **CLC 67, 231**
See also CA 138; CANR 114, 175; CWW
2; DLB 299; EWL 3; RGHL; WLIT 6

Grossman, Vasilii Semenovich
See Grossman, Vasily (Semenovich)

Grossman, Vasily (Semenovich)
1905-1964 .... **CLC 41**
See also CA 124; 130; DLB 272; MTCW 1;
RGHL

Grove, Frederick Philip
See Greve, Felix Paul (Berthold Friedrich)

Grubb
See Crumb, R.

Grumbach, Doris 1918- .... **CLC 13, 22, 64**
See also CA 5-8R; CAAS 2; CANR 9, 42,
70, 127; CN 6, 7; INT CANR-9; MTCW
2; MTFW 2005

Grundtvig, Nikolai Frederik Severin
1783-1872 .... **NCLC 1, 158**
See also DLB 300

Grunge
See Crumb, R.

Grunwald, Lisa 1959- .... **CLC 44**
See also CA 120; CANR 148

Gryphius, Andreas 1616-1664 .... **LC 89**
See also CDWLB 2; DLB 164; RGWL 2, 3

Guare, John 1938- .... **CLC 8, 14, 29, 67; DC**
20
See also CA 73-76; CAD; CANR 21, 69,
118; CD 5, 6; DAM DRAM; DFS 8, 13;
DLB 7, 249; EWL 3; MAL 5; MTCW 1,
2; RGAL 4

Guarini, Battista 1538-1612 .... **LC 102**
See also DLB 339

Gubar, Susan 1944- .... **CLC 145**
See also CA 108; CANR 45, 70, 139, 179;
FW; MTCW 1; RGAL 4

Gubar, Susan David
See Gubar, Susan

Gudjonsson, Halldor Kiljan
1902-1998 .... **CLC 25**
See also CA 103; 164; CWW 2; DLB 293,
331; EW 12; EWL 3; RGWL 2, 3

Guedes, Vincente
See Pessoa, Fernando

Guenter, Erich
See Eich, Gunter

Guest, Barbara 1920-2006 ... **CLC 34; PC 55**
See also BG 1:2; CA 25-28R; 248; CANR
11, 44, 84; CP 1, 2, 3, 4, 5, 6, 7; CWP;
DLB 5, 193

Guest, Edgar A(lbert) 1881-1959 ... **TCLC 95**
See also CA 112; 168

Guest, Judith 1936- .... **CLC 8, 30**
See also AAYA 7, 66; CA 77-80; CANR
15, 75, 138; DA3; DAM NOV, POP;
EXPN; INT CANR-15; LAIT 5; MTCW
1, 2; MTFW 2005; NFS 1

Guevara, Che
See Guevara (Serna), Ernesto

Guevara (Serna), Ernesto
1928-1967 .... **CLC 87; HLC 1**
See also CA 127; 111; CANR 56; DAM
MULT; HW 1

Guicciardini, Francesco 1483-1540 ..... **LC 49**

Guido delle Colonne c. 1215-c.
1290 .... **CMLC 90**

Guild, Nicholas M. 1944- .... **CLC 33**
See also CA 93-96

Guillemin, Jacques
See Sartre, Jean-Paul

Guillen, Jorge 1893-1984 . **CLC 11; HLCS 1;**
PC 35
See also CA 89-92; 112; DAM MULT,
POET; DLB 108; EWL 3; HW 1; RGWL
2, 3

Guillen, Nicolas (Cristobal)
1902-1989 .... **BLC 1:2; CLC 48, 79;**
HLC 1; PC 23
See also BW 2; CA 116; 125; 129; CANR
84; DAM MST, MULT, POET; DLB 283;
EWL 3; HW 1; LAW; RGWL 2, 3; WP

Guillen y Alvarez, Jorge
See Guillen, Jorge

Guillevic, (Eugene) 1907-1997 .... **CLC 33**
See also CA 93-96; CWW 2

Guillois
See Desnos, Robert

Guillois, Valentin
See Desnos, Robert

Guimaraes Rosa, Joao 1908-1967 ... **CLC 23;**
HLCS 1
See also CA 175; 89-92; DLB 113, 307;
EWL 3; LAW; RGSF 2; RGWL 2, 3;
WLIT 1

Guiney, Louise Imogen
1861-1920 .... **TCLC 41**
See also CA 160; DLB 54; RGAL 4

Guinizelli, Guido c. 1230-1276 ...... **CMLC 49**
See also WLIT 7

Guinizzelli, Guido
See Guinizelli, Guido

Guiraldes, Ricardo (Guillermo)
1886-1927 .... **TCLC 39**
See also CA 131; EWL 3; HW 1; LAW;
MTCW 1

Gumilev, Nikolai (Stepanovich)
1886-1921 .... **TCLC 60**
See also CA 165; DLB 295; EWL 3

Gumilyov, Nikolay Stepanovich
See Gumilev, Nikolai (Stepanovich)

Gump, P. Q.
See Card, Orson Scott

Gump, P.Q.
See Card, Orson Scott

Gunesekera, Romesh 1954- .... **CLC 91**
See also BRWS 10; CA 159; CANR 140,
172; CN 6, 7; DLB 267, 323

Gunn, Bill
See Gunn, William Harrison

Gunn, Thom(son William)
1929-2004 . **CLC 3, 6, 18, 32, 81; PC 26**
See also BRWS 4; CA 17-20R; 227; CANR
9, 33, 116; CDBLB 1960 to Present; CP
1, 2, 3, 4, 5, 6, 7; DAM POET; DLB 27;
INT CANR-33; MTCW 1; PFS 9; RGEL
2

Gunn, William Harrison
1934(?)-1989 .... **CLC 5**
See also AITN 1; BW 1, 3; CA 13-16R;
128; CANR 12, 25, 76; DLB 38

Gunn Allen, Paula
See Allen, Paula Gunn

Gunnars, Kristjana 1948- .... **CLC 69**
See also CA 113; CCA 1; CP 6, 7; CWP;
DLB 60

Gunter, Erich
See Eich, Gunter

Gurdjieff, G(eorgei) I(vanovich)
1877(?)-1949 .... **TCLC 71**
See also CA 157

Gurganus, Allan 1947- .... **CLC 70**
See also BEST 90:1; CA 135; CANR 114;
CN 6, 7; CPW; CSW; DAM POP; GLL 1

Gurney, A. R.
See Gurney, A(lbert) R(amsdell), Jr.

Gurney, A(lbert) R(amsdell), Jr.
1930- .... **CLC 32, 50, 54**
See also AMWS 5; CA 77-80; CAD; CANR
32, 64, 121; CD 5, 6; DAM DRAM; DLB
266; EWL 3

Gurney, Ivor (Bertie) 1890-1937 ... **TCLC 33**
See also BRW 6; CA 167; DLBY 2002;
PAB; RGEL 2

Gurney, Peter
See Gurney, A(lbert) R(amsdell), Jr.

Guro, Elena (Genrikhovna)
1877-1913 .... **TCLC 56**
See also DLB 295

Gustafson, James M(oody) 1925- ... **CLC 100**
See also CA 25-28R; CANR 37

Gustafson, Ralph (Barker)
1909-1995 .... CLC 36
See also CA 21-24R; CANR 8, 45, 84; CP
1, 2, 3, 4, 5, 6; DLB 88; RGEL 2

Gut, Gom
See Simenon, Georges (Jacques Christian)

Guterson, David 1956- .... CLC 91
See also CA 132; CANR 73, 126; CN 7;
DLB 292; MTCW 2; MTFW 2005; NFS
13

Guthrie, A(lfred) B(ertram), Jr.
1901-1991 .... CLC 23
See also CA 57-60; 134; CANR 24; CN 1,
2, 3; DLB 6, 212; MAL 5; SATA 62;
SATA-Obit 67; TCWW 1, 2

Guthrie, Isobel
See Grieve, C(hristopher) M(urray)

Gutierrez Najera, Manuel
1859-1895 .... HLCS 2; NCLC 133
See also DLB 290; LAW

Guy, Rosa (Cuthbert) 1925- .... CLC 26
See also AAYA 4, 37; BW 2; CA 17-20R;
CANR 14, 34, 83; CLR 13, 137; DLB 33;
DNFS 1; JRDA; MAICYA 1, 2; SATA 14,
62, 122; YAW

Gwendolyn
See Bennett, (Enoch) Arnold

H. D.
See Doolittle, Hilda

H. de V.
See Buchan, John

Haavikko, Paavo Juhani 1931- .. CLC 18, 34
See also CA 106; CWW 2; EWL 3

Habbema, Koos
See Heijermans, Herman

Habermas, Juergen 1929- .... CLC 104
See also CA 109; CANR 85, 162; DLB 242

Habermas, Jurgen
See Habermas, Juergen

Hacker, Marilyn 1942- ...... CLC 5, 9, 23, 72,
91; PC 47
See also CA 77-80; CANR 68, 129; CP 3,
4, 5, 6, 7; CWP; DAM POET; DLB 120,
282; FW; GLL 2; MAL 5; PFS 19

Hadewijch of Antwerp fl. 1250- ... CMLC 61
See also RGWL 3

Hadrian 76-138 .... CMLC 52

Haeckel, Ernst Heinrich (Philipp August)
1834-1919 .... TCLC 83
See also CA 157

Hafiz c. 1326-1389(?) .... CMLC 34
See also RGWL 2, 3; WLIT 6

Hagedorn, Jessica T(arahata)
1949- .... CLC 185
See also CA 139; CANR 69; CWP; DLB
312; RGAL 4

Haggard, H(enry) Rider
1856-1925 .... TCLC 11
See also BRWS 3; BYA 4, 5; CA 108; 148;
CANR 112; DLB 70, 156, 174, 178;
FANT; LMFS 1; MTCW 2; RGEL 2;
RHW; SATA 16; SCFW 1, 2; SFW 4;
SUFW 1; WLIT 4

Hagiosy, L.
See Larbaud, Valery (Nicolas)

Hagiwara, Sakutaro 1886-1942 .... PC 18;
TCLC 60
See also CA 154; EWL 3; RGWL 3

Hagiwara Sakutaro
See Hagiwara, Sakutaro

Haig, Fenil
See Ford, Ford Madox

Haig-Brown, Roderick (Langmere)
1908-1976 .... CLC 21
See also CA 5-8R; 69-72; CANR 4, 38, 83;
CLR 31; CWRI 5; DLB 88; MAICYA 1,
2; SATA 12; TCWW 2

Haight, Rip
See Carpenter, John (Howard)

Haij, Vera
See Jansson, Tove (Marika)

Hailey, Arthur 1920-2004 .... CLC 5
See also AITN 2; BEST 90:3; BPFB 2; CA
1-4R; 233; CANR 2, 36, 75; CCA 1; CN
1, 2, 3, 4, 5, 6, 7; CPW; DAM NOV, POP;
DLB 88; DLBY 1982; MTCW 1, 2;
MTFW 2005

Hailey, Elizabeth Forsythe 1938- ..... CLC 40
See also CA 93-96, 188; CAAE 188; CAAS
1; CANR 15, 48; INT CANR-15

Haines, John (Meade) 1924- .... CLC 58
See also AMWS 12; CA 17-20R; CANR
13, 34; CP 1, 2, 3, 4, 5; CSW; DLB 5,
212; TCLE 1:1

Ha Jin
See Jin, Xuefei

Hakluyt, Richard 1552-1616 .... LC 31
See also DLB 136; RGEL 2

Haldeman, Joe 1943- .... CLC 61
See also AAYA 38; CA 53-56, 179; CAAE
179; CAAS 25; CANR 6, 70, 72, 130,
171; DLB 8; INT CANR-6; SCFW 2;
SFW 4

Haldeman, Joe William
See Haldeman, Joe

Hale, Janet Campbell 1947- .... NNAL
See also CA 49-52; CANR 45, 75; DAM
MULT; DLB 175; MTCW 2; MTFW 2005

Hale, Sarah Josepha (Buell)
1788-1879 .... NCLC 75
See also DLB 1, 42, 73, 243

Halevy, Elie 1870-1937 .... TCLC 104

Haley, Alex(ander Murray Palmer)
1921-1992 ...... BLC 1:2; CLC 8, 12, 76;
TCLC 147
See also AAYA 26; BPFB 2; BW 2, 3; CA
77-80; 136; CANR 61; CDALBS; CPW;
CSW; DA; DA3; DAB; DAC; DAM MST,
MULT, POP; DLB 38; LAIT 5; MTCW
1, 2; NFS 9

Haliburton, Thomas Chandler
1796-1865 .... NCLC 15, 149
See also DLB 11, 99; RGEL 2; RGSF 2

Hall, Donald 1928- ... CLC 1, 13, 37, 59, 151,
240; PC 70
See also AAYA 63; CA 5-8R; CAAS 7;
CANR 2, 44, 64, 106, 133; CP 1, 2, 3, 4,
5, 6, 7; DAM POET; DLB 5, 342; MAL
5; MTCW 2; MTFW 2005; RGAL 4;
SATA 23, 97

Hall, Donald Andrew, Jr.
See Hall, Donald

Hall, Frederic Sauser
See Sauser-Hall, Frederic

Hall, James
See Kuttner, Henry

Hall, James Norman 1887-1951 ..... TCLC 23
See also CA 123; 173; LAIT 1; RHW 1;
SATA 21

Hall, Joseph 1574-1656 .... LC 91
See also DLB 121, 151; RGEL 2

Hall, Marguerite Radclyffe
See Hall, Radclyffe

Hall, Radclyffe 1880-1943 ...... TCLC 12, 215
See also BRWS 6; CA 110; 150; CANR 83;
DLB 191; MTCW 2; MTFW 2005; RGEL
2; RHW

Hall, Rodney 1935- .... CLC 51
See also CA 109; CANR 69; CN 6, 7; CP
1, 2, 3, 4, 5, 6, 7; DLB 289

Hallam, Arthur Henry
1811-1833 .... NCLC 110
See also DLB 32

Halldor Laxness
See Gudjonsson, Halldor Kiljan

Halleck, Fitz-Greene 1790-1867 .... NCLC 47
See also DLB 3, 250; RGAL 4

Halliday, Michael
See Creasey, John

Halpern, Daniel 1945- .... CLC 14
See also CA 33-36R; CANR 93, 174; CP 3,
4, 5, 6, 7

Hamburger, Michael 1924-2007 ... CLC 5, 14
See also CA 5-8R, 196; 261; CAAE 196;
CAAS 4; CANR 2, 47; CP 1, 2, 3, 4, 5, 6,
7; DLB 27

Hamburger, Michael Peter Leopold
See Hamburger, Michael

Hamill, Pete 1935- .... CLC 10, 261
See also CA 25-28R; CANR 18, 71, 127,
180

Hamill, William Peter
See Hamill, Pete

Hamilton, Alexander 1712-1756 .... LC 150
See also DLB 31

Hamilton, Alexander
1755(?)-1804 .... NCLC 49
See also DLB 37

Hamilton, Clive
See Lewis, C.S.

Hamilton, Edmond 1904-1977 .... CLC 1
See also CA 1-4R; CANR 3, 84; DLB 8;
SATA 118; SFW 4

Hamilton, Elizabeth 1758-1816 ... NCLC 153
See also DLB 116, 158

Hamilton, Eugene (Jacob) Lee
See Lee-Hamilton, Eugene (Jacob)

Hamilton, Franklin
See Silverberg, Robert

Hamilton, Gail
See Corcoran, Barbara (Asenath)

Hamilton, (Robert) Ian 1938-2001 . CLC 191
See also CA 106; 203; CANR 41, 67; CP 1,
2, 3, 4, 5, 6, 7; DLB 40, 155

Hamilton, Jane 1957- .... CLC 179
See also CA 147; CANR 85, 128; CN 7;
MTFW 2005

Hamilton, Mollie
See Kaye, M.M.

Hamilton, (Anthony Walter) Patrick
1904-1962 .... CLC 51
See also CA 176; 113; DLB 10, 191

Hamilton, Virginia 1936-2002 .... CLC 26
See also AAYA 2, 21; BW 2, 3; BYA 1, 2,
8; CA 25-28R; 206; CANR 20, 37, 73,
126; CLR 1, 11, 40, 127; DAM MULT;
DLB 33, 52; DLBY 2001; INT CANR-
20; JRDA; LAIT 5; MAICYA 1, 2; MAI-
CYAS 1; MTCW 1, 2; MTFW 2005;
SATA 4, 56, 79, 123; SATA-Obit 132;
WYA; YAW

Hammett, (Samuel) Dashiell
1894-1961 .... CLC 3, 5, 10, 19, 47; SSC
17; TCLC 187
See also AAYA 59; AITN 1; AMWS 4;
BPFB 2; CA 81-84; CANR 42; CDALB
1929-1941; CMW 4; DA3; DLB 226, 280;
DLBD 6; DLBY 1996; EWL 3; LAIT 3;
MAL 5; MSW; MTCW 1, 2; MTFW
2005; NFS 21; RGAL 4; RGSF 2; TUS

Hammon, Jupiter 1720(?)-1800(?) . BLC 1:2;
NCLC 5; PC 16
See also DAM MULT, POET; DLB 31, 50

Hammond, Keith
See Kuttner, Henry

Hamner, Earl (Henry), Jr. 1923- ...... CLC 12
See also AITN 2; CA 73-76; DLB 6

Hampton, Christopher 1946- .... CLC 4
See also CA 25-28R; CD 5, 6; DLB 13;
MTCW 1

Hampton, Christopher James
See Hampton, Christopher

Hamsun, Knut
See Pedersen, Knut

Hamsund, Knut Pedersen
See Pedersen, Knut

Handke, Peter 1942- .... **CLC 5, 8, 10, 15, 38, 134; DC 17**
See also CA 77-80; CANR 33, 75, 104, 133, 180; CWW 2; DAM DRAM, NOV; DLB 85, 124; EWL 3; MTCW 1, 2; MTFW 2005; TWA

Handler, Chelsea 1976(?)- .... **CLC 269**
See also CA 243

Handy, W(illiam) C(hristopher)
1873-1958 .... **TCLC 97**
See also BW 3; CA 121; 167

Hanley, James 1901-1985 ..... **CLC 3, 5, 8, 13**
See also CA 73-76; 117; CANR 36; CBD; CN 1, 2, 3; DLB 191; EWL 3; MTCW 1; RGEL 2

Hannah, Barry 1942- .. **CLC 23, 38, 90, 270; SSC 94**
See also BPFB 2; CA 108; 110; CANR 43, 68, 113; CN 4, 5, 6, 7; CSW; DLB 6, 234; INT CA-110; MTCW 1; RGSF 2

Hannon, Ezra
See Hunter, Evan

Hanrahan, Barbara 1939-1991 .... **TCLC 219**
See also CA 121; 127; CN 4, 5; DLB 289

Hansberry, Lorraine (Vivian)
1930-1965 ... **BLC 1:2, 2:2; CLC 17, 62; DC 2; TCLC 192**
See also AAYA 25; AFAW 1, 2; AMWS 4; BW 1, 3; CA 109; 25-28R; CABS 3; CAD; CANR 58; CDALB 1941-1968; CWD; DA; DA3; DAB; DAC; DAM DRAM, MST, MULT; DFS 2; DLB 7, 38; EWL 3; FL 1:6; FW; LAIT 4; MAL 5; MTCW 1, 2; MTFW 2005; RGAL 4; TUS

Hansen, Joseph 1923-2004 .... **CLC 38**
See also BPFB 2; CA 29-32R; 233; CAAS 17; CANR 16, 44, 66, 125; CMW 4; DLB 226; GLL 1; INT CANR-16

Hansen, Karen V. 1955- .... **CLC 65**
See also CA 149; CANR 102

Hansen, Martin A(lfred)
1909-1955 .... **TCLC 32**
See also CA 167; DLB 214; EWL 3

Hanson, Kenneth O(stlin) 1922- .... **CLC 13**
See also CA 53-56; CANR 7; CP 1, 2, 3, 4, 5

Hardwick, Elizabeth 1916-2007 .... **CLC 13**
See also AMWS 3; CA 5-8R; 267; CANR 3, 32, 70, 100, 139; CN 4, 5, 6; CSW; DA3; DAM NOV; DLB 6; MBL; MTCW 1, 2; MTFW 2005; TCLE 1:1

Hardwick, Elizabeth Bruce
See Hardwick, Elizabeth

Hardwick, Elizabeth Bruce
See Hardwick, Elizabeth

Hardy, Thomas 1840-1928 . **PC 8, 92; SSC 2, 60, 113; TCLC 4, 10, 18, 32, 48, 53, 72, 143, 153; WLC 3**
See also AAYA 69; BRW 6; BRWC 1, 2; BRWR 1; CA 104; 123; CDBLB 1890-1914; DA; DA3; DAB; DAC; DAM MST, NOV, POET; DLB 18, 19, 135, 284; EWL 3; EXPN; EXPP; LAIT 2; MTCW 1, 2; MTFW 2005; NFS 3, 11, 15, 19; PFS 3, 4, 18; RGEL 2; RGSF 2; TEA; WLIT 4

Hare, David 1947- . **CLC 29, 58, 136; DC 26**
See also BRWS 4; CA 97-100; CANR 39, 91; CBD; CD 5, 6; DFS 4, 7, 16; DLB 13, 310; MTCW 1; TEA

Harewood, John
See Van Druten, John (William)

Harford, Henry
See Hudson, W(illiam) H(enry)

Hargrave, Leonie
See Disch, Thomas M.

Hariri, Al- al-Qasim ibn 'Ali Abu Muhammad al-Basri
See al-Hariri, al-Qasim ibn 'Ali Abu Muhammad al-Basri

Harjo, Joy 1951- ..... **CLC 83; NNAL; PC 27**
See also AMWS 12; CA 114; CANR 35, 67, 91, 129; CP 6, 7; CWP; DAM MULT; DLB 120, 175, 342; EWL 3; MTCW 2; MTFW 2005; PFS 15; RGAL 4

Harlan, Louis R(udolph) 1922- .... **CLC 34**
See also CA 21-24R; CANR 25, 55, 80

Harling, Robert 1951(?)- .... **CLC 53**
See also CA 147

Harmon, William (Ruth) 1938- .... **CLC 38**
See also CA 33-36R; CANR 14, 32, 35; SATA 65

Harper, F. E. W.
See Harper, Frances Ellen Watkins

Harper, Frances E. W.
See Harper, Frances Ellen Watkins

Harper, Frances E. Watkins
See Harper, Frances Ellen Watkins

Harper, Frances Ellen
See Harper, Frances Ellen Watkins

Harper, Frances Ellen Watkins
1825-1911 . **BLC 1:2; PC 21; TCLC 14, 217**
See also AFAW 1, 2; BW 1, 3; CA 111; 125; CANR 79; DAM MULT, POET; DLB 50, 221; MBL; RGAL 4

Harper, Michael S(teven) 1938- ..... **BLC 2:2; CLC 7, 22**
See also AFAW 2; BW 1; CA 33-36R; 224; CAAE 224; CANR 24, 108; CP 2, 3, 4, 5, 6, 7; DLB 41; RGAL 4; TCLE 1:1

Harper, Mrs. F. E. W.
See Harper, Frances Ellen Watkins

Harpur, Charles 1813-1868 .... **NCLC 114**
See also DLB 230; RGEL 2

Harris, Christie
See Harris, Christie (Lucy) Irwin

Harris, Christie (Lucy) Irwin
1907-2002 .... **CLC 12**
See also CA 5-8R; CANR 6, 83; CLR 47; DLB 88; JRDA; MAICYA 1, 2; SAAS 10; SATA 6, 74; SATA-Essay 116

Harris, Frank 1856-1931 .... **TCLC 24**
See also CA 109; 150; CANR 80; DLB 156, 197; RGEL 2

Harris, George Washington
1814-1869 .... **NCLC 23, 165**
See also DLB 3, 11, 248; RGAL 4

Harris, Joel Chandler 1848-1908 ..... **SSC 19, 103; TCLC 2**
See also CA 104; 137; CANR 80; CLR 49, 128; DLB 11, 23, 42, 78, 91; LAIT 2; MAICYA 1, 2; RGSF 2; SATA 100; WCH; YABC 1

Harris, John (Wyndham Parkes Lucas)
Beynon 1903-1969 .... **CLC 19**
See also BRWS 13; CA 102; 89-92; CANR 84; DLB 255; SATA 118; SCFW 1, 2; SFW 4

Harris, MacDonald
See Heiney, Donald (William)

Harris, Mark 1922-2007 .... **CLC 19**
See also CA 5-8R; 260; CAAS 3; CANR 2, 55, 83; CN 1, 2, 3, 4, 5, 6, 7; DLB 2; DLBY 1980

Harris, Norman .... **CLC 65**

Harris, (Theodore) Wilson 1921- ... **BLC 2:2; CLC 25, 159**
See also BRWS 5; BW 2, 3; CA 65-68; CAAS 16; CANR 11, 27, 69, 114; CD-WLB 3; CN 1, 2, 3, 4, 5, 6, 7; CP 1, 2, 3, 4, 5, 6, 7; DLB 117; EWL 3; MTCW 1; RGEL 2

Harrison, Barbara Grizzuti
1934-2002 .... **CLC 144**
See also CA 77-80; 205; CANR 15, 48; INT CANR-15

Harrison, Elizabeth (Allen) Cavanna
1909-2001 .... **CLC 12**
See also CA 9-12R; 200; CANR 6, 27, 85, 104, 121; JRDA; MAICYA 1; SAAS 4; SATA 1, 30; YAW

Harrison, Harry 1925- .... **CLC 42**
See also CA 1-4R; CANR 5, 21, 84; DLB 8; SATA 4; SCFW 2; SFW 4

Harrison, Harry Max
See Harrison, Harry

Harrison, James
See Harrison, Jim

Harrison, James Thomas
See Harrison, Jim

Harrison, Jim 1937- .... **CLC 6, 14, 33, 66, 143; SSC 19**
See also AMWS 8; CA 13-16R; CANR 8, 51, 79, 142; CN 5, 6; CP 1, 2, 3, 4, 5, 6; DLBY 1982; INT CANR-8; RGAL 4; TCWW 2; TUS

Harrison, Kathryn 1961- .... **CLC 70, 151**
See also CA 144; CANR 68, 122

Harrison, Tony 1937- .... **CLC 43, 129**
See also BRWS 5; CA 65-68; CANR 44, 98; CBD; CD 5, 6; CP 2, 3, 4, 5, 6, 7; DLB 40, 245; MTCW 1; RGEL 2

Harriss, Will(ard Irvin) 1922- .... **CLC 34**
See also CA 111

Hart, Ellis
See Ellison, Harlan

Hart, Josephine 1942(?)- .... **CLC 70**
See also CA 138; CANR 70, 149; CPW; DAM POP

Hart, Moss 1904-1961 .... **CLC 66**
See also CA 109; 89-92; CANR 84; DAM DRAM; DFS 1; DLB 7, 266; RGAL 4

Harte, (Francis) Bret(t)
1836(?)-1902 ... **SSC 8, 59; TCLC 1, 25; WLC 3**
See also AMWS 2; CA 104; 140; CANR 80; CDALB 1865-1917; DA; DA3; DAC; DAM MST; DLB 12, 64, 74, 79, 186; EXPS; LAIT 2; RGAL 4; RGSF 2; SATA 26; SSFS 3; TUS

Hartley, L(eslie) P(oles) 1895-1972 ... **CLC 2, 22**
See also BRWS 7; CA 45-48; 37-40R; CANR 33; CN 1; DLB 15, 139; EWL 3; HGG; MTCW 1, 2; MTFW 2005; RGEL 2; RGSF 2; SUFW 1

Hartman, Geoffrey H. 1929- .... **CLC 27**
See also CA 117; 125; CANR 79; DLB 67

Hartmann, Sadakichi 1869-1944 ... **TCLC 73**
See also CA 157; DLB 54

Hartmann von Aue c. 1170-c.
1210 .... **CMLC 15**
See also CDWLB 2; DLB 138; RGWL 2, 3

Hartog, Jan de
See de Hartog, Jan

Haruf, Kent 1943- .... **CLC 34**
See also AAYA 44; CA 149; CANR 91, 131

Harvey, Caroline
See Trollope, Joanna

Harvey, Gabriel 1550(?)-1631 .... **LC 88**
See also DLB 167, 213, 281

Harvey, Jack
See Rankin, Ian

Harwood, Ronald 1934- .... **CLC 32**
See also CA 1-4R; CANR 4, 55, 150; CBD; CD 5, 6; DAM DRAM, MST; DLB 13

Hasegawa Tatsunosuke
See Futabatei, Shimei

Hasek, Jaroslav (Matej Frantisek)
1883-1923 .... **SSC 69; TCLC 4**
See also CA 104; 129; CDWLB 4; DLB 215; EW 9; EWL 3; MTCW 1, 2; RGSF 2; RGWL 2, 3

Higgins, Aidan 1927- .... **SSC 68**
See also CA 9-12R; CANR 70, 115, 148; CN 1, 2, 3, 4, 5, 6, 7; DLB 14

Higgins, George V(incent)
1939-1999 .... **CLC 4, 7, 10, 18**
See also BPFB 2; CA 77-80; 186; CAAS 5; CANR 17, 51, 89, 96; CMW 4; CN 2, 3, 4, 5, 6; DLB 2; DLBY 1981, 1998; INT CANR-17; MSW; MTCW 1

Higginson, Thomas Wentworth
1823-1911 .... **TCLC 36**
See also CA 162; DLB 1, 64, 243

Higgonet, Margaret .... **CLC 65**

Highet, Helen
See MacInnes, Helen (Clark)

Highsmith, Patricia 1921-1995 ...... **CLC 2, 4, 14, 42, 102**
See also AAYA 48; BRWS 5; CA 1-4R; 147; CANR 1, 20, 48, 62, 108; CMW 4; CN 1, 2, 3, 4, 5; CPW; DA3; DAM NOV, POP; DLB 306; GLL 1; MSW; MTCW 1, 2; MTFW 2005; NFS 27; SSFS 25

Highwater, Jamake (Mamake)
1942(?)-2001 .... **CLC 12**
See also AAYA 7, 69; BPFB 2; BYA 4; CA 65-68; 199; CAAS 7; CANR 10, 34, 84; CLR 17; CWRI 5; DLB 52; DLBY 1985; JRDA; MAICYA 1, 2; SATA 32, 69; SATA-Brief 30

Highway, Tomson 1951- ..... **CLC 92; DC 33; NNAL**
See also CA 151; CANR 75; CCA 1; CD 5, 6; CN 7; DAC; DAM MULT; DFS 2; DLB 334; MTCW 2

Hijuelos, Oscar 1951- .... **CLC 65; HLC 1**
See also AAYA 25; AMWS 8; BEST 90:1; CA 123; CANR 50, 75, 125; CPW; DA3; DAM MULT, POP; DLB 145; HW 1, 2; LLW; MAL 5; MTCW 2; MTFW 2005; NFS 17; RGAL 4; WLIT 1

Hikmet, Nazim 1902-1963 .... **CLC 40**
See Nizami of Ganja
See also CA 141; 93-96; EWL 3; WLIT 6

Hildegard von Bingen 1098-1179 . **CMLC 20**
See also DLB 148

Hildesheimer, Wolfgang 1916-1991 .. **CLC 49**
See also CA 101; 135; DLB 69, 124; EWL 3; RGHL

Hill, Aaron 1685-1750 .... **LC 148**
See also DLB 84; RGEL 2

Hill, Geoffrey (William) 1932- ...... **CLC 5, 8, 18, 45, 251**
See also BRWS 5; CA 81-84; CANR 21, 89; CDBLB 1960 to Present; CP 1, 2, 3, 4, 5, 6, 7; DAM POET; DLB 40; EWL 3; MTCW 1; RGEL 2; RGHL

Hill, George Roy 1921-2002 .... **CLC 26**
See also CA 110; 122; 213

Hill, John
See Koontz, Dean R.

Hill, Susan 1942- .... **CLC 4, 113**
See also BRWS 14; CA 33-36R; CANR 29, 69, 129, 172; CN 2, 3, 4, 5, 6, 7; DAB; DAM MST, NOV; DLB 14, 139; HGG; MTCW 1; RHW; SATA 183

Hill, Susan Elizabeth
See Hill, Susan

Hillard, Asa G. III .... **CLC 70**

Hillerman, Anthony Grove
See Hillerman, Tony

Hillerman, Tony 1925-2008 ...... **CLC 62, 170**
See also AAYA 40; BEST 89:1; BPFB 2; CA 29-32R; 278; CANR 21, 42, 65, 97, 134; CMW 4; CPW; DA3; DAM POP; DLB 206, 306; MAL 5; MSW; MTCW 2; MTFW 2005; RGAL 4; SATA 6; SATA-Obit 198; TCWW 2; YAW

Hillesum, Etty 1914-1943 .... **TCLC 49**
See also CA 137; RGHL

Hilliard, Noel (Harvey) 1929-1996 ... **CLC 15**
See also CA 9-12R; CANR 7, 69; CN 1, 2, 3, 4, 5, 6

Hillis, Rick 1956- .... **CLC 66**
See also CA 134

Hilton, James 1900-1954 .... **TCLC 21**
See also AAYA 76; CA 108; 169; DLB 34, 77; FANT; SATA 34

Hilton, Walter (?)-1396 .... **CMLC 58**
See also DLB 146; RGEL 2

Himes, Chester (Bomar)
1909-1984 .... **BLC 1:2; CLC 2, 4, 7, 18, 58, 108; TCLC 139**
See also AFAW 2; AMWS 16; BPFB 2; BW 2; CA 25-28R; 114; CANR 22, 89; CMW 4; CN 1, 2, 3; DAM MULT; DLB 2, 76, 143, 226; EWL 3; MAL 5; MSW; MTCW 1, 2; MTFW 2005; RGAL 4

Himmelfarb, Gertrude 1922- .... **CLC 202**
See also CA 49-52; CANR 28, 66, 102, 166

Hinde, Thomas
See Chitty, Thomas Willes

Hine, (William) Daryl 1936- .... **CLC 15**
See also CA 1-4R; CAAS 15; CANR 1, 20; CP 1, 2, 3, 4, 5, 6, 7; DLB 60

Hinkson, Katharine Tynan
See Tynan, Katharine

Hinojosa, Rolando 1929- .... **HLC 1**
See also CA 131; CAAS 16; CANR 62; DAM MULT; DLB 82; EWL 3; HW 1, 2; LLW; MTCW 2; MTFW 2005; RGAL 4

Hinton, S.E. 1950- .... **CLC 30, 111**
See also AAYA 2, 33; BPFB 2; BYA 2, 3; CA 81-84; CANR 32, 62, 92, 133; CDALBS; CLR 3, 23; CPW; DA; DA3; DAB; DAC; DAM MST, NOV; JRDA; LAIT 5; MAICYA 1, 2; MTCW 1, 2; MTFW 2005; NFS 5, 9, 15, 16; SATA 19, 58, 115, 160; WYA; YAW

Hippius, Zinaida (Nikolaevna)
See Gippius, Zinaida (Nikolaevna)

Hiraoka, Kimitake 1925-1970 ... **CLC 2, 4, 6, 9, 27; DC 1; SSC 4; TCLC 161; WLC 4**
See also AAYA 50; BPFB 2; CA 97-100; 29-32R; DA3; DAM DRAM; DLB 182; EWL 3; GLL 1; MJW; MTCW 1, 2; RGSF 2; RGWL 2, 3; SSFS 5, 12

Hirsch, E.D., Jr. 1928- .... **CLC 79**
See also CA 25-28R; CANR 27, 51, 146, 181; DLB 67; INT CANR-27; MTCW 1

Hirsch, Edward 1950- .... **CLC 31, 50**
See also CA 104; CANR 20, 42, 102, 167; CP 6, 7; DLB 120; PFS 22

Hirsch, Eric Donald, Jr.
See Hirsch, E.D., Jr.

Hitchcock, Alfred (Joseph)
1899-1980 .... **CLC 16**
See also AAYA 22; CA 159; 97-100; SATA 27; SATA-Obit 24

Hitchens, Christopher 1949- .... **CLC 157**
See also CA 152; CANR 89, 155

Hitchens, Christopher Eric
See Hitchens, Christopher

Hitler, Adolf 1889-1945 .... **TCLC 53**
See also CA 117; 147

Hoagland, Edward (Morley) 1932- .. **CLC 28**
See also ANW; CA 1-4R; CANR 2, 31, 57, 107; CN 1, 2, 3, 4, 5, 6, 7; DLB 6; SATA 51; TCWW 2

Hoban, Russell 1925- .... **CLC 7, 25**
See also BPFB 2; CA 5-8R; CANR 23, 37, 66, 114, 138; CLR 3, 69, 139; CN 4, 5, 6, 7; CWRI 5; DAM NOV; DLB 52; FANT; MAICYA 1, 2; MTCW 1, 2; MTFW 2005; SATA 1, 40, 78, 136; SFW 4; SUFW 2; TCLE 1:1

Hobbes, Thomas 1588-1679 .... **LC 36, 142**
See also DLB 151, 252, 281; RGEL 2

Hobbs, Perry
See Blackmur, R(ichard) P(almer)

Hobson, Laura Z(ametkin)
1900-1986 .... **CLC 7, 25**
See also BPFB 2; CA 17-20R; 118; CANR 55; CN 1, 2, 3, 4; DLB 28; SATA 52

Hoccleve, Thomas c. 1368-c. 1437 ...... **LC 75**
See also DLB 146; RGEL 2

Hoch, Edward D. 1930-2008 .... **SSC 119**
See also CA 29-32R; CANR 11, 27, 51, 97; CMW 4; DLB 306; SFW 4

Hoch, Edward Dentinger
See Hoch, Edward D.

Hochhuth, Rolf 1931- .... **CLC 4, 11, 18**
See also CA 5-8R; CANR 33, 75, 136; CWW 2; DAM DRAM; DLB 124; EWL 3; MTCW 1, 2; MTFW 2005; RGHL

Hochman, Sandra 1936- .... **CLC 3, 8**
See also CA 5-8R; CP 1, 2, 3, 4, 5; DLB 5

Hochwaelder, Fritz 1911-1986 .... **CLC 36**
See also CA 29-32R; 120; CANR 42; DAM DRAM; EWL 3; MTCW 1; RGWL 2, 3

Hochwalder, Fritz
See Hochwaelder, Fritz

Hocking, Mary (Eunice) 1921- .... **CLC 13**
See also CA 101; CANR 18, 40

Hodge, Merle 1944- .... **BLC 2:2**
See also EWL 3

Hodgins, Jack 1938- .... **CLC 23**
See also CA 93-96; CN 4, 5, 6, 7; DLB 60

Hodgson, William Hope
1877(?)-1918 .... **TCLC 13**
See also CA 111; 164; CMW 4; DLB 70, 153, 156, 178; HGG; MTCW 2; SFW 4; SUFW 1

Hoeg, Peter 1957- .... **CLC 95, 156**
See also CA 151; CANR 75; CMW 4; DA3; DLB 214; EWL 3; MTCW 2; MTFW 2005; NFS 17; RGWL 3; SSFS 18

Hoffman, Alice 1952- .... **CLC 51**
See also AAYA 37; AMWS 10; CA 77-80; CANR 34, 66, 100, 138, 170; CN 4, 5, 6, 7; CPW; DAM NOV; DLB 292; MAL 5; MTCW 1, 2; MTFW 2005; TCLE 1:1

Hoffman, Daniel (Gerard) 1923- . **CLC 6, 13, 23**
See also CA 1-4R; CANR 4, 142; CP 1, 2, 3, 4, 5, 6, 7; DLB 5; TCLE 1:1

Hoffman, Eva 1945- .... **CLC 182**
See also AMWS 16; CA 132; CANR 146

Hoffman, Stanley 1944- .... **CLC 5**
See also CA 77-80

Hoffman, William 1925- .... **CLC 141**
See also AMWS 18; CA 21-24R; CANR 9, 103; CSW; DLB 234; TCLE 1:1

Hoffman, William M.
See Hoffman, William M(oses)

Hoffman, William M(oses) 1939- ..... **CLC 40**
See also CA 57-60; CAD; CANR 11, 71; CD 5, 6

Hoffmann, E(rnst) T(heodor) A(madeus)
1776-1822 ..... **NCLC 2, 183; SSC 13, 92**
See also CDWLB 2; CLR 133; DLB 90; EW 5; GL 2; RGSF 2; RGWL 2, 3; SATA 27; SUFW 1; WCH

Hofmann, Gert 1931-1993 .... **CLC 54**
See also CA 128; CANR 145; EWL 3; RGHL

Hofmannsthal, Hugo von 1874-1929 ... **DC 4; TCLC 11**
See also CA 106; 153; CDWLB 2; DAM DRAM; DFS 17; DLB 81, 118; EW 9; EWL 3; RGWL 2, 3

Hogan, Linda 1947- ..... **CLC 73; NNAL; PC 35**
See also AMWS 4; ANW; BYA 12; CA 120, 226; CAAE 226; CANR 45, 73, 129; CWP; DAM MULT; DLB 175; SATA 132; TCWW 2

Jelakowitch, Ivan
See Heijermans, Herman

Jelinek, Elfriede 1946- .... **CLC 169**
See also AAYA 68; CA 154; CANR 169; DLB 85, 330; FW

Jellicoe, (Patricia) Ann 1927- .... **CLC 27**
See also CA 85-88; CBD; CD 5, 6; CWD; CWRI 5; DLB 13, 233; FW

Jelloun, Tahar ben
See Ben Jelloun, Tahar

Jemyma
See Holley, Marietta

Jen, Gish
See Jen, Lillian

Jen, Lillian 1955- .... **AAL; CLC 70, 198, 260**
See also AMWC 2; CA 135; CANR 89, 130; CN 7; DLB 312

Jenkins, (John) Robin 1912- .... **CLC 52**
See also CA 1-4R; CANR 1, 135; CN 1, 2, 3, 4, 5, 6, 7; DLB 14, 271

Jennings, Elizabeth (Joan)
1926-2001 .... **CLC 5, 14, 131**
See also BRWS 5; CA 61-64; 200; CAAS 5; CANR 8, 39, 66, 127; CP 1, 2, 3, 4, 5, 6, 7; CWP; DLB 27; EWL 3; MTCW 1; SATA 66

Jennings, Waylon 1937-2002 .... **CLC 21**

Jensen, Johannes V(ilhelm)
1873-1950 .... **TCLC 41**
See also CA 170; DLB 214, 330; EWL 3; RGWL 3

Jensen, Laura (Linnea) 1948- .... **CLC 37**
See also CA 103

Jerome, Saint 345-420 .... **CMLC 30**
See also RGWL 3

Jerome, Jerome K(lapka)
1859-1927 .... **TCLC 23**
See also CA 119; 177; DLB 10, 34, 135; RGEL 2

Jerrold, Douglas William
1803-1857 .... **NCLC 2**
See also DLB 158, 159, 344; RGEL 2

Jewett, (Theodora) Sarah Orne
1849-1909 . **SSC 6, 44, 110; TCLC 1, 22**
See also AAYA 76; AMW; AMWC 2; AMWR 2; CA 108; 127; CANR 71; DLB 12, 74, 221; EXPS; FL 1:3; FW; MAL 5; MBL; NFS 15; RGAL 4; RGSF 2; SATA 15; SSFS 4

Jewsbury, Geraldine (Endsor)
1812-1880 .... **NCLC 22**
See also DLB 21

Jhabvala, Ruth Prawer 1927- . **CLC 4, 8, 29, 94, 138; SSC 91**
See also BRWS 5; CA 1-4R; CANR 2, 29, 51, 74, 91, 128; CN 1, 2, 3, 4, 5, 6, 7; DAB; DAM NOV; DLB 139, 194, 323, 326; EWL 3; IDFW 3, 4; INT CANR-29; MTCW 1, 2; MTFW 2005; RGSF 2; RGWL 2; RHW; TEA

Jibran, Kahlil
See Gibran, Kahlil

Jibran, Khalil
See Gibran, Kahlil

Jiles, Paulette 1943- .... **CLC 13, 58**
See also CA 101; CANR 70, 124, 170; CP 5; CWP

Jimenez (Mantecon), Juan Ramon
1881-1958 .... **HLC 1; PC 7; TCLC 4, 183**
See also CA 104; 131; CANR 74; DAM MULT, POET; DLB 134, 330; EW 9; EWL 3; HW 1; MTCW 1, 2; MTFW 2005; RGWL 2, 3

Jimenez, Ramon
See Jimenez (Mantecon), Juan Ramon

Jimenez Mantecon, Juan
See Jimenez (Mantecon), Juan Ramon

Jin, Ba 1904-2005 .... **CLC 18**
See also CA 244; CWW 2; DLB 328; EWL 3

Jin, Ha
See Jin, Xuefei

Jin, Xuefei 1956- .... **CLC 109, 262**
See also CA 152; CANR 91, 130, 184; DLB 244, 292; MTFW 2005; NFS 25; SSFS 17

Jodelle, Etienne 1532-1573 .... **LC 119**
See also DLB 327; GFL Beginnings to 1789

Joel, Billy
See Joel, William Martin

Joel, William Martin 1949- .... **CLC 26**
See also CA 108

John, St.
See John of Damascus, St.

John of Damascus, St. c.
675-749 .... **CMLC 27, 95**

John of Salisbury c. 1115-1180 ..... **CMLC 63**

John of the Cross, St. 1542-1591 .... **LC 18, 146**
See also RGWL 2, 3

John Paul II, Pope 1920-2005 .... **CLC 128**
See also CA 106; 133; 238

Johnson, B(ryan) S(tanley William)
1933-1973 .... **CLC 6, 9**
See also CA 9-12R; 53-56; CANR 9; CN 1; CP 1, 2; DLB 14, 40; EWL 3; RGEL 2

Johnson, Benjamin F., of Boone
See Riley, James Whitcomb

Johnson, Charles (Richard) 1948- . **BLC 1:2, 2:2; CLC 7, 51, 65, 163**
See also AFAW 2; AMWS 6; BW 2, 3; CA 116; CAAS 18; CANR 42, 66, 82, 129; CN 5, 6, 7; DAM MULT; DLB 33, 278; MAL 5; MTCW 2; MTFW 2005; RGAL 4; SSFS 16

Johnson, Charles S(purgeon)
1893-1956 .... **HR 1:3**
See also BW 1, 3; CA 125; CANR 82; DLB 51, 91

Johnson, Denis 1949- . **CLC 52, 160; SSC 56**
See also CA 117; 121; CANR 71, 99, 178; CN 4, 5, 6, 7; DLB 120

Johnson, Diane 1934- ...... **CLC 5, 13, 48, 244**
See also BPFB 2; CA 41-44R; CANR 17, 40, 62, 95, 155; CN 4, 5, 6, 7; DLBY 1980; INT CANR-17; MTCW 1

Johnson, E(mily) Pauline 1861-1913 . **NNAL**
See also CA 150; CCA 1; DAC; DAM MULT; DLB 92, 175; TCWW 2

Johnson, Eyvind (Olof Verner)
1900-1976 .... **CLC 14**
See also CA 73-76; 69-72; CANR 34, 101; DLB 259, 330; EW 12; EWL 3

Johnson, Fenton 1888-1958 .... **BLC 1:2**
See also BW 1; CA 118; 124; DAM MULT; DLB 45, 50

Johnson, Georgia Douglas (Camp)
1880-1966 .... **HR 1:3**
See also BW 1; CA 125; DLB 51, 249; WP

Johnson, Helene 1907-1995 .... **HR 1:3**
See also CA 181; DLB 51; WP

Johnson, J. R.
See James, C(yril) L(ionel) R(obert)

Johnson, James Weldon
1871-1938 .... **BLC 1:2; HR 1:3; PC 24; TCLC 3, 19, 175**
See also AAYA 73; AFAW 1, 2; BW 1, 3; CA 104; 125; CANR 82; CDALB 1917-1929; CLR 32; DA3; DAM MULT, POET; DLB 51; EWL 3; EXPP; LMFS 2; MAL 5; MTCW 1, 2; MTFW 2005; NFS 22; PFS 1; RGAL 4; SATA 31; TUS

Johnson, Joyce 1935- .... **CLC 58**
See also BG 1:3; CA 125; 129; CANR 102

Johnson, Judith (Emlyn) 1936- .... **CLC 7, 15**
See also CA 25-28R; 153; CANR 34, 85; CP 2, 3, 4, 5, 6, 7; CWP

Johnson, Lionel (Pigot)
1867-1902 .... **TCLC 19**
See also CA 117; 209; DLB 19; RGEL 2

Johnson, Marguerite Annie
See Angelou, Maya

Johnson, Mel
See Malzberg, Barry N(athaniel)

Johnson, Pamela Hansford
1912-1981 .... **CLC 1, 7, 27**
See also CA 1-4R; 104; CANR 2, 28; CN 1, 2, 3; DLB 15; MTCW 1, 2; MTFW 2005; RGEL 2

Johnson, Paul 1928- .... **CLC 147**
See also BEST 89:4; CA 17-20R; CANR 34, 62, 100, 155

Johnson, Paul Bede
See Johnson, Paul

Johnson, Robert .... **CLC 70**

Johnson, Robert 1911(?)-1938 .... **TCLC 69**
See also BW 3; CA 174

Johnson, Samuel 1709-1784 . **LC 15, 52, 128; PC 81; WLC 3**
See also BRW 3; BRWR 1; CDBLB 1660-1789; DA; DAB; DAC; DAM MST; DLB 39, 95, 104, 142, 213; LMFS 1; RGEL 2; TEA

Johnson, Stacie
See Myers, Walter Dean

Johnson, Uwe 1934-1984 .. **CLC 5, 10, 15, 40**
See also CA 1-4R; 112; CANR 1, 39; CD-WLB 2; DLB 75; EWL 3; MTCW 1; RGWL 2, 3

Johnston, Basil H. 1929- .... **NNAL**
See also CA 69-72; CANR 11, 28, 66; DAC; DAM MULT; DLB 60

Johnston, George (Benson) 1913- .... **CLC 51**
See also CA 1-4R; CANR 5, 20; CP 1, 2, 3, 4, 5, 6, 7; DLB 88

Johnston, Jennifer (Prudence)
1930- .... **CLC 7, 150, 228**
See also CA 85-88; CANR 92; CN 4, 5, 6, 7; DLB 14

Joinville, Jean de 1224(?)-1317 ..... **CMLC 38**

Jolley, Elizabeth 1923-2007 ..... **CLC 46, 256, 260; SSC 19**
See also CA 127; 257; CAAS 13; CANR 59; CN 4, 5, 6, 7; DLB 325; EWL 3; RGSF 2

Jolley, Monica Elizabeth
See Jolley, Elizabeth

Jones, Arthur Llewellyn 1863-1947 . **SSC 20; TCLC 4**
See Machen, Arthur
See also CA 104; 179; DLB 36; HGG; RGEL 2; SUFW 1

Jones, D(ouglas) G(ordon) 1929- ..... **CLC 10**
See also CA 29-32R; CANR 13, 90; CP 1, 2, 3, 4, 5, 6, 7; DLB 53

Jones, David (Michael) 1895-1974 .... **CLC 2, 4, 7, 13, 42**
See also BRW 6; BRWS 7; CA 9-12R; 53-56; CANR 28; CDBLB 1945-1960; CP 1, 2; DLB 20, 100; EWL 3; MTCW 1; PAB; RGEL 2

Jones, David Robert 1947- .... **CLC 17**
See also CA 103; CANR 104

Jones, Diana Wynne 1934- .... **CLC 26**
See also AAYA 12; BYA 6, 7, 9, 11, 13, 16; CA 49-52; CANR 4, 26, 56, 120, 167; CLR 23, 120; DLB 161; FANT; JRDA; MAICYA 1, 2; MTFW 2005; SAAS 7; SATA 9, 70, 108, 160; SFW 4; SUFW 2; YAW

Jones, Edward P. 1950- .. **BLC 2:2; CLC 76, 223**
See also AAYA 71; BW 2, 3; CA 142; CANR 79, 134; CSW; MTFW 2005; NFS 26

Kandinsky, Wassily 1866-1944 .... **TCLC 92**
  See also AAYA 64; CA 118; 155
Kane, Francis
  See Robbins, Harold
Kane, Paul
  See Simon, Paul
Kane, Sarah 1971-1999 .... **DC 31**
  See also BRWS 8; CA 190; CD 5, 6; DLB
   310
Kanin, Garson 1912-1999 .... **CLC 22**
  See also AITN 1; CA 5-8R; 177; CAD;
   CANR 7, 78; DLB 7; IDFW 3, 4
Kaniuk, Yoram 1930- .... **CLC 19**
  See also CA 134; DLB 299; RGHL
Kant, Immanuel 1724-1804 ..... **NCLC 27, 67**
  See also DLB 94
Kantor, MacKinlay 1904-1977 .... **CLC 7**
  See also CA 61-64; 73-76; CANR 60, 63;
   CN 1, 2; DLB 9, 102; MAL 5; MTCW 2;
   RHW; TCWW 1, 2
Kanze Motokiyo
  See Zeami
Kaplan, David Michael 1946- .... **CLC 50**
  See also CA 187
Kaplan, James 1951- .... **CLC 59**
  See also CA 135; CANR 121
Karadzic, Vuk Stefanovic
  1787-1864 .... **NCLC 115**
  See also CDWLB 4; DLB 147
Karageorge, Michael
  See Anderson, Poul
Karamzin, Nikolai Mikhailovich
  1766-1826 .... **NCLC 3, 173**
  See also DLB 150; RGSF 2
Karapanou, Margarita 1946- .... **CLC 13**
  See also CA 101
Karinthy, Frigyes 1887-1938 .... **TCLC 47**
  See also CA 170; DLB 215; EWL 3
Karl, Frederick R(obert)
  1927-2004 .... **CLC 34**
  See also CA 5-8R; 226; CANR 3, 44, 143
Karr, Mary 1955- .... **CLC 188**
  See also AMWS 11; CA 151; CANR 100;
   MTFW 2005; NCFS 5
Kastel, Warren
  See Silverberg, Robert
Kataev, Evgeny Petrovich
  1903-1942 .... **TCLC 21**
  See also CA 120; DLB 272
Kataphusin
  See Ruskin, John
Katz, Steve 1935- .... **CLC 47**
  See also CA 25-28R; CAAS 14, 64; CANR
   12; CN 4, 5, 6, 7; DLBY 1983
Kauffman, Janet 1945- .... **CLC 42**
  See also CA 117; CANR 43, 84; DLB 218;
   DLBY 1986
Kaufman, Bob (Garnell)
  1925-1986 .... **CLC 49; PC 74**
  See also BG 1:3; BW 1; CA 41-44R; 118;
   CANR 22; CP 1; DLB 16, 41
Kaufman, George S. 1889-1961 ...... **CLC 38;**
  DC 17
  See also CA 108; 93-96; DAM DRAM;
   DFS 1, 10; DLB 7; INT CA-108; MTCW
   2; MTFW 2005; RGAL 4; TUS
Kaufman, Moises 1964- .... **DC 26**
  See also CA 211; DFS 22; MTFW 2005
Kaufman, Sue
  See Barondess, Sue K(aufman)
Kavafis, Konstantinos Petrou
  1863-1933 .... **PC 36; TCLC 2, 7**
  See also CA 104; 148; DA3; DAM POET;
   EW 8; EWL 3; MTCW 2; PFS 19; RGWL
   2, 3; WP
Kavan, Anna 1901-1968 .... **CLC 5, 13, 82**
  See also BRWS 7; CA 5-8R; CANR 6, 57;
   DLB 255; MTCW 1; RGEL 2; SFW 4

Kavanagh, Dan
  See Barnes, Julian
Kavanagh, Julie 1952- .... **CLC 119**
  See also CA 163; CANR 186
Kavanagh, Patrick (Joseph)
  1904-1967 .... **CLC 22; PC 33**
  See also BRWS 7; CA 123; 25-28R; DLB
   15, 20; EWL 3; MTCW 1; RGEL 2
Kawabata, Yasunari 1899-1972 ..... **CLC 2, 5,**
  9, 18, 107; SSC 17
  See also CA 93-96; 33-36R; CANR 88;
   DAM MULT; DLB 180, 330; EWL 3;
   MJW; MTCW 2; MTFW 2005; RGSF 2;
   RGWL 2, 3
Kawabata Yasunari
  See Kawabata, Yasunari
Kaye, Mary Margaret
  See Kaye, M.M.
Kaye, M.M. 1908-2004 .... **CLC 28**
  See also CA 89-92; 223; CANR 24, 60, 102,
   142; MTCW 1, 2; MTFW 2005; RHW;
   SATA 62; SATA-Obit 152
Kaye, Mollie
  See Kaye, M.M.
Kaye-Smith, Sheila 1887-1956 .... **TCLC 20**
  See also CA 118; 203; DLB 36
Kaymor, Patrice Maguilene
  See Senghor, Leopold Sedar
Kazakov, Iurii Pavlovich
  See Kazakov, Yuri Pavlovich
Kazakov, Yuri Pavlovich 1927-1982 . **SSC 43**
  See also CA 5-8R; CANR 36; DLB 302;
   EWL 3; MTCW 1; RGSF 2
Kazakov, Yury
  See Kazakov, Yuri Pavlovich
Kazan, Elia 1909-2003 .... **CLC 6, 16, 63**
  See also CA 21-24R; 220; CANR 32, 78
Kazantzakis, Nikos 1883(?)-1957 .... **TCLC 2,**
  5, 33, 181
  See also BPFB 2; CA 105; 132; DA3; EW
   9; EWL 3; MTCW 1, 2; MTFW 2005;
   RGWL 2, 3
Kazin, Alfred 1915-1998 ..... **CLC 34, 38, 119**
  See also AMWS 8; CA 1-4R; CAAS 7;
   CANR 1, 45, 79; DLB 67; EWL 3
Keane, Mary Nesta (Skrine)
  1904-1996 .... **CLC 31**
  See also CA 108; 114; 151; CN 5, 6; INT
   CA-114; RHW; TCLE 1:1
Keane, Molly
  See Keane, Mary Nesta (Skrine)
Keates, Jonathan 1946(?)- .... **CLC 34**
  See also CA 163; CANR 126
Keaton, Buster 1895-1966 .... **CLC 20**
  See also AAYA 79; CA 194
Keats, John 1795-1821 ...... **NCLC 8, 73, 121;**
  PC 1, 96; WLC 3
  See also AAYA 58; BRW 4; BRWR 1; CD-
   BLB 1789-1832; DA; DA3; DAB; DAC;
   DAM MST, POET; DLB 96, 110; EXPP;
   LMFS 1; PAB; PFS 1, 2, 3, 9, 17; RGEL
   2; TEA; WLIT 3; WP
Keble, John 1792-1866 .... **NCLC 87**
  See also DLB 32, 55; RGEL 2
Keene, Donald 1922- .... **CLC 34**
  See also CA 1-4R; CANR 5, 119
Keillor, Garrison 1942- ..... **CLC 40, 115, 222**
  See also AAYA 2, 62; AMWS 16; BEST
   89:3; BPFB 2; CA 111; 117; CANR 36,
   59, 124, 180; CPW; DA3; DAM POP;
   DLBY 1987; EWL 3; MTCW 1, 2; MTFW
   2005; SATA 58; TUS
Keith, Carlos
  See Lewton, Val
Keith, Michael
  See Hubbard, L. Ron
Kell, Joseph
  See Burgess, Anthony

Keller, Gottfried 1819-1890 .... **NCLC 2; SSC**
  26, 107
  See also CDWLB 2; DLB 129; EW; RGSF
   2; RGWL 2, 3
Keller, Nora Okja 1965- .... **CLC 109**
  See also CA 187
Kellerman, Jonathan 1949- .... **CLC 44**
  See also AAYA 35; BEST 90:1; CA 106;
   CANR 29, 51, 150, 183; CMW 4; CPW;
   DA3; DAM POP; INT CANR-29
Kelley, William Melvin 1937- .... **BLC 2:2;**
  CLC 22
  See also BW 1; CA 77-80; CANR 27, 83;
   CN 1, 2, 3, 4, 5, 6, 7; DLB 33; EWL 3
Kellock, Archibald P.
  See Mavor, Osborne Henry
Kellogg, Marjorie 1922-2005 .... **CLC 2**
  See also CA 81-84; 246
Kellow, Kathleen
  See Hibbert, Eleanor Alice Burford
Kelly, Lauren
  See Oates, Joyce Carol
Kelly, M(ilton) T(errence) 1947- ...... **CLC 55**
  See also CA 97-100; CAAS 22; CANR 19,
   43, 84; CN 6
Kelly, Robert 1935- .... **SSC 50**
  See also CA 17-20R; CAAS 19; CANR 47;
   CP 1, 2, 3, 4, 5, 6, 7; DLB 5, 130, 165
Kelman, James 1946- .... **CLC 58, 86**
  See also BRWS 5; CA 148; CANR 85, 130;
   CN 5, 6, 7; DLB 194, 319, 326; RGSF 2;
   WLIT 4
Kemal, Yasar
  See Kemal, Yashar
Kemal, Yashar 1923(?)- .... **CLC 14, 29**
  See also CA 89-92; CANR 44; CWW 2;
   EWL 3; WLIT 6
Kemble, Fanny 1809-1893 .... **NCLC 18**
  See also DLB 32
Kemelman, Harry 1908-1996 .... **CLC 2**
  See also AITN 1; BPFB 2; CA 9-12R; 155;
   CANR 6, 71; CMW 4; DLB 28
Kempe, Margery 1373(?)-1440(?) ... **LC 6, 56**
  See also BRWS 12; DLB 146; FL 1:1;
   RGEL 2
Kempis, Thomas a 1380-1471 .... **LC 11**
Kenan, Randall (G.) 1963- .... **BLC 2:2**
  See also BW 2, 3; CA 142; CANR 86; CN
   7; CSW; DLB 292; GLL 1
Kendall, Henry 1839-1882 .... **NCLC 12**
  See also DLB 230
Keneally, Thomas 1935- .... **CLC 5, 8, 10, 14,**
  19, 27, 43, 117
  See also BRWS 4; CA 85-88; CANR 10,
   50, 74, 130, 165; CN 1, 2, 3, 4, 5, 6, 7;
   CPW; DA3; DAM NOV; DLB 289, 299,
   326; EWL 3; MTCW 1, 2; MTFW 2005;
   NFS 17; RGEL 2; RGHL; RHW
Keneally, Thomas Michael
  See Keneally, Thomas
Kennedy, A. L. 1965- .... **CLC 188**
  See also CA 168, 213; CAAE 213; CANR
   108; CD 5, 6; CN 6, 7; DLB 271; RGSF
   2
Kennedy, Adrienne (Lita) 1931- .... **BLC 1:2;**
  CLC 66; DC 5
  See also AFAW 2; BW 2, 3; CA 103; CAAS
   20; CABS 3; CAD; CANR 26, 53, 82;
   CD 5, 6; DAM MULT; DFS 9; DLB 38,
   341; FW; MAL 5
Kennedy, Alison Louise
  See Kennedy, A. L.
Kennedy, John Pendleton
  1795-1870 .... **NCLC 2**
  See also DLB 3, 248, 254; RGAL 4

Author Index

CANR-34; MAL 5; MTCW 1, 2; MTFW
2005; PAB; PFS 9, 26; RGAL 4; TCLE
1:1; WP

Kinsella, Thomas 1928- .... **CLC 4, 19, 138,
274; PC 69**
See also BRWS 5; CA 17-20R; CANR 15,
122; CP 1, 2, 3, 4, 5, 6, 7; DLB 27; EWL
3; MTCW 1, 2; MTFW 2005; RGEL 2;
TEA

Kinsella, W.P. 1935- .... **CLC 27, 43, 166**
See also AAYA 7, 60; BPFB 2; CA 97-100,
222; CAAE 222; CAAS 7; CANR 21, 35,
66, 75, 129; CN 4, 5, 6, 7; CPW; DAC;
DAM NOV, POP; FANT; INT CANR-21;
LAIT 5; MTCW 1, 2; MTFW 2005; NFS
15; RGSF 2

Kinsey, Alfred C(harles)
1894-1956 .... **TCLC 91**
See also CA 115; 170; MTCW 2

Kipling, (Joseph) Rudyard 1865-1936 . **PC 3,
91; SSC 5, 54, 110; TCLC 8, 17, 167;
WLC 3**
See also AAYA 32; BRW 6; BRWC 1, 2;
BYA 4; CA 105; 120; CANR 33; CDBLB
1890-1914; CLR 39, 65; CWRI 5; DA;
DA3; DAB; DAC; DAM MST, POET;
DLB 19, 34, 141, 156, 330; EWL 3;
EXPS; FANT; LAIT 3; LMFS 1; MAI-
CYA 1, 2; MTCW 1, 2; MTFW 2005;
NFS 21; PFS 22; RGEL 2; RGSF 2; SATA
100; SFW 4; SSFS 8, 21, 22; SUFW 1;
TEA; WCH; WLIT 4; YABC 2

Kircher, Athanasius 1602-1680 .... **LC 121**
See also DLB 164

Kirk, Russell (Amos) 1918-1994 .. **TCLC 119**
See also AITN 1; CA 1-4R; 145; CAAS 9;
CANR 1, 20, 60; HGG; INT CANR-20;
MTCW 1, 2

Kirkham, Dinah
See Card, Orson Scott

Kirkland, Caroline M. 1801-1864 . **NCLC 85**
See also DLB 3, 73, 74, 250, 254; DLBD
13

Kirkup, James 1918- .... **CLC 1**
See also CA 1-4R; CAAS 4; CANR 2; CP
1, 2, 3, 4, 5, 6, 7; DLB 27; SATA 12

Kirkwood, James 1930(?)-1989 .... **CLC 9**
See also AITN 2; CA 1-4R; 128; CANR 6,
40; GLL 2

Kirsch, Sarah 1935- .... **CLC 176**
See also CA 178; CWW 2; DLB 75; EWL
3

Kirshner, Sidney
See Kingsley, Sidney

Kis, Danilo 1935-1989 .... **CLC 57**
See also CA 109; 118; 129; CANR 61; CD-
WLB 4; DLB 181; EWL 3; MTCW 1;
RGSF 2; RGWL 2, 3

Kissinger, Henry A(lfred) 1923- ..... **CLC 137**
See also CA 1-4R; CANR 2, 33, 66, 109;
MTCW 1

Kittel, Frederick August
See Wilson, August

Kivi, Aleksis 1834-1872 .... **NCLC 30**

Kizer, Carolyn 1925- ..... **CLC 15, 39, 80; PC
66**
See also CA 65-68; CAAS 5; CANR 24,
70, 134; CP 1, 2, 3, 4, 5, 6, 7; CWP; DAM
POET; DLB 5, 169; EWL 3; MAL 5;
MTCW 2; MTFW 2005; PFS 18; TCLE
1:1

Klabund 1890-1928 .... **TCLC 44**
See also CA 162; DLB 66

Klappert, Peter 1942- .... **CLC 57**
See also CA 33-36R; CSW; DLB 5

Klausner, Amos
See Oz, Amos

Klein, A(braham) M(oses)
1909-1972 .... **CLC 19**
See also CA 101; 37-40R; CP 1; DAB;
DAC; DAM MST; DLB 68; EWL 3;
RGEL 2; RGHL

Klein, Joe
See Klein, Joseph

Klein, Joseph 1946- .... **CLC 154**
See also CA 85-88; CANR 55, 164

Klein, Norma 1938-1989 .... **CLC 30**
See also AAYA 2, 35; BPFB 2; BYA 6, 7,
8; CA 41-44R; 128; CANR 15, 37; CLR
2, 19; INT CANR-15; JRDA; MAICYA
1, 2; SAAS 1; SATA 7, 57; WYA; YAW

Klein, T.E.D. 1947- .... **CLC 34**
See also CA 119; CANR 44, 75, 167; HGG

Klein, Theodore Eibon Donald
See Klein, T.E.D.

Kleist, Heinrich von 1777-1811 .... **DC 29;
NCLC 2, 37; SSC 22**
See also CDWLB 2; DAM DRAM; DLB
90; EW 5; RGSF 2; RGWL 2, 3

Klima, Ivan 1931- .... **CLC 56, 172**
See also CA 25-28R; CANR 17, 50, 91;
CDWLB 4; CWW 2; DAM NOV; DLB
232; EWL 3; RGWL 3

Klimentev, Andrei Platonovich
See Klimentov, Andrei Platonovich

Klimentov, Andrei Platonovich
1899-1951 .... **SSC 42; TCLC 14**
See also CA 108; 232; DLB 272; EWL 3

Klinger, Friedrich Maximilian von
1752-1831 .... **NCLC 1**
See also DLB 94

Klingsor the Magician
See Hartmann, Sadakichi

Klopstock, Friedrich Gottlieb
1724-1803 .... **NCLC 11**
See also DLB 97; EW 4; RGWL 2, 3

Kluge, Alexander 1932- .... **SSC 61**
See also CA 81-84; CANR 163; DLB 75

Knapp, Caroline 1959-2002 .... **CLC 99**
See also CA 154; 207

Knebel, Fletcher 1911-1993 .... **CLC 14**
See also AITN 1; CA 1-4R; 140; CAAS 3;
CANR 1, 36; CN 1, 2, 3, 4, 5; SATA 36;
SATA-Obit 75

Knickerbocker, Diedrich
See Irving, Washington

Knight, Etheridge 1931-1991 .... **BLC 1:2;
CLC 40; PC 14**
See also BW 1, 3; CA 21-24R; 133; CANR
23, 82; CP 1, 2, 3, 4, 5; DAM POET; DLB
41; MTCW 2; MTFW 2005; RGAL 4;
TCLE 1:1

Knight, Sarah Kemble 1666-1727 .... **LC 7**
See also DLB 24, 200

Knister, Raymond 1899-1932 .... **TCLC 56**
See also CA 186; DLB 68; RGEL 2

Knowles, John 1926-2001 ... **CLC 1, 4, 10, 26**
See also AAYA 10, 72; AMWS 12; BPFB
2; BYA 3; CA 17-20R; 203; CANR 40,
74, 76, 132; CDALB 1968-1988; CLR 98;
CN 1, 2, 3, 4, 5, 6, 7; DA; DAC; DAM
MST, NOV; DLB 6; EXPN; MTCW 1, 2;
MTFW 2005; NFS 2; RGAL 4; SATA 8,
89; SATA-Obit 134; YAW

Knox, Calvin M.
See Silverberg, Robert

Knox, John c. 1505-1572 .... **LC 37**
See also DLB 132

Knye, Cassandra
See Disch, Thomas M.

Koch, C(hristopher) J(ohn) 1932- .... **CLC 42**
See also CA 127; CANR 84; CN 3, 4, 5, 6,
7; DLB 289

Koch, Christopher
See Koch, C(hristopher) J(ohn)

Koch, Kenneth 1925-2002 .... **CLC 5, 8, 44;
PC 80**
See also AMWS 15; CA 1-4R; 207; CAD;
CANR 6, 36, 57, 97, 131; CD 5, 6; CP 1,
2, 3, 4, 5, 6, 7; DAM POET; DLB 5; INT
CANR-36; MAL 5; MTCW 2; MTFW
2005; PFS 20; SATA 65; WP

Kochanowski, Jan 1530-1584 .... **LC 10**
See also RGWL 2, 3

Kock, Charles Paul de 1794-1871 . **NCLC 16**

Koda Rohan
See Koda Shigeyuki

Koda Rohan
See Koda Shigeyuki

Koda Shigeyuki 1867-1947 .... **TCLC 22**
See also CA 121; 183; DLB 180

Koestler, Arthur 1905-1983 ... **CLC 1, 3, 6, 8,
15, 33**
See also BRWS 1; CA 1-4R; 109; CANR 1,
33; CDBLB 1945-1960; CN 1, 2, 3;
DLBY 1983; EWL 3; MTCW 1, 2; MTFW
2005; NFS 19; RGEL 2

Kogawa, Joy Nozomi 1935- ..... **CLC 78, 129,
262, 268**
See also AAYA 47; CA 101; CANR 19, 62,
126; CN 6, 7; CP 1; CWP; DAC; DAM
MST, MULT; DLB 334; FW; MTCW 2;
MTFW 2005; NFS 3; SATA 99

Kohout, Pavel 1928- .... **CLC 13**
See also CA 45-48; CANR 3

Koizumi, Yakumo
See Hearn, (Patricio) Lafcadio (Tessima
Carlos)

Kolmar, Gertrud 1894-1943 .... **TCLC 40**
See also CA 167; EWL 3; RGHL

Komunyakaa, Yusef 1947- . **BLC 2:2; BLCS;
CLC 86, 94, 207; PC 51**
See also AFAW 2; AMWS 13; CA 147;
CANR 83, 164; CP 6, 7; CSW; DLB 120;
EWL 3; PFS 5, 20, 30; RGAL 4

Konigsberg, Alan Stewart
See Allen, Woody

Konrad, George
See Konrad, Gyorgy

Konrad, George
See Konrad, Gyorgy

Konrad, Gyorgy 1933- .... **CLC 4, 10, 73**
See also CA 85-88; CANR 97, 171; CD-
WLB 4; CWW 2; DLB 232; EWL 3

Konwicki, Tadeusz 1926- .... **CLC 8, 28, 54,
117**
See also CA 101; CAAS 9; CANR 39, 59;
CWW 2; DLB 232; EWL 3; IDFW 3;
MTCW 1

Koontz, Dean
See Koontz, Dean R.

Koontz, Dean R. 1945- .... **CLC 78, 206**
See also AAYA 9, 31; BEST 89:3, 90:2; CA
108; CANR 19, 36, 52, 95, 138, 176;
CMW 4; CPW; DA3; DAM NOV, POP;
DLB 292; HGG; MTCW 1; MTFW 2005;
SATA 92, 165; SFW 4; SUFW 2; YAW

Koontz, Dean Ray
See Koontz, Dean R.

Kopernik, Mikolaj
See Copernicus, Nicolaus

Kopit, Arthur (Lee) 1937- ...... **CLC 1, 18, 33**
See also AITN 1; CA 81-84; CABS 3;
CAD; CD 5, 6; DAM DRAM; DFS 7, 14,
24; DLB 7; MAL 5; MTCW 1; RGAL 4

Kopitar, Jernej (Bartholomaus)
1780-1844 .... **NCLC 117**

Kops, Bernard 1926- .... **CLC 4**
See also CA 5-8R; CANR 84, 159; CBD;
CN 1, 2, 3, 4, 5, 6, 7; CP 1, 2, 3, 4, 5, 6,
7; DLB 13; RGHL

Kornbluth, C(yril) M. 1923-1958 .... **TCLC 8**
See also CA 105; 160; DLB 8; SCFW 1, 2;
SFW 4

La Fontaine, Jean de 1621-1695 .... **LC 50**
See also DLB 268; EW 3; GFL Beginnings to 1789; MAICYA 1, 2; RGWL 2, 3; SATA 18

LaForet, Carmen 1921-2004 .... **CLC 219**
See also CA 246; CWW 2; DLB 322; EWL 3

LaForet Diaz, Carmen
See LaForet, Carmen

Laforgue, Jules 1860-1887 . **NCLC 5, 53; PC 14; SSC 20**
See also DLB 217; EW 7; GFL 1789 to the Present; RGWL 2, 3

Lagerkvist, Paer (Fabian) 1891-1974 .. **CLC 7, 10, 13, 54; SSC 12; TCLC 144**
See also CA 85-88; 49-52; DA3; DAM DRAM, NOV; DLB 259, 331; EW 10; EWL 3; MTCW 1, 2; MTFW 2005; RGSF 2; RGWL 2, 3; TWA

Lagerkvist, Par
See Lagerkvist, Paer (Fabian)

Lagerloef, Selma (Ottiliana Lovisa)
See Lagerlof, Selma (Ottiliana Lovisa)

Lagerlof, Selma (Ottiliana Lovisa) 1858-1940 .... **TCLC 4, 36**
See also CA 108; 188; CLR 7; DLB 259, 331; MTCW 2; RGWL 2, 3; SATA 15; SSFS 18

La Guma, Alex 1925-1985 .. **BLCS; CLC 19; TCLC 140**
See also AFW; BW 1, 3; CA 49-52; 118; CANR 25, 81; CDWLB 3; CN 1, 2, 3; CP 1; DAM NOV; DLB 117, 225; EWL 3; MTCW 1, 2; MTFW 2005; WLIT 2; WWE 1

Lahiri, Jhumpa 1967- .... **SSC 96**
See also AAYA 56; CA 193; CANR 134, 184; DLB 323; MTFW 2005; SSFS 19, 27

Laidlaw, A. K.
See Grieve, C(hristopher) M(urray)

Lainez, Manuel Mujica
See Mujica Lainez, Manuel

Laing, R(onald) D(avid) 1927-1989 . **CLC 95**
See also CA 107; 129; CANR 34; MTCW 1

Laishley, Alex
See Booth, Martin

Lamartine, Alphonse (Marie Louis Prat) de 1790-1869 .... **NCLC 11, 190; PC 16**
See also DAM POET; DLB 217; GFL 1789 to the Present; RGWL 2, 3

Lamb, Charles 1775-1834 ..... **NCLC 10, 113; SSC 112; WLC 3**
See also BRW 4; CDBLB 1789-1832; DA; DAB; DAC; DAM MST; DLB 93, 107, 163; RGEL 2; SATA 17; TEA

Lamb, Lady Caroline 1785-1828 ... **NCLC 38**
See also DLB 116

Lamb, Mary Ann 1764-1847 ...... **NCLC 125; SSC 112**
See also DLB 163; SATA 17

Lame Deer 1903(?)-1976 .... **NNAL**
See also CA 69-72

Lamming, George (William) 1927- . **BLC 1:2, 2:2; CLC 2, 4, 66, 144**
See also BW 2, 3; CA 85-88; CANR 26, 76; CDWLB 3; CN 1, 2, 3, 4, 5, 6, 7; CP 1; DAM MULT; DLB 125; EWL 3; MTCW 1, 2; MTFW 2005; NFS 15; RGEL 2

L'Amour, Louis 1908-1988 .... **CLC 25, 55**
See also AAYA 16; AITN 2; BEST 89:2; BPFB 2; CA 1-4R; 125; CANR 3, 25, 40; CPW; DA3; DAM NOV, POP; DLB 206; DLBY 1980; MTCW 1, 2; MTFW 2005; RGAL 4; TCWW 1, 2

Lampedusa, Giuseppe (Tomasi) di
See Tomasi di Lampedusa, Giuseppe

Lampman, Archibald 1861-1899 .. **NCLC 25, 194**
See also DLB 92; RGEL 2; TWA

Lancaster, Bruce 1896-1963 .... **CLC 36**
See also CA 9-10; CANR 70; CAP 1; SATA 9

Lanchester, John 1962- .... **CLC 99**
See also CA 194; DLB 267

Landau, Mark Alexandrovich
See Aldanov, Mark (Alexandrovich)

Landau-Aldanov, Mark Alexandrovich
See Aldanov, Mark (Alexandrovich)

Landis, Jerry
See Simon, Paul

Landis, John 1950- .... **CLC 26**
See also CA 112; 122; CANR 128

Landolfi, Tommaso 1908-1979 .... **CLC 11, 49**
See also CA 127; 117; DLB 177; EWL 3

Landon, Letitia Elizabeth 1802-1838 .... **NCLC 15**
See also DLB 96

Landor, Walter Savage 1775-1864 .... **NCLC 14**
See also BRW 4; DLB 93, 107; RGEL 2

Landwirth, Heinz
See Lind, Jakov

Lane, Patrick 1939- .... **CLC 25**
See also CA 97-100; CANR 54; CP 3, 4, 5, 6, 7; DAM POET; DLB 53; INT CA-97-100

Lane, Rose Wilder 1887-1968 ...... **TCLC 177**
See also CA 102; CANR 63; SATA 29; SATA-Brief 28; TCWW 2

Lang, Andrew 1844-1912 .... **TCLC 16**
See also CA 114; 137; CANR 85; CLR 101; DLB 98, 141, 184; FANT; MAICYA 1, 2; RGEL 2; SATA 16; WCH

Lang, Fritz 1890-1976 .... **CLC 20, 103**
See also AAYA 65; CA 77-80; 69-72; CANR 30

Lange, John
See Crichton, Michael

Langer, Elinor 1939- .... **CLC 34**
See also CA 121

Langland, William 1332(?)-1400(?) .... **LC 19, 120**
See also BRW 1; DA; DAB; DAC; DAM MST, POET; DLB 146; RGEL 2; TEA; WLIT 3

Langstaff, Launcelot
See Irving, Washington

Lanier, Sidney 1842-1881 . **NCLC 6, 118; PC 50**
See also AMWS 1; DAM POET; DLB 64; DLBD 13; EXPP; MAICYA 1; PFS 14; RGAL 4; SATA 18

Lanyer, Aemilia 1569-1645 .... **LC 10, 30, 83; PC 60**
See also DLB 121

Lao-Tzu
See Lao Tzu

Lao Tzu c. 6th cent. B.C.-3rd cent. B.C. .... **CMLC 7**

Lapine, James (Elliot) 1949- .... **CLC 39**
See also CA 123; 130; CANR 54, 128; DFS 25; DLB 341; INT CA-130

Larbaud, Valery (Nicolas) 1881-1957 .... **TCLC 9**
See also CA 106; 152; EWL 3; GFL 1789 to the Present

Larcom, Lucy 1824-1893 .... **NCLC 179**
See also AMWS 13; DLB 221, 243

Lardner, Ring
See Lardner, Ring(gold) W(ilmer)

Lardner, Ring W., Jr.
See Lardner, Ring(gold) W(ilmer)

Lardner, Ring(gold) W(ilmer) 1885-1933 ..... **SSC 32, 118; TCLC 2, 14**
See also AMW; BPFB 2; CA 104; 131; CDALB 1917-1929; DLB 11, 25, 86, 171; DLBD 16; MAL 5; MTCW 1, 2; MTFW 2005; RGAL 4; RGSF 2; TUS

Laredo, Betty
See Codrescu, Andrei

Larkin, Maia
See Wojciechowska, Maia (Teresa)

Larkin, Philip (Arthur) 1922-1985 ... **CLC 3, 5, 8, 9, 13, 18, 33, 39, 64; PC 21**
See also BRWS 1; CA 5-8R; 117; CANR 24, 62; CDBLB 1960 to Present; CP 1, 2, 3, 4; DA3; DAB; DAM MST, POET; DLB 27; EWL 3; MTCW 1, 2; MTFW 2005; PFS 3, 4, 12; RGEL 2

La Roche, Sophie von 1730-1807 .... **NCLC 121**
See also DLB 94

La Rochefoucauld, Francois 1613-1680 .... **LC 108**
See also DLB 268; EW 3; GFL Beginnings to 1789; RGWL 2, 3

Larra (y Sanchez de Castro), Mariano Jose de 1809-1837 .... **NCLC 17, 130**

Larsen, Eric 1941- .... **CLC 55**
See also CA 132

Larsen, Nella 1893(?)-1963 ... **BLC 1:2; CLC 37; HR 1:3; TCLC 200**
See also AFAW 1, 2; AMWS 18; BW 1; CA 125; CANR 83; DAM MULT; DLB 51; FW; LATS 1:1; LMFS 2

Larson, Charles R(aymond) 1938- ... **CLC 31**
See also CA 53-56; CANR 4, 121

Larson, Jonathan 1960-1996 .... **CLC 99**
See also AAYA 28; CA 156; DFS 23; MTFW 2005

La Sale, Antoine de c. 1386-1460(?) . **LC 104**
See also DLB 208

Las Casas, Bartolome de 1474-1566 .... **HLCS; LC 31**
See also DLB 318; LAW; WLIT 1

Lasch, Christopher 1932-1994 .... **CLC 102**
See also CA 73-76; 144; CANR 25, 118; DLB 246; MTCW 1, 2; MTFW 2005

Lasker-Schueler, Else 1869-1945 ... **TCLC 57**
See also CA 183; DLB 66, 124; EWL 3

Lasker-Schuler, Else
See Lasker-Schueler, Else

Laski, Harold J(oseph) 1893-1950 . **TCLC 79**
See also CA 188

Latham, Jean Lee 1902-1995 .... **CLC 12**
See also AITN 1; BYA 1; CA 5-8R; CANR 7, 84; CLR 50; MAICYA 1, 2; SATA 2, 68; YAW

Latham, Mavis
See Clark, Mavis Thorpe

Lathen, Emma
See Hennissart, Martha

Lathrop, Francis
See Leiber, Fritz (Reuter, Jr.)

Lattany, Kristin
See Lattany, Kristin (Elaine Eggleston) Hunter

Lattany, Kristin (Elaine Eggleston) Hunter 1931- .... **CLC 35**
See also AITN 1; BW 1; BYA 3; CA 13-16R; CANR 13, 108; CLR 3; CN 1, 2, 3, 4, 5, 6; DLB 33; INT CANR-13; MAICYA 1, 2; SAAS 10; SATA 12, 132; YAW

Lattimore, Richmond (Alexander) 1906-1984 .... **CLC 3**
See also CA 1-4R; 112; CANR 1; CP 1, 2, 3; MAL 5

Laughlin, James 1914-1997 .... **CLC 49**
See also CA 21-24R; 162; CAAS 22; CANR 9, 47; CP 1, 2, 3, 4, 5, 6; DLB 48; DLBY 1996, 1997

Leger, Alexis
    See Leger, (Marie-Rene Auguste) Alexis
      Saint-Leger
**Leger, (Marie-Rene Auguste) Alexis
    Saint-Leger** 1887-1975 .. **CLC 4, 11, 46;
    PC 23**
    See also CA 13-16R; 61-64; CANR 43;
      DAM POET; DLB 258, 331; EW 10;
      EWL 3; GFL 1789 to the Present; MTCW
      1; RGWL 2, 3
Leger, Saintleger
    See Leger, (Marie-Rene Auguste) Alexis
      Saint-Leger
Le Guin, Ursula K. 1929- ...... **CLC 8, 13, 22,
    45, 71, 136; SSC 12, 69**
    See also AAYA 9, 27; AITN 1; BPFB 2;
      BYA 5, 8, 11, 14; CA 21-24R; CANR 9,
      32, 52, 74, 132; CDALB 1968-1988; CLR
      3, 28, 91; CN 2, 3, 4, 5, 6, 7; CPW; DA3;
      DAB; DAC; DAM MST, POP; DLB 8,
      52, 256, 275; EXPS; FANT; FW; INT
      CANR-32; JRDA; LAIT 5; MAICYA 1,
      2; MAL 5; MTCW 1, 2; MTFW 2005;
      NFS 6, 9; SATA 4, 52, 99, 149, 194;
      SCFW 1, 2; SFW 4; SSFS 2; SUFW 1, 2;
      WYA; YAW
Lehmann, Rosamond (Nina)
    1901-1990 .... **CLC 5**
    See also CA 77-80; 131; CANR 8, 73; CN
      1, 2, 3, 4; DLB 15; MTCW 2; RGEL 2;
      RHW
Leiber, Fritz (Reuter, Jr.)
    1910-1992 .... **CLC 25**
    See also AAYA 65; BPFB 2; CA 45-48; 139;
      CANR 2, 40, 86; CN 2, 3, 4, 5; DLB 8;
      FANT; HGG; MTCW 1, 2; MTFW 2005;
      SATA 45; SATA-Obit 73; SCFW 1, 2;
      SFW 4; SUFW 1, 2
Leibniz, Gottfried Wilhelm von
    1646-1716 .... **LC 35**
    See also DLB 168
Leino, Eino
    See Lonnbohm, Armas Eino Leopold
Leiris, Michel (Julien) 1901-1990 ..... **CLC 61**
    See also CA 119; 128; 132; EWL 3; GFL
      1789 to the Present
Leithauser, Brad 1953- .... **CLC 27**
    See also CA 107; CANR 27, 81, 171; CP 5,
      6, 7; DLB 120, 282
le Jars de Gournay, Marie
    See de Gournay, Marie le Jars
Lelchuk, Alan 1938- .... **CLC 5**
    See also CA 45-48; CAAS 20; CANR 1,
      70, 152; CN 3, 4, 5, 6, 7
Lem, Stanislaw 1921-2006 ..... **CLC 8, 15, 40,
    149**
    See also AAYA 75; CA 105; 249; CAAS 1;
      CANR 32; CWW 2; MTCW 1; SCFW 1,
      2; SFW 4
Lemann, Nancy (Elise) 1956- .... **CLC 39**
    See also CA 118; 136; CANR 121
Lemonnier, (Antoine Louis) Camille
    1844-1913 .... **TCLC 22**
    See also CA 121
Lenau, Nikolaus 1802-1850 .... **NCLC 16**
L'Engle, Madeleine 1918-2007 .... **CLC 12**
    See also AAYA 28; AITN 2; BPFB 2; BYA
      2, 4, 5, 7; CA 1-4R; 264; CANR 3, 21,
      39, 66, 107; CLR 1, 14, 57; CPW; CWRI
      5; DA3; DAM POP; DLB 52; JRDA;
      MAICYA 1, 2; MTCW 1, 2; MTFW 2005;
      SAAS 15; SATA 1, 27, 75, 128; SATA-
      Obit 186; SFW 4; WYA; YAW
L'Engle, Madeleine Camp Franklin
    See L'Engle, Madeleine
Lengyel, Jozsef 1896-1975 .... **CLC 7**
    See also CA 85-88; 57-60; CANR 71;
      RGSF 2
Lenin 1870-1924 .... **TCLC 67**
    See also CA 121; 168

Lenin, N.
    See Lenin
Lenin, Nikolai
    See Lenin
Lenin, V. I.
    See Lenin
Lenin, Vladimir I.
    See Lenin
Lenin, Vladimir Ilyich
    See Lenin
Lennon, John (Ono) 1940-1980 .. **CLC 12, 35**
    See also CA 102; SATA 114
Lennox, Charlotte Ramsay
    1729(?)-1804 .... **NCLC 23, 134**
    See also DLB 39; RGEL 2
Lentricchia, Frank, Jr.
    See Lentricchia, Frank
Lentricchia, Frank 1940- .... **CLC 34**
    See also CA 25-28R; CANR 19, 106, 148;
      DLB 246
Lenz, Gunter .... **CLC 65**
Lenz, Jakob Michael Reinhold
    1751-1792 .... **LC 100**
    See also DLB 94; RGWL 2, 3
Lenz, Siegfried 1926- .... **CLC 27; SSC 33**
    See also CA 89-92; CANR 80, 149; CWW
      2; DLB 75; EWL 3; RGSF 2; RGWL 2, 3
Leon, David
    See Jacob, (Cyprien-)Max
Leonard, Dutch
    See Leonard, Elmore
Leonard, Elmore 1925- .... **CLC 28, 34, 71,
    120, 222**
    See also AAYA 22, 59; AITN 1; BEST 89:1,
      90:4; BPFB 2; CA 81-84; CANR 12, 28,
      53, 76, 96, 133, 176; CMW 4; CN 5, 6, 7;
      CPW; DA3; DAM POP; DLB 173, 226;
      INT CANR-28; MSW; MTCW 1, 2;
      MTFW 2005; RGAL 4; SATA 163;
      TCWW 1, 2
Leonard, Elmore John, Jr.
    See Leonard, Elmore
Leonard, Hugh
    See Byrne, John Keyes
Leonov, Leonid (Maximovich)
    1899-1994 .... **CLC 92**
    See also CA 129; CANR 76; DAM NOV;
      DLB 272; EWL 3; MTCW 1, 2; MTFW
      2005
Leonov, Leonid Maksimovich
    See Leonov, Leonid (Maximovich)
Leopardi, (Conte) Giacomo
    1798-1837 .... **NCLC 22, 129; PC 37**
    See also EW 5; RGWL 2, 3; WLIT 7; WP
Le Reveler
    See Artaud, Antonin (Marie Joseph)
Lerman, Eleanor 1952- .... **CLC 9**
    See also CA 85-88; CANR 69, 124, 184
Lerman, Rhoda 1936- .... **CLC 56**
    See also CA 49-52; CANR 70
Lermontov, Mikhail Iur'evich
    See Lermontov, Mikhail Yuryevich
Lermontov, Mikhail Yuryevich
    1814-1841 .... **NCLC 5, 47, 126; PC 18**
    See also DLB 205; EW 6; RGWL 2, 3;
      TWA
Leroux, Gaston 1868-1927 .... **TCLC 25**
    See also CA 108; 136; CANR 69; CMW 4;
      MTFW 2005; NFS 20; SATA 65
Lesage, Alain-Rene 1668-1747 .... **LC 2, 28**
    See also DLB 313; EW 3; GFL Beginnings
      to 1789; RGWL 2, 3
Leskov, N(ikolai) S(emenovich) 1831-1895
    See Leskov, Nikolai (Semyonovich)
Leskov, Nikolai (Semyonovich)
    1831-1895 ... **NCLC 25, 174; SSC 34, 96**
    See also DLB 238

Leskov, Nikolai Semenovich
    See Leskov, Nikolai (Semyonovich)
Lesser, Milton
    See Marlowe, Stephen
Lessing, Doris 1919- .. **CLC 1, 2, 3, 6, 10, 15,
    22, 40, 94, 170, 254; SSC 6, 61; WLCS**
    See also AAYA 57; AFW; BRWS 1; CA
      9-12R; CAAS 14; CANR 33, 54, 76, 122,
      179; CBD; CD 5, 6; CDBLB 1960 to
      Present; CN 1, 2, 3, 4, 5, 6, 7; CWD; DA;
      DA3; DAB; DAC; DAM MST, NOV;
      DFS 20; DLB 15, 139; DLBY 1985; EWL
      3; EXPS; FL 1:6; FW; LAIT 4; MTCW 1,
      2; MTFW 2005; NFS 27; RGEL 2; RGSF
      2; SFW 4; SSFS 1, 12, 20, 26; TEA;
      WLIT 2, 4
Lessing, Doris May
    See Lessing, Doris
Lessing, Gotthold Ephraim
    1729-1781 .... **DC 26; LC 8, 124, 162**
    See also CDWLB 2; DLB 97; EW 4; RGWL
      2, 3
Lester, Julius 1939- .... **BLC 2:2**
    See also AAYA 12, 51; BW 2; BYA 3, 9,
      11, 12; CA 17-20R; CANR 8, 23, 43, 129,
      174; CLR 2, 41, 143; JRDA; MAICYA 1,
      2; MAICYAS 1; MTFW 2005; SATA 12,
      74, 112, 157; YAW
Lester, Richard 1932- .... **CLC 20**
Levenson, Jay .... **CLC 70**
Lever, Charles (James)
    1806-1872 .... **NCLC 23**
    See also DLB 21; RGEL 2
Leverson, Ada Esther
    1862(?)-1933(?) .... **TCLC 18**
    See also CA 117; 202; DLB 153; RGEL 2
Levertov, Denise 1923-1997 .. **CLC 1, 2, 3, 5,
    8, 15, 28, 66; PC 11**
    See also AMWS 3; CA 1-4R, 178; 163;
      CAAE 178; CAAS 19; CANR 3, 29, 50,
      108; CDALBS; CP 1, 2, 3, 4, 5, 6; CWP;
      DAM POET; DLB 5, 165, 342; EWL 3;
      EXPP; FW; INT CANR-29; MAL 5;
      MTCW 1, 2; PAB; PFS 7, 17; RGAL 4;
      RGHL; TUS; WP
Levi, Carlo 1902-1975 .... **TCLC 125**
    See also CA 65-68; 53-56; CANR 10; EWL
      3; RGWL 2, 3
Levi, Jonathan .... **CLC 76**
    See also CA 197
Levi, Peter (Chad Tigar)
    1931-2000 .... **CLC 41**
    See also CA 5-8R; 187; CANR 34, 80; CP
      1, 2, 3, 4, 5, 6, 7; DLB 40
Levi, Primo 1919-1987 ...... **CLC 37, 50; SSC
    12, 122; TCLC 109**
    See also CA 13-16R; 122; CANR 12, 33,
      61, 70, 132, 171; DLB 177, 299; EWL 3;
      MTCW 1, 2; MTFW 2005; RGHL;
      RGWL 2, 3; WLIT 7
Levin, Ira 1929-2007 .... **CLC 3, 6**
    See also CA 21-24R; 266; CANR 17, 44,
      74, 139; CMW 4; CN 1, 2, 3, 4, 5, 6, 7;
      CPW; DA3; DAM POP; HGG; MTCW 1,
      2; MTFW 2005; SATA 66; SATA-Obit
      187; SFW 4
Levin, Ira Marvin
    See Levin, Ira
Levin, Ira Marvin
    See Levin, Ira
Levin, Meyer 1905-1981 .... **CLC 7**
    See also AITN 1; CA 9-12R; 104; CANR
      15; CN 1, 2, 3; DAM POP; DLB 9, 28;
      DLBY 1981; MAL 5; RGHL; SATA 21;
      SATA-Obit 27
Levine, Albert Norman
    See Levine, Norman

Lively, Penelope 1933- .... **CLC 32, 50**
　　See also BPFB 2; CA 41-44R; CANR 29,
　　67, 79, 131, 172; CLR 7; CN 5, 6, 7;
　　CWRI 5; DAM NOV; DLB 14, 161, 207,
　　326; FANT; JRDA; MAICYA 1, 2;
　　MTCW 1, 2; MTFW 2005; SATA 7, 60,
　　101, 164; TEA
Lively, Penelope Margaret
　　See Lively, Penelope
Livesay, Dorothy (Kathleen)
　　1909-1996 .... **CLC 4, 15, 79**
　　See also AITN 2; CA 25-28R; CAAS 8;
　　CANR 36, 67; CP 1, 2, 3, 4, 5; DAC;
　　DAM MST, POET; DLB 68; FW; MTCW
　　1; RGEL 2; TWA
Livius Andronicus c. 284B.C.-c.
　　204B.C. .... **CMLC 102**
Livy c. 59B.C.-c. 12 .... **CMLC 11**
　　See also AW 2; CDWLB 1; DLB 211;
　　RGWL 2, 3; WLIT 8
Li Yaotang
　　See Jin, Ba
Lizardi, Jose Joaquin Fernandez de
　　1776-1827 .... **NCLC 30**
　　See also LAW
Llewellyn, Richard
　　See Llewellyn Lloyd, Richard Dafydd Viv-
　　ian
Llewellyn Lloyd, Richard Dafydd Vivian
　　1906-1983 .... **CLC 7, 80**
　　See also CA 53-56; 111; CANR 7, 71; DLB
　　15; SATA 11; SATA-Obit 37
Llosa, Jorge Mario Pedro Vargas
　　See Vargas Llosa, Mario
Llosa, Mario Vargas
　　See Vargas Llosa, Mario
Lloyd, Manda
　　See Mander, (Mary) Jane
Lloyd Webber, Andrew 1948- .... **CLC 21**
　　See also AAYA 1, 38; CA 116; 149; DAM
　　DRAM; DFS 7; SATA 56
Llull, Ramon c. 1235-c. 1316 .... **CMLC 12**
Lobb, Ebenezer
　　See Upward, Allen
Locke, Alain (Le Roy)
　　1886-1954 .... **BLCS; HR 1:3; TCLC 43**
　　See also AMWS 14; BW 1, 3; CA 106; 124;
　　CANR 79; DLB 51; LMFS 2; MAL 5;
　　RGAL 4
Locke, John 1632-1704 .... **LC 7, 35, 135**
　　See also DLB 31, 101, 213, 252; RGEL 2;
　　WLIT 3
Locke-Elliott, Sumner
　　See Elliott, Sumner Locke
Lockhart, John Gibson 1794-1854 .. **NCLC 6**
　　See also DLB 110, 116, 144
Lockridge, Ross (Franklin), Jr.
　　1914-1948 .... **TCLC 111**
　　See also CA 108; 145; CANR 79; DLB 143;
　　DLBY 1980; MAL 5; RGAL 4; RHW
Lockwood, Robert
　　See Johnson, Robert
Lodge, David 1935- .... **CLC 36, 141**
　　See also BEST 90:1; BRWS 4; CA 17-20R;
　　CANR 19, 53, 92, 139; CN 1, 2, 3, 4, 5,
　　6, 7; CPW; DAM POP; DLB 14, 194;
　　EWL 3; INT CANR-19; MTCW 1, 2;
　　MTFW 2005
Lodge, Thomas 1558-1625 .... **LC 41**
　　See also DLB 172; RGEL 2
Loewinsohn, Ron(ald William)
　　1937- .... **CLC 52**
　　See also CA 25-28R; CANR 71; CP 1, 2, 3,
　　4
Logan, Jake
　　See Smith, Martin Cruz
Logan, John (Burton) 1923-1987 .... **CLC 5**
　　See also CA 77-80; 124; CANR 45; CP 1,
　　2, 3, 4; DLB 5

Lo-Johansson, (Karl) Ivar
　　1901-1990 .... **TCLC 216**
　　See also CA 102; CANR 20, 79, 137;
　　DLB 259; EWL 3; RGWL 2, 3
Lo Kuan-chung 1330(?)-1400(?) .... **LC 12**
Lomax, Pearl
　　See Cleage, Pearl
Lomax, Pearl Cleage
　　See Cleage, Pearl
Lombard, Nap
　　See Johnson, Pamela Hansford
Lombard, Peter 1100(?)-1160(?) ... **CMLC 72**
Lombino, Salvatore
　　See Hunter, Evan
London, Jack 1876-1916
　　See London, John Griffith
London, John Griffith 1876-1916 .... **SSC 4,
　　49; TCLC 9, 15, 39; WLC 4**
　　See also AAYA 13, 75; AITN 2; AMW;
　　BPFB 2; BYA 4, 13; CA 110; 119; CANR
　　73; CDALB 1865-1917; CLR 108; DA;
　　DA3; DAB; DAC; DAM MST, NOV;
　　DLB 8, 12, 78, 212; EWL 3; EXPS;
　　JRDA; LAIT 3; MAICYA 1, 2,; MAL 5;
　　MTCW 1, 2; MTFW 2005; NFS 8, 19;
　　RGAL 4; RGSF 2; SATA 18; SFW 4;
　　SSFS 7; TCWW 1, 2; TUS; WYA; YAW
Long, Emmett
　　See Leonard, Elmore
Longbaugh, Harry
　　See Goldman, William
Longfellow, Henry Wadsworth
　　1807-1882 .... **NCLC 2, 45, 101, 103; PC
　　30; WLCS**
　　See also AMW; AMWR 2; CDALB 1640-
　　1865; CLR 99; DA; DA3; DAB; DAC;
　　DAM MST, POET; DLB 1, 59, 235;
　　EXPP; PAB; PFS 2, 7, 17; RGAL 4;
　　SATA 19; TUS; WP
Longinus c. 1st cent. - .... **CMLC 27**
　　See also AW 2; DLB 176
Longley, Michael 1939- .... **CLC 29**
　　See also BRWS 8; CA 102; CP 1, 2, 3, 4, 5,
　　6, 7; DLB 40
Longstreet, Augustus Baldwin
　　1790-1870 .... **NCLC 159**
　　See also DLB 3, 11, 74, 248; RGAL 4
Longus fl. c. 2nd cent. - .... **CMLC 7**
Longway, A. Hugh
　　See Lang, Andrew
Lonnbohm, Armas Eino Leopold
　　See Lonnbohm, Armas Eino Leopold
Lonnbohm, Armas Eino Leopold
　　1878-1926 .... **TCLC 24**
　　See also CA 123; EWL 3
Lonnrot, Elias 1802-1884 .... **NCLC 53**
　　See also EFS 3
Lonsdale, Roger .... **CLC 65**
Lopate, Phillip 1943- .... **CLC 29**
　　See also CA 97-100; CANR 88, 157; DLBY
　　1980; INT CA-97-100
Lopez, Barry (Holstun) 1945- .... **CLC 70**
　　See also AAYA 9, 63; ANW; CA 65-68;
　　CANR 7, 23, 47, 68, 92; DLB 256, 275,
　　335; INT CANR-7, CANR-23; MTCW 1;
　　RGAL 4; SATA 67
Lopez de Mendoza, Inigo
　　See Santillana, Inigo Lopez de Mendoza,
　　Marques de
Lopez Portillo (y Pacheco), Jose
　　1920-2004 .... **CLC 46**
　　See also CA 129; 224; HW 1
Lopez y Fuentes, Gregorio
　　1897(?)-1966 .... **CLC 32**
　　See also CA 131; EWL 3; HW 1
Lorca, Federico Garcia
　　See Garcia Lorca, Federico
Lord, Audre
　　See Lorde, Audre

Lord, Bette Bao 1938- .... **AAL; CLC 23**
　　See also BEST 90:3; BPFB 2; CA 107;
　　CANR 41, 79; INT CA-107; SATA 58
Lord Auch
　　See Bataille, Georges
Lord Brooke
　　See Greville, Fulke
Lord Byron
　　See Byron, George Gordon (Noel)
Lord Dunsany
　　See Dunsany, Edward John Moreton Drax
　　Plunkett
Lorde, Audre 1934-1992 .... **BLC 1:2, 2:2;
　　CLC 18, 71; PC 12; TCLC 173**
　　See also AFAW 1, 2; BW 1, 3; CA 25-28R;
　　142; CANR 16, 26, 46, 82; CP 2, 3, 4, 5;
　　DA3; DAM MULT, POET; DLB 41; EWL
　　3; FW; GLL 1; MAL 5; MTCW 1, 2;
　　MTFW 2005; PFS 16; RGAL 4
Lorde, Audre Geraldine
　　See Lorde, Audre
Lord Houghton
　　See Milnes, Richard Monckton
Lord Jeffrey
　　See Jeffrey, Francis
Loreaux, Nichol .... **CLC 65**
Lorenzini, Carlo 1826-1890 .... **NCLC 54**
　　See also CLR 5, 120; MAICYA 1, 2; SATA
　　29, 100; WCH; WLIT 7
Lorenzo, Heberto Padilla
　　See Padilla (Lorenzo), Heberto
Loris
　　See Hofmannsthal, Hugo von
Loti, Pierre
　　See Viaud, (Louis Marie) Julien
Lottie
　　See Grimke, Charlotte L(ottie) Forten
Lou, Henri
　　See Andreas-Salome, Lou
Louie, David Wong 1954- .... **CLC 70**
　　See also CA 139; CANR 120
Louis, Adrian C. .... **NNAL**
　　See also CA 223
Louis, Father M.
　　See Merton, Thomas (James)
Louise, Heidi
　　See Erdrich, Louise
Lovecraft, H. P. 1890-1937 .... **SSC 3, 52;
　　TCLC 4, 22**
　　See also AAYA 14; BPFB 2; CA 104; 133;
　　CANR 106; DA3; DAM POP; HGG;
　　MTCW 1, 2; MTFW 2005; RGAL 4;
　　SCFW 1, 2; SFW 4; SUFW
Lovecraft, Howard Phillips
　　See Lovecraft, H. P.
Lovelace, Earl 1935- .... **CLC 51**
　　See also BW 2; CA 77-80; CANR 41, 72,
　　114; CD 5, 6; CDWLB 3; CN 1, 2, 3, 4,
　　5, 6, 7; DLB 125; EWL 3; MTCW 1
Lovelace, Richard 1618-1658 ..... **LC 24, 158;
　　PC 69**
　　See also BRW 2; DLB 131; EXPP; PAB;
　　RGEL 2
Low, Penelope Margaret
　　See Lively, Penelope
Lowe, Pardee 1904- .... **AAL**
Lowell, Amy 1874-1925 ... **PC 13; TCLC 1, 8**
　　See also AAYA 57; AMW; CA 104; 151;
　　DAM POET; DLB 54, 140; EWL 3;
　　EXPP; LMFS 2; MAL 5; MBL; MTCW
　　2; MTFW 2005; PFS 30; RGAL 4; TUS
Lowell, James Russell 1819-1891 ... **NCLC 2,
　　90**
　　See also AMWS 1; CDALB 1640-1865;
　　DLB 1, 11, 64, 79, 189, 235; RGAL 4

Marques, Rene 1919-1979 .. **CLC 96; HLC 2**
See also CA 97-100; 85-88; CANR 78;
DAM MULT; DLB 305; EWL 3; HW 1,
2; LAW; RGSF 2

Marquez, Gabriel Garcia
See Garcia Marquez, Gabriel

Marquis, Don(ald Robert Perry)
1878-1937 .... **TCLC 7**
See also CA 104; 166; DLB 11, 25; MAL
5; RGAL 4

Marquis de Sade
See Sade, Donatien Alphonse Francois

Marric, J. J.
See Creasey, John

Marryat, Frederick 1792-1848 .... **NCLC 3**
See also DLB 21, 163; RGEL 2; WCH

Marsden, James
See Creasey, John

Marsh, Edward 1872-1953 .... **TCLC 99**

Marsh, (Edith) Ngaio 1895-1982 .. **CLC 7, 53**
See also CA 9-12R; CANR 6, 58; CMW 4;
CN 1, 2, 3; CPW; DAM POP; DLB 77;
MSW; MTCW 1, 2; RGEL 2; TEA

Marshall, Alan
See Westlake, Donald E.

Marshall, Allen
See Westlake, Donald E.

Marshall, Garry 1934- .... **CLC 17**
See also AAYA 3; CA 111; SATA 60

Marshall, Paule 1929- .... **BLC 1:3, 2:3; CLC
27, 72, 253; SSC 3**
See also AFAW 1, 2; AMWS 11; BPFB 2;
BW 2, 3; CA 77-80; CANR 25, 73, 129;
CN 1, 2, 3, 4, 5, 6, 7; DA3; DAM MULT;
DLB 33, 157, 227; EWL 3; LATS 1:2;
MAL 5; MTCW 1, 2; MTFW 2005;
RGAL 4; SSFS 15

Marshallik
See Zangwill, Israel

Marsilius of Inghen c.
1340-1396 .... **CMLC 106**

Marsten, Richard
See Hunter, Evan

Marston, John 1576-1634 .... **LC 33**
See also BRW 2; DAM DRAM; DLB 58,
172; RGEL 2

Martel, Yann 1963- .... **CLC 192**
See also AAYA 67; CA 146; CANR 114;
DLB 326, 334; MTFW 2005; NFS 27

Martens, Adolphe-Adhemar
See Ghelderode, Michel de

Martha, Henry
See Harris, Mark

Marti, Jose
See Marti (y Perez), Jose (Julian)

Marti (y Perez), Jose (Julian)
1853-1895 ..... **HLC 2; NCLC 63; PC 76**
See also DAM MULT; DLB 290; HW 2;
LAW; RGWL 2, 3; WLIT 1

Martial c. 40-c. 104 .... **CMLC 35; PC 10**
See also AW 2; CDWLB 1; DLB 211;
RGWL 2, 3

Martin, Ken
See Hubbard, L. Ron

Martin, Richard
See Creasey, John

Martin, Steve 1945- .... **CLC 30, 217**
See also AAYA 53; CA 97-100; CANR 30,
100, 140; DFS 19; MTCW 1; MTFW
2005

Martin, Valerie 1948- .... **CLC 89**
See also BEST 90:2; CA 85-88; CANR 49,
89, 165

Martin, Violet Florence 1862-1915 .. **SSC 56;
TCLC 51**

Martin, Webber
See Silverberg, Robert

Martindale, Patrick Victor
See White, Patrick (Victor Martindale)

Martin du Gard, Roger
1881-1958 .... **TCLC 24**
See also CA 118; CANR 94; DLB 65, 331;
EWL 3; GFL 1789 to the Present; RGWL
2, 3

Martineau, Harriet 1802-1876 ...... **NCLC 26,
137**
See also DLB 21, 55, 159, 163, 166, 190;
FW; RGEL 2; YABC 2

Martines, Julia
See O'Faolain, Julia

Martinez, Enrique Gonzalez
See Gonzalez Martinez, Enrique

Martinez, Jacinto Benavente y
See Benavente (y Martinez), Jacinto

Martinez de la Rosa, Francisco de Paula
1787-1862 .... **NCLC 102**
See also TWA

Martinez Ruiz, Jose 1873-1967 .... **CLC 11**
See also CA 93-96; DLB 322; EW 3; EWL
3; HW 1

Martinez Sierra, Gregorio
See Martinez Sierra, Maria

Martinez Sierra, Gregorio
1881-1947 .... **TCLC 6**
See also CA 115; EWL 3

Martinez Sierra, Maria 1874-1974 .. **TCLC 6**
See also CA 250; 115; EWL 3

Martinsen, Martin
See Follett, Ken

Martinson, Harry (Edmund)
1904-1978 .... **CLC 14**
See also CA 77-80; CANR 34, 130; DLB
259, 331; EWL 3

Martyn, Edward 1859-1923 .... **TCLC 131**
See also CA 179; DLB 10; RGEL 2

Marut, Ret
See Traven, B.

Marut, Robert
See Traven, B.

Marvell, Andrew 1621-1678 .... **LC 4, 43; PC
10, 86; WLC 4**
See also BRW 2; BRWR 2; CDBLB 1660-
1789; DA; DAB; DAC; DAM MST,
POET; DLB 131; EXPP; PFS 5; RGEL 2;
TEA; WP

Marx, Karl (Heinrich)
1818-1883 .... **NCLC 17, 114**
See also DLB 129; LATS 1:1; TWA

Masaoka, Shiki -1902
See Masaoka, Tsunenori

Masaoka, Tsunenori 1867-1902 ..... **TCLC 18**
See also CA 117; 191; EWL 3; RGWL 3;
TWA

Masaoka Shiki
See Masaoka, Tsunenori

Masefield, John (Edward)
1878-1967 .... **CLC 11, 47; PC 78**
See also CA 19-20; 25-28R; CANR 33;
CAP 2; CDBLB 1890-1914; DAM POET;
DLB 10, 19, 153, 160; EWL 3; EXPP;
FANT; MTCW 1, 2; PFS 5; RGEL 2;
SATA 19

Maso, Carole 1955(?)- .... **CLC 44**
See also CA 170; CANR 148; CN 7; GLL
2; RGAL 4

Mason, Bobbie Ann 1940- ... **CLC 28, 43, 82,
154; SSC 4, 101**
See also AAYA 5, 42; AMWS 8; BPFB 2;
CA 53-56; CANR 11, 31, 58, 83, 125,
169; CDALBS; CN 5, 6, 7; CSW; DA3;
DLB 173; DLBY 1987; EWL 3; EXPS;
INT CANR-31; MAL 5; MTCW 1, 2;
MTFW 2005; NFS 4; RGAL 4; RGSF 2;
SSFS 3, 8, 20; TCLE 1:2; YAW

Mason, Ernst
See Pohl, Frederik

Mason, Hunni B.
See Sternheim, (William Adolf) Carl

Mason, Lee W.
See Malzberg, Barry N(athaniel)

Mason, Nick 1945- .... **CLC 35**

Mason, Tally
See Derleth, August (William)

Mass, Anna .... **CLC 59**

Mass, William
See Gibson, William

Massinger, Philip 1583-1640 .... **LC 70**
See also BRWS 11; DLB 58; RGEL 2

Master Lao
See Lao Tzu

Masters, Edgar Lee 1868-1950 ...... **PC 1, 36;
TCLC 2, 25; WLCS**
See also AMWS 1; CA 104; 133; CDALB
1865-1917; DA; DAC; DAM MST,
POET; DLB 54; EWL 3; EXPP; MAL 5;
MTCW 1, 2; MTFW 2005; RGAL 4;
TUS; WP

Masters, Hilary 1928- .... **CLC 48**
See also CA 25-28R; 217; CAAE 217;
CANR 13, 47, 97, 171; CN 6, 7; DLB
244

Masters, Hilary Thomas
See Masters, Hilary

Mastrosimone, William 1947- .... **CLC 36**
See also CA 186; CAD; CD 5, 6

Mathe, Albert
See Camus, Albert

Mather, Cotton 1663-1728 .... **LC 38**
See also AMWS 2; CDALB 1640-1865;
DLB 24, 30, 140; RGAL 4; TUS

Mather, Increase 1639-1723 .... **LC 38, 161**
See also DLB 24

Mathers, Marshall
See Eminem

Mathers, Marshall Bruce
See Eminem

Matheson, Richard 1926- .... **CLC 37, 267**
See also AAYA 31; CA 97-100; CANR 88,
99; DLB 8, 44; HGG; INT CA-97-100;
SCFW 1, 2; SFW 4; SUFW 2

Matheson, Richard Burton
See Matheson, Richard

Mathews, Harry 1930- .... **CLC 6, 52**
See also CA 21-24R; CAAS 6; CANR 18,
40, 98, 160; CN 5, 6, 7

Mathews, John Joseph 1894-1979 .. **CLC 84;
NNAL**
See also CA 19-20; 142; CANR 45; CAP 2;
DAM MULT; DLB 175; TCWW 1, 2

Mathias, Roland 1915-2007 .... **CLC 45**
See also CA 97-100; 263; CANR 19, 41;
CP 1, 2, 3, 4, 5, 6, 7; DLB 27

Mathias, Roland Glyn
See Mathias, Roland

Matsuo Basho 1644(?)-1694 ...... **LC 62; PC 3**
See also DAM POET; PFS 2, 7, 18; RGWL
2, 3; WP

Mattheson, Rodney
See Creasey, John

Matthew of Vendome c. 1130-c.
1200 .... **CMLC 99**
See also DLB 208

Matthews, (James) Brander
1852-1929 .... **TCLC 95**
See also CA 181; DLB 71, 78; DLBD 13

Matthews, Greg 1949- .... **CLC 45**
See also CA 135

Matthews, William (Procter III)
1942-1997 .... **CLC 40**
See also AMWS 9; CA 29-32R; 162; CAAS
18; CANR 12, 57; CP 2, 3, 4, 5, 6; DLB
5

McGahern, John 1934-2006 .... **CLC 5, 9, 48, 156; SSC 17**
See also CA 17-20R; 249; CANR 29, 68, 113; CN 1, 2, 3, 4, 5, 6, 7; DLB 14, 231, 319; MTCW 1

McGinley, Patrick (Anthony) 1937- . **CLC 41**
See also CA 120; 127; CANR 56; INT CA-127

McGinley, Phyllis 1905-1978 .... **CLC 14**
See also CA 9-12R; 77-80; CANR 19; CP 1, 2; CWRI 5; DLB 11, 48; MAL 5; PFS 9, 13; SATA 2, 44; SATA-Obit 24

McGinniss, Joe 1942- .... **CLC 32**
See also AITN 2; BEST 89:2; CA 25-28R; CANR 26, 70, 152; CPW; DLB 185; INT CANR-26

McGivern, Maureen Daly
See Daly, Maureen

McGivern, Maureen Patricia Daly
See Daly, Maureen

McGrath, Patrick 1950- .... **CLC 55**
See also CA 136; CANR 65, 148; CN 5, 6, 7; DLB 231; HGG; SUFW 2

McGrath, Thomas (Matthew)
1916-1990 .... **CLC 28, 59**
See also AMWS 10; CA 9-12R; 132; CANR 6, 33, 95; CP 1, 2, 3, 4, 5; DAM POET; MAL 5; MTCW 1; SATA 41; SATA-Obit 66

McGuane, Thomas 1939- .. **CLC 3, 7, 18, 45, 127**
See also AITN 2; BPFB 2; CA 49-52; CANR 5, 24, 49, 94, 164; CN 1, 2, 3, 4, 5, 6, 7; DLB 2, 212; DLBY 1980; EWL 3; INT CANR-24; MAL 5; MTCW 1; MTFW 2005; TCWW 1, 2

McGuane, Thomas Francis III
See McGuane, Thomas

McGuckian, Medbh 1950- .... **CLC 48, 174; PC 27**
See also BRWS 5; CA 143; CP 4, 5, 6, 7; CWP; DAM POET; DLB 40

McHale, Tom 1942(?)-1982 .... **CLC 3, 5**
See also AITN 1; CA 77-80; 106; CN 1, 2, 3

McHugh, Heather 1948- .... **PC 61**
See also CA 69-72; CANR 11, 28, 55, 92; CP 4, 5, 6, 7; CWP; PFS 24

McIlvanney, William 1936- .... **CLC 42**
See also CA 25-28R; CANR 61; CMW 4; DLB 14, 207

McIlwraith, Maureen Mollie Hunter
See Hunter, Mollie

McInerney, Jay 1955- .... **CLC 34, 112**
See also AAYA 18; BPFB 2; CA 116; 123; CANR 45, 68, 116, 176; CN 5, 6, 7; CPW; DA3; DAM POP; DLB 292; INT CA-123; MAL 5; MTCW 2; MTFW 2005

McIntyre, Vonda N. 1948- .... **CLC 18**
See also CA 81-84; CANR 17, 34, 69; MTCW 1; SFW 4; YAW

McIntyre, Vonda Neel
See McIntyre, Vonda N.

McKay, Claude
See McKay, Festus Claudius

McKay, Festus Claudius
1889-1948 ...... **BLC 1:3; HR 1:3; PC 2; TCLC 7, 41; WLC 4**
See also AFAW 1, 2; AMWS 10; BW 1, 3; CA 104; 124; CANR 73; DA; DAB; DAC; DAM MST, MULT, NOV, POET; DLB 4, 45, 51, 117; EWL 3; EXPP; GLL 2; LAIT 3; LMFS 2; MAL 5; MTCW 1, 2; MTFW 2005; PAB; PFS 4; RGAL 4; TUS; WP

McKuen, Rod 1933- .... **CLC 1, 3**
See also AITN 1; CA 41-44R; CANR 40; CP 1

McLoughlin, R. B.
See Mencken, H(enry) L(ouis)

McLuhan, (Herbert) Marshall
1911-1980 .... **CLC 37, 83**
See also CA 9-12R; 102; CANR 12, 34, 61; DLB 88; INT CANR-12; MTCW 1, 2; MTFW 2005

McMahon, Pat
See Hoch, Edward D.

McManus, Declan Patrick Aloysius
See Costello, Elvis

McMillan, Terry 1951- .. **BLCS; CLC 50, 61, 112**
See also AAYA 21; AMWS 13; BPFB 2; BW 2, 3; CA 140; CANR 60, 104, 131; CN 7; CPW; DA3; DAM MULT, NOV, POP; MAL 5; MTCW 2; MTFW 2005; RGAL 4; YAW

McMurtry, Larry 1936- .... **CLC 2, 3, 7, 11, 27, 44, 127, 250**
See also AAYA 15; AITN 2; AMWS 5; BEST 89:2; BPFB 2; CA 5-8R; CANR 19, 43, 64, 103, 170; CDALB 1968-1988; CN 2, 3, 4, 5, 6, 7; CPW; CSW; DA3; DAM NOV, POP; DLB 2, 143, 256; DLBY 1980, 1987; EWL 3; MAL 5; MTCW 1, 2; MTFW 2005; RGAL 4; TCWW 1, 2

McMurtry, Larry Jeff
See McMurtry, Larry

McNally, Terrence 1939- ... **CLC 4, 7, 41, 91, 252; DC 27**
See also AAYA 62; AMWS 13; CA 45-48; CAD; CANR 2, 56, 116; CD 5, 6; DA3; DAM DRAM; DFS 16, 19; DLB 7, 249; EWL 3; GLL 1; MTCW 2; MTFW 2005

McNally, Thomas Michael
See McNally, T.M.

McNally, T.M. 1961- .... **CLC 82**
See also CA 246

McNamer, Deirdre 1950- .... **CLC 70**
See also CA 188; CANR 163

McNeal, Tom .... **CLC 119**
See also CA 252; CANR 185; SATA 194

McNeile, Herman Cyril
1888-1937 .... **TCLC 44**
See also CA 184; CMW 4; DLB 77

McNickle, (William) D'Arcy
1904-1977 .... **CLC 89; NNAL**
See also CA 9-12R; 85-88; CANR 5, 45; DAM MULT; DLB 175, 212; RGAL 4; SATA-Obit 22; TCWW 1, 2

McPhee, John 1931- .... **CLC 36**
See also AAYA 61; AMWS 3; ANW; BEST 90:1; CA 65-68; CANR 20, 46, 64, 69, 121, 165; CPW; DLB 185, 275; MTCW 1, 2; MTFW 2005; TUS

McPhee, John Angus
See McPhee, John

McPherson, James Alan, Jr.
See McPherson, James Alan

McPherson, James Alan 1943- . **BLCS; CLC 19, 77; SSC 95**
See also BW 1, 3; CA 25-28R; 273; CAAE 273; CAAS 17; CANR 24, 74, 140; CN 3, 4, 5, 6; CSW; DLB 38, 244; EWL 3; MTCW 1, 2; MTFW 2005; RGAL 4; RGSF 2; SSFS 23

McPherson, William (Alexander)
1933- .... **CLC 34**
See also CA 69-72; CANR 28; INT CANR-28

McTaggart, J. McT. Ellis
See McTaggart, John McTaggart Ellis

McTaggart, John McTaggart Ellis
1866-1925 .... **TCLC 105**
See also CA 120; DLB 262

Mda, Zakes 1948- .... **BLC 2:3; CLC 262**
See also CA 205; CANR 151, 185; CD 5, 6; DLB 225

Mda, Zanemvula
See Mda, Zakes

Mda, Zanemvula Kizito Gatyeni
See Mda, Zakes

Mead, George Herbert 1863-1931 . **TCLC 89**
See also CA 212; DLB 270

Mead, Margaret 1901-1978 .... **CLC 37**
See also AITN 1; CA 1-4R; 81-84; CANR 4; DA3; FW; MTCW 1, 2; SATA-Obit 20

Meaker, M. J.
See Meaker, Marijane

Meaker, Marijane 1927- .... **CLC 12, 35**
See also AAYA 2, 23; BYA 1, 7, 8; CA 107; CANR 37, 63, 145, 180; CLR 29; GLL 2; INT CA-107; JRDA; MAICYA 1, 2; MAICYAS 1; MTCW 1; SAAS 1; SATA 20, 61, 99, 160; SATA-Essay 111; WYA; YAW

Meaker, Marijane Agnes
See Meaker, Marijane

Mechthild von Magdeburg c. 1207-c. 1282 .... **CMLC 91**
See also DLB 138

Medoff, Mark (Howard) 1940- ... **CLC 6, 23**
See also AITN 1; CA 53-56; CAD; CANR 5; CD 5, 6; DAM DRAM; DFS 4; DLB 7; INT CANR-5

Medvedev, P. N.
See Bakhtin, Mikhail Mikhailovich

Meged, Aharon
See Megged, Aharon

Meged, Aron
See Megged, Aharon

Megged, Aharon 1920- .... **CLC 9**
See also CA 49-52; CAAS 13; CANR 1, 140; EWL 3; RGHL

Mehta, Deepa 1950- .... **CLC 208**

Mehta, Gita 1943- .... **CLC 179**
See also CA 225; CN 7; DNFS 2

Mehta, Ved 1934- .... **CLC 37**
See also CA 1-4R, 212; CAAE 212; CANR 2, 23, 69; DLB 323; MTCW 1; MTFW 2005

Melanchthon, Philipp 1497-1560 .... **LC 90**
See also DLB 179

Melanter
See Blackmore, R(ichard) D(oddridge)

Meleager c. 140B.C.-c. 70B.C. ...... **CMLC 53**

Melies, Georges 1861-1938 .... **TCLC 81**

Melikow, Loris
See Hofmannsthal, Hugo von

Melmoth, Sebastian
See Wilde, Oscar

Melo Neto, Joao Cabral de
See Cabral de Melo Neto, Joao

Meltzer, Milton 1915- .... **CLC 26**
See also AAYA 8, 45; BYA 2, 6; CA 13-16R; CANR 38, 92, 107; CLR 13; DLB 61; JRDA; MAICYA 1, 2; SAAS 1; SATA 1, 50, 80, 128; SATA-Essay 124; WYA; YAW

Melville, Herman 1819-1891 ..... **NCLC 3, 12, 29, 45, 49, 91, 93, 123, 157, 181, 193; PC 82; SSC 1, 17, 46, 95; WLC 4**
See also AAYA 25; AMW; AMWR 1; CDALB 1640-1865; DA; DA3; DAB; DAC; DAM MST, NOV; DLB 3, 74, 250, 254; EXPN; EXPS; GL 3; LAIT 1, 2; NFS 7, 9; RGAL 4; RGSF 2; SATA 59; SSFS 3; TUS

Members, Mark
See Powell, Anthony

Membreno, Alejandro .... **CLC 59**

Menand, Louis 1952- .... **CLC 208**
See also CA 200

Menander c. 342B.C.-c. 293B.C. .... **CMLC 9, 51, 101; DC 3**
See also AW 1; CDWLB 1; DAM DRAM; DLB 176; LMFS 1; RGWL 2, 3

Menchu, Rigoberta 1959- .. **CLC 160; HLCS 2**
See also CA 175; CANR 135; DNFS 1; WLIT 1

Mencken, H(enry) L(ouis)
1880-1956 .... **TCLC 13, 18**
See also AMW; CA 105; 125; CDALB 1917-1929; DLB 11, 29, 63, 137, 222; EWL 3; MAL 5; MTCW 1, 2; MTFW 2005; NCFS 4; RGAL 4; TUS

Mendelsohn, Jane 1965- .... **CLC 99**
See also CA 154; CANR 94

Mendelssohn, Moses 1729-1786 .... **LC 142**
See also DLB 97

Mendoza, Inigo Lopez de
See Santillana, Inigo Lopez de Mendoza, Marques de

Menton, Francisco de
See Chin, Frank (Chew, Jr.)

Mercer, David 1928-1980 .... **CLC 5**
See also CA 9-12R; 102; CANR 23; CBD; DAM DRAM; DLB 13, 310; MTCW 1; RGEL 2

Merchant, Paul
See Ellison, Harlan

Meredith, George 1828-1909 .. **PC 60; TCLC 17, 43**
See also CA 117; 153; CANR 80; CDBLB 1832-1890; DAM POET; DLB 18, 35, 57, 159; RGEL 2; TEA

Meredith, William 1919-2007 ...... **CLC 4, 13, 22, 55; PC 28**
See also CA 9-12R; 260; CAAS 14; CANR 6, 40, 129; CP 1, 2, 3, 4, 5, 6, 7; DAM POET; DLB 5; MAL 5

Meredith, William Morris
See Meredith, William

Merezhkovsky, Dmitrii Sergeevich
See Merezhkovsky, Dmitry Sergeyevich

Merezhkovsky, Dmitry Sergeevich
See Merezhkovsky, Dmitry Sergeyevich

Merezhkovsky, Dmitry Sergeyevich
1865-1941 .... **TCLC 29**
See also CA 169; DLB 295; EWL 3

Merezhkovsky, Zinaida
See Gippius, Zinaida (Nikolaevna)

Merimee, Prosper 1803-1870 . **DC 33; NCLC 6, 65; SSC 7, 77**
See also DLB 119, 192; EW 6; EXPS; GFL 1789 to the Present; RGSF 2; RGWL 2, 3; SSFS 8; SUFW

Merkin, Daphne 1954- .... **CLC 44**
See also CA 123

Merleau-Ponty, Maurice
1908-1961 .... **TCLC 156**
See also CA 114; 89-92; DLB 296; GFL 1789 to the Present

Merlin, Arthur
See Blish, James (Benjamin)

Mernissi, Fatima 1940- .... **CLC 171**
See also CA 152; DLB 346; FW

Merrill, James 1926-1995 ...... **CLC 2, 3, 6, 8, 13, 18, 34, 91; PC 28; TCLC 173**
See also AMWS 3; CA 13-16R; 147; CANR 10, 49, 63, 108; CP 1, 2, 3, 4; DA3; DAM POET; DLB 5, 165; DLBY 1985; EWL 3; INT CANR-10; MAL 5; MTCW 1, 2; MTFW 2005; PAB; PFS 23; RGAL 4

Merrill, James Ingram
See Merrill, James

Merriman, Alex
See Silverberg, Robert

Merriman, Brian 1747-1805 .... **NCLC 70**

Merritt, E. B.
See Waddington, Miriam

Merton, Thomas (James)
1915-1968 . **CLC 1, 3, 11, 34, 83; PC 10**
See also AAYA 61; AMWS 8; CA 5-8R; 25-28R; CANR 22, 53, 111, 131; DA3; DLB 48; DLBY 1981; MAL 5; MTCW 1, 2; MTFW 2005

Merwin, W.S. 1927- ..... **CLC 1, 2, 3, 5, 8, 13, 18, 45, 88; PC 45**
See also AMWS 3; CA 13-16R; CANR 15, 51, 112, 140; CP 1, 2, 3, 4, 5, 6, 7; DA3; DAM POET; DLB 5, 169, 342; EWL 3; INT CANR-15; MAL 5; MTCW 1, 2; MTFW 2005; PAB; PFS 5, 15; RGAL 4

Metastasio, Pietro 1698-1782 .... **LC 115**
See also RGWL 2, 3

Metcalf, John 1938- .... **CLC 37; SSC 43**
See also CA 113; CN 4, 5, 6, 7; DLB 60; RGSF 2; TWA

Metcalf, Suzanne
See Baum, L(yman) Frank

Mew, Charlotte (Mary) 1870-1928 .. **TCLC 8**
See also CA 105; 189; DLB 19, 135; RGEL 2

Mewshaw, Michael 1943- .... **CLC 9**
See also CA 53-56; CANR 7, 47, 147; DLBY 1980

Meyer, Conrad Ferdinand
1825-1898 .... **NCLC 81; SSC 30**
See also DLB 129; EW; RGWL 2, 3

Meyer, Gustav 1868-1932 .... **TCLC 21**
See also CA 117; 190; DLB 81; EWL 3

Meyer, June
See Jordan, June

Meyer, Lynn
See Slavitt, David R.

Meyer-Meyrink, Gustav
See Meyer, Gustav

Meyers, Jeffrey 1939- .... **CLC 39**
See also CA 73-76, 186; CAAE 186; CANR 54, 102, 159; DLB 111

Meynell, Alice (Christina Gertrude Thompson) 1847-1922 .... **TCLC 6**
See also CA 104; 177; DLB 19, 98; RGEL 2

Meyrink, Gustav
See Meyer, Gustav

Mhlophe, Gcina 1960- .... **BLC 2:3**

Michaels, Leonard 1933-2003 ..... **CLC 6, 25; SSC 16**
See also AMWS 16; CA 61-64; 216; CANR 21, 62, 119, 179; CN 3, 45, 6, 7; DLB 130; MTCW 1; TCLE 1:2

Michaux, Henri 1899-1984 .... **CLC 8, 19**
See also CA 85-88; 114; DLB 258; EWL 3; GFL 1789 to the Present; RGWL 2, 3

Micheaux, Oscar (Devereaux)
1884-1951 .... **TCLC 76**
See also BW 3; CA 174; DLB 50; TCWW 2

Michelangelo 1475-1564 .... **LC 12**
See also AAYA 43

Michelet, Jules 1798-1874 .... **NCLC 31**
See also EW 5; GFL 1789 to the Present

Michels, Robert 1876-1936 .... **TCLC 88**
See also CA 212

Michener, James A. 1907(?)-1997 . **CLC 1, 5, 11, 29, 60, 109**
See also AAYA 27; AITN 1; BEST 90:1; BPFB 2; CA 5-8R; 161; CANR 21, 45, 68; CN 1, 2, 3, 4, 5, 6; CPW; DA3; DAM NOV, POP; DLB 6; MAL 5; MTCW 1, 2; MTFW 2005; RHW; TCWW 1, 2

Mickiewicz, Adam 1798-1855 . **NCLC 3, 101; PC 38**
See also EW 5; RGWL 2, 3

Middleton, (John) Christopher
1926- .... **CLC 13**
See also CA 13-16R; CANR 29, 54, 117; CP 1, 2, 3, 4, 5, 6, 7; DLB 40

Middleton, Richard (Barham)
1882-1911 .... **TCLC 56**
See also CA 187; DLB 156; HGG

Middleton, Stanley 1919- .... **CLC 7, 38**
See also CA 25-28R; CAAS 23; CANR 21, 46, 81, 157; CN 1, 2, 3, 4, 5, 6, 7; DLB 14, 326

Middleton, Thomas 1580-1627 ...... **DC 5; LC 33, 123**
See also BRW 2; DAM DRAM, MST; DFS 18, 22; DLB 58; RGEL 2

Mieville, China 1972(?)- .... **CLC 235**
See also AAYA 52; CA 196; CANR 138; MTFW 2005

Migueis, Jose Rodrigues 1901-1980 . **CLC 10**
See also DLB 287

Mihura, Miguel 1905-1977 .... **DC 34**
See also CA 214

Mikszath, Kalman 1847-1910 .... **TCLC 31**
See also CA 170

Miles, Jack .... **CLC 100**
See also CA 200

Miles, John Russiano
See Miles, Jack

Miles, Josephine (Louise)
1911-1985 .... **CLC 1, 2, 14, 34, 39**
See also CA 1-4R; 116; CANR 2, 55; CP 1, 2, 3, 4; DAM POET; DLB 48; MAL 5; TCLE 1:2

Militant
See Sandburg, Carl (August)

Mill, Harriet (Hardy) Taylor
1807-1858 .... **NCLC 102**
See also FW

Mill, John Stuart 1806-1873 ... **NCLC 11, 58, 179**
See also CDBLB 1832-1890; DLB 55, 190, 262; FW 1; RGEL 2; TEA

Millar, Kenneth 1915-1983 .. **CLC 1, 2, 3, 14, 34, 41**
See also AMWS 4; BPFB 2; CA 9-12R; 110; CANR 16, 63, 107; CMW 4; CN 1, 2, 3; CPW; DA3; DAM POP; DLB 2, 226; DLBD 6; DLBY 1983; MAL 5; MSW; MTCW 1, 2; MTFW 2005; RGAL 4

Millay, E. Vincent
See Millay, Edna St. Vincent

Millay, Edna St. Vincent 1892-1950 ..... **PC 6, 61; TCLC 4, 49, 169; WLCS**
See also AMW; CA 104; 130; CDALB 1917-1929; DA; DA3; DAB; DAC; DAM MST, POET; DLB 45, 249; EWL 3; EXPP; FL 1:6; GLL 1; MAL 5; MBL; MTCW 1, 2; MTFW 2005; PAB; PFS 3, 17; RGAL 4; TUS; WP

Miller, Arthur 1915-2005 ..... **CLC 1, 2, 6, 10, 15, 26, 47, 78, 179; DC 1, 31; WLC 4**
See also AAYA 15; AITN 1; AMW; AMWC 1; CA 1-4R; 236; CABS 3; CAD; CANR 2, 30, 54, 76, 132; CD 5, 6; CDALB 1941-1968; DA; DA3; DAB; DAC; DAM DRAM, MST; DFS 1, 3, 8; DLB 7, 266; EWL 3; LAIT 1, 4; LATS 1:2; MAL 5; MTCW 1, 2; MTFW 2005; RGAL 4; RGHL; TUS; WYAS 1

Miller, Henry (Valentine)
1891-1980 .... **CLC 1, 2, 4, 9, 14, 43, 84; TCLC 213; WLC 4**
See also AMW; BPFB 2; CA 9-12R; 97-100; CANR 33, 64; CDALB 1929-1941; CN 1, 2; DA; DA3; DAB; DAC; DAM MST, NOV; DLB 4, 9; DLBY 1980; EWL 3; MAL 5; MTCW 1, 2; MTFW 2005; RGAL 4; TUS

Miller, Hugh 1802-1856 .... **NCLC 143**
See also DLB 190

Miller, Jason 1939(?)-2001 .... **CLC 2**
See also AITN 1; CA 73-76; 197; CAD; CANR 130; DFS 12; DLB 7

Miller, Sue 1943- .... **CLC 44**
   See also AMWS 12; BEST 90:3; CA 139;
   CANR 59, 91, 128; DA3; DAM POP;
   DLB 143

Miller, Walter M(ichael, Jr.)
   1923-1996 .... **CLC 4, 30**
   See also BPFB 2; CA 85-88; CANR 108;
   DLB 8; SCFW 1, 2; SFW 4

Millett, Kate 1934- .... **CLC 67**
   See also AITN 1; CA 73-76; CANR 32, 53,
   76, 110; DA3; DLB 246; FW; GLL 1;
   MTCW 1, 2; MTFW 2005

Millhauser, Steven 1943- ... **CLC 21, 54, 109;**
   SSC 57
   See also AAYA 76; CA 110; 111; CANR
   63, 114, 133; CN 6, 7; DA3; DLB 2;
   FANT; INT CA-111; MAL 5; MTCW 2;
   MTFW 2005

Millhauser, Steven Lewis
   See Millhauser, Steven

Millin, Sarah Gertrude 1889-1968 ... **CLC 49**
   See also CA 102; 93-96; DLB 225; EWL 3

Milne, A. A. 1882-1956 .... **TCLC 6, 88**
   See also BRWS 5; CA 104; 133; CLR 1,
   26, 108; CMW 4; CWRI 5; DA3; DAB;
   DAC; DAM MST; DLB 10, 77, 100, 160;
   FANT; MAICYA 1, 2; MTCW 1, 2;
   MTFW 2005; RGEL 2; SATA 100; WCH;
   YABC 1

Milne, Alan Alexander
   See Milne, A. A.

Milner, Ron(ald) 1938-2004 .. **BLC 1:3; CLC**
   56
   See also AITN 1; BW 1; CA 73-76; 230;
   CAD; CANR 24, 81; CD 5, 6; DAM
   MULT; DLB 38; MAL 5; MTCW 1

Milnes, Richard Monckton
   1809-1885 .... **NCLC 61**
   See also DLB 32, 184

Milosz, Czeslaw 1911-2004 .... **CLC 5, 11, 22,**
   31, 56, 82, 253; PC 8; WLCS
   See also AAYA 62; CA 81-84; 230; CANR
   23, 51, 91, 126; CDWLB 4; CWW 2;
   DA3; DAM MST, POET; DLB 215, 331;
   EW 13; EWL 3; MTCW 1, 2; MTFW
   2005; PFS 16, 29; RGHL; RGWL 2, 3

Milton, John 1608-1674 ..... **LC 9, 43, 92; PC**
   19, 29; WLC 4
   See also AAYA 65; BRW 2; BRWR 2; CD-
   BLB 1660-1789; DA; DA3; DAB; DAC;
   DAM MST, POET; DLB 131, 151, 281;
   EFS 1; EXPP; LAIT 1; PAB; PFS 3, 17;
   RGEL 2; TEA; WLIT 3; WP

Min, Anchee 1957- .... **CLC 86**
   See also CA 146; CANR 94, 137; MTFW
   2005

Minehaha, Cornelius
   See Wedekind, Frank

Miner, Valerie 1947- .... **CLC 40**
   See also CA 97-100; CANR 59, 177; FW;
   GLL 2

Minimo, Duca
   See D'Annunzio, Gabriele

Minot, Susan (Anderson) 1956- ...... **CLC 44,**
   159
   See also AMWS 6; CA 134; CANR 118;
   CN 6, 7

Minus, Ed 1938- .... **CLC 39**
   See also CA 185

Mirabai 1498(?)-1550(?) .... **LC 143; PC 48**
   See also PFS 24

Miranda, Javier
   See Bioy Casares, Adolfo

Mirbeau, Octave 1848-1917 .... **TCLC 55**
   See also CA 216; DLB 123, 192; GFL 1789
   to the Present

Mirikitani, Janice 1942- .... **AAL**
   See also CA 211; DLB 312; RGAL 4

Mirk, John (?)-c. 1414 .... **LC 105**
   See also DLB 146

Miro (Ferrer), Gabriel (Francisco Victor)
   1879-1930 .... **TCLC 5**
   See also CA 104; 185; DLB 322; EWL 3

Misharin, Alexandr .... **CLC 59**

Mishima, Yukio
   See Hiraoka, Kimitake

Mishima Yukio
   See Hiraoka, Kimitake

Miss C. L. F.
   See Grimke, Charlotte L(ottie) Forten

Mister X
   See Hoch, Edward D.

Mistral, Frederic 1830-1914 .... **TCLC 51**
   See also CA 122; 213; DLB 331; GFL 1789
   to the Present

Mistral, Gabriela
   See Godoy Alcayaga, Lucila

Mistry, Rohinton 1952- ... **CLC 71, 196, 274;**
   SSC 73
   See also BRWS 10; CA 141; CANR 86,
   114; CCA 1; CN 6, 7; DAC; DLB 334;
   SSFS 6

Mitchell, Clyde
   See Ellison, Harlan; Silverberg, Robert

Mitchell, Emerson Blackhorse Barney
   1945- .... **NNAL**
   See also CA 45-48

Mitchell, James Leslie 1901-1935 .... **TCLC 4**
   See also BRWS 14; CA 104; 188; DLB 15;
   RGEL 2

Mitchell, Joni 1943- .... **CLC 12**
   See also CA 112; CCA 1

Mitchell, Joseph (Quincy)
   1908-1996 .... **CLC 98**
   See also CA 77-80; 152; CANR 69; CN 1,
   2, 3, 4, 5, 6; CSW; DLB 185; DLBY 1996

Mitchell, Margaret (Munnerlyn)
   1900-1949 .... **TCLC 11, 170**
   See also AAYA 23; BPFB 2; BYA 1; CA
   109; 125; CANR 55, 94; CDALBS; DA3;
   DAM NOV, POP; DLB 9; LAIT 2; MAL
   5; MTCW 1, 2; MTFW 2005; NFS 9;
   RGAL 4; RHW; TUS; WYAS 1; YAW

Mitchell, Peggy
   See Mitchell, Margaret (Munnerlyn)

Mitchell, S(ilas) Weir 1829-1914 .... **TCLC 36**
   See also CA 165; DLB 202; RGAL 4

Mitchell, W(illiam) O(rmond)
   1914-1998 .... **CLC 25**
   See also CA 77-80; 165; CANR 15, 43; CN
   1, 2, 3, 4, 5, 6; DAC; DAM MST; DLB
   88; TCLE 1:2

Mitchell, William (Lendrum)
   1879-1936 .... **TCLC 81**
   See also CA 213

Mitford, Mary Russell 1787-1855 ... **NCLC 4**
   See also DLB 110, 116; RGEL 2

Mitford, Nancy 1904-1973 .... **CLC 44**
   See also BRWS 10; CA 9-12R; CN 1; DLB
   191; RGEL 2

Miyamoto, (Chujo) Yuriko
   1899-1951 .... **TCLC 37**
   See also CA 170, 174; DLB 180

Miyamoto Yuriko
   See Miyamoto, (Chujo) Yuriko

Miyazawa, Kenji 1896-1933 .... **TCLC 76**
   See also CA 157; EWL 3; RGWL 3

Miyazawa Kenji
   See Miyazawa, Kenji

Mizoguchi, Kenji 1898-1956 .... **TCLC 72**
   See also CA 167

Mo, Timothy (Peter) 1950- .... **CLC 46, 134**
   See also CA 117; CANR 128; CN 5, 6, 7;
   DLB 194; MTCW 1; WLIT 4; WWE 1

Modarressi, Taghi (M.) 1931-1997 ... **CLC 44**
   See also CA 121; 134; INT CA-134

Modiano, Patrick (Jean) 1945- .... **CLC 18,**
   218
   See also CA 85-88; CANR 17, 40, 115;
   CWW 2; DLB 83, 299; EWL 3; RGHL

Mofolo, Thomas (Mokopu)
   1875(?)-1948 .... **BLC 1:3; TCLC 22**
   See also AFW; CA 121; 153; CANR 83;
   DAM MULT; DLB 225; EWL 3; MTCW
   2; MTFW 2005; WLIT 2

Mohr, Nicholasa 1938- .... **CLC 12; HLC 2**
   See also AAYA 8, 46; CA 49-52; CANR 1,
   32, 64; CLR 22; DAM MULT; DLB 145;
   HW 1, 2; JRDA; LAIT 5; LLW; MAICYA
   2; MAICYAS 1; RGAL 4; SAAS 8; SATA
   8, 97; SATA-Essay 113; WYA; YAW

Moi, Toril 1953- .... **CLC 172**
   See also CA 154; CANR 102; FW

Mojtabai, A(nn) G(race) 1938- ..... **CLC 5, 9,**
   15, 29
   See also CA 85-88; CANR 88

Moliere 1622-1673 ..... **DC 13; LC 10, 28, 64,**
   125, 127; WLC 4
   See also DA; DA3; DAB; DAC; DAM
   DRAM, MST; DFS 13, 18, 20; DLB 268;
   EW 3; GFL Beginnings to 1789; LATS
   1:1; RGWL 2, 3; TWA

Molin, Charles
   See Mayne, William (James Carter)

Molnar, Ferenc 1878-1952 .... **TCLC 20**
   See also CA 109; 153; CANR 83; CDWLB
   4; DAM DRAM; DLB 215; EWL 3;
   RGWL 2, 3

Momaday, N. Scott 1934- ...... **CLC 2, 19, 85,**
   95, 160; NNAL; PC 25; WLCS
   See also AAYA 11, 64; AMWS 4; ANW;
   BPFB 2; BYA 12; CA 25-28R; CANR 14,
   34, 68, 134; CDALBS; CN 2, 3, 4, 5, 6,
   7; CPW; DA; DA3; DAB; DAC; DAM
   MST, MULT, NOV, POP; DLB 143, 175,
   256; EWL 3; EXPP; INT CANR-14;
   LAIT 4; LATS 1:2; MAL 5; MTCW 1, 2;
   MTFW 2005; NFS 10; PFS 2, 11; RGAL
   4; SATA 48; SATA-Brief 30; TCWW 1,
   2; WP; YAW

Monette, Paul 1945-1995 .... **CLC 82**
   See also AMWS 10; CA 139; 147; CN 6;
   GLL 1

Monroe, Harriet 1860-1936 .... **TCLC 12**
   See also CA 109; 204; DLB 54, 91

Monroe, Lyle
   See Heinlein, Robert A.

Montagu, Elizabeth 1720-1800 .... **NCLC 7,**
   117
   See also FW

Montagu, Mary (Pierrepont) Wortley
   1689-1762 .... **LC 9, 57; PC 16**
   See also DLB 95, 101; FL 1:1; RGEL 2

Montagu, W. H.
   See Coleridge, Samuel Taylor

Montague, John (Patrick) 1929- ..... **CLC 13,**
   46
   See also CA 9-12R; CANR 9, 69, 121; CP
   1, 2, 3, 4, 5, 6, 7; DLB 40; EWL 3;
   MTCW 1; PFS 12; RGEL 2; TCLE 1:2

Montaigne, Michel (Eyquem) de
   1533-1592 .... **LC 8, 105; WLC 4**
   See also DA; DAB; DAC; DAM MST;
   DLB 327; EW 2; GFL Beginnings to
   1789; LMFS 1; RGWL 2, 3; TWA

Montale, Eugenio 1896-1981 ... **CLC 7, 9, 18;**
   PC 13
   See also CA 17-20R; 104; CANR 30; DLB
   114, 331; EW 11; EWL 3; MTCW 1; PFS
   22; RGWL 2, 3; TWA; WLIT 7

Montesquieu, Charles-Louis de Secondat
   1689-1755 .... **LC 7, 69**
   See also DLB 314; EW 3; GFL Beginnings
   to 1789; TWA

Montessori, Maria 1870-1952 .... **TCLC 103**
   See also CA 115; 147

2; MAL 5; MBL; MTCW 1, 2; MTFW 2005; NFS 1, 6, 8, 14; RGAL 4; RHW; SATA 57, 144; SSFS 5; TCLE 1:2; TUS; YAW

Morrison, Van 1945- .... **CLC 21**
See also CA 116; 168

Morrissy, Mary 1957- .... **CLC 99**
See also CA 205; DLB 267

Mortimer, John 1923-2009 .... **CLC 28, 43**
See also CA 13-16R; CANR 21, 69, 109, 172; CBD; CD 5, 6; CDBLB 1960 to Present; CMW 4; CN 5, 6, 7; CPW; DA3; DAM DRAM, POP; DLB 13, 245, 271; INT CANR-21; MSW; MTCW 1, 2; MTFW 2005; RGEL 2

Mortimer, John Clifford
See Mortimer, John

Mortimer, Penelope (Ruth)
1918-1999 .... **CLC 5**
See also CA 57-60; 187; CANR 45, 88; CN 1, 2, 3, 4, 5, 6

Mortimer, Sir John
See Mortimer, John

Morton, Anthony
See Creasey, John

Morton, Thomas 1579(?)-1647(?) .... **LC 72**
See also DLB 24; RGEL 2

Mosca, Gaetano 1858-1941 .... **TCLC 75**

Moses, Daniel David 1952- .... **NNAL**
See also CA 186; CANR 160; DLB 334

Mosher, Howard Frank 1943- .... **CLC 62**
See also CA 139; CANR 65, 115, 181

Mosley, Nicholas 1923- .... **CLC 43, 70**
See also CA 69-72; CANR 41, 60, 108, 158; CN 1, 2, 3, 4, 5, 6, 7; DLB 14, 207

Mosley, Walter 1952- .... **BLCS; CLC 97, 184**
See also AAYA 57; AMWS 13; BPFB 2; BW 2; CA 142; CANR 57, 92, 136, 172; CMW 4; CN 7; CPW; DA3; DAM MULT, POP; DLB 306; MSW; MTCW 2; MTFW 2005

Moss, Howard 1922-1987 . **CLC 7, 14, 45, 50**
See also CA 1-4R; 123; CANR 1, 44; CP 1, 2, 3, 4; DAM POET; DLB 5

Mossgiel, Rab
See Burns, Robert

Motion, Andrew 1952- .... **CLC 47**
See also BRWS 7; CA 146; CANR 90, 142; CP 4, 5, 6, 7; DLB 40; MTFW 2005

Motion, Andrew Peter
See Motion, Andrew

Motley, Willard (Francis)
1909-1965 .... **CLC 18**
See also AMWS 17; BW 1; CA 117; 106; CANR 88; DLB 76, 143

Motoori, Norinaga 1730-1801 .... **NCLC 45**

Mott, Michael (Charles Alston)
1930- .... **CLC 15, 34**
See also CA 5-8R; CAAS 7; CANR 7, 29

Mountain Wolf Woman 1884-1960 . **CLC 92; NNAL**
See also CA 144; CANR 90

Moure, Erin 1955- .... **CLC 88**
See also CA 113; CP 5, 6, 7; CWP; DLB 60

Mourning Dove 1885(?)-1936 .... **NNAL**
See also CA 144; CANR 90; DAM MULT; DLB 175, 221

Mowat, Farley 1921- .... **CLC 26**
See also AAYA 1, 50; BYA 2; CA 1-4R; CANR 4, 24, 42, 68, 108; CLR 20; CPW; DAC; DAM MST; DLB 68; INT CANR-24; JRDA; MAICYA 1, 2; MTCW 1, 2; MTFW 2005; SATA 3, 55; YAW

Mowat, Farley McGill
See Mowat, Farley

Mowatt, Anna Cora 1819-1870 ..... **NCLC 74**
See also RGAL 4

Mo Yan
See Moye, Guan

Moye, Guan 1956(?)- .... **CLC 257**
See also CA 201; EWL 3; RGWL 3

Mo Yen
See Moye, Guan

Moyers, Bill 1934- .... **CLC 74**
See also AITN 2; CA 61-64; CANR 31, 52, 148

Mphahlele, Es'kia 1919-2008 .... **BLC 1:3; CLC 25, 133**
See also AFW; BW 2, 3; CA 81-84; 278; CANR 26, 76; CDWLB 3; CN 4, 5, 6; DA3; DAM MULT; DLB 125, 225; EWL 3; MTCW 2; MTFW 2005; RGSF 2; SATA 119; SATA-Obit 198; SSFS 11

Mphahlele, Ezekiel
See Mphahlele, Es'kia

Mphahlele, Zeke
See Mphahlele, Es'kia

Mqhayi, S(amuel) E(dward) K(rune Loliwe)
1875-1945 .... **BLC 1:3; TCLC 25**
See also CA 153; CANR 87; DAM MULT

Mrozek, Slawomir 1930- .... **CLC 3, 13**
See also CA 13-16R; CAAS 10; CANR 29; CDWLB 4; CWW 2; DLB 232; EWL 3; MTCW 1

Mrs. Belloc-Lowndes
See Lowndes, Marie Adelaide (Belloc)

Mrs. Fairstar
See Horne, Richard Henry Hengist

M'Taggart, John M'Taggart Ellis
See McTaggart, John McTaggart Ellis

Mtwa, Percy (?)- .... **CLC 47**
See also CD 6

Mueller, Lisel 1924- .... **CLC 13, 51; PC 33**
See also CA 93-96; CP 6, 7; DLB 105; PFS 9, 13

Muggeridge, Malcolm (Thomas)
1903-1990 .... **TCLC 120**
See also AITN 1; CA 101; CANR 33, 63; MTCW 1, 2

Muhammad 570-632 .... **WLCS**
See also DA; DAB; DAC; DAM MST; DLB 311

Muir, Edwin 1887-1959 . **PC 49; TCLC 2, 87**
See also BRWS 6; CA 104; 193; DLB 20, 100, 191; EWL 3; RGEL 2

Muir, John 1838-1914 .... **TCLC 28**
See also AMWS 9; ANW; CA 165; DLB 186, 275

Mujica Lainez, Manuel 1910-1984 ... **CLC 31**
See also CA 81-84; 112; CANR 32; EWL 3; HW 1

Mukherjee, Bharati 1940- ..... **AAL; CLC 53, 115, 235; SSC 38**
See also AAYA 46; BEST 89:2; CA 107, 232; CAAE 232; CANR 45, 72, 128; CN 5, 6, 7; DAM NOV; DLB 60, 218, 323; DNFS 1, 2; EWL 3; FW; MAL 5; MTCW 1, 2; MTFW 2005; RGAL 4; RGSF 2; SSFS 7, 24; TUS; WWE 1

Muldoon, Paul 1951- .... **CLC 32, 72, 166**
See also BRWS 4; CA 113; 129; CANR 52, 91, 176; CP 2, 3, 4, 5, 6, 7; DAM POET; DLB 40; INT CA-129; PFS 7, 22; TCLE 1:2

Mulisch, Harry (Kurt Victor)
1927- .... **CLC 42, 270**
See also CA 9-12R; CANR 6, 26, 56, 110; CWW 2; DLB 299; EWL 3

Mull, Martin 1943- .... **CLC 17**
See also CA 105

Muller, Wilhelm .... **NCLC 73**

Mulock, Dinah Maria
See Craik, Dinah Maria (Mulock)

Multatuli 1820-1881 .... **NCLC 165**
See also RGWL 2, 3

Munday, Anthony 1560-1633 .... **LC 87**
See also DLB 62, 172; RGEL 2

Munford, Robert 1737(?)-1783 .... **LC 5**
See also DLB 31

Mungo, Raymond 1946- .... **CLC 72**
See also CA 49-52; CANR 2

Munro, Alice 1931- .... **CLC 6, 10, 19, 50, 95, 222; SSC 3, 95; WLCS**
See also AITN 2; BPFB 2; CA 33-36R; CANR 33, 53, 75, 114, 177; CCA 1; CN 1, 2, 3, 4, 5, 6, 7; DA3; DAC; DAM MST, NOV; DLB 53; EWL 3; MTCW 1, 2; MTFW 2005; NFS 27; RGEL 2; RGSF 2; SATA 29; SSFS 5, 13, 19; TCLE 1:2; WWE 1

Munro, H(ector) H(ugh) 1870-1916 . **SSC 12, 115; TCLC 3; WLC 5**
See also AAYA 56; BRWS 6; BYA 11; CA 104; 130; CANR 104; CDBLB 1890-1914; DA; DA3; DAB; DAC; DAM MST, NOV; DLB 34, 162; EXPS; LAIT 2; MTCW 1, 2; MTFW 2005; RGEL 2; SSFS 1, 15; SUFW

Munro, Hector H.
See Munro, H(ector) H(ugh)

Murakami, Haruki 1949- .... **CLC 150, 274**
See also CA 165; CANR 102, 146; CWW 2; DLB 182; EWL 3; MJW; RGWL 3; SFW 4; SSFS 23

Murakami Haruki
See Murakami, Haruki

Murasaki, Lady
See Murasaki Shikibu

Murasaki Shikibu 978(?)-1026(?) .. **CMLC 1, 79**
See also EFS 2; LATS 1:1; RGWL 2, 3

Murdoch, Iris 1919-1999 .. **CLC 1, 2, 3, 4, 6, 8, 11, 15, 22, 31, 51; TCLC 171**
See also BRWS 1; CA 13-16R; 179; CANR 8, 43, 68, 103, 142; CBD; CDBLB 1960 to Present; CN 1, 2, 3, 4, 5, 6; CWD; DA3; DAB; DAC; DAM MST, NOV; DLB 14, 194, 233, 326; EWL 3; INT CANR-8; MTCW 1, 2; MTFW 2005; NFS 18; RGEL 2; TCLE 1:2; TEA; WLIT 4

Murfree, Mary Noailles 1850-1922 .. **SSC 22; TCLC 135**
See also CA 122; 176; DLB 12, 74; RGAL 4

Murglie
See Murnau, F.W.

Murnau, Friedrich Wilhelm
See Murnau, F.W.

Murnau, F.W. 1888-1931 .... **TCLC 53**
See also CA 112

Murphy, Richard 1927- .... **CLC 41**
See also BRWS 5; CA 29-32R; CP 1, 2, 3, 4, 5, 6, 7; DLB 40; EWL 3

Murphy, Sylvia 1937- .... **CLC 34**
See also CA 121

Murphy, Thomas (Bernard) 1935- ... **CLC 51**
See also CA 101; DLB 310

Murphy, Tom
See Murphy, Thomas (Bernard)

Murray, Albert 1916- .... **BLC 2:3; CLC 73**
See also BW 2; CA 49-52; CANR 26, 52, 78, 160; CN 7; CSW; DLB 38; MTFW 2005

Murray, Albert L.
See Murray, Albert

Murray, James Augustus Henry
1837-1915 ....**TCLC 117**

Murray, Judith Sargent
1751-1820 .... **NCLC 63**
See also DLB 37, 200

Murray, Les(lie Allan) 1938- .... **CLC 40**
See also BRWS 7; CA 21-24R; CANR 11,
27, 56, 103; CP 1, 2, 3, 4, 5, 6, 7; DAM
POET; DLB 289; DLBY 2001; EWL 3;
RGEL 2

Murry, J. Middleton
See Murry, John Middleton

Murry, John Middleton
1889-1957 .... **TCLC 16**
See also CA 118; 217; DLB 149

Musgrave, Susan 1951- .... **CLC 13, 54**
See also CA 69-72; CANR 45, 84, 181;
CCA 1; CP 2, 3, 4, 5, 6, 7; CWP

Musil, Robert (Edler von)
1880-1942 ... **SSC 18; TCLC 12, 68, 213**
See also CA 109; CANR 55, 84; CDWLB
2; DLB 81, 124; EW 9; EWL 3; MTCW
2; RGSF 2; RGWL 2, 3

Muske, Carol
See Muske-Dukes, Carol

Muske, Carol Anne
See Muske-Dukes, Carol

Muske-Dukes, Carol 1945- .... **CLC 90**
See also CA 65-68, 203; CAAE 203; CANR
32, 70, 181; CWP; PFS 24

Muske-Dukes, Carol Ann
See Muske-Dukes, Carol

Muske-Dukes, Carol Anne
See Muske-Dukes, Carol

Musset, Alfred de 1810-1857 . **DC 27; NCLC
7, 150**
See also DLB 192, 217; EW 6; GFL 1789
to the Present; RGWL 2, 3; TWA

Musset, Louis Charles Alfred de
See Musset, Alfred de

Mussolini, Benito (Amilcare Andrea)
1883-1945 .... **TCLC 96**
See also CA 116

Mutanabbi, Al-
See al-Mutanabbi, Ahmad ibn al-Husayn
Abu al-Tayyib al-Jufi al-Kindi

My Brother's Brother
See Chekhov, Anton (Pavlovich)

Myers, L(eopold) H(amilton)
1881-1944 .... **TCLC 59**
See also CA 157; DLB 15; EWL 3; RGEL
2

Myers, Walter Dean 1937- ...... **BLC 1:3, 2:3;
CLC 35**
See also AAYA 4, 23; BW 2; BYA 6, 8, 11;
CA 33-36R; CANR 20, 42, 67, 108, 184;
CLR 4, 16, 35, 110; DAM MULT, NOV;
DLB 33; INT CANR-20; JRDA; LAIT 5;
MAICYA 1, 2; MAICYAS 1; MTCW 2;
MTFW 2005; SAAS 2; SATA 41, 71, 109,
157, 193; SATA-Brief 27; WYA; YAW

Myers, Walter M.
See Myers, Walter Dean

Myles, Symon
See Follett, Ken

Nabokov, Vladimir (Vladimirovich)
1899-1977 .... **CLC 1, 2, 3, 6, 8, 11, 15,
23, 44, 46, 64; SSC 11, 86; TCLC 108,
189; WLC 4**
See also AAYA 45; AMW; AMWC 1;
AMWR 1; BPFB 2; CA 5-8R; 69-72;
CANR 20, 102; CDALB 1941-1968; CN
1, 2; CP 2; DA; DA3; DAB; DAC; DAM
MST, NOV; DLB 2, 244, 278, 317; DLBD
3; DLBY 1980, 1991; EWL 3; EXPS;
LATS 1:2; MAL 5; MTCW 1, 2; MTFW
2005; NCFS 4; NFS 9; RGAL 4; RGSF
2; SSFS 6, 15; TUS

Naevius c. 265B.C.-201B.C. .... **CMLC 37**
See also DLB 211

Nagai, Kafu 1879-1959 .... **TCLC 51**
See also CA 117; 276; DLB 180; EWL 3;
MJW

Nagai, Sokichi
See Nagai, Kafu

Nagai Kafu
See Nagai, Kafu

na gCopaleen, Myles
See O Nuallain, Brian

na Gopaleen, Myles
See O Nuallain, Brian

Nagy, Laszlo 1925-1978 .... **CLC 7**
See also CA 129; 112

Naidu, Sarojini 1879-1949 .... **TCLC 80**
See also EWL 3; RGEL 2

Naipaul, Shiva 1945-1985 .... **CLC 32, 39;
TCLC 153**
See also CA 110; 112; 116; CANR 33; CN
2, 3; DA3; DAM NOV; DLB 157; DLBY
1985; EWL 3; MTCW 1, 2; MTFW 2005

Naipaul, Shivadhar Srinivasa
See Naipaul, Shiva

Naipaul, V.S. 1932- .. **CLC 4, 7, 9, 13, 18, 37,
105, 199; SSC 38, 121**
See also BPFB 2; BRWS 1; CA 1-4R;
CANR 1, 33, 51, 91, 126; CDBLB 1960
to Present; CDWLB 3; CN 1, 2, 3, 4, 5,
6, 7; DA3; DAB; DAC; DAM MST,
NOV; DLB 125, 204, 207, 326, 331;
DLBY 1985, 2001; EWL 3; LATS 1:2;
MTCW 1, 2; MTFW 2005; RGEL 2;
RGSF 2; TWA; WLIT 4; WWE 1

Nakos, Lilika 1903(?)-1989 .... **CLC 29**

Napoleon
See Yamamoto, Hisaye

Narayan, R.K. 1906-2001 ...... **CLC 7, 28, 47,
121, 211; SSC 25**
See also BPFB 2; CA 81-84; 196; CANR
33, 61, 112; CN 1, 2, 3, 4, 5, 6, 7; DA3;
DAM NOV; DLB 323; DNFS 1; EWL 3;
MTCW 1, 2; MTFW 2005; RGEL 2;
RGSF 2; SATA 62; SSFS 5; WWE 1

Nash, Fredric Ogden
See Nash, Ogden

Nash, Ogden 1902-1971 ...... **CLC 23; PC 21;
TCLC 109**
See also CA 13-14; 29-32R; CANR 34, 61,
185; CAP 1; CP 1; DAM POET; DLB 11;
MAICYA 1, 2; MAL 5; MTCW 1, 2;
RGAL 4; SATA 2, 46; WP

Nashe, Thomas 1567-1601(?) . **LC 41, 89; PC
82**
See also DLB 167; RGEL 2

Nathan, Daniel
See Dannay, Frederic

Nathan, George Jean 1882-1958 .... **TCLC 18**
See also CA 114; 169; DLB 137; MAL 5

Natsume, Kinnosuke
See Natsume, Soseki

Natsume, Soseki 1867-1916 .... **TCLC 2, 10**
See also CA 104; 195; DLB 180; EWL 3;
MJW; RGWL 2, 3; TWA

Natsume Soseki
See Natsume, Soseki

Natti, (Mary) Lee 1919- .... **CLC 17**
See also CA 5-8R; CANR 2; CWRI 5;
SAAS 3; SATA 1, 67

Navarre, Marguerite de
See de Navarre, Marguerite

Naylor, Gloria 1950- . **BLC 1:3; CLC 28, 52,
156, 261; WLCS**
See also AAYA 6, 39; AFAW 1, 2; AMWS
8; BW 2, 3; CA 107; CANR 27, 51, 74,
130; CN 4, 5, 6, 7; CPW; DA; DA3;
DAC; DAM MST, MULT, NOV, POP;
DLB 173; EWL 3; FW; MAL 5; MTCW
1, 2; MTFW 2005; NFS 4, 7; RGAL 4;
TCLE 1:2; TUS

Neal, John 1793-1876 .... **NCLC 161**
See also DLB 1, 59, 243; FW; RGAL 4

Neff, Debra .... **CLC 59**

Neihardt, John Gneisenau
1881-1973 .... **CLC 32**
See also CA 13-14; CANR 65; CAP 1; DLB
9, 54, 256; LAIT 2; TCWW 1, 2

Nekrasov, Nikolai Alekseevich
1821-1878 .... **NCLC 11**
See also DLB 277

Nelligan, Emile 1879-1941 .... **TCLC 14**
See also CA 114; 204; DLB 92; EWL 3

Nelson, Alice Ruth Moore Dunbar
1875-1935 .... **HR 1:2**
See also BW 1, 3; CA 122; 124; CANR 82;
DLB 50; FW; MTCW 1

Nelson, Willie 1933- .... **CLC 17**
See also CA 107; CANR 114, 178

Nemerov, Howard 1920-1991 .... **CLC 2, 6, 9,
36; PC 24; TCLC 124**
See also AMW; CA 1-4R; 134; CABS 2;
CANR 1, 27, 53; CN 1, 2, 3; CP 1, 2, 3,
4, 5; DAM POET; DLB 5, 6; DLBY 1983;
EWL 3; INT CANR-27; MAL 5; MTCW
1, 2; MTFW 2005; PFS 10, 14; RGAL 4

Nepos, Cornelius c. 99B.C.-c.
24B.C. .... **CMLC 89**
See also DLB 211

Neruda, Pablo 1904-1973 .. **CLC 1, 2, 5, 7, 9,
28, 62; HLC 2; PC 4, 64; WLC 4**
See also CA 19-20; 45-48; CANR 131; CAP
2; DA; DA3; DAB; DAC; DAM MST,
MULT, POET; DLB 283, 331; DNFS 2;
EWL 3; HW 1; LAW; MTCW 1, 2;
MTFW 2005; PFS 11, 28; RGWL 2, 3;
TWA; WLIT 1; WP

Nerval, Gerard de 1808-1855 ... **NCLC 1, 67;
PC 13; SSC 18**
See also DLB 217; EW 6; GFL 1789 to the
Present; RGSF 2; RGWL 2, 3

Nervo, (Jose) Amado (Ruiz de)
1870-1919 .... **HLCS 2; TCLC 11**
See also CA 109; 131; DLB 290; EWL 3;
HW 1; LAW

Nesbit, Malcolm
See Chester, Alfred

Nessi, Pio Baroja y
See Baroja, Pio

Nestroy, Johann 1801-1862 .... **NCLC 42**
See also DLB 133; RGWL 2, 3

Netterville, Luke
See O'Grady, Standish (James)

Neufeld, John (Arthur) 1938- .... **CLC 17**
See also AAYA 11; CA 25-28R; CANR 11,
37, 56; CLR 52; MAICYA 1, 2; SAAS 3;
SATA 6, 81, 131; SATA-Essay 131; YAW

Neumann, Alfred 1895-1952 .... **TCLC 100**
See also CA 183; DLB 56

Neumann, Ferenc
See Molnar, Ferenc

Neville, Emily Cheney 1919- .... **CLC 12**
See also BYA 2; CA 5-8R; CANR 3, 37,
85; JRDA; MAICYA 1, 2; SAAS 2; SATA
1; YAW

Newbound, Bernard Slade 1930- .... **CLC 11,
46**
See also CA 81-84; CAAS 9; CANR 49;
CCA 1; CD 5, 6; DAM DRAM; DLB 53

Newby, P(ercy) H(oward)
1918-1997 .... **CLC 2, 13**
See also CA 5-8R; 161; CANR 32, 67; CN
1, 2, 3, 4, 5, 6; DAM NOV; DLB 15, 326;
MTCW 1; RGEL 2

Newcastle
See Cavendish, Margaret Lucas

Newlove, Donald 1928- .... **CLC 6**
See also CA 29-32R; CANR 25

Newlove, John (Herbert) 1938- .... **CLC 14**
See also CA 21-24R; CANR 9, 25; CP 1, 2,
3, 4, 5, 6, 7

Newman, Charles 1938-2006 .... **CLC 2, 8**
See also CA 21-24R; 249; CANR 84; CN
3, 4, 5, 6
Newman, Charles Hamilton
See Newman, Charles
Newman, Edwin (Harold) 1919- ...... **CLC 14**
See also AITN 1; CA 69-72; CANR 5
Newman, John Henry 1801-1890 . **NCLC 38,**
99
See also BRWS 7; DLB 18, 32, 55; RGEL
2
Newton, (Sir) Isaac 1642-1727 ...... **LC 35, 53**
See also DLB 252
Newton, Suzanne 1936- .... **CLC 35**
See also BYA 7; CA 41-44R; CANR 14;
JRDA; SATA 5, 77
New York Dept. of Ed. .... **CLC 70**
Nexo, Martin Andersen
1869-1954 .... **TCLC 43**
See also CA 202; DLB 214; EWL 3
Nezval, Vitezslav 1900-1958 .... **TCLC 44**
See also CA 123; CDWLB 4; DLB 215;
EWL 3
Ng, Fae Myenne 1956- .... **CLC 81**
See also BYA 11; CA 146
Ngcobo, Lauretta 1931- .... **BLC 2:3**
See also CA 165
Ngema, Mbongeni 1955- .... **CLC 57**
See also BW 2; CA 143; CANR 84; CD 5,
6
Ngugi, James T.
See Ngugi wa Thiong'o
Ngugi, James Thiong'o
See Ngugi wa Thiong'o
Ngugi wa Thiong'o 1938- .... **BLC 1:3, 2:3;**
CLC 3, 7, 13, 36, 182, 275
See also AFW; BRWS 8; BW 2; CA 81-84;
CANR 27, 58, 164; CD 3, 4, 5, 6, 7; CD-
WLB 3; CN 1, 2; DAM MULT, NOV;
DLB 125; DNFS 2; EWL 3; MTCW 1, 2;
MTFW 2005; RGEL 2; WWE 1
Niatum, Duane 1938- .... **NNAL**
See also CA 41-44R; CANR 21, 45, 83;
DLB 175
Nichol, B(arrie) P(hillip) 1944-1988 . **CLC 18**
See also CA 53-56; CP 1, 2, 3, 4; DLB 53;
SATA 66
Nicholas of Autrecourt c.
1298-1369 .... **CMLC 108**
Nicholas of Cusa 1401-1464 .... **LC 80**
See also DLB 115
Nichols, John 1940- .... **CLC 38**
See also AMWS 13; CA 9-12R, 190; CAAE
190; CAAS 2; CANR 6, 70, 121, 185;
DLBY 1982; LATS 1:2; MTFW 2005;
TCWW 1, 2
Nichols, Leigh
See Koontz, Dean R.
Nichols, Peter (Richard) 1927- .... **CLC 5, 36,**
65
See also CA 104; CANR 33, 86; CBD; CD
5, 6; DLB 13, 245; MTCW 1
Nicholson, Linda .... **CLC 65**
Ni Chuilleanain, Eilean 1942- .... **PC 34**
See also CA 126; CANR 53, 83; CP 5, 6, 7;
CWP; DLB 40
Nicolas, F. R. E.
See Freeling, Nicolas
Niedecker, Lorine 1903-1970 ..... **CLC 10, 42;**
PC 42
See also CA 25-28; CAP 2; DAM POET;
DLB 48
Nietzsche, Friedrich (Wilhelm)
1844-1900 .... **TCLC 10, 18, 55**
See also CA 107; 121; CDWLB 2; DLB
129; EW 7; RGWL 2, 3; TWA
Nievo, Ippolito 1831-1861 .... **NCLC 22**
Nightingale, Anne Redmon 1943- .... **CLC 22**
See also CA 103; DLBY 1986

Nightingale, Florence 1820-1910 ... **TCLC 85**
See also CA 188; DLB 166
Nijo Yoshimoto 1320-1388 .... **CMLC 49**
See also DLB 203
Nik. T. O.
See Annensky, Innokenty (Fyodorovich)
Nin, Anais 1903-1977 ..... **CLC 1, 4, 8, 11, 14,**
60, 127; SSC 10
See also AITN 2; AMWS 10; BPFB 2; CA
13-16R; 69-72; CANR 22, 53; CN 1, 2;
DAM NOV, POP; DLB 2, 4, 152; EWL
3; GLL 2; MAL 5; MBL; MTCW 1, 2;
MTFW 2005; RGAL 4; RGSF 2
Nisbet, Robert A(lexander)
1913-1996 .... **TCLC 117**
See also CA 25-28R; 153; CANR 17; INT
CANR-17
Nishida, Kitaro 1870-1945 .... **TCLC 83**
Nishiwaki, Junzaburo 1894-1982 .... **PC 15**
See also CA 194; 107; EWL 3; MJW;
RGWL 3
Nissenson, Hugh 1933- .... **CLC 4, 9**
See also CA 17-20R; CANR 27, 108, 151;
CN 5, 6; DLB 28, 335
Nister, Der
See Der Nister
Niven, Larry 1938- .... **CLC 8**
See also AAYA 27; BPFB 2; BYA 10; CA
21-24R, 207; CAAE 207; CAAS 12;
CANR 14, 44, 66, 113, 155; CPW; DAM
POP; DLB 8; MTCW 1, 2; SATA 95, 171;
SCFW 1, 2; SFW 4
Niven, Laurence VanCott
See Niven, Larry
Nixon, Agnes Eckhardt 1927- .... **CLC 21**
See also CA 110
Nizan, Paul 1905-1940 .... **TCLC 40**
See also CA 161; DLB 72; EWL 3; GFL
1789 to the Present
Nkosi, Lewis 1936- .... **BLC 1:3; CLC 45**
See also BW 1, 3; CA 65-68; CANR 27,
81; CBD; CD 5, 6; DAM MULT; DLB
157, 225; WWE 1
Nodier, (Jean) Charles (Emmanuel)
1780-1844 .... **NCLC 19**
See also DLB 119; GFL 1789 to the Present
Noguchi, Yone 1875-1947 .... **TCLC 80**
Nolan, Brian
See O Nuallain, Brian
Nolan, Christopher 1965-2009 .... **CLC 58**
See also CA 111; CANR 88
Noon, Jeff 1957- .... **CLC 91**
See also CA 148; CANR 83; DLB 267;
SFW 4
Norden, Charles
See Durrell, Lawrence (George)
Nordhoff, Charles Bernard
1887-1947 .... **TCLC 23**
See also CA 108; 211; DLB 9; LAIT 1;
RHW; SATA 23
Norfolk, Lawrence 1963- .... **CLC 76**
See also CA 144; CANR 85; CN 6, 7; DLB
267
Norman, Marsha (Williams) 1947- . **CLC 28,**
186; DC 8
See also CA 105; CABS 3; CAD; CANR
41, 131; CD 5, 6; CSW; CWD; DAM
DRAM; DFS 2; DLB 266; DLBY 1984;
FW; MAL 5
Normyx
See Douglas, (George) Norman
Norris, (Benjamin) Frank(lin, Jr.)
1870-1902 . **SSC 28; TCLC 24, 155, 211**
See also AAYA 57; AMW; AMWC 2; BPFB
2; CA 110; 160; CDALB 1865-1917; DLB
12, 71, 186; LMFS 2; MAL 5; NFS 12;
RGAL 4; TCWW 1, 2; TUS
Norris, Kathleen 1947- .... **CLC 248**
See also CA 160; CANR 113

Norris, Leslie 1921-2006 .... **CLC 14**
See also CA 11-12; 251; CANR 14, 117;
CAP 1; CP 1, 2, 3, 4, 5, 6, 7; DLB 27,
256
North, Andrew
See Norton, Andre
North, Anthony
See Koontz, Dean R.
North, Captain George
See Stevenson, Robert Louis (Balfour)
North, Captain George
See Stevenson, Robert Louis (Balfour)
North, Milou
See Erdrich, Louise
Northrup, B. A.
See Hubbard, L. Ron
North Staffs
See Hulme, T(homas) E(rnest)
Northup, Solomon 1808-1863 ...... **NCLC 105**
Norton, Alice Mary
See Norton, Andre
Norton, Andre 1912-2005 .... **CLC 12**
See also AAYA 14; BPFB 2; BYA 4, 10,
12; CA 1-4R; 237; CANR 2, 31, 68, 108,
149; CLR 50; DLB 8, 52; JRDA; MAI-
CYA 1, 2; MTCW 1; SATA 1, 43, 91;
SUFW 1, 2; YAW
Norton, Caroline 1808-1877 .. **NCLC 47, 205**
See also DLB 21, 159, 199
Norway, Nevil Shute 1899-1960 .... **CLC 30**
See also BPFB 3; CA 102; 93-96; CANR
85; DLB 255; MTCW 2; NFS 9; RHW 4;
SFW 4
Norwid, Cyprian Kamil
1821-1883 .... **NCLC 17**
See also RGWL 3
Nosille, Nabrah
See Ellison, Harlan
Nossack, Hans Erich 1901-1977 .... **CLC 6**
See also CA 93-96; 85-88; CANR 156;
DLB 69; EWL 3
Nostradamus 1503-1566 .... **LC 27**
Nosu, Chuji
See Ozu, Yasujiro
Notenburg, Eleanora (Genrikhovna) von
See Guro, Elena (Genrikhovna)
Nova, Craig 1945- .... **CLC 7, 31**
See also CA 45-48; CANR 2, 53, 127
Novak, Joseph
See Kosinski, Jerzy
Novalis 1772-1801 .... **NCLC 13, 178**
See also CDWLB 2; DLB 90; EW 5; RGWL
2, 3
Novick, Peter 1934- .... **CLC 164**
See also CA 188
Novis, Emile
See Weil, Simone (Adolphine)
Nowlan, Alden (Albert) 1933-1983 ... **CLC 15**
See also CA 9-12R; CANR 5; CP 1, 2, 3;
DAC; DAM MST; DLB 53; PFS 12
Noyes, Alfred 1880-1958 ...... **PC 27; TCLC 7**
See also CA 104; 188; DLB 20; EXPP;
FANT; PFS 4; RGEL 2
Nugent, Richard Bruce
1906(?)-1987 .... **HR 1:3**
See also BW 1; CA 125; DLB 51; GLL 2
Nunez, Elizabeth 1944- .... **BLC 2:3**
See also CA 223
Nunn, Kem .... **CLC 34**
See also CA 159
Nussbaum, Martha Craven 1947- .. **CLC 203**
See also CA 134; CANR 102, 176
Nwapa, Flora (Nwanzuruaha)
1931-1993 .... **BLCS; CLC 133**
See also BW 2; CA 143; CANR 83; CD-
WLB 3; CWRI 5; DLB 125; EWL 3;
WLIT 2

Olson, Toby 1937- .... **CLC 28**
See also CA 65-68; CAAS 11; CANR 9,
31, 84, 175; CP 3, 4, 5, 6, 7
Olyesha, Yuri
See Olesha, Yuri (Karlovich)
Olympiodorus of Thebes c. 375-c.
430 .... **CMLC 59**
Omar Khayyam
See Khayyam, Omar
Ondaatje, Michael 1943- ..... **CLC 14, 29, 51,
76, 180, 258; PC 28**
See also AAYA 66; CA 77-80; CANR 42,
74, 109, 133, 172; CN 5, 6, 7; CP 1, 2, 3,
4, 5, 6, 7; DA3; DAB; DAC; DAM MST;
DLB 60, 323, 326; EWL 3; LATS 1:2;
LMFS 2; MTCW 2; MTFW 2005; NFS
23; PFS 8, 19; TCLE 1:2; TWA; WWE 1
Ondaatje, Philip Michael
See Ondaatje, Michael
Oneal, Elizabeth 1934- .... **CLC 30**
See also AAYA 5, 41; BYA 13; CA 106;
CANR 28, 84; CLR 13; JRDA; MAICYA
1, 2; SATA 30, 82; WYA; YAW
Oneal, Zibby
See Oneal, Elizabeth
O'Neill, Eugene (Gladstone)
1888-1953 ... **DC 20; TCLC 1, 6, 27, 49;
WLC 4**
See also AAYA 54; AITN 1; AMW; AMWC
1; CA 110; 132; CAD; CANR 131;
CDALB 1929-1941; DA; DA3; DAB;
DAC; DAM DRAM, MST; DFS 2, 4, 5,
6, 9, 11, 12, 16, 20, 26; DLB 7, 331; EWL
3; LAIT 3; LMFS 2; MAL 5; MTCW 1,
2; MTFW 2005; RGAL 4; TUS
Onetti, Juan Carlos 1909-1994 ... **CLC 7, 10;
HLCS 2; SSC 23; TCLC 131**
See also CA 85-88; 145; CANR 32, 63; CD-
WLB 3; CWW 2; DAM MULT, NOV;
DLB 113; EWL 3; HW 1, 2; LAW;
MTCW 1, 2; MTFW 2005; RGSF 2
O'Nolan, Brian
See O Nuallain, Brian
O Nuallain, Brian 1911-1966 .... **CLC 1, 4, 5,
7, 10, 47**
See also BRWS 2; CA 21-22; 25-28R; CAP
2; DLB 231; EWL 3; FANT; RGEL 2;
TEA
Ophuls, Max
See Ophuls, Max
Ophuls, Max 1902-1957 .... **TCLC 79**
See also CA 113
Opie, Amelia 1769-1853 .... **NCLC 65**
See also DLB 116, 159; RGEL 2
Oppen, George 1908-1984 ..... **CLC 7, 13, 34;
PC 35; TCLC 107**
See also CA 13-16R; 113; CANR 8, 82; CP
1, 2, 3; DLB 5, 165
Oppenheim, E(dward) Phillips
1866-1946 .... **TCLC 45**
See also CA 111; 202; CMW 4; DLB 70
Oppenheimer, Max
See Ophuls, Max
Opuls, Max
See Ophuls, Max
Orage, A(lfred) R(ichard)
1873-1934 .... **TCLC 157**
See also CA 122
Origen c. 185-c. 254 .... **CMLC 19**
Orlovitz, Gil 1918-1973 .... **CLC 22**
See also CA 77-80; 45-48; CN 1; CP 1, 2;
DLB 2, 5
Orosius c. 385-c. 420 .... **CMLC 100**
O'Rourke, Patrick Jake
See O'Rourke, P.J.
O'Rourke, P.J. 1947- .... **CLC 209**
See also CA 77-80; CANR 13, 41, 67, 111,
155; CPW; DAM POP; DLB 185

Orris
See Ingelow, Jean
Ortega y Gasset, Jose 1883-1955 ...... **HLC 2;
TCLC 9**
See also CA 106; 130; DAM MULT; EW 9;
EWL 3; HW 1, 2; MTCW 1, 2; MTFW
2005
Ortese, Anna Maria 1914-1998 .... **CLC 89**
See also DLB 177; EWL 3
Ortiz, Simon
See Ortiz, Simon J.
Ortiz, Simon J. 1941- . **CLC 45, 208; NNAL;
PC 17**
See also AMWS 4; CA 134; CANR 69, 118,
164; CP 3, 4, 5, 6, 7; DAM MULT, POET;
DLB 120, 175, 256, 342; EXPP; MAL 5;
PFS 4, 16; RGAL 4; SSFS 2; TCWW 2
Ortiz, Simon Joseph
See Ortiz, Simon J.
Orton, Joe
See Orton, John Kingsley
Orton, John Kingsley 1933-1967 .... **CLC 4,
13, 43; DC 3; TCLC 157**
See also BRWS 5; CA 85-88; CANR 35,
66; CBD; CDBLB 1960 to Present; DAM
DRAM; DFS 3, 6; DLB 13, 310; GLL 1;
MTCW 1, 2; MTFW 2005; RGEL 2;
TEA; WLIT 4
Orwell, George
See Blair, Eric (Arthur)
Osborne, David
See Silverberg, Robert
Osborne, Dorothy 1627-1695 .... **LC 141**
Osborne, George
See Silverberg, Robert
Osborne, John 1929-1994 .... **CLC 1, 2, 5, 11,
45; TCLC 153; WLC 4**
See also BRWS 1; CA 13-16R; 147; CANR
21, 56; CBD; CDBLB 1945-1960; DA;
DAB; DAC; DAM DRAM, MST; DFS 4,
19, 24; DLB 13; EWL 3; MTCW 1, 2;
MTFW 2005; RGEL 2
Osborne, Lawrence 1958- .... **CLC 50**
See also CA 189; CANR 152
Osbourne, Lloyd 1868-1947 .... **TCLC 93**
Osceola
See Blixen, Karen (Christentze Dinesen)
Osgood, Frances Sargent
1811-1850 .... **NCLC 141**
See also DLB 250
Oshima, Nagisa 1932- .... **CLC 20**
See also CA 116; 121; CANR 78
Oskison, John Milton
1874-1947 .... **NNAL; TCLC 35**
See also CA 144; CANR 84; DAM MULT;
DLB 175
Ossoli, Sarah Margaret (Fuller)
1810-1850 .... **NCLC 5, 50, 211**
See also AMWS 2; CDALB 1640-1865;
DLB 1, 59, 73, 183, 223, 239; FW; LMFS
1; SATA 25
Ostriker, Alicia 1937- .... **CLC 132**
See also CA 25-28R; CAAS 24; CANR 10,
30, 62, 99, 167; CWP; DLB 120; EXPP;
PFS 19, 26
Ostriker, Alicia Suskin
See Ostriker, Alicia
Ostrovsky, Aleksandr Nikolaevich
See Ostrovsky, Alexander
Ostrovsky, Alexander 1823-1886 .. **NCLC 30,
57**
See also DLB 277
Osundare, Niyi 1947- .... **BLC 2:3**
See also AFW; BW 3; CA 176; CDWLB 3;
CP 7; DLB 157
Otero, Blas de 1916-1979 .... **CLC 11**
See also CA 89-92; DLB 134; EWL 3
O'Trigger, Sir Lucius
See Horne, Richard Henry Hengist

Otto, Rudolf 1869-1937 .... **TCLC 85**
Otto, Whitney 1955- .... **CLC 70**
See also CA 140; CANR 120
Otway, Thomas 1652-1685 ... **DC 24; LC 106**
See also DAM DRAM; DLB 80; RGEL 2
Ouida
See De La Ramee, Marie Louise
Ouologuem, Yambo 1940- .... **CLC 146**
See also CA 111; 176
Ousmane, Sembene 1923-2007 .... **BLC 1:3,
2:3; CLC 66**
See also AFW; BW 1, 3; CA 117; 125; 261;
CANR 81; CWW 2; EWL 3; MTCW 1;
WLIT 2
Ovid 43B.C.-17 .... **CMLC 7, 108; PC 2**
See also AW 2; CDWLB 1; DA3; DAM
POET; DLB 211; PFS 22; RGWL 2, 3;
WLIT 8; WP
Owen, Hugh
See Faust, Frederick (Schiller)
Owen, Wilfred (Edward Salter)
1893-1918 ... **PC 19; TCLC 5, 27; WLC
4**
See also BRW 6; CA 104; 141; CDBLB
1914-1945; DA; DAB; DAC; DAM MST,
POET; DLB 20; EWL 3; EXPP; MTCW
2; MTFW 2005; PFS 10; RGEL 2; WLIT
4
Owens, Louis (Dean) 1948-2002 .... **NNAL**
See also CA 137; 179; 207; CAAE 179;
CAAS 24; CANR 71
Owens, Rochelle 1936- .... **CLC 8**
See also CA 17-20R; CAAS 2; CAD;
CANR 39; CD 5, 6; CP 1, 2, 3, 4, 5, 6, 7;
CWD; CWP
Oz, Amos 1939- ...... **CLC 5, 8, 11, 27, 33, 54;
SSC 66**
See also CA 53-56; CANR 27, 47, 65, 113,
138, 175; CWW 2; DAM NOV; EWL 3;
MTCW 1, 2; MTFW 2005; RGHL; RGSF
2; RGWL 3; WLIT 6
Ozick, Cynthia 1928- . **CLC 3, 7, 28, 62, 155,
262; SSC 15, 60, 123**
See also AMWS 5; BEST 90:1; CA 17-20R;
CANR 23, 58, 116, 160, 187; CN 3, 4, 5,
6, 7; CPW; DA3; DAM NOV, POP; DLB
28, 152, 299; DLBY 1982; EWL 3; EXPS;
INT CANR-23; MAL 5; MTCW 1, 2;
MTFW 2005; RGAL 4; RGHL; RGSF 2;
SSFS 3, 12, 22
Ozu, Yasujiro 1903-1963 .... **CLC 16**
See also CA 112
Pabst, G. W. 1885-1967 .... **TCLC 127**
Pacheco, C.
See Pessoa, Fernando
Pacheco, Jose Emilio 1939- .... **HLC 2**
See also CA 111; 131; CANR 65; CWW 2;
DAM MULT; DLB 290; EWL 3; HW 1,
2; RGSF 2
Pa Chin
See Jin, Ba
Pack, Robert 1929- .... **CLC 13**
See also CA 1-4R; CANR 3, 44, 82; CP 1,
2, 3, 4, 5, 6, 7; DLB 5; SATA 118
Packer, Vin
See Meaker, Marijane
Padgett, Lewis
See Kuttner, Henry
Padilla (Lorenzo), Heberto
1932-2000 .... **CLC 38**
See also AITN 1; CA 123; 131; 189; CWW
2; EWL 3; HW 1
Paerdurabo, Frater
See Crowley, Edward Alexander
Page, James Patrick 1944- .... **CLC 12**
See also CA 204
Page, Jimmy 1944-
See Page, James Patrick

Paterson, Katherine 1932- .... **CLC 12, 30**
See also AAYA 1, 31; BYA 1, 2, 7; CA 21-24R; CANR 28, 59, 111, 173; CLR 7, 50, 127; CWRI 5; DLB 52; JRDA; LAIT 4; MAICYA 1, 2; MAICYAS 1; MTCW 1; SATA 13, 53, 92, 133; WYA; YAW

Paterson, Katherine Womeldorf
See Paterson, Katherine

Patmore, Coventry Kersey Dighton
1823-1896 .... **NCLC 9; PC 59**
See also DLB 35, 98; RGEL 2; TEA

Paton, Alan 1903-1988 ..... **CLC 4, 10, 25, 55, 106; TCLC 165; WLC 4**
See also AAYA 26; AFW; BPFB 3; BRWS 2; BYA 1; CA 13-16; 125; CANR 22; CAP 1; CN 1, 2, 3, 4; DA; DA3; DAB; DAC; DAM MST, NOV; DLB 225; DLBD 17; EWL 3; EXPN; LAIT 4; MTCW 1, 2; MTFW 2005; NFS 3, 12; RGEL 2; SATA 11; SATA-Obit 56; TWA; WLIT 2; WWE 1

Paton Walsh, Gillian
See Paton Walsh, Jill

Paton Walsh, Jill 1937- .... **CLC 35**
See also AAYA 11, 47; BYA 1, 8; CA 262; CAAE 262; CANR 38, 83, 158; CLR 2, 6, 128; DLB 161; JRDA; MAICYA 1, 2; SAAS 3; SATA 4, 72, 109, 190; SATA-Essay 190; WYA; YAW

Patsauq, Markoosie 1942- .... **NNAL**
See also CA 101; CLR 23; CWRI 5; DAM MULT

Patterson, (Horace) Orlando (Lloyd)
1940- .... **BLCS**
See also BW 1; CA 65-68; CANR 27, 84; CN 1, 2, 3, 4, 5, 6

Patton, George S(mith), Jr.
1885-1945 .... **TCLC 79**
See also CA 189

Paulding, James Kirke 1778-1860 ... **NCLC 2**
See also DLB 3, 59, 74, 250; RGAL 4

Paulin, Thomas Neilson
See Paulin, Tom

Paulin, Tom 1949- .... **CLC 37, 177**
See also CA 123; 128; CANR 98; CP 3, 4, 5, 6, 7; DLB 40

Pausanias c. 1st cent. - .... **CMLC 36**

Paustovsky, Konstantin (Georgievich)
1892-1968 .... **CLC 40**
See also CA 93-96; 25-28R; DLB 272; EWL 3

Pavese, Cesare 1908-1950 .... **PC 13; SSC 19; TCLC 3**
See also CA 104; 169; DLB 128, 177; EW 12; EWL 3; PFS 20; RGSF 2; RGWL 2, 3; TWA; WLIT 7

Pavic, Milorad 1929- .... **CLC 60**
See also CA 136; CDWLB 4; CWW 2; DLB 181; EWL 3; RGWL 3

Pavlov, Ivan Petrovich 1849-1936 . **TCLC 91**
See also CA 118; 180

Pavlova, Karolina Karlovna
1807-1893 .... **NCLC 138**
See also DLB 205

Payne, Alan
See Jakes, John

Payne, Rachel Ann
See Jakes, John

Paz, Gil
See Lugones, Leopoldo

Paz, Octavio 1914-1998 . **CLC 3, 4, 6, 10, 19, 51, 65, 119; HLC 2; PC 1, 48; TCLC 211; WLC 4**
See also AAYA 50; CA 73-76; 165; CANR 32, 65, 104; CWW 2; DA; DA3; DAB; DAC; DAM MST, MULT, POET; DLB 290, 331; DLBY 1990, 1998; DNFS 1;

EWL 3; HW 1, 2; LAW; LAWS 1; MTCW 1, 2; MTFW 2005; PFS 18, 30; RGWL 2, 3; SSFS 13; TWA; WLIT 1

p'Bitek, Okot 1931-1982 . **BLC 1:3; CLC 96; TCLC 149**
See also AFW; BW 2, 3; CA 124; 107; CANR 82; CP 1, 2, 3; DAM MULT; DLB 125; EWL 3; MTCW 1, 2; MTFW 2005; RGEL 2; WLIT 2

Peabody, Elizabeth Palmer
1804-1894 .... **NCLC 169**
See also DLB 1, 223

Peacham, Henry 1578-1644(?) .... **LC 119**
See also DLB 151

Peacock, Molly 1947- .... **CLC 60**
See also CA 103, 262; CAAE 262; CAAS 21; CANR 52, 84; CP 5, 6, 7; CWP; DLB 120, 282

Peacock, Thomas Love
1785-1866 .... **NCLC 22; PC 87**
See also BRW 4; DLB 96, 116; RGEL 2; RGSF 2

Peake, Mervyn 1911-1968 .... **CLC 7, 54**
See also CA 5-8R; 25-28R; CANR 3; DLB 15, 160, 255; FANT; MTCW 1; RGEL 2; SATA 23; SFW 4

Pearce, Ann Philippa
See Pearce, Philippa

Pearce, Philippa 1920-2006 .... **CLC 21**
See also BYA 5; CA 5-8R; 255; CANR 4, 109; CLR 9; CWRI 5; DLB 161; FANT; MAICYA 1; SATA 1, 67, 129; SATA-Obit 179

Pearl, Eric
See Elman, Richard (Martin)

Pearson, Jean Mary
See Gardam, Jane

Pearson, Thomas Reid
See Pearson, T.R.

Pearson, T.R. 1956- .... **CLC 39**
See also CA 120; 130; CANR 97, 147, 185; CSW; INT CA-130

Peck, Dale 1967- .... **CLC 81**
See also CA 146; CANR 72, 127, 180; GLL 2

Peck, John (Frederick) 1941- .... **CLC 3**
See also CA 49-52; CANR 3, 100; CP 4, 5, 6, 7

Peck, Richard 1934- .... **CLC 21**
See also AAYA 1, 24; BYA 1, 6, 8, 11; CA 85-88; CANR 19, 38, 129, 178; CLR 15, 142; INT CANR-19; JRDA; MAICYA 1, 2; SAAS 2; SATA 18, 55, 97, 110, 158, 190; SATA-Essay 110; WYA; YAW

Peck, Richard Wayne
See Peck, Richard

Peck, Robert Newton 1928- .... **CLC 17**
See also AAYA 3, 43; BYA 1, 6; CA 81-84; 182; CAAE 182; CANR 31, 63, 127; CLR 45; DA; DAC; DAM MST; JRDA; LAIT 3; MAICYA 1, 2; NFS 29; SAAS 1; SATA 21, 62, 111, 156; SATA-Essay 108; WYA; YAW

Peckinpah, David Samuel
See Peckinpah, Sam

Peckinpah, Sam 1925-1984 .... **CLC 20**
See also CA 109; 114; CANR 82

Pedersen, Knut 1859-1952 .. **TCLC 2, 14, 49, 151, 203**
See also AAYA 79; CA 104; 119; CANR 63; DLB 297, 330; EW 8; EWL 8; MTCW 1, 2; RGWL 2, 3

Peele, George 1556-1596 .... **DC 27; LC 115**
See also BRW 1; DLB 62, 167; RGEL 2

Peeslake, Gaffer
See Durrell, Lawrence (George)

Peguy, Charles (Pierre)
1873-1914 .... **TCLC 10**
See also CA 107; 193; DLB 258; EWL 3; GFL 1789 to the Present

Peirce, Charles Sanders
1839-1914 .... **TCLC 81**
See also CA 194; DLB 270

Pelagius c. 350-c. 418 .... **CMLC 112**

Pelecanos, George P. 1957- .... **CLC 236**
See also CA 138; CANR 122, 165; DLB 306

Pelevin, Victor 1962- .... **CLC 238**
See also CA 154; CANR 88, 159; DLB 285

Pelevin, Viktor Olegovich
See Pelevin, Victor

Pellicer, Carlos 1897(?)-1977 .... **HLCS 2**
See also CA 153; 69-72; DLB 290; EWL 3; HW 1

Pena, Ramon del Valle y
See Valle-Inclan, Ramon (Maria) del

Pendennis, Arthur Esquir
See Thackeray, William Makepeace

Penn, Arthur
See Matthews, (James) Brander

Penn, William 1644-1718 .... **LC 25**
See also DLB 24

PEPECE
See Prado (Calvo), Pedro

Pepys, Samuel 1633-1703 ... **LC 11, 58; WLC 4**
See also BRW 2; CDBLB 1660-1789; DA; DA3; DAB; DAC; DAM MST; DLB 101, 213; NCFS 4; RGEL 2; TEA; WLIT 3

Percy, Thomas 1729-1811 .... **NCLC 95**
See also DLB 104

Percy, Walker 1916-1990 .... **CLC 2, 3, 6, 8, 14, 18, 47, 65**
See also AMWS 3; BPFB 3; CA 1-4R; 131; CANR 1, 23, 64; CN 1, 2, 3, 4; CPW; CSW; DA3; DAM NOV, POP; DLB 2; DLBY 1980, 1990; EWL 3; MAL 5; MTCW 1, 2; MTFW 2005; RGAL 4; TUS

Percy, William Alexander
1885-1942 .... **TCLC 84**
See also CA 163; MTCW 2

Perdurabo, Frater
See Crowley, Edward Alexander

Perec, Georges 1936-1982 .... **CLC 56, 116**
See also CA 141; DLB 83, 299; EWL 3; GFL 1789 to the Present; RGHL; RGWL 3

Pereda (y Sanchez de Porrua), Jose Maria de 1833-1906 .... **TCLC 16**
See also CA 117

Pereda y Porrua, Jose Maria de
See Pereda (y Sanchez de Porrua), Jose Maria de

Peregoy, George Weems
See Mencken, H(enry) L(ouis)

Perelman, S(idney) J(oseph)
1904-1979 .. **CLC 3, 5, 9, 15, 23, 44, 49; SSC 32**
See also AAYA 79; AITN 1, 2; BPFB 3; CA 73-76; 89-92; CANR 18; DAM DRAM; DLB 11, 44; MTCW 1, 2; MTFW 2005; RGAL 4

Peret, Benjamin 1899-1959 .... **PC 33; TCLC 20**
See also CA 117; 186; GFL 1789 to the Present

Peretz, Isaac Leib
See Peretz, Isaac Loeb

Peretz, Isaac Loeb 1851(?)-1915 ...... **SSC 26; TCLC 16**
See also CA 109; 201; DLB 333

Peretz, Yitzhok Leibush
See Peretz, Isaac Loeb

Pirandello, Luigi 1867-1936 .. **DC 5; SSC 22; TCLC 4, 29, 172; WLC 4**
See also CA 104; 153; CANR 103; DA; DA3; DAB; DAC; DAM DRAM, MST; DFS 4, 9; DLB 264, 331; EW 8; EWL 3; MTCW 2; MTFW 2005; RGSF 2; RGWL 2, 3; WLIT 7

Pirdousi
See Ferdowsi, Abu'l Qasem

Pirdousi, Abu-l-Qasim
See Ferdowsi, Abu'l Qasem

Pirsig, Robert M(aynard) 1928- ... **CLC 4, 6, 73**
See also CA 53-56; CANR 42, 74; CPW 1; DA3; DAM POP; MTCW 1, 2; MTFW 2005; SATA 39

Pisan, Christine de
See Christine de Pizan

Pisarev, Dmitrii Ivanovich
See Pisarev, Dmitry Ivanovich

Pisarev, Dmitry Ivanovich
1840-1868 .... **NCLC 25**
See also DLB 277

Pix, Mary (Griffith) 1666-1709 ..... **LC 8, 149**
See also DLB 80

Pixerecourt, (Rene Charles) Guilbert de
1773-1844 .... **NCLC 39**
See also DLB 192; GFL 1789 to the Present

Plaatje, Sol(omon) T(shekisho)
1878-1932 .... **BLCS; TCLC 73**
See also BW 2, 3; CA 141; CANR 79; DLB 125, 225

Plaidy, Jean
See Hibbert, Eleanor Alice Burford

Planche, James Robinson
1796-1880 .... **NCLC 42**
See also RGEL 2

Plant, Robert 1948- .... **CLC 12**

Plante, David 1940- .... **CLC 7, 23, 38**
See also CA 37-40R; CANR 12, 36, 58, 82, 152; CN 2, 3, 4, 5, 6, 7; DAM NOV; DLBY 1983; INT CANR-12; MTCW 1

Plante, David Robert
See Plante, David

Plath, Sylvia 1932-1963 ..... **CLC 1, 2, 3, 5, 9, 11, 14, 17, 50, 51, 62, 111; PC 1, 37; WLC 4**
See also AAYA 13; AMWR 2; AMWS 1; BPFB 3; CA 19-20; CANR 34, 101; CAP 2; CDALB 1941-1968; DA; DA3; DAB; DAC; DAM MST, POET; DLB 5, 6, 152; EWL 3; EXPN; EXPP; FL 1:6; FW; LAIT 4; MAL 5; MBL; MTCW 1, 2; MTFW 2005; NFS 1; PAB; PFS 1, 15, 28; RGAL 4; SATA 96; TUS; WP; YAW

Plato c. 428B.C.-347B.C. .... **CMLC 8, 75, 98; WLCS**
See also AW 1; CDWLB 1; DA; DA3; DAB; DAC; DAM MST; DLB 176; LAIT 1; LATS 1:1; RGWL 2, 3; WLIT 8

Platonov, Andrei
See Klimentov, Andrei Platonovich

Platonov, Andrei Platonovich
See Klimentov, Andrei Platonovich

Platonov, Andrey Platonovich
See Klimentov, Andrei Platonovich

Platt, Kin 1911- .... **CLC 26**
See also AAYA 11; CA 17-20R; CANR 11; JRDA; SAAS 17; SATA 21, 86; WYA

Plautus c. 254B.C.-c. 184B.C. .... **CMLC 24, 92; DC 6**
See also AW 1; CDWLB 1; DLB 211; RGWL 2, 3; WLIT 8

Plick et Plock
See Simenon, Georges (Jacques Christian)

Plieksans, Janis
See Rainis, Janis

Plimpton, George 1927-2003 .... **CLC 36**
See also AITN 1; AMWS 16; CA 21-24R; 224; CANR 32, 70, 103, 133; DLB 185, 241; MTCW 1, 2; MTFW 2005; SATA 10; SATA-Obit 150

Pliny the Elder c. 23-79 .... **CMLC 23**
See also DLB 211

Pliny the Younger c. 61-c. 112 ...... **CMLC 62**
See also AW 2; DLB 211

Plomer, William Charles Franklin
1903-1973 .... **CLC 4, 8**
See also AFW; BRWS 11; CA 21-22; CANR 34; CAP 2; CN 1; CP 1, 2; DLB 20, 162, 191, 225; EWL 3; MTCW 1; RGEL 2; RGSF 2; SATA 24

Plotinus 204-270 .... **CMLC 46**
See also CDWLB 1; DLB 176

Plowman, Piers
See Kavanagh, Patrick (Joseph)

Plum, J.
See Wodehouse, P(elham) G(renville)

Plumly, Stanley 1939- .... **CLC 33**
See also CA 108; 110; CANR 97, 185; CP 3, 4, 5, 6, 7; DLB 5, 193; INT CA-110

Plumly, Stanley Ross
See Plumly, Stanley

Plumpe, Friedrich Wilhelm
See Murnau, F.W.

Plutarch c. 46-c. 120 .... **CMLC 60**
See also AW 2; CDWLB 1; DLB 176; RGWL 2, 3; TWA; WLIT 8

Po Chu-i 772-846 .... **CMLC 24**

Podhoretz, Norman 1930- .... **CLC 189**
See also AMWS 8; CA 9-12R; CANR 7, 78, 135, 179

Poe, Edgar Allan 1809-1849 ..... **NCLC 1, 16, 55, 78, 94, 97, 117, 211; PC 1, 54; SSC 1, 22, 34, 35, 54, 88, 111; WLC 4**
See also AAYA 14; AMW; AMWC 1; AMWR 2; BPFB 3; BYA 5, 11; CDALB 1640-1865; CMW 4; DA; DA3; DAB; DAC; DAM MST, POET; DLB 3, 59, 73, 74, 248, 254; EXPP; EXPS; GL 3; HGG; LAIT 2; LATS 1:1; LMFS 1; MSW; PAB; PFS 1, 3, 9; RGAL 4; RGSF 2; SATA 23; SCFW 1, 2; SFW 4; SSFS 2, 4, 7, 8, 16, 26; SUFW; TUS; WP; WYA

Poet of Titchfield Street, The
See Pound, Ezra (Weston Loomis)

Poggio Bracciolini, Gian Francesco
1380-1459 .... **LC 125**

Pohl, Frederik 1919- .... **CLC 18; SSC 25**
See also AAYA 24; CA 61-64, 188; CAAE 188; CAAS 1; CANR 11, 37, 81, 140; CN 1, 2, 3, 4, 5, 6; DLB 8; INT CANR-11; MTCW 1, 2; MTFW 2005; SATA 24; SCFW 1, 2; SFW 4

Poirier, Louis
See Gracq, Julien

Poitier, Sidney 1927- .... **CLC 26**
See also AAYA 60; BW 1; CA 117; CANR 94

Pokagon, Simon 1830-1899 .... **NNAL**
See also DAM MULT

Polanski, Roman 1933- .... **CLC 16, 178**
See also CA 77-80

Poliakoff, Stephen 1952- .... **CLC 38**
See also CA 106; CANR 116; CBD; CD 5, 6; DLB 13

Police, The
See Copeland, Stewart (Armstrong); Sting; Summers, Andy

Polidori, John William
1795-1821 .... **NCLC 51; SSC 97**
See also DLB 116; HGG

Poliziano, Angelo 1454-1494 .... **LC 120**
See also WLIT 7

Pollitt, Katha 1949- .... **CLC 28, 122**
See also CA 120; 122; CANR 66, 108, 164; MTCW 1, 2; MTFW 2005

Pollock, (Mary) Sharon 1936- .... **CLC 50**
See also CA 141; CANR 132; CD 5; CWD; DAC; DAM DRAM, MST; DFS 3; DLB 60; FW

Pollock, Sharon 1936- .... **DC 20**
See also CD 6

Polo, Marco 1254-1324 .... **CMLC 15**
See also WLIT 7

Polonsky, Abraham (Lincoln)
1910-1999 .... **CLC 92**
See also CA 104; 187; DLB 26; INT CA-104

Polybius c. 200B.C.-c. 118B.C. ...... **CMLC 17**
See also AW 1; DLB 176; RGWL 2, 3

Pomerance, Bernard 1940- .... **CLC 13**
See also CA 101; CAD; CANR 49, 134; CD 5, 6; DAM DRAM; DFS 9; LAIT 2

Ponge, Francis 1899-1988 .... **CLC 6, 18**
See also CA 85-88; 126; CANR 40, 86; DAM POET; DLBY 2002; EWL 3; GFL 1789 to the Present; RGWL 2, 3

Poniatowska, Elena 1932- . **CLC 140; HLC 2**
See also CA 101; CANR 32, 66, 107, 156; CDWLB 3; CWW 2; DAM MULT; DLB 113; EWL 3; HW 1, 2; LAWS 1; WLIT 1

Pontoppidan, Henrik 1857-1943 .... **TCLC 29**
See also CA 170; DLB 300, 331

Ponty, Maurice Merleau
See Merleau-Ponty, Maurice

Poole, (Jane Penelope) Josephine
See Helyar, Jane Penelope Josephine

Poole, Josephine
See Helyar, Jane Penelope Josephine

Popa, Vasko 1922-1991 . **CLC 19; TCLC 167**
See also CA 112; 148; CDWLB 4; DLB 181; EWL 3; RGWL 2, 3

Pope, Alexander 1688-1744 ...... **LC 3, 58, 60, 64, 164; PC 26; WLC 5**
See also BRW 3; BRWC 1; BRWR 1; CD-BLB 1660-1789; DA; DA3; DAB; DAC; DAM MST, POET; DLB 95, 101, 213; EXPP; PAB; PFS 12; RGEL 2; WLIT 3; WP

Popov, Evgenii Anatol'evich
See Popov, Yevgeny

Popov, Yevgeny .... **CLC 59**
See also DLB 285

Poquelin, Jean-Baptiste
See Moliere

Porete, Marguerite (?)-1310 .... **CMLC 73**
See also DLB 208

Porphyry c. 233-c. 305 .... **CMLC 71**

Porter, Connie (Rose) 1959(?)- .... **CLC 70**
See also AAYA 65; BW 2, 3; CA 142; CANR 90, 109; SATA 81, 129

Porter, Gene(va Grace) Stratton
See Stratton-Porter, Gene(va Grace)

Porter, Katherine Anne 1890-1980 ... **CLC 1, 3, 7, 10, 13, 15, 27, 101; SSC 4, 31, 43, 108**
See also AAYA 42; AITN 2; AMW; BPFB 3; CA 1-4R; 101; CANR 1, 65; CDALBS; CN 1, 2; DA; DA3; DAB; DAC; DAM MST, NOV; DLB 4, 9, 102; DLBD 12; DLBY 1980; EWL 3; EXPS; LAIT 3; MAL 5; MBL; MTCW 1, 2; MTFW 2005; NFS 14; RGAL 4; RGSF 2; SATA 39; SATA-Obit 23; SSFS 1, 8, 11, 16, 23; TCWW 2; TUS

Porter, Peter (Neville Frederick)
1929- .... **CLC 5, 13, 33**
See also CA 85-88; CP 1, 2, 3, 4, 5, 6, 7; DLB 40, 289; WWE 1

Porter, William Sydney
See Henry, O.

Romains, Jules 1885-1972 .... **CLC 7**
　See also CA 85-88; CANR 34; DLB 65,
　321; EWL 3; GFL 1789 to the Present;
　MTCW 1

Romero, Jose Ruben 1890-1952 .... **TCLC 14**
　See also CA 114; 131; EWL 3; HW 1; LAW

Ronsard, Pierre de 1524-1585 . **LC 6, 54; PC 11**
　See also DLB 327; EW 2; GFL Beginnings
　to 1789; RGWL 2, 3; TWA

Rooke, Leon 1934- .... **CLC 25, 34**
　See also CA 25-28R; CANR 23, 53; CCA
　1; CPW; DAM POP

Roosevelt, Franklin Delano
　　1882-1945 .... **TCLC 93**
　See also CA 116; 173; LAIT 3

Roosevelt, Theodore 1858-1919 ..... **TCLC 69**
　See also CA 115; 170; DLB 47, 186, 275

Roper, Margaret c. 1505-1544 .... **LC 147**

Roper, William 1498-1578 .... **LC 10**

Roquelaure, A. N.
　See Rice, Anne

Rosa, Joao Guimaraes 1908-1967
　See Guimaraes Rosa, Joao

Rose, Wendy 1948- . **CLC 85; NNAL; PC 13**
　See also CA 53-56; CANR 5, 51; CWP;
　DAM MULT; DLB 175; PFS 13; RGAL
　4; SATA 12

Rosen, R.D. 1949- .... **CLC 39**
　See also CA 77-80; CANR 62, 120, 175;
　CMW 4; INT CANR-30

Rosen, Richard
　See Rosen, R.D.

Rosen, Richard Dean
　See Rosen, R.D.

Rosenberg, Isaac 1890-1918 .... **TCLC 12**
　See also BRW 6; CA 107; 188; DLB 20,
　216; EWL 3; PAB; RGEL 2

Rosenblatt, Joe
　See Rosenblatt, Joseph

Rosenblatt, Joseph 1933- .... **CLC 15**
　See also CA 89-92; CP 3, 4, 5, 6, 7; INT
　CA-89-92

Rosenfeld, Samuel
　See Tzara, Tristan

Rosenstock, Sami
　See Tzara, Tristan

Rosenstock, Samuel
　See Tzara, Tristan

Rosenthal, M(acha) L(ouis)
　　1917-1996 .... **CLC 28**
　See also CA 1-4R; 152; CAAS 6; CANR 4,
　51; CP 1, 2, 3, 4, 5, 6; DLB 5; SATA 59

Ross, Barnaby
　See Dannay, Frederic; Lee, Manfred B.

Ross, Bernard L.
　See Follett, Ken

Ross, J. H.
　See Lawrence, T(homas) E(dward)

Ross, John Hume
　See Lawrence, T(homas) E(dward)

Ross, Martin 1862-1915
　See Martin, Violet Florence
　See also DLB 135; GLL 2; RGEL 2; RGSF
　2

Ross, (James) Sinclair 1908-1996 ... **CLC 13; SSC 24**
　See also CA 73-76; CANR 81; CN 1, 2, 3,
　4, 5, 6; DAC; DAM MST; DLB 88;
　RGEL 2; RGSF 2; TCWW 1, 2

Rossetti, Christina 1830-1894 ... **NCLC 2, 50, 66, 186; PC 7; WLC 5**
　See also AAYA 51; BRW 5; BYA 4; CLR
　115; DA; DA3; DAB; DAC; DAM MST;
　POET; DLB 35, 163, 240; EXPP; FL 1:3;
　LATS 1:1; MAICYA 1, 2; PFS 10, 14, 27;
　RGEL 2; SATA 20; TEA; WCH

Rossetti, Christina Georgina
　See Rossetti, Christina

Rossetti, Dante Gabriel 1828-1882 . **NCLC 4, 77; PC 44; WLC 5**
　See also AAYA 51; BRW 5; CDBLB 1832-
　1890; DA; DAB; DAC; DAM MST,
　POET; DLB 35; EXPP; RGEL 2; TEA

Rossi, Cristina Peri
　See Peri Rossi, Cristina

Rossi, Jean-Baptiste 1931-2003 .... **CLC 90**
　See also CA 201; 215; CMW 4; NFS 18

Rossner, Judith 1935-2005 .... **CLC 6, 9, 29**
　See also AITN 2; BEST 90:3; BPFB 3; CA
　17-20R; 242; CANR 18, 51, 73; CN 4, 5,
　6, 7; DLB 6; INT CANR-18; MAL 5;
　MTCW 1, 2; MTFW 2005

Rossner, Judith Perelman
　See Rossner, Judith

Rostand, Edmond (Eugene Alexis)
　　1868-1918 .... **DC 10; TCLC 6, 37**
　See also CA 104; 126; DA; DA3; DAB;
　DAC; DAM DRAM, MST; DFS 1; DLB
　192; LAIT 1; MTCW 1; RGWL 2, 3;
　TWA

Roth, Henry 1906-1995 ..... **CLC 2, 6, 11, 104**
　See also AMWS 9; CA 11-12; 149; CANR
　38, 63; CAP 1; CN 1, 2, 3, 4, 5, 6; DA3;
　DLB 28; EWL 3; MAL 5; MTCW 1, 2;
　MTFW 2005; RGAL 4

Roth, (Moses) Joseph 1894-1939 ... **TCLC 33**
　See also CA 160; DLB 85; EWL 3; RGWL
　2, 3

Roth, Philip 1933- ... **CLC 1, 2, 3, 4, 6, 9, 15, 22, 31, 47, 66, 86, 119, 201; SSC 26, 102; WLC 5**
　See also AAYA 67; AMWR 2; AMWS 3;
　BEST 90:3; BPFB 3; CA 1-4R; CANR 1,
　22, 36, 55, 89, 132, 170; CDALB 1968-
　1988; CN 3, 4, 5, 6, 7; CPW 1; DA; DA3;
　DAB; DAC; DAM MST, NOV, POP;
　DLB 2, 28, 173; DLBY 1982; EWL 3;
　MAL 5; MTCW 1, 2; MTFW 2005; NFS
　25; RGAL 4; RGHL; RGSF 2; SSFS 12,
　18; TUS

Roth, Philip Milton
　See Roth, Philip

Rothenberg, Jerome 1931- .... **CLC 6, 57**
　See also CA 45-48; CANR 1, 106; CP 1, 2,
　3, 4, 5, 6, 7; DLB 5, 193

Rotter, Pat .... **CLC 65**

Roumain, Jacques (Jean Baptiste)
　　1907-1944 .... **BLC 1:3; TCLC 19**
　See also BW 1; CA 117; 125; DAM MULT;
　EWL 3

Rourke, Constance Mayfield
　　1885-1941 .... **TCLC 12**
　See also CA 107; 200; MAL 5; YABC 1

Rousseau, Jean-Baptiste 1671-1741 ...... **LC 9**

Rousseau, Jean-Jacques 1712-1778 .... **LC 14, 36, 122; WLC 5**
　See also DA; DA3; DAB; DAC; DAM
　MST; DLB 314; EW 4; GFL Beginnings
　to 1789; LMFS 1; RGWL 2, 3; TWA

Roussel, Raymond 1877-1933 .... **TCLC 20**
　See also CA 117; 201; EWL 3; GFL 1789
　to the Present

Rovit, Earl (Herbert) 1927- .... **CLC 7**
　See also CA 5-8R; CANR 12

Rowe, Elizabeth Singer 1674-1737 ..... **LC 44**
　See also DLB 39, 95

Rowe, Nicholas 1674-1718 .... **LC 8**
　See also DLB 84; RGEL 2

Rowlandson, Mary 1637(?)-1678 .... **LC 66**
　See also DLB 24, 200; RGAL 4

Rowley, Ames Dorrance
　See Lovecraft, H. P.

Rowley, William 1585(?)-1626 ... **LC 100, 123**
　See also DFS 22; DLB 58; RGEL 2

Rowling, J.K. 1965- .... **CLC 137, 217**
　See also AAYA 34; BYA 11, 13, 14; CA
　173; CANR 128, 157; CLR 66, 80, 112;
　MAICYA 2; MTFW 2005; SATA 109,
　174; SUFW 2

Rowling, Joanne Kathleen
　See Rowling, J.K.

Rowson, Susanna Haswell
　　1762(?)-1824 .... **NCLC 5, 69, 182**
　See also AMWS 15; DLB 37, 200; RGAL 4

Roy, Arundhati 1960(?)- .... **CLC 109, 210**
　See also CA 163; CANR 90, 126; CN 7;
　DLB 323, 326; DLBY 1997; EWL 3;
　LATS 1:2; MTFW 2005; NFS 22; WWE
　1

Roy, Gabrielle 1909-1983 .... **CLC 10, 14**
　See also CA 53-56; 110; CANR 5, 61; CCA
　1; DAB; DAC; DAM MST; DLB 68;
　EWL 3; MTCW 1; RGWL 2, 3; SATA
　104; TCLE 1:2

Royko, Mike 1932-1997 .... **CLC 109**
　See also CA 89-92; 157; CANR 26, 111;
　CPW

Rozanov, Vasilii Vasil'evich
　See Rozanov, Vassili

Rozanov, Vasily Vasilyevich
　See Rozanov, Vassili

Rozanov, Vassili 1856-1919 .... **TCLC 104**
　See also DLB 295; EWL 3

Rozewicz, Tadeusz 1921- .... **CLC 9, 23, 139**
　See also CA 108; CANR 36, 66; CWW 2;
　DA3; DAM POET; DLB 232; EWL 3;
　MTCW 1, 2; MTFW 2005; RGHL;
　RGWL 3

Ruark, Gibbons 1941- .... **CLC 3**
　See also CA 33-36R; CAAS 23; CANR 14,
　31, 57; DLB 120

Rubens, Bernice (Ruth) 1923-2004 . **CLC 19, 31**
　See also CA 25-28R; 232; CANR 33, 65,
　128; CN 1, 2, 3, 4, 5, 6, 7; DLB 14, 207,
　326; MTCW 1

Rubin, Harold
　See Robbins, Harold

Rudkin, (James) David 1936- .... **CLC 14**
　See also CA 89-92; CBD; CD 5, 6; DLB 13

Rudnik, Raphael 1933- .... **CLC 7**
　See also CA 29-32R

Ruffian, M.
　See Hasek, Jaroslav (Matej Frantisek)

Rufinus c. 345-410 .... **CMLC 111**

Ruiz, Jose Martinez
　See Martinez Ruiz, Jose

Ruiz, Juan c. 1283-c. 1350 .... **CMLC 66**

Rukeyser, Muriel 1913-1980 . **CLC 6, 10, 15, 27; PC 12**
　See also AMWS 6; CA 5-8R; 93-96; CANR
　26, 60; CP 1, 2, 3; DA3; DAM POET;
　DLB 48; EWL 3; FW; GLL 2; MAL 5;
　MTCW 1, 2; PFS 10, 29; RGAL 4; SATA-
　Obit 22

Rule, Jane 1931-2007 .... **CLC 27, 265**
　See also CA 25-28R; 266; CAAS 18; CANR
　12, 87; CN 4, 5, 6, 7; DLB 60; FW

Rule, Jane Vance
　See Rule, Jane

Rulfo, Juan 1918-1986 .. **CLC 8, 80; HLC 2; SSC 25**
　See also CA 85-88; 118; CANR 26; CD-
　WLB 3; DAM MULT; DLB 113; EWL 3;
　HW 1, 2; LAW; MTCW 1, 2; RGSF 2;
　RGWL 2, 3; WLIT 1

Rumi, Jalal al-Din 1207-1273 ...... **CMLC 20; PC 45**
　See also AAYA 64; RGWL 2, 3; WLIT 6;
　WP

Runeberg, Johan 1804-1877 .... **NCLC 41**

EWL 3; EXPN; LAIT 4; MAICYA 1, 2; MAL 5; MTCW 1, 2; MTFW 2005; NFS 1; RGAL 4; RGSF 2; SATA 67; SSFS 17; TUS; WYA; YAW

Salisbury, John
 See Caute, (John) David

Sallust c. 86B.C.-35B.C. .... **CMLC 68**
 See also AW 2; CDWLB 1; DLB 211; RGWL 2, 3

Salter, James 1925- .... **CLC 7, 52, 59, 275; SSC 58**
 See also AMWS 9; CA 73-76; CANR 107, 160; DLB 130; SSFS 25

Saltus, Edgar (Everton) 1855-1921 . **TCLC 8**
 See also CA 105; DLB 202; RGAL 4

Saltykov, Mikhail Evgrafovich 1826-1889 .... **NCLC 16**
 See also DLB 238:

Saltykov-Shchedrin, N.
 See Saltykov, Mikhail Evgrafovich

Samarakis, Andonis
 See Samarakis, Antonis

Samarakis, Antonis 1919-2003 .... **CLC 5**
 See also CA 25-28R; 224; CAAS 16; CANR 36; EWL 3

Samigli, E.
 See Schmitz, Aron Hector

Sanchez, Florencio 1875-1910 .... **TCLC 37**
 See also CA 153; DLB 305; EWL 3; HW 1; LAW

Sanchez, Luis Rafael 1936- .... **CLC 23**
 See also CA 128; DLB 305; EWL 3; HW 1; WLIT 1

Sanchez, Sonia 1934- . **BLC 1:3, 2:3; CLC 5, 116, 215; PC 9**
 See also BW 2, 3; CA 33-36R; CANR 24, 49, 74, 115; CLR 18; CP 2, 3, 4, 5, 6, 7; CSW; CWP; DA3; DAM MULT; DLB 41; DLBD 8; EWL 3; MAICYA 1, 2; MAL 5; MTCW 1, 2; MTFW 2005; PFS 26; SATA 22, 136; WP

Sancho, Ignatius 1729-1780 .... **LC 84**

Sand, George 1804-1876 .... **DC 29; NCLC 2, 42, 57, 174; WLC 5**
 See also DA; DA3; DAB; DAC; DAM MST, NOV; DLB 119, 192; EW 6; FL 1:3; FW; GFL 1789 to the Present; RGWL 2, 3; TWA

Sandburg, Carl (August) 1878-1967 . **CLC 1, 4, 10, 15, 35; PC 2, 41; WLC 5**
 See also AAYA 24; AMW; BYA 1, 3; CA 5-8R; 25-28R; CANR 35; CDALB 1865-1917; CLR 67; DA; DA3; DAB; DAC; DAM MST, POET; DLB 17, 54, 284; EWL 3; EXPP; LAIT 2; MAICYA 1, 2; MAL 5; MTCW 1, 2; MTFW 2005; PAB; PFS 3, 6, 12; RGAL 4; SATA 8; TUS; WCH; WP; WYA

Sandburg, Charles
 See Sandburg, Carl (August)

Sandburg, Charles A.
 See Sandburg, Carl (August)

Sanders, (James) Ed(ward) 1939- .... **CLC 53**
 See also BG 1:3; CA 13-16R; CAAS 21; CANR 13, 44, 78; CP 1, 2, 3, 4, 5, 6, 7; DAM POET; DLB 16, 244

Sanders, Edward
 See Sanders, (James) Ed(ward)

Sanders, Lawrence 1920-1998 .... **CLC 41**
 See also BEST 89:4; BPFB 3; CA 81-84; 165; CANR 33, 62; CMW 4; CPW; DA3; DAM POP; MTCW 1

Sanders, Noah
 See Blount, Roy, Jr.

Sanders, Winston P.
 See Anderson, Poul

Sandoz, Mari(e Susette) 1900-1966 .. **CLC 28**
 See also CA 1-4R; 25-28R; CANR 17, 64; DLB 9, 212; LAIT 2; MTCW 1, 2; SATA 5; TCWW 1, 2

Sandys, George 1578-1644 .... **LC 80**
 See also DLB 24, 121

Saner, Reg(inald Anthony) 1931- .... **CLC 9**
 See also CA 65-68; CP 3, 4, 5, 6, 7

Sankara 788-820 .... **CMLC 32**

Sannazaro, Jacopo 1456(?)-1530 .... **LC 8**
 See also RGWL 2, 3; WLIT 7

Sansom, William 1912-1976 . **CLC 2, 6; SSC 21**
 See also CA 5-8R; 65-68; CANR 42; CN 1, 2; DAM NOV; DLB 139; EWL 3; MTCW 1; RGEL 2; RGSF 2

Santayana, George 1863-1952 .... **TCLC 40**
 See also AMW; CA 115; 194; DLB 54, 71, 246, 270; DLBD 13; EWL 3; MAL 5; RGAL 4; TUS

Santiago, Danny
 See James, Daniel (Lewis)

Santillana, Inigo Lopez de Mendoza, Marques de 1398-1458 .... **LC 111**
 See also DLB 286

Santmyer, Helen Hooven 1895-1986 .... **CLC 33; TCLC 133**
 See also CA 1-4R; 118; CANR 15, 33; DLBY 1984; MTCW 1; RHW

Santoka, Taneda 1882-1940 .... **TCLC 72**

Santos, Bienvenido N(uqui) 1911-1996 ... **AAL; CLC 22; TCLC 156**
 See also CA 101; 151; CANR 19, 46; CP 1; DAM MULT; DLB 312, 348; EWL; RGAL 4; SSFS 19

Santos, Miguel
 See Mihura, Miguel

Sapir, Edward 1884-1939 .... **TCLC 108**
 See also CA 211; DLB 92

Sapper
 See McNeile, Herman Cyril

Sapphire 1950- .... **CLC 99**
 See also CA 262

Sapphire, Brenda
 See Sapphire

Sappho fl. 6th cent. B.C.- ... **CMLC 3, 67; PC 5**
 See also CDWLB 1; DA3; DAM POET; DLB 176; FL 1:1; PFS 20; RGWL 2, 3; WLIT 8; WP

Saramago, Jose 1922- .... **CLC 119, 275; HLCS 1**
 See also CA 153; CANR 96, 164; CWW 2; DLB 287, 332; EWL 3; LATS 1:2; NFS 27; SSFS 23

Sarduy, Severo 1937-1993 .... **CLC 6, 97; HLCS 2; TCLC 167**
 See also CA 89-92; 142; CANR 58, 81; CWW 2; DLB 113; EWL 3; HW 1, 2; LAW

Sargeson, Frank 1903-1982 ..... **CLC 31; SSC 99**
 See also CA 25-28R; 106; CANR 38, 79; CN 1, 2, 3; EWL 3; GLL 2; RGEL 2; RGSF 2; SSFS 20

Sarmiento, Domingo Faustino 1811-1888 .... **HLCS 2; NCLC 123**
 See also LAW; WLIT 1

Sarmiento, Felix Ruben Garcia
 See Dario, Ruben

Saro-Wiwa, Ken(ule Beeson) 1941-1995 .... **CLC 114; TCLC 200**
 See also BW 2; CA 142; 150; CANR 60; DLB 157

Saroyan, William 1908-1981 ... **CLC 1, 8, 10, 29, 34, 56; DC 28; SSC 21; TCLC 137; WLC 5**
 See also AAYA 66; CA 5-8R; 103; CAD; CANR 30; CDALBS; CN 1, 2; DA; DA3; DAB; DAC; DAM DRAM, MST, NOV;

DFS 17; DLB 7, 9, 86; DLBY 1981; EWL 3; LAIT 4; MAL 5; MTCW 1, 2; MTFW 2005; RGAL 4; RGSF 2; SATA 23; SATA-Obit 24; SSFS 14; TUS

Sarraute, Nathalie 1900-1999 .... **CLC 1, 2, 4, 8, 10, 31, 80; TCLC 145**
 See also BPFB 3; CA 9-12R; 187; CANR 23, 66, 134; CWW 2; DLB 83, 321; EW 12; EWL 3; GFL 1789 to the Present; MTCW 1, 2; MTFW 2005; RGWL 2, 3

Sarton, May 1912-1995 ... **CLC 4, 14, 49, 91; PC 39; TCLC 120**
 See also AMWS 8; CA 1-4R; 149; CANR 1, 34, 55, 116; CN 1, 2, 3, 4, 5, 6; CP 1, 2, 3, 4, 5, 6; DAM POET; DLB 48; DLBY 1981; EWL 3; FW; INT CANR-34; MAL 5; MTCW 1, 2; MTFW 2005; RGAL 4; SATA 36; SATA-Obit 86; TUS

Sartre, Jean-Paul 1905-1980 . **CLC 1, 4, 7, 9, 13, 18, 24, 44, 50, 52; DC 3; SSC 32; WLC 5**
 See also AAYA 62; CA 9-12R; 97-100; CANR 21; DA; DA3; DAB; DAC; DAM DRAM, MST, NOV; DFS 5, 26; DLB 72, 296, 321, 332; EW 12; EWL 3; GFL 1789 to the Present; LMFS 2; MTCW 1, 2; MTFW 2005; NFS 21; RGHL; RGSF 2; RGWL 2, 3; SSFS 9; TWA

Sassoon, Siegfried (Lorraine) 1886-1967 .... **CLC 36, 130; PC 12**
 See also BRW 6; CA 104; 25-28R; CANR 36; DAB; DAM MST, NOV, POET; DLB 20, 191; DLBD 18; EWL 3; MTCW 1, 2; MTFW 2005; PAB; PFS 28; RGEL 2; TEA

Satterfield, Charles
 See Pohl, Frederik

Satyremont
 See Peret, Benjamin

Saul, John III
 See Saul, John

Saul, John 1942- .... **CLC 46**
 See also AAYA 10, 62; BEST 90:4; CA 81-84; CANR 16, 40, 81, 176; CPW; DAM NOV, POP; HGG; SATA 98

Saul, John W.
 See Saul, John

Saul, John W. III
 See Saul, John

Saul, John Woodruff III
 See Saul, John

Saunders, Caleb
 See Heinlein, Robert A.

Saura (Atares), Carlos 1932-1998 .... **CLC 20**
 See also CA 114; 131; CANR 79; HW 1

Sauser, Frederic Louis
 See Sauser-Hall, Frederic

Sauser-Hall, Frederic 1887-1961 ..... **CLC 18, 106**
 See also CA 102; 93-96; CANR 36, 62; DLB 258; EWL 3; GFL 1789 to the Present; MTCW 1; WP

Saussure, Ferdinand de 1857-1913 .... **TCLC 49**
 See also DLB 242

Savage, Catharine
 See Brosman, Catharine Savage

Savage, Richard 1697(?)-1743 .... **LC 96**
 See also DLB 95; RGEL 2

Savage, Thomas 1915-2003 .... **CLC 40**
 See also CA 126; 132; 218; CAAS 15; CN 6, 7; INT CA-132; SATA-Obit 147; TCWW 2

Savan, Glenn 1953-2003 .... **CLC 50**
 See also CA 225

Savonarola, Girolamo 1452-1498 ...... **LC 152**
 See also LMFS 1

Sax, Robert
 See Johnson, Robert

Scott, Sir Walter 1771-1832 .... **NCLC 15, 69, 110, 209; PC 13; SSC 32; WLC 5**
See also AAYA 22; BRW 4; BYA 2; CD-BLB 1789-1832; DA; DAB; DAC; DAM MST, NOV, POET; DLB 93, 107, 116, 144, 159; GL 3; HGG; LAIT 1; RGEL 2; RGSF 2; SSFS 10; SUFW 1; TEA; WLIT 3; YABC 2

Scribe, (Augustin) Eugene 1791-1861 . **DC 5; NCLC 16**
See also DAM DRAM; DLB 192; GFL 1789 to the Present; RGWL 2, 3

Scrum, R.
See Crumb, R.

Scudery, Georges de 1601-1667 .... **LC 75**
See also GFL Beginnings to 1789

Scudery, Madeleine de 1607-1701 .. **LC 2, 58**
See also DLB 268; GFL Beginnings to 1789

Scum
See Crumb, R.

Scumbag, Little Bobby
See Crumb, R.

Seabrook, John
See Hubbard, L. Ron

Seacole, Mary Jane Grant
1805-1881 .... **NCLC 147**
See also DLB 166

Sealy, I(rwin) Allan 1951- .... **CLC 55**
See also CA 136; CN 6, 7

Search, Alexander
See Pessoa, Fernando

Seare, Nicholas
See Whitaker, Rod

Sebald, W(infried) G(eorg)
1944-2001 .... **CLC 194**
See also BRWS 8; CA 159; 202; CANR 98; MTFW 2005; RGHL

Sebastian, Lee
See Silverberg, Robert

Sebastian Owl
See Thompson, Hunter S.

Sebestyen, Igen
See Sebestyen, Ouida

Sebestyen, Ouida 1924- .... **CLC 30**
See also AAYA 8; BYA 7; CA 107; CANR 40, 114; CLR 17; JRDA; MAICYA 1, 2; SAAS 10; SATA 39, 140; WYA; YAW

Sebold, Alice 1963- .... **CLC 193**
See also AAYA 56; CA 203; CANR 181; MTFW 2005

Second Duke of Buckingham
See Villiers, George

Secundus, H. Scriblerus
See Fielding, Henry

Sedges, John
See Buck, Pearl S(ydenstricker)

Sedgwick, Catharine Maria
1789-1867 .... **NCLC 19, 98**
See also DLB 1, 74, 183, 239, 243, 254; FL 1:3; RGAL 4

Sedulius Scottus 9th cent. -c. 874 .. **CMLC 86**

Seebohm, Victoria
See Glendinning, Victoria

Seelye, John (Douglas) 1931- .... **CLC 7**
See also CA 97-100; CANR 70; INT CA-97-100; TCWW 1, 2

Seferiades, Giorgos Stylianou
1900-1971 .... **CLC 5, 11; TCLC 213**
See also CA 5-8R; 33-36R; CANR 5, 36; DLB 332; EW 12; EWL 3; MTCW 1; RGWL 2, 3

Seferis, George
See Seferiades, Giorgos Stylianou

Segal, Erich (Wolf) 1937- .... **CLC 3, 10**
See also BEST 89:1; BPFB 3; CA 25-28R; CANR 20, 36, 65, 113; CPW; DAM POP; DLBY 1986; INT CANR-20; MTCW 1

Seger, Bob 1945- .... **CLC 35**

Seghers
See Radvanyi, Netty

Seghers, Anna
See Radvanyi, Netty

Seidel, Frederick 1936- .... **CLC 18**
See also CA 13-16R; CANR 8, 99, 180; CP 1, 2, 3, 4, 5, 6, 7; DLBY 1984

Seidel, Frederick Lewis
See Seidel, Frederick

Seifert, Jaroslav 1901-1986 . **CLC 34, 44, 93; PC 47**
See also CA 127; CDWLB 4; DLB 215, 332; EWL 3; MTCW 1, 2

Sei Shonagon c. 966-1017(?) ..... **CMLC 6, 89**

Sejour, Victor 1817-1874 .... **DC 10**
See also DLB 50

Sejour Marcou et Ferrand, Juan Victor
See Sejour, Victor

Selby, Hubert, Jr. 1928-2004 ..... **CLC 1, 2, 4, 8; SSC 20**
See also CA 13-16R; 226; CANR 33, 85; CN 1, 2, 3, 4, 5, 6, 7; DLB 2, 227; MAL 5

Selzer, Richard 1928- .... **CLC 74**
See also CA 65-68; CANR 14, 106

Sembene, Ousmane
See Ousmane, Sembene

Senancour, Etienne Pivert de
1770-1846 .... **NCLC 16**
See also DLB 119; GFL 1789 to the Present

Sender, Ramon (Jose) 1902-1982 ...... **CLC 8; HLC 2; TCLC 136**
See also CA 5-8R; 105; CANR 8; DAM MULT; DLB 322; EWL 3; HW 1; MTCW 1; RGWL 2, 3

Seneca, Lucius Annaeus c. 1B.C.-c. 65 .... **CMLC 6, 107; DC 5**
See also AW 2; CDWLB 1; DAM DRAM; DLB 211; RGWL 2, 3; TWA; WLIT 8

Senghor, Leopold Sedar
1906-2001 .. **BLC 1:3; CLC 54, 130; PC 25**
See also AFW; BW 2; CA 116; 125; 203; CANR 47, 74, 134; CWW 2; DAM MULT, POET; DNFS 2; EWL 3; GFL 1789 to the Present; MTCW 1, 2; MTFW 2005; TWA

Senior, Olive (Marjorie) 1941- .... **SSC 78**
See also BW 3; CA 154; CANR 86, 126; CN 6; CP 6, 7; CWP; DLB 157; EWL 3; RGSF 2

Senna, Danzy 1970- .... **CLC 119**
See also CA 169; CANR 130, 184

Sepheriades, Georgios
See Seferiades, Giorgos Stylianou

Serling, (Edward) Rod(man)
1924-1975 .... **CLC 30**
See also AAYA 14; AITN 1; CA 162; 57-60; DLB 26; SFW 4

Serna, Ramon Gomez de la
See Gomez de la Serna, Ramon

Serpieres
See Guillevic, (Eugene)

Service, Robert
See Service, Robert W(illiam)

Service, Robert W(illiam)
1874(?)-1958 ... **PC 70; TCLC 15; WLC 5**
See also BYA 4; CA 115; 140; CANR 84; DA; DAB; DAC; DAM MST, POET; DLB 92; PFS 10; RGEL 2; SATA 20

Seth, Vikram 1952- .... **CLC 43, 90**
See also BRWS 10; CA 121; 127; CANR 50, 74, 131; CN 6, 7; CP 5, 6, 7; DA3; DAM MULT; DLB 120, 271, 282, 323; EWL 3; INT CA-127; MTCW 2; MTFW 2005; WWE 1

Setien, Miguel Delibes
See Delibes Setien, Miguel

Seton, Cynthia Propper 1926-1982 .. **CLC 27**
See also CA 5-8R; 108; CANR 7

Seton, Ernest (Evan) Thompson
1860-1946 .... **TCLC 31**
See also ANW; BYA 3; CA 109; 204; CLR 59; DLB 92; DLBD 13; JRDA; SATA 18

Seton-Thompson, Ernest
See Seton, Ernest (Evan) Thompson

Settle, Mary Lee 1918-2005 .... **CLC 19, 61, 273**
See also BPFB 3; CA 89-92; 243; CAAS 1; CANR 44, 87, 126, 182; CN 6, 7; CSW; DLB 6; INT CA-89-92

Seuphor, Michel
See Arp, Jean

Sevigne, Marie (de Rabutin-Chantal)
1626-1696 .... **LC 11, 144**
See also DLB 268; GFL Beginnings to 1789; TWA

Sevigne, Marie de Rabutin Chantal
See Sevigne, Marie (de Rabutin-Chantal)

Sewall, Samuel 1652-1730 .... **LC 38**
See also DLB 24; RGAL 4

Sexton, Anne (Harvey) 1928-1974 ..... **CLC 2, 4, 6, 8, 10, 15, 53, 123; PC 2, 79; WLC 5**
See also AMWS 2; CA 1-4R; 53-56; CABS 2; CANR 3, 36; CDALB 1941-1968; CP 1, 2; DA; DA3; DAB; DAC; DAM MST, POET; DLB 5, 169; EWL 3; EXPP; FL 1:6; FW; MAL 5; MBL; MTCW 1, 2; MTFW 2005; PAB; PFS 4, 14, 30; RGAL 4; RGHL; SATA 10; TUS

Shaara, Jeff 1952- .... **CLC 119**
See also AAYA 70; CA 163; CANR 109, 172; CN 7; MTFW 2005

Shaara, Michael 1929-1988 .... **CLC 15**
See also AAYA 71; AITN 1; BPFB 3; CA 102; 125; CANR 52, 85; DAM POP; DLBY 1983; MTFW 2005; NFS 26

Shackleton, C.C.
See Aldiss, Brian W.

Shacochis, Bob
See Shacochis, Robert G.

Shacochis, Robert G. 1951- .... **CLC 39**
See also CA 119; 124; CANR 100; INT CA-124

Shadwell, Thomas 1641(?)-1692 .... **LC 114**
See also DLB 80; IDTP; RGEL 2

Shaffer, Anthony 1926-2001 .... **CLC 19**
See also CA 110; 116; 200; CBD; CD 5, 6; DAM DRAM; DFS 13; DLB 13

Shaffer, Anthony Joshua
See Shaffer, Anthony

Shaffer, Peter 1926- ... **CLC 5, 14, 18, 37, 60; DC 7**
See also BRWS 1; CA 25-28R; CANR 25, 47, 74, 118; CBD; CD 5, 6; CDBLB 1960 to Present; DA3; DAB; DAM DRAM, MST; DFS 5, 13; DLB 13, 233; EWL 3; MTCW 1, 2; MTFW 2005; RGEL 2; TEA

Shakespeare, William 1564-1616 . **PC 84, 89, 98; WLC 5**
See also AAYA 35; BRW 1; CDBLB Before 1660; DA; DA3; DAB; DAC; DAM DRAM, MST, POET; DFS 20, 21; DLB 62, 172, 263; EXPP; LAIT 1; LATS 1:1; LMFS 1; PAB; PFS 1, 2, 3, 4, 5, 8, 9; RGEL 2; TEA; WLIT 3; WP; WS; WYA

Shakey, Bernard
See Young, Neil

Shalamov, Varlam (Tikhonovich)
1907-1982 .... **CLC 18**
See also CA 129; 105; DLB 302; RGSF 2

Shamloo, Ahmad
See Shamlu, Ahmad

Shamlou, Ahmad
See Shamlu, Ahmad

Sidhwa, Bapsy (N.) 1938- .... **CLC 168**
   See also CA 108; CANR 25, 57; CN 6, 7;
   DLB 323; FW
Sidney, Mary 1561-1621 .... **LC 19, 39**
   See also DLB 167
Sidney, Sir Philip 1554-1586 .... **LC 19, 39,**
   131; PC 32
   See also BRW 1; BRWR 2; CDBLB Before
   1660; DA; DA3; DAB; DAC; DAM MST,
   POET; DLB 167; EXPP; PAB; PFS 30;
   RGEL 2; TEA; WP
Sidney Herbert, Mary
   See Sidney, Mary
Siegel, Jerome 1914-1996 .... **CLC 21**
   See also AAYA 50; CA 116; 169; 151
Siegel, Jerry
   See Siegel, Jerome
Sienkiewicz, Henryk (Adam Alexander Pius)
   1846-1916 .... **TCLC 3**
   See also CA 104; 134; CANR 84; DLB 332;
   EWL 3; RGSF 2; RGWL 2, 3
Sierra, Gregorio Martinez
   See Martinez Sierra, Gregorio
Sierra, Maria de la O'LeJarraga Martinez
   See Martinez Sierra, Maria
Sigal, Clancy 1926- .... **CLC 7**
   See also CA 1-4R; CANR 85, 184; CN 1,
   2, 3, 4, 5, 6, 7
Siger of Brabant 1240(?)-1284(?) . **CMLC 69**
   See also DLB 115
Sigourney, Lydia H.
   See Sigourney, Lydia Howard (Huntley)
   See also DLB 73, 183
Sigourney, Lydia Howard (Huntley)
   1791-1865 .... **NCLC 21, 87**
   See Sigourney, Lydia H.
   See also DLB 1, 42, 239, 243
Sigourney, Lydia Huntley
   See Sigourney, Lydia Howard (Huntley)
Siguenza y Gongora, Carlos de
   1645-1700 .... **HLCS 2; LC 8**
   See also LAW
Sigurjonsson, Johann
   See Sigurjonsson, Johann
Sigurjonsson, Johann 1880-1919 ... **TCLC 27**
   See also CA 170; DLB 293; EWL 3
Sikelianos, Angelos 1884-1951 .... **PC 29;**
   TCLC 39
   See also EWL 3; RGWL 2, 3
Silkin, Jon 1930-1997 .... **CLC 2, 6, 43**
   See also CA 5-8R; CAAS 5; CANR 89; CP
   1, 2, 3, 4, 5, 6; DLB 27
Silko, Leslie 1948- ...... **CLC 23, 74, 114, 211;**
   NNAL; SSC 37, 66; WLCS
   See also AAYA 14; AMWS 4; ANW; BYA
   12; CA 115; 122; CANR 45, 65, 118; CN
   4, 5, 6, 7; CP 4, 5, 6, 7; CPW 1; CWP;
   DA; DA3; DAC; DAM MST, MULT,
   POP; DLB 143, 175, 256, 275; EWL 3;
   EXPP; EXPS; LAIT 4; MAL 5; MTCW
   2; MTFW 2005; NFS 4; PFS 9, 16; RGAL
   4; RGSF 2; SSFS 4, 8, 10, 11; TCWW 1,
   2
Sillanpaa, Frans Eemil 1888-1964 ... **CLC 19**
   See also CA 129; 93-96; DLB 332; EWL 3;
   MTCW 1
Sillitoe, Alan 1928- .. **CLC 1, 3, 6, 10, 19, 57,**
   148
   See also AITN 1; BRWS 5; CA 9-12R, 191;
   CAAE 191; CAAS 2; CANR 8, 26, 55,
   139; CDBLB 1960 to Present; CN 1, 2, 3,
   4, 5, 6; CP 1, 2, 3, 4, 5; DLB 14, 139;
   EWL 3; MTCW 1, 2; MTFW 2005; RGEL
   2; RGSF 2; SATA 61
Silone, Ignazio 1900-1978 .... **CLC 4**
   See also CA 25-28; 81-84; CANR 34; CAP
   2; DLB 264; EW 12; EWL 3; MTCW 1;
   RGSF 2; RGWL 2, 3

Silone, Ignazione
   See Silone, Ignazio
Siluriensis, Leolinus
   See Jones, Arthur Llewellyn
Silver, Joan Micklin 1935- .... **CLC 20**
   See also CA 114; 121; INT CA-121
Silver, Nicholas
   See Faust, Frederick (Schiller)
Silverberg, Robert 1935- .... **CLC 7, 140**
   See also AAYA 24; BPFB 3; BYA 7, 9; CA
   1-4R, 186; CAAE 186; CAAS 3; CANR
   1, 20, 36, 85, 140, 175; CLR 59; CN 6, 7;
   CPW; DAM POP; DLB 8; INT CANR-
   20; MAICYA 1, 2; MTCW 1, 2; MTFW
   2005; SATA 13, 91; SATA-Essay 104;
   SCFW 1, 2; SFW 4; SUFW 2
Silverstein, Alvin 1933- .... **CLC 17**
   See also CA 49-52; CANR 2; CLR 25;
   JRDA; MAICYA 1, 2; SATA 8, 69, 124
Silverstein, Shel 1932-1999 .... **PC 49**
   See also AAYA 40; BW 3; CA 107; 179;
   CANR 47, 74, 81; CLR 5, 96; CWRI 5;
   JRDA; MAICYA 1, 2; MTCW 2; MTFW
   2005; SATA 33, 92; SATA-Brief 27;
   SATA-Obit 116
Silverstein, Virginia B(arbara Opshelor)
   1937- .... **CLC 17**
   See also CA 49-52; CANR 2; CLR 25;
   JRDA; MAICYA 1, 2; SATA 8, 69, 124
Sim, Georges
   See Simenon, Georges (Jacques Christian)
Simak, Clifford D(onald) 1904-1988 . **CLC 1,**
   55
   See also CA 1-4R; 125; CANR 1, 35; DLB
   8; MTCW 1; SATA-Obit 56; SCFW 1, 2;
   SFW 4
Simenon, Georges (Jacques Christian)
   1903-1989 .... **CLC 1, 2, 3, 8, 18, 47**
   See also BPFB 3; CA 85-88; 129; CANR
   35; CMW 4; DA3; DAM POP; DLB 72;
   DLBY 1989; EW 12; EWL 3; GFL 1789
   to the Present; MSW; MTCW 1, 2; MTFW
   2005; RGWL 2, 3
Simic, Charles 1938- .... **CLC 6, 9, 22, 49, 68,**
   130, 256; PC 69
   See also AAYA 78; AMWS 8; CA 29-32R;
   CAAS 4; CANR 12, 33, 52, 61, 96, 140;
   CP 2, 3, 4, 5, 6, 7; DA3; DAM POET;
   DLB 105; MAL 5; MTCW 2; MTFW
   2005; PFS 7; RGAL 4; WP
Simmel, Georg 1858-1918 .... **TCLC 64**
   See also CA 157; DLB 296
Simmons, Charles (Paul) 1924- .... **CLC 57**
   See also CA 89-92; INT CA-89-92
Simmons, Dan 1948- .... **CLC 44**
   See also AAYA 16, 54; CA 138; CANR 53,
   81, 126, 174; CPW; DAM POP; HGG;
   SUFW 2
Simmons, James (Stewart Alexander)
   1933- .... **CLC 43**
   See also CA 105; CAAS 21; CP 1, 2, 3, 4,
   5, 6, 7; DLB 40
Simmons, Richard
   See Simmons, Dan
Simms, William Gilmore
   1806-1870 .... **NCLC 3**
   See also DLB 3, 30, 59, 73, 248, 254;
   RGAL 4
Simon, Carly 1945- .... **CLC 26**
   See also CA 105
Simon, Claude 1913-2005 ... **CLC 4, 9, 15, 39**
   See also CA 89-92; 241; CANR 33, 117;
   CWW 2; DAM NOV; DLB 83, 332; EW
   13; EWL 3; GFL 1789 to the Present;
   MTCW 1
Simon, Claude Eugene Henri
   See Simon, Claude
Simon, Claude Henri Eugene
   See Simon, Claude

Simon, Marvin Neil
   See Simon, Neil
Simon, Myles
   See Follett, Ken
Simon, Neil 1927- .... **CLC 6, 11, 31, 39, 70,**
   233; DC 14
   See also AAYA 32; AITN 1; AMWS 4; CA
   21-24R; CAD; CANR 26, 54, 87, 126;
   CD 5, 6; DA3; DAM DRAM; DFS 2, 6,
   12, 18,, 24; DLB 7, 266; LAIT 4; MAL 5;
   MTCW 1, 2; MTFW 2005; RGAL 4; TUS
Simon, Paul 1941(?)- .... **CLC 17**
   See also CA 116; 153; CANR 152
Simon, Paul Frederick
   See Simon, Paul
Simonon, Paul 1956(?)- .... **CLC 30**
Simonson, Rick .... **CLC 70**
Simpson, Harriette
   See Arnow, Harriette (Louisa) Simpson
Simpson, Louis 1923- ... **CLC 4, 7, 9, 32, 149**
   See also AMWS 9; CA 1-4R; CAAS 4;
   CANR 1, 61, 140; CP 1, 2, 3, 4, 5, 6, 7;
   DAM POET; DLB 5; MAL 5; MTCW 1,
   2; MTFW 2005; PFS 7, 11, 14; RGAL 4
Simpson, Mona 1957- .... **CLC 44, 146**
   See also CA 122; 135; CANR 68, 103; CN
   6, 7; EWL 3
Simpson, Mona Elizabeth
   See Simpson, Mona
Simpson, N(orman) F(rederick)
   1919- .... **CLC 29**
   See also CA 13-16R; CBD; DLB 13; RGEL
   2
Sinclair, Andrew (Annandale) 1935- . **CLC 2,**
   14
   See also CA 9-12R; CAAS 5; CANR 14,
   38, 91; CN 1, 2, 3, 4, 5, 6, 7; DLB 14;
   FANT; MTCW 1
Sinclair, Emil
   See Hesse, Hermann
Sinclair, Iain 1943- .... **CLC 76**
   See also BRWS 14; CA 132; CANR 81,
   157; CP 5, 6, 7; HGG
Sinclair, Iain MacGregor
   See Sinclair, Iain
Sinclair, Irene
   See Griffith, D.W.
Sinclair, Julian
   See Sinclair, May
Sinclair, Mary Amelia St. Clair (?)-
   See Sinclair, May
Sinclair, May 1865-1946 .... **TCLC 3, 11**
   See also CA 104; 166; DLB 36, 135; EWL
   3; HGG; RGEL 2; RHW; SUFW
Sinclair, Roy
   See Griffith, D.W.
Sinclair, Upton 1878-1968 ...... **CLC 1, 11, 15,**
   63; TCLC 160; WLC 5
   See also AAYA 63; AMWS 5; BPFB 3;
   BYA 2; CA 5-8R; 25-28R; CANR 7;
   CDALB 1929-1941; DA; DA3; DAB;
   DAC; DAM MST, NOV; DLB 9; EWL 3;
   INT CANR-7; LAIT 3; MAL 5; MTCW
   1, 2; MTFW 2005; NFS 6; RGAL 4;
   SATA 9; TUS; YAW
Sinclair, Upton Beall
   See Sinclair, Upton
Singe, (Edmund) J(ohn) M(illington)
   1871-1909 .... **WLC**
Singer, Isaac
   See Singer, Isaac Bashevis
Singer, Isaac Bashevis 1904-1991 .. **CLC 1, 3,**
   6, 9, 11, 15, 23, 38, 69, 111; SSC 3, 53,
   80; WLC 5
   See also AAYA 32; AITN 1, 2; AMW;
   AMWR 2; BPFB 3; BYA 1, 4; CA 1-4R;
   134; CANR 1, 39, 106; CDALB 1941-
   1968; CLR 1; CN 1, 2, 3, 4; CWRI 5;
   DA; DA3; DAB; DAC; DAM MST, NOV;

DLB 6, 28, 52, 278, 332, 333; DLBY
1991; EWL 3; EXPS; HGG; JRDA; LAIT
3; MAICYA 1, 2; MAL 5; MTCW 1, 2;
MTFW 2005; RGAL 4; RGHL; RGSF 2;
SATA 3, 27; SATA-Obit 68; SSFS 2, 12,
16, 27; TUS; TWA

Singer, Israel Joshua 1893-1944 .... **TCLC 33**
See also CA 169; DLB 333; EWL 3

Singh, Khushwant 1915- .... **CLC 11**
See also CA 9-12R; CAAS 9; CANR 6, 84;
CN 1, 2, 3, 4, 5, 6, 7; DLB 323; EWL 3;
RGEL 2

Singleton, Ann
See Benedict, Ruth

Singleton, John 1968(?)- .... **CLC 156**
See also AAYA 50; BW 2, 3; CA 138;
CANR 67, 82; DAM MULT

Siniavskii, Andrei
See Sinyavsky, Andrei (Donatevich)

Sinibaldi, Fosco
See Kacew, Romain

Sinjohn, John
See Galsworthy, John

Sinyavsky, Andrei (Donatevich)
1925-1997 .... **CLC 8**
See also CA 85-88; 159; CWW 2; EWL 3;
RGSF 2

Sinyavsky, Andrey Donatovich
See Sinyavsky, Andrei (Donatevich)

Sirin, V.
See Nabokov, Vladimir (Vladimirovich)

Sissman, L(ouis) E(dward)
1928-1976 .... **CLC 9, 18**
See also CA 21-24R; 65-68; CANR 13; CP
2; DLB 5

Sisson, C(harles) H(ubert)
1914-2003 .... **CLC 8**
See also BRWS 11; CA 1-4R; 220; CAAS
3; CANR 3, 48, 84; CP 1, 2, 3, 4, 5, 6, 7;
DLB 27

Sitting Bull 1831(?)-1890 .... **NNAL**
See also DA3; DAM MULT

Sitwell, Dame Edith 1887-1964 ..... **CLC 2, 9,
67; PC 3**
See also BRW 7; CA 9-12R; CANR 35;
CDBLB 1945-1960; DAM POET; DLB
20; EWL 3; MTCW 1, 2; MTFW 2005;
RGEL 2; TEA

Siwaarmill, H. P.
See Sharp, William

Sjoewall, Maj 1935- .... **CLC 7**
See also BPFB 3; CA 65-68; CANR 73;
CMW 4; MSW

Sjowall, Maj
See Sjoewall, Maj

Skelton, John 1460(?)-1529 ..... **LC 71; PC 25**
See also BRW 1; DLB 136; RGEL 2

Skelton, Robin 1925-1997 .... **CLC 13**
See also AITN 2; CA 5-8R; 160; CAAS 5;
CANR 28, 89; CCA 1; CP 1, 2, 3, 4, 5, 6;
DLB 27, 53

Skolimowski, Jerzy 1938- .... **CLC 20**
See also CA 128

Skram, Amalie (Bertha)
1847-1905 .... **TCLC 25**
See also CA 165

Skvorecky, Josef 1924- . **CLC 15, 39, 69, 152**
See also CA 61-64; CAAS 1; CANR 10,
34, 63, 108; CDWLB 4; CWW 2; DA3;
DAC; DAM NOV; DLB 232; EWL 3;
MTCW 1, 2; MTFW 2005

Slade, Bernard 1930-
See Newbound, Bernard Slade

Slaughter, Carolyn 1946- .... **CLC 56**
See also CA 85-88; CANR 85, 169; CN 5,
6, 7

Slaughter, Frank G(ill) 1908-2001 ... **CLC 29**
See also AITN 2; CA 5-8R; 197; CANR 5,
85; INT CANR-5; RHW

Slavitt, David R. 1935- .... **CLC 5, 14**
See also CA 21-24R; CAAS 3; CANR 41,
83, 166; CN 1, 2; CP 1, 2, 3, 4, 5, 6, 7;
DLB 5, 6

Slavitt, David Rytman
See Slavitt, David R.

Slesinger, Tess 1905-1945 .... **TCLC 10**
See also CA 107; 199; DLB 102

Slessor, Kenneth 1901-1971 .... **CLC 14**
See also CA 102; 89-92; DLB 260; RGEL
2

Slowacki, Juliusz 1809-1849 .... **NCLC 15**
See also RGWL 3

Smart, Christopher 1722-1771 .... **LC 3, 134;
PC 13**
See also DAM POET; DLB 109; RGEL 2

Smart, Elizabeth 1913-1986 .... **CLC 54**
See also CA 81-84; 118; CN 4; DLB 88

Smiley, Jane 1949- ...... **CLC 53, 76, 144, 236**
See also AAYA 66; AMWS 6; BPFB 3; CA
104; CANR 30, 50, 74, 96, 158; CN 6, 7;
CPW 1; DA3; DAM POP; DLB 227, 234;
EWL 3; INT CANR-30; MAL 5; MTFW
2005; SSFS 19

Smiley, Jane Graves
See Smiley, Jane

Smith, A(rthur) J(ames) M(arshall)
1902-1980 .... **CLC 15**
See also CA 1-4R; 102; CANR 4; CP 1, 2,
3; DAC; DLB 88; RGEL 2

Smith, Adam 1723(?)-1790 .... **LC 36**
See also DLB 104, 252, 336; RGEL 2

Smith, Alexander 1829-1867 .... **NCLC 59**
See also DLB 32, 55

Smith, Alexander McCall 1948- ..... **CLC 268**
See also CA 215; CANR 154; SATA 73,
179

Smith, Anna Deavere 1950- ...... **CLC 86, 241**
See also CA 133; CANR 103; CD 5, 6; DFS
2, 22; DLB 341

Smith, Betty (Wehner) 1904-1972 .... **CLC 19**
See also AAYA 72; BPFB 3; BYA 3; CA
5-8R; 33-36R; DLBY 1982; LAIT 3;
RGAL 4; SATA 6

Smith, Charlotte (Turner)
1749-1806 .... **NCLC 23, 115**
See also DLB 39, 109; RGEL 2; TEA

Smith, Clark Ashton 1893-1961 .... **CLC 43**
See also AAYA 76; CA 143; CANR 81;
FANT; HGG; MTCW 2; SCFW 1, 2; SFW
4; SUFW

Smith, Dave
See Smith, David (Jeddie)

Smith, David (Jeddie) 1942- .... **CLC 22, 42**
See also CA 49-52; CAAS 7; CANR 1, 59,
120; CP 3, 4, 5, 6, 7; CSW; DAM POET;
DLB 5

Smith, Iain Crichton 1928-1998 .... **CLC 64**
See also BRWS 9; CA 21-24R; 171; CN 1,
2, 3, 4, 5, 6; CP 1, 2, 3, 4, 5, 6; DLB 40,
139, 319; RGSF 2

Smith, John 1580(?)-1631 .... **LC 9**
See also DLB 24, 30; TUS

Smith, Johnston
See Crane, Stephen (Townley)

Smith, Joseph, Jr. 1805-1844 .... **NCLC 53**

Smith, Kevin 1970- .... **CLC 223**
See also AAYA 37; CA 166; CANR 131

Smith, Lee 1944- .... **CLC 25, 73, 258**
See also CA 114; 119; CANR 46, 118, 173;
CN 7; CSW; DLB 143; DLBY 1983;
EWL 3; INT CA-119; RGAL 4

Smith, Martin
See Smith, Martin Cruz

Smith, Martin Cruz 1942- .. **CLC 25; NNAL**
See Smith, Martin Cruz
See also BEST 89:4; BPFB 3; CA 85-88;
CANR 6, 23, 43, 65, 119, 184; CMW 4;
CPW; DAM MULT; POP; HGG; INT
CANR-23; MTCW 2; MTFW 2005;
RGAL 4

Smith, Patti 1946- .... **CLC 12**
See also CA 93-96; CANR 63, 168

Smith, Pauline (Urmson)
1882-1959 .... **TCLC 25**
See also DLB 225; EWL 3

Smith, R. Alexander McCall
See Smith, Alexander McCall

Smith, Rosamond
See Oates, Joyce Carol

Smith, Seba 1792-1868 .... **NCLC 187**
See also DLB 1, 11, 243

Smith, Sheila Kaye
See Kaye-Smith, Sheila

Smith, Stevie 1902-1971 .... **CLC 3, 8, 25, 44;
PC 12**
See also BRWS 2; CA 17-18; 29-32R;
CANR 35; CAP 2; CP 1; DAM POET;
DLB 20; EWL 3; MTCW 1, 2; PAB; PFS
3; RGEL 2; TEA

Smith, Wilbur 1933- .... **CLC 33**
See also CA 13-16R; CANR 7, 46, 66, 134,
180; CPW; MTCW 1, 2; MTFW 2005

Smith, Wilbur Addison
See Smith, Wilbur

Smith, William Jay 1918- .... **CLC 6**
See also AMWS 13; CA 5-8R; CANR 44,
106; CP 1, 2, 3, 4, 5, 6, 7; CSW; CWRI
5; DLB 5; MAICYA 1, 2; SAAS 22;
SATA 2, 68, 154; SATA-Essay 154; TCLE
1:2

Smith, Woodrow Wilson
See Kuttner, Henry

Smith, Zadie 1975- .... **CLC 158**
See also AAYA 50; CA 193; DLB 347;
MTFW 2005

Smolenskin, Peretz 1842-1885 .... **NCLC 30**

Smollett, Tobias (George) 1721-1771 ... **LC 2,
46**
See also BRW 3; CDBLB 1660-1789; DLB
39, 104; RGEL 2; TEA

Snodgrass, Quentin Curtius
See Twain, Mark

Snodgrass, Thomas Jefferson
See Twain, Mark

Snodgrass, W. D. 1926-2009 .... **CLC 2, 6, 10,
18, 68; PC 74**
See also AMWS 6; CA 1-4R; CANR 6, 36,
65, 85, 185; CP 1, 2, 3, 4, 5, 6, 7; DAM
POET; DLB 5; MAL 5; MTCW 1, 2;
MTFW 2005; PFS 29; RGAL 4; TCLE
1:2

Snodgrass, William De Witt
See Snodgrass, W. D.

Snorri Sturluson 1179-1241 .... **CMLC 56**
See also RGWL 2, 3

Snow, C(harles) P(ercy) 1905-1980 ... **CLC 1,
4, 6, 9, 13, 19**
See also BRW 7; CA 5-8R; 101; CANR 28;
CDBLB 1945-1960; CN 1, 2; DAM NOV;
DLB 15, 77; DLBD 17; EWL 3; MTCW
1, 2; MTFW 2005; RGEL 2; TEA

Snow, Frances Compton
See Adams, Henry (Brooks)

Snyder, Gary 1930- . **CLC 1, 2, 5, 9, 32, 120;
PC 21**
See also AAYA 72; AMWS 8; ANW; BG
1:3; CA 17-20R; CANR 30, 60, 125; CP
1, 2, 3, 4, 5, 6, 7; DA3; DAM POET; DLB
5, 16, 165, 212, 237, 275, 342; EWL 3;
MAL 5; MTCW 2; MTFW 2005; PFS 9,
19; RGAL 4; WP

Snyder, Zilpha Keatley 1927- .... **CLC 17**
See also AAYA 15; BYA 1; CA 9-12R, 252;
CAAE 252; CANR 38; CLR 31, 121;
JRDA; MAICYA 1, 2; SAAS 2; SATA 1,
28, 75, 110, 163; SATA-Essay 112, 163;
YAW

Soares, Bernardo
See Pessoa, Fernando

Sobh, A.
See Shamlu, Ahmad

Sobh, Alef
See Shamlu, Ahmad

Sobol, Joshua 1939- .... **CLC 60**
See also CA 200; CWW 2; RGHL

Sobol, Yehoshua 1939-
See Sobol, Joshua

Socrates 470B.C.-399B.C. .... **CMLC 27**

Soderberg, Hjalmar 1869-1941 ...... **TCLC 39**
See also DLB 259; EWL 3; RGSF 2

Soderbergh, Steven 1963- .... **CLC 154**
See also AAYA 43; CA 243

Soderbergh, Steven Andrew
See Soderbergh, Steven

Sodergran, Edith (Irene) 1892-1923
See Soedergran, Edith (Irene)

Soedergran, Edith (Irene)
1892-1923 .... **TCLC 31**
See also CA 202; DLB 259; EW 11; EWL
3; RGWL 2, 3

Softly, Edgar
See Lovecraft, H. P.

Softly, Edward
See Lovecraft, H. P.

Sokolov, Alexander V(sevolodovich)
1943- .... **CLC 59**
See also CA 73-76; CWW 2; DLB 285;
EWL 3; RGWL 2, 3

Sokolov, Raymond 1941- .... **CLC 7**
See also CA 85-88

Sokolov, Sasha
See Sokolov, Alexander V(sevolodovich)

Solo, Jay
See Ellison, Harlan

Sologub, Fedor
See Teternikov, Fyodor Kuzmich

Sologub, Feodor
See Teternikov, Fyodor Kuzmich

Sologub, Fyodor
See Teternikov, Fyodor Kuzmich

Solomons, Ikey Esquir
See Thackeray, William Makepeace

Solomos, Dionysios 1798-1857 .... **NCLC 15**

Solwoska, Mara
See French, Marilyn

Solzhenitsyn, Aleksandr 1918-2008 ... **CLC 1,
2, 4, 7, 9, 10, 18, 26, 34, 78, 134, 235;
SSC 32, 105; WLC 5**
See also AAYA 49; AITN 1; BPFB 3; CA
69-72; CANR 40, 65, 116; CWW 2; DA;
DA3; DAB; DAC; DAM MST, NOV;
DLB 302, 332; EW 13; EWL 3; EXPS;
LAIT 4; MTCW 1, 2; MTFW 2005; NFS
6; RGSF 2; RGWL 2, 3; SSFS 9; TWA

Solzhenitsyn, Aleksandr I.
See Solzhenitsyn, Aleksandr

Solzhenitsyn, Aleksandr Isayevich
See Solzhenitsyn, Aleksandr

Somers, Jane
See Lessing, Doris

Somerville, Edith Oenone
1858-1949 .... **SSC 56; TCLC 51**
See also CA 196; DLB 135; RGEL 2; RGSF
2

Somerville & Ross
See Martin, Violet Florence; Somerville,
Edith Oenone

Sommer, Scott 1951- .... **CLC 25**
See also CA 106

Sommers, Christina Hoff 1950- ...... **CLC 197**
See also CA 153; CANR 95

Sondheim, Stephen 1930- .. **CLC 30, 39, 147;
DC 22**
See also AAYA 11, 66; CA 103; CANR 47,
67, 125; DAM DRAM; DFS 25; LAIT 4

Sondheim, Stephen Joshua
See Sondheim, Stephen

Sone, Monica 1919- .... **AAL**
See also DLB 312

Song, Cathy 1955- .... **AAL; PC 21**
See also CA 154; CANR 118; CWP; DLB
169, 312; EXPP; FW; PFS 5

Sontag, Susan 1933-2004 ... **CLC 1, 2, 10, 13,
31, 105, 195**
See also AMWS 3; CA 17-20R; 234; CANR
25, 51, 74, 97, 184; CN 1, 2, 3, 4, 5, 6, 7;
CPW; DA3; DAM POP; DLB 2, 67; EWL
3; MAL 5; MBL; MTCW 1, 2; MTFW
2005; RGAL 4; RHW; SSFS 10

Sophocles 496(?)B.C.-406(?)B.C. .... **CMLC 2,
47, 51, 86; DC 1; WLCS**
See also AW 1; CDWLB 1; DA; DA3;
DAB; DAC; DAM DRAM, MST; DFS 1,
4, 8, 24; DLB 176; LAIT 1; LATS 1:1;
LMFS 1; RGWL 2, 3; TWA; WLIT 8

Sordello 1189-1269 .... **CMLC 15**

Sorel, Georges 1847-1922 .... **TCLC 91**
See also CA 118; 188

Sorel, Julia
See Drexler, Rosalyn

Sorokin, Vladimir .... **CLC 59**
See also CA 258; DLB 285

Sorokin, Vladimir Georgievich
See Sorokin, Vladimir

Sorrentino, Gilbert 1929-2006 .... **CLC 3, 7,
14, 22, 40, 247**
See also CA 77-80; 250; CANR 14, 33, 115,
157; CN 3, 4, 5, 6, 7; CP 1, 2, 3, 4, 5, 6,
7; DLB 5, 173; DLBY 1980; INT
CANR-14

Soseki
See Natsume, Soseki

Soto, Gary 1952- ... **CLC 32, 80; HLC 2; PC
28**
See also AAYA 10, 37; BYA 11; CA 119;
125; CANR 50, 74, 107, 157; CLR 38;
CP 4, 5, 6, 7; DAM MULT; DFS 26; DLB
82; EWL 3; EXPP; HW 1, 2; INT CA-
125; JRDA; LLW; MAICYA 2; MAIC-
YAS 1; MAL 5; MTCW 2; MTFW 2005;
PFS 7, 30; RGAL 4; SATA 80, 120, 174;
WYA; YAW

Soupault, Philippe 1897-1990 .... **CLC 68**
See also CA 116; 147; 131; EWL 3; GFL
1789 to the Present; LMFS 2

Souster, (Holmes) Raymond 1921- .... **CLC 5,
14**
See also CA 13-16R; CAAS 14; CANR 13,
29, 53; CP 1, 2, 3, 4, 5, 6, 7; DA3; DAC;
DAM POET; DLB 88; RGEL 2; SATA 63

Southern, Terry 1924(?)-1995 .... **CLC 7**
See also AMWS 11; BPFB 3; CA 1-4R;
150; CANR 1, 55, 107; CN 1, 2, 3, 4, 5,
6; DLB 2; IDFW 3, 4

Southerne, Thomas 1660-1746 .... **LC 99**
See also DLB 80; RGEL 2

Southey, Robert 1774-1843 .... **NCLC 8, 97**
See also BRW 4; DLB 93, 107, 142; RGEL
2; SATA 54

Southwell, Robert 1561(?)-1595 .... **LC 108**
See also DLB 167; RGEL 2; TEA

Southworth, Emma Dorothy Eliza Nevitte
1819-1899 .... **NCLC 26**
See also DLB 239

Souza, Ernest
See Scott, Evelyn

Soyinka, Wole 1934- .. **BLC 1:3, 2:3; CLC 3,
5, 14, 36, 44, 179; DC 2; WLC 5**
See also AFW; BW 2, 3; CA 13-16R;
CANR 27, 39, 82, 136; CD 5, 6; CDWLB
3; CN 6, 7; CP 1, 2, 3, 4, 5, 6 ,7; DA;
DA3; DAB; DAC; DAM DRAM, MST,
MULT; DFS 10, 26; DLB 125, 332; EWL
3; MTCW 1, 2; MTFW 2005; PFS 27;
RGEL 2; TWA; WLIT 2; WWE 1

Spackman, W(illiam) M(ode)
1905-1990 .... **CLC 46**
See also CA 81-84; 132

Spacks, Barry (Bernard) 1931- .... **CLC 14**
See also CA 154; CANR 33, 109; CP 3, 4,
5, 6, 7; DLB 105

Spanidou, Irini 1946- .... **CLC 44**
See also CA 185; CANR 179

Spark, Muriel 1918-2006 .... **CLC 2, 3, 5, 8,
13, 18, 40, 94, 242; PC 72; SSC 10, 115**
See also BRWS 1; CA 5-8R; 251; CANR
12, 36, 76, 89, 131; CDBLB 1945-1960;
CN 1, 2, 3, 4, 5, 6, 7; CP 1, 2, 3, 4, 5, 6,
7; DA3; DAB; DAC; DAM MST, NOV;
DLB 15, 139; EWL 3; FW; INT CANR-
12; LAIT 4; MTCW 1, 2; MTFW 2005;
NFS 22; RGEL 2; TEA; WLIT 4; YAW

Spark, Muriel Sarah
See Spark, Muriel

Spaulding, Douglas
See Bradbury, Ray

Spaulding, Leonard
See Bradbury, Ray

Speght, Rachel 1597-c. 1630 .... **LC 97**
See also DLB 126

Spence, J. A. D.
See Eliot, T(homas) S(tearns)

Spencer, Anne 1882-1975 .... **HR 1:3; PC 77**
See also BW 2; CA 161; DLB 51, 54

Spencer, Elizabeth 1921- .... **CLC 22; SSC 57**
See also CA 13-16R; CANR 32, 65, 87; CN
1, 2, 3, 4, 5, 6, 7; CSW; DLB 6, 218;
EWL 3; MTCW 1; RGAL 4; SATA 14

Spencer, Leonard G.
See Silverberg, Robert

Spencer, Scott 1945- .... **CLC 30**
See also CA 113; CANR 51, 148; DLBY
1986

Spender, Stephen 1909-1995 ..... **CLC 1, 2, 5,
10, 41, 91; PC 71**
See also BRWS 2; CA 9-12R; 149; CANR
31, 54; CDBLB 1945-1960; CP 1, 2, 3, 4,
5, 6; DA3; DAM POET; DLB 20; EWL
3; MTCW 1, 2; MTFW 2005; PAB; PFS
23; RGEL 2; TEA

Spengler, Oswald (Arnold Gottfried)
1880-1936 .... **TCLC 25**
See also CA 118; 189

Spenser, Edmund 1552(?)-1599 ...... **LC 5, 39,
117; PC 8, 42; WLC 5**
See also AAYA 60; BRW 1; CDBLB Be-
fore 1660; DA; DA3; DAB; DAC; DAM
MST, POET; DLB 167; EFS 2; EXPP;
PAB; RGEL 2; TEA; WLIT 3; WP

Spicer, Jack 1925-1965 .... **CLC 8, 18, 72**
See also BG 1:3; CA 85-88; DAM POET;
DLB 5, 16, 193; GLL 1; WP

Spiegelman, Art 1948- .... **CLC 76, 178**
See also AAYA 10, 46; CA 125; CANR 41,
55, 74, 124; DLB 299; MTCW 2; MTFW
2005; RGHL; SATA 109, 158; YAW

Spielberg, Peter 1929- .... **CLC 6**
See also CA 5-8R; CANR 4, 48; DLBY
1981

Spielberg, Steven 1947- .... **CLC 20, 188**
See also AAYA 8, 24; CA 77-80; CANR
32; SATA 32

Spillane, Frank Morrison
See Spillane, Mickey

Sternberg, Josef von 1894-1969 .... **CLC 20**
   See also CA 81-84
Sterne, Laurence 1713-1768 .. **LC 2, 48, 156;**
   WLC 5
      See also BRW 3; BRWC 1; CDBLB 1660-
      1789; DA; DAB; DAC; DAM MST, NOV;
      DLB 39; RGEL 2; TEA
Sternheim, (William Adolf) Carl
   1878-1942 .... **TCLC 8**
      See also CA 105; 193; DLB 56, 118; EWL
      3; IDTP; RGWL 2, 3
Stevens, Margaret Dean
   See Aldrich, Bess Streeter
Stevens, Mark 1951- .... **CLC 34**
   See also CA 122
Stevens, R. L.
   See Hoch, Edward D.
Stevens, Wallace 1879-1955 . **PC 6; TCLC 3,**
   12, 45; WLC 5
      See also AMW; AMWR 1; CA 104; 124;
      CANR 181; CDALB 1929-1941; DA;
      DA3; DAB; DAC; DAM MST, POET;
      DLB 54, 342; EWL 3; EXPP; MAL 5;
      MTCW 1, 2; PAB; PFS 13, 16; RGAL 4;
      TUS; WP
Stevenson, Anne (Katharine) 1933- .. **CLC 7,**
   33
      See also BRWS 6; CA 17-20R; CAAS 9;
      CANR 9, 33, 123; CP 3, 4, 5, 6, 7; CWP;
      DLB 40; MTCW 1; RHW
Stevenson, Robert Louis (Balfour)
   1850-1894 ...... **NCLC 5, 14, 63, 193; PC**
   84; SSC 11, 51; WLC 5
      See also AAYA 24; BPFB 3; BRW 5;
      BRWC 1; BRWR 1; BYA 1, 2, 4, 13; CD-
      BLB 1890-1914; CLR 10, 11, 107; DA;
      DA3; DAB; DAC; DAM MST, NOV;
      DLB 18, 57, 141, 156, 174; DLBD 13;
      GL 3; HGG; JRDA; LAIT 1, 3; MAICYA
      1, 2; NFS 11, 20; RGEL 2; RGSF 2;
      SATA 100; SUFW; TEA; WCH; WLIT 4;
      WYA; YABC 2; YAW
Stewart, J(ohn) I(nnes) M(ackintosh)
   1906-1994 .... **CLC 7, 14, 32**
      See also CA 85-88; 147; CAAS 3; CANR
      47; CMW 4; CN 1, 2, 3, 4, 5; DLB 276;
      MSW; MTCW 1, 2
Stewart, Mary (Florence Elinor)
   1916- .... **CLC 7, 35, 117**
      See also AAYA 29, 73; BPFB 3; CA 1-4R;
      CANR 1, 59, 130; CMW 4; CPW; DAB;
      FANT; RHW; SATA 12; YAW
Stewart, Mary Rainbow
   See Stewart, Mary (Florence Elinor)
Stewart, Will
   See Williamson, John Stewart
Stifle, June
   See Campbell, Maria
Stifter, Adalbert 1805-1868 ... **NCLC 41, 198;**
   SSC 28
      See also CDWLB 2; DLB 133; RGSF 2;
      RGWL 2, 3
Still, James 1906-2001 .... **CLC 49**
      See also CA 65-68; 195; CAAS 17; CANR
      10, 26; CSW; DLB 9; DLBY 01; SATA
      29; SATA-Obit 127
Sting 1951- .... **CLC 26**
   See also CA 167
Stirling, Arthur
   See Sinclair, Upton
Stitt, Milan 1941-2009 .... **CLC 29**
   See also CA 69-72
Stockton, Francis Richard
   1834-1902 .... **TCLC 47**
      See also AAYA 68; BYA 4, 13; CA 108;
      137; DLB 42, 74; DLBD 13; EXPS; MAI-
      CYA 1, 2; SATA 44; SATA-Brief 32; SFW
      4; SSFS 3; SUFW; WCH
Stockton, Frank R.
   See Stockton, Francis Richard

Stoddard, Charles
   See Kuttner, Henry
Stoker, Abraham 1847-1912 . **SSC 62; TCLC**
   8, 144; WLC 6
      See also AAYA 23; BPFB 3; BRWS 3; BYA
      5; CA 105; 150; CDBLB 1890-1914; DA;
      DA3; DAB; DAC; DAM MST, NOV;
      DLB 304; GL 3; HGG; LATS 1:1; MTFW
      2005; NFS 18; RGEL 2; SATA 29; SUFW;
      TEA; WLIT 4
Stoker, Bram
   See Stoker, Abraham
Stolz, Mary 1920-2006 .... **CLC 12**
      See also AAYA 8, 73; AITN 1; CA 5-8R;
      255; CANR 13, 41, 112; JRDA; MAICYA
      1, 2; SAAS 3; SATA 10, 71, 133; SATA-
      Obit 180; YAW
Stolz, Mary Slattery
   See Stolz, Mary
Stone, Irving 1903-1989 .... **CLC 7**
      See also AITN 1; BPFB 3; CA 1-4R; 129;
      CAAS 3; CANR 1, 23; CN 1, 2, 3, 4;
      CPW; DA3; DAM POP; INT CANR-23;
      MTCW 1, 2; MTFW 2005; RHW; SATA
      3; SATA-Obit 64
Stone, Oliver 1946- .... **CLC 73**
      See also AAYA 15, 64; CA 110; CANR 55,
      125
Stone, Oliver William
   See Stone, Oliver
Stone, Robert 1937- .... **CLC 5, 23, 42, 175**
      See also AMWS 5; BPFB 3; CA 85-88;
      CANR 23, 66, 95, 173; CN 4, 5, 6, 7;
      DLB 152; EWL 3; INT CANR-23; MAL
      5; MTCW 1; MTFW 2005
Stone, Robert Anthony
   See Stone, Robert
Stone, Ruth 1915- .... **PC 53**
      See also CA 45-48; CANR 2, 91; CP 5, 6,
      7; CSW; DLB 105; PFS 19
Stone, Zachary
   See Follett, Ken
Stoppard, Tom 1937- ... **CLC 1, 3, 4, 5, 8, 15,**
   29, 34, 63, 91; DC 6, 30; WLC 6
      See also AAYA 63; BRWC 1; BRWR 2;
      BRWS 1; CA 81-84; CANR 39, 67, 125;
      CBD; CD 5, 6; CDBLB 1960 to Present;
      DA; DA3; DAB; DAC; DAM DRAM,
      MST; DFS 2, 5, 8, 11, 13, 16; DLB 13,
      233; DLBY 1985; EWL 3; LATS 1:2;
      MTCW 1, 2; MTFW 2005; RGEL 2;
      TEA; WLIT 4
Storey, David (Malcolm) 1933- . **CLC 2, 4, 5,**
   8
      See also BRWS 1; CA 81-84; CANR 36;
      CBD; CD 5, 6; CN 1, 2, 3, 4, 5, 6; DAM
      DRAM; DLB 13, 14, 207, 245, 326; EWL
      3; MTCW 1; RGEL 2
Storm, Hyemeyohsts 1935- ... **CLC 3; NNAL**
      See also CA 81-84; CANR 45; DAM MULT
Storm, (Hans) Theodor (Woldsen)
   1817-1888 ... **NCLC 1, 195; SSC 27, 106**
      See also CDWLB 2; DLB 129; EW; RGSF
      2; RGWL 2, 3
Storni, Alfonsina 1892-1938 . **HLC 2; PC 33;**
   TCLC 5
      See also CA 104; 131; DAM MULT; DLB
      283; HW 1; LAW
Stoughton, William 1631-1701 .... **LC 38**
   See also DLB 24
Stout, Rex (Todhunter) 1886-1975 ..... **CLC 3**
      See also AAYA 79; AITN 2; BPFB 3; CA
      61-64; CANR 71; CMW 4; CN 2; DLB
      306; MSW; RGAL 4
Stow, (Julian) Randolph 1935- ... **CLC 23, 48**
      See also CA 13-16R; CANR 33; CN 1, 2,
      3, 4, 5, 6, 7; CP 1, 2, 3, 4; DLB 260;
      MTCW 1; RGEL 2

Stowe, Harriet (Elizabeth) Beecher
   1811-1896 .... **NCLC 3, 50, 133, 195;**
   WLC 6
      See also AAYA 53; AMWS 1; CDALB
      1865-1917; CLR 131; DA; DA3; DAB;
      DAC; DAM MST, NOV; DLB 1, 12, 42,
      74, 189, 239, 243; EXPN; FL 1:3; JRDA;
      LAIT 2; MAICYA 1, 2; NFS 6; RGAL 4;
      TUS; YABC 1
Strabo c. 64B.C.-c. 25 .... **CMLC 37**
   See also DLB 176
Strachey, (Giles) Lytton
   1880-1932 .... **TCLC 12**
      See also BRWS 2; CA 110; 178; DLB 149;
      DLBD 10; EWL 3; MTCW 2; NCFS 4
Stramm, August 1874-1915 .... **PC 50**
      See also CA 195; EWL 3
Strand, Mark 1934- .. **CLC 6, 18, 41, 71; PC**
   63
      See also AMWS 4; CA 21-24R; CANR 40,
      65, 100; CP 1, 2, 3, 4, 5, 6, 7; DAM
      POET; DLB 5; EWL 3; MAL 5; PAB;
      PFS 9, 18; RGAL 4; SATA 41; TCLE 1:2
Stratton-Porter, Gene(va Grace)
   1863-1924 .... **TCLC 21**
      See also ANW; BPFB 3; CA 112; 137; CLR
      87; CWRI 5; DLB 221; DLBD 14; MAI-
      CYA 1, 2; RHW; SATA 15
Straub, Peter 1943- .... **CLC 28, 107**
      See also BEST 89:1; BPFB 3; CA 85-88;
      CANR 28, 65, 109; CPW; DAM POP;
      DLBY 1984; HGG; MTCW 1, 2; MTFW
      2005; SUFW 2
Straub, Peter Francis
   See Straub, Peter
Strauss, Botho 1944- .... **CLC 22**
   See also CA 157; CWW 2; DLB 124
Strauss, Leo 1899-1973 .... **TCLC 141**
   See also CA 101; 45-48; CANR 122
Streatfeild, Mary Noel
   See Streatfeild, Noel
Streatfeild, Noel 1897(?)-1986 .... **CLC 21**
      See also CA 81-84; 120; CANR 31; CLR
      17, 83; CWRI 5; DLB 160; MAICYA 1,
      2; SATA 20; SATA-Obit 48
Stribling, T(homas) S(igismund)
   1881-1965 .... **CLC 23**
      See also CA 189; 107; CMW 4; DLB 9;
      RGAL 4
Strindberg, (Johan) August
   1849-1912 ... **DC 18; TCLC 1, 8, 21, 47;**
   WLC 6
      See also CA 104; 135; DA; DA3; DAB;
      DAC; DAM DRAM, MST; DFS 4, 9;
      DLB 259; EW 7; EWL 3; IDTP; LMFS
      2; MTCW 2; MTFW 2005; RGWL 2, 3;
      TWA
Stringer, Arthur 1874-1950 .... **TCLC 37**
   See also CA 161; DLB 92
Stringer, David
   See Roberts, Keith (John Kingston)
Stroheim, Erich von 1885-1957 ..... **TCLC 71**
Strugatskii, Arkadii (Natanovich)
   1925-1991 .... **CLC 27**
      See also CA 106; 135; DLB 302; SFW 4
Strugatskii, Boris (Natanovich)
   1933- .... **CLC 27**
      See also CA 106; DLB 302; SFW 4
Strugatsky, Arkadii Natanovich
   See Strugatskii, Arkadii (Natanovich)
Strugatsky, Boris (Natanovich)
   See Strugatskii, Boris (Natanovich)
Strummer, Joe 1952-2002 .... **CLC 30**
Strunk, William, Jr. 1869-1946 ...... **TCLC 92**
   See also CA 118; 164; NCFS 5
Stryk, Lucien 1924- .... **PC 27**
      See also CA 13-16R; CANR 10, 28, 55,
      110; CP 1, 2, 3, 4, 5, 6, 7

Tesich, Steve 1943(?)-1996 .... **CLC 40, 69**
See also CA 105; 152; CAD; DLBY 1983

Tesla, Nikola 1856-1943 .... **TCLC 88**

Teternikov, Fyodor Kuzmich
1863-1927 .... **TCLC 9**
See also CA 104; DLB 295; EWL 3

Tevis, Walter 1928-1984 .... **CLC 42**
See also CA 113; SFW 4

Tey, Josephine
See Mackintosh, Elizabeth

Thackeray, William Makepeace
1811-1863 ...... **NCLC 5, 14, 22, 43, 169,
213; WLC 6**
See also BRW 5; BRWC 2; CDBLB 1832-
1890; DA; DA3; DAB; DAC; DAM MST,
NOV; DLB 21, 55, 159, 163; NFS 13;
RGEL 2; SATA 23; TEA; WLIT 3

Thakura, Ravindranatha
See Tagore, Rabindranath

Thames, C. H.
See Marlowe, Stephen

Tharoor, Shashi 1956- .... **CLC 70**
See also CA 141; CANR 91; CN 6, 7

Thelwall, John 1764-1834 .... **NCLC 162**
See also DLB 93, 158

Thelwell, Michael Miles 1939- .... **CLC 22**
See also BW 2; CA 101

Theo, Ion
See Theodorescu, Ion N.

Theobald, Lewis, Jr.
See Lovecraft, H. P.

Theocritus c. 310B.C.- .... **CMLC 45**
See also AW 1; DLB 176; RGWL 2, 3

Theodorescu, Ion N. 1880-1967 .... **CLC 80**
See also CA 167; 116; CDWLB 4; DLB
220; EWL 3

Theriault, Yves 1915-1983 .... **CLC 79**
See also CA 102; CANR 150; CCA 1;
DAC; DAM MST; DLB 88; EWL 3

Therion, Master
See Crowley, Edward Alexander

Theroux, Alexander 1939- .... **CLC 2, 25**
See also CA 85-88; CANR 20, 63; CN 4, 5,
6, 7

Theroux, Alexander Louis
See Theroux, Alexander

Theroux, Paul 1941- .... **CLC 5, 8, 11, 15, 28,
46, 159**
See also AAYA 28; AMWS 8; BEST 89:4;
BPFB 3; CA 33-36R; CANR 20, 45, 74,
133, 179; CDALBS; CN 1, 2, 3, 4, 5, 6,
7; CP 1; CPW 1; DA3; DAM POP; DLB
2, 218; EWL 3; HGG; MAL 5; MTCW 1,
2; MTFW 2005; RGAL 4; SATA 44, 109;
TUS

Theroux, Paul Edward
See Theroux, Paul

Thesen, Sharon 1946- .... **CLC 56**
See also CA 163; CANR 125; CP 5, 6, 7;
CWP

Thespis fl. 6th cent. B.C.- .... **CMLC 51**
See also LMFS 1

Thevenin, Denis
See Duhamel, Georges

Thibault, Jacques Anatole Francois
1844-1924 .... **TCLC 9**
See also CA 106; 127; DA3; DAM NOV;
DLB 123, 330; EWL 3; GFL 1789 to the
Present; MTCW 1, 2; RGWL 2, 3; SUFW
1; TWA

Thiele, Colin 1920-2006 .... **CLC 17**
See also CA 29-32R; CANR 12, 28, 53,
105; CLR 27; CP 1, 2; DLB 289; MAI-
CYA 1, 2; SAAS 2; SATA 14, 72, 125;
YAW

Thiong'o, Ngugi Wa
See Ngugi wa Thiong'o

Thistlethwaite, Bel
See Wetherald, Agnes Ethelwyn

Thomas, Audrey (Callahan) 1935- .... **CLC 7,
13, 37, 107; SSC 20**
See also AITN 2; CA 21-24R, 237; CAAE
237; CAAS 19; CANR 36, 58; CN 2, 3,
4, 5, 6, 7; DLB 60; MTCW 1; RGSF 2

Thomas, Augustus 1857-1934 .... **TCLC 97**
See also MAL 5

Thomas, D.M. 1935- ..... **CLC 13, 22, 31, 132**
See also BPFB 3; BRWS 4; CA 61-64;
CAAS 11; CANR 17, 45, 75; CDBLB
1960 to Present; CN 4, 5, 6, 7; CP 1, 2, 3,
4, 5, 6, 7; DA3; DLB 40, 207, 299; HGG;
INT CANR-17; MTCW 1, 2; MTFW
2005; RGHL; SFW 4

Thomas, Dylan (Marlais) 1914-1953 .... **PC 2,
52; SSC 3, 44; TCLC 1, 8, 45, 105;
WLC 6**
See also AAYA 45; BRWS 1; CA 104; 120;
CANR 65; CDBLB 1945-1960; DA; DA3;
DAB; DAC; DAM DRAM, MST, POET;
DLB 13, 20, 139; EWL 3; EXPP; LAIT
3; MTCW 1, 2; MTFW 2005; PAB; PFS
1, 3, 8; RGEL 2; RGSF 2; SATA 60; TEA;
WLIT 4; WP

Thomas, (Philip) Edward 1878-1917 . **PC 53;
TCLC 10**
See also BRW 6; BRWS 3; CA 106; 153;
DAM POET; DLB 19, 98, 156, 216; EWL
3; PAB; RGEL 2

Thomas, J.F.
See Fleming, Thomas

Thomas, Joyce Carol 1938- .... **CLC 35**
See also AAYA 12, 54; BW 2, 3; CA 113;
116; CANR 48, 114, 135; CLR 19; DLB
33; INT CA-116; JRDA; MAICYA 1, 2;
MTCW 1, 2; MTFW 2005; SAAS 7;
SATA 40, 78, 123, 137; SATA-Essay 137;
WYA; YAW

Thomas, Lewis 1913-1993 .... **CLC 35**
See also ANW; CA 85-88; 143; CANR 38,
60; DLB 275; MTCW 1, 2

Thomas, M. Carey 1857-1935 .... **TCLC 89**
See also FW

Thomas, Paul
See Mann, (Paul) Thomas

Thomas, Piri 1928- .... **CLC 17; HLCS 2**
See also CA 73-76; HW 1; LLW

Thomas, R(onald) S(tuart)
1913-2000 .... **CLC 6, 13, 48**
See also BRWS 12; CA 89-92; 189; CAAS
4; CANR 30; CDBLB 1960 to Present;
CP 1, 2, 3, 4, 5, 6, 7; DAB; DAM POET;
DLB 27; EWL 3; MTCW 1; RGEL 2

Thomas, Ross (Elmore) 1926-1995 .. **CLC 39**
See also CA 33-36R; 150; CANR 22, 63;
CMW 4

Thompson, Francis (Joseph)
1859-1907 .... **TCLC 4**
See also BRW 5; CA 104; 189; CDBLB
1890-1914; DLB 19; RGEL 2; TEA

Thompson, Francis Clegg
See Mencken, H(enry) L(ouis)

Thompson, Hunter S. 1937(?)-2005 .. **CLC 9,
17, 40, 104, 229**
See also AAYA 45; BEST 89:1; BPFB 3;
CA 17-20R; 236; CANR 23, 46, 74, 77,
111, 133; CPW; CSW; DA3; DAM POP;
DLB 185; MTCW 1, 2; MTFW 2005;
TUS

Thompson, James Myers
See Thompson, Jim

Thompson, Jim 1906-1977 .... **CLC 69**
See also BPFB 3; CA 140; CMW 4; CPW;
DLB 226; MSW

Thompson, Judith (Clare Francesca)
1954- .... **CLC 39**
See also CA 143; CD 5, 6; CWD; DFS 22;
DLB 334

Thomson, James 1700-1748 .... **LC 16, 29, 40**
See also BRWS 3; DAM POET; DLB 95;
RGEL 2

Thomson, James 1834-1882 .... **NCLC 18**
See also DAM POET; DLB 35; RGEL 2

Thoreau, Henry David 1817-1862 .. **NCLC 7,
21, 61, 138, 207; PC 30; WLC 6**
See also AAYA 42; AMW; ANW; BYA 3;
CDALB 1640-1865; DA; DA3; DAB;
DAC; DAM MST; DLB 1, 183, 223, 270,
298; LAIT 2; LMFS 1; NCFS 3; RGAL
4; TUS

Thorndike, E. L.
See Thorndike, Edward L(ee)

Thorndike, Edward L(ee)
1874-1949 .... **TCLC 107**
See also CA 121

Thornton, Hall
See Silverberg, Robert

Thorpe, Adam 1956- .... **CLC 176**
See also CA 129; CANR 92, 160; DLB 231

Thorpe, Thomas Bangs
1815-1878 .... **NCLC 183**
See also DLB 3, 11, 248; RGAL 4

Thubron, Colin 1939- .... **CLC 163**
See also CA 25-28R; CANR 12, 29, 59, 95,
171; CN 5, 6, 7; DLB 204, 231

Thubron, Colin Gerald Dryden
See Thubron, Colin

Thucydides c. 455B.C.-c. 395B.C. . **CMLC 17**
See also AW 1; DLB 176; RGWL 2, 3;
WLIT 8

Thumboo, Edwin Nadason 1933- .... **PC 30**
See also CA 194; CP 1

Thurber, James (Grover)
1894-1961 .. **CLC 5, 11, 25, 125; SSC 1,
47**
See also AAYA 56; AMWS 1; BPFB 3;
BYA 5; CA 73-76; CANR 17, 39; CDALB
1929-1941; CWRI 5; DA; DA3; DAB;
DAC; DAM DRAM, MST, NOV; DLB 4,
11, 22, 102; EWL 3; EXPS; FANT; LAIT
3; MAICYA 1, 2; MAL 5; MTCW 1, 2;
MTFW 2005; RGAL 4; RGSF 2; SATA
13; SSFS 1, 10, 19; SUFW; TUS

Thurman, Wallace (Henry)
1902-1934 .. **BLC 1:3; HR 1:3; TCLC 6**
See also BW 1, 3; CA 104; 124; CANR 81;
DAM MULT; DLB 51

Tibullus c. 54B.C.-c. 18B.C. .... **CMLC 36**
See also AW 2; DLB 211; RGWL 2, 3;
WLIT 8

Ticheburn, Cheviot
See Ainsworth, William Harrison

Tieck, (Johann) Ludwig
1773-1853 ..... **NCLC 5, 46; SSC 31, 100**
See also CDWLB 2; DLB 90; EW 5; IDTP;
RGSF 2; RGWL 2, 3; SUFW

Tiger, Derry
See Ellison, Harlan

Tilghman, Christopher 1946- .... **CLC 65**
See also CA 159; CANR 135, 151; CSW;
DLB 244

Tillich, Paul (Johannes)
1886-1965 .... **CLC 131**
See also CA 5-8R; 25-28R; CANR 33;
MTCW 1, 2

Tillinghast, Richard (Williford)
1940- .... **CLC 29**
See also CA 29-32R; CAAS 23; CANR 26,
51, 96; CP 2, 3, 4, 5, 6, 7; CSW

Tillman, Lynne (?)- .... **CLC 231**
See also CA 173; CANR 144, 172

Timrod, Henry 1828-1867 .... **NCLC 25**
See also DLB 3, 248; RGAL 4

Tindall, Gillian (Elizabeth) 1938- ...... **CLC 7**
See also CA 21-24R; CANR 11, 65, 107;
CN 1, 2, 3, 4, 5, 6, 7

Ting Ling
See Chiang, Pin-chin

Tiptree, James, Jr.
See Sheldon, Alice Hastings Bradley

Tirone Smith, Mary-Ann 1944- .... **CLC 39**
See also CA 118; 136; CANR 113; SATA 143

Tirso de Molina 1580(?)-1648 .... **DC 13; HLCS 2; LC 73**
See also RGWL 2, 3

Titmarsh, Michael Angelo
See Thackeray, William Makepeace

Tocqueville, Alexis (Charles Henri Maurice Clerel Comte) de 1805-1859 .. **NCLC 7, 63**
See also EW 6; GFL 1789 to the Present; TWA

Toe, Tucker
See Westlake, Donald E.

Toer, Pramoedya Ananta 1925-2006 .... **CLC 186**
See also CA 197; 251; CANR 170; DLB 348; RGWL 3

Toffler, Alvin 1928- .... **CLC 168**
See also CA 13-16R; CANR 15, 46, 67, 183; CPW; DAM POP; MTCW 1, 2

Toibin, Colm 1955- .... **CLC 162**
See also CA 142; CANR 81, 149; CN 7; DLB 271

Tolkien, John Ronald Reuel
See Tolkien, J.R.R

Tolkien, J.R.R 1892-1973 ...... **CLC 1, 2, 3, 8, 12, 38; TCLC 137; WLC 6**
See also AAYA 10; AITN 1; BPFB 3; BRWC 2; BRWS 2; CA 17-18; 45-48; CANR 36, 134; CAP 2; CDBLB 1914-1945; CLR 56; CN 1; CPW 1; CWRI 5; DA; DA3; DAB; DAC; DAM MST, NOV, POP; DLB 15, 160, 255; EFS 2; EWL 3; FANT; JRDA; LAIT 1; LATS 1:2; LMFS 2; MAICYA 1, 2; MTCW 1, 2; MTFW 2005; NFS 8, 26; RGEL 2; SATA 2, 32, 100; SATA-Obit 24; SFW 4; SUFW; TEA; WCH; WYA; YAW

Toller, Ernst 1893-1939 .... **TCLC 10**
See also CA 107; 186; DLB 124; EWL 3; RGWL 2, 3

Tolson, M. B.
See Tolson, Melvin B(eaunorus)

Tolson, Melvin B(eaunorus) 1898(?)-1966 .... **BLC 1:3; CLC 36, 105; PC 88**
See also AFAW 1, 2; BW 1, 3; CA 124; 89-92; CANR 80; DAM MULT, POET; DLB 48, 76; MAL 5; RGAL 4

Tolstoi, Aleksei Nikolaevich
See Tolstoy, Alexey Nikolaevich

Tolstoi, Lev
See Tolstoy, Leo (Nikolaevich)

Tolstoy, Aleksei Nikolaevich
See Tolstoy, Alexey Nikolaevich

Tolstoy, Alexey Nikolaevich 1882-1945 .... **TCLC 18**
See also CA 107; 158; DLB 272; EWL 3; SFW 4

Tolstoy, Leo (Nikolaevich) 1828-1910 . **SSC 9, 30, 45, 54; TCLC 4, 11, 17, 28, 44, 79, 173; WLC 6**
See also AAYA 56; CA 104; 123; DA; DA3; DAB; DAC; DAM MST, NOV; DLB 238; EFS 2; EW 7; EXPS; IDTP; LAIT 2; LATS 1:1; LMFS 1; NFS 10, 28; RGSF 2; RGWL 2, 3; SATA 26; SSFS 5; TWA

Tolstoy, Count Leo
See Tolstoy, Leo (Nikolaevich)

Tomalin, Claire 1933- .... **CLC 166**
See also CA 89-92; CANR 52, 88, 165; DLB 155

Tomasi di Lampedusa, Giuseppe 1896-1957 .... **TCLC 13**
See also CA 111; 164; DLB 177; EW 11; EWL 3; MTCW 2; MTFW 2005; RGWL 2, 3; WLIT 7

Tomlin, Lily 1939(?)- .... **CLC 17**
See also CA 117

Tomlin, Mary Jane
See Tomlin, Lily

Tomlin, Mary Jean
See Tomlin, Lily

Tomline, F. Latour
See Gilbert, W(illiam) S(chwenck)

Tomlinson, (Alfred) Charles 1927- .... **CLC 2, 4, 6, 13, 45; PC 17**
See also CA 5-8R; CANR 33; CP 1, 2, 3, 4, 5, 6, 7; DAM POET; DLB 40; TCLE 1:2

Tomlinson, H(enry) M(ajor) 1873-1958 .... **TCLC 71**
See also CA 118; 161; DLB 36, 100, 195

Tomlinson, Mary Jane
See Tomlin, Lily

Tonna, Charlotte Elizabeth 1790-1846 .... **NCLC 135**
See also DLB 163

Tonson, Jacob fl. 1655(?)-1736 .... **LC 86**
See also DLB 170

Toole, John Kennedy 1937-1969 ..... **CLC 19, 64**
See also BPFB 3; CA 104; DLBY 1981; MTCW 2; MTFW 2005

Toomer, Eugene
See Toomer, Jean

Toomer, Eugene Pinchback
See Toomer, Jean

Toomer, Jean 1894-1967 ... **BLC 1:3; CLC 1, 4, 13, 22; HR 1:3; PC 7; SSC 1, 45; TCLC 172; WLCS**
See also AFAW 1, 2; AMWS 3, 9; BW 1; CA 85-88; CDALB 1917-1929; DA3; DAM MULT; DLB 45, 51; EWL 3; EXPP; EXPS; LMFS 2; MAL 5; MTCW 1, 2; MTFW 2005; NFS 11; RGAL 4; RGSF 2; SSFS 5

Toomer, Nathan Jean
See Toomer, Jean

Toomer, Nathan Pinchback
See Toomer, Jean

Torley, Luke
See Blish, James (Benjamin)

Tornimparte, Alessandra
See Ginzburg, Natalia

Torre, Raoul della
See Mencken, H(enry) L(ouis)

Torrence, Ridgely 1874-1950 .... **TCLC 97**
See also DLB 54, 249; MAL 5

Torrey, E. Fuller 1937- .... **CLC 34**
See also CA 119; CANR 71, 158

Torrey, Edwin Fuller
See Torrey, E. Fuller

Torsvan, Ben Traven
See Traven, B.

Torsvan, Benno Traven
See Traven, B.

Torsvan, Berick Traven
See Traven, B.

Torsvan, Berwick Traven
See Traven, B.

Torsvan, Bruno Traven
See Traven, B.

Torsvan, Traven
See Traven, B.

Toson
See Shimazaki, Haruki

Tourneur, Cyril 1575(?)-1626 .... **LC 66**
See also BRW 2; DAM DRAM; DLB 58; RGEL 2

Tournier, Michel 1924- .... **CLC 6, 23, 36, 95, 249; SSC 88**
See also CA 49-52; CANR 3, 36, 74, 149; CWW 2; DLB 83; EWL 3; GFL 1789 to the Present; MTCW 1, 2; SATA 23

Tournier, Michel Edouard
See Tournier, Michel

Tournimparte, Alessandra
See Ginzburg, Natalia

Towers, Ivar
See Kornbluth, C(yril) M.

Towne, Robert (Burton) 1936(?)- ..... **CLC 87**
See also CA 108; DLB 44; IDFW 3, 4

Townsend, Sue
See Townsend, Susan Lilian

Townsend, Susan Lilian 1946- .... **CLC 61**
See also AAYA 28; CA 119; 127; CANR 65, 107; CBD; CD 5, 6; CPW; CWD; DAB; DAC; DAM MST; DLB 271; INT CA-127; SATA 55, 93; SATA-Brief 48; YAW

Townshend, Pete
See Townshend, Peter

Townshend, Peter 1945- .... **CLC 17, 42**
See also CA 107

Townshend, Peter Dennis Blandford
See Townshend, Peter

Tozzi, Federigo 1883-1920 .... **TCLC 31**
See also CA 160; CANR 110; DLB 264; EWL 3; WLIT 7

Trafford, F. G.
See Riddell, Charlotte

Traherne, Thomas 1637(?)-1674 .. **LC 99; PC 70**
See also BRW 2; BRWS 11; DLB 131; PAB; RGEL 2

Traill, Catharine Parr 1802-1899 .. **NCLC 31**
See also DLB 99

Trakl, Georg 1887-1914 .... **PC 20; TCLC 5**
See also CA 104; 165; EW 10; EWL 3; LMFS 2; MTCW 2; RGWL 2, 3

Trambley, Estela Portillo
See Portillo Trambley, Estela

Tranquilli, Secondino
See Silone, Ignazio

Transtroemer, Tomas Gosta
See Transtromer, Tomas

Transtromer, Tomas (Gosta)
See Transtromer, Tomas

Transtromer, Tomas 1931- .... **CLC 52, 65**
See also CA 117; 129; CAAS 17; CANR 115, 172; CWW 2; DAM POET; DLB 257; EWL 3; PFS 21

Transtromer, Tomas Goesta
See Transtromer, Tomas

Transtromer, Tomas Gosta
See Transtromer, Tomas

Transtromer, Tomas Gosta
See Transtromer, Tomas

Traven, B. 1882(?)-1969 .... **CLC 8, 11**
See also CA 19-20; 25-28R; CAP 2; DLB 9, 56; EWL 3; MTCW 1; RGAL 4

Trediakovsky, Vasilii Kirillovich 1703-1769 .... **LC 68**
See also DLB 150

Treitel, Jonathan 1959- .... **CLC 70**
See also CA 210; DLB 267

Trelawny, Edward John 1792-1881 .... **NCLC 85**
See also DLB 110, 116, 144

Tremain, Rose 1943- .... **CLC 42**
See also CA 97-100; CANR 44, 95, 186; CN 4, 5, 6, 7; DLB 14, 271; RGSF 2; RHW

Tremblay, Michel 1942- .... **CLC 29, 102, 225**
See also CA 116; 128; CCA 1; CWW 2; DAC; DAM MST; DLB 60; EWL 3; GLL 1; MTCW 1, 2; MTFW 2005

Underwood, Miles
See Glassco, John

Undset, Sigrid 1882-1949 .... **TCLC 3, 197; WLC 6**
See also AAYA 77; CA 104; 129; DA; DA3; DAB; DAC; DAM MST, NOV; DLB 293, 332; EW 9; EWL 3; FW; MTCW 1, 2; MTFW 2005; RGWL 2, 3

Ungaretti, Giuseppe 1888-1970 ... **CLC 7, 11, 15; PC 57; TCLC 200**
See also CA 19-20; 25-28R; CAP 2; DLB 114; EW 10; EWL 3; PFS 20; RGWL 2, 3; WLIT 7

Unger, Douglas 1952- .... **CLC 34**
See also CA 130; CANR 94, 155

Unsworth, Barry 1930- .... **CLC 76, 127**
See also BRWS 7; CA 25-28R; CANR 30, 54, 125, 171; CN 6, 7; DLB 194, 326

Unsworth, Barry Forster
See Unsworth, Barry

Updike, John 1932-2009 .... **CLC 1, 2, 3, 5, 7, 9, 13, 15, 23, 34, 43, 70, 139, 214; PC 90; SSC 13, 27, 103; WLC 6**
See also AAYA 36; AMW; AMWC 1; AMWR 1; BPFB 3; BYA 12; CA 1-4R; CABS 1; CANR 4, 33, 51, 94, 133; CDALB 1968-1988; CN 1, 2, 3, 4, 5, 6, 7; CP 1, 2, 3, 4, 5, 6, 7; CPW 1; DA; DA3; DAB; DAC; DAM MST, NOV, POET, POP; DLB 2, 5, 143, 218, 227; DLBD 3; DLBY 1980, 1982, 1997; EWL 3; EXPP; HGG; MAL 5; MTCW 1, 2; MTFW 2005; NFS 12, 24; RGAL 4; RGSF 2; SSFS 3, 19; TUS

Updike, John Hoyer
See Updike, John

Upshaw, Margaret Mitchell
See Mitchell, Margaret (Munnerlyn)

Upton, Mark
See Sanders, Lawrence

Upward, Allen 1863-1926 .... **TCLC 85**
See also CA 117; 187; DLB 36

Urdang, Constance (Henriette)
1922-1996 .... **CLC 47**
See also CA 21-24R; CANR 9, 24; CP 1, 2, 3, 4, 5, 6; CWP

Urfe, Honore d' 1567(?)-1625 .... **LC 132**
See also DLB 268; GFL Beginnings to 1789; RGWL 2, 3

Uriel, Henry
See Faust, Frederick (Schiller)

Uris, Leon 1924-2003 .... **CLC 7, 32**
See also AITN 1, 2; BEST 89:2; BPFB 3; CA 1-4R; 217; CANR 1, 40, 65, 123; CN 1, 2, 3, 4, 5, 6; CPW 1; DA3; DAM NOV, POP; MTCW 1, 2; MTFW 2005; RGHL; SATA 49; SATA-Obit 146

Urista (Heredia), Alberto (Baltazar)
1947- .... **HLCS 1; PC 34**
See also CA 45-48R; CANR 2, 32; DLB 82; HW 1; LLW

Urmuz
See Codrescu, Andrei

Urquhart, Guy
See McAlmon, Robert (Menzies)

Urquhart, Jane 1949- .... **CLC 90, 242**
See also CA 113; CANR 32, 68, 116, 157; CCA 1; DAC; DLB 334

Usigli, Rodolfo 1905-1979 .... **HLCS 1**
See also CA 131; DLB 305; EWL 3; HW 1; LAW

Usk, Thomas (?)-1388 .... **CMLC 76**
See also DLB 146

Ustinov, Peter (Alexander)
1921-2004 .... **CLC 1**
See also AITN 1; CA 13-16R; 225; CANR 25, 51; CBD; CD 5, 6; DLB 13; MTCW 2

U Tam'si, Gerald Felix Tchicaya
See Tchicaya, Gerald Felix

U Tam'si, Tchicaya
See Tchicaya, Gerald Felix

Vachss, Andrew 1942- .... **CLC 106**
See also CA 118, 214; CAAE 214; CANR 44, 95, 153; CMW 4

Vachss, Andrew H.
See Vachss, Andrew

Vachss, Andrew Henry
See Vachss, Andrew

Vaculik, Ludvik 1926- .... **CLC 7**
See also CA 53-56; CANR 72; CWW 2; DLB 232; EWL 3

Vaihinger, Hans 1852-1933 .... **TCLC 71**
See also CA 116; 166

Valdez, Luis (Miguel) 1940- ..... **CLC 84; DC 10; HLC 2**
See also CA 101; CAD; CANR 32, 81; CD 5, 6; DAM MULT; DFS 5; DLB 122; EWL 3; HW 1; LAIT 4; LLW

Valenzuela, Luisa 1938- .... **CLC 31, 104; HLCS 2; SSC 14, 82**
See also CA 101; CANR 32, 65, 123; CD-WLB 3; CWW 2; DAM MULT; DLB 113; EWL 3; FW; HW 1, 2; LAW; RGSF 2; RGWL 3

Valera y Alcala-Galiano, Juan
1824-1905 .... **TCLC 10**
See also CA 106

Valerius Maximus .... **CMLC 64**
See also DLB 211

Valery, (Ambroise) Paul (Toussaint Jules)
1871-1945 .... **PC 9; TCLC 4, 15**
See also CA 104; 122; DA3; DAM POET; DLB 258; EW 8; EWL 3; GFL 1789 to the Present; MTCW 1, 2; MTFW 2005; RGWL 2, 3; TWA

Valle-Inclan, Ramon (Maria) del
1866-1936 .... **HLC 2; TCLC 5**
See also CA 106; 153; CANR 80; DAM MULT; DLB 134, 322; EW 8; EWL 3; HW 2; RGSF 2; RGWL 2, 3

Vallejo, Antonio Buero
See Buero Vallejo, Antonio

Vallejo, Cesar (Abraham)
1892-1938 .... **HLC 2; TCLC 3, 56**
See also CA 105; 153; DAM MULT; DLB 290; EWL 3; HW 1; LAW; PFS 26; RGWL 2, 3

Valles, Jules 1832-1885 .... **NCLC 71**
See also DLB 123; GFL 1789 to the Present

Vallette, Marguerite Eymery
1860-1953 .... **TCLC 67**
See also CA 182; DLB 123, 192; EWL 3

Valle Y Pena, Ramon del
See Valle-Inclan, Ramon (Maria) del

Van Ash, Cay 1918-1994 .... **CLC 34**
See also CA 220

Vanbrugh, Sir John 1664-1726 .... **LC 21**
See also BRW 2; DAM DRAM; DLB 80; IDTP; RGEL 2

Van Campen, Karl
See Campbell, John W(ood, Jr.)

Vance, Gerald
See Silverberg, Robert

Vance, Jack 1916- .... **CLC 35**
See also CA 29-32R; CANR 17, 65, 154; CMW 4; DLB 8; FANT; MTCW 1; SCFW 1, 2; SFW 4; SUFW 1, 2

Vance, John Holbrook
See Vance, Jack

Van Den Bogarde, Derek Jules Gaspard Ulric Niven 1921-1999 .... **CLC 14**
See also CA 77-80; 179; DLB 14

Vandenburgh, Jane .... **CLC 59**
See also CA 168

Vanderhaeghe, Guy 1951- .... **CLC 41**
See also BPFB 3; CA 113; CANR 72, 145; CN 7; DLB 334

van der Post, Laurens (Jan)
1906-1996 .... **CLC 5**
See also AFW; CA 5-8R; 155; CANR 35; CN 1, 2, 3, 4, 5, 6; DLB 204; RGEL 2

van de Wetering, Janwillem
1931-2008 .... **CLC 47**
See also CA 49-52; 274; CANR 4, 62, 90; CMW 4

Van Dine, S. S.
See Wright, Willard Huntington

Van Doren, Carl (Clinton)
1885-1950 .... **TCLC 18**
See also CA 111; 168

Van Doren, Mark 1894-1972 .... **CLC 6, 10**
See also CA 1-4R; 37-40R; CANR 3; CN 1; CP 1; DLB 45, 284, 335; MAL 5; MTCW 1, 2; RGAL 4

Van Druten, John (William)
1901-1957 .... **TCLC 2**
See also CA 104; 161; DLB 10; MAL 5; RGAL 4

Van Duyn, Mona 1921-2004 .... **CLC 3, 7, 63, 116**
See also CA 9-12R; 234; CANR 7, 38, 60, 116; CP 1, 2, 3, 4, 5, 6, 7; CWP; DAM POET; DLB 5; MAL 5; MTFW 2005; PFS 20

Van Dyne, Edith
See Baum, L(yman) Frank

van Herk, Aritha 1954- .... **CLC 249**
See also CA 101; CANR 94; DLB 334

van Itallie, Jean-Claude 1936- .... **CLC 3**
See also CA 45-48; CAAS 2; CAD; CANR 1, 48; CD 5, 6; DLB 7

Van Loot, Cornelius Obenchain
See Roberts, Kenneth (Lewis)

van Ostaijen, Paul 1896-1928 .... **TCLC 33**
See also CA 163

Van Peebles, Melvin 1932- .... **CLC 2, 20**
See also BW 2, 3; CA 85-88; CANR 27, 67, 82; DAM MULT

van Schendel, Arthur(-Francois-Emile)
1874-1946 .... **TCLC 56**
See also EWL 3

Van See, John
See Vance, Jack

Vansittart, Peter 1920-2008 .... **CLC 42**
See also CA 1-4R; 278; CANR 3, 49, 90; CN 4, 5, 6, 7; RHW

Van Vechten, Carl 1880-1964 ... **CLC 33; HR 1:3**
See also AMWS 2; CA 183; 89-92; DLB 4, 9, 51; RGAL 4

van Vogt, A(lfred) E(lton) 1912-2000 . **CLC 1**
See also BPFB 3; BYA 13, 14; CA 21-24R; 190; CANR 28; DLB 8, 251; SATA 14; SATA-Obit 124; SCFW 1, 2; SFW 4

Vara, Madeleine
See Jackson, Laura (Riding)

Varda, Agnes 1928- .... **CLC 16**
See also CA 116; 122

Vargas Llosa, Jorge Mario Pedro
See Vargas Llosa, Mario

Vargas Llosa, Mario 1936- .. **CLC 3, 6, 9, 10, 15, 31, 42, 85, 181; HLC 2**
See also BPFB 3; CA 73-76; CANR 18, 32, 42, 67, 116, 140, 173; CDWLB 3; CWW 2; DA; DA3; DAB; DAC; DAM MST, MULT, NOV; DLB 145; DNFS 2; EWL 3; HW 1, 2; LAIT 5; LATS 1:2; LAW; LAWS 1; MTCW 1, 2; MTFW 2005; RGWL 2, 3; SSFS 14; TWA; WLIT 1

Varnhagen von Ense, Rahel
1771-1833 .... **NCLC 130**
See also DLB 90

Vasari, Giorgio 1511-1574 .... **LC 114**

von Daniken, Erich
See von Daeniken, Erich

von Eschenbach, Wolfram c. 1170-c.
1220 .... **CMLC 5**
See also CDWLB 2; DLB 138; EW 1;
RGWL 2, 3

von Hartmann, Eduard
1842-1906 .... **TCLC 96**

von Hayek, Friedrich August
See Hayek, F(riedrich) A(ugust von)

von Heidenstam, (Carl Gustaf) Verner
See Heidenstam, (Carl Gustaf) Verner von

von Heyse, Paul (Johann Ludwig)
See Heyse, Paul (Johann Ludwig von)

von Hofmannsthal, Hugo
See Hofmannsthal, Hugo von

von Horvath, Odon
See von Horvath, Odon

von Horvath, Odon
See von Horvath, Odon

von Horvath, Odon 1901-1938 .... **TCLC 45**
See also CA 118; 184, 194; DLB 85, 124;
RGWL 2, 3

von Horvath, Oedoen
See von Horvath, Odon

von Kleist, Heinrich
See Kleist, Heinrich von

Vonnegut, Kurt, Jr.
See Vonnegut, Kurt

Vonnegut, Kurt 1922-2007 .... **CLC 1, 2, 3, 4,**
5, 8, 12, 22, 40, 60, 111, 212, 254; SSC
8; WLC 6
See also AAYA 6, 44; AITN 1; AMWS 2;
BEST 90:4; BPFB 3; BYA 3, 14; CA
1-4R; 259; CANR 1, 25, 49, 75, 92;
CDALB 1968-1988; CN 1, 2, 3, 4, 5, 6,
7; CPW 1; DA; DA3; DAB; DAC; DAM
MST, NOV, POP; DLB 2, 8, 152; DLBD
3; DLBY 1980; EWL 3; EXPN; EXPS;
LAIT 4; LMFS 2; MAL 5; MTCW 1, 2;
MTFW 2005; NFS 3, 28; RGAL 4;
SCFW; SFW 4; SSFS 5; TUS; YAW

Von Rachen, Kurt
See Hubbard, L. Ron

von Sternberg, Josef
See Sternberg, Josef von

Vorster, Gordon 1924- .... **CLC 34**
See also CA 133

Vosce, Trudie
See Ozick, Cynthia

Voznesensky, Andrei (Andreievich)
1933- .... **CLC 1, 15, 57**
See also CA 89-92; CANR 37; CWW 2;
DAM POET; EWL 3; MTCW 1

Voznesensky, Andrey
See Voznesensky, Andrei (Andreievich)

Wace, Robert c. 1100-c. 1175 .... **CMLC 55**
See also DLB 146

Waddington, Miriam 1917-2004 .... **CLC 28**
See also CA 21-24R; 225; CANR 12, 30;
CCA 1; CP 1, 2, 3, 4, 5, 6, 7; DLB 68

Wade, Alan
See Vance, Jack

Wagman, Fredrica 1937- .... **CLC 7**
See also CA 97-100; CANR 166; INT CA-
97-100

Wagner, Linda W.
See Wagner-Martin, Linda (C.)

Wagner, Linda Welshimer
See Wagner-Martin, Linda (C.)

Wagner, Richard 1813-1883 ..... **NCLC 9, 119**
See also DLB 129; EW 6

Wagner-Martin, Linda (C.) 1936- .... **CLC 50**
See also CA 159; CANR 135

Wagoner, David (Russell) 1926- .... **CLC 3, 5,**
15; PC 33
See also AMWS 9; CA 1-4R; CAAS 3;
CANR 2, 71; CN 1, 2, 3, 4, 5, 6, 7; CP 1,
2, 3, 4, 5, 6, 7; DLB 5, 256; SATA 14;
TCWW 1, 2

Wah, Fred(erick James) 1939- .... **CLC 44**
See also CA 107; 141; CP 1, 6, 7; DLB 60

Wahloo, Per 1926-1975 .... **CLC 7**
See also BPFB 3; CA 61-64; CANR 73;
CMW 4; MSW

Wahloo, Peter
See Wahloo, Per

Wain, John (Barrington) 1925-1994 . **CLC 2,**
11, 15, 46
See also CA 5-8R; 145; CAAS 4; CANR
23, 54; CDBLB 1960 to Present; CN 1, 2,
3, 4, 5; CP 1, 2, 3, 4, 5; DLB 15, 27, 139,
155; EWL 3; MTCW 1, 2; MTFW 2005

Wajda, Andrzej 1926- .... **CLC 16, 219**
See also CA 102

Wakefield, Dan 1932- .... **CLC 7**
See also CA 21-24R, 211; CAAE 211;
CAAS 7; CN 4, 5, 6, 7

Wakefield, Herbert Russell
1888-1965 .... **TCLC 120**
See also CA 5-8R; CANR 77; HGG; SUFW

Wakoski, Diane 1937- ...... **CLC 2, 4, 7, 9, 11,**
40; PC 15
See also CA 13-16R, 216; CAAE 216;
CAAS 1; CANR 9, 60, 106; CP 1, 2, 3, 4,
5, 6, 7; CWP; DAM POET; DLB 5; INT
CANR-9; MAL 5; MTCW 2; MTFW
2005

Wakoski-Sherbell, Diane
See Wakoski, Diane

Walcott, Derek 1930- . **BLC 1:3, 2:3; CLC 2,**
4, 9, 14, 25, 42, 67, 76, 160; DC 7; PC
46
See also BW 2; CA 89-92; CANR 26, 47,
75, 80, 130; CBD; CD 5, 6; CDWLB 3;
CP 1, 2, 3, 4, 5, 6, 7; DA3; DAB; DAC;
DAM MST, MULT, POET; DLB 117,
332; DLBY 1981; DNFS 1; EFS 1; EWL
3; LMFS 2; MTCW 1, 2; MTFW 2005;
PFS 6; RGEL 2; TWA; WWE 1

Waldman, Anne (Lesley) 1945- .... **CLC 7**
See also BG 1:3; CA 37-40R; CAAS 17;
CANR 34, 69, 116; CP 1, 2, 3, 4, 5, 6, 7;
CWP; DLB 16

Waldo, E. Hunter
See Sturgeon, Theodore (Hamilton)

Waldo, Edward Hamilton
See Sturgeon, Theodore (Hamilton)

Walker, Alice 1944- .... **BLC 1:3, 2:3; CLC 5,**
6, 9, 19, 27, 46, 58, 103, 167; PC 30;
SSC 5; WLCS
See also AAYA 3, 33; AFAW 1, 2; AMWS
3; BEST 89:4; BPFB 3; BW 2, 3; CA 37-
40R; CANR 9, 27, 49, 66, 82, 131;
CDALB 1968-1988; CN 4, 5, 6, 7; CPW;
CSW; DA; DA3; DAB; DAC; DAM MST,
MULT, NOV, POET, POP; DLB 6, 33,
143; EWL 3; EXPN; EXPS; FL 1:6; FW;
INT CANR-27; LAIT 3; MAL 5; MBL;
MTCW 1, 2; MTFW 2005; NFS 5; PFS
30; RGAL 4; RGSF 2; SATA 31; SSFS 2,
11; TUS; YAW

Walker, Alice Malsenior
See Walker, Alice

Walker, David Harry 1911-1992 ...... **CLC 14**
See also CA 1-4R; 137; CANR 1; CN 1, 2;
CWRI 5; SATA 8; SATA-Obit 71

Walker, Edward Joseph 1934-2004 .. **CLC 13**
See also CA 21-24R; 226; CANR 12, 28,
53; CP 1, 2, 3, 4, 5, 6, 7; DLB 40

Walker, George F(rederick) 1947- .. **CLC 44,**
61
See also CA 103; CANR 21, 43, 59; CD 5,
6; DAB; DAC; DAM MST; DLB 60

Walker, Joseph A. 1935-2003 .... **CLC 19**
See also BW 1, 3; CA 89-92; CAD; CANR
26, 143; CD 5, 6; DAM DRAM, MST;
DFS 12; DLB 38

Walker, Margaret 1915-1998 .... **BLC 1:3;**
CLC 1, 6; PC 20; TCLC 129
See also AFAW 1, 2; BW 2, 3; CA 73-76;
172; CANR 26, 54, 76, 136; CN 1, 2, 3,
4, 5, 6; CP 1, 2, 3, 4, 5, 6; CSW; DAM
MULT; DLB 76, 152; EXPP; FW; MAL
5; MTCW 1, 2; MTFW 2005; RGAL 4;
RHW

Walker, Ted
See Walker, Edward Joseph

Wallace, David Foster 1962-2008 .... **CLC 50,**
114, 271; SSC 68
See also AAYA 50; AMWS 10; CA 132;
277; CANR 59, 133; CN 7; DA3; MTCW
2; MTFW 2005

Wallace, Dexter
See Masters, Edgar Lee

Wallace, (Richard Horatio) Edgar
1875-1932 .... **TCLC 57**
See also CA 115; 218; CMW 4; DLB 70;
MSW; RGEL 2

Wallace, Irving 1916-1990 .... **CLC 7, 13**
See also AITN 1; BPFB 3; CA 1-4R; 132;
CAAS 1; CANR 1, 27; CPW; DAM NOV,
POP; INT CANR-27; MTCW 1, 2

Wallant, Edward Lewis 1926-1962 ... **CLC 5,**
10
See also CA 1-4R; CANR 22; DLB 2, 28,
143, 299; EWL 3; MAL 5; MTCW 1, 2;
RGAL 4; RGHL

Wallas, Graham 1858-1932 .... **TCLC 91**

Waller, Edmund 1606-1687 .... **LC 86; PC 72**
See also BRW 2; DAM POET; DLB 126;
PAB; RGEL 2

Walley, Byron
See Card, Orson Scott

Walpole, Horace 1717-1797 ..... **LC 2, 49, 152**
See also BRW 3; DLB 39, 104, 213; GL 3;
HGG; LMFS 1; RGEL 2; SUFW 1; TEA

Walpole, Hugh (Seymour)
1884-1941 .... **TCLC 5**
See also CA 104; 165; DLB 34; HGG;
MTCW 2; RGEL 2; RHW

Walrond, Eric (Derwent) 1898-1966 . **HR 1:3**
See also BW 1; CA 125; DLB 51

Walser, Martin 1927- .... **CLC 27, 183**
See also CA 57-60; CANR 8, 46, 145;
CWW 2; DLB 75, 124; EWL 3

Walser, Robert 1878-1956 ..... **SSC 20; TCLC**
18
See also CA 118; 165; CANR 100; DLB
66; EWL 3

Walsh, Gillian Paton
See Paton Walsh, Jill

Walsh, Jill Paton
See Paton Walsh, Jill

Walter, Villiam Christian
See Andersen, Hans Christian

Walter of Chatillon c. 1135-c.
1202 .... **CMLC 111**

Walters, Anna L(ee) 1946- .... **NNAL**
See also CA 73-76

Walther von der Vogelweide c.
1170-1228 .... **CMLC 56**

Walton, Izaak 1593-1683 .... **LC 72**
See also BRW 2; CDBLB Before 1660;
DLB 151, 213; RGEL 2

Walzer, Michael (Laban) 1935- ...... **CLC 238**
See also CA 37-40R; CANR 15, 48, 127

Wambaugh, Joseph, Jr. 1937- ...... **CLC 3, 18**
See also AITN 1; BEST 89:3; BPFB 3; CA
33-36R; CANR 42, 65, 115, 167; CMW
4; CPW 1; DA3; DAM NOV, POP; DLB
6; DLBY 1983; MSW; MTCW 1, 2

Wambaugh, Joseph Aloysius
See Wambaugh, Joseph, Jr.
Wang Wei 699(?)-761(?) . **CMLC 100; PC 18**
See also TWA
Warburton, William 1698-1779 .... **LC 97**
See also DLB 104
Ward, Arthur Henry Sarsfield
1883-1959 .... **TCLC 28**
See also CA 108; 173; CMW 4; DLB 70;
HGG; MSW; SUFW
Ward, Douglas Turner 1930- .... **CLC 19**
See also BW 1; CA 81-84; CAD; CANR
27; CD 5, 6; DLB 7, 38
Ward, E. D.
See Lucas, E(dward) V(errall)
Ward, Mrs. Humphry 1851-1920
See Ward, Mary Augusta
See also RGEL 2
Ward, Mary Augusta 1851-1920 ... **TCLC 55**
See Ward, Mrs. Humphry
See also DLB 18
Ward, Nathaniel 1578(?)-1652 .... **LC 114**
See also DLB 24
Ward, Peter
See Faust, Frederick (Schiller)
Warhol, Andy 1928(?)-1987 .... **CLC 20**
See also AAYA 12; BEST 89:4; CA 89-92;
121; CANR 34
Warner, Francis (Robert Le Plastrier)
1937- .... **CLC 14**
See also CA 53-56; CANR 11; CP 1, 2, 3, 4
Warner, Marina 1946- .... **CLC 59, 231**
See also CA 65-68; CANR 21, 55, 118; CN
5, 6, 7; DLB 194; MTFW 2005
Warner, Rex (Ernest) 1905-1986 ...... **CLC 45**
See also CA 89-92; 119; CN 1, 2, 3, 4; CP
1, 2, 3, 4; DLB 15; RGEL 2; RHW
Warner, Susan (Bogert)
1819-1885 .... **NCLC 31, 146**
See also AMWS 18; DLB 3, 42, 239, 250,
254
Warner, Sylvia (Constance) Ashton
See Ashton-Warner, Sylvia (Constance)
Warner, Sylvia Townsend
1893-1978 .. **CLC 7, 19; SSC 23; TCLC
131**
See also BRWS 7; CA 61-64; 77-80; CANR
16, 60, 104; CN 1, 2; DLB 34, 139; EWL
3; FANT; FW; MTCW 1, 2; RGEL 2;
RGSF 2; RHW
Warren, Mercy Otis 1728-1814 ..... **NCLC 13**
See also DLB 31, 200; RGAL 4; TUS
Warren, Robert Penn 1905-1989 .. **CLC 1, 4,
6, 8, 10, 13, 18, 39, 53, 59; PC 37; SSC
4, 58; WLC 6**
See also AITN 1; AMW; AMWC 2; BPFB
3; BYA 1; CA 13-16R; 129; CANR 10,
47; CDALB 1968-1988; CN 1, 2, 3, 4;
CP 1, 2, 3, 4; DA; DA3; DAB; DAC;
DAM MST, NOV, POET; DLB 2, 48, 152,
320; DLBY 1980, 1989; EWL 3; INT
CANR-10; MAL 5; MTCW 1, 2; MTFW
2005; NFS 13; RGAL 4; RGSF 2; RHW;
SATA 46; SATA-Obit 63; SSFS 8; TUS
Warrigal, Jack
See Furphy, Joseph
Warshofsky, Isaac
See Singer, Isaac Bashevis
Warton, Joseph 1722-1800 ... **LC 128; NCLC
118**
See also DLB 104, 109; RGEL 2
Warton, Thomas 1728-1790 .... **LC 15, 82**
See also DAM POET; DLB 104, 109, 336;
RGEL 2
Waruk, Kona
See Harris, (Theodore) Wilson
Warung, Price
See Astley, William

Warwick, Jarvis
See Garner, Hugh
Washington, Alex
See Harris, Mark
Washington, Booker T(aliaferro)
1856-1915 .... **BLC 1:3; TCLC 10**
See also BW 1; CA 114; 125; DA3; DAM
MULT; DLB 345; LAIT 2; RGAL 4;
SATA 28
Washington, George 1732-1799 .... **LC 25**
See also DLB 31
Wassermann, (Karl) Jakob
1873-1934 .... **TCLC 6**
See also CA 104; 163; DLB 66; EWL 3
Wasserstein, Wendy 1950-2006 . **CLC 32, 59,
90, 183; DC 4**
See also AAYA 73; AMWS 15; CA 121;
129; 247; CABS 3; CAD; CANR 53, 75,
128; CD 5, 6; CWD; DA3; DAM DRAM;
DFS 5, 17; DLB 228; EWL 3; FW; INT
CA-129; MAL 5; MTCW 2; MTFW 2005;
SATA 94; SATA-Obit 174
Waterhouse, Keith (Spencer) 1929- . **CLC 47**
See also BRWS 13; CA 5-8R; CANR 38,
67, 109; CBD; CD 6; CN 1, 2, 3, 4, 5, 6,
7; DLB 13, 15; MTCW 1, 2; MTFW 2005
Waters, Frank (Joseph) 1902-1995 .. **CLC 88**
See also CA 5-8R; 149; CAAS 13; CANR
3, 18, 63, 121; DLB 212; DLBY 1986;
RGAL 4; TCWW 1, 2
Waters, Mary C. .... **CLC 70**
Waters, Roger 1944- .... **CLC 35**
Watkins, Frances Ellen
See Harper, Frances Ellen Watkins
Watkins, Gerrold
See Malzberg, Barry N(athaniel)
Watkins, Gloria Jean
See hooks, bell
Watkins, Paul 1964- .... **CLC 55**
See also CA 132; CANR 62, 98
Watkins, Vernon Phillips
1906-1967 .... **CLC 43**
See also CA 9-10; 25-28R; CAP 1; DLB
20; EWL 3; RGEL 2
Watson, Irving S.
See Mencken, H(enry) L(ouis)
Watson, John H.
See Farmer, Philip Jose
Watson, Richard F.
See Silverberg, Robert
Watts, Ephraim
See Horne, Richard Henry Hengist
Watts, Isaac 1674-1748 .... **LC 98**
See also DLB 95; RGEL 2; SATA 52
Waugh, Auberon (Alexander)
1939-2001 .... **CLC 7**
See also CA 45-48; 192; CANR 6, 22, 92;
CN 1, 2, 3; DLB 14, 194
Waugh, Evelyn 1903-1966 ... **CLC 1, 3, 8, 13,
19, 27, 44, 107; SSC 41; WLC 6**
See also AAYA 78; BPFB 3; BRW 7; CA
85-88; 25-28R; CANR 22; CDBLB 1914-
1945; DA; DA3; DAB; DAC; DAM MST,
NOV, POP; DLB 15, 162, 195; EWL 3;
MTCW 1, 2; MTFW 2005; NFS 13, 17;
RGEL 2; RGSF 2; TEA; WLIT 4
Waugh, Evelyn Arthur St. John
See Waugh, Evelyn
Waugh, Harriet 1944- .... **CLC 6**
See also CA 85-88; CANR 22
Ways, C.R.
See Blount, Roy, Jr.
Waystaff, Simon
See Swift, Jonathan
Webb, Beatrice (Martha Potter)
1858-1943 .... **TCLC 22**
See also CA 117; 162; DLB 190; FW
Webb, Charles 1939- .... **CLC 7**
See also CA 25-28R; CANR 114, 188

Webb, Charles Richard
See Webb, Charles
Webb, Frank J. .... **NCLC 143**
See also DLB 50
Webb, James, Jr.
See Webb, James
Webb, James 1946- .... **CLC 22**
See also CA 81-84; CANR 156
Webb, James H.
See Webb, James
Webb, James Henry
See Webb, James
Webb, Mary Gladys (Meredith)
1881-1927 .... **TCLC 24**
See also CA 182; 123; DLB 34; FW; RGEL
2
Webb, Mrs. Sidney
See Webb, Beatrice (Martha Potter)
Webb, Phyllis 1927- .... **CLC 18**
See also CA 104; CANR 23; CCA 1; CP 1,
2, 3, 4, 5, 6, 7; CWP; DLB 53
Webb, Sidney (James) 1859-1947 .. **TCLC 22**
See also CA 117; 163; DLB 190
Webber, Andrew Lloyd
See Lloyd Webber, Andrew
Weber, Lenora Mattingly
1895-1971 .... **CLC 12**
See also CA 19-20; 29-32R; CAP 1; SATA
2; SATA-Obit 26
Weber, Max 1864-1920 .... **TCLC 69**
See also CA 109; 189; DLB 296
Webster, John 1580(?)-1634(?) ...... **DC 2; LC
33, 84, 124; WLC 6**
See also BRW 2; CDBLB Before 1660; DA;
DAB; DAC; DAM DRAM, MST; DFS
17, 19; DLB 58; IDTP; RGEL 2; WLIT 3
Webster, Noah 1758-1843 .... **NCLC 30**
See also DLB 1, 37, 42, 43, 73, 243
Wedekind, Benjamin Franklin
See Wedekind, Frank
Wedekind, Frank 1864-1918 .... **TCLC 7**
See also CA 104; 153; CANR 121, 122;
CDWLB 2; DAM DRAM; DLB 118; EW
8; EWL 3; LMFS 2; RGWL 2, 3
Wehr, Demaris .... **CLC 65**
Weidman, Jerome 1913-1998 .... **CLC 7**
See also AITN 2; CA 1-4R; 171; CAD;
CANR 1; CD 1, 2, 3, 4, 5; DLB 28
Weil, Simone (Adolphine)
1909-1943 .... **TCLC 23**
See also CA 117; 159; EW 12; EWL 3; FW;
GFL 1789 to the Present; MTCW 2
Weininger, Otto 1880-1903 .... **TCLC 84**
Weinstein, Nathan
See West, Nathanael
Weinstein, Nathan von Wallenstein
See West, Nathanael
Weir, Peter (Lindsay) 1944- .... **CLC 20**
See also CA 113; 123
Weiss, Peter (Ulrich) 1916-1982 .. **CLC 3, 15,
51; TCLC 152**
See also CA 45-48; 106; CANR 3; DAM
DRAM; DFS 3; DLB 69, 124; EWL 3;
RGHL; RGWL 2, 3
Weiss, Theodore (Russell)
1916-2003 .... **CLC 3, 8, 14**
See also CA 9-12R; 189; 216; CAAE 189;
CAAS 2; CANR 46, 94; CP 1, 2, 3, 4, 5,
6, 7; DLB 5; TCLE 1:2
Welch, (Maurice) Denton
1915-1948 .... **TCLC 22**
See also BRWS 8, 9; CA 121; 148; RGEL
2
Welch, James (Phillip) 1940-2003 ..... **CLC 6,
14, 52, 249; NNAL; PC 62**
See also CA 85-88; 219; CANR 42, 66, 107;
CN 5, 6, 7; CP 2, 3, 4, 5, 6, 7; CPW;
DAM MULT, POP; DLB 175, 256; LATS
1:1; NFS 23; RGAL 4; TCWW 1, 2

Williams, Ben Ames 1889-1953 ..... **TCLC 89**
See also CA 183; DLB 102
Williams, Charles
See Collier, James Lincoln
Williams, Charles (Walter Stansby)
1886-1945 .... **TCLC 1, 11**
See also BRWS 9; CA 104; 163; DLB 100,
153, 255; FANT; RGEL 2; SUFW 1
Williams, C.K. 1936- .... **CLC 33, 56, 148**
See also CA 37-40R; CAAS 26; CANR 57,
106; CP 1, 2, 3, 4, 5, 6, 7; DAM POET;
DLB 5; MAL 5
Williams, Ella Gwendolen Rees
See Rhys, Jean
Williams, (George) Emlyn
1905-1987 .... **CLC 15**
See also CA 104; 123; CANR 36; DAM
DRAM; DLB 10, 77; IDTP; MTCW 1
Williams, Hank 1923-1953 .... **TCLC 81**
See also CA 188
Williams, Helen Maria
1761-1827 .... **NCLC 135**
See also DLB 158
Williams, Hiram Hank
See Williams, Hank
Williams, Hiram King
See Williams, Hank
Williams, Hugo (Mordaunt) 1942- ... **CLC 42**
See also CA 17-20R; CANR 45, 119; CP 1,
2, 3, 4, 5, 6, 7; DLB 40
Williams, J. Walker
See Wodehouse, P(elham) G(renville)
Williams, John A(lfred) 1925- .... **BLC 1:3;**
CLC 5, 13
See also AFAW 2; BW 2, 3; CA 53-56, 195;
CAAE 195; CAAS 3; CANR 6, 26, 51,
118; CN 1, 2, 3, 4, 5, 6, 7; CSW; DAM
MULT; DLB 2, 33; EWL 3; INT CANR-6;
MAL 5; RGAL 4; SFW 4
Williams, Jonathan 1929-2008 .... **CLC 13**
See also CA 9-12R; 270; CAAS 12; CANR
8, 108; CP 1, 2, 3, 4, 5, 6, 7; DLB 5
Williams, Jonathan Chamberlain
See Williams, Jonathan
Williams, Joy 1944- .... **CLC 31**
See also CA 41-44R; CANR 22, 48, 97,
168; DLB 335; SSFS 25
Williams, Norman 1952- .... **CLC 39**
See also CA 118
Williams, Roger 1603(?)-1683 .... **LC 129**
See also DLB 24
Williams, Sherley Anne
1944-1999 .... **BLC 1:3; CLC 89**
See also AFAW 2; BW 2, 3; CA 73-76; 185;
CANR 25, 82; DAM MULT, POET; DLB
41; INT CANR-25; SATA 78; SATA-Obit
116
Williams, Shirley
See Williams, Sherley Anne
Williams, Tennessee 1911-1983 . **CLC 1, 2, 5,**
7, 8, 11, 15, 19, 30, 39, 45, 71, 111; DC
4; SSC 81; WLC 6
See also AAYA 31; AITN 1, 2; AMW;
AMWC 1; CA 5-8R; 108; CABS 3; CAD;
CANR 31, 132, 174; CDALB 1941-1968;
CN 1, 2, 3; DA; DA3; DAB; DAC; DAM
DRAM, MST; DFS 17; DLB 7, 341;
DLBD 4; DLBY 1983; EWL 3; GLL 1;
LAIT 4; LATS 1:2; MAL 5; MTCW 1, 2;
MTFW 2005; RGAL 4; TUS
Williams, Thomas (Alonzo)
1926-1990 .... **CLC 14**
See also CA 1-4R; 132; CANR 2
Williams, Thomas Lanier
See Williams, Tennessee
Williams, William C.
See Williams, William Carlos

Williams, William Carlos
1883-1963 .... **CLC 1, 2, 5, 9, 13, 22, 42,**
67; PC 7; SSC 31; WLC 6
See also AAYA 46; AMW; AMWR 1; CA
89-92; CANR 34; CDALB 1917-1929;
DA; DA3; DAB; DAC; DAM MST,
POET; DLB 4, 16, 54, 86; EWL 3; EXPP;
MAL 5; MTCW 1, 2; MTFW 2005; NCFS
4; PAB; PFS 1, 6, 11; RGAL 4; RGSF 2;
SSFS 27; TUS; WP
Williamson, David (Keith) 1942- ..... **CLC 56**
See also CA 103; CANR 41; CD 5, 6; DLB
289
Williamson, Jack
See Williamson, John Stewart
Williamson, John Stewart
1908-2006 .... **CLC 29**
See also AAYA 76; CA 17-20R; 255; CAAS
8; CANR 23, 70, 153; DLB 8; SCFW 1,
2; SFW 4
Willie, Frederick
See Lovecraft, H. P.
Willingham, Calder (Baynard, Jr.)
1922-1995 .... **CLC 5, 51**
See also CA 5-8R; 147; CANR 3; CN 1, 2,
3, 4, 5; CSW; DLB 2, 44; IDFW 3, 4;
MTCW 1
Willis, Charles
See Clarke, Arthur C.
Willis, Nathaniel Parker
1806-1867 .... **NCLC 194**
See also DLB 3, 59, 73, 74, 183, 250;
DLBD 13; RGAL 4
Willy
See Colette, (Sidonie-Gabrielle)
Willy, Colette
See Colette, (Sidonie-Gabrielle)
Wilmot, John 1647-1680 .... **LC 75; PC 66**
See also BRW 2; DLB 131; PAB; RGEL 2
Wilson, A.N. 1950- .... **CLC 33**
See also BRWS 6; CA 112; 122; CANR
156; CN 4, 5, 6, 7; DLB 14, 155, 194;
MTCW 2
Wilson, Andrew Norman
See Wilson, A.N.
Wilson, Angus (Frank Johnstone)
1913-1991 . **CLC 2, 3, 5, 25, 34; SSC 21**
See also BRWS 1; CA 5-8R; 134; CANR
21; CN 1, 2, 3, 4; DLB 15, 139, 155;
EWL 3; MTCW 1, 2; MTFW 2005; RGEL
2; RGSF 2
Wilson, August 1945-2005 .... **BLC 1:3, 2:3;**
CLC 39, 50, 63, 118, 222; DC 2, 31;
WLCS
See also AAYA 16; AFAW 2; AMWS 8; BW
2, 3; CA 115; 122; 244; CAD; CANR 42,
54, 76, 128; CD 5, 6; DA; DA3; DAB;
DAC; DAM DRAM, MST, MULT; DFS
3, 7, 15, 17, 24; DLB 228; EWL 3; LAIT
4; LATS 1:2; MAL 5; MTCW 1, 2;
MTFW 2005; RGAL 4
Wilson, Brian 1942- .... **CLC 12**
Wilson, Colin (Henry) 1931- .... **CLC 3, 14**
See also CA 1-4R; CAAS 5; CANR 1, 22,
33, 77; CMW 4; CN 1, 2, 3, 4, 5, 6; DLB
14, 194; HGG; MTCW 1; SFW 4
Wilson, Dirk
See Pohl, Frederik
Wilson, Edmund 1895-1972 .. **CLC 1, 2, 3, 8,**
24
See also AMW; CA 1-4R; 37-40R; CANR
1, 46, 110; CN 1; DLB 63; EWL 3; MAL
5; MTCW 1, 2; MTFW 2005; RGAL 4;
TUS
Wilson, Ethel Davis (Bryant)
1888(?)-1980 .... **CLC 13**
See also CA 102; CN 1, 2; DAC; DAM
POET; DLB 68; MTCW 1; RGEL 2
Wilson, Harriet
See Wilson, Harriet E. Adams

Wilson, Harriet E.
See Wilson, Harriet E. Adams
Wilson, Harriet E. Adams
1827(?)-1863(?) ...... **BLC 1:3; NCLC 78**
See also DAM MULT; DLB 50, 239, 243
Wilson, John 1785-1854 .... **NCLC 5**
See also DLB 110
Wilson, John (Anthony) Burgess
See Burgess, Anthony
Wilson, Katharina .... **CLC 65**
Wilson, Lanford 1937- .. **CLC 7, 14, 36, 197;**
DC 19
See also CA 17-20R; CABS 3; CAD; CANR
45, 96; CD 5, 6; DAM DRAM; DFS 4, 9,
12, 16, 20; DLB 7, 341; EWL 3; MAL 5;
TUS
Wilson, Robert M. 1941- .... **CLC 7, 9**
See also CA 49-52; CAD; CANR 2, 41; CD
5, 6; MTCW 1
Wilson, Robert McLiam 1964- .... **CLC 59**
See also CA 132; DLB 267
Wilson, Sloan 1920-2003 .... **CLC 32**
See also CA 1-4R; 216; CANR 1, 44; CN
1, 2, 3, 4, 5, 6
Wilson, Snoo 1948- .... **CLC 33**
See also CA 69-72; CBD; CD 5, 6
Wilson, William S(mith) 1932- .... **CLC 49**
See also CA 81-84
Wilson, (Thomas) Woodrow
1856-1924 .... **TCLC 79**
See also CA 166; DLB 47
Winchester, Simon 1944- .... **CLC 257**
See also AAYA 66; CA 107; CANR 90, 130
Winchilsea, Anne (Kingsmill) Finch
1661-1720
See Finch, Anne
See also RGEL 2
Winckelmann, Johann Joachim
1717-1768 .... **LC 129**
See also DLB 97
Windham, Basil
See Wodehouse, P(elham) G(renville)
Wingrove, David 1954- .... **CLC 68**
See also CA 133; SFW 4
Winnemucca, Sarah 1844-1891 .... **NCLC 79;**
NNAL
See also DAM MULT; DLB 175; RGAL 4
Winstanley, Gerrard 1609-1676 .... **LC 52**
Wintergreen, Jane
See Duncan, Sara Jeannette
Winters, Arthur Yvor
See Winters, Yvor
Winters, Janet Lewis
See Lewis, Janet
Winters, Yvor 1900-1968 .. **CLC 4, 8, 32; PC**
82
See also AMWS 2; CA 11-12; 25-28R; CAP
1; DLB 48; EWL 3; MAL 5; MTCW 1;
RGAL 4
Winterson, Jeanette 1959- .... **CLC 64, 158**
See also BRWS 4; CA 136; CANR 58, 116,
181; CN 5, 6, 7; CPW; DA3; DAM POP;
DLB 207, 261; FANT; FW; GLL 1;
MTCW 2; MTFW 2005; RHW; SATA 190
Winthrop, John 1588-1649 .... **LC 31, 107**
See also DLB 24, 30
Winthrop, Theodore 1828-1861 ... **NCLC 210**
See also DLB 202
Winton, Tim 1960- .... **CLC 251; SSC 119**
See also AAYA 34; CA 152; CANR 118;
CN 6, 7; DLB 325; SATA 98
Wirth, Louis 1897-1952 .... **TCLC 92**
See also CA 210
Wiseman, Frederick 1930- .... **CLC 20**
See also CA 159

Wister, Owen 1860-1938 ..... **SSC 100; TCLC 21**
See also BPFB 3; CA 108; 162; DLB 9, 78, 186; RGAL 4; SATA 62; TCWW 1, 2

Wither, George 1588-1667 .... **LC 96**
See also DLB 121; RGEL 2

Witkacy
See Witkiewicz, Stanislaw Ignacy

Witkiewicz, Stanislaw Ignacy
1885-1939 .... **TCLC 8**
See also CA 105; 162; CDWLB 4; DLB 215; EW 10; EWL 3; RGWL 2, 3; SFW 4

Wittgenstein, Ludwig (Josef Johann)
1889-1951 .... **TCLC 59**
See also CA 113; 164; DLB 262; MTCW 2

Wittig, Monique 1935-2003 .... **CLC 22**
See also CA 116; 135; 212; CANR 143; CWW 2; DLB 83; EWL 3; FW; GLL 1

Wittlin, Jozef 1896-1976 .... **CLC 25**
See also CA 49-52; 65-68; CANR 3; EWL 3

Wodehouse, P(elham) G(renville)
1881-1975 .. **CLC 1, 2, 5, 10, 22; SSC 2, 115; TCLC 108**
See also AAYA 65; AITN 2; BRWS 3; CA 45-48; 57-60; CANR 3, 33; CDBLB 1914-1945; CN 1, 2; CPW 1; DA3; DAB; DAC; DAM NOV; DLB 34, 162; EWL 3; MTCW 1, 2; MTFW 2005; RGEL 2; RGSF 2; SATA 22; SSFS 10

Woiwode, L.
See Woiwode, Larry (Alfred)

Woiwode, Larry (Alfred) 1941- ... **CLC 6, 10**
See also CA 73-76; CANR 16, 94; CN 3, 4, 5, 6, 7; DLB 6; INT CANR-16

Wojciechowska, Maia (Teresa)
1927-2002 .... **CLC 26**
See also AAYA 8, 46; BYA 3; CA 9-12R; 183; 209; CAAE 183; CANR 4, 41; CLR 1; JRDA; MAICYA 1, 2; SAAS 1; SATA 1, 28, 83; SATA-Essay 104; SATA-Obit 134; YAW

Wojtyla, Karol (Jozef)
See John Paul II, Pope

Wojtyla, Karol (Josef)
See John Paul II, Pope

Wolf, Christa 1929- ...... **CLC 14, 29, 58, 150, 261**
See also CA 85-88; CANR 45, 123; CDWLB 2; CWW 2; DLB 75; EWL 3; FW; MTCW 1; RGWL 2, 3; SSFS 14

Wolf, Naomi 1962- .... **CLC 157**
See also CA 141; CANR 110; FW; MTFW 2005

Wolfe, Gene 1931- .... **CLC 25**
See also AAYA 35; CA 57-60; CAAS 9; CANR 6, 32, 60, 152; CPW; DAM POP; DLB 8; FANT; MTCW 2; MTFW 2005; SATA 118, 165; SCFW 2; SFW 4; SUFW 2

Wolfe, Gene Rodman
See Wolfe, Gene

Wolfe, George C. 1954- .... **BLCS; CLC 49**
See also CA 149; CAD; CD 5, 6

Wolfe, Thomas (Clayton)
1900-1938 .... **SSC 33, 113; TCLC 4, 13, 29, 61; WLC 6**
See also AMW; BPFB 3; CA 104; 132; CANR 102; CDALB 1929-1941; DA; DA3; DAB; DAC; DAM MST, NOV; DLB 9, 102, 229; DLBD 2, 16; DLBY 1985, 1997; EWL 3; MAL 5; MTCW 1, 2; NFS 18; RGAL 4; SSFS 18; TUS

Wolfe, Thomas Kennerly, Jr. 1931- .. **CLC 1, 2, 9, 15, 35, 51, 147**
See also AAYA 8, 67; AITN 2; AMWS 3; BEST 89:1; BPFB 3; CA 13-16R; CANR 9, 33, 70, 104; CN 5, 6, 7; CPW; CSW;

DA3; DAM POP; DLB 152, 185 185; EWL 3; INT CANR-9; LAIT 5; MTCW 1, 2; MTFW 2005; RGAL 4; TUS

Wolfe, Tom
See Wolfe, Thomas Kennerly, Jr.

Wolff, Geoffrey 1937- .... **CLC 41**
See also CA 29-32R; CANR 29, 43, 78, 154

Wolff, Geoffrey Ansell
See Wolff, Geoffrey

Wolff, Sonia
See Levitin, Sonia

Wolff, Tobias 1945- .... **CLC 39, 64, 172; SSC 63**
See also AAYA 16; AMWS 7; BEST 90:2; BYA 12; CA 114; 117; CAAS 22; CANR 54, 76, 96; CN 5, 6, 7; CSW; DA3; DLB 130; EWL 3; INT CA-117; MTCW 2; MTFW 2005; RGAL 4; RGSF 2; SSFS 4, 11

Wolitzer, Hilma 1930- .... **CLC 17**
See also CA 65-68; CANR 18, 40, 172; INT CANR-18; SATA 31; YAW

Wollstonecraft, Mary 1759-1797 .... **LC 5, 50, 90, 147**
See also BRWS 3; CDBLB 1789-1832; DLB 39, 104, 158, 252; FL 1:1; FW; LAIT 1; RGEL 2; TEA; WLIT 3

Wonder, Stevie 1950- .... **CLC 12**
See also CA 111

Wong, Jade Snow 1922-2006 .... **CLC 17**
See also CA 109; 249; CANR 91; SATA 112; SATA-Obit 175

Wood, Ellen Price
See Wood, Mrs. Henry

Wood, Mrs. Henry 1814-1887 ...... **NCLC 178**
See also CMW 4; DLB 18; SUFW

Wood, James 1965- .... **CLC 238**
See also CA 235

Woodberry, George Edward
1855-1930 .... **TCLC 73**
See also CA 165; DLB 71, 103

Woodcott, Keith
See Brunner, John (Kilian Houston)

Woodruff, Robert W.
See Mencken, H(enry) L(ouis)

Woodward, Bob 1943- .... **CLC 240**
See also CA 69-72; CANR 31, 67, 107, 176; MTCW 1

Woodward, Robert Upshur
See Woodward, Bob

Woolf, (Adeline) Virginia 1882-1941 .. **SSC 7, 79; TCLC 1, 5, 20, 43, 56, 101, 123, 128; WLC 6**
See also AAYA 44; BPFB 3; BRW 7; BRWC 2; BRWR 1; CA 104; 130; CANR 64, 132; CDBLB 1914-1945; DA; DA3; DAB; DAC; DAM MST, NOV; DLB 36, 100, 162; DLBD 10; EWL 3; EXPS; FL 1:6; FW; LAIT 3; LATS 1:1; LMFS 1; MTCW 1, 2; MTFW 2005; NCFS 2; NFS 8, 12, 28; RGEL 2; RGSF 2; SSFS 4, 12; TEA; WLIT 4

Woollcott, Alexander (Humphreys)
1887-1943 .... **TCLC 5**
See also CA 105; 161; DLB 29

Woolman, John 1720-1772 .... **LC 155**
See also DLB 31

Woolrich, Cornell
See Hopley-Woolrich, Cornell George

Woolson, Constance Fenimore
1840-1894 .... **NCLC 82; SSC 90**
See also DLB 12, 74, 189, 221; RGAL 4

Wordsworth, Dorothy 1771-1855 . **NCLC 25, 138**
See also DLB 107

Wordsworth, William 1770-1850 .. **NCLC 12, 38, 111, 166, 206; PC 4, 67; WLC 6**
See also AAYA 70; BRW 4; BRWC 1; CD-BLB 1789-1832; DA; DA3; DAB; DAC; DAM MST, POET; DLB 93, 107; EXPP; LATS 1:1; LMFS 1; PAB; PFS 2; RGEL 2; TEA; WLIT 3

Wotton, Sir Henry 1568-1639 .... **LC 68**
See also DLB 121; RGEL 2

Wouk, Herman 1915- .... **CLC 1, 9, 38**
See also BPFB 2, 3; CA 5-8R; CANR 6, 33, 67, 146; CDALBS; CN 1, 2, 3, 4, 5, 6; CPW; DA3; DAM NOV, POP; DLBY 1982; INT CANR-6; LAIT 4; MAL 5; MTCW 1, 2; MTFW 2005; NFS 7; TUS

Wright, Charles 1932-2008 ... **BLC 1:3; CLC 49**
See also BW 1; CA 9-12R; 278; CANR 26; CN 1, 2, 3, 4, 5, 6, 7; DAM MULT, POET; DLB 33

Wright, Charles 1935- ... **CLC 6, 13, 28, 119, 146**
See also AMWS 5; CA 29-32R; CAAS 7; CANR 23, 36, 62, 88, 135, 180; CP 3, 4, 5, 6, 7; DLB 165; DLBY 1982; EWL 3; MTCW 1, 2; MTFW 2005; PFS 10

Wright, Charles Penzel, Jr.
See Wright, Charles

Wright, Charles Stevenson
See Wright, Charles

Wright, Frances 1795-1852 .... **NCLC 74**
See also DLB 73

Wright, Frank Lloyd 1867-1959 .... **TCLC 95**
See also AAYA 33; CA 174

Wright, Harold Bell 1872-1944 .... **TCLC 183**
See also BPFB 3; CA 110; DLB 9; TCWW 2

Wright, Jack R.
See Harris, Mark

Wright, James (Arlington)
1927-1980 .... **CLC 3, 5, 10, 28; PC 36**
See also AITN 2; AMWS 3; CA 49-52; 97-100; CANR 4, 34, 64; CDALBS; CP 1, 2; DAM POET; DLB 5, 169, 342; EWL 3; EXPP; MAL 5; MTCW 1, 2; MTFW 2005; PFS 7, 8; RGAL 4; TUS; WP

Wright, Judith 1915-2000 ... **CLC 11, 53; PC 14**
See also CA 13-16R; 188; CANR 31, 76, 93; CP 1, 2, 3, 4, 5, 6, 7; CWP; DLB 260; EWL 3; MTCW 1, 2; MTFW 2005; PFS 8; RGEL 2; SATA 14; SATA-Obit 121

Wright, L(aurali) R. 1939- .... **CLC 44**
See also CA 138; CMW 4

Wright, Richard 1908-1960 .. **BLC 1:3; CLC 1, 3, 4, 9, 14, 21, 48, 74; SSC 2, 109; TCLC 136, 180; WLC 6**
See also AAYA 5, 42; AFAW 1, 2; AMW; BPFB 3; BW 1; BYA 2; CA 108; CANR 64; CDALB 1929-1941; DA; DA3; DAB; DAC; DAM MST, MULT, NOV; DLB 76, 102; DLBD 2; EWL 3; EXPN; LAIT 3, 4; MAL 5; MTCW 1, 2; MTFW 2005; NCFS 1; NFS 1, 7; RGAL 4; RGSF 2; SSFS 3, 9, 15, 20; TUS; YAW

Wright, Richard B. 1937- .... **CLC 6**
See also CA 85-88; CANR 120; DLB 53

Wright, Richard Bruce
See Wright, Richard B.

Wright, Richard Nathaniel
See Wright, Richard

Wright, Rick 1945- .... **CLC 35**

Wright, Rowland
See Wells, Carolyn

Wright, Stephen 1946- .... **CLC 33**
See also CA 237

Wright, Willard Huntington
1888-1939 .... **TCLC 23**
See also CA 115; 189; CMW 4; DLB 306;
DLBD 16; MSW

Wright, William 1930- .... **CLC 44**
See also CA 53-56; CANR 7, 23, 154

Wroth, Lady Mary 1587-1653(?) .... **LC 30,
139; PC 38**
See also DLB 121

Wu Ch'eng-en 1500(?)-1582(?) .... **LC 7**

Wu Ching-tzu 1701-1754 .... **LC 2**

Wulfstan c. 10th cent. -1023 .... **CMLC 59**

Wurlitzer, Rudolph 1938(?)- .... **CLC 2, 4, 15**
See also CA 85-88; CN 4, 5, 6, 7; DLB 173

Wyatt, Sir Thomas c. 1503-1542 . **LC 70; PC
27**
See also BRW 1; DLB 132; EXPP; PFS 25;
RGEL 2; TEA

Wycherley, William 1640-1716 .... **LC 8, 21,
102, 136**
See also BRW 2; CDBLB 1660-1789; DAM
DRAM; DLB 80; RGEL 2

Wyclif, John c. 1330-1384 .... **CMLC 70**
See also DLB 146

Wylie, Elinor (Morton Hoyt)
1885-1928 .... **PC 23; TCLC 8**
See also AMWS 1; CA 105; 162; DLB 9,
45; EXPP; MAL 5; RGAL 4

Wylie, Philip (Gordon) 1902-1971 ... **CLC 43**
See also CA 21-22; 33-36R; CAP 2; CN 1;
DLB 9; SFW 4

Wyndham, John
See Harris, John (Wyndham Parkes Lucas)
Beynon

Wyss, Johann David Von
1743-1818 .... **NCLC 10**
See also CLR 92; JRDA; MAICYA 1, 2;
SATA 29; SATA-Brief 27

Xenophon c. 430B.C.-c. 354B.C. ... **CMLC 17**
See also AW 1; DLB 176; RGWL 2, 3;
WLIT 8

Xingjian, Gao 1940- .... **CLC 167**
See also CA 193; DFS 21; DLB 330;
MTFW 2005; RGWL 3

Yakamochi 718-785 .... **CMLC 45; PC 48**

Yakumo Koizumi
See Hearn, (Patricio) Lafcadio (Tessima
Carlos)

Yamada, Mitsuye (May) 1923- .... **PC 44**
See also CA 77-80

Yamamoto, Hisaye 1921- .... **AAL; SSC 34**
See also CA 214; DAM MULT; DLB 312;
LAIT 4; SSFS 14

Yamauchi, Wakako 1924- .... **AAL**
See also CA 214; DLB 312

Yan, Mo
See Moye, Guan

Yanez, Jose Donoso
See Donoso (Yanez), Jose

Yanovsky, Basile S.
See Yanovsky, V(assily) S(emenovich)

Yanovsky, V(assily) S(emenovich)
1906-1989 .... **CLC 2, 18**
See also CA 97-100; 129

Yates, Richard 1926-1992 .... **CLC 7, 8, 23**
See also AMWS 11; CA 5-8R; 139; CANR
10, 43; CN 1, 2, 3, 4, 5; DLB 2, 234;
DLBY 1981, 1992; INT CANR-10; SSFS
24

Yau, John 1950- .... **PC 61**
See also CA 154; CANR 89; CP 4, 5, 6, 7;
DLB 234, 312; PFS 26

Yearsley, Ann 1753-1806 .... **NCLC 174**
See also DLB 109

Yeats, W. B.
See Yeats, William Butler

Yeats, William Butler 1865-1939 . **DC 33; PC
20, 51; TCLC 1, 11, 18, 31, 93, 116;
WLC 6**
See also AAYA 48; BRW 6; BRWR 1; CA
104; 127; CANR 45; CDBLB 1890-1914;
DA; DA3; DAB; DAC; DAM DRAM,
MST, POET; DLB 10, 19, 98, 156, 332;
EWL 3; EXPP; MTCW 1, 2; MTFW
2005; NCFS 3; PAB; PFS 1, 2, 5, 7, 13,
15; RGEL 2; TEA; WLIT 4; WP

Yehoshua, A.B. 1936- .... **CLC 13, 31, 243**
See also CA 33-36R; CANR 43, 90, 145;
CWW 2; EWL 3; RGHL; RGSF 2; RGWL
3; WLIT 6

Yehoshua, Abraham B.
See Yehoshua, A.B.

Yellow Bird
See Ridge, John Rollin

Yep, Laurence 1948- .... **CLC 35**
See also AAYA 5, 31; BYA 7; CA 49-52;
CANR 1, 46, 92, 161; CLR 3, 17, 54, 132;
DLB 52, 312; FANT; JRDA; MAICYA 1,
2; MAICYAS 1; SATA 7, 69, 123, 176;
WYA; YAW

Yep, Laurence Michael
See Yep, Laurence

Yerby, Frank G(arvin) 1916-1991 . **BLC 1:3;
CLC 1, 7, 22**
See also BPFB 3; BW 1, 3; CA 9-12R; 136;
CANR 16, 52; CN 1, 2, 3, 4, 5; DAM
MULT; DLB 76; INT CANR-16; MTCW
1; RGAL 4; RHW

Yesenin, Sergei Aleksandrovich
See Esenin, Sergei

Yevtushenko, Yevgeny (Alexandrovich)
1933- ...... **CLC 1, 3, 13, 26, 51, 126; PC
40**
See also CA 81-84; CANR 33, 54; CWW
2; DAM POET; EWL 3; MTCW 1; PFS
29; RGHL; RGWL 2, 3

Yezierska, Anzia 1885(?)-1970 .... **CLC 46;
TCLC 205**
See also CA 126; 89-92; DLB 28, 221; FW;
MTCW 1; NFS 29; RGAL 4; SSFS 15

Yglesias, Helen 1915-2008 .... **CLC 7, 22**
See also CA 37-40R; 272; CAAS 20; CANR
15, 65, 95; CN 4, 5, 6, 7; INT CANR-15;
MTCW 1

Y.O.
See Russell, George William

Yokomitsu, Riichi 1898-1947 .... **TCLC 47**
See also CA 170; EWL 3

Yolen, Jane 1939- .... **CLC 256**
See also AAYA 4, 22; BPFB 3; BYA 9, 10,
11, 14, 16; CA 13-16R; CANR 11, 29, 56,
91, 126, 185; CLR 4, 44; CWRI 5; DLB
52; FANT; INT CANR-29; JRDA; MAI-
CYA 1, 2; MTFW 2005; SAAS 1; SATA
4, 40, 75, 112, 158, 194; SATA-Essay 111;
SFW 4; SUFW 2; WYA; YAW

Yonge, Charlotte (Mary)
1823-1901 .... **TCLC 48**
See also CA 109; 163; DLB 18, 163; RGEL
2; SATA 17; WCH

York, Jeremy
See Creasey, John

York, Simon
See Heinlein, Robert A.

Yorke, Henry Vincent 1905-1974 ...... **CLC 2,
13, 97**
See also BRWS 2; CA 85-88, 175; 49-52;
DLB 15; EWL 3; RGEL 2

Yosano, Akiko 1878-1942 ... **PC 11; TCLC 59**
See also CA 161; EWL 3; RGWL 3

Yoshimoto, Banana
See Yoshimoto, Mahoko

Yoshimoto, Mahoko 1964- .... **CLC 84**
See also AAYA 50; CA 144; CANR 98, 160;
NFS 7; SSFS 16

Young, Al(bert James) 1939- .... **BLC 1:3;
CLC 19**
See also BW 2, 3; CA 29-32R; CANR 26,
65, 109; CN 2, 3, 4, 5, 6, 7; CP 1, 2, 3, 4,
5, 6, 7; DAM MULT; DLB 33

Young, Andrew (John) 1885-1971 ...... **CLC 5**
See also CA 5-8R; CANR 7, 29; CP 1;
RGEL 2

Young, Collier
See Bloch, Robert (Albert)

Young, Edward 1683-1765 .... **LC 3, 40**
See also DLB 95; RGEL 2

Young, Marguerite (Vivian)
1909-1995 .... **CLC 82**
See also CA 13-16; 150; CAP 1; CN 1, 2,
3, 4, 5, 6

Young, Neil 1945- .... **CLC 17**
See also CA 110; CCA 1

Young Bear, Ray A. 1950- ... **CLC 94; NNAL**
See also CA 146; DAM MULT; DLB 175;
MAL 5

Yourcenar, Marguerite 1903-1987 ... **CLC 19,
38, 50, 87; TCLC 193**
See also BPFB 3; CA 69-72; CANR 23, 60,
93; DAM NOV; DLB 72; DLBY 1988;
EW 12; EWL 3; GFL 1789 to the Present;
GLL 1; MTCW 1, 2; MTFW 2005;
RGWL 2, 3

Yuan, Chu 340(?)B.C.-278(?)B.C. . **CMLC 36**

Yu Dafu 1896-1945 .... **SSC 122**
See also DLB 328; RGSF 2

Yurick, Sol 1925- .... **CLC 6**
See also CA 13-16R; CANR 25; CN 1, 2,
3, 4, 5, 6, 7; MAL 5

Zabolotsky, Nikolai Alekseevich
1903-1958 .... **TCLC 52**
See also CA 116; 164; EWL 3

Zabolotsky, Nikolay Alekseevich
See Zabolotsky, Nikolai Alekseevich

Zagajewski, Adam 1945- .... **PC 27**
See also CA 186; DLB 232; EWL 3; PFS
25

Zakaria, Fareed 1964- .... **CLC 269**
See also CA 171; CANR 151, 188

Zalygin, Sergei -2000 .... **CLC 59**

Zalygin, Sergei (Pavlovich)
1913-2000 .... **CLC 59**
See also DLB 302

Zamiatin, Evgenii
See Zamyatin, Evgeny Ivanovich

Zamiatin, Evgenii Ivanovich
See Zamyatin, Evgeny Ivanovich

Zamiatin, Yevgenii
See Zamyatin, Evgeny Ivanovich

Zamora, Bernice (B. Ortiz) 1938- .. **CLC 89;
HLC 2**
See also CA 151; CANR 80; DAM MULT;
DLB 82; HW 1, 2

Zamyatin, Evgeny Ivanovich
1884-1937 .... **SSC 89; TCLC 8, 37**
See also CA 105; 166; DLB 272; EW 10;
EWL 3; RGSF 2; RGWL 2, 3; SFW 4

Zamyatin, Yevgeny Ivanovich
See Zamyatin, Evgeny Ivanovich

Zangwill, Israel 1864-1926 ... **SSC 44; TCLC
16**
See also CA 109; 167; CMW 4; DLB 10,
135, 197; RGEL 2

Zanzotto, Andrea 1921- .... **PC 65**
See also CA 208; CWW 2; DLB 128; EWL
3

Zappa, Francis Vincent, Jr. 1940-1993
See Zappa, Frank
See also CA 108; 143; CANR 57

Zappa, Frank .... **CLC 17**
See Zappa, Francis Vincent, Jr.

Zaturenska, Marya 1902-1982 ..... **CLC 6, 11**
See also CA 13-16R; 105; CANR 22; CP 1,
2, 3

Literary Criticism Series
Cumulative Topic Index

This index lists all topic entries in Gale's *Children's Literature Review* (CLR), *Classical and Medieval Literature Criticism* (CMLC), *Contemporary Literary Criticism* (CLC), *Drama Criticism* (DC), *Literature Criticism from 1400 to 1800* (LC), *Nineteenth-Century Literature Criticism* (NCLC), *Short Story Criticism* (SSC), and *Twentieth-Century Literary Criticism* (TCLC). The index also lists topic entries in the Gale Critical Companion Collection, which includes the following publications: *The Beat Generation* (BG), *Feminism in Literature* (FL), *Gothic Literature* (GL), and *Harlem Renaissance* (HR).

Abbey Theatre in the Irish Literary Renaissance TCLC 154: 1-114
origins and development, 2-14
major figures, 14-30
plays and controversies, 30-59
artistic vision and significance, 59-114

Abolitionist Literature of Cuba and Brazil, Nineteenth-Century NCLC 132: 1-94
overviews, 2-11
origins and development, 11-23
sociopolitical concerns, 23-39
poetry, 39-47
prose, 47-93

The Aborigine in Nineteenth-Century Australian Literature NCLC 120: 1-88
overviews, 2-27
representations of the Aborigine in Australian literature, 27-58
Aboriginal myth, literature, and oral tradition, 58-88

Acting on the Restoration and Eighteenth-Century English Stage LC 148: 1-116
overviews 2-23
acting styles 23-43
influential actors 43-70
introduction of actresses 70-86
influence of the actress 86-115

Adventure Literature TCLC 202: 1-89
overviews and general studies 2-32
juvenile adventure narratives 32-8
adventure literature and imperialism 38-57
war and adventure 57-88

The Aesopic Fable LC 51: 1-100
the British Aesopic Fable, 1-54
the Aesopic tradition in non-English-speaking cultures, 55-66
political uses of the Aesopic fable, 67-88
the evolution of the Aesopic fable, 89-99

African-American Folklore and Literature TCLC 126: 1-67
African-American folk tradition, 1-16
representative writers, 16-34
hallmark works, 35-48
the study of African-American literature and folklore, 48-64

Age of al-Andalus CMLC 81: 1-174
overviews, 1-48

history, society, and culture, 48-127
Andalusī poetry, 127-73

Age of Johnson LC 15: 1-87
Johnson's London, 3-15
aesthetics of neoclassicism, 15-36
"age of prose and reason," 36-45
clubmen and bluestockings, 45-56
printing technology, 56-62
periodicals: "a map of busy life," 62-74
transition, 74-86

The Age of King Alfred the Great CMLC 79: 1-141
overviews and historical background, 4-17
the Alfredian translations, 17-43
King Alfred's prefaces, 43-84
Alfred and Boethius, 84-140

Age of Spenser LC 39: 1-70
overviews and general studies, 2-21
literary style, 22-34
poets and the crown, 34-70

AIDS in Literature CLC 81: 365-416

Alchemy in Seventeenth-Century England LC 148: 117-241
overviews 118-47
the last alchemists 147-69
Ben Jonson and *The Alchemist* 169-88
alchemy and poetry 188-239

Alcohol and Literature TCLC 70: 1-58
overview, 2-8
fiction, 8-48
poetry and drama, 48-58

Alexander the Great in Literature CMLC 112: 1-255
overviews and major works, 2-57
Alexander according to Greek and Roman historians, 57-178
the Medieval Alexander, 178-255

American Abolitionism NCLC 44: 1-73
overviews and general studies, 2-26
abolitionist ideals, 26-46
the literature of abolitionism, 46-72

American Autobiography TCLC 86: 1-115
overviews and general studies, 3-36
American authors and autobiography, 36-82
African-American autobiography, 82-114

American Black Humor Fiction TCLC 54: 1-85
characteristics of black humor, 2-13
origins and development, 13-38
black humor distinguished from related literary trends, 38-60
black humor and society, 60-75
black humor reconsidered, 75-83

American Civil War in Literature NCLC 32: 1-109
overviews and general studies, 2-20
regional perspectives, 20-54
fiction popular during the war, 54-79
the historical novel, 79-108
NCLC 212: 1-148
overviews, 4-32
gender roles, 32-70
race and slavery, 70-104
physicality and mortality, 104-47

The American Dream in Literature TCLC 210: 1-105
overviews, 2-11
the American Dream and popular culture, 11-27
the immigrant experience and the American Dream, 27-40
American authors and the American Dream, 40-105

American Frontier in Literature NCLC 28: 1-103
definitions, 2-12
development, 12-17
nonfiction writing about the frontier, 17-30
frontier fiction, 30-45
frontier protagonists, 45-66
portrayals of Native Americans, 66-86
feminist readings, 86-98
twentieth-century reaction against frontier literature, 98-100

American Humor Writing NCLC 52: 1-59
overviews and general studies, 2-12
the Old Southwest, 12-42
broader impacts, 42-5
women humorists, 45-58

American Immigrant Literature TCLC 206: 1-131
overviews and general studies, 2-33
cultural displacement, 33-78
stereotypes, identity, representation, 78-104

NCLC Cumulative Nationality Index

AMERICAN

Adams, John **106**
Adams, John Quincy **175**
Alcott, Amos Bronson **1, 167**
Alcott, Louisa May **6, 58, 83**
Alger, Horatio Jr. **8, 83**
Allston, Washington **2**
Apess, William **73**
Audubon, John James **47**
Barlow, Joel **23**
Bartram, William **145**
Beecher, Catharine Esther **30**
Bellamy, Edward **4, 86, 147**
Bird, Robert Montgomery **1, 197**
Boker, George Henry **125**
Boyesen, Hjalmar Hjorth **135**
Brackenridge, Hugh Henry **7**
Brentano, Clemens (Maria) **1, 191**
Brown, Charles Brockden **22, 74, 122**
Brown, William Wells **2, 89**
Brownson, Orestes Augustus **50**
Bryant, William Cullen **6, 46**
Calhoun, John Caldwell **15**
Channing, William Ellery **17**
Child, Francis James **173**
Child, Lydia Maria **6, 73**
Chivers, Thomas Holley **49**
Cooke, John Esten **5**
Cooke, Rose Terry **110**
Cooper, James Fenimore **1, 27, 54, 203**
Cooper, Susan Fenimore **129**
Cranch, Christopher Pearse **115**
Crèvecoeur, Michel Guillaume Jean de **105**
Crockett, David **8**
Cummins, Maria Susanna **139**
Dana, Richard Henry Sr. **53**
Delany, Martin Robinson **93**
Dickinson, Emily (Elizabeth) **21, 77, 171**
Douglass, Frederick **7, 55, 141**
Dunlap, William **2**
Dwight, Timothy **13**
Emerson, Mary Moody **66**
Emerson, Ralph Waldo **1, 38, 98**
Field, Eugene **3**
Foster, Hannah Webster **99**
Foster, Stephen Collins **26**
Fuller, Margaret **5, 50, 211**
Frederic, Harold **10, 175**
Freneau, Philip Morin **1, 111**
Garrison, William Lloyd **149**
Hale, Sarah Josepha (Buell) **75**
Halleck, Fitz-Greene **47**
Hamilton, Alexander **49**
Hammon, Jupiter **5**
Harris, George Washington **23, 165**
Hawthorne, Nathaniel **2, 10, 17, 23, 39, 79, 95, 158, 171, 191**
Hawthorne, Sophia Peabody **150**
Hayne, Paul Hamilton **94**
Holmes, Oliver Wendell **14, 81**
Hooper, Johnson Jones **177**
Horton, George Moses **87**

Irving, Washington **2, 19, 95**
Jackson, Helen Hunt **90**
Jacobs, Harriet A(nn) **67, 162**
James, Alice **206**
James, Henry Sr. **53**
Jefferson, Thomas **11, 103**
Kennedy, John Pendleton **2**
Kirkland, Caroline M. **85**
Lanier, Sidney **6, 118**
Larcom, Lucy **179**
Lazarus, Emma **8, 109**
Lincoln, Abraham **18, 201**
Lippard, George **198**
Longfellow, Henry Wadsworth **2, 45, 101, 103**
Longstreet, Augustus Baldwin **159**
Lowell, James Russell **2, 90**
Madison, James **126**
Melville, Herman **3, 12, 29, 45, 49, 91, 93, 123, 157, 181, 193**
Mowatt, Anna Cora **74**
Murray, Judith Sargent **63**
Neal, John **161**
Osgood, Frances Sargent **141**
Parker, Theodore **186**
Parkman, Francis Jr. **12**
Parton, Sara Payson Willis **86**
Paulding, James Kirke **2**
Peabody, Elizabeth Palmer **169**
Pinkney, Edward **31**
Poe, Edgar Allan **1, 16, 55, 78, 94, 97, 117, 211**
Prescott, William Hickling **163**
Rowson, Susanna Haswell **5, 69, 182**
Sedgwick, Catharine Maria **19, 98**
Shaw, Henry Wheeler **15**
Sigourney, Lydia Howard (Huntley) **21, 87**
Simms, William Gilmore **3**
Smith, Joseph Jr. **53**
Smith, Seba **187**
Solomon, Northup **105**
Southworth, Emma Dorothy Eliza Nevitte **26**
Stowe, Harriet (Elizabeth) Beecher **3, 50, 133, 195**
Taylor, Bayard **89**
Tenney, Tabitha Gilman **122**
Thoreau, Henry David **7, 21, 61, 138, 207**
Thorpe, Thomas Bangs **183**
Timrod, Henry **25**
Trumbull, John **30**
Truth, Sojourner **94**
Tyler, Royall **3**
Very, Jones **9**
Warner, Susan (Bogert) **31, 146**
Warren, Mercy Otis **13**
Webster, Noah **30**
Webb, Frank J. **143**
Whitman, Sarah Helen (Power) **19**
Whitman, Walt(er) **4, 31, 81, 205**
Whittier, John Greenleaf **8, 59**
Willis, Nathaniel Parker **194**
Wilson, Harriet E. Adams **78**

Winnemucca, Sarah **79**
Winthrop, Theodore **210**

ARGENTINIAN

Echeverria, (Jose) Esteban (Antonino) **18**
Hernández, José **17**
Sarmiento, Domingo Faustino **123**

AUSTRALIAN

Adams, Francis **33**
Clarke, Marcus (Andrew Hislop) **19**
Gordon, Adam Lindsay **21**
Harpur, Charles **114**
Kendall, Henry **12**

AUSTRIAN

Grillparzer, Franz **1, 102**
Lenau, Nikolaus **16**
Nestroy, Johann **42**
Raimund, Ferdinand Jakob **69**
Sacher-Masoch, Leopold von **31**
Stifter, Adalbert **41, 198**

BRAZILIAN

Alencar, Jose de **157**
Alves, Antônio de Castro **205**

CANADIAN

Crawford, Isabella Valancy **12, 127**
De Mille, James **123**
Haliburton, Thomas Chandler **15, 149**
Lampman, Archibald **25, 194**
Moodie, Susanna (Strickland) **14, 113**
Richardson, John **55**
Traill, Catharine Parr **31**

CHINESE

Li Ju-chen **137**

COLOMBIAN

Isaacs, Jorge Ricardo **70**
Silva, José Asunción **114**

CUBAN

Avellaneda, Gertrudis Gómez de **111**
Casal, Julián del **131**
Heredia, José Maráa **209**
Manzano, Juan Francisco **155**
Martí (y Pérez), José (Julian) **63**
Villaverde, Cirilo **121**

CZECH

Macha, Karel Hynek **46**

DANISH

Andersen, Hans Christian **7, 79, 214**
Grundtvig, Nicolai Frederik Severin **1, 158**
Jacobsen, Jens Peter **34**
Kierkegaard, Søren **34, 78, 125**

ISBN-13: 978-1-4144-3513-8
ISBN-10: 1-4144-3513-4

90000

9 781414 435138